S 1.1:964-

W9-BXA-055

FEDERAL
PUBLICATION

Foreign Relations of the
United States, 1964–1968

Volume XXV

South Asia

Editors	Gabrielle S. Mallon
	Louis J. Smith
General Editor	David S. Patterson

United States Government Printing Office
Washington
2000

DEPARTMENT OF STATE PUBLICATION 10689

OFFICE OF THE HISTORIAN

BUREAU OF PUBLIC AFFAIRS

For sale by the U.S. Government Printing Office
Superintendent of Documents, Mail Stop: SSOP, Washington, DC 20402-9328

ISBN 0-16-049945-3

Preface

The *Foreign Relations of the United States* series presents the official documentary historical record of major foreign policy decisions and significant diplomatic activity of the United States Government. The series documents the facts and events that contributed to the formulation of policies and includes evidence of supporting and alternative views to the policy positions ultimately adopted.

The Historian of the Department of State is charged with the responsibility for the preparation of the *Foreign Relations* series. The staff of the Office of the Historian, Bureau of Public Affairs, plans, researches, compiles, and edits the volumes in the series. This documentary editing proceeds in full accord with the generally accepted standards of historical scholarship. Official regulations codifying specific standards for the selection and editing of documents for the series were first promulgated by Secretary of State Frank B. Kellogg on March 26, 1925. These regulations, with minor modifications, guided the series through 1991.

A new statutory charter for the preparation of the series was established by Public Law 102–138, the Foreign Relations Authorization Act, Fiscal Years 1992 and 1993, which was signed by President George Bush on October 28, 1991. Section 198 of P.L. 102–138 added a new Title IV to the Department of State's Basic Authorities Act of 1956 (22 USC 4351, *et seq.*).

The statute requires that the *Foreign Relations* series be a thorough, accurate, and reliable record of major United States foreign policy decisions and significant United States diplomatic activity. The volumes of the series should include all records needed to provide comprehensive documentation of major foreign policy decisions and actions of the United States Government. The statute also confirms the editing principles established by Secretary Kellogg: the *Foreign Relations* series is guided by the principles of historical objectivity and accuracy; records should not be altered or deletions made without indicating in the published text that a deletion has been made; the published record should omit no facts that were of major importance in reaching a decision; and nothing should be omitted for the purposes of concealing a defect in policy. The statute also requires that the *Foreign Relations* series be published not more than 30 years after the events recorded. The editor is convinced that this volume, which was compiled in 1994–1996, meets all regulatory, statutory, and scholarly standards of selection and editing.

Structure and Scope of the Foreign Relations Series

This volume is part of a subseries of volumes of the *Foreign Relations* series that documents the most important issues in the foreign policy of the 5 years (1964–1968) of the administration of Lyndon B. Johnson. The subseries presents in 34 volumes a documentary record of major foreign policy decisions and actions of President Johnson's administration. This volume documents U.S. policy toward India, Pakistan, and Afghanistan.

Principles of Document Selection for the Foreign Relations Series

In preparing each volume of the *Foreign Relations* series, the editors are guided by some general principles for the selection of documents. Each editor, in consultation with the General Editor and other senior editors, determines the particular issues and topics to be documented either in detail, in brief, or in summary.

The following general selection criteria are used in preparing volumes in the *Foreign Relations* series. Individual compiler-editors vary these criteria in accordance with the particular issues and the available documentation. The editors also apply these selection criteria in accordance with their own interpretation of the generally accepted standards of scholarship. In selecting documentation for publication, the editors gave priority to unpublished classified records, rather than previously published records (which are accounted for in appropriate bibliographical notes).

Selection Criteria (in general order of priority):

1. Major foreign affairs commitments made on behalf of the United States to other governments, including those that define or identify the principal foreign affairs interests of the United States;

2. Major foreign affairs issues and activities, including dissenting or alternative opinions to the process ultimately adopted, undertaken on behalf of the United States by government officials and representatives in all agencies in the foreign affairs community;

3. The decisions, discussions, actions, and considerations of the President, as the official constitutionally responsible for the direction of foreign policy, including important information that attended Presidential decisions;

4. The discussions and actions of the National Security Council, the Cabinet, and special Presidential policy groups, including the policy options brought before these bodies or their individual members;

5. The policy options adopted by or considered by the Secretary of State and the most important actions taken to implement Presidential decisions or policies;

6. Diplomatic negotiations and conferences, official correspondence, and other exchanges between U.S. representatives and those of other governments that demonstrate the main lines of policy implementation on major issues;

7. The main policy lines of intelligence activities if they constituted major aspects of U.S. foreign policy toward a nation or region or if they provided key information in the formulation of major U.S. policies;

8. The role of the Congress in the preparation and execution of particular foreign policies or foreign affairs actions;

9. Economic aspects of foreign policy;

10. The main policy lines of U.S. military and economic assistance as well as other types of assistance;

11. The political-military recommendations, decisions, and activities of the military establishment and major regional military commands as they bear upon the formulation or execution of major U.S. foreign policies;

12. Diplomatic appointments that reflect major policies or affect policy changes.

Sources for the Foreign Relations Series

The *Foreign Relations* statute requires that the published record in the *Foreign Relations* series include all records needed to provide comprehensive documentation on major U.S. foreign policy decisions and significant U.S. diplomatic activity. It further requires that government agencies, departments, and other entities of the U.S. Government engaged in foreign policy formulation, execution, or support cooperate with the Department of State Historian by providing full and complete access to records pertinent to foreign policy decisions and actions and by providing copies of selected records. Many of the sources consulted in the preparation of this volume have been declassified and are available for review at the National Archives and Records Administration. The declassification review and opening for public review of all Department of State records no later than 30 years after the events is mandated by the *Foreign Relations* statute. The Department of State and other record sources used in the volume are described in detail in the section on Sources below.

Focus of Research and Principles of Selection for Foreign Relations, 1964–1968, Volume XXV

The editors of the volume sought to present documentation illuminating responsibility for major foreign policy decisions in the U.S. Government, with emphasis on the President and his advisers. The documents include memoranda and records of discussions that set forth policy issues and options and show decisions or actions taken. The emphasis is on the development of U.S. policy and on major aspects and repercussions of its execution rather than on the details of policy execution.

Major topics covered in this volume include: 1) U.S. military assistance to India and Pakistan; 2) U.S. efforts to counter Chinese influence in Pakistan and Soviet influence in India; 3) the U.S. reaction to the crises in the Rann of Kutch and Kashmir and the hostilities between India and Pakistan in 1965; 4) the U.S. reaction to the food crisis on the subcontinent; 5) the U.S. response to the decision by Pakistan not to renew the agreement with the United States governing facilities at Peshawar; and 6) U.S. efforts in Afghanistan to use limited economic assistance to promote economic development and to limit Soviet influence.

Lyndon Johnson's personal involvement in the making of foreign policy decisions relating to South Asia was second only to his involvement in decisions relating to the fighting in Southeast Asia. Johnson's involvement is particularly evident during the 1965 crises over Kashmir and the Rann of Kutch and in the U.S. response to the threat of famine in India in 1965–1967. The editors sought to document the President's role as far as possible.

Editorial Methodology

The documents are presented chronologically according to Washington time or, in the case of conferences, in the order of individual meetings. Memoranda of conversation are placed according to the time and date of the conversation, rather than the date the memorandum was drafted.

Editorial treatment of the documents published in the *Foreign Relations* series follows Office style guidelines, supplemented by guidance from the General Editor and the chief technical editor. The source text is reproduced as exactly as possible, including marginalia or other notations, which are described in the footnotes. Texts are transcribed and printed according to accepted conventions for the publication of historical documents in the limitations of modern typography. A heading has been supplied by the editors for each document included in the volume. Spelling, capitalization, and punctuation are retained as found in the source text, except that obvious typographical errors are silently corrected. Other mistakes and omissions in the source text are corrected by bracketed insertions: a correction is set in italic type; an addition in roman type. Words or phrases underlined in the source text are printed in italics. Abbreviations and contractions are preserved as found in the source text, and a list of abbreviations is included in the front matter of each volume.

Bracketed insertions are also used to indicate omitted text that deals with an unrelated subject (in roman type) or that remains classified after declassification review (in italic type). The amount of material not declassified has been noted by indicating the number of lines or pages of source text that were omitted. Entire documents withheld for declassification purposes have been accounted for and are listed by headings, source notes, and number of pages not declassified in their chronological place. The amount of material omitted from the selected documents because it was unrelated to the subject of the volume, however, has not been delineated. All brackets that appear in the source text are so identified by footnotes.

The first footnote to each document indicates the document's source, original classification, distribution, and drafting information. This note also provides the background of important documents and policies and indicates whether the President or his major policy advisers read the document. Every effort has been made to determine if a document has been previously published, and, if so, this information has been included in the source footnote.

Editorial notes and additional annotation summarize pertinent material not printed in the volume, indicate the location of additional documentary sources, provide references to important related documents printed in other volumes, describe key events, and provide summaries of and citations to public statements that supplement and elucidate the printed documents. Information derived from memoirs and other first-hand accounts has been used when appropriate to supplement or explicate the official record.

Advisory Committee on Historical Diplomatic Documentation

The Advisory Committee on Historical Diplomatic Documentation, established under the *Foreign Relations* statute, reviews records, advises, and makes recommendations concerning the *Foreign Relations* series. The Advisory Committee monitors the overall compilation and editorial process of the series and advises on all aspects of the preparation and declassification of the series. Although the Advisory Committee does not attempt to review the contents of individual volumes in the series, it does monitor the overall process and makes recommendations on particular problems that come to its attention.

The Advisory Committee has not reviewed this volume.

Declassification Review

The Information Response Branch of the Office of IRM Programs and Services, Bureau of Administration, Department of State, conducted the declassification review of the documents published in this volume. The review was conducted in accordance with the standards set forth in Executive Order 12958 on Classified National Security Information and applicable laws.

Under Executive Order 12958, specific information may be exempt from automatic declassification after 25 years if its release could be expected to:

1) reveal the identity of a confidential human source, or reveal information about the application of an intelligence source or method,

or reveal the identity of a human intelligence source when the unauthorized disclosure of that source would clearly and demonstrably damage the national security interests of the United States;

2) reveal information that would assist in the development or use of weapons of mass destruction;

3) reveal information that would impair U.S. cryptologic systems or activities;

4) reveal information that would impair the application of state of the art technology within the U.S. weapon system;

5) reveal actual U.S. military war plans that remain in effect;

6) reveal information that would seriously and demonstrably impair relations between the United States and a foreign government, or seriously and demonstrably undermine ongoing diplomatic activities of the United States;

7) reveal information that would clearly and demonstrably impair the current ability of U.S. Government officials to protect the President, Vice President, and other officials for whom protection services, in the interest of national security, are authorized;

8) reveal information that would seriously and demonstrably impair current national security emergency preparedness plans; or

9) violate a statute, treaty, or international agreement.

The principle guiding declassification review is to release all information, subject only to the current requirements of national security as embodied in law and regulation. Declassification decisions entailed concurrence of the appropriate geographic and functional bureaus in the Department of State, other concerned agencies of the U.S. Government, and the appropriate foreign governments regarding specific documents of those governments.

The final declassification review of this volume, which began in 1996 and was completed in 1999, resulted in the decision to withhold about .8 percent of the documentation proposed for publication; 5 documents were denied in full. The decision on two intelligence issues was appealed to a High-Level Panel consisting of senior representatives from the Department of State, the National Security Council, and the Central Intelligence Agency, established in 1998 to determine whether or not a covert activity could be acknowledged by the United States. The Panel arrived at a determination to release additional information on one issue and to approve an issue statement (Document 77) on the other.

The Office of the Historian is confident, on the basis of the research conducted in preparing this volume and as a result of the declassification review process described above, that the documentation and editorial notes presented here provide an accurate account of U.S. policy toward South Asia during the 1964–1968 period.

Acknowledgments

The editor wishes to acknowledge the assistance of officials at the Lyndon B. Johnson Library of the National Archives and Records Administration, especially Regina Greenwell, and Charlaine Burgess, who provided key research assistance. The editor also wishes to acknowledge the assistance of historians at the Central Intelligence Agency.

Louis J. Smith collected documentation for the compilation on South Asia and selected and edited it, under the supervision of Harriet Dashiell Schwar and the general supervision of former General Editor Glenn W. LaFantasie and current General Editor David S. Patterson. Gabrielle Mallon prepared the compilation on Afghanistan, as well as the lists of names, sources, and abbreviations. Vicki E. Futscher and Rita M. Baker did the copy and technical editing, and Susan C. Weetman coordinated the final declassification review. Juniee Oneida prepared the index.

William Slany
The Historian
Bureau of Public Affairs

June 2000

Johnson Administration Volumes

Following is a list of the volumes in the *Foreign Relations* series for the administration of President Lyndon B. Johnson. The titles of individual volumes may change. The year of publication is in parentheses after the title.

I	Vietnam, 1964 (1992)
II	Vietnam, January–June 1965 (1996)
III	Vietnam, July–December 1965 (1996)
IV	Vietnam, 1966 (1998)
V	Vietnam, 1967
VI	Vietnam, January–August 1968
VII	Vietnam, September 1968–January 1969
VIII	International Monetary and Trade Policy (1998)
IX	International Development and Economic Defense Policy; Commodities (1997)
X	National Security Policy
XI	Arms Control and Disarmament (1997)
XII	Western Europe
XIII	Western Europe Region (1995)
XIV	Soviet Union
XV	Germany and Berlin (1999)
XVI	Cyprus; Greece; Turkey (2000)
XVII	Eastern Europe; Austria; Finland (1996)
XVIII	Arab-Israeli Dispute, 1964–1967 (2000)
XIX	Six-Day War
XX	Arab-Israeli Dispute, 1967–1968
XXI	Near East Region; Arabian Peninsula (2000)
XXII	Iran (1999)
XXIII	Congo
XXIV	Africa (1999)
XXV	South Asia (2000)
XXVI	Indonesia; Malaysia-Singapore; Philippines
XXVII	Mainland Southeast Asia; Regional Affairs (2000)
XXVIII	Laos (1998)
XXIX	Part 1, Korea (2000)
XXIX	Part 2, Japan
XXX	China (1998)
XXXI	South and Central America; Mexico
XXXII	Dominican Crisis; Cuba; Caribbean
XXXIII	Organization of Foreign Policy; United Nations
XXXIV	Energy Diplomacy and Global Issues (1999)

Contents

Sources

The editors of the *Foreign Relations* series have complete access to all the retired records and papers of the Department of State: the central files of the Department; the special decentralized files ("lot files") of the Department at the bureau, office, and division levels; the files of the Department's Executive Secretariat, which contain the records of international conferences and high-level official visits, correspondence with foreign leaders by the President and Secretary of State, and memoranda of conversations between the President and Secretary of State and foreign officials; and the files of overseas diplomatic posts. All the Department's indexed central files for these years have been permanently transferred to the National Archives and Records Administration (Archives II) at College Park, Maryland. Many of the Department's decentralized office (or lot) files covering this period, which the National Archives deems worthy of permanent retention, have been transferred or are in the process of being transferred from the Department's custody to Archives II.

The editors of the *Foreign Relations* series also have full access to the papers of President Johnson and other White House foreign policy records. Presidential papers maintained and preserved at the Presidential libraries include some of the most significant foreign affairs-related documentation from the Department of State and other Federal agencies including the National Security Council, the Central Intelligence Agency, the Department of Defense, and the Joint Chiefs of Staff.

Department of State historians also have access to records of the Department of Defense, particularly the records of the Joint Chiefs of Staff and the Secretaries of Defense and their major assistants.

In preparing this volume, the editor made extensive use of Presidential papers and other White House records at the Lyndon B. Johnson Library, which proved the richest source of documentation on President Johnson's role in the South Asia region. Within the National Security File, the Country Files, the Head of State Correspondence Files, the file of Memos to the President, and the files of McGeorge Bundy, Robert Komer, Walt Rostow, and Harold Saunders were particularly valuable. The President's Office file within the White House Central File is similarly valuable. The National Security Council history on the food crisis on the subcontinent, and the supporting collection of documents, prepared by Harold Saunders, which is within the National Security File, is uniquely valuable for the role of President Johnson and his principal advisers, such as Secretary of Agriculture Orville Freeman.

Thanks to the leadership of the Johnson Library, the Department of State historians had full access to the audiotapes of President Johnson's telephone conversations. These audiotapes include substantial numbers of telephone conversations between President Johnson and Secretary of State Rusk, Secretary of Defense McNamara, the President's Special Assistant for National Security Affairs McGeorge Bundy, and key members of Congress. The editor of this volume found these perhaps the most valuable collection at the Johnson Library for the purpose of illuminating the role of President Johnson and his principal advisers. The tape recordings were especially important in documenting President Johnson's outlook and role in managing the food crisis. Although the transcripts give the substance of the conversations, readers are urged to consult the recordings for a full appreciation of those dimensions that cannot be captured fully in a transcription, such as the speakers' inflections and emphases that may convey nuances of meaning.

Second in importance to the records at the Johnson Library were the records of the Department of State. The central files of the Department of State provide rich detail on the crises that developed in 1965 over the Rann of Kutch and Kashmir. They are augmented in this regard by the lot files of the Department and by the files of the Secretary of Defense and the Assistant Secretary of Defense for International Security Affairs.

The Central Intelligence Agency provides the Department of State historians access to intelligence documents from records in its custody and at the Presidential libraries. This access is arranged and facilitated by the CIA's History Staff, part of the Center for the Study of Intelligence, pursuant to a May 1992 memorandum of understanding.

The editor included a selection of intelligence estimates and analyses seen by high-level policymakers, especially those that were made available to President Johnson. Among the intelligence records reviewed for the volume were those in country and intelligence files at the Johnson Library, the files of the Directors of Central Intelligence, especially John McCone, CIA intelligence reports and summaries, retired files of the Department of State's Bureau of Intelligence and Research containing National Intelligence Estimates, and the INR Historical Files.

Almost all of this documentation has been made available for use in the *Foreign Relations* series thanks to the consent of the agencies mentioned, the assistance of their staffs, and the cooperation and support of the National Archives and Records Administration.

The following list identifies the particular files and collections used in the preparation of this volume. The declassification and transfer to the National Archives of the Department of State records is in process, and many of those records are already available for public review at the National Archives. The declassification review of other records is going forward in accordance with the provisions of Executive Order 12958, under which all records over 25 years old, except file series exemptions requested by agencies and approved by the President, should be reviewed for declassification by 2002.

Unpublished Sources

Department of State

Central Files. See National Archives and Records Administration below.

Lot Files. These files have been transferred or will be transferred to the National Archives and Records Administration at College Park, Maryland, Record Group 59.

INR/IL Historical Files

Files of the Office of Intelligence Coordination, containing records from the 1940s through the 1970s, maintained by the Office of Intelligence Liaison, Bureau of Intelligence and Research.

NEA Files: Lot 71 D 79

Subject files of the Assistant Secretary of State for Near Eastern and South Asian Affairs, 1967–1969.

NEA/INC Files: Lot 71 D 174

India economic subject files for 1967, maintained by the Office of India, Nepal, and Ceylon Affairs, Bureau of Near Eastern and South Asian Affairs.

NEA/INC Files: Lot 72 D 132

India economic subject files for 1968, maintained by the Office of India, Nepal, and Ceylon Affairs, Bureau of Near Eastern and South Asian Affairs.

NEA/INC Files: Lot 73 D 24

India political subject files for 1968, maintained by the Office of India, Nepal, and Ceylon Affairs, Bureau of Near Eastern and South Asian Affairs.

NEA/INS Files: Lot 73 D 349

India political files for 1945–1970, maintained by the Office of India, Nepal, and Sri Lanka Affairs, Bureau of Near Eastern and South Asian Affairs.

NEA/INS Files: Lot 76 D 30

India political subject files for 1968 and 1971, maintained by the Office of India, Nepal, and Sri Lanka Affairs, Bureau of Near Eastern and South Asian Affairs.

NEA/INS Files: Lot 78 D 60

NEA/INS Country Director's files for 1963–1974, maintained by the Bureau of Near Eastern and South Asian Affairs.

NEA/PAB Files: Lot 74 D 145

Afghanistan political and economic subject files for 1967 and 1969, maintained by the Office of Pakistan, Afghanistan and Bangladesh Affairs, Bureau of Near Eastern and South Asian Affairs.

NEA/PAB Files: Lot 75 D 87

Pakistan defense subject files for 1967–1969, maintained by the Office of Pakistan, Afghanistan, and Bangladesh Affairs, Bureau of Near Eastern and South Asian Affairs.

NEA/PAB Files: Lot 75 D 129

Afghanistan political subject files for 1964–1968, maintained by the Office of Pakistan, Afghanistan, and Bangladesh Affairs, Bureau of Near Eastern and South Asian Affairs.

NEA/PAB Files: Lot 78 D 186

Pakistan political subject files for 1961–1967, maintained by the Office of Pakistan, Afghanistan, and Bangladesh Affairs, Bureau of Near Eastern and South Asian Affairs.

NEA/PAF Files: Lot 71 D 386

Pakistan political subject files for 1967, maintained by the Office of Pakistan and Afghanistan Affairs, Bureau of Near Eastern and South Asian Affairs.

NEA/PAF Files: Lot 72 D 71

Pakistan political subject files for 1968, maintained by the Office of Pakistan and Afghanistan Affairs, Bureau of Near Eastern and South Asian Affairs.

National Archives and Records Administration, College Park, MD

Record Group 59, Records of the Department of State

Central Files

AGR 1 INDIA: general agriculture policy and plans, India
AGR 12 INDIA: crop production and consumption, India
AGR 12 PAK: crop production and consumption, Pakistan
AID 9 INDIA: loans for economic development, India
AID 9 PAK: loans for economic development, Pakistan
AID (IBRD) 9 INDIA: IBRD economic development loans to India
AID (US) INDIA: general policy, U.S. aid to India
AID (US) PAK: general policy, U.S. aid to Pakistan
AID (US) 1 PAK: general policy, plans, coordination, U.S. aid to Pakistan
AID (US) 5: U.S. aid laws and regulations
AID (US) 8 AFG: U.S. grants and technical assistance to Afghanistan
AID (US) 9 AFG: U.S. loans for economic development, Afghanistan
AID (US) 9 PAK: U.S. loans for economic development, Pakistan
AID (US) 15 AFG: PL 480, Food for Peace Programs, Afghanistan
AID (US) 15 INDIA: PL 480, Food for Peace Programs, India
AID (US) 15 PAK: PL 480, Food for Peace Programs, Pakistan
AID (US) 15–4 INDIA: PL 480 Agreements, India
AID (US) 15–8 AFG: PL 480, Title I commodity Sales, Afghanistan
AID (US) 15–8 INDIA: PL 480, Title I commodity sales, India
AID (US) 15–8 PAK: PL 480, Title I commodity sales, Pakistan
AID (US) AFG: general policy, U.S. aid to Afghanistan
DEF 1 INDIA: defense policy, India
DEF 1 PAK: defense policy, Pakistan
DEF 1 PAK–US: defense policy, Pakistan–U.S.
DEF 1–1 INDIA–US: contingency planning, India–US
DEF 12 CHEROKEE; exclusive communications channel between the
DEF 12 INDIA: armaments, India
DEF 12 PAK: armaments, Pakistan
DEF 12–1 CHICOM: research and development, Communist China
DEF 12–1 INDIA: research and development, India
DEF 12–5 INDIA: procurement and sale of armaments, India
DEF 12–5 PAK: procurement and sale of armaments, Pakistan
DEF 15 PAK–US: bases and installations, Pakistan–U.S.
DEF 15–1 PAK: bases and installations policy and plans, Pakistan

DEF 15–10 PAK–US: establishment, construction, and termination of bases and installations, Pakistan–U.S.

DEF 15–4 PAK–US: bases and installations agreements and leases, Pakistan–U.S.

DEF 18 UN: arms control and disarmament, UN

DEF 18–8 INDIA: testing and detection of nuclear explosions, India

DEF 18–8 PAK: testing and detection of nuclear explosions, Pakistan

DEF 18–8 US: testing and detection of nuclear explosions, U.S.

DEF 19 US–INDIA: military assistance, U.S.–India

DEF 19 US–PAK: military assistance, U.S.–Pakistan

DEF 19–3 INDIA: defense organizations and conferences, India

DEF 19–3 US–INDIA: defense organizations and conferences, U.S.–India

DEF 19–3 US–PAK: defense organizations and conferences, U.S.–Pakistan

DEF 19–4 US–INDIA: military assistance agreements, U.S.–India

DEF 19–6 USSR: military assistance supplied by the U.S.S.R.

DEF 19–6 USSR–INDIA: U.S.S.R. military assistance to India

DEF 19–6 USSR–PAK: U.S.S.R. military assistance to Pakistan

DEF 19–8 BEL–PAK: Belgian military assistance to Pakistan

DEF 19–8 US–BEL: U.S. military assistance to Belgium

DEF 19–8 US–GERW: U.S. military assistance to West Germany

DEF 19–8 US–INDIA: defense equipment and supplies, U.S.–India

DEF 19–8 US–IRAN: defense equipment and supplies, U.S.–Iran

DEF 19–8 US–PAK: defense equipment and supplies, U.S.–Pakistan

E 5 AFG/FIVE YEAR PLAN: economic development, Afghanistan

E 8–1 INDIA: prices, cost of living, India

FN 9 PAK–US: foreign investment, Pakistan–U.S.

FSE 13 INDIA: nuclear power, reactors, India

IT 7–16 AFG: highway and transportation network, Afghanistan

LEG 7 POAG: legislative and legal affairs, visits by Congressman Poage

ORG 7 AGR: organization and administration, Agriculture visits

ORG 7 JCS: organization and administration, JCS visits

ORG 7 NEA: organization and administration, NEA visits

ORG CIA: organization and administration, CIA

POL AFG–US: political affairs and relations, Afghanistan–US

POL INDIA–PAK: political affairs and relations, India–Pakistan

POL INDIA–US: political affairs and relations, India–U.S.

POL PAK: political affairs and relations, Pakistan

POL PAK–US: political affairs and relations, Pakistan–US

POL US–USSR: political affairs and relations, U.S.–U.S.S.R. rivers and seaways, Afghanistan–Iran–Helmand Valley

POL 1 AFG: general policy and background, Afghanistan

POL 1 AFG–US: general policy, Afghanistan–US

POL 1 INDIA–PAK: general policy, India–Pakistan

POL 1 INDIA–US: general policy, India–U.S.

POL 1 INDIA–USSR: general policy, India–U.S.S.R.

POL 1 PAK: general policy and background, Pakistan

POL 2 AFG: general reports and statistics, Afghanistan

POL 2 ASIA SE: general reports and statistics, Southeast Asia

POL 2 ASIA: general reports and statistics, Asia

POL 2 INDIA: general reports and statistics, India

POL 2 PAK: general reports and statistics, Pakistan

POL 7 AFG: visits, meetings with Afghan leaders

POL 7 CHICOM: visits, meetings with Chinese Communist leaders

POL 7 INDIA: visits, meetings with Indian leaders

POL 7 PAK: visits, meetings with Pakistani leaders

POL 7 PAK–US: visits, meetings, Pakistani–U.S. leaders
POL 7 US/FREEMAN: visits, meetings of Orville L. Freeman
POL 7 US/HARRIMAN: visits, meetings of W. Averell Harriman
POL 7 US/HUMPHREY: visits, meetings of Vice President Humphrey
POL 7 US/JOHNSON: visits, meetings of President Lyndon B. Johnson
POL 7 US/ROSTOW: visits, meetings of Eugene V. Rostow
POL 7 US/SHRIVER: visits, meetings of W. Sargent Shriver
POL 7 USSR: visits, meetings with Soviet leaders
POL 10 INDIA: colonialism, imperialism, India
POL 12–5 PAK: political parties, laws and statutes, Pakistan
POL 15–1 AFG: Afghanistan Head of State
POL 15–1 INDIA: Indian head of state
POL 15–1 PAK: Pakistan head of state
POL 17 INDIA–PAK: diplomatic and consular representation, India–Pakistan
POL 17–4 US: ceremonial and social affairs, U.S.
POL 18 INDIA: provincial, municipal and state government, India
POL 23–8 INDIA: demonstrations, riots, protests, India
POL 23–8 PAK: demonstrations, riots, protests, Pakistan
POL 27 CHICOM–INDIA: military operations, Chinese Communists–India
POL 27 INDIA–PAK: military operations, India–Pakistan
POL 27 VIET S: military operations, South Vietnam
POL 27–14 INDIA–PAK: truce, cease-fire, armistice, India–Pakistan
POL 27–14 VIET: truce, cease-fire, armistice, Vietnam
POL 27–3 VIET S: use of foreign country forces, South Vietnam
POL 28–8 INDIA: occupied areas
POL 29 INDIA: political prisoners, India
POL 31–1 INDIA–PAK: air disputes and violations, India–Pakistan
POL 32–1 INDIA/PAK/UN: territory and boundary disputes, India, Pakistan/U.N
POL 32–1 INDIA–PAK: India–Pakistan border conflicts
POL 33–1 AFG–IRAN/HELMAND: waters, boundaries, international
SCI 7 US: science and technology, visits and missions, U.S. Secretary of State and an Ambassador
SOC 10 INDIA: disasters and disaster relief, India

Lot Files

Ball Files: Lot 74 D 272

Files of Under Secretary of State George Ball, 1961–1966.

Conference Files: Lot 66 D 110

Records of official visits by heads of government and foreign ministers to the United States and international conferences attended by the President, the Secretary of State, and other U.S. officials, 1961–1964, maintained by the Executive Secretariat.

Conference Files: Lot 66 D 347

Records of official visits by heads of government and foreign ministers to the United States, and international conferences attended by the President, Vice President, or Secretary of State for 1965, maintained by the Executive Secretariat.

Conference Files: Lot 67 D 305

Collection of documentation on visits to the United States by ranking foreign officials and on major conferences attended by the Secretary of State, January–October 8, 1966, maintained by the Executive Secretariat.

Conference Files: Lot 67 D 587

Records of official visits, October 1966–May 10, 1967, maintained by the Executive Secretariat.

Conference Files: Lot 69 D 182

Collection of documentation on visits to the United States by ranking foreign officials and on major conferences attended by the Secretary of State, January–November 1968, maintained by the Executive Secretariat.

Harriman Files: Lot 71 D 461

Files of Ambassador at Large W. Averell Harriman for 1967 and 1968, maintained by the Executive Secretariat.

Katzenbach Files: Lot 74 D 271

Files of Under Secretary of State Nicholas deB. Katzenbach, September 1966–January 1969, maintained by the Executive Secretariat.

NEA Files: Lot 67 D 410

Subject files of the Assistant Secretary of State for Near Eastern and South Asian Affairs for 1965.

NEA/INC Files: Lot 66 D 415

Miscellaneous Kashmir files, maintained by the Office of India, Nepal, and Ceylon Affairs, Bureau of Near Eastern and South Asian Affairs.

NEA/INC Files: Lot 68 D 49

India economic subject files for 1964, maintained by the Office of India, Nepal, and Ceylon Affairs, Bureau of Near Eastern and South Asian Affairs

NEA/INC Files: Lot 68 D 207

India political subject files for 1964, maintained by the Office of India, Nepal, and Ceylon Affairs, Bureau of Near Eastern and South Asian Affairs.

NEA/INC Files: Lot 69 D 29

India economic subject files for 1965, maintained by the Office of India, Nepal, and Ceylon Affairs, Bureau of Near Eastern and South Asian Affairs.

NEA/INC Files: Lot 69 D 52

India political subject files for 1965, maintained by the Office of India, Nepal, and Ceylon Affairs, Bureau of Near Eastern and South Asian Affairs.

NEA/INC Files: Lot 69 D 483

India economic subject files for 1966, maintained by the Office of India, Nepal, and Ceylon Affairs, Bureau of Near Eastern and South Asian Affairs.

NEA/INC Files: Lot 70 D 314

India political subject files for 1966, maintained by the Office of India, Nepal, and Ceylon Affairs, Bureau of Near Eastern and South Asian Affairs.

NEA/INC Files: Lot 70 D 316

India political subject files for 1967, maintained by the Office of India, Nepal, and Ceylon Affairs, Bureau of Near Eastern and South Asian Affairs.

NEA/RA Files: Lot 67 D 210

Political-military subject files for 1963–1965, maintained by the Office of Regional Affairs, Bureau of Near Eastern and South Asian Affairs.

Presidential Correspondence: Lot 66 D 294

Exchanges of correspondence between the President and Secretary of State and heads of foreign governments and foreign ministers, 1961–1965, maintained by the Executive Secretariat.

Presidential Correspondence: Lot 66 D 476

Correspondence of the President with various heads of state, 1961–1966, maintained by the Executive Secretariat.

Presidential Correspondence: Lot 67 D 262

Official exchanges of correspondence of the President and the Secretary of State with various heads of state and other foreign officials for 1966, maintained by the Executive Secretariat.

Presidential Memoranda of Conversation: Lot 66 D 149

Memoranda of conversations between the President and foreign visitors, 1956–1964, maintained by the Executive Secretariat.

Rusk Files: Lot 72 D 192

Files of Secretary of State Dean Rusk, 1961–1969, including texts of speeches and public statements, miscellaneous correspondence files, White House correspondence, chronological files, and memoranda of telephone conversations.

S/S–NSC Files: Lot 70 D 265

Master set of papers pertaining to National Security Council meetings, including policy papers, position papers, administrative documents, but not minutes of the meetings themselves, for 1961–1966, maintained by the Executive Secretariat.

S/S–NSC Files: Lot 72 D 316

Master file of National Security Action Memoranda (NSAMs), 1961–1968, maintained by the Executive Secretariat.

Central Intelligence Agency

Job 79–R01012A, ODDI Registry of NIE and SNIE Files
Job 80–B01285A, DCI (Helms) Files, Memos for the Record
Job 80–B01285A, DCI (McCone) Files, Memos for the Record
Job 77–0055R, DDO/NE Files

Washington National Records Center, Suitland, MD

Record Group 84, Records of Foreign Service Posts of the United States

Kabul Embassy Files: FRC 70 A 4844

Classified and unclassified files of the Embassy in Kabul for 1964–1965, formerly Lot 69 F 92.

Karachi Embassy Files: FRC 68 A 1814

> Classified files of the Embassy in Karachi for 1962–1964, formerly Lot 67 F 74.

Karachi Embassy Files: FRC 69 A 3876

> Classified files of the Embassy in Karachi for 1965, formerly Lot 68 F 100.

New Delhi Embassy Files: FRC 69 A 3876

> Classified and unclassified files of the Embassy in New Delhi for 1959–1965, formerly Lot 68 F 115.

Record Group 330, Records of the Office of the Secretary of Defense

OASD/ISA Files: FRC 68 A 306

> Secret and lower-classified general files of the Assistant Secretary of Defense for International Security Affairs, 1964.

OASD/ISA Files: FRC 70 A 3717

> Secret files of the Assistant Secretary of Defense for International Security Affairs, 1965.

OASD/ISA Files: FRC 70 A 5127

> Secret files of the Assistant Secretary of Defense for International Security Affairs, 1965.

OASD/ISA Files: FRC 70 A 6648

> Secret files of the Assistant Secretary of Defense for International Security Affairs, 1966.

OASD/ISA Files: FRC 72 A 1498

> Secret files of the Assistant Secretary of Defense for International Security Affairs, 1968.

OSD Files: FRC 69 A 7425

> Top Secret files of the Secretary of Defense, Deputy Assistant Secretary of Defense, and Special Assistants, 1964.

OSD Files: FRC 70 A 1266

> Secret files of the Secretary of Defense, Deputy Assistant Secretary of Defense, and Special Assistants, 1965.

OSD Files: FRC 70 A 4443

> Secret files of the Secretary of Defense, Deputy Assistant Secretary of Defense, and Special Assistants, 1966.

OSD Files: FRC 70 A 4662

> Top Secret files of the Secretary of Defense, the Deputy Assistant Secretary of Defense, and Special Assistants, 1966.

OSD Files: FRC 72 A 2468

> Secret files of the Secretary of Defense, Deputy Assistant Secretary of Defense, and Special Assistants, 1967.

OSD Files: FRC 73 A 1250
   Secret files of the Secretary of Defense, Deputy Assistant Secretary of Defense, and
   Special Assistants, 1968.

OSD Files: FRC 77–0075
   Memoranda of conversations between Secretary of Defense McNamara and Heads
   of State (other than NATO).

Lyndon B. Johnson Library, Austin, TX

Papers of President Lyndon B. Johnson

National Security File

   Country File
   Committee File
   Files of McGeorge Bundy
   Files of C.D. Clifton
   Files of Robert W. Komer
   Files of Walt W. Rostow
   Files of Harold H. Saunders
   Head of State Correspondence File
   Intelligence File
   Memos to the President
   Name File
   National Security Action Memorandums
   National Security Council Histories
   National Security Council Meetings File
   Special Head of State Correspondence File

Special Files
   Office of the President File
   President's Daily Diary
   Rusk Appointment Book
   Recordings and Transcripts of Telephone Conversations and Meetings
   Tom Johnson's Notes of Meetings

White House Central Files
   Confidential File
   Subject File

Other Personal Papers

George Ball Papers

Thomas Mann Papers

Published Sources

U.S. Government Documentary Collections

U.S. Department of State. Department of State *Bulletin*, 1964–1968 (Volumes LI–LIX). Washington: U.S. Government Printing Office, 1964–1968.

————. *American Foreign Policy: Current Documents, 1964, 1965, 1966, 1967.* Washington: U.S. Government Printing Office, 1967–1969.

U.S. National Archives and Records Administration. *Public Papers of the Presidents of the United States: Lyndon B. Johnson, 1963–64, 1965, 1966, 1967, 1968, 1968–69.* Washington: U.S. Government Printing Office, 1965–1970.

Memoirs

Ayub Khan, Mohammed. *Friends Not Masters.* London: Oxford University Press, 1967.

Ball, George. *The Past Has Another Pattern: Memoirs.* New York: W.W. Norton & Company, 1982.

Bhutto, Zulfikar Ali. *The Myth of Independence.* London: Oxford University Press, 1969.

Bowles, Chester. *Promises to Keep.* New York: Harper and Row, 1971.

Desai, Morarji. *The Story of My Life.* Volume II. New Delhi: Macmillan, 1974.

Gopal, Sarvepalli. *Jawaharlal Nehru.* Volume III. London: Jonathan Cape, 1984.

Johnson, Lyndon B. *The Vantage Point.* New York: Holt, Rinehart and Winston, 1971.

Rusk, Dean. *As I Saw It.* New York: Norton, 1990.

Abbreviations

ACDA, Arms Control and Disarmament Agency
ACU, Afghan Construction Unit
AEC, Atomic Energy Commission
AEDS, Atomic Energy Detection Station
AID, Agency for International Development
AID/A, Office of the Administrator, Agency for International Development
AID/NESA, Agency for International Development/Bureau for Near East and South Asia
Amb, Ambassador
APC, armored personnel carrier
ASA, Afghan Student Association
ASAP, as soon as possible

BNA, Office of British Commonwealth and Northern European Affairs, Bureau of European Affairs, Department of State
BOQ, Bachelor Officers Quarters
BuRec, Bureau of Reclamation (Afghanistan)

CA, circular airgram
CAAG, Civil Air Advisory Group
CAP, Civil Air Project
CARE, Cooperatives for American Relief Everywhere, Inc.
CAS, Controlled American Source
CCC, Commodity Credit Corporation
CENTO, Central Treaty Organization
CFL, Cease-Fire Line
CGUSAMC, Commanding General, U.S. Air Matériel Command
ChiCom, Chinese Communist(s)
CHMAAG, Chief, Military Assistance Advisory Group
CHUSMSMI, Chief, U.S. Military Supply Mission to India
CIA, Central Intelligence Agency
CIB, Central Intelligence Bureau (India)
CINCEUR, Commander in Chief, Europe
CINCMEAFSA, Commander in Chief, Middle East/South Asia and Africa South of the Sahara
CINCPAC, Commander in Chief, Pacific
CINCSTRIKE, Commander in Chief, Strike Command
CIR, Canada India Reactor
CJCS, Chairman, Joint Chiefs of Staff
COMSAT, Communications Satellite Corporation
CONUS, Continental United States
CRO, Commonwealth Relations Office (UK)
CT, Country Team
CUSASEC MAAGChief, U.S. Army Section, Military Advisory Group
CY, calendar year

DAO, Defense Attaché Office
DATT, Defense Attaché
DCM, Deputy Chief of Mission
DepSecDef, Deputy Secretary of Defense
Deptel, Department of State telegram

DGS, Director General of Security (India)
DIA, Defense Intelligence Agency
DOD, Department of Defense
DOD/ISA, Department of Defense, International Security Affairs

Embtel, Embassy telegram
ESSGA, Emergency Special Session of the General Assembly (United Nations)
EUR, Bureau of European Affairs, Department of State
Exdis, exclusive distribution (acronym indicating extremely limited distribution or dissemination)
EXIM, Export-Import Bank

FAO, Food and Agriculture Organization (UN)
FCI, Fertilizer Corporation of India
FE, Far East; Bureau of Far Eastern Affairs, Department of State
FinMin, Finance Minister
FonMin, Foreign Minister
FonOff, Foreign Office
FonSec, Foreign Secretary
FRC, Federal Records Center
FRG, Federal Republic of Germany
FY, fiscal year
FYI, for your information

G-2, Army Intelligence
GNP, Gross National Product
GOA, Government of Afghanistan
GOB, Government of Belgium
GOI, Government of India
GOJ, Government of Japan
GON, Government of Nigeria
GOP, Government of Pakistan
GOT, Government of Turkey
G/PM, Deputy Assistant Secretary of State for Politico-Military Affairs
GRC, Government of the Republic of China
GROMET, code name for Indian rain augmentation project initiated at the end of 1966

HICOM, High Commissioner
HIQ, Herat-Islam-Qala Road (Afghanistan)
HMG, Her Majesty's Government
HVA, Helmand Valley Authority

IAF, Indian Air Force
IB, Intelligence Bureau (India)
IBRD, International Bank for Reconstruction and Development (World Bank)
ICC, International Commodity Clearinghouse
IDA, International Development Association
IMF, International Monetary Fund
INR, Bureau of Intelligence and Research, Department of State
IO, Bureau of International Organization Affairs, Department of State
IRBM, Intermediate range ballistic missile
ISID, Indian equivalent of CIA

JCS, Joint Chiefs of Staff
JCSM, Joint Chiefs of Staff Memorandum

LDC, less developed countries
Limdis, Limited Distribution (acronym indicating very limited distribution or dissemination)
L/NEA, Assistant Legal Adviser for Near Eastern and South Asian Affairs, Department of State

M, Office of the Under Secretary of State for Economic Affairs
MAAG, Military Assistance Advisory Group
MAP, Military Assistance Program
MEA, Minister of External Affairs
MFA, Minister of Foreign Affairs
MIG, A.I. Mikoyan i M.I. Gurevich (Soviet fighter aircraft named for designers Mikoyan and Gurevich)
Min, Minister
MinAg, Minister of Agriculture
MinFin, Minister of Finance
MinInt, Minister of the Interior
MinPlan, Minister of Planning
MK, Morrison-Knudson, Inc.
MLF, multilateral force
MOD, Minister of Defense
MP, Member of Parliament; Madhya Pradesh, a state in India
MRBM, medium-range ballistic missile

NATO, North Atlantic Treaty Organization
NEA, Bureau of Near Eastern and South Asian Affairs, Department of State
NEA/INC, Office of India, Nepal, and Ceylon Affairs, Bureau of Near Eastern and South Asian Affairs, Department of State
NEA/NR, Office of Near Eastern, South Asian Regional Affairs, Bureau of Near Eastern and South Asian Affairs, Department of State
NEA/PAF, Office of Pakistan-Afghanistan Affairs, Bureau of Near Eastern and South Asian Affairs, Department of State
NEA/SOA, Office of South Asian Affairs, Bureau of Near Eastern and South Asian Affairs, Department of State
NIE, National Intelligence Estimate
Nodis, No dissemination or distribution (other than to persons indicated)
Noforn, no foreign dissemination (acronym indicating that the document may not be disseminated to any foreigner, either in the U.S. or overseas)
Notal, not received by all addressees
NPT, Nuclear Non-Proliferation Treaty
NSA, National Security Agency
NSAM, National Security Action Memorandum
NSC, National Security Council
NSCIG/NEA, National Security Council Interdepartmental Group for Near East and South Asia
NVN, North Vietnam
NYT, *New York Times*

OASD/ISA, Office of the Assistant Secretary of Defense for International Security Affairs
OAU, Organization of African Unity
ODDI, Office of the Directorate of Intelligence, Central Intelligence Agency

ODR, Office of the U.S. Defense Representative, India; succeeded the U.S. Military Supply Mission in 1967
OSD, Office of the Secretary of Defense

PA, Purchase Authorization
PAF, Pakistan Air Force
Pak, Pakistan; Pakistani
Pindi, abbreviated form of Rawalpindi
P.L., Public Law
PM, Prime Minister
POL, petroleum, oil, and lubricants
POLAD, Political Adviser
PriMin, Prime Minister

RCA, Radio Corporation of America
reftel, reference telegram
reps, representatives
RG, Record Group
RGA, Royal Government of Afghanistan

SAM, surface to air missiles
SC, Security Council (UN)
SEA, Southeast Asia; Office of Southeast Asian Affairs, Bureau of Far Eastern Affairs, Department of State
SEATO, Southeast Asia Treaty Organization
SecGen, Secretary-General (UN)
Secto, series indicator for telegrams from the Secretary of State to the Department of State
septel, separate telegram
SFRC, Senate Foreign Relations Committee
SIG, Senior Interdepartmental Group
SNIE, Special National Intelligence Estimate
SOA, Office of South Asian Affairs, Bureau of Near Eastern and South Asian Affairs, Department of State
SOV, Soviet(s); also, Office of Soviet Union Affairs, Bureau of European Affairs, Department of State
S/S, Executive Secretariat, Department of State
SVN, South Vietnam
SYG, Secretary-General (UN)

TD, Tashkent Declaration
Tosec, series indicator for telegrams from the Department of State to the Secretary of State
TTK, initials of T.T. Krishnamachari, Indian Minister of Economic and Defense Coordination

UAR, United Arab Republic
UK, United Kingdom
UN, United Nations
UNCTAD, United Nations Conference on Trade and Development
UNGA, United Nations General Assembly
UNIPOM, United Nations India-Pakistan Observation Mission
UNMOGIP, United Nations Military Observer Group for India and Pakistan
UNSC, United Nations Security Council
UP, Uttar Pradesh, a state in India
UPI, United Press International

USAF, United States Air Force
USDA, United States Department of Agriculture
USDel, United States Delegation
USG, United States Government
USIA, United States Information Agency
USIB, United States Intelligence Board
USIS, United States Information Service (overseas branches of USIA)
USMSMI, United States Military Supply Mission to India
USSR, Union of Soviet Socialist Republics
UST, United States Treaties and Other International Agreements
USUN, United States Mission to the United Nations
UW, unconventional warfare

VOA, Voice of America
VP, Vice President

WAPDA, Water and Power Development Authority of West Pakistan
WH, White House

Persons

Adams, General Paul D., Commander in Chief, Strike Command (CINCSTRIKE), until November 1966; also Commander in Chief, Middle East/South Asia and Africa South of the Sahara (CINCMEAFSA), until November 1966

Ahmed, Aziz, Foreign Secretary of Pakistan until June 1966

Ahmed, Ghulam, Pakistani Ambassador to the United States until September 1966

Ayub Khan, Field Marshal Mohammad, President of Pakistan and Minister of Defense

Ball, George W., Under Secretary of State until September 1966; Representative to the United Nations, June–September 1968

Battle, Lucius D., Ambassador to the United Arab Republic, September 1964–March 1967; Assistant Secretary of State for Near Eastern and South Asian Affairs, April 1967–September 1968

Bell, David E., Administrator of the Agency for International Development until June 1966

Bhabha, Dr. Homi J., Secretary of the Indian Department of Atomic Energy until January 1966

Bhagat, Bali Ram, Indian Minister of State for External Affairs from November 1967

Bhutto, Zulfikar Ali, Foreign Minister of Pakistan until June 1966

Bohlen, Charles E., Ambassador to France until February 1968; thereafter Deputy Under Secretary of State for Political Affairs

Bowles, Chester A., Ambassador to India

Buffum, William B., Director, Office of United Nations Political and Security Affairs, Bureau of International Organization Affairs, Department of State, until August 1965; Deputy Assistant Secretary of State for International Organization Affairs, September 1965–December 1966; thereafter Deputy Representative to the United Nations

Bundy, McGeorge, Special Assistant to the President for National Security Affairs until February 1966

Bunker, Ellsworth, Ambassador at Large, October 1966–March 1967; thereafter Ambassador to Vietnam

Butterfield, Alexander, Deputy Assistant to the President

Califano, Joseph, Special Assistant to the President from July 1965

Cameron, Turner C., Director, Office of South Asian Affairs, Bureau of Near Eastern and South Asian Affairs, Department of State, until July 1965

Cargo, William I., Deputy Chief of Mission in Pakistan until August 1967

Chadhury, General J.N., Chief of Staff of the Indian Army

Chagla, Mohammad Ali Currim, Indian Minister of Education, Scientific Research and Cultural Affairs, July 1964–November 1966; Minister of External Affairs, November 1966–September 1967

Chaudhuri, Sachindra Nath, Indian Minister of Finance, December 1965–March 1967

Chavan, Y.B. (Yashwantrao Balwantrao), Indian Minister of Defense, June 1964–November 1966; thereafter Minister of Home Affairs

Clifford, Clark M., lawyer and one of the "Wise Men" who served as unofficial advisers to President Johnson; Secretary of Defense from March 1968

Coon, Carleton S., Jr., Officer in Charge of India, Nepal, and Ceylon Affairs, Bureau of Near Eastern and South Asian Affairs, Department of State, September 1965–July 1968

Davies, Rodger P., Deputy Assistant Secretary of State for Near Eastern and South Asian Affairs from October 1965

Dayal, Rajeshwar, Foreign Secretary of the Indian Minister of External Affairs from 1967

Dean, Arthur H., lawyer and one of the "Wise Men" who served as unofficial advisers to President Johnson; served in this capacity after October 1965

Desai, Morarji Ranchhodji, Deputy Prime Minister and Finance Minister of India from March 1967

Dole, Robert J., Republican Congressman from Kansas

Ellender, Allen J., Democratic Senator from Louisiana

Eskildsen, Clarence, Deputy Administrator, Foreign Agricultural Service, Department of Agriculture

Etemadi, Nur Ahmad, Minister of Foreign Affairs of Afghanistan, November 1965–October 1967; thereafter Prime Minister

Farhadi, Abdul Ghafur Rawan, Secretary, Afghan Council of Ministers, and Director General for Political Affairs, Ministry of Foreign Affairs, from August 1964

Fowler, Henry H., Secretary of the Treasury, April 1965–December 1968

Freeman, Orville L., Secretary of Agriculture

Gandhi, Indira, Indian Minister of Information and Broadcasting from 1964 until January 1966; Prime Minister and Minister of Atomic Energy from January 1966; also Foreign Minister and Chairman of the Planning Commission from November 1967

Gaud, William S., Assistant Administrator, Bureau for Near East and South Asia, Agency for International Development, February 1964–August 1966; thereafter Administrator

Goldberg, Arthur J., Representative to the United Nations, July 1965–June 1968

Grant, James P., Deputy Assistant Secretary of State for Near Eastern and South Asian Affairs until September 1964

Hamilton, Edward K., Member of the National Security Council Staff, October 1965–December 1968

Handley, William J., Deputy Assistant Secretary of State for Near Eastern and South Asian Affairs from September 1964

Hare, Raymond A., Assistant Secretary of State for Near Eastern and South Asian Affairs, September 1965–November 1966

Harriman, W. Averell, Under Secretary of State for Political Affairs until March 1965; thereafter Ambassador at Large

Hart, Parker T., Ambassador to Saudi Arabia until May 1965; Ambassador to Turkey, October 1965–October 1968; thereafter Assistant Secretary of State for Near Eastern and South Asian Affairs

Heck, L. Douglas, Country Director for India, Ceylon, and Nepal–Maldive Affairs, Bureau of Near Eastern and South Asian Affairs, Department of State, October 1966–July 1968

Helms, Richard M., Deputy Director of Central Intelligence, April 1965–June 1966; thereafter Director

Hilaly, Agha, Pakistani Ambassador to the United States from October 1966

Hoopes, Townsend W., Deputy Assistant Secretary of Defense for International Security Affairs, 1965–1968

Hughes, Thomas L., Director of the Bureau of Intelligence and Research, Department of State

Humphrey, Hubert H., Vice President of the United States

Husain, M. Arshad, Pakistani High Commissioner in India until May 1968; thereafter Foreign Minister

Husain, Zakir, Vice President of India until May 1967; thereafter President

Jacobsen, Jake, Special Counsel to the President, 1965–1967
Jernegan, John D., Deputy Assistant Secretary of State for Near Eastern and South Asian Affairs until July 1965
Jha, Chandra Shekhar, Foreign Secretary of Indian Ministry of Foreign Affairs from February 1965
Jha, Lakshmi Kant, Secretary to the Indian Prime Minister, July 1964–July 1967; thereafter Governor of the Reserve Bank of India
Johnson, Major General Charles E., III, Chief, United States Military Supply Mission to India, from January 1965
Johnson, Lyndon B., President of the United States
Johnson, U. Alexis, Deputy Under Secretary of State for Political Affairs until July 1964; Deputy Ambassador to Vietnam, July 1964–September 1965; Deputy Under Secretary of State for Political Affairs, November 1965–October 1966; thereafter Ambassador to Japan
Johnson, W. Thomas, White House Deputy Press Secretary
Jones, Jim R., Assistant to the President, February 1965–January 1968; Deputy Special Assistant to the President, January–May 1968; Special Assistant to the President from May 1968; also from January 1968 served as President's Appointments Secretary
Jung, Nawab Ali Javar, Indian Ambassador to the United States from January 1968

Katzenbach, Nicholas deB., Deputy Attorney General until February 1965; Attorney General, February 1965–October 1966; thereafter Under Secretary of State
Khan, Admiral A.R., Pakistani Minister of Defense from October 1966
Khan, Air Marshal Asghar, Commander in Chief of the Pakistani Air Force until July 1965
Khan, Air Marshal Malik Nur, Commander in Chief of the Pakistani Air Force from July 1965
Kohler, Foy D., Deputy Under Secretary of State for Political Affairs, November 1966–December 1967
Komer, Robert W., Member of the National Security Council Staff until September 1965; Deputy Special Assistant to the President for National Security Affairs, October 1965–March 1966; Special Assistant to the President, March 1966–May 1967; appointed Ambassador to Turkey December 3, 1968
Krishnamachari, T.T. (Tiruvallur Thattai), Indian Minister of Finance, August 1963–December 1965
Krishna Menon, V.K. (Vengalil Krishnan), Indian political leader; former Minister of Defense; member of the Lok Sabha (Parliament) until 1967
Kuznetsov, Vasiliy V., First Deputy Minister of Foreign Affairs, Union of Soviet Socialist Republics

Laingen, L. Bruce, Officer in Charge of Pakistan–Afghanistan Affairs, Bureau of Near Eastern and South Asian Affairs, Department of State, September 1964–August 1967
Laise, Carol C., Director, Office of South Asian Affairs, Bureau of Near Eastern and South Asian Affairs, Department of State, August 1965–July 1966; Country Director for India, Ceylon, Nepal, and Maldive Islands, July–September 1966; thereafter Ambassador to Nepal
Lewis, John P., AID Director in New Delhi, India, from September 1964
Locke, Eugene M., Ambassador to Pakistan, June 1966–April 1967; Deputy Ambassador to Vietnam, May 1967–January 1968

Macomber, William B., Assistant Administrator for Near East and South Asia, Agency for International Development, February 1964–March 1967; thereafter Assistant Secretary of State for Congressional Relations

Maiwandwal, Mohammad Hashim, Prime Minister of Afghanistan, October 1965–October 1967

Majid, Abdul, Afghan Ambassador to the United States until January 1967

Malikyar, Abdullah, First Deputy Prime Minister of Afghanistan until February 1964; Minister of Finance until June 1964; Acting Prime Minister, February–June 1964; Afghan Ambassador to the United Kingdom, October 1964–March 1967; thereafter Ambassador to the United States

Mann, Thomas C., Under Secretary of State for Economic Affairs, March 1965–May 1966

McConaughy, Walter P., Jr., Ambassador to Pakistan until May 1966; thereafter Ambassador to China

McCone, John A., Director of Central Intelligence until April 1965

McGee, Gale, Democratic Senator from Wyoming

McNamara, Robert S., Secretary of Defense until February 1968; thereafter President of the International Bank for Reconstruction and Development (World Bank)

McNaughton, John T., Assistant Secretary of Defense for International Security Affairs, July 1964–July 1967

Mehta, Asoka, Indian Minister of Planning and Social Welfare until November 1967; thereafter Minister of Petroleum and Chemicals and Social Welfare

Miller, Jack R., Republican Senator from Iowa

Moyers, Bill D., Special Assistant to the President and Chief of Staff at the White House, October 1964–January 1967; also White House Press Secretary, July 1965–January 1967

Naas, Charles W., Pakistan Desk Officer, Bureau of Near Eastern and South Asian Affairs, Department of State, until July 1964

Nanda, Gulzarilal, Indian Minister of Home Affairs until November 1966; also Interim Prime Minister, May 27–June 9, 1964

Nehru, B.K. (Braj Kumar), Indian Ambassador to the United States until December 1967

Nehru, Jawaharlal, Prime Minister of India until his death on May 27, 1964

Neumann, Robert G., Ambassador to Afghanistan from February 1967

Nimmo, Lieutenant General Robert H., Chief Military Observer, United Nations Military Observer Group in India and Pakistan until his death in January 1966

Nitze, Paul H., Deputy Secretary of Defense from July 1967

Oehlert, Benjamin H., Jr., Ambassador to Pakistan from August 1967

Parthasarathi, Gopalaswami, Indian Permanent Representative to the United Nations

Pickard, Cyril, Superintending Under-Secretary, Asia and Atlantic Division, British Commonwealth Relations Office, until May 1966; thereafter British High Commissioner in Pakistan

Pirzada, Sharifuddin, Attorney General of Pakistan until July 1966; Foreign Minister, July 1966–May 1968; thereafter Attorney General

Poage, William R., Democratic Congressman from Texas

Raborn, Vice Admiral William F., Jr., Director of Central Intelligence, April 1965–June 1966

Radhakrishnan, Dr. Sarvepalli, President of India until May 1967

Ram, Jagjivan, Indian Minister of Labor, Employment, and Rehabilitation until March 1967; Minister of Food and Agriculture from March 1967

Rao, P.V.R., Indian Defense Secretary

Read, Benjamin H., Special Assistant to the Secretary of State and Executive Secretary of the Department of State

Rishtiya, Sayyid Mohammed Kasim, Afghan Minister of Press and Information until July 1964; First Deputy Prime Minister and Minister of Finance, July 1964–November 1965

Rockwell, Stuart W., Deputy Assistant Secretary of State for Near Eastern and South Asian Affairs from September 1966
Rostow, Eugene V., Under Secretary of State for Political Affairs from October 1966
Rostow, Walt W., Counselor of the Department of State and Chairman of the Policy Planning Council until March 1966; thereafter Special Assistant to the President
Rusk, Dean, Secretary of State

Sarabhai, Dr. V.A. (Vikram Ambalal), Chairman of India's Atomic Energy Commission, and Secretary to the Department of Atomic Energy from May 1966
Saunders, Harold H., Member of the National Security Council Staff
Scali, John A., Special Consultant to the President
Schneider, David T., Officer in Charge of India, Ceylon, and Nepal Affairs, Bureau of Near Eastern and South Asian Affairs, Department of State, until July 1965; Deputy Director, Office of South Asian Affairs, August 1965–August 1966; thereafter Deputy Chief of Mission in Pakistan
Schnittker, John A., Under Secretary of Agriculture, 1965–1968
Schultze, Charles L., Director, Bureau of the Budget, until January 1968
Shastri, Lal Bahadur, Indian Minister Without Portfolio until June 1964; Prime Minister, Minister of External Affairs, and Minister of Atomic Energy from June 1964 until his death on January 11, 1966
Shoaib, Mohammed, Pakistani Minister of Finance until September 1966; thereafter Vice President of the International Bank for Reconstruction and Development (World Bank)
Shriver, R. Sargent, Jr., Director of the Peace Corps until 1966
Singh, Air Marshal Arjan, Chief of Staff, Indian Air Force
Singh, Swaran, Indian Minister of External Affairs, July 1964–November 1966; thereafter Minister of Defense
Sisco, Joseph J., Assistant Secretary of State for International Organization Affairs from September 1965
Smith, Bromley K., Executive Secretary of the National Security Council
Solbert, Peter O.A., Deputy Assistant Secretary of Defense for International Security Affairs until December 1965
Spain, James W., Director, Office of Research and Analysis for Near East and South Asia, Bureau of Intelligence and Research, Department of State, March 1964–June 1966; thereafter Country Director for Pakistan–Afghanistan
Steeves, John M., Ambassador to Afghanistan until July 1966
Stevenson, Adlai E., Representative to the United Nations until his death in July 1965
Stoddart, Jonathan D., Deputy Director, Near East and South Asia Region, Office of the Assistant Secretary of Defense for International Security Affairs
Subramaniam, Chidambara, Indian Minister of Food and Agriculture, June 1964–March 1967

Talbot, Phillips, Assistant Secretary of State for Near Eastern and South Asian Affairs until September 1965
Taylor, General Maxwell D., Chairman of the Joint Chiefs of Staff until July 1964; Ambassador to Vietnam, July 1964–July 1965
Thant, U, Secretary-General of the United Nations
Thompson, Llewellyn E., Ambassador at Large until December 1966; also Acting Deputy Under Secretary of State for Political Affairs

Uquaili, N.M. (Nabi Babash Mohammad Sidique), Pakistani Minister of Finance from July 1966

Warnke, Paul C., Assistant Secretary of Defense for International Security Affairs from August 1967

Watson, Marvin, Special Assistant to the President, January 1965–April 1968

Wilson, Harold, British Prime Minister from October 1964

Woods, George D., President of the International Bank for Reconstruction and Development (World Bank) until 1968

Wriggins, W. Howard, Member of the National Security Council Staff, 1966–1967

Yaftali, Abdullah, Afghan Minister of Finance, November 1965–November 1967; Minister of Planning until November 1967; thereafter Second Deputy Prime Minister

Yahya Khan, General A.M., Chief of Staff of the Pakistani Army from March 1966

Yung, Nawab Ali Yavar, Indian Ambassador to the United States from March 1968

Yusuf, Mohammed, Prime Minister and Minister of Foreign Affairs of Afghanistan until October 1965

Yusuf, S.M., Pakistani Foreign Secretary from June 1966

Zahir Shah, Mohammed, King of Afghanistan

Zahir, Dr. Abdul, Deputy Prime Minister of Afghanistan from April 1964

Zwick, Charles J., Director, Bureau of the Budget, from January 1968

South Asia

India and Pakistan

1. Editorial Note

On January 6, 1964, Indian Prime Minister Jawaharlal Nehru suffered a stroke that affected his ability to discharge his responsibilities as head of the Indian Government. Nehru's illness prompted speculation within the U.S. Government concerning its impact upon India and upon negotiations with the Indian Government. It also opened speculation concerning Nehru's likely successor. On January 9 Department of State Executive Secretary Benjamin H. Read sent a memorandum to Special Assistant for National Security Affairs McGeorge Bundy assessing the consequences of Nehru's illness. (Johnson Library, National Security File, Country File, India, Vol. I, Memos and Misc, 12/63–3/64) On January 16 Assistant Secretary of State for Near Eastern and South Asian Affairs Phillips Talbot sent a memorandum to Secretary of State Rusk analyzing the likely successors to Nehru from the perspective of U.S. policy. (National Archives and Records Administration, RG 59, Central Files 1964–66, POL 15–1 INDIA)

---

2. Memorandum of Conversation[1]

Washington, January 8, 1964, 10:30 a.m.

SUBJECT

Pakistan–Indian Relations

PARTICIPANTS

The Secretary
His Excellency G. Ahmed, Ambassador of Pakistan
M. Masood, Minister of Pakistan
M. Jafri, First Secretary of Embassy
Mr. Talbot, Assistant Secretary for NEA
Mr. Naas, SOA

---

[1] Source: National Archives and Records Administration, RG 59, Central Files 1964–66, POL INDIA–PAK. Confidential. Drafted by Charles W. Naas on January 9 and approved in S on January 19.

1

Integration of Kashmir

Ambassador Ahmed called on the Secretary under instructions to express the concern of the GOP over Indian actions to integrate Kashmir into India. The Ambassador reviewed briefly the proposals made by former Prime Minister Bakshi in October 1963,[2] the subsequent discussion in early October between Under Secretary Ball and Foreign Minister Bhutto,[3] and Pakistan's protests to India and its letters to the Security Council. The Ambassador stated that the GOP was particularly disturbed by the November 27, 1963 debate in the Lok Sabha over the integration of Kashmir. Although the GOI has decided not to repeal Article 370[4] at this time, integration is proceeding apace. Continued steps toward complete integration could create a serious situation in the area and he hoped the U.S. could intercede in some way.

Mr. Talbot told the Ambassador that we have made it perfectly clear to the GOI that the U.S. position was governed by the January 24, 1957 U.N. resolution.[5] The Ambassador remarked that it was only a small comfort to Pakistan to know that other nations did not recognize India's actions; integration was nevertheless taking place and India was consolidating its position in Kashmir.

The Ambassador said that overall Indo–Pak relations were bad. At the recent Jaipur meeting of the Congress Party a resolution was passed which linked the Chinese Communists and Pakistan, charging that they were committing aggression against India. He quoted GOI Minister Subramaniam as stating that the GOI was taking steps to contain and to vacate this aggression. If these words are applied to Kashmir, he said, they are very ominous.

The Secretary inquired whether there might be any benefit from informal, unofficial talks between knowledgeable Indians and Pakistanis on the problems besetting the two nations. Such talks might be one step toward improving relations. The Ambassador expressed doubt that talks of this nature could be fruitful; they would not carry much weight with either government.

---

[2] On October 3, 1963, G.M. Bakshi, outgoing Prime Minister of Kashmir, announced to the legislature of Kashmir a number of proposed constitutional changes designed to further the integration of Kashmir into the Indian Union. The United States expressed deep concern to the Indian Government over Bakshi's announcement, which was viewed as likely to complicate the task of promoting a climate in which progress could be made toward reducing tensions on the subcontinent. See *Foreign Relations,* 1961–1963, vol. XIX, Document 344.

[3] See ibid., Document 332.

[4] Article 370 of the Indian Constitution outlined the relationship between the State of Jammu and Kashmir and the Indian Union.

[5] UN doc. S/3779, printed in Department of State *Bulletin,* February 11, 1957, p. 232.

The Secretary asked whether the Ambassador had read Chairman Khrushchev's "peace proposals"[6] carefully, and whether the Ambassador saw in them any indication of possible changes in the Soviet position on Kashmir. He noted that we were examining the statement from many different vantage points; frankly, he said, we do not yet know whether the document is primarily propagandistic but it deserves careful attention. The Ambassador replied that he had not thoroughly studied Khrushchev's paper, but he had not seen any indication in it of a change in Soviet policy on Kashmir.

U.S. Military Aid to India; Chicom Intentions

The Ambassador stated that it appeared to him that the "regional military situation" in South Asia had changed somewhat in the last few months. He said it was fairly clear that the Chinese did not intend to attack India; in fact, it appeared that the Chinese were moving some of their forces to the Sinkiang border area. President Ayub's assessment of the Chinese threat had proved correct, he said. In view of the changed situation, the Ambassador asked, is there any possibility the U.S. might review its policy with respect to arms aid for India. The Secretary stated that our position had not changed since General Taylor had talked with President Ayub. He agreed, on the basis of his own experience in the area in World War II, that an invasion of the subcontinent from the north was not in the cards. It also appeared, he added, that the Chinese may refrain from military efforts of any kind against India in the near future. The Chinese, however, had the capacity in place to take limited actions. More importantly, the Secretary said, we have seen no changes in the basic attitude of the Chinese Communists. They were violating the Geneva accord, sponsoring terrorism in Latin America, had refused to sign the Test Ban Treaty, were stepping up the war in Viet Nam by supplying large quantities of Chinese matériel (recently 7 tons of Chinese equipment were captured in the Delta), and were continuing to take the same belligerent line in the Moscow–Peiping dispute. In sum, he said, we see no evidence that the Chinese want to live in peace with their neighbors. We believe it is definitely possible that in the months ahead the Chinese will provoke further trouble somewhere along their perimeter.

In closing, the Secretary stated that he would discuss with his colleagues the matters raised by the Ambassador and would talk to him again.

---

[6] Reference is to a letter sent by Khrushchev to various Heads of State on December 31, 1963, concerning the peaceful settlement of territorial disputes. For text of the letter, as received in Washington, see *American Foreign Policy: Current Documents, 1963*, pp. 938–940.

3.   Memorandum From Secretary of State Rusk to President Johnson[1]

Washington, January 16, 1964.

SUBJECT

Military Assistance to India and Pakistan: General Taylor's Report[2]

I have reviewed with General Taylor the results of his trip to India and Pakistan. He has come back with excellent ideas about future military assistance to those two countries. These supplement and refine the basic approach worked out by the Standing Group and embodied in my recommendations to you of December 11.[3]

General Taylor would fix responsibility on the Indians for coming up with a satisfactory five-year defense plan which would limit their force goals, hold down procurement from the Soviets and hold to a minimum the diversion of their resources from economic development. Within such a plan it would be up to the Indians to set the priorities among the competing needs of their own services. Such a plan might include a limited number of high performance aircraft from Free World sources.

I believe the foregoing course of action would permit us to follow the roughly parallel course with India and Pakistan on high performance aircraft which we believe to be quite essential for political reasons.

I recommend that you authorize us to proceed along the lines of my proposal to you as refined by General Taylor's findings.

To move this matter ahead, the following steps are in order:

1. Inform the British and other Commonwealth aid donors fully about our military assistance planning for both India and Pakistan and obtain their continued cooperation and participation.

2. Tell the Indians that:

—we are willing to provide longer run military assistance if they work out a satisfactory five-year defense plan, as defined above;
—this plan would assume a mutually acceptable political framework (i.e., Indian policies towards Pakistan and China);

---

[1] Source: Johnson Library, National Security File, NSAMs, NSAM 279, Military Assistance to India and Pakistan. Secret.

[2] For the report submitted by Chairman of the Joint Chiefs of Staff Maxwell Taylor on December 23, 1963, to Secretary of Defense McNamara concerning his trip to India and Pakistan in December, see *Foreign Relations, 1961–1963*, vol. XIX, Document 348.

[3] See ibid., Document 342.

—for the purpose of preparing their plan they could use a planning figure of about $50 million MAP annually[4] from the United States which, of course, is subject to Congressional appropriations;

—we look to them to make the initial decision on priorities among the competing needs of their services, bearing in mind that an acceptable plan must not excessively strain Indian resources;

—we intend to continue with an interim program over the next year at roughly current levels while they work out their plan.

3. Tell the Pakistanis that:

—we are willing to support a satisfactory five-year Pakistani military plan within a mutually acceptable political framework (i.e., fulfillment by Pakistan of its obligations to CENTO, SEATO and the United States);

—we are willing to work with the Pakistanis in developing the priorities of this plan;

—we want to resume discussions looking towards the expansion of our facilities.

4. Keep both the Indians and Pakistanis generally informed of our assistance activities in each country. General Taylor has already done much of this job with Ayub, drawing a surprisingly mild reaction. However, a long-term military program for India, including possibly some supersonics, and the provision of additional supersonics to Pakistan will very possibly create an initial storm in each country about our policy in the other. We shall have to find ways of riding this out.

Dean Rusk

---

[4] In his report to McNamara, Taylor proposed a planning figure of $50–$60 million. In an assessment of Taylor's recommendations, submitted in a January 13 memorandum to McNamara, the Joint Chiefs of Staff concluded that in view of the decreasing military assistance funds available, a planning assumption of not more than $50 million per year for each country was preferred. (JCSM–15–64; Washington National Records Center, RG 330, OSD Files: FRC 69 A 7425, 381 India) Peter Solbert, Deputy Assistant Secretary of Defense for International Security Affairs, concurred in the JCS conclusion in a January 14 memorandum to McNamara. (Ibid.) McNamara noted his approval of the revised planning figure on Solbert's memorandum. On January 15 Robert Komer of the NSC Staff sent a memorandum to McGeorge Bundy in which he argued for holding to the original $50–$60 million proposal as offering more potential for influencing Indian policy. (Johnson Library, National Security File, Country File, India, Vol. VI, Cables/Memos/ Misc, 9/65–1/66)

4.   **Memorandum From the Executive Secretary of the Department of State (Read) to the President's Special Assistant for National Security Affairs (Bundy)[1]**

Washington, January 16, 1964.

SUBJECT

Hindu–Muslim Rioting in India and Pakistan

Current Situation

The major scene of the Hindu–Muslim rioting has shifted to Pakistan where at Narayanganj, a few miles south of Dacca in East Pakistan, a minimum of 300 Hindus were killed on January 13–14.[2] Calcutta is calming down under rigid army and police control. Deaths are estimated in the neighborhood of 175 in the city and surrounding areas but the total may be three times this number. We cannot discount the possibility of a resurgence of violence in the Calcutta area or new outbreaks elsewhere in India in reaction to the deaths near Dacca.

The principal danger to India and Pakistan from the riots is that they may start up again a massive flow of refugees between the two countries like those which took place in 1947 and 1950. President Ayub, in a strong letter sent to President Radhakrishnan January 13,[3] said that already 20,000 Indian Muslims had crossed into East Pakistan since the Calcutta riots began. There are still 10 million Hindus in East Pakistan and over 44 million Muslims in India. The migration of even a small proportion of these would put enormous economic and political burdens on these two countries and do much to deepen the enmity which exist between them.

Background

The current cycle of religious and communal disturbances began in Indian Kashmir in late December when Kashmiri Muslims demonstrated over the theft of a relic of the Prophet. The Pakistan Government and press cited these events in Kashmir as evidence of Indian failure to protect the rights of Muslims in Kashmir. This led to protest demonstrations all over Pakistan. One such demonstration in Khulna, East

---

[1] Source: Johnson Library, National Security File, Country File, Pakistan, Vol. I, Memos, 11/63–5/64. Confidential.

[2] Extensive reporting on these communal riots, which were triggered by the theft of a Muslim relic at Srinagar in Kashmir, is in National Archives and Records Administration, RG 59, Central Files 1964–66, POL 23–8 INDIA.

[3] The text of this letter was sent to Washington in telegram 1303 from Karachi, January 14. (Ibid.)

Pakistan, deteriorated into anti-Hindu riots in which at least 27 persons died. A factor which undoubtedly contributed to the atmosphere in which these riots took place was the Indian policy of expulsion from Assam of Muslim immigrants from East Pakistan.

The press in Calcutta made much of the East Pakistan disturbances and Indian political leaders, particularly Krishna Menon, strongly attacked Pakistan on the issue of the Khulna riots at the Congress Party Conference in early January. Exaggerated reports by Hindu refugees from East Pakistan contributed to the inflammatory atmosphere in which the Calcutta riots broke out.

Clearly, resumption of large scale migration would present a great setback to economic development and political stability in both countries. They undoubtedly realize this. The history of their relations indicates that at a time such as this, when the interest of both countries is so deeply involved, they have frequently managed to get together and work out ways of dealing with mutual problems. For example, Nehru and Pakistan Prime Minister, Liaquat Ali Khan, met in 1950 and agreed upon a pact which stemmed the last major tide of migration. We believe some similar kind of joint Indo–Pak action may be necessary to end the present cycle of disturbances. It is unfortunate that Nehru's illness removes his restraining hand from the scene at this time.

What We Are Doing

We believe that the Governments of India and Pakistan will get together only when each is convinced that its interest requires joint action. Our influence to precipitate such a meeting is limited. We have proposed to the British that they use the Commonwealth framework to encourage joint Indo–Pak action.[4] If the British take this initiative, as we hope they will, we will strongly support them. We feel that our action should be informal and behind the scenes. Prospects for effective joint action would be damaged if the governments and peoples of India and Pakistan considered that it was being taken in response to Western pressure rather than the compulsions of the communal situation itself. We have already instructed our posts in India and Pakistan to urge restraint on both governments and, in particular, to suggest that India and Pakistan take steps to limit inflammatory press reporting on the riots.[4]

There is also a need for emergency relief, which will grow if the disturbances and migrations continue. U.S. voluntary agencies are already providing foodgrains and powdered milk in Calcutta, where our Consulate General reports there are no shortages of food for immediate

---

[4] In telegram 4267 to London, January 15, also sent to New Delhi as telegram 1425 and to Karachi as telegram 921. (Ibid.)

relief work. We are studying what additional steps we might take to help. We believe we should be in a position to respond to governmental requests for emergency assistance, rather than take the initiative at this stage, since each country probably would prefer to handle this problem in its own way without having to call for help from foreign governments.

Dan T. Christensen[5]

---

[5] Christensen signed for Read above Read's typed signature.

---

5.   Telegram From the Embassy in Pakistan to the Department of State[1]

Karachi, January 16, 1964, 9 p.m.

1323. I saw President in Karachi for a half hour early evening Jan 14 at my request, for general exchange of views. FonOff DirGen Salman Ali present as very industrious note taker, which made atmosphere slightly less informal and relaxed than on some other occasions.

1. I expressed our concern at outbreak and spread of communal disturbances West Bengal and East Pakistan. Voiced earnest hope that everything possible would be done by leaders of both countries to extinguish communal passions and restore law and order. I expressed satisfaction at the useful instructions and the moderating effect of the President's message to the people of Pakistan of Jan 13.

I also noted the several good points in his message of Jan 13 to Indian Pres Radhakrishnan,[2] text of which just released by press.

2. President was incensed at West Bengal excesses against Muslims but his anger was well contained. He said his govt recognized importance of curbing natural retaliatory feelings of people of Pakistan and assured me every effort would continue be made to this end. He felt the thousands of refugees pouring into East Pakistan could not be prevented from telling their tales of horror and he feared the spread of these stories would compound the difficulties of restraining the

---

[1] Source: National Archives and Records Administration, RG 59, Central Files 1964–66, POL 32–1 INDIA–PAK. Secret; Priority; Limdis. Repeated to New Delhi and London.
[2] See footnote 2, Document 4.

people. He thought the prospects were good that the situation would not get out of hand in East Pakistan unless there should be new outrages against Muslims on a wide scale in West Bengal.

3. I told President that evidence available to us indicated Indian authorities both central and local, civil and military, were making honest and energetic efforts to restore law and order in Calcutta and throughout West Bengal. Five battalions of army troops said to have been brought in and signs indicated situation rapidly being brought under control. I said Amb Bowles was in close touch with GOI and was urging effective police and relief action by authorities, that they refrain from inflammatory public statements, and that Indian public be urged not to react violently to unfortunate communal incidents in Khulna and elsewhere in East Pakistan.

4. President doubted that Indian steps to restore law and order would be efficacious. He said GOP was seriously considering taking to UN entire question of mistreatment of Muslims by GOI in Kashmir, and in West Bengal and Assam. He expressed skepticism that Western countries would support a Pakistan UN complaint along this line and I did not comment on this speculation.

5. President in common with other Pakistani officials was inclined to dismiss outbreaks in East Pakistan against Hindus as relatively inconsequential and not to be mentioned in same breath with mass attacks on life, property and residence rights of Muslims in India. His posture was one of suppressed but deep indignation.

6. On prospective deployment of Indian Ocean task force,[3] I found President technically noncommittal but privately still clearly critical of the concept. I could only get his assent that his govt will not take any public position on proposal before it is fully and officially defined. I called attention to various ways in which the proposal had been exaggerated and otherwise distorted by the press and some govts following the unfortunate premature and inaccurate publicity. I expressed confidence that GOP would perceive stabilizing and deterrent value small independent task force could have in area and would agree that its intermittent presence on high seas in area would pose no problems on any consequence for GOP. I said the force if activated would not have to put into ports of area in order to carry out its role, and we would not need any permission from any other govt for it to operate on high seas, but naturally we sought approval and cooperation of friendly countries and would like to feel that the vessels would be

---

[3] Documentation on the proposal to deploy a U.S. Naval task force in the Indian Ocean, which was developed and discussed during 1963, is in *Foreign Relations, 1961–1963*, volume XIX.

welcome as in past for periodic courtesy calls at friendly ports, including Karachi, and possibly Chittagong.

7. President said he still felt that task force could not fulfill role we envisage for it. It would be too far removed to have any effect on China and it would not be useful in dealing with what he called "local squabbles" of area, would create more problems than it would solve, and would certainly tend to spread any conflict. He thought there would be a better chance of avoiding intervention by other powers and of containing and liquidating local squabbles, if GOP forces were enabled with proper equipment to do job themselves. I observed that the primary objective of task force would be prevention rather than cure. I noted that his apparent discounting of the stabilizing and deterrent effect of such a naval presence did not seem very compatible with the deep misgivings frequently expressed to us by GOP about the possibility of aggression in area. The President said the harm resulting from the upsetting of established ratio of power in subcontinent by our arms aid program for India could not be offset by operations of a carrier task force. I asked the President to keep an open mind on task force and to continue to refrain from taking a negative position on task force until all point ramifications could be more fully explored and he indicated his assent.

8. Chou En-lai visit. I took oblique approach to impending visit of Chinese Communist leaders, Chou En-lai and Chen Yi. President had asked me about my travel plans for the next few weeks, and I mentioned likelihood that I would be in Lahore for horse show in early March. I half-humorously expressed the hope that I would not encounter Chinese Communists as guests at horse show. (This was prompted by persistent but unverified rumors that Chou En-lai may delay his travel here by a couple of weeks in order to compel Pakistanis to make him chief guest at Lahore horse show.) The President responded by minimizing any embarrassment if Chou En-lai were at horse show. He argued that the presence or absence of Chou En-lai would not be matter of any great significance.

9. With this opening, I told the President that in the view of myself and my government the pitch in which the visit was played would make considerable difference. I knew the GOP would feel the visit to Pakistan could not be cancelled now, and, of course, we know that the essential requirements of protocol and courtesy would have to be met. But there were many degrees of cordiality and recognition above this necessary minimum which could be invoked or withheld, depending on the desires of the host government. We hoped that visit would be played in as low a key as possible in order to minimize the harm. I remarked that the treatment accorded the Chinese Communist visitors in Pakistan would be closely observed in Washington.

10. The President said the traditions of hospitality in Pakistan went beyond minimum customary diplomatic requirements, and Pakistani tradition of special hospitality would have to be maintained. He hoped that not too much would be read into this. I said we know that a certain amount of red carpet would have to be rolled out, but we hoped the red carpet would be no wider than necessary and the pile of the carpet no deeper than necessary.

11. In response to some light probing, the President acknowledged that Chou En-lai would visit various places in Pakistan and would be exposed to the public on various occasions. I expressed the hope that he would not be given wide scope for public speeches or other good sounding boards for his propaganda efforts. The President said the effectiveness of Chou En-lai's contacts with the people of Pakistan would be up to the people themselves. The government could not control reaction of the people, and if they wished to respond enthusiastically to Mr. Chou En-lai that could not be helped.

12. The President said he felt it would be a mistake to get excited about a visit which was in the normal tradition of exchanges of official missions by neighboring governments maintaining diplomatic relations. There was nothing unusual about it, and he hoped we would not react unduly.

13. President assured me that his only objective was to "hold back the Chinese and keep them on their side of the line." He felt the pursuit of "normalization" was the best way of avoiding provocation and ensuring that the Chinese would stay where they belonged. He thought his method of dealing with them would be more successful than the Indian had been.

14. I told him that any opportunities offered Chinese which they could exploit were unfortunate at this time. We could not be happy about any evidences of acceptance of the Chinese Communists, considering their record.

15. Other topics of less urgent nature are being reported by airgram.

McConaughy

6.   Telegram From the Department of State to the Embassy in Pakistan[1]

Washington, January 17, 1964, 10:25 a.m.

931. Embtel 1281.[2] We agree that meeting between President and Ayub could be important for future course US–Pakistan relations. For meeting to have this impact, believe we must be sure Ayub will come prepared for constructive discussions of common policies for future, not to rehash old concerns and grievances. Therefore we would see meeting not as culmination past series high level discussions but as occasion for writing new chapter in US–Pakistan relations.

During past year we have repeatedly put to Ayub and his principal lieutenants our analysis of situation in South Asia and requirements for action which this analysis imposes. Likewise Pakistanis have explained their position to us in detail and have supplemented these official expositions with public statements such as *Foreign Affairs* article.[3]

At conclusion of these exchanges we have impression that Ayub is beginning to move more realistically to accommodate himself to minimum requirements on subcontinent as we see them. We on our side are also moving to accommodate him in two principal ways. First, we are close to decisions on longer term military aid for his forces. Second, we recognize that we can live with some improvement of Pakistan–Chinese Communist relations and we understand that this is important element in Ayub's increasing domestic strength. We have thrown up danger signals from time to time, but over longer run we believe Ayub's continued need for US military and economic assistance will place acceptable limits to his "normalization" policy.

Months ahead will give us opportunities to test these assumptions and to see just how far Ayub is adjusting to new relationship. By his

---

[1] Source: National Archives and Records Administration, RG 59, Central Files 1964–66, POL 7 PAK. Secret; Priority; Exdis. Drafted by Turner C. Cameron, Jr., on January 13; cleared by Phillips Talbot, David Dean (FE), Deputy Assistant Secretary for Politico-Military Affairs Jeffrey C. Kitchen, Solbert, Harriman, and McGeorge Bundy; and approved and initialed by Secretary Rusk.

[2] In telegram 1281 from Karachi, January 9, Ambassador McConaughy reported that Foreign Minister Bhutto had informally broached the possibility of a meeting between President Ayub and President Johnson, and he indicated that Ayub would be receptive to an invitation to visit Washington. McConaughy judged that Bhutto's feeler intimated that Ayub was preparing himself to accept the implications of a continued program of U.S. arms assistance to India. Given Ayub's predilection for president-to-president dealing, McConaughy recommended extending an invitation to Ayub "because of important favorable bearing it might well have on our relations at this troublous juncture." (Ibid.)

[3] Reference is to Mohammad Ayub Khan, "Pakistan-American Alliance," *Foreign Affairs*, vol. 42, pp. 195–203.

handling of Chou En-lai visit Ayub can signal to us that he indeed understands dangers of going too far in his relations with Communist China. His reaction to our military assistance package can be a signal that he is indeed swallowing, though with difficulty, our continued military assistance to India. His reactions to suggested joint military exercise plan will be another signal. His reactions to a weakened Nehru will add another dimension to our assessment of how he sees future role of Pakistan in subcontinent.

When we have made these and other readings we will be in a better position to say that a meeting of two Presidents will advance our common understandings and US national interests. Therefore we do not believe that you should follow up Bhutto's feeler in your next meeting with Ayub. We do agree that you and we should remain closely in touch on this subject.

Because he made it clear that his feeler was without authorization, we assume that Bhutto may not want a negative indication from you which might involve his or Ayub's prestige. If, however, he does return to question, you should try to deflect him from his notion of an early meeting with President. You might say that you have taken informal soundings in Washington which indicate that while a friend like Ayub is of course welcome, reading of Washington scene is that it would be better to postpone consideration of specific date until later.

Rusk

---

7.   **Letter From President Johnson to the Ambassador to India (Bowles)**[1]

Washington, January 21, 1964.

Dear Chet:

I appreciate both your good wishes and your thoughtful words on India and Pakistan.[2] Depend on it that I am fully aware of the importance of consolidating the gains we have made vis-à-vis India. You in turn will agree, I am sure, that we must do so in ways which will minimize the risks to our relationship with Pakistan.

---

[1] Source: Johnson Library, National Security File, Country File, India, Exchanges with Bowles (cont.). Secret. Drafted by Komer and Johnson.

[2] Reference is to Bowles' letter to the President on December 27, 1963; see *Foreign Relations, 1961–1963*, vol. XIX, Document 350.

Thus I share your feeling that we must move ahead with "the building of a new relationship with India which will bring her growing industrial and military potential into focus against the Chinese Communists." But you—and all of our key ambassadors—must bear with the limits of the possible in terms of what I can get the Congress to do back here. The attack on foreign aid restricts our freedom of maneuver until we can get the aid tangle straightened out. In fact, the problem of the moment is as much that of protecting the sizable aid investment we already make in India—by far the largest anywhere—as that of getting new military aid on the scale you suggest. We will simply have to stretch the resources of diplomacy to restrain Indian appetites, while still getting the forward movement we seek.

For this, I count heavily on you. With your experience, you are the right man in the right spot at the right time. So I look to you to carry on the crucially important task of maintaining and strengthening our ties with India at a time when we may be temporarily unable to meet many justifiable needs. I shall expect you to let me know personally any time you feel our affairs are badly off the rails.

With all good wishes,

Lyndon[3]

---

[3] Printed from a copy that indicates the President signed the original.

8.   **Memorandum From Robert Komer of the National Security
Council Staff to President Johnson[1]**

Washington, January 21, 1964.

Tab A is Secretary Rusk's proposal on how to handle MAP for
India and Pakistan.[2] It is based on Taylor's recommendations following
his December trip, and concurred in by McNamara and Bell.

In essence, they say let's put the bee on the Indians to come up
with a sensible five-year anti-China program, telling them that *if* it is
satisfactory India can plan on around $50 million MAP per annum
from us. Bowles thinks this sum much too small given the strategic
stakes involved (Tab B).[3] State, Bundy and I wanted to go a bit
more his way; even with only $1 billion annual MAP we could easily
find another $10 million by marginal cuts in other countries which
are far less important. But we caved when DOD was adamant on
$50 million.

We'd also work out a 5-year plan with the Paks, as a means of
protecting our Pak assets. Of course, neither proposal really involves
a big new outlay we wouldn't be undertaking otherwise. As long as
we have a MAP, we'd presumably want to invest so much in India
and Pakistan. So all that is really proposed is to package our MAP in
five-year terms rather than annual increments in order to maximize
the needed impact and get the most leverage.

Moreover, we suggest in both cases only an opening gambit. Then
we check our bets until we see their responses. And even if both agree
to our terms, we'd make clear there can be no irrevocable five-year
"commitments." We'd of course declare our Executive Branch intent,
but make clear it is dependent on annual Hill action *and* Pak/Indian performance.

The options are to: (1) remand the proposal again for further study
if you have reservations; (2) simply delay action further on grounds
that time is not ripe; (3) approve going ahead with initial approaches.
The chief reasons arguing for (3) are to get a handle on the Indian
buildup and to show India, now in disarray over Nehru's illness, that
we're still backing it against China. The post-Nehru leadership could
be far more pro-US than Nehru. These are big stakes. And if we go
ahead with India, we also want to protect our flank with the Paks.

---

[1] Source: Johnson Library, National Security File, National Security Action Memorandums, NSAM 279, Military Assistance to India and Pakistan. Secret.
[2] Document 3.
[3] Telegram 2140 from New Delhi, January 14, not printed.

You could either have a meeting or, in view of inter-agency agreement, just sign off along the lines of Tab C[4] (which embodies certain cautionary words I think you'd want).

R. W. Komer

---

[4] Attached at Tab C was a draft of NSAM No. 279, Document 13.

---

9.   Telegram From the Department of State to the Embassy in Pakistan[1]

Washington, January 21, 1964, 6:50 p.m.

960. At his request Pak Ambassador called on Governor Harriman January 21. Grant of NEA and Sisco of IO also present. Ambassador briefly reviewed developments last few months respecting Kashmir leading to GOP decision refer issue to SC.[2] He said GOP very concerned by rising tension in Azad Kashmir and believed Indian moves annex Kashmir must be stopped. He asked for full and positive US support in SC and assistance behind the scene.

Governor Harriman replied that we believe GOP decision take issue to SC, a decision on which we had not been consulted, was unwise, could achieve little, and might be very harmful in present tense communal situation. He recalled strong US support in 1962 which followed President Kennedy–Ayub discussions in July 1961, but said we were not in position offer same support this time. US would vote

---

[1] Source: National Archives and Records Administration, RG 59, Central Files 1964–66, POL 32–1 INDIA–PAK. Confidential; Priority. Drafted by Naas; cleared by James P. Grant, Carol C. Laise, and Joseph J. Sisco; and approved by Harriman. Repeated to London, New Delhi, Embassy Office Rawalpindi, and USUN.

[2] On January 16, Foreign Minister Bhutto sent a letter to the President of the UN Security Council requesting an urgent meeting of the Council to deal with the Kashmir issue. The text of the letter was conveyed to Washington as an enclosure to airgram A–585 from Karachi, January 18. (Ibid.) Foreign Secretary Aziz Ahmed informed McConaughy on January 17 of the decision to take the Kashmir dispute to the Security Council. (Telegram 1331 from Karachi, January 17; ibid.)

for right kind resolution (if resolution proves desirable), but would refrain from active role in view our belief SC debate is wrong approach to problem. US believes bilateral talks to dampen current communal troubles necessary and best step take at this time. Ambassador was informed that we are very concerned that acrimonious debate on Kashmir and inevitable discussion communal strife could spark further massive disorders. (Ahmed appeared genuinely surprised learn scale East Pak disorders.) Also Nehru's illness contributes our view this is very bad time raise Kashmir in SC and Pakistan cannot expect our support if it moves ahead without getting our judgment in advance. Governor stated that over-all GOP policy of trying bring many pressures bear on India was increasing tension in area and would make solution problems more difficult. For example, Pak moves toward Chicoms last year helped scuttle bilateral talks.

Ahmed stated that bilateral talks on Kashmir could achieve nothing. Bilateral talks on communal trouble could proceed at same time SC debate but essential thing was get at root of problem—Kashmir. SC debate, he said, would help cool atmosphere. He said he did not know anything about GOP plans or tactics for handling issue in Security Council.

Governor repeated our view that SC debate unwise at this time but emphasized that we do not condone India's integration moves and had so informed GOI. Also, it is firm unswerving US policy help find solution Kashmir problem; we simply disagree with current Pak tactics. In our view solution more likely in atmosphere of goodwill than strain.

Comment: Strong line here was necessary as we fear from Embtels 1354 and 1360[3] GOP may be under misapprehension about extent of assistance we will give them in SC. Ambassador's reaction confirmed this impression. We hope Embassy will continue make clear to GOP as instructed Deptel 940[4] that we will not play previous leading role. Both Karachi and Delhi should avoid indicating specific nature of any proposal we would be prepared support in SC since USUN will require

---

[3] In telegram 1354 from Karachi, January 20, McConaughy reported that, in accordance with instructions from the Department, he informed Aziz Ahmed that the United States would not actively support Pakistan's appeal to the Security Council. McConaughy observed, however, that the Foreign Secretary's response made clear that Pakistan was determined to highlight the need for progress on the Kashmir issue. Telegram 1360 from Karachi, January 21, reported another conversation between McConaughy and Aziz Ahmed on Pakistan's appeal to the United Nations. Ahmed expressed confidence that U.S. influence on the issue would be exercised on behalf of a constructive solution, but McConaughy noted that the United States could not be expected to get out in front in support of the independent Pakistani initiative. (Both ibid.)

[4] Dated January 18. (Ibid., POL 32–1 INDIA–PAK/UN)

flexibility in its discussions with principal parties and other members of SC. Further guidance re SC handling will follow.[5]

Rusk

---

[5] McConaughy reported on January 23 that he raised the matter of the referral of the Kashmir issue to the United Nations with President Ayub that morning. McConaughy questioned the wisdom of the course, pointing out that it would antagonize India without producing any progress if India did not wish to cooperate. Ayub remained firm in his determination. (Telegram 128 from Rawalpindi to Karachi, repeated to Washington, January 23; ibid.)

---

10.   Memorandum From the Executive Secretary of the Department of State (Read) to the President's Special Assistant for National Security Affairs (Bundy)[1]

Washington, January 27, 1964.

SUBJECT

    Pakistan's Referral of Kashmir to Security Council

Pakistan has requested an immediate meeting of the Security Council to consider "the grave situation that has arisen in the states of Jammu and Kashmir" and "the danger that it poses to peace in the region." Pakistan's case encompasses the steps taken by India to integrate Kashmir into the Indian Union.[2] These steps, Pakistan claims, violate the resolutions of the Security Council. Pakistan's case also emphasizes Indian denial of human rights in Kashmir and Indian failure to bring under control the communal riots in Calcutta.

Events Leading Up to Referral to Security Council

The present series of events leading up to Pakistan's return to the Security Council began with the failure of bilateral talks in the spring of 1963 and the rejection by both India and Pakistan of the U.S./ U.K. mediation proposal. Thereafter, both sides reverted to previous

---

[1] Source: Johnson Library, National Security File, Country File, Kashmir, Vol. I, 12/63–7/64. Secret.

[2] On January 21, President Ayub sent a letter to President Johnson arguing the necessity for Pakistan to take the Kashmir issue to the UN Security Council. (Ibid., Head of State Correspondence File, Pakistan, Vol. 1, President Ayub Correspondence, 12/15/ 63–12/31/65)

uncompromising positions on Kashmir and Pakistan started its quest for new ways of "leaning on India." When, last fall, the Indians announced the latest in a long series of moves to integrate Kashmir into the Indian Union, Pakistan protested vigorously. India remained undeterred. Pakistan then sought to dramatize its case by playing up incidents along the cease-fire line at Chaknot and near Poonch. India carefully avoided being provoked. Pakistan also alleged the Indians were misusing U.S. arms along the cease-fire line.

India, in the east, resumed the eviction of Muslims, many of whom had entered India illegally, from Assam into East Pakistan. Inconclusive discussions took place regarding possible Indo–Pak talks on this issue. Pakistan ordered the closing of the Indian consular office at Rajshahi, despite the adverse effect this had on the prospects for negotiations on the eviction issue. India continued a policy of relative restraint and did not retaliate.

Against this background, the Kashmir demonstrations over the theft of a relic of the Prophet broke out in late December. (See our memorandum of December 31, 1963.)[3] This mass display of feeling clearly indicated a lack of confidence in the local Kashmir Government, dominated by the Bakshi family, on which the Government of India had depended for ten years. Although information is scanty because of tight Indian control, available reports indicate, however, that the demonstrations were not in support of Pakistan.

Triggered by the furor in Pakistan over the Kashmir demonstrations and the Indian Muslim eviction policy, communal rioting in East Pakistan followed. The rioting spread across the border to Calcutta, where it became much more serious, and then back to East Pakistan in Dacca and Narayanganj. (See our memorandum of January 16, 1964.)[4]

United States Action

When the Indians announced their moves further to integrate Kashmir into the Indian Union we told them we considered such action unfortunate. As tension increased along the cease-fire line we urged both sides to exercise restraint and informally discussed the situation with the United Nations Secretariat. When the demonstrations over the theft of the relic took place in Kashmir we urged both countries to avoid making this a new issue between them. As communal rioting became serious we persuaded the British to propose Indo–Pak talks and we supported their initiative. This action was, however, overtaken by the Pak decision to go to the Security Council. Although we doubted we could dissuade the Paks from this course, we supported a British

---

[3] Printed in *Foreign Relations,* 1961–1963, vol. XIX, Document 351.
[4] Document 4.

initiative to reverse this decision on the grounds that the best way to deal with the serious communal disturbances was to hold bilateral talks leading to joint action.

Our experience during this period has thus shown that our leverage has been slight on these issues.

Pakistan's Referral to the Security Council

In coming to the Security Council at this time, Pakistan is continuing its policy of "leaning on India." As will be indicated in more detail below, India's position has been weakened by a number of factors, some related and some unrelated to its quarrel with Pakistan. By contrast, Ayub currently enjoys a strong political position and so probably feels he is in good shape to exploit India's weakness, although he probably finds the Dacca riots an embarrassment.

Pakistan is probably seeking many of the same objectives in the Security Council it has in previous debates. These include focusing world attention on Kashmir and India's failure to carry out the U.N. resolutions, obtaining a reaffirmation of the Security Council's position on Kashmir, and reminding Kashmiris that there is hope for a change in status in Kashmir.

There are new factors which form a background for Pakistan's move in the Security Council, however. Pakistan is concerned over the new U.S. relationship with India. It has begun a "normalization" of its relations particularly with Communist China but also with the Soviet Union and other bloc countries and initiated an effort to exert a more influential role in the Afro-Asian bloc.

Pakistan did not consult us prior to its referral to the Security Council and it apparently was aware that our support might be considerably less active than in the past. It may be that Pakistan is considering how, without abandoning its present legal position, it can move the Kashmir issue into a new framework so that greater Afro-Asian support can be gained. The emphasis that Pakistan is giving to the human rights aspects of the question suggests such a possible new framework, one which might also be effective in the General Assembly. Pakistan may also be interested in testing Western and Soviet attitudes on Kashmir prior to Chou En-lai's visit. This is a factor we shall have to keep in mind in developing our strategy in the Security Council.

India's Position

Pakistan has brought India to the Security Council at a time of particular Indian weakness. India is greatly embarrassed by its troubles in Kashmir where the Indian-supported regime has been repudiated by the people. Its policy of expelling Muslims from Assam which was a contributing factor to the riots in Bengal, has the appearance of being inconsistent with India's own concept of a secular state. In Calcutta India has suffered the worst communal rioting at least since 1950.

India has additional unrelated troubles to worry about. Its economy has become sluggish. It is anxiously eyeing the peregrinations of Chou En-lai, fearful that he may convince India's erstwhile Afro-Asian friends to support China's position regarding Sino-Indian border talks. The popularity of the Congress Party is declining. Finally, just at this time, India has been deprived of effective leadership by Nehru's illness, and is undergoing an intense domestic power struggle. (The appointment of Lal Bahadur Shastri to the Cabinet is not likely to lessen this struggle.)

Under these conditions, it is difficult to predict how India will react to Pakistan's taking Kashmir to the Security Council. It seems most unlikely that India will respond with concessions on Kashmir. Rather, the danger is that India may feel impelled to take strong action to recoup its position in Kashmir. It might try to accomplish this by political moves to increase central control over Kashmir and by a strong, emotional line in the U.N. debate. Such moves could cause a resumption of communal rioting.

Lurking in the background in India will be Krishna Menon, who has always made great political capital by attacking Pakistan. He will be quick to seize upon any opportunity, presented either by apparent Western support of the Pak position, or by too moderate an Indian defense, in order to continue to rebuild his political position.

The manner in which various GOI leaders handle this question may noticeably affect their position in the struggle to succeed Nehru, which is now going on in India. This may both limit their flexibility and increase temptations to resort to demagoguery. It follows, therefore, that from the standpoint of India's future, and our relationship with India, we are entering a very critical period, and every action the U.S. takes must be calculated with this in view.

United States Stance

We believe we should "back off" somewhat from our previous active substantive role on the Kashmir issue in the Security Council, at least until we see more clearly what the GOP and GOI strategy will be and whether the climate of debate will admit of constructive action. Pakistan made its decision to take the issue to the U.N. without consulting us. We believe the move ill-advised and more likely to stimulate further rioting than to stem it. We discharged our obligation to Ayub to support him on Kashmir in the Security Council when the issue came up in the Security Council in the winter and spring of 1962. At that time it was only as the result of President Kennedy's personal intercession with the Irish Ambassador that we were able to obtain a sponsor for a resolution acceptable to Pakistan. Since that time developments in the bilateral talks and our abortive mediation efforts gave us opportunities to reiterate to the GOP that we saw quiet diplomacy as the only constructive way to move ahead but the GOP and the GOI were unreceptive. We certainly do not intend to abandon our previous position in support of Security Council resolutions on Kashmir, but neither do we see any purpose served by mere reaffirmation since it has become clear that this will not advance but instead, might retard a solution. In the bilateral talks Pakistan signified willingness to consider approaches other than a plebiscite and India recognized that the status of Kashmir was in dispute and territorial adjustments might be necessary.

We see little or no prospect for progress toward a Kashmir settlement under the present conditions. Security Council consideration is likely to stiffen India's position at least for the time being. Our leverage is demonstrably low. The Chinese military pressure on India has eased. The Pak–Chicom relationship has become such that the Indians question what benefit they would get in terms of their national security from the major concessions they would have to make to reach agreement on Kashmir.

The immediate problem which must be faced on the subcontinent is the communal tensions and the dislocations caused by the recent riots which still smolder under heavy military and police control. Interlarded is the festering problem of Kashmir which is the focus of the Pakistan Security Council complaint. Unless a satisfactory arrangement is made on the communal problem, massive migration could take place which could affect our interest in the area as well as those of India and Pakistan. The communal disturbances appear to be under control for the present, although they could erupt again at any time.

We are working quietly behind the scenes to try to moderate the forthcoming debate in the Security Council, which otherwise might exacerbate the situation. We hope the debate can be brought to a rapid conclusion without passage of a resolution and that the Indians and the Pakistanis can be brought together in talks.

The Secretary-General has indicated to Governor Stevenson his willingness to offer his good offices to the parties in whatever manner they might feel useful, but we do not yet know the results of the Secretary-General's efforts in this regard. At the same time, we expect our Embassies in Karachi and New Delhi to continue quietly urging talks leading to joint Indo–Pak action. Underlying our strategy is our view that the Hindu–Muslim problem is a deep-rooted one which must be faced squarely by India and Pakistan and that we should not inject ourselves in such a way that either party looks to us to bring about a solution.

John McKesson[5]

---

[5] McKesson signed for Read above Read's typed signature.

11.   Telegram [*text not declassified*] to the Department of State[1]

Washington, January 30, 1964, 2126Z.

98158. For Under Secretary Harriman eyes only. The following message was received [*less than 1 line of source text not declassified*] on 30 Jan 1964 from Ambassador Bowles for Under Secretary Harriman with information copies for Mr. McGeorge Bundy and Mr. John McCone. Copies are being sent to Mr. Bundy and Mr. McCone.

"When I left Washington late November, understanding was that Department would take initiative aimed at winning support, first in India and then in Pakistan, for autonomous Kashmir. You will recall that this decision was to be taken at high level, and not to be referred to in any but most tightly controlled communications. Need for this program has if anything become even greater in light developments of past six weeks. Deterioration in Indo-Pak relations so serious that chance of winning support in both countries for steps leading to modus vivendi has actually improved. During same period Indian Government has been forced consider seriously, as one means restoring popular rule Jammu and Kashmir, the release of Sheikh Abdullah, which would mean entire acceptance in principle of ultimate autonomy in some form. Time is ripe for careful covert campaign to bolster possibility such a step. Please let me know [*less than 1 line of source text not declassified*] present status of my November request."

---

[1] Source: National Archives and Records Administration, RG 59, Central Files 1964–66, POL 32–1 INDIA–PAK. Secret; Exdis.

12.   Telegram From the Embassy in Pakistan to the Department of State[1]

Karachi, February 1, 1964, 3 p.m.

1456. Bhutto Nov 29 meeting with President.[2]

1. After dinner which I gave in Rawalpindi evening Jan 25, FonMin Bhutto in relaxed and confiding mood told me in strict secrecy of what he termed hitherto unrevealed aspect of his Nov 29 conversation with Pres in Washington.

2. He said that he had been given highly important oral message by Pres Ayub to convey directly and personally to Pres Johnson. This was distinct from the routine written communication which he delivered.[3] Bhutto said he had planned to convey this oral message near end of the meeting. Bhutto said that before he got around to delivering the message, Pres Johnson tackled him on the matter of the invitation to Chou En-lai to visit Pakistan. He said that frankly he had not expected to be reproached on this subject at that time considering the circumstances of his visit to the US and he was taken aback.

3. Although his instructions from Pres Ayub were unequivocal that the message should be delivered, he made a quick decision not to convey the message feeling that the atmosphere was not right for the conveyance of his message in the wake of the President's remarks about the GOP invitation to the Chinese Communists. He thought the delivery of the message would seem inappropriate under the circumstances, and its impact would be lost. He said he even felt that it might seem like a weak, unauthorized and improvised defense against the criticism levelled at the GOP action.

4. He said he had told Pres Ayub of his non-delivery of the message, and the reason therefor, as soon as he returned to Pakistan. He did not state Pres Ayub's reaction, but the inference was that Ayub had at least tacitly approved his action, since no further effort has been made to deliver the message.

---

[1] Source: National Archives and Records Administration, RG 59, Central Files 1964–66, POL 1 PAK. Secret; Exdis.

[2] Bhutto's meeting with President Johnson on November 29 was summarized in telegram 755 to Karachi, December 2, 1963; see Foreign Relations, 1961–1963, vol. XIX, Document 341.

[3] The written message cited by Bhutto expressed Ayub's friendship and best wishes to the new President. The text of the message was transmitted to Karachi in telegram 756, December 2. (National Archives and Records Administration, RG 59, Central Files 1964–66, POL 15–1 US/JOHNSON)

5. He then said he would summarize the message to me. Message in words as close to those actually used by Bhutto as I can recall them, was as follows:

"My President (Pres Ayub) has instructed me to inform you (Pres Johnson) that you can consider yourself relieved of one worry, for my government will not under any circumstances reverse its present foreign policy. No government headed by me (Ayub) will enter into an alignment with the Communists or otherwise undermine the existing alliance relationships."

6. Bhutto said that this assurance was to be categorical. It did not have any escape clause. It was unqualified so long as Ayub remained at the head of the GOP.

7. I agreed that message was of great significance and told Bhutto that I considered it most unfortunate that a means had not been found to transmit the message as an actual statement of prevailing policy.

8. It was quite clear that Bhutto did not consider that he was giving the assurance to me now as current Pakistan policy approved by the Pres. He considers that the matter is back in the hands of Pres Ayub and if the Pres wishes to state this to the US as a binding commitment, it will be up to him to decide on the means of transmitting it to the US Government.

9. *Comment:* Following my return from Rawalpindi, I with my senior staff have given serious consideration to authenticity and implications of this purported message of assurance. In general, we have some very serious reservations and are not prepared to accept Bhutto's version at face value. More specifically our tentative conclusions are:

A) Ayub probably gave Bhutto instructions to give some sort of assurances to Pres Johnson but Bhutto, who probably had doubts as to wisdom of this action, seized on circumstances in meeting to justify not delivering message. We doubt Bhutto would tell me of message if none actually existed since I could check directly with Ayub. Furthermore, there is Bhutto's request for meeting with Pres on grounds he had very important message from Ayub which was not in fact forthcoming. Our review of memcon also leads to conclusion Bhutto had more than adequate opportunity deliver message, but hesitated and then seized on exchange regarding Chou En-lai visit to rationalize its non-delivery.

B) Assurances quoted to me have no binding force and we suspect that Bhutto may be seeking get best of both worlds, trying to ease our concern by this backhanded quotation of intended message and yet avoiding putting assurances in form of actual commitment. Such action would be consistent with Bhutto's posture in recent months.

C) In any event, Ayub had subsequent opportunities during Taylor and Shriver visits and during my Jan 14 meeting to give us those assurances and did not choose to do so.

D) There may well be element of threat in implication by Bhutto he not certain same assurances will be reauthorized by Ayub.

10. It is highly important that we probe in some discreet manner to ascertain what is back of this recital, and to see if Ayub now willing to give us assurance in categorical terms quoted by Bhutto. But this needs to be done without destroying my relationship with Bhutto. I will make recommendations after short further reflection.

McConaughy

---

13.   National Security Action Memorandum No. 279[1]

Washington, February 8, 1964.

MEMORANDUM FOR

The Secretary of State
The Secretary of Defense

SUBJECT

Military Assistance to India and Pakistan

I have no objection to going forward with exploratory approaches looking toward possible five year MAP programs for India and Pakistan under the conditions described in the Secretary of State's 16 January memorandum to me.[2]

However, I do not believe that we should yet discuss MAP levels with either country. Until we have a clearer idea of the prospect for the FY 1965 aid program, it seems to me premature to indicate to India or Pakistan how much military aid they might be able to count upon, regardless of how tentatively we put it. Instead, we should indicate to both governments that they should prepare austere minimum five year programs. Then, as their plans mature and as we get a better reading on Congressional attitudes, we can make a final decision on what MAP to provide.

Furthermore, in the course of these discussions I desire that the following precautions be observed:

---

[1] Source: Johnson Library, National Security File, NSAMs, NSAM 279, Military Assistance to India and Pakistan. Secret. Copies were sent to the AID Administrator and the Director of Central Intelligence.

[2] Document 3.

1. We should make clear to both countries what we expect of them in return for prospective long-term military aid. As to India, we particularly want it to hold foreign exchange diversions from development to defense to a reasonable level, lest we end up indirectly helping finance an excessive defense effort via aid which we provide for quite another purpose.

2. In the case of Pakistan, our MAP help should be appropriately linked to satisfactory performance with respect to its alliance obligations and to our intelligence facilities.

3. Both governments must be made to understand that no irrevocable five year MAP commitments can be undertaken by the US, both because aid levels each year will depend on Congress and because our actual aid each year will depend on continuing Pakistani and Indian performance.

4. Our approaches to India and Pakistan should be timed for optimum impact. For example, I do not believe that we should initially approach Pakistan until we have assessed the results of the Chou En-lai visit.

With these caveats, I approve proceeding along the lines of the Secretary of State's 16 January proposals.

L.B.J.

---

14.   Telegram From the Department of State to the Mission to the United Nations[1]

Washington, February 12, 1964, 12:10 p.m.

2174. Following summary for information only and contents should not be disclosed to foreign officials. It is uncleared and subject to amendment upon review of memcon.

On very short notice FonMin Bhutto and Agha Shahi[2] came to Washington February 10 for small working dinner at Secretary's invitation. SC Kashmir debate predominated. Bhutto made strong pitch for

---

[1] Source: National Archives and Records Administration, RG 59, Central Files 1964–66, POL 32–1 INDIA–PAK. Confidential; Priority; Limdis. Drafted by Laise on February 11 and approved by Talbot. Also sent to Karachi and repeated to New Delhi and London. A memorandum of this conversation is ibid., POL INDIA–PAK.

[2] Bhutto was in the United States to participate in the Security Council debate on Kashmir. Shahi was an official of the Pakistani Foreign Ministry.

necessity of having current SC consideration terminate with resolution even if Soviets vetoed. He stressed importance of this: (1) to hearten people of Kashmir in new situation presented by recent demonstrations; (2) to continue to bring force of world opinion to bear on Indian actions; (3) to avoid deterioration in US–Pakistan relations. Secretary sought to make clear that US attitude toward Pakistan or Kashmir issue has not changed but that touchstone of our policy is Peiping. Our overriding concern is general war and necessity for curbing Peiping's aggressiveness. This is reason for our sensitivity to French moves, but more particularly Pakistan's[3] because latter is power in Asia. Bhutto stated that if there were an honorable settlement of Kashmir, Ayub's 1959 offer[4] could prevail, though he did not want this revealed to Indians. Secretary also told Bhutto our influence is limited both Pindi and Delhi and that requirement for solution of Kashmir in long run is desire of two countries for good relations. World opinion not likely to influence India any more than Pakistan. It is "mistake of lifetime" to think that India can be coerced. There is need for informal discussions among rational elements on both sides; with changing leadership in India, Pakistan has an opportunity to build climate favorable to reduction of tensions.

In course of this discussion Bhutto claimed Ayub domestic position stronger in 1964 than in 1959. Appropos of nothing he warned that US was wrong to think it could separate individuals in GOP; he stated that as FonMin he spoke for Ayub and US must have confidence in GOP as whole.

Bhutto seemed willing to consider consensus[5] if it injected SYG and made it clear past SC resolutions are binding. However, Ambassador Ahmed continued to stress setback to US-Pak relations to point Bhutto chided him with observation US-Pak relations are more abiding than this.

In post-mortem following dinner Secretary stated we should try to strengthen Ivory Coast consensus; that there is no point in being even-handed on substance of Kashmir in view our basic position; but

---

[3] Reference is to French and Pakistani initiatives to normalize relations with China.

[4] Apparent reference to the offer Ayub made on December 22, 1959, at the urging of Ambassador Rountree, to issue a joint declaration with India that all questions between India and Pakistan would be settled for the indefinite future by peaceful negotiations, provided that prior agreement had been reached on basic principles, including settlement of the Kashmir dispute. See *Foreign Relations, 1958–1960*, vol. XV, pp. 197–201.

[5] Reference is to a proposed consensus statement advanced by the Ivory Coast Representative to the Security Council to substitute for a resolution on Kashmir viewed as certain to be vetoed by the Soviet Union. Extensive reporting on the debate on Kashmir in the Security Council is in National Archives and Records Administration, RG 59, Central Files 1964–66, POL 32–1 INDIA–PAK.

that resolution should not be crammed down our throats with Chou visit coming up.

Invitation extended by Secretary to Indian rep Chagla for working dinner February 14 turned down; efforts to find mutually acceptable time for appointment February 11 failed owing to prior engagements and weather.[6]

Rusk

---

[6] On February 12, Ambassador Bowles reported on a meeting he had that day with Lal Bahadur Shastri, Minister Without Portfolio charged by the Indian Government with responsibility for seeking to lower the level of tension in Kashmir. Shastri expressed deep concern over the course of the UN debate concerning Kashmir and stated that without U.S. neutrality in the debate, he would face great difficulties in achieving his mission in Kashmir. (Telegram 2391 from New Delhi, February 12; ibid.)

---

15.   Telegram From the Embassy in Pakistan to the Department of State[1]

Karachi, February 13, 1964, 5:30 p.m.

1520. Kashmir.

1. I saw President for forty minutes in his Karachi office this morning. FonSec Aziz Ahmed also present. Pres was in good and responsive mood, although naturally concerned about various difficult foreign policy problems before him. Principal topic was Security Council consideration of Kashmir issue which is reported herein. Other topics reported separately.[2]

I first delivered Mrs. Kennedy's Jan 23 letter of appreciation for Pakistani sympathy and support after death of Pres Kennedy.[3] Pres read letter in my presence and responded feelingly.

---

[1] Source: National Archives and Records Administration, RG 59, Central Files 1964–66, POL 32–1 INDIA–PAK. Secret; Immediate; Limdis. Repeated to New Delhi, USUN, and London and passed to the White House.

[2] In telegram 1529 from Karachi, February 14, McConaughy reported on that part of his conversation with Ayub in which they briefly discussed the visit to Pakistan by Chinese Premier Chou En-lai, which was scheduled to begin on February 18. (Ibid.) McConaughy reported in telegram 1530 from Karachi, February 14, on the part of the discussion relating to the military assistance program. (Ibid., DEF 19–3 US–PAK)

[3] Not found.

2. Pres turned to Kashmir debate in SC, urging that US support strong UN resolution, notwithstanding certainty of Soviet veto. He felt resolution would have strong effect regardless of Soviet opposition, meaning of which would not be lost on people of Pakistan or the world. On other hand he thought "consensus statement," especially in watered-down version and lacking unanimous support, would not have any propulsive effect, would not be interpreted as a meaningful action by the people of Pakistan, and would not give UN SecGen needed strong encouragement to enter Kashmir scene in an intermediary role.

3. President expressed particular unhappiness with reports he said he was still receiving from New York indicating that US was actively working against resolution and was pushing for diluted type of consensus statement as suggested by Ivory Coast representative. He understood that Ivory Coast draft would play into Indian hands by mingling Kashmir issue with other disputes between Pakistan and India in way which would prevent UN concentration on Kashmir and would enable Indians to divert attention from Kashmir and go through form of general bilateral discussions without ever having to face up to Kashmir question.

4. President said if these reports were accurate he wanted to plead earnestly with us to reconsider US position. He felt that GOI could perhaps be moved by resolution but not by fuzzy consensus. He said "Hindu are naturally bullies," but he said it was also characteristic of them to trim their sails quickly when they saw it was expedient to do so. He felt a resolute US position would be the best way of constraining the Indians to see where their best interests lay.

5. President hoped we would see that our broad objective of protection and security of subcontinent hinged entirely on Kashmir settlement. He argued that defense of every sector of subcontinent closely interrelated and penetration of any sector by either Soviet or Chinese Communism would pave the way for ultimate fall of entire subcontinent. As long as Kashmir remained source of fundamental discord and open wound on body of subcontinent, way was open for Communist infection of whole subcontinent by Communists. A strong cooperative defense of the subcontinent would be automatically established once the vulnerable Kashmir exposure is healed. The President professed his dismay that we could not see that our heavy expenditure on military assistance to India was wasted so long as Kashmir remained unsolved. Even from narrow standpoint our security concern would be best served by Kashmir settlement and he could not understand why we did not make such settlement the highest and most urgent objective of US policy in subcontinent.

6. I told President that Kashmir solution stood high on our priority list as it had for many years. I recalled our consistent support of UN resolutions and told him this position unchanged and that our differ-

ences at this moment over how to proceed in SC were essentially tactical rather than substantive. I urged President to look objectively at merits of strong consensus statement making essential points about (1) UN history of dispute and (2) importance of respecting will of Kashmir people, as against hunting up a resolution which would have no operative or Parliamentary validity because of inevitable Soviet veto. I said that a good consensus statement embodying the essential points and confirmed by SC President as representing views of preponderant majority of SC might well have less abrasive effect on Indians and have more potential for moving Kashmir negotiation forward than repetition of traditional resolution exercise. I thought that the significance and the hope in a good consensus statement could be explained to people of Pakistan in terms they would understand as a more realistic UN effort under present conditions than more repetition of ill-fated resolution attempt.

7. President said if consensus statement would in actuality carry more weight than a vetoed resolution, GOP would of course have to consider it but he doubted whether there was any real tangible potential in a consensus statement. He said if the consensus statement strongly covered the two points I had mentioned plus a third point, namely definite recommendation that UN SecGen U Thant or his nominee come into Kashmir picture in some sort of intermediary role, and if general assent to consensus statement by SC members could be obtained, then GOP possibly could go along. But not otherwise. He said he thought it was very important to find out what it would take to get U Thant actively into the Kashmir picture and he hoped our delegation would promptly explore this point in connection with its consideration of consensus versus resolution. He was worried about effect on US image among Pak people if for first time we do not promote resolution and he thought we would see the merit of putting Soviet Union rather than US in a blameworthy position in the eyes of Pak people. Also worried about effect on GOP position with Pak people of first failure to get impressive SC vote on a formal resolution. He said specifically that GOP understands certainty of Soviet veto and is prepared to live with that situation. Vetoed resolution would be better than a diluted consensus statement and better than a questionable consensus which might be rendered meaningless by non-concurrence of various members.

8. I mentioned Bhutto's working dinner with Secretary in Washington Feb 10 and told him that extended exchange on this issue had taken place. I stressed our view that voluntary Indian participation in Kashmir settlement effort was essential and that coercion of India on the issue would not lead to a viable Kashmir solution and was out of the question.

9. President agreed that India could not be coerced but he felt that Indian inertia on the question might be overcome by discreet US push.

As Indians gain momentum perhaps they could be brought to see that Kashmir settlement is in their own immediate vital security interest. President maintained that other Indo-Pak issues, including joint defense, evictions, communal tension, trade and transit would wither away in light of Kashmir accord.

10. I told President that his statement that GOP might consider strong consensus statement commanding overwhelming support of SC membership was encouraging, and that we would continue to explore the possibilities. I indicated my assumption that Bhutto would keep in close touch with USDel.

McConaughy

16.   Telegram From the Embassy in India to the Department of State[1]

New Delhi, February 20, 1964, 11:30 a.m.

2445. Department pass White House. Security Council debate on Kashmir[2] has touched off predictable emotional outburst in both Indian official and public circles which has damaged UK-U.S.-Indian relations and further widened gap between India and Pakistan.

On basis of discussions with MPs now in Delhi for current Lok Sabha session and with GOI officials and diplomatic colleagues, it is clear feeling now runs deep. Although British bearing full brunt of Indian indignation and resentment, U.S. is in strong runner-up position.

In Calcutta press conference last Friday attended by some fifty newsmen, questioning on U.S. position in regard to Kashmir–Pakistan was more relentless than anything I had previously experienced in India. I refused to comment on U.S. position in regard to Kashmir on grounds Stevenson had not yet spoken and underscored as on similar occasions urgent need for some solution to Pak-India impasse acceptable to both sides. When anti-British statements became extreme I

[1] Source: National Archives and Records Administration, RG 59, Central Files 1964–66, POL 32–1 INDIA–PAK. Confidential. Repeated to London, Karachi, and USUN and passed to the White House.
[2] On February 17, Foreign Minister Bhutto asked for and received a postponement of the Security Council debate on Kashmir to allow him to return to Karachi for consultations and new instructions. (Telegram 3114 from USUN, February 17; ibid.) Bhutto joined Chou En-lai and his party when they began their visit to Pakistan on February 18. (Telegram 1588 from Karachi, February 25; ibid.)

reminded press reps that UK as well as U.S. had been quick to come to India's aid when ChiComs attacked while USSR was unable to make up its mind. Even more moderate Indian press reps suggested afterwards that my remarks were beyond call of duty.

At small stag dinner at my home last night attended by Ashoka Mehta, Lakshmi Jain of Indian Cooperative Union, S.K. Dey, Minister of State for Community Development and Cooperation, Vkrv Rao, Pitamber Pant and Raj Krishna, all of Planning Commission, subject of Kashmir-Pakistan-U.S. relationship wholly absorbed an evening that had been set aside for economic discussions. Even these firm friends of U.S. with their deep understanding of what we have done to bolster Indian economy were, with single exception of Ashoka Mehta, emotional and unreasonable.

General theme running through discussion was that while Indians are appreciative for our economic and military assistance matters of national pride have become so involved in Kashmir-Pak situation that Indians can no longer afford to be taken for granted.

Mood was both strongly anti-Communist and anti-Chinese with no suggestion of compromise on either position. However, heavy emphasis was placed on fact that Nehru era is drawing to close and regardless of efforts of presumably sober people like themselves India which had been denied close relations it wanted with U.S. would now find itself drifting further from West and towards admittedly rambunctious and unappealing role which they assert has been practiced successfully by other nations.

Against this background following is our estimate of four factors which have contributed to this widespread emotional reaction. However unreasonable they may appear to us it is important that we understand them if we are to act realistically and effectively.

1. Factors that apply in general to India's relationship to what is loosely known as "the West":

Following ChiCom aggression in Oct 1962 and Pak flirtation with our major Asian enemy there was deep conviction within GOI and among Indian people that their relations with West would now be on new and much closer footing. They felt this assumption was particularly valid in view of their efforts to maintain moderate response to what they genuinely believe to be accelerated Pak effort to stir up subcontinent and thereby prevent closer India–U.S. relations.

Efforts to which they refer include decision of year ago, against their better judgment, to hold talks on Kashmir and to offer what they believed to be important concessions; agreement in December not to close Shillong in retaliation for Rajshahi; restraint following second wave of Pak riots on Jan 18 and 20; Nanda–Shastri proposal for joint

review of communal riots by Home Ministers; GOI willingness to negotiate question of illegal Muslim settlers in Assam and Tripura at Ministerial level as requested by GOP (if those meetings went well they asserted
that they would agree to discuss Kashmir itself), etc.

When Pakistan failed to respond to these GOI efforts to ease tensions and took issue to SC Indians were keenly aware that we deplored
this action, and therefore jumped to conclusion that UK–US position
would at best favor GOI and at worse remain neutral.

2. Factors involving their own internal problems:

GOI is embittered over fact that following Nehru's illness Pakistan
had seemed to take ruthless advantage of period of political uncertainty
which is now aggravated by Chou En-lai's State visit to Pakistan.

Further to feed GOI frustration is embarrassment caused by their
belated recognition that Kashmir govt which they built around Bakshi
in addition to being corrupt had no public support whatsoever. At
same time they are resentful of what they believe to be deliberate
appeals by Paks to arouse religious antagonism previous to and following theft of sacred relic, appeals which they feel gravely threatened
their vision of secular state in India in which all religions can live
peacefully together.

Finally new group headed by Shastri and Kamaraj which is gradually moving into leadership of GOI was itself persuaded of need for
finding some basis for settlement Kashmir dispute and now finds itself
badgered by extremists with little hope of meaningful discussions for
some time to come.

3. Factors which produced particularly strong anti-British reaction:

Ever since turn of century most Indians have been persuaded that
British deliberately backed Muslim minority against Hindu majority
as basic means of forestalling Indian independence. They feel that this
British policy was thereby responsible for final partition which in their
view unnecessarily split continent wide open and led to present difficulties.

Indians look on British Conservative Party with particularly deep
distrust. Duncan Sandys and Home are considered lineal descendants
of British Viceroys who supported by Conservative govts in London
were responsible for putting almost every member of present GOI in
prison for at least one or two terms. Against this background they were
infuriated by British SC suggestion that original accession of Kashmir
to India in 1947 approved by Viceroy and by act of Parliament was
irrelevant. Moreover in endorsing past SC resolutions both British and
ourselves have emphasized self determination features of August 1948
resolution which Indians know have great appeal to people all over

world while failing to mention related reference in same resolution that Paks must agree to withdraw from Azad Kashmir as prerequisite of self-determination process.

4. Factors which relate to Indian criticisms of U.S.:

In India President Kennedy was looked upon as special friend who was author of Indian resolution in Congress, who had frequently spoken in behalf of Indian aid, and who had singled out India as great experiment in democracy. With loss of this friend, Indians now believe we favor Pakistan in its disagreement with India and discount India's importance.

From this basic assumption have stemmed two further reactions. First of these is belief that military assistance program which after my return from Washington in Nov and particularly following Max Taylor's visit here two weeks later was assumed to be forthcoming was held up because of pressure by Paks on Johnson administration and second, feeling that Paks would not have taken Kashmir issue to SC if not convinced that new administration was oriented favorably in their direction. However unjust this may appear to people in Washington it must be realized that this is deep-seated conviction that runs through Indian Govt, press, Lok Sabha and informed citizens generally.

In this framework Chagla's[3] reports that U.S. had pushed Great Britain into forward role and quietly urged Ivory Coast to put forward formula that supported Pak position received credence which it did not deserve.

Although these reactions may appear unreasonable and distorted we should not minimize their implications. In spite of great personal influence and prestige of Gore-Booth British ability to exercise constructive influence here will be circumscribed for some time.

Krishna Menon has been given platform and equipped with issue on which he excels. His Feb 14 speech was effective and received reaction from sizable majority of Lok Sabha. Civil servants such as Gundevia who have preached futility of dealing with Paks and need for firm line have been strengthened, while moderates are being forced to get on bandwagon.

After Congress Parliamentary Party executive indignation meeting on Feb 14 fifty-one Congress MPs issued statement sharply critical of pro-Pakistan stand of British. Signatories included such staunch pro-U.S. moderates as Tyagi K.C. Pant, Raghunath Singh and Ravindra Varma.

Another element in general worsening situation is hardening of views of West Bengal politicians on status of East Pak Hindus and

---

[3] M.C. Chagla, Indian Minister of Education, was representing India in the Security Council debate on Kashmir.

increasing communal attitude towards refugee problem which I encountered in Calcutta.

Most distressing of all is fact that throughout India, Pakistan controversy once again dominates news and China for first time in over year is off front page. In addition Indians have again been forcefully reminded of Soviet contribution to GOI's position on Kashmir and of importance of non-alignment in order to insure continued Soviet support at very moment when MIG–21s and SAMs are under discussion with USSR.

Although situation to put it mildly is unhappy one, it is no time for discouragement. In every way available to us we will strive to calm down GOI officials and to encourage more sober reaction from press. If Paks do not indulge in further provocative actions in connection with Chou En-lai visit or otherwise we may be able to resume in due course constructive dialogue with GOI which will underscore overriding need for Indians and Paks to seek some means by which they can live together in rational manner.

Lest we lose perspective I think I should report that difficult dinner of last evening followed busy day in and around Kanpur where I encountered strong pro American sentiment at Engineering College and in two nearby villages where several hundred cultivators assured me that "Indians and Americans are brothers".

Bowles

---

17.   Telegram From the Department of State to the Embassy in Pakistan[1]

Washington, February 21, 1964, 6:51 p.m.

1086. We are transmitting by separate messages Secretary's January 16 Memorandum to the President on "Military Assistance to India and Pakistan" and National Security Action Memorandum of February 8[2]

---

[1] Source: National Archives and Records Administration, RG 59, Central Files 1964–66, DEF 19–3 US–INDIA. Secret; Priority; Limdis. Drafted by Cameron; cleared by Deputy Director of the Office of Near Eastern and South Asian Regional Affairs John P. Walsh, Solbert, Harriman, and Komer, and in draft by Dean, Frazier Meade (BNA), Joseph Norbury (SOV), Howard Meyers (G/PM), William S. Gaud (AID/NESA), and Hirshberg (AID/PC); and approved by Talbot. Repeated to London, New Delhi, CINCSTRIKE, and Hong Kong.

[2] In telegram 1084 to Karachi, also sent to New Delhi as telegram 1687, and telegram 1083 to Karachi, also sent to New Delhi as telegram 1686, both February 21. (Both ibid.)

giving President's approval with certain caveats. Following represents our thoughts how best proceed within above policy guidelines. (Separate instructions being sent Embassy New Delhi.)[3]

In view para 4 of NSAM, we can go no further now than to pass to you our preliminary thoughts about communicating our decisions to Ayub. As we see it, this process involves four distinct steps:

1. A signal to Ayub that our thinking on military aid is well along and that we hope to be able to talk in greater detail before end of March. Deptel 1045[4] authorized you to take this step with Ayub in your conversation on Feb. 13 and we see from Embtel 1530[5] that you have done so. Our thoughts behind this instruction were:

(a) Since we plan convey our decisions to GOI within near future but to GOP only after estimating effect Chou visit, it was urgent to give a signal to Ayub that we still planned to move ahead roughly in parallel.

(b) In the event info of our approach to GOI reaches GOP, the fact that we had given a signal to GOP could be helpful in dampening its reaction. If leak occurs you could also remind GOP of statements about US military aid to India made by General Taylor to Ayub (Embtel 1189).[6]

(c) Conceivably our signal could exert some moderating influence on GOP during Chou visit.

2. An assessment of the results of the Chou visit in terms of US-Pak-Chicom relations would be second step.

3. Third step would be a formal approach to Ayub setting forth the political framework within which we are prepared to engage in long-term military assistance to Pakistan. This step would take place as soon as practicable after completion of step two and certainly before visit to Pakistan by General Adams (JCS 4526 from CJCS for MG Ruhlen).[7] Intent of formal approach will be to use prospect of continued military assistance both as a carrot to demonstrate value of continued alliance relationship and as a lever to get from Pakistan the necessary assurances that it will limit its relationship with Peiping and pursue policies in general which will not be adverse to US interests. We expect to insist on a genuine meeting of minds on these issues, and continuing performance, as the condition for this aid.

4. The fourth step would be technical discussions on military level about planning for five year program. Believe General Adams might initiate these discussions.

---

[3] Document 18.

[4] Dated February 12. (National Archives and Records Administration, RG 59, Central Files 1964–66, POL 32–1 INDIA–PAK)

[5] See footnote 2, Document 15.

[6] Dated December 21, 1963. (National Archives and Records Administration, RG 59, Central Files 1961–63, ORG 7 JCS)

[7] Not found.

We will count on you and Hong Kong to give us your best judgment on results Chou visit. We shall then send you instructions on
carrying out steps 3 and 4.

FYI. We have already told Paks in December that we intend going
ahead with longer term aid. In fact, by our indicating general magnitude
of $50 million, the Paks now know more of our intentions than we are
as yet able to tell Indians.

Therefore, if US-GOI talks raised with you before you are able to
have full discussion with Ayub, you should take line that (1) GOP
already informed in December that we are going ahead with military
aid program for India and general thinking within Executive Branch
about its scope, (2) we are having discussions this future program,
(3) GOP will be kept informed when talks with GOI come into clear
focus, and (4) we hope to hold parallel discussions with GOP on appropriate occasion before end of March. End FYI.

Ball

---

18.   **Telegram From the Department of State to the Embassy in
India**[1]

Washington, February 21, 1964, 6:52 p.m.

1690. New Delhi's 2221 to Department.[2] We are now in position
to make exploratory approaches to GOI looking toward possible five-
year MAP program for India. We have transmitted separately text of
President's decision on military assistance for India and Pakistan as
well as text Secretary's memorandum to President of Jan. 16.[3] You will
understand requirement to observe most carefully caveats on NSAM.
These documents, plus General Taylor's report[4] and Secretary's memorandum to President of Dec. 11,[5] which you already have, provide
framework for your approach.

---

[1] Source: National Archives and Records Administration, RG 59, Central Files 1964–
66, DEF 19–3 US–INDIA. Secret; Priority; Limdis. Drafted by David T. Schneider and
Franklin J. Crawford (NEA/SOA); cleared in draft by Walsh, Gaud, Norbury, and Meade
and by Warren, Dean, Komer, Solbert, Hirshberg, and Harriman; and approved by Talbot.
Repeated to Karachi, London, and CINCSTRIKE/CINCMEAFSA.

[2] Not found.

[3] See footnote 2, Document 17.

[4] See footnote 2, Document 3.

[5] Printed in *Foreign Relations*, 1961–1963, vol. XIX, Document 342.

While package has changed during its consideration here, which will complicate your task of negotiating it in Delhi, our willingness in principle to go forward on a long-term MAP program marks a major step forward, significance of which should not be lost on Indians. Moreover, it represents potential program of considerable magnitude. Your extensive talks with Indian leaders have laid excellent groundwork for gaining Indian acceptance concepts upon which our proposals based. As indicated below we are adding one and possibly two elements which may make Indians more receptive to your approach: our willingness to place all aid on grant basis and possibly some dollar military sales on favorable terms under an export promotion program.

It seems to us General Taylor's approach provides us with best point of departure from which to follow-up, and get Indians make policy decisions which we consider sound as part their own plan. Thus, rather than seeking understandings from Indians re force levels, diversion of foreign exchange, etc., we would look to them to prepare their own austere plan which would satisfactorily deal with these factors.

In this approach to GOI you should take following line:

1. Since Chicom invasion in fall of 1962 USG has been fully cognizant of India's determination build its defenses against continuing Chicom threat and its need for external assistance. To this end we first extended emergency Nassau aid. We are now following this up with roughly similar amounts of assistance for FY '64. It has now become more evident that India will require assistance over an additional period of years. Our assistance has been based upon our careful examination of the threat to Indian security, India's military requirements to defend itself over the long-term against this threat, Indian absorptive capacity and availability of US resources. Our latest studies of this question have included extensive consultation in New Delhi and Washington and have encompassed a review of the over-all situation at highest levels of USG.

2. However, central to India's own defense planning is need for inter-ministerial decisions by which Indian Government establishes sensible long-term military program, and achieves balanced relationship between this and its economic programs. General Taylor made this point clear in December, and we have been waiting for further word as to firming up of Indian plans.

3. To move this process forward, US now ready to discuss possible five-year military assistance program to India provided GOI works out austere minimum five-year plan for defense against Chinese Communist threat, taking into account needs of its military services. For purposes of preparing their plan GOI should assume minimum levels of assistance which it considers it requires and can obtain from foreign sources.

It must be made clear that US assistance will, of course, be subject to availability of funds. No irrevocable commitments can be undertaken because Congressional appropriations will rule. Moreover, we want to make clear that actual level of our aid must depend on continued joint understanding as to purposes for which provided and effective utilization.

4. We realize planning of kind outlined above is time-consuming process. Consequently, if necessary, we are prepared to continue our military assistance during FY '65 at approximately current levels (FYI. As you know FY '64 program level is $50 million. End FYI.) until detailed Indian plan can be worked out.

5. A satisfactory Indian military plan should cover following factors:

(A) *Allocation of Scarce Resources Between Development and Defense.* We are confident that Indians are aware of need to avoid stripping their economic development program to pay for a military build-up. In countering Chicom threat, continued economic growth is at least as important over long run as military strength. A satisfactory plan would hold to minimum diversion of resources, particularly foreign exchange, from economic development. We feel this point especially keenly because US is largest provider of scarce foreign exchange to Indian 5-Year Plans. US does not want both to provide MAP to meet what we regard as legitimate Indian needs and simultaneously to see additional hard currency which we provide for quite another purpose, diverted from it.

(B) *Allocation of Resources Among Indian Military Services.* Just as any Indian defense plan would reflect decision on allocation of resources between defense and economic development, it would also set priorities among competing needs of Indian military services. It follows, therefore, that we would look to GOI to make initial decision on priorities for use of US assistance as between ground and air defenses, to meet Chicom threat.

Should Indians inquire concerning our reaction if they include high performance aircraft from Free World sources in their plan, you should reply it up to them to establish relative priorities and individual items will be considered in our review of the overall plan. FYI. We see these coming later rather than sooner in plan for reasons of pricing, availability, Indian capacity to absorb, and, of course, reaction in Pakistan. End FYI. We obviously see number of MIGs and SAMs which Indians acquire from Soviets as affecting extent to which it necessary for US to fill Indian needs.

(C) *Force Levels.* Satisfactory Indian plan would include time phased levels of force goals which were realistic in terms of limited resources available to India for defense purposes.

(D) *Soviet Military Assistance.* Any Indian defense plan will, of course, take into account military assistance from all sources. In deciding on extent to which we can support such plan US will naturally be interested in extent and types of Soviet assistance GOI contemplates. We are aware that India has already made certain military purchase arrangements with Soviet Union. We recognize that Indians will be accepting some Soviet aid. We do, however, proceed from assumption that West is clearly more reliable source of support to India against Chicoms. Our specific judgment on significance of Soviet military assistance would be determined by number of factors including following: quantities and types of Soviet aid accepted, effect on security US equipment, compatibility of differing types equipment, extent to which Soviet assistance requires introduction Soviet technicians, impact of Soviet aid, degree of Indian dependence on Soviets, and U.S. Congressional attitudes. (See Deptels 1281 December 23, 1963[6] and 96 July 10, 1963.[7])

6. In sum, we presume among other elements Indians would wish include following in their five-year plan:

a. Their estimate of threat, to include most probable scale of Chinese Communist attack, if any.

b. Statement of Indian resources available during period for military purposes, expressed in terms of internal expenditures and foreign exchange outlays.

c. Assumption for planning purposes of minimum foreign assistance required and obtainable from all countries.

d. Decision on force levels supportable by application of foregoing resources.

e. Assessment of impact of this military program on economic development (including an assessment of total external assistance required to support this plan together with economic development plans).

f. Decisions on defense production.

7. GOI will understand that US has been assisting India within context of broad agreement on certain aspects of foreign policy. Our assistance is provided to strengthen India against possibility of renewed Chinese Communist aggression. This assistance has greatly complicated our relations with Pakistan, and has become a new factor in Indo–Pak relations. You should drive home point that if we agree to support an Indian five-year plan we would assume India would in its national interest continue to explore ways of improving its relations with Pakistan. Furthermore, we would naturally expect India and US would continue in broad agreement regarding their assessment of Chicom threat to Asia and strategy required to meet it.

---

[6] Printed ibid., Document 349.

[7] Not found.

8. As further support to India's defense effort, US has under consideration new program of military sales so that certain high priority items not covered by MAP could be purchased from US on favorable credit terms. FYI. We wish emphasize still contingent status of this program. Since India will continue to make substantial military purchases abroad from own resources, we see considerable merit to military sales program for our balance of payments purposes. If program approved, terms will be such as to allow us to compete effectively for this foreign exchange. End FYI.

9. In response Indian request we are now willing to provide all our MAP aid on grant basis, provided that satisfactory arrangements are made for meeting USMSMI rupee expenses by GOI. FYI. Suggest you use this as bargaining tool to obtain Indian agreement to Memorandum of Understanding I. We will send further instructions regarding Memorandum of Understanding II. End FYI.

10. We realize defense planning of the kind we believe India should do may tax Indian capabilities. Should GOI desire, we stand ready to provide advice in defense planning techniques. (FYI. This is delicate area. Any assistance rendered would be only in techniques, and US planners would not participate in decision as to content of Indian plan. You are authorized use this opportunity renew our invitation to Defense Minister Chavan visit US, accompanied by appropriate military and civilian officers, to study our techniques for defense planning. You may also wish explore concept of permanent national security planning organization with full time staff, which we believe India needs. End FYI.)

We plan have discussion with Ambassador B.K. Nehru here along above lines. We will also go over our plans with British Embassy. We know you will wish have similar talks with British in Delhi but we believe you should refrain from wide discussion (e.g., in Coordination Committee) for the present. Particularly since we have not yet had discussions with Paks on our MAP plans there it is important that we do utmost to keep info on our plans for India closely held. You should not approach GOI prior departure Chou En-lai from Pakistan.

Ball

19.   **Memorandum From the Deputy Director of the Bureau of Intelligence and Research (Denney) to Secretary of State Rusk**[1]

Washington, February 24, 1964.

SUBJECT

Possible Indian Nuclear Weapons Development

New information has recently come to hand on the Indian reactor and plutonium separation facilities which suggests that within four to six months India will be able and may intend to produce weapons-grade plutonium free of any safeguards. While we have no other evidence that they are starting a nuclear weapons program, they are now in a position to put together a crude device within one to three years of the start up of their plutonium facility, scheduled for May of this year.[2]

While the psychological and political barriers to a weapons program remain strong in India, the Chinese threat makes somewhat less easy any confident assumptions on this score. We think it unlikely that the Indians would test a weapon barring further changes in its internal political or international position—for example a Chinese communist nuclear test or good evidence of Chicom intent to test. On the other hand, there might be some attractiveness to the Indians in a vigorous weapons research program stopping short of an actual test. Mounting a test, if it seemed politic to do so, could be quickly arranged if a device were at hand, and if preparation of a test site had gone forward during the weapon development period. It should be noted that the high capital cost of the fissionable materials component of a nuclear weapon has now been met.

Discussion. India has established a fairly advanced nuclear energy program which has been publicly described as being confined to nuclear research, the exploitation of basic nuclear raw materials, and the development of nuclear power. In addition to two small research reactors, India has a 40 MW(thermal) research reactor—the so-called Canada India Reactor (CIR)—which is capable of producing sufficient quantities of plutonium for one or two weapons a year. This reactor, which went critical in mid-1960, is no longer under safeguards, since Canadian fuel has been replaced with domestic uranium and U.S.-

---

[1] Source: Johnson Library, National Security File, Country File, India, Vol. I, Memos & Miscellaneous, 12/63–3/64. Secret; Noforn. No drafting information appears on the memorandum. A stamp indicates it was received at the NSC on February 25.

[2] McGeorge Bundy highlighted the final sentence of the first paragraph for Komer's attention and noted in the margin: "RWK Interesting?"

supplied heavy water was sold outright without controls. The Director of the Indian plutonium separation facility has stated that the CIR fuel load is changed approximately every six months. This is an exceptionally short period for normal research reactor operation. At the design power level of 40 MW(thermal), which has only been reached in the last few months of operation, this recharging cycle would result in plutonium of weapons grade, rather than the usual research reactor products.

The plutonium separation plant at Trombay is scheduled to start test operations this month, and will begin separation of its first active load from the CIR reactor in mid-May. Its capacity is such that an entire CIR fuel loading could be processed in about one month.

India has more than adequate fuel supplies to operate the CIR for the production of weapon-grade plutonium. In addition, the domestic production of uranium is being increased and the uranium metal plant and fuel element fabrication facility are being expanded.[3]

The first nuclear power station, Tarapur, being constructed with U.S. assistance, will not contribute to an Indian nuclear weapon capability. Its large plutonium production will be entirely under US safeguards. Two more power reactors are presently planned. The extent to which they will add to Indian weapons potential will depend entirely on safeguard arrangements.

---

[3] On May 14, INR Director Thomas Hughes sent a memorandum to Rusk offering a further assessment of the prospects for Indian nuclear weapons development. The Canadian-Indian reactor at Trombay had begun operations and the INR report noted that the core of the reactor was being changed every 6 months. "This six months cycle is unusually short for a research reactor of the CIR type. While training or some other technical reason may explain this short cycle, it is appropriate for production of weapons-grade plutonium." Hughes noted that there was no evidence of a weapons research and development program, but concluded that the political environment in India for such a program was more favorable than it had been a year before. (National Archives and Records Administration, RG 59, Central Files 1964–66, FSE 13 (INDIA)

20.   Memorandum From Robert Komer of the National Security
        Council Staff to President Johnson[1]

Washington, February 26, 1964.

You may want to read attached two cables from Bowles.[2] Despite his wordiness, they bring into sharp relief how our India affairs are sliding backwards from the high point of our vigorous response to the Chicom attack in October 1962. This trend is largely inevitable, as the Chicom attack recedes and the more normal factors which plague our relations like Kashmir assume their usual place. But as Bowles points out, it is costing us.

The Soviets faltered when Peiping attacked India, while we responded magnificently. But as the Sino-Soviet split widens, Moscow has been making up for lost time. Soviets are now doing more than we to woo the India military establishment. Meanwhile, our Pak friends are doing their best to prove their thesis that India isn't serious about China, by forcing India to focus on Pak–Indian issues. The more they distract Delhi from Peking the more they hurt us.

This is not a trend likely to create great complications for us this year, or maybe next. Only if the Paks press Kashmir to the point of open violence is a crisis likely. But it is a trend of great long term significance. India, as the largest and potentially most powerful non-Communist Asian nation, is in fact the major prize in Asia.

We have already invested $4.7 billion in the long-term economic buildup of a hopefully democratic power. But our politico-military policy has never matched our economic investment, partly because Pakistan shrewdly signed two alliances with us as a means of reinsurance against India. For this Pakistan has gotten some $700 million in US military aid, all of which has in fact gone to protect it against India. Per capita, the Paks have got much more aid from us than the Indians. We can and should protect Pakistan against India, but we cannot permit our ties—or our taste for Ayub against Nehru—to stand in the way of

---

[1] Source: Johnson Library, National Security File, Memos to the President, McGeorge Bundy, Vol. I, 11/63–2/64. Secret.

[2] Attached were telegram 2445 from New Delhi (Document 16), and telegram 2457 from New Delhi, February 20. In the latter Bowles sounded the alarm on what he saw as the steadily increasing role of the Soviet Union in Indian military procurement plans. Bowles noted that 3 months had passed since General Taylor had visited New Delhi and encouraged Indian officals to expect that U.S. agreement to a long-term military assistance program was imminent. With no subsequent word on that agreement, the Indian Government had begun to turn toward the Soviet Union to meet its needs. Bowles felt that the situation could still be salvaged and urged a rapid decision on military assistance.

a strong Indian policy. This would permit the tail to wag the dog, which is just what Paks are trying to do.

With India heading into a succession crisis, we have to keep a sharp eye out. If India falls apart we are the losers. If India goes Communist, it will be a disaster comparable only to the loss of China. Even if India reverts to pro-Soviet neutralism, our policy in Asia will be compromised. These risks are real, and the irony is that they are dangerous for Pakistan as well.

Bowles makes wordy sense on this problem, we think.

Bob Komer[3]

---

[3] Both Bundy's and Komer's typed signatures appear on the memorandum, but only Komer signed it.

---

21.   Message From Robert Komer of the National Security Council Staff to the Ambassador to India (Bowles)[1]

Washington, February 27, 1964.

Bundy and I can't help but feel that Orpheus engine for HF–24[2] is our secret weapon for sidetracking Soviet MIG and possibly SAM deals.[3] You yourself have pointed out how going ahead with HF–24 would also pander to Indian nationalism, while being the course least painful to the Paks. This track is also a lot easier than SAMs from here, which are out.

We understand that if UK would only get Bristol to put two of the test engines into flyable conditions, it should cost less than $1 million. Bristol of course is holding out for commitment on full develop-

---

[1] Source: Johnson Library, National Security File, Country File, India, Exchanges with Bowles. Secret. Notes on the message indicate that it was sent priority [text not declassified] as CAP 64063.

[2] HF–24 was a fighter aircraft manufactured in India.

[3] In a February 27 memorandum to Assistant Secretary of Defense for International Security Affairs William Bundy, Komer noted that President Johnson had read telegram 2457 from New Delhi (see footnote 2, Document 20) and was concerned about the inroads the Soviet Union was making in the Indian military establishment. (Washington National Records Center, RG 330, OASD/ISA Files: FRC 68 A 306, India, 091.31–320.2)

ment and tooling up cost first but surely HMG could make them see the light. Why shouldn't this be top priority claim on UK military aid? We've been touting this here, and have gotten DOD to raise in London. But it badly needs another big push from you and Gore-Booth now, if we're not to shut the barn door just after the horse is gone. Needless to say, our intervention is private to you.[4]

[4] The last sentence was added in Komer's handwriting. Bowles reported on February 28 that he had discussed U.S. concern over Soviet military sales to India with Defense Minister Chavan in the context of a possible 5-year military assistance program. Chavan indicated that Indian withdrawal from the agreement concerning the MIGs would be difficult, and he asked if the United States could provide some high-performance aircraft to fill the gap until the MIGs and improved HF–24s became available in 1967. (Telegram 2544 from New Delhi; National Archives and Records Administration, RG 59, Central Files 1964–66, DEF 19–3 US–INDIA) On March 5 the Department instructed the Embassy to make certain that the Indian Government understood the circumstances under which they might obtain assistance for the Indian Air Force from the West, and also instructed the Embassy to ensure that the Indians understood the problems they would encounter if they relied on the Soviet Union. (Telegram 1782 to New Delhi; ibid.)

22.   Telegram From the Embassy in Pakistan to the Department of State[1]

Karachi, March 3, 1964, 8 p.m.

1654. Kashmir.

1. I had 45-minute breakfast appointment with President Ayub in Dacca March 2. Principal Secretary Farooqui only other person present. About half of conversation devoted to Kashmir issue and upcoming GOP tactics related thereto. President said his government has made firm decision to return to Security Council this month. Said FonMin Bhutto would leave March 9 for New York. He did not seem worried about sponsorship of item in SC or outcome.

2. Without making frontal attack on his decision, I raised question as to wisdom of hurried resort to SC again without full consultation with friends. I noted possibility that some SC members might be antagonized by Pak tactics and that voting prospect might be somewhat less

[1] Source: National Archives and Records Administration, RG 59, Central Files 1964–66, POL 15–1 PAK. Secret; Priority. Repeated to USUN, Hong Kong, London, and New Delhi.

favorable for Pakistan now than in February. Some difficulty might be encountered in mustering affirmative votes for usual type of resolution by all non-Communist SC members. The tactical situation might argue strongly for different type of approach or at least a delay in renewal of Security Council effort.

3. President said GOP really had no alternative since it was fully committed to SC effort which was merely recessed last month. Abandonment now would be misinterpreted at home and abroad. President indicated he was aware that GRC would be in chair during March and apparently assumed continued fairly benevolent ChiNat posture.

4. I told President that if die was cast on reopening of matter in SC, further consideration should certainly be given procedure best calculated to enlist GOI cooperation in settlement effort. We still thought consensus approach least abrasive and offered better prospects [than resolution?] opposed by GOI and certain to be vetoed by USSR. We thought that a consensus statement making three essential points stressed by GOP (reaffirmation of standing UN position, confirmation of validity of self-determination principle, and invocation of some mediatory effort with assistance of UN SecGen), might again be sought.

5. President said a good consensus statement would be acceptable to Pakistan as substitute for resolution if Soviets and Indians could be induced not to oppose it. But he was convinced that it would be impossible to avoid Soviet and Indian opposition. In that event the GOP would prefer traditional type of resolution, even though vetoed by the USSR. The force of a resolution blocked only by Soviet misuse of veto would be understood by all, whereas a consensus statement probably somewhat watered down, and still objected to by Indians and Soviets, would not have much weight or meaning.

6. I paraphrased language used by Secretary in his recent Washington meeting with Bhutto to effect that India could not be coerced into Kashmir settlement. A durable settlement could only be attained by voluntary agreement of interested parties.

7. President said that GOP has sought voluntary agreement with India for many years without success. His government must question whether a purely conciliatory approach will have any effect on the GOI. He did not imply that the threat of force should be invoked, but he felt that more energetic diplomatic action by Pakistan was only course open in present situation. He did agree up to a point about the futility of coercion, but he clearly felt that activist measures short of that must be resorted to in order to compel the Indians to see that a solution must be achieved.

8. President said deliberately and with emphasis that his government was now determined to press continuously on the Kashmir issue

until settlement reached. He said his government will not give GOI any rest until then.

9. Other principal topic of conversation was recent Chou En-lai visit on which I obtained illuminating though not new or surprising background. This is covered in separate tel.[2]

McConaughy

[2] McConaughy concluded from his discussion of the Chou En-lai visit with Ayub that Ayub wanted to play the role of honest broker in establishing more effective communication between the United States and China, but was coming to recognize the stumbling blocks in the way of any détente. (Telegram 1665 from Karachi, March 5; ibid.) The Embassy's overall assessment of the effect of the Chou visit, provided in telegram 1589 from Karachi, February 25, was that the visit, which concluded on February 26, had not substantially altered the character of relations between Pakistan and China. The process of "normalization" continued but ties had not been visibly broadened in the economic, cultural, or political realms, and Ayub and Bhutto had publicly reaffirmed Pakistan's adherence to its Western alliances during the visit. (Ibid., POL 7 CHICOM)

23. Memorandum From the President's Special Assistant for National Security Affairs (Bundy) and Robert Komer of the National Security Council Staff to President Johnson[1]

Washington, March 8, 1964.

Two Pak/Indian matters pose immediate problems. Recent evidence suggests that Ayub smells blood in his effort to lean on India over Kashmir, at a time when India is weak. He just told McConaughy he wouldn't let up until he got a settlement (Karachi 1654).[2] We see his tactics as totally miscast. India's weakness will just lead it to dig its heels in harder, so the only result may be a big Kashmir crisis, perhaps this summer, which could reduce rather than enhance the prospects for settlement and catch us in the middle again to boot.

Even more worrisome, that tough bargainer Ayub seems to think he has us on the run, given our mild reaction to the Ayub–Chou love feast and our continued benign tolerance of constant flaying of us by the Pak press, plus public criticisms by Ayub himself. He'll be convinced

[1] Source: Johnson Library, National Security File, Country File, Pakistan, Vol. I, Memos, 11/63–5/64. Secret.

[2] Document 22.

of it if we now go in and dangle a five-year Military Assistance carrot before him, without simultaneous blunt talk about having reached the limits of our tolerance over his playing with Peiping at the very time when it is squeezing us in Southeast Asia. Indeed, we planned the five-year package (which as you recall has been kept free of any price tag) for the very purpose of permitting us to talk bluntly.

We here believe Ayub fully realizes how his utter dependence on us sets limits of tolerance beyond which he cannot go. But State's intelligence chief[3] (just back from Karachi) says that the Paks are very pleased that these limits are so flexible, and will keep stretching them as far as they can.

So it's time for us to do a bit of hard bargaining with Ayub by setting out firmly to him the terms on which we will continue US military and, implicitly, economic aid (several hundred million dollars a year). A five-year MAP approach (even on a no-commitment basis) is such a big carrot that unless we put the quid pro quo clear on it he may see it as another evidence we're caving. This will only encourage him to step up his pressure on India thus putting us on a direct collision course.

Talbot, our Near East Assistant Secretary, will see Ayub Wednesday,[4] which is the time for setting out where we stand. Only if Talbot is clearly speaking for you, however, will he carry the necessary weight. As you know, Ayub believes in direct dealing at the top. So we suggest that you arm Talbot with the attached message which is carefully calculated for effect.[5]

McGB
RWK

---

[3] Thomas L. Hughes.

[4] March 11. Talbot was scheduled to visit India and Pakistan as part of a tour of posts in the Middle East and South Asia.

[5] Bundy sent this joint memorandum and the attached draft message to President Johnson on March 8 under cover of a shorter memorandum in which he made the point that they were designed to begin the job of "staightening out Ayub Khan, which will take a lot of time." Johnson checked the option line that reads: "Speak to me." He added a handwritten note that reads: "I'm against sending message to Talbot. If I know Ayub it will only incense him." (Johnson Library, National Security File, Country File, Pakistan, Vol. I, Memos, 11/63–5/64) Bundy discussed the proposed message in a telephone conversation with Johnson on March 9. Johnson reiterated that he felt it would be a mistake to send a stiff message to Ayub in his name which Ayub would be certain to resent. Bundy agreed but repeated the case for taking a firm line: "The reason for talking firmly is that if we don't change the signals our man is going in there with a military assistance package, and we do not want them to think that we come right around with more cookies." Johnson approved sending a firm message through Talbot, one he anticipated would "make him [Ayub] come to us." (Ibid., Recordings and Transcripts, Recording of a telephone conversation between President Johnson and McGeorge Bundy, March 9, 1964, 4:27 p.m., Tape F64.16, Side B, PNO 1)

24.   **Letter From the President's Special Assistant for National Security Affairs (Bundy) to the Ambassador to India (Bowles)**[1]

Washington, March 9, 1964.

Dear Chet:

We here have reacted with lively sympathy to your paeans of woe from Delhi, and have been doing all we can to help.[2]

For what it's worth, my feeling (and Bob Komer's, too) is that we're the victims of an inevitable falling off in US/Indian relations from the high point of Winter 1962. There's no use blaming ourselves unduly that neither Washington nor Delhi can sustain the high pitch of collaboration which emerged from the Chicom attack. We've had trouble on our side sustaining the momentum of our relationship, but the Indian slate is by no means clean either. VOA was a fiasco, Bokaro failed at least partly because of Indian stickiness, and Delhi's handling of its military program has been so tediously slow as to damp much of our enthusiasm here. These are facts with which we must live.

As I see it, we're also going through the painful transition of disengaging from the out and out pro-Pak policy of the 1950's, and shifting to one more consonant with our real strategic interests. This is not an easy process at best, and I must say that neither our Pak nor our Indian friends make it any easier.

Of one thing you may be sure—the President too sees your problem with lively sympathy. His actions to date should lay to rest any unfounded Indian (or Pak) suspicions that he sees matters differently from his predecessor, and I may add that he is annoyed by these suspicions. His authorization of five-year MAP approaches (which marks much more of a departure in the case of India than in that of Pakistan) is ample evidence of his position.

But you in turn will understand that the struggle over AID is critical here. The President cannot expose his flank right now by promis-

---

[1] Source: Johnson Library, National Security File, Country File, India, Exchanges with Bowles (cont.). Secret.

[2] On March 9, Bowles sent a [text not declassified] cable to Bundy and Komer stating his desire to return to Washington and express his concerns about South Asian policy directly to President Johnson. (Telegram 901600Z from New Delhi; ibid.) Bundy responded [text not declassified] and reassured Bowles that his cables were reaching the President and receiving serious consideration. Bundy added that he and Komer did not see "any far-reaching decisions on Kashmir, aid to India, or pre-empting Soviets being made quite yet, and frankly doubt whether your return just now would prove especially satisfying." (White House telegram CAP 64069 to New Delhi, from Bundy to Bowles, March 9; ibid.)

ing amounts on which he may be unable to perform. I'm sure you realize this. And I know from what he's said that he counts on you to get this across in Delhi as no one else really could.

On top of all this, we have an election year; the moratorium on politics is over, and we're going to have to steel ourselves for a lot of silly fuss. So if we're a little slow in answering your mail or in responding to your counsel, bear with us. Once every four years Washington is on the firing line and we're going to have to get through November before we can turn as fully to our foreign concerns as our far-flung viceroys would like. So be of good cheer.

Sincerely,

McGeorge Bundy[3]

---

[3] Printed from a copy that bears this typed signature.

---

25.   Telegram From the Department of State to the Embassy in Pakistan[1]

Washington, March 9, 1964, 8:55 p.m.

1182. For Talbot and Ambassador. The President is deeply concerned over the indication that Ayub intends to continue his policy of leaning on India (and on us), using the Chicoms as a lever. He desires that before opening five-year MAP discussions with the Paks we seek to reach the necessary degree of understanding on future US/Pak relations.

To this end President wants Talbot to make frank, straightforward exposition of the obligations as well as benefits of Pakistan's alliance with the US. Ayub must be made to understand that there are limits of US tolerance beyond which he cannot go if he wants continued US support and that he is close to these limits.

Talbot should make presentation as his own and should not state it as direct message from President, but he is authorized to say he is

---

[1] Source: National Archives and Records Administration, RG 59, Central Files 1964–66, POL PAK–US. Secret; Immediate; Exdis. Drafted in the White House and approved by Don T. Christensen (S/S). A draft of the telegram, March 9, 6 p.m., was initialed by Rusk. (Ibid.)

expressing opinion of entire USG and not just his own view or even that of Department on importance of preserving the basic Pakistani-US relationship which has served us both so well in the past. We fully aware of Pak unhappiness over our policy toward India, but believe Paks are now fully aware that for reasons of global anti-Communist strategy we are determined to help India.

Despite our differences, we on our side have continued our full support of Pakistan's vital economic development, we have sought to help bring about a Kashmir settlement, we have tried in a number of ways to reassure Paks of our support against any aggression—including one from India. But we cannot continue to sustain past close US/Pak relationship if it becomes more and more of a one-way street. In effect, while continuing to give lip service to alliance, Paks are adopting tactics quite inconsistent with overall US anti-Communist strategy in Asia, which necessarily focussing largely on Chicom threat. We are determined to face squarely our responsibility for helping to maintain the security of free Asia against the Chinese Communists until the nations concerned are strong enough to preserve it themselves. Pak policy cuts across this grain. When we are trying to stop Chinese Communist infiltration in Southeast Asia, Paks in effect seem to be encouraging them to make hay in South Asia.

Moreover, though we understand Pak motivations in using China to help them lean on India, we gravely doubt that it will produce the results Paks want. The Free World cannot afford to let India, any more than Pakistan, succumb to Communism or fall apart. As to Kashmir, we see Pak pressure tactics as forcing India to dig in its heels at a time of weakness, whereas making common cause with India against China could be far more productive.

Nor is it consonant with the spirit of our alliance to find ourselves the object of constant public harassment in Pakistan, even including high-level pronouncements.

You may say that President himself, who feels he knows Ayub well and admires what he has done for Pakistan, has expressed confidence Ayub will appreciate straight talk from us, and not misconstrue our candor. It is President's own earnest desire to see end to mutual back-biting, and reaffirmation of those strong mutual interests which still underlie US/Pak relationship, in order prevent this relationship from slipping further downhill.

We do not want you to mention five-year MAP approach till we have had chance to sort out Pak reactions to your political approach. Nor do we want you to link our failure to be forthcoming yet on MAP to our concerns above. We prefer to let Paks make this link themselves. If Paks raise MAP question you may say that we had hoped to be able start talking about ongoing MAP, but general atmosphere in USG (including sentiment on Capitol Hill) is such that pending further sorting out of foreign aid prospects and other matters we feel it better hold off. Should Ayub raise Indian discussions, you can reply that all we are telling Indians as yet is to come up with austere longer-term defense plans so we can have basis for later MAP decisions here too.

This message supplements Deptel 1174 to Karachi[2] and should of course supersede it in event of any conflict.

Rusk

---

[2] Telegram 1174 to Karachi, March 7, provided guidance for Talbot's impending discussions with Ayub. The Department stated that the principal objectives of the conversations should be to get a fresh assessment of the results of the Chou visit, and to establish a framework of political understanding within which it would be possible to move into a discussion of long-term military assistance to Pakistan. (Ibid., POL 7 PAK–US)

---

26.   Telegram From the Embassy in India to the Department of State[1]

New Delhi, March 10, 1964, 1 p.m.

2646. Embtel 2639.[2] In followup conversation with Desai evening March 8, Talbot explained US view of question SC Kashmir debate as set out Deptel 1806 and as also reflected Deptel 1807.[3] Desai heard him out and then set out GOI position even more sharply than it had emerged previous day. He said GOI is not going to concur or participate in resumption SC debate at present time and under circumstances of Pak request.

---

[1] Source: National Archives and Records Administration, RG 59, Central Files 1964–66, POL 32–1 INDIA–PAK. Confidential; Priority. Repeated to Karachi, London, and USUN.

[2] Telegram 2639 from New Delhi, March 9, reported on the initial meeting Talbot and Bowles had on March 7 with M. J. Desai, Secretary General of the Ministry of External Affairs. Desai laid out India's objections to a resumption of the Secretary Council debate on Kashmir, and accepted Talbot's point that the United States could not oppose a request made by any UN member for Security Council consideration of a pressing problem. (Ibid.)

[3] Talbot visited India March 6–10. In telegrams 1806 and 1807 to New Delhi, both March 7, the Department suggested to Talbot that the best line to take with Indian officials concerning the resumption of Security Council debate on Kashmir was that a rapid crystallization of a consensus statement that would not damage the interests of either party would be the best way to minimize debate and avoid further heightening of tension between India and Pakistan. (Telegram 1806 is ibid., telegram 1807 is ibid., POL 7 CHICOM)

Furthermore, GOI is not going to discuss Kashmir with GOP at least until communal questions discussed and communal tensions tranquilized. He sought to dramatize importance this matter by citing, among other things, issuance 120,000 migration certificates to residents East Pakistan for removal to India.

On the Kashmir question, Desai said British High Commissioner Gore-Booth had on last day previous debate come to him with proposition India accept reference either in resolution or consensus to past resolutions calling them any name that would suit India. Desai said he had explained that India could take references to resolutions of August 13, 1948[4] and Jan. 5, 1949,[5] but no others; and of course full compliance with all recommendations of these resolutions would be precondition for progress on substance of issue.

Talbot said it would help USG's thinking in all this to know how far GOI intends to carry integration of Kashmir, public discussion of which in India does not help. Desai said that there is no intention or prospect of repeal of Article 370 of Indian Constitution but he gave impression steps short of this by Kashmir government itself, such as adopting titles chief minister and governor, will probably go ahead.[6]

Bowles

---

[4] Printed in *U.S. Participation in the United Nations: Report by the President to the Congress for the Year 1948* (Department of State Publication 3437, 1949).

[5] UN doc. S/1196.

[6] Talbot also discussed the Kashmir issue with Shastri, whom he found to be moderate and impressive in a way that reminded him of former President Truman. (Telegram 2662 from New Delhi, March 11; National Archives and Records Administration, RG 59, Central Files 1964–66, POL 32–1 INDIA–PAK) Talbot discussed the proposed military assistance agreement with Defense Minister Chavan, and emphasized the need for an Indian defense plan that gave primacy to the needs of economic development. (Telegram 2637 from New Delhi, March 9; Johnson Library, National Security Files, Country File, India, Cables, Vol. I, 12/63–11/64) On March 9 Talbot and Bowles paid a courtesy visit to Prime Minister Nehru. Talbot was shocked by Nehru's mental and psychological deterioration, and reported that "it was quite impossible to communicate with him." (Telegram 2659 from New Delhi, March 11; ibid.)

27.   Telegram From the Embassy Office in Pakistan to the Department of State[1]

Rawalpindi, March 11, 1964, 2145Z.

47. Dept to determine distribution if any to other posts. Ref: Deptels 1182 and 1174.[2]

1. Assistant Secretary Talbot and I met with President Ayub March 11 at Lahore for one hour and 35 minutes.[3] Discussion covered fundamental aspects US–Pak relations with Talbot setting forth in clear terms deep US Govt. concern over current GOP policies toward Communist China and India as set forth Deptel 1182. Ayub was cordial, gave Talbot full hearing but responded in firm terms expounding familiar Pak position on these issues.

2. In preliminary discussion Ayub expressed his admiration for President Johnson and asked particularly that his personal regards be sent to President and Mrs. Johnson and to Mrs. Kennedy. He questioned Talbot on impressions gained at previous stops during Talbot's current trip and was particularly interested in Talbot's appraisal of Nehru's health. Talbot told Ayub Nehru not at all well although others in Delhi say he much improved. Talbot said he found in Delhi a mood on impending change in leadership but it quite uncertain how long it will take for change to take place and could be weeks, months or even year or two. He found Shastri impressive, quiet, serious and as man willing reach beyond set patterns. He mentioned Shastri prepared start talks on communal, refugee and eviction problems at whatever level desired. Ayub pointed out that he had offered such talks and GOI had avoided reply.

---

[1] Source: National Archives and Records Administration, RG 59, Central Files 1964–66, POL PAK–US. Secret; Immediate; Exdis. Passed to the White House at 7:11 a.m. The telegram is a joint telegram from CUSASEC MAAG and the Embassy Office in Rawalpindi.

[2] See Document 25 and footnote 2 thereto.

[3] Talbot visited Pakistan March 10–13. On March 11 he met briefly with Foreign Minister Bhutto in Lahore where they discussed the Kashmir issue and U.S. concerns about Pakistan's relationship with China. In discussing Kashmir, Bhutto said that Pakistan would be prepared to accept a consensus statement as the result of the Security Council debate if the statement did not dilute Pakistan's position under prior UN resolutions. (Telegram 46 from Rawalpindi, March 11; National Archives and Records Administration, RG 59, Central Files 1964–66, POL 32–1 INDIA–PAK) On March 13 Talbot and McConaughy met with Finance Minister Shoaib. McConaughy had to leave the meeting before it was concluded and reported on the conversation in telegram 1724 from Karachi, March 13. (Ibid., ORG 7 NEA) Talbot reported on the conclusion of the conversation in telegram 51 from Rawalpindi, March 13. (Ibid., POL 2 PAK) Talbot and McConaughy repeated the concerns they had earlier expressed to Ayub in their conversation with Shoaib. Shoaib told them that Ayub's government intended to make a strong effort to reduce the dangerously high level of tension between Pakistan and India. Shoaib also said that he felt that Pakistan had "turned the corner" in its attitude toward the United States and he anticipated that relations would improve.

3. Following preliminaries, Talbot stated he wished to discuss with President Ayub basic state US–Pak relationship and how relationship can be reaffirmed and strengthened. US understood quite fully Pak concern over US policy toward India and we think Paks likewise recognize both strong efforts assure military aid to India will not have adverse effects feared by Pakistan as well as role played by aid to India in our basic anti-Communist posture in Asia. Naturally in this part of world our anti-Communist efforts directed against Communist China. Although we are also concerned by Soviet maneuvering, as we making clear in India. We are determined to help threatened countries in Asia to protect their security until they are strong enough protect themselves. US policy is to contain the Chinese Communist threat and do what is necessary to keep ChiComs from breaking out.

4. Talbot said that while US did not regard Chou En-lai visit by itself as necessarily damaging to US–Pak relations, Washington is increasingly anxious over indications that US and Pakistan approaches to Communist China issue are growing further and further apart. While we try to confine ChiComs in Southeast Asia, Pak actions seem to enable them to make hay in South Asia. He could report that USG as whole profoundly disturbed by this situation.

5. Talbot said US obviously has stake in stability and security of subcontinent. We would still like to pursue an overall subcontinental policy but until this possible in future we are working with India and Pakistan individually. However, US fearful that current differences in US–Pakistan tactical and strategic actions will cause at minimum confusion and doubt and at maximum much more serious problems. Talbot went on to point out that US assumes there are several things GOP desires from us: (a) credible assurances—which have been given, and are subject to refinement to assist Pakistan if attacked; (b) US continued commitment to its obligations under regional pacts; (c) continuation of US military and economic assistance; and (d) assistance in seeking resolution of Kashmir issue. US has met all of these requirements of Pakistan.

6. Talbot pointed out that in return US has certain requirements from Pakistan: (a) maintenance of its commitments to CENTO and SEATO which Ayub has recently reaffirmed; (b) assurances that Pak–ChiCom relations will not be permitted to develop in such way as to affect adversely US–Pak relations or disrupt US efforts to support and prop up countries in Asia resisting ChiComs (Talbot noted for example we would take amiss any Pak support for ChiCom initiatives with Afro–Asian nations against US security interests); (c) rejection of use of force against India. On substance of Kashmir issue, US stand is clear as restated recently by Secretary Rusk. We wish to be helpful. However, when we differ on tactics to gain this end, US must reserve to itself

choice of means whose pursuit it will support. US is persuaded that unremitting pressure against India over Kashmir at this stage will have more adverse than favorable effects, for several reasons. First, political transition from Nehru is now at hand in India and pressure now on Kashmir would give leg up to anti-Pakistan extremists in resulting struggle for power. Secondly, within Kashmir current ferment could in itself produce real change but chances of this desired end far better if process allowed to develop without external pressures. US recognizes it differs with Pak on this issue but feels there is firm basis for its judgment.

7. In summing up, Talbot emphasized US anxious that it and Pakistan enjoy full, solid relationship which to benefit of both. We disturbed that Pak actions undermining our efforts to be helpful. As one example, we would like to see Pak restraint on criticism of US actions particularly since we feel we have exercised restraint towards Pakistan. With respect to China we know that Ayub perceives long-range ChiCom threat, but unhappily we differ on how to deal with Communist China. Concluding, Talbot said that President Johnson, who feels he knows Ayub well and who admires what Ayub has done for Pakistan, had felt that Ayub would appreciate candid statement of what is troubling us. Certainly President looks to strengthening of our relationship in spirit of mutual confidence.

8. Ayub then responded with restatement basic Pak position. First he stressed that Pakistan considers us its "natural friend" and, in fact, the "natural friend" of all small countries of Asia. In every instance where trouble arises from powerful neighbors—Soviet Union, Communist China and India—Asian countries look for friendship. Country most interested in their future is US. He reaffirmed Paks intended to continue membership in pacts. CENTO he especially considered vital for GOP protection; GOP also will remain in SEATO, which it joined mainly for sake of friendship with US, since it has no basic national interest of its own in Southeast Asia. Furthermore, Pakistan will not interfere with US actions to protect Asia and, in fact, Pakistan wants to promote strength and prestige of US.

9. Ayub said, however, that while GOP understands and appreciates reasons for US aid to India, it differs from US on this issue. Neither India nor Pakistan can be defended by itself and all invasions into subcontinent have succeeded when people in area divided. Therefore, defense of subcontinent needs some sort of Indo–Pak settlement, but US does not further this objective by its aid to India.

10. Ayub then set forth his concerns over Indian military buildup, over US failure point out to India danger of internecine war with Pakistan, and over US unwillingness to press India for Indo–Pak settlement. He said GOP had examined time and again Indian military

requirements for defense against Communist China. At most ChiComs could use 16 brigades in northern area with one or two more in reserve. Therefore, he questioned where India could use 16, let alone 21, divisions and 45 Air Force squadrons. Ayub pointed out even Chinese railroad to Lhasa will not drastically improve Chinese logic position since railroad will not be open during winter months and at best will have capacity for maintaining two or three divisions. GOP has concluded India intends to revert to its initial focus on Pakistan as no. 1 enemy and there will be no further hostilities between China and India. Indian military build-up is constant threat to Pakistan and while GOP has US guarantee it feels in last resort it will have to depend on own resources. Furthermore, Indian military build-up has hardened Indian stance generally. This has had upsetting effect on Pak public and has contributed to difficulties such as eviction of Muslims and border firings. Therefore, while US is helping India as part of its worldwide involvements, Pakistan is more anxious about effect on it of India's military build-up.

11. Ayub then went on to defend Pak–ChiCom border agreement stating Paks merely wished to avoid very situation India faced. He felt that, given difficult terrain in north and untenable military situation from Pak viewpoint vis-à-vis, Communist China, there was legitimate basis for border demarcation.

12. Ayub recognized it tragic that US–Pak relationship had become strained but what could we expect except that Pakistanis would be unhappy over US aid to India. He reiterated GOP has no intention of interfering with US actions in Asia and in fact wants to see US influence stay in area. He had made this point repeatedly in his trips to Burma, Ceylon and Malaysia. However, US–Pak relations had eroded due to US and Indian actions and Pakistan must decrease its military and political commitments in order to be free to deal with trouble from India.

13. On Chou En-lai's visit, Ayub said Chinese had asked to come several times before Paks agreed. During visit he had spent half of discussion time urging settlement with US and pressing ChiComs not to do anything which would aggravate situation in Asia since Paks feel any turmoil in Asia will affect US interests.

14. Ayub thought basic difference between US and Paks is attitude toward India and assessment Indian intentions. GOP, having tried conciliatory policy without success, feels moderate approach will not achieve results. Ayub said there no statesmanship in India today and Pak people feel US siding with India against Pakistan. This is deplorable situation and prospect is, while US policy in India continues on present course, US–Pak relations will encounter difficulties. Ayub said he will continue endeavor to keep things in check and not let events be taken

out of context. This will not be simple task since he under great amount of pressure. He is one who must defend established policy, and our present course in India throws added load on him here.

15. Talbot and Ayub then engaged in spirited exchange with Talbot continually pressing Ayub particularly on questions of Pak–ChiCom relations and Pak views regarding India.

16. In discussing Indo–Pak relations Talbot raised further points:

(A) US feels its involvement in military assistance to India helpful and useful to Pakistan in part because of restraining influence it enables us to exert on Indian program. Ayub acknowledged US role is not entirely fruitless.

(B) US feels Pak tactics of harassment of India are troublesome and against Paks' own long-range interests, and complaints against our aid to India not helpful. Ayub responded that Paks should at least have right to complain even if they could not change the course of US policy. GOP feels it has been restrained in view of public reaction to US military aid to India.

(C) US feels Pak–ChiCom relationship as means of leaning of US on India is making our task of seeking settlement in subcontinent more complicated. Ayub responded that US asking too much if it wishes reduction of pressure on India. India for years has been maintaining overwhelming pressures on Pakistan seeking its isolation, neutralization and surrender. In response Paks must "keep India engaged." GOP is not asking ChiComs to support it in this venture. GOP continues to exclude ChiCom influence from Pakistan, and has no capability to affect ChiCom efforts elsewhere. If India wants Pak–ChiCom relationship ended, it can achieve this by agreeing to Indo–Pak settlement. GOP is prepared to search for "honorable peace," but it will not surrender or in current circumstances give up its right to keep India "engaged." Pakistan today has no alternative but steady counter-pressure on India. It considers India aggressor and sees no basis for Indian fears of Pakistan since India is five times as strong as Pakistan.

(D) Talbot stressed US can be helpful only if there is reduction in Indo–Pak tensions. Ayub responded that reduction of tension can only take place at "power house" where generated. Pakistan only reflects emissions beamed on it by India. India continuing pressure on Pakistan as indicated by evictions, integration of Kashmir, etc. However, if India takes half step toward reduction of tensions GOP prepared to take full step. Ayub said he would give his personal guarantee in writing on this point. Talbot pointed out GOP actions however have effect of cancelling out efforts to decrease pressures.

(E) Ayub urged that we discuss first with Pakistan any initiatives we wish to take in India to reduce tensions and promised to give his best advice and lend full assistance. Talbot said all our efforts directed toward peace, security and progress in subcontinent.

17. Talbot returned to Pak–ChiCom relations, reiterating that these of major concern to us. He pointed out Pak–ChiCom relationship not only troubles us, but makes it more difficult for those Indians interested in Indo–Pak reconciliation to be helpful. Ayub responded "Let them be troubled." However, he again assured Talbot that GOP will do nothing that will jeopardize US interests. Talbot responded that Chi-Coms gaining opening in South Asia through Pak relationship which in fact cuts sharply across US policy.

18. When we pressed him, Ayub said that GOP seeking only "very limited relationship" with ChiComs based on three main requirements:

(A) A neighborly relationship with ChiComs but not developing beyond this point; (B) a window on Peking; and (C) Chinese markets for Pak exports since restrictive import policies of ECM and US hamper exports of manufactured goods to these areas. Ayub indicated Paks not prepared to cut back this relationship as thus defined, since GOP has other enemies besides Communists, e.g. India. When Talbot observed extension of Pak–ChiCom relationship would be of grave concern to us, Ayub replied that when Chou En-lai in Pakistan, Paks refused to discuss even innocuous cultural agreements because US is "touchy." Pressed further about intentions Ayub said that while relationship strictly limited today no absolute guarantee can be given about future. Ayub said Pakistan wants no changed policy and sees no need to shift from present limited relationships unless US should further compromise Pakistan's position, which would be great tragedy. Ayub also felt it against US interests not to have tentacles in Communist China while at same time viewing ChiCom policy toward US as "very foolish."

19. In somewhat repetitious final go-around on our concerns and Pak reactions, Talbot emphasized that US shaping its policies in South Asia with great care to assure minimum provocation and maximum helpfulness to both Pakistan and India. On military aid to India, for example, he could imagine no other country directly attacked by Chi-Coms which would have received so little US aid as it braced itself against possible invasion. We had limited our response to Indian requests primarily out of deference to Pak anxieties arising out of unresolved Pak–Indian disputes. Ayub described himself as grateful for this. Talbot continued with hope GOP in turn would understand US anxieties, foremost among them ChiComs breaking out through South Asia thanks to Paks. He wanted be sure Ayub understood depth of US feeling on this point. Ayub did not budge in his response. He said Paks do not wish to dictate US policy toward ChiComs but must have right to reduce tensions with other neighbors while India's power expanding. For good measure he added that while US has given assurances of

support to GOP, Paks feel US might have difficulty delivering on these assurances. If it did Soviets might threaten to join in on India's side, thus escalating the struggle. Pakistan would prefer to fight its own battles.

As conversation shifted to general topics and meeting came to close, Ayub again asked that his highest respects be conveyed to the President.

Comments will follow in separate message.[4]

Spielman

_____

[4] Document 28.

_____

28.   Telegram From the Embassy Office in Pakistan to the Department of State[1]

Rawalpindi, March 12, 1964, 1946Z.

48. Dept to determine any further distribution. Ref: Emboff tel 47.[2] Fm Talbot. Ambassador McConaughy and I share several major impressions of Ayub's responses to my representation. We read his statements as again demonstrating that the American connection is fundamental to his policy. He sees no alternative to this for Pakistan, nor indeed any alternative to an American presence in free Asia if latter is to survive. Equally, I felt, he is directing Pak policies with assurance of a man persuaded that the US is reciprocally reliant on its Pakistan connection in an Asia awash in neutralism.

Ambassador suggests Ayub is also increasingly influenced by evidence that US is "allowing" other allies—e.g., France, Britain, and now Turkey and Greece—substantially greater latitude than previously to take independent and even disruptive actions without destroying alliance relations, and applies this lesson to what he sees as his political needs in Pakistan.

It was in this context, I believe, that Ayub replied to our démarche for restraint in his dealings with ChiComs and India. Paks feeling virtuous after having demonstrated capability of restraint during

_____

[1] Source: National Archives and Records Administration, RG 59, Cental Files 1964–66, POL PAK–US. Secret; Immediate. Passed to the White House at 6:33 p.m. The telegram is a joint telegram from CUSASEC MAAG and the Embassy Office in Rawalpindi.
[2] Document 27.

Chou's visit from which, they point out, emerged not even previously expected cultural agreement. Paks therefore feel we should be satisfied with their performance in dealing with ChiComs at no cost to West, leaving them free at will to use their new ChiCom connections as pressure against India. I am uncertain how far our talk led Ayud away from this comfortable assumption, but at minimum it should intensify debate that has recently occupied top echelons here over American limits of tolerance. Ayub obviously gave very little ground in conversation. Ambassador and I feel, however that he and his advisors might now consider that their actions have carried them closer to our toleration limits than some may heretofore have believed. This should increase their anxiety over effect on US of further "normalization" moves proposed by ChiComs and also their caution in openly using ChiCom relationship for ploys against India.

On India Ayub's line is even more defiant than last year. I made no visible dent on his expressed determination to put unremitting pressure on India until something gives on Kashmir. He scorned idea that a more cooperative posture would be more persuasive with those blessed Hindus. Repeatedly he brushed aside my argument that Pakistan's hard line, like its dalliance with China, renders ineffective US efforts to influence India toward compromise on Indo–Pak issues. He appraises Indian position on these, especially Kashmir, as adamant and reciprocates heartily by equal adamacy. If this is in part a posture assumed for our benefit, it obviously also carries explosive potentials. Ayub's attitude may rest on several separate judgments. In circumstances of today he feels he has more latitude than last year to press publicly and deliberately against India without damage to Pak interests. He presumably believes Pak's relations with other Afro–Asian countries stronger than last year while India's prestige has dropped. His philosophy of use of power clearly impels him to strive for settlement of dispute by pressing hard on opponent, taking full advantage of situations of weakness. This leads him to judgment Pakistan relatively stronger now vis-à-vis India than likely to be several years hence. Finally, in strong stand on Kashmir he appeals to emotions of Pakistani patriotism and solidarity which are mainsprings of support to his regime.

Ayub appears to be playing complicated game in mixed atmosphere of frustration and self confidence. Several recent actions, such as return to Security Council, suggest Paks in mood to follow impulses to act, but then anxious to try to bring US aboard. Object, of course, is to make every effort keep Kashmir question in motion, but not lose Americans in process. Meanwhile, it is increasingly clear that Ayub, for reasons of dignity or otherwise, has put out instruction that Paks shall not make any assistance requests. Paks have never mentioned deferred Dacca airport loan. General LeMay said nobody raised MAP questions with him, nor have I encountered any such request. It would seem evident Paks unwilling get themselves in begging position while sorting our present troubles in overall relationship with US.

At same time Ambassador points out Ayub's references to "cutting commitments" reflect his current unwillingness to commit troops outside Pakistan for CENTO or SEATO purposes, as well as evident reluctance to take on any new or expanded commitments.

Before leaving subcontinent I hope to send you some comments on our policy dilemmas in South Asia. Meanwhile it is apparent our problems in Pakistan have not been resolved.[3]

---

[3] The telegram was transmitted via military channels and bears no signature.

---

29.   Memorandum From the Director of the Office of United Nations Political Affairs (Buffum) to the Deputy Assistant Secretary of State for International Organization Affairs (Gardner)[1]

Washington, March 23, 1964.

SUBJECT

Kashmir Debate in UN Security Council

In response to your inquiry, the following is a digest of recent Security Council consideration of the Kashmir problem.

At the request of the Indian Representative (which was moved to a vote by the Czech Representative), the Security Council on March 20 agreed to adjourn debate on the Kashmir question until May 5. The non-communist "nine" of the Security Council subscribed to a statement made to the Council by Brazil's Ambassador Bernardes which inter alia reserved the right of the Security Council President or any Member to reconvene the Council before May 5 should new developments of a military or political nature alter or worsen the situation prevailing in Jammu and Kashmir. Bernardes also appealed to the parties to "refrain from any action or threat of action capable of endan-

---

[1] Source: National Archives and Records Administration, RG 59, Central Files 1964–66, POL 32–1 INDIA–PAK. Limited Official Use. Drafted by John W. Kimball of UNP.

gering international peace and security or likely to make this already complex and delicate problem still more intractable."

As you know, Pakistan first requested the Security Council to deal with what it termed in January a worsening situation in Kashmir. The Council met between February 3 and 17 to hear Pakistani Foreign Minister Bhutto and Indian Minister for Education Chagla exchange views on this problem.

During these sessions in February, the United States did not assume its previous overtly-active role in the negotiations and tried to avoid the introduction of a resolution which we believed would be vetoed by the USSR. We wished instead to quietly arrange a consensus statement by the Council to the effect that communal harmony in the subcontinent should be restored, that the parties should resume negotiations to settle their outstanding differences, including Kashmir, and the possibility of third-party mediation, with some sort of assistance from the UN Secretary-General, should be considered. Although the "nine" favored this approach, the Indians rejected any mention of "past actions" or "past proceedings" (referring to past UN resolutions) in the operative paragraphs of the consensus and subsequently the Pakistanis withdrew their earlier agreement to a consensus, stating that a resolution, even if vetoed, would be preferable. At this point, Bhutto abruptly moved an adjournment, ostensibly to enable him to return home for further consultations, but apparently to play host to Chou En Lai.

After Chou left, Pakistan requested the Security Council to resume its consideration of the Kashmir issue, but India, in its turn, found it desirable to oppose this move, arguing that its ministerial-level personnel were occupied in budget matters before the Indian Parliament and could not travel to New York before late April.

Eventually, however, the Council met again on March 17, with Pakistan represented by Bhutto and India by its Permanent Representative, Chakravarty. After a moderate statement by Bhutto outlining his government's views on the situation in Kashmir, Chakravarty asked for an adjournment of the Council to late April or early May to enable India to be properly represented before the Council. The Czech Representative supported this call for adjournment and requested a vote under Rule 33 (3) for adjournment to May 5. Ambassador Bernardes, however, persuaded the Czech to withdraw his motion and suggested instead that the Council suspend discussion for several days in order to permit consultations among the Members on the question of adjournment for the longer period.

Between March 17 and 20, there was considerable activity in New York among the "nine" to see in what ways India's request for adjournment could be "conditioned" to show the Council's continuing interest in progress on the Kashmir question as well as to meet, at least in part, the desire of Mr. Bhutto to hold the line against further Indian moves (which were also contrary to the spirit of the UN's previous resolutions) to integrate Kashmir into the Indian Union.

Although the US tended to favor adjournment at this time in order to relieve the Indian domestic scene of as much pressure as possible during a difficult transition period, we were also reluctant to have Mr. Bhutto leave New York after such a short and inconclusive Security Council session. It was apparent that the non-permanent members of the Security Council were hopeful of achieving some progress on the Kashmir issue and somewhat irked at the manner in which India's Chakravarty was demonstrating a lack of cooperation in this regard. We further believed it desirable from the standpoint of Indo–Pak relations to leave as little "vacuum" as possible between the two SC meetings (March and May) on the Kashmir problem.

We thus encouraged and supported Ambassador Bernardes in his efforts to draft and obtain agreement for another consensus statement which would have been read by the SC President on March 20 when the Czech motion to adjourn was considered. However, the Soviets and Czechs, presumably at the behest of India, did not agree to placing "conditions" on the adjournment, arguing that no such conditions had been imposed on the earlier Pakistani request for adjournment. It was finally arranged for Ambassador Bernardes to read his own statement during discussion of the motion, and that like-minded members of the "nine" would subscribe to it in short statements of their own.

In an interesting exchange on March 20 after the SC Members had spoken, Foreign Minister Bhutto took the floor and praised Bernardes' efforts while at the same time noting that if events required a new Security Council meeting before May 5, it was his understanding and the understanding of a majority of Security Council Members that such a meeting could be called at any time. Bhutto pledged that no political, military, administrative, or judicial steps would be taken by Pakistan to alter the existing situation in the area, and asked for similar assurances from the Indian Representative. Chakravarty surprised the Council Members by responding that Jammu–Kashmir is an integral part of India, regardless of the opinion of the Pakistani Foreign Minister or SC Members, and that India would continue its integration moves, notwithstanding the feelings of the Pakistanis, Council Members, or anyone else.[2]

---

[2] The Embassy in New Delhi reported on March 26 that Lal Bahadur Shastri told the Lok Sabha that the Security Council had not placed any restrictions on India regarding the full integration of Jammu and Kashmir with India. He doubted that it would be possible to take action regarding Article 370 during the current session of the Kashmir state assembly, since the assembly was about to adjourn. But he added: "The Foreign Minister of Pakistan can say what he likes. We will do what we want." (Telegram 2841 from New Delhi; ibid., POL 10 INDIA)

This last exchange, reports USUN, dismayed members of the "nine" and led Benhima (Morocco) to tell Ambassador Yost after the SC Session that, should India persist in its integration moves in Jammu and Kashmir, he (Benhima) would call for a new Council meeting before the May 5 date.

30. Telegram From the Embassy in the United Kingdom to the Department of State[1]

London, March 25, 1964, 2 p.m.

4705. For the Secretary from Talbot.

1. Since leaving subcontinent I have been pondering grave deterioration of Indo–Pak relations and implications for our policies, on which I should now like to comment.

2. As usual situation includes many conflicting strands. Compared to several years ago, both countries show substantial modernization and development, especially in cities and towns. Recent tours of Ambassador Bowles in South India and Ambassador McConaughy in East Pakistan yielded warm and friendly receptions. It is clear that in both countries our long-term policies are having beneficial effects; it is US which is looked to first for understanding and support.

3. Internal dynamics of India and Pakistan are, however, in sharpest contrast in years. With Nehru dessicated, Indian top leadership is defensive and defiant in face of farm shortfalls, rising prices, bankruptcy of Kashmir policy, conviction that Paks and ChiComs are making common cause, and evident reduction of Indian influence in Afro–Asian and world councils. Despite impact in economy and development, therefore, Indians now scheduling annual military outlays of nearly $2 billion, with emphasis on defense production and fascination with sophisticated weaponry.

4. Moreover, Indian focus on ChiComs as prime enemy has in recent months been befogged by Pak policies which have also refur-

---

[1] Source: National Archives and Records Administration, RG 59, Central Files 1964–66, POL INDIA–PAK. Secret; Immediate; Exdis. Repeated to New Delhi and Karachi for the Ambassadors only and passed to the White House at 1:15 p.m.

bished position of Pak haters in India. Last year's confidence US would help India against China has consequently now been diluted by doubts US would similarly be available to restrain Paks if they should cause trouble alone or in association with ChiComs. Indians therefore are increasingly of mood to hedge position by finding alternative sources of military equipment. As fears of Pakistan have risen, earlier reluctance to become dependent on Soviet supplies has been dropping. Now many Indians seem pleased at prospect that in military procurement as in political field, they can play different options against one another.

5. Pakistan, by contrast, today shows mixture of basic anxieties and new-found buoyancy. While still driven to foreign policy extremes by fear and distrust of India, Paks are sufficiently pleased with prospects of making gains from current Indian weakness so there is risk they will badly over-estimate their tactical advantages. Nonetheless, I believe Shoaib is not alone in recognizing Paks have been suckered by ChiComs and now need to restore balance by greater caution with Peiping and more careful cultivation of US relations. Surprising warm-up of Pak delegation in recent CENTO economic meeting may have meaning in this connection.

6. However, in view centrality of India in Pak perspective we can anticipate Paks like Indians will welcome alternative options to full dependence on US. Assuming they now recognize they cannot cross permissible limits of alliance with ChiComs, Paks could become easy targets of those like De Gaulle and current Iraqi visitor who advocate neutralism in Asia and argue US will live with that.

7. Thus Soviets, ChiComs, neutralists and West—each with own objectives—are kibitzers and to some extent actors in present Indo–Pak turmoil.

8. It is in this context that some Indo–Pak climax is slowly approaching. Kashmir fever, armed clashes on borders, and refugee followers are spreading viruses that erupt in communal killings. These generated high tempers, naked distrust and intransigence on both sides. Most hopeful thing I can see is that situation may be producing its own anti-toxins. In similar crises in past both sides have finally pulled back for negotiations. Sometimes periods of relative calm and constructive activity have ensued. Both countries remain under control today of men who went through 1947 cataclysm. I found several on each side remembering those days and determined not to permit similar disintegration now.

9. Our stakes in subcontinent remain very high. At one level is our interest in preserving and if possible expanding our cooperation with Paks against Soviets and with Indians against ChiComs. At another is importance of preserving and strengthening freedom and viability of this region of 550 million which, if taken over by Communists,

would represent setback of dimensions comparable to ChiCom victory of 1949. India and Pakistan are so intertwined we cannot expect either to remain healthy if other disintegrates. With these thoughts in mind, I suggest following policy lines for consideration:

A. An over-all stance of sympathy and reserve on most explosive Indo–Pak issues. These conflicts are corrosive and costly, and deserve our understanding. They are also hot issues, and our counsels of restraint are likely have little impact until parties themselves see wisdom in pulling back from brink. Plethora of tactical advice sometimes reduces impact of our interventions at really crucial moments. It also tempts each party to use our readiness for immediate interventions in ploys against other. While I am somewhat out of touch at moment, I suspect this applies just now to refugee movements and communal rioting, for example.

B. On Kashmir, a posture of limited diplomatic but, so far as possible, no public activity. For their own reasons Pakistan requires continued external involvement in Kashmir issue and India rejects any. I doubt any external enticement or pressure (within limits tolerable to maintenance of our overall interests in sub-continent) will soon loosen Indian grip on Kashmir. Certainly none will have effect at this moment of defiant weakness. I doubt equally that Ayub can afford to give up political dividends of continuous attack on Kashmir status quo; indeed, pressures on him to permit military pin-pricks and Algeria-type penetrations into Kashmir in absence of progress on diplomatic front may be real. Since this is not an obsolescent issue I believe outside powers involved in sub-continent cannot escape it. Our goal therefore should be to acknowledge it but to tamp it down. Best ploy I can think of is to encourage secret talks outside sub-continent, as privately advocated by Munuddin and B. K. Nehru but not yet by their governments. This would have advantage of being an operation process to keep heat on India but not a public circus.

C. On military aid to India, prompt progress toward detailed and intimate discussion of Indian military plans in context of our five-year assistance proposals. To protect its economy as well as to avoid unnecessary provocation of Pakistan, India needs to re-examine its $2 billion military planning figure, with 15%–18% required in foreign exchange. Probably only US can substantially influence it in this direction, and then only if we are genuine participants in its defense build-up. Also, probably only US can press focus on ChiComs as real enemy. Considering our difficulty in applying restraints to ambitions in such countries as Iran and Pakistan, where we have provided bulk of military hardware available to armed forces, we can expect extremely difficult task in peddling advantages of restraint to Indians to whom even $50 million aid level will be only peripheral. Yet costs of failure so significant that major effort will be worthwhile.

D. On economic aid to India, continuation of present policies. Need continues great; indeed, as economy grows balance of payments strains also grow, and our interests would be as adversely affected as in part by Indian inability to meet its problems. Even so, we can hardly increase economic aid to India while military expenditures are out of balance.

E. On aid to Pakistan, a frank business as usual approach. In recent past we have sought to register our unhappiness with Paks by dragging our feet on aid projects and planning. It has not worked. It is now evident prideful Paks under Ayub's instructions are not raising aid questions with us. Hold-up of Dacca Airport loan, for example, makes us look picayune and a little silly. Economic aid considerations are the same for Pakistan as for India. On military aid, we ought to start talking promptly and with no fanfare about possible five-year planning. Paks know we are entering this phase with India, and as they examine alternative options in immediate future their estimate of our interest in them will be important. I incline to treat Paks in next stage as if Shoaib's assertion they want to improve relations with us were correct. If it is not, we can drag feet later. If it is, we do not want to lose this turn in their thinking by refusing to believe it is true.

F. On weaponry, an effort to de-emphasize symbolism of supersonics. At present it seems crux of our military aid posture is yea or nay on supersonics. But rest of world has crossed this bridge and if such little fellows as Iraq and Syria have MIG 21's while we are about to give or sell supersonics to such countries as Iran and Lebanon, both India and Pakistan will find ways to develop supersonic fleets soon. If we could de-emphasize their symbolism and threat them like weaponry our military aid program in both India and Pakistan would be easier to handle.

10. My apologies for length of this message. I have not found time on this trip to distill it further.[2]

Jones

---

[2] McGeorge Bundy sent a copy of this telegram to Komer for comment, noting in the margin, "He's coocoo on the way to treat Ayub." (Johnson Library, National Security File, Country File, India, Cables, Vol. II, 4/64–6/64)

31. **Memorandum From Robert Komer of the National Security Council Staff to the President's Special Assistant for National Security Affairs (Bundy)[1]**

Washington, March 26, 1964.

Mac—

Phil Talbot's long cable (London 4705)[2] strikes me as penetrating in its analysis but feeble in the responses it proposes.

Agreed that our stake in the subcontinent remains "very high." Agreed that "some Indo–Pak climax is slowly approaching." Phil's policy recipe for dealing with the matter is, characteristically, not to get too involved and to continue business as usual (i.e. aid).

There's much to be said for this recipe. But one major flaw is the assumption that we can stand aloof—if real trouble develops the very fact that our stake is so "high" will tend to drag us in. Most active preventive diplomacy might at least minimize the likelihood of a galloping crisis in which our interests almost inevitably suffer. Cyprus is a case in point. And as in Cyprus, we face a double dilemma on the subcontinent—not only is a risky crisis likely *but we are friends with both sides.* So we're forced to carry water on both shoulders, to pursue a middle course, to satisfy neither of our suitors, while the Soviets and Chinese take the easy road of backing one side or the other.

For these reasons I favor a more active effort to turn aside a Kashmir crisis. Phil himself admits we can't avoid being involved, but his "ploy" of encouraging secret talks will only be accepted if we do a lot of arm-twisting and above all make clear to the "aggressor"—at this point Pakistan—that continued escalation might cost it dearly.

I also see compelling reasons for not returning to "a frank business as usual approach" to Ayub on such a slim basis as Shoaib's private assurance that the Paks are coming around. We'll remain trapped on the horns of the Pak/Indian dilemma until we get across to the Paks that they have only a limited partnership with us. We can subsidize their development, protect them against Indian aggression, continue to seek a Kashmir compromise, but we cannot back them in leaning on India.

Moreover, we've never had a better opportunity for the necessary readjustment of our Pak relations (to rectify the overcommitment we slid into in 1954–60). Mao's attack awakened the Indians, while Ayub's

---

[1] Source: Johnson Library, National Security File, Name File, Komer Memos, Vol. I. Secret.

[2] Document 30.

flirtation with the ChiComs has belatedly made all of us realize that Pakistan's overriding concern is to use us against India. This is wholly understandable, but hardly a mutual US/Pak interest. Moreover, Pakistan's utter—and irreplaceable—dependence on us means we can, with skill, bring it around to accepting our terms, and still giving us the one thing we really want.

I feel that if we revert to "business as usual" with Ayub now it will simply convince him that he can have his cake and eat it too. It will embolden him more than deter him. Phil argues that the alternative of registering "our unhappiness with Paks by dragging our feet on aid projects and planning . . . has not worked." I flatly disagree. In the first place this hasn't been a consistent policy—we've wobbled all over the lot. Only in the last few weeks have we begun to growl (even here we had to get Harriman to say what Talbot didn't)[3] and more important, to show by actions as well as words that we're unhappy (Kashmir SC postponement, not talking 5 year MAP).

So what's the risk in waiting at least a few more weeks to see if we've registered before starting to talk MAP. I want more to go on than Shoaib's siren song; I don't think we'll "lose this turn in their thinking" by waiting (it may make them turn more). And I doubt that "we can drag feet later" if we're wrong—it's been all too difficult to get even the half-baked foot-dragging we're doing now.[4]

In sum, I urge (1) holding off till we get a few more signals on five-year MAP approach to Paks; (2) developing a scenario for US/UK preventive action to forestall a major Kashmir crisis this year (let's at least get an option to look at); (3) developing some kind of package to forestall Soviet pre-emption of all aid to the Indian air force (we were hot on this in mid-1962 but no one even heeds Bowles' pleas today).

---

[3] On March 16 Under Secretary Harriman called in Pakistani Ambassador Ghulam Ahmed to emphasize U.S. concern about Pakistan's relations with China. Harriman stated that Pakistan's policy added to China's prestige and undermined U.S. interests. He added "we find this distasteful." He expressed the hope that Pakistan would recognize U.S. concerns and would do nothing more to harm U.S. interests. He also admonished Ahmed about the pressure Pakistan was exerting on India on the Kashmir issue, which Harriman stated was counter-productive and undercut U.S. ability to play a constructive role in India. (Telegram 1232 to Karachi, March 17; National Archives and Records Administration, RG 59, Central Files 1964–66, POL 7 PAK–US) On March 31 Foreign Secretary Aziz Ahmed called in Ambassador McConaughy and registered an emphatic objection to the tone and content of Harriman's remarks to Ambassador Ahmed. (Telegram 1838 from Karachi, March 31; ibid.)

[4] McGeorge Bundy made a marginal notation next to this paragraph which reads: "I agree strongly and so does LBJ."

With these amendments, I'd buy Talbot policy lines (otherwise excellent) and see in Bowles' return a real opportunity to get top level focus on them.[5]

RWK

---

[5] Bundy added another handwritten note at the end of the memorandum which reads: "I agree, except I'm less scared and so less activist on Kashmir; I think Talbot's tamp-down is fairly good."

---

32. Memorandum for the Record[1]

Washington, March 31, 1964.

SUBJECT

Conference between Secretary McNamara and Ambassador Bowles March 31, 1964 at 4:30 pm

1. General Discussion.

Ambassador Bowles discussed the Indian Five Year Defense Plan[2] and there was agreement that this plan was too large from the point of view of budget, force levels, and number of personnel in the armed forces, and foreign exchange. Ambassador Bowles estimated that the proposed budget would run at about 5.9% of the GNP which was definitely too high.

2. Aircraft Package.

Ambassador Bowles recommended that we offer to the Indians, under our Military Assistance Program something on the order of 70 F6A aircraft for relatively quick delivery and also offer to explore with the Indians the possibility of developing the HF–24. Ambassador Bowles stated that he was sure the Indians would proceed with the HF–24 whether or not we assisted. It was his hope that the foregoing package would be helpful in causing the Indians to reduce or discontinue their proposed MIG production.

---

[1] Source: Washington National Records Center, RG 330, OASD/ISA Files: FRC 68 A 306, 333 India. Secret. Prepared by Peter Solbert.

[2] A copy of the 110-page Indian Five-Year Defense Plan, covering the years 1964–1969, which was presented to the Embassy in New Delhi on March 21, is ibid., 381 India.

3. Conclusions.

Mr. McNamara agreed that we could offer the F6A under our Military Assistance Program to India. He also agreed that we could explore with the Indians the practicality of development of the HF–24, possibly with the Rolls Royce engine. Mr. McNamara also stated that our military assistance for India would have to include substantially more defense production (with the result that we might well have to do the same thing for Pakistan).

Mr. McNamara also agreed to the proposed Chavan visit in May and will send a letter to Chavan via Ambassador Bowles inviting him to Washington.

4. Future Action.

a. *Study of the Chinese Air Force.* Ambassador Bowles is very anxious to have a detailed study of the Chinese air force as a threat against India. The purpose of this study is to permit Ambassador Bowles to point out the capabilities and weaknesses of the Chinese air threat to India. Ambassador Bowles is leaving for New Delhi on Friday and it is doubtful whether such a study can be prepared by DIA in that time. However, we should collect for Ambassador Bowles a set of presently existing intelligence studies on the Chinese air force. If these studies contain information which Ambassador Bowles should not pass on the Indians we must so indicate to him.

b. *Comparison of Aircraft.* Mr. McNamara would like to have an analysis prepared which will compare the Chinese aircraft capabilities with the capabilities of the F6A, the F5A, the F–104 A/B, the F–104G, the HF–24 in all versions including estimates on Mark II, and MIG 21. The table should also include similar information for certain aircraft in the Indian air force, namely, the Vampire NF–54, Mystere 4A, Hunter F Mark 56, Gnat F Mark I, Toofani, and Vampire FB–52. On a separate sheet information should be set forth concerning the capabilities of aircraft in the Pakistani air force so that a similar comparison can be made between the threat constituted by the Pakistani air force and the above name aircraft.

c. *Development of the HF–24.* Arrangements should be made promptly to send U.S. representatives to India to look into the HF–24 development. A thorough investigation should be made as to the fitness of the Rolls Royce engine for the HF–24; the changes which would have to be made in the airframe design to accommodate the Rolls Royce engine; and the changes which would have to be made in the engine manufacturing plant in order to construct the Rolls Royce engine in India. If necessary U.S. representatives should be sent to England to look into the Rolls Royce engine further. If we need to go outside the armed forces and obtain people from industry to review such matters as the aircraft production plant in India, this should be done. The courses of action on this point would appear to be: (i) a cable to the British confirming our interest in this project and our desire to proceed promptly with the above investigation; (ii) the selection of the right people to go to India and possibly the UK and if necessary, Germany to review the availability of the engine with the Germans; (iii) alerting them so that they can carry out their investigation and be back with a report in the U.S. prior to Chavan's arrival in May; and (iv) obtain from Ambassador Bowles, on his return to New Delhi, assurance that the Indians will cooperate with the U.S. representatives and make all necessary information available to them to prepare their report.

d. *The F6A.* We should be in touch with Douglas Aircraft Corporation to let them know that we are interested in presenting a package to the Indians which would include the rehabilitated F6A. It would be desirable if material comparable to that given to us at the briefing two weeks ago could be prepared for Ambassador Bowles to take back this coming Friday. In the meantime, we should obtain promptly the refined pricing of the F6A and the related spares and training equipment. This will involve determining from Navy what portion of the spares are surplus stock and what portion of the spares would have to be sold by Douglas to India.

e. *Sidewinders.* Steps should be taken to obtain the necessary clearance to release to the Indians the F6A and Sidewinder missiles. This may prove somewhat sticky and should be started immediately so that problems can be ironed out as soon as possible and permission obtained.

Peter Solbert

33.   Memorandum From Robert Komer of the National Security Council Staff to President Johnson[1]

Washington, April 2, 1964.

Chester Bowles, whom you're seeing at 5:30, is in good spirits and should be no problem. We've met his immediate needs within the guidelines you laid down earlier, and he's not asking for anything more. So a friendly hearing and reassurance you're backing him will fill the bill.

The Navy's current phasing out of the old F–6A interceptor has fortuitously permitted McNamara to put together a minimal air package as a means of at least partly pre-empting Soviet SAM and MIG offers. It involves mainly 75 surplus F–6As. While not as good as the F–104s the Paks have (which will mute their reaction), the F–6 is plenty good enough to meet the Chicom air threat. Total cost with spares, etc. would be only $15–25 million out of planned MAP (not extra). Alternatively, Indians can have two squadrons of F–5As, *but not till 1965–67*. We and UK will also try to find an engine to power India's homegrown HF–24 fighter, as an alternative to their producing MIG–21s in India.

Bowles is happy; he thinks this package good enough to show the Indians we genuinely want to help, though there's only a fighting chance they'll actually bite. Beyond this, he's made three points back here:

1. With Nehru on his last legs, this is a time of maximum weakness and indecision in Delhi. The emerging leadership, especially Shastri—the heir apparent, looks good from our viewpoint. Now is the time to encourage them, and to minimize the risk of a swing back toward Menonism.

2. It's also no time for the Paks to lean on India over Kashmir. First, this tactic won't work, because Indians will just crawl into their shells. Second, it diverts Indian eyes from the Chicom threat and back toward Pakistan as Enemy No. 1, which is just what we don't want.

3. The Indians feel we drew back after our first spurt of help to them when the Chicoms attacked. But our new MAP program should help recapture lost ground.

The first draft of the *Indian five year defense plan* we asked for is, as expected, grossly inflated. But it's an asking price, not a final one, and Bowles will go back hard to get it trimmed. Even if cut back to what we think reasonable, however, it will entail more foreign exchange outlays than we and UK are willing to cover under military aid. So to pick up some of this business and help our gold flow, we'll offer reasonable credit terms for some dollar sales.

---

[1] Source: Johnson Library, National Security File, Country File, India, Vol. II, Cables, 4/64–6/64. Secret.

Bowles has a scheme for using a large chunk of the over $300 million in surplus rupees we're holding to set up a *bi-national foundation* for all sorts of people-to-people programs.[2] Since these rupees are valueless to us, we can't lose. The only real problem is to shepherd this through Congress, on which a friendly word from you may be needed.

Attached is a State background piece.[3] I'll sit in, if you've no objection, as the usual precaution against visitors overstating what is said.[4]

R. W. Komer[5]

---

[2] Bowles laid out his proposal for a binational educational and cultural foundation in India in airgram A–864 from New Delhi, March 11. (Ibid., Exchanges with Bowles)

[3] Not attached.

[4] No record of the meeting between Bowles and Johnson, nor of a previous meeting scheduled for the day before between Rusk and Bowles, has been found.

[5] Printed from a copy that bears this typed signature.

---

34. Memorandum of Conversation[1]

Washington, April 9, 1964, 4:30–5:15 p.m.

SUBJECT

General State of MAP for Pakistan and Letter of General Musa

PARTICIPANTS

Pakistan Side
Ambassador to the United States—Gulam Ahmed
Military Attaché—Brigadier M. Ismail Khan
Second Secretary—T. Y. Mahtab

United States Side
Secretary of Defense—Robert S. McNamara
Deputy Assistant Secretary of Defense (ISA)—Peter Solbert
Assistant for South Asian Affairs—Robert J. Murray

---

[1] Source: Washington National Records Center, RG 330, OSD Files: FRC 77–0075, Memo of Conversations Between Sec. McNamara and Heads of State (other than NATO). Secret. Prepared by Robert J. Murray on April 22. The meeting was held in McNamara's office.

The Ambassador opened the meeting by indicating that he would like to discuss the letter of General Musa[2] and the general state of MAP. The Secretary replied that he found the Musa letter one of the most upsetting he had ever read and indicated that it contained a number of misrepresentations. The Secretary said there was ample room for discussion of future performance but little for past performance.

The Ambassador said that two major problems seemed to be slow induction of equipment and ammunition. Inadequate ammunition reserves and defective ammunition seemed to be causing the Pakistan Army great difficulty. The Secretary said that the ammunition was continuously being delivered and that we had taken steps to correct the defective ammunition. In any case these were the types of things that should be discussed between our respective military people in Pakistan, and the letter indicated to him a complete breakdown of communications on the scene. The Secretary said that if we are at fault we'll change, but "I don't think we are." The Secretary said we could not run the program in this detail from Washington.

Ambassador Ahmed stated that President Ayub would like to know if this was a communications problem or whether the MAP difficulties arose from something else. The Secretary replied that it certainly was a communications problem, not anything else—not our unhappiness at Pakistan's current relations with the Chinese.

Ambassador Ahmed mentioned that he would like to review a few items in the Musa letter:

1. *Parachute Companies.* Ambassador Ahmed said the record on this seemed unclear. The Secretary suggested that the record be looked at again: We had promised to increase the battalion from seven to nine companies, five of which were to receive parachute training. This training was now going on. Ambassador Ahmed asked if we could not consider this further and discuss it with General Musa when he is in the United States for the CENTO meetings. The Secretary replied that we could certainly talk about it but that unless new facts had come to light, he did not think the decision would be changed.

2. *Hawk Battalions.* The Secretary indicated that we had clearly been at fault on this one; we had asked the GOP to organize the necessary battalion personnel and that upon subsequent review of our MAP plans decided that for the limited defense offered and the high cost involved, it was inappropriate to supply one Hawk battalion. It was a question of cost-effectiveness. We should either make a much greater investment than the funds would allow or we should not pro-

---

[2] This letter from the Commander-in-Chief of the Army of Pakistan has not been found.

gram any Hawks at all. Ambassador Ahmed asked if that was where the matter now stands, and the Secretary said it was. The Secretary then reviewed the problem of air defense in general, indicating that in Europe they have just decided that a complete air defense was not worth the price. The Secretary noted that the Soviets had spent billions of dollars on their air defense and we can still penetrate them at any time, and that even U.S. air defenses are not 100% effective.

3. *Defense Production Assistance.* The Secretary noted that we were going ahead with defense production assistance and that we hoped this would resolve some of the outstanding difficulties we have on ammunition to our mutual satisfaction.

4. *H–34 Helicopters.* Ambassador Ahmed noted the Musa letter mentioned one squadron and asked where this stood at the moment and he was advised that six helicopters of a similar type had already been delivered in accord with the Secretary's commitment.

5. *Modernization of Artillery.* Ambassador Ahmed indicated that the slow modernization of our artillery seemed to be causing the armored brigade substantial difficulties. The Secretary stated that self-propelled artillery was being introduced gradually but that we don't have our own army entirely equipped. We have to modernize on a gradual basis even for ourselves.

Ambassador Ahmed said that "these things struck me as important, and I thought I would bring them to your attention. I hope that General Musa can talk further with you when he arrives later this month. One further point that I thought valid concerned the $5\frac{1}{2}$ division force base and the two categories of 'modernization' and 'meeting deficiencies' being considered separately." The Secretary replied that while they are separate, they were considered concurrently. "It must be understood that no army can complete its modernization process overnight—we do not do it, the Soviets do not do it, no other country in the world does it, and certainly Pakistan cannot do it." The Secretary said that he was glad that the Commander-in-Chief, General Musa, was coming as we would have an opportunity to discuss some of these things. They should have been discussed in Pakistan. He reiterated his earlier statement that this was a most upsetting letter, that he thought some of the statements in it were irresponsible, that it erroneously implied that he had failed to meet his commitments and that it certainly indicated a breakdown of communications. Ambassador Ahmed replied that he will want to tell President Ayub, that this was a communications problem and not a problem of another sort. Mr. McNamara asked that he also tell the President that "when I make a commitment, I keep it." The Secretary also indicated that if this communications problem was not resolved, he would like Ambassador Ahmed to call him at any time to discuss the matter.

35.   Telegram From the Embassy in Pakistan to the Department of State[1]

Karachi, April 11, 1964, 6 p.m.

1935. Indo-Pak relations.

1. As we survey coming months, period of unusual fluidity on subcontinent fraught with potential dangers to US interests must be anticipated. Conversely, months ahead could provide singular opportunity to take major steps toward stability and peace to subcontinent. While anyone surveying long and tragic history of subcontinent intolerance, hatred, strife, and inhumanity could not rate high prospects for resolving Indo-Pak differences, rewards of subcontinent peace would be so great that we cannot afford to neglect full exploitation any possible avenues which may emerge from increasingly fluid situation.

2. Status quo on subcontinent will be virtually impossible to retain under impact of successive developments foreshadowing basic readjustments. These developments summarized as:

A) Gradual relinquishment of Nehru's leadership in India;

B) Heightened communal tensions which pose alternatives of further mass upheavals or considerable degree of Indo-Pak cooperation to calm situation;

C) India's proposed new 5-year military program, which, if not substantially modified in concept as well as degree, will herald such a radical alteration of balance of power on subcontinent as to drive GOP toward reckless counteracting measures; and

D) Release of Sheikh Abdullah,[2] throwing to Kashmiris large share of initiative on future status of Kashmir and seemingly making virtually impossible preservation of Kashmir status quo without most serious repressive action by GOI.

3. It is clear that Paks have not yet come fully to grips with implications of these newly emerging forces on subcontinent. Typically Abdullah's release has left Paks indecisive as to their next moves. While Paks have officially welcomed action in anticipation basic change in Kashmir's status, there is note of real caution as they recognize unpredictable Abdullah might come up with Kashmir settlement proposal

---

[1] Source: National Archives and Records Administration, RG 59, Central Files 1964–66, POL 1 INDIA–PAK. Secret; Priority; Limdis. Repeated to New Delhi, London, USUN, and CINCMEAFSA for POLAD.

[2] Sheikh Mohammed Abdullah, head of the Jammu and Kashmir National Conference, was a nationalist leader jailed by India almost continuously from August 1953 until his release on April 8, 1964.

generally acceptable to Kashmiris but unpalatable to some elements here, and without Pak participation in preliminary negotiations.

4. For present, Pak reaction to recent developments has been to continue pushing policy lines adopted after outbreak Sino-Indian hostilities, because this is most convenient alternative open to them and because these policies have in their view paid dividends. Paks thus have pursued policy of keeping strong ties to West and retaining benefits therefrom, while broadening their base outside, both among Afro-Asians and Communists—principally Peiping—with objective of keeping pressure on India. Transient successes of this policy have exhilarated some Paks and led to some cockiness.

5. Beneath surface, however, there are signs of ferment and dispute within Pak policy circles. Transition from Nehru and developments inside Kashmir have stimulated moderate elements such as Pak HICOM in Delhi, FinMin Shoaib, and former establishment Secretary Muenuddin to look for new and more restrained approaches to Indo-Pak issues. Essentially same forces also sense that current bifurcated policy has virtually reached limits of US tolerance and point where its inner contradictions can no longer be ignored; they are urging buttressing of Western alignment. But, hard-liners led by Foreign Ministry are holding to their ground and in fact ready to advocate some further and more significant steps away from West, notwithstanding risk of aid reduction. Ayub sits in center of this policy conflict and has not chosen. While inclined toward pro-Western policy, he has at least acquiesced in alienating actions proposed by Foreign Ministry elements. While Ayub apparently sees some value in continuation this dual policy for present, essentially he is marking time while waiting to see the course of impending developments, and in first instance US reaction to them. Thus, we may be facing precarious period in US-Pak relations, with Pak foreign policy delicately balanced in increasingly fluid environment.

6. Clearly, US and Indian interest lie in tipping the balance towards moderate elements in Pak inner circle and bringing weight of Ayub's authority fully on this side of scale. US retains sufficient position in Pakistan to influence heavily the crucial decision, but we cannot do it alone. In the final analysis, Indian policy will have far greater bearing on Paks, and I recognize our influence in India may be even more peripheral than in Pakistan.

7. The key area lies as always in Kashmir with essential question whether Abdullah's release can be exploited to fashion Kashmir settlement which serves as a bridge between India and Pakistan. Understandably, Indians would find far easier a solution worked out directly with Abdullah, excluding Pakistani participation or advice. Drawback is serious doubt that any solution thus arrived at would be acceptable

or lasting, let alone conducive to Indo-Pak reconciliation. Most important, a unilateral Kashmir settlement by India with a softened-up Abdullah, along with major Indian military buildup and new increments of US MAP to India, most critically delivery of 72 F–6As, would be likely move Paks right out of Western alignment.

8. The months ahead could face us with formidable problems and difficult decisions. Pak actions of recent past do not merit any effort on our part seeming to reward their conduct, and would deserve stern warnings if by such tactics we could retrieve lost ground with Paks. But such demonstrations on our part have failed in past and it is my judgment that if "pushed to wall" as he defines the term, Ayub may—however rash the decision may seem to us—follow hard-liners advice and elect course of non-alignment, with all its consequences, including reduction in aid.

9. There is good chance we can avoid Ayub's being "pushed to wall" even by his distorted definition of term. Alternative is carrot and stick approach to both Pakistan and India in a major effort to exploit current developments to achieve an Indo-Pak reconciliation through settlement of the Kashmir question on basis internationalization formula which I believe we all feel has best prospect for mutual albeit reluctant acceptance all parties concerned. I realize enormous psychological obstacles in both countries but very fluidity of current situation may serve to damp down past prejudices. Furthermore, it is inconceivable to me that almost one billion dollars of economic and military aid on subcontinent annually does not offer us significant invisible leverage in both countries as distasteful as this fact may be to them.

10. In mounting such an effort, I am not necessarily suggesting direct pressures or even at this stage direct involvement in Kashmir negotiations. Indirect pressures would probably be more effective. I recommend, therefore, initially combination of following tactics:

A) In Pakistan, giving discreet support for moderate elements, pointing out more emphatically counterproductive effect at this stage of pressure tactics on India;

B) Slowing down temporarily any commitments to long-range economic and military programs (beyond fiscal 1965) for either India or Pakistan until we can judge their effect on prospects for Kashmir settlement, triggered by Abdullah's release; and,

C) In India, emphasizing imperative requirement for settlement as only means of closing ranks against pressure on subcontinent from north and frustrating ChiCom machinations in South Asia.

McConaughy

36. **Telegram From the Department of State to the Embassy in Pakistan[1]**

Washington, April 16, 1964, 3:56 p.m.

1380. We have been examining carefully our future policy respecting MAP policy for Pakistan in light of framework established by: General Taylor's report,[2] Secretary's January 16 memorandum to President,[3] NSAM 279 of February 8,[4] instructions to Talbot (Deptels 1174 and 1182)[5] and discussions which you and Talbot have had with Ayub and other Pak leaders. We have decided upon following course of action:

1. We will not raise with GOP at this time (April, May) subject multi-year MAP.

In our view, discussions on "political framework" with Pak leaders have not produced fully satisfactory responses. Recent Pak signals tend to point to less cooperation rather than more. Our main concern centers on possible secret understandings between Paks and Chicoms. Until we have clearer picture of these and can judge possible effect on our over-all position in subcontinent, we will wish reserve our positions on longer term military aid questions.

2. We will proceed with discussions on FY 1965 MAP.

We recognize necessity signal to GOP our intention and desire maintain present ties. Continued silence on our part in important MAP field, when it clear we are talking MAP to Indians, could lead GOP to make serious errors in judgment about our intentions. We have significant interests in Pakistan, some of which directly linked at least in Pak mind with MAP. We believe we must, in current situation, take some steps conserve these interests and head off Paks from taking actions inimical to them.

3. Therefore, we shall initiate discussions on FY 1965 MAP with General Musa in Washington later this month.[6]

As we see it, timing of initial conversations on MAP is very important. GOP aware in general way of our Indian MAP intentions and

---

[1] Source: National Archives and Records Administration, RG 59, Central Files 1964–66, DEF 19 US–PAK. Secret; Limdis. Drafted by Naas; cleared by Talbot and Cameron, and in draft by Walsh, Komer, Lang (DOD/ISA), Warren (G/PM), Wriggins (S/P), Macomber (AID/NESA), and Hirschberg (AID/PC); and approved by Harriman. Repeated to New Delhi, London, and CINCSTRIKE for POLAD.

[2] See footnote 2, Document 3.

[3] Document 3.

[4] Document 13.

[5] Document 25 and footnote 2 thereto.

[6] General Musa was scheduled to attend CENTO meetings in Washington.

that Chavan and defense team are coming here in May. We believe our talks with GOP should come before Chavan visit and not appear as attempt mollify GOP after Chavan departs. Musa visit provides excellent opportunity do this.

4. We shall inform Musa that FY 1965 program will not include additional aircraft but that we shall be in position to deliver additional F104As in FY 1966 provided that political climate at that time is right.

We recognize that GOP will be very concerned over our getting into aircraft field with India and that we should not continue avoid question supersonics for Pakistan. We envisage reference to possible delivery in 1966 as important double purpose step. It should help keep Pakistan reaction to Indian air package within tolerable bounds, and also serve as signal to Ayub that, if he is prepared be mindful our concerns, we shall be mindful of his. Also, breaking ice on supersonic question may provide framework for pursuing discussion on one of our key concerns.

5. We shall continue keep GOP informed about our future MAP plans for India.

You will receive instructions following Chavan visit to bring GOP up to date on our thinking on our MAP for India. During conversations here with Musa we shall inform him that we intend continue to give moderate military assistance to India and that this aid will be related to India's development of a sound defense plan.

6. We shall keep under constant review question of whether we should at later date proceed with multi-year Pak program.

We view discussion on one-year program as interim measure and realize that by time we are ready firm up our five-year program with India, we may have to be more forthcoming with GOP to avoid serious imbalance in our military relations with India and Pakistan.

Appreciate your 1935[7] and 1936,[8] which received after above decisions taken. Believe approach outlined here should help meet some of your concerns.

Ball

---

[7] Document 35.

[8] In telegram 1936 from Karachi, April 11, McConaughy warned that a decision to provide 72 F–6A aircraft to India would have "far reaching and immediate negative effect" on U.S. relations with Pakistan. (National Archives and Records Administration, RG 59, Central Files 1964–66, DEF 19–3 US–INDIA)

37.   Telegram From the Embassy in India to the Department of
State[1]

New Delhi, April 20, 1964, 3 p.m.

3122. Dept pass Defense. Deptel 2085 sent April 15[2] was delayed
in transmission and did not reach us until Saturday. While we are
in agreement with general principles laid down, we believe careful
coordination between New Delhi and Washington is essential. In this
regard, we are concerned about Dept's intention of spelling out US
position to BK Nehru before our presentation to GOI has been more
fully developed here. Following is report of our activities and plans in
preparing GOI for Chavan visit and suggestions for future actions:

1. Immediately upon my return from Washington on April 9, I
held preliminary talks with Shastri, T.T. Krishnamachari and Chavan.
Since all three individuals were in highly emotional state as result of
Abdullah situation, I spoke in general terms about size of military
budget and its effect on Indian development, the need to distinguish
more clearly between Chinese intentions which are evil and Chinese
capacity which is limited, and on our desire to work out close relationships on military matters similar to relationships on economic development. In this initial talk I felt it important to leave generally hopeful
impression in regard to US assistance side-by-side with expression of
deep concern that budgetary situation might be getting out of hand.

2. Simultaneously, DCM held meetings with Kaul and other members of Secretariat, while Gen Kelly talked with Chavan expressing
same general views and then inaugurated series of more detailed meetings with Indian military. This completed what we consider to be first
stage of our effort here in Delhi to give Indians sense of general direction
we are likely to take.

3. The second stage of our New Delhi operation is comprehensive
memorandum which I am directing to Prime Minister on India's defense problem and US relationship to it. Although I doubt PM has

---

[1] Source: National Archives and Records Administration, RG 59, Central Files 1964–
66, DEF 1 INDIA. Secret; Priority. Repeated to Karachi, London, and CINCSTRIKE for
POLAD and passed to Defense.
[2] Telegram 2085 to New Delhi, April 15, outlined the approach officials in Washington
planned to take in discussing military assistance and the Indian 5-year plan with Defense
Minister Chavan and his party when they visited Washington in May. The focus of the
discussions would be on attempting to demonstrate how India could achieve a reasonably
satisfactory defense within a limited resource ceiling. To pave the way for this approach,
the Department felt that preliminary work was necessary in Washington and in New
Delhi. The Embassy was instructed to encourage the Indian Government to impose a
more austere limit on defense expenditures than that envisaged in the 5-year plan, and
to do so prior to Chavan's visit. (Ibid., POL 7 INDIA)

capacity or desire to discuss this memorandum, copies are going to TTK, Shastri and Chavan and I expect to discuss it with them in detail Wednesday or Thursday[3] of this week. Copies of the memorandum are being airgrammed Dept. It contains the following points:

A. Over period of time, close working partnership has developed between USG and GOI regarding India's economic development. Our present task is to develop similar relationship in military field. This requires us frankly to explore security problems which India faces, her own capacity to meet them, amount and type of assistance that is required and ways USG can be most helpful.

B. US and India are generally agreed on the Chinese Communist intentions which are obviously aggressive and expansionist. It is also clear that Chinese military capacity under certain conditions is substantial.

However, key question is manner in which Chinese may be expected to pursue their aggressive intents and their capacity to bring their potential strength to bear against India in particular.

Comment: It is critically important to avoid appearing to water down the menace that China holds for India and Asia. We have been trying to persuade India for years that China is aggressive and dangerous power. A blunt USG effort to minimize Chinese threat at this stage would be considered first as inconsistent with what we have said before and second as transparent reaction to Pak pressure to reduce aid to India. Even if it should succeed, this approach would only play into hands of Communists, Menonites and Hindu extremists who are following precisely this same line in effort to substitute Pakistan for China as India's number one enemy. Our approach should be to play up evil intent of Chinese and then distinguish between the intent on one hand and capacity on the other of Chinese to bring their strength to bear. Even here we must be careful not to undermine the Indian confidence in our motivation and judgment.

C. Therefore, we see India's defense problem as two dimensional: (1) an adequate military defense shield and (2) the building of vigorous, dynamic society which is impervious to covert Chinese Communist infiltration. Although we feel defense shield is of vital importance, USG's experience in other areas has demonstrated that even strongest and most expensively equipped armies are ineffective unless they are vigorously supported by people who feel sense of progress. On this score, we have made our share of mistakes and we do not want to see India repeat them.

D. Against this background, we must say in all frankness that we do not believe India's defense projection is properly balanced between

---

[3] April 22 and 23.

military-political-economic factors; indeed we doubt that India's economic development can proceed at an adequate pace unless foreign exchange allocated to defense is reduced. Although we strongly favor India saving her foreign exchange by producing items such as small arms ammunition, etc., we would warn against domestic production which puts too heavy drain on foreign exchange and capital and trained personnel.

E. Although these questions will require definition and discussion, we are aware of India's need for more modern interceptors and hopeful we can be helpful in this regard; also in aiding domestic production which saves foreign exchange while not placing undue drain on India's domestic industrial growth, plus assistance along present lines for Indian army.

4. We have carefully avoided all references to Soviet equipment or specific ways that money can be saved. At this stage we believe it is far better to let Indians think situation out themselves. If we can once persuade them to cut down size of plan and foreign exchange that goes with it, pressure may be focussed on SAMs and MIGs which is where we want it. However, if we go too far in appearing to direct Indian foreign policy, they will dig in their heels regardless of effect of such actions on their relations with us. Indians, whatever their weaknesses, are bright people and we do not have to pound the desk and repeat our points ad infinitum for them to understand them.

5. Third stage here will be personal talks I expect to have with Shastri, Chavan and TTK. Hopefully these discussions will be completed by Thursday night; will promptly cable results. Until these talks are completed, I strongly urge that discussions between Department and BK Nehru be postponed.

When Nehru was here in Delhi he was in an emotional and frustrated mood, and unpleasantly irritated at USG. Although this mood may be explained by concern over father, it was sufficiently noticeable for MJ Desai to comment on it to me. While I believe Department is correct that BK Nehru sees situation much as we do, I would not trust him at this point to report Department's views to GOI in balanced manner. If distorted interpretation of his talks with Dept suggesting somewhat different US position should arrive before we have completed our own presentation considerable crockery may be unnecessarily broken.

6. In any event, following my talks with Shastri, TTK and Chavan, which I hope will be reflected in tone and content in discussions with Nehru in Washington, we will follow through here to pick up loose ends.

7. In regard to Indian defense progress itself, we believe, as reported in Embtel 3052,[4] that we are approaching moment of truth in

---

[4] Dated April 14. (National Archives and Records Administration, RG 59, Central Files 1964–66, DEF 19 US–INDIA)

our military relations with Indian Government. Although our long delay and indecision is understandable, we are now close to being dealt out of meaningful role in Indian defense situation, at a time when political situation here is in a state of flux and Soviet Union increasingly freed of its inhibitions in regard to China may be prepared to take much more forthcoming role in regard to military assistance. At present, we are in position of denying India sophisticated ground force equipment, dragging feet on domestic military production and offering them airplanes which they consider obsolescent.

In our opinion, Gen Adams' message to JCS[5] which arrived this morning is wholly sound; indeed it is along precise lines of our own recommendations in Embtel 3052.

As Gen Adams properly states, anything less than a program of this kind will leave us sitting on side lines with only marginal influence over Indian military policy at time when Indian military may be called on for an increasing political role.

One final word: since my arrival here last July, we have been faced with long list of difficult situations ranging from VOA to Bokaro to Kashmir wrangle, to failure last fall to go through with military assistance-political package, to need to explain USG position in SC which Indians considered antagonistic and unfair.

If we are now planning to move ahead with Indian military program it is important that US Mission in New Delhi appear to GOI as primary means of communication and of US action. Therefore, if Department's and Pentagon response to our recommendations is positive, I recommend that we be authorized before Chavan group leaves for US to give top Indian officials preliminary knowledge of positive contributions that we have in mind, with whatever caveats may be required. This will greatly strengthen our ability to deal effectively with GOI on future questions in a particularly critical and difficult time.[6]

Bowles

---

[5] Not found.

[6] In telegram 2144 to New Delhi, April 21, the Department concurred with the tactics proposed by Bowles of gradually moving into progressively expanding discussions regarding the Indian 5-year plan, but questioned the wisdom of a written exchange with the Indian Government concerning it, for fear of a leak, which might prejudice the negotiations. (National Archives and Records Administration, RG 59, Central Files 1964–66, DEF 1 INDIA) On the same day, Bowles sent an 8-page memorandum to the Prime Minister entitled "India's National Defense and American Assistance." A copy of this memorandum was transmitted to Washington as an enclosure to airgram A–1049 from New Delhi, April 22; ibid.

38.   **Letter From Robert Komer of the National Security Council Staff to the Ambassador to India (Bowles)**[1]

Washington, April 24, 1964.

Dear Chet:

I'm concerned by a number of developments, or the lack of them, which have tended to cloud the highly favorable atmosphere upon your departure.

First is the lack, to my knowledge, of a major effort to get across to the GOI as yet about the grossly inflated size of their five-year plan. Any program of this magnitude would inevitably be at the expense of economic development and we've got to get across as soon as possible that this would be robbing Peter to pay Paul. AID is quite unhappy, and will become more so when the extent of diversion contemplated sinks in. Moreover, pressure against undue diversion of foreign exchange from the development program is a good indirect means of getting the Indians to focus on the need to cut down their elaborate hardware demands, especially in the air defense field.

Chavan's visit and then TTK's will simply be a flop if we have to spend all our time pressing them to squeeze the water out of their plan. If we let this issue become later a major bone of contention between the US and India it will do neither country any good. By all odds the best thing, therefore, is to get the Indian Finance Ministry to do our dirty work for us. We're relying on you for this.

I don't know what you did to General Adams (all to the good nonetheless), but it's highly premature to start plugging 104s. We barely got an F6A plus HF–24 engine program going, with a few squadrons of F5s as a possible alternative, when you come back changing the bidding again. Mind you, I think it makes political sense to give India 104s *if necessary,* but this must emerge as the logical outcome of a prolonged discussion in which we successively discard other options. Again, we here have seen nothing firm about whether you have ever even tried out the original package on the Indians yet.

I hate to badger you like this, but we scored rather a breakthrough when you were here and it's dangerous to attempt to improve on what we got without even trying it out. As I know you realize, there are strong suspicions here that indeed you did try out the package and got nowhere, so are coming back for more. If this is the case, tell us

---

[1] Source: Johnson Library, National Security File, Country File, India, Exchanges with Bowles (cont.). Secret; Via Classified Pouch; Eyes Only for the Ambassador.

so because only if you tried and failed will we be able to argue effectively for trying something else.

I've just heard you have the amoebic bug. All best wishes for a quick recovery. It's also best for cosmetic reasons that you postpone your return in May as late as possible.

Meanwhile, do try to warn off Chavan and others from coming with any exaggerated expections of the US cornucopia. Big ideas which are then disappointed will only set back our Indian enterprise at a time when we finally got it moving forward again.

Once again my apologies for these admonitory words. But you know they come from a friend. All the best for an early recovery.

Sincerely,

R. W. Komer[2]

P.S. Since writing this, I just saw your talk with TTK.[3] Good stuff!

---

[2] Printed from a copy that bears this typed signature.

[3] Reference is to a conversation that Bowles had with Finance Minister Krishnamachari on April 23, which was reported in telegram 3158 from New Delhi, April 23. Bowles found Krishnamachari in an emotional state anticipating a joint attack on India by China and Pakistan within 3 months, an attack he feared would have to be met without U.S. military assistance, which the United States would be unable to provide in an election year. Bowles reminded Krishnamachari that the United States had come to India's defense in 1962, and assured him that in similar circumstances it would do so again. Bowles then turned the conversation to the issue of military assistance, and stated that the United States had decided on a longer range program provided that the Indian budgetary situation was worked out in a rational manner with a minimum drain on foreign exchange. He noted that the proposed 5-year plan called for a doubling of foreign exchange defense expenditures as compared with figures discussed the previous fall. Bowles said that such expenditure was more than India could afford given her need for more rapid economic growth. (National Archives and Records Administration, RG 59, Central Files 1964–66, DEF 19 US–INDIA)

39.   Memorandum of Conversation[1]

Washington, April 27, 1964, 11:06 a.m.

SUBJECT

Meeting of President with Mrs. Indira Gandhi[2]

PARTICIPANTS

Mrs. Indira Gandhi   The President
Ambassador B.K. Nehru   Assistant Secretary Phillips Talbot
                                      R.W. Komer

The President greeted Mrs. Gandhi cordially, remarking on his previous meetings with her and with her father. It was because he regarded himself as such a strong friend of India that he was surprised at Mrs. Gandhi's referring to US favoritism toward Pakistan on Kashmir as she had in a recent interview with the *New York Times*. The President stressed that we were firm in our determination to have the most friendly relations with India. So, he said smilingly, he could not accept any implication of partisanship.

Mrs. Gandhi reassured the President that India understood and appreciated US policy and US help. She and her father personally knew of the President's strong friendship for India, and she had merely been referring to one part of US policy, that toward Kashmir, on which we did not seem sympathetic to the Indian point of view. Ambassador Nehru interjected that two great powers could certainly disagree on one among many questions without any diminution in the overall friendly relations between them.

The President came back again on the issue of US friendship for India and decried any suggestion of partisanship on any issue between us. As for the Indians being disturbed at our relations with Pakistan, they should realize that the Pakistani were far more angry with us. The Paks were much more unhappy about our policy toward India than India seemed to be about our policy toward Pakistan.

The President went on to describe how the US was not only seeking to help nations abroad develop themselves but to deal with the problems of poverty and discrimination in the US. He outlined his own

---

[1] Source: National Archives and Records Administration, RG 59, Presidential Memoranda of Conversation: Lot 66 D 149. Secret. Drafted by Talbot and Komer on April 30 and approved in the White House on May 11. The conversation was held at the White House. The time of the meeting is taken from the President's Daily Diary. (Johnson Library)

[2] Prime Minister Nehru's daughter was visiting the United States for the inaugural ceremonies of the World's Fair.

recent efforts to this end citing various statistics. He mentioned, for example, that 49% of draft-age Americans failed to meet minimum physical standards for the draft. Ambassador Nehru was shocked that this figure should be so high, but Mrs. Gandhi pointed out that India had had similar difficulties in recruitment after the Chinese attack.

Mrs. Gandhi then presented a letter from Prime Minister Nehru to the President.[3] The latter read it carefully and commented on how much he appreciated the friendly sentiments it contained. India could count on US friendship and on continued US help.

The President remarked on how many friends India has in his Administration. We sent Ambassadors to India who seemed to spend every day thinking of new ways in which we could be helpful.

Mentioning his particular affection for Mr. Nehru, the President asked about his current health. Mrs. Gandhi replied that he was better and up and around a bit more. The President remarked upon how people had counted him out at the time of his own heart attack. But two months later he was back in shape again and had been ever since. No one should count Mr. Nehru out either. He urged Mrs. Gandhi to carry this message back to Prime Minister Nehru and to give him the President's affectionate regards.

After pictures were taken, the President showed Mrs. Gandhi and the Ambassador the rose garden.

---

[3] In his April 14 letter to President Johnson, Prime Minister Nehru referred, inter alia, to the continuing differences that troubled relations between India and Pakistan. He pledged that India's efforts to reach an understanding with Pakistan with regard to Kashmir and the communal problems would continue. Nehru noted that India faced a constant threat from China, and added that he was glad that Defense Minister Chavan would be coming to the United States to discuss India's defense requirements. He expressed his gratitude for all of the military and economic assistance the United States had provided to India. (Johnson Library, National Security File, Country File, India, Nehru Correspondence)

40.   Memorandum of Conversation[1]

Washington, April 29, 1964, 4 p.m.

PRESENT

General Taylor, Chairman, Joint Chiefs of Staff
General Musa, Pakistan
Brigadier Gul Hassan Khan, Pakistan
Brigadier Ismail Khan, Pakistan

1. The conversation began with General Taylor asking General Musa whether he had been able to see all the US officials whom he had hoped to see during his visit. General Musa stated that he had seen Mr. McNaughton, Mr. Solbert and General Wood.[2] The latter had spent two hours with him and they were able to discuss "the letter."[3] General Musa reported that General Wood gave him a general indication of the 64–65 MAP which included no increase in the current ceiling. General Wood also emphasized that the entire program was contingent on the availability of funds and as a result General Musa felt little progress had been made.

2. General Taylor observed that he was glad General Musa had had the opportunity to make the same points to General Wood as he had made earlier to General Taylor. That even though General Musa might feel no progress had been made an exchange of frank views was usually helpful.

3. General Musa advised General Taylor that during his frank discussion with General Wood the latter informed him of the US intent to provide two squadrons of F 104's during the period CY 1965–1966, provided the political climate was satisfactory at the time. General Musa then told General Taylor that he was not happy with the condition now being attached to a military program. He felt that it removed the

---

[1] Source: Washington National Records Center, RG 330, OSD Files: FRC 69 A 7425, Pakistan 091.112. Secret. Prepared by Commander John J. Shanahan of the Chairman's Staff Group on April 30. The conversation was held in General Taylor's office.

[2] General Robert J. Wood, USA, Director for Military Assistance under the Assistant Secretary of Defense for International Security Affairs.

[3] Reference is to a letter from General Musa to General Taylor concerning the military assistance program for Pakistan. This letter, which has not been found, was discussed in a meeting between Taylor and Musa on April 22. Musa stated that the letter was intended to offer constructive suggestions and was not meant to criticize U.S. efforts. Musa added, however, that the fact that India had received as much military assistance during the past 7 months as Pakistan had received in 7 years was creating political problems for President Ayub. (Washington National Records Center, RG 330, OSD Files: FRC 69 A 7425, Pakistan 091.112)

charm and grace which exists between the military in our two countries. General Musa was so concerned about this that he had discussed it with FM Bhutto who in turn agreed and said he would take the matter up with Secretary Rusk later in the day.

4. General Taylor advised General Musa that this was not really a condition in the sense described by General Musa but was a fact of life. As General Musa should by now be well aware, US Congressional reaction to MAP is influenced significantly by the political actions of our friends.

5. General Musa raised the subject of the "7th Fleet Units" currently in the Indian Ocean and stated that Pakistan's position on this subject is apparently misunderstood in Washington. General Musa said that there was never any intent on the part of Pakistan to give the impression that the "7th Fleet" was not welcome in the area.

6. General Taylor agreed that he thought the official Pakistan position had been factually reported to Washington, however it was entirely possible that the Pak press had confused the issue for some people.

7. General Musa reported that General Adams had been very kind to him and had spent considerable time over a two day period discussing the "exercise."[4] General Musa has decided that the US is apprehensive on two points concerning advance planning for this exercise and that this explains our reluctance to agree to planning. He described the two points as:

a. "We want you to plan against India."
b. "The forces agreed to in the plan would mean a commitment of US forces."

General Musa then emphasized that planning does not mean a commitment. The upshot of his meetings with General Adams is that he will take the exercise scenario home for discussions with his President.

8. General Taylor suggested that in view of the short time remaining it might be best to postpone the exercise, that such exercises are normally arranged and budgeted for at least a year ahead. General Taylor asked General Musa to make it entirely clear that the US is not pressing this exercise on Pakistan.

---

[4] Reference is to a proposed joint U.S.-Pakistan military exercise described by Pentagon planners as a mobility exercise. The proposal was discussed by General Taylor during his visit to Pakistan in December 1963, and again by General Taylor and General Musa during their conversation on April 22. The intent underlying the proposal was to help relieve Pakistani concerns about the U.S. commitment to Pakistan's security.

9. The conversation ended with General Musa advising that he has hopes of seeing the Secretary of Defense, in fact he had postponed his departure for two additional days in this endeavor.

10. General Taylor said he knew the Secretary of Defense would be pleased to see General Musa provided the Secretary's schedule would allow.

---

41. Telegram From the Department of State to the Embassy in Pakistan[1]

Washington, May 1, 1964, 6:13 p.m.

1456. Kashmir. Following summary FYI and Noforn. It is uncleared and subject to amendment upon review of memcon.

Secretary met with Foreign Secretary Bhutto April 29.[2] Bhutto accompanied by Ambassador G. Ahmed and Minister Iftikar Ali. Assistant Secretary Talbot also present.

Secretary opened conversation by expressing appreciation for Bhutto's help in getting agreement on CENTO communiqué.

Bhutto said he would like to start with Kashmir situation. UN Rep Bunche had talked to Ayub during his recent visit subcontinent and told Ayub he had not known how critical situation was until he had visited Kashmir. He had been struck by intensity of feeling on issue. Ayub replied he hoped Bunche appreciated GOP's problem of keeping lid on those who demand action on Kashmir problem.

GOP viewed release of Sheikh Abdullah as due to two factors, upsurge of feeling in Indian-held Kashmir following the loss of the Sacred Relic, and "our modest efforts in the Security Council." Credit goes, however, to Security Council itself and its members.

Bhutto noted that US had had reservations about timing of Security Council debates in February and March and added "time has shown debates were helpful." Climax is now approaching. Security Council

---

[1] Source: National Archives and Records Administration, RG 59, Central Files 1964–66, POL 32–1 INDIA–PAK. Secret; Limdis. Drafted by Officer in Charge of Pakistan-Afghanistan Affairs Harold Josif on April 30, cleared by Special Assistant for UN Planning Elmore Jackson in IO, and approved by Grant. Also sent to New Delhi, London, and USUN.

[2] Bhutto was in Washington for the CENTO Ministerial meetings.

can assist in arriving at settlement of issue.[3] One could not expect anything miraculous but could expect some action to bring together parties to dispute to discuss problem, i.e., Sheikh Abdullah, Nehru and Ayub. It would be difficult for any of parties to take initiative however. This would not be true if Security Council requested talks. Bhutto personally out of touch due recent travels but his "tentative ideas" were as follows: There should be Security Council session. Short speeches would be necessary to bring record up to date. Council should then take some action to inject its authority into situation. Would be premature to send out SYG as mediator. However he could visit subcontinent personally and encourage talks between parties. Bhutto said he had discussed this idea with Butler[4] who thought it was reasonable. Bhutto then asked, "Does this appeal to you?"

Secretary asked what clues GOP had as to influence of Nehru's illness on situation. He assumed it was considerable. Bhutto replied "So they say." Secretary remarked he had impression Shastri now more influential in foreign affairs. Bhutto replied, "Yes, but Security Council could strengthen his hands." A fair proposal coming from Security Council would do this and would bring world opinion to bear. On other hand, inaction would provide Indians with further opportunity to proceed with integration of Kashmir. Secretary noted release of Sheikh Abdullah must have introduced major new element into situation and Indians must have recognized this. Secretary asked for Bhutto's assessment of why Abdullah was released at this time. Bhutto replied Indians had probably released him to let off some of steam built up in Kashmir; his release sooner or later was inevitable. One theory was Sadiq[5] had timed release so as to have Sheikh Abdullah eclipse Bakshi, Sadiq's personal rival. Of course Sadiq could also take credit for a popular measure. Another theory was that the release was planned to coincide with passage of a bill further integrating Kashmir into India. Personally he believed first theory more plausible.

Secretary said he thought SYG had standing authority to go out to subcontinent if he were willing. Bhutto replied it would depend on members of Security Council. Talbot added "and parties to dispute." Bhutto said no, only members. India and Pakistan not members of Council and India has opposed past resolutions. Repeated he not asking for mediation by SYG, just that he get in touch with parties and go and assess situation which threatens peace of area. Ambassador Ahmed added India would not object; it could not object. Requirement now

---

[3] The UN Security Council was scheduled to begin reconsideration of the Kashmir issue on May 5.

[4] British Foreign Secretary R.A. Butler.

[5] G.M. Sadiq, Prime Minister of Kashmir, succeeded G.M. Bakshi in October 1963.

was to lend authority of Security Council to SYG role. He should act under new authority, not under continuing authority.

Secretary inquired about expectation at last SC meeting of what next session would do. Bhutto replied that effort to reach consensus had broken down on language in operative part. The phrase "UN action" had not been acceptable to his Government. Said that if Council goes back to consensus route his instructions were to procure a reference to "wishes of the Kashmiri people in accordance with UN resolutions." Bhutto also expressed view that if SYG visits subcontinent he should certainly see Sheikh Abdullah. In reply to a question Bhutto also said it was not clear whether Sheikh Abdullah was talking about self-determination for *all* of Kashmir, though he seemed to have made an oblique reference to Azad Kashmir as one of the four regions of Kashmir.

Secretary asked if Paks sufficiently confident about results of any plebiscite to agree to any number of options being put to people of Kashmir so long as one is accession to Pakistan? Bhutto replied yes. There is hope in Sheikh Abdullah's statements but he is vague as to what he wants. This is not true of people of Kashmir, even in Jammu.

Secretary noted situation now in motion and offers opportunities, but this probably not due so much to Security Council as Bhutto seemed believe. Bhutto replied "We cannot get solution only with Security Council, nor without Security Council." Secretary said he would talk with Ambassador Stevenson and work out our position,[6] also we should hear from New Delhi on Sheikh Abdullah's talk with Nehru. At close of conversation he added it would be hard to find any question whose solution would give us greater satisfaction.

Remainder of conversation was on other topics and is being reported in separate telegrams.

Rusk

---

[6] In the wake of Rusk's conversation with Bhutto, the Department sent a message to USUN informing the Mission that the consensus statement approach followed before the Security Council adjourned no longer seemed viable. The Department felt that the minimum Pakistan could reasonably expect from the renewed Security Council debate was an outcome reminding the Indian Government that they were not conducting negotiations with Sheikh Abdullah in a vacuum nor with unlimited time. (Telegram 2833 to USUN, May 2; National Archives and Records Administration, RG 59, Central Files 1964–66, POL 32–1, INDIA–PAK/UN)

42.   Memorandum From the Deputy Assistant Secretary of Defense for International Security Affairs (Solbert) to Secretary of Defense McNamara[1]

Washington, May 6, 1964.

SUBJECT

Long Term Military Assistance for India

1. *Discussions with the Indians.* We will be reviewing the Indian Five-Year Defense Plan with the Indian experts on May 11–15 and with Defense Minister Chavan on May 19–21.

2. *General Approach.* The main purpose of these discussions will be to persuade the Indians to revise their Plan downward. At the same time we will review the FY 65 program with the Indians. We also plan to be forthcoming (on a credit sales or grant basis) on certain specific items which we can agree are reasonable and have a high priority, such as aircraft as discussed below, which might be funded subsequent to FY 65. While this is a deviation from the JCS recommendation (Tab A)[2] that we should not make any commitments beyond the FY 65 plan until the Indians revise their Plan, it seems a desirable step to evidence our good faith in the current negotiations.

3. *Military Assistance Credit Sales.* We would hope that during the meeting with Minister Chavan we might be sufficiently forthcoming in the credit sales area to arrive at a Memorandum of Understanding to be signed by yourself and the Minister on an initial sales package using FY 64, and possibly FY 65, money to finance the credit terms. We anticipate that the major portion of credit sales which could be agreed upon at this time would be in the area of defense production machinery but might also include such items as vehicles, tanks, materials handling equipment, communications equipment, raw materials and road construction equipment. We understand that the Indians consider defense production as a most important field.

In the longer run, upon agreement as to a more reasonable Indian Plan, a military assistance sales program can be established for India involving both cash and credit sales. This could provide over a 5-year period an annual credit line of $35–$50 million, repayable over a 5 to

---

[1] Source: Washington National Records Center, RG 330, OSD Files: FRC 69 A 7425, India 091.3 MSP. Secret. Received in the Office of the Secretary of Defense on May 7 at 10:52 a.m.

[2] Not found attached. The attachment was apparently a draft of the memorandum dealing with air defense aircraft for India that the JCS sent to McNamara as JCSM–396–64 on May 8. (Ibid., India 452)

10 year period at an interest rate not exceeding 5% as the initial U.S. negotiating position. Henry Kuss has in mind for consideration later some of the items in the Indian Plan such as transport aircraft (C–130s), supersonic aircraft (such as F–104s), and possibly Hawk missiles. While we may come to some of these items for India some day, they are not presently justified by the Chicom threat and their excessive expense is inconsistent with our pressures for reduction of Indian defense spending and our support of the Indian economic program.

We plan at present to aim for a credit sales program for FY 64, and possibly FY 65, covering low cost but high priority items and not discuss at this time the above-mentioned more expensive items.

4. *Air Defense Aircraft.* As you recall, when Ambassador Bowles was here it was agreed that we would discuss with the Indians the capability, cost, and availability of F–6A and F–5 aircraft and offer to assist in development of the HF–24. Since the Ambassador has returned to India, he has reverted to his original position that supplying several squadrons of F–104s is the only method to achieve his objective of minimizing Soviet influence in the Indian Air Force. In our judgment, and that of State, supplying F–104s to India in the present time frame will cause serious problems with the Pakistanis and is not presently required by the Chicom threat (though there is now increasing evidence that the Chicoms have some MIG 21s).

Accordingly, I recommend that F–104s not be offered to the Indians on any basis at present, though this would not necessarily preclude some future cash or credit sales arrangement if our efforts involving the HF–24 are not successful. In lieu thereof I recommend that we offer as alternatives F–6A aircraft on a grant aid basis or F–5 aircraft on a grant aid or credit sales basis, along with the assistance on the HF–24, as discussed below.[3]

While we will make every effort to persuade the Indians to accept our F–6A or F–5 aircraft, along with development of the HF–24, the general feeling of the Country Team in India is that this aircraft package will be unacceptable to the Indians. If this turns out to be the case, we can consider possible alternatives during Chavan's discussions with you. One alternative, proposed by the State Department, is for the U.S. to say to the Indians that if, after an examination of technical feasibility, the UK and the U.S. agree with India to collaborate in the production of the HF–24, and if this collaboration fails to produce a supersonic interceptor adequate to meet the Chicom threat, at such time as this failure is determined the U.S. will assist in finding other means to meet the Indian need for supersonic aircraft. I regard this as a commitment

---

[3] McNamara initialed his approval on May 8.

to make available to the Indians, on a credit or cash purchase basis, a Mach 2 aircraft some two or three years from now if the HF–24 project fails. While this proposition has some merit, it is an extremely vague commitment and I recommend we defer any action on such a statement to the Indians pending our assessment of the Indian experts' reactions to the presently proposed aircraft package.[4]

HF–24. Our exploration of the feasibility of assisting the Indians with the development of an engine for the HF–24 has been held up because the Indians have not granted permission for the US–UK team to visit the plant in India. The Embassy in New Delhi believes this is because of current negotiations with the UAR for an engine. The Indians have, however, offered to send drawings of the airframe to Rolls Royce in London. The project still seems feasible, and accordingly we will suggest to the Indians when they are in Washington that they permit a team of US–UK personnel to visit India as soon as possible to study the problems of adapting the HF–24 airframe to the Rolls Royce engine and the problems of manufacturing the aircraft and engine in India.

5. *Sparrow.* I understand that the Navy has as of this date determined that the Sparrow missile should not be released to India. So far Sparrow III, which we have been considering giving to India for the F–6A, has not been given to any other country (including NATO), and the Navy feels that release would result in serious risk of compromising Sparrow III–6B which is used on our first line fighters. (We do have clearance on Sidewinder.)

Peter Solbert

---

[4] McNamara initialed his approval on May 8.

43. **Memorandum From Samuel E. Belk of the National Security Council Staff to the President's Special Assistant for National Security Affairs (Bundy)[1]**

Washington, May 18, 1964.

SUBJECT

Security Council Consideration of (1) Kashmir and (2) the Cambodian Complaint

Kashmir: As you probably are aware, the Council has had this problem under consideration since mid-March when, after several inconclusive meetings, it adjourned until last week and has since met on the problem five times. It has been an extremely "ho-hum" exercise. The Paks originally believed they could push through a strong resolution condemning the Indians for not complying with the previous UN requests in connection with a plebiscite, troop withdrawals, etc.; but when it became evident that they could not get the votes, they asked for an adjournment. In the interim, we and other Council members tried unsuccessfully to get the Paks to agree to drop the matter entirely, but they felt they had committed themselves so heavily at home that it was necessary to come back to the Council. The situation now is that the Paks have abandoned hope of getting a resolution or even a consensus, and will be satisfied with a statement by the Chairman of the Council (Seydoux of France) which will sum up the views expressed during the Council meetings and which will note especially that the majority of the Council would like to see the SYG more strongly involved in the dispute than he now is. The USSR and Czechoslovakia, on behalf of the Indians, have come out strongly against this position. Seydoux convened a caucus of the Council members at 1130 today to try to work out final language and, having failed, he will convene another caucus at 1500 this afternoon. If he is successful, he may well hold what everyone hopes will be the final Council meeting on the problem still later in the day.[2] The problem is the degree of SYG involvement desired. At this morning's meeting, the Russians seemed to be taking a harder line than the Indians against a role for the SYG. For

---

[1] Source: Johnson Library, National Security File, Country File, Kashmir, Vol. I, 12/63–7/64. Confidential.

[2] The summary statement by Security Council President Roger Seydoux at the conclusion of debate on Kashmir on May 18 was forwarded to the Department in telegram 4182 from USUN, May 19. On the issue of the proposed involvement of the Secretary-General in facilitating negotiations between India and Pakistan on the issue, Seydoux noted that some members of the Council supported such a role for the Secretary-General and other members opposed it. (National Archives and Records Administration, RG 59, Central Files 1964–66, POL 32–1 INDIA–PAK/UN)

our own part, we would like to see the SYG in a procedural role which would allow him to explore quietly new methods of approach with the Indians and the Paks, e.g., is it feasible to seek out a third party who might be able to make some progress; perhaps even the SYG himself could play this role.[3]

[Here follows discussion of Security Council consideration of a complaint lodged by Camdodia.]

Sam

_____

[3] USUN reported that the mood of Foreign Minister Bhutto and his delegation as they left New York following the debate was one of bitter disappointment. Bhutto felt that Pakistan's two major allies had failed to support it during the debate. (Telegram 3185 from USUN, May 19; ibid.) On May 21, Ayub told McConaughy that he felt India would "take succor" from the Security Council debate because the United States and the United Kingdom had "kept quiet" while the Soviet Union had actively supported India. He anticipated that this would make the Indians less inclined to settle the Kashmir dispute by negotiation. (Telegram 71 from Rawalpindi, May 21; ibid., POL 32–1 INDIA–PAK) The Embassy in India reported that while the popular reaction to the outcome of the debate was generally positive, credit for the outcome went to the Soviet Union. There was widespread resentment of U.S. and U.K. support for Pakistan during the debate. (Telegram 3466 from New Delhi, May 20; ibid., POL 32–1 INDIA–PAK/UN)

_____

44.   Memorandum From Robert Komer of the National Security Council Staff to the President's Special Assistant for National Security Affairs (Bundy)[1]

Washington, May 21, 1964.

Mac—

Indian Defense Team talks[2] here have boiled down to two issues, which may be decided when McNamara talks with Chavan tomorrow morning.

_____

[1] Source: Johnson Library, National Security File, Country File, India,Vol. II, Cables, 4/64–6/64. Secret. A note in Komer's handwriting at the top of the first page reads, "Urgent."

[2] Talks with a team of Indian Defense experts, headed by Defense Secretary P.V.R. Rao and Lieutenant General Moti Sagar, Chief of Staff of the Indian Army, began in Washington on May 11. Documentation on the talks is in the National Archives and Records Administration, RG 59, Central Files 1964–66, DEF 1 INDIA and Washington National Records Center, RG 330, OASD/ISA Files: FRC 68 A 306, 381 India.

A. *FY'65 arms credit ceiling.* Indian 5-Year Defense Plan called for $1.9 billion foreign exchange outlays 1965–69. By some tall talking about how to get more defense for less and overriding need to protect development program, we've brought Indians down to $1.5. We think proper level ought to be about $1.3 billion, a cool one-third cut (but we can probably get Indian Finance Ministry to do this).

Issue turns on whether we should now offer Indians up to $50 million in FY'65 *MAP credit sales* (on top of $50 million MAP grants we plan). Since Indians will spend foreign exchange anyway, credit offers mean they'll buy from us rather than Sovs (or Brits, etc.) thus limiting purchases they can make from Sovs (pre-emption in fact). DOD wants to tell Indians now, so they can plan properly. State wants to hold off firm credit offer as lever to bring Indian ceiling down from $1.5 to $1.3. I don't feel strongly but lean toward State, especially since we could give 3/4% terms which makes Indian mouths water.

B. *Should we offer F–104s?* We're convinced Indians won't buy our aid package of 75 surplus F–6As plus help on HF–24 designed to pre-empt MIG deal. If not, McNamara would like to offer his favorite F–5. But Indians don't want it; like everyone else they want flashy 104s (Lockheed went out and sold them again). Bob says "never!" From a purely military viewpoint he's dead right. F–5 or F–6A is cheaper, easier to handle, maintain, etc.

But issue turns on political grounds (and NEA hopes to get Rusk to talk to Bob). NEA would like to tell Indians let's see if HF–24 deal can be worked out in lieu of MIGs. If not, we'll help you get alternate 2–3 squadrons of 104s within next 3–4 years, provided you don't build MIGs. Argument runs:

a. This gives fighting chance of blocking MIG production (1 in 5 is my guess). But if Indians don't bite, as all too likely, *then we at least get the credit for having been forthcoming.* We've convinced them at least that we don't regard them as second-rate citizens vis-à-vis the Paks (who get 104s). So we get a free ride.

b. True, 104s are "wasteful," but they involve *no extra out-of-pocket cost to us.* All we'd do is substitute 104s for other items, not add them on. Since *Indians are going to waste money on supersonics anyway,* why not let it flow back to us rather than to Soviets?

c. Bowles *is* right, after all, that Sovs are mounting a major new Indian aid effort (in response to ours, by the way). We'll have to live with it, and it partly serves our purpose, but after the big upward push of 1961–63 why let the Soviets gain too much kudos by picking up every option—supersonics, BOKARO, new VOA transmitter—we let drop.

d. We know we're going to give Paks two more squadrons of 104s, even though we're playing hard to get just now. Are 104s for Paks more sensible than for Indians? Hell no.

I've carried this as far as I can with DOD. Would you entertain calling Bob on this before he sees Chavan tomorrow? Bob's right that 104s are wasteful, but I think you'll agree that's not the point.

At minimum I'd like to see Bob avoid saying "no" till you, he and Rusk could talk with LBJ next Tuesday[3] lunchtime. LBJ sees Chavan Thursday. He could make some real Indian mileage by offering 104s in lieu of MIGs, an offer which probably wouldn't be picked up, which wouldn't cost extra if it was, and which is no more than we're already doing for no better reason for Pakistan.

Bob K.

---

[3] May 26.

---

45.   Telegram From the Department of State to the Embassy in India[1]

Washington, May 22, 1964, 9:04 p.m.

2398. Following summary FYI only and Noforn. It is uncleared and subject to amendment upon review of memcon.

Indian DefMin Chavan and Amb BK Nehru met with Secretary and Talbot May 21.[2] Chavan opened up discussion saying talks between Indian Defense team and DOD indicated US and India were in substantial agreement on Chicom threat, which had increased somewhat since 1962. While there is apparently little imminent danger of attack, this cannot be ruled out. In order be prepared for this eventuality and make most careful use of resources, GOI has prepared Five-Year Defense Plan. Although defense effort under Plan sizeable, it will have no adverse effect on economic development. Plan places priority on building defense production base and securing combat aircraft. Chavan requested US support to Five-Year Defense Plan, consisting of MAP at the same levels as last two years and credit sales assistance.

---

[1] Source: National Archives and Records Administration, RG 59, Central Files 1964–66, POL 27 CHICOM–INDIA. Secret; Limdis. Drafted and approved by Schneider in NEA/SOA.

[2] Chavan also met with Harriman on May 21. The conversation is summarized in telegram 2400 to New Delhi, May 23. (Ibid., DEF 19–2 US–INDIA)

Indicating specific reply on these matters up to Secretary McNamara and President, Secretary described difficulties we have already had with Congress this year concerning long-term military aid. Also stated President may be reluctant make commitments extending beyond his present term.

Turning to Indo–Pak problems Secretary described circumstances under which CENTO established in order meet Soviet threat and under which US extended military aid to Pakistan. Now India was threatened by China and was also obtaining US military aid. India and Pakistan, however, are "looking over their shoulders at each other" and we must examine how we have unwittingly gotten into supporting arms race on subcontinent. When we think of possibilities for subcontinental defense we agonize at Indo–Pak enmity.

Chavan replied India also wished resolve problems with Pakistan but must avoid actions which, instead of solving problems, might multiply them. Explained Abdullah's activities constitute new factor in Kashmir situation; India wishes him well.

Secretary inquired how far Indians believed Pak–Chicom relationship has progressed. Chavan replied there apparently no Pak–Chicom military agreement but if Chicoms attack India GOI fearful Paks will take action to tie down Indian forces.

Re China threat, Chavan repeated line that 1966–67 critical period because Katmandu Road and possibly Lhasa Railroad would be completed. Secretary inquired regarding effect in India of Chicom explosion of nuclear device. Chavan saw effect considerably greater in smaller Asian countries than in India although fact of explosion would also cause psychological reaction in India. Secretary commented he saw explosion possible within next year although Soviets had told us it not likely for 4–5 years. Remarked Asian countries could take little comfort from Chicom's lack of sophisticated delivery system since general lack sophisticated air defense in free Asia meant such delivery system unnecessary. Secretary also said, judging on basis his wartime experiences in eastern India, in his view Chinese unlikely attack through Burma because of logistic difficulties.

When, in response question, Chavan commented on lasting character Sino–Soviet rift, Secretary said we have, nevertheless, assumed neither Soviets nor Chicoms could afford see other punished in conflict with capitalist nations. Therefore, we assumed alliance would not be dissolved. Secretary wondered if opportunity bring India under Communist control presented to Soviets and Chicoms, it might possibly draw the two together. He concluded Sino–Soviet split important but not complete enough for either US or India to rely upon.

At conclusion of discussion Secretary said India could be assured US much concerned about any attempt by Chicoms break out into rest of Asia. Entirely aside from our concern for Indian development and security, basic US interest requires peace and security in both Atlantic and Pacific. If Peiping continues down course of aggression there will be serious trouble. Referring to great burden we bear in world, Secretary once more noted US distress at contrast between what could be achieved on subcontinent through Indo–Pak cooperation and what is being accomplished. This is tragedy for India as well as US.

Rusk

---

46.   Memorandum of Conversation[1]

Washington, May 22, 1964, 8:30–9:30 a.m.

SUBJECT

Indian Military Assistance

PARTICIPANTS

Indian Side
Minister of Defense, Y.B. Chavan
Ambassador B.K. Nehru
Defense Secretary, P.V.R. Rao
Mr. S. Soundararajan, Deputy Secretary to MOD
Mr. R.D. Pradhan, Secretary to the Minister of Defense

United States Side
Secretary of Defense—Robert S. McNamara
Deputy Assistant Secretary of State—James P. Grant
Deputy Assistant Secretary of Defense (ISA)—Peter Solbert

1. *Foreign Exchange Expenditures.* The Secretary opened the meeting by asking Mr. Chavan whether he had any comments to make on the progress of the past week's negotiations. Mr. Chavan responded by stating that he understood the level of foreign exchange expenditures under the Plan was a point of difference between us, and suggested that a solution might be reached if we could increase our military assistance from $50 million a year to $60 million a year. In fact, he said

---

[1] Source: Washington National Records Center, RG 330, OSD Files: FRC 77–0075, Memos of Conversation Between Sec. McNamara and Heads of State (Other than NATO). Secret. Approved by Peter Solbert on May 22. A stamped note on the memorandum reads, "Mr. Vance has seen."

he had understood before coming here that we were planning on a continuation of the Nassau level of $60 million a year.

2. *Military Credit Sales for FY 65.* Mr. McNamara responded by raising the question of our providing military assistance credit in the amount of $50 million for FY 65. He stated that he was willing to provide this credit if the Indians would reduce the foreign exchange expenditures under the Plan to a level of 682 crores ($1,435 million) and to try to work toward a level of 650 crores ($1,365 million). This would be regarded as an Indian declaration of intention. He went on to say that this figure of 682 crores of foreign exchange would include all of India's defense foreign exchange requirements, including the purchase of any aircraft.

3. *Long Term Military Assistance.* The Ambassador pointed out that unless the United States is prepared to declare its intentions over the five-year period, this would require the Indians to give a commitment to keep their foreign exchange at the 682 crores level for the five-year period against a one-year commitment by the United States to provide $50 million of military grant aid assistance and $50 million of military credit sales. Mr. McNamara agreed that this was the proposition, but that he would also be willing to agree to five-year military assistance of the Indian Plan, subject to the availability of funds, if the Indians would:

a. Agree to limit their foreign exchange expenditures to 682 crores or less;

b. Make corresponding reductions in their rupee defense budget; and

c. Support reasonable force levels during the Five Year Plan, particularly in the air defense field.

In response to Ambassador Nehru's point that this appeared to be a five-year commitment by the Indians as against a one-year commitment by the United States at this time, Mr. McNamara pointed out that if it became necessary for the Indians to go beyond the 682 crores foreign exchange level, one way was for them to pay back the U.S. $50 million loan and then be free of their commitment on foreign exchange expenditures.

It was agreed that for the purpose of computations necessary to arrive at the 682 crores level of foreign exchange expenditures, $50 million of U.S. military assistance grant aid annually could be assumed over the period of the Plan. Mr. McNamara made it clear that this was not a commitment on our part to provide that amount of assistance over the period of the Plan.

4. *Memorandum of Understanding.* It was agreed that the best way to resolve the general question under discussion was to postpone commitments until Mr. Chavan returns to Washington on May 28th to see the President. In the meantime Secretary Rao will work with us to

prepare a memorandum of understanding[2] to set forth clearly what we have in mind. Mr. Rao said that he would reduce the Plan to 682 crores and make the corresponding reductions.

5. *Air Defense.* Mr. Chavan asked the Secretary's advice as to what should be done in the area of air defense. Mr. McNamara responded by saying that his Air Force people believed that the Chinese Communists have a limited offensive potential. They have obsolete aircraft with spare parts problems and limitations on pilot training, with no prospects for an improvement over the next 3 to 5 years. He did not feel that it was wise for nations on the perimeter of Communist China to expend excessive sums for air defense against such a limited air threat. Specifically, he believed the Indians should reduce their number of squadrons from the 45 level and that they should phase out as rapidly as possible the obsolete aircraft which they had in their aircraft inventory.

6. *Aircraft.* In response to Ambassador Nehru's comment that the Indians needed to look to replacement aircraft before removing obsolete aircraft, the Secretary responded that having a large number of obsolete aircraft results in a drain on the effectiveness of the other aircraft and that some reduction would improve the combat effectiveness of the Indian Air Force.

With respect to the question of more modern aircraft, the Secretary said that he could not advise them specifically on this problem at this time. He said he knew that they had HF–24 problems, the question of MIG production, their desire for 104's, etc. He felt this would take some time to sort out, possibly weeks or even months.

Ambassador Nehru and Secretary Rao commented that the Chinese Communist Air Force could bomb India today without successful interception and for this reason they needed Mach 2 aircraft. The Secretary of Defense stated that he did not agree with the need for a Mach 2 aircraft. This led to a discussion of details of the appropriate response to the Communist air threat to India and our view that subsonic aircraft, including F–6A, were nearly as effective at this time as Mach 2 aircraft.

Ambassador Nehru then asked Secretary McNamara as to the correctness of his information that we had F–104s coming into surplus availability. Mr. McNamara pointed out that we were phasing F–104A/Bs from our Air Force into our National Guard, and that in any event only a limited number of about three squadrons were in our inventory at present.

---

[2] Rao prepared a draft memorandum of understanding, drawn up on the basis of the discussion between McNamara and Chavan, and sent copies to James Grant and Peter Solbert later in the day on May 22. (National Archives and Records Administration, RG 59, Central Files 1964–66, DEF 1 INDIA)

47.   Editorial Note

The tenth meeting of the India consortium, organized by the International Bank for Reconstruction and Development, took place in Washington on May 26, 1964. The meeting was attended by representatives of Austria, Belgium, Canada, France, Germany, Italy, Japan, the Netherlands, the United Kingdom, the United States, the International Bank for Reconstruction and Development, and the International Development Association. The International Monetary Fund sent an observer. The purpose of the meeting was to consider aid for the fourth year of India's Third Five-Year Plan, covering the period April 1964–March 1965. The communiqué issued at the end of the pledging session indicated that members of the consortium had agreed to undertake commitments totaling $1,028,000. The U.S. share of the overall commitment was $435 million. Approximately one-half of the aid pledged at the meeting took the form of non-project aid intended to be used to finance the imports required for the maintenance of the Indian economy. (Telegram 7761 to London, May 26; National Archives and Records Administration, RG 59, Central Files 1964–66, AID 9 INDIA)

48.   Memorandum From Robert Komer of the National Security Council Staff to the President's Special Assistant for National Security Affairs (Bundy)[1]

Washington, May 27, 1964.

Mac—

While Bob McNamara is dead right that F–104s are too rich for India's blood (and that F–5 is far better suited than F–104 to most of our indigent clients), I suspect he'd agree that issue really turns on political grounds:

1. Indians are determined to get supersonics somewhere, most likely MIGs. To have a fighting chance of pre-empting them we have to offer something they think comparable.

2. All of us except Bowles feel that India is already so signed on to MIG deal that it couldn't back out now. Thus odds are we'd get the

---

[1] Source: Johnson Library, National Security File, Country File, India, Vol. II, Cables, 4/64–6/64. Secret.

political credit for being forthcoming without really having to give. All-important here is not to make Indians feel they're second-class citizens, i.e. they can't have F–104s when Paks already have them.

3. True, F–104s are wasteful but they need *involve no extra out-of-pocket cost to us.* We'd merely substitute 104s for other credit items. Since Indians are going to waste money on supersonics anyway why not let it flow back to us?

4. While pre-empting MIG production isn't absolutely crucial, it is a sensitive sector. More important, since Indians are passionate about 104s (Chavan was simply afraid to raise it with Bob), it would put capstone on a highly successful Pentagon exercise in which we've brought Indians a long way.

5. Soviets are picking up too many options we let drop—Bokaro, VOA transmitter, supersonics, etc. An F–104 offer is about only big gesture we have currently available—at a crucial time of indecision following Nehru's death.

On all these scores, I'd argue for a package proposal of: (a) F–6As as interim help; (b) all-out help on HF–24; (c) if this doesn't pan out, 2–3 squadrons of F–104s a few years from now—all predicated on India not going ahead with MIGs (except rounding out one squadron they have). I'll bet this offer (which probably wouldn't be taken up) would produce enough real political plus to justify the military loss.[2] And Paks, though mighty unhappy, couldn't complain too much; they're getting F–104s too, and they'd face supersonics in any case—better our 104s than a lot more MIGs.[3]

R.W. Komer[4]

---

[2] Bundy sent a copy of this memorandum to McNamara with a covering note that reads, in part: "Bob—While I know how flinthearted you are on fancy birds for the underdeveloped, let me try out on you the political side of the case. Here's a note to me from Bob Komer, which I find quite persuasive." (Ibid., Vol. II, Memos and Miscellaneous, 4/64–6/64)

[3] Foreign Minister Bhutto called McConaughy in on May 26 and stated that Ayub had instructed him to stress the mounting Pakistani concern over reports of the likelihood of increased U.S. military assistance to India. Bhutto said that if the Indian threat to Pakistan was enhanced by such assistance, Pakistan would be forced to reduce its involvement in "free world concerns and interests in Asia" and concentrate on the preservation of its own vital national interests. (Telegram 2293 from Karachi, May 26; National Archives and Records Administration, RG 59, Central Files 1964–66, DEF 19–3 US–INDIA)

[4] Printed from a copy that bears this typed signature.

49.   Telegram From the Embassy in India to the Department of State[1]

New Delhi, May 29, 1964, 0530Z.

Secto 11. Personal for President and Acting Secretary from Secretary. It is quite clear as seen from here that it was indeed important for me to come to represent the President at Nehru's funeral.[2] Rank of dignitaries here from other countries and obvious appreciation of Indian leadership are both indicative. I have been invited to speak briefly at [garble] open-air meeting here in commemoration of Nehru presided over by President Radhakrishnan.

In brief private call which Bowles and I made on Radhakrishnan last evening, he showed great strength and determination as India faces the future. He believes that the new India will be "more pro-West than ever." He believes new government will be constituted very quickly, no later than Saturday, and that Congress Party Parliamentary Group will probably cast about three hundred votes for Shastri and about one hundred for Morarji Desai. Curious combinations between far right (Morarji Desai) and far left (Krishna Menon) are complicating factor. Despite Shastri's apparent large lead, it could develop that Congress Party will attempt to find unanimity and turn to someone like Nanda, temporary Prime Minister.

I am seeing Kosygin this afternoon and will do my best to underline the importance of Soviet Union and US working together for peace in Southeast Asia, especially in Laos.

I am also calling on Japanese Foreign Minister this afternoon and will emphasize need for caution on Japan's part in building up its relations with Peiping at time when latter's militancy is threatening war in the Pacific.

During my brief stop in Tehran, I learned that Shah is prepared to make contribution to South Vietnam.

Bowles

---

[1] Source: National Archives and Records Administration, RG 59, Central Files 1964–66, POL 15–1 INDIA. Secret; Immediate; Nodis.

[2] Prime Minister Nehru died on May 27. Minister of Home Affairs Gulzarilal Nanda became Acting Prime Minister on Nehru's death. Secretary of State Rusk headed the U.S. delegation that attended Nehru's funeral. Nehru's death interrupted the talks Defense Minister Chavan was having in Washington, and Chavan and his party returned to India in Rusk's plane. Chavan sent a message from the plane to President Johnson regretting the fact that tragic circumstances precluded the meeting he was scheduled to have with the President. (Johnson Library, National Security File, Country File, India, Vol. II, Cables, 4/64–6/64)

50.   Telegram From the Embassy in India to the Department of State[1]

New Delhi, May 30, 1964, midnight.

3577. Secretary pre-occupied with Southeast Asia and was inclined during plane trip from US to New Delhi to postpone decision on military aid to India. However, believe he was impressed with obvious political opportunity facing us with a new government coming in and the rapidly increasing GOI fear of Chinese breakthrough in Southeast Asia. As a result he seemed cautiously favorable to procedures and substantive recommendations which I have since his departure described in a comprehensive cabled proposal (Embtel 3572).[2] This will reach him in Saigon Sunday and should be in your hands and McNamara's hopefully before McNamara leaves for Honolulu.

If the President can be persuaded to read our cable[3] I think he will have clearer perspective of the current opportunities for US in India.

Measures needed to button up the military aid situation here and to take advantage of dramatic opportunity with a new government are as follows:

1. Secure USG concurrence in modest adjustments requested by GOI in the agreement between Chavan and ourselves so that memorandum of understanding[4] can promptly go to new Cabinet for final approval.

---

[1] Source: National Archives and Records Administration, RG 59, Conference Files: Lot 66 D 110, CF 2405B. Secret. Also sent to the White House for McGeorge Bundy.

[2] In telegram 3572 from New Delhi, May 30, Bowles strongly endorsed McNamara's desire to expedite a military assistance agreement. He argued that the best way for the United States to associate itself with the new government in India would be to follow up on the favorable outcome of the Chavan talks. Bowles proposed that the agreement discussed in Washington should be finalized and initialed by Chavan and himself as soon as possible. When the new government was formed, Bowles would negotiate implementation of the agreement. (Johnson Library, National Security File, Country File, India, Vol. II, Cables, 4/64–6/64)

[3] Komer commented on telegram 3572 in a June 3 memorandum to McGeorge Bundy. Komer found Bowles' proposals persuasive, but added: "you and I are among the few people in this town who read Bowles' epistles for sense. He's so drawn down his credit that neither DOD nor the Seventh Floor in State really focus on his mail anymore. Even the President seems to react adversely to Chet's overbidding." Komer concluded that "the real issue is not whether Bowles is right but whether we can sell his wares to a harassed President over the niggling objections of Rusk and Defense." (Ibid.)

[4] A draft memorandum of understanding, based on the one provided by Rao to Solbert, was furnished by Solbert to Rao on May 27 prior to the departure of the Indian delegation. The text of this draft was transmitted to New Delhi on May 28 in joint State/Defense telegram DA 970998. (Washington National Records Center, RG 330, OSD Files: FRC 69 A 7425, India 091.112)

2. Authorize me to secure approval of new government of press statement included in Embtel 3572[5] or some genuinely meaningful substitute. If I can get such a statement in the papers here within a day or two after the formation of the new government the political effect in what will inevitably be rather wobbly situation might well be both profound and dramatic. If I can be authorized to say that military loans in addition to grants will be in neighborhood of 50 million dollars this will further strengthen our position. After all, this will leak sooner or later in any event.

It is particularly important to get the story published before we are hit by leaks and distortions that can confuse the situation with added possibility of military aid proposals from Moscow to new Indian government.

3. Authorize me to proceed at once to negotiate package air agreement along lines proposed Embtel 3572 with whatever caveats may be required to secure approval. I believe it is essential that we include some reference to F–104s and the stronger the reference the greater the possibility of persuading the new government to limit MIGs to acceptable numbers. If technical questions arise that are beyond our capacities here experts should be sent from Washington.

If you can manage this I will be greatly in your debt and the next message you can expect from me will be a Christmas card.

Bowles

---

[5] The press release Bowles proposed in telegram 3572 emphasized the positive outcome of the discussions between Chavan and McNamara. It noted that the United States agreed that India's 5-year plan provided a sound basis for defense assistance and referred to discussions to develop plans for U.S. assistance in meeting India's need for high-performance aircraft.

51.   Memorandum From Robert Komer of the National Security Council Staff to the President's Special Assistant for National Security Affairs (Bundy)[1]

Washington, June 2, 1964.

Mac—

Shastri's victory[2] is a definite plus for our side. He was the guy who had the guts to vote for letting Abdullah out of the clink. What remains to be seen, however, is whether Shastri can make that inchoate mass known as the Congress Party pull together, and whether he has the ability to lead.

Ayub's conciliatory noises yesterday[3] are also a plus.

Meanwhile Talbot says Rusk wants to go slow on arms aid to India, till we see how Indians *and Paks* perform on SEA. In other words, let's not offend the Paks just now. Do you agree? I'm more inclined to agree with Bowles that now's the time for a gesture toward Indians.

RWK[4]

---

[1] Source: Johnson Library, National Security File, Country File, India, Vol. II, Cables, 4/64–6/64. Secret.

[2] Lal Bahadur Shastri was elected leader of the Congress Parliamentary Party on June 2. He was sworn in as Prime Minister, Minister of External Affairs, and Minister of Atomic Energy on June 9.

[3] Ayub responded to Shastri's election by urging a "fresh look" at relations between Pakistan and India. Shastri stated at a June 2 press conference that he was "much impressed" by Ayub's statement. (Telegram 3633 from New Delhi, June 3; National Archives and Records Administration, RG 59, Central Files 1964–66, POL 32–1 INDIA–PAK)

[4] Bundy wrote a note to Komer beneath his initials: "speak to me on this."

52.   Letter From Secretary of Defense McNamara to Minister of Defense Chavan[1]

Washington, June 3, 1964.

Dear Mr. Minister:

I am very pleased that our recent discussions concerning the Indian Five-Year Defense Plan reached general agreement, but the event which terminated them has caused us all great sorrow. Prime Minister Nehru's sudden death has brought to a close a remarkable career, devoted throughout as it was to the service of India. All of us here join in sending you our sympathy on such a loss.

I know that we are both interested in the momentum of our talks in Washington carrying on. I agree with your suggestion to Assistant Secretary Talbot that we omit from the Memorandum the sentence referring to the Rs. 650 crores level of foreign exchange.[2] As you recall, at our meeting I indicated my feeling that moving toward the Rs. 650 crores level would constitute a less severe drain on India's economic development, but I see no necessity to include this in the Memorandum.

I understand that your other point related to the Indian force plans referred to in Article 3 of the Memorandum. Here again I agree with your suggested revision of the Memorandum so that the second and third sentences of Article 3 of the Memorandum read as follows:

"Minister Chavan said that Indian Defense Representatives would determine the specific items in the Plan to be deferred to come within the above-mentioned foreign exchange level and would determine appropriate readjustments in the Plan. Projection by the United States of its military assistance, both grant aid and credit sales, on a multi-year basis will depend on these determinations."

As you can well appreciate, any multi-year projection of United States military assistance to India must rest on a general understanding between us with respect to proposed defense foreign exchange expenditures, rupee military budget, and force plans which such assistance would go to support. Your Defense Plan, including the force plans, will certainly continue to be a topic of mutual discussions between us.

---

[1] Source: Washington National Records Center, RG 330, OASD/ISA Files: FRC 68 A 306, India 381. Secret. Drafted by Solbert. The text of this letter was transmitted to New Delhi on June 3 in telegram DEF 971909. (Ibid., OSD Files: FRC 69 A 7425)

[2] Both of the changes proposed by Chavan in the language of the memorandum of understanding were explained in a June 3 memorandum from Solbert to McNamara. Solbert noted that Chavan felt that the Rs. 650 crores objective in the memorandum of understanding would be difficult to sell to the Indian Cabinet, and the language relating to force levels would be read by the Shastri government as an unacceptable abrogation of decision-making authority to an external power. (Ibid.)

I hope that these suggestions are helpful in putting the Memorandum of Understanding into appropriate form for execution.[3] I am very pleased by the tenor of the discussions which we had over the past few weeks here in Washington on your Defense Plan and I look forward to agreement on longer term arrangements between our Governments in this respect.

Sincerely yours,

Robert S. McNamara[4]

---

[3] Bowles reported in telegram 3626 from New Delhi, June 3, that Chavan had secured Cabinet approval for the memorandum of understanding, subject to the two changes he had proposed. (National Archives and Records Administration, RG 59, Central Files 1964–66, DEF 19 US–INDIA)

[4] Printed from a copy that bears this signature and an indication that the original was signed.

---

53.   Memorandum From Robert Komer of the National Security Council Staff and the President's Special Assistant for National Security Affairs (Bundy) to President Johnson[1]

Washington, June 4, 1964.

McNamara's talks with Indian Defense Minister Chavan went quite well, until interrupted by Nehru's death. Indians had produced a 5-Year Defense Plan at our request, and we managed to squeeze the key foreign exchange component down $332 million (about 20%) on grounds deleted items were militarily unnecessary and too great a burden on the economy.

In turn McNamara has agreed to $50 million MAP in FY'65 for mountain warfare equipment, communications, and defense production. He has withheld any 5-year MAP promises until he can work over their plan some more, especially on the air side. We did, however, tell Indians they could assume for planning purposes roughly same level in future years.

---

[1] Source: Johnson Library, National Security File, Country File, India, Vol. II, Cables, 4/64–6/64. Secret.

McNamara also agreed to sell on credit terms up to $10 million in FY'64 and $50 million FY'65 certain items to be agreed. Since the Indians intend to spend some of their own hard currency anyway, this neat device meant that much of it will flow to us rather than to the Soviets or UK.

Both we and Indians regard this exercise to date as successful and want to tape it down in a Memorandum of Understanding (Tab A),[2] which McNamara has OKed. Chavan has himself appealed to us to OK it, so that he can run it through Indian cabinet, and we can put out a brief announcement on success of talks, a good gesture in India just now.

The Memo, and proposed bland press release (Tab B),[3] fall far short of what Bowles wants (but will be a plus in India even so). For example, it does *not* include any US jet offer designed to pre-empt Indian MIG deal with Soviets. Bundy and I hope you'll hear argument on this separately later.

We simply want to give you the final word on this before going ahead.[4] It's only an early stage in a long and painful dialogue with the Indians but both sides are happy with progress to date. Nor will Paks be too unhappy, because we haven't given much (we've kept them clued).

Recommend your early approval. Indians hope to get it so their cabinet can act before it goes Saturday to bury Nehru's ashes.[5]

R.W. Komer
McG. B.

---

[2] Not printed. This revised draft, dated May 27, the essentials of which are summarized in this memorandum, was signed by Bowles and Chavan on June 6 as a memorandum of understanding on military assistance. The text of the agreement, as signed, was transmitted to the Department in airgram A–1290 from New Delhi, June 18. (National Archives and Records Administration, RG 59, Central Files 1964–66, DEF 19–4 US–INDIA)

[3] Not printed. The text of the press release was transmitted to New Delhi on June 5 in telegram 2534, with authorization for the Embassy to release it. (Ibid., DEF 19–3 US–INDIA)

[4] Bundy received preliminary approval for the agreement from President Johnson in a telephone conversation the previous evening. (Johnson Library, Transcripts of Telephone Conversations, Alpha Series, McGeorge Bundy)

[5] President Johnson checked the approval line.

54.   Telegram From the Embassy in India to the Department of State[1]

New Delhi, June 6, 1964, 1300Z.

3686. Late Friday afternoon I met with Lal Bahadur Shastri for forty-five minutes. The new PriMin was calm, cordial and relaxed. The talk which included some pointed references to military assistance agreement developed along following lines:

1. Shastri opened conversation with an emotional and extended reference to Nehru in course of which he reviewed his 37-year personal relationship, the unique influence that Nehru had on the Indian people, his moral and physical courage, etc. through his efforts a strong national political foundation has been built. The new Indian Govt was determined to build on that foundation and he was personally encouraged by the initial response of Congress Party and Indian public.

2. I stressed world-wide implications of Indian democratic experiment, growing understanding in US of Nehru's personal qualities and historic role, warm press and public reaction to his own recent election, and continuing determination of USG to back Indian economic development and military defense with greatest vigor.

3. Picking up my last point, Shastri reminded me of our last conversation in which he had expressed view that outcome of Chavan visit to US was of profound importance. He was delighted to hear that negotiations had been successful. Although Chavan had shown him agreement he had been so harried that he had not had opportunity to study it.

4. At his request I outlined main points, stressing need for balance between the economic growth which is essential to national unity and motivation and an adequate force with which to defend Indian borders.

Shastri asked incisive questions about US help for domestic military production, nature of grant aid arrangements, likely magnitude of our assistance plans, prospects for continuing congressional support, etc., and next step in regard to air force negotiations which he understood had not been completed.

5. In regard to latter point I expressed the hope that discussions would soon be resumed and that decision satisfactory to both of us could be reached in near future.

---

[1] Source: National Archives and Records Administration, RG 59, Central Files 1964–66, POL 1 INDIA–US. Confidential. Repeated to the White House, Defense Department, London, and CINCMEAFSA for POLAD.

Perhaps more than any other nation we shared India's concern over long range implications of China's political objectives and military capacity. Although we felt that Indian Defense Ministry was inclined to overrate China's present air capacity and to underrate her potential missile capacity, we fully agreed that India needs an effective air defense system with a number of high performance aircraft, and we expressed our willingness to provide such aircraft.

Our difficulties lie along two lines (1) our belief that the Indian defense authorities as in every other govt have failed to balance questions of financial costs against practical requirements and (2) our concern over growing dependence of Indian Air Force on USSR. If in addition to transport planes, SAMs and some MIG–21s this should now be expanded by the addition of a large MIG–21 assembly line, major US assistance to Indian air force would not only be unnecessary but would also create many security problems for us.

While we welcome lessening of tensions with USSR we cannot forget that less than two years ago Mr. Khrushchev's government had surreptitiously attempted to place forty missiles in Cuba armed with nuclear warheads and aimed at forty US cities. If India could visualize a Chinese attempt to place similar installations in Bhutan or Burma she would understand our reaction.

In any event it is important that the Prime Minister and his key associates understand our view of India's actual air defense needs based on many years of experience in similar situations. In initial stage we believed that India needs reasonably effective airplane with high rate of climb that could be delivered here quickly and at low cost. Over longer haul India needs a supersonic plane perferably produced or assembled in this country.

In regard to first need we had discussed with Mr. Chavan F6As, a proven plane with fast rate of climb, and an extremely low cost, relatively easy to fly and available promptly.

In regard to second need, we had expressed our willingness during Washington discussions to help India in every practical way to find suitable engine for her HF–24 (Mach II). Naturally the question had arisen: but what if our combined efforts should fail?

The Indian Air Force had expressed an eagerness for US F–104Gs. Although this is an outstanding plane we had stressed that it is extremely costly, hard to fly and prone to accidents. Moreover present assembly lines in Japan, Germany and Canada are likely to be closed down before end of next year.

We had also discussed the F–5 which although not as fast as the F–104 is fully capable of handling Chinese bombers and much less expensive although more so than the F–6A.

In any event the situation was still hanging fire. Indian Air Force like every other air force naturally wanted the best regardless of cost. We on other hand are deeply concerned about unbalancing the defense budget with unnecessarily sophisticated weapons.

If we did decide to backup HF–24 project with supersonic plane acceptable to Indians we would do so on assumption that India would not feel that a major MIG–21 production effort was also required in addition to our contribution plus the expensive Soviet SAMs which we understood had already been contracted for.

6. Shastri listened attentively to this presentation and asked pertinent questions; his final one being "Does Chavan agree with your views?" I replied that although Mr. Chavan had seen all three planes and undoubtedly had formed some opinion he was probably waiting for US decision as to what we are willing to do.

The Indian Air Force was greatly taken with F–104 which we all agreed was an outstanding plane. In the end, however, such decisions as in our own govt would have to be taken by the civilian ministries; in doing so I only hoped they would not forget that the added cost of the Air Force proposals would probably be enough to build two or three new Indian universities or dam over one of India's greatest rivers.

Although PriMin might assume he was not a military expert I could assure him that he would soon be forced by such situations to become one. He would find that it is a rare occasion when he will be provided by wholly right or wholly wrong alternatives; on questions of defense as elsewhere the available policy choices are bound to be unsatisfactory in one way or another.

7. Shastri then asked me about procedure. I replied that the classified general agreement was all set and in Mr. Chavan's hands and that as soon as he approved it we would issue joint press statement.

I said that press statement that we had prepared was deliberately in low key and rather vague on key questions because from Indian point of view and our own it was essential not to upset the Pakistanis.

As PriMin himself had pointed out, Ayub Khan had taken moderate and encouraging position in regard to India. If this mood is adequately encouraged we may expect further weakening of the Sino–Pak relationship which will serve our common interests.

Shastri agreed with this and commented that he was glad general agreement had been reached, that he was grateful for my explanation of air force question which he had not previously understood, and that in meantime Chavan had full authority to sign agreement.

8. I closed my end of conversation with remarks on overriding importance of the US–Indian relationship, our heavy stake in India's economic and political success and in her military defense, and the

fact that as India's new Prime Minister he could count on President Johnson, Dean Rusk, me and everyone else in our govt for understanding and support in good times or in bad.

Shastri replied that he hoped we could talk frequently about many things, that he was particularly conscious of my long interest in Indian development, and that he would like to feel free to discuss with me some special problems in that regard. For instance, he shared my conviction that India's political future would be determined in her villages, and added that new land reform measures were high on Congress Party agenda and that he hoped to talk with me about them soon.

His final comment at the door was a request that I personally thank Dean Rusk for interrupting his busy Washington schedule to come all the way to New Delhi for Nehru's funeral.

Bowles

---

55.   Telegram From the Department of Defense to the Embassy in Pakistan[1]

Washington, June 7, 1964, 0008Z.

DEF 972285. From OASD/ISA. This is a joint State/Defense message. Reference Deptel 2374.[2] As indicated in our cables to New Delhi on the need for cautious press play on the McNamara–Chavan understanding, we recognize that Paks will have difficulty in swallowing new stage of US military assistance to India. The Indian military buildup inevitably is changing the military power balance in the subcontinent and we recognize that Pak unhappiness over this is compounded by our significant assistance role with the Indians. It is extremely important therefore that both India's buildup and most particularly our role be kept in as accurate a perspective as possible by the Paks. Following

---

[1] Source: National Archives and Records Administration, RG 59, Central Files 1964–66, DEF 19 US–INDIA. Secret. Repeated to New Delhi, London, CINCMEAFSA, and State Department Operations Center.

[2] The reference is in error. The correct reference is telegram 2374 from Karachi, June 5, in which the Embassy expressed concern about the memorandum of understanding on military assistance to India that was about to be signed. Although the agreement did not embrace the sensitive issue of supersonic aircraft for India, the Embassy was deeply concerned about the impact of the agreement upon the balance of military power on the subcontinent, upon prospects for an Indo–Pak reconciliation, and upon the U.S. position in Pakistan. (Ibid., DEF 19–3 US–INDIA)

should be helpful in clarifying for your information what has been agreed to with the Indians as reftel has indicated some misunderstanding.

Our discussions with the Indians resulted in a cut back of their program for offshore defense acquisitions during five years from a total of $1911 million including aircraft to $1432 million averaging $286 million annually. The latter includes all identifiable offshore acquisitions including US, UK and Soviet assistance as well as those from India's own foreign exchange (do not understand source of your erroneous figure of $400 million for the annual level of Indian offshore acquisitions). The offshore procurement ceiling of $1432 million includes not only all direct procurement for the armed forces but also many of the indirect foreign exchange charges, e.g., raw material for Indian ordnance factories (does not however include certain other indirect foreign exchange costs such as POL).

The $286 million annual rate is about the average for the past two Indian fiscal years including all foreign military aid. The result, therefore, of our $50 million credit in FY 65 will be to reduce the use of India's own foreign exchange for military procurement to a level well below that of the past two years and primarily result in channeling increased procurement to US market. We realize that this is a difficult point to convince the Paks on; however, given the ceiling we have agreed to with the Indians, it is valid and needs to be reiterated to the Paks.

Our assistance to Indian defense production has been concentrated on infantry requirements, particularly ammo production and not, as Paks may fear, in major equipment production. For example, the Ambajhari ordnance plant is to produce primarily ammunition for mortars, pack 75's and recoilless rifles which are particularly required for mountain divisions even though also used for the regular infantry divisions.

You can indicate to the Paks that our review of the Indian five year plan has resulted both in substantial reduction in Indian plans and also in increased concentration of their buildup to respond to the Communist threat. (FYI. e.g., Indian plans for naval modernization were cut back drastically by some 75 per cent. End FYI)

You will note from McNamara letter to Chavan[3] and memorandum of understanding that in fact US has agreed only to FY 1964 and FY 1965 programs. Longer term projection of our assistance will depend upon India satisfying certain conditions as listed in McNamara letter.

---

[3] Document 52.

We anticipate that as a minimum it will take several months before we are in position make long term projection should we decide at that time such a course is appropriate.[4]

---

[4] On June 15 the Embassy reported that Foreign Minister Bhutto expressed sharp criticism of the U.S. military assistance agreement with India. Bhutto stated in a press conference that the agreement would aggravate tension on the subcontinent and make a settlement between India and Pakistan more difficult. (Telegram 2459 from Karachi; National Archives and Records Administration, RG 59, Central Files 1964–66, DEF 19–3 US–INDIA) The Embassy noted in telegram 2498 from Karachi, June 19, that Bhutto's attitude reflected the concerns of the rest of the Pakistani Government. Since the United States was held to be largely responsible for what the Ayub government saw as an increasingly dangerous situation, the Embassy felt there was a need to restore the U.S. position in Pakistan and to give Pakistan a greater sense of confidence in its security. (Ibid.)

---

56.   Telegram From the Department of State to the Embassy in India[1]

Washington, June 10, 1964, 9:40 p.m.

2573. New Delhi's 3685 to Dept,[2] repeated Karachi 1631, CINC-MEAFSA unnumbered.

Air Defense Assistance. During year and half of Indo–Pak tensions since Chicom attack we have not permitted Pak objections to stand in way of larger US interest in strengthening Indian forces against threat Chicom aggression. At same time we have done what possible to encourage Pak–Indian accommodation in realization that any lasting security of subcontinent requires Indo–Pak cooperation. Nehru's death, accession of moderate Shastri government, and friendly reaction of Ayub has opened new vista of possible Pak–Indian accommodation. Under these circumstances believe main play of USG for coming weeks should be to leave field open for possible development of forces leading toward accommodation and avoid actions which might tend rekindle

---

[1] Source: National Archives and Records Administration, RG 59, Central Files 1964–66, DEF 19–3 US–INDIA. Secret; Immediate. Drafted by Schneider; cleared by Talbot, Cameron, Solbert (substance), and Freshman (G/PM) (substance); and approved and initialed by Rusk. Repeated to Karachi, London, and CINCSTRIKE for POLAD.

[2] In telegram 3685 from New Delhi, June 6, Bowles argued for building upon the success achieved with the memorandum of understanding on military assistance by negotiating an agreement to meet the Indian Government's desire to upgrade the Indian Air Force. (Ibid.)

flames of subcontinent controversy. Underlying this policy is thesis that as prospects for Indo–Pak accommodation improve, long run security of subcontinent requires that major determinant US policy be what will contribute to proper climate for accommodation.

Judged against this background, we believe Memorandum of Understanding recently concluded with GOI is about as far as we can go at this moment without risking injecting new disruptive factor into Indo–Pak relations. Therefore, while we believe we should meet our commitment to continue discussing air defense assistance with Indians, we should defer for time being presenting comprehensive package for air assistance. Accordingly, Embassy should delay continuation of current talks on comprehensive aircraft assistance. We will follow-up in later message with strategy by which we propose to meet commitment to continue discussions while deferring any new offer. FYI: We are planning continue our initiative with Indians for comprehensive feasibility study of HF–24 while deferring discussion with Indians of possible backup of project with US supersonic aircraft.[3] End FYI.

We believe Memorandum of Understanding has already effectively demonstrated for the present our support of new government. Your reports show that Indian officials are quite pleased results Chavan mission. Moreover, talks with Rao and Khera indicate Indians may be further down MIG–21 road than we had previously realized. Under circumstances described above seems our best tactic now would be to do what we can to encourage Indians keep available options open (i.e., MIG–21 and HF–24) until they have facts which would enable them in making decisions to take into account technical and military factors, as well as their evident preference for domestic production. Feasibility study of HF–24 is essential ingredient of this tactic.

We count on you to help reduce sense of immediacy which has been built up around this subject. Your return to US would in itself contribute to this.

Rusk

---

[3] On June 17 the Department instructed the Embassy to implement this strategy in discussing the requirements of the Indian Air Force. (Telegram 2624 to New Delhi; ibid., DEF 19–3 US–INDIA)

57.   Memorandum From Robert Komer of the National Security Council Staff to President Johnson[1]

Washington, June 16, 1964.

Chet Bowles is back full of vim and vigor. He's quite optimistic about the new *Shastri* cabinet, which he sees as more practical and less woolly-minded than Nehru's. You should get his slant.

The chief pending item of Indian business is whether we should include in our longer term military program an air defense package designed to preempt their MIG deal with Moscow. Proposal is that we offer to sell or grant India (within proposed MAP ceilings—so no added cost to us): (a) 72 surplus F–6As; (b) help in making their own homegrown HF–24 supersonic; and (c) if HF–24 doesn't pan out, we'd provide 24–36 F–104s a few years from now; *all this only on condition that India give up MIG–21 production.*

Most of us are convinced that India is much too far down the road to renege on MIG deal (only Bowles differs—and he's climbing down now too). Thus we'd get all the political benefit of showing the Indians they're not second-class citizens (i.e. we're willing to give F–104s to them as well as Paks) without ever having our offer taken up. Or, if we were all wrong, and Indians bit, then we have the great plus of getting non-aligned India to reject MIGs. This would also protect the Paks, since a few squadrons of Indian F–104s would be less dangerous than a whole MIG production line.

McNamara has come around to buying this deal. He says let's offer F–104s to *both* India and Pakistan or to neither. *State,* however, is more equivocal; it sees an air offer to India as upsetting the Paks just when Ayub is coming around to a conciliatory policy. So State says let's hold off awhile (see their brief attached).[2]

But one of the factors bringing Paks around (aside from Nehru's death) is that we're finally getting through to them that they can't have a veto on our Indian policy. Also this air offer is a non-starter anyway, so why all the worry? At any rate, you might hear argument from Bowles, and then take issue up at lunch if you see a case.[3]

Only other issue is State's proposal you give Shastri an open-ended visit invite. I *told* them you couldn't do this before election, but

---

[1] Source: Johnson Library, National Security File, Country File, India, Vol. III, Cables, 6/64–11/64. Secret.

[2] Not printed. The brief on the air defense assistance package took the form of a June 16 memorandum from Talbot to Rusk, passed to the White House.

[3] No record of Bowles' meeting with President Johnson has been found.

suggest instead you allow Bowles to tell Shastri this, and to say that if elected you'd much look forward to seeing him at some mutually convenient time thereafter.[4]

R.W. Komer[5]

---

[4] A handwritten note by Talbot on the June 16 memorandum to Rusk cited in footnote 2 above indicates that President Johnson discussed this issue with Bowles on June 15 and authorized him to tell Shastri that if the November elections went well Johnson hoped that he and Shastri would find the opportunity to meet.

[5] Bundy initialed below Komer's signature.

---

58. **Letter From Secretary of State Rusk to Secretary of Defense McNamara[1]**

Washington, June 17, 1964.

Dear Bob:

We may be close enough to agreement on the contents of a comprehensive U.S. air defense package for India so that it would be worthwhile for me to try to set them down in writing. My objective is to secure Executive Branch agreement on this now. As you probably know, for the immediate present we are deferring presentation of any comprehensive air package in order to avoid introducing a jarring note during the Indo-Pak honeymoon which seems to be in process. In this regard I might add that Pak Foreign Minister Bhutto has already publicly criticized our recent announcement to the press of additional military assistance to India at a time when Pakistan is trying to improve its relations with India. He has done this despite the obvious restraint imposed by his government on critical press reaction to the announcement.

So that we will be in a position to move when the time is ripe—and we have our eyes very much on possible Soviet moves and the timing of any Indian military mission to Moscow—I suggest an air package on the following order:

---

[1] Source: Washington National Records Center, RG 330, OSD Files: FRC 69 A 7425, India 381. Secret. Received in the Office of the Secretary of Defense on June 18 at 11:22 a.m. A stamped notation on the letter reads: "SecDef has seen, 20 June 1964."

1. *F6A's.* Three squadrons of (72) F6A's. (We have, of course, already discussed these with the Indians. I should express our strong view that we should not go in with the F6A's alone but that they should be only a part of a comprehensive package.)

2. *HF–24.* If our feasibility studies are positive, we would be willing to provide technical assistance in adapting a Western engine to the HF–24 airframe, and other technical assistance in developing this airplane into an operational Mach 2 interceptor.

3. *Supersonics.* If, after a year or so of joint efforts to develop the HF–24, this aircraft does not seem likely to become an operational Mach 2 interceptor, we would be prepared to help the Indians find suitable Western supersonics. We now see our way clear to offering some 36 of these. We would tell the Indians this when we present the comprehensive air package. If the Indians should come back and say that this package is not responsive to their desire for some sort of domestic assembly—which the MIG deal would permit—I should hope that we would be prepared to look most closely into what could be done to meet this point.

For planning purposes I believe we need now an Executive Branch determination that these 36 aircraft could be F–104G's, although I would hope that we could get the Indians to settle on some other interceptor, such as the F5A or F–104 A/B. (We have gone beyond the 24 F–104's which you suggested as we don't believe we could sell the package at this level; at 36 we would have something which would give us a chance with the Indians. We would not expect in any event that deliveries of U.S. supersonics to India over the next five years would get ahead of deliveries to Pakistan.)

I am particularly persuaded that this entire package, including individual components such as the F6A's, should be offered only on the condition that India drop its plans for obtaining MIG 21's beyond rounding out a single squadron of no more than 24 aircraft. Our position with Pakistan would be greatly weakened if the Indians were able to secure substantial combat air assistance from both blocs. Furthermore, I am greatly concerned regarding the reaction on the Hill should we help the Indians with combat air while they build up their stock of MIG 21's. Reaction on the Hill may be hard enough to deal with after an Indian MIG deal even if we do not help the Indians in the combat air field.

I hope you agree that we can move forward with our planning on this basis.

Sincerely,

Dean

59.   Memorandum From Robert Komer of the National Security Council Staff to the President's Special Assistant for National Security Affairs (Bundy)[1]

Washington, June 23, 1964.

McGB:

It looks as though Mikoyan's surprise stopover in Delhi (en route to Djakarta) may have clinched MIG deal. Our DCM was told (Delhi 3851)[2] that it was "confirmed" by Mikoyan. DCM regards die as cast, but a few of us here still hope there may be some F–104 play left for us. In any case, we can keep plugging HF–24 engine, in hopes that if it pans out we'll have new case for limiting MIG purchases.

Meanwhile Paks seem to be whomping up another anti-US MAP for India campaign (note attached).[3] To me, this is *not* yet the time to start being nice to Paks, but to growl back at them a while longer. Paks claim long-term US aid prevents India/Pak reconciliation, but in point of fact unless we keep them in suspense it is *they* who lose incentive for compromise with Shastri.

RWK

---

[1] Source: Johnson Library, National Security File, Country File, Pakistan, Vol. II, 6/64–11/64. Secret.

[2] Dated June 22. (National Archives and Records Administration, RG 59, Central Files 1964–66, POL 7 INDIA)

[3] Two telegrams were attached. Telegram 2523 from Karachi, June 23, reported that Foreign Minister Bhutto told the National Assembly on June 22 that in light of the new U.S.–Indian military assistance agreement, the "time has come for Pakistan to undertake a reappraisal of its foreign policy and review her political and military commitments." Telegram 2528 from Karachi, June 24, cited a local press report of that day that quoted President Ayub as charging the United States with basing its policy toward South Asia on opportunism and not hesitating to "let down friends."

60.   Letter From President Ayub to President Johnson[1]

Rawalpindi, July 1, 1964.

My dear President Johnson,

I am asking my Ambassador to call on you and apprise you of the likely repercussions of the recent decision of your Administration concerning military aid to India. I think the time has come for me to make a personal approach to you.

We have, over the last two years, repeatedly represented to the United States Government the dangers implicit in their policy of massive arms aid to India. From the very beginning we have held the view that the arming of India on the scale chosen by the United States was uncalled for. Time has proved that we were right. It must now be clear to everyone that China does not plan to invade India and there is no likelihood of recrudescence of even a limited arms conflict between India and China.

On the other hand, this aid imperils the security of Pakistan, your ally; it prevents an Indo-Pakistan rapproachment over Kashmir which immobilises the bulk of their armed forces in a dangerous confrontation; it must lead to an arms race between India and Pakistan and thereby place a crushing burden on their economies. Surely this is no way of preventing the inroads of Communism into the sub-continent—if this is the United States objective. On the contrary, it would facilitate them.

Further, by continuing to build India's armed might, the United States might well force India's smaller neighbours already deeply mistrustful of India—to seek the protection of China.

In short, the policy the United States is following in this area is self-defeating.

The foregoing considerations have been put before the United States Government time and again. If I am restating them, it is because I have a feeling that these considerations have not been given the weight they deserve.

On May 26 my Foreign Minister explained to Ambassador McConaughy Pakistan's growing concern at the continued arming of India. He also stated that if this policy continued, Pakistan would be compelled to reconsider its commitments to her allies.

---

[1] Source: National Archives and Records Administration, RG 59, Central Files 1964–66, DEF 19 US–PAK. Secret; Exdis. The classification marking was added in the Department of State. The text of this letter was transmitted to the Embassy in Karachi in telegram 25, July 9. (Ibid., DEF 19–3 US–INDIA) Ambassador Ahmed delivered the letter to President Johnson on July 7; see Document 63.

Your Government has since decided not merely to continue to arm India; it has offered India twice as much arms aid in FY 1965 as in previous years. India has also been given to understand that she may expect to receive military aid of this order for the next five years.

Not to mention the timing of previous decisions to arm India which have all contributed towards complicating Indo-Pakistan relations, the present decision, in particular, has been singularly ill-timed. Latterly, we were moving towards a relaxation of tension in our relations with India. There was some hope that the Shastri Government recognised the importance of improving relations with Pakistan and, to that end, might be willing to settle the Kashmir dispute. That hope has now been rudely shaken.

This latest manifestation of US Administration's resolve to continue to give long term military aid to India has caused deep misgivings in Pakistan. Faced with the resultant growing peril to our security, because of the enormous Indian arms build up with US support, I am writing to you in the hope that you will please look personally into the issues I have mentioned and take suitable corrective action in the interest of Pakistan–United States relationship which has so far been cordial and warm. And to my way of thinking very little effort is required to maintain it so. I am saying this as I have belief in your wisdom and sagacity. I also believe that this is not only necessary in the interest of Pakistan but also very much in the global interest of the United States relating to Asia.

With warm personal regards,

Yours sincerely,

Mohammad Ayub Khan

---

61.   Letter From Secretary of Defense McNamara to Secretary of State Rusk[1]

Washington, July 2, 1964.

Dear Dean:

I agree with the proposal for an air defense package for India as set forth in your letter of June 17, 1964,[2] with the exception that I think

---

[1] Source: National Archives and Records Administration, RG 59, Central Files 1964–66, DEF 19–8 US–INDIA. Secret.

[2] Document 58.

we should limit the number of F–5 or F–104G aircraft which we offer to India to a total of 24 aircraft. These aircraft would presumably be supplied to India primarily on a credit sales basis. I think we should maintain a balance between the high performance aircraft offered to India and those offered to Pakistan, and accordingly the present 12 F–104A/B's in Pakistan should be augmented by not more than an additional 12 F–104's through grant aid, bringing Pakistan's total of F–104 aircraft to 24.

I believe we should make every effort to limit the Indians to the acquisition of about a dozen MIG–21's rather than permitting them to go to two dozen aircraft. I think our package, with the offer of up to 72 F–6 aircraft and support for the HF–24 included, is sufficiently attractive to warrant a firm U.S. position in limiting the Indians to the smallest number of MIG's possible. I would like to emphasize that any agreement with respect to our assistance in connection with the HF–24 should be limited at this stage solely to technical assistance.

Sincerely,

Bob

---

62.   Telegram From the Department of State to the Embassy in India[1]

Washington, July 2, 1964, 8:45 p.m.

17. Embtel 3851.[2] During call on Assistant Secretary Talbot June 30 Cabinet Secretary Khera said he had pretty clear impression India not likely obtain combat aircraft from US as long as it committed to MIG deal. Wanted to know if this actually the case. Talbot asked about MIG developments during Mikoyan's visit, was told commitment for production facilities (not assembly) made some two years ago and had been "reinforced" during Mikoyan's visit. He added many technical details remained to be worked out but basic deal firm and it hard to imagine could be changed now. In response question whether this meant India would be embarking on two supersonic production lines he replied this apparently the case. Talbot said we considered this too

---

[1] Source: National Archives and Records Administration, RG 59, Central Files 1964–66, DEF 19–3 US–INDIA. Secret. Drafted by Crawford in NEA/SOA, cleared by Laise, and approved by Talbot. Repeated to London, Karachi, and CINCMEAFSA for POLAD.

[2] See footnote 2, Document 59.

much of foreign exchange burden. We had wanted be responsive to India's request for help on HF–24 in hope this would ultimately meet need for supersonics, but question of two supersonic production lines would cause us serious trouble. Grant, who also present, remarked we recognized GOI would have political problems with Soviets depending on how far MIG deal had gone but that we thought it might be possible for US to help in combat aircraft field if GOI could phase out MIG program with a squadron of planes. Khera said he understood our position on problems MIG production caused us and would convey it to GOI. He wondered if this ruled out US help on jigs and tools for HF–24 production line. Talbot replied we would have to look at this very carefully.

Khera asked for reduction military credit sales interest from 3 per cent to 3/4 of 1 per cent on grounds India's debt servicing load increasing greatly. He was told possibility putting military credit sales on same basis economic aid would be examined.

Reporting on London talks, Khera said he talked about HF–24 engine to Rolls Royce who now studying drawings and might possibly be in India in fortnight for on-the-ground look at plane.

Rusk

---

63.   Memorandum of Conversation[1]

Washington, July 7, 1964, 5:48–5:58 p.m.

SUBJECT

U.S. Military Assistance to India

PARTICIPANTS

The President
His Excellency Ghulam Ahmed, Ambassador of Pakistan
Mr. Tayeb-Uddin Mahtab, Second Secretary, Embassy of Pakistan
Assistant Secretary Phillips Talbot (NEA)

Ambassador Ahmed congratulated the President on the passage of the Civil Rights Act, and expressed the admiration of the Pakistani

---

[1] Source: Johnson Library, National Security File, Country File, Pakistan, Vol. II, 6/64–11/64. Secret; Exdis. Drafted by Talbot. The meeting was held at the White House. The time of the meeting is taken from the President's Daily Diary. (Ibid.) Another copy of this memorandum is in National Archives and Records Administration, RG 59, Central Files 1964–66, DEF 19–8 US–INDIA.

people for the President's courage and skill in successfully carrying through legislation of such historic importance. He then handed over a letter from President Ayub.[2]

When the President had read the letter, the Ambassador suggested that from its contents the President would recognize the depth of President Ayub's anxiety about United States military assistance to India. Pakistan had hoped the time had come when this aid would be stopped, since the Chinese threat to India had clearly receded. Instead, United States military assistance to India had been doubled. There was also now a long-term understanding on arms aid. He was sorry to have to say that these regrettable developments had definitely upset the balance of power in the subcontinent, and, in addition, had clearly eroded Pakistan's ability to meet its obligations to its allies.

The President interrupted to ask if this were why President Ayub had not replied to requests for some assistance to Vietnam. He had been shocked at President Ayub's silence, especially as Pakistan had once before offered troops to assist in protecting Southeast Asia. He had thought that now President Ayub would at least put the Pakistan flag there.

The Ambassador, clearly uninformed on this question, said he did not know about other assistance but, of course, Pakistan could not now put any soldiers there. Pakistan faced a difficult threat. Its neighbor, India, was completely non-aligned and had made no commitment whatsoever to any free world cause. As President Ayub had pointed out before, Pakistan could foresee that a militarily strong India would oust the American presence from Southeast Asia. President Ayub had great respect for President Johnson and trusted that, with his knowledge of the situation in the area, he would be able to understand the situation and rectify the steps that were being taken.

After a quiet pause, the President said he would study President Ayub's letter carefully and talk with his associates about it. However, he did not share President Ayub's feeling that because the United States has helped India, Pakistan should ignore its alliance obligations. Obviously Pakistan would have to decide its course. He himself did not think it would be in Pakistan's interest to leave the alliances, but that would have to be Pakistan's decision.

The Ambassador, visibly concerned at the President's reaction, interposed that President Ayub had not said he would leave the alliances. In response the President read from the Ayub letter, saying he had inferred the President was thinking of this possibility from such phrases as the following:

---

[2] Document 60.

"On May 26 my Foreign Minister explained to Ambassador McConaughy Pakistan's growing concern at the continued arming of India. He also stated that if this policy continued, Pakistan would be compelled to reconsider the commitments to her allies."

The Ambassador asserted that what President Ayub hoped was that this United States policy would not continue. The President then read another quotation from the letter:

"Further, by continuing to build India's armed might, the United States might well force India's smaller neighbors—already deeply mistrustful of India—to seek the protection of China."

The Ambassador responded that this could happen. Without referring to Pakistan's relations with China, he said that after all Nepal was already almost in the mouth of China; Burma was under considerable pressure; Ceylon, as everyone knew, was going wildly from policy to policy; and there were difficulties in Sikkim and Bhutan.

Speaking slowly and seriously, the President expressed great admiration for President Ayub and great affection for the people of Pakistan. He knew that the Ambassador was about to go to London to see President Ayub,[3] and asked him to give President Ayub his warm personal regards. However, he added soberly, he did not agree with what President Ayub had written about the necessity of the United States following the course President Ayub recommended. In light of the way President Ayub seemed to feel, he guessed we were coming to the point at which we would all have to re-evaluate the condition of our relationship. This troubled him deeply, he concluded, because there was no people for whom he had greater regard then for the Pakistani people.

After a pause, when it became clear that the President had no more to say, the Ambassador, who appeared shaken by the tone and content of the President's comments, said he would carry the President's message to President Ayub, and took his leave.

---

[3] Ayub was attending the Commonwealth Conference in London.

64.   Memorandum From Robert Komer of the National Security Council Staff to President Johnson[1]

Washington, July 15, 1964.

You've so shaken all of us on India/Pak policy that we want to be sure you know in advance about tomorrow's pledging session for the 1964/65 share of the Pak Consortium. We and our friends will announce pledges of $420–430 million (about $212 million US),[2] which will get a little play in Friday's papers.

This just makes public an AID commitment already given; in fact, we've gotten the Paks in return to make some very sensible moves to liberalize their private sector. But we'll also have McConaughy make the point to Ayub that we and our allies are continuing to give him major aid at the very time when he's slanging us.

R. W. Komer[3]

---

[1] Source: Johnson Library, National Security File, Country File, Pakistan, Vol. II, Cables, 6/64–11/64. Secret; Exdis. A handwritten "L" on the memorandum indicates that it was seen by the President.

[2] The sixth meeting of the Pakistan consortium took place in Washington on July 16 at the initiative of the International Bank for Reconstruction and Development. The meeting was attended by representatives of Belgium, Canada, France, Germany, Italy, Japan, the Netherlands, the United Kingdom, the United States, the International Bank for Reconstruction and Development, and the International Development Association. The purpose of the meeting was to consider aid for the fifth year of Pakistan's Second Five-Year Plan, covering the period July 1964–June 1965. A total of $431 million was pledged, of which the United States pledged $212.5 million.

[3] Bundy initialed below Komer's signature.

65.   Memorandum of Conversation[1]

Washington, July 15, 1964, 1:38 p.m.

SUBJECT

President's Conversation with Ambassador McConaughy[2]

PARTICIPANTS

The President
Ambassador Walter McConaughy
Mr. Phillips Talbot, Assistant Secretary of State, NEA
Mr. R. W. Komer, White House

Ambassador McConaughy said Ayub has manifested strong feelings of rapport with President Johnson, especially after his visit to the Texas ranch in 1961. Ayub had been disappointed with what he felt was a failure by President Kennedy to understand fully Pakistan's problem with arms assistance to India and had counted on a more sympathetic hearing from President Johnson. Ayub felt that we were not taking Pakistani views enough into account. The Ambassador thought it would be most useful to build on the great respect which Ayub had for the President by inviting Ayub here for a face-to-face talk after the U.S. elections. This would please Ayub and give him a chance to get things off his chest, even though we might have to agree to disagree again. The Department had incorporated a suggestion for such a meeting in the draft Presidential letter for the Ambassador to take back with him, if the President approved.

After rereading President Ayub's July 1, 1964 letter[3] and reading the proposed reply, the President outlined a different type of reply he wished to have made to Ayub. Instead of taking a letter, Ambassador McConaughy should give an oral response when he next saw Ayub. The President did not want to give Ayub an invitation to Washington now, or anytime before the November election. He did not see much point in another session of unproductive argument with Ayub.

---

[1] Source: Johnson Library, National Security File, Country File, Pakistan, Vol. II, Cables, 6/64–11/64. Secret; Exdis. Drafted by Talbot on July 20. The meeting was held at the White House. The time of the meeting is taken from the President's Daily Diary. (Ibid.)

[2] Ambassador McConaughy was in Washington on home leave and was scheduled to return to Pakistan on July 21. In an undated note to President Johnson concerning his scheduled meeting with McConaughy, Secreatry Rusk noted that McConaughy should be in a position to respond to President Ayub's July 1 letter when he returned to Pakistan. Rusk attached a draft letter to Ayub that he recommended the President sign as a basis for McConaughy's discussion with Ayub. (Ibid., National Security File, Country File, Pakistan, Vol. II, Cables)

[3] Document 60.

The President said that the Ambassador should restate the President's highest personal regard for President Ayub. The Ambassador should then say that the President had read President Ayub's letter with a great deal of interest and considerable distress. The President had little to add to what he had already told Pakistan Ambassador G. Ahmed when the letter was presented. He did not share President Ayub's viewpoint that he was being disloyal to the Alliance by trying to work with India in what he considers to be our interest and also Ayub's. Moreover he was distressed that such an old and valued ally of ours as President Ayub should want to give the attention he has given to Communist China. Ayub must know we Americans felt strongly about China; we were having all sorts of trouble with China in Southeast Asia right now. As for President's Ayub's suggestion that he might have to reappraise Pakistan's commitments to the Alliances, the President could not see that this would be in Pakistan's interest or in ours, but it was a decision that only President Ayub could make. We valued the Pakistan alliance. As he had said to Ambassador Ahmed, we recognized Pakistan's right as a sovereign country to re-examine its policies. Regrettable as it might be, we would have to re-examine ours also, if Pakistan did so.

Commenting on these statements to be made to President Ayub, the President said he did not wish to provoke Ayub. Ayub, who is about as able, tough and ruthless as anyone the President had known, was enough of a dictator so that if the President were to respond to the letter by inviting Ayub to Washington, Ayub would think we were admitting we had been wrong in our policy toward India. After the election, the President would see if he wanted to have Ayub here for a debating contest, or let Pakistan go its own way. If Pakistan wanted to change its course, there wasn't much we could do about it. We were giving Pakistan more than double the per capita aid that we gave India. If Ayub wanted to jeopardize this, it was up to him. The President doubted that Pakistan could get much from either Communist China or the Soviet Union.

Ambassador McConaughy estimated that as long as Ayub was in control in Pakistan, he wasn't about to commit suicide by reversing Pakistan foreign policy and risking the loss of U.S. aid. Ayub was very conscious of the value of his U.S. ties, and while a shrewd bargainer was unlikely to go over the brink. In fact, Pakistan was continuing to work with us in many fields and had just recently offered to share any intelligence they collected on the new air route to Communist China. However, Ayub was very disillusioned with what he saw as a shift in U.S. policy and in the sub-continent power balance at the expense of Pakistan. We should try to bring Ayub around, seeking to avoid any action which might cause him to think he was being forced to the brink.

The President wondered how much we were getting for the very large amounts of aid we were giving to India as well as Pakistan. He asked how much our aid to Pakistan was running; when told that it was over $400 million including PL–480, he commented that the question of aid to Pakistan would certainly be settled if the Morse Amendment were passed. The President said that when Ayub was willing to send men to Laos, he thought our aid was worthwhile. But now that the Pakistanis refused to help us in Viet Nam, he didn't know whether we were getting very much for our money. Mr. Komer and the others present noted the special facilities available to the U.S. and cooperation in various intelligence fields, but agreed that the price was high in terms of specific benefits.

Ambassador McConaughy thought that a Kashmir settlement would contribute more than anything else to the solution of our dilemma on the subcontinent. Ayub had made clear that if only Kashmir could be settled, he would again offer joint defense to India. Pakistan and India would not have to deploy against each other and they could release forces for use elsewhere. The President didn't think that either side would settle Kashmir. The President observed that what we did for many countries was repaid by their involving us in their own ancient feuds—not only Kashmir between India and Pakistan, but the Arabs and Israel and now the Greeks and Turks over Cyprus.

The President had endured what Ayub had written without questioning his loyalty to our cause, but he did not share Ayub's view that while we were giving twice as much aid per capita to Pakistan as to India we ought to be precluded from doing with India what we thought to be in our interest and the over-all interest as well. He was not sure that all our actions with India have been the wisest possible, but we were set on that course and would see it through. After the election we should take a "long look" at our Indian policy over the next four years.

The President then reiterated that he didn't want to set up a meeting with Ayub now. As the President put it, "Ayub says he'll take a look at his hole card. Let's wait till he does so and then we will look at ours. Isn't this good poker?" Mr. Talbot agreed.

Summing up, the President requested Ambassador McConaughy to restate to Ayub the position the President himself had taken with G. Ahmed on July 7. He should tell Ayub that the President had read his letter with interest but with distress. He regretted Ayub's feeling that it was necessary to re-evaluate the desirability of Pakistan's alliance. But he recognized that this was a decision for Ayub himself to make. In this case, we would have to re-examine our policy toward Pakistan, too. The President then repeated that he wasn't sure about all aspects of our India policy either and we should take another look at our policy after the election.

66.   Letter From the Ambassador to India (Bowles) to the President's Special Assistant for National Security Affairs (Bundy)[1]

New Delhi, July 18, 1964.

Dear Mac:

By the time you receive this letter you will perhaps have read and digested our Embtel 143[2] in which I outlined the situation I found on my return to India in regard to military assistance in general and the proposed Air Force package in particular.

Although the GOI was greatly pleased by our willingness to provide grant and loan assistance on a five year basis, they became convinced some time in late June that we are not prepared to provide the assistance to the Indian Air Force which was the primary item on Chavan's shopping list.[3] At the same time, they decided that the British, to whom we referred them, would not come up with a submarine to match the one we gave the Pakistanis.

This gives the USSR the opportunity to enter the Indian defense situation by the dramatic measures which we had sought to deny them. Khera will be in Moscow sometime in August and the Chavan mission arrives there on August 28. In the normal course of events, we may expect announcements in the Indian and United States press in early September stating that the Soviet Union has agreed to provide surface-to-air missiles for the protection of north Indian cities, twelve additional MIG–21s to make an active squadron of sixteen, an assembly line to produce MIG–21s here in India, and possibly one or more submarines.

Such announcements in the midst of a particularly bitter United States election debate on foreign policy will provide an open invitation to the more irresponsible elements at home, and consequently our

---

[1] Source: Johnson Library, National Security File, Country File, India, Vol. III, Cables, 7/64–11/64. Secret; Eyes Only. Bundy sent this letter to Komer on July 24 with a handwritten note that reads: "What can we do for him?"

[2] Bowles used telegram 143 from New Delhi, July 16, to express in more detail the concerns and proposed solutions set forth in this letter. (National Archives and Records Administration, RG 59, Central Files 1964–66, DEF 19 US–INDIA)

[3] India Desk Officer Anthony Lakeland discussed the Chavan visit with Chavan in Bombay on July 7 and drew a different conclusion concerning Chavan's view of potential U.S. assistance for the Indian Air Force. According to Lakeland's record of the conversation, Chavan considered the question of India's requirement for a supersonic fighter to be still open for discussion and he urged that it remain so. (Memorandum of conversation, July 7; ibid., NEA/INC Files: Lot 68 D 207, POL 15–1, Y.B. Chavan Defense Minister)

difficulties in dealing rationally with the Indian subcontinent will be further compounded.

As you know, this is precisely the kind of situation that we have been warning against for months. Indeed you may find it worthwhile to reread the memorandum which I prepared on November 12[4] for my visit to Washington just before Jack Kennedy died. (There is a copy in your files.)

I think you will be impressed all over again with the opportunity which we had then to evolve a realistic South Asian military-political policy which would take into account our relations with India and Pakistan, reconcile the defense needs of each nation in a balanced fashion, encourage a greater Indian involvement in South Asia and keep the Soviets away from the more sensitive and dramatic military areas—all at a modest cost to ourselves.

If we had been free to offer at an earlier date the five year $50 million grant–$50 million loan military program outlined in the McNamara–Chavan exchange plus the aircraft proposal which Rusk recommended to McNamara (and which he largely accepted) we could have largely pre-empted the military situation in India in a way that would be greatly to our advantage and that of the Paks.

Although I am most appreciative of your support and that of Bob Komer and Jim Grant, I am deeply distressed over my own failure to break through the wall of timidity and inertia that I encountered in other quarters.

However, this is water over the dam; our task now is to consider what we can do to make the best of a situation which still contains many major elements of strength.

As soon as T.T. Krishnamachari has a chance to settle down after his visit to London, I shall describe to him the implications of this situation in our forthcoming election and stress the importance (a) of making sure that the Khera–Chavan purchases in the Soviet Union do not result in India's exceeding our agreed ceiling on foreign exchange expenditures and (b) the advisability of keeping publicity regarding whatever agreements may be reached with the USSR to an absolute minimum, and, if at all possible, of spreading these agreements over a period of several months in order to cushion the public impact here and in the United States.

---

[4] This memorandum, entitled "Toward a Balance of Political and Military Forces in South Asia," is in the Kennedy Library, National Security Files, Countries Series, India, Security, 1963. The memorandum is summarized in a November 12, 1963, memorandum from Komer to President Kennedy, printed in Foreign Relations, 1961–1963, vol. XIX, Document 337.

I will see that this message comes through loud and clear to TTK and to Shastri. However, it is important that the United States Government at this stage avoid any appearance of petulance or frustration in India and so I plan to limit myself to casual comments on this particular subject in discussions with other members of the Cabinet and the press.

For the time being this is about all we can expect to accomplish here within our present authority. However, to establish the optimum tactical position a further step is *essential*, i.e., well in advance of Chavan's visit to the USSR we should casually establish the fact that if the GOI had chosen to follow a different course, we would have been prepared to provide India with a comprehensive and fully adequate Air Force defense program including some arrangement for F–104s.

With a little elbow room and a few well placed but hazy conversations, I believe I can establish the impression that the present situation was India's deliberate choice. This may help persuade the Indians to keep their present air defense dealings with the Soviets in a low key; above all it will prepare the ground first with the Indian Government and later, if necessary, with key members of the Indian press when the announcement comes that the Pakistanis are getting their additional squadron of F–104s.

It is particularly important, Mac, that I quietly establish this point *soon;* otherwise it will look like the comment of a petulant loser on the eve of the Soviet-Indian negotiations in Moscow. I'll be deeply grateful for your support and help.

In the meantime, we are proceeding vigorously with our analysis of the overlapping interests of Pakistan and India in economic, military and political fields, which I am hopeful can be used effectively in our dealings with both governments.

I am also embarking on a renewed effort to persuade the GOI and key members of the Indian press not only of India's stake in keeping the communists out of Southeast Asia (which they already accept) but also the similarity of United States-Indian interests in this area and the expedient character of the whole Soviet operation there (witness USSR support for Sukarno against Malaysia). With a little luck perhaps I can bring them into some degree of conflict with the Soviets on this question and eventually persuade them to take a somewhat more active role.

It is folly for either the United States or the Indians to assume that they can count on Soviet policies in Asia paralleling our own interests. To be sure, there may be occasions when for tactical reasons we will momentarily find ourselves on the same side of the table. But a little more than three years ago Khrushchev was threatening Jack Kennedy with oblivion if we failed to get out of Berlin and less than two years ago he was busily planting missiles in Cuba. The Indians must gradu-ally be convinced of these realities.[5]

In the meantime, United States influence is bound to suffer in some degree because of the deep concern over the news of the Goldwater nomination. The fact that he was nominated by the Senate minority leader and seconded by the leader of the House and that all the other Republican candidates promptly moved to make the nomination unani-mous has compounded the impression that a major segment of the American people actually favor a program of reckless adventurism in world affairs, and the abandonment of our present efforts in the developing nations.

The possibilities are rather frightening and I only hope that our good Republican business friends such as Jack McCloy, as well as Nelson Rockefeller and other political leaders, will see the urgent need to help us assure not only Goldwater's defeat but his political de-struction.

Warmest regards.

Sincerely,

Chester Bowles[6]

---

[5] Joint State/Defense telegram 190, July 24, replied to Bowles that the conclusions drawn in Washington from the military assistance negotiations with the Indians differed from his. Washington officials thought India had achieved most of what it had sought in the Chavan talks and was not likely to abandon the possibility of air defense assistance from the West, whatever the outcome of negotiations in Moscow. They expected India, as a non-aligned power, to shop broadly for military supplies and assistance. The tele-gram concluded: "So long as we demonstrate responsiveness and steady support for principal Indian requirements in military field, we do not see Soviet aid, including that in the military field, as seriously threatening over the long term our present basic level of influence in India or India's capability to maintain its independence and integrity." (National Archives and Records Administration, RG 59, Central Files 1964–66, DEF 19 US–INDIA)

[6] Printed from a copy that bears this typed signature.

67. Telegram From the Embassy in Pakistan to the Department of State[1]

Karachi, August 11, 1964, 6 p.m.

301. Deptel 108.[2]

1. August 10 at Murree I had first meeting with President Ayub since my return. Meeting lasted about 90 minutes. Only others present were FonSec Aziz Ahmed, and FonOff note-taker. Ayub was in warm responsive mood, despite serious aspects of occasion. He showed lively interest in my account of Washington consultations, with marked degree of personal affability.

2. I started with recital of favorable developments on economic front which took place during period of consultations, including impressive consortium outcome and hopeful outlook for Karachi steel mill and for Indus River dam studies by World Bank.

3. I then delivered President's oral reply to Ayub letter of July 1. After stressing President's message of greeting and high personal regard, I made the three substantive points clearly and directly, although as considerately and non-abrasively as I could. I expounded the reasoning supporting the President's position, spelling out the variety and the depth of the strong assurances, and safeguards which Pakistan enjoys and inescapable responsibility resting on US as nation bearing heaviest share of burden of ChiCom containment to determine for itself how it could best contribute to countering of rising ChiCom pressures on India, which threatened all of South Asia.

4. Ayub took this exposition in good spirit, and heartily reciprocated President's expression of good will and high personal regard. Although he could not break down all of premises underlying US exposition, he recognized the predominant share of the load which US bears for preserving freedom and stability in Asia. He acknowledged that we have the right and obligation to make our own independent decisions after we have listened to our friends and allies.

He still urges US to weigh seriously and point-by-point his argument that China has no motivation to move militarily against India, that India has no legitimate justification for the huge military establishment she is acquiring, and that India's disproportionate military establishment will actually play into Communist hands by: (A) breaking

---

[1] Source: National Archives and Records Administration, RG 59, Central Files 1964–66, POL 7 PAK–US. Secret; Priority; Limdis. Repeated to London and New Delhi.

[2] Telegram 108 to Karachi, July 29, reviewed for Ambassador McConaughy the instructions he had received from President Johnson during their July 15 meeting; see Document 65.

India economically (witness the current food riots as one small forerunner) and (B) driving her distrustful small neighbors toward China as
a make-weight against an overbearing India in an unbalanced situation.

5. I then made use of most of the remaining material contained
in reftel. I laid particular stress on the seriousness with which whole
American nation regarded ChiComs challenge, even before last week's
Gulf of Tonkin crisis. I told him why we considered that ChiCom
shadow would be even longer and more ominous than the Soviet
one for next few years. I described the conviction of the American
Government and people that we are entitled to ask our allies and
indeed every free country to stand up and be counted in the current
dangerous confluence of events. I indicated the disappointment in the
highest quarters of our government that the GOP had not yet seen fit
to make even a token non-strategic contribution in Viet Nam.

6. Ayub confirmed that the GOP was not making a contribution in
Viet Nam. He expressed his regret at inability to do so and said reason
was "impossibility of enlarging Pakistan's political or military commitments in that area" owing to increased vulnerability of Pakistan vis-à-
vis India. I asked Ayub if he thought a token contribution in the non-
military field would represent any enlarged political or military commitment. He said in his opinion it would, and furthermore "people would
not understand." I replied that undoubtedly the Chinese Communists
would profess not to understand. Ayub said his own people would not
understand either. I surmised that if so, it would be because of the conditioning they had received in recent months from official and other public
news media. Ayub then made puzzling remark that if there was any contribution from Pakistan to the US which we needed or thought might be
useful, we should let him know. He would want to comply and would
make every effort to do so. But a contribution to some other government
in the Southeast Asia area he would have to rule out.

7. I probed for precise meaning of GOP intimation that it might
be obliged to "re-examine its policy." This was in the light of my
unvarnished presentation of the President's position that in such regrettable event we would correspondingly have to re-evaluate our policy.
Ayub then gave me most significant pronouncement of meeting. He
said that what he had had in mind as a possibility was a re-examination
of Pakistan's tie to SEATO. Only this and nothing more. He said that
Pakistan had never had a deep intrinsic interest of its own in SEATO
anyway. Pakistan had joined in 1954 only as a cooperative gesture to
the US. (He turned aside my observation that East Pakistan was very
close to the treaty area with the remark that East Pakistan was surrounded by India.) Pakistan had been prepared through 1961 to contribute armed forces in fulfillment of her treaty obligations. Pakistan was
embarrassed by her current inability to pull her weight in the organiza-

tion because of liabilities nearer home and therefore it might be the most honorable and realistic course for Pakistan to withdraw. He did not intend for any "re-appraisal" to go beyond this.

8. I gave him the background for our action in Tonkin Gulf crisis, building it around the President's statement in his Syracuse University speech that "aggression unchallenged is aggression unleashed." I told him that although it might seem a paradox at first blush, the course we had followed was actually the most prudent and the one best calculated to preserve the peace. Ayub was clearly sympathetic to our case in Viet Nam, but he voiced a neutralist line of thinking, stressing the importance of immediate conciliation and negotiation with a view to prompt compromise agreement with the Communists. This neutralist stance was unnatural and out of character for President Ayub and I told him so. I told him that it would not work to negotiate with the Communists from a position of disadvantage. The Communists would not abide by any agreement unless they had to, or unless it served their interests. This meant that an agreement with the Communists must be virtually self-enforcing in order to survive. Unhappily the forces of freedom are not yet in that position of strength in Southeast Asia. This was the reason that we were opposing a neutralist-slanted 14-nation conference now, and this was why we regretted the hasty and public GOP endorsement of such a conference without any consultation with us. Ayub almost admitted that he agreed with our reasoning, saying rather defensively that he had thought perhaps we could conduct a conference negotiation while still carrying on the war.

9. I told Ayub that we regret the rather unfavorable press treatment in Pakistan so far on the Tonkin Gulf incidents. The government news media had been carefully correct and impartial in their publicity over the radio and elsewhere, but the private press generally had made considerable use of Communist propaganda releases, and had ranged from unsympathetic to hostile in its news and editorial treatment of the US action. I thought that the press attitude, combined with the recent government policy of attentiveness to Communist China, had confused the public, and had caused the Pakistani people to take a distorted view of the fundamental confrontation in Southeast Asia, the successful outcome of which was vital to the freedom and national integrity of Pakistan, as of all other peoples of Asia. I thought that this distorted view might have contributed to the regrettable attack on the USIS Library in Dacca by a student [garble] August 6 and the anti-US demonstrations in Chittagong on August 7. I mentioned the apparent lack of alertness on the part of the Daiw police in dealing with the Dacca incident. Ayub said he greatly regretted these incidents and he was investigating the reported shortcomings of the police. He thought the East Pakistan troubles were fomented by organized Communist agitators operating in Dacca with guidance and support

from Calcutta. In response to my observation that it was a tragic irony that the Pak public seemed to be extending its sympathies to the wrong side when Pak freedom would eventually be jeopardized by the loss of freedom in Viet Nam, Ayub thought the Pak public was confused by the authoritarian and hard-fisted nature of the present GVN, and by apparent intervention of the USG as an outside government in favor of an unpopular and unrepresentative government of General Khanh. I asked if the GOP could not do some educative work over the radio and in the press so that the people would understand which side their vital interests were really identified with. But he was skeptical that his government could do anything effective along this line.

10. In referring to India, I expressed the Department's commendation of the constructive and conciliatory words and actions of the GOP toward India at the time of Nehru's death, Shastri's accession, and thereafter. I expressed guarded optimism that notwithstanding the setback of Shastri's illness, favorable developments might be in the offing, with some ferment still in process in Kashmir, and with the Indians clearly groping for some positive initiatives. I said we fully recognized the decisive part that a Kashmir settlement could play in an Indo-Pak détente and the frustrations of ChiCom machinations on the sub-continent (an aspect which Ayub had broadly hinted at early in the conversation). Without being coercive, we would continue to encourage the search for a settlement. Ayub said he had had a frank talk with TTK at the London Prime Ministers conference. TTK had invited Ayub to pay an official visit to India soon. Ayub told him he was ready for a meeting with Shastri as soon as Shastri was physically able, provided there was first tangible evidence of a genuine Indian disposition to mend relations. Ayub indicated a dislike of TTK's idea that he (Ayub) should do a lot of traveling about India on his visit to make himself known and "sell" the Indian people on the need for a settlement. Ayub felt that the selling was a job for the Indians to do for themselves and that he should not pay a visit until there was some positive prospect for real accomplishment. He felt that an unsuccessful or inconclusive visit would do more harm than good. But he told me he is ready for a visit when he gets a meaningful Indian signal, with or without a preparatory meeting at the Ministerial level. FonSec Aziz Ahmed made his only contribution to the conversation at this point, interjecting that he had just heard from the GOI that Swaran Singh was agreeable to a preliminary Foreign Ministers meeting with Bhutto. Aziz Ahmed obviously favored this.

The President bade me goodbye very cordially. He and I agreed that the meeting had been a useful one and had cleared the atmosphere considerably, although problems remain which have not been fully plumbed. A few additional subsidiary items from conversation and comments will follow.

McConaughy

68.   Telegram From the Department of State to the Embassy in
Pakistan[1]

Washington, August 16, 1964, 5:31 p.m.

194. Karachi's 301.[2] Definitive assessment of appropriate response
to Ayub must, of course, await your comment.[3] Initially we read his
conversation with you as confirmation of two already apparent trends
in Pak foreign policy: a pulling away from alliances, and a narrowing
of a Pak relationship with U.S. to bilateral interchange. At same time
we are puzzled that his response shows no comprehension that his
"reappraisal" will necessarily lead to similar action on our part.

Whatever his professed willingness to do anything for U.S. (as
contrasted to third country in SE Asia) may mean, we are more concerned at this juncture with Ayub's pronouncement that in talking of
reappraising GOP policies he "only had had in mind a possibility of
re-examination of Pakistan's tie to SEATO." Such threat is of course
not new and we find it difficult to believe Ayub would judge in his
interest to move precipitously to follow through on this threat as he
would obviously forfeit his bargaining counter and in process run risk
of seriously jeopardizing aspects of U.S.-Pak relationship in which Ayub
remains interested. Nevertheless, in our present confrontation with
Chicoms, we must guard against sudden GOP move to withdraw from
SEATO and we consider we must respond quickly and firmly to Ayub's
observation. We have following series of steps in mind:

1. You would be instructed see Ayub without delay. You would
state that we of course do not question GOP's sovereign right to determine where its national interests lie. However, we have same right.
We want Ayub to know that we would regard GOP withdrawal from
SEATO during our present critical confrontation with Chicoms as adversely and seriously affecting our national interest and such action
could not but affect adversely U.S.-Pak relations. He must realize that

---

[1] Source: National Archives and Records Administration, RG 59, Central Files 1964–
66, POL 1 PAK. Secret; Priority; Limdis. Drafted by Laise and Cameron, cleared by
Director of the Office of Regional Affairs in EUR Joseph A. Mendenhall and Harriman,
and approved by Talbot. Repeated to London and New Delhi.

[2] Document 67.

[3] McConaughy provided his assessment of his August 10 conversation with Ayub
in telegram 347 from Karachi, August 18. McConaughy viewed the conversation as
further evidence that Ayub had deliberately charted a course of limited disengagement
from Pakistan's ties with the United States. McConaughy felt that Ayub had made clear
that as long as he considered U.S. policies toward India inimical to Pakistan's national
interest, Pakistan would pursue a China policy that interfered with U.S. objectives in
Asia. McConaughy feared that Pakistan's ties with the West were slowly ending. (National
Archives and Records Administration, RG 59, Central Files 1964–66, POL 1 PAK)

any actions appearing to support Chicom position will elicit profoundly adverse reaction from Congress and U.S. public. Since we cannot believe President Ayub would knowingly launch upon a course that is bound to have such serious consequences for Pakistan, we wish to request that before GOP decides to initiate action to terminate its SEATO membership we be consulted to ensure that there is a full mutual understanding of the consequences of this action for Pakistan before it is taken.

2. Simultaneously with your approach we would call Ambassador Ahmed in to get across same points. We also would plan to give Ambassador additional food for thought by recalling to his mind general lines of Secretary's talk with Bhutto on April 29.[4] You will recall that in this talk Secretary described "political climate" which could affect our delivery of additional 104s in terms of developments in our confrontation with Chicoms. We would want the Pakistanis to draw the conclusion that Pak actions which adversely affect our posture against Chicoms will inevitably affect our ability to continue same quality of assistance to Paks. We shall also find way to get across to Ambassador that course of action and reaction such as this will unfortunately prejudice continuation of personal exchanges at the highest level which have characterized our relations with Pak and which we had looked forward to continuing at appropriate opportunity in future.

3. When Shoaib arrives in September we would take soundings to ensure that our exchange of signals is understood and hopefully to arrest any further deterioration of our relationship.

Your views on above course of action urgently requested.[5]

Rusk

---

[4] See Document 41.

[5] McConaughy replied in telegram 348 from Karachi, August 18. Although he did not view Ayub's threat to leave SEATO as implying an imminent move, he felt that Pakistan's policies in Asia were running sufficently counter to U.S. interests to warrant the type of firm response outlined in telegram 194. He was slightly more optimistic about Ayub's mood and intentions than the Department, however, and suggested that the response be tempered by probing for what Ayub meant when he offered to do anything to help the United States. (National Archives and Records Administration, RG 59, Central Files 1964–66, POL 1 PAK)

69.   Telegram From the Embassy in India to the Department of
State[1]

New Delhi, August 27, 1964, 9 p.m.

677. On August 26 at 6 PM I met with Lal Bahadur Shastri for 45 minutes. Shastri opened conversation by apologizing for having postponed our meeting which was originally planned for noon of that day. He had decided, at the last moment, to have frank meeting with all top civil servants and meeting had lasted for over two hours. He had emphasized need for much greater administrative effort, longer hours, elimination of red tape, courage to make decisions, etc.

The primary purpose of my visit was to communicate our views on military aid situation before Chavan's departure for Moscow August 28. On this subject conversation developed along following lines:

1. Since previous conversations with Chavan, Patil and TTK had made it clear that right now GOI feels itself to be under particular pressure from us in regard to economic, military and other matters, I opened discussion by frankly acknowledging difficulties that exist when one country gives another major sums of money.

However, we did not see the situation as a one way street. Although our aid might be important to India, her success was vital to our security and hopes for a more rational world. Such a relationship called for frankness in discussing our respective problems.

I then reviewed original military aid discussions last October and my understanding that if our assistance was reasonably large and maintained over period of years, GOI would not find it necessary to rely in any significant way on USSR in defense area.

US military aid program which was finally agreed to in June represented substantial sum with assurances, with certain qualifications, that it will be continued for five years. Shortly thereafter Khera told us that the MIG deal, on which we had had much contradictory information, was settled, and we also heard that two Soviet SAM complexes were agreed to. All of this plus Chavan's departure for Moscow created certain complications for all of us which I wanted PriMin to understand.

I was not questioning India's policy of nonalignment which we understood. I was, however, concerned that India was putting too much trust in a nation which Shastri, as a former Home Minister, knew did not necessarily have India's best interests at heart.

---

[1] Source: National Archives and Records Administration, RG 59, Central Files 1964–66, DEF 19 US–INDIA. Secret. Repeated to Cairo, Karachi, London, Moscow, Kathmandu, Bombay, Calcutta, and Madras, and also sent to CINCMEAFSA/POLAD.

I added that there was no need for him to comment on a subject which probably involved certain difficulties for him. I simply wanted him to understand our reasoning and particularly my own reaction in view of long negotiations which I had been conducting with his government for last ten months.

2. Shastri replied that I had clarified several questions which he had not thoroughly understood. He was particularly disturbed that we had not been told more precisely about MIG decision which had been made personally by former PriMin Nehru and April in face of some differences of opinion within GOI.

Although under these conditions he would find it impossible to revise this decision unless Soviets themselves reneged, he would talk further with Chavan before he left and do all he could to handle situation in a way that would cause the least possible embarrassment.

3. Shastri then turned to question of HF–24 which he said was creating all kinds of difficulties for India with UAR. He described his Ambassador in Cairo as an emotional man who sent back messages stating that unless India did precisely what UAR wanted her to do, present friendly relations between UAR and India might be destroyed.

This impressed Shastri as unreasonable since as far as he knew UAR was in no position to provide fully acceptable engine within reasonable period of time. Furthermore UAR proposal called for the engine to be built in Cairo and the air frame in Bangalore. This was contrary to India's interests since her major objective was to produce an indigenous plane.

Nevertheless with nonaligned conference coming up in October, situation did create a formidable political problem and it would be necessary to mark time until dust settled.

4. I suggested that all nations face somewhat similar political problems in regard to development of their defenses. For instance, many of our cities and states bring heavy pressure to bear on federal government to continue production of obsolete and semi-obsolete equipment on grounds that curtailment would create local unemployment and political difficulties. A major achievement of present US administration has been its willingness to face up to these pressures and to insist on best possible defense for smallest amount of money.

India, facing huge economic requests, could not afford to build her armed forces on a political basis. The MIG deal was primarily based on the questionable hope that it would involve Russians on Indian side in case Chinese attacked. An agreement with the UAR in regard to HF–24 was in India's interest if it provided better plane, but if it were designed to placate Nasser it might prove to be an expensive undertaking.

Shastri accepted this and I believe over a period of time, he will act in accordance with it. In the present situation, he is involved with decisions made by the already legendary Jawaharlal Nehru which, barring a fumble by the Soviets which we have no reason to anticipate, he cannot be expected to reverse.

Throughout discussion Shastri acted very much like the PriMin of India and once again I was impressed with his intellectual capacity and his direct, earthy approach. If he keeps his health, he will do well, perhaps very well.

Bowles

70. **Memorandum From Robert Komer of the National Security Council Staff to the President's Special Assistant for National Security Affairs (Bundy)[1]**

Washington, September 10, 1964.

Mac—

Have been holding open option of President announcing new one-year PL 480 agreement for India, which will probably be signed 16 September (it doesn't depend on new law). Agreement involves $398 million worth of wheat (4 million tons) and rice (306,000 tons) and vegetable oils. This ain't hay, and could be tied to other US actions to meet Indian food crisis[2] (stepping up wheat shipments from 400,000 tons per month to 600,000 etc.).

Much of this has already been made public by Freeman, Bowles and others, but only NYT has made much of it from what I've seen. So there's still play. All I'd have in mind would be WH statement unless press conference happened to fall that day.

---

[1] Source: Johnson Library, National Security File, Country File, India, Vol. III, Cables & Memos, 7/64–11/64. Secret.

[2] In a July 30 memorandum to Rusk, Talbot described a "major political-economic problem" confronting the Indian Government as a result of a sharp rise in foodgrain prices. Prices had risen steadily throughout 1964 and were one-third higher than a year previous. NEA's assessment was that the high prices were due to poor distribution rather than a shortage of grain. (National Archives and Records Administration, RG 59, Central Files 1964–66, E 8–1 INDIA)

If this doesn't excite you, I'd like to remove block from story now.[3]

RWK

---

[3] Bundy's handwritten note at the end of the memorandum instructed Komer to postpone a press release until after the P.L. 480 legislation had passed. On September 30 a Title I P.L. 480 sales agreement and two loan agreements were concluded and signed in New Delhi. A press release was issued at the time of the signing. The texts of the agreements and the press release were transmitted to the Department as attachments to airgram A–365 from New Delhi, October 5; National Archives and Records Administration, RG 59, Central Files 1964–66, AID (US) 15–8 INDIA.

---

71.   Letter From the Ambassador to India (Bowles) to the President's Special Assistant for National Security Affairs (Bundy)[1]

New Delhi, September 16, 1964.

Dear Mac:

I believe we are faced with an important question of tactics in regard to the handling of questions involving nuclear power here in India.[2]

It has been our view that while the development of Chinese nuclear weapons is an ominous development it can with skilled handling be made to serve our political purposes here in India.

With this in mind I have discussed with Shastri, TTK, Chavan and Desai in the last several months, the possibility that the Chinese may be able to develop not only a crude nuclear bomb but also intermediate range missiles with nuclear war-heads. In developing this possibility I referred vaguely to information about a testing installation in West China which has come to us from [less than 1 line of source text not declassified] and other sources.

I have pointed out that when and if these weapons are fully developed, India will find herself faced with the choice of three courses of action.

---

[1] Source: Johnson Library, National Security File, Country File, India, Vol. IV, Cables, 12/64–6/65. Top Secret.

[2] In late August the Committee on Nuclear Weapons Capabilities, chaired by Llewellyn Thompson, was formed to consider the question of the proliferation of national nuclear weapons capabilities, particularly with respect to India. Documentation on the activities of the Thompson Committee is in Foreign Relations, 1964–1968, volume XI.

(1) India could take a position similar to that which we took regarding Cuba, i.e. an ultimatum to the Chinese to remove such installations from Tibet or to see them blown up by the Indian Airforce. This involves obvious risks in brinkmanship.

(2) India could proceed to develop her own nuclear deterrent capacity. This, I suggested, would not only run contrary to India's clear commitment in the United Nations and elsewhere, but it would also be a losing game both technologically and financially. While the Chinese could reach the major northern Indian cities with relatively few short-range missiles, the Indians would require many more weapons of greater range and precision to reach comparable targets in China. Clearly it would make no sense for a country facing India's vast economic problems and financial difficulties to embark on a program of this nature.

(3) India could reach a quiet understanding with the United States under which we would undertake to provide India with the same type of nuclear umbrella that has enabled Japan, the Scandinavian countries and other nations to maintain an effective defense at a reasonable cost.

I believe that these three or four discussions have done much to make some Indian leaders think in broader terms about questions of nuclear defense. If carried somewhat further I believe they might also provide an arresting influence on India's plans to build up a major supersonic airforce which clearly has no relevance to India's air defense vis-à-vis the potential threat from China.

Against this background I recently sent a message to John McCone[3] suggesting that his briefing team which met here last weekend with the GOI be authorized to discuss Chinese nuclear installations and potentialities and the ultimate need for further information on their development. John took a rather dim view of this on the ground that if India becomes too aware of this possibility she may move into the development of nuclear weapons herself.

This impresses me as miscalculation. The more opportunity we have to talk to the Indians about this situation the more likely we are to persuade them that the nuclear deterrent that could provide a real threat to Chinese cities was beyond their capacity and that the ultimate solution may be some kind of understanding with us.

The question I may add goes beyond this particular point. [2 *lines of source text not declassified*] If we fail to come clean the Indians will

---

[3] Not found. McCone discussed the proposal to brief Shastri about the progress of the Chinese nuclear weapons program with Richard Helms on September 8. His concern about such a briefing was that it might stimulate a similar weapons program in India. (Memorandum for the record by McCone, September 8; Central Intelligence Agency, Job 80–B01285A, DCI (McCone) Files, Memos for the Record, 9 Jul–10 Sept 1964)

eventually discover through their own sources (and very possibly from the Russians) precisely what the Chinese have been doing. At that point we will appear in their eyes to either have been inept in our own intelligence work or to have withheld vital information from them.

I will be grateful if you will think about this complex problem, discuss it with John and also whoever you may feel should be involved and then give me your considered views.

Warmest regards,

Sincerely,

Chester Bowles[4]

---

[4] Printed from a copy that bears this typed signature.

---

72.   Telegram From the Embassy Office in Pakistan to the Department of State[1]

Rawalpindi, September 19, 1964, 7 p.m.

2. I had fifty minute meeting with Pres Ayub morning Sept 18 Rawalpindi. FonOff note taker only other person present. Personal atmosphere cordial and results substantially satisfactory within limitations to be expected.

1. SEATO

I obtained the assurances we required on continuation Pak membership in SEATO. In effect we have highest level corroboration of what Bhutto told me Sept 9. After my exposition of intensified need for united front of SEATO allies in view acute confrontation taking place in Southeast Asia, Pres indicated his govts distaste for staying in the organization where it was unable to carry out the commitments and obligations normally associated with membership. He said that Pakistan unable carry out those commitments because of increased military capability which has been given Pakistan's neighbor, said this increased capability had "created great difficulties for Pakistan" and had "put Pakistan under severe pressure." He asked me if US neverthe-

---

[1] Source: National Archives and Records Administration, RG 59, Central Files 1964–66, POL 15–1 PAK. Secret; Immediate. Repeated to New Delhi, London, Bangkok, Hong Kong, USUN, Kabul, Moscow, and Karachi and passed to the White House.

less preferred that Pakistan retain her SEATO membership. I replied that we could not concede the validity of the premises he had spelled out, but in any event we consider it of high importance that a solid alliance front be maintained with Pakistan remaining in SEATO and identifying herself with objectives and spirit of the organization.

Pres said in that case Pakistan would retain her membership. He added that this was being done solely out of regard for the US and in consideration the recognized need to avoid any action which in the US view would interfere with the implementation of broad US policy.

2. ChiRep issues in UN

After I had set forth in pessimistic terms the unpredictable but certainly adverse effect which could be expected to flow from any favorable vote on the admission of Communist China to the General Assembly this autumn, Ayub assured me that Pakistan had no reason to get out in front on the Communist China issue in the UN and said he saw no reason why Pakistan needed to do anything other than cast affirmative ballot if issue came to vote. He agreed that Chinese Communists are carrying out disruptive operations in various places, although he did not know much about Chinese Communist subversive activities in Africa and wanted to know more about that, especially about the interplay of Chinese Communist and Soviet subversive efforts in the Congo.

I told him in a general way of assurances I had from Bhutto on ChiRep issue. The Pres did not indicate any disagreement with Bhutto's position and said the GOP had no occasion to actually push for admission of Communist China this year. He seemed to assume that the vote could not be so close that Pakistan can some day be an honest broker in bringing about some sort of détente between US and Communist China and that it might be better to postpone any showdown on Chinese Communist membership in the UN. He said he believed that some US-Chinese Communist relations would have to be established. When I said there would have to be some changes made in Peiping first, he heartily concurred but noted there would need to be some adjustments of view in Washington also.

3. Exchanges of good-will gesture with Communist China

I made the President aware of the difficulties that are caused by unnecessary and unfortunate gestures of friendship and goodwill between Pakistan and Communist China, especially during this trying period. I said the gestures were particularly regrettable when there was an appearance of some possible negotiations of a secret nature. I cited the recent extended and rather private Pak hospitality accorded Chi-Com Vice Minister of Defense Air Marshal Liu, in Peshawar and Karachi as an example.

President defended good-will gesture as necessary part of new Pak policy of good neighborliness. He assured me that absolutely no substantive talks of sensitive nature were held with Liu, and he chided us for hyper-sensitiveness and over-suspiciousness. He said Marshal Liu was received only as routine good-will gesture. Pak Air Marshal Asghar Khan had just that morning reported on the visit to him; and had reconfirmed that nothing of any significance took place during visit. He said visit lasted as long as it did only because of infrequency of flights from Pakistan to China. Liu had to wait for next scheduled PIA weekly flight. He urged that we trust GOP good intentions as a friend of the US and that we have confidence in Pak ability to deal with Chinese Communist without falling into any traps or giving anything away. He thought that some useful information and some Pak leverage on Chinese Communists might be developed out of Pak associations with Chinese Communists. I told Pres that appearances had to be considered and general impression gained by Americans was bound to be adverse. Chinese Communists were able to exploit their apparent gains in Pakistan. It was natural for Americans reading the headlines to take a dim view of what seemed to be going on. I said inexplicable Pak actions made it difficult for American friends of Pakistan in a better position to explain in comprehensive terms Pak courses of action. I told him high-level visits between Pakistan and Chinese Communist leaders, exchanges of good-will missions composed prominent people, and Pak senior level participation in Chinese Communist national occasions were all unfortunate and harmful to our relations in present circumstance.

Pres said he wanted me to believe that his government did not intend to do anything inconsistent with her friendship with the United States or contrary to basic American interests. "We do not want to do anything that would hurt you." He said he was in favor of drawing closer to Communist China.

4. Indo-Pak relations and Narayan[2] visit

I probed for further information on results recent visit of Narayan.

Ayub said Narayan was "the best Hindu I have ever dealt with." He felt talks had been worthwhile, although only exploratory. He attributed influence and stature to Narayan in India even absence government position or mandate from Shastri government. He said he had given Narayan full Pak position that fundamental issue in Indo-Pak relations (Kashmir) would not be postponed or subordinated, and that any meeting of the two heads of government which did not produce tangible results would be a mistake. He said Narayan had spoken well of Shastri's intentions. In regard to a Pakistan settlement, Narayan was

---

[2] Jayaprakash Narayan.

not certain Shastri considered himself in a sufficiently strong domestic position to take the unpopular steps that would be necessary to produce tangible progress with Narayan from summit meeting. Ayub said that the main result of his sessions with Narayan was apparently clear and sympathetic comprehension by Narayan of the Pak position and an undertaking by Narayan to find out from Shastri whether latter felt that he could open the way for a really substantive development at a summit conference this year.

Ayub said Narayan is to give an assessment as soon as Narayan obtains Shastri's reaction. Ayub indicated that his decision is whether to go to Delhi would be influenced by Narayan's report.

I told Ayub that I believed it was the estimate of Amb Bowles and his staff in Delhi that Shastri was genuinely disposed to press for constructive steps and that perhaps Shastri would be inclined to reciprocate affirmative moves by Pres Ayub, possibly including the return of a summit level visit. Ayub took note of this and perhaps took some encouragement from it. He seemed appreciative of our desire to facilitate a settlement, but again expressed dignified regret that we had not found a way of working our assistance to India into a framework of conciliation on the part of India. He accepted my statement that we could not force the GOI, but added that he believed our resources should be sufficient to find a way of inducing India without force.

5. GOP suspicions of US activities in Pakistan

I told Pres that in view of systematic efforts of elements unfriendly to us to propagate fabricated stories of US official sympathy with opposition parties in Pakistan, I was going to give him an assurance which ought to be, and probably was, unnecessary. This assurance was that US reps would be fully circumspect in all their contacts to insure that none of their actions or relationships could be plausibly misconstrued as giving aid and comfort to anti-govt elements, or as constituting intervention in the forthcoming election campaign or in any aspect of the domestic affairs of Pakistan. I said that our people had not been guilty of any such impropriety but I knew that allegations to this effect had been manufactured out of the whole cloth and that unfortunately they seemed to have been given some degree of credence.

Pres said he welcomed and appreciated this statement. He confirmed that reports along lines indicated had come to his ears, especially in reference to East Pakistan. He said the reports charged US reps with maintaining prejudicial contacts with such opposition leaders as Mujibur Rahman, disaffected student groups and othr dissident elements. He said the reports included assertions that money had changed hands. I told him that it was incredible that such preposterous insinuations could be seriously entertained by anyone who knew anything about American policy. I said that as he knew Americans were mostly gregarious people who liked to get acquainted with all manner of people among whom they lived. Some of personnel might not inquire too closely about all the connections of people with whom they struck up a casual acquaintance. Americans could not be expected to hole up and isolate themselves and see no one except govt officials and those in East Pakistan could not be expected to confine their casual day to day contacts exclusively to other foreigners and govt officials. Pres had earlier said that GOP rep could not be expected to "go into purdah" so far as contacts with Chinese Communists were concerned. At this point I tossed the phrase back at him, saying that Americans could not be expected to "go into purdah" as far as casual social contacts with non-official Bengalese in East Pakistan were concerned. But I assured him that I had issued new instructions to all our people to use the greatest circumspection so as to avoid any even half-way reasonable inference that they were consorting improperly with anti-govt elements.

Pres said he was very pleased to hear this and he accepted my assurances. However he picked up book on his desk which he said he had been reading with surprise and shock at its title "The Invisible Government."[3] He hoped nothing like the operations described in the book were going on.

I told him I assumed no one would take as gospel truth everything appearing in that mischievous and irresponsible book. (N.B. I understand on good authority the Pak Foreign Office has systematically distributed copies of this book among most of the officials in Pakistan.)

I told the President that, of course, we were not assisting and would not assist in any opposition element in Pakistan. By the same token, although we recognized the key importance of Pres Ayub to the stability and welfare of Pakistan, we were, of course, not in any way intervening in his behalf either in the election campaign. Our posture was completely "hands off." Pres immediately expressed his approval, saying "I want to be judged by my own people."

6. Rail spur to Afghanistan

I mentioned apparent Pak delay in signing agreement covering engineering survey for the rail extension from Chaman to Spin Baldak. I told him that we had a direct interest since AID was providing the financing through a development loan. We understood Afghans had already done their part and we were ready to make the loan. The absence of Pak signature to the agreement was holding up the survey. I knew he was interested in the early completion of the rail extension as an important element improvement of Pak-Afghan ties and a means

---

[3] Apparent reference to David Wise and Thomas Ross, *The Invisible Government* (London: Jonathan Cape, 1964).

of strengthening the Yusuf government. Pres responded that he did not want any delay and promised he would investigate immediately reasons for inaction on the Pak side. He made handwritten notation of this matter on his own pad.

7. Soviet role on sub-continent

We discussed Chavan trip to Soviet Union and resultant announcement of substantial new Soviet military assistance to India.[4] I noted that publicity on this development had been received quite mildly by Pak Government, press and people, in sharp contrast to strong outburst which greeted every modest installment of Western arms assistance to India. Pres said reason for this was that US was a friend of Pakistan. Pakistan expected nothing from her enemies, but expected much of her friends.

Pres expressed some puzzlement at double standard apparently applied by US to Soviet Union and Communist China. I explained why short-run threat from Communist China seemed greater, and therefore called for stricter immediate measures of deterrence, including tighter trade controls.

Pres referred to overall ceiling on Indian arms procurement from all sources which he understood had been agreed to by Chavan in Washington last summer, and inquired if Soviet arms included in recent Indo-Soviet announcement would in US view come within this ceiling.

I said I would want consult Washington before replying definitely, but it was my offhand impression that Soviet offer was a credit arrangement which would be includable.

Pres said this was an important question to him, and asked [me to?] ascertain Washington interpretation urgently.[5]

McConaughy

---

[4] Defense Minister Chavan reported to the Lok Sabha on September 21 on the military assistance for India which had resulted from his trips to the United States, United Kingdom, and Soviet Union. The text of Chavan's statement was transmitted to Washington in airgram A–332, September 23; National Archives and Records Administration, RG 59, Central Files 1964–66, DEF 19 US–INDIA. Komer summed up the agreement reached in Moscow in a September 21 memorandum to President Johnson. Beyond military credits, Komer felt that the most significant new element in the agreement was India's purchase of 90 Soviet amphibious tanks, which, he noted, "gives the Soviets their first foothold in the Indian army." (Johnson Library, National Security File, Country File, Pakistan, Vol. II, 6/64–11/64) Talbot assessed the agreement in a September 11 memorandum to Secretary Rusk and concluded that the understanding reached with Chavan in June, which called for a ceiling on Indian military procurement abroad, should hold down Indian purchases from the Soviet Union. (National Archives and Records Administration, RG 59, NEA/INC Files: Lot 68 D 207, DEF 19–6, Communist Bloc Assistance)

[5] In telegram 13 to Rawalpindi, September 22, the Department confirmed McConaughy's impression that the agreed ceiling on Indian foreign procurement applied to Soviet purchases. (Ibid., Central Files 1964–66, DEF 19–3 INDIA)

73.   Memorandum for the Record[1]

Washington, September 24, 1964.

McGeorge Bundy's 45-minute talk with Pakistan Finance Minister Shoaib was most cordial throughout. Shoaib explained that he was passing through from the Tokyo IMF/IB meeting and stopped off to talk financial matters with his old friends in Washington.[2] He had just hit George Woods for a $25 million "balance of payments" loan. Since Pakistan had taken a deliberate laissez-faire tack and was liberalizing imports, it needed some more money to finance these.

He and Bundy exchanged thoughts on the differences between Pakistan and US views of Communist China and India. In effect, Shoaib admitted that the Pakistanis couldn't quite understand why we felt as strongly as we did about Peiping. However, he continued, Americans seem unable to understand how strongly they feel about India. These differences were probably based more on emotion and geography than on reason, but they were realities nonetheless.

For example, Ayub and the Pak military simply didn't think that the Indians would ever fight China. Delhi would soon reach an accommodation with Peiping; then, of course, the future weight of India's defense buildup would be directed against Pakistan. Bundy refused to argue the merits of this Pakistan view, but he couldn't understand why, if the Indians were too "cowardly" to fight the Chinese, the Paks were so scared of India.

Shoaib recalled his meeting with President Kennedy in 1963; he said that, just as he had assured the President then, Pakistan had made no serious moves toward China. They were just keeping on good terms so as to minimize any possible future difficulties. There was nothing in Pak/Chicom relations that was not in the newspapers. He described the circumstances surrounding the $60 million Chicom loan offer.

Komer thought that, even accepting Shoaib's contention that nothing serious had happened, there was little question that Pakistan-US relations had soured noticeably in the months since the Shoaib/Kennedy interview. The combination of Pak needling and US defensive

---

[1] Source: Johnson Library, National Security File, Country File, Pakistan, Vol. II 6/64–11/64. Secret. A copy was sent to Talbot marked "Personal."

[2] While in Washington Shoaib also met with Talbot, Harriman, Rusk, and McNamara. A record of Talbot's September 21 conversation with Shoaib is in the National Archives and Records Administration, RG 59, Central Files 1964–66, POL PAK–US. Records of Shoaib's meetings on September 21 with Harriman and on September 24 with Rusk are ibid., POL 7 PAK. A record of Shoaib's meeting on September 21 with McNamara is in the Washington National Records Center, RG 330, OSD Files: FRC 69 A 7425, Pakistan 091.112.

reactions was leading to a gradual shift in attitudes on both sides. Our fear was that Ayub might be boxing himself in—if he let Pakistan public opinion get so exercised that he would lose his freedom of action.

Bundy philosophized a bit about the US-Pak alliance. When originally laid on, it had seemed doubly useful to both countries. First, there was the real common interest which we had in strengthening a vulnerable flank. Second, it had political salability in both countries. Our politicians could justify it as a move against the Communists; Pak politicians could justify it as reinsurance against India. Historic circumstance, rather than any shift in our own intentions, had tended to change this situation. Now, politicians here found it hard to defend our Pak alliance because of Pak moves toward China, while Ayub's political sense required him to complain about his US ally aiding India.

But the Paks must understand that we had not changed our position—we had never envisaged our relationship as aimed at India. We still wanted to be on the best of terms with Pakistan, unless the Paks themselves made this impossible.

Bundy probed on President Ayub's own attitude. So long as we were satisfied that Ayub himself had a clear sense of the desirability of maintaining our relationship, we could both sustain a fair amount of political sniping. We wanted to be sure that Ayub was solid on the continued value of the tie. It rather bothered us when Ayub himself used the respected pages of *Foreign Affairs* to tell us we were foolishly naive about India (Shoaib said "misguided" was a better word) or when he called the President's policy opportunistic in the *Daily Mail*.

Shoaib insisted that Ayub had no intention of switching away from the US. True, he had certain political requirements which as a politician he must meet. But he knew he needed the US. To clear the air, and to make sure that Johnson and Ayub got through clearly to each other, the two Presidents must get together at the summit as soon as possible and talk this matter over. This was the best, indeed the only, way to avoid misunderstanding. It couldn't happen too soon. He had also mentioned this to Secretary Rusk. Bundy agreed that a summit would be useful; there was no one for whom President Johnson had more respect than Ayub. A meeting would rank high on our future agenda.

Bundy stressed, however, that neither Ayub nor any other Pakistani should be under any illusion that leaning on the US or making noises toward China would change our determination to help India against China. This was a major aspect of our foreign policy. The Paks might disagree with our judgment as to the reliability of India and whether the Indians would ever fight China. But this was not the issue. We regarded India as a very important place and were determined to avoid the critical vacuum which would be created by India's collapse. This was also in Pakistan's interest. Did Shoaib, for example, want to see

India fall apart in 15 years or so? Shoaib asserted, "Not in 15 years, nor in 50."

Nonetheless, he feared that India could fall apart if it bankrupted itself by such huge military expenditures. The Indian military budget was now up to $2 billion. India couldn't afford this kind of military establishment. He, Shoaib, had firmly resisted this sort of thing in Pakistan. When the service chiefs had recently gone to Ayub and insisted that Pak foreign exchange be used for military purchases, Ayub had vetoed it on Shoaib's plea. Ayub has told Musa and Asghar Khan that he knew they could put up a jolly good scrap without the additional hardware.

Yet we should understand that Musa and Ayub and many others were very unhappy about US military aid to India. Our decision last June to go ahead with a further program had had a bad effect, mainly because in the talks with General Taylor the previous December they had gotten the impression that they had convinced us there was no need for longer term MAP for India since the Chinese weren't going to attack again. Moreover, they had expected us to offer some compensatory military aid to Pakistan to preserve the previous three-to-one military balance on which the Pak military counted so heavily. Now the balance seemed to be going heavily against them. When the Indians made their peace with China, Pakistan would face this whole new Indian military machine. We should do what we could to butter up the Pak military.

Komer interjected that we found the Pak military a bit too emotional and not coldly professional enough about our aid to India. Regardless of the comparable dollar value, we were sending a lot more fighting value to the Paks. As an example of how Pak emotionalism could work against its own interests, he recounted how we had considered suggesting to the Paks that a US offer of a few supersonics to India on condition that India not buy or build a much larger number of MIGs would actually serve Pak interests. But we concluded that the Paks just wouldn't think this through.

Shoaib and Bundy fenced briefly on Kashmir. The former recounted how TTK had told him in Tokyo that Nehru wanted to settle Kashmir before his death. Shastri was an unknown quantity, and Shoaib was convinced that there was no likelihood of movement on Kashmir just now. Bundy assured him that we still thought a settlement essential, and would do what we could when the time was ripe.

At several points Shoaib made allusions to the problem with Bhutto and the MEA. He subsequently told Komer that he was aware we knew that Bhutto was at one extreme among Pak policy-makers. Ayub deliberately kept in the middle, and didn't take all Bhutto's advice. He repeated what he had told Phil Talbot, i.e. that he had inspired the

RCD gambit[3] as an alternative to Bhutto's pressure for new gestures toward China.

RWK

---

[3] Reference is to a proposal Shoaib explained to Talbot on September 21 that he had made to Ayub for a regional grouping of Muslim states to include Turkey, Iran, Pakistan, and possibly Afghanistan. Shoaib's idea was to create a security arrangement among the non-Communist Muslim states of the area that would shore up Pakistan's security position without requiring it to turn, as Bhutto preferred, to China for support.

---

74.   Memorandum of Conversation[1]

Washington, November 3, 1964.

SUBJECT

    Chinese Nuclear Explosion

PARTICIPANTS

    B.K. Nehru, Ambassador of India
    William C. Foster, Director, U.S. Arms Control and Disarmament Agency

Ambassador Nehru called at his request primarily to discuss the situation arising out of the explosion of the Chinese nuclear device.[2] He stated that, as we knew, the Indian Government had made a formal decision prior to the explosion not to engage in the development of nuclear weapons no matter what any other country did. A formal reconsideration of this policy was undertaken after the Chinese explosion and the government confirmed its earlier decision not to go this route. The Ambassador recalled with satisfaction the comments that I

---

[1] Source: National Archives and Records Administration, RG 59, Central Files 1964–66, DEF 12–1 CHICOM. Confidential. Drafted by Foster.

[2] China detonated a nuclear device on October 16. On October 28 Secretary of Defense McNamara transmitted to Secretary Rusk an October 23 JCS paper that commented on a Thompson Committee report entitled "The Indian Nuclear Problem: Proposed Course of Action." McNamara and the JCS concurred with offering general assurances to non-nuclear states in light of the Chinese nuclear explosion. The JCS recommended, however, that if discussions with India were begun, no action be taken that would alienate Pakistan. (Ibid., DEF 19 US–INDIA; also available on the Internet, National Security Archive (www.gwu.edu/~nsarchiv), Electronic Briefing Book No. 6, "India and Pakistan—On the Nuclear Threshold," Document 2)

had made at Geneva, the comments by the Secretary of State, and the comments by the President commending the Indian action. He said there was no intention to change this decision, but there were strong pressures in India to have the government explode a nuclear device so as to offset the genuine psychological advantages which the Chinese had obtained in Southeast Asia by virtue of their explosion. He said that this act of theirs, instead of being condemned by most of the non-aligned nations, was actually being commended to some extent on the basis of showing that the white world was no better than they and that the United States, at least in the Far East and Africa, was not the super power it used to be.

He said that Dr. Bhabha[3] had estimated that India could develop a reasonable nuclear capability for $20 million. He said that, on the other hand, in the course of a year or two China probably could work out a makeshift capability by which they could drop a nuclear bomb on New Delhi without much fear of Indian defense against it. He spoke feelingly of what had been interpreted as a defeat of India by China in the land attack of a couple of years ago. In his opinion, it was really not a defeat since India had chosen to defend wrong positions to begin with, but based on withdrawal to better and more appropriate positions would have been able to repel any later Chinese attack.

The nuclear explosion, however, had the potential for seriously degrading India's position in the Far East and therefore political pressures within India might indeed build up so that it would be politically impossible to resist proposals for an Indian bomb. He asked our thinking with reference to these questions.

I told the Ambassador we understood the pressures which might build up and yet his government must recognize that if India were to make the decision to produce nuclear weapons, this would be a long step toward proliferation of such weapons throughout the world. It seemed to us a much better decision, both from the viewpoint of best utilization of economic resources and indeed the security of the world, to devote the Indian influence to non-proliferation. I said that the United States is planning active attempts to achieve some sort of universal non-proliferation agreement, that this was a continuation of our proposals at Geneva, and the Soviet Union appeared to have a genuine interest in this, which interest had been stated by them to be blocked by the Multilateral Force.

I said we do not agree with the Russians' appraisal. We feel that the MLF actually can contribute to non-proliferation by our retaining veto power in the multilateral group. It is also planned that no single

---

[3] Homi J. Bhabha, Secretary of the Indian Department of Atomic Energy.

nation in the group will have the option of utilizing the nuclear weapons assigned to it. I stated we could well understand why Germany and indeed all of Western Europe wished to participate in offsetting the hundreds of Soviet IRBM's and MRBM's pointed at Western Europe, and the Multilateral Force was designed to meet this desire.

I called attention to President Johnson's statement of a week ago Sunday as to the United States support of nations which would be subjected to nuclear aggression or blackmail. He said, "But the United States would not come to our aid by attacking China if at the same time the Soviet Union said that it would assist China under such an attack." I said I could not speculate on such a contingency, but we had commitments with many nations in the North Atlantic Alliance to come to their aid, even though the United States was not attacked in the particular situation where North Atlantic countries were attacked by the Soviet Union. He said that the informal offer of aid could not be made formal since India because of its non-alignment policy could not enter a firm defense agreement with the United States.

He expressed an interest in our plans for non-proliferation. I outlined some of these briefly. I said that India could be of great influence in helping to promote non-proliferation at the General Assembly and I hoped his government would support these efforts.

Moving on to another question, he asked our intention concerning a meeting with China in response to the U Thant proposal for a five power nuclear conference. I said we thought that the Chinese proposal was for propaganda purposes only since they had shown no serious interest in disarmament questions; that a proposal by China for a conference to discuss the destruction of all nuclear weapons with China sitting in as a nuclear power was somewhat ridiculous in that they had exploded their one device and had suggested we discuss giving up all of ours in exchange for the meager demonstration China had given.

The Ambassador said that the important point to keep in mind is that any participation by China in a five power conference concerned with nuclear weapons, which conference had been approved by the U.S. with the implication that China is a nuclear power, and excluding India, would be the end of Indian influence in Asia. In view of India's status in Asia and her peaceful nuclear achievements, such a meeting without her would be a disastrous blow psychologically and every other way to the Indian Government. Any such conference, therefore, in his opinion, should include all nations capable of nuclear weapons development of which India is one.

In leaving, he said that India was deeply interested in any findings we had concerning the technology and so forth of the Chinese explosion, and I said that the Indian Government's request for this information had been forwarded by the State Department to the suitable agencies and whatever could be given to them I was sure he would hear about in the reasonably near future. I said the analysis of these events sometimes took considerable time, however, and there might not be detailed information available for some time.[4]

In response to my question concerning Krishna Menon's new activities, he said that, in his opinion, Menon did not have any additional influence and the comments made about Menon's participation in the All India Party Congress referred only to an internal policy statement which had no bearing on the governmental position.

The discussion, which began at 3:30, ended at 4:45.

---

[4] Telegram 918 to New Delhi, November 2, informed the Embassy of a telegram received by the Chairman of the AEC, John G. Palfrey, on October 23 from Minister Babha, in which Babha requested an arrangement to exchange information on the effects of the Chinese explosions. The Embassy was instructed to deliver Palfrey's response, which informed Babha that arrangements should be made through Ambassador Bowles since "a number of agencies of the USG would likely be involved." (National Archives and Records Administration, RG 59, Central Files 1964–66, DEF 12–1 CHICOM; also available on the Internet, National Security Archive (www.gwu.edu/~nsarchive), Electronic Briefing Book No. 6, "India and Pakistan—On the Nuclear Threshold," Document 4) Ray Cline, CIA Deputy Director for Intelligence, briefed Prime Minister Shastri in New Delhi on October 27 about the Chinese nuclear program. (Telegram 1297 from New Delhi, October 27; National Archives and Records Administration, RG 59, Central Files 1964–66, DEF 12–1 CHICOM)

---

75.   Memorandum From the Assistant for Counterinsurgency, Department of Defense (Carroll) to the Deputy Director of the Near East and South Asia Region, Department of Defense (Stoddart)

Washington, November 23, 1964.

[Source: Washington National Records Center, RG 330, OASD/ ISA Files: FRC 68 A 306, 452.1 India. Secret. 2 pages of source text not declassified.]

76. **Memorandum From the Deputy Director for Plans, Central Intelligence Agency (Helms) to Director of Central Intelligence McCone**

CSDB–312/012201–64   Washington, November 27, 1964.

[Source: Johnson Library, National Security File, Country File, Pakistan, Vol. II, 6/64–11/64. Secret; No Foreign Dissem/Controlled Dissem; No Dissem Abroad/Background Use Only. 2 pages of source text not declassified.]

---

77. **Editorial Note**

In late 1964, Special Assistant to the President for National Security Affairs McGeorge Bundy was advised of information indicating that the Pakistani Government had a secret commitment from China that established a significantly closer relationship between the two countries than had been publicly acknowledged, although the details of such commitment were not available to the United States Government.

---

78. **National Intelligence Estimate[1]**

NIE 31–64   Washington, December 10, 1964.

THE PROSPECTS FOR INDIA

The Problem

To estimate probable developments in India during the next three to four years.

---

[1] Source: Central Intelligence Agency, Job 79–R01012A, ODDI Registry of NIE and SNIE Files. Secret; Controlled Dissem. Prepared by the Central Intelligence Agency and the intelligence organizations of the Departments of State and Defense and the National Security Agency. All members of the U.S. Intelligence Board concurred in the estimate on December 10 except the Assistant to the Director of the Federal Bureau of Investigation, who abstained because the subject was outside his jurisdiction.

Conclusions

A. India has survived the experience of the loss of Nehru with considerable initial success. We cannot yet be certain about the quality of Prime Minister Shastri's leadership. Clearly he lacks Nehru's prestige and authority, and thus far he has governed primarily by compromise and concensus. But in past posts he proved himself a generally effective leader, and we believe that he will gradually exert a firmer control. In domestic policy, he is unlikely to depart substantially from Nehru's line, though in practice his socialism may prove more flexible and pragmatic. (Paras. 1–2, 5, 13–15)

B. The Congress Party, now led by a coalition of state leaders, will probably provide India with stable and orderly government for the next several years. However, continued jockeying for power between the center and the states, as well as strains within the central government itself, are likely at times to generate indecision and inefficiency. Prospects for Congress unity would be clouded were Shastri to depart from the scene in the near future, but the Congress leadership could probably agree on a successor. There are no effective nationwide opposition parties, and in the 1967 elections Congress will probably continue in its dominant position at the national level and in all but one or two states. (Paras. 4, 6, 8–12, 18)

C. The pace of economic growth has slowed considerably during the past three years. In particular, agriculture has shown no increase in output. Industrial growth has been better, and industrial production is likely to grow by 40 to 50 percent during the Third Five-Year Plan (1961–1966). Over the five year period, GNP, instead of rising by the planned 30 percent, will probably increase by no more than 18 to 20 percent, or about the same amount it increased during each of the first two plans. The still tentative Fourth Five-Year Plan (1966–1971) sets forth even more ambitious goals, including much larger investments in the agricultural sector. India is unlikely to achieve these goals, though food grain production will probably increase significantly by the late 1960s. In any case, increased foreign aid will be needed, as import requirements and debt servicing charges will rise faster than exports. (Paras. 19–31)

D. The Shastri government's foreign policies will probably be less concerned with broad international questions and more devoted to specific issues involving India's self interest. India will continue its policy of nonalignment, which in recent years has come to be focused on the need for support from both the US and USSR in the confrontation with Communist China. Between India and China, we foresee neither a general settlement nor an outbreak of major fighting. A prerequisite of any substantial easing of Indo-Pakistani tensions is a settlement of the Kashmir dispute, and of this there is no early prospect. However, major hostilities between the two countries are not likely, and some specific problems may be resolved. India will devote more attention than in the past to its other neighbors, seeking to reduce possible Communist Chinese influence. In the nonaligned world as a whole, India will probably play a generally moderating, but on the whole less influential, role than it did in earlier years. (Paras. 32–42)

E. India's leaders want armed forces capable of containing both Pakistan and Communist China and to this end have sharply increased defense spending under a $10–12 billion Five-Year Defense Plan (1964–1969). This, combined with military aid from the US, the USSR, and the UK, is enabling India to further expand and modernize its forces, but the plan is likely to take seven years to complete. Though the army still suffers from deficiencies of leadership and training, its combat effectiveness is improving and it could probably overwhelm its smaller Pakistani foe. While the Chinese would initially have the advantage of terrain in any conflict, the Indian army could probably stop a Chinese invasion before it reached the plains. (Paras. 43–49)

F. India has the capability for developing nuclear weapons, and the government is under considerable domestic pressure to do so. We believe that at a minimum India will continue to build up its nuclear capability, and this will enable it to start a weapons program promptly after a decision to do so. Whether the Indians decide to do so will depend on such questions as the cost of a nuclear weapons program and of a delivery system, the pace and scope of the Chinese program, and the importance the Indians attach to assurances from the US and other nuclear powers. (Paras. 50–51)

[Here follows the 16-page Discussion section.]

---

79.   Telegram From the Department of State to the Embassy in India[1]

Washington, December 12, 1964, 1:28 p.m.

1185. This relates to your plans to see Shastri soon for further discussion of Indian nuclear problem. Since your last talk he has

---

[1] Source: National Archives and Records Administration, RG 59, Central Files 1964–66, FSE 13 INDIA. Secret; Priority; Limdis. Drafted by Schneider in NEA/SOA; cleared by Officer in Charge of Atomic Energy Affairs in SCI Charles W. Thomas, Hall of AEC, Wreatham B. Gathright and W. Howard Wriggins of S/P, Samuel DePalma of ACDA, and Raymond L. Garthoff of G/PM; and approved by William J. Handley. Repeated to London and Ottawa.

presumably had opportunity reflect on problem and climate may therefore be good for moving further along course we have charted. We hope, and his statements suggest, his exposure in London to variety of views and questions on nuclear matters may have stimulated more thought about what India needs to do to reinforce its present nuclear policy.

We believe our focus with Indians should be on problem of building prestige of Indian science and technology, but first you will need to find out extent to which Indians have reflected on this question and ideas they have about coping with it. It seems to us that time at which we can offer assistance designed to increase Indian prestige depends upon the extent to which GOI thinking has developed.

Consequently, our first need is to probe and if necessary to direct GOI thoughts in this area. If GOI has recognized and weighed full dimensions of their prestige problem, they are probably looking for ways to deal with it and may be receptive to our help. If their analysis of their situation and alternatives has not reached this stage, however, an immediate offer from us might either make them suspicious of our motives or cause them to think we are trying to buy their adherence to a peaceful uses only policy, thereby increasing their leverage over us. You are, of course, best judge of proper timing of raising subject possible US assistance with them.

As you know, we still believe it is quite important that Indians take initiative and we play responding role.

We note that during and immediately after Shastri's London visit there has been some public talk about assurances of support to India in event of Chicom nuclear attack.[2] As you know, we do not wish to proceed at present beyond general statement of assurances included in President's statement of October 16 and his speech of

---

[2] The Reuters news agency reported from London on December 4 that Shastri had publicly urged the world's atomic powers to consider how they could guarantee the security of the non-nuclear nations against attack. (Johnson Library, National Security File, Committee File, Committee on Nuclear Proliferation, India) British Prime Minister Wilson told President Johnson in a conversation in Washington on December 8 that Shastri had told him that he was under strong domestic pressure to authorize the development of a nuclear weapon. Shastri stated that he preferred not to, but the Chinese bomb had shifted the balance of power in Asia, and the only alternative he saw to an Indian nuclear program was a protective nuclear umbrella provided by the existing nuclear powers with the Soviet Union playing an important role. Wilson said that Shastri had asked him to pass his concerns to Washington. (National Archives and Records Administration, RG 59, Presidential Memoranda of Conversation: Lot 66 D 149)

October 18.[3] We are therefore in position of wanting to know what Shastri may have in mind of not wanting to take any initiative to explore subject with GOI.

When you believe time appropriate to discuss with Shastri possible US assistance to Indian science and technology you may draw as appropriate on following points:

1. We are impressed by achievements Indian science and technology which we believe exceed those of Communist Chinese.
2. We agree with Indians that world should know more about these achievements.
3. We wonder what plans Indians have for making known Indian progress and for further scientific endeavor.
4. (In response Indian request) USG would be pleased to talk over any plans Indians may have to achieve these objectives to see how we can appropriately assist.
We have in mind jointly exploring possibility of developing one or more ventures in fields peaceful uses nuclear energy and space technology that would serve highlight India's capabilities.
5. We recognize that Indian need is to demonstrate Indian progress. Any possible US assistance would therefore be directed toward clearly identifiable Indian projects with US role unobtrusive.

When discussions reach this point would appreciate your suggestions for next step. Before taking such step, know you agree on need to have established general framework with Indian political leaders for any expansion of cooperation in peaceful uses or space field. We see this as essential preliminary for making the most of discussions with Bhabha during his visit here next February.

Ball

---

[3] President Johnson issued a statement to the press concerning the Chinese detonation of a nuclear device on October 16, the day of the test. On October 18 he made a radio and television address to the nation in which he offered the following assurance to non-nuclear nations: "The nations that do not seek national nuclear weapons can be sure that, if they need our strong support against some threat of nuclear blackmail, then they will have it." The October 16 statement is printed in *Public Papers of the Presidents of the United States: Lyndon B. Johnson, 1963–64*, Book II, p. 1357. For text of the October 18 address, see Department of State *Bulletin*, November 2, 1964, pp. 610–614.

80.   Telegram From the Department of State to the Embassy in Pakistan[1]

Washington, December 14, 1964, 7:40 p.m.

639. At his request Pak Ambassador G. Ahmed saw Governor Harriman December 11 to express grave concern of GOP at announcement December 4 by GOI Minister Nanda of GOI intention to extend the constitutional provision of President's rule to Kashmir.[2] Points made by Ambassador Ahmed were: (1) by this action, even fiction of separateness of Kashmir is being destroyed; (2) this action, coming at a time when President Ayub had sought to be conciliatory and on heels of an Ayub–Shastri meeting, has special significance and indicates that India does not want peaceful settlement; (3) effect of this action on Kashmir itself might very well be explosive; (4) things are bound to become steadily more and more difficult; (5) GOP continues to believe that military aid to India is responsible for this stiffening Indian attitude; (6) because of India's dependence on US aid, US has a whip hand and nothing will stop India in its move to integrate Kashmir unless US threatens to stop aid; (7) GOP will certainly protest to the UN, but Ambassador was uncertain what GOP might do beyond that; (8) purpose of Ambassador's call was to ask US what GOP should do since earlier this year US chided Pakistan for taking issue to Security Council without prior consultation with US.

In reply Governor Harriman, noting his custom of always being quite frank with both Pakistan and India, stated: (1) we agree with GOP's position on Indian actions to integrate Kashmir, and consider Pakistanis have right to be concerned; personally Governor was shocked; (2) we continue to regard Kashmir as disputed territory and do not recognize right of India to change its status unilaterally; (3) we registered our position December 10 with Indians and must await their response; (4) question of GOP going to Security Council is within

---

[1] Source: National Archives and Records Administration, RG 59, Central Files 1964–66, POL 32–1 INDIA–PAK. Secret. Drafted by Laise on December 11, cleared by Kimball in IO and Handley, and approved and initialed by Harriman. Repeated to New Delhi, London, and USUN.

[2] Home Minister Nanda's announcement concerning the application of President's rule to Kashmir was made during a debate in the Lok Sabha on December 4 on an opposition motion calling for the deletion of Article 370 from the Indian Constitution, which would have had the effect of fully integrating Kashmir into the Indian Union. The motion was ultimately defeated. In the course of the debate, Nanda stated that the government had decided to apply to Kashmir the provisions of Articles 356 and 357 of the Constitution, which provided for President's rule in the event of a breakdown of constitutional government, and enabled the central parliament to legislate for the state during President's rule. (Airgram A–566 from New Delhi, December 9; ibid., POL 18 INDIA)

competence of GOP to decide but we appreciate GOP informing us frankly of problem and they should feel free to discuss it with us; (5) reason for Indian action at this time is difficult to assess. We did not believe there was any relationship between military aid and Indian actions on Kashmir. Prime Minister Shastri had demonstrated a constructive attitude in past toward India–Pakistan problems and US still believes there is a reason to hope he will move in constructive direction. However, his illness and many problems have slowed momentum in establishing his position and pressures on him, particularly on Kashmir, by opposition and within Congress to exist; (6) US ability to bring pressure to bear upon India is limited by our confrontation with Chicom threat and activities in area and elsewhere around the world. (Adverse effect of Pak-Chicom relationship also noted.)

Ambassador Ahmed pressed hard on what US advice was to Pakistan and what US would do, stating that, if subcontinent is to be secured against external threats, it can only be done by arrangements between India and Pakistan. However, US actions contribute to deterioration of this relationship by not making military aid conditional on a Kashmir settlement. Governor stated he was not in position to offer any further comment on question raised by Ambassador but he would consult with his colleagues and keep in touch with Ambassador if there were anything further to say. He fully concurred that agreement between Pak and India essential for security of subcontinent and had so stated on numerous occasions.

Ball

---

81. **Telegram From the Department of State to the Embassy in Pakistan**[1]

Washington, December 24, 1964, 4:04 p.m.

676. Assistant Secretary Talbot called in Pak Ambassador Ahmed December 24 to follow up on Ambassador's December 11 conversation with Governor Harriman on Kashmir integration moves by GOI.[2] Talbot

---

[1] Source: National Archives and Records Administration, RG 59, Central Files 1964–66, POL 32–1 INDIA–PAK. Secret. Drafted by Simmons (NEA/SOA), cleared by Cameron and Kimball (IO/UNP), and approved by Talbot. Also sent to New Delhi, London, and USUN.

[2] See Document 80.

said we have made firm diplomatic representations to Indians regarding our attitude towards recent Indian action extending provisions of Articles 356 and 357 to Kashmir.[3] He noted that we have seen Pakistan's letter to SC which seemed to us an appropriate way to deal with the matter. Talbot reiterated our long standing legal position that we do not recognize validity of unilateral actions to change the status of Kashmir. He affirmed US had made this legal position clear to Indians. He pointed out on other hand US feels that such deep international dispute as Kashmir is unlikely to be resolved solely in terms of legal considerations. Talbot cited our extensive and unsuccessful efforts to help resolve problem, most recently in 1963. He stated that it seemed to us afterwards neither side regarded substantial compromises in its positions as in its national interest. Only with such compromise can movement toward a settlement occur. As US ponders current situation we do not see how outside powers can be helpful until disputants decide themselves to make such concessions.

Talbot expressed concern over sharpening tensions over Kashmir and within Kashmir noting Azad Kashmir President Hamid Khan's statement that his government considered itself relieved of its CFL obligations because of latest GOI measures. We were also aware of escalation of CFL incidents. US failed to see how rising tensions would improve chances for settlement. However US hopeful that tentative beginnings of a dialogue which began in 1964 between Shastri and Ayub could be carried forward in the new year.

Talbot said Pakistan knows our concern for stability and security of subcontinent and our desire to maintain closest possible relations with Pakistan. But, Pakistan must also be aware of our deepening confrontation with Communist China. This confrontation must affect and color our policies in Asia at this stage.

Ambassador Ahmed in reply said GOP was quite appreciative of US position concerning recent Indian action. But in Pakistan's opinion asking for substantial compromises is asking too much. Fundamentals of an issue cannot be disregarded summarily because party in the wrong is adamant on facing facts squarely. Facts are Kashmir is held against wishes of its people and this condition is recognized by world opinion. Ayub had said that if plebiscite impossible, he was prepared to listen to any other ideas. GOI response has been to strengthen its

---

[3] Talbot called in Ambassador Nehru on December 18 to express U.S. disagreement with and disapproval of the Kashmir integration decisions announced by Nanda on December 4. He said the United States was surprised and disappointed over India's latest moves with respect to Kashmir, and would not recognize any Indian action to settle the Kashmir dispute unilaterally by changing Kashmir's status with respect to the Indian Union. (Telegram 1250 to New Delhi, December 18; National Archives and Records Administration, RG 59, Central Files 1964–66, POL 32–1 INDIA–PAK)

stranglehold on Kashmir at time when atmosphere of good will had been built up at least from Pakistan side.

Increased tensions were inevitable results of India's action and explosive situation may develop in Kashmir whose leaders must now be restive. With respect to Azad Kashmir President's statement this reflects his own view and does not commit the GOP.

Talbot commented that one factor increasing turbulence in the subcontinent and Indo-Pak relations is political and military pressure by Chicoms. This was not a factor in the pre-1962 Kashmir situation. Chicom policies however now are important factor and have made Indo-Pak relations more difficult. Ahmed agreed that this argument has been used with good effect by US and India. But he stated argument should not cloud US judgment. Every question is now being pivoted around China which is new factor in calculus but impasse on Kashmir has existed 15 years.

Ahmed said that Pakistan appreciates our difficulties in Far East. GOP has maintained for two years there would be no Chinese attack on India and that China and India will settle their differences. Therefore China should not be considered major factor in Indo-Pak problem. Nonetheless the US, UK, and USSR arms build up in India goes on encouraging Indian intransigence. This is why the US is getting nowhere on Kashmir.

Assuming subcontinent defense is an American objective, the USG should tell GOI that until it does come to terms on Kashmir, India will not receive American aid. "The US has whiphand but refuses to crack the whip."

Ahmed said he would like to hear not only that US deplored GOI action but also that US would do something about it. US should use leverage with India. This was his suggested solution; he believed that US should consider others. US position should not rest solely that India and Pakistan must make substantial concessions which is both Indian and Soviet position. Ahmed said he was not happy with this posture which in effect meant no decisions.

Ambassador Ahmed then asked if Indians had given us any explanation for their action. Talbot responded that whatever their reasons may have been Indians had been left in no doubt as to our attitude.

Amassador Ahmed expressed his puzzlement over Shastri's consent to recent Indian action. Shastri had reputation of being man of conciliation and did not give impression he was under pressure to take hard line on Pakistan. In closing he reiterated his view that Kashmir problem was not only problem for GOI and GOP but USG had interest in its resolution and should and could play more active role in subcontinent.

Rusk

82.   Telegram From the Embassy in India to the Department of State[1]

New Delhi, December 31, 1964, 1 p.m.

1862. Two days ago [1 line of source text not declassified], told Emb officer, in strictest confidence that Cabinet had instructed Bhabha to proceed with first stages of producing atomic bomb.

Bhabha had previously reported that eighteen months would be required to produce bomb and once initial explosion had occurred, he could produce fifty in five years. According to [less than 1 line of source text not declassified], Bhabha was then instructed to proceed with first twelve months of necessary work. At end of that period GOI would review situation and decide whether or not to push project to completion.

Factors influencing final decision would include progress during this twelve month period by nuclear powers to bring ChiCom nuclear bomb production under control and additional amount of prestige ChiComs would have acquired by having bomb. Bhabha had assured Cabinet that final test could be handled underground and hence there would be no violation of Moscow agreement.[2]

Although efforts of mission officers [less than 1 line of source text not declassified] to check this story have produced no further evidence, [less than 1 line of source text not declassified] has thus far been accurate reporter and because procedure he described could be rationalized however painfully in Indian mind as not violating previous agreements or contradicting stated policy, we have been concerned.

Therefore at completion of my regular business with Swaran Singh in yesterday's meeting I expressed serious distress over what I described (in order to divert suspicion from [less than 1 line of source text not declassified]) as two apparently well authenticated stories from Bombay that indicated Cabinet had decided to move ahead with program as described above.

Swaran Singh asserted flatly that rumor was unfounded, that such effort would be breach of public understanding and that I should accept his assurance that no such plan was in wind.

I replied that I was reassured by what he said since it would be impossible for GOI to prepare for setting off atomic device without it

---

[1] Source: National Archives and Records Administration, RG 59, Central Files 1964–66, DEF 18–8 INDIA. Secret; Limdis. Received at 4:19 a.m.

[2] Reference is to the Limited Test Ban Treaty signed in Moscow on August 5, 1963. (14 UST (Part 2) 1313)

becoming generally known, and this in turn would greatly undercut India's present forthright position.

Swaran Singh remarked that while I must realize GOI is under great pressure from various groups in country to go ahead with bomb, PriMin was adamant on this subject. We could rest assured that if GOI should change its mind we would be so informed.

I said it has been suggested to me that story might have been floated deliberately by someone interested in pressuring U.S. into guarantee of India's security so that building of Indian bomb would not be necessary. I reminded Swaran Singh of President's statement of assurance on Oct 16 and said we had deliberately avoided further reference to nuclear umbrellas because we did not want to appear to be pressing them into relationship with us which they might not be prepared to undertake.[3] Furthermore, public comment about U.S. nuclear support for India at this time would tend to frighten off Russians who otherwise might conceivably be persuaded to undertake parallel if not joint approach.

Swaran Singh expressed his appreciation of our sensitivity to his political problems but made no comment on my suggestion that story might have been deliberately planted.

Comment: [less than 1 line of source text not declassified] statement to Emb officer was made on highly confidential basis and it is of vital importance that his name be protected within Dept and elsewhere. Otherwise we will lose good friend who in past has been excellent source.

Bowles

---

[3] Ambassador at Large Llewellyn Thompson sent a memorandum to Rusk on December 31 expressing his concern that Bowles was encouraging the Indians to think that the United States would be prepared to offer a unilateral guarantee to India against nuclear attack, or be prepared to enter into a joint guarantee with the Soviet Union. Thompson noted that he was unaware that any such policy had been discussed in Washington and added that he did not see how such a specific guarantee could be offered to a non-aligned country and not offered to all of the allies of the United States. He also observed that the Joint Chiefs of Staff had serious reservations about the concept of a joint guarantee with the Soviet Union. (National Archives and Records Administration, RG 59, Central Files 1964–66, DEF 18–8 INDIA; also available on the Internet, National Security Archive (www.gwu.edu/~nsarchive), Electronic Briefing Book No. 6, "India and Pakistan—On the Nuclear Threshold," Document 5)

83.   Telegram From the Ambassador to India (Bowles) to Robert Komer of the National Security Council Staff[1]

New Delhi, January 8, 1965, 1220Z.

When I left Washington on December 7 I felt we were all agreed on both critical importance of persuading India not to produce nuclear weapons and also on best means of achieving this.

In my meetings with President, Secretary, Mac, Phil, you, etc. I suggested that this could be best accomplished by (A) creating sense of pride on part of Indian Govt and people in their own scientific capacity and as contributing factor, demonstrate to people all over world India's scientific prowess; (B) encouraging India to take lead not only in condemning China's disregard of Moscow Treaty but in leading fight against further proliferation; and (C) being alert to any opportunities that might come our way to assure India that if she were blackmailed or attacked by China with or without nuclear weapons, we would not stand on sidelines. Since my return here, I sense that these objectives are not as clear in some peoples' minds as I assumed them to be.

Indians are still eager to take major role on proliferation issue and as I stressed with no negative reactions in Washington, we should be trying in every way to encourage them. If they will take lead position as non-nuclear country that is easily capable of producing weapons, our interests will be far better served than by teaming up with white nation of four million people with no such nuclear potential or political weight.

In regard to deterrent question and US position in support of India, I do not think we need to do anything at present moment. Indians are aware of President's Oct 16 statement. However we should be flexible enough to grab any opportunity that comes along, conceivably by some kind of parallel action with Russians.

Purpose of this message is to alert you to opportunities we see here outside flow of traffic through State Dept.

Jerry Wiesner[2] can be extraordinarily persuasive in educating such high Indian officials as Shastri, in background discussions with Indian

---

[1] Source: Johnson Library, National Security File, Country File, India, Exchanges with Bowles. Confidential. [text not declassified]

[2] On December 21 Bowles discussed with Prime Minister Shastri the possibility of a visit to India by Dr. Jerome Wiesner of the Massachusetts Institute of Technology to review the status of Indian science and to discuss with Indian scientists the peaceful uses of nuclear energy. Shastri welcomed such a visit. (Telegram 1778 from New Delhi, December 21, 1964; National Archives and Records Administration, RG 59, Central Files 1964–66, SCI 7 US) On January 12, the Department informed the Embassy in New Delhi that Wiesner had agreed to undertake the mission. The Department anticipated that Wiesner might be influential in helping to strengthen the Indian resolve to limit the Indian nuclear program to peaceful purposes. (Telegram 1393 to New Delhi; ibid.)

press, in exploring scientific projects on which we can cooperate, in coming up with fresh ideas and on his return home in presenting these ideas to people in Washington.

I know as always that you will give us all help you can.

---

84.   Telegram From the Embassy in Pakistan to the Department of State[1]

Karachi, January 14, 1965, 8 p.m.

1323. Deptel 733.[2] My meeting with Ayub in Rawalpindi this morning was the best in over a year. In response to an intimation from me, the usual Foreign Office note-taker was omitted and we met alone for entire 50-minute period. Feeling post-election euphoria, he was in relaxed, communicative mood and seemed full of good will toward US. He responded with warmth to my reiteration of our congratulations and sense of satisfaction at his impressive election success. He drew friendly analogy between President Johnson's electoral triumph and impending inauguration, and his own. I had definite impression that he considers he has a freer hand and more latitude of action now that election stresses and uncertainties are over, and that he will feel less constraint about seeking some improvement of his relations with US.

Early in conversation I extended President's invitation for Washington visit latter half April, recalling that it had been over two years since Ayub was last in the US and 3-1/2 years since his last full-fledged visit, emphasizing importance and urgency we attach to wide range of bilateral and regional issues which call for consideration Chief of State level.

Ayub concurred heartily in urgent requirement for face-to-face meeting with President Johnson to consider many pressing matters and spelled out in warm, even affectionate, terms his eagerness to see President and his family again. He said "President Johnson knows depth of my friendship and regard for him which is so evident it does not even need to be restated." He said only difficulty with suggested latter part of April date was the heavy program of major engagements

---

[1] Source: National Archives and Records Administration, RG 59, Central Files 1964–66, POL 7 PAK. Secret; Priority; Limdis.

[2] In telegram 733 to Karachi, January 12, the Department, responding to a suggestion made by Shoaib to Rusk in September, authorized McConaughy to extend an invitation to Ayub to visit Washington to meet with the President in the latter half of April. (Ibid.)

already laid on for him throughout entire spring period March through June. He mentioned Afro-Asian conference at Algiers, prospective visits to Communist China and Soviet Union, National Assembly elections, budget session of National Assembly, Commonwealth Ministers conference in London and possible State visit to UK.

He asked if it might be feasible to postpone US visit to latter half of 1965 in view of this problem. Then he inquired if, better yet, the President could not visit Pakistan? He indicated that with any encouragement at all he would like to extend the invitation. I discouraged the latter suggestion mentioning the most formidable schedule of visits and trips already in prospect for the President throughout 1965. I then questioned the wisdom of postponing Ayub visit to US to late 1965. I pointed out that our continuing assistance programs, both economic and military, needed to be planned ahead and that while we did not tie our assistance directly to political considerations, we needed to be sure that the broad policy framework within which our programs operated was appropriately set and reciprocally understood. His visit was important and urgent from this standpoint. The entire spectrum of problems relating to our interests, programs and presence in Pakistan, the position of Pakistan in the free alliances, the paramount issues between Pakistan and India, Pakistan in the Afro-Asian context, and the Pak relationship with Communist China and the Soviet Union, needed top level attention sooner rather than later. We would prefer to consult with him as our ally before our consideration of current problems in South Asia went much further.

This gave the President pause and he said he would like to have a short time to consider further the timing of a visit. He expressed his wish to arrange the visit at the time mentioned if it were in any way possible. I told him that if necessary the visit could be limited to the suggested two days in Washington, although we would be disappointed if he could not make a week's tour of the country. I added that it might be possible for him to combine the short visit to Washington with some other scheduled trip in a westerly direction. He replied he would give me a definite reply within two weeks at the outside. I accepted this. It was evident from a later portion of the conversation, which I will report separately, that his current idea of trying to moderate and restrain the aggressive tendencies of Communist China during his forthcoming visit to Peiping looms large in his mind and that he would like to discuss with the President and Secretary Rusk before he goes to Peiping tactics and arguments he might use in seeking to influence the Chinese Communists. While I did not encourage him in this quixotic concept, I infer that this may be an additional reason for him to try to squeeze in the visit to Washington at the time we have offered, notwithstanding the undoubted difficulties for him.

Other principal topics covered in our wide ranging discussion were: (1) Bhutto's current visit to Moscow and Pak-Soviet relations in general, (2) Nature of Pak relationship with Communist China, (3) Chicom policy in South and Southeast Asia, (4) Post-election domestic situation here, (5) Indian negotiating attitude toward Pakistan, (6) need for periodic US Naval task force presence in Indian Ocean, (7) slanderous election charges by Pak official against local US representatives, and (8) requirement for permission to rent housing in Rawalpindi to enable US Mission personnel to make the move from Karachi to Rawalpindi. On all these matters the President's reaction ranged from slightly better to materially better than my expectations. Separate telegram covers all these topics.[3]

Tone of President's attitude can be summarized in his statement that "Pakistan remains in alliance relationship with you and nothing has changed that."

McConaughy

---

[3] These topics were reported on in telegrams 1336 and 1343 from Karachi, January 15 and 16 respectively. (Ibid., POL 15–1 PAK)

---

85.   Telegram From the Embassy in India to the Department of State[1]

New Delhi, January 21, 1965, 11 a.m.

2054. Message to Secretary from Dr. Wiesner. Pass to White House. Before leaving New Delhi Wednesday[2] evening for home I left following report for John Palfrey, AEC,[3] who will be in New Delhi on Thursday.

---

[1] Source: Johnson Library, National Security File, Subject File, Nuclear Weapons, India, Vol. I. Secret; Immediate. Repeated to the White House for Bundy.

[2] January 20. Wiesner arrived in India on January 14. In telegram 2055 from New Delhi, January 21, Bowles reported that during a week divided between New Delhi and Bombay, Wiesner met with Shastri and other senior officials of the government. Bowles noted that Wiesner was very favorably received and that, during the course of his visit, Shastri stated that if nuclear weapons were ever made in India it would not be during a Ministry headed by him. (National Archives and Records Administration, RG 59, Central Files 1964–66, SCI 7 US)

[3] John G. Palfrey, Chairman of the Atomic Energy Commission, visited India to attend the inauguration of a plutonium plant at Trombay on January 22.

I have asked to have it sent on to you in the thought it may be helpful in evaluation situation here. Report is as follows.

"There has been a very considerable debate here both in public and private regarding the possibility and desirability of making an Indian nuclear weapon. The main motivation to date is political, but there is also some desire for a deterrent against China and some vague feeling that if a nuclear mine field makes sense in Europe it could be useful on India–China border.

The issue here was confused by Bhabha's quotations from the AEC report on Plowshare[4] presented at Geneva that gave a cost of $600,000 for a 2 MT explosion. This was generally interpreted to mean that India could carry out a nuclear explosion for such a sum. In particular this is what the PriMin seems to have believed at one point. Many scientists have complained to the PriMin about this and Bhabha has clarified the point.

Nonetheless I believe that he is still underestimating the cost of carrying out a nuclear explosion. He told me that he could make and test a crude nuclear device for approximately ten million dollars. Incidentally I think it would be helpful if the AEC could provide a cost estimate having some solidity. The estimate should be based on the assumption that the Indians have plutonium available but must develop everything else.[5]

Bhabha is still saying that it would be possible to make a nuclear explosion in 18 months. Many of the scientists object to this optimistic figure and at least two have written to the PriMin stating that it was too optimistic. Bhabha apparently wants authority and resources to move forward without final decison regarding actual explosion.

No one has estimated what a real weapon system would cost or understands what will be done with it.

On the constructive side there are several possibilities. Best of all would be to support the Indian resolution,[6] or some variant of it, in

---

[4] The report has not been further identified. Plowshare was a program initiated by the Atomic Energy Commission during the Kennedy administration to explore the possibilities of peaceful nuclear explosions. The program continued during the Johnson administration. Documentation on Plowshare is in *Foreign Relations, 1961–1963*, volume VII, and 1964–1968, volume XI.

[5] Telegram 425 to Bombay, for Palfrey, January 21, forwarded the assessment of the U.S. intelligence community that it would take 1–3 years and would cost India $30–$40 million to develop a modest weapons program. Palfrey was authorized to share that information with Bhabha, and to discuss Plowshare-type projects with him. (Johnson Library, National Security File, Country File, India, Cables, Vol. IV, 12/64–6/65)

[6] Apparent reference to the resolution submitted on September 14, 1964, to the Eighteen-Nation Disarmament Committee in Geneva by the delegations of Brazil, Burma, Ethiopia, India, Mexico, Nigeria, Sweden, and the UAR calling for a cessation of nuclear testing. See *Documents on Disarmament, 1964*, pp. 428–429.

the UN. The Indian resolution would put the Indians squarely on record against acquisition of weapons and certainly would be a powerful deterrent to any bomb movement here.

Of a more limited scope are the various technical things that could be done. I have discussed the possibility of a small satellite, Plowshare experiments, tropical weather studies, Asian-region ground water development, collaborative research on thorium fuel and fast reactors and further cooperative activities on technical education.

Bhabha is anxious to explore availability of Plowshare with you. He is interested in the possibility of making harbors and water reservoirs. He also raised the question of the exchange of radioactive sampling data obtained from Chinese tests.

It would help the Indians politically if some test data could be made available. I don't know what the restrictions would be but believe that some could be given to them quickly without any harm. I made no statement regarding the possibility but said that he should explore the matter with you and I would look into it at home.

Bhabha is also interested in talking about nuclear desalinization. We touched on this briefly but without reaching any judgment regarding the desirability of doing anything at the present time.

I did not explore the question of an AEC representative in Bombay."

End of report of Dr. Wiesner to John Palfrey.[7]

Bowles

---

[7] A January 30 memorandum from Llewellyn Thompson to Secretary Rusk, Under Secretary Ball, Assistant Secretary Talbot, and Walt Rostow, on the subject of "Indian Nuclear Weapons Capability," considered alternatives to U.S. assurances to India. Thompson proposed suggesting that India make a unilateral statement that it would not submit to nuclear threats "from anyone" and that the Indian Government was confident that the major nuclear powers would take "appropriate action" if India were attacked with nuclear weapons. The U.S. response to such an Indian statement would reserve U.S. freedom of action in such a case but note that the "heavy price" any country would pay if it considered using nuclear weapons against India made such a contingency "highly unlikely." (National Archives and Records Administration, RG 59, Central Files 1964–66, DEF 12 INDIA; also available on the Internet, National Security Archive (www.gwu.edu/~nsarchive), Electronic Briefing Book No. 6, "India and Pakistan—On the Nuclear Threshold," Document 6)

86.   Telegram From the Embassy in India to the Department of State[1]

New Delhi, January 29, 1965, 1:30 p.m.

2113. A new development has occurred in Indian military planning which we believe to be of significant importance. First indication occurred last Friday[2] during courtesy call on Defense Minister Chavan on which I accompanied General Johnson.[3]

After usual pleasantries Chavan stated that important changes had occurred in GOI thinking in regard to Air Force. As result he would like to renew at future meeting his request for American assistance on somewhat different basis. Consequently on January 28 Gen Johnson, John Millar[4] and I met with Chavan and Secy of Ministry of Defense PVR Rao for three-quarters hour. Exchange developed along following lines:

1. Chavan stated that after several months consideration he and his colleagues are now ready to accept analysis which Secy McNamara advanced in their Washington conversations last May; i.e., that India should cut down her present wide variety of planes, that F104G was expensive toy which India could not afford, that India had urgent need for ground support aircraft to defend itself against China, that F5 was ideal plane for this purpose to complement Indian-produced HF–24 Mark I and that it would be long time if ever before HF–24 Mark II would become reality.

Based on this review GOI would therefore like to request assistance in procuring minimum of three squadrons and maximum of six squadrons of F5As to be spread over two or three years. He explained this to mean 16 aircraft per squadron plus spares.

2. In response to my inquiry about current GOI plans in regard to MIG–21s Chavan stated that they expected to receive 24–36 MIG–21s from Soviets. In reply to my further question about MIG–21 production in India, Chavan said that while project was proceeding satisfactorily it would be at least ten years before this production line could contribute significantly to India's defense.

Rao added that there was no security threat to U.S. equipment since Soviets were limited to two sites—Chandigarh and Nasik—and

---

[1] Source: National Archives and Records Administration, RG 59, Central Files 1964–66, DEF 19–3 US–INDIA. Confidential; Priority. Repeated to DOD, CINCMEAFSA, London, and Karachi.
[2] January 22.
[3] Major General Charles E. Johnson, Chief of the U.S. Supply Mission to India.
[4] John Y. Millar, First Secretary of Embassy.

were forbidden to leave them. The last Russians to visit Hindustan Aircraft Limited were Bulganin and Khrushchev.

In regard to plans for HF–24 Mark I Chavan stated that he and his colleagues believed that with our help this plane could be made into effective ground support aircraft. They would greatly appreciate help of U.S. experts in solving technical problems and any advice for improving plane generally. They would also appreciate modest amount of U.S. financial assistance to which we referred in previous cables. Rao added that a successful HF–24 (model unspecified) would eliminate the need to produce MIGs.

3. In response to Defense Minister's presentation I stated that while we were prepared to help India in every reasonable way to strengthen her defense against China, we were concerned by relationship of Soviet Union to Indian Air Force. If India had not decided to proceed with MIG–21 production line willy-nilly we would have been willing last June to go a long way towards meeting India's needs for more modern air force.

Although we had no desire to carry on cold war here in India or anywhere else, we were faced with practical problems which involved not only our security but also India's. U.S. and Soviet Union were both agreed that primary need is to avoid nuclear war. However, once we move beyond that first priority U.S. and USSR national objectives varied profoundly.

For instance our second highest priority is to develop working relationship with Soviets which will enable us to lower tensions and to cooperate in solving many disturbing problems which now threaten peace. In contrast, second highest priority of Soviet Union is to lessen tensions between Moscow and Peking and ultimately to create effective basis for cooperation between Russia and China.

Although it is now clear that fulfillment of Soviet objectives is impossible as long as aging Long March veterans are running China, Kremlin hopes that once Chinese leadership role has passed to younger men the two nations can coordinate their efforts in economic, political and military fields.

In meantime we Americans cannot expect any profound changes in Moscow's attitude towards us. India should also realize that as long as this situation exists, USSR will be at best uncertain friend. Indeed if Soviets ever have opportunity to choose between China and India, they will surely pick China since China is potential threat to Soviet security and India is not.

4. Chavan stated that he understood our position and thought it was reasonable. India was fully determined to stand up to Chinese political or military aggression. However, he was faced with practical

day-to-day problem of building India's defense on month-to-month and year-to-year basis.

I closed this exchange by remarking that planes we were discussing had ten year life span and during this period we must face possibility of profound changes in Soviet-Chinese relationship. However I would carefully consider his request with my associates here in Delhi and then transmit it with my recommendations to Washington.

Comment: Gen Johnson, Millar and I came away with clear impression that Chavan was not only reversing position his Air Force people had pushed him into last spring and putting in an order for American planes that he rejected at that time but also that he was easing away from Soviet Union as source of military procurement and towards US.

In effect he accepted our position on present costly proliferation of IAF, impracticality and extravagance of F104 cost and performance advantages of F5A, and practical difficulties in way of building HF–24 Mark II. Only item on which he did not fall in line was MIG assembly line on which GOI is publicly committed and from which it would be difficult for them suddenly to pull back.

We here are agreed that it is politically and militarily sound to provide Indian Air Force with a combat aircraft of characteristics of the F5A, for following reasons:

A. Since F5A could be used as interceptor provision of significant number would at least sharply improve chances that MIG project will fade out if not fall through entirely.
B. If we do not provide F5As we see no likely alternative to vigorous continuation of MIG project. Since there would be no controls on MIG production or use this would be to the disadvantage of Pakistan as well as US.
C. F5A would replace multiple makes of obsolescent aircraft and should permit reduction in total Indian requirements.
D. They would strengthen Indian defenses against Chinese and hence would be serving US interests.[5']

Bowles

---

[5] On February 2 Peter Solbert, Deputy Assistant Secretary of Defense, ISA, sent a memorandum to the Chairman of the Joint Chiefs of Staff asking for the Joint Chiefs' assessment of the request put to Bowles by Chavan as reported in this telegram. Solbert noted that, in his view, the Indian request for F–5 aircraft might provide an opportunity not only to limit the Indian acquisition of MIGs, but might to bring about a substantial restructuring of the Indian Air Force. (Washington National Records Center, RG 330, OASD/ISA Files: FRC 70 A 3717, 452.1 India)

87.   Telegram From the Embassy in India to the Department of State[1]

New Delhi, February 19, 1965, 4 p.m.

2351. M.J. Desai has privately informed me that a new crisis in Pak-India relationship may soon erupt in area of Kutch.

According to his report number of Pak police, perhaps company or two, have taken possession of old fort several miles within established Indo-Pak border. Desai stated that border in this area is based on agreements made many years before partition and is clearly marked by high ground on Pak side and desert on India side. Consequently in his view there could be no possibility of mistake.

In answer to my question as to why Paks would be interested in occupying exposed desert fort on Indian territory, Desai suggested that prospects for oil in this region are excellent and Paks may be preparing to stake out their claim.

I expressed hope that Indians would use greatest care in dealing with situation since any incident might readily escalate to which Desai agreed.

Although we have no way accurately to assess this, Embassy Karachi should know about it. Desai spoke to me in confidence and it is therefore essential that my source be protected.

Bowles

---

[1] Source: National Archives and Records Administration, RG 59, Central Files 1964–66, POL 32–1 INDIA–PAK. Secret; Priority. Repeated to Karachi.

---

88.   Memorandum of Conversation[1]

Washington, February 22, 1965.

SUBJECT

Indian Nuclear Energy Program

---

[1] Source: National Archives and Records Administration, RG 59, Central Files 1964–66, DEF 12–1 INDIA. Secret. Drafted by Schneider on February 25 and approved in U on March 8.

PARTICIPANTS

His Excellency B. K. Nehru, Ambassador of India
Dr. Homi Bhabha, Secretary of the Department of Atomic Energy, Government of India

Mr. Ball, Under Secretary of State
Robert Anderson, U
David T. Schneider, NEA/SOA

Calling at his own request, Dr. Bhabha opened the conversation with a description of India's nuclear power reactor program. Analyzing the economics of nuclear power plants he concluded that although capital costs were somewhat high, in areas where hydroelectric power potential was fully exploited or did not exist and where the sources of coal were remote, nuclear power was very much less expensive in India than coal power.

Dr. Bhabha then directed the conversation to what he called the dilemma India faced regarding what to do to counteract the "noise" of Communist China's nuclear explosion. He explained that India needed to make some dramatic "peaceful" achievement to offset the prestige gained by Communist China among Africans and Asians.[2] Mr. Ball noted however that African opinion on the Communist Chinese detonation was divided. The Africans had been impressed but they were also disturbed regarding the possible effects of fallout. Dr. Bhabha granted that this may be so but said very few Africans had been willing to join in criticism of Communist China. He believed that if any of these countries could secure nuclear weapons they would. Mr. Ball replied that the problem was to get the major non-nuclear countries to agree to forego nuclear weapons; then the way would be clear for other nations to follow. Dr. Bhabha said that in order to do this a way must be found so that a nation will gain as much by not going for nuclear weapons as it might by developing them. It was not helpful to differentiate between members of the "nuclear club" and non-nuclear nations. Mr. Ball agreed and said that we want to prevent countries from gaining status by developing nuclear weapons.

Dr. Bhabha then examined India's accomplishments in the area of nuclear energy and contrasted them with those of China. He noted there were really only two nuclear powers in the world, the United States and the USSR. Britain and France were on quite a different level;

---

[2] On November 23, 1964, AEC Commissioner John G. Palfrey wrote to Llewellyn E. Thompson suggesting discussing with Bhabha during his February visit U.S.-Indian cooperation in the peaceful uses of atomic energy. Palfrey attached to his letter a "Discussion Paper on Prospects for Intensifying Peaceful Atomic Cooperation With India." (Ibid., Thompson Files: Lot 67 D 2; also available on the Internet, National Security Archive (www.gwu.edu/~nsarchiv), Electronic Briefing Book No. 6, "India and Pakistan—On the Nuclear Threshold," Document 3)

still at a much lower level was Communist China. India could quite easily have achieved China's capability.

Dr. Bhabha explained that the Chinese were greatly indebted to the USSR for helping them on their weapons program. At the end of the five-year period of Soviet assistance (about 1959 or 1960) the Soviets had been putting up a diffusion plant, which was not completed, however. The Chinese had asked for a model nuclear bomb but the Soviets had refused; the Chinese had then alleged that the Soviets were backing out of an agreement with them. The Soviet Union must nevertheless have left the blueprints for a nuclear device with Communist China.

Dr. Bhabha explained that if India went all out, it could produce a device in 18 months; with a U.S. blueprint it could do the job in six months. It was clear from this analysis how the Chinese gained time because of the Soviet help. In fact the Chinese in 1958 had admitted to the Indians that their first nuclear reactor was Soviet-built and that only the Soviets were fully acquainted with its operation. When Chou En-lai had visited the Indian Atomic Energy establishment at Trombay some years ago, he had said it would take China 15 years to accomplish what India had. Dr. Bhabha noted that even if this was exaggerated, China at that time was at least three years behind India.

Dr. Bhabha noted that even today we do not know if all of the U–235 used in the Chinese device was produced in China. He said that an Indonesian representative at the recent inauguration of the Indian plutonium separation plant at Bombay had said she had learned in Peiping recently that the Chinese reactor there was operated only when VIP's visited it. "What other reason except shortage of fuel could there be for this?" asked Dr. Bhabha.

Dr. Bhabha explained that if India is to maintain its prestige relative to the Chinese in the fields of science and technology two things should be done: (1) ways must be found for it to demonstrate to other Asian and African countries India's scientific achievements, (2) a greater awareness of Chinese indebtedness to the Soviet Union for its nuclear achievements must be created. Mr. Ball responded that the Department should look into what could be done about it.

Concluding his presentation, Dr. Bhabha said that during the next four or five years there were very few countries which had the capability of developing a nuclear device. Even Japan and Germany had no plutonium separation plants and so were some four years away from being able to produce a device. In fact India was much the closest. India's plutonium separation plant is quite large, large enough to process all of the plutonium from the reactors India is now building. In five years India could produce 100 nuclear bombs per year.

Dr. Bhabha stated that it was the policy of his government, with which he agreed, not to seek nuclear weapons. If his government is to justify this policy, however, ways must be found by which his country can gain at least as much by sticking to peaceful uses as it could by embarking on a weapons program.

---

89.   Information Memorandum From the Assistant Secretary of State for Near Eastern and South Asian Affairs (Talbot) to Secretary of State Rusk[1]

Washington, February 23, 1965.

SUBJECT

Supersonic Aircraft for India and Pakistan

This is to alert you that we will probably have to make important decisions regarding the supply of supersonic aircraft to both Pakistan and India before the Ayub visit in April and the Shastri visit some time thereafter. You should also know that the Vice President indicated he was interested in this question when I saw him just before my Jordan trip.

India

In an apparent policy shift, Defense Minister Chavan asked Ambassador Bowles for F–5's on January 22. (See New Delhi's 2113[2] at Tab A.) We have asked the Ambassador if he can get more information about what is behind this request, particularly if it indicates the Indians are backing away from their MIG–21 agreement with the Soviets. (See Deptel 1584[3] at Tab B.)

Also, we have received a report of undetermined reliability from a covert source to the effect that Chavan believes that the Soviets have reneged on an oral commitment they made to him to provide production facilities for an advanced version of the MIG–21. Now they insist that all

---

[1] Source: National Archives and Records Administration, RG 59, Central Files 1964–66, DEF 19–3 US–INDIA. Secret. Drafted by Schneider on February 17, and cleared in draft by Edward A. Padelford (NEA/NR), A.J. Moses (G/PM), Thomas P. Thornton (INR/RNA), and Joseph B Norbury, Jr. (EUR/SOV).

[2] Document 86.

[3] In telegram 1584 to New Delhi, February 5, a joint State/Defense message, the two Departments expressed interest in Chavan's request for F–5 aircraft, and listed a number of questions for the Embassy to pose in probing for the motivation behind Chavan's request. The response to the request would depend on a clearer reading of what prompted the request. (National Archives and Records Administration, RG 59, Central Files 1964–66, DEF 19–3 US–INDIA)

India can have is facilities for producing a version of the MIG–21 that will be obsolete by the time it is produced. The report also indicates that Chavan believes the Soviets are lagging on deliveries of finished MIG–21's. (Deliveries now, however, seem in fact to be underway.)

Pakistan

On April 27, 1964 we told General Musa we would provide Pakistan with two additional squadrons of F–104's in FY 1966 if the political climate was right at the time. Our long-run modernization plan for the Pakistan Air Force calls for the two squadrons of 104's followed by F–5's in FY 1967, of course, subject to our political decision to do so. (During the winter we had some indications that we might be able to get by with only one squadron of F–104's.)

We believe it is best that we reserve judgment for the present on both of these questions. In the case of India, we will need much more information regarding the factors behind the Indian request. In the case of Pakistan, we will wish to make a careful review of "political climate" as the time for President Ayub's visit approaches. We will, of course, want to consider carefully the effect of providing supersonic aircraft to each country on our relations with the other. In this regard we may wish to consider not only providing aircraft to both countries but also denying them to both.

---

90.   Memorandum to Holders of NIE 4–2–64 and NIE 31–64[1]

Washington, February 25, 1965.

LIKELIHOOD OF INDIAN DEVELOPMENT OF
NUCLEAR WEAPONS

1. Despite the October 1964 Communist Chinese explosion, the Indian Government has publicly reaffirmed its intent not to produce

---

[1] Source: Central Intelligence Agency, Job 79–R01012A, ODDI Registry of NIE and SNIE Files. Secret; Controlled Dissem. According to a note on the cover sheet, the memorandum was prepared by the Central Intelligence Agency and the intelligence organizations of the Departments of State and Defense, the AEC, and NSA. All members of the U.S. Intelligence Board concurred on February 25, except the Assistant to the Director of the Federal Bureau of Investigation, who abstained because the subject was outside of his jurisdiction.

NIE 4–2–64, "Prospects for a Proliferation of Nuclear Weapons Over the Next Decade," October 21, 1964, is ibid. For the conclusions of NIE 31–64, "The Prospects for India," see Document 78.

nuclear weapons. In addition, the Congress Party, at Shastri's behest, formally adopted a statement of policy against the production of such weapons. Moreover, the Indian Government has recently acknowledged to the Canadians that they had originally agreed that the Canadian-Indian Reactor—the only one presently capable of producing plutonium—should be used only for peaceful purposes. On the other hand, domestic pressures to build nuclear weapons have increased considerably since the Chinese detonation.

2. India can proceed with a number of the steps which are prerequisites to a weapons program without making a firm decision to develop nuclear weapons. It is probably now producing small quantities of plutonium metal, which could be used in the planned reactor program but also would be needed in a weapons program. Its atomic energy organization and its military establishment are big enough to absorb such activities as development of weapons designs and the necessary electronics. It could delay its final decision on the making of weapons for about a year, and could still have its first weapon at about the same time as if such a decision were made now. There is some evidence that the Indian Government has decided to proceed with work preliminary to a weapons program, and we believe this is the course which it will follow during the next year or so.

3. Indian policy over the longer run will depend on a number of factors. Important considerations will include the pace and scope of the Chinese program, the nature of Chinese policy, and the impact which the Indians consider that China's actions have on India's prestige and political position. If the Chinese carry out a vigorous test program and appear to be moving successfully toward an operational weapons capability, and if they continue their truculent foreign policy, the pressures within India for a weapons program will grow stronger. The Indian Government will continue to seek international agreement on nonproliferation and, more importantly, on arms control in order to reduce the Chinese threat. It is not optimistic that such agreements can be reached soon, if at all, and meanwhile its policy decisions will be influenced by its prospects for obtaining assurances of protection from the US, the USSR, and the UK, and the degree of confidence which it places in any such assurances.

4. The Indian Government is concerned with the cost of a nuclear weapons program and of an adequate delivery system. However, we do not believe costs will be the decisive element in India's decision. India has increased its annual defense budget fourfold—to nearly $2 billion—in the last eight years, and, in the course of the next several years, could undertake a modest weapons program and probably acquire a more advanced aircraft delivery system with only a moderate increase in its defense budget. India might indeed, during the next

decade, be able to acquire, at an acceptable cost, a missile delivery system suitable to carry the warheads it could manufacture. The Indians regard their country as a potential if not actual great power, and when faced with disputes in the past their policy has been to build up their military strength.

5. We cannot estimate with confidence how the various internal and external factors will interact to determine India's ultimate course. However, we believe that unless the Indian Government considers that it has international guarantees which adequately protect its security, the chances are better than even that within the next several years India will decide to develop nuclear weapons.

---

91.   Telegram From the Embassy in India to the Department of State[1]

New Delhi, March 5, 1965, 9 p.m.

2504. Governor Harriman called on Prime Minister Shastri evening March 4. Greene, L.K. Jha and MEA note-takers also present.[2]

Harriman conveyed cordial greetings from President to PM and expressed gratification that Prime Minister will be visiting President June 1 and 2[3] and assured him of warm welcome.

Shastri expressed pleasure at prospect. Harriman outlined progressive nature of President's domestic program with benefit to people and strength of U.S. economy. In response direct question by Jha on whether President was so preoccupied with domestic program he was not as concerned with foreign affairs, Harriman reassured him that although President had concentrated on getting his domestic program started in Congress, his attention to and concern for international issues has high priority.

---

[1] Source: National Archives and Records Administration, RG 59, Central Files 1964–66, POL 15–1 INDIA. Secret; Limdis. Repeated to Moscow and Saigon.

[2] Under Secretary Harriman visited India March 3–7 following visits to Israel and Afghanistan and prior to attending a Far Eastern Chiefs of Mission conference in Manila. Deputy Chief of Mission Joseph N. Greene hosted the Harriman mission until Bowles returned from another commitment on March 6. In telegram 926 to Karachi, February 25, the Embassy was informed that the Department did not object to having the Pakistan Government draw the conclusion that Harriman's failure to stop in Pakistan was related to Ayub's forthcoming visit to Peking. (Ibid., POL 7 PAK)

[3] Bowles was instructed on January 12 to extend an invitation from President Johnson to Prime Minister Shastri to visit Washington. (Telegram 1387 to New Delhi; ibid., POL 7 INDIA)

Harriman said one of President's major concerns is to protect against proliferation of nuclear weapons, and he asked for Shastri's assistance to this end. Shastri's position is admired and problems of Indian security are understood in Washington. U.S. has been glad to share with Shastri all information it has about Chinese capabilities and hopes Shastri will let us know if there is any further information he would like to have. Governor Harriman alluded to President's October 18 statement, emphasizing our determination to reassure Asian nations who may be subject to blackmail.[4]

Shastri agreed non-proliferation of vital importance and said major nuclear powers must figure out how to assure it. He said India is not going to make nuclear weapons, and this makes it most important for GOI to figure out how to assure India's defenses if India subject to nuclear threat, although India cannot join military pact.

Harriman recalled that at the time negotiation of partial test ban treaty, Khrushchev would not discuss non-proliferation agreement but had wanted universal commitment to test ban treaty and indicated desire isolate China. (Shastri concurred in this.) U.S. would like to proceed to comprehensive test ban agreement, but Soviets not yet willing to give necessary inspection. In this connection, we hope for resumption ENDC meetings in April and that GOI will agree, but Soviets have not responded to this suggestion.

Harriman expressed USG willingness discuss India's nuclear security problem at any time GOI wished to raise it, and asked about Shastri's talk with Wilson which it had been reported dealt with shield or umbrella. Shastri said he had had to deny public reports that he had asked Wilson for any such thing; he had told Wilson it was all right with him if Wilson discussed matter with President Johnson but it would be unwise for India, as only one of the non-nuclear powers, to seek a shield for itself alone. Thus the problem is for present nuclear powers to devise reassurances to all non-nuclear states against Chinese threat.

In reply to question, Shastri said he had no precise formula for accomplishing this; perhaps reassurance could take the form of joint statement that any threat from any nuclear power would be met, that there should be no further proliferation and that test ban should be total. He thought there might be other ways, and Governor Harriman invited him to let us have any ideas he had and in any event to help assure non-proliferation now.

---

[4] Rusk sent Harriman instructions for his and Bowles' discussion with Shastri of Indian nuclear security in telegram 840 to Tel Aviv, February 27. (Ibid., POL 7 US/HARRIMAN; also available on the Internet, National Security Archive (www.gwu.edu/~nsarchive), Electronic Briefing Book No. 6, "India and Pakistan—On the Nuclear Threshold," Document 7)

In reply query, Harriman said we have no indications of change in Soviet policy on disarmament since Khrushchev's ouster. We hope, and believe new Soviet leaders do too, that bilateral US-Soviet dialogue will continue. In this connection it would be most helpful to get from Shastri when he comes to Washington the information he obtained in Moscow on Soviet thinking on these matters. Shastri agreed.

Shastri asked what indications we have of ChiCom intentions regarding India. Harriman said we have nothing specific although ChiComs are generally more aggressive as they try to take from Moscow leadership of international Communist movement. They appear determined to support liberation movements and guerrilla actions rather than open warfare at present time. Shastri said he did not anticipate ChiCom atttack on India in immediate future but there has been build up and logistic improvement in border areas.

Jha interjected that India is still weak in the air and Shastri said he would also look forward to talking to the President about U.S. military assistance. He thought our help in aircraft had not been coming along as scheduled;[5] Jha corrected this to note that agreement has not yet been reached. In reply to query, Shastri said Soviets had not been fully coming through either. He and Jha said MIG production project is, however, going ahead.

Shastri turned to Southeast Asia, noting that discussions in Washington would have to be in light of circumstances at the time. Harriman recapitulated U.S. White Paper[6] and stressed our hope escalation by North Vietnam would stop but equally our determination to stay with the job until North Vietnam lays off interference in South Vietnam. He stressed our conviction there is nothing to talk about at a conference until they do. He urged Shastri to get our latest views on this question just before he goes to Moscow, stressed we consider De Gaulle's support of Soviet call for conference as unhelpful and hoped Shastri would not join with Soviets in that approach. Shastri indicated he understood.

In answer query, Shastri thought Kosygin had gone to Hanoi at least to offset ChiCom influence and possibly to seek a solution. He thought new Soviet leaders want to exercise moderating influence in SEA, where disillusionment with ChiComs is spreading, even including Ne Win but excluding Sukarno.

---

[5] Indian Army Chief of Staff General Chadhury reinforced this point in a conversation with Harriman on March 6, expressing the hope that the United States would agree to supply India with F-5A fighters. (Memorandum of conversation, March 6; National Archives and Records Administration, RG 59, NEA Files: Lot 67 D 410, New Delhi)

[6] Reference is to the report issued by the Department of State on February 27, 1965, entitled *Aggression From the North: The Record of North Viet-Nam's Campaign To Conquer South Viet-Nam*. The report, without its attached photographs and appendixes, is printed in Department of State *Bulletin*, March 22, 1965, pp. 404–427.

Shastri also anticipated discussing with President India's economic affairs. Harriman noted there has been good progress but India's needs will doubtless continue and increased investment both public and private, foreign and domestic, will be important. He expressed certainty GOI could get more foreign private investment with a little more understanding of the requirements of American businessmen regarding the investment climate; important element in this is U.S. businessman's reluctance to let government, any government, control his investments. He added he was heartened in these respects by Prime Minister's statement in Parliament March 2 (Embtel 2452).[7]

Shastri and Jha said that foreign private collaboration with domestic Indian private sector always welcome and point Governor had raised only relevant in respect of collaboration in public sector. Shastri said visiting American businessmen had recently expressed to him willingness to sell their equity to Indian public after say ten years.

Referring to his recent visit to Israel, Harriman described importance Israelis attach to water resources, akin to protecting national territory itself, and urged Shastri to keep an eye on outrageous and spiteful Arab diversion projects.

In brief reference to UAR, Harriman noted Nasser and Ben Bella are fishing for trouble, e.g., by passing Soviet equipment to rebels in Congo. Shastri said he thought Nasser has "succumbed to pressure" and seemed disenchanted with him.

In leaving, Harriman expressed confidence in Shastri's leadership and in expanding cooperation between our two countries.[8]

Bowles

---

[7] Telegram 2452 from New Delhi, March 3, reported that in a debate in the Lok Sabha, Shastri stated that, in general, majority Indian share-holding would be required in most businesses established with foreign participation, but the Indian Government would allow majority foreign share-holding in selected cases where there was a lack of either local technical knowledge or adequate foreign exchange. (National Archives and Records Administration, RG 59, Central Files 1964–66, POL 15–1 INDIA)

[8] Harriman's meeting with Finance Minister Krishnamachari on March 4 was reported in telegram 2482 from New Delhi, March 4. (Ibid., POL 7 US/HARRIMAN) On March 5 Harriman met in the morning with Foreign Secretary C.S. Jha and Commonwealth Secretary Rajeshwar Dayal. That conversation was reported in telegram 2511 from New Delhi, March 6. (Ibid., POL 1 INDIA–US) On the evening of March 5 Harriman met with Swaran Singh, who became Minister of External Affairs in July 1964. In contrast to his earlier meeting with Jha and Dayal, Harriman's conversation with Singh, which ranged over such issues as nuclear policy, the Arab-Israeli conflict, the Congo, and Southeast Asia, was reported to have included a number of sharp exchanges. (Telegram 2512 from New Delhi, March 6; ibid., POL 7 US/HARRIMAN)

92. Telegram From the Embassy in the Philippines to the Department of State[1]

Manila, March 7, 1965, 10 p.m.

1641. For the President and SecState from Harriman. Following is summary of major impressions gained in 3-1/2 days concentrated discussions.[2]

I have visited India four times in the last six years, the last time in 1962 in connection with India's emergency arms needs.

I feel today quite a new attitude towards US and the world situation reflected by Indian officials as well as press. I almost felt I was in a different country. With one exception, discussions with Indian Ministers and officials were relaxed and frank with full agreement on such matters as aggressive intents of Red China, need to prevent Reds' take-over in South Vietnam and SEA, willingness to consider objectively our policies and work with us for common objectives in other areas of world. They show greater confidence in their ability to solve India's economic problems with increased production in agriculture and industry and have greater understanding of need to develop private sector by both domestic and foreign investment, although not yet taking all necessary actions.

On other hand, Indians still are over-hopeful of Soviet Union's good intents, fear effects our tougher attitude toward Soviets, and are concerned that our policies toward Hanoi will bring Moscow and Peiping together again. They want to continue play non-aligned role although they are considerably disillusioned with Sukarno and Nasser.

They want to work with us on nuclear controls but don't want to spoil their non-aligned image by bilateral security arrangements. They show a more pragmatic and less doctrinaire approach to political and economic matters, but are somewhat held in check by loyalty to interpretations of Nehru's principles and purposes.

I had the feeling that I could talk freely with them without fear of being misunderstood and that we could reach understandings on a much broader area. They are, of course, still suspicious and fearful of some of our policies and methods, i.e., that we will fail to take advantage of what they consider Moscow's willingness to come to agreements on

---

[1] Source: National Archives and Records Administration, RG 59, Central Files 1964–66, POL 7 US/HARRIMAN. Secret; Priority; Exdis. Repeated to New Delhi and passed to the White House.

[2] Harriman subsequently submitted a report on his trip to President Johnson, which included a 1-page summary of his visit to India. (Memorandum for the President, March 15; Johnson Library, National Security File, Country File, Israel, Harriman Israeli Mission (II))

nuclear and arms controls, political settlements in Europe, etc. and although they don't want us to leave South Vietnam before an effective agreement, they fear we may overly react against Hanoi and thereby bring Red China and Soviet Union into the conflict.

I feel our economic and military assistance is beginning to pay off, but if we don't continue, economy will not expand to breakthrough to self sufficiency, and military capability will not be sufficient to act as deterrent to Red Chinese aggression—first in Nepal and Bhutan and later Assam.

Ambassador's absence first two days gave me better opportunity to get to know country team. I was favorably impressed by all— political, economic, information and military, and by the coordination under Bowles' vigorous and spirited leadership. Gen. Johnson, who was with me in 1962 has excellent relations with Indian Military. Chief of Staff General Chadhury spoke highly of him and our cooperation in general. There is no doubt army has made good progress in every way during last two years but air force is dangerously weak. Indians are prepared to emphasize air requirements in next year's aid program requests and I hope we can fill them.

Indians are still stubborn over Kashmir settlement and relations with Pakistan are most unsatisfactory. Indo-Pak settlement is still number one problem and should have our continued attention in concert with British.

The one exception to my generally favorable reaction in talks with officials was with Swaran Singh, Minister External Affairs. I felt I was arguing with Krishna Menon again. Not that he is Communist-inclined but because he took critical attitude on most all our policies. Bowles tells me Swaran Singh has little influence and hopes he will be replaced. Bowles does his business with Prime Minister and capable Foreign Office officials, as well as other Ministers direct.

Press reaction to my visit was generally good with understanding editorials on our policies in Vietnam and fair reporting on my blunt statements.

Surveys show public have increasing respect for and confidence in US.

All in all, I am much more hopeful of India and feel we can expect her to play more effective role towards free world objectives.[3]

Blair

---

[3] McGeorge Bundy forwarded a copy of this telegram to President Johnson on March 10 with a covering note in which he made the following comment: "I think it is good and accurate. We all feel that between now and the Shastri visit we shall have to look hard at our policy toward India." (Ibid., Memos to the President, McGeorge Bundy, Vol. 9, 3/3/65–6/30/65)

93.   **Telegram From the Embassy in Pakistan to the Department of State[1]**

Karachi, March 16, 1965, 6 p.m.

1730. Embtel 1679.[2] Ayub's Communist China Visit.[3]

1. Emb evaluation of Ayub's visit to Communist China reaffirms our initial appraisal that on balance visit represents significant consolidation of Pak–ChiCom relationship and poses fundamental policy issues for US.

2. ChiComs once again outmaneuvered Paks and scored major propaganda victory both in Pakistan and internationally. Ayub's repeated expressions of admiration for and confidence in ChiCom leaders, identification of ChiCom achievements as providing model for other Afro-Asian countries, and enthusiastic references during trip to ChiCom desire for peace has created unfortunate image of close and increasingly amicable and cooperative Pak relationship with ChiComs in Afro-Asian context. Propagation of this image in Pakistan greatly abetted by Pak press play undoubtedly with general encouragement from GOP Ministry of Information. There is absence of any visible appreciation of problems which ChiCom aggressive challenge creates for US and other countries in FE and SEA. Moreover, joint communiqué[4] and Ayub's speeches sharpen growing contrast between private assurances and remarks by Ayub to Ambassador, and public stance not only of Bhutto and other Pak leaders but of Ayub himself.

3. Paks, however, have not come back empty-handed from visit. Their gains appear primarily psychological rather than tangible. Communiqué reference to threat to peace presented by Kashmir problem goes beyond previous Pak–ChiCom formulations in stressing urgency

---

[1] Source: National Archives and Records Administration, RG 59, Central Files 1964–66, POL 7 PAK. Secret. Repeated to New Delhi, Hong Kong, London, Moscow, and CINCMEAFSA and CINCPAC for POLADs.

[2] Telegram 1679 from Karachi, March 10, summarized the joint communiqué issued in Peking on March 7 by Bhutto and Chinese Foreign Minister Chen I. The Embassy reported that the communiqué reflected the closer ties developing between the two countries. (Ibid.)

[3] Ayub paid a State visit to China March 2–9. He was accompanied by Foreign Minister Bhutto.

[4] A copy of the joint communiqué issued on March 7 is attached to a March 9 memorandum to Talbot from Turner Cameron assessing the significance of the Ayub visit to China. (National Archives and Records Administration, RG 59, Central Files 1964–66, POL 7 PAK) Komer commented on Cameron's critical assessment in a March 20 memorandum to Bundy: "State is finally getting fed up with our Pak friends. This is a useful precursor to what I think is an essential showdown with him here in April." (Johnson Library, National Security File, Country File, Pakistan, Vol. III, 12/64–7/65)

of problem although there no indication of more specific ChiCom commitment of support to Paks.

Secondly, Ayub has probably enhanced both his domestic image and international stature as leading Afro-Asian voice who able and willing to act independently of Western influences and who important enough to merit top-level treatment by ChiComs. Perhaps most vital to Paks, visit tended to place new pressures on India by emphasizing solidity of Pak–ChiCom ties. To achieve these objectives, Pak apparently prepared to pay price of accepting ChiCom formulations on several acute international issues and to bury their differences over approach to A–A conf.

4. Greatest potential risk to Paks lies in impact of visit on US–Pak relations. FonMin Shoaib clearly recognized this danger in conversation with me March 10 (Embtel 1726).[5] Ayub may have felt that as long as he steered clear of sensitive Vietnam issue he could avoid stirring up US. Another consideration was undoubtedly MFA estimate that US is unprepared exert strong pressure on GOP to limit Pak–ChiCom relationship through restriction of economic and military aid programs.

5. As Ayub visit to US draws closer, we must therefore face the fundamental issue of how far we are prepared to support Pakistan in the face of some policies running counter to our interests. I will be submitting in the near future my recommendations for Ayub visit and our posture during interval preceding visit. To set the stage, I believe that it is essential to shake Pakistani confidence that continued full US support can be taken for granted, irrespective of GOP international posturing. We wish to bring Ayub to Washington genuinely concerned about the future of US-Pakistani ties. I have already started this process in my talks with Shoaib and intend to continue to plant seeds of misgiving. However, I strongly urge against any public US Govt remonstrations. These would only provoke a defensive reaction making it more difficult for Ayub to climb back from the limb.

McConaughy

---

[5] Dated March 15. (National Archives and Records Administration, RG 59, Central Files 1964–66, POL 7 PAK)

94.   National Intelligence Estimate[1]

NIE 32–65   Washington, March 24, 1965.

THE PROSPECTS FOR PAKISTAN

The Problem

To assess the situation in Pakistan, and estimate developments over the next few years.

Conclusions

A. President Ayub is almost certain to retain his dominant position for the foreseeable future. Fairly effective economic management, if accompanied by continued large-scale foreign aid, probably would permit Pakistan to maintain its impressive annual GNP growth of five percent or so for the next two or three years at least. This will nevertheless leave Pakistan beset with numerous economic problems. (Paras. 1–15)

B. Tensions between Pakistan and India are likely to increase in the next few years over the issues of Kashmir, communal violence, and refugees. Nevertheless, we think the leaders of both countries will be able to prevent major hostilities. (Paras. 18–20)

C. Ayub sees little chance of persuading the US to alter its policies toward India and is, therefore, probably unwilling to change the basic direction of his foreign policies. Despite the growing divergence of US and Pakistani policies in Asia, Ayub probably believes that the US, because of its many interests in Pakistan, will continue to supply it with military and economic assistance. The initial Pakistani response to a direct US threat to reduce military and/or economic aid unless Pakistan modified its relations with China would probably be reciprocal threats against the alliances and the US special facilities. Nevertheless, if Ayub were convinced that the US really intended to reduce its support of Pakistan substantially, there is a better than even chance that he would mute though not abandon his China policy—at least until he could develop adequate alternative sources for US aid. (Paras. 23–28)

D. Ayub probably now regards a working relationship with Communist China as one of the key elements in Pakistan's security against

---

[1] Source: Central Intelligence Agency, Job 79–R01012A, ODDI Registry of NIE and SNIE Files. Secret; Controlled Dissem. According to a note on the cover sheet, the estimate was prepared by the Central Intelligence Agency and the intelligence organizations of the Departments of State and Defense and NSA. All the members of the U.S. Intelligence Board concurred in the estimate on March 24 except the representatives of the Atomic Energy Commission and the Federal Bureau of Investigation, who abstained because the subject was outside their jurisdiction.

India. Ayub will continue his recent efforts to improve relations with the Afro-Asian states, keeping in line with the mainstream of Afro-Asian views on most issues—a policy which has great political appeal within Pakistan. He will also seek better relations with the USSR as a supplement to the main lines of his foreign policy. (Paras. 21–22, 29, 31)

[Here follows the 14-page Discussion section of the estimate.]

95. Memorandum From Robert Komer of the National Security Council Staff to President Johnson[1]

Washington, April 2, 1965.

Foreign Minister Bhutto's latest effusion on Pakistan/Chicom relations is a harbinger of the line you'll get from Ayub on 26 April (see attached).[2] Bhutto had the gall to say publicly there's no inconsistency in Pakistan being friends with both the US and Chicoms, since both are "peace-loving" states. Nor do we like Bhutto's remark that US aid to India after the 1962 Chicom attack "shattered" the whole concept of alliances with the US (SEATO and CENTO). These alliances were never at any time aimed against India (as the Paks well know, because they've been trying for the last 10 years to get them changed).

In essence, the Paks seem to have arrived at the conclusion they can have their cake and eat it too. Actually, Pakistan is being a lot more friendly to Peiping than to Washington, despite the fact that we still pay all the bills (about $450 million in FY 64).

We're getting back quiet word that this casual equating of the US and Chicoms goes down like a lead balloon here. We're also making known our slight annoyance that when Rusk goes all the way to Tehran for the CENTO ministerial meeting next week Ayub and Bhutto go to *Moscow* instead of meeting with their allies. This, of course, after Ayub's recent well-publicized trip to Peiping.

I'm still convinced that Ayub knows at heart he can't do without us, but is going to play the Chicoms off against India (and us) so long as he thinks he can get away with it. Our best Pak friend, Finance

---

[1] Source: Johnson Library, National Security File, Country File, Pakistan, Ayub Khan Visit, 4/65. Secret.
[2] The attachment was telegram 1840 from Karachi, March 29, which reported on a press conference held by Foreign Minister Bhutto. (Ibid.)

Minister Shoaib, says flatly that Aziz Ahmed (ex-Ambassador here) keeps telling Ayub that the Pak accommodation with Peiping can be carried much further *without jeopardizing the flow of US aid.*

So the real problem is how to get across to Ayub that he can't cozy up to our Chicom enemies and pursue an anti-US line on most issues of concern to us (Vietnam, Malaysia), while still getting the second largest chunk of US aid. Unless he pulls back, present trends will carry Pakistan beyond the point of no return, and then Congress may not even allow us to provide $400–500 million per year. At that point we'll lose our crucial intelligence facility at Peshawar to boot.

We've failed so far to get through to Ayub along these lines, partly because he's surrounded by people who tell him we're only bluffing. Thus his visit here provides our best opportunity (and perhaps our last). And only the President of the US can say such things to Ayub in a credible way.[3]

R. W. Komer

---

[3] McGeorge Bundy passed Komer's memorandum to the President under cover of a memorandum in which he stated that he agreed with Komer. He added that "we ought to begin to blow the whistle on him" and agreed that the best time to do so would be during Ayub's scheduled visit to Washington. (Ibid., Memos to the President, McGeorge Bundy, Vol. 9, March–April 14, 1965)

---

96.   Telegram From the Embassy in Pakistan to the Department of State[1]

Karachi, April 4, 1965, 7 p.m.

1894. Re: Deptel 1072.[2] Conversation with President Ayub.

1. I met for one hour with Ayub early evening April 1 in Karachi. Appointment made as result brief private chat I had with him at morn-

---

[1] Source: National Archives and Records Administration, RG 59, Central Files 1964–66, POL 15–1 PAK. Secret; Limdis.

[2] Telegram 1072 to Karachi, March 30, contained an overview of U.S. policy toward the Soviet Union for McConaughy's use in his discussion with Ayub prior to Ayub's trip to Moscow. Ayub was scheduled to make a State visit to the Soviet Union April 3–11. The Department instructed McConaughy to express the surprise felt in Washington at the timing of Ayub's trip, which coincided with the CENTO Ministerial Meeting in Tehran April 7–8. Since Bhutto was planning to accompany Ayub to Moscow, Pakistan would not be represented at the CENTO meeting at the Foreign Minister level. (Ibid.)

ing ceremony, after FonOff had attempted to frustrate projected appointment, apparently without President's knowledge. Meeting took place on veranda President's house in outwardly relaxed and personally friendly atmosphere, with no other person present.

2. I spelled out our views on current Soviet foreign policy orientation and tactics in line reftel. President manifested unusual interest in our assessment and jotted down principal points. Said he would find it useful in making his own estimate after his Moscow visit. Promised to give us his corresponding evaluation after his return. He spoke as an ally working in close concert with US. He stated his belief that "Soviet menace far greater than Chinese" and reiterated his conviction that Soviet aspiration was undiminished to reach warm water at Arabian Sea at Karachi as well as through Caspian to Eastern Mediterranean and Persian Gulf.

3. I had a plausible opening at this point to seek reassurance on continuation our facilities at Peshawar (a matter which Soviets are certain to press) but they [he?] made no mention of subject, and I decided not to broach it either.

4. I turned conversation to Sino-Pak affairs, expressing concern at rapidly developing course of relations. I said it was my estimate that the downhill momentum was getting close to roller coaster velocity and that I would be lacking in candor if I did not tell him that the many gestures of Pakistan in the direction of Communist China at this juncture were coming under the serious scrutiny of USG. I cited various indications of a relationship of special closeness between GOP and CPR which have been played out before a national and world audience here in recent weeks following his visit to Communist China with its various unfortunate implications and repercussions. I told him that I had received a circumstantial but not entirely adequate explanation from FonOff Addl Sec Agha Shahi of the joint communiqué.

5. Ayub said earnestly that I was magnifying unduly the extent and significance of Pak gestures toward Communist China. His only purpose in his limited dealings with CPR was to pursue policy of good neighborly relations, and to preserve peace in Asia. Present explosive situation might lead to outbreak of hostilities involving Communist China, which would create a situation very dangerous for security of Pakistan as well as other countries. His object was merely to seek to abate tensions, which was in interest of all. He then gave me following points on his own talks with Chou En-lai, Chen Yi and other top Chinese leaders.

A. Joint communiqué:

Joint communiqués were the bane of his existence when he made foreign visits. They consumed an inordinate amount of time and energy, resulted in endless haggling, created trouble and misunderstanding.

He said they were not binding and therefore they did not really mean anything anyway and we should not take the verbiage too seriously. He wished they could be abolished. He said certain gestures of accommodation had to be made by a visitor to the host government, especially when the reception was so stirring as in his case. He said that Vietnam was the most significant item that had come up in the joint communiqué discussions and he reminded me that he had held a firm line against the Chinese on this, resulting in an impasse and a conspicuous omission of any reference to Vietnam.

B. Vietnam:

Ayub said the Chinese gave him their standard version of the situation and issues in Vietnam, arguing that the US had prevented a plebiscite in Vietnam, and in many ways had violated the letter and spirit of 1954 Geneva Accords. They described US as direct successor of French as colonialist exploiters of Vietnam and portrayed insurgency of Viet Cong as essentially a nationalist, internally-based, patriotic uprising of South Vietnamese people against neo-colonialists and their puppets. Asserted war was continuation of "liberation struggle" which had begun against the French. Ayub said he did obtain an important admission from the ChiComs as a result of his probing questions, that they had "formerly" supplied arms and other military weapons to North Vietnam for use of Viet Cong. But ChiComs denied that they were currently extending support, alleging that it was now unnecessary in view of increased capability of Viet Cong themselves. In response to further Ayub questions about role of North Vietnam, ChiComs said they "supposed" North Vietnamese were "helping" Viet Cong to some extent. Ayub said that ChiComs were absolutely adamant in resisting his urging that they agree to third party recommendations for a conference on Vietnam without pre-conditions. They were uncompromising in their demands for full US withdrawal before any consideration given to conference possibility. Ayub said he told them that of course Americans could never agree to this and he could not associate himself with any such extreme ChiCom demand. Ayub also told me that ChiComs were explicit in their threat to enter the fray openly and directly if widened US participation made it necessary. Ayub saw no prospect for narrowing the gulf and expressed deep pessimism as to the prospects. He did not believe the ChiComs would even consider accepting a US requirement for prior withdrawal of outside Communist support of Viet Cong and he said the dilemma appeared insoluble.

C. GRC, Taiwan and two Chinas:

Ayub said Chinese took soft tactical line in response to his statement of US position as to GRC and Taiwan as he understood it. Apparently he stated the position in terms fairly sympathetic to US, putting it to ChiComs that US had assumed solemn defense obligations to GRC which no one could expect us to abrogate. He said the ChiComs replied that they understood difficulty for US which was inherent in its mutual defense obligations and that they were in no hurry about taking control of Taiwan. They intimated to Ayub that a long transition period probably of indefinite duration could be arranged if US would only accept general principle that Taiwan was part of China and that established Chinese Government on Mainland was entitled to exercise sovereignty over Taiwan. On this principle they would never yield. Ayub said ChiComs assured him that they had nothing against us other than Vietnam and Taiwan issues.

D. SEATO and CENTO:

Ayub told me that he had informed ChiComs at outset that GOP could not let down its allies with whom it was aligned and that his government expected to remain in both SEATO and CENTO. He said he told Chinese that since these pacts were entirely defensive and could not be invoked ("would be non-fructifying" was the phrase he used) in the absense of aggression, the Chinese had nothing to worry about. Ayub said that the Chinese, while perhaps not liking this too much, did not argue the point and tacitly accepted his position.

E. US presence in Asia:

Ayub told me that while he thought he had acted consistently with his obligations in presenting the foregoing points, the most significant act he had performed in US behalf was his statement in his speech in Shanghai that while China had a role in Asia which the US should recognize and accept, the US also had a role and responsibilities in Asia which China should recognize and accept. Ayub said that it was most difficult to take this position before a vast throng of Chinese, especially after the massive welcome he had received. But he thought it needed to be done and he had done it. He did not think any other visiting Chief of State could or would have done it under similar circumstances. The Chinese did not like this statement but it is now on the record and personally heard by a great Chinese audience. He hoped it would do some good.

F. Essential character of ChiCom revolution:

Ayub stated it was Pak firm conviction that ChiCom revolution is primarily nationalistic and internal. He was impressed with the profound absorption of the ChiComs with their own domestic problems and progress. He thought they were primarily interested in social and economic reforms at home and the prosecution of their economic development programs. He felt they had accomplished a lot already but they obviously had much more to do in the welfare and development field and he was inclined to credit the view that their ambitious goals at home consume most of their energies leaving little interest in foreign adventurism. He said the Chinese posture seems to him to be increasingly nationalistic. They are deeply aware of their national history before the advent of Communism and they frequently cite it. He said the Chinese told him that as part of their self-examination process they are continually reminding and admonishing themselves against the danger of the CPR itself falling into the error of "big nation chauvinism." They said their self-discipline saves them from this error. He quoted the Chinese leaders as saying that China throughout her history had suffered heavily from every involvement in foreign wars, and their leaders did not intend to be drawn into any more foreign wars which could be avoided.

G. ChiCom attitude toward Communist insurgency in other countries:

Ayub told me of a very significant and flagrantly contradictory position stated by ChiComs on above topic. Full import apparently not realized by Ayub. This enunciation by ChiComs was to effect they "were committed to assist, and would assist, 'national liberation' movements or uprising against oppressive governments all over the world—whether in Asia, Africa, or Latin America."

H. ChiCom attitude toward Ayub's US visit:

Ayub said he had told ChiComs that he had not any authorization to speak for US in Peiping and he, of course, would not presume to speak for the Chinese in Washington. He had then told them that his objective was to further the prospects for peace between the two countries and that if he could "lower the temperature" even [garble—a little?] in both Peiping and Washington he would have served in some modest way the cause of peace. He said the Chinese endorsed this point of view, telling him that they wanted the temperature lowered in both countries and wishing him well on his Washington visit.

6. I expressed appreciation for comprehensive rundown given me by the President, giving him full credit for not yielding to ChiComs on Vietnam question, and implying I considered his dismissal of joint communiqué as meaningless, to signify that visit had not actually changed established Pak position on any of questions mentioned in communiqué. I then said that while there was some reassurance in what he had told me as to posture he had assumed with ChiComs during his visit, other aspects of Pak relationship with ChiComs remained deeply disquieting. I did not see how he could be so charitable in his interpretation of ChiCom motivations and I assumed he could see the inconsistency and the irreconcilability of various postures assumed by ChiComs. I asked him to postulate for a moment the contingency of a strengthened pro-Chinese Communist organization in East Pakistan which GOP had taken steps to curb. I asked him if he did not agree with me that by the ChiComs' own declaration of policy, they would find it necessary to support and incite such a movement

against the GOP? Ayub conceded ChiCom support of such a subversive group would probably have been assumed.

7. Responding to my expressions of foreboding at the general trend of Pak–ChiCom relations, Ayub said with some fervor that relationship was strictly limited and did not undermine Pak internal security or Pak–US relationship. He said that if he had any desire or intention to enter into an entangling relationship with ChiComs he could easily have negotiated either open or secret agreements with them. He had done neither and there had been no agreements other than the innocuous cultural and economic ones which we knew about. He took issue with my anxiety that the Chinese already had a useful opening wedge for expanding their influence in this country. He thought that the strong Islamic faith of Pakistan was a certain bulwark against the penetration of Communist ideology. When I told him of the first hand evidence I saw on all hands that the press and people of Pakistan are assuming and accepting a more intimate association between Pakistan and Communist China as "the wave of the future," and are inferring that the US presence in Pakistan is in gradual retreat, he discounted such evidence by saying "a lot of our prominent people who should know better get wrong ideas" and by branding the entire Pakistan press and journalistic fraternity as unprincipled and irresponsible.

8. I wondered out loud if he exempted from the foregoing journalistic indictment Mr. Altaf Husain, the rabidly anti-American editor of *Dawn*, and outspoken advocate of a close Pakistani alignment with Communist China, whom he had just taken into his Cabinet as Minister of Industry. Ayub's reply was that he had taken Altaf Husain into his Cabinet only because of the acute lack of qualified Bengalis and the necessity for equal representation from East Pakistan in the Cabinet. He said that he would be able to control Altaf Husain as a member of his government whereas he could not control him as a newspaper editor. He had exacted an understanding from Altaf Husain and he thought I would see revised behavior from him as a Minister. He also thought that *Dawn*'s editorial policy would be less objectionable to US with Altaf Husain out of the picture.

9. Ayub said that unavoidably the American position in Pakistan and Pak–US relations had suffered some damage. "That is not your fault and it is not my fault." He seemed to feel that intermediate level policy makers in Washington had persuaded the American leadership of the merits of a policy of US military assistance to India. This policy was responsible for all the mischief. He spoke with the deepest rancor of unalterable Hindu rejection of Pakistan's right to exist. He predicted with fatalism the eventual outbreak of a clash between Pakistan and India. Pakistanis could not then accept the

assistance of US ground forces, even if offered, because Pakistanis would lose their self-respect (which was essential for national survival) if they did not fight their own battles. The Pakistanis would be overwhelmed and they would die, he said with mounting bitterness, but "every Pakistani would account for four Indians before he died." I endeavored to calm down such talk but he insisted that our support of India had emboldened the GOI to provocations beyond the danger point. He had been certain all along that there was no prospect of either China or India initiating a renewal of late 1962, and his recent talks in Peiping with the Chinese leaders had fully confirmed this estimate. The danger was between India and Pakistan, not between China and India. He knew the Indians had no intention of fighting, even if he was wrong about Chinese intentions. He accused the Indians of mounting a series of provocative incidents, citing the Indian pressure against the Dahagram enclave and "the increasing killings along the Kashmir cease fire line every day and every night." He said the Indian philosophy called for the expulsion of American presence and influence from the Sub-continent as soon as India could take care of Pakistan, and the US would see that its tooling up of the Indians would accelerate its own departure from this part of Asia. He pointed out that of the four large countries which come together in the northern part of the Sub-continent, Pakistan was the only one which naturally and logically welcomes American presence and American influence. Yet by taking the plunge in India, the US has deliberately alienated Pakistan and would in the end have nothing or less than nothing in return. He defined Indian known expansionist ambitions as extending from the Hindukush mountains in the west to Indo-China and Malaysia in the east. He predicted that the US would pay a heavy price in terms of its regional and global interests for feeding indirect expansionist ambitions. It was an American policy error of great magnitude, the full extent of which would be revealed only with the passage of time.

10. I told the President he knew the reasons we could not agree with him on the effects of our policy, and I did not go over that ground again. The President said the immediate bilateral and regional interests of Pakistan which the GOP considered vital to its national security and very existence would have to be reconciled with or worked into US global policy and global interests if the US wanted to preserve its position here. Pakistan could not accept a US position that the US global struggle against Communism must override everything else, if this meant making Pakistan a satellite of India. When I demurred at any suggestion that the US had any such thing in mind he said that he had been told by American official visitors that Pakistan's own security from India must be subordinated to global US interests, since "the US was in the business of fighting Communism."

Ayub said, "We would be willing if necessary to be a satellite of the US if we remained secure from India, but we can never accept a relationship which would expose us to being a satellite of India."

11. After regretting the use of the term satellite in any such context, I returned to the topic of fraternization with Red China. I recalled the President's speech in Urdu to the Pakistan Armed Forces he reviewed on March 23. I told him that standing before Pakistan Army and Air Force entirely equipped with American arms and equipment intended for defense against the Communist threat, he had gone out of his way to extol Communist China. He had expressed confidence on the basis of his recent visit that China was peace loving and that the Pak forces had nothing to fear from that quarter. That speech had been made on the [garble—very day?] that the Chinese Communists had openly threatened to start another Korea-type of intervention in Vietnam. I asked him what he expected the American people to make of such a speech. I recalled that almost every newspaper, in both news columns and editorials, is frequently full of adulation to Chinese Communist policy and acts. There is equally enthusiastic abuse of the US, including excoriation of US employment of routine police gasses which do no organic harm and which are identical with what the police of Pakistan are using every week. A point had been reached where even the chairman of the Pakistan Red Cross, Mr. Wajid Ali, that very morning in the presence of both of us had found it necessary to insert praise of Communist China in his speech at the annual meeting. I said some of his assurances sounded soothing but the American people do not know how to take them when they look at the events. I mentioned a rapid fire succession of visits to Pakistan by ChiCom VIP's and growing exploitation of Pakistan contacts by ChiCom leaders for propaganda, tactical and prestige purposes. I mentioned the return of Chen Yi for a 5-day visit and the hurriedly arranged and seemingly triumphal re-visit of Chou En-lai, scheduled to arrive the next day with great fanfare.

12. I said that even if the Executive branch of the USG should be willing to set aside some of its misgivings for the time being and try to defend before the US Congress the appropriations request necessary to carry forward US programs in Pakistan. I didn't know how effective explanation or rationalization of current GOP foreign policy could be made, especially in the shadow of the deepening crisis fomented by Communist China in Southeast Asia.

13. President Ayub paused before he replied he could see that things looked worse than they really were. He recognized that the problem would need to be discussed when he went to Washington.

14. We had a pleasant exchange on President's preferences as to use of his free time while in US. This will follow in separate message.

15. Comments and assessment of conversation will follow by telegram near future.

McConaughy

97. Telegram From the Department of State to Secretary of State Rusk in Tehran[1]

Washington, April 6, 1965, 7:55 p.m.

Tosec 13. For Secretary from Ball. At lunch today President took extremely strong stand on postponement of Ayub and Shastri visits. He feels that appearance of Ayub on April 26–27 and Shastri on June 2–3 would jeopardize passage foreign assistance legislation. Ayub's visit would focus attention on activities his Peiping and Moscow trips and recent unfortunate statements. Both would almost certainly feel compelled to make statements regarding Vietnamese problem that would cause trouble with press and in Congress.

Ayub does not return from Moscow until April 11 so we have few days in which to consider how to best handle situation. Talk today was of sending Harriman to Pakistan to see Ayub and having Bunker talk with Shastri late next week in order to arrange postponement both visits.

One difficulty is that President does not intend to delay Moro visit April 20–21 or visit of Wilson on April 15 and is still planning to invite Erhard again this spring. In addition Kenyatta has been asked to come in May and Park is also coming May 17–18.

One possibility would be to postpone Ayub visit first but let Shastri visit stand at least for the time being. We could simply tell Ayub quietly that in view of his recent visits to Peiping and Moscow a visit to Washington at the present time could result only in confusion and would seriously jeopardize Pak foreign aid. This has some risks but at the same time asking Ayub quietly to postpone his visit might provide useful shock treatment since indications are he is being regularly advised by Aziz Ahmed and Bhutto that he can push US further without seriously endangering his foreign aid.

---

[1] Source: Johnson Library, National Security File, Country File, India, Vol. IV, Cables, 12/64–6/65. Secret; Immediate; Nodis. Drafted and initialed by Acting Secretary Ball.

On the other hand it may be better if we are going to postpone Ayub to try to postpone Shastri also. Personally, I doubt it but both solutions have their problems.

I should greatly appreciate your advice as to what recommendation to make to the President. You may wish to have a private talk with Shoaib indicating the very real possibility that an Ayub visit at this time would not be healthy from the point of view of our aid program for Pakistan.[2]

Ball

---

[2] Rusk responded with a personal message for the President on April 8. He urged that any message to Ayub postponing his visit be deferred until after Ayub returned from the Soviet Union. Rusk stated that he planned to have a private talk with Shoaib and would discuss with him the difficulties posed by Ayub's impending visit to Washington. (Telegram Secto 20 from Tehran; National Archives and Records Administration, RG 59, Central Files 1964–66, POL 7 PAK) President Johnson accepted Rusk's recommendation. (Telegram Tosec 43 to Tehran, April 8; ibid.)

---

98.   **Telegram From Secretary of State Rusk to the Department of State**[1]

Tehran, April 8, 1965, 11 p.m.

Secto 32. Eyes only President and Ball from Secretary. I had a very frank and private discussion with Pakistan Finance Minister Shoaib this afternoon about general state of our relations. Will be reporting full details later. I did, as though on my own responsibility, explore with him fully the dangers and disadvantages of an Ayub visit at this time. I explained both the complications with regard to the final stages of foreign aid legislation and the understandable preoccupation we have with South Viet Nam. I told him quite frankly I thought this was a very poor time for such a visit because Ayub might become embroiled in controversies which he would not relish and to which he could by inadvertence contribute. Shoaib's first reaction was one of considerable concern, for all of the obvious reasons. When I asked him directly however at the end of the conversation what the effect would be in

---

[1] Source: National Archives and Records Administration, RG 59, Central Files 1964–66, POL 7 PAK. Secret; Immediate; Eyes Only; Nodis.

Pakistan if the visit were postponed, he said that "it would not be too serious if it were made clear to President Ayub that Shastri's visit was also being postponed." He added that of course it would be entirely appropriate to inform Shastri that Ayub visit was off.

I am not certain because of the very personal character of our conversation and the personal politics of Pakistan that Shoaib will report my conversation before Ayub returns to Pakistan. If he does, I am sure he will report it as expressions of my own concern rather than any decision already taken.

I still believe that it is very important not to seek out Ayub in the Soviet Union with a request for postponement for reason I have already expressed. I do believe it would be advisable for the President to have a personal report from me on my talk with Shoaib as well as a fresh assessment of domestic and international political factors before the final button is pushed on postponement. My own assessment from this vantage point is that the President's Hopkins speech[2] was a major contribution to international understanding of the American purpose in South Viet Nam.

Rusk

---

[2] Reference is to the speech President Johnson made at Johns Hopkins University on April 7 in which he expressed the readiness of the United States for unconditional discussions leading to a peaceful settlement in Vietnam. For text, see Department of State *Bulletin*, April 26, 1965, pp. 606–610.

---

99.   Telegram From the Department of State to the Embassy in India[1]

Washington, April 14, 1965, 10:02 p.m.

2155. For Ambassador from the Secretary. Because of the delicate and pressing situation in Viet Nam the President feels strongly that both the Ayub and Shastri visits should be postponed. The President was looking forward to a fruitful talk with Shastri but he thinks it likely that early in June he will be preoccupied with Southeast Asia as

---

[1] Source: National Archives and Records Administration, RG 59, Central Files 1964–66, POL 7 PAK. Secret; Immediate; Nodis. Drafted by Ball, cleared by McGeorge Bundy, and approved by Rusk. Repeated to Karachi.

well as with the legislative program that is likely to reach a crunch about that time. With these thoughts in mind he is reviewing his entire schedule to see how the load can be lightened. Thus he is planning to postpone a visit from Kenyatta as well as Ayub and Shastri.

In view of the fact that the Ayub visit is scheduled to take place in less than a fortnight the President is sending a letter to Ayub[2] that is being repeated to you. If you feel a Presidential letter to Shastri should follow up your initial approach such a letter can be sent.

I hope that you can approach Shastri in such a way as to lead him to feel that a postponement of his visit until fall is in the interests of India. In our view it would not be useful for him to come while the aid bill is pending in spite of the fact that the Indian attitude regarding South Viet Nam has been generally helpful. There are still substantial differences of emphasis between us regarding sensitive issues, including Southeast Asia, and Shastri would almost certainly find it necessary to make statements that could lead to adverse comment in the press and in Congress.

You should also be aware that continuing failure of India and Pakistan to resolve their differences has been picked up and referred to most critically in executive sessions of congressional committees.

I would appreciate it if you would coordinate your appointment with Shastri so that you and Ambassador McConaughy will be going in at approximately the same time. We are anxious to avoid having news of action in one capital reach the other before the appropriate approach has been made. You are of course at liberty to tell Shastri that we are suggesting to Ayub that his visit also be postponed.

Rusk

---

[2] See Document 100.

100. Telegram From the Department of State to the Embassy in Pakistan[1]

Washington, April 14, 1965, 10:35 a.m.

1145. For Ambassador McConaughy from Secretary. You should seek private appointment with Ayub soonest and deliver following message from President: [2]

"Dear Mr. President:

I need not tell you of the importance which the Government and the people of the United States have steadfastly attached to relationships between our two countries. These relationships have been good for both of us and strong enough to allow the frankest of discussions on matters where we do not share the same views.

It was for this reason that I have been looking forward to your visit to Washington so that we might profit from our confidence in each other to discuss frankly our common problems and to chart our courses together for the troublesome months and years that lie ahead.

The fact that you and I have both recently received unmistakably clear and strong mandates from our electorates to pursue our national and international goals has made this meeting seem even more opportune and desirable.

What I now propose, therefore, comes only after the most serious reflection during the past few days and with our common interests foremost in mind. I have in fact reluctantly come to the view that this month is not a good time for the two of us to meet in Washington.

Our foreign aid legislation is now before the Congress, and my years of political experience in Congress, as Vice President and President, have led me to the conclusion that your visit at this time would focus public attention on the differences between Pakistani and United States policy toward Communist China. This I fear might gravely affect

---

[1] Source: Johnson Library, National Security File, Head of State Correspondence File, Pakistan, Vol. I, Pres. Ayub Correspondence, 12/15/63–12/31/65. Secret; Immediate; Nodis. Drafted by Ball and Handley, cleared with McGeorge Bundy, and approved by Rusk. Repeated to New Delhi.

[2] Rusk sent an accompanying personal message to McConaughy explaining that there was no give in the President's decision to postpone Ayub's visit. He encouraged McConaughy to stress to Ayub that the mood of Congress was such that his presence in Washington would seriously jeopardize foreign assistance for Pakistan. McConaughy was authorized to tell Ayub that Shastri's visit was also being postponed. (Telegram 1143 to Karachi, April 14; National Archives and Records Administration, RG 59, Central Files 1964–66, POL 7 PAK)

our ability to assist your Government in the economic and defense programs on which you are embarked and would work against the shared interests of the United States and Pakistan.

I cannot overstate the full depth of American feeling about Communist China. The mounting number of American casualties in South Vietnam is having a profound effect upon American opinion. This is being felt in Congress just at the time when our foreign aid legislation is at the most sensitive point in the legislative cycle.

Under these circumstances I think it would be in the interests of both our countries and contribute to the assurance of close and mutually helpful relations between us if we could postpone our meeting until later this year—perhaps early in the fall.

Certainly there is much for us to talk about when we do meet. While some of our [*your?*] policies have caused concern to us, our mutual interests unquestionably outweigh our differences. For my part, I shall continue to seek the most friendly and constructive alliance relationship with you and your country.

I shall, therefore, look forward to a full, frank and friendly discussion, but I do think it can be more profitable in a few months than at the moment. I would appreciate your judgment on this matter and I would be guided by your thoughts as to how a postponement can best be worked out with a minimum of awkwardness on both sides."

Rusk

---

101.   Telegram From the White House to the Embassy in India[1]

Washington, April 15, 1965, 5:30 p.m.

CAP 65102. Eyes Only for Bowles from Bundy. President and all rest of us here can well understand your distress at Shastri postpone-

---

[1] Source: Johnson Library, National Security File, Country File, India, Exchanges with Bowles. Secret; Immediate. [*text not declassified*] Drafted by Komer. The fourth and fifth paragraphs of the telegram were revised by hand by Bundy. The final paragraph was revised and expanded by Komer.

ment,[2] but I can assure you that this decision taken with best interests India as well as US thoroughly in mind. It is not to be construed as merely a conditioned reflex to decision disinvite Ayub.

In point of fact USG, with Vietnam and host of other problems on its plate over next few months, and with aid bill having rocky passage through Congress, is in no position talk turkey with Shastri just now. Nor for that matter does Shastri seem from here to be as yet in any position to say much to us. So rather than have merely a polite get-together with neither party yet ready for constructive palaver, the President prefers that we both do our homework and get aid bill passed first.

You should know that President feels deeply a Shastri visit here could focus unwelcome attention on the fact that we're spending biggest single chunk of our aid money on an enterprise which isn't going anywhere fast. Add to this the risk of undue focus on the fact that our two largest clients don't seem able to live on the same continent with each other without constant bickering. Regardless of the causes, this doesn't go down well here.

It also makes the time most unpropitious for those here who feel that US interests dictate consideration of a package of major help for India in return for some quite far-reaching understandings with respect to: (a) non-proliferation; (b) more sensible economic policies; and (c) movement toward Pak/Indian reconciliation. As we see it, Indians are not ready to talk sensibly about this yet.

So larger interests, as well as immediate problems, argue for accepting any short term affront to Indian amour propre in the interest of a more productive visit later. Am sure you see this loud and clear.

Thus our chore at this point is to find ways and means of softening the blow. Very much will also depend on your own ability to say convincingly that postponement must not be read as any more than what it is—a feeling on the President's own part plus that of all his advisers that the time would simply be riper in the fall. In

---

[2] Bowles reacted to the instruction to inform Shastri that his visit to Washington was being postponed in a telegram for the President and the Secretary in which he emphasized the consequences he felt would follow. He wrote of the "profound shock and resentment which will be felt by Shastri personally and which will be reflected throughout GOI and in press if he is disinvited under these conditions." Given Ayub's recent dealings with China, Bowles could appreciate the reasons for postponing Ayub's visit, but he felt that if the objective was to be tough with Ayub there was all the more reason to encourage Shastri's visit. Canceling both visits, he concluded, would be viewed in India as appeasement of Pakistan and an affront to India. (Telegram 2920 from New Delhi, April 15; ibid., Memos to the President, McGeorge Bundy, Vol. 10, April 15–May 31, 1965)

short, the President says he respects your understanding of the Indians but wants you to respect his understanding of the Congress. Good luck.[3]

---

[3] Rusk reinforced this message with a personal cable to Bowles the same day emphasizing that it was important for Bowles to see Shastri with news of the postponement in coordination with McConaughy's approach to Ayub, lest the Indian Government receive the news indirectly. (Telegram 2161 to New Delhi, April 15; ibid.)

---

102.   Telegram From the Department of State to the Embassy in India[1]

Washington, April 15, 1965, 8:57 p.m.

2162. As indicated in immediately preceding instructions,[2] there follows Presidential message to Shastri which you may deliver in your discretion:

Dear Mr. Prime Minister:

You know how much I have been looking forward to your visit here as an opportunity for the two of us to share our thoughts on the efforts we are making to give our peoples a better life. As the date approaches, I have realized that circumstances have combined to deprive us of the atmosphere in which we could most profitably do this. The Viet-Nam crisis has focused the attentions of my Government, as I am sure it has yours, on immediate issues related to our security in the Far East. Ambassador Lodge will give you my views on this and I hope you will speak to him most frankly regarding yours.

Furthermore, the future of the United States aid program has been called into question in the Congress, and the coming weeks promise to be ones of intense debate. In these circumstances the long-term interests of our two countries, and our ability to pursue them jointly,

---

[1] Source: Johnson Library, National Security File, Country File, India, Vol. IV, Cables, 12/64–6/65. Secret; Flash; Nodis. Drafted by Schneider; cleared by Handley, Rusk (substance), and McGeorge Bundy; and approved by Blaine C. Tueller (S/S). Repeated to Karachi.

[2] See footnote 3, Document 101.

would be better served in my judgment if you came in the fall after the Congress has adjourned than in June. I have, therefore, reluctantly come to the conclusion that the next month or two would not be right time for us to exchange thoughts on our long-range plans and aspirations. I hope that you will not find it too inconvenient to defer your visit here until early this fall.

Our countries have long been closely associated in many common endeavors. In this association I believe we have developed the confidence in each other which allows me to suggest a new time for us to meet.

With warm regards.

Sincerely, Lyndon B. Johnson

Rusk

103.   Telegram From the Embassy Office in Pakistan to the Department of State[1]

Rawalpindi, April 15, 1965.

37. For the Secretary from McConaughy. Deptel 1143 to Karachi.[2] I had 50-minute meeting with President Ayub in Rawalpindi beginning at 6:30 this evening. FonSec Aziz Ahmed only other person present. I set forth President's reasons for suggesting postponement of visit in non-abrasive terms, indicating his belief that such action was in best interests of Pakistan. I informed Ayub that corresponding postponement suggestion being made to Shastri. I presented President's letter of April 14[3] which President read carefully in my presence.

I affirmed that suggestion for postponement was not a cancellation and that President would want visit rescheduled when time was opportune.

President took the postponement suggestions well and responded in amicable vain, although he seemed slightly taken aback. He did not

[1] Source: National Archives and Records Administration, RG 59, Central Files 1964–66, POL 7 PAK. Secret; Immediate; Nodis. Repeated to Karachi and New Delhi. No time of transmission is on the telegram; it was received at 4:06 p.m.
[2] See footnote 2, Document 100.
[3] See Document 100.

give any evidence of having had any forewarning from Shoaib or any other source.

President said that he would never wish to take any action which might embarrass the President or complicate his grave problems in this serious hour. He would want to accommodate to any viewpoint of the President on the projected visit and he could understand how criticism could be arising in the Congress and with the US public. He stated that of course he would agree to the postponement of the visit. At the same time he wanted to express his disappointment that he would not have the opportunity of consulting and exchanging views with the President his assessment of the Chinese Communist and Soviet attitudes toward the United States, especially in relation to Southeast Asia, based on his recent visits.

President good-naturally reminded me that he had not suggested April date for visit, and that this date had been put to him as the time most convenient to President Johnson. He said he had then adjusted his tight schedule with some difficulty to meet what he understood were the preferences of the USG. However, he recognized that circumstances could change and he knew that the current problems of the United States administration with Congress as well as in other respects had to be reckoned with.

While President's acceptance of postponement was unconditional he clearly attached considerable weight to the parallel postponement suggestion to Shastri. This was saving element in our presentation. Prompted somewhat by Aziz Ahmed, he said that he would like for announcement of postponement his visit to be timed to coincide with release of news of Shastri postponement.

He suggested that I work with FonSec Aziz Ahmed on phraseology of postponement announcement, which he thought might be issued jointly. He did not seem unduly concerned about explanation of postponement, indicating only that he thought it could be plausibly attributed to heavy preoccupations of President Johnson with Southeast Asia and other issues, both foreign and domestic. He would like announcement to emphasize that action was more postponement, with hope expressed that meeting could take place later in 1965.[4]

President said that he had tried to do all he could in general cause, both in Peking and Moscow. While his success was limited, he believed

---

[4] President Johnson issued a statement on April 16 from Johnson City, Texas, indicating that because of the situation in Vietnam and the press of business in Congress he had to reduce his schedule and postpone a number of visits to Washington by foreign leaders. He noted that President Ayub and Prime Minister Shastri had graciously agreed to postpone their visits. (Telegram 1158 to Karachi, April 16; National Archives and Records Administration, RG 59, Central Files 1964–66, POL 7 INDIA)

he had made a reasonably effective exposition of positions opposed to the Communists, and had gained a fairly revealing insight into Chinese and Soviet attitudes and approaches to current critical issues, which could be of some background value to US.[5]

FonSec Aziz Ahmed is to take up draft postponement announcement with me as soon as word is received that Shastri also has agreed to postponement. I would welcome Department's proposed text of announcement by return cable.

Brief general conversation with Ayub unrelated to foregoing will be reported separately tomorrow.[6]

McConaughy

---

[5] McConaughy reported in more detail about Ayub's discussion of his trip to the Soviet Union in telegram 1970 from Karachi, April 17. (Ibid., POL 7 PAK)

[6] McConaughy also reported that during his April 15 conversation with Ayub, he had expressed strong concern over the succession of inflammatory incidents which had recently been exacerbating relations between Pakistan and India. He pointed in particular to the fighting which had developed in the Rann of Kutch. Ayub assured him that Pakistani soldiers had not gone beyond and did not intend to go beyond their traditional patrol routes in the disputed area. (Telegram 1971 from Karachi, April 18; ibid., POL 32–1 INDIA–PAK)

---

104.   Telgram From the Embassy in India to the Department of State[1]

New Delhi, April 16, 1965, 0812Z.

2932. Deptels 2161,[2] 2165,[3] Rawalpindi's 37[4] to Dept. Since PriMin Shastri is out of town until Sunday evening I delivered President's

---

[1] Source: National Archives and Records Administration, RG 59, Central Files 1964–66, POL 7 INDIA. Secret; Flash; Limdis. Repeated to Karachi and passed to White House.

[2] See footnote 3, Document 101.

[3] In telegram 2165 to New Delhi, repeated to Karachi as telegram 1152, April 15, the Department warned that news of the postponement of the Ayub and Shastri visits was leaking in Washington. It was therefore "imperative" for both countries to agree quickly upon press statements relating to the postponements. The Department transmitted proposed drafts to be used as models. (National Archives and Records Administration, RG 59, Central Files 1964–66, POL 7 PAK)

[4] Document 103.

letter to L. K. Jha. I also noted that postponement of Shastri and Ayub visit has leaked in Washington.

Jha read letter and expressed his disappointment and concern. His concern was compounded as we assumed it would be by linking of withdrawal of Ayub Khan invitation with that of Shastri.

I stressed that only reason why two actions appeared to be coupled was that both visits happened to fall in same time span and President found it essential to clear his schedule because of crisis in Southeast Asia. Indeed all engagements that did not deal directly with urgent domestic questions or Southeast Asia were being simultaneously cancelled or postponed.

Jha replied that he could readily understand pressures to which President referred. However fact that Ayub Khan and Shastri visit were being cancelled simultaneously would surely lead to feeling within India and abroad that Shastri, who was opposing Chinese both militarily and politically, has been linked with Ayub Khan who has been cooperating with Chinese, and that Americans are indifferent to this distinction.

Misunderstanding in India will be compounded by leak to which I referred and fact that Paks armed with American weapons are pressing in Kutch border area will lead further to confusion. I admitted that there are bound to be some misunderstandings and confusion in press. However it is our task to minimize this confusion and to make sure that postponement which I believe to be wise under circumstances did not lead to unnecessary difficulties for all of us.

Although President and administration understood India's unaligned position, fact of matter was the GOI had often mishandled its public relations in such way as to create misunderstandings and in some cases resentment.

For instance, we knew Indians had worked most effectively behind scenes in regard to Southeast Asia situation at Belgrade and elsewhere and we were hopeful that they would continue to do so. However their failure publicly to recognize that we are in fact fighting their battles as well as our own creates a sense of disappointment. In that regard I was hopeful that PriMin would be able to make strong case in Moscow for more forthcoming Soviet position in support of some form of Johnson plan.

Jha picked up my reference to Moscow by stating that PriMin had always linked Moscow and US visits together and had deliberately arranged to go to Moscow before going to Washington so he could report to President progress that he had hoped to make there. Under present conditions Jha felt sure PriMin would wish he were not going to Moscow.

We then turned to problem of how best to handle situation here in India. Jha said he would get PriMin on telephone in next few hours. We agreed to coordinate with GOI as best we could press handling both in Washington and here in India. Admittedly leak had created serious difficulties for us all but we would do our best to ease problems for both govts. Jha particularly asked USG hold its announcement until he has talked to Shastri.[5]

Bowles

---

[5] After a telephone call to Shastri, Jha reported to Bowles that Shastri was deeply disappointed. Jha indicated that the Indian Government would issue a press release stating that the postponement was agreed upon as a result of President Johnson's heavy schedule, and that there would be further discussions concerning rescheduling the visit. (Telegram 2934 from New Delhi, April 16; National Archives and Records Administration, RG 59, Central Files 1964–66, POL 7 INDIA) In Washington, Rusk called in Ambassador Nehru, gave him a copy of the letter to Shastri, and explained the reasons for the postponement. Nehru's reaction was that postponement of the visit on such short notice was "an act of discourtesy" certain to cause resentment in New Delhi. (Telegram 2175 to New Delhi, April 17; ibid.)

---

105.   Telegram From the Embassy in Pakistan to the Department of State[1]

Karachi, April 21, 1965.

1995. 1. When I saw Foreign Secretary Aziz Ahmed April 19 (Embassy telegram 1981)[2] he said he wanted to mention off the record another matter, namely "US communications installations." He had five requests to make, enumerated below.

(A) He wanted full statement from me in near future as to recent, current and prospective expansion of facilities at Peshawar installation. He said this report should cover both equipment and buildings. Said he had studied 1959 agreement and realized that expansion now taking place did not contravene "letter" of agreement since area not being

---

[1] Source: National Archives and Records Administration, RG 59, Central Files 1964–66, DEF 15 PAK–US. Secret; Priority; [*classification designator not declassified*]. No time of transmission is given on the telegram, which was received at 3:39 p.m.

[2] McConaughy's meeting with Ahmed on April 19 was devoted in large part to a discussion of Ayub's visit to the Soviet Union. (Telegram 1981 from Karachi, April 19; ibid., POL 7 PAK)

expanded. However, GOP felt that any additional buildings or equipment not authorized by it violated the "spirit" of the agreement, especially since we had sought and failed to obtain President Ayub's agreement to certain expansion proposals some time back.

(B) He wanted information as to when we could close down the "three smaller installations" (not otherwise identified, but obviously referring to [2 *lines of source text not declassified*]). He said if we were not prepared to close them down soon, GOP would want explanation as to why they could not be closed down and would have to insist on negotiation of agreements to provide for their continued operation. He said the three facilities appeared not to be covered by any written agreements at present, and GOP understood they had been installed as "ad hoc" arrangements for short term period. He said GOP was not well informed about functions of these units and would like better access. I commented that we had not considered installations to be on ad hoc or temporary basis but rather for indefinite period. I noted that [*less than 1 line of source text not declassified*] had full access, and had personally inspected some or all of them, as I recalled it. I asked if he was suggesting blanketing of small installations under 1959 Peshawar agreement. He said if small installations could not be closed in near future GOP would expect separate agreements to be negotiated for each. He did not refer to 1964 discussion of "regularization" of status these units [*less than 1 line of source text not declassified*].

(C) [*10 lines of source text not declassified*]

(D) He wanted full and unlimited access to every sector Peshawar installation granted for a [*1 line of source text not declassified*]. While he was vague I gather he was asking for blanket clearance for any person who might be designated by [*less than 1 line of source text not declassified*] to inspect on his behalf at any time, and not necessarily the individual who has the official title of [*less than 1 line of source text not declassified*].

(E) He wanted us to exclude from Peshawar installation any naturalized American citizen of Indian origin. He complained strongly about a naturalized non-commissioned officer of American Air Force named Singh, formerly stationed at Peshawar, who he said had returned occasionally for unexplained visits and had also visited India after his Peshawar trips. He said there was "another Sikh" with American papers who also had visited the installation and who was a source of concern to Pak intelligence.

2. I was noncommittal with Aziz Ahmed, only stating that I would be in touch with him later as to the general subject. I questioned his invocation of "spirit" as a workable basis for interpretation of the explicit provision of an international agreement.

3. When I saw Finance Minister Shoaib privately on April 20 I made guarded reference to Aziz Ahmed's attempt to intrude the For-

eign Office into this delicate intelligence field. Shoaib confirmed my surmise that nothing transpired during Moscow visit which would seem to jeopardize existence of our facilities and that Aziz Ahmed probably was free-wheeling to some extent in an effort to make trouble for us. (It would be a major coup for Aziz Ahmed if he could seize complete control of negotiations and operations in this field [less than 1 line of source text not declassified], capitalizing on continued Russian diplomatic pressure and threats, and on undoubted desire of President and entire GOP to get maximum mileage out of their cards.) Shoaib advised me strongly to resist Pak Foreign Office intrusion into this subject if I possibly could, since it would at a minimum greatly complicate our difficulties. But he did not know offhand the best means of handling this tough, tactical problem.

4. I expect to transmit further thoughts and recommendations when I have considered matter further and examined it more completely with Shaffter. Meanwhile, I request Hughes to inform Secretary, [less than 1 line of source text not declassified].

5. I plan to request renewal of my consultation orders near future and this will be one of major subjects I will expect to take up in Washington, hopefully early May.

McConaughy

106. Telegram From the Embassy in India to the Department of State[1]

New Delhi, April 21, 1965.

2970. Tuesday[2] evening at 9 PM I met for one and half hours with PriMin Shastri who was accompanied by L. K. Jha. Mrs. Pandit had warned me earlier in evening that PriMin was deeply and personally offended but I was unprepared for painful and difficult discussion which followed.

I opened exchange by emphasizing President's, Secretary's and my own deep regret that visit had not gone through on schedule and by expressing hope that postponement which President had suggested

---

[1] Source: National Archives and Records Administration, RG 59, Central Files 1964–66, POL 7 INDIA. Secret; Priority; Limdis. Repeated to the White House. No time of transmission is on the telegram; it was received at 4:15 a.m.

[2] April 20.

would not create too many difficulties for him. I then filled in silence that followed with description of massive pressures on President generated by Vietnam crisis, adding that charges which would have been leveled at India by Ayub Khan during his Washington visit however unjust would have created difficulties for all of us, especially in light of delicacy of legislative situation, etc.

After further silence Shastri responded with stream of comments which reflected profound sense of personal hurt. These comments included following:

He had been personally embarrassed before his country, his party and world at time when India had been striving diligently to cooperate with us in bringing peace to South Vietnam; if President had wanted to postpone or cancel visit he would have been glad to cooperate and why was he not given opportunity to withdraw his acceptance with dignity. His capacity to influence events for India in Moscow, Algiers and Commonwealth had been greatly diminished, while in India extreme left would accuse him of having been too subservient to US while extreme right would say he had not been subservient enough.

Manner in which invitation had been cancelled indicated deep psychological gap between India and US which he was afraid could never be bridged. He in any case was at loss to know how mutual confidence could be restored. For instance, if US gives India aid under present circumstances it would be said we were attempting to buy her good will and if we refuse her assistance it would be said that [we?] were punishing India for failure to follow American line.

Although PriMin listened politely to my rebuttal in which I touched on our strong support for India's fight for freedom when he, Gandhi and Nehru were in prison, our encouragement to India in days of her constitution building, our willingness to provide substantial economic aid even through difficult Krishna Menon era without political strings, etc. I can't say that I accomplished much.

However illogical and unreasonable Shastri's reactions may appear in Washington it is essential that we understand that we are now dealing with deeply hurt man. Under normal circumstances he is sensitive person, often unsure of himself, but he has been striving for a more affirmative foreign policy role which he had felt, according to Jha, was almost within his grasp.

In India I am afraid we are in for some difficult times and it will be some months before situation is back where it was ten days ago. Best thing we can do is quietly to go about our business and resist temptation publicly to trade criticisms or to create new grounds for debate.

Present situation is most serious I have encountered in my many years in dealing with Indian people and government. However, it is vitally important that we remember that a strong common ground between Indians and ourselves has been built up over years. Although it may be dented and scarred it will not disappear overnight.[3]

Bowles

---

[3] Bowles sent another cable to Washington on April 21, for Rusk and McNamara, in which he stated that he felt the atmosphere in New Delhi could be improved if he were authorized to tell Shastri and Chavan privately that the response to the Indian request for F–5 fighters was favorable, and that an announcement to that effect would be made at a time mutually satisfactory to the two governments. (Telegram 2978 from New Delhi; Johnson Library, National Security File, Country File, India, Vol. IV, Cables, 12/64–6/65)

---

107. Memorandum From the Executive Secretary of the Department of State (Read) to the President's Special Assistant for National Security Affairs (Bundy)[1]

Washington, April 24, 1965.

SUBJECT

Fighting in the Rann of Kutch Between India and Pakistan

Enclosed is a memorandum surveying the background and implications of developments in the Rann of Kutch. The highlights are:

—Indo-Pak border negotiations in 1960 could not sort out the conflicting claims in this sector of the border, but both countries acknowledged that there was a dispute.

—Hard evidence on what is actually taking place is limited. The present train of events began in January of this year when Indian patrols discovered that Pakistani posts had been established in area claimed by India.

—The terrain gives Pakistan a military advantage which it appears to have exploited in the escalating series of incidents that have occurred in recent weeks.

—Regular military units have recently been deployed by both sides.

---

[1] Source: Johnson Library, National Security File, Country File, India, Vol. IV, Memos & Miscellaneous, 12/64–6/65. Secret.

—Pakistan is bringing in troops from MAP-supported units.

—There is danger that the fighting will intensify and spread.

—The dispute has assumed major political significance in both Delhi and Rawalpindi, and has serious implications for our policies and programs in the subcontinent. Both parties are seeking to draw us into an emotion-laden dispute at a difficult time in our relationships with both countries.

Benjamin H. Read[2]

Enclosure[3]

RANN OF KUTCH DISPUTE

Background

The area in dispute, extending out from the old fort of Kanjarkot, lies on the northern edge of the Rann of Kutch, a desolate area in Western India on the Arabian Sea. It is alternately salt flats and tidal basin. (The inundation lasts from June to November.) The area was admitted by both sides to be in dispute at the time of the Indo-Pakistani border negotiations of 1960. It was agreed at that time that further discussions would be held to explore the validity of the conflicting claims, but so far as we know these have not taken place.

The current difficulties apparently began in January 1965, when the Indians became aware that Pakistani border police were patrolling below the Indian claim line. India lodged a protest and increased its own patrolling activity. In mid-February, Pakistani forces dug themselves in around Kanjarkot, which may have been previously unoccupied, although Ayub claims that Pakistan had "long" occupied it. Both sides have since built up the forces available to them in the area, manned strong points, and shifted defense responsibility from border units to the army.

During April, a series of incidents has occurred with both sides blaming the other. The Pakistanis, enjoying a militarily superior position, have moved forcefully against Indian outposts near the border fort of Kanjarkot and most recently staged a "preemptive" attack at Biar Bet, deeper within the disputed area. The Indians have been mainly on the defensive but, according to Pakistan, have established outposts within undisputed Pakistani territory.

---

[2] Another member of the Secretariat signed for Read above his typed signature in an illegible hand.

[3] Secret; Noforn.

Both sides allege that the other has employed armor. The Indians have denied the charge and we have no evidence to support it. Although firm proof is lacking, there are reports supporting the Indian claim that Pakistan has moved armor to the Kutch area and that it may be engaged in action. The unit concerned, according to Embassy Karachi, is MAP-equipped. Casualties have been reported by both sides, shooting continues between patrols and strong points, and public opinion—especially in India—has been aroused sharply.

Pakistani patrolling south of Kanjarkot may have been going on for quite some time without the Indians knowing it. There is little doubt, however, that Pakistani occupation of Kanjarkot would have upset a long-standing status quo. The Indian response of occupying other posts near the frontier and, reportedly, building an airstrip nearby brought the latent crisis to a head.

It will probably not be possible to determine who began firing, and since the area involved is legitimately in dispute between Pakistan and India, it is difficult to ascertain that either side committed aggression against the territory of the other. (All action thus far has, however, been much closer to the Indian claim line than to that of Pakistan.)

Both sides have engaged in sparring over negotiations to ameliorate the situation. The Indians accepted a Pakistani ceasefire offer on April 15, but it has never been implemented. The Pakistanis demand a demilitarization of the entire disputed area as a precondition to talks, and the Indians would require a restoration of the status quo ante, including Pakistani withdrawal from Kanjarkot. Pakistan claims that Kanjarkot is not within the disputed area and India would be understandably loath to evacuate all the way down to the 24th parallel, so the prospects for a ceasefire and negotiations are dim.

Political Implications

a) *India:* In an atmosphere colored by India's military humiliation by the Chinese in 1962, strong public resentment over Pakistan's developing relationship with Peiping and the hurt feelings over the postponement of Shastri's visit, the already beleaguered GOI cannot afford domestically to be gotten the better of by Pakistan in a military confrontation. The Indian Foreign Secretary has told our DCM that "the country is in no mood to take any more pushing in the Rann of Kutch and the GOI may be constrained to retaliate elsewhere, where conditions are more favorable to Indian forces". The GOI's domestic political discomfort is increased by aspects of the Kutch dispute which are analogous to the pre-1962 situation in Ladakh—e.g. the belated discovery by Indian patrols of foreign military posts in a neglected area of Indian-claimed territory.

Even before the activization of the Kutch dispute, the moderate Shastri government proved to be most vulnerable politically to charges of weakness and indecision. Pakistan's apparent utilization of U.S.-supplied MAP equipment in the dispute further complicates the situation domestically for the GOI by providing additional grounds for criticism to extremists of both the left and right who can exploit traditional Indian resentments over U.S.-Pakistan security agreements of the 1950's and India's acceptance in 1962 of more rigid constraints on the use of U.S. military equipment.

b) *Pakistan:* The Kutch dispute, occurring in an area of Pak military superiority, provides the GOP with several opportunities. Diplomatically, it provides Pakistan an opportunity to damage Indo-U.S. relations, through the use of MAP equipment in a situation where there is some ambiguity over the justification of its use. Additionally, the Kutch dispute provides Pakistan, in the weeks just before Bandung II, with an opportunity to brand India as an aggressor in Afro-Asian eyes. This objective will be further advanced if Pak actions in Kutch cause India to retaliate elsewhere, especially if India should move into an area generally recognized as Pak territory. Domestically, the Kutch confrontation enables the GOP to score over India, despite India's overall military superiority, particularly in Kashmir and along the East Pak border.

Finally, Pakistan undoubtedly calculates that India's response to the Kutch situation will lend a plausibility to the basic Pak contention that India would use its military strength enhanced by our military assistance to intimidate Pakistan and stick to an intransigent policy on Kashmir, rather than in combatting Communist China.

c) *United States:* The fighting in Kutch, particularly Pakistan's probable use of MAP equipment, has propelled us once more into the center of a subcontinental dispute at a moment when our leverage in both countries is at a low point. Our relations with India, already exacerbated by the postponement of Shastri's visit, will be further strained by public charges of Pakistan's use of MAP equipment. Moreover, our problems with the GOI will be complicated by the fact that we have imposed more stringent conditions on Indian use of MAP equipment (i.e. only against Communist China) than the conditions imposed on Pakistan. This discrepancy may assume exaggerated significance in view of the fact that the Soviets have imposed no conditions whatsoever on use of the military assistance they have supplied India. This complicating aspect of the situation may be highlighted by Shastri's imminent departure for Moscow in an atmosphere of resentment over the postponement of his visit to the United States.

In recent years, India's preoccupation with the China threat has led the GOI to rely heavily on our ability to restrain Pakistan whenever

Indo-Pak tensions have threatened to get out of hand. In the present situations, the Indians have indicated they would like help in promoting a ceasefire.

---

108.   Telegram From the Embassy in India to the Department of State[1]

New Delhi, April 24, 1965, 1305Z.

3018. References Embtels 3015,[2] 3016.[3] DCM called on Foreign Secretary Jha afternoon April 24 to solicit facts and statement of GOI policy into which Chaudhury's presentation fits. Jha's comments boiled down to effort to place on U.S. onus for restraining further Pak "aggression." He also seemed to be fishing for offer of good offices in getting cease-fire and talks. Finally, it apparent that all or most of this will be in tomorrow morning's papers.

Efforts to illuminate facts added little to previous knowledge and Chaudhury's presentation. Tank attack had occurred at 7 A.M. this morning and in Jha's view fits into growing pattern of Pak aggressiveness. This is compounded by fact attack took place while GOP was presumably awaiting GOI response to latest formulation of proposal for cease-fire. Jha several times used the phrases "grave situation" and "general war," saying in latter connection that the country is in no mood to take any more pushing around in Rann of Kutch and Government of India may be constrained retaliate elsewhere, where conditions more favorable to Indian forces. He said this has not been decided by GOI.

Jha summarized exchanges between himself and Pak High Commissioner over last several weeks on cease-fire and talks. He said he thought both GOP and GOI had agreed on desirability of cease-fire

---

[1] Source: Johnson Library, National Security File, Country File, India, Vol. IV, Cables, 12/64–6/65. Secret; Immediate. Repeated to DOD for DIA, CINCMEAFSA, Karachi, and London, and passed to the White House.

[2] In telegram 3015 from New Delhi, April 24, the Embassy reported that the Chief of the Indian Army Staff, General J.N. Chadhury, had requested U.S. assistance in restraining the escalation of what he described as an attack by Pakistani tanks of U.S. origin supported by infantry in the Rann of Kutch. (Ibid.)

[3] Telegram 3016 from New Delhi, April 24, reported on Chadhury's request in greater detail. Chadhury said that he had irrefutable evidence that the tanks being used in the Pakistani attack were of U.S. origin. It was his understanding, he said, that the United States had promised to intervene if either India or Pakistan used MAP equipment against the other. (Ibid.)

and that problem arises over search for agreed formulation. Jha gave DCM text which he said has been given to GOP and remains GOI position:

"1. There should be a cease-fire effective from (date to be agreed);

"2. Immediately thereafter, there should be an official level meeting to determine the status quo ante which should be restored; and

"3. Thereafter, there should be a high level meeting to discuss the Kutch–Sind border question.

"Both governments have assured each other of their sincere desire and determination to find a peaceful solution to the Kutch–Sind border problem and to avoid the use of force."

Latest Pak proposal he described as serious retrogression even from previous Pak proposals, and supplied text as follows:

"1. There should be a cease-fire effective from (date);

"2. Immediately thereafter the armed forces of both India and Pakistan whether civil or military shall be completely withdrawn from the disputed territory namely the area which extends from a line running south of Kanjarkot to the disputed Sind–Kutch boundary which runs roughly along 24 degree latitude;

"3. Thereafter there should be a high level meeting to resolve the dispute relating to the above-mentioned territory.

"Both governments have expressed their desire to reach an early settlement of this dispute through peaceful means."

Jha said that although there may be something to talk about in respect of precise location of boundary, and small disputed area "around Kanjarkot," it is quite intolerable to identify disputed territory as reaching to 24th parallel in ground rules for talks. He would be telling Pak High Commissioner so immediately following this conversation.

DCM deplored possibility of escalation hostilities and repeated importance of getting cease-fire. Jha continued insist there is no doubt who is aggressor and reiterated it should be matter of deep concern to USG that GOP is using U.S. weapons in face of Eisenhower–Nehru and subsequent assurances to GOI.

Leaving aside question of weapons, DCM stuck to importance of cease-fire and, speaking entirely personally, wondered whether it would help any if friend or friends of India and Pakistan were publicly to call on both to cease-fire. Jha said he had been trying to demonstrate that GOI wants cease-fire and he hopes GOP does too. He also threw out point about good offices, making clear, however, that these should not go to substance of dispute (e.g., mediation or arbitration) but only to getting agreed formula for talk. He clearly did not think GOP is receptive to this sort of proposition. In fact, at one point, elaborating on dangers of "general war," he speculated that GOP and Chicoms are in collusion to try provoke GOI. DCM said this was a grave accusation, or better hypothesis, to which Jha replied "accusation" would do.

In reply DCM query whether GOI would be turning to United Nations, Jha disparaged capacity of UN to do anything constructive in this situation.

Conversation concluded with Jha's assertion that one cannot keep out of the press either the "fact" that U.S. tanks have been used by Paks or that GOI has brought USG into this issue.

Comments follow.[4]

Bowles

----

[4] In the comments that followed in telegram 3019 from New Delhi, April 24, the Embassy concluded that unless the United States could disprove that U.S. equipment was being used in the Pakistani attack, the Indian Government and populace would expect the United States to take effective action to stop such use. (Ibid.)

----

109.   Telegram From the Department of State to the Embassy in Pakistan[1]

Washington, April 24, 1965, 9 a.m.

1195. Delhi's 3015 repeated Karachi 628.[2] Since Paks have already confirmed to us that their forces have attacked in Biar Bet area and that this well within disputed area (Karachi's 2003 repeated Delhi 699),[3] and since you report that these are MAP supplied forces, you should seek appointment soonest with Forn Minister or Forn Secretary to express our strong concern over what appears be worsening situation Rann of Kutch. You should recall assurances given you by Ayub (Karachi's 1971 repeated Delhi 687)[4] that Paks had not and did not intend to go beyond traditional patrol routes in disputed areas and that Pak forces would not use any more force than necessary to repel force

----

[1] Source: Johnson Library, National Security File, Country File, Pakistan, Vol. III, Cables, 12/64–7/65. Secret; Immediate. Drafted by Laingen and Laise, cleared in substance by Stoddard in DOD/ISA, and approved by Handley. Also sent to New Delhi as telegram 2222, and repeated to CINCMEAFSA and London.

[2] See footnote 2, Document 108.

[3] Dated April 22. (National Archives and Records Administration, RG 59, Central Files 1964–66, POL 32–1 INDIA–PAK)

[4] See footnote 6, Document 103.

resorted to by Indian side. Moreover Ayub recognized something had to be done to relieve worsening situation and that Pakistan shared responsibility for this. Pak action confirmed by MFA Director Akhund would appear inconsistent with these assurances and we must now ask what Pak intentions are.

In making representations you should cite accusation re use of MAP equipment made by General Chaudhri and seek confirmation.[5] Since we assume there little doubt that accusations well founded, believe you should sound warning that use of our MAP equipment in this type of situation could jeopardize MAP program.

You should also say that we are expressing our strong concern over Kutch situation to Indians.

For Delhi: In whatever followup steps Embassy takes with MEA noted reftel, assume Ambassador will register our increasing concern. Ambassador should inform MEA we are making representations to GOP.

Agree with Delhi on importance of coordinating closely with British, who we would hope also bringing their influence to bear on both parties.

Rusk

---

[5] In telegram 2015 from Karachi, April 25, the Embassy reported that a Defense Ministry spokesman had emphatically denied the Indian allegations. (Johnson Library, National Security File, Country File, Pakistan, Vol. III, Cables, 12/64–7/65)

---

110.   Memorandum From Robert Komer of the National Security Council Staff to the President's Special Assistant for National Security Affairs (Bundy)[1]

Washington, April 26, 1965.

Mac—

This *Rann of Kutch* business could build up to a real mess.

To oversimplify, the Paks found a good new place to lean on Indians—one where the terrain favored Pak side. The Indians reacted

---

[1] Source: Johnson Library, National Security File, Country File, Pakistan, Vol. III, 12/64–7/65. Secret.

with their usual ineptitude, but at any rate both sides have built up to 6–7000 men and the Paks hold the forward position in the disputed area.

What worries State is that Indians are building up to a binge. They are determined not to let the Paks of all people get away with a Ladakh-type humiliation. So there's a strong chance of *Indian retaliation elsewhere,* where the odds favor them more.

If this occurs, who knows what will happen. An Indian deputy foreign minister told the new UK High Commissioner, Freeman, that it might mean a major Pak/Indian war.[2]

We're hesitant to weigh in too hard because neither Paks nor Indians are very friendly to us at the moment. Ergo, I'm plugging for UK,[3] Commonwealth, and UN admonitory noises with us in a supporting role. If things take a turn for the worse, however, we may have to buy a share.

RWK

---

[2] In response to news reports that Pakistan had ordered the mobilization of its armed forces, the Department of State sent instructions to Karachi and New Delhi on April 25 to approach the governments and counsel restraint. (Telegram 1201 to Karachi, also sent to New Delhi as telegram 2228; National Archives and Records Administration, RG 59, Central Files 1964–66, POL 32–1 INDIA–PAK)

[3] On April 27 Komer sent a note to Bundy to report that British Prime Minister Wilson had weighed in personally with Ayub and Shastri and proposed a cease-fire. (Johnson Library, National Security File, Country File, Pakistan, Vol. III, Memos, 12/64–7/65) The British démarche was reported in telegram 2033 from Karachi, April 27, and in telegram 3069 from New Delhi, April 28. (Ibid., Cables, 12/64–7/65; National Archives and Records Administration, RG 59, Central Files 1964–66, POL 32–1 INDIA–PAK)

111.   Telegram From the Embassy in Pakistan to the Department of State[1]

Karachi, April 27, 1965, 1530Z.

2040. Embtel 2039.[2]

1. Events relating to Rann of Kutch clash seem to be propelling us toward milestone in US relations with Pakistan and India. Thanks to needlessly belligerent and self-centered actions of both countries, not only are we faced with a major crisis in Indo-Pak relations, but major crises in US-Indian and US-Pak relations. Immediate issues are of course fighting in Rann of Kutch and use of MAP equipment there by Paks.

But, in fact, much broader issues involving our position on Subcontinent are actually at stake. Rann of Kutch has made it clear that US and UK cannot safely remain aloof from intramural Indo-Pak disputes although they are not of our making. US assistance is significant factor in enhanced military capabilities of both countries. In case of Pakistan five and one-half of its seven and one-half divisions are MAP supported. In the case of India, US military aid and US assistance in defense production area serve indirectly if not directly to upgrade appreciably India's ability to sustain operations like Rann of Kutch engagements. This broadest context of issue posed by Rann of Kutch is how to avoid frustration of US efforts, undertaken in both countries at enormous cost, which would surely result from enlarged and prolonged hostilities.

2. Regardless of merits India's claim that Paks are employing MAP equipment in Rann of Kutch for aggression or Pakistani contention that its actions are justifiable defensive reactions to Indian encroachments disrupting long established equilibrium in upper half of Rann, present situation is not tolerable for us in terms our essential interests in Subcontinent.

We are faced thus by a most crucial dilemma. To withdraw MAP support from Pakistan, however justifiable in the abstract would be to open here a Pandora's box of outright neutralism and sweeping policy reorientation. MAP is lifeblood of Pak national security. If Paks are cut off from MAP because of its use in disputes with India, where facts

---

[1] Source: Johnson Library, National Security File, Country File, Pakistan, Vol. III, Cables, 12/64–7/65. Secret; Immediate; Limdis. Repeated to New Delhi and CINCMEAFSA for POLAD, and passed to the White House, DOD, and CIA at 1:50 p.m.

[2] In telegram 2039 from Karachi, April 27, McConaughy reported on a conversation with Foreign Secretary Aziz Ahmed in which Ahmed told him that India rejected Pakistan's proposal for a cease-fire. Ahmed said that in light of the Indian rejection, Pakistani forces in the Rann of Kutch would have to "stay put." (National Archives and Records Administration, RG 59, Central Files 1964–66, POL 32–1 INDIA–PAK)

(other than shared culpability both sides) have always been almost impossible to sort out and with Indians still benefitting from US military equipment while still not entirely dependent on it, Paks will consider that they have no choice but to look elsewhere for military support and guarantees against aggression. In our view, it would be difficult to over-estimate the emotional impact of this issue in Pakistan, or the adverse effect on the American presence here, including without doubt status of our special facilities, that would flow from a rupture of the Military Assistance Program. Yet, to decline to control in some effective way, improper or questionable Pak employment of MAP equipment would be impossible to defend not only before Congress and in India, but in terms our ability to exercise influence through MAP on Paks.

3. We see no clear answer to this dilemma. To move all the way to either of these alternatives would have far-reaching ominous implications, forcing very choice between India and Pakstan we wish to avoid. In the case before us, we consider that the only course we can readily live with is one which makes the choice unnecessary in present inflamed circumstances [garble] one of either reversion to 1960 arrangements in Rann of Kutch, including agreed ground rules, or an immediate and unconditional cease fire. We might thus avoid involvement in merits of case or need for decision for the present on the MAP issue—although we probably must face up to latter over longer run. We urge full weight of US Government be put behind British good offices effort (Embtel 2033),[3] both here and in Delhi.

4. To reinforce this effort, Paks must be admonished again at highest level that US MAP programs, apart from legal interpretations, clearly jeopardized as a defensible practical proposition by continuation of Rann of Kutch fighting. I believe I can get this across to President Ayub in a form that he will comprehend without undue resentment.

At same time, responsibility for concoction and vigorous stirring of Rann of Kutch witches' brew rests equally on Pak and Indian shoulders. Our warning to GOP therefore should be matched with similar emphatic warning to GOI, particularly in view GOI threats to extend conflict to other areas, apparent Indian interest in compounding our difficulties in Pakistan, and Indian exploitation of [garble—closer?] Soviet ties. Both GOP and GOI must be faced with fact that aid to both will be imperiled if they do not buckle down to business of arranging immediate cease fire.

McConaughy

---

[3] See footnote 3, Document 109.

112.   Telegram From the Department of State to the Embassy in Pakistan[1]

Washington, April 27, 1965, 8:02 p.m.

1217. Rann of Kutch. Talbot called in Pak Ambassador Ghulam Ahmed today to reinforce Ambassador McConaughy's earlier representations of U.S. concern re Rann to GOP Foreign Secretary. Talbot said that we are also having talks in New Delhi.[2] He said that what troubles us most is that apparently for first time since Kashmir cease fire, military forces of two countries are engaged in organized conflict. We see very considerable risks and dangers ahead in this situation.

As Ambassador knew, Senate recently reduced FY–66 MAP by $115 million. This decision was reversed after intensive efforts. Cut was assigned to India, Pakistan, Greece and Turkey. This mood is fed by present situation, and implications for subcontinent cannot be ignored. Aziz Ahmed told Ambassador McConaughy MAP-supplied tanks were being used in conflict. Aziz Ahmed also indicated that GOP would welcome clarification from U.S. of interpretation our military assistance agreement regarding use of MAP equipment in such dispute. Talbot said he wished state our position in response to Aziz's request and covered points in Deptel 1200 to Karachi.[3] He said it was quite evident Pakistan's attack on Biar Bet is inconsistent with maintaining "legitimate self-defense."

Our larger concern is to bring this situation to an end before it assumes importance of another Kashmir, creating deep frictions between two nations. We earnestly hope both countries can find way to arrange cease fire.

---

[1] Source: National Archives and Records Administration, RG 59, Central Files 1964–66, POL 32–1 INDIA–PAK. Secret; Immediate. Drafted by William L. Simmons in NEA/SOA, and approved by Handley. Repeated to London, New Delhi, and CINCMEAFSA.

[2] Talbot also discussed the Rann of Kutch situation with Indian Ambassador Nehru on April 27, and argued for the wisdom of a cease-fire agreement. (Telegram 2245 to New Delhi, April 27; Johnson Library, National Security File, Country File, India, Vol. IV, Cables, 12/64–6/65)

[3] Telegram 1200 to Karachi, April 24, defined the U.S. legal position regarding the use of MAP equipment in disputed territories, such as the Rann of Kutch. MAP equipment was furnished with the clear understanding that it was required for internal security, legitimate self-defense, or collective security. The Department concluded that the United States could not unilaterally determine where the disputed border was for the purpose of establishing the right or wrong of the use of equipment supplied under MAP agreements. The Department also did not feel that either Pakistan or India could offer assurances that the equipment was being used for internal security or legitimate self-defense. Therefore the United States was not willing to countenance the use of MAP equipment in disputed areas such as the Rann of Kutch. (National Archives and Records Administration, RG 59, Central Files 1964–66, POL 32–1 INDIA–PAK)

Ambassador said he was not familiar with latest Karachi talks. However as he understood it Bhutto's April 15 statement and GOP's letter to Security Council stood as basis Pakistan's position. He recalled that area above 24th Parallel was regarded in pre-partition days as part of Sind. Therefore in his view not correct to say that this territory disputed and question of use of MAP equipment in disputed territory did not arise. What was important was to define what is disputed territory.

He continued that war talk had been coming from Indian side. Indian allegations of Pakistani mobilization have been categorically denied while GOI has admitted to mobilization. Ambassador noted Ayub's Dacca speech and contrasted President's peaceful remarks with Indian statements relating alleged Pak casualties. Looking at it from Washington, Kashmir incidents, Dahagram and Rann of Kutch seemed to fall into pattern of planned Indian aggression.

Ambassador stated that this is a case where U.S. should firmly come to Pakistan's aid. He recalled Under Secretary Ball's assurances of U.S. assistance to Pakistan in event of Indian aggression.[4] Pakistan obviously cannot match India in duplicity. Already India has presented better case internationally than Pakistan. Ambassador asked for Talbot's views on what U.S. would do.

Talbot said that in first instance cease fire should be arranged. He said it should not be beyond ingenuity of disputants to find way to bring prompt end to fighting, particularly since both countries are in agreement on desirability of cease fire as well as negotiations to resolve impasse. Following cease fire both sides might set up machinery to settle disputes of this type.

Ambassador commented that such machinery does exist with regard to West Pakistan-Indian frontier. Pakistan certainly wants peaceful solution but India charges of Pakistan wanting to broaden the conflict and Chinese-Pakistan collusion indicate opposite view holds for India.

Ambassador said that apart from tanks he was not aware of what other MAP equipment may be in use. He thought that it might be useful to examine "at leisure" 1961 Kennedy–Ayub Communiqué[5] which he believed had extended scope of use of MAP equipment.

---

[4] In a conversation with Ayub in Rawalpindi on September 5, 1963, Ball reiterated the assurance that the United States would come to Pakistan's assistance in the event of aggression from any source. The conversation was reported in telegram 236 from Tehran, September 5; for text, see Foreign Relations, 1961–1963, vol. XIX, Document 328.

[5] For the joint communiqué issued on July 31, 1961, at the conclusion of the Washington portion of a State visit to the United States by Ayub, see Department of State Bulletin, August 7, 1961, pp. 240–241.

Talbot closed by noting U.S. can foresee very serious consequences both on subcontinent and outside unless there is cessation in present hostilities.

Rusk

---

113. Telegram From the White House to the Embassy in India[1]

Washington, April 28, 1965, 11 a.m.

CAP 65138. Eyes Only for Bowles from Bundy. Have just seen your 3057[2] asking help on pending matters before you return here mid-May. We are fully and sympathetically aware of hectic situation in subcontinent and will do our best to push some of these matters forward. However, with all the candor you have come to expect via this channel, let me warn against great expectations just now. With Vietnam in the forefront of all minds, there is simply not likely to be the kind of constructive focus on the issues you raise which is necessary to push them through.

Moreover, while tactical considerations may argue for early gestures before Shastri goes to Moscow, we still see merit in reserving some of the items you propose till we can fit them better into package approach being considered here, rather than dishing them out piecemeal. Two-year PL 480 commitment now, for example, might deprive us of major leverage before we have fully worked out what we want Indians to do in return, at least in agriculture sector. A one-year, frankly interim, agreement might suffice for our immediate purpose.

---

[1] Source: Johnson Library, National Security File, Country File, India, Exchanges with Bowles. Secret; Immediate. [*text not declassified*]

[2] In telegram 3057 from New Delhi, April 27, Bowles raised the question of pending decisions on three issues he felt it was important to move forward on before his return to Washington in mid-May. The two most important related to the Indian requests for a 2-year agreement on P.L. 480 assistance and for F–5 fighter aircraft. Bowles urged positive decisions on both, although he recognized that in view of the fighting in the Rann of Kutch it would not be possible to announce a decision to provide F–5s to India for some time. He also urged action on his proposal for the creation of a binational cultural foundation, noting that a decision had been pending for more than a year. (Ibid., Vol. IV, Cables, 12/64–6/65)

As for F–5A, we see little chance of promising aircraft now when Paks and perhaps Indians are using our MAP for purposes far afield from what we intended.[3]

In sum, my reading of Washington end is that the way of wisdom is not to push too hard on big new programs till we can revalidate our Indian enterprise and get the aid bill through. Here we must grant the President's own unparalleled sense of the rocky road the aid bill is travelling and his strong desire not to rock the boat till he knows what's in his pocket. Nor does Vietnam, where the course we have to take will not win us many short term plaudits overseas, ease the problem.

So timing is everything just now. On this score, Komer and I strongly urge that you postpone your home leave for six weeks or so. When we heard you were coming, we thought it wise on your behalf to check with the President, and this is his own distinct preference. Aside from the value of having you at the helm in Delhi during a ticklish period in US/Indian relations, we may need your guiding hand in handling Vietnam affairs with the Indians. Equally important, you could not come back now without talking India and it is simply not a propitious time to do so. You would inevitably be caught in the backwash of the Shastri affair, and have to answer embarrassing queries. Even strictly home leave might be misconstrued, and you couldn't really come back without a Washington leg.

These are difficult times, not least for you, and we all appreciate your gallant handling of affairs at your end. I also realize how difficult it is in Delhi to get the full flavor of the situation here. However, I'm sure you will understand the President's own judgment as to why the timing would be better, and your presence here more productive, when our own affairs on the Hill and in Vietnam are more fully sorted out.

---

[3] On May 8, Rusk informed Bowles, in a personal cable, that the decision had been made to defer a response to the Indian request for F–5 aircraft. (Telegram 2348 to New Delhi; National Archives and Records Administration, RG 59, Central Files 1964–66, DEF 19–8 US–INDIA)

114. Telegram From the Embassy Office in Pakistan to the Department of State[1]

Rawalpindi, April 30, 1965.

43. Deptel 1230[2] and 1231[3] and Rawalpindi's 42[4] to Department.

1. Just after I left my noon meeting April 30 with Foreign Minister Bhutto, he requested me to see him again at 4 p.m. When I returned for second meeting, I found Foreign Minister Bhutto and Foreign Secretary Aziz Ahmed noticeably agitated. Bhutto explained that they had received, just after my noon call, message from Ambassador G. Ahmed reporting his conversation with Talbot on April 27 (Deptel 1217)[5] at which Talbot had set forth our position that MAP equipment not to be used in disputed areas (Deptel 1200).[6] Bhutto pointed out question had profound implications for GOP since bulk of its military equipment is MAP-supplied and probably any military action by India against Pakistan would be launched from or against disputed area, such as Kashmir or Rann of Kutch. Paks under this reasoning could not use MAP where it would be needed and would be in impossible position.

2. I clarified our position in accordance with Deptel 1230 stressing that we were not laying out rigid generalized rule necessarily applicable to all disputed territories. We would expect to make determination on each issue based on merits or case. In case of Rann of Kutch we considered facts and circumstances murky, legitimate self-defense not established, and therefore use of MAP equipment by either side not justified. Situation here readily susceptible to settlement without dangerous resort to force and cease-fire should be pursued. Furthermore, question

---

[1] Source: National Archives and Records Administration, RG 59, Central Files 1964–66, POL 32–1 INDIA–PAK. Secret; Immediate. Repeated to New Delhi, London, Karachi, CINCMEAFSA, and DOD. No time of transmission is given on the telegram, which was received at 4:34 p.m. Passed to the White House and CIA.

[2] In telegram 1230 to Karachi, April 29, the Department clarified its position with respect to the acceptable use of MAP equipment. The legal position outlined in telegram 1200 to Karachi, April 24, was intended to apply to the situation in the Rann of Kutch, and was not meant to imply that a case for legitimate self-defense could never be made in connection with a disputed border. (Ibid.)

[3] Telegram 1231 to Karachi, April 29, instructed McConaughy to make clear the U.S. position with respect to the use of MAP equipment in his scheduled meeting with Bhutto on April 30. (Ibid.)

[4] Telegram 42 from Rawalpindi, April 30, reported on McConaughy's first meeting with Bhutto on April 30. Bhutto, on instructions from Ayub, asked McConaughy to ascertain what the U.S. position would be in the event that "unmistakable Indian threats" led to general warfare between India and Pakistan. Bhutto described the situation as the gravest in the history of Indo-Pakistani relations and reviewed the history of U.S. assurances to protect Pakistan in the event of Indian aggression. (Ibid.)

[5] Document 112.

[6] See footnote 3, Document 112.

of use of MAP equipment in Rann of Kutch area would be merely academic point if cease-fire achieved. At later points in conversation, I hammered away at this point in order to emphasize necessity of Pak agreement to cease-fire.

3. Bhutto and Aziz Ahmed were at once relieved by clarification that no far-reaching generalized principle automatically to all disputed areas had been set up, and still deeply concerned by implications of our postulation as applied to Rann of Kutch situation. Two main points made by Bhutto and Aziz Ahmed in commenting on our position re use of MAP equipment were: (a) Before US attempted to make unilateral decision as to whether legitimate self-defense involved in Rann of Kutch or in other areas, further extensive consideration facts and full consultations between us should be held. (b) Since most Pak military equipment MAP-supplied, while Indians not dependent to any comparable extent on US sources, Paks would be more heavily penalized by US withholding from both sides, and Indians would be emboldened if Paks relatively disadvantaged. Under present circumstances in Rann of Kutch, GOP would be forced to withdraw all its forces onesidedly, since they mainly MAP-supplied, while Indians not thus handicapped.

4. Aziz Ahmed also presented Pak justification that use of MAP in Rann of Kutch in fact "legitimate self-defense" involving defense of territory properly claimed by GOP and wrongfully attacked by India. He pointed to following facts: (a) GOP maintained post at Chad Bet until 1956, at which time Indian forces came in with air cover and took over post by force, which GOP did not resist; (b) in 1960 when territorial dispute last discussed, it was agreed that neither side would disturb status quo; (c) beginning in January 1965 India in fact disturbed status quo by establishing a series of new posts in disputed territory and by moving in first police and then strong military forces; and (d) GOP did not move troops into disputed area until 18 April after Indians hit Pak post at Ding preemptorily, demanded Pak evacuation of Kanjarkot and took over other posts.

5. In reply, I stressed first that facts still murky, given strong Indian presentation of its conflicting position, that US taking openminded position in absence of basis for judgment, that pressing objective at moment is to achieve cease-fire, and that problem involved in this case clearly dictated closer consultations at early stage on any comparable threatening situation in future. I assured Paks that, in taking stance on Rann of Kutch, we are applying terms of standing agreement to particular existing situation rather than redefining this agreement or establishing any general restriction indiscriminately applicable to all disputed territories.

6. Bhutto came back to question he raised at earlier meeting on US assurances, drawing analogy between US determination on use of

MAP equipment and US determination on whether aggression involved. He recalled that, during his discussions with Under Secretary Ball in Washington in October 1963, he had foreseen the very possibility that, in a murky situation, aggression could not be readily determined and that our assurances to GOP on aggression by India would be difficult to invoke quickly enough to help Pakistan. For this reason, Bhutto said, he had urged further definition and strengthening of our assurances. Instead, the US reaction in the Rann of Kutch crisis would appear to confirm Pak misgivings and to dilute the force and dependability of US assurances. Bhutto urged an early response to his inquiry of this morning on US reaction in event Indian threats of retaliation carried out. He also proposed that urgent problem of right to use MAP equipment be accorded further exhaustive consideration and analysis by two governments, even [*given?*] its far-reaching implications.

7. I told Bhutto that I was doubtful that reply would be received to his question about US assurances before he left for London evening May 2 but this was matter he might take up with Secretary at London. I also indicated again that it seemed unlikely that we would be able comment on hypothetical situations relating to recent Indian vague threats which we hope and believe India will not carry out. Bhutto argued that current Indian threat not hypothetical given statements made by Shastri and other recent Indian actions.

8. During discussion, in response my pressing on need for immediate cease-fire, Bhutto reiterated that Paks prepared for cease-fire as outlined to UK. He also informed me of gist of Ayub reply to Wilson letter of April 30 setting basis for "de facto" cease-fire. He informed me that Pak forces have been restrained from taking further action so as not to aggravate situation further in Rann of Kutch area. Pak forces in area are therefore not taking advantage of superior military position which would now permit them readily to reach 24th parallel, and to take over Chad Bet and cut off whole GOI force from its line of retreat.

Comment: It quite clear at conclusion our meeting, which lasted almost one hour, that Bhutto and Aziz Ahmed quite shaken by definition of our position in context of actual Rann of Kutch situation, and also in context of how it might affect US MAP support and defense assistance in event of future fuzzed over aggression by India.

9. I would not recommend immediate response to Bhutto reassuring GOP on effectiveness of past assurances against aggression, since a little uncertainty on their part for next few days could provide the additional leverage needed to achieve cease-fire. However, I do not think that we can postpone providing these reassurances very long without risking very serious damage to our position here. At same time, I strongly urge that GOI be reminded immediately of the standing explicit US assurances to Pakistan as a further deterrent against an

Indian contemplation of retaliatory action against Pakistan in another area, such as East Pakistan.

McConaughy

115. Telegram From the Embassy in India to the Department of State[1]

New Delhi, May 1, 1965, 0400Z.

3111. Ambassadors Bowles and Lodge[2] this evening called on Prime Minister Shastri who was obviously preoccupied with the situation in the Rann of Kutch. PM asked Lodge to convey the following message to President Johnson: the Government of India has no objections to discussions concerning boundary demarcations in Kutch area. GOI has agreed to British proposals for cease-fire and discussions. If Pakistan does not accept a cease-fire he "shudders" to think what position GOI might have to adopt. Not only is there a danger of a large conflict, internal difficulties are also possible (he mentioned specifically the possibility of communal disturbances in both countries).

Pakistani propaganda concerning Indian attack is preposterous since, if India had planned an attack, it would never have chosen such an unfavorable area.

Shastri further stated that on April 13 Pakistan had made proposals consisting of (1) a cease-fire, (2) return to the status quo ante, (3) further discussions. The next day GOI accepted. Immediately thereafter Pakistan withdrew the original proposal and made further demands.

Lodge agreed to deliver the message to President Johnson. The conversation then turned to the situation in Vietnam. Lodge outlined the reasons why Vietnam is an important issue and described the nature of the struggle. He concluded with a request for any advice Shastri might want to proffer and suggested the possibility that GOI might

---

[1] Source: National Archives and Records Administration, RG 59, Central Files 1964–66, POL 32–1 INDIA–PAK. Secret. Also sent to the White House, and repeated to Saigon and CINCPAC for POLAD.

[2] Ambassador Henry Cabot Lodge stopped at New Delhi on the way to Vietnam at President Johnson's request to assure Prime Minister Shastri that Johnson had meant no discourtesy in postponing Shastri's visit. Lodge was instructed to explain the reasons for the postponement again, and to tell Shastri that Johnson was anxious to reschedule the visit. (Telegram CAP 65137 to New Delhi, April 27; ibid., POL 7 INDIA)

want to assist the GVN in some concrete manner such as by sending ambulances and personnel.

Shastri then commented that he appreciated the clear description of the situation and remarked that the U.S. was the best judge of what should be done. He stated somewhat wistfully that there seemed little chance for talks. In describing his position that conflict should cease, he stressed that the North Vietnamese and the Vietcong must cease their activities as part of an agreement.

The meeting ended with a brief discussion of the degree to which Communist China is failing to gain complete support in Africa and the nonaligned countries.

Bowles

---

116. Telegram From the Embassy in Pakistan to the Department of State[1]

Karachi, May 4, 1965, 1700Z.

2125. Rann of Kutch.

1. I had a concentrated 15-minute conversation with President Ayub in Karachi today at a tea following investiture ceremony. He showed conciliatory attitude toward resolution Rann of Kutch dispute, but extremely tough posture toward Indians in event they attack Pakistan in new area. He said public opinion in this country would never condone a passive reaction to an unprovoked Indian strike at some new point along Pakistan border. In that event Pakistan would hit back without pulling the punch and he felt no other government could blame her. He noted that Pakistani forces had held back in the Rann. Could easily have pushed south to the 24th parallel and beyond. This restraint had been in deference to the views of their friends and to the fact that the situation was a confused one. The same restraints would not apply in the event of outright and flagrant Indian aggression in a new place unrelated to the Rann of Kutch.

2. I told President that we were strongly hopeful that Indians would not strike elsewhere. We felt that some of the strong statements

---

[1] Source: Johnson Library, National Security File, Country File, Pakistan, Vol. III, Cables, 12/64–7/65. Secret; Immediate. Repeated to London, New Delhi, CINCMEAFSA for POLAD, and DOD. Passed to the White House and CIA.

made by Prime Minister Shastri in the Lok Sabha were dictated by domestic political requirements and should not be taken literally at face value. We were counseling restraint just as earnestly on the Indian side as on the Pakistani side. We thought that threatening talk on either side made the already dangerous situation more inflammable, and we hoped such talk could be avoided.

3. President said he was sympathetic with settlement efforts which British are making and he was cooperating to the best of his ability. Pakistan had been glad to do its part in virtual cease-fire now in effect.[2] He was rather worried that there had been some light artillery firing on May 2, significance of which was obscure. He said he had already agreed in principle to arbitration or mediation of substance of the dispute by impartial authorities of third countries. He would be willing to grant them every facility and to pledge the GOP to abide by their findings and their award. He hoped it would be possible to proceed promptly to this conclusive stage. He reiterated that Pakistan would agree to make the arbitration binding.

4. I raised the problem of intermediate stages, presumably involving a formalized cease-fire, disengagement, restoration of some sort of status quo ante and possible negotiation or discussion of substance of dispute between representatives of interested parties. The President was distrustful of Indian good faith during intermediate stages and expressed the view that any restoration of status quo ante during interim period should be dispensed with. He also thought bilateral substantive negotiation between the two sides would probably be useless or worse, with Indians inclined to take advantage of any intermediate sites to consolidate their position in upper Rann and then refuse to budge or admit existence of dispute, regardless of recommendations of any outside impartial body, as in case of previous Indo-Pak disputes. The President said he thought withdrawal by both sides from disputed zone was only necessary preliminary to arbitration or mediation effort. If Indians distrusted Pakistan observance of withdrawal agreement because of relatively higher terrain on Pak side of disputed area, he would be glad to agree to impartial military observers coming into disputed area to insure that neither side violated withdrawal terms while arbitral group was deliberating. He reaffirmed that Pakistan would accept arbitral award even if it was entirely unfavorable to Pakistan.

---

[2] In telegram 2097 from Karachi, May 2, McConaughy reported on a conversation the previous night with Bhutto in which Bhutto said that his government had decided to observe a cease-fire, if India did the same. Bhutto stated that the paramount consideration in the government's decision had been the special relationship with the United States. (Ibid.)

5. I told President that I regretted GOP decision not to allow visit of our MAAG representatives to that part of Rann which Paks hold. I had thought it would be useful for officers to see exact situation and extent of use of MAP and other military material. Especially in view Indian permission for our officers in New Delhi to visit Indian side, I thought negative Pak decision was regrettable. I noted that Paks had assured us they had nothing to hide and I thought a policy of free MAAG access to the combat area would be more compatible with Pak position that there is nothing to hide. It would also be more consonant with general [garble—nature?] of full confidence between GOP forces and our MAAG, which was implicit in the mutual defense relationship.

6. President said it was idea true [sic] that Pak Army had nothing to hide. He had felt that there was no particular point in military visits since Paks freely state and acknowledge that they are using MAP equipment and MAAG knows exactly what each Pak unit has. Forces committed to the area are all MAP supported and he pointed out that of course troops in combat use whatever equipment they have, regardless of origin.

7. President then astounded me by saying that he had approved turn [down?] of US suggestion for military visit to Rann area because he understood that it was proposed to bring out officers from the United States for this purpose. He did not see the necessity of this when there were highly-qualified MAAG officers in Pakistan who knew the situation better than any outside officers could.

8. President, in turn, was astounded when I told him he evidently had been misinformed by his people; that we had never suggested or even thought of bringing out officers from the US to make the inspection. I told him that of course we had proposed to use only resident MAAG officers. President replied that he had no objection to visit by MAAG officers and that he would give appropriate orders to facilitate immediate visit, if I wanted this done.

9. I told him I thought it would be a good idea, assuming he perceived no substantial objection. President said he had absolutely no objection although he doubted if anything new would be established as a result of the visit.

10. He then called Brigadier Riaz Hussain, Chief of ISID (who was standing nearby) over to join us and instructed him, in my presence, to arrange visit of two MAAG officers immediately. He turned to me to say that General Ruhlen, MAAG Chief, knew the score completely and he would like for him to go personally. I said we had thought in terms of the Colonel who was chief of the Army section under General Ruhlen and perhaps an artillery officer. But I had no objection to General Ruhlen going and I would ask him to go if the President wanted him included. The President told Riaz Hussain to arrange for General

Ruhlen and one other MAAG officer, named by me or General Ruhlen, to go immediately. He said they should go first to Badin, then to Eighth Division headquarters and then as far down in the combat area under Pak control as they cared to go.

11. I am now consulting with General Ruhlen as to details with a view to laying the trip on for Thursday, May 6.

McConaughy

---

117. Memorandum of Conversation[1]

Washington, May 8, 1965.

SUBJECT

Use of U.S. Arms in Rann of Kutch

PARTICIPANTS

The Secretary
His Excellency B. K. Nehru, Ambassador of India
NEA—William J. Handley, Deputy Assistant Secretary
NEA/SOA—David T. Schneider, India Desk

Ambassador Nehru came in at his request to discuss Indo-Pakistan relations. The Ambassador said he did not want to discuss so much the pros and cons of the Kutch issue as the question of the use of U.S. arms by Pakistan in the Rann of Kutch. He said that there was "incontrovertible proof" that Pakistan had used U.S. tanks against India in the Rann. The Ambassador presented the Secretary with nine pictures of tanks, trucks and soldiers which he said had been taken at Biar Bet by a low flying aircraft. The Ambassador read from a Reuters report which said that President Ayub had indicated Pakistan was using U.S. arms and was entitled to the use of all arms in its possession. He said that the Pakistani units involved in Kutch were MAP-supplied units. Summarizing his position, the Ambassador said it was "incontrovertible" that Pakistan had taken action against India to alter the status quo in the Rann and had used U.S. arms in contravention of U.S. assurances to India given by President Eisenhower, Secretary Dulles, and Ambassador Bunker.

---

[1] Source: National Archives and Records Administration, RG 59, Central Files 1964–66, DEF 12 INDIA. Secret. Drafted by Schneider and approved in S on May 17.

The Secretary said we had expressed our position on use of U.S. equipment quite strongly to both India and Pakistan. Ambassador Nehru asked what the Secretary meant by both sides. India had not used U.S. equipment. The Secretary said Pakistan claims to have captured U.S.-made 106 mm recoilless rifles. Our inspectors who visited the Indian lines, however, have not seen such equipment. It was on the basis of the claims of both sides that we made statements to both India and Pakistan.

Continuing, the Secretary informed Ambassador Nehru that we did not have the full story yet from our military observers but Pakistan had not denied it had used U.S. equipment. We had made it clear to Pakistan that we were not willing that such equipment be used. We have expressed our views strongly—very strongly. When the Pakistanis raised the question of our assurances to them in connection with a possible Indian retaliatory attack, we replied that we considered such a question hypothetical. We believe our representations have had something to do with the Pakistani decision not to escalate hostilities further in the Rann. We hope the British peace efforts will succeed in taking this dispute out of the military area to the conference table.

Ambassador Nehru said that while India hopes the Kutch question will be resolved, a more important question of principle is involved. U.S. assurances to India had been the foundation of Indian defense policy. If these assurances were eroded, it would be a very serious matter. The Secretary asked what Ambassador Nehru would have us do. At first, the Ambassador said this was not for him to say except that, as far as India was concerned, the U.S. reaction had been inadequate. When further pressed by the Secretary, he said an adequate action would be to tell Pakistan that the U.S. would not provide any more arms. He said he was without instructions on this point, however. The Secretary suggested the alternative of stopping use of U.S. arms in the Kutch area. Ambassador Nehru commented, "If you can."

The Secretary asked Ambassador Nehru what he could say about Indian troop movements. Indicating he did not know the details on this subject, the Ambassador said what movement had taken place was of troops without U.S. arms. He then returned to the theme that Indian defense policy was based upon the assumption that U.S. assurances were enforceable, mentioning that a substantial part of the GOI had been committed to this belief. He said he had argued with the Finance Minister years ago against increased defense expenditures on the grounds that U.S. assurances would be carried out.

The Ambassador said one aspect of the problem regarding U.S. assurances was public and political. Mentioning a Selig Harrison article in the *Washington Post* and a speech by A.B. Vajpayee in Parliament, he described the great criticism of the U.S. in India for permitting

Pakistan to use U.S. arms in violation of U.S. assurances. He then charged that the U.S. was merely equating India with Pakistan saying, "Every time Pakistan hits us, you must hit both sides." The Secretary referred to reports he had heard of the movement of Indian mountain divisions, which he thought were MAP supplied. Mr. Handley noted that the 50th para brigade which India had used in Kutch had been furnished limited MAP equipment, but that it was not known if it had taken any MAP items with them.

The Secretary said that the test of the adequacy of our actions with Pakistan was the result, i.e., the end of the fighting. Ambassador Nehru said, however, something also must be done in public to help take care of India's Parliamentary problem. The Secretary responded that what we say publicly should be related to the British peace effort. Ambassador Nehru agreed we should do nothing to interfere with that.

Looking to the future, the Secretary said we would get complete information on use of U.S. equipment shortly. Our people have already visited Indian forces and report they had not found any U.S. equipment. We have not had any report from the Pak side, but we suppose our inspectors will find U.S. arms. Then we will go to the Pak Government and ask that our understandings be complied with. At what point this becomes public depends upon the British peace-making effort.

Mr. Handley said that we had spoken most strongly to Pakistan, as Ambassador Bowles has told the GOI. The Ambassador responded that Pakistan's use of the equipment nonetheless went on. When Mr. Handley pointed out that the proof of the effectiveness of our action was the cessation of hostilities, Ambassador Nehru said that India had also stopped and Pakistanis were still in Indian territory. The Secretary countered by saying that MAP equipment was not being used today to fire on Indians. Terming this a good argument but unsatisfying, the Ambassador said the credibility of U.S. assurances is in question and must be re-established. The Secretary repeated that the effectiveness of U.S. assurances and the cessation of hostilities were very closely related. The test of our fulfilling our assurances is in what happens. Taking issue with the Secretary, the Ambassador said the test was not whether the fighting stopped, but was whether Pakistan was prevented from using U.S. equipment. Under present circumstances, Pakistan can use the equipment at some other place again. The Secretary responded that if the Ambassador was suggesting that we take punitive action far beyond what is needed, such as a break with Pakistan, he should know we will not do this. The Ambassador replied he was not asking this and agreed with the Secretary that what we do is our problem regarding which he could not advise us.

Mr. Handley asked that since the GOI knows we have taken a very strong position with Pakistan and this had had a favorable result, was there anything that could be done in Delhi to tone down the public reaction? The Ambassador dismissed this question by saying that he did not believe his Government considered the U.S. has taken adequate measures. The Prime Minister had said as much. When the Secretary asked what the result of the British effort would be, the Ambassador replied that it would succeed but only because India would make compromises.

Returning to the subject of U.S. assurances, the Secretary said our objective was to end the fighting; then the question of use of U.S. equipment would not arise. If the problem of use of U.S. equipment came up again, we would deal with it at that time. The Ambassador replied this was not enough. It would not give India any assurance regarding the future. The Secretary said he should think that the cessation of the fighting was a demonstration that we considered our commitments to both India and Pakistan seriously.

The Ambassador reacted strongly to this comment asking why the U.S. insists on considering India and Pakistan together. India observes its commitments scrupulously; to equate it with Pakistan was wrong. One party has obeyed the law, the other has not. Why this equation? The Secretary again asked about Indian troop movements. He ended the conversation saying that we had made representations to both sides on the basis of charges made by both India and Pakistan. We would continue to try to get more information regarding use of U.S. arms. Ambassador Nehru concluded saying India had given full facilities to U.S. observers who had found no U.S. equipment. Therefore, the U.S. should not equate India and Pakistan when "the other side" is guilty.

118. **Telegram From the Department of State to the Embassy in India**[1]

Washington, May 8, 1965, 2:34 p.m.

2349. Eyes Only Ambassador From Secretary. I would greatly appreciate your personal estimate as to whether Shastri's political weakness may not be major element of danger in present situation. Reports just received of arrest of Sheik Abdullah[2] and rioting in Srinagar[3] are further signs that he may be too weak to be wise. His attempt in parliament yesterday to lay blame on us, despite his knowledge of strongest possible efforts we have made in Pakistan on MAP problem is another. Reports of troop movements in India involving units equipped with MAP are relevant. So is London's 208 repeated to you.[4] Please let us know whether there is more we should do to support UK peacemaking effort. B.K. Nehru saw me and made it clear he wanted more than pull back or stand down of MAP equipment in Rann of Kutch; he wanted us to punish Pakistan by cutting off all aid. Public impression here that India moved to change a status quo in Rann of Kutch, that India refuses to acknowledge that a dispute exists, that India threatens to widen the conflict into other areas and that India is exploiting MAP to blame us for a difficulty with Pakistan. Regards.

Rusk

---

[1] Source: National Archives and Records Administration, RG 59, Central Files 1964–66, POL 32–1 INDIA–PAK. Secret; Immediate; Nodis. Drafted and approved by Rusk. A handwritten notation on the telegram reads "OK/L," indicating that it was cleared by President Johnson.

[2] The arrest of Abdullah on May 8 was reported in telegram 3199 from New Delhi, May 8. (Ibid., POL 29 INDIA)

[3] According to an official government spokesman in New Delhi, four people were killed by police in Srinagar in demonstrations protesting the arrest of Sheikh Abdullah. (Telegram 3205 from New Delhi, May 8; ibid., POL 28–8 INDIA)

[4] The reference is in error; the telegram has not been further identified.

119.   Telegram From the Embassy in India to the Department of State[1]

New Delhi, May 10, 1965, 0930Z.

3210. For Secretary Rusk. Deptel 2349.[2] I shall comment on questions posed in your personal cable as briefly and precisely as I can.

1. I agree that Shastri in dealing with present crisis has been weak, unsophisticated and needlessly fearful of his Parliamentary opposition. Because Parliament has been in session this has further complicated already complex situation and added to dangers. (*Note:* Parliament recesses this week until August.)

2. In present heavily charged atmosphere it would have been serious mistake for Abdullah to have returned to Srinagar; riots encouraged by Pak and/or ChiCom agitators could readily have got out of hand. However I believe Sheikh could have been persuaded voluntarily to stay away from Kashmir until dust settles. Fact that GOI instead of attempting so to persuade him arbitrarily sent him off to South India under house arrest reflects their present state of jitters.

3. In regard to US protest to Paks on use of US equipment, GOI has had only your statements to B.K. Nehru and my guarded off the record statements here to go on, and these did not help them in dealing with agitated oppositionists on floor of Parliament. Moreover unchallenged Pak insistence that USG had in fact made no protest further confused our public position and left us open to bitter attacks from leftwingers and suspicion from moderates.

In this context Shastri's impatient reaction to taunt in Parliament (apparently based on leak from Talbot's talk with B.K. Nehru) that we had warned India against attacking Pakistan reflects Indian resentment at being bracketed with Pakistan in situation where they genuinely believe themselves to be victim. Nevertheless Shastri's comment was uncalled for and I shall so state when I see L.K. Jha this afternoon.

4. We believe US equipped Indian troops now in vicinity of West Pakistan border are limited to two brigades. We have asked clearance for USMSMI officer to visit area and ascertain facts.

Most immediate danger lies in fact that both armies which by common consent had been five miles back from each side of border are now directly on border. UK HICOMM has expressed agreement with my suggestion that when and if we get ceasefire UK should

---

[1] Source: National Archives and Records Administration, RG 59, Central Files 1964–66, POL 32–1 INDIA–PAK. Secret; Immediate; Nodis.

[2] Document 118.

continue in its mediating role to press for return to their former positions.

5. If we were publicly to chastise Paks for misuse of US equipment as urged by B.K. Nehru we would greatly ease public resentment against us here in India, which would make our lives easier, but we might also destroy hope for negotiated agreement. Under these circumstances, I agree with our position and have supported it vigorously with Indian press, members of Cabinet and other opinion makers.

6. In regard to border dispute itself Pak-India border was accepted at time of partition in all British official agreements and maps as the border between old state of Sind which went to Pakistan and old state of Kutch which went to India and is so registered on all US maps. Consequently it is difficult for either US or British, who were originally responsible for establishing border, to see how Indians could lose the case before impartial tribunal.

India does not, however deny that disagreement exists as to precise location of this border since it was never demarcated by British and hence may run few hundred yards north or south of present line as shown on map. However not until 1954 did Paks introduce proposition that Kutch was inland sea and that hence they were entitled to half of it; i.e., down to 24th parallel.

7. In regard to who started Kutch squabble no one can be sure. Blow-up may have been result of deliberate Pak push to make Indians look foolish; if so, mission was accomplished. It is also conceivable that there was some tie with Chinese. However it seems to me more likely that fight started by accident as in case of two small boys pushing each other on playground after school.

In any event, India with her deep concern over China which until three weeks ago was uppermost in minds of most Indians had nothing whatsoever to gain from attack on Pakistan. Moreover if India should in fact have plotted attack on Pakistan it surely would not have chosen area where Indian armed forces are at such disadvantage in regard to terrain and logistics. India had only police in area. Nearest Indian military was battalion sixty miles away on other side of sandy waste.

8. India right now is in angry, unreasonable, and indeed irrational mood due to combination of reasons: i.e., lingering humiliation from Chinese attack, Chinese prestige gain with nuclear bomb which India could also produce, Indian Army's alleged defeat at hands of Pak Army in Kutch, and frustrated feeling that US, whom six out of seven Indians according to our public opinion poll of few months ago considered India's best friend, does not understand their position.

While Shastri has been responsive to this mood, and at times even contributed to it, he has thus far firmly retained power of decision at each step along way toward cease fire.

Barring some accident there is no reason to assume that war is at hand. British HICOMM John Freeman believes that cease fire agreement may be reached before adjournment of Parliament Tuesday night. Shastri leaves for Moscow Wednesday and has extended his visit which had previously been cut to three days to comply with his original schedule. He will also leave on schedule for London, Ottawa and Algiers as planned.

9. In regard to how USG can best support British John Freeman believes that our most effective move would be to make it clear to Paks that US arms are not to be used against Indians except in clear case of Indian invasion of Pak territory. Barring this private reiteration of our previous statement we both feel US should stay on sidelines.

In meantime we have made most vigorous effort to impress Indian leaders and opinion makers with total folly of retaliatory attack on Pakistan, to warn of Chinese plot designed to wreck both Pakistan and India, and to explain our unaligned position as best we can, etc.

10. Even though situation settles down as we feel it is likely to do, considerable ground will have been lost in India. I can foresee two particularly unhappy possibilities and one potentially favorable one.

A. Whether or not we believe it to be justified Indians have been genuinely and deeply disturbed. As long as we describe ourselves as an ally of Pakistan they will not henceforth trust our guaranties. In view of their fear combined attack by both China and Pakistan this lack of confidence may lead them into costly and foolhardy guns ahead of butter approach with possibility of decision to proceed with nuclear explosion regardless of implications to US aid or to economic progress.

B. If Soviets want to make big play for India, door is now wide open; even many normally sober and pro-American Indians for moment at least are easy target for Soviet blandishments.

It is open question, of course, as to how Soviets may choose to use their opportunity. Soviet resources are limited and too close a relationship with still democratic India would confuse their Leninist role as revolutionary leader. I would expect them, however, to go considerable distance in Moscow meeting with Shastri, perhaps very great distance.

C. One positive element that I can see at present is possibility that present eyeball to eyeball confrontation may have same sobering effect on Pakistan and India that Cuban confrontation had on US and USSR. If so, it could open range of more favorable possibilities.

This, I hope, answers your specific questions. I am preparing more complete cable which will provide background in depth which I believe is urgently needed if we are to prevent rapid and disastrous erosion of US position in South Asia which we have been laboriously building up for last decade.

Bowles

---

120. Letter From the Ambassador of Pakistan (Ahmed) to Secretary of State Rusk[1]

Washington, May 11, 1965.

My dear Mr. Secretary,

I have received the following message from the President of Pakistan for transmission to the President of the United States:

Begins "Dear Mr. President,

I write to inform you of the grave situation that has arisen in the sub-continent as a result of India's aggressive actions in recent months: First, the forcible occuption of Pakistan's enclave of Dahagram, then an aggressive march into disputed territory of the Rann of Kutch and now concentration of virtually the entire striking power of the Indian armed forces on Pakistan borders. Dahagram was restored to us only after the Indians came to realise that their action was wholly untenable and it was impossible for them to continue to stay there; India's attempt to take over disputed Rann of Kutch territory by force was foiled only by counter military measures which we, under the circumstances, were compelled to take, and, now, we too have had to deploy our forces in defensive positions on the India-Pakistan border to meet the threat that arises from India's latest action.

2. As you know Kashmir has been the prime source of this conflict between India and Pakistan. Even as I write, reports are pouring in from Srinagar and other places in Indian-occupied Kashmir of wholesale arrests of Kashmiri leaders and firing by Indian forces on the unfortunate Kashmiri people whose only crime is that they are struggling to free themselves of Indian military yoke and are protesting against the imprisonment by India for the third time of their leader Sheikh Abdullah. This is yet another instance of India's cynical disre-

---

[1] Source: Johnson Library, National Security File, Head of State Correspondence File, Pakistan, Vol. I, Pres. Ayub Correspondence, 12/15/63–12/31/64. No classification marking. The letter was forwarded to the White House on May 12, under cover of a memorandum from Executive Secretary Read to McGeorge Bundy. (Ibid.)

gard of the need for a peaceful settlement of her disputes with Pakistan on a just and honourable basis.

3. This same attitude is demonstrated by the Indian stand in regard to the Rann of Kutch dispute. Here again, as in the case of Kashmir, the Government of India now claims that the disputed territory is Indian territory. In actual fact the dispute concerning this territory has been previously discussed between India and Pakistan on several occasions—the latest in 1960 when the two Governments agreed that pending further consideration of this dispute, neither side would disturb the status quo. India accuses Pakistan of aggression in the Rann of Kutch. In fact it was India that moved large forces into the disputed territory during months of January–April this year, established forward military posts therein and carried out full-scale land, sea and air manoeuvres in its vicinity, thus forcibly demolishing the status quo. It was only on April 8th when the Indian forces attacked a Pakistan outpost at Ding in an endeavour to complete a military take over of the territory to present Pakistan with a fait accompli that the Pakistan forces went into action for the first time, and it was on April 19th after patiently watching India's aggressive actions in the Rann of Kutch for three and a half months that Pakistan forces went into the disputed territory for the first time. Subsequent military developments in the Rann are known to your Government.

4. Foiled in her attempt to seize the disputed territory by force, the Indian Prime Minister proceeded publicly to threaten Pakistan that India would attack Pakistan on other points of our border of her own choosing if we refused to accept solution dictated by India. These were: a cease-fire and return to status quo ante, which meant that India would stay in possession of the disputed territory while we would have to clear out, and that the dispute would be settled only on the basis that the border needed to be demarcated and there was no territory in dispute. We could scarcely be expected to accept such a demand at the point of the gun.

5. Even in face of this I have exercised the greatest restraint. On April 29th I stopped our troops in the Rann of Kutch from exploiting a favourable tactical situation when after the capture of Biar Bet they were in a position to cut right through to the Indian forces on the 24th parallel and destroy from the rear the two Indian Brigades located in the disputed territory. Furthermore on April 30th I unilaterally ordered our troops in the Rann of Kutch not to do anything that might aggravate the situation, which ultimately led to a de facto cease-fire there. All this was done in face of considerable opposition and in the hope India may thus be convinced of our sincere desire to settle disputes by the sensible method available, i.e., by peaceful means.

6. Following these truculent declarations India has massed practically the entire Indian Army and Air Force, including all Indian armour,

on Pakistan's borders in offensive formations. Pakistan has naturally had to deploy her own forces in defensive positions to meet this new threat. We have also informed the Security Council of the threat to peace that has thus arisen in this region.

7. The armies of Pakistan and India now stand poised against each other. The situation is one of the utmost gravity. A trial of armed strength between India and Pakistan will be a war without frontiers. It could engulf the entire six hundred million people of this sub-continent with all its terrible consequences. But we trust that even at this late hour it may be possible for the Indian leaders to pause and consider where India's true interests lie and that she may refrain from seeking a military decision.

8. As you know Mr. President we have time and again warned your Government that arming of India by the U.S. on the scale on which it has proceeded during the last two years could only lead to situations such as the present, that India would be encouraged to settle her disputes with Pakistan by force, that she was building two armies—one allegedly to fight the Chinese and the other to contain Pakistan—but that when she found a suitable opportunity she would employ both these armies against Pakistan. Your Government continued to believe that India had no such aggressive intentions, and has continued to arm India even though the Chinese military threat has admittedly receded. While defending this policy spokesmen of your Government have time and again reminded us of American assurances to come to our assistance in the event of aggression. At one time Mr. Harriman even expressed surprise to our Ambassador that Pakistan should not have been satisfied with those assurances. That India should have followed her aggressive actions in the Rann of Kutch by proceeding to mass against Pakistan practically her entire army—and a large part of forces allegedly facing China—regardless of your diplomatic persuasions to the contrary, and that the two countries should now be on the brink of war confirms fears we have repeatedly expressed about the unwisdom of arming an aggressive and unreliable India.

9. Explaining the explosive situation arising out of the massing of Indian troops on our borders we have suggested to your Ambassador that your Government consider reminding Mr. Shastri of the existence of American assurances in the event of aggression against Pakistan in the hope that such a reminder may help to deter Mr. Shastri and the other fire-eating Indian leaders from involving the sub-continent in a war which could do irreparable damage to the cause of freedom and peace in this region.

With warm personal regards,

Yours sincerely,

Mohammad Ayub Khan." Ends.

I should be grateful if the above message is conveyed to the President.

Please accept, Mr. Secretary, the assurances of my highest consideration.[2]

G. Ahmed

---

[2] Ahmed delivered the letter to Rusk on May 11. After reading the letter, Rusk commented that according to a Reuters report just received from Karachi, the two sides appeared to have reached agreement on British proposals relating to the dispute in the Rann of Kutch. If that were the case, the concerns mentioned in Ayub's letter became moot. Ahmed agreed but reiterated that until a settlement was effected the situation along the border was volatile. (Telegram 1288 to Karachi, May 11; National Archives and Records Administration, RG 59, Central Files 1964–66, POL 32–1 INDIA–PAK)

---

121. Telegram From the Department of State to the Embassy in Pakistan[1]

Washington, May 14, 1965, 8:09 p.m.

1305. Pak Ambassador G. Ahmed called on Acting Assistant Secretary Handley at former's initiative May 14. Ambassador said he had very urgent message from his Government following up conversation he had had with Secretary May 11.[2]

Ambassador prefaced his remarks by saying British were now at most critical stage of negotiations and that as he understood it there were two main points of difference. First related to definition of issue itself and on this GOP view was that it of utmost importance that issue be clearly described as dispute that it is. This particularly important because next and important step was arbitration. Second point of difference related to re-establishment status quo. Indians insisting on reversion in Kutch to status quo as of January 1, 1965 and Ambassador said it seemed GOP prepared accept this. In view of much more serious

---

[1] Source: National Archives and Records Administration, RG 59, Central Files 1964–66, POL 32–1 INDIA–PAK. Secret; Immediate. Drafted by Laingen; cleared in substance by Murray in OSD/ISA, and Officer in Charge of UK Affairs Thomas M. Judd; and approved by Handley. Also sent to New Delhi and London, and repeated to CINCMEAFSA.

[2] See footnote 2, Document 120.

problem however of present concentration forces along other areas Pak-Indian border, his Government felt it of extreme importance that agreement also provide for withdrawal forces all along Indian border. In response question from Handley, Ambassador said Paks had made this proposal a condition to agreement to British proposals but he unaware of any Indian response.

Ambassador then said he under instructions inform U.S. that GOP regarded this condition of very great importance, particularly because of recent serious violations Pak air space. On May 12 unidentified Indian aircraft had overflown Suleimanki; on May 14 Indian Canberra had overflown Kharian, headquarters Pak armored strength. Ambassador said that ordinarily of course such planes would have been shot down but such action not taken because of Ayub's firm instructions up to now avoid any retaliatory action that ran risk broader conflict. His Government had now informed him however that because of latest overflights, PAF now under instructions take whatever action necessary deter further such violations. Ambassador said this emphasized extreme urgency of some agreement that would result in disentanglement of armies now facing each other along borders.

Handley said Ambassador well aware that we supporting British efforts. As Secretary said May 11 greatest possible prudence on both sides now essential and he wanted to re-emphasize what Secretary had said. He was sure Ambassador aware of tremendous costs to both countries should conflict ensue. He hoped strongly that agreement could be reached on cease fire so that both sides rather than risking pounding each other in battle would pound negotiating table across from each other. Said that alleged Indian overflights and possible Pak response highlighted extreme delicacy of situation and essentiality prudence and restraint on both sides. Handley said he would of course ensure that Ambassador's comments brought to attention all concerned.

Ambassador said Paks already exercising restraint but this had to be considered against facts involved. Facts were that Indians now more seriously violating Pak air space. In East Pakistan at Lathitilla Indians were engaged in heavy firing at Pak positions that could have serious consequences. In West Pakistan India had four Divisions, including armored Division, drawn up as close as 150 yards and at 25-mile depth. In East Pakistan Indians had available seven Divisions, three of which near Sikkim facing Chinese but other four already poised at various places along East Pakistan border. All of these facts in Pak view emphasized need for U.S. to use its influence help ensure that there be speedy disentanglement of forces along borders and urgent steps to stop any further violations Pak air space.

In subsequent telephone conversation Handley asked whether Pakistan had informed India of stronger position it now taking on alleged overflights. Ambassador said he did not know. Handley stressed urgent importance Pakistan doing so. We would of course inform our Embassy Delhi and GOI of what Ambassador had told us[3] but this clearly no substitute Paks taking steps immediately ensure that Indians aware instructions Pak forces now operating under.

Comment: We see G. Ahmed's approach combined with Ayub letter[4] as Pak effort designed enlist our aid in applying pressure on Indians at crucial point in British cease-fire negotiations. Their intent seems to be to try to shift our attention from Kutch and use of MAP there to broader question of possible Indian action elsewhere and our assurances relating thereto. We do not intend see GOP turn tables to keep our feet to fire instead of other way on.

For London: Please pass this urgently to Pickard.

Ball

---

[3] After his meeting with Ahmed, Handley called in Indian Minister Banerjee and conveyed to him the warning concerning Indian overflights of Pakistan territory that Ahmed had passed on to Handley. The Embassy in New Delhi was instructed to make a similar approach to the Ministry of Foreign Affairs. (Telegram 2408 to New Delhi, May 14; National Archives and Records Administration, RG 59, Central Files 1964–66, POL 31–1 INDIA–PAK)

[4] See Document 120.

---

122.   Memorandum From Robert Komer of the National Security Council Staff to President Johnson[1]

Washington, May 20, 1965.

Here is a new pitch from Dave Bell[2] on the importance of going ahead with the remaining *already authorized* loans to India and Pakistan plus the advance program loans to both.

AID and State see a strong foreign policy argument for going ahead in a normal businesslike way, especially so as to avoid suspicion

---

[1] Source: Johnson Library, National Security File, Name File, Komer Memos, Vol. I. Limited Official Use.

[2] Reference is to a May 20 memorandum from David E. Bell, Administrator of the Agency for International Development, to President Johnson. In the memorandum, Bell outlined the pending loans to India and Pakistan that would fulfill consortia commitments made to each country. (Ibid., NSC History, Indian Famine, Aug 1966–Feb 1967, Vol. IV)

that there was a major policy change implicit in the postponement of the Ayub and Shastri visits.

Beyond this, however, Bell is quite concerned over his domestic budgetary problem. All of the money involved, including the advances, *is from already appropriated FY'65 aid funds.* If we don't go ahead and obligate some of this before 30 May, it will look as though AID is crowding an unusually large amount of obligations into the last month of the fiscal year.

Worse yet, if we don't approve any of these loans before the end of the fiscal year, AID will have about $250 million left over on 30 June. Since we presented the FY'65 aid program to Congress last year as a minimum figure, we will have some explaining to do if this large an amount is left unspent. A carryover of this size might also affect Congressional willingness to approve the full amount you've requested for FY 1966.

Therefore, Bundy and I would join State and AID in urging that you approve going ahead with this program. *If we desire to exert pressure on Pakistan and/or India by holding off on various aid loans we can easily do so with FY 1966 money,* where we will not be under the same end of the fiscal year time pressure. Should you still have questions, Dave Bell is eager to talk with you on this matter.

R. W. Komer

Approve

See me[3]

---

[3] Johnson checked this option line. Komer sent another memorandum to the President on this issue on May 25 urging a positive decision. Johnson responded with a handwritten note on the memorandum that reads as follows: "Bob—Don't press me or pressure me—I'll get to this when I can, I hope today." (Ibid., Memos to the President, McGeorge Bundy, Vol. 10, Apr 15–May 31, 1965)

123. Letter From Prime Minister Shastri to President Johnson[1]

New Delhi, May 23, 1965.

Dear Mr. President,

On April 16, 1965 Ambassador Chester Bowles conveyed to me your message[2] informing me that for various reasons it would not be convenient for you to receive me in Washington on the 2nd June as previously arranged. In deference to your wishes, I had naturally, and I must confess with some sense of disappointment, to cancel the visit to the United States which was scheduled for early June. You have suggested that I should visit the USA in autumn. I am, however, not able to say at present whether my parliamentary and other commitments will permit me to do so.

You have referred to our close association in many common endeavours. We greatly value this association and trust that it will continue undiminished in a spirit of mutual understanding.

I was happy to meet Ambassador Henry Cabot Lodge who also handed me your letter of April 15. I was interested to learn from him about the Vietnam situation. The situation is really depressing and dangerous. I hope that it might be possible for circumstances to arise which will permit of a dialogue and a peaceful solution of the Vietnam problem. I know the same thought must be uppermost in your mind also. In today's situation when China is pursuing an aggressive policy, it is difficult to anticipate with any degree of certainty, the likely course of events. But believe me Mr. President, I do feel sincerely that the more rational elements might possibly respond well if it were possible for you to consider a cessation of the air strikes. In any case it would greatly strengthen the chances of a peaceful solution. Such a decision on your part would be a significant contribution towards the promotion of world peace and would be in keeping with the high statesmanship which the United States has displayed in moments of crisis.

We ourselves have been passing through a difficult situation. You are no doubt informed of the recent attack on us by Pakistan in the Kutch–Sind border area. This has roused a great deal of feeling. We are a peaceful nation wedded to the pursuit of peace and economic development but it seems our neighbours China and Pakistan are determined to provoke us. We are exercising a great deal of patience and we have responded positively to Prime Minister Harold Wilson's initia-

---

[1] Source: Johnson Library, National Security File, Country File, India, Shastri Correspondence. No classification marking.

[2] See Document 102.

tive to bring about a ceasefire and restoration of status quo ante. I am afraid Pakistan has been raising all kinds of difficulties regarding ceasefire and restoration of status quo as on 1st January, 1965 which have prevented an agreement being reached. The fact that Pakistan has been using United States armour and equipment against us has naturally caused much concern in our country. I know, however, that your Government has already taken up this matter with the Government of Pakistan.

With warmest personal regards,

Yours sincerely,

Lal Bahadur

---

124.   Memorandum From Robert Komer of the National Security Council Staff to the President's Special Assistant for National Security Affairs (Bundy)[1]

Washington, May 28, 1965.

McGB:

FYI we face two other *India–Pak aid problems,* which we haven't dared put up to the President yet:[2]

1. The pre-pledging session of the *Pak consortium* meets next *Tuesday.* Normally, we'd tell the other donors what we plan to put in, as an incentive to them. AID would normally lobby during this session to line up pledges for the next. The Paks are asking for $500 million (an economically sound step up from $435 last year), so the main issue will be who ups the ante how much.

But this time we'll simply say we haven't made up our minds. This lack of our usual enthusiasm will signal to the Paks that we're not doing business as usual, even though we'll say the increased Pak request is justified. There's enough uncertainty in this kind of signal (since we've already done some lobbying with the Germans) not to provoke a sharp Pak reaction, but it will make Ayub wonder. This might provide some restraint on his performance at the Algiers confer-

---

[1] Source: Johnson Library, National Security File, Name File, Komer Memos, Vol. I. Confidential.

[2] Bundy added a handwritten note to the end of the memorandum that reads: "Don't be scared—let's get ready to talk it out with him."

ence. Then, we'll have to make up our minds before pledging meeting at end of July.

2. We have to negotiate a new *PL 480 agreement for India* in June. The present one expires 30 June, and the pipeline will begin running out in July unless the Indians can place new orders mid-June. Meanwhile, there are a lot of technical details to be ironed out here and then negotiated with the Indians. We've told the State and AID not to ask the President's approval until they've taken comprehensive Congressional soundings. They'll finish that process and be in with their request for go-ahead late next week.

In sum, we can probably get through next week's Pak consortium session without going to LBJ, though we'll need his guidance before the end of July meeting. But Indian PL 480 is more urgent, since we really have to get going now to keep the food moving.

RWK

---

125. Telegram From the Department of State to the Embassy in India[1]

Washington, June 3, 1965, 10:52 a.m.

2518. Ref New Delhi's 3523, info London 909, Karachi 805.[2] Despite disappointing Indian response to latest British proposals and British discouragement in Delhi at near impasse reached there, it looks to us that British are far from dead end in current negotiating effort. While Indian position is more rigid, we note from complete rundown given by British here that Paks continue to be more flexible on points of difference, i.e., patrolling and disengagement. (This confirmed by NPR 793.)[3] British here also indicate CRO considering alternate ways of

---

[1] Source: National Archives and Records Administration, RG 59, Central Files 1964–66, POL 32–1 INDIA–PAK. Secret; Priority; Limdis. Drafted by Schneider on June 2, cleared by Cameron, and approved and initialed by Talbot. Repeated to Karachi and London.

[2] In telegram 3523 from New Delhi, June 2, the Embassy noted that the military confrontation between India and Pakistan was likely to become more dangerous if allowed to drift. Arguing that U.S. interests in the subcontinent would compel the United States to become involved if the situation became more heated, the Embassy proposed direct U.S. involvement in the search for a settlement before a more dangerous confrontation developed. (Ibid.)

[3] Not found.

resolving disengagement impasse and that James[4] has specifically recommended that USG not intervene at this time. James says U.S. might help push agreement on disengagement later on but should do so in support of British proposals and not as separate initiative.

We continue to see prospect that British effort may continue for some time with considerable hope for success. While Shastri may not have authority to negotiate with Ayub in London, we doubt either side will burn bridges before then especially as there are signs that both appear to be genuinely concerned about avoiding misstep that could have serious consequences for both. Following Commonwealth Conference there will be visits by Wilson to subcontinent later in summer. Knowledge of forthcoming visits should help prevent either side from breaking off discussions and visits should be occasion for further negotiation. In short, there seems to be time for further British efforts; two parties seem to want to find a way out of escalating conflict; and therefore there is room for further progress toward agreement.

We doubt that US would be in better position than UK to bring Indians and Paks to agreement on disengagement at this time. In fact, we believe that so long as British effort continues, our participation in separate initiative would complicate British diplomatic task and lessen prospect for their success. US intervention on this issue in both capitals (particularly in Delhi) is not likely to be very effective at this time; even our bona fides are sometimes questioned. For example, Embassy suggests we use security assurances and military aid as leverage. Credibility of assurances has been seriously challenged in both countries (e.g. see Embtel 3518)[5] and Indians, whose negotiating position would suffer most by disengagement, are already questioning value of our military aid. Finally it seems quite unlikely that US initiative could be kept secret. Leak would put great political pressure on Shastri, particularly because of current attitudes about US in India.

In light of above we have reached conclusion that US should not take up separate initiative on subcontinent at present time.

Ambassador Bowles concurs.

Rusk

---

[4] Sir Morrice James.
[5] Dated June 1. (National Archives and Records Administration, RG 59, Central Files 1964–66, DEF 18 UN)

126. Memorandum From Robert Komer of the National Security Council Staff to President Johnson[1]

Washington, June 5, 1965.

I hesitate to bring this matter up again, but a new wrinkle has developed on remaining *FY 65 aid loans to India and Pakistan*. Otto Passman[2] is pressing Dave Bell on how much money AID expects to have left over at the end of this fiscal year. Bell seeks guidance as he feels he can't delay answering Passman beyond next week or the latter will begin to smell a rat.

A lesser problem is that the Indians and Paks are beginning to ask insistently how soon some of these loans will be released. They are *not* aware to date of any hold order; instead we think the Indians in particular are worried because their foreign exchange reserves have dropped to a record low of $162 million (they've even been forced to draw a $125 million standby from the IMF).

To recap, AID and State seek a go-ahead on three categories of aid: (a) Some $227 million in loans to India and $18.5 million to Pakistan, which have already been approved, authorized, and announced, and where only formal loan agreements remain to be signed; (b) some $76 million in loan applications for India and $51 million for Pakistan—AID would like to authorize those which pass muster; and (c) new program loans of up to $100 million for India and up to $70 million for Pakistan as a first installment on this year's pledges. All but the new $70 million for Pakistan is covered by pledges already made.[3]

Bell expects to obligate fully all other AID funds, so his answer to Passman depends essentially on the India/Pak items above. There seem to be three options:

A. Authorize Bell to proceed to the extent necessary to obligate all FY 1965 aid funds before 30 June, but to continue holding off on anything beyond. This is the course which State and AID recommend on foreign policy grounds, and to meet existing commitments. It would also permit Bell to meet the Passman problem.

B. Authorize proceeding on all previously announced loans and other feasible project loans, but not the new program loans for India

---

[1] Source: Johnson Library, National Security File, Memos to the President, McGeorge Bundy, Vol. 11, June 1965. Secret.

[2] Otto E. Passman, Representative from Louisiana, Chairman of the House Subcommittee on Foreign Aid.

[3] At the twelfth meeting of the India consortium, held in Washington on April 21, the United States pledged $435 million of the $1,027,160,000 pledged by the consortium to support India for FY 1965–66. (Circular airgram CA–12756, May 28; National Archives and Records Administration, RG 59, Central Files 1964–66, AID 9 INDIA)

or Pakistan. In this case Bell sees us falling short on obligating FY 65 funds by about $125–175 million.

C. Hold off on all further loans to India and Pakistan in which case AID will have about $250–300 million in Development Loan funds left over.[4]

R. W. K.[5]

Approve Course A, B, C. (check your choice), or

Tell Bell to keep stalling Passman until we can discuss the matter further

or

Speak to me[6]

---

[4] Bundy sent this memorandum to Johnson on June 5 with a covering memorandum in which he explained that Komer had prepared his memorandum at Bundy's request. Bundy noted that he strongly favored alternative A of those listed in Komer's memorandum. (Ibid.)

[5] Bundy initialed below Komer's initials.

[6] This option is checked.

---

127.   Letter From President Johnson to Prime Minister Shastri[1]

Washington, June 5, 1965.

Dear Mr. Prime Minister:

Your letter of May 23[2] arrived as I was writing to send my best wishes on the first anniversary of your assuming the office of Prime Minister. The year has been a difficult one for both of us, but I know that our faith in the democratic way of doing things will bear fruit.

---

[1] Source: National Archives and Records Administration, RG 59, Presidential Correspondence: Lot 66 D 294, Johnson/India, 1964–1965. Secret; Exdis. A typewritten note at the end of the letter reads: "Handed to Mr. David Schneider, NEA, 6–11–65 for delivery to Ambassador Nehru to be hand carried to PM Shastri in Canada." The text of the letter was transmitted to New Delhi in telegram 2540, June 5, for delivery to Shastri prior to his departure for Canada. (Johnson Library, National Security File, Country File, India, Shastri Correspondence)

[2] Document 123.

We have also been deeply concerned over the unhappy events in the Rann of Kutch and the use of U.S. military equipment in this dispute. The role of a friend to both parties is not easy and often misunderstood. But I believe our efforts to put a stop to the use of our military equipment were helpful in getting the fighting stopped. Now the problem becomes one of finding a formula for peaceful settlement as a substitute for settlement by force. Despite the problems you mention, I deeply hope that you can reach an agreement, and thereby reduce the awesome possibility of larger conflict.

I fully share your desire that you and I, and our two governments, should act always in a spirit of mutual understanding. In that spirit, let me respond very frankly to your suggestion that the search for peace in Vietnam might be furthered by a cessation of the air strikes being conducted against North Vietnam by the South Vietnamese and U.S. air forces. You know the importance we attach to a solution to the Vietnam problem. To us, the Chinese Communist-supported aggression in Vietnam poses the same kind of threat to Free World interests as Communist China's attack on India in 1962.

I wish to tell you in utmost privacy of the effort we have already made to induce a response from Hanoi by a suspension of air strikes, and the depressing lack of any response. I enclose an informal and confidential memorandum[3] which candidly describes our efforts to date, and our current thinking as to certain future possibilities. It reflects my own deep desire to find a road to peace in Vietnam, and to share my thinking with you fully to this end.

Let me assure you that we will continue prayerfully to explore any hopeful opening. There is no step I would not take if in my judgment it offered real prospect of the peaceful settlement we both want.

I deeply regret that your parliamentary and other commitments may not permit an autumn visit. I assure you we would welcome a visit at any future date you should conclude would be desirable and convenient to you.[4]

With warm personal regards.

Sincerely,

Lyndon B. Johnson

---

[3] Not printed. The text of this memorandum was also transmitted to New Delhi in telegram 2540.

[4] The Embassy reported that the text of President Johnson's letter was delivered to the Ministry of Foreign Affairs on June 6 and was received with the assurance that it would be passed on to Shastri before he departed for Canada. (Telegram 3567 from New Delhi, June 6; National Archives and Records Administration, RG 59, Central Files 1964–66, POL 15–1 INDIA)

128.   Memorandum From Robert Komer of the National Security Council Staff to President Johnson[1]

Washington, June 8, 1965.

SUBJECT

Meeting on Pak/Indian Aid Decisions, Noon 9 June 1965

Rusk, McNamara, Mann and Bell have been asked to attend.

This memo summarizes the current situation. Much of it is familiar ground but Bundy and I thought you'd like a recap.

US aid an incentive to other donors. The precedents on economic aid to India/Pakistan go back almost to the end of World War II, basically as part of our effort to shore up the threatened nations on the borders of the Communist Bloc. Then in 1958, we organized a World Bank consortium for *India* as a device to get other Western countries to bear more of the aid burden. Each year since we've used a US pledge as a lever on them. This has proven quite successful—in FY 1965 for example we got total pledges of over $1 billion, of which our share was around 40%.

In 1961 we did the same thing for *Pakistan;* here our share has run somewhat higher (around 50% in the last two years), but we've gotten other donors and the Bank heavily involved. So Bell is naturally concerned lest, if we begin to backtrack, our UK, Japanese, German and other friends will too.

Administration clearance of FY'65 India/Pak aid. After being worked out among the agencies, the FY'65 figures went through the regular vetting procedure; (a) BOB reviewed the forward projections provided by AID for consistency with Administration guidelines; (b) the regular budget submission was reviewed by BOB, and then discussed with you; (c) the annual foreign aid message was cleared; and (d) the Congressional presentation was then checked with BOB. The Bundy shop participated throughout. I think it fair to say that all AID decisions and authorizations during FY'65, including consortium pledges, have been within these Administration guidelines.

In late April, following your call to Tom Mann about our pending FY'66 pledge to the Indian consortium, we put out a special White House request that *all* pending Pak/Indian aid decisions be cleared here first. We've been operating on this basis to the present.

---

[1] Source: Johnson Library, National Security File, Memos to the President, McGeorge Bundy, Vol. 10, Apr. 15–May 31, 1965. Secret. Two pages of statistics detailing economic and military assistance provided to India and Pakistan, 1946–1965, were attached but are not printed.

Issues for Decision. Mostly because of circumstance, but partly because of our hold order, we have an end of fiscal year logjam. Since we've already disbursed most of Pakistan's FY'65 aid, the logjam mostly affects India:

A. Some $227 million in loans to India and $18.5 million to Pakistan which have already been approved, authorized and announced. Only the actual signing of the loan agreements remains. The biggest item is a $190 million program loan to India under last year's consortium pledge. For Passman purposes this money is regarded as already committed (it will not show up as an end-FY 65 shortfall); of course, it is also regarded as committed by the Indians and Paks.

B. Some $76 million in loan applications for India and $61 million for Pakistan. AID would like to authorize those which are ready before 30 June to utilize FY'65 funds, *but not all will be ready.*

C. For the last two years we have given *India* an advance program loan for a fraction of our new consortium pledge, to keep aid flowing *since the Indian fiscal year begins two months earlier than ours.* This year State and AID want to give up to $100 million to India and start the same procedure for Pakistan with *up to $70 million.* Aside from being good economics, this is essential to commit FY'65 funds which otherwise would be haggled about by Passman on specious grounds. It does not deprive us of much FY'66 leverage, since it covers only a fifth to a third of what we'd normally give. Nor does this money flow till we actually sign the loan, it would only be authorized now.

D. The Indian *PL 480 agreement* also expires 30 June, and the pipeline will begin running out this July. To forestall hoarding and then hunger in India, we need approval to make a new *one-year* agreement.

The case for going ahead with the above items is threefold:

A. It forestalls a sterile debate with Passman over why we couldn't even commit the allegedly minimum amount requested for FY 1965. If we hold up all new commitments beyond June 30, we'll run $250–300 million short.

B. It avoids the risk of a major to-do with Paks and Indians over whether we are backing away from pledges and commitments already made. Both now strongly suspect we're holding out on them, but haven't been able to pin it on us yet. If we hold up past 30 June, however, this will be impossible to conceal.

C. The story will inevitably be played up in the US press. Among other things, it will revive speculation about the real purpose of the Ayub and Shastri postponements.

D. The backlash might affect current aid appropriations, if Congress gets a sense that the Administration is backing off on India/Pak aid.

Recommendations. You can use tomorrow's meeting both to forestall the above kind of unnecessary trouble and to put State, AID and Defense on notice that you're highly sceptical about our current Pak/Indian policies and (a) want a hard new look at them before we spend a lot more money; (b) want to keep the Paks and Indians worried lest Uncle Sam become a lot less generous. Essentially, the trick would be to do the necessary to limit the risk to our FY 66 aid appropriation, but simultaneously instruct State and AID that we want to play a lot harder to get with the Indians and Paks. The following scenario would serve this purpose:

1. You'll go ahead reluctantly on using up FY 65 money only because we're too far down the pike to pull back gracefully without (a) accusations that we're backing off on pledges; or (b) giving Passman a handle to cut FY 66 money.

2. *But you seriously question whether we're getting our money's worth from this huge investment,* and intend to continue personally vetting all major new commitments until we've done a basic policy review which satisfies you and which you can use persuasively on the Congress. Rusk should take leadership on this.

3. *You don't want to have Ayub or Shastri here* till we've worked out our new policy line, and have softened both up to the point where they want to come for help rather than come tell you how to run Vietnam, etc. So you want much clearer signals to both Paks and Indians first (perhaps via special emissaries).

4. Despite Pakistan's fine economic performance, let's get across quietly but clearly to Ayub that *he can't play China's game while being banked by the US.*

5. Let's tell the Indians we're not very happy with them either, especially their tendency to take our aid for granted without doing enough to help themselves or to recognize that we're fighting their war in Vietnam.

6. In effect you fully recognize the central importance of India/Pakistan, but when we're investing as much AID money there as in the Alianza, you see a need for tighter control and greater emphasis on results.[2]

R. W. Komer[3]

---

[2] Bundy sent this memorandum to Johnson on June 8 under cover of a brief memorandum in which he stated: "I think he makes a very good case for authorizing the immediate public decisions, while insisting on a hard new look at our Indian/Pak policy." (Ibid.) Johnson responded with a handwritten note on Bundy's covering memorandum that reads: "I'm not for allocating or approving $1 now unless I have already signed and agreed—If I have, show me when and where."

[3] McGeorge Bundy initialed below Komer's signature.

129.   Memorandum by the President's Special Assistant for National Security Affairs (Bundy)[1]

Washington, June 9, 1965.

MEMORANDUM FOR
The Secretary of State
The Secretary of Defense
The Administrator, the Agency for International Development

SUBJECT
Presidential Decisions on Aid to India/Pakistan, 9 June 1965

After reviewing and discussing a memorandum from Messrs. Bell and Mann,[2] the President:

1. Agreed that AID could proceed with those loans already authorized and announced, plus certain loans which are close to completion (these loans are detailed in the attachment to the 9 June Bell/Mann Memorandum).

2. Directed that there be no additional decisions, authorizations or announcements on loans to India or Pakistan without his approval, pending passage of the FY 1966 foreign aid appropriation.

3. Disapproved advance program loans to India and Pakistan, even if as a result we had to ask Congress to reappropriate the money involved.

4. Requested an early review of economic aid to India and Pakistan by State and AID, in the context of our global pattern of use of aid resources. It should cover such issues as: (a) whether the US should be spending such large sums in either country; and (b) how to achieve more leverage for our money, in terms both of more effective self-help and of our political purposes.

5. Requested early recommendations on (a) a new PL 480 agreement with India; (b) what US pledge, if any, should be made at the Pakistan Consortium pledging session in late July.

McG. Bundy

---

[1] Source: Johnson Library, National Security File, Country File, Pakistan, Vol. III, Memos, 12/64–7/65. Secret; Limit Distribution. Copies were sent to the Under Secretary of State, the Under Secretary of State for Economic Affairs, and the Director of the Bureau of the Budget.
[2] Reference is to a memorandum from Bell to the President, dated June 9, dealing with AID loans to India and Pakistan. A copy is ibid., NSC History, Indian Famine, Aug 66–Feb 67, Vol I.

130. **Information Memorandum From the Assistant Secretary of State for Near Eastern and South Asian Affairs (Talbot) to Secretary of State Rusk[1]**

Washington, June 10, 1965.

SUBJECT

Kashmir Ceasefire Line Incident at Kargil

According to reports from United Nations Observer Group (UNMOGIP) sources, on the night of May 16–17 Indian troops attacked and occupied two Pak outposts near Kargil on the Pak side of the Kashmir ceasefire line. On June 6 the Indians reportedly extended their salient by twenty to twenty-five miles to the west of Kargil. The Indians thus far have refused to give up the territory they have occupied. General Nimmo has not yet reported the Indian violation to UN Headquarters in the hope that he will be able to persuade the Indians to withdraw. The Pak posts occupied by the Indians overlooked the strategic Srinagar-to-Leh road, India's only land link to its forces in Ladakh. The Indians for some time have been concerned over possible Sino-Pak cooperation directed against India in sensitive areas.

The incidents near Kargil are clearly related to the sharp increase in recent months of the number and intensity of incidents all along the ceasefire line; and the escalation of fighting along the ceasefire line is itself a symptom of the very serious deterioration of Indo-Pak relations evidenced by the fighting in the Rann of Kutch and the subsequent forward deployment of the armies of both countries at key points all along the Indo-Pak border.

We are asking New Delhi's comments on the report from UNMOGIP sources (see Karachi's 2363 at Tab A)[2] that the Indians are using American ammunition against the Paks in Kashmir. USUN has been asked to initiate discussions with Ralph Bunche regarding the capabilities of UNMOGIP to carry out its assigned functions (see Deptel 2896 at Tab B).[2]

---

[1] Source: National Archives and Records Administration, RG 59, Central Files 1964–66, POL 32–1 INDIA–PAK. Secret. Drafted by India Desk Officer Albert A. Lakeland. A handwritten "Saw" next to the Secretary's name on the memorandum indicates that Rusk saw it.

[2] Dated June 9; not printed.

**131.   Memorandum From Robert Komer of the National Security
Council Staff to the President's Special Assistant for
National Security Affairs (Bundy)**[1]

Washington, June 11, 1965.

Mac—

Leaning on the Paks. Lest anyone should think we're utterly immo-
bile, we've already done a few things (though I've had an uphill fight
all the way):

1. We've stalled two years, and are still, on two squadrons F–104s,
for which Paks are bleeding.

2. At recent Consortium pre-pledging session, we didn't even
mention a figure, but instead joined World Bank, UK, and Germans in
beating up Paks on certain economic conditions.

3. We didn't come through with new PL 480 agreement Paks
wanted but simply extended present one six months with no add-ons
(because Paks haven't complied with reporting provisions).

4. We turned down $25–30 million Roopur atomic power plant
(on technical grounds that Paks couldn't market that much power).

5. We're stalling on $120 million Karachi steel mill (for which Paks
are panting). Real grounds are that ExIm refused so much as a 2/3
share, so AID got cold feet and is doing a new survey.

Fascinating thing is that all the above have apparently been taken
by the Paks as *political* signals, when in fact the last three were straight
economic in origin (so was the second in large part). This just shows
you the perils of heliographing to parties that don't speak the same
language. At any rate I've told AID that, whatever they may have
intended, they did a swell job.

New signals. Instead of special envoys, or tough talk just now, I
favor keeping up the above line. For ostensibly legitimate *economic*
reasons, we keep stalling and diddling. The Paks take it all as really
political, but it's that much harder for them to confront us:

1. Postpone Pak pledging session a month, on grounds we need
a better answer to US and IB queries. This will rock the Paks, and buy
us another month to see if they come around. It also buys more time
to decide how much we'll pledge.

2. Keep stalling on Karachi steel mill, new PL 480 agreement, etc.

3. Hold up deliveries on other MAP items besides planes. Stalling
on tanks and APCs would painfully remind Ayub we don't want him

---

[1] Source: Johnson Library, National Security File, Country File, Pakistan, Vol. III,
Memos, 12/64–7/65. Secret.

using US-supplied armor in places like the Rann of Kutch. Also, Rusk just approved selling some *ammo* to the Paks.[2] Why?

4. Now that McNamara has spoken his golden words, why not operate on the most sensitive nerve of all—Peshawar? *If we cut back a little on personnel or new construction there, it would shake Pak confidence in what they regard as their hole card.* They'd really be shaken if they thought we were getting ready to pull out. Such a signal would have to be carefully handled, lest the Paks think Aziz Ahmed's recent approach scared us off. What say we clue Raborn/Helms on LBJ's strong views, and ask them to look into this.

We're embarked on a risky course, and it will take steady nerves, because Ayub will probably growl back before retreating. But we have a clear mandate now, and I'm really using it now to move the way we should have long since.

RWK

---

[2] Next to this sentence in the margin, Komer wrote: "Gawd!"

---

132. Telegram From the Embassy Office in Pakistan to the Department of State[1]

Rawalpindi, June 11, 1965.

58. (1) I had 70-minute meeting with President in Rawalpindi this morning, with Foreign Minister Bhutto and Foreign Office notetaker also present. Prevailing atmosphere was frank and favorable, with dominant note of seriousness. General environment confirmed recent impression there has been some limited GOP re-evaluation of foreign policy situation to our advantage.

(2) We opened with discussion Indo-Pak confrontation crisis. On Rann of Kutch, I expressed our emphatic backing of UK Good Offices effort, and stated our earnest hope that search for settlement formula

---

[1] Source: National Archives and Records Administration, RG 59, Central Files 1964–66, POL 15–1 PAK. Secret; Priority. Repeated to Karachi, New Delhi, Algiers, London, and CINCMEAFSA for POLAD.

would be pursued diligently and non-stop until agreement reached. Indicated our disappointment that impasse so protracted. Suggested that if no agreement reached earlier, talks be pursued at London while Ayub and Shastri both at Commonwealth Prime Ministers Conference. Urged Ayub as leader in stronger and more prestigious political position be prepared to go the extra mile of conciliation if necessary in order to achieve agreement. Noted that two sides had already reached agreement in principle substantive question, and that remaining points of disagreement seemed to involve more tactics and supposed face-saving than substance. Ayub responded that he was indeed disposed to go the limit on conciliation and felt that he had already done so. It was Shastri who had refused to agree to immediate termination of dangerous deployment of forces along Pak border which GOI had initiated. And it was Shastri who refused accept an impartial formula for patrol routes in Rann of Kutch during interim period. Ayub said contemptuously that Shastri was "talking through his Dhoti" in his immoderate claims, demands, and threats. Ayub assured me he would continue diligently in the search for agreement and he spoke highly of British efforts.

(3) On larger question of Indo-Pak confrontation outside the Rann, Ayub concurred with deep conviction in my statement of dangerous flammability of situation and wasteful, burdensome cost in economic and development terms of protracted deployment of forces along borders. He stressed Pak anxiety to normalize military posture immediately and deplored Indian refusal. He deprecated Indian HICOM's recent statement to him that Pak insistence on withdrawal of forces from borders was a challenge of Indian sovereignty. Stated he could not fathom such distorted reasoning, especially since Paks were not even suggesting where Indian forces should be stationed once they are removed from their present unnatural and threatening deployment in immediate border area. Ayub referred to Indian incursions in Kargil area of Kashmir cease-fire line. He said five lightly manned posts well over on Pak side have been completely overrun by overwhelming Indian force and continue to be held by Indians. Said he supposed this was implementation of Indian threat to respond to Rann of Kutch incident at unrelated place "of their own choosing." Ayub regretted inability of UN military observer group to prevent violations. Said he thought Commanding General Nimmo entirely too senile and feeble to be effective. When I speculated on the desirability of considering a strengthening of UNMOGIP as a means of keeping the peace, he indicated that he would be inclined to give sympathetic consideration to any UN proposal along such lines.

[Here follows discussion of the forthcoming African-Asian Conference at Algiers and an assessment of developments in Southeast Asia.]

7. Ayub appeal for certain additional MAP by grant or credit sale being reported separately.[2]

McConaughy

---

[2] In telegram 2416 from Karachi, June 18, McConaughy reported that during a June 11 conversation, Ayub made an appeal for limited additional military assistance. Ayub said he had carefully selected a few high-performance items designed to have a deterrent effect on a potential aggressor. He asked for a "moderate" number of higher performance planes to replace the aging F–86 fighters of the Air Force. McConaughy noted that when Ayub referred to higher performance aircraft, presumably he meant F–104s. Ayub also asked for a number of tanks and four submarines. (Ibid., DEF 19–3 US–PAK)

---

133. Telegram From the Department of State to the Embassy in India[1]

Washington, June 15, 1965, 10:51 a.m.

2590. Following summary is FYI and Noforn. It is uncleared and subject to amendment upon review of memcon.

Following return from Ottawa where he had seen Prime Minister Shastri, Amb. B.K. Nehru came in to see Secretary June 14. Said Shastri had asked him raise extremely serious matter at highest possible level in USG. Shastri wished inform us that if friends of India and Pakistan desired peace on subcontinent they should exert maximum possible pressure on Pakistan to evacuate Rann of Kutch. India had accepted initial British proposal for negotiations and had thereafter accepted number of changes proposed by Paks. India could make no further concessions and could not tolerate Pak occupation Indian territory. If diplomacy fails, India must use force to drive out Pakistan. GOI is quite aware of political, economic and social consequences of war. It has however reached point at which it can make no further concessions.

In response Secretary commented on appalling consequences of subcontinental war which could not be limited to clash between armed forces. Said casualties would be comparable to those of nuclear exchange. Because of this India and Pakistan almost compelled approach

---

[1] Source: National Archives and Records Administration, RG 59, Central Files 1964–66, POL 32–1 INDIA–PAK. Secret; Immediate; Limdis. Drafted by Schneider on June 14, cleared by Judd in BNA, and approved by Talbot. Also sent to London, and repeated to Karachi, USUN, and CINCMEAFSA for POLAD.

idea of war as inconceivable. Since points of difference regarding British proposal small, Secretary saw great imbalance between nature of differences and consequences of war. Recalling difficult year and a half of discussions he had had with Gromyko following the 1961 Kennedy–Khrushchev meeting Secretary observed it easy to start war; alternative of working out peaceful solutions much more difficult. India and Pakistan should bear this in mind since consequences of war so enormous.

Secretary said we strongly support British negotiating effort. We will be in touch with British as well as Paks and Indians, but obviously solution this problem not to be found in Washington.

Nehru repeated that India fully aware consequences of war but could not make further concessions. Said Indian view was that President Ayub does not want war but Bhutto and Aziz Ahmed wish avoid settlement and are relying on Communist Chinese support. Shastri was concerned about possibility direct Chicom intervention. Secretary said he was not in position comment with assurance regarding this. In view of Ayub's attitude Secretary asked if there could be contact between Pak President and Shastri in London. Nehru said Shastri was committed to Cabinet to avoid discussion Rann of Kutch in London, although subordinate officials may take up question. Nehru also commented on great Indian political pressures on Kutch issue and said if Shastri doesn't take action his successor will do so.

Asked about situation on Kashmir ceasefire line near Kargil, Nehru responded Indian action there did not represent government policy. Local Indian commander had taken action in disobedience of orders. This was not Indian countermove.[2] Indians will clear up this matter, but it may take a few days. Nehru said we could tell Paks we had Indian assurance Kargil situation would be "cleared up".

During conversation earlier in day, Nehru had made similar presentation to Talbot. In addition Nehru said L.K. Jha had told him Cabinet had agreed permit Kutch situation remain as is until Shastri's return. If matter not resolved by then there would be nothing to do but employ force. In response Talbot focused on narrow margin of differences separating India and Pakistan and great need for further effort reach agreement in order to avoid disaster.

Talbot conveyed above to British Minister (Stewart) June 14. Stewart queried whether Indian approach was tactical maneuver to involve US

---

[2] On June 16, Indian Chargé Banerjee called on Talbot and presented a paper giving the Indian position concerning Kargil, which differed sharply from that conveyed by Nehru to Rusk on June 14. The paper alleged that Pakistani forces had initiated the conflict in the Kargil region and had been repulsed by Indian forces, which were "obliged" to occupy two posts on the Pakistan side of the cease-fire line. Nehru was with Shastri in London and unavailable for comment. (Telegram 2604 to New Delhi, June 16; ibid.)

or whether Shastri's position really as weak as this suggests. Talbot replied Indian position sounds unbelievable but cannot be discounted. Said this next week in London would be of crucial importance. British may wish consider what influence they can bring to bear. Also noted we had told Indians we support British negotiating effort and consequently we wish avoid getting into substance. Talbot made it clear that any action we might take with Paks would await UK reaction Indian approach.

Stewart said he would inform London of above tonight and we could expect London's reactions June 15.

Rusk

---

134. Memorandum From Robert Komer of the National Security Council Staff to President Johnson[1]

Washington, June 21, 1965, 1:45 p.m.

We have set in train the following actions to flesh out your new tactical line designed to soften up the Paks and Indians, and make them come to us:

1. *Stalling on MAP.* Though matters referred to you recently have involved only economic aid and PL 480, we're operating on the assumption that you want well-orchestrated action across the board. So we've told DOD that, while not suspending everything, we should delay action on certain key MAP and sales items to make both Paks and Indians come to us. In India's case this means chiefly continued stalling on F–5s; in Pakistan's case on F–104s, ammo, and perhaps armor.

Since there is a higher risk of a Pak/Indian flareup than any time since 1947, our stalling on MAP makes sense as a warning here too. A major risk, however, is that we're driving the Indian military to get more from the Soviets, which doesn't serve our longer term interest.

2. *Intelligence.* Since Ayub thinks the Peshawar[2] facility is his top card, we're looking at ways and means of convincing him it isn't all that important to us. For example, we could halt new construction. This would make the intelligence community scream, but is probably worth it. We're also planning to use [*less than 1 line of source text not*

---

[1] Source: Johnson Library, National Security File, Memos to the President, McGeorge Bundy, Vol. 11, June 1965. Top Secret.
[2] Johnson circled Peshawar and noted in the margin: "get Raborn opinion."

declassified] to get across indirectly to Ayub that we're close to giving up on the Paks.

3. *Stalling on Pak Consortium.* So far our hold-up on economic aid is hurting the Indians more than the Paks (for the simple reason that more Indian matters have been pending). But the next big occasion will be the FY 1966 pledge to the Pak Consortium, due 27 July. We favor telling the Paks *now* that we want to postpone this a month, ostensibly for economic reasons. Our thought is to have George Woods go to London and tell Ayub. This will shake Ayub, and buy us more time to see whether our signals are getting through.[3]

Are we on the right track on the above? Our new tough-minded Pak/Indian tactics are causing much anguish in the town, especially from those who see their programs endangered. It would help if you'd tell Rusk in particular[4] (he missed the June meeting), so that we'll have State with us, instead of dragging its feet on such matters.

R. W. Komer[5]

Yes[6]

No

---

[3] Komer added a handwritten note in the margin at this point that reads: "Too late! Woods got back today. He did say U.S. was *considering* this."

[4] Bundy added a handwritten note in the margin at this point which reads: "(or I can)".

[5] McGeorge Bundy initialed below Komer's signature.

[6] Johnson checked the "Yes" option line.

---

135.   Memorandum of Telephone Conversation Between President Johnson and the Under Secretary of State for Economic Affairs (Mann)[1]

Washington, June 28, 1965, 1:20 p.m.

[Here follows discussion unrelated to South Asia.]

Mr. Mann told the President that he was working on a draft concerning India and Pakistan.[2] He told the President that Mr. Woods had

---

[1] Source: Johnson Library, Mann Papers, Telephone Conversations with LBJ, May 2, 1965–June 2, 1966. No classification marking. Transcribed in Mann's office.

[2] Not found.

talked to Ayub in London and had told him that we were uncertain as to what we were going to do on the consortium July 27. Mr. Mann said that in essence Mr. Woods had said that our relations were not of the best; that we were sort of tired of being like a cow that is kicked in the side when milk is wanted and then kicked in the side to let it know that no more milk was needed at the moment.

Mr. Mann told the President what Mr. Woods had said and said he thought that Mr. Woods had done a good job. Mr. Mann said we have a different situation with the Indians. They have not been insulting us as much—particularly in the past ten days.

Mr. Mann said that he hoped to have the memo ready by tomorrow. He said he was suggesting that we begin a dialogue with India and Pakistan in which we say in effect that we do not mind cooperating but we expect the same kind of respect everyone else does and say if we cannot establish the kind of understanding the people of this country have a right to expect and want, then we cannot go ahead. If we can reach an understanding then we can go ahead. Mr. Mann said all this would be in the memo and he hoped the President would buy it. He said he would like to see the President send somebody over to talk with Shastri—not at a high level—but quietly. He suggested Mr. Bell.

The President said he did not wish to send anybody over and that he thought our Ambassadors should go and talk to these people. Mr. Mann said that the Ambassador to India (Bowles) was here. The President said that the Chargé should do it. The President said that he should go in and say that we understand that they are not going to be able to come to America and our President cannot go there and the reason for the postponement was because of the heavy feeling and that we would be glad to discuss it if they want to send somebody over. If they do not wish to do this we will understand. Mr. Mann asked the President if he wanted these men to come over on State visits and the President said he did not but he also did not want to be sending his people over there to give money away. He said he thought that we should tell our Ambassadors in these two countries, that in a dignified and reserved way they should say that we regret very much but we completely understand Mr. Shastri's inability to come. We regret we have to postpone it, but in the President's judgment sentiment is such that he would have no bill at all and that there is a different attitude in our country now on the part of the people and the President (after spending 40 billion in Asia) and we had hoped we would be able to talk it out, but since he could not come, if he wanted to send someone else, or have his Ambassador talk with us about it, that will be fine. The President said that we could let Nehru come in. We then tell him we understand but we are not going to be able to go along on economic basis.

Mr. Mann said he thought that on the Pakistan side, Mr. Woods had already made the first steps towards getting a representative over here. The President told Mr. Mann to go ahead and draft whatever he wanted to but that he would like to talk to him about it. He said he would prefer to discuss this with Mr. Mann. Mr. Mann said he understood and that he would draft a paper and then talk to the President about it.

The President said that we should let these people know, through our Ambassadors, that we have pulled up business for a while. Mr. Mann said o.k.

136. Memorandum From the President's Special Assistant for National Security Affairs (Bundy) to President Johnson[1]

Washington, June 28, 1965, 7:45 p.m.

Agenda for Tuesday Lunch

There are a number of special issues which need brief discussion in order to have your guidance clearly understood, and it may save you time to list them this evening.

[Here follow background summaries of unrelated agenda items.]

3. The India–Pakistan problem.

Both on Pakistan and India, it is time for specific guidance from you. In the case of the Paks, what is now needed is decision to postpone the Pak consortium scheduled for July 27. You have approved this postponement in principle, but we have not made a direct instruction on it, and that is what will be needed. There is also a smaller matter of Pakistan year-end arms purchases which Dean Rusk may bring up for decision. This is an $8 million straight sale which could go either way, depending on whether you want the foreign exchange or the signal to the Paks.

On the Indian side, the principal problem is PL–480. The program is held up, in accordance with your instructions, but the Indians have been fobbed off with a series of stories about technical difficulties, and they simply do not understand that the United States Government is not going to come forward with any proposal at all until they come in and ask us for it in a serious political way. As a practical matter, they may not get this signal unless we make sure that it is communicated to

---

[1] Source: Johnson Library, National Security File, Files of McGeorge Bundy, Luncheons with the President, Vol. I (Part 1). Secret.

them, and I think it may be time for you to authorize such a communication. It would have to be very skillfully done, and I think Rusk himself may be the man to do it. But you and he should have a very clear understanding of exactly what is to be communicated. Are we talking about not having a PL–480 agreement? Or is there a particular condition attached to it which Rusk should know about?

[Here follow summaries of unrelated agenda items.]

McG. B.

---

137. **Memorandum From the President's Special Assistant for National Security Affairs (Bundy) to President Johnson**[1]

Washington, June 30, 1965, 1:30 p.m.

SUBJECT

Progress on the Pak-Indian front

1. I have talked with Tom Mann this morning, and I think, as a result of your talk with him, the State Department for the first time has really got the signal. As Tom said to me, there has been great reluctance to believe over there that the White House meant what it said, but Tom himself has now taken hold, and I think the results will be very constructive.

2. Three major steps are being taken now:

A. The first is definite notice to George Woods that we want the July consortium on Pakistan postponed. This will clear the decks for serious talk with the Pakistani representative who is likely to turn up here quite soon.

B. Tom Mann is talking to B.K. Nehru and will make it very clear to him that we think the time is ripe for a very serious talk with the Indians about the whole range of our relationships, which are a very great expense to us. Tom's conversations will be careful and courteous, but thorough, and he will suggest to B.K. that he himself go back to India and get Shastri to designate a really high-level visitor to come over here for very serious talks.

---

[1] Source: Johnson Library, National Security File, Memos to the President, McGeorge Bundy, Vol. 11, June 1965. Secret.

C. Bob McNamara is having a full review of the MAP pipeline and will have alternatives for the handling of that for discussion next Tuesday. Meanwhile there will be technical delays on all deliveries in that field. This has been the hardest spigot to get turned off, and Bob thinks there are some tough choices in the handling of it, pending the serious talks that are now in prospect with both countries. But he will have suggestions on that next week.

3. My own conversations with State, AID and Defense make it clear to me that the message is now getting across and that Mann, McNamara and Bell all mean to conduct their business in accordance with your basic desire. This is an important change for the good.

4. There does remain one special case which may require special treatment before we really finish talking turkey with these two governments—that is the question of food for India. I don't see how we can reach any general agreement with the Indians in the next week or two. Yet if we do not make some interim arrangement for shipments of wheat within that time-frame, there may well be a real problem of food shortage in India which the Indians could successfully blame on us. That could bring us a lot of violent and quite unnecessary criticism, and might even give the Soviets a chance to make emergency deliveries and make us look foolish. This is what we just avoided in Egypt a couple of weeks ago.

I have told Bob Komer to prepare a contingency plan for interim wheat deliveries on a very limited basis. This plan will not be marketed around the city, but it will be available for a prompt decision in the light of what Tom Mann learns from his first hard talk with Nehru.

McG. B.

---

138. **Editorial Note**

On June 30, 1965, India and Pakistan signed an agreement that ended the fighting in the Rann of Kutch. The agreement, which was facilitated through the good offices of the United Kingdom, was signed separately in Karachi and New Delhi. (Telegrams 2496 from Karachi and 3788 from New Delhi, both June 30; National Archives and Records Administration, RG 59, Central Files 1964–66, POL 32–1 INDIA–PAK) President Ayub of Pakistan issued a statement on June 30 welcoming not only the agreement relating to the Rann of Kutch, but also a second agreement signed by India and Pakistan which called for the withdrawal of troops from both sides of the entire border between India and Pakistan. (Telegram 6 from Karachi, July 1; ibid.) President Johnson sent a personal message to British Prime Minister Wilson on June 30 congratulating him on his success in bringing the conflict to a peaceful solution. (Telegram 8235 to London; ibid.)

The agreement signed by India and Pakistan called for the dispute to be settled on the basis of binding arbitration, by an arbitral tribunal to be established with the cooperation of the Secretary-General of the United Nations. India subsequently appointed a Yugoslav arbitrator to the tribunal, Pakistan appointed an Iranian arbitrator, and UN Secretary-General U Thant chose a Swede as the chairman. The tribunal did not reach agreement on a final award until February 1968. The award gave approximately 10 percent of the disputed territory to Pakistan, including much of the high ground where the heaviest fighting took place. The award was reluctantly accepted by Pakistan, but bitterly resented in India, where it was generally felt that India had a strong case for sovereignty over the entire Rann of Kutch. (Memorandum from Thomas L. Hughes to Rusk, February 20, 1968; ibid.)

---

139. Telegram From the Department of State to the Embassy in Pakistan[1]

Washington, June 30, 1965, 6:56 p.m.

1485. Please inform Minister Finance Shoaib, and in your discretion President Ayub, that given fact that US Congress has not yet completed its authorization action on aid bill, given fact that after authorization process is completed it will be necessary to go through a separate appropriation procedure in the Congress, given reluctance of the Administration to make a pledge in advance of action by the Congress, and in view of certain other problems which we would be prepared to discuss with GOP should it wish, US is suggesting to World Bank that date of consortium meeting be postponed until after Congress adjourns. US thinking is that date of 27 September would allow adequate leeway and is so proposing to Bank.

You should also say that while postponement of consortium meeting will ultimately become public knowledge, our suggestion is that both USG and GOP should avoid premature publicity.

Rusk

---

[1] Source: National Archives and Records Administration, RG 59, Central Files 1964–66, AID 9 PAK. Secret; Limdis. Drafted by Mann, cleared by Komer, and approved by Mann.

140. Memorandum From Robert Komer of the National Security Council Staff to the President's Special Assistant for National Security Affairs (Bundy)[1]

Washington, July 2, 1965.

Mac—

I've asked Talbot to goose Rusk to join in on Indian PL 480.

Let me recap that we've already cut down the new Indian request from a two-year 16 million ton deal to a one year 7 million ton one.

Second, we've *just* had a new high level appeal from Indian Food Minister, Subramaniam, who says they need help *now* to "avoid crisis shortage." His "particular concern arises from fact that lean months are August and September" before the new Indian crop is in.

Agriculture is our best source. Its key man tells me that to prevent interruption in food shipments, new shipments have to start by 1 September; this means contracts have to be made by 15 August; this means Indians have to have a PA by 15 July; this means we've got to allow say a minimum week before 15 July to negotiate the deal with India. Hence *6 July or so.*

Indian stocks are quite low (two months). If shipments are interrupted, word always leaks out. Once the public becomes aware hoarding starts almost immediately (we've been through this before). Traders hold out of the market to wait for higher prices. The experts are convinced that Indian opinion won't understand *why* we didn't come through, and Indian officialdom will try to shift the blame to us. We'll have a lot of flak in the US press too about why we're "starving" Indians.[2]

The way out is *a simple two-month extension of the current agreement* (only one million tons). If done by 6 July or so, it would buy time, avoid a political explosion, and still keep India on a mighty short rein. We'd insist on all the new tough PL 480 provisions, e.g. dollars for ocean freight, 20% US uses (up from 5%), and 4-1/4% interest.

If we don't come through India will have to *use its own scarce foreign exchange to buy wheat elsewhere* as the UAR did. In this case our

---

[1] Source: Johnson Library, National Security File, Country File, India, Vol. V, Cables, 6/65–9/65. Secret.

[2] In a July 2 memorandum to Rusk, AID Administrator Bell warned: "I cannot emphasize too strongly the serious consequences that would follow from a cessation of wheat shipments—or even from publicity about the possibility of such a cessation. There were food riots in India last year and they could easily occur again." (National Archives and Records Administration, RG 59, Central Files 1964–66, AID (US) 15–8 INDIA)

own *aid dollars* would be indirectly subsidizing Indian wheat purchases to help out someone else's balance of payments.

RWK

---

141.   Telegram From the Embassy in Pakistan to the Department of State[1]

Karachi, July 4, 1965, 2020Z.

13. Dept pass AID. Deptel 1485.[2] Postponement of Pak consortium pledging session.

1. I personally delivered information contained reftel to President Ayub in Murree July 3. In consultation with Macdonald, I had decided it would be preferable to go straight to Ayub first with this news, thus relieving Shoaib of onus of having to carry and explain to Ayub this unwelcome message.

2. I set forth almost verbatim content of reftel. Ayub took the news quite hard—worse than I had anticipated. His first question was whether pledging action for India had also been postponed. Negative response to this seemed to embitter him. He noted that postponement now would cause maximum embarrassment for GOP, which had just come out with numerous policy statements and actions in economic field which would be prejudiced by US action. He complained that unexpected action left his government in vulnerable position.

3. Ayub asked with air of complete innocence, what were "certain other problems" referred to? Said blandly that so far as he knew, everything was set for consortium meeting and he was unable to identify the problems. I identified general foreign policy problem area for him, without getting down to specific complaints.

4. Ayub observed that he had not had any intimation from World Bank President George Woods in London last week that there might be difficulties in relation to consortium pledging session. He said emphatically that Woods had not hinted at any timing problems on part of US and he ventured the opinion that Woods, "being a man with common sense," would not agree with or want to approve the postponement suggestion.

---

[1] Source: National Archives and Records Administration, RG 59, Central Files 1964–66, AID 9 PAK. Secret; Priority; Limdis.
[2] Document 139.

5. Ayub said that he did not see how the postponement news could be kept confidential for any length of time. It could not be kept quiet and the effects of the news would be unfortunate.

6. Ayub opined that the postponement decision clearly represented the beginnings of a new US policy toward Pakistan. He interpreted the announcement as the first stage of the implementation. He said, "Anyone can see that this amounts to more than a mere delay."

7. Ayub did not anticipate any policy development which could be expected to change the position between now and September. He said he had done his best to persuade the US to see the argument for Pakistan's "independent" foreign policy. The US had not been inclined to heed him as to this, or as to the dangers of US arms aid to India. He did not see that there was much more he could try to do.

8. His immediate reaction was that Pakistan would have to "look elsewhere" for economic development assistance. If GOP was unable to find other sources of assistance, Pakistan would simply have to retrench. The people had been through adversity before and could do it again. "We will have to cut the coat according to the cloth."

9. Ayub was non-responsive as to whether he planned to pursue our invitation to discuss the "other problems." He did not register any noticeable interest in sending a representative to the US. He thought that no great interest in an exchange had been shown on US side, noting that his last letter to President on threat to Pak security from India[3] was unacknowledged after more than a month.

10. I made effort to damp down Ayub's disturbing over-reaction without diluting the force of our message. I told him that the message did not foreclose anything and that the way remained entirely open for a constructive plenary session the end of September.

A delay of few weeks did not have to constitute any major setback. I said the situation was entirely recoverable and he should not consider that anything irretrievable had happened. The GOP had the means of readily restoring the situation, and giving US a case which we could effectively put before the Congress. I told him that I and my associates would be available day and night to assist the GOP in getting the program back on the tracks. However, Ayub gave no sign that as of today he is prepared to bring about any GOP policy modifications in response to postponement move.

11. The President thanked me for conveying the message to him privately. He said he would want to handle it in his own way and he asked me not to pass the information to any of his Ministers or other GOP officials.

---

[3] The letter was dated May 11; see Document 120.

12. Since there was no note-taker present and since he showed an interest in having an accurate summary of the message for reference, I wrote out in long hand for him a summary of reftel.

I urged the President not to misread message, and assured him that I was here to do everything humanly possible to bring about a meeting of minds and to restore the old harmony of foreign policy outlook.

13. Separate message will follow tomorrow on discussion initiated by President and pursued at his request as to intent and significance of recent GOP foreign policy moves and their relationship to essential US interests in Asia.[4]

14. *Comment:* It seems evident that reftel will precipitate a considerable stir and possibly an actual full-blown crisis in our relations with Pakistan. Ayub seems to feel that our postponement move challenges him, and strikes at self respect of country by seeking to penalize Pakistan publicly for pursuing "independent" foreign policy. While he may calm down after he has thought through the issues and consulted some of the fairly cool heads in his Cabinet, at the moment he is in a state of repressed anger at what he considers an unjustified punitive action, and the application of a double standard of international conduct to Pakistan and India. There is some danger of his reacting as if he has been "driven to the wall." Macdonald and I in consultation with senior staff will submit further comments and recommendations tomorrow.

McConaughy

---

[4] Telegram 15 from Karachi, July 4, described the tenor of Ayub's remarks in the extended discussion during his July 3 meeting with McConaughy. His remarks reflected disappointment at what he saw as his inability to make the United States see the validity of the reasons for Pakistan's "independent" foreign policy. Pakistan, he insisted, had to face the continuing hostility of India, and could not afford to incur the avoidable enmity of large Communist neighbors in addition to India's. (National Archives and Records Administration, RG 59, Central Files 1964–66, AID 9 PAK)

142.   Memorandum From Robert Komer of the National Security Council Staff to President Johnson[1]

Washington, July 6, 1965.

Postponement on Pak Consortium, which McConaughy personally told Ayub about on 3 July, was quite a shock. Ayub apparently took the Congressional argument quite well but asked about the "other problems" mentioned. McConaughy mentioned the general foreign policy area, at which Ayub launched into a defense of Pakistan's "independent" foreign policy. His Chicom policy was aimed solely at avoiding provocation of China. As for Vietnam, Ayub looked on this as essentially an example of "big-power rivalries." He said that the US wanted its associates to be "only satellites—non-thinking followers who blindly acquiesce to US policy." Ayub opined that the postponement clearly represented the beginning of a new US policy toward Pakistan. He said that anyone could see that this amounted to more than a mere delay. His immediate reaction was that Pakistan would have to look elsewhere for development aid; if this proved impossible the Paks would simply have to retrench. He did not register any interest in sending someone to the US.

Ayub's foreign policy explanations were so thin that even McConaughy went back at him sharply. To characterize Vietnam as "big power rivalry" was far from the mark. The issue was the freedom of Asian countries to exist free from Communist intrusion. This was more important to the free Asian countries than it was to the US. He made a strong plea for Pakistan to declare itself on Vietnam. As to the allegation that we were only looking for satellites, McConaughy invited Ayub to look at some of the Asian countries that were standing foursquare behind us—such as Turkey, Iran, Thailand or the Philippines. Would he brand these countries as satellites?

McConaughy's judgment is that Ayub considers the US is taking a fundamental decision to force him to make a clear-cut choice between the US and an "independent" policy.[2] Ayub almost certainly sees our position as creating a tough problem for him either way he turns, succumbing to US pressure or sustaining loss of US aid. Either could undermine confidence in his leadership and provide a major issue for his opponents. As McConaughy points out, Ayub has been riding high and undoubtedly considers consortium postponement as a US effort

---

[1] Source: Johnson Library, National Security File, Memos to the President, McGeorge Bundy, Vol. 12, July 1965. Secret.

[2] McConaughy conveyed this assessment in telegram 19 from Karachi, July 5. (National Archives and Records Administration, RG 59, Central Files 1964–66, AID 9 PAK)

to whittle him down. So "a fundamental showdown with Pakistan is thus abruptly looming for us."

McConaughy comments that he noted a distressing contrast to Ayub's previous line of thinking; Ayub sounded at some points like an appeaser, an opportunist, an Afro-Asian extremist, and an advocate of full non-alignment. Our Ambassador sees this change as in part a result of Ayub's adverse reactions to our policy, but notes that the "malign and near-hypnotic influence of Bhutto is probably the chief contributing factor."

McConaughy's best guess is that Ayub will make a cautious probe to explore our position more fully, but may not be disposed to send any emissary lest this be interpreted as a first step in surrendering to US pressures. He sees the most dangerous risk as a public crisis, which could be precipitated quickly by premature leaks leading to an outraged emotional reaction against US attachment of political strings to aid. He pleads that we avoid any Washington leaks suggesting pressure tactics, since the Paks would then feel compelled to come back with anti-US blasts.

Our best bet is to sit tight and wait for Ayub's next move. Meanwhile we are working up contingency guidance to forestall any public spat. When the consortium postponement gets out, we can simply say that we want to wait until Congress appropriates the money and certain technical issues are resolved. All this will take delicate handling, but my hunch is that Ayub is too smart to jeopardize his meal ticket by lashing back too hard just yet.

R. W. Komer[3]

---

[3] McGeorge Bundy initialed below Komer's signature.

143.   Memorandum From the President's Special Assistant for National Security Affairs (Bundy)[1]

Washington, July 6, 1965.

MEMORANDUM FOR
The Secretary of State
The Secretary of Defense
The Director of Central Intelligence

Pursuant to the President's desire for an orchestrated US Government effort to convince Pakistan of our dissatisfaction with its current posture, it seems worthwhile to explore the possibilities for appropriate supporting action in the intelligence field. One possibility would be to convey the impression that the US is taking positive measures to reduce its dependence on US intelligence facilities in Pakistan, because of its loss of confidence in Pakistani policy. The following options might be explored:

(a) Suspend currently planned action to expand or improve our facilities, especially those actions which are non-essential (e.g. housing).

(b) Reduce US personnel strength at our Pakistani facilities. Perhaps this could be done as a temporary measure and one involving non-essential personnel.

(c) Proceed on a high priority basis to develop alternate facilities in Iran [less than 1 line of source text not declassified] to the extent feasible. This step might be desirable as insurance in any case.

Since actions along these lines could prove costly in terms of intelligence and dollars, it seems essential that both pros and cons be carefully explored. I suggest we prepare to submit recommendations to the President by about 20 July.

McGeorge Bundy

---

[1] Source: Washington National Records Center, RG 330, OASD/ISA Files: FRC 70 A 5127, 350.09 Pakistan. Top Secret/Sensitive.

144. Telegram From the Department of State to the Embassy in Pakistan[1]

Washington, July 8, 1965, 5:25 p.m.

36. For Ambassador. Our position is that USG does not think it should make aid commitments until Congress has authorized and appropriated funds necessary to carry out commitment.

FYI. Pledging was made in Indian consortium some time ago and was related to last year of five year plan. Pakistan consortium faces question of new five year plan.

US position has nothing to do with problems between India and Pakistan. Our position remains the same as it was before, namely, we hope that these problems can be solved and we have no desire take sides. End FYI.

You should, as appropriate occasions present themselves, make it clear that we do not agree that our inability to make pledge until after US Congress has acted can properly be called "pressure". It simply means US not in a position to make any commitments until after Congress has acted.

FYI. We have not suggested (Embtel 19)[2] that Shoaib visit US. Understand President of World Bank has suggested to Ayub that Shoaib visit might be useful. While, if Shoaib decides to come to Washington, we would be happy to discuss problems with him, decision on whether Shoaib comes is entirely in the hands of GOP.

FYI. We do have number of problems which should be discussed and believe these should be discussed in a frank and friendly fashion. However again this is separate from Congressional question mentioned above.[3] End FYI.

Rusk

---

[1] Source: National Archives and Records Administration, RG 59, Central Files 1964–66, AID 9 PAK. Secret; Immediate; Exdis. Drafted by Mann and cleared by Talbot and in AID by Bell.

[2] See footnote 2, Document 142.

[3] In telegram 38 to Karachi, July 8, McConaughy was instructed to be governed by the guidance in this telegram in his discussions with Pakistani officials concerning the postponement of the consortium meeting. Once a dialogue was opened, the Department anticipated that there would be a number of issues that could be usefully discussed. Chief among these was the conviction in Washington that "Pakistan and US must find better way to work together towards common goals while avoiding unnecessary attacks on each other over matters on which we are in disagreement." (National Archives and Records Administration, RG 59, Central Files 1964–66, POL PAK–US)

145. Memorandum From Robert Komer of the National Security Council Staff to President Johnson[1]

Washington, July 9, 1965, 11:15 a.m.

MAP for India and Pakistan. Attached is a longish memo from Secretary McNamara describing our current programs.[2] It breaks down into three categories: (a) FY 65 and prior programs still undelivered—roughly $50 million for Pakistan and $70 million for India; (b) FY 66 programs (roughly $46 million for Pakistan and $50 million for India), which have *not* yet been approved by DOD and passed as firm to the recipients; and (c) various other requests such as Ayub's recent plea for submarines, F–104s, and tanks. There are also certain dollar credit sales, which I presume we would not want to interfere with (e.g. the sale of $8 million in ammo to the Paks which you recently approved).

There are political risks in holding up MAP. It has traditionally been most sensitive to the Paks, who regard it as essential vis-à-vis India, and whose military are a major political force. As to the Indians, we could spook them to buy more from the USSR. There is also a real question of whether we want or need to hit either Paks or Indians harder than we have already, lest we trigger an open confrontation by pushing too hard.

Thus there is a case for continuing business as usual, except for continuing to hold off on key items such as F–5s for India and F–104s or submarines for the Paks.

A second alternative would be to handle MAP as you have economic aid: (a) continue with deliveries under FY 65 and prior grant programs for which the funds have been appropriated and commitments in effect made; (b) defer telling either we approve the FY 1966 programs, on the grounds that the funds have not yet been appropriated; (c) simply not respond on major additional requests until we have better indications as to the future attitudes of India and Pakistan.

We are not recommending any action till we can get the views of State and Defense. In the meantime, however, DOD will hold off telling the Paks and Indians about any FY 66 program approvals.[3]

R. W. Komer[4]

---

[1] Source: Johnson Library, National Security File, Memos to the President, McGeorge Bundy, Vol. 12, July 1965. Secret.

[2] The memorandum to the President is dated July 6; not printed. (Ibid., 7/1/65–9/22/65)

[3] Johnson responded with a handwritten note on the memorandum that reads: "I would hold everything military etc in abeyance—see me for details."

[4] McGeorge Bundy initialed below Komer's signature.

146. Memorandum From Robert Komer of the National Security Council Staff to the President's Special Assistant for National Security Affairs (Bundy)[1]

Washington, July 9, 1965.

Mac—

Paks are continuing their one-upmanship on consortium postponement.

G. Ahmed braced Rusk this noon with attached bristling "oral message from his government"[2] (no doubt drafted by brother Aziz and Bhutto). In effect it says stop trying to push us.

When Rusk pleaded Congressional problems, G. Ahmed brusquely told him everything was fine on Capitol Hill. He told Talbot after the session that "this game is not worth the candle" and that this was the first time in the history of US/Pak relationship that economic aid had been used for political purposes.

I'm sure State is quivering but I hope that President will insist on simply staring the Paks down. The State experts' hunch and mine is that the Paks are probing to see how far they can rock us. Since one can't return an oral note, I hope we'll give the Paks the silent treatment. They have to come to us in the last analysis.

RWK

---

[1] Source: Johnson Library, National Security File, Country File, Pakistan, Vol. III, Memos, 12/64–7/65. Secret.

[2] Ahmed's meeting with Rusk was reported to Karachi in telegram 51, July 10. (National Archives and Records Administration, RG 59, Central Files 1964–66, AID 9 PAK) The text of the oral message, a copy of which Ahmed left with Rusk, was repeated to Karachi in telegram 44, July 9. The message stated that the Ayub government considered the U.S. proposal ill-advised. The proposed postponement of the consortium meeting was described as invidious and motivated by political rather than economic grounds. The fact that the Pakistan consortium was being postponed and the Indian consortium was not was bound to inflame public opinion in Pakistan, the message warned. (Ibid.)

147.   Telegram From the Embassy in Pakistan to the Department of State[1]

Karachi, July 10, 1965.

50. Personal for the Secretary. When FinMin Shoaib saw me this morning about postponement consortium pledging session,[2] he said that you had offered him the use of our telegraphic facilities if he ever had a message of special importance and sensitivity which he wished to convey urgently to you. He said he thought the current situation called for such a message and asked that I transmit the following to you on his behalf:

Begin message: In the context of the recent Ayub–Woods conversation in London, favorable policy developments were under way here, which are threatened by the shift in the US Govt approach to the consortium pledging session. I ask your help in finding some way out so that a crisis does not arise. *End message.*

McConaughy

---

[1] Source: Johnson Library, National Security File, Country File, Pakistan, Vol. III, Cables, 12/64–7/65. Secret; Priority; Exdis. No time of transmission is given on the telegram, which was received at 8:16 a.m.

[2] The IBRD advised the Department on July 9 that in view of the U.S. inability to take a positive position in the pledging session scheduled for July 27, the Pakistan consortium pledging session was being rescheduled to September 23. (Telegram 153 to London, July 9; National Archives and Records Administration, RG 59, Central Files 1964–66, AID 9 PAK)

148.   Memorandum of Telephone Conversation Between President Johnson and the Under Secretary of State for Economic Affairs (Mann)[1]

Washington, July 13, 1965, 10:50 a.m.

The President said he had received Mr. Mann's note.[2] He said that he thought it was a little late to get the letter[3] changed. The President said he would be glad to see him when he wishes to come. The President said he would like Mr. Mann to get the best economic people thinking about the food shortage—make a special case out of it—there is starvation and famine—and then submit a recommendation to the Congress saying here is the situation, here is what they are asking for, here is a real serious situation and ask Congress to consider it, act on it and dispose of it. The President said he would like to send a special case up rather than taking the responsibility himself.

Mr. Mann said the thing that bothered him was that the Indians might not realize that the timing of this visit may be important. He said he had not said anything to the Indians but he thought that somehow they ought to be made aware of this. Mr. Mann admitted that it may be too late this morning to try to get the letter changed and perhaps we should be working on some kind of talk between the President and Shastri and the President and Ayub. Mr. Mann said if they did not lose their heads over there, we might be able to really accomplish something.

The President said that Mr. Mann should tell Nehru that Bhutto had announced this morning the postponement of the consortium, and that the President was hoping to see Ayub before the consortium was held at the end of September. The President said they might not want to be definite about next year in these circumstances. Mr. Mann said that was his idea exactly. He said he had no intention to press the Ambassador but only to make him aware. The President said he did not want to take the responsibility personally for this. Mr. Mann asked what would happen if these visits came through and we worked out some kind of a sensible arrangement with both countries. He said he did not know if this was possible with Pakistan but he thought it was possible with India. He said in this case, we might go ahead with the original program. The President repeated that he did not want to take this responsibility—he wished the Con-

---

[1] Source: Johnson Library, Mann Papers, Telephone Conversations with LBJ, May 2, 1965–June 2, 1966. No classification marking. Transcribed in Mann's office.
[2] Not found.
[3] Not further identified.

gress to pass on it. Mr. Mann said he would pass the message on in an oblique way to Nehru.

The President said he would be most happy to see him as soon as the appropriation bill gets through the House. Mr. Mann said he understood. He said he was not going to urge the Ambassador to do anything. He is just going to make him conscious of the situation.

[Here follows discussion unrelated to South Asia.]

---

149.   Memorandum for the Record[1]

Washington, July 13, 1965, 5:26 p.m.

SUBJECT

President's Talk with Ambassador B. K. Nehru, July 13, 1965

PRESENT

The President
H.E. B. K. Nehru, Indian Ambassador
Under Secretary Thomas Mann
Mr. R. W. Komer

The President greeted Ambassador Nehru cordially. After some small talk, the President asked about Shastri's trip to Canada and Europe. Nehru thought it had been quite successful. He described how Shastri had asked him in Ottawa how Vietnam was ever going to be settled. He had replied there was no easy way to settle Vietnam, but constant Indian comments didn't help the situation any. In effect Shastri should keep quiet about Vietnam.

---

[1] Source: Johnson Library, National Security File, Country File, India, Vol. V, Memos and Miscellaneous, 6/65–9/65. Secret. Drafted by Komer on July 16. The time of the meeting, which took place at the White House, is taken from the President's Daily Diary. (Ibid.)

Nehru then presented a letter from Prime Minister Shastri,[2] which he described as a response to President Johnson's letter of 5 June.[3] The President read it carefully, remarking that he was very pleased that the Rann of Kutch issue had been settled. Nehru agreed that it was a "great relief."

The President expressed his appreciation for Mr. Shastri's letter. As for Shastri's request that he see Finance Minister Khrishnamachari during the latter's visit in September, he would be delighted to do so.

Then the President noted Shastri's emphasis on food. He was considering a message to Congress on the Asian food problem so that Congress itself could become more fully involved. There was some feeling in the Congress against so much aid to other countries. Aside from the many complaints about aid in general, some Congressmen didn't understand why countries like India should go for steel mills instead of fertilizer. The President's idea was to get the House and Senate to debate out the issue of whether we should provide "food for famine", and decide on what position they wanted to take. The President himself was strongly for providing such help. He kept rereading Barbara Ward's book "Rich Nations and Poor Nations", and felt deeply the moral obligation of rich nations like the United States to help others. So he had told Secretary Rusk just today that he wanted a food for famine proposal put before the Congress as soon as possible.

The President mentioned that because of the Congressional problem he had also held up a new pledge to the Pakistan consortium until the appropriation had been acted upon. He commented on the difficulties of getting the aid bill through, pointing out that the Administration had lost 12–8 on the bill in the Foreign Relations Committee, which simply shouldn't have happened. But the Indians kept telling us how to solve Vietnam and Ayub was off receiving Chou En-lai. This sort of thing certainly affected the vote. We had had to get the proxy

---

[2] Shastri's July 9 letter to Johnson was devoted largely to prospects for India's economic development. He expressed gratitude for U.S. economic assistance, which had contributed importantly to India's development. Shastri noted that India was in the process of drafting its Fourth Five-Year Plan, which was scheduled to commence on April 1, 1966, and he asked if Johnson would discuss the draft plan with Finance Minister T.T. Krishnamachari when he visited Washington in September. Of more pressing importance, Shastri noted that the P.L. 480 agreement, which governed the flow of needed food grains to India, had expired on June 30. He asked Johnson to intervene personally to expedite the negotiation of a new agreement so that the movement of grain would not be interrupted. Finally, Shastri expressed appreciation for the renewed invitation to visit the United States and indicated that, although he would not be able to come until the next calendar year, he looked forward to a visit at a mutually convenient date. (Ibid., National Security File, Special Head of State Correspondence File, India, 4/15/65–2/28/66)

[3] Document 127.

of Senator Symington who was ill in Bethesda, but finally got the vote reversed 10–8.

The President then described his current difficulties with conference on the authorization bill. Fulbright wanted a two year bill; the House was adamant on one year. Their positions were irreconcilable. Besides all this, the Senate had gotten tired and one afternoon had let $200 million get cut off the barebones request he had sent up. In an exchange with Nehru, the President indicated that he'd like to get the $200 million from the Senate side and the two year bill from the House side; but the House wouldn't budge.

Then came the appropriation process. The President asked Nehru whether he had ever met Otto Passman. He described his next "easy job" was that of taking on Passman, who was always a tough customer. If he could only get by Passman, he was willing to gamble on the Senate in order to move ahead with discussions on aid to Pakistan.

On India's food needs, the President felt that we should promptly send a food-for-famine message to the Hill. He described the difficulties on the agricultural bill this year—on which he thought we would probably get licked. When Nehru praised his record to date, the President philosophized about his increasing difficulties with the Congress. In his judgment a Presidential mandate lasted only about six months under the US system. The Administration was having increasing difficulty with the mass media, with the muttering of the "diplomats", and with the Congress. So he was due for some reversals. It would become more difficult for the Administration to lead here and to lead abroad. He had no illusions about being able to maintain the present pace; in fact, he expected some reversals within the next 45 days. So he asked Nehru to give us any help he could in convincing the Congress about India's food needs. The President insisted that Congress must share this responsibility.

Nehru, referring to the Shastri letter, indicated that India's needs fell into two categories; first was the immediate need for food to avert great difficulty because India's food stocks were exhausted; second was a longer range aid need for the next 5 year plan. Commenting on India's immediate needs, the President said he certainly didn't want people to starve but wanted the Congress to be in partnership on whatever we did. So he told Messrs. Mann and Komer to get busy on a message to the Congress. Meanwhile, he said, we could do what needed to be done if necessary to avert catastrophe.

The President then described "in confidence" the difficulties the US was having in Vietnam, and what we were going to have to do. We were going to have to put in more people—at least 100,000 and perhaps double that number. We would also have to go for several billion dollars more in additional defense expenditures this year, and probably call up reserves, postpone the discharges of people serving in Vietnam, even increase the draft—perhaps calling up married men. McNamara was going to Vietnam to get the facts on which to base any such decisions. As an added problem, the Republicans were beginning to criticize our Vietnam policy. People like Congressman Ford wanted the President to do reckless things, but he would not do so. We were not bombing Hanoi nor were we crossing the Chinese frontier. So the President was mystified by the Chinese accusation that we had done so; he speculated that perhaps the Chinese were seeking to provide an excuse to cover some move that they planned. As Nehru knew, we had also tried in every way possible to get the North Vietnamese to talk but had failed. Now the latest effort, Wilson's sending Davies to Hanoi, had flopped too. The President ended up by indicating that he wasn't pessimistic. He didn't think we would lose out in Vietnam but it would be a long hard struggle. However, in view of the way the Indians seemed compelled to comment so often on Vietnam, we would certainly like to know India's solution. If Shastri knew how to settle Vietnam, we wished he would tell us.

As an example of how things could turn out better than they seemed at the low point, the President cited the Dominican Republic situation. He thought that it was steadily improving. There would have been a Castro regime in another 24 hours if we hadn't moved in. The Dominican Republic might yet go in this direction in the next election, but at least this would be a free choice.

At this point the President was informed that Ambassador Lodge was waiting, so he invited Nehru to stay and visit for a few moments with Lodge. After a brief discussion of the problems Lodge would confront in Vietnam, the President showed the group the Rose Garden.

R. W. Komer[4]

---

[4] Printed from a copy that bears this typed signature.

150. Telegram From the Department of State to the Embassy in Pakistan[1]

Washington, July 14, 1965, 6:17 p.m.

64. Embtel 50.[2] For Ambassador. You should thank Shoaib on behalf Secretary for personal message conveyed reftel and say that Secretary appreciates confidence in our relations on which it rests. Secretary strongly shares Shoaib's desire that crisis be avoided. Whole objective our actions and talks we seek with GOP is to avoid such crisis developing. He is confident that Shoaib will do everything he can to achieve same end. You should tell Shoaib however that considerations affecting our position on timing Consortium afford U.S. no alternative and we hope he can get Ayub to see this in proper perspective so that we can proceed to examine our problems and find a better way to work together toward common goals.

Rusk

[1] Source: National Archives and Records Administration, RG 59, Central Files 1964–66, AID 9 PAK. Secret; Priority; Exdis. Drafted by Laingen and Laise on July 13, cleared by Talbot and Mann, and approved and initialed by Rusk. Also sent to Rawalpindi.
[2] Document 147.

151. Telegram From the Department of State to the Embassy in Pakistan[1]

Washington, July 15, 1965, 5:14 p.m.

72. Following summary FYI and Noforn. It is uncleared and subject to amendment upon review.

Secretary met briefly with Pak Ambassador Ahmed this afternoon[2]

[1] Source: National Archives and Records Administration, RG 59, Central Files 1964–66, AID 9 PAK. Secret; Immediate; Limdis. Drafted by Laingen and approved by Talbot. Also sent to Rawalpindi and repeated to London in New Delhi.
[2] The Embassy in Pakistan reported on July 15 that Ahmed's scheduled July 15 meeting with Rusk was viewed as being of such significance that a Cabinet meeting was being deferred until a report of the meeting could be received. (Telegram 6 from Rawalpindi; ibid.)

but did not get substance of our differences with Pakistan because meeting cut short by Secretary's departure for airport to meet Amb. Stevenson's funeral cortege. Talk to be resumed July 16 at 4 p.m. Talbot also present as well as note takers both sides.

Ambassador referred to report he had received of Ambassador McConaughy's conversation with Shoaib July 11 from which he had concluded it view USG that political issues should not be linked with Consortium developments. Amb Ahmed said if this true this was sound position because it had after all been consistent USG policy not to link economic aid with political considerations. If however, USG should conclude on objective grounds that it must cut back commitment to Third Plan it only fair GOP should know soon so it could begin adjusting its own thinking. For present GOP must continue assume on basis preliminary Consortium meeting June that all members believed Pak Third Plan soundly based.

Secretary's response emphasized three points. First, he did not want Ambassador to conclude from Consortium developments that we now tying aid to all sorts of political considerations. What we were doing was part of our way of dealing with facts of life on Hill. Secretary not sure that GOP fully appreciated depth of re-examination future aid legislation now under way, especially in Senate. House also had reservations, though of different kind. Conference committee on authorization bill deadlocked. In such situation it obviously important have better idea how things will work out before US makes major additional commitments in aid field.[3]

Second point Secretary emphasized was that if we are perhaps a bit difficult to live with these days, our friends abroad should recognize why. Fact was that we faced in Southeast Asia life-or-death issues involving danger of general war in Pacific. Situation highly dangerous because other side has shown no sign of wanting peace—which could come within 48 hours if they were ready. Our friends should recognize that when we faced with issues of this dimension we naturally deeply sensitive.

Third, Secretary said he wanted emphasize again cumulative adverse effect on Congress over recent years of differences between India and Pakistan and implication this could have for US policy. If India and Pakistan were at peace, subcontinent would be impregnable, arms race could be avoided and resources applied rationally across subconti-

---

[3] AID Administrator Bell made similar points on July 14 in a discussion with Ahmed of economic issues bearing on U.S. relations with Pakistan. (Telegram Aidto 97 to Karachi, July 15; ibid., Ball Files: Lot 74 D 272, Pakistan)

nent. Indo-Pak tensions clearly had resulted in net added burden on all concerned including USG.[4]

Ambassador said he wanted to respond to Pak actions cited by Secretary previous conversation, namely Pak–Chicom communiqué and Bhutto talk with North Vietnam FonMin Algiers. Ambassador said latter was in pursuance understanding Ayub had with PM Wilson that he would do what he could behind the scenes to improve outlook for Commonwealth Vietnam peace mission. Ayub had instructed Bhutto get in touch with North Vietnam FonMin at Algiers and Bhutto had done so but had run into stone wall. As for Peiping communiqué, reference to "imperialism" therein clearly not directed at US; to Pakistanis "imperialists" are Indians in Kashmir. Secretary said we accepted this explanation but when Communist regimes use this word in joint communiqués, it amounts to word of propaganda inevitably meaning US.

Rusk

---

[4] Telegram 79 to Karachi, July 17, expanded the reporting on Rusk's July 15 conversation with Ahmed. Touching on the problem of differences between India and Pakistan, Rusk suggested that the improved atmosphere following the settlement of the dispute over the Rann of Kutch might provide a basis for secret talks on the Kashmir issue. Ahmed agreed to relay the suggestion to his government. (Ibid., Central Files 1964–66, AID 9 PAK)

152.   Telegram From the Office of the Secretary of Defense to the Commander in Chief, Middle East, South Asia, and Africa South of the Sahara (Adams)[1]

Washington, July 15, 1965, 1928Z.

5899. From OASD/ISA. Message in Three Parts.

Part I for All.

1. The Secretary of Defense has issued the following instructions regarding Military Assistance to Pakistan and India: Without disclosing the decision to the Paks or the Indians, defer until further notice approval of any portions of the FY 66 program of military assistance to those countries. This issue will be reviewed on or about 15 August 1965.

Part II for CINCMEAFSA

2. Procedure to implement this decision influenced by following: FY 66 CRA MAP Orders were issued on 6 July 1965 and pursuant to this authority actions are under way to implement these orders. These actions include: (a) requisitions for spare parts initiated by host country personnel; (b) country personnel being selected and ordered to CONUS for training. Hence it must be assumed that this CRA element of the FY 66 Program has been communicated to Paks and Indians. Therefore, to preclude disclosure to Paks and Indians, implementation of all actions authorized by CRA will continue.

3. Further discussions in New Delhi and Karachi with host country personnel on FY 66 MAP should not be initiated, but, if requested on Pak or Indian initiative, discussions may be conducted on a low key "business as usual" basis without commitment. Other than CRA MAP Orders already issued, approval of additional FY 66 MAP will be deferred.

4. Regarding GOI FY 66 credit sales USMSMI should proceed with its review of GOI submission. USMSMI should limit its contacts or consultations with GOI representatives to minimum and limit such contacts to low level business as usual approach. Any GOI requests for urgent processing of items under FY 66 credit sales program should be accepted without comment or commitment by USMSMI and forwarded through usual channels with its recommendations.

---

[1] Source: Johnson Library, National Security File, Country File, Pakistan, Vol. V, Cables, 9/65–1/66. Secret; Priority; Noforn Def. Drafted by Colonel Lincoln A. Simon, USA, of the Office of Military Assistance, DOD/ISA, and approved by General Robert J. Wood, USA, Director of Military Assistance, DOD/ISA. Also sent to Department of the Army, Chief of Naval Operations, and Chief of Staff of the Air Force, and repeated to CMAAG Karachi, CUSMSMI New Delhi, Department of State, and the White House.

Part III for Military Departments

5. Continue delivery of programs approved and funded in FY 65 and prior years MAP Orders.

---

153.   Memorandum From Robert Komer of the National Security Council Staff to President Johnson[1]

Washington, July 15, 1965.

Pak reactions to consortium postponement. The Paks have apparently decided to take a tough line (perhaps to test how serious we are). After appeals to us not to postpone the consortium, Bhutto then announced our request[2] (he expressed doubt that the US actually intended to cut off aid "or that it would dare do so even if it wanted to, in view of uniformly adverse and violent Afro-Asian reaction which could be expected.")

The result is that the postponement *has* now become a public issue. McConaughy says "our position in Pakistan is rapidly assuming crisis proportions."[3] Ayub himself in a speech said Pakistan seeks "friends not masters" and that the US has been acting in a manner prejudicial to Pakistan's interests in Indo/Pak disputes. It is not unusual, he said, that big powers become overbearing in their attitudes. The Pak press is taking this line.

Earlier, Bhutto gave McConaughy a tough time, saying that Pakistan not the US was really the injured party. Hence, we should come to them, not they to us.[4] Then on 9 July Pak Ambassador Ahmed delivered a tough oral message to Rusk calling the postponement "ill-advised"; its "invidious nature" would not be lost on the Pak people.[5]

---

[1] Source: Johnson Library, National Security File, Memos to the President, McGeorge Bundy, Vol. 12, July 1965. Secret.

[2] Bhutto announced the U.S. decision to request a postponement of the Pakistan consortium meeting during a debate on foreign policy in the National Assembly on July 13. (Telegram 3 from Rawalpindi, July 13; National Archives and Records Administration, RG 59, Central Files 1964–66, AID 9 PAK)

[3] McConaughy made this assessment in telegram 8 from Rawalpindi, July 15. He noted that through press articles and speeches the country was being aroused to unite behind the government's resistance to alleged U.S. attempts to suborn Pakistani sovereignty and national pride. (Ibid.)

[4] McConaughy reported this July 12 conversation in telegram 2 from Rawalpindi, July 13. (Ibid.)

[5] See footnote 2, Document 146.

Rusk talked briefly with Ahmed today, but asked Ahmed to come back tomorrow, because he had to meet the Stevenson plane. *Rusk's main reason was that he wants to talk with you first.* He and Talbot are deeply troubled that we're approaching an open confrontation with the Paks, and are inclined to play it cautiously. Rusk emphasized to Ahmed that our Hill troubles were real, citing the conference deadlock as evidence of a deeper malaise. In answer to Ahmed's question as to whether we still intended to make a pledge in September, Rusk told him this was our present intention.

We're in for a rough ride, but there are even greater risks in backwatering in the face of the foolhardy Pak decision to create a public spat. Since we hold the better cards, we can afford to sit tight and keep quiet for a while longer, and see if they'll come to us.[6]

R. W. Komer[7]

_____

[6] Bundy added a handwritten note that reads: "strongly agree."
[7] Bundy initialed below Komer's signature.

---

154. Memorandum From the President's Special Assistant for National Security Affairs (Bundy) to President Johnson[1]

Washington, July 16, 1965, 11:05 a.m.

SUBJECT

Food for the Hungry, the Hill, and the Indians

The best way of meeting your objectives has been studied by Komer, Bator, Schultze, AID, Agriculture, and State (Freeman is away, but Schnittker has signed on).

The basic problem is to steer a course that will endorse food for India, and open the way for a broad new food program next year, *without* undermining or attempting to replace your existing PL 480 authority this year. (To seek small changes in the present law would merely open Pandora's box for the Committees, and to put a whole

_____

[1] Source: Johnson Library, National Security File, Country File, India, Vol. V, Memos and Miscellaneous, 6/65–9/65. Confidential.

new program forward for legislation this year is just not practicable, according to Budget and Agriculture.)

The best arrangement we can think of is as follows:

First, to give turn-around time, authorize an interim food program for India, redesigned to meet as many as possible of the new criteria. This is purely a standby operation and we recommend four months instead of two simply to avoid useless nervousness both in the bureaucracy and in India. We also believe it may be better not to use a short-fuse deadline on the Congress, but you will have a better judgment on this point.

Four Months

Two Months

Speak to me[2]

Second, send up a message asking for a joint Congressional resolution with the following components: [3]

1. An endorsement of this brief extension of the PL 480 agreement with India.

2. A further endorsement of other interim programs that will be necessary in the months between now and the new legislative proposal.

3. A broader endorsement (after the manner of the Vandenberg Resolution of 1948) of your intent to develop a basic new program to provide food for the hungry in cooperation with the governments of the hungry nations and the other food-producing countries—a new world-wide war against hunger. The components of the resolution would be framed to match the following position, which would be set out in an accompanying message:

a. Stress your concern over the dangerous *food problem* facing the world and particularly Asia in the coming years.

b. State your conviction that our *Food for Peace program* will require major redirection if we are to help the developing nations cope with this problem.

c. Announce that you are now studying ways of redirecting these programs so that US food aid will:

---

[2] There is no indication on the memorandum that Johnson responded to any of the options.

[3] Komer prepared a draft of such a message on July 15. (Johnson Library, National Security File, Country File, India, Vol. V, Memos and Miscellaneous, 6/65–9/65)

—be contingent upon effective *self-help* efforts by the recipient nation, particularly those aimed at securing an *expansion in* agricultural output.

—maximize the contribution of food aid to *overall economic development goals.*

—meet the *nutritional needs* and prevent famine among the peoples of the recipient countries.

—encourage the *cooperative participation of other food exporting countries* in this whole effort.

d. Emphasize the connection between the *food problem* and the *population problem* and reiterate your willingness to work with LDC's on programs to moderate the population explosion.

e. State your intention to submit major changes in PL 480 legislation at the next session, once your intensive study has been completed.

The attached outline message shows the skeleton of what could be done. There are plenty of statistics and lots of eloquence which can be supplied in support of this basic argument.

What we need to know now is whether this basic approach meets your requirements. If it does, we can produce a fleshed-out resolution and a draft message over the weekend with help from Goodwin and Galbraith, both of whom are in town.

Yes

No

Speak to me

McG. B.

155. Telegram From the Department of State to the Embassy in Pakistan[1]

Washington, July 16, 1965, 8:39 p.m.

78. Deptel 72.[2] Following summary based on uncleared memcon; FYI, Noforn and subject to revision on review:

Secretary met with Pakistan Ambassador July 16 to continue conversation reported reftel. Secretary told Ambassador he had seen press reports Ayub PML speech July 14 sharply critical US; thought it desirable resume discussion after full text available. Secretary wondered, however, on basis apparent GOP public reaction to date what GOP had in mind and where we went from here.

Ambassador said reaction in Pakistan had been foreshadowed in oral message he had communicated earlier. He understood GOP stance to be it sought no confrontation with USG but still believed postponement Consortium session provocative and discriminatory. General policy GOP remained one of supporting principles moderation, peaceful settlement disputes and good neighborliness (even with India if it would agree). GOP felt in pursuit this course it had made contributions to moderation and responsibility Afro-Asian world. Even where there had been differences with Allies, especially on continuing arms aid to India, Pakistan had not gone off deep end. He thought it fair to say that in matters vital to US Pakistan as ally and friend had been very mindful US requirements. Ambassador cited as examples Ayub's speech Peiping advocating a negotiated settlement South Viet-Nam that recognized US interests and Ayub's firm refusal go along with Chicom and Soviet demands to include condemnatory paragraphs against US policy Viet-Nam in joint communiqués after visits those countries.

After both visits US Ambassador Karachi had been given detailed briefing GOP actions. Nevertheless, Ambassador Ahmed doubted whether USG fully appreciated how Pakistan, even though "in lion's den itself," had sought to protect US interests. There may have been isolated instances, particularly where Pak politicians had said one thing or another, where US could take exception to Pak actions. But even so there was sharp contrast between Pak actions and those of India. India constantly made statements critical US policies South Viet-Nam but India seemed to be able to get away with almost anything.

---

[1] Source: National Archives and Records Administration, RG 59, Central Files 1964–66, AID 9 PAK. Secret; Immediate; Limdis. Drafted by Laingen, cleared by Laise, and approved by Talbot. Also sent to Rawalpindi and repeated to New Delhi and London.

[2] Document 151.

Ambassador said essential point was whether or not Pakistan had joined with forces inimical to US. He was authorized to say in categorical terms that answer was no and he could say this with full authority his Government. Secretary interjected this was very important statement. Secretary found statement particularly interesting in light of fact he had recently felt it necessary to say in response query from Congressional friend that he really could not say what Pakistan would do should there be general conflict in Pacific. Ambassador said: "Well you have my answer."

Ambassador observed U.S. of course could not expect Pak support on every issue. Secretary emphasized last thing in world we wanted was satellite relationship; wondered, however, if Pakistan wanted U.S. to be satellite of Pakistan. Ambassador said this out of question. Secretary said he not so sure; noted we had concluded at time Chicom attack on India 1962 that it in our vital national interest come to India's support. From that point on U.S.–Pak relations ran into difficulty. Since then U.S. did not really know what Pakistan asking of us in our relationship.

In response, Ambassador discoursed on GOP disagreement U.S. policy toward India; emphasized view arms aid India could only be directed at Pakistan. In response Secretary's earlier query about where we went from here, Ambassador said that if U.S. wanted discussions GOP ready have them whenever U.S. desired.

Secretary asked if it would be unfair to say that one source long-standing misunderstanding between U.S. and Pakistan had been different view from very outset as to objective our alliance relationship. We saw it directed against communist aggression; Pakistan apparently saw alliances as source strength against India. Ambassador said he could not really say; he assumed objective in any event was strong Pakistan that would not fall prey to anyone.

Secretary reaffirmed our interest in continuing discussion; said objective should be to identify both our common interests and points of divergence and see how we can circumscribe those differences. It possible that most of our problems had arisen out of misunderstanding and he thought there was good chance they could be cleared up.

During conversation Secretary said he wanted take opportunity inquire of Ambassador about report we had heard from Indonesian source that Indonesia getting C–130 spares from Paks. Indonesians had gotten C–130's from us in past but we had suspended program after Indonesia began using them against Malaysia and one or two shot down. He assumed only C–130 equipment Paks had was from U.S. MAP. Ambassador said he uninformed but would check, adding comment Pak C–130's "falling apart too."

Rusk

156. Memorandum From the President's Special Assistant for National Security Affairs (Bundy) to President Johnson[1]

Washington, July 18, 1965, 10:30 a.m.

SUBJECT

Pakistan

Yesterday you told me that you would like to get a message to the Paks either through a letter to Ayub or a talk with the Ambassador—making it very clear indeed that you do not propose to talk about assistance programs until they have been authorized and appropriated by the Congress. I spoke to Dean Rusk about it. He said that this message had been communicated over and over, but that he thought it would be good to do it again. He is drafting a Presidential letter to Ayub, and he will make the point again to Ahmed next week himself. He and Ahmed had an unsatisfactory conversation Friday,[2] and the Secretary is very fearful that the Paks may "overreact" in the next few days. My own impression is that there is a contest between the bad Bhutto and the good Shoaib, and that Ayub will not do anything final in the next little while.

Meanwhile, I think it is getting more urgent that we get beyond the immediate tactical point—that we can't do business until the Congress has acted—and get as clear an understanding as we can of what you really want from the Paks. McConaughy certainly, and Rusk probably, do not really know what you want, and with the best will in the world, their ignorance may lead to complicate the problem. Even your White House troops may fall into the same error.

For this reason I venture to offer for your consideration the attached paper prepared by Bob Komer's very bright Asian hand, Hal Saunders.[3] The first four pages are all you really need to read, although the supporting papers on Pakistan behavior in the last three years is instructive. If the policy Saunders outlines is somewhere near your own view, it might well be wise for us to draft a memorandum from you to the

---

[1] Source: Johnson Library, National Security File, Memos to the President, McGeorge Bundy, Vol. 12, 7/1/65–9/65. No classification marking. A handwritten note on the memorandum reads, "ret'd from Pres. Has seen 7:45 a.m. 19 July 65."

[2] July 16.

[3] Reference is to a 4-page memorandum, dated July 16, entitled "What Do We Want In Pakistan." Saunders supplemented his memorandum with a 14-page chronology, also dated July 16, entitled "Pakistani Transgressions of US Friendship." (Johnson Library, National Security File, Country File, Pakistan, Vol. III, Memos and Miscellaneous, 12/64–7/65)

Secretary of State which would spell out your views. If Saunders is way off base, then we need to know it.

I don't quite know how to offer a set of choices for your answer on this one. If you could write just one line of your own views, it would be a great help, or, alternatively, I can ask you for a reaction sometime in the coming week.

McG. B.

---

157.   Memorandum From Secretary of State Rusk to President Johnson[1]

Washington, July 19, 1965.

In response to Mr. Bundy's memorandum of July 6,[2] I have explored the suggested options which might be taken in the intelligence field pursuant to your desire for an orchestrated U.S. Government effort to convince Pakistan of our dissatisfaction with its current posture. The Director of Intelligence and Research, Department of State, has also participated fully in USIB deliberations on this subject. A copy of the current USIB study,[3] together with the State Department's comment on it, will be available to you separately.

I agree with you that the whole question of our intelligence relationships with Pakistan must be subject to the most searching examination. This question involves a variety of complex and interrelated factors. I believe, for example, the Government of Pakistan puts great weight on the importance of our intelligence facilities in terms of our massive assistance program and that their official statements on the discomfiture which they feel over these installations are designed to increase their leverage with us. Nevertheless, the possibility of an ouster remains.

I welcome the view expressed in the USIB paper that all elements of the Government should bend their efforts in close cooperation to develop any feasible alternatives for our intelligence installations in Pakistan. I believe this effort should include thorough exploration of

---

[1] Source: Johnson Library, National Security File, Country File, Pakistan, Vol. III, 12/64–7/65. Top Secret/Sensitive. Received in McGeorge Bundy's office at 1:19 p.m.

[2] Document 143.

[3] Not found.

the possibilities for space and seaborne facilities, as well as installations in Iran [*less than 1 line of source text not declassified*].[4] Despite the formidable technological and budgetary problems involved, it seems to me that the development of alternatives is a matter of the highest importance which must be pursued vigorously irrespective of our current problem with Pakistan.

I can conceive of circumstances (especially as we get further along in our development of alternatives) in which it may be possible and useful to use our intelligence facilities in Pakistan to help convey a message to that Government. This might, depending on circumstances, be done by either reducing or expanding present activities. However, in view of (1) the actions we are taking or considering in the political, military, and economic fields, (2) Pakistan's reaction to these to date, and (3) the importance of the intelligence acquired from the facilities, I do not consider it necessary or desirable for us to reduce existing facilities at this time.

We also face the question of whether or not currently planned improvements at existing facilities in Pakistan should be carried out according to the present schedule. We will want to make certain that any such improvements will not re-emphasize to the Pakistanis our dependence on the Peshawar complex. Such an interpretation could complicate our efforts in other fields to establish a more desirable relationship with Pakistan. I recommend therefore that no further additions or improvements to the facilities be undertaken at this time.

There is a final problem. I understand that one major improvement, i.e., construction of an addition to the operations building and new dormitories at the Peshawar installation, is already underway. This work, which was authorized before our present policy initiative was undertaken, is likely to be conspicuous. We will need to examine carefully whether or not it too should be suspended temporarily. I believe a final decision on this subject should be reached after the Secretary of Defense and the Director of Central Intelligence have had a chance to present their views on it to you.

Dean Rusk

---

[4] On July 27 Ambassador Bowles discussed with DCI Raborn the possibility of [*text not declassified*]. (Central Intelligence Agency, Job 80–B01285A, DCI Files, DCI Memos for the Record, 22 July–3 Nov 1965)

158.   Telegram From the Department of State to the Embassy in Pakistan[1]

Washington, July 23, 1965, 3:11 p.m.

105. For Ambassador.

1. We regret that GOP has over-reacted to notice that USG was unable to pledge at consortium meeting scheduled for July. It would appear that Ayub, at least initially, followed the anti-American line of Bhutto and other extremists.

2. To the extent that GOP intention is to apply pressure on us—and this would appear to be motive of Bhutto and his associates—USG wishes to continue at all times treat GOP with courtesy and politeness while making it clear tactic of abuse and attack will not cause USG to change its policies or decisions. It is important that the Paks know of the extremely bad impression Pakistan's behavior is creating from top to bottom in the US.

3. We are concerned, however, that Ayub may have been led to believe that US is embarked on a specific course to force Pakistan acceptance of a subservient role to India. When you next see Ayub you should make clear to him this is totally false. Our position was and is that we do not want to take sides in dispute between India and Pakistan; that we have hoped and continue to hope for a peaceful solution of the Kashmir and other issues between the two countries; and that we do not consider that US friendship with one is incompatible with friendship with other.

4. You should also make clear US has no desire compromise Pak sovereignty or force Paks to abjure normal relations with any country, including Red China. Instead, what is largely at issue is obligations of alliances freely entered into by Pakistan and which Ayub himself has repeatedly said have been of great benefit to it. As Paks well know, we have construed SEATO and CENTO as directed specificially and exclusively against the Communist threat. US has taken these alliances into account in providing truly massive investment in Pak viability and security, an investment which on any proportionate basis far greater than that which US has made in India, for example. Indeed, Pakistan second largest recipient US aid in world. Yet, as focus of US effort resist Communist expansion has shifted increasingly to Southeast Asia, it has received less and less cooperation from its Pak allies. This,

---

[1] Source: National Archives and Records Administration, RG 59, Central Files 1964–66, AID 9 PAK. Secret; Priority; Limdis. Drafted by Mann and Komer, cleared by Talbot, and approved and initialed by Rusk. Also sent to Rawalpindi.

despite fact that US defending flank of South Asia, including Pakistan. We deeply disappointed.

5. Even so, we have always respected the sovereignty and independence of Pakistan and its right to conduct its domestic and foreign policies in the way which, in the opinion of the GOP, best meets the requirements of the Pakistani people. We shall continue to do so. But by the same token we expect all other countries to treat decisions of the USG with the same mutual respect. A USG decision, for example, to devote a larger or a smaller portion of its resources to foreign economic or military assistance or to allocate the amount made available in a particular way is certainly an appropriate subject for quiet and constructive discussion between countries such as the US and Pakistan, which have enjoyed friendly relations over a period of years. Yet with all due respect we cannot agree that there is any obligation to maintain a particular level of aid in any country or, indeed, any aid at all. The allocation and use of US resources is a matter which ultimately must be decided by the USG. The supplying of foreign aid is a privilege not an obligation, just as the receipt of concessional loans and other types of assistance is a privilege rather than a right. We cannot therefore accept the suggestion that our attitude in a consortium can properly be called "pressure."

6. The GOP is doubtless aware of the propensity of some US aid recipients to attack US policy and motives in an extreme and unfair fashion, particularly in public forums. Quite apart and separate from Pakistan, the attacks in various parts of the world have created resentment among the people of the US and in our Congress. This and other problems related to aid (including inadequate self-help measures in some countries and the gold outflow from the US) have recently resulted in increasing opposition to the level of US foreign aid as well as to its allocation. This opposition, while not new, is greater than before and constitutes a real problem. Even a brief study of recent Congressional debates and proposals on this subject should be sufficient to demonstrate current temper of US public and congressional attitudes.

7. We believe that it is reasonable to expect that problems of this kind—indeed, any problems which either US or Pakistani government wishes to raise—should be discussed in a quiet, dignified and constructive manner. Anytime after House of Representatives has completed its action on current aid bill would be satisfactory from our point of view. This should occur in two to three weeks, although the exact date is not within Department's control. As for channel for conducting meaningful dialogue, in view of strong and unfriendly reaction of GOP we have no plans at this time to send any high official to Pakistan. We gather the GOP plans send no one here. Perhaps best and most effective communication channel for time being is through US Ambassador.

8. You are authorized convey as much of foregoing to Ayub as you deem helpful. Our position should on the one hand be dignified and courteous and even friendly and, on other, should indicate US does not consider either its motives or its action improper or harmful to Pakistan's sovereignty or dignity in any respect.

Rusk

---

159. Telegram From the Embassy Office in Pakistan to the Department of State[1]

Rawalpindi, July 30, 1965, 1600Z.

29. Re Rawalpindi's 27 to Dept[2]—Consortium Postponement.

1. My overall conclusion at close of rather frustrating 18-day stay in Pindi is that Paks remain bitterly resentful of consortium postponement action; determined to adhere to posture of injured innocence; disinclined to take any initiative toward reconciliatory talks with US at this time; and dead set against any gesture toward adjustment of present GOP foreign policy orientation in remaining weeks before September 23 consortium meeting.

2. I have encountered no disposition on part of any GOP leaders to take advantage of my extended presence in Pindi to get any preliminary meaningful dialogue under way. I have had to take initiative for every appointment I have had, and I have invariably had to do the steering to get the conversation around to the critical subject, except, of course, in case of Shoaib. All Ministers to whom I have talked have seemed generally well disposed, but timid on this issue, and evidently powerless to exert any decisive influence. They are disposed to assume that any modification of posture required to get relations back on its track will be taken by the US. Clearly, the President himself is calling the shots aided and advised by Bhutto. FinMin Shoaib is doing his best to keep GOP rational but is increasingly feeling pressure of his critics and is so much on defensive that he is wary of seeing me with any frequency.

---

[1] Source: National Archives and Records Administration, RG 59, Central Files 1964–66, AID 9 PAK. Secret; Priority; Limdis. Repeated to Karachi.

[2] Not found.

3. President's mood toward US is amalgam of shocked disappointment, angry outrage and some degree of plain spitefulness and animosity. He has evaded on flimsy pretext my request made on July 21 for a quiet, private, personal and informal talk with him aimed at restoring a good cooperative working relationship. I am bound to conclude that President in his present heated mood does not wish to open any meaningful dialogue with US.

4. Immoderate trend of President's thinking can be seen in his decision to allow Bhutto to reveal and distort in inflammatory terms before National Assembly our interest in discussion of "certain other matters" during waiting period consortium meeting; and in his refusal to allow Shoaib in his July 24 speech to National Assembly to dwell on bona fide Congressional reasons for postponement of pledging session.

5. President undoubtedly feels that our renewed appeal for support of Vietnam is related to consortium postponement, which he envisages as power play to bring him into line. I hear on good authority that he resents omission of any reference to consortium pledging problem in US appeal for GOP assistance to Vietnam. He is also hurt by continued absence of any reply to his Presidential letter of last spring regarding Indian belligerence.[3]

6. Paks by and large remain suspicious that US plans for them to play second fiddle to India in containment of Communist China on this flank. They are increasingly convinced we will not use our growing leverage on India (resulting from increased Indian economic dependence on US) to induce Kashmir settlement which would solve whole problem of subcontinental solidarity. With U.S. consortium pledge to India already made they consider that we are blind both to India's military trafficking with Soviet Russia and to India's abysmally poor economic performance. They consider that either of these circumstances should result in India's getting short shrift from US instead of—as they see it—far better treatment than Pakistan.

7. GOP as of this moment evidently does not envisage any circumstances under which it would be willing to [garble—bend?] on so-called "independent" policy of non-provocation of Communist countries and substantial improvement of relations with them. Paks have industriously worked themselves into a public position where they could hardly live with an abrupt change of policy stance now, even if they wanted to. Both Chinese Communists and USSR are working assiduously to enlarge their opening.

8. We can only stand steady on our present position for the next two or three weeks. We need to show great forbearance and keep

---

[3] See Document 120.

the way open for any possible Pak change of heart about starting a meaningful dialogue.[4] I have let it be known widely that I am ready to return from Karachi for this purpose on a few hours' notice. I am leaving now for a talk with Bhutto enroute to airport.

9. Further analysis and recommendation will follow from Karachi.

McConaughy

---

[4] The Department concurred with McConaughy's analysis in telegram 129 to Karachi, July 31. (National Archives and Records Administration, RG 59, Central Files 1964–66, AID 9 PAK)

---

160. Editorial Note

On August 2, 1965, President Johnson discussed the contretemps that had developed with Pakistan over the postponement of the Pakistan consortium meeting in a telephone conversation with Secretary of State Rusk. Johnson was at his ranch in Texas and Rusk was in his office in the Department of State. In a conversation that also dealt with Vietnam, Rusk assured Johnson that the pledge the United States had made in the Indian consortium meeting in June represented the fulfillment of a prior commitment, and differed in that respect from the new commitment contemplated with respect to the Pakistan consortium. After some additional discussion of the problem, relating in good part to an assessment of the Pakistani response to the postponement and the steps that could be taken to restore relations to a more normal basis, Johnson referred to a number of suggestions made to him by William B. Macomber, Assistant Administrator of the Bureau of Near Eastern and South Asian Affairs in the Agency for International Development. In response to those suggestions, Johnson said he had decided "we ought to take every means, direct and indirect, one, to tell him [Ayub] to quit trying us in the newspapers with his speeches, two, to stop the construction [of additional facilities at Peshawar] if that was the judgment of the government, three, to tell them that they were welcome and we were ready to talk to them as soon as the Congress had acted, fourth, that we have not played any different policy with them than we have with any other government, that while we had tentative commitments before, we had not cancelled them and we were not cancelling his for this year but we were not making any new ones." (Johnson Library, Recordings and Transcripts, Recording of a Telephone

Conversation Between President Johnson and Secretary Rusk, August 2, 1965, 10:33 a.m. (Texas time), Tape F65.01, Side A, PNO 137. A transcript of this conversation is ibid., Transcripts of Telephone Conversations, Alpha Series, Dean Rusk. The transcript bears the heading "President Johnson's Notes on Conversation with Secretary Rusk." A slightly different transcript, bearing the same heading, but misdated July 31, is ibid.

---

161.   Telegram From the Embassy in Pakistan to the Department of State[1]

Karachi, August 2, 1965.

152. Ref: Rawalpindi's 29.[2] FonMin Bhutto on consortium postponement.

1. I saw Bhutto at my request just before my departure from Rawalpindi afternoon July 30. He was in personally cordial mood but substance his remarks reflected hard GOP position encased in velvet glove.

2. He expressed regret that President Ayub had so far been unable to meet my request for an appointment. He gave a new and apparently candid reason for Ayub's avoidance of appointment, namely that Ayub feared that in his anger he would lose control of himself and make some undiplomatic statement to me. Bhutto quoted Ayub as saying he would rather wait until situation had jelled somewhat before he saw me. I told Bhutto that I was accustomed to plain language and President need have no fear of speaking to me as bluntly as he wished. I felt dialogue should have been started, before now, and no inhibitions about diplomatic niceties should stand in the way. Bhutto said he would pass this to President. He said President had authorized him to inform me that he (Bhutto) was fully empowered to make and to receive all representations on behalf of the President in the current crisis.

3. I told Bhutto of our great regret at GOP decision to publicize current difficulties, arousing public opinion and making reestablishment of understanding far more difficult. I specifically deplored Bhutto's decision to stress (and in our view overstress) to the Assembly

---

[1] Source: National Archives and Records Administration, RG 59, Central Files 1964–66, AID 9 PAK. Secret; Priority; Limdis. Repeated to Rawalpindi. No time of transmission is given on the telegram, which was received at 2:29 p.m.

[2] Document 159.

the relationship of "certain other matters" to the consortium postponement. I felt this was a fateful decision which called into question the
real interest of the GOP in a quiet search for an amicable understanding.
In the inflamed and emotional atmosphere now created it was hard to
see how any diplomatic dialogue could have much chance of achieving
concrete results. Bhutto responded that tradition of complete candor in
foreign policy debate in National Assembly made necessary a complete
exposure of any issue as fundamental as consortium postponement.
The postponement would have leaked out soon anyway and GOP
would have been in untenable position with NA if the matter had not
been discussed first in Assembly. When I observed that he could have
divulged fact of postponement without making inflammatory political
charges which were bound to arouse strong emotions, he said GOP
had to give its own interpretation of the event to the Assembly. He
said patriotic emotions were undoubtedly aroused, but he did not think
this would lead to anti-US violence, and government was determined
to extend full protection to American nationals and properties. He cited
painful action of Dacca police in tear-gassing demonstration university
students as evidence of the resolve of the government to keep down
anti-American disorders.

4. Bhutto said that Ayub's deep sense of grievance against US was
aggravated by a second look in retrospect at postponement of his
projected visit to US last April. With benefit of hindsight, abrupt postponement looked more offensive to Paks now than it did at the time. He
said Ayub is convinced that postponement of visit and postponement of
consortium are part of some pattern of unsympathetic and indifferent
US attitude toward GOP essential interests and views.

5. There was extended discussion of Indian affairs, with Bhutto
showing a particular interest in the Indian public record on the confrontation in Viet Nam, and in the US evaluation of Indian record. Obviously
Bhutto believes that the Indian position on Viet Nam is less helpful
from our standpoint than is the record of Pakistan, and he would like
to document this if he can. He would like a list of Indian statements
and actions and the American assessment thereof.

6. I told Bhutto in confidence of the deferral of any commitment
on Fiscal 1966 aid funds for India, the same as for Pakistan. This meant
there was no discrimination in practice, even though India consortium
pledging session had been held before present Congressional question
arose. He said he had not understood this before and he would inform
the President.

7. I told Bhutto candidly that GOP decision to create a public crisis
in our relations over consortium postponement issue, and the resultant
stir of highly charged and misguided sentiment against the US had
created an exceedingly unfavorable impression in the US which is

not confined to any one sector of our government or people. The unwillingness of the GOP to get a meaningful dialogue started or do anything else to mend the situation has compounded the GOP mistake as we see it; he [I] said that the way the GOP was handling the problem would strengthen sentiment in the US for seeking a very clear and explicit understanding with Pakistan. Bhutto immediately interpreted this as a threat to take a hard line, and said if the US did take a hard line, Pakistan would immediately take a harder line. He said he knew this could result in a still harder US line, and then Pakistan would have to take a yet harder line. He said there could be an "escalation" in Pakistan as in Viet Nam, except that it would be a "peaceful escalation" here and not a warlike one.

8. Bhutto revealed full knowledge of President Johnson's message of July 25 to Ayub regarding Viet Nam.[3] He said reply would be forthcoming within next few days. Bhutto showed considerable interest in military situation in Viet Nam and asked in detail about USAF bombing of missile sites near Hanoi and whether we had evidence that Soviet personnel were present at sites. He reminded me that GOP had informed US some time back that ChiComs had agreed to permit Soviets to ship military material to North Viet Nam through Chinese territory.

9. Bhutto said GOP would be glad to transmit for us any messages to ChiComs or others in regard to Vietnamese crisis. He said GOP wanted to be helpful. However, it was evident he was only thinking of GOP good offices role as neutral friendly to both sides.

10. Bhutto remained amiable and even somewhat complimentary throughout. Said he would be coming to Karachi about August 5 and would like to have dinner with me there.

McConaughy

---

[3] Johnson sent a message to Ayub on July 25 explaining the decision to expand the U.S. military role in South Vietnam and asking for the support of Ayub's government. (Johnson Library, National Security File, Special Head of State Correspondence, Pakistan–Presidential Correspondence, Part I)

162. Memorandum From Robert Komer of the National Security Council Staff to Secretary of State Rusk[1]

Washington, August 2, 1965.

The President wanted me to pass on the points I made to him over the weekend on *Pakistan*. I was pointing out the problems inherent in the apparent Pak decision to wait us out on our consortium, meanwhile mobilizing counterpressures on us.

The risk in sitting tight under these circumstances was that if the Paks didn't get the word, and start coming to us, we'd face a tough decision on 23 September. If we then made the pledge they wanted, it would look as though we'd capitulated to Pak pressures. If we didn't make a pledge, it would trigger a far worse crisis with the Paks. Since we'd no longer be able to use the Congressional argument, it would appear as a straight political pressure play. The Paks might then feel compelled to put the squeeze on Peshawar, for example.

So I suggested stepping up our effort to make Ayub come to us before 23 September by a series of steps designed to shake him loose. These wouldn't involve chasing after him but rather making quite clear that he was skating on thin ice: (1) Pass the word via direct and indirect means that by making such a public to-do over our request for consortium postponement, he'd changed the name of the game. Therefore, unless the Paks changed their tune we might not be able to make any pledge at all. (2) Shaking Pak confidence that they had an ace up their sleeve in Peshawar by suspending all new construction (thus making them think we might pull out). (3) Then passing word that we wouldn't run after the Paks and ask them to let us give them aid. If Ayub valued US support he'd be wise to pick up our "standing invitation" and himself suggest a visit here soon.

My understanding is that the President is inclined to agree on suspending new construction in Peshawar, but wishes to have your views first. This might be worth discussing at your Tuesday lunch with him, and I attach a memo to him summarizing the matter to this end.[2]

R. W. Komer

---

[1] Source: National Archives and Records Administration, RG 59, Central Files 1964–66, DEF 15 PAK–US. Secret. Also sent to McNamara.

[2] The August 2 memorandum from Komer to Johnson, not printed, is headed "Intelligence Leverage on Pakistan."

163. Memorandum for the Record[1]

Washington, August 4, 1965.

President's Meeting with John Bonny

Mr. John Bonny, President of Morrison Knudson, came in on 4 August at his request to give the President an "oral message" from President Ayub. Messrs. Califano and Komer sat in.

When Mr. Bonny transitted Pakistan en route home from Vietnam, he'd been invited by Ghulam Faruq, an old friend and a Pak cabinet minister,[2] to see Ayub. Ayub had asked him to deliver a personal message expressing his highest regard for President Johnson and his deepest gratitude for the hospitality which both President and Mrs. Johnson had shown him at their ranch. Regardless of the US decision on the consortium, Pakistan would remain a friend of the US and considered itself irrevocably tied to the future of the West.

Bonny then discussed the highlights of his almost hour-long talk with Ayub. He told Ayub he had just arrived from Vietnam, where M–K was doing military construction work. In Bonny's opinion the only nations which had stood up and been counted on the US side were Australia and New Zealand. It was time for other countries to stand up and be counted too. Ayub commented if he had the hydrogen bomb, he would adopt exactly the same policies as the US.

Ayub then brought up his visit to Peiping (Bonny commented that all of Ayub's statements were subsequently confirmed by Ghulam Faruq, who had accompanied Ayub). Chou En-lai attempted to influence Ayub to withdraw from SEATO. However, Ayub replied that SEATO was a defensive alliance. If the Chicoms didn't violate the territory of other nations, they had nothing to fear from SEATO. If they did, Pakistan would do all in its limited power to defeat this aggression.

Ayub said there was in his opinion a misunderstanding of his apparent appeasement of the Communists. Pakistan was weak so wanted to keep on good terms with its two powerful neighbors.

The President broke in to say that that was Ayub's business. What concerned the President was his public attacks on us and his general assumption that our money grew on trees. The President had said that we could make no commitments to any country until we got the money

---

[1] Source: National Archives and Records Administration, RG 59, Central Files 1964–66, POL PAK–US. Secret. Prepared by Komer.

[2] Minister of Commerce.

(he described his Congressional problems). When he proposed that Ayub postpone his visit till Congress passed the aid bill, the first thing Ayub did was to leak it—thus causing us trouble with the Indians. Also, Ayub's own Foreign Minister was working against him and against us. Then Ayub said he would have to have a consortium meeting on 27 July, even though we had explained why we would be unable to pledge until after Congress acted.

The President pointed out that he didn't have a "penny" of authority to spend until then. However, the minute the bill was through, he would be prepared to talk with Ayub. Then he would decide what to do in our national interest. At the moment he thought that providing aid to Pakistan was in our national interest. But if Ayub wanted to "try this case in the papers," he could take the consequences. Ayub couldn't "pressure" us. A host still had the right to say when he wanted a guest to come. Moreover, the President thought Ayub was wise enough that he ought to know that if he wanted a showdown, he wouldn't be able to pressure us. Who was he to tell us that we wanted to be "masters" of Pakistan? The President went on to say that if there was a pro-Pak man in town, it was Lyndon Johnson. But he didn't like being bullied. Bonny interjected that he didn't think Ayub felt that way. Ayub had an opposition party and a bad Foreign Minister. The President reiterated that he was Ayub's friend; he would sit down with Ayub when he got his money. Bonny could tell him that he had an open invite the day the aid bill was signed.

Komer spoke further with Bonny after his meeting with the President. Bonny stressed that Ghulam Faruq, whom he described as the #2 minister in Pakistan, was an extremely close friend. In fact, Bonny was probably his closest American friend. Bonny suggested that if we wanted him to send back a message he could do so through Ghulam Faruq. M–K had a good code which it used repeatedly for communicating with its top man in Pakistan (the only one who knew it). If we thought it advisable, he would be happy to use this channel to Faruq. Bonny felt very strongly that the best way to resolve the crisis was to get Ayub here for a face-to-face talk; so he would be happy to send such a message. He agreed that he would call me next Wednesday upon his return to Washington to find out what we would prefer. He also agreed to have his notes typed up and send them to the President.

Bonny felt that if Ayub came here we could get him to send perhaps even a division to Vietnam. Ayub had described how Chou told him the Chicoms had used less than one division in the border fight with India in late 1962. Chou told Ayub he was astounded by the way the Indians collapsed. Ayub commented that he had always believed one Pakistani division to be worth three Indian divisions, but after hearing

Chou he was convinced that one Pak division was equal to at least five Indian divisions.

R. W. Komer[3]

---

[3] Printed from a copy that bears this typed signature.

---

164. Telegram From the Department of State to the Embassy in India[1]

Washington, August 8, 1965, 8:33 p.m.

177. Eyes only for the Ambassador from the Secretary. I have just been informed by UK Ambassador that Indian Government has reported to UK, US and Soviet Union that large-scale Pakistani infiltrations under way in Kashmir and that if this is not stopped GOI must take strong countermeasures. Please let us have your assessment most urgently.[2]

Rusk

---

[1] Source: National Archives and Records Administration, RG 59, Central Files 1964–66, POL 32–1 INDIA–PAK. Secret; Flash; Exdis. Drafted and approved by Rusk.

[2] Bowles responded that C.S. Jha had told him and British High Commissioner Freeman on August 8 that Pakistani penetrations of Indian territory had started on August 5 and involved at least 4 groups of 50–60 men who had infiltrated Indian territory as much as 30 miles. According to Jha, captured infiltrators admitted to being members of a paramilitary organization trained by the Pakistani army. Jha stated that his government would take whatever measures were necessary to stop such infiltration, and asked the U.S. and British Governments to bring pressure to bear on Pakistan to halt the provocation. Bowles felt that if the situation was as Jha represented it could lead to a major reaction against Pakistan in India. (Telegram 225 from New Delhi, August 9; ibid.)

165. **Memorandum From Robert Komer of the National Security Council Staff to President Johnson[1]**

Washington, August 9, 1965.

Pakistan Roundup. Our Embassy says the Paks are at it again criticising the consortium postponement (Karachi 193 attached).[2] Bhutto just gave another speech criticising our aid to India over Pak protests. He blamed the US for the aid "stoppage," but said it wasn't aid anyway because it was loans which had to be repaid with heavy interest.

Since in fact we haven't stopped aid, only postponed new FY'66 commitments, would you see merit in discreetly letting out this fact (we have almost $300 million in old aid in the pipeline, are still shipping last year's wheat, etc.)?

Canada's High Commissioner, who saw Ayub recently, is slightly more optimistic than our Embassy (Karachi 183 attached).[3] He sees Ayub as at least admitting Pakistan might have been "guilty of some excesses."

Pak pressure on Kashmir. We have good evidence that the Paks are stepping up infiltration into Kashmir, which could build up to a good-sized flap. The Indians are again threatening "strong countermeasures." This could be the Rann of Kutch all over again, with each side alleging the other is misusing our MAP arms.

Iran's Ambassador to Pakistan, a shrewd observer, says that Bhutto admitted his policy is based on the assumption that the US will be forced out of Vietnam and that Pakistan had better accommodate to an increasingly powerful Red China.

Suspending Peshawar Construction. Bundy and I have pushed this, but our intelligence people claim it wouldn't be understood. It's up to Rusk and McNamara.

Ayub Visit. Shoaib told the Australian Hicom that it was up to the big power, not the little one, to take the initiative for improving relations. We've sent your "message" via John Bonny, Goldberg has talked

---

[1] Source: Johnson Library, National Security File, Memos to the President, McGeorge Bundy, Vol. 13, August 1965. Secret. McGeorge Bundy sent this memorandum to the President under cover of a memorandum in which he noted that the roundup on Pakistan might be out of date in that Komer was unaware of Johnson's conversation with Rusk about sending Harriman to Pakistan. (Ibid., 7/1/65–9/22/65)
[2] Dated August 8; not printed.
[3] Dated August 6; not printed.

with the Pak at the UN,[4] and we are waiting for Rusk to activate the promising UK circuit. You may want to raise this at Tuesday lunch.

In sum, it's too early yet to tell whether we're moving the Paks. If we don't get some indications in the next week or so, however, we may want to step up our effort another notch.

R. W. Komer

---

[4] UN Ambassador Arthur Goldberg met in New York on August 7 with Amjad Ali, Pakistani Permanent Representative to the United Nations. Goldberg told Ali that he came at President Johnson's request following a conversation at Johnson's ranch. The President wanted President Ayub to know that he meant exactly what he said on U.S. aid to Pakistan, which was that a decision on such aid would have to wait until after there had been progress in Congress on the overall aid bill. Distortion of the reasoning underlying this decision in the Pakistani press had made things extremely difficult, and Johnson wanted Ayub to know that continuation of such distortions was not conducive to the good relations between Pakistan and the United States that had prevailed for so long. (Memorandum of conversation, August 7; Johnson Library, National Security File, Country File, Pakistan, Vol. III, Memos, 12/64–7/65)

---

166.   Minutes of Meeting of the 303 Committee[1]

Washington, August 9, 1965.

SUBJECT

Minutes of the Meeting of the 303 Committee, 9 August 1965

PRESENT

Mr. Bundy, Ambassador Thompson, and Admiral Raborn

Also present were Lt. General Marshall S. Carter (NSA), Lt. General Joseph F. Carroll (DIA), Mr. Robert W. Komer, and Dr. Huntington Sheldon

1. Pakistan

a. Mr. Bundy asked Mr. Komer to provide the committee with a brief summary of the Pakistan problem. Mr. Komer pointed out that we were seeking ways to persuade Ayub—the only person one can do business with in Pakistan—to come to us before the 23rd of September, the consortium deadline. Among the few visible means of leverage would be suspension of construction on the U.S. [*less than 1 line of*

---

[1] Source: Department of State, INR/IL Historical Files, 303 C.24, August 26, 1965. Secret; Eyes Only. Prepared on August 10 by Peter Jessup of the National Security Council Staff. Copies were sent to Ambassador Thompson, Vance, and Admiral Raborn.

source text not declassified] installations in Peshawar. Mr. Komer pointed out that the Paks regarded Peshawar as their hole card; if we could shake their confidence that this was so by such a gesture (while not affecting intelligence collection per se), it could indicate to Ayub that the U.S. meant business.

b. Ambassador Thompson stated that he had discussed these matters with Secretary Rusk, who wanted to talk further with Secretary McNamara. He also suggested that the suspension of construction ploy could have the opposite effect of that intended: instead of "shaking up" the Pakistanis, they might interpret that we were being deferential towards them.

c. The earlier suggestion of Mr. Vance that [*less than 1 line of source text not declassified*] was also thought to contain backfire possibilities: it might be difficult to get them back in at a later date, and it might be read as an admission that [*less than 1 line of source text not declassified*] did not constitute a priority project.

d. Admiral Raborn felt that stopping the construction was a minimal gesture at best that would only muddy waters and could set in motion more undesirable events.

e. On the question of alternate sites, Mr. Komer pointed out that presumably the Pakistanis could publicize any moves we make in the direction of Iran [*less than 1 line of source text not declassified*] with unfortunate results. Mr. Komer emphasized that ways to test the reliability of our ally were few and far between. He suggested [*1 line of source text not declassified*].

f. Admiral Raborn stated that he looked with little optimism on the alternate site [*less than 1 line of source text not declassified*] as long-range risks and that Pakistan was, in effect, a bonded ally and all methods of negotiating should be explored. He felt the threat of suspension of foreign aid was the single strongest weapon in our arsenal and reiterated that the suspension of construction threat was a minor tactic.

g. Mr. Komer warned that higher authority was unlikely to respond to blackmail tactics by Pakistan. With the Pakistanis lambasting us on a regular basis it was going to be difficult when we reached the deadline of the 23rd of September to feed the hand that bites us. If we were then unable to make a pledge because it would seem like caving to Pak public pressures, the risks of Pak retaliation against Peshawar would go up.

h. Mr. Bundy summarized the disparate views and stated that we must all search for quiet ways to convince Ayub in the next six weeks. We sought to produce a tactical situation to reopen talks with Ayub and to indicate our state of mind. He concluded that agreement could not be reached in this meeting, and the matter would be referred back to the Secretaries of State and Defense. He emphasized that we want to avoid creating an atmosphere of haggle.

i. Generals Carroll and Carter summarized the exact status of the building program.

j. Mr. Komer indicated the spiraling nature of the situation down to 23 September and repeated that even small efforts could be worth trying now.

k. The Committee did agree to the following:

(1) to proceed rapidly with all preliminary planning for alternate sites;
(2) not to break ground for the construction of the BOQ at Peshawar (new construction, as opposed to work in progress);
(3) not to use [less than 1 line of source text not declassified] for approaches to Ayub in view of certain recent changes, [1 line of source text not declassified];
(4) the results of this discussion would be brought to the attention of Secretaries Rusk and McNamara as possible assistance in their deliberations.

[Here follows discussion unrelated to Pakistan.]

Peter Jessup

---

167.   Telegram From the Department of State to the Embassy in Pakistan[1]

Washington, August 10, 1965, 9:48 a.m.

163. Embtel 193.[2] We are in full agreement your view that restored communication with Ayub at earliest moment is essential to get Paks clearly to see risks to their own interests that their current public campaign against us is creating. However in war of nerves Ayub has chosen to wage, it clearly also important we not appear be succumbing to pressure tactics he using against us.

Therefore we believe for present it best you defer making formal request for appointment, leaving your previous request for appointment on the record and allowing time for countervailing pressures of kind you and we are seeking stimulate hopefully begin having some effect on Ayub's public stance.

---

[1] Source: National Archives and Records Administration, RG 59, Central Files 1964–66, POL PAK–US. Secret; Immediate; Limdis. Drafted by Laingen on August 9; cleared by Handley, Macomber in AID/NESA, Judd in BNA, and Komer; and approved and initialed by Rusk. Repeated to New Delhi and London.
[2] Summarized in Document 165.

For our part, after weighing several alternative courses action here, we have concluded we should concentrate for moment on asking U.K. to help us to get through to Ayub, since visit of neither George Woods nor Eugene Black is presently in the cards. Therefore we plan call in British Ambassador in next day or two to suggest HMG make renewed effort try to get Ayub to see seriousness present situation and encourage him to take steps necessary to break current impasse.[3] We want to convey through this channel that: (a) we will not succumb to pressure campaign of kind Ayub has mounted against us; (b) only way this can be straightened out is if GOP stops public criticism and anti-U.S. campaign and climate is created for better talks; and (c) that there is standing invitation for Ayub to come here in early fall and this could be dusted off and moved up if Ayub were disposed come here for Presidential talks. Our plans with British should not be revealed to U.K. Hicom.

FYI. Ambassador Goldberg has expressed to Amjad Ali our concern over current GOP tactics. We also envisage calling in Ambassador Ahmed again soon. End FYI.

Rusk

---

[3] Rusk had a conversation along these lines on August 13 with Ambassador Sir Patrick Dean. (Telegram 834 to London, August 13; National Archives and Records Administration, RG 59, Central Files 1964–66, POL PAK–US)

---

168.   National Security Action Memorandum No. 337[1]

Washington, August 10, 1965.

MEMORANDUM TO

The Secretary of State
The Secretary of Defense
The Director of Central Intelligence

SUBJECT

US Intelligence Facilities in Pakistan

In the light of your responses to my memorandum of July 6 on this subject, the President approves your unanimous recommendation

---

[1] Source: Johnson Library, National Security File, NSAMs, NSAM 337. Top Secret; COMINT. Prepared by McGeorge Bundy. A copy was sent to the Director of the Budget.

that we proceed as a matter of urgency to devevlop alternate facilities, and requests a firm recommendation on this matter as soon as feasible.[2]

He also approves the Secretary of State's recommendation that no further additions or improvements to the facilities be undertaken at this time.

Finally, he asks that the agencies concerned keep this matter under continuous review and prepare, on a contingency basis, a list of measures they would recommend if it were decided to use this means of convincing Pakistan of our dissatisfaction with its current posture.[3]

McGeorge Bundy

---

[2] On August 21 the Department asked the Embassy in [text not declassified] to comment [text not declassified]. (Telegram [text not declassified] to [text not declassified]; Department of State, INR/IL Historical Files, [text not declassified] Cables, [text not declassified]) On August 25 the Department requested a similar assessment from the Embassy in Tehran; see Foreign Relations, 1964–1968, vol. XXII, Document 94.

[3] The Department transmitted the conclusions of NSAM No. 337 to Ambassador McConaughy on August 19. (Telegram 28 to Rawalpindi; Department of State, INR/IL Historical Files, [text not declassified] Cables, Rawalpindi)

---

169.   Telegram From the Mission at the United Nations to the Department of State[1]

New York, August 17, 1965, 2110Z.

399. Re: Consortium aid to Pakistan—US relations.

Amjad Ali (Pakistan) called on Goldberg today to reply to informal suggestions made by latter, on behalf of Pres Johnson, to improve Pakistan-US understanding (memcon Aug. 7).[2]

---

[1] Source: National Archives and Records Administration, RG 59, Central Files 1964–66, AID 9 PAK. Secret; Immediate; Exdis. Passed to the White House.

[2] See footnote 4, Document 165.

Amjad Ali said Ayub highly pleased at friendly contact established through Goldberg and wants latter to convey his "warm personal friendship for Pres Johnson." (Amjad Ali recalled Ayub visited Pres at LBJ Ranch.) Ayub was reassured on US reasons for postponement of commitments on aid. News of postponement came at very sensitive time, day after issuance by Pakistan Govt of semi-annual announcement of import policy. Announcement included estimates of imports, which depend in part on aid. Since legislature in session, Ayub had to bring matter to their attention and this inevitably created unfavorable impression. US move had come as unpleasant surprise to those (including Amjad Ali) who had worked for closer relations between two countries.

Ayub believed that any temporary deterioration in relations between two countries can, "with objectivity," be put right. Any doubts US had re Pakistan foreign policy could be discussed in Wash. Ayub certain misunderstandings would thus be cleared up. Ayub noted further that there is large area of agreement in general orientation of policy of Pakistan and US and Pakistan intended continue such orientation. Pakistan cherished friendships with West in general and US in particular. Always prepared to hold bilateral talks and believes they be useful.

Having conveyed foregoing message from Ayub, Amjad Ali made, apparently, on his own initiative, several alternative procedural suggestions: 1) perhaps Justice Goldberg could take hand in talks by going to Pakistan; 2) alternatively George Woods, Pres of IBRD, who also well regarded by Ayub might go to Karachi (Woods met with Ayub during last Commonwealth meetings in London); 3) high-powered "envoy" be sent from Karachi to Washington.

Goldberg welcomed the spirit of Ayub response. As *New York Times* reported today, conf comite appears virtually to have resolved differences between House and Senate foreign aid bills and early passage likely. He was sure Pres Ayub would receive cordial welcome. He was particularly gratified at Ayub's assurances Pakistan orientation will continue as in past; he had no doubts himself about Pakistan's orientation and was glad misunderstanding in process of being cleared up.

Re suggestions he go to Karachi, Goldberg said he would talk to both Pres and Secy of State about Amjad Ali's three procedural suggestions, including visit by high level Pakistan envoy to Washington. Would respond after consultations in Washington.

Comment: Most striking element of Ayub message as conveyed by Amjad Ali was firm restatement of (a) friendship with West and US in particular and (b) continuance of its traditional foreign policy orientation. Presumably this implies continuing membership in SEATO and alliance with US.[3]

Plimpton

---

[3] McGeorge Bundy sent a copy of this telegram to President Johnson on August 18 under cover of a memorandum in which he sought Johnson's reaction to the suggestion that Goldberg, Woods, or some other high-level envoy be sent to Ayub. Johnson wrote on Bundy's memorandum "Forget it!! Tell Goldberg we are out of travel cards." Bundy noted that the possibility of a visit to Pakistan by Harriman had been discussed with the Department of State, and Johnson also ruled that out. (Johnson Library, National Security File, Memos to the President, McGeorge Bundy, Vol. 13, August 1965)

---

170. Memorandum From Robert Komer of the National Security Council Staff to President Johnson[1]

Washington, August 19, 1965, 5 p.m.

Pak/Indian Roundup. Karachi 255[2] at Tab A is a fascinating talk between Bhutto and McConaughy, which makes clear that the Pak tactic is to wait us out until they see if we make a consortium pledge. Then Ayub might be willing to come (perhaps before he goes to the UK in mid-October). *Bhutto* is clearly angling for a prior visit, and Rusk at least will have to see him because he's coming to the UNGA. Bhutto clearly has the wind up that we think him the enemy, so we'll have to treat him with kid gloves. We might even be able to softsoap him into being the conciliator.

Goldberg–Amjad Ali. At Tab B is Goldberg's report on the reply he got,[3] which he says he discussed with you. We've asked him to go back at Amjad, stressing that only the two Presidents can make the real decisions needed, so an early summit is far better than special envoys.[4]

---

[1] Source: Johnson Library, National Security File, Name File, Komer Memos, Vol. I. Secret.

[2] Dated August 18; attached but not printed.

[3] Reference is to telegram 399 from USUN, Document 169.

[4] Johnson added a handwritten note at the end of the memorandum which reads: "We will await Cong action before commitments. Then we will await their visit before participating in consortium. Goldberg goes too far in assuming as soon as Cong acts all is well. We will determine what is in our natl interest & act accordingly after Ayub visit. Get this word to him loud, clear, & unequivocal. L."

The UK Approach. We've finally given the British a brief,[5] which makes clear to them at least our feeling that if Ayub can't come we can't pledge. They say they'll do their best, but their experts and ours agree that Ayub will regard coming so close to 23 September as negotiating under the gun. So they doubt we can possibly get Ayub here before October. Bundy and I keep saying "try!"

Shastri Visit. Tom Mann and I have stressed to B.K. Nehru the desirability of Shastri coming here in October. Bowles also took up the matter with Shastri's chief aide again. My hunch is Shastri will come; if so, it's imperative this not leak till we've told Ayub.

Kashmir crisis. This mess may yet get much worse, which could change the whole bidding on visits. The Pak infiltration effort to stir up a local revolt seems to have failed so far, but the Paks are still at it and the Indians are retaliating.

R. W. Komer[6]

---

[5] A paper entitled "Guidelines for British Talks With President Ayub" was given to Cyril Pickard of the Commonwealth Relations Office on August 19 at the conclusion of his visit to Washington for talks on the Pakistan consortium problem. The text of the paper was transmitted to Karachi in telegram 220, August 20. (National Archives and Records Administration, RG 59, Central Files 1964–66, AID 9 PAK)

[6] McGeorge Bundy initialed below Komer's signature.

---

171.   Telegram From the Department of State to the Mission at the United Nations[1]

Washington, August 19, 1965, 7:56 p.m.

278. For Ambassador Goldberg. President desires that you go back at Amjad Ali to reinforce idea that Ayub visit here highly desirable, since new situation created by violent Pak attacks on US makes highest level meeting of minds almost essential if Pak/US relations to be unfrozen.

Suggest you tell Amjad you have checked with Washington and found President greatly appreciative Ayub's friendly sentiments and

---

[1] Source: National Archives and Records Administration, RG 59, Central Files 1964–66, POL PAK–US. Secret; Exdis. Drafted by Komer, cleared by Talbot and Michael V. Connors in IO, and approved by Mann. Repeated to Karachi.

assurances our ties still strong, but frankly found them hard to square with public stance taken by Paks, including Ayub himself.

Even so, the President clearly reciprocates Ayub's "warm personal friendship" and believes that the two of them could quickly reach an understanding. So he welcomes the idea of highest level dialogue in Washington. You raised the question of someone like yourself going out to pave the way—but it's clear that you or George Woods or a high-powered Pak envoy couldn't settle matters. Only the two Presidents could. That's why an early direct meeting of minds at the top seems the best way to put Pak/US relations back on the tracks. The President regards Ayub as having a cordial standing invite for early fall, but you assume he'd be quite prepared to reinvite Ayub if the latter were receptive. As Secretary Ball told Bhutto in London, we had hoped the visit could be rescheduled for September.

Therefore, your own personal instinct is to urge that the two Presidents get together soonest. In fact, your hunch is that it's hard to see how Pak/US relations can be unfrozen in the way the Paks want otherwise. FYI, though we are most unlikely to make a pledge until Ayub comes, we do not want to give any direct ultimatum to the Paks, lest it freeze their position. End FYI.[2]

Rusk

------

[2] Goldberg passed the message to Amjad Ali as instructed on August 20. Ali expressed appreciation for the cordial remarks and the renewed invitation, but he pointed out that it might be difficult for Ayub to leave Pakistan because of the tense situation developing over Kashmir. (Telegram 453 from USUN, August 20; ibid.)

172.   Editorial Note

On August 19, 1965, Ambassador Chester Bowles sent a 10-page memorandum to President Johnson entitled "Observations on Military Aid to the Indian Subcontinent." He sent it under cover of a letter in which he described the issue of military assistance as "one of the most complex and difficult on our Asian agenda." Bowles devoted part of his memorandum to tracing the history of what he saw as an opportunity wasted in the wake of the 1962 border war between India and China to establish the United States as the principal source of military assistance to India. The failure to do so, Bowles pointed out, had opened the door to increasing Soviet military assistance and influence in India.

Bowles painted a picture of India evolving into an Asian Yugoslavia, but he argued that it was not too late to reverse the trend. He proposed that the United States should continue the 5-year $50 million grant and $50 million sales assistance support program for India, while at the same time opening the way for India's procurement of the weapons it needed for its defense, including F–5 fighters. He recognized that such a program would prompt an adverse reaction from Pakistan, but he argued that the United States should face up to the Pakistani reaction and cushion it with the economic assistance upon which Pakistan was dependent. (Johnson Library, National Security File, Country File, India, Exchanges with Bowles)

On August 28 President Johnson sent a note to McGeorge Bundy and Bromley Smith which reads: "I have read Chester Bowles' memo and I would like the best analysis I can get. In my judgment we ought to get out of military aid to both Pakistan and India. I want to see Rusk about it." (Ibid.)

---

173. Memorandum From Robert Komer of the National Security Council Staff to the President's Special Assistant for National Security Affairs (Bundy)[1]

Washington, August 20, 1965.

Mac—

Other mood music on Pak problem is as follows:

1. Mann is opposed to looking nervous by too much frantic diplomacy to get Ayub here shortly. He fears that we'll cave at the last minute on pledging so doesn't want to see us get out on too much of a limb till we've looked all the way down the road. He wants to be sure the President is really prepared to see 23 September go by without a pledge, even at the cost of considerably increased risk to Peshawar (about which the whole intelligence lobby will scream). He thinks we must make a deliberate choice as to whether we're willing to lose it, if necessary. Tom says he's seen too many cases in which we got chicken at the last minute.

2. Talbot and the experts (powerfully abetted by Pickard) are leading the chickens, with an assist from Ball. They are genuinely fearful

---

[1] Source: Johnson Library, National Security File, Name File, Komer Memos, Vol. I. Secret.

that we can push the psychotic Paks too far, with the result that: (a) a major crisis could be precipitated in the subcontinent, maybe even a rash Pak attack on India; and/or (b) the Paks could tell us to go jump, and take Peshawar with us. The Paks are playing with fire by their continued major infiltration into Kashmir; if the Indians decide to strike back elsewhere or Hindu–Moslem riots occur, we'll have a *big* mess. I think they overstate the risks, but am the first to admit that the stakes are big. Perhaps we should give the President a reminder as to the risks, however.

3. The experts also argue against softening up Ayub with counter-threats. A soft sell is better calculated to get him here, as well as some US gesture which will help him to save face (e.g. sending someone out or inviting Bhutto here).

4. In any case they also see the odds as strongly against Ayub coming here before 23 September. He won't come to Canossa on such short notice. Talbot says that to come just before 23 September would make Ayub seem to be negotiating under the gun. But he and Pickard see the odds as good that we could get Ayub to come later (earliest would be October), *if* we're careful not to crowd him too much.

5. No one has an answer to what we'd then do on 23 September. Mann says just "sweet talk" but no aid or at best a partial pledge. I'd agree. So just in case, we're now actively looking at ways to slide past 23 September with a minimum of fireworks.

RWK

---

174.   **Memorandum From Harold Saunders of the National Security Council Staff to the President's Special Assistant for National Security Affairs (Bundy)[1]**

Washington, August 23, 1965.

McGB:

In case the President should quiz you about Selig Harrison's piece on Indian famine (attached),[2] it's too early to tell whether India faces

---

[1] Source: Johnson Library, National Security File, Name File, Saunders Memos. Confidential.

[2] Not attached. In an article datelined New Delhi, August 21, Harrison wrote that India appeared to be facing its worst food crisis since 1951 as a result of a persistent drought. (*Washington Post*, August 22, 1965, p. A25)

a crop disaster. We won't have an accurate measure of the summer crop until mid-October. But if dry weather continues another 10 days, the crop will probably fall well short of last year's.

The one thing that may trigger LBJ reaction is Harrison's putting the finger right on the President for holding up a full-scale extension of PL 480. He doesn't link it with Shastri's visit.

Bell had hoped to send over this week his proposal for a 10-month agreement. However, the President's disapproval of Title III has thrown him off stride, and he'll probably wait until he finds out what the President wants. He'll propose an agreement of the remaining 5 million tons of wheat (plus minor commodities) originally planned. Bowles hopes to back this up with a memo from Subramaniam laying out India's plans to improve agricultural performance, and we'd weave these in as informal conditions.

Hal

---

175. Memorandum From Robert Komer of the National Security Council Staff to President Johnson[1]

Washington, August 28, 1965, 10:30 a.m.

Pak/Indian Roundup. Kashmir is still bubbling merrily and could blow up. U Thant fears the whole 1949 cease-fire agreement may collapse. He wanted to report blaming the Paks for starting the mess, but the Paks threatened to withdraw from the UN if he did. Nor are the Indians too eager to take Kashmir to the UN lest the whole question of its status be reopened (which is what the Paks want).

Bowles sees mounting pressures for Indian retaliation and urges we call the Pak bluff that they aren't involved, lest they be encouraged to think they are getting away with the game. In fact, we have [*less than 1 line of source text not declassified*] a most reliable report that both the Kashmir infiltration and the earlier Rann of Kutch affair are part of a "well-organized plan" to force a Kashmir settlement. This plan was checked out with both the Chicoms and Indos. Worth reading (Tab A).[2]

---

[1] Source: Johnson Library, National Security File, Memos to the President, McGeorge Bundy, Vol. 13, August 1965. Secret.

[2] Reference is to Intelligence Information Cable [*number not declassified*], August 26, 1965.

The UK gambit. Wilson sent a rather bland letter to Ayub (Tab B),[3] as an opener to get Ayub to see his envoy next week. We think we frightened the Brits enough to get them to try hard, but I suspect that after they sound out Ayub Harold Wilson will be back at you.

Meanwhile the true extent of our disillusionment with the Paks is being gotten out through various quiet channels (the Pak Ambassador here is highly chastened, whatever his demeanor on the *Sequoia*). Even if Ayub doesn't come till October or so, all this will help insure that he comes in the right mood.

Ayub and Shastri Visits. The Kashmir flare-up makes it difficult for either to firm up plans now, though I'll wager we could land Shastri if you wrote him directly, reminding him we'd love to have him though we realized Kashmir might get in the way. My hunch still is that this would also help move along Ayub.

Wednesday Meeting. Though we've scheduled a Wednesday[4] morning meeting of Rusk, Mann, and Bell with you on Title III feeding programs, Bundy and I suggest we broaden it to include Pak/Indian problems in general. We keep putting out the word "no meeting no pledge"; but getting it directly from you would be quite useful at this point.

R.W. Komer

---

[3] An undated copy of Wilson's letter to Ayub, offering British help with the Pakistan consortium problem, is attached at Tab B.

[4] September 1.

---

176.   Memorandum From Robert Komer of the National Security Council Staff to President Johnson[1]

Washington, August 31, 1965, 4 p.m.

We just got some very disturbing reports that *Paks have decided to escalate in Kashmir* by throwing in regulars, because they can't otherwise cope with Indian retaliation across the cease-fire line.

---

[1] Source: Johnson Library, National Security File, Name File, Komer Memos, Vol. I. Secret.

The rationale is that the Paks, having failed to spark a "war of liberation" via a Kashmiri uprising, may now feel they've got to enter the lists directly to forestall a humiliating failure. CIA believes that the Pak generals are very unhappy with their bum intelligence and with the failure of the Ayub/Bhutto gambit to stir up Kashmir.

But Pak escalation would trigger a critical Pak/Indian crisis—though still one big step short of a Pak/Indian war. There's a case for sitting back a while longer and letting both Paks and Indians face up to the awesome risks involved. These might make both more malleable vis-à-vis us. On the other hand, the chances of an explosion are great enough so that we ought to push the UN hardest to intervene—and perhaps the UK too. We could supplement by *private* blasts at both Paks and Indians. My impression is that we're *not* moving fast enough on this one (Goldberg was to see U Thant today, but we didn't yet have the new alarming reports).

R. W. Komer

---

177. Telegram From the Embassy in India to the Department of State[1]

New Delhi, September 1, 1965, 1635Z.

446. At 2000 hrs Delhi time today I called on ForMin Swaran Singh and Foreign Secy C.J. Jha and registered urgent plea for Indian restraint in dealing with Pakistan armored attack which was launched this morning north of Jammu.[2] I made following points:

1. Paks were clearly guilty of training large number of guerrilla infiltrators and sending them across cease-fire line and deep into Kashmir Valley.

---

[1] Source: National Archives and Records Administration, RG 59, Central Files 1964–66, POL 32–1 INDIA–PAK. Secret; Immediate. Passed to the White House, DOD, and CIA.

[2] Four hours earlier, General Chadhury, Chief of the Indian Army Staff, had called in General Johnson, Chief of the U.S. Military Supply Mission in India, and informed him that Pakistan had launched an attack spearheaded by a regiment of MAP-supplied M–48 Patton tanks in the Chhamb area at the juncture of the cease-fire line in Kashmir and the international border between the two countries. Chadhury stated that India was not using any U.S.-supplied military equipment in the conflict. At the time of Chadhury's report, Pakistani forces were about 3 miles across the cease-fire line. (Telegram 444 from New Delhi, September 1; ibid.) When Defense Minister Chavan reported the attack in the Indian Parliament at noon on the following day, he indicated that Pakistani forces had driven 5 miles across the cease-fire line. (Telegram 455 from New Delhi, September 2; ibid.)

2. Although India's action in seizing control of key infiltration points and breaking up supply lines on Pak side of cease-fire line may have been logical from purely military point of view it was serious political mistake. Paks already embarrassed by failure of their guerrilla effort were almost bound to react elsewhere and this they have now done.

3. India now faces historic decision which will affect her future and that of South Asia for generation to come. Counter thrust by India at some more favorable point either on cease-fire line or international boundary, will almost certainly touch off war that would soon be out of control. If on other hand India makes it clear that it has no desire to extend fighting and earnestly seeks peaceful solution, situation may still be brought under control.

Swaran Singh, while defending India's thrust across cease-fire line as militarily necessary to stop infiltration, accepted my analysis, and asserted that India has no further moves in mind and is prepared to meet Pakistan more than half way.

However, supported by C.S. Jha, he strongly protested use by Paks of US Patton tanks, and asked what we would do to carry out our assurances that we would not permit US military equipment to be used against India unless India were clearly the aggressor. I replied I had fully informed my government and I was certain that situation would be carefully investigated.

Swaran Singh continued to press his point, asserting that only US was in position to restrain Pak Army which thanks to its American equipment had certain advantages over Indians particularly in tanks and planes.

I then switched conversation back to central point, i.e. that India had big decision to make; counter thrust in response to today's action by Paks or reasonable posture that could save subcontinent from bitter conflict. Whatever arguments of tactical military necessity might be advanced, I was profoundly hopeful that political judgments would be overriding. Even if Paks refuse to negotiate and choose path toward war, India's position at least would be clear and world-wide support would be assured in whatever might follow.

Bowles

178.   Memorandum for the Record[1]

Washington, September 2, 1965, 9:30 a.m.

SUBJECT

Meeting with the President on Kashmir, 2 September 1965, 9:30 am

PRESENT

The President
Secretary Rusk
Mr. Talbot
Mr. Sisco
Mr. Handley
Secretary Vance
General Taylor
General Wheeler
Admiral Raborn
Mr. Cline
Mr. McG. Bundy
Mr. Moyers
Mr. Komer

Secretary Rusk described how Kashmir could erupt into a major fracas; perhaps the most serious problem could be communal rioting; there was a risk that millions could be killed. So every effort must be made to stop the fighting. The Pakistanis had started the current affair with a massive infiltration of several thousand men. Then the Indians crossed the CFL in a mop-up operation, especially to pinch off a dangerous salient. Now the Paks had escalated by throwing in their regular army in an apparent attempt to cut the road to Srinagar.

The Secretary saw the key as being to restore the CFL, including against Pak infiltration. Yesterday we thought direct US intervention and threat of MAP suspension might be necessary. Now U Thant had issued an appeal,[2] so we'd put out a strong supporting statement. The Secretary had talked to the Paks and Indians. Our next step depended on the answer to the SYG's appeal. For example, if one side said yes and the other no, a new situation would be created. So Secretary Rusk

---

[1] Source: Johnson Library, National Security File, Country File, Kashmir, Vol. II, 9/65–10/65. Secret. Prepared by Komer.

[2] On September 1, UN Secretary-General U Thant issued an appeal to President Ayub and Prime Minister Shastri for an immediate cease-fire in the conflict. U Thant offered his services in helping to reestablish peace and in seeking a solution to the Kashmir dispute. (Telegram 595 from USUN, September 1; ibid.) Ambassador Goldberg issued a statement shortly thereafter fully endorsing the Secretary-General's appeal. (Telegram 601 from USUN, September 1; ibid.) In Washington, Rusk called in the Indian and Pakistani Ambassadors and stated that the U.S. Government strongly supported U Thant's appeal. (Telegram 261 to Karachi, September 1; ibid.)

proposed a more limited démarche than yesterday, principally asking the Paks about their use of US equipment. In response to the President's query he indicated that the UK plans to put out a statement this morning.

The President wanted to be very cautious about anything we said. First, both sides wanted us to threaten them so they could be martyrs. Second, both would use US equipment if they needed it, regardless of what we said. So the President wanted to get someone else in—as in PM Wilson's last intervention. We should "get behind a log and sleep a bit." The President said he had found out over the last few months how little influence we had with the Paks or Indians. We had never threatened them, but they kept saying so. Thus the President's view was to let the SYG do it or let PM Wilson do it. The President did not want to intervene personally. He'd like to sit it out a little bit. The President questioned Paragraph 4 of the draft telegram[3] before him. Wasn't this a subtle threat?

Secretary Rusk felt our own position was involved on the issue of the use of MAP-supplied arms. We'd told both the Indians and Paks that our equipment was not for this purpose. So we were on a spot.

When the President asked when the pledging session was, Bundy told him 23 September, but pointed out that it was likely to be overshadowed by Kashmir. At some point we'd have to say we were not the quartermasters for two armies fighting each other.

Secretary Rusk pointed out that once Pak use of US equipment was confirmed we'd begin getting strong Indian complaints.

The President repeated that we should confine ourselves to supporting the UN. We should "hide behind that log." He disapproved of Paras. 3 and 4 and the first sentence of Para. 5 in the draft telegram[4] before him. He also desired that we tell the Paks we intended to speak equally strongly to the Indians.

The meeting then took up Dominican Republic items.

RWK

---

[3] Apparent reference to a draft of the telegram sent on September 2 as telegram 266 to Karachi and 327 to New Delhi. The draft has not been found. For text of the telegram as sent, see Document 179.

[4] Paragraph 5 was apparently deleted before the telegram was sent.

179. **Telegram From the Department of State to the Embassy in Pakistan[1]**

Washington, September 2, 1965, 6:58 p.m.

266. From the Secretary. Situation Kashmir has now clearly reached point of major Pak-Indian military confrontation, involving use of U.S. MAP equipment. It therefore urgent both Karachi and Delhi reiterate our very strong concern to highest appropriate authorities, coordinating closely with British. At this immediate point, however, we do not believe we should make any démarche to either side as to what we might have to do if fighting escalates but rather restrict our position essentially to full support for efforts UNSYG. What we do in future will depend on variety factors, especially situation as we see it after two parties have indicated nature their response SYG's appeal.

Your approach should therefore rest on following points:

1. We are seriously concerned that situation which has developed in Kashmir will lead to major war between India and Pakistan.

2. We have given our full support to UNSYG's appeal of September 1 and have urged full, sympathetic and prompt response by both parties.

3. We could only view any further escalation of hostilities by either side in light UNSYG's appeal as seriously prejudicial to peaceful settlement.

4. We are speaking equally strongly to both GOI and GOP about complying with SYG's appeal.

For Delhi: Above responds your 458.[2] Re Para C your 444,[3] we consider we have given to GOI and GOP sufficient assurances for

---

[1] Source: National Archives and Records Administration, RG 59, Central Files 1964–66, POL 32–1 INDIA–PAK. Secret; Immediate; Limdis. Drafted by Laise; cleared by Talbot, Captain Asbury Coward, USN, in G/PM, Assistant Legal Adviser for Near Eastern and South Asian Affairs Donald A. Wehmeyer, Deputy Assistant Secretary of Defense for International Security Affairs William E. Lang, Sisco, Mann, and Komer; and approved and initialed by Rusk. Also sent to New Delhi as telegram 327, and repeated to USUN, London, Bonn for the Under Secretary, Ankara, and Tehran.

[2] In telegram 458 from New Delhi, September 2, Bowles urgently suggested the need for direct U.S. pressure on both sides to respond to the Secretary-General's appeal. If India accepted the appeal for a cease-fire and Pakistan did not, Bowles requested authority to tell Shastri that the United States would promptly cut off all military assistance to Pakistan. (Ibid.) Bowles was informed, in telegram 330 to New Delhi, September 2, that a decision had been taken at the highest level not to engage in direct pressure on either India or Pakistan for the time being, but to place primary reliance on the United Nations. (Ibid.)

[3] Telegram 444 from New Delhi is summarized in footnote 2, Document 177. In paragraph C, Bowles urged that both parties to the conflict should be informed that should either side be attacked by a Communist country, the United States would use all available constitutional powers to come to the defense of the side attacked.

dealing with Communist attack and do not expect nor wish to reiterate them in present circumstances.

Rusk

---

180.   Telegram From the Department of State to the Embassy in India[1]

Washington, September 3, 1965, 6:38 p.m.

343. Following summary FYI and Noforn based on uncleared memcon and subject to revision upon review.

Ambassador Nehru called on Secretary September 3 under instructions discuss Kashmir situation and Pak use of MAP equipment in fighting. Nehru's opening presentation made following points: a) he reviewed development current fighting in Kashmir, as seen by GOI, beginning with infiltration Pak guerrillas; said Paks apparently trying cut both Jammu–Poonch road and Jammu–Srinagar road. If former road cut, India would lose contact with major segment of cease-fire line (CFL); if latter road cut GOI would lose contact with whole of Kashmir. Nehru said GOI could not allow Paks to cut road to Srinagar. If Paks do, India will have to move across international boundary in Punjab to cut off Pak forces on Srinagar road; b) Nehru said he had not yet received word on GOI reply to SYG's appeal; added that his general instructions this regard are that GOI quite prepared to respect CFL if Paks do. However, GOI cannot accept distinction between "forces in civilian clothes and regular forces." Nehru then said GOI cannot withdraw unless Paks do; c) re Pak use of MAP equipment Nehru reviewed discussions he had had on this subject with Secretary and Assistant Secretary Talbot during Kutch dispute. Nehru said "We have to know where we stand on this once and for all. Here is clear cut case of your assurances not being fulfilled." He said questions of assurances is a matter between India and US, and not between India and Pakistan.

Nehru then said, speaking personally rather than under instructions, "How are we to get a cease-fire? They (i.e. Paks) have your equipment and probably military advantage in Kashmir. If Paks do not

---

[1] Source: National Archives and Records Administration, RG 59, Central Files 1964–66, POL 32–1 INDIA–PAK. Secret; Immediate; Noforn. Drafted by Lakeland, cleared by Sisco, and approved by Talbot. Also sent to Karachi, London, USUN, and CINCMEAFSA for POLAD.

stop, as we told them years back, India will attack across international border. We will have to do that unless you can stop them."

In reply Secretary said USG very much aware of MAP aspect of problem; said he had been talking to the President about this and we have discussed it with GOP. Secretary said he did not want to give off cuff reply on MAP assurances questions. Secretary then said larger problem is to get peace established regardless of weapons being used. That is why we are supporting the SYG's appeal for cease-fire. When Nehru interjected that MAP assurances question was related but separate issue, Secretary acknowledged point but said if fighting continues both sides are going to use whatever equipment they have. Secretary added that MAP equipment now in US ports not relevant to question of fighting. Secretary then said that if larger problem of fighting solved in context SYG's appeal, smaller problems will fall into place. Secretary expressed hope that GOI will announce publicly today acceptance of SYG's appeal. He notes that SYG's private report and General Nimmo's report included question of infiltrators. Secretary said it very important for Delhi to make it clear that GOI accepts SYG's appeal.

Nehru asked how peace could be achieved unless Paks accept SYG's appeal; said Paks have not yet done so. Secretary said if GOI accepts and Paks do not then UN machinery comes into play to get acceptance and compliance on the ground. Nehru asked how sanctions would be applied to Paks if they only say yes to SYG's appeal and do not actually comply. Secretary responded that for seventeen years neither India nor Pakistan has heeded our advice on Kashmir dispute and said we cannot control tanks from ten thousand miles away. Secretary said he could not be more precise at this time as to what USG would do if Paks do not comply with SYG's appeal; said if it gets to that point where he could be more precise he would let Nehru know.

Secretary then asked whether infiltrators had expected popular uprising in Kashmir and said it our understanding that infiltrators were rather easily blunted and contained by GOI. If this the case, why did India move across CFL? Nefru replied that India had moved across CFL at main infiltration points to prevent further infiltration and cut off those infiltrators already on Indian side of CFL. Nehru said India had no intention of invading Azad Kashmir to re-occupy territory and that moves only designed to protect against infiltration.

Nehru asked for clarification of news report he had seen that USG investigating reports of use of MAP equipment by both sides. Secretary replied we have had allegations concerning both sides and added we had sent couple of observers to investigate.

Secretary returned to question of SYG's appeal, saying it would put GOI in strong position to come back promptly with affirmative reply. He added that if only one side accepts SYG's appeal this would not adversely affect its position on ground but in terms of UN and international machinery it would tend to shift things in favor of the side which accepts SYG appeal.

Rusk

181. **Telegram From the Embassy in India to the Department of State**[1]

New Delhi, September 4, 1965, 1237Z.

478. At 1215 hrs Saturday I called on PriMin who was accompanied by L.K. Jha. PriMin was cool, collected, articulate and very clear in his views throughout conversation which lasted about 35 minutes. British HICOMM Freeman who saw him yesterday had similar impression.

At least it is clear that we are not dealing with a mad man who is about to fly off on an emotional tangent. Although this does not mean that Shastri will necessarily come up with wise decisions, it does mean he is unlikely to act in blind anger.

Conversation developed along following lines:

1. I stated I was speaking not only as American Amb but as established friend of India who has watched her development over long period of years, who has been deeply encouraged recent months by positive factors which are now beginning to contribute to India's faster growth, and who is looking forward with keen anticipation to major economic breakthrough here in India within next few years which could have tremendous implications for entire world.

2. I then took chance in regard to his mood based on previous conversations with him that involved historic parallels and delivered a bit of a lecture, i.e., PriMin is facing kind of fateful historic decision that had been faced by scores of other leaders in different parts of

---

[1] Source: National Archives and Records Administration, RG 59, Central Files 1964–66, POL 32–1 INDIA–PAK. Secret; Immediate. Repeated to Karachi, London, CINC-MEAFSA for POLAD, USUN, and the White House. Received at 9:35 a.m., and passed to the White House, DOD, and CIA at 10:30 a.m.

world in last several hundred years. Some had met challenge with courage and imagination, others under pressure had taken what turned out to be wrong path with heavy cost to everyone involved. For instance in Europe in late July and early August 1914 leaders of key countries found themselves locked in by previous speeches and pronouncements and what they assumed were demands of public opinion. In spite of fact that each one recognized in his heart that the powers were on military collision course, no man had courage and imagination to interrupt the deadly process.

3. In present situation one point at least was clear. Regardless of what his govt did now, it may be that Paks themselves have decided to push situation into all-out war; if so, there is nothing he could do to stop them. But what he can do is to make a war-like course on part of Pakistan much more difficult by establishing a strong case for India before world opinion by his own restraint. If under those circumstances Paks should decide in favor of war, Shastri's own personal role and that of India would be clear beyond question and thoughtful men throughout world would support him.

4. I stated I realized he was under heavy political pressure not only from opposition but from people within Congress Party who would criticize any compromise on his part at this time designed to establish peace. I reminded PriMin however, of situation in 1961 when our own relations with Soviet Union were at particularly explosive stage and President of US went before UN to state that although US was prepared to defend its interests whatever the cost, it was anxious above all for peaceful solution and would meet Soviet Union more than half-way in seeking such a solution.

President's speech was warmly received throughout world and strongly supported by overwhelming majority of American people who took pride in fact that their President and govt were doing everything in their power to ease world tensions and to create basis for new and friendlier relationships.

5. Shastri expressed appreciation and agreement with principles I laid down. He stated, however, that our situation in 1961 and that of India in 1965 are very different. No one questions military and economic power of USA. However, world considers India weak, wobbly and divided nation. Pakistan seemed to be basing its current aggressive policy on this false assumption. In view of developments of last three weeks this greatly complicates his own problems at home and abroad.

6. I made obvious reply that it took strong man to make peace, while very weakest leader could start a war, and then asked Shastri how he intended to reply to SYG's appeal for ceasefire. He replied that three points were in his opinion of utmost importance:

A. Nimmo report[2] must be made public. UN border observers had no police power, i.e. no authority to stop fighting by physical means. Therefore it has been clear from outset that their role is to inform SYG and world as whole what is actually going on in Kashmir so that there is no need to depend on conflicting propaganda claims of the two nations.

Most direct way to achieve this objective would be to have SYG himself based on observers' report decide where blame should be placed and then publicly state his findings.

Since SYG had decided to take neutral position in order to enhance his own peace-making powers, it was essential that report at least should become public knowledge even though in some respects it was critical of India so that world opinion could be brought to bear. If UN observers could not fulfill this function, what was purpose of sending them to Kashmir?

B. Following publication of the report Pakistan must agree to withdraw remaining 2,000–3,000 infiltrators who had crossed border starting August 5. Until infiltrators are withdrawn by Pakistan, there can be no hope for peaceful solution. (*Note:* He was not clear whether this withdrawal should be part of general withdrawal of all forces or precede withdrawal of uniformed forces.)

C. In order to prevent repeat performance UN observer team's staff should be greatly expanded to give them effective coverage of whole area.

7. Shastri then said he hoped US and other nations would not assume that this was good time to discuss long-term settlement of Kashmir problem. At present he said we are close to war brought on by Pak aggression.

He earnestly hoped atmosphere could ultimately be created that would permit thoughtful discussions about problems that have in last seventeen years blocked good relationship between the two neighbors. Some day if Ayub Khan had change of heart and got rid of Bhutto, then essential broader agreement might become possible; if not, perhaps after Ayub Khan has gone.

However it should be clear that current mood prohibited any such effort now and he hoped that US and other govts would not press India to discuss subject which, in present upheaval, was not ready for discussion.

---

[2] On September 3 Secretary-General U Thant submitted a report to the Security Council on the situation in Kashmir which was based upon a report prepared by General Robert H. Nimmo, Chief Military Observer of the United Nations Military Observer Group in India and Pakistan. (UN doc. S/6651) An excerpt of the report is printed in *American Foreign Policy: Current Documents, 1965*, pp. 797–800.

8. In reply to Shastri's questions about use of American military equipment by Paks, I stated that observers which we had sent to area at Gen Chadhury's suggestion were unable to get close enough to fighting to see. It was my understanding that we are now making determined effort to get at facts from Pakistan side. I admitted that tanks and planes used by Pak Army may well have come from US, and that if so this would be violation of our agreements which we would view with great concern. However way to settle primary problem now is to stop all fighting. If fighting continued in face of SYG appeal with American equipment being used aggressively as distinguished from defensively by either Paks or Indians, we would have to consider measures that might be taken.

9. In final ten minutes of discussion we went over same points in various ways. I ended exchange by strong personal plea for moderate and affirmative response to SYG's appeal and by expressing hope that Shastri would seize this historic opportunity to establish himself as man of peace in Nehru–Gandhi tradition and at same time to win respect of hundreds of millions of people throughout the world who had learned at heavy cost what destruction modern war could bring.

Shastri followed me to door and expressed his appreciation in warm, friendly and yet confident manner for what he described as helpful exchange.

Comment: I do not dare predict how Indians in last analysis will react. In spite of Shastri's calm appearance, mood here in Delhi is one of frustrated militance; there is strong feeling even among normally sober people that once new ceasefire is established, Paks will turn to some new form of military harassment and that process will go on indefinitely.

Faced with this situation Shastri has taken strong and not unreasonable position, i.e., that Nimmo report which makes no bones about Pakistan's responsibility for training and sending in large guerrilla unit should be made public and that based on facts established by this report, Paks should then agree to remove infiltrators from Valley and from Jammu. Indians and Pak troops should at such stage be withdrawn to their own side of ceasefire line, and then some new policing system involving adequate personnel and perhaps establishment of mile wide neutral belt would be set up in place of present ineffective system.

However this combination is admittedly difficult one for Paks to swallow since they have officially denied there are any infiltrators from Pakistan on Indian-held territory and are still insisting that whole Valley is in wild revolt against Indians under leadership of non-existent Kashmir revolutionary govt.

I again suggest that if Indians come through with reasonable presentation at Security Council as I earnestly hope they will, Paks can be persuaded to agree to ceasefire only by application of some kind of sanctions by US, by US and UK, or by UN generally.

Bowles

---

182.   Memorandum From Robert Komer of the National Security Council Staff to President Johnson[1]

Washington, September 4, 1965, 4 p.m.

Pak/Indian SitRep. While the Pak Army thrust toward the only key road into Kashmir was halted temporarily, they seem to be resuming their drive. Meanwhile both nations are in effect mobilizing. Another issue is whether the Indians will retaliate or try the UN cease-fire route.

Bowles is doing a bang-up job of pleading restraint with the Indians. He's telling them that war would set back both countries for a generation. The Indian reply to the SYG's cease-fire appeal is fuzzy and argumentative, but it does seem largely responsive to the SYG so long as the withdrawal includes the Pak infiltrators who started the affair.

Meanwhile the Indians are raising a public storm over Pakistan's "US-supplied" tanks and planes. This is inevitable, and will build up quite a head of steam. We'll get insistent queries in the SC on it.

As for the Paks, they seem hell bent on forcing a Kashmir negotiation—whatever the cost. They see themselves as compelled to this desperate gamble by their inability to get any negotiated settlement over the last 17 years. Thus the odds are that the Paks *won't* accept the cease-fire appeal unless it includes a new Kashmir negotiation. It is essentially an exercise in brinkmanship. All this seems clear from Bhutto's hortatory speech saying this is hour of reckoning, and in effect rejecting the 1949 CFL which the UN and the rest of us are frantically attempting to restore.

State may propose you send a friendly reply to Ayub's letter,[2] for delivery by McConaughy when he sees Ayub *Monday*.[3] It would urge

---

[1] Source: Johnson Library, National Security File, Country File, Pakistan, Vol. IV, 8/65–9/65. Secret.

[2] Ayub sent a letter to Johnson on September 2 providing a detailed justification for Pakistan's involvement in the Kashmir dispute. The text of the letter, as conveyed by Ambassador Ahmed to Secretary Rusk on September 2, is in National Archives and Records Administration, RG 59, Presidential Correspondence: Lot 66 D 476, Lebanon through Pakistan.

[3] September 6.

compliance with the SYG's appeal. This makes sense, but the real issue is whether McConaughy should also take a vigorous stand on use of our MAP equipment and US/Pak relations, or should simply listen.

The State experts now fear that a vigorous stand might drive the Paks to even more desperate action. I wouldn't underestimate these risks; there's a good case for playing it cautiously at a time when passions are running so high. But my own sense is that one reason the Paks are causing such trouble is that they don't yet realize what thin ice they're on with us. Thus sobering words from McConaughy and then the British (who see Ayub Tuesday) would serve more as a restraint than as a goad. So my instinct would be for McConaughy to hit Ayub at least on US/Pak relations, as an indirect means of sobering him on Kashmir. But playing it cautiously at a moment of high tension may be the safer course.

R.W. Komer

---

183. **Telegram From the Department of State to the Embassy in Pakistan**[1]

Washington, September 4, 1965, 9:05 p.m.

283. Deliver soonest following letter from President in response Ayub letter September 2.[2]

"Dear Mr. President:

Thank you for your letter of September 2 concerning the critical situation in Kashmir.

I share most earnestly the concern you express over the threat in the current situation to the continued maintenance of peaceful relations between Pakistan and India. The consequences of war would be so serious and so sweeping as to undermine all of the impressive progress that your country and India have made in the short years since independence. On this we can all agree.

---

[1] Source: National Archives and Records Administration, RG 59, Central Files 1964–66, POL 32–1 INDIA–PAK. Confidential, Immediate. Drafted by Laingen and Laise; cleared by Handley, Sisco, and Bundy; and approved and initialed by Rusk. Repeated to USUN, New Delhi, London, and Paris for Ball; and pouched to CINCSTRIKE/CINCMEAFSA.

[2] See footnote 2, Document 182.

It therefore seems to me that you and India, and indeed all of us, have an immediate interest in bringing the current fighting to an end. Secretary General U Thant has urgently appealed for an immediate cease fire and other steps to restore normal conditions along the Cease-Fire Line.

The UN Security Council has now also unanimously called for an immediate cease fire.[3] Those appeals merit prompt and wide support if the peace is to be kept. We are giving the Secretary General our full backing. We will continue to do so. I profoundly hope that your Government, as well as India, will not hesitate in offering him the support and cooperation necessary so that peace and calm can be restored.

I am well aware that a restoration of normal conditions along the Cease-Fire Line will not in itself bring an end to this dispute. And I know of the depth of feeling of your countrymen regarding Kashmir. But I am convinced that a real settlement of that difficult problem cannot be had by resort to force or unilateral action by either side. Whatever the merits of the dispute there can be no real settlement except through peaceful means and through redoubled efforts by men of good will to reason together in both your country and India and to find a way, as you say, to settle this and other disputes in an honorable and mutually beneficial manner. It will continue to be the policy of my country to do whatever we can to encourage and support efforts toward that end.

I would welcome any suggestions you might have on what could usefully be done. This could perhaps best be discussed in the personal talks which I hope we shall be able to have soon.

Sincerely, Lyndon B. Johnson."

Rusk

---

[3] Security Council Resolution 209, adopted September 4. (UN doc. S/RES/209)

184.   Telegram From the Department of State to the Embassy in
       Pakistan[1]

Washington, September 5, 1965, 1:21 p.m.

284. For Ambassador from Secretary. The following are your instructions for your meeting with Ayub on Monday.[2] They are framed
in the light of our information from the British that the Paks apparently
still think we will go ahead and pledge on 23 September.

1. You should say you are speaking under instructions.

2. Paks will notice we have so far refrained from public apportion-
ment of blame in current Kashmir crisis. But whatever the merits of
Kashmir dispute itself, US cannot condone attempt to compel its settlement by use of force.

3. Therefore, US strongly supports SYG's appeal for cease-fire and
will of course have to take whatever steps are indicated to support him.

4. For example, Paks should have been well aware—from Rann
of Kutch episode—of spot in which US placed by Pak use of MAP
equipment provided as part of defensive anti-communist alliance and
not for purposes of local wars among neighbors. So we hope Pakistan
will understand our problem and act in accordance with our agreement.

5. The violent Pak reaction to what began as a simple US request
for two month postponement of our aid pledge was deeply regrettable.
It was inconsistent with the mutual respect expected among allies, and
the continued massive flow of US aid. Its predictable effect was to
surface all the basic concerns about US/Pak relations which were growing in minds of people of America.

6. We see little point in a sterile debate over who is the "aggrieved"
party. The US feels it has nothing to apologize for. We have consistently
given Pakistan highly preferential treatment over far larger India in
the allocation of our aid. Even after the apparent community of interest
between Pakistan and the US began declining, we continued and even
increased such assistance in the hope that matters could be sorted out.

7. But current situation has persuaded President there must be a
basic examination of Pak/US relations. The President believes these
fundamental issues can and must be thrashed out only between the
two key people and feels that until this can be arranged US will not

---

[1] Source: National Archives and Records Administration, RG 59, Central Files 1964–
66, POL 32–1 INDIA–PAK. Secret; Immediate; Exdis. Drafted by Bundy, and approved
and initialed by Rusk. Also sent to Rawalpindi, and repeated to London and to Paris
for Ball.

[2] September 6.

attempt to take any far-reaching decisions on bilateral matters (if Ayub asks whether this means no pledge, you should answer that you simply don't know but that that is the way you would interpret it yourself). The President believes that a mutually beneficial relationship would likely grow out of this meeting.

8. Meanwhile, we appeal to Ayub's statesmanship not to risk Pakistan's future on a set of risky gambles which could easily prove disastrous. We see Pakistan at a major crossroads. It will determine for itself the future course of its policy. We naturally hope it will remain basically disposed toward US, and the President hopes to discuss this whole matter personally with Ayub. However, we do not feel able to act as if nothing has happened until the basic issues have been discussed at summit.

Finally, you should inform Ayub that early this week the US Government will be forced by American public opinion to state whether it is continuing military supplies to countries which have not accepted UN appeal for cease-fire. You should make it clear that when this question is posed the US will have to answer that no military assistance is being supplied to any such country. You should say that you do not know just when or how this statement will become necessary, but that our Government has asked you to give this private notice in advance that such a statement is sure to be necessary soon unless there is a very prompt and affirmative response to the UN appeal. You should not respond to any question from Ayub as to whether this same message is going to India, on which you are "without instructions".

For London: Please inform CRO substance this instruction.

Rusk

---

185. **Telegram From the Department of State to the Embassy in Pakistan**[1]

Washington, September 5, 1965, 3:57 p.m.

285. Joint State–Defense message. In effort to avoid embarrassment to USG during Kashmir conflict delivery of certain major end items

---

[1] Source: National Archives and Records Administration, RG 59, Central Files 1964–66, DEF 19–8 US–PAK. Secret; Limdis. Drafted by Colonel C.P. Miller (DOD/ISA) on September 4. Cleared by Sisco, Mann, Handley, and in substance by Meyers and Komer, and approved and initialed by Rusk. Also sent to New Delhi, CUSMSMI New Delhi, and CMAAG Karachi, and repeated to USUN, CINCSTRIKE, CGAFLC DAYTON OHIO, CGUSAMC, and CGMTMTS.

enroute or pending shipment is being suspended for the time being. Specifically these are: 1) For Pakistan—Three T–33 aircraft in France, approximately 160 Sidewinders in Germany, 47 M–48 tanks in CONUS, and ammunition on board SS *Victory* (MSTS) now at sea, and 2) For India—rebuilt engines for C–119 aircraft in CONUS.

No other impact shipments of this nature known here as due to arrive either country within 30 days. If other deliveries this nature known to addressees, please report immediately.

No publicity is to attend these suspensions and local governments should not be informed. If queried, respond in non-abrasive manner that delay is for administrative reasons.

Rusk

---

186.   Memorandum Prepared in the Office of Current Intelligence, Central Intelligence Agency[1]

OCI No. 2316/65   Washington, September 6, 1965.

POSSIBLE SINO-PAKISTANI MILITARY ARRANGEMENT

1. A series of clandestine reports received since early 1964 indicates a possible secret Sino-Pakistani mutual defense agreement of some kind. It seems probable, however, that any such understanding would be very loose and cast in terms which provide Peiping maximum latitude in deciding when or whether it might come into force.

2. It appears from the reports that US involvement in support of Indian military operations would be a key element in any Chinese undertaking to help Pakistan. China's behavior toward Pakistan, although very friendly, has been marked by caution in matters which involve mutual defense questions. Chinese commentary on the Rann of Kutch crisis appeared calculated to provide political backing for Pakistan while avoiding any commitment of Chinese military support. In the present Kashmir fighting, Chinese commentary has so far been

---

[1] Source: Johnson Library, National Security File, Country File, Pakistan, Vol. IV, Memos and Miscellaneous, 8/65–9/65. Secret; No Foreign Dissem/Controlled Dissem; No Dissem Abroad/Background Use Only.

largely limited to reportorial accounts of the clashes which are slanted to show that the Indians are the culpable party.[2]

3. We believe, nonetheless, that some secret understanding exists between Peiping and Rawalpindi. Moreover, we foresee that however loose and "uncommitted" the Chinese may have kept themselves, the understanding gives Pakistan something which Rawalpindi can consider an "ace in the hole" in the present confrontation. At minimum, this could produce a feeling of greater confidence in Rawalpindi than is warranted either by the terms of the understanding or Pakistan's present military advantage in the Jammu area. At worst, it could make Pakistan utterly foolhardy.

4. A chronological record of the reporting on this subject is at annex.[3]

---

[2] On September 4 visiting Chinese Foreign Minister Chen Yi stated at a press conference in Karachi that China supported the "just struggle of Kashmir people against tyrannical domination of India." He condemned Indian violations of the cease-fire line for provoking the conflict, and he noted that China supported the "just" actions of Pakistan to repel Indian armed provocation. (Unnumbered telegram from Karachi, September 6; National Archives and Records Administration, RG 59, Central Files 1964–66, POL 7 CHICOM)

[3] The 4-page annex is not printed.

---

187. Telegram From the Embassy Office in Pakistan to the Department of State[1]

Rawalpindi, September 6, 1965, 1430Z.

38. I met one hour this morning with Pres Ayub and FornMin Bhutto. I asked Pres if report of large scale Indian attack true.[2] His reply affirmative; at map he pointed out four areas current Indian activities: 1) Dara Nanak against Jassar; 2) Lahore–Macbulpura enclave; 3) south east of Lahore against Bedian Link Canal where Pak/

---

[1] Source: National Archives and Records Administration, RG 59, Central Files 1964–66, POL 32–1 INDIA–PAK. Secret; Flash. Received at 11:45 a.m., and passed to the White House at 11:47 a.m. Repeated to Karachi, London, New Delhi, DOD, CINCMEAFSA, and USUN. The telegram was also passed to USIB agencies.

[2] On the morning of September 6 Indian forces launched a four-pronged attack across the border between India and Pakistan in the vicinity of Lahore in the Punjab. (Telegram 409 to USUN, September 6; ibid., POL 27 INDIA–PAK)

Indian forces currently engaged east of canal; 4) north east of Lahore, air action against rail line. Said Indians have considerable concentrations of troops in Jammu and Pathankot areas with total 75 battalions near Kharian. Maintained this concentration was what forced Pakistan undertake Bhimber–Chhamb operation. Said Indians have offensive capabilities north from Akhnar which "we are watching," and around Jammu. Estimated Indians want to go for Lahore, acted in hurry pushed by politicians. Rest of Indian armed forces closing in on area and probably expected be committed later. Said main military access route current Indian movements is along Patti, Harike and Mabul road. Responding my observation this appeared by major military undertaking Pres said, "Yes sir, it is catastrophic and we are getting ready for desperate fight."

I observed both sides had sown wind and now reaping whirlwind of disaster. What with Mujahideen operations since August 5, Paks not clear of responsibility. Pres agreed but pointed to constant Indian harassments in area, and Bhutto interjected GOI since death Nehru has treated Kashmir as closed question refusing even discuss it. I stressed it nonetheless difficult for us understand Pak resort force, even granted it was on smaller scale than that which appears to have just overtaken them. Pres acknowledged point but commented events boiling this direction for some time. Ayub replied it quite clear Indians have now invaded Pak proper. There nothing else to do but prepare for fight to finish. Said friends have obligations to Pak. U.S. has obligations and GOP going to ask fulfillment. We also going ask other friends, "or so-called friends." Added GOP must now ask you what U.S. proposes do. Said U.S. has great responsibility. Quite clear India got American arms only to fight against Pak. GOP warned United States, now it has come to pass. Ayub pointed to record of unilateral Indian action against the original U.N. resolution and against people of Kashmir.

I pointed to evidently clear Pak use of U.S. military equipment in Kashmir. Pres asked how could he deny those people arms. I pointed out bluntly that U.S. arms made available against Communist aggression not for local wars. Said I cannot predict how American government and people will react their use now. I stressed need Pak acceptance in principle UNSYG's appeal and underlined this very pressing matter. Pointed out if GOP could accept appeal in principle, it should have greatest importance now as move toward cessation of hostilities. Ayub replied Pak had accepted original (1948) cease fire with understanding other things to follow leading toward settlement, but through all the years nothing had happened. I replied simple cease fire now essential first step any solution. Ayub said if there a package deal, GOP be prepared to consider. I stressed it first necessary put out conflagration and hardly possible discuss permanent settlement while house burning down. Ayub said GOP response Sec Gen's appeal delivered today but now there new situation. Said let there be cease fire by all means but some sense must come of it too. I reiterated unlikely substance of matter could be fruitfully discussed in heat conflict and stressed first requirement now is stop shooting. Pres said, "First you honor your commitment to us. As to cease fire, if India ready talk, we can have cease fire in place, call it armistice if you like." Bhutto interjected, would be possible have mutual Indian/Pak complete military withdrawal from all Kashmir. Ayub agreed. When I observed India likely to reject such a proposal, Pres agreed and maintained then it would be question of bringing pressure to bear. UN forces could maintain law and order in interim period if necessary.

I drew Pres's attention to fact American people would now feel pulled squarely forward [toward?] middle destructive sub-continental conflict and tremendous pressures would arise not to contribute to internecine warfare and to suspend military assistance both sides. Bhutto declared no country outside sub-continent has such stake as U.S. this matter. Neither India nor Pak are Communist. U.S. has heavy investment both countries. U.S. occupies special position sub-continent. These fundamental considerations. I told Pres I wished he could meet face to face with Pres Johnson. I realized obstacles which new situation placed before any such meeting. I had intended renew suggestion two chiefs of state meet for discussion. Pres Johnson had wanted mutually beneficial discussion so things could be worked out by two leaders. Ayub responded would like take first opportunity such a meeting. Personally, believed there very little differences between us, only petty misunderstandings, but nothing real. Understood U.S. under pressure Vietnam and Pak under pressure also. Said differences will arise but basically impossible change geography and basic need both sides for understanding. I noted need for understanding higher now than ever. Ayub said "Whether you believe us or not, wherever we go we plead for U.S., because we are allies and you have helped us. I am chiefly responsible and very interested in U.S. alliance. It based not on whim but on sound factors."

Pres said Pak only could assure security by alliance with U.S. He pleaded for understanding that given state Pak relations India, Pak cannot take risk of opposing massive ChiCom/Soviet power. Said, "If you wish us do anything which concerns us only, we will go the limit. But if it impinges on our relationships with others, we must weigh limits our possibilities. As long as you understand these two fundamentals, I cannot see serious difficulties arising between us. When I have opportunity see President Johnson, will explain this in detail." Pres said GOP "has cause complain over U.S. support to India. We have right as friends and allies to complain to you. We do not complain to Indians.

That would be pointless. you must understand we in difficult situation."

Bhutto said it now necessary go back to basics. If one thinks only of cease fire, fundamental problem only gets worse and tangled upon charges and counter charges, actions and counter actions. Said now is time for honorable settlement. Said this is time when we "can use not pressure but realities of situation to press for honorable settlement." Ayub said U.S. hopes not to come into middle of current Indo-Pak crisis and stressed in chorus with Bhutto, that nonetheless U.S. is in middle. President said U.N. weakened and won't work. Said, however despite U.N., there are bilateral obligations. Said "You can warn us and India too, but you cannot avoid responsibility. You are on trial. You cannot hedge or hide from this obligation. Otherwise, dispute will go on interminably."

I said we must try for solution through U.N. President replied, "All right, try but you have a bilateral obligation and we are going demand fulfillment." I stressed case hardly clear, certainly not black and white. President said, "All right, all right." I referred to provocations and counter-provocations on mounting scale by each side alternately. President responded Kashmir disputed territory, and GOP has not aggressed against Indian territory. I stressed dispute cannot be settled by force. President agreed.

I asked President whether I might with confidence report to Washington, GOP has no arrangement or understanding with Chinese Communists or Soviet Union. Ayub replied, "I can say, how will Soviets assist us, how can they? ChiComs will only do what suits them. If they could assist us, India could not have withdrawn troops from that northern border and thrown them against us. We have no obligation with USSR and they have none with us. We have not approached Chinese. We do not want them, for Russians and U.S. forces would come in. We do not want that." I asked whether he expected ChiCom diversionary action. Ayub replied, "What Chinese or Soviets will do in future, I do not know. We have not heard anything of such intention. Naturally, they won't waste any advantage." I asked President whether he anticipated current crisis would stimulate communal disturbances. He said did not know, GOP had taken all reasonable precautions but in India that possibility endemic. I asked whether President anticipated GOP would be able maintain internal law and order. President replied, "Yes, it our duty and will do very best."

Ayub said "You have role to play. You must and can play it. If sub-continent goes up in flames, as it will, what then? There are irresponsible men in Indian Cabinet." I reiterated plea for positive GOP response SecGen appeal. I pointed out GOP would then be in strong moral and legal position in contrast previously defensive position regarding infiltrators. GOP could put itself on side of peace and put India on moral defensive if India failed to respond and GOP did. It historic decision and GOP stands at crossroads.

President said, "We will give them damn good battle. We not over optimistic, but we not pessimistic. As to cease fire, where does it get us?" Bhutto interjected, that resolution basic question would subsume question U.S. arms to both sides.

I pointed out consortium meeting question seemed overtaken although it remains for later consideration. At moment house on fire. I noted that with war, all bets off concerning consortium meeting. We naturally hope won't be war when that date comes but who can say now.

Bhutto handed me aide-mémoire invoking our defense agreement reported Embtel 37 to Dept.[3] Full text my discussion with President follows separate tel.[4]

McConaughy

---

[3] Telegram 37 from Rawalpindi, September 6, transmitted the text of the aide-mémoire. The aide-mémoire alleged that India had unleashed a war of aggression against Pakistan, and called upon the United States to fulfill the terms of the agreement entered into in 1959. Under the terms of that agreement, the United States would view any threat to the security, independence, and territorial integrity of Pakistan with the utmost gravity, and would take effective action to assist Pakistan to suppress aggression. (Ibid., POL 32–1 INDIA–PAK)

[4] Telegram 41 from Rawalpindi, September 6. (Ibid.) McConaughy reported his impressions of the conversation in telegram 43 from Rawalpindi, September 6. He noted that Ayub showed signs of strain but gave the impression of determination, and Bhutto made "occasional emotional and provocative interjections." McConaughy quoted one such comment by Bhutto: "India commits aggression and Pak aid consortium is postponed." McConaughy felt that while Ayub leaned on Bhutto's counsel to some extent, he was master of his own house. And he noted that Ayub had given every indication of being anxious to improve his relations with the United States. (Ibid.)

188. Telegram From the Department of State to the Embassy in Pakistan[1]

Washington, September 6, 1965, 2:28 p.m.

290. Rawalpindi's 37.[2] You should respond as follows to GOP request for USG action pursuant our assurances to Pakistan:

(1) Like Ayub, we are deeply disturbed at most drastic and grave turn that has occurred in the situation between India and Pakistan. Point has now been reached that risks disaster for both Pakistan and India. Situation requires most sober reassessments both Pakistan and Indian leadership before it too late;

(2) In accordance with our assurances to Pakistan we are acting urgently, as we said we would, to meet this common danger by full support for immediate UN action to end the hostilities; that must be first objective of all concerned;

(3) We regard Indian military strike across Punjab frontier as most serious development. To meet situation effectively, however, Paks and we need to be completely frank with each other. We must view India's attacks across Pak border in over-all context events past few weeks. It clear from UNSYG report[3] that immediate crisis began with substantial infiltration of armed men from the Pakistan side. We aware India first put regular forces across CFL but Pak responses thereto in Chhamb area struck at points India considered vital, and Indians have long asserted (a) they could not tolerate continued Pak offensive, and (b) if Pakistan should strike India's vital interests, India would have no choice but to respond in area of its own choosing. GOP must have been well aware of risk involved in its own actions in Jammu and Kashmir;

(4) To have any chance of averting immediate prospect of sheer disaster for both Pakistan and India, which would also have grave repercussions for Free World security in Asia, appeal of UNSC must be honored by both parties. We urgently ask Pakistan's cooperation by immediate and full acceptance of UNSC's resolutions.[4] This will assist us to act effectively.

---

[1] Source: National Archives and Records Administration, RG 59, Central Files 1964–66, POL 32–1 INDIA–PAK. Secret; Immediate. Drafted by Laingen and Talbot; cleared by Sisco, Deputy Legal Adviser Richard D. Kearny, Townsend Hoopes, and Komer; and approved and initialed by Rusk. Also sent to Rawalpindi, and repeated to New Delhi, London, USUN, CINCMEAFSA, Tehran, Ankara, Paris for Ball and DOD.

[2] See footnote 3, Document 187.

[3] See footnote 2, Document 181.

[4] The UN Security Council adopted Resolution 210 on September 6, renewing its earlier call for a cease-fire. (UN doc. S/RES/210)

(5) We are fully aware, as President indicated in his letter to Ayub,[5] relationship unresolved Kashmir dispute to present tension. But neither we nor any other friends both parties can assist in coping with this or other root causes of Indo-Pak tensions without immediate and respected cease-fire and withdrawal of forces both sides.

(6) We have appealed to Shastri for India's immediate cooperation with UN efforts.

(7) Our subsequent actions will depend in first instance on response both countries to UN efforts.[6]

Rusk

---

[5] See Document 183.

[6] Rusk sent a personal message to McConaughy and Bowles on September 6 in which he noted that both India and Pakistan would be making a major effort to gain U.S. support, and each would develop its own brand of disappointment and resentment toward the United States. In the face of pressure and recrimination, the Ambassadors and their staffs "should be ready to explain firmly but sympathetically why the U.S. is not moving in to participate in the way each might wish." Essentially, Rusk stated, "we are being asked to come in on the crash landing where we had no chance to be in on the take-off." (Telegram 293 to Karachi also sent as telegram 364 to New Delhi; National Archives and Records Administration, RG 59, Central Files 1964–66, POL 32–1 INDIA–PAK)

---

189.   **Telegram From the Department of State to the Embassy in India**[1]

Washington, September 6, 1965, 2:22 p.m.

359. You are requested to seek appointment at highest possible level to convey following views of USG:

(1) The United States is deeply concerned by the growing escalation of the fighting between India and Pakistan. We cannot believe that these two great nations wish to hurl themselves into disaster which threatens them as a result of present developments.

---

[1] Source: National Archives and Records Administration, RG 59, Central Files 1964–66, POL 32–1 INDIA–PAK. Secret; Immediate. Drafted by Schneider; cleared by Talbot, Sisco, Kearney, Lang (DOD/ISA) and Komer; and approved and initialed by Rusk. Repeated to Karachi, London, Rawalpindi, Ankara, Tehran, USUN, CINCSTRIKE/ CINCMEAFSA, Paris for the Under Secretary, and DOD.

(2) Also of great concern is danger of involvement (politically and or militarily) of Communist Chinese. Continuation of conflict likely plunge India more deeply into cross currents of cold war and internal Communist bloc conflicts. Chicoms will be certain winners; it difficult see how either India or Pakistan could benefit regardless of outcome.

(3) If there is to be any chance of averting immediate prospect of sheer disaster for both India and Pakistan, it is extremely important that UNSC appeals be honored by both.

(4) We therefore earnestly appeal to GOI to accept the call of the United Nations Secretary General and the Security Council for an immediate cease fire and withdrawal of all armed personnel.

(5) We are addressing similar appeal to Pakistan for cease fire in accordance with call of SYG and Security Council.

Rusk

---

190. Memorandum From Robert Komer of the National Security Council Staff to President Johnson[1]

Washington, September 7, 1965, 7:30 p.m.

Rusk drafted the attached statement,[2] which he and Bell request you authorize Mahon[3] to put out tomorrow. It is primarily an effort to forestall restrictive Pak/Indian amendments to the aid appropriation. Mahon is strongly so urging.

You'll see that it not only covers the halt in MAP deliveries but mentions the holdup on new economic aid commitments. This no more

---

[1] Source: Johnson Library, National Security File, Memos to the President, McGeorge Bundy, Vol. 14, 7/1/65–9/22/65. Confidential.

[2] The statement indicated that in view of the conflict between India and Pakistan the United States had suspended military assistance shipments to both countries, and that, pending action on the foreign assistance appropriations bill, the United States had not been making new economic commitments since the new fiscal year began, including India and Pakistan.

[3] George H. Mahon, Representative from Texas, Chairman of the House Appropriations Committee, made the statement in the debate in the House on September 8. He indicated that the positions with respect to military and economic assistance had been outlined for him by Secretary of State Rusk as administration policy, and he urged legislative support for that policy, as well as for the administration's policy of supporting the UN efforts to seek a resolution to the conflict on the subcontinent of South Asia. (*Congressional Record*, Vol. 111, pt. 17, p. 23141) The text of the statement was transmitted on September 8 to Karachi as telegram 310 and to New Delhi as telegram 379. (National Archives and Records Administration, RG 59, Central Files 1964–66, POL 27 INDIA–PAK)

than accords with the facts of life, and helps establish our case for postponing any Pak consortium pledge.

But there is no easy solution to the underlying policy issues involved in aid suspension. It will certainly be highly resented in both India and Pakistan, and risks pushing both even further off the deep end. On the other hand, it may well help bring home to both the consequences of their folly. So Bundy and I think the argument is swung by the point that the importance of protecting the aid bill outweighs the risk of further affront to India and Pakistan.

Rusk wants your clearance tonight, but you may want to discuss the matter at the leadership breakfast. Bundy is available at home this evening if needed, and I can be reached through the Sit Room.[4]

R. W. Komer

---

[4] Johnson wrote "OK" at the end of the memorandum.

---

191. Memorandum From Robert Komer of the National Security Council Staff to President Johnson[1]

Washington, September 7, 1965, 7:30 p.m.

Pak/Indian Roundup. The military situation remains confused. Apparently the Paks have held the Indian thrust into the Punjab. An Indian thrust into East Pakistan seems imminent, if not underway.[2] Neither party shows any signs of response to cease-fire appeals as yet.

The Chicoms have announced "firm support" of Pakistan, but there are no signs yet that this means more than words. The USSR has come out strongly in favor of the UN cease-fire appeal.

---

[1] Source: Johnson Library, National Security File, Memos to the President, McGeorge Bundy, Vol. 14, 7/1/65–9/22/65. Secret. A handwritten "L" on the memorandum indicates that the President saw it.

[2] Intelligence reports as of September 6 indicated a build-up of Indian forces all along the border with East Pakistan. (White House telegram CAP 65565 to the LBJ Ranch in Texas, September 7; ibid., Country File, India, Vol. V, Cables, 6/65–9/65)

U Thant leaves this evening. We've offered him logistic support, including use of our attaché aircraft for travel around the area and planes to bring in more UN observers if needed.

Attached are two cables (Delhi 503[3] and Karachi 398[4]) which give important insights into the current mood of both parties. Our announcement of aid suspension tomorrow will lead to howls from both, but it should also help bring home to them the consequences of their folly.

When UK High Commissioner James saw Ayub today, the latter was apparently now more fully aware of the mess he's in. We infer this from Ayub's willingness to accept Pearson[5] as mediator. James felt it was *not* the time to bring up how we were unlikely to pledge.

Shastri has just written you a letter, which BK Nehru asks to deliver personally. We don't know the contents but suspect it is a defense of India's position.

R. W. Komer

---

[3] In telegram 503 from New Delhi, September 7, Bowles reported on a conversation that morning with L.K. Jha, Secretary to the Prime Minister. He asked Jha if the situation was beyond recovery or if diplomatic efforts might yet prevent full-blown war. Jha responded that a cease-fire was possible if the Pakistani infiltrators were removed from Kashmir, if the cease-fire line and the UN apparatus to enforce it were revamped to avoid further violations, and if Pakistan agreed to take the pressure off the Kashmir issue until an atmosphere could be reestablished in which reasonable negotiations were possible. Jha also noted that after the border war with China in 1962 and subsequent Chinese and Pakistani propaganda about the fighting qualities of the Indian army, Shastri was determined in the present conflict to establish India as a nation of vitality, purpose, and strength. (National Archives and Records Administration, RG 59, Central Files 1964–66, POL 27 INDIA–PAK)

[4] Telegram 398 from Karachi, September 7, reported on a message from Finance Minister Shoaib, which McConaughy felt merited high-level consideration. Shoaib noted that Bhutto had arranged the call upon the United States to fulfill its pledges to Pakistan knowing that it would not be able to respond in a clear and conclusive manner. The war therefore offered the opportunity in Bhutto's words to "silence once and for all the American party." Shoaib worried that attacks on the United States would increase and the misunderstanding between the two countries would grow. He asked for some gesture of U.S. support to offset the negative atmosphere building in Pakistan, preferably a statement that the United States intended to make the scheduled consortium pledge. (Ibid., POL PAK–US)

[5] Lester Pearson, Prime Minister of Canada.

192. Telegram From the Department of State to the Embassy in India[1]

Washington, September 8, 1965, 1:57 p.m.

383. Personal for the Ambassador from the Secretary. As seen from here there are very urgent reasons why we should attempt to prevent Indo-Pak fighting from expanding into the Bengal–East Pakistan area. Quite apart from strong humanitarian reasons for not extending ground and air operations in area of massed populations, the military situation in the West still appears to be somewhat tentative and possibilities of getting cease-fire and pullback still exist. Opening up of front in the Eastern subcontinent would be further major inflammation and would substantially increase risks of Chinese involvement. Surely, given threatening noises out of Peiping,[2] Indian authorities can see the point of conserving their resources in the East to meet a possible Chinese move rather than catch up East Pakistan in the step by step escalation which becomes increasingly difficult for either of two governments or the UN to control. Further factor is our own national interest against spreading of fighting into areas in which reasonable care of foreign residents will be extremely difficult. Unless you see strong objections, in which case we would wish your prompt comments, you are authorized to take this matter up urgently with highest Indian authorities. If they are responsive, we would make immediate and similar approach to Pakistan to get their agreement not to expand the violence into the East. You should make it clear that this is in no sense an endorsement by us of the validity of the fighting in the West and that this is without prejudice to our full support of UN SYG. But if both countries are to avoid a catastrophe some restraint must begin to enter the picture and,

---

[1] Source: National Archives and Records Administration, RG 59, Central Files 1964–66, POL 27 INDIA–PAK. Secret; Immediate. Drafted by Rusk, cleared by Talbot and Bundy, and approved and initialed by Rusk. Repeated to Karachi.

[2] On September 8 China sent a note to India protesting serious violations of Chinese territory by Indian troops and warning that if the violations did not cease, "India must bear responsibility for all consequences arising therefrom." (Telegram 573 from New Delhi, September 11; ibid.) In Washington, the Chinese threat was taken seriously. Komer wrote a memorandum on September 8 entitled "US Policy at the Crossroads in the Subcontinent" in which he concluded that if China became militarily involved in the war between India and Pakistan, the United States would have little choice other than to become similarly involved since "the whole Western power position in Asia may be at stake." (Johnson Library, National Security File, Country File, India, Agenda Points, 9/17/65)

given the menacing threats from Peiping, peace in the East is at least a beginning.[3]

Rusk

---

[3] Bowles responded on September 9 that he agreed with Rusk's message and instructed his staff to make the points with senior members of the Ministry of Foreign Affairs and the Ministry of Defense. He did not feel the issue needed to be pressed at the highest levels of the government since Defense Minister Chavan had just made a statement in the Indian Parliament indicating that India had no plans to escalate the war into East Pakistan. (Telegram 541 from New Delhi; National Archives and Records Administration, RG 59, Central Files 1964–66, POL 27 INDIA–PAK) Ambassador McConaughy reported in telegram 459 from Karachi, September 12, that he delivered a note to the Pakistani Foreign Ministry expressing U.S. concern that every effort be made to avoid expanding the war into East Pakistan. (Ibid.)

---

193. Editorial Note

In a telephone conversation on September 8, 1965, President Johnson and Secretary of Defense McNamara discussed what they saw as dangerous possibilities developing as a result of the conflict between India and Pakistan. McNamara noted that he was concerned about a number of contingencies that might develop which the United States was not fully prepared to deal with, the most serious of which was the possibility that China might initiate military operations against India. McNamara observed that the Chinese threat to India posed a very serious problem. The danger that China might move against India had become immediate in light of the note China had sent to India earlier in the day.

Referring to the Chinese note, Johnson said: "And looked like she was threatening to today, didn't she?"

McNamara responded: "She'll threaten and we ought to know what we'd do if she did move. We'd be in a terrible jam if she did and we didn't have plans. So we'll be working on that."

Johnson asked what McNamara thought the Soviet Union would do in the event that China entered the conflict, and when McNamara indicated that he didn't know, Johnson answered his own question: "I think they'd move too."

McNamara expressed his concern about what the British would do in the event the conflict mushroomed to include China and possibly the Soviet Union.

Johnson commented: "They're going to run out, as they usually do."

McNamara agreed: "I think so. And I think we've got to have some plans for that. So these are some of the projects we'll be working on." (Johnson Library, Recordings and Transcripts, Recording of Telephone Conversation Between President Johnson and Secretary of Defense McNamara, September 8, 1965, 6 p.m., Tape F65.02, Side A, PNO 1)

---

194. Telegram From the Department of State to the Embassy in India[1]

Washington, September 8, 1965, 7:12 p.m.

390. For Ambassadors from the Secretary. Deptel 382 to New Delhi repeated 312 to Karachi.[2] I have just returned from two and one-half hour session with Senate Appropriations Committee that is considering Aid bill. Sentiment in that Committee and on Hill against continuing not only military but also economic aid to India and Pakistan unless hostilities are halted is even more violent than I had anticipated it would be. There is also talk on Hill of amendments to halt all arms and aid to India and Pakistan outright instead of just suspending it and to condition all further economic assistance on a cessation of fighting.

I am informing you of this situation as it is important that Indian and Pakistani Governments not underestimate extent of Congressional reaction and are aware that continuing hostilities are jeopardizing future aid programs for both countries.

Rusk

---

[1] Source: National Archives and Records Administration, RG 59, Central Files 1964–66, POL 27 INDIA–PAK. Confidential; Priority; Limdis. Drafted by MacArthur and approved and initialed by Rusk. Also sent to Karachi as telegram 322.

[2] Telegram 382 to New Delhi, also sent as telegram 312 to Karachi, September 8, instructed the two Embassies to give their host governments the text of the proposed statement by Mahan, noting that it had been approved by the Johnson administration. For a summary of the statement, see footnote 3, Document 190. The Embassies were instructed to make clear that the announced action was not meant as a punishment or threat, but was what U.S. opinion required in a situation of de facto war. The United States could not support the UN appeal for a cease-fire and, at the same time, provide the equipment that might be used to pursue that conflict. (National Archives and Records Administration, RG 59, Central Files 1964–66, POL 27 INDIA–PAK)

195.   Memorandum for the Record[1]

Washington, September 9, 1965.

The President's Meeting with Indian Ambassador B. K. Nehru, 6 p.m. 9 September 1965 (off the record)

Ambassador Nehru gave the President a letter dated 7 September 1965 from Prime Minister Shastri.[2] After the President had read it, Nehru explained that he had asked for a meeting so that he could stress certain points in the letter. First, "we want peace not war". Second, "The only way to stop Pakistan's attack in Kashmir had been to counterattack in the Punjab." This was the only reason why India had responded as it did. Third, India genuinely wanted a cease fire and withdrawal; its reply to U Thant's appeal had been badly "misunderstood". But India had to have all of the people shooting at Indians up there in Kashmir stop firing and withdraw. It couldn't just be the uniformed forces. India had to cross the cease-fire line in the first place to stop such infiltrators from causing havoc.

Nehru then gave the President a copy of Defense Minister Chavan's 8 September speech[3] with certain passages marked, saying these indicated that India acted purely as a defensive measure. For example, India would not take any action to escalate the war in East Pakistan. He also showed the President a copy of the Secretary General's report[4] with passages marked citing Pak infiltration into Kashmir. He said that he wished to make such points clear at the top level to the President.

Nehru went on to say that two additional points disturbed India. One was the use of US arms against them. India had based its whole defense policy on US assurances that it would not permit Pakistan to use US arms against India. Otherwise it would have armed much more heavily. This assurance had not been honored, but Nehru admitted he didn't see what could be done about it. Then he complained that the State Department kept saying that both sides were using US arms. This was just not so up to the present. Mr. Komer mentioned, in response to the President's inquiry, that this had occurred once but that he believed that it was inadvertent and had not been repeated.

---

[1] Source: Johnson Library, National Security File, Country File, India, Vol. V, Cables, 6/65–9/65. Secret. Prepared by Komer.

[2] In the letter, Shastri reviewed the conflict with Pakistan and argued that India's involvement was a defensive reaction to deliberate provocation. (Ibid., Shastri Correspondence)

[3] See footnote 3, Document 192.

[4] See footnote 2, Document 181.

The President stated with vigor that this war must be halted somehow. Neither side could win anything in any way commensurate with the risks involved. The stakes were far bigger than Kashmir now. We were going to "put all our chips behind U Thant." We had also made strong representations to Pakistan about the use of US equipment. We had made clear that we could not accept this.

Nehru asked about the China problem. He said that his government had no firm evidence, but that it felt there was a clear Chinese-Pakistani-Indonesian understanding "to put a triple squeeze on us." Perhaps the Chinese would not go to war, but at least they would use political pressure. If the Chicoms did come in, what do we do?

The President said this was "giving us gray hairs right now." We were worried, but we just didn't know what the Chicoms would do. The cardinal point was, however, to keep Pakistan from going the Chinese route. For all we knew, Pakistan might have some kind of agreement with China. Nehru interjected that India thought the Indonesian contribution might be to take the Andaman and Nicobar Islands. India couldn't stop this; it had no navy.

The President reiterated that we must all back U Thant in order to get peace. The whole future of Asia was at stake. However, stronger US public noises about the Chinese Communist threat might only provoke Peiping.

Raising the Kashmir question, Nehru said that a nation under attack could not even talk about a Kashmir settlement at such a time. That would mean surrender. "We can not let them shoot their way into getting Kashmir." At this point the President raised the question of our aid bill. He was afraid that the India-Pak mess might kill the aid bill. He had managed to ram it through the House, but the Senate was another matter. Other countries didn't seem to realize our problems on these matters. Those who criticized our lack of sophistication or our policies didn't realize that Congress might just listen to them and stop aid.

Then the President described how Shastri and Ayub visits last spring would have been at precisely the wrong time. Congress was always looking for awkward statements by foreign leaders or for the President himself to make mistakes which would permit them to cut aid. Then recently we were within one week of passing the aid bill when war broke out. He regretted that the delays in postponing the earlier visit scheduled for Ayub, and then the leak, had made it difficult for us to notify Shastri in time. Nehru assured him that there was "no ill will left" about the visit postponement. The President had no need to worry. Indeed Shastri had hoped to come in October, but this was probably impossible now because of the war.

The President summed up by saying that what was urgently needed was (1) all-out support for the Syg; (2) rush the aid bill through;

(3) tell both sides not to use our equipment; and (d) watch the Chinese. He had spent two hours on this problem today, and stressed that we "must find the solution". We would do everything we could. The future of Asia is at stake. Recalling his 1962 visit with pleasure, he said he had the warmest feeling for the people of India. We were anxious to do everything we could in the hope that India one hundred years from now would be like the United States.

The President said that "what I am doing in this country this year, I would like to do worldwide. My foreign policy is the Great Society." He described how there were only four bills left of all those that he hoped to get passed this year. When he got these passed, his domestic job would be largely done. Foreign aid was the toughest, though. The US had spent $800 billion on armaments since the end of World War II. One could remake the world with $800 billion. The President then took Nehru to meet various members of his staff.

RWK

196. Memorandum From Secretary of State Rusk to President Johnson[1]

Washington, September 9, 1965.

SUBJECT

India and Pakistan

I

Events just down the road in the subcontinent can have the most complex and farreaching consequences for the United States. We don't yet know how far the Chinese Communists will involve themselves. However, their strident "demands" on India yesterday (which give color to reports of a Pakistan-Chinese Communist understanding and Shoaib's warning that Bhutto would play the Chinese Communist card)

---

[1] Source: Johnson Library, National Security File, Country File, India, Memos and Miscellaneous, 6/65–9/65. Secret. McGeorge Bundy sent this memorandum to the President on September 10 under cover of a note that reads: "Here is an important paper from the Secretary of State giving his current thinking on the South Asian crisis. He is clearly moving toward a position of heavier engagement—as I think we all are. But his thinking is not very concrete—and neither is anyone else's yet." (Ibid.)

make it a clear contingency. This could convert the Pakistan-Indian war into a Free World-Communist confrontation.

In any event, Pakistani-Indian warfare bites deeply into American interests. U Thant's mission offers a chance for the two countries to pull back from the abyss. Its success could get us back to the disagreeably bumpy, but relatively safe, verbal hassling over Kashmir with each country still seeking maximum United States support for its position. Otherwise, the prospect is grim. Fighting could exhaust one country or both, and subject the 50 million Moslems in India and upwards of 10 million Hindus in Pakistan to unbelievable blood baths. Collapse and communal chaos would call into question the future of the subcontinent itself and would certainly negate our effort to build there a viable counterweight to Communist China.

II

If Kashmir were the only issue, the U.S. could reasonably hope to stand aside. However, the whole Western power position in Asia may shortly be at stake.

So far, with an investment of nearly $12 billion, we have helped move the 600 million people of India and Pakistan along a line that has frustrated Communist ambitions. India along with Japan is the only power potential in Asia comparable to China. Were it now to go down the drain, we would face a new situation in many ways as serious as the loss of China. And as India goes, so eventually will Pakistan.

The effects would be directly felt all along the Asian rim:

—The Shah, sympathizing with Ayub and pressed by him for help, sees this as a question of how in a pinch the United States meets its assurances. So to a degree does Turkey.

—As Indonesia drifts toward greater hostility, and probably Communist domination, our position in Southeast Asia is directly affected, and South Asia becomes even more important.

—Latent Japanese neutralist tendencies could bloom disturbingly in the wake of a major humiliation of India and of what would be seen as a Chinese Communist victory over the U.S.

—Chinese Communist involvement would make South Asia and Vietnam actually two parts of the same basic problem: that of containing Peiping's outward thrust, and thus reasonably add to our burdens.

—Finally, if the Chicoms get involved or this conflict runs its present course, Pakistan will wind up deeply committed to the Chinese Communists while India, feeling let down by the West and its national prestige at stake, would almost certainly go for the nuclear bomb.

III

Against risks this great, the question is whether the U.S. can afford or even maintain non-involvement. There is a strong Congressional urge that we get out of South Asia. Should this succeed in tying your hand, there can be no crisis management but only crisis drift, since whether acting indirectly (through the U.N., the U.K., the Commonwealth or Pearson) or directly, only the U.S. has at its disposal the essential carrots and sticks to influence the situation in the long run.

IV

There are risks in crisis management but also opportunities. Ayub seems fearful of all-out war with India, as he has reason to be. Shastri should fear the Chinese factor as well as domestic disruption arising from communal explosions. Continuing warfare will bankrupt both. In this moment of truth, both may realize their need to be more responsive than heretofore. The shifting Soviet position holds possibilities of less interference than usual if we should bear down.

We might get both countries to stop hostilities if we were prepared to give full support to efforts towards a negotiation of their outstanding disputes, including Kashmir. Our involvement would also improve the chances of keeping both India and Pakistan reasonably linked to the West and reasonably firm against Chinese Communist encroachment into the subcontinent.

Pakistan-Indian bitterness makes it extraordinarily difficult to keep good relations with both. If at the end of the day we were forced to choose between them, India with its much larger population, industrial base, rudimentary democracy, and other potentials would probably be a better bet. However, we could never fully support policy goals of either India or Pakistan. The best protection of American interests rests in maintaining adequate, though probably not intimate, links with both.

Dean Rusk

197. Telegram From the Embassy in India to the Department of State[1]

New Delhi, September 9, 1965, 0620Z.

531. Embtel 330.[2] We are now reviewing our ongoing programs in light of effect of current hostilities. Over course of next week we shall be sending Dept series of separate messages covering economic aid, military aid, Peace Corps and USIS programs.

It is our belief that most new loan action as well as fourth plan dialogue should be suspended at least for duration of fighting although monitoring of past loans and existing and developing technical assistance projects should continue normally as possible. Cable reviewing this subject is now in preparation.

Most urgent decision we require is on PL 480.

GOI estimates that supplies wheat available under current PL 480 agreement (including July 26 60 day amendment) would be completely shipped by about Oct 25. If break in supply line is to be avoided, we would have to conclude new agreement within next two weeks to allow sufficient time for Indian supply mission Washington to begin purchases and arrange shipping for additional supplies after shipments under current agreement are completed.

Even if fighting should peter out, food shortage in India is likely to be serious to desperate in next 12 months, though too early to make firm estimates, prospects are that delay in monsoon will result in harvests significantly below level of last year. Pressure on foodstocks, already great, will be accentuated by current hostilities which bound to stimulate increased speculation and hoarding.

If in addition there should be a gap in arrivals of wheat and other commodities from US, it would be impossible to make it up by accelerating subsequent shipments since current GOI import requirements are already very near capacity of ports and internal transport system when scheduled on regular basis. Continued flow imports is necessary to enable GOI prevent breakdown existing distribution arrangements and to plan efficient utilization wheat and rice on yearly basis, and to avoid disastrous consequence for Indian people.

---

[1] Source: National Archives and Records Administration, RG 59, Central Files 1964–66, AID (US) 15 INDIA. Confidential; Immediate; Limdis. Received at 4:13 a.m., and passed to the White House, DOD, CIA, and USIA at 4:40 a.m. Repeated to Bombay, Calcutta, London, USUN, Karachi, and Madras.

[2] In telegram 330 from New Delhi, August 19, the Embassy questioned the wisdom of using food assistance as a lever to promote agricultural policy decisions promoted by the United States. The telegram discussed the issues still in question with respect to negotiating a new P.L. 480 agreement. (Ibid.)

I wish to emphasize that if we should fail maintain shipments, effects on India and our position here would be drastic. Though Indians could get by for little while on indigenous supplies, existing stocks and some new cash purchases, they would quickly run into major catastrophe affecting tens of millions of people. Present stocks are meager and Indians lack foreign exchange for substantial cash purchases abroad. Indians would thus soon be running out of food and inability meet rationing commitments would result severe repercussions in major metropolitan area.

Moreover our unique ability assist in easing food shortages will do much improve our political position here which has been severely damaged by use of US planes and tanks by Paks. Equally important, when hostilities terminated hopefully in near future, adequate food will be primary requisite for economic stability and continuance development.

I assume there may be objectives under present circumstances to negotiating new agreement along lines recommended Embtel 330. If this is case I urge, for reasons indicated above, immediate authorization to conclude further amendment of Sept 30, 1964, agreement for additional million tons of wheat plus available rice and non-fat dry milk with assurances to GOI that we intend continue to help feed people.

Bowles

---

198. Telegram From the Embassy in Pakistan to the Department of State[1]

Karachi, September 9, 1965, 1245Z.

428. Subject: Kashmir. Deptel 290.[2] I met for 45 minutes today with FonMin Bhutto to present US response GOP request for invocation defense agreement. I paraphrased reftel and later sent FonMin minute. I added US concerting all our resources behind Security Council and SecGen. We cannot say what next step would be if current initiative should not work. We do not even want to envisage possibility of it not

---

[1] Source: National Archives and Records Administration, RG 59, Central Files 1964–66, POL 27 INDIA–PAK. Secret; Immediate. Received at 8:41 p.m., and passed to the White House, DOD, and CIA at 9 p.m. Repeated to London, New Delhi, and CINCMEAFSA for POLAD.
[2] Document 188.

working, and assume FonMin would agree on this. Bhutto replied if UN were only means of securing justice and meeting armed aggression, there would be no need for bilateral alliances.

If only reason for bilateral agreement with US were to refer to UN then Pakistan might as well not have that agreement. US/Pak agreement is special arrangement and obligation US with respect Pakistan. To refer GOP now to UN is to say US not willing fulfill its obligations. Situation all the more complicated than heretofore since UN has done nothing effective over 18 years re Kashmir. This was Indian intention and if [it?] is base your reply, we might as well [have?] listened to Indians. Fear GOP must make special note of that. US/Pak bilateral agreement not dependent upon UN blessing. If that, however, US approach, must say it causes disappointment GOP. I pointed out I had not said current UN approach the full extent our reaction. It first step and hopefully enough lay basis for settlement acceptable GOP but obviously must get cease fire and withdrawal forces both sides. We have said that "depends upon responses both sides." We recognize our responsibility to go beyond first step if that does not work. If you cooperate in good faith and clarity, US has responsibility. Bhutto said time is of essence. We cannot go by stages when fate of nation hangs in balance. India has violated pledges and promises to people of Kashmir and violated UN resolution. India has embarked on aggression, in East Pakistan by economic aggression, expelling Muslims, infiltrating Jammu. India has perhaps over-reacted. India has committed aggression against Kashmir. Pakistan cannot commit aggression there, they are our own people. India reoccupied Kargil posts August 30, and on August 24 undertook Poonch offensive. GOP had to react but only did so in disputed territory. At every stage India has escalated; by crossing CFL, by launching Uri–Poonch offensive. But nobody, even our allies, came to us and acknowledged those actions as provocative. As self-respecting people we had react. India then determined to react anew and invade Pak territory. I asked about GOP position of implementation cease fire and withdrawal as first step. Bhutto replied this happened in past with very same language, cease fire, UN resolution and promises to bring full weight to bear. Now people have made sacrifices and India has committed aggression. With all that should we repeat mistakes of past and accept cease fire? What is different element to assure India would take different position? Eighteen years ago it was easier accept cease fire, now it much more complicated. We want cease fire but are not going to permit surrender our vital interest. India has no vital interest in Kashmir. Pakistan has vital moral, ethnic, religious interest. Am afraid matter not being looked at objectively. Cease fire must form part of final Kashmir settlement along lines: a) India and Pakistan vacate territory, b) UN administration of law and order for period approximately six months, c) plebiscite within precisely stipulated time. Without that there can be no solution. I said India not able to agree to that now and Bhutto responded, "Then let them destroy Pakistan!" I observed FonMin must be aware there new sense of urgency concerning Kashmir problem compared that past 18 years. Not possible now treat issue passively. Impossible with new situation fail seek acceptable solution. Bhutto said, "People of Kashmir alone must decide, and no solution is complete without people of Kashmir expressing right of self determination. This is battle of survival for Pakistan. We must be either degraded as nation or prevail. We prepared fight to finish. Pakistan is small country but morality is on our side and Pak people united. You cannot destroy a people and their spirit by one battle in Lahore." I interjected that force no ultimate answer. Bhutto retorted, "What has happened over past 18 years?"

I pointed out to FonMin his position amounted to saying GOP not willing abandon use of force even if other side withdrew. He replied Pakistan has been invaded. I asked if invader withdraws, would that not be better than throwing him out? Bhutto replied, "Yes, if he also withdrew from Jammu and Kashmir." I said it new position that Jammu and Kashmir part of Pakistan. Bhutto said no, it goes back at least a year. I asked does not plebiscite come first, and Bhutto responded with, "Why has there not been a plebiscite last 18 years?" I said Amb Bowles making urgent representation New Delhi today, and I hoped India would agree to cease fire and withdraw, albeit, I did not expect that would include Jammu and Kashmir. I pointed out that all our persuasiveness has been brought to bear beyond any other thought possible before. Bhutto observed US position India of special character but with Pakistan US has special moral and contractual obligations. Commented surely US can do more than direct GOP to UN.

I asked FonMin about GOP position concerning visit UN SecGen. Bhutto said GOP did not object to welcoming him so he might see for himself. He expressed facetious hope Article 19 question sufficiently resolved to permit UN pay SecGen air fare. Noting that question and other UN problems, Bhutto said please take such indications (of weakness) into account before putting all US might behind UN. Said valuable time has been lost with possibly far-reaching consequences. Stressed bilateral obligations not superseded by UN.

I acknowledged US bilateral responsibilities go beyond appeal to UN if that should not work. However, as our treaties usually indicate, we seek work within UN if possible. Bhutto said late Secretary Dulles had promised immediate US action event Indian aggression. Said Under Secretary Ball became irritated when Bhutto pointed out US would not intervene promptly enough. Cited late President Kennedy's saying US would break relations with India in event aggression. Amb Harriman had asserted US simply would not permit Indian attack. Bhutto commented now GOP fears being realized.

I pointed out to FonMin US using its might right now, and I was not saying if present efforts do not work that we will not try other ways. I said that if GOP could only cooperate, likelihood was more serious effort than ever before seek acceptable solution. Bhutto retorted that people of Kashmir most concerned, suffering as they do from genocide, expulsion and violation from India. I observed India must be brought to accept any agreement of her own free will. To be [garble— viable?] all three parties must be willing to accept, i.e., Pakistan, India, and Kashmir.

Bhutto responded, "We not bartering over piece of territory but are concerned with fate five million people. If they want Indian, okay. If they wish to be part of Pakistan, that's fine. If they wish something else, that's all right too. Whatever they want."

I told FonMin US hoped GOP can see way clear accept UN initiative as outlined by me if Indians accept. Said such acceptance would buy time. Valuable time in which to work toward agreement. Observed that in unfortunate case India should not accept, GOP would be in strong diplomatic position and thus could not lose either way. Bhutto said GOP had tried UN and been humiliated, been treated there as naïve and stupid, subjected to cynical discussion and told to be realistic. Said he had told UN representatives sub-continent could take fire in absence settlement, but they said that impossible. Bhutto claimed GOP had tried very hard obtain peaceful settlement. GOP had accepted all 14 proposals made, as well as UN resolution, Commonwealth initiative, GOP had refrained from taking advantage in Sino-Indian crisis, listened to intermediaries, participated in discussions in Geneva, FonMin maintained GOP had always taken initiatives in seeking peaceful solution. Reiterated it necessary study totality of problem.

I suggested GOP receptivity possible visit SecGen signified to me that GOP not prepared abandon peaceful solution and is keeping mind open. Bhutto replied, "Open mind, yes! But a positive cease fire, cease fire which means settlement, plebiscite." Bhutto pointed to Pak locale on crossroads of Asia, asking how can Paks as Oriental people prevent visit their country SecGen who also Asian. Said GOP of course has no objection but if SecGen thinks he not going to address self to heart of matter but simply put forth Indian position, his visit can serve no useful purpose. I observed SecGen certainly not going present GOI position, and I reiterated necessity both sides stop shooting and seek agreement. Bhutto replied that matter of formality. Said cease fire without larger agreement not possible.

I asked FonMin if any further intelligence available concerning Indian movements last few hours.

He replied no, he then referred Peenion Vielt, calling him old friend of Pakistan, and saying such visit would also be welcome but in same way and manner as the UN SecGen. Reiterated that to be meaningful any discussion must [be] addressed to main problem. Said this matter for US more than any other country.

McConaughy

199. Memorandum From Robert Komer of the National Security Council Staff to President Johnson[1]

Washington, September 10, 1965, 6:45 p.m.

Pak/Indian Roundup. Still no clear picture of the situation on the only really active front in the Punjab below Kashmir. Pak counterattacks in the Lahore area have taken them well into India, and Delhi seems quite worried.

The SYG doesn't seem to have gotten very far in his talks with the Paks, who are still insisting on a Kashmir settlement as part of any cease-fire agreement. Nor does McConaughy's latest talk with Bhutto (Karachi 428[2] attached) show much give.

The much more guarded tone of Indian statements suggests that Delhi is getting worried over Pak counterattacks. Chavan's denial India was attacking East Pakistan is the first bright move they've made so far. But Delhi's 564[3] from an excellent source shows little give as yet either.

The consensus here is that neither side will begin to negotiate seriously until more blood has been let. Many of us feel that the Paks will do quite well militarily in the next week or so in the key Punjab sector. But this would only humiliate the Indians and probably make them *less* likely to stop shooting. The Paks are already beginning to worry about running out of ammo, etc. at which time Indian weight would begin to tell.

---

[1] Source: Johnson Library, National Security File, Country File, Pakistan, Vol. IV, Memos and Miscellaneous, 8/65–9/65. Secret.

[2] Document 198.

[3] In telegram 564 from New Delhi, September 10, the Embassy reported on a conversation with Sarvepalli Gopal, Director of the Historical Division of the Ministry of External Affairs and son of President Radhakrishnan. According to Gopal, India had no territorial ambitions in Pakistan, but had established the objective in the war of destroying the Pakistani military capability, thereby also finally settling the Kashmir issue. (National Archives and Records Administration, RG 59, Central Files 1964–66, POL 27 INDIA–PAK)

Our Muslim friends (Iran, Turkey, and Saudi Arabia especially) are eager to show their sympathy to the Paks.[4] We don't think we ought to growl at them too much because they won't provide significant support and it helps for the Paks to think they have at least a few anchors left to Westward.

PM Wilson told the Paks he saw a solution emerging in four stages: (a) cease fire; (b) return to status quo; (c) neutralize and quiet Kashmir; and (d) a Kashmir settlement. U Thant too says the UN would probably have to take on the Kashmir issue again. The Brits apparently envisage some Commonwealth initiative if U Thant fails, and are probing Moscow's view.

Nothing from the Chicoms so far except more noise. But Delhi fears the Paks may try to incite India to attack East Pakistan, because this would trigger the Chicoms.

R. W. Komer[5]

---

[4] The Embassy in Tehran reported on September 9 that the Shah had received a telephone call from Ayub with an urgent request for help. Ayub reportedly said that the ally capable of providing the most effective assistance was the United States, which was failing to respond probably because of a desire to see Pakistan destroyed and one Indian nation emerge on the subcontinent. (Telegram 313 from Tehran; ibid.) On September 10 Iran and Turkey issued a joint communiqué, which fixed responsibility for the war on the subcontinent on India, and expressed their readiness to support Pakistan. They also endorsed the appeal of the UN Secretary-General for a cease-fire, and indicated that they were prepared to put contingents of their armed forces at the disposal of the United Nations as peacekeeping forces. (Telegram 274 from Ankara, September 10; ibid.)

[5] Printed from a copy that bears this typed signature.

200. Telegram From the Embassy Office in Pakistan to the Department of State[1]

Rawalpindi, September 10, 1965, 1005Z.

52. Deptel 312 to Karachi.[2] Suspension military aid shipments to Pakistan and India.

I saw FornMin Bhutto in Rawalpindi 5:30 p.m. Sept 9 to deliver text Mahon Congressional statement (Deptel 310 to Karachi).[3] Transmittal this report on meeting delayed by difficulties of night work and movement owing to blackout and curfew with added handicaps incident to removal of 500-lb. Indian dud bomb from environs Embassy residence last night.

Bhutto read full text which I delivered to him and listened attentively to my exposition of what the action did and did not signify.[4] After long pause he described our action in tone of foreboding as a fateful one which adhered to, would mean that Pak–U.S. relations could not be the same again. He termed the decision an act not of an ally and not even that of a neutral. Rather, it was an act which would be of net benefit to the Indian side. He argued that India with its varied sources of foreign supply, its larger domestic armaments industry and its greater industrial capacity and reserves could stand the loss of U.S. supply flow far better than could Pakistan, which had placed all of its reliance on the U.S. and was almost totally dependent on this one source. Attrition was already becoming a problem for the Pak forces and attrition would soon have a ruinous effect on Pakistan's ability to defend itself if U.S. decision not reversed. Said Paks would fight on to finish with sticks and stones and with bare hands if necessary, but their ability to hold back Indian attack would be vitally undermined by this U.S. blow. He asked to convey the earnest plea of the GOP for reconsideration.

---

[1] Source: National Archives and Records Administration, RG 59, Central Files 1964–66, POL 27 INDIA–PAK. Secret; Immediate. Repeated to Karachi, London, New Delhi, USUN, and CINCMEAFSA for POLAD, and passed to the White House, USIA, DOD, and CIA.

[2] See footnote 2, Document 194.

[3] See footnote 3, Document 190.

[4] On September 10 the Department also sent notice to Karachi and New Delhi that effective September 10 no further commercial licenses for the export of munitions to India and Pakistan were to be issued. In addition, all shipments of munitions to the two countries for which valid licenses had been issued but which had not left the United States were stopped. (Telegram 350 to Karachi, also sent as telegram 427 to New Delhi; National Archives and Records Administration, RG 59, Central Files 1964–66, POL 27 INDIA–PAK)

Bhutto said that if U.S. intent by this action was to put pressure on Pakistan to compel it to accept UNSYG's proposals, we would be disappointed, for pressure effort would have exact oppsite effect. GOP would now be even less inclined than before to accept proposals which would not contain assured provision for withdrawal of Indian armed forces from Kashmir and exercise of self-determination right by Kashmiris. Pakistan would not respond to the kind of pressure inherent in the U.S. action.

Bhutto gave an impassioned account of history of Kashmir troubles with India over last four months beginning with May 15 Indian occupation of posts on Pak territory near Kargil and ending with outright Indian invasion of territory of Pakistan proper across international border on Sept 6, which had introduced an entirely new dimension into the conflict. This was a deliberate act of aggressive war which had to be treated apart from the Kashmir fighting. Pakistan stood at a historic crossroads and was fighting for its very existence against a total Indian challenge. It was crucial for allies and friends of Pakistan, among which the U.S. came first, to understand this and to respond. Pakistan could not fathom U.S. refusal to see the case of her ally in the hour of that ally's trial and victimization by Indian aggressor, an aggressor that had never had any regard for the U.S. and had never assumed any commitments to or done anything for the U.S. He pled with us to stop the Indian aggression by cutting off economic assistance to India, including PL–480 food, until India terminated the aggression against Pakistan. Argued that action just announced by U.S. would be of only minor consequence to Indians, but a disastrous reverse to Pakistan. It would reward the aggressor and brand the U.S. as unwilling even to follow a neutral course toward a beleaguered ally. No one could deny that Pakistan had been attacked on her own undisputed territory on Sept 6 and was engaged in a fight for her national existence. Was this not an exercise of legitimate self-defense?

Bhutto bitterly recounted Indian cruelties and repressions against Kashmiris on both sides of CFL, stating that Shastri govt far more vicious than Nehru govt in exterminating and deporting Muslims, facilitating influx of Hindu migrants, trying to rub out distinctive indigenous character Kashmir state and people, and re-introducing worst aspects of old Dogra regime.

I sought to stem Bhutto tirade by pointing out that we were convinced that action was for preservation of Pakistan as well as subcontinent as a whole; that unconditional acceptance now by Pakistan of Security Council's and SYG's proposals would in any event protect Pakistan from victimization by superior military power of India; that our action was not punitive or threatening, but an unwillingness (demanded by U.S. public opinion and feelings of humanitarianism) to fuel a destructive conflict totally irreconcilable with the principles of peaceful negotiation and settlement which we believed were the only ones which would work. I told Bhutto it seemed to us that GOP was refusing to abandon the resort to force unless it attained in advance full agreement to its basic objectives as to Kashmir. It was not sensible to assume that this most intractable of world issues that has defied all solution efforts for 18 years could be settled now by the attachment of a Pakistani-prescribed rider to a cease-fire agreement. It would not be politically conceivable for any Indian government to concede the whole basic issue in relation to cease-fire agreement. The cease-fire and withdrawal by both sides would have to come first and Pakistan would need to take it on faith that a most resolute and concentrated multilateral effort to achieve a negotiated peaceful settlement would be mounted immediately thereafter.

Bhutto said with conviction that it would not be possible to ask the brave Pakistani soldiers or the Kashmir freedom fighters who had sacrificed so much to accept a capitulation by the GOP to the old status quo which would certainly mean a repetition of the intolerable delays, defiances, and deceptions of the Indians over the last 18 years, with even greater ruthlessness and intransigence to be expected from the Indians after their success. The Indians were demanding cease-fire terms which would fully consolidate their strangle hold on Kashmir. Pakistan could never accede to such terms, or accept a formula which would render meaningless all the sacrifices of those patriots standing fast against India oppression. I said the GOP must be aware of the fact that our decision not to fuel the conflagration on either side was not only the decision of the Executive branch but of the Legislative branch and the U.S. people as well, a decision which the GOP should not expect to be changed in present situation. If unhappy contingency arose where India would be in position of defying UN after Pakistan accepted SC and UNSYG proposals, an entirely new situation would be created which would have to be examined on its merits.

Bhutto put in a plea for permission for Pakistan to buy for cash the necessary military supplies from the U.S. to keep its defense machine going, if the U.S. adhered to its position that it could not continue the flow on the usual grant basis. He said the Pakistanis would sell all their possessions, even their family heirlooms in order to get the means to continue the struggle until the Indian invasion repulsed and Kashmiri rights established. Pakistan would somehow obtain the necessary means of continuing the struggle by one means or another.

I told him he knew the matter with us was not one of dollars and cents in this hour of trial but of doing the best we could to stop the holocaust and start the search for a peaceful settlement which could endure.

The difficult meeting ended on a somber note with an oppressive feeling on my part that more ominous developments may be in the air.[5]

McConaughy

---

[5] McConaughy sent a more detailed account of the conversation to the Department on September 11 in telegram 444. (Ibid.)

---

201.   Telegram From the Embassy in India to the Department of State[1]

New Delhi, September 11, 1965.

576. In response to what he described as urgent request I called on Pres Radhakrishnan Saturday afternoon at 5. He said he had great deal on his mind and covered wide variety of subjects. Following are highlights:

1. At session with U Thant tomorrow India is prepared to say at outset that it fully accepts Security Council resolution to pull back its troops all along line providing Pakistan pulls back theirs including infiltrators they have introduced into Kashmir. Since infiltrators have been returning in large numbers to Azad Kashmir during last few days latter question seemed more manageable than it might have been week ago.

President added that there might be some continuing negotiations in regard to few sections of Azad Kashmir including Kargil and Haji Pir Pass which controls strategic transportation routes into Kashmir Valley, or within Valley. However he did not think this needed to be sticking point.

Solution might lie in adjustments along ceasefire line where India could compensate Pakistan for strategic areas they have in mind. Or if this were not acceptable to Pakistan he thought India would agree to accept guarantee of more adequate controls by UN.

President added that U Thant was staying with him, and that he looked forward to some good talks.

---

[1] Source: National Archives and Records Administration, RG 59, Central Files 1964–66, POL 27 INDIA–PAK. Secret; Immediate. Repeated to USUN, Karachi, London, and the White House. The telegram does not indicate the time of transmission; it was received at 2:55 p.m.

In response I stated that we welcomed willingness of Indians to accept Security Council resolution, and I understood India's conviction that military question be detached at this stage from Kashmir political problem. However I wondered if India could not offer Pakistan some concession in political field such as proposal for two year cooling off period during which each country would seek to improve atmosphere on subcontinent through cultural exchanges, elimination of propaganda and radio attacks, etc. At end of this cooling off period it could be agreed that outstanding economic and political questions would be discussed by series of committees and commissions.

Radhakrishnan replied that he personally could see no objection to this suggestion although he did not think that it was possible to agree to the Kashmir adjustments that Pakistan has in mind. Best solution would be changes in present ceasefire line, but even this could not be tackled in present heated atmosphere; no Indian govt could survive that agreed to give up any Kashmir soil under these conditions.

2. Against background of Swaran Singh's statement last night that India was trying to keep fighting at minimum during U Thant visit, I asked about reports seeping into Delhi of heavy casualties and losses on both sides. Radhakrishnan stated that Swaran Singh was correct in that India was not attempting to advance but rather was fighting from strong defensive positions. Paks had attacked persistently with heavy commitment of their armored strength and except for one small area had been repulsed. He added that morale in Pak army seemed to be deteriorating rapidly. Twelve Patton tanks had been captured today when their crews deserted; two others had surrendered.

I asked the President if any casualty figures were available and he said confidentially that Indians had lost 8,000 killed. When I expressed surprise at this high figure, he said the Pak losses had been significantly heavier. When I pressed to get count of prisoners, wounded, etc., he retreated from his original estimate, saying that he might have been wrong. (*Note:* This is much higher than any other figure we have had thus far.)

3. President stated he was worried about what seemed to him clearly provocative action Pak Air Force was now taking in East Pakistan. It was to India's obvious interest to neutralize East Pakistan and confine fighting to western front. However hotheads in Pak Air Force were doing their best to stir up Indian military on grounds that major fighting in East Pakistan would help to bring Chinese into war.

I made strong plea for India to exercise moderation, pointing out that most important thing right now is to be sure politicians control military and that India is not led into blunders by military men who were oblivious to political realities.

At this point Radhakrishnan rang bell by his chair and when one of his military aides entered room, he said, "Please ask the Air Marshal (meaning Arjan Singh) to call on me at 6 pm." I remarked that President seemed to be exercising his prerogatives as CIC. President replied that although he was not directly involved in military questions he was in position to play moderating role and he knew that Arjan Singh would listen to him.

4. Conversation turned to question of China. Radhakrishnan said Indian Govt is deeply worried about possibility of Chinese attack, particularly because language of recent Chinese note was reminiscent of threats India had received in early fall of 1962. If attack should come, what could India expect from US?

I responded that our actions would no doubt depend on conditions existing at that time. In view of our long efforts to contain ComChina over last twenty years we obviously had no desire to see them overrun Assam or any part of India. At same time we had no desire to underwrite total war on subcontinent. Therefore much would depend on genuineness of India's efforts to reach agreement with Pakistan so that bulk of her resources could be used against China. I stressed that I could not speak for President, that I was only giving him my offhand personal view. Radhakrishnan stated that he fully understood and thought that my analysis was fair.

5. President stated India was also worried about Indonesia, Turkey and Iran. In case of Indonesia Indians had made official request to Soviet Union to cut off spare parts, ammunition and other supplies as we had done in case of India and Pakistan. So far GOI had not received reply.

In regard to Turkey and Iran, India hoped that we would not permit shipment of arms obtained under CENTO.[2] He understood that Iran was also intending to supply Pakistan with petroleum products.

He then repeated Swaran Singh's request of last evening that we publicly urge all nations not to send equipment to either Pakistan or India on grounds that by supplying belligerents war would be more likely to spread.

6. Pres Radhakrishnan then brought up submarine which we have loaned to Pakistan. What could we do to stop Paks from using our submarine to blow up Indian shipping?

---

[2] Ambassador Nehru called on Secretary Rusk on September 11 with an urgent request for a U.S. public statement opposing outside intervention in the conflict. Nehru cited reports that Turkey and Iran might supply Pakistan with military equipment obtained from the United States. (Telegram 429 to New Delhi, September 11; ibid.)

I explained that we were in dilemma because Pakistan could just as easily argue that we should withdraw radar equipment which we had previously loaned to Indians. Under circumstances we thought best thing to do was to steer clear of whole subject since we are unable to enforce original agreements with either govt.

7. President asked whether I thought Paks could be persuaded to accept Security Council resolution as India intended to do. I replied that from all indications Paks intended to push hard for Kashmir political agreement as condition for ceasefire.

Radhakrishnan said GOI had unverified reports that Ayub Khan was being pushed out or at least into background and that Bhutto and Musa might seize power with purpose of continuing war to bitter end. He earnestly hoped that this rumor was false.

Comment: I gather that President's general purpose was to inform me that India was prepared to accept U Thant's proposals and he was hoping that I might have something to tell him about intentions Pakistan.

Bowles

---

202. Editorial Note

On September 12, 1965, President Johnson and Secretary of Defense McNamara again discussed developments on the subcontinent during a telephone conversation.

Johnson: "What do you think about the India–Pakistan thing?"

McNamara: "I'm pleased that it hasn't erupted to a higher level of military action than it has. I really don't know how it's getting along. Our intelligence is—I don't mean CIA necessarily—I mean information we get through our military sources and diplomatic. That's really not very good. I don't know exactly how the battle is going. What little information I do have on it indicates to me that the Paks are ahead at this point."

Johnson: "Yes, that's the way it appears."

McNamara: "And my own impression of the relative military strengths of the two countries is that the Paks could continue to achieve military advantage for a period of, I'd just guess off-hand 4 weeks.

And then at the end of that period I would think that the total strength of the Indians in terms of men and equipment, which is roughly four times that of the Paks, would begin to be felt. And then by the end of say 12 weeks, if the conflict continues that long, I would expect the Indians to reverse the trend and then be in a militarily advantageous position."

Johnson: "What about the Chinese? That's the 64 dollar . . . ."

McNamara: "We don't have any real evidence, and I think we would have if there had been substantial moves. We don't have any real evidence that they're building up strength on that Northeast Frontier Agency border. And we've been very anxious to get more intelligence, we've worked out a plan to do it with some U–2s. I think this will give us advance notice of any movement of men or equipment up there. And there has to be some movement before they can effectively intervene. They can intervene with a few advance days of preparation on their part, and I think they would just clean up that area—push the Indians out if they chose to do so. I rather doubt they'll choose to do it. It's very dangerous for them to do so. My own view is that it almost certainly would involve Western support to India, which China would like to avoid. The great danger here, it seems to me, is the weakening, if not destruction of the Indian political institutions as a result of this."

Johnson and McNamara then briefly discussed the threat to Indian political institutions.

Johnson: "What about our continuing to send in economic help, food to both of them while they're fighting?"

McNamara: "I'd put it off a little while, Mr. President. I think you're going to have to send the food a week from now, or two weeks from now, but you don't have to do it today. I just don't see how you can avoid sending food to really starving people."

Johnson: "Well, you know damn well as Napoleon says, an army runs on its belly. And you know that they're going to go right to the army."

McNamara: "No. No, I don't think so. The food's going to the army anyhow. There's not going to be any food shortage in the army, whether you send food or not. But on the food, as I said, you don't have to decide today. You probably don't even have to decide it a week from today." (Johnson Library, Recordings and Transcripts, Recording of Telephone Conversation Between President Johnson and Secretary of Defense McNamara, September 12, 1965, 9:26 a.m., Tape F65.02, Side B, PNO 1)

203. Memorandum From Robert Komer of the National Security Council Staff to the President's Special Assistant for National Security Affairs (Bundy)[1]

Washington, September 13, 1965.

Mac—

Pak/India Food. You wanted a reminder before meeting with President.

I'm solid with State/AID and embassies in believing that if Pak and Indian public came to believe we were using food as an instrument of pressure, it would be a real setback to our influence.

We can tell roughly when an actual pinch might occur—*but the real problem is psychological.* At what point, in their current emotional state, will the Paks and Indians start accusing us of using food as a weapon? Bowles thinks this could "blow sky high in another week or so," and I'd stick with the judgment of the man in the field in this case.[2]

The trick is to keep on using food as leverage by only dribbling it out slowly, but to do so in time to forestall *public* reactions. Thus we keep the GOI and GOP worried (as they already are by our stalling), yet don't give them or anyone else a handle to accuse us of using starvation as a weapon. It could also help trigger communal riots.

State/AID recommend a million ton (two month) extension for India and 350,000 tons (under existing agreement) for Paks, which would carry them till about December—mostly for East Pakistan. *I'd favor just cutting both in half—but doing it now!*

RWK

---

[1] Source: Johnson Library, National Security File, Name File, Komer Memos, Vol. II. Secret.

[2] When Bowles saw Subramaniam on September 12 the latter warned that if a disastrous situation affecting the welfare of millions of people in India was to be avoided the Indian Government had to know what to expect from the United States in the way of P.L. 480 grain shipments. (Telegram 580 from New Delhi, September 12; ibid.) Bowles underlined Subramaniam's warning in a personal cable to Komer the same day, in which he cautioned: "We must know soon where we stand on PL 480 as this situation can blow sky high in another week or so." (Telegram 121340Z from New Delhi; ibid., Country File, India, Exchanges with Bowles)

204. Editorial Note

On September 15, 1965, President Ayub sent a letter to President Johnson explaining Pakistan's response to the cease-fire proposal made to India and Pakistan by UN Secretary-General U Thant on September 12. Thant's proposal called for a UN-supervised cease-fire to take effect on September 14. Thant asserted that the Security Council would then explore, as a matter of urgency, means and methods of achieving an enduring peace between India and Pakistan. Ayub explained in his letter to Johnson that Pakistan did not oppose a cease-fire. But he argued that a cease-fire that did not provide for a self-executing arrangement for a final settlement of the Kashmir dispute would merely reestablish an unacceptable status quo, and would have the effect of rewarding Indian aggression. (National Archives and Records Administration, RG 59, Central Files 1964–66, POL 27 INDIA–PAK) Accordingly, Pakistan rejected the cease-fire proposal on September 15. (Telegram 72 from Rawalpindi, September 15; ibid.)

In a press conference for foreign correspondents on September 15, Ayub called on President Johnson to bring the influence of the United States to bear on the conflict to bring it to a halt. (Telegram 69 from Rawalpindi, September 15; Johnson Library, National Security File, Country File, India, Agenda Points, September 17, 1965)

India responded to the Secretary-General's cease-fire proposal on September 14. The Indian response, in the form of a letter from Shastri to Thant, constituted a qualified acceptance of the cease-fire proposal. India was prepared to accept the proposal as put forward by U Thant, but only if it was amended to deal with the problem of armed infiltrators into Kashmir. India alleged that Pakistan had triggered the crisis by training and introducing infiltrators into Kashmir, and Shastri's letter stated that any cease-fire that did not mandate the removal of all such infiltrators and provide for India to deal with any subsequent infiltrators, would not settle the crisis and would not be acceptable. (Telegram 643 from New Delhi, September 15; National Archives and Records Administration, RG 59, Central Files 1964–66, POL 27 INDIA–PAK)

205. Special National Intelligence Estimate[1]

SNIE 13–10–65   Washington, September 16, 1965.

PROSPECTS OF CHINESE COMMUNIST INVOLVEMENT IN THE
INDO-PAKISTAN WAR

Conclusion

We believe that China will avoid direct, large-scale, military involvement in the Indo-Pakistan war. An impending Pakistani defeat would, however, substantially increase the pressures for Chinese entry. Even in this circumstance we believe the chances are better than even that the logistic problems involved and the primacy of Vietnam in China's interests would keep China from undertaking a major military venture against India. In addition to propaganda, political support, and military gestures, China will probably offer material aid, but it probably cannot deliver more than token amounts. It will make threats and there is an even chance it will make small-scale military probes across the Indian frontier; the odds that it might launch a limited-objective attack similar to that of 1962 are somewhat lower. In either case it would expect to produce political and psychological effects far greater than the military importance would justify.

[Here follows the 11-page Discussion portion of the Estimate.]

---

[1] Source: Central Intelligence Agency, Job 79–R01012A, ODDI Registry of NIE and SNIE Files. Secret; Controlled Dissem; Sensitive. According to a note on the cover sheet, the estimate was prepared by the CIA and the intelligence organizations of the Departments of State and Defense, and the NSA. All members of the U.S. Intelligence Board concurred in the estimate on September 16 except the representatives of the Atomic Energy Commission and the Federal Bureau of Investigation, who abstained because the subject matter was outside of their jurisdiction.

206.   Letter From Prime Minister Shastri to President Johnson[1]

New Delhi, September 16, 1965.

Dear Mr. President:

Ambassador Nehru has reported to me the sympathetic hearing which you gave him when he delivered my last message to you regarding the present conflict between India and Pakistan.[2] I am sending this further communication to you to keep you informed of subsequent developments and to share with you, on a personal level, my thoughts and concerns about the trend of events.

2. As you doubtless know by now, I indicated to the Secretary-General the willingness of my Government to agree to an immediate cease-fire without any pre-conditions, while acquainting him with our stand on certain issues. One of the features of the Pakistani invasion is that it includes large numbers of armed personnel who are not in uniform for whom Pakistan disowns responsibility, although there is unquestionable evidence to show that they have, in fact, been equipped, organised and directed by Pakistan. This is a new technique of aggression to deal with which no effective weapons have yet been designed by the international community. Even so, as I have said, I was agreeable to a cease-fire if Pakistan also agreed to it. While I do not know the precise nature of President Ayub's reply to U Thant, the fact remains that there has been no cease-fire and the fighting continues.

3. I notice from President Ayub's press conference that he regards Pakistan to be engaged in a life and death struggle with India. All I can say is that so far as we are concerned, we consider it to be in our interests to see the people of Pakistan prosper and to live in friendship with India. We are not out to destroy Pakistan, but to protect our own territory from repeated attacks.

4. President Ayub, in his press conference, also stated that what he really wants the U.N. Security Council to do is not to deal with the issues raised by Pakistani invasion, overt and covert, but to lend support to Pakistan's fantastic claim over the State of Jammu & Kashmir. This claim is based on Pakistan's assertion that since the majority of the inhabitants of the State of Jammu & Kashmir are Muslims, the State should have acceded to Pakistan and not to India.

5. The Indian nation consists of people who subscribe to different religious beliefs—Hindus, Muslims, Sikhs, Christians, Parsees, as well

---

[1] Source: Johnson Library, National Security File, Country File, India, Shastri Correspondence. No classification marking. The letter was sent to the White House on September 17 under cover of a note from Ambassador Nehru.

[2] See footnote 2, Document 195.

as tribal peoples living in this country from prehistoric times, who speak different languages, almost as many as are spoken on the continent of Europe. We have, in fact, as many Muslims in India as there are in West Pakistan. In India, as in the United States of America, people of different origins, different races, different colours and different religions, live together as citizens of a state in which, despite the stresses and strains which do develop in a mixed society, the Constitution and the laws guarantee equal rights to all citizens. You yourself, Mr President, have made, in recent months, a tremendous contribution in your own country to the task of giving adequate legal protection to a racial minority. It is through national solidarity, rather than through the mischievous doctrine of self-determination, the minorities can find their fulfilment.

6. The reason why, when in 1947, we first went to the Security Council with a complaint of aggression against Pakistan, we made a unilateral promise of having a plebiscite in the State of Jammu & Kashmir, was that, at that time, the State had no democracy, having been under the rule of a prince in the British days, and we were anxious ourselves to be satisfied that the people, as distinct from the ruler, genuinely favoured accession to India. Ever since the accession of the State, we have been building up democratic institutions. There have been three general elections in conditions of freedom. The results of these elections have demonstrated clearly that the people of Jammu & Kashmir have accepted their place in the Indian Union. I should like to state quite categorically that there can be no further question of any plebiscite to ascertain the wishes of the people of Jammu & Kashmir. Furthermore, I would assert that the relationship between a federal government and its constituent states is no matter for any other country or for the Security Council. If President Ayub feels that by launching an invasion on the State of Jammu & Kashmir, he will pressurize us into ceding any part of the State of Jammu & Kashmir, all I can say is that he is grievously mistaken. Much though we love peace, we shall not buy it by selling our territory.

7. The real question before the U.N., the Security Council and the international community, as a whole, is not of the State of Jammu & Kashmir, but that of restoring peace which was broken once again by Pakistan, and of ensuring that the boundary line between India and Pakistan is not repeatedly violated either by regular troops or by those in disguise.

8. President Ayub has made an appeal to the United States to use its influence for the restoration of peace. I very much hope, Mr President, that the United States will do so. I think the first essential for this is to prevent the conflict from spreading. Pakistan, as you know, has appealed to many nations for help: to western powers in the name

of its alliances, to middle-east and Arab countries in the name of religion, as well as to Indonesia and China on the basis of the philosophy of which these two countries are the main exponents. I hope, Mr President, you will find it possible to make it clear to Pakistan that the neutrality which you have, for understandable reasons, maintained in this conflict so far, will have to be modified if other powers begin to join it directly or indirectly. That Pakistan is anxious to spread the conflict is evident from the fact that despite further declaration that we do not want to see any fighting start in East Pakistan, it is making repeated air attacks from East Bengal on Indian air bases, particularly those which are vital for our defence against China.

9. Before leaving India, the Secretary-General left with me a letter throwing out various suggestions for the restoration of peace, his efforts to bring about a cease-fire having failed. One of them is a meeting between President Ayub and me. I do not see how, while the armies of the two countries are locked in combat, the heads of two governments could start a dialogue across the table. You can imagine the effect it would have on the morale of our troops and our people who are solidly behind them. Quite apart from that, I cannot quite see what such a meeting might possibly lead to. As you know, in 1962 there was a meeting between President Ayub Khan and Pandit Jawaharlal Nehru when it was agreed that there should be meetings between ministers followed by a summit. We did have a number of meetings between the foreign ministers of two countries, but their positions were so far apart that it became pointless to think of a meeting at the level of heads of government.

10. The Secretary-General has also put forward the idea of mediation by the Secretary-General himself, or by any power friendly to both countries. The difficulty about this too is that what Pakistan wants is not a mediation to bring about an end to fighting and to restore peace without losing face, but mediation in respect of Pakistan's claim to the State of Jammu & Kashmir which we cannot possibly accept.

11. I do not question that even after the present fighting has come to an end, there will remain many issues between the two countries which will continue to create ill-feeling and give rise to friction. We have always felt that this is an unfortunate state of affairs and with better relationship and greater cooperation between the two countries, their economic progress, which is the prime task before them, and in which your great country has been helping so much, will be accelerated. Such an improvement in the relationship between the two countries is eminently desirable, but it would need at least a couple of years of real peace on the borders and a willingness on the part of Pakistan not to align itself in any way with the main threat against India, namely

China, before any efforts to improve overall relations between two countries can really become fruitful.

Yours sincerely,

Lal Bahadur[3]

---

[3] Printed from a copy that bears this typed signature and an indication that the original was signed.

---

207. Telegram From the Embassy in India to the White House[1]

New Delhi, September 16, 1965, 1027Z.

655. For President Johnson. In view of many difficult problems that are crowding your plate I hesitate to communicate with you directly except under most urgent circumstances. However we have thus far had no reply to numerous messages on future PL 480 shipments and since we have now reached crisis point I believe such communication is justified.

PL 480 shipments to India have been coming in under sixty-day agreement signed July 26. Under this authorization the last shipments of foodgrains is scheduled to stop by end of October. Even if we should sign renewal agreement today, there would already be a gap between this date and arrival of shipments under new authorization.

In spite of massive increase in India's foodgrain production of nearly 11 percent last year, situation in regard to food supplies and food prices has been serious. Increases in purchasing power, burdens on transportation system plus whisperings of hold-up in US supplied grains are starting to lead to scare buying, hoarding and rise in prices.

If under these circumstances PL 480 shipments were to stop, be curtailed or delayed, situation could quickly get out of hand. Food riots in major cities managed by Communists would be inevitable. As they put out word that growing shortages were caused by sudden stoppage of food shipments from USA to low income Indian families public antagonism would become dangerously inflamed.

---

[1] Source: Johnson Library, National Security File, Country File, India, Vol. V, Cables, 6/65–9/65. Secret; Immediate; Exdis. Repeated to the Department of State, with the request that it be passed to the Department of Agriculture for Freeman.

Although agitation against US would not affect abilities of Indian Army in Punjab it would profoundly affect USG in Delhi and all that we have been working for here since India became independent.

Ever since fighting started on August 5 I and members of US Mission in Delhi have been bringing to bear every argument and every pressure to influence India toward course of moderation in regard to a Pakistan settlement while at same time seeking to buttress their faith in USA. Yesterday Indian Govt in spite of its growing military advantage agreed unconditionally to an immediate ceasefire. If following the all-out effort our Mission has been making here and GOIs affirmative response to U Thant request, USG should hold up urgently needed food shipments, our influence in India will [be] grievously eroded and Soviet influence increased.

With Soviet SAMs protecting Delhi and other cities from attack by Pak MAP-procured B–57s, Soviet tanks fighting US tanks in Punjab and additional MIGs apparently on their way, Soviets have already made deep inroads.

In my previous messages I had strongly recommended a 15 month extension, since this would enable Indians to make major advances in their agricultural policies which we have been supporting. In view of importance of helping India become self-sufficient in food I still believe this is proper decision. However, if USG feels that now is not the appropriate time to conclude such a long-term and substantial agreement I strongly urge you to authorize me to sign sixty-day contract. This would assure flow of food ships until latter part of December.

I have already been pressed hard for our decision by able, dedicated, highly pro-American officials who are responsible for Indian agricultural policy and who recently sent communication to Secy Freeman expressing determination to make India self-supporting in regard to foodgrains by 1971. Following GOI action yesterday in unconditionally accepting U Thant's proposal for ceasefire these pressures will now be redoubled.

Because I did not know whether you were familiar with the problem I have gone into some detail. I assure you, however, that I am not crying wolf.

Bowles

208.   Telegram From the Department of State to the Embassy in India[1]

Washington, September 17, 1965, 6:13 p.m.

498. Following based on uncleared memorandum of conversation and is FYI, Noforn and subject to revision upon review.

Indian Ambassador Nehru called on Secretary September 17 to deliver letter from Shastri to President[2] regarding Indo-Pak fighting. In addition, based on phone call he had had from Foreign Minister Swaran Singh, Nehru requested:

1) That USG make formal statement warning Chicoms that US will intervene if Chicoms attack India; said formal warning desired to supplement helpful informal statement already made by Secretary.[3] Nehru said GOI hopes such formal warning by US would prevent Chicom intervention.

2) That US come to India's assistance if Chicoms attack; said nature of such assistance would be for US to decide. Secretary said request for formal US statement warning Chicoms re intervention involves major US decision and said that decision make formal warning statement would subsume decision provide assistance in event of Chicom attack, since warning would have no credible deterrent effect if not backed by decision to act. Secretary said only President can make this decision, and told Nehru he would discuss matter with President as soon as possible. Secretary said that, in context Indian request for US warning statement and decision intervene in event of Chicom attack, in our view it of greatest importance that fighting between India and Pakistan be stopped somehow.

3) That as requested in Shastri letter US "neutrality" re Indo-Pak fighting will be modified if other outside powers intervene. Nehru said that India's unconditional acceptance of U Thant's appeal for unconditional ceasefire puts India in the clear and GOI feels it has now gone along with Security Council resolution. Nehru added that Foreign Minister Singh told him to request that US posture in Security Council

---

[1] Source: National Archives and Records Administration, RG 59, Central Files 1964–66, POL 27 INDIA–PAK. Secret; Immediate; Exdis. Drafted by Lakeland, cleared by Laise, and approved by Handley. Repeated to Karachi, London, Hong Kong, Moscow, USUN, CINCSTRIKE/CINCMEAFSA, DOD, CIA, and the White House.

[2] Document 206.

[3] On September 15 Rusk made a statement at a press conference warning China to stay out of the conflict between India and Pakistan. See *The Washington Post*, September 16, 1965.

take into account threat posed to India in latest Chicom note,[4] and that US modify "neutral" position it thus far has adopted re Indo-Pak fighting.

Secretary asked whether it was GOI position that Kashmir not even discussible, and to what extent settlement of Kashmir problem is war aim of both India and Pakistan. Nehru replied that settlement of Kashmir issue not an Indian war aim. He said, however, GOI cannot discuss anything with Pakistan at this time and GOI cannot agree as condition to any settlement ending fighting that it will discuss status of Kashmir; said situation must go back to status quo ante bellum and Paks must get their forces out of Kashmir. Nehru said there no man in India today who can agree to discuss Kashmir.

In response to question whether in requesting US assistance in event of Chicom attack India invoking Air Defense Agreement, Nehru replied he had no specific instructions as to nature of assistance US might provide.

In reply to question whether GOI thinks Chicoms would violate demarcated international boundary in Sikkim, Nehru replied that Chicom ultimatum "raised everything—the whole border."

Referring to request for formal statement warning Chicoms against intervention, Secretary told Nehru we had used occasion of last Cabot–Wang talks in Warsaw to warn Peking about interfering in Indo-Pak fighting.[5]

In closing Secretary said he would discuss Shastri letter and Indian requests for formal warning statement, and for US agreement provide assistance in event of Chicom attack, with President and get in touch with Nehru as soon as possible. Nehru reminded Secretary that time limit on Chicom ultimatum runs out on Sunday.[6]

Comment: It apparent Shastri letter written before receipt Chicom note; Nehru request for US support vis-à-vis Chicoms made orally, based on his conversation with Foreign Minister this morning.

Rusk

---

[4] Reference is to a September 16 note from the Chinese Ministry of Foreign Affairs to the Indian Embassy in Peking. The note reiterated China's support for "the right of the Kashmiri people to self-determination" and China's support for Pakistan in its fight against the "unbridled aggression" of India. The note reviewed the boundary dispute along the border between China and Sikkim and closed with a demand that India dismantle all of its military works along that border within 3 days of the delivery of the note. The text of the note is printed in *American Foreign Policy: Current Documents, 1965,* pp. 752–754.

[5] The meeting between U.S. Ambassador to Poland John M. Cabot and Chinese Ambassador to Poland Wang Kuo-chuan took place on September 15. For a report of the meeting, see *Foreign Relations,* 1964–1968, vol. XXX, Document 101.

[6] September 19.

209.   Record of Meeting[1]

Washington, September 17, 1965, 6 p.m.

UNCLEARED SUMMARY OF WHITE HOUSE MEETING ON SOUTH ASIAN PROBLEMS

PARTICIPANTS

    The President
    Secretary Rusk
    Secretary McNamara
    Under Secretary Ball
    Mr. Raborn
    Ambassador Thompson
    Assistant Secretary Sisco
    Mr. McGeorge Bundy

The President decided the following on the Indian-Pakistan situation:

1) We would continue to give the strongest support to the Secretary General and the Security Council. He approved the current draft of the resolution.[2] In general we are to emphasize publicly the efforts that we are making through the UN here at the Department and in New York.

2) No messages would go from the President to Ayub and Shastri for the time being. This might be reviewed in light of whatever Security Council action is taken.

3) Both Defense and State should develop contingency plans on possible next steps for the President's review.

4) No preparatory military moves should now be made in the area.

5) George Ball is to prepare a memorandum giving the pros and cons on whether we should cut off food supplies.

6) [8 lines of source text not declassified]

With respect to the three questions the Indians have put to us[3] and which have now become public knowledge, George Ball will brief Greenfield on the following line: That the Indians have discussed with us their concern over the Chicom development; we have discussed with them our concern in this regard; and that we will take note of these as we pursue our policy within the Security Council.

---

[1] Source: National Archives and Records Administration, RG 59, Central Files 1964–66, POL 27 INDIA–PAK. Secret; Sensitive; Exdis. Drafted by Sisco in IO.

[2] Apparent reference to a draft of the resolution adopted by the Security Council on September 20 which demanded that a cease-fire between India and Pakistan take effect on September 22. (UN doc. S/RES/211)

[3] See Document 208.

210.   Circular Telegram From the Department of State to Certain Posts[1]

Washington, September 17, 1965, 5:22 p.m.

420. Joint State/AID Message. Pakistan Consortium.[2]

1. *World Bank Position.* Bank has been querying Consortium members this week on their views and plans concerning pledging session scheduled September 23. The Bank leadership had previously informed the Department on most confidential basis that it did not see how the Bank/IDA could make a pledge until the situation in the subcontinent is clarified.

2. *UK Position.* British Embassy informs us that London considers atmosphere for September 23 meeting basically affected by the hostilities; basis on which Pakistan aid requirements previously discussed has been altered; therefore it believes it would not be advisable hold Consortium meeting next week; hopes Bank will agree and so inform GOP.

3. *US Position.* Our most critical concern at this time is to obtain ceasefire. To that end we giving all support to efforts of UNSYG under UNSC resolutions September 4 and September 6. On September 8 we suspended military aid shipments to both India and Pakistan and informed both Governments accordingly. Subsequently, we have suspended all licenses for commercial shipments of military items to both countries. However, shipments are continuing in accordance existing agreements under economic aid program, including PL 480.

Pending enactment FY 66 aid appropriation, the Administration has in general not been making any new economic aid loans or grants since beginning FY 66, and both India and Pakistan have been affected. Current hostilities raise important new issues. Secretary has assured Congress that Administration would consult with appropriate members of Congress on situation in subcontinent in connection with making new economic loans or grants to either India or Pakistan. (Representative Mahon, Appropriation Committee Chairman, read out the Secretary's assurances during House debate aid bill September 8.)

---

[1] Source: National Archives and Records Administration, RG 59, Central Files 1964–66, AID 9 PAK. Confidential; Priority. Drafted by Sidney Sober, cleared by Mann's staff assistant James D. Johnston and Macomber, and approved by Handley. Sent to Bonn, Brussels, The Hague, London, Ottawa, Paris, Rome, and Tokyo, and repeated to Canberra, Karachi, New Delhi, and Rawalpindi.

[2] In telegram 530 from Karachi, September 17, the Embassy emphasized the importance of the scheduled consortium meeting. Because of the Kashmir crisis and the growing sense of isolation from Western support felt in Pakistan, the Embassy warned that the decisions taken with respect to the consortium meeting would be magnified in importance in terms of U.S. relations with Pakistan and Pakistan's foreign policy orientation. (Ibid.)

We have come to conclusion that under present circumstances we not yet in position make pledge on current year's aid level for Pakistan. Present US position does not in any way indicate lessening our interest in economic development of Pakistan. We hope for an early return to situation in which we could again pledge our support for its economic development program.

4. Subsequent to British approach to us, AID Regional Assistant Administrator Macomber on September 16 informally indicated to representatives major Consortium member countries our concurrence with British position and explained US thinking as outlined 3. above.

5. Believe Macomber's discussions have met our general requirements for consultation with Consortium members. However, in addition, if you deem desirable in light queries addressed to you, you may inform host government that US has given very serious consideration to question of pledge and draw on above to describe situation as we see it. Any approach you make should be in low key so as avoid impression we applying pressure other Consortium members.

6. Will inform you further developments soonest.[3]

7. Separate instruction will follow for Karachi/Rawalpindi.

Rusk

---

[3] On September 22 the Department sent a circular telegram to the same posts indicating that the World Bank had decided to postpone the Pakistan consortium meeting scheduled for September 23. (Circular telegram 459; ibid.)

---

211.   Telegram From the Embassy in India to the Department of State[1]

New Delhi, September 18, 1965, 1255Z.

698. L.K. Jha reports that Chinese movements in battalion strength on Eastern border of Ladakh and in Chumbi Valley indicate that Peking is getting ready for military action. GOI therefore asks if we would be

---

[1] Source: National Archives and Records Administration, RG 59, Central Files 1964–66, DEF 1–1 INDIA–US. Secret; Immediate; Limdis. Repeated to USUN, DOD, Karachi, London, Hong Kong, CINCMEAFSA, and the White House and passed to DOD, CIA, and USIA.

willing on strictly covert basis to authorize US personnel to consult with Indian military planners on contingency basis.

Jha stressed that this action need not imply favorable US response to India's request for help if Chinese attack. However, if an attack should come it could speed up effective assistance by several days.

We have personnel here who are qualified to open such discussions. I recommend that we be authorized to proceed with strict understanding that no US commitment is involved.[2]

Bowles

---

[2] The Department responded that the United States was not prepared to initiate contingency planning. A decision taken at the "highest level" was to avoid commitment of any sort pending the unfolding of the situation. In discussions with the Indian Government, the Embassy was instructed to indicate that the U.S. commitment in Vietnam was heavy and increasing. Effective defense of the subcontinent, from the U.S. perspective, depended on the internal strength of India and Pakistan, and the conflict between the two countries undermined that strength. It was essential that India move toward a rational solution to the problems, including Kashmir, that divided and weakened the subcontinent so that it could face the major threat from China. (Telegram 513 to New Delhi, September 18; ibid., POL 27 INDIA–PAK)

---

212.   Telegram From the Embassy Office in Pakistan to the Department of State[1]

Rawalpindi, September 18, 1965, 1128Z.

82. For immediate personal attention of the Secretary. I flew back Rawalpindi this morning on urgent intimation from Shoaib he needed see me. With new Pak restrictions on activities of all diplomats, he was not supposed to receive me without official being present to record conversation. To evade this he had to telescope private and sensitive part of conversation into about four minutes when we were alone while note-taking officer was being summoned.

His message was to effect that Ayub wants to reject Chinese overtures and come down on U.S. side in confrontation now shaping up.

---

[1] Source: National Archives and Records Administration, RG 59, Central Files 1964–66, POL 27 INDIA–PAK. Secret; Flash; Exdis. Repeated to Karachi, and passed to the White House, DOD, and CIA. McGeorge Bundy sent a copy to the President at 10:30 a.m. under cover of a note that reads: "This is the despatch I mentioned on the phone." (Johnson Library, National Security File, Country File, Pakistan, Vol. V, Cables, 9/65–1/66)

But Ayub must have some high-level U.S. statement which he can use as basis for his decision. Recurring theme voiced by President last night was "Why do U.S. actions seem designed to push me toward the Chinese? I don't want to sit in Chinese lap, and I won't do so if it can be avoided. But if U.S. can't give me any help, I'll have no choice."

Shoaib said a "gesture" from the U.S. would be sufficient to turn the tide at this moment. When I pressed him to identify the kind of "gesture" that he had in mind, he indicated that an authoritative U.S. statement attaching responsibility to India for original violation international border on September 6 would suffice. In a vaguer vein he indicated that some U.S. public statement of intention to use its influence to bring about an actual implementation of Kashmir position traditionally taken by U.S., as that position was outlined by Secretary Rusk September 14, would also give President Ayub the basis he feels he needs. Shoaib said he felt that action was required in about next 24 hours, which would point to a relationship between Pak decision and expiry of ChiCom ultimatum to GOI.

With fateful consequences depending on U.S. and Pak decisions next 36 hours, this hasty, incomplete and second-level statement of far-reaching request is not adequate. I urge that I be given instructions by return Flash message from the President to have it out with Ayub as to precisely what he seeks from us and where he stands.

It will be crucially important for me to be instructed as to what if anything I can say by way of private assurances to Ayub that India will be required to show some flexibility in considering a political solution of the Kashmir question, as a condition of any prospective U.S. assistance against Communist China. It is doubtful that Pakistan can be held in line without some assurance to this effect.

McConaughy

213. Editorial Note

During the course of a conversation on September 18, 1965, with Ambassador Goldberg concerning efforts being made by the UN Security Council to bring an end to the conflict in South Asia, President Johnson outlined the U.S. position he wanted emphasized at the United Nations.

Johnson: "We think the Pakistani people ought to have a cease-fire 'til we can pull this thing—we think India ought to do it. What's sauce for the goose is sauce for the gander. Hold the two of them, be equal to both, strictly neutral, pull them together, no threats. But they just can't afford to have this World War III. . . . They can't have that kind of crime around their necks."

Johnson indicated that he wanted Goldberg to make it very clear that the United States was fully behind the United Nations in its efforts to deal with the crisis.

Later in the conversation, Johnson ruminated about the Kashmir crisis and its bearing on the decision he had to make concerning the provision of grain supplies to offset drought on the subcontinent.

Johnson: "I've got to make up my mind whether I'm going to send about 35 million a month in giveaway food to India. And if I do, I've got to continue to Pakistan. It runs about 475 million people, it involves about a million tons for every two months. I think that we oughtn't to be shipping munitions or food or anything else to them while they are in this difficulty. Furthermore, I think until they come here, and we sit down and have an agreement, India's got 470 million worth of reserves, and there's no reason why they can't pay for their wheat if they can pay for munitions. Napoleon said an army fights on its belly, and I don't see any reason for doing it, although State Department and all the people want us to continue to give away. They say there'll be a bunch of riots if we don't. But I think it might be—I don't know if we got an obligation the rest of our lives just to ship them 10% of what they eat. And not without even having agreement or discussions, or tying in any alliance, or to be sure of serving our national interests. They say if you don't, they'll go to Russia. Well, I think it might be a good thing if Russia did a little of it for a while. . . . But they're pressing me a good deal, and I've got to make a decision in the next few hours."

Goldberg, in response to the President's question, advised against cutting off the flow of food to the subcontinent. Instead, he proposed an oil embargo to bring an end to the fighting. Johnson did not respond to Goldberg's suggestion. He reverted to the decision he had on his desk concerning food for India.

Johnson: "I'm humane, but I don't have to feed the world. I'll sell them anything they want to buy. I haven't got any inherent or constitutional requirement that I know of to furnish it to them ad infinitum. On July 27, I said now I'll give you a million tons extra, which will give you two months. And you come here and we'll talk about our national interests and your national interests. That two months is up September 27. This is September 19. [sic] And of that million tons that I gave them on July 27, 630,000 have been shipped to India. The balance will be shipped next month. But additional wheat must be authorized or purchased now if the flow of the pipeline is not to be interrupted, since it takes at least 10 days or two weeks to contract for the wheat. An additional month for ocean transport. We are therefore in a position where delay beyond four or five more days in authorizing an extension of P.L. 480 shipments would mean a break in the supply line and a shortfall of supplies later this fall."

Near the end of the conversation, Goldberg speculated that, in light of the Indian acceptance of the cease-fire proposal, there was the possibility that a cease-fire could be achieved within the next 48 hours. Johnson therefore concluded that his decision concerning food for India could wait for 2 or 3 days. (Johnson Library, Recordings and Transcripts, Recording of Telephone Conversation Between President Johnson and Ambassador Goldberg, September 18, 1965, 1:27 p.m., Tape F65.04, Side A, PNO 1)

---

214. Telegram From the Department of State to the Embassy Office in Pakistan[1]

Washington, September 18, 1965, 6:21 p.m.

83. For Ambassador from Secretary. Ref: Your 82.[2] You should not seek an interview with Ayub, but you should convey clearly to Bhutto, Shoaib and to any others whom you think useful, and who would communicate accurately to Ayub the following:

1. The Chinese ultimatum and the rumors of Chinese troop movements puts Ayub squarely against a critical problem of choice. If he should encourage, or even—by failing to agree to a cease-fire—create the situation that produces Chicom intervention, he will have alienated himself from the West. This is not a threat but a reality. If the Chicoms do intervene,[3] the world will place the blame for that action on Ayub's failure to agree to the cease-fire.

---

[1] Source: National Archives and Records Administration, RG 59, Central Files 1964–66, POL 27 INDIA–PAK. Secret; Flash; Exdis. Drafted by Ball, cleared by McGeorge Bundy, and approved by Rusk. Repeated to London, New Delhi, USUN, DOD, CIA, and the White House.

[2] Document 212.

[3] Komer told Ball in a telephone conversation on September 19 that the President was pleased to learn that the Chinese had extended the deadline in their ultimatum to September 22. Johnson intimated that the Chinese extension was due to U.S. pressure, an apparent reference to warnings against Chinese involvement in the conflict on the subcontinent passed by Cabot to Wang and by Rusk in his September 15 statement to the press. (Johnson Library, Ball Papers, Pakistan, 4/1/64–8/16/66)

2. At the same time, the threat of Chinese intervention provides Ayub the opportunity to move off his present position of rejecting a cease-fire. He can take the position that the dangers of escalation involved in these Chinese moves make it imperative that the Indo-Pak conflict be stopped. Such a declaration should not result in any loss of face on the part of Pakistan since Pakistan is not threatened directly by the Chicoms. The world would tend to view such action as statesmanlike.

3. At the same time we recognize that the basic causes of the conflict cannot be disregarded. For that reason we are helping to obtain Security Council action calling for India and Pakistan to utilize all peaceful means including those listed in Article 33 of the Charter to bring about a permanent solution of the political problems underlying the conflict and supporting the proposal made by the Secretary General calling for a meeting of the two heads of government including the possibility of using the good offices of the Secretary General and other third parties under the auspices of the UN.

4. While this matter is under consideration in the Security Council, it is of utmost importance that Pakistan put itself in as favorable position as possible in world opinion. India so far has the political advantage because it has unconditionally agreed to the cease-fire. The threat of Chicom escalation affords Ayub the opportunity to move toward the same position without sacrifice of dignity. If he does so, the possibility for serious Security Council action toward a permanent solution of the problem will be greatly enhanced.

5. The Pakistanis will undoubtedly raise with you their wish for U.S. assistance in pushing Indians toward negotiations on Kashmir, and their "need" for some form of U.S. reassurances on continuation of aid. You should say on both of these points that you are without official instructions and that you are concerned[4] that Washington cannot make any useful comment on these matters until it has some clear indication that Ayub is not casting his lot with Communist Chinese at a moment of decisive importance for the future of the free subcontinent. You should add as your personal opinion that it is your judgment and the judgment of men close to the President, with whom you have been in touch, that once the firing is stopped and President Johnson is convinced that renewed U.S. assistance will be used to help the people of Pakistan and not to support military adventures, you believe that close and mutually helpful relations between the U.S. and Pakistan can quickly be restored. But you should express your absolute conviction that President Johnson is not the sort of man who will ever give his

---

[4] The Embassy was instructed, in telegram 84 to Rawalpindi, September 19, to change "concerned" to "convinced." (National Archives and Records Administration, RG 59, Central Files 1964–66, POL 27 INDIA–PAK)

approval to one thin dime for a country which supports or encourages the aggressive pressures of Red China.[5]

For USUN: We would like to have the same position conveyed privately and in confidence by Ambassador Goldberg to Amjad Ali.

Rusk

[5] Since Ambassador Ahmed was in New York, Ball and Komer called Pakistani Minister of Embassy Iftikhar Ali off the golf course on September 19 to convey the message outlined in telegram 83. (Memorandum from Komer to Bundy, September 19; Johnson Library, National Security File, Name File, Komer Memos, Vol. II; Memorandum of telephone conversation between Ball and Komer, September 19; ibid., Ball Papers, Pakistan, 4/1/64–8/16/66)

215. Telegram From the Embassy Office in Pakistan to the Department of State[1]

Rawalpindi, September 19, 1965, 1400Z.

84. Indo-Pak crisis—SC Kashmir. I have just come from private meeting this afternoon with Shoaib, which we arranged at home of mutual Pakistani friend, where we were able to talk freely, escaping restrictions on calls at government offices where in Shoaib's words, "semi-police state atmosphere now prevails." Shoaib told me he had a long private session with President last night and he is greatly encouraged by increasing moderation of President's attitude. He described President as disenchanted with Bhutto's reckless adventurism, grieved at Pak losses, strongly averse to entering any Chicom association and open to a sensible compromise way out. Shoaib said President growingly aware of Bhutto's extremism though Bhutto's job not now in jeopardy. Shoaib said President vetoed Bhutto's projected trip to New York for current SC session because he felt Bhutto would not show sufficient balance.

Shoaib said much as President wants to compromise issue with India quickly, he cannot give an accounting to the people of Pakistan with nothing to show for the sacrifices entailed. President believes he would fall if he had to admit to failure, and Shoaib agrees with him.

[1] Source: National Archives and Records Administration, RG 59, Central Files 1964–66, POL 27 INDIA–PAK. Secret; Immediate; Limdis. Received at 12:17 p.m., and passed to the White House, DOD, CIA, and USIA at 1:10 p.m. Repeated to London, New Delhi, USUN, Karachi, and CINCMEAFSA.

Shoaib said GOP recognized that problem was to find a fair median position on the operative paragraph in SC resolution on Kashmir[2]—a compromise which both Pakistan and India could live with. He recognized that India could not live with unqualified provision now for plebiscite and withdrawal of all forces from occupied Kashmir. Pakistan could not live with simple cease-fire and freeze in status quo ante.

Shoaib recommendation as minimum alternative which he believes President could buy and then sell to Pak people, is as follows: a provision in operative paragraph of the Security Council resolution which would call for settlement of all principal outstanding issues between India and Pakistan, "including Kashmir" or "such as Kashmir."[3] He said Pakistan could accept provision along this line with a mere illustrative reference to Kashmir. He felt confident India could also accept this, since Kashmir had been mentioned before by agreement in joint documents, announcements, and resolutions.

I told Shoaib of my earlier conversation with Bhutto and how far out and unrealistic his proposals were.[4] I was greatly encouraged to hear of Shoaib's far more sensible approach, which gives us something to work on which is inside the park at least. I told him I would send off an urgent message on this and would hope the suggestion would provide a new take-off point.

I believe this really modest proposal by Shoaib which undoubtedly has President's tacit approval, gives us new hope for saving the situation here. It offers the modicum of nourishment which Paks must have to enable them to back off from the brink. I urge its most careful, sympathetic and (for all believers) prayerful consideration.

McConaughy

---

[2] Reference is to Resolution 211 adopted by the Security Council on September 20. For text, see *American Foreign Policy: Current Documents, 1965*, pp. 805–806.

[3] Resolution 211 included the following language: "Convinced that an early cessation of hostilities is essential as a first step towards a peaceful settlement of the outstanding differences between the two countries on Kashmir and other related matters." (Ibid.)

[4] McConaughy reported on his conversation with Bhutto and Aziz Ahmed on the morning of September 19 in telegram 85 from Rawalpindi, September 19. McConaughy stated U.S. views as instructed (see Document 214). According to McConaughy, Bhutto's response was "hard-nosed and disquieting." He indicated that Pakistan would not agree to a simple cease-fire without some undertaking on the merits of the dispute or some action to liquidate Indian aggression. Bhutto stated categorically that Pakistan had no secret understanding with China, and he denied that the Chinese ultimatum imposed any obligation on Pakistan to accept a cease-fire agreement. He offered Pakistani acceptance of an immediate cease-fire on the basis of an agreement by India and Pakistan to withdraw all their armed forces from Kashmir, an agreement underwritten by the United States. McConaughy said that it was not realistic to put such a proposal forward seriously, and Bhutto responded that it was meant seriously. (National Archives and Records Administration, RG 59, Central Files 1964–66, INDIA–PAK)

216.   Telegram From the Department of State to the Embassy in India[1]

Washington, September 19, 1965, 7:19 p.m.

518. Deptel 513 to New Delhi.[2] Following based upon uncleared memcon. It is FYI, Noforn and subject to amendment upon review.

Under Secretary Ball called in Amb B.K. Nehru Sept 19 to respond to GOI requests which Ambassador had put to Secretary Sept 17 (Deptel 498)[3] and which L.K. Jha had made to Amb. Bowles Sept 18.

After discussion state of play in New York, Amb. Nehru asked if USG had decided upon course following SC action. Under Secretary replied US placing great emphasis upon giving UNSC every chance work out subcontinent crisis. Said this was case in which bilateral diplomacy has great limitations particularly since US has friendly relations with both India and Pakistan. Said he would not wish predict future US course.

Under Secretary commented that Indians had replied to Chicom note in statesmanlike manner. Chicom response now gives more time. Remarked that there may be some benefit in Indian admission of existence "structures".

Amb Nehru admitted there were such "structures" and claimed they had been unoccupied for 3 years. Said there seemed be difference between Indian estimate of Chicom forces deployed along Indian border (his figure was 150,000) and considerably lower US estimate. We replied our estimate was about 67,000 in Tibet including 5–6,000 in Ladakh plus about 20,000 in Sinkiang. Nehru said India not particularly concerned about Chicom attacks through Chumbi Valley, but was worried about possible Chicom move through Karakoram Pass into Pak held Kashmir. From this side Chicoms could attack in vicinity Kargil and cut off India division in Ladakh by cutting Srinagar–Leh road. Amb Nehru said GOI convinced there was Pak–Chicom collusion.

Under Secretary read from Tass story reporting that Kosygin had invited Shastri and Ayub meet on Soviet soil to discuss conflict.[4] Nehru

---

[1] Source: National Archives and Records Administration, RG 59, Central Files 1964–66, POL 27 INDIA–PAK. Secret; Immediate; Limdis. Drafted by Schneider and approved by Handley. Repeated to Karachi, London, USUN, CINCMEAFSA, Hong Kong, Rawalpindi, the White House, DOD, and CIA.

[2] See footnote 2, Document 211.

[3] Document 208.

[4] Kosygin sent letters on September 17 to Shastri and Ayub, which were published in *Pravda*, inviting them to meet on Soviet territory to resolve the conflict, with the participation of Kosygin if desired. (Telegram 948 from Moscow, September 21; National Archives and Records Administration, RG 59, Central Files 1964–66, POL 27 INDIA–PAK)

explained this offer, which was for meeting at Tashkent, had been made some time ago. Did not indicate nature Indian reply.

Under Secretary then referred to GOI request USG give warning against Chicom attacks. Stated we believe there would be grave dangers in such action since Chicoms might consider this challenge they would have to take up. We had raised matter at Warsaw talks and Chicoms have undoubtedly taken our probable reaction into consideration.

Under Secretary mentioned heavy US commitments in Southeast Asia. Said defense of subcontinent had been weakened by Indo-Pak conflict. Consequently we were concentrating on ending fighting so Indo-Pak differences can be sorted out. Sorting out will depend upon GOI's willingness talk about outstanding problems.

Nehru interjected this hard for GOI to do. When Paks "hold gun" to India, it can't agree such proposal. Under Secretary replied Paks asking for plebiscite; we recognize this would be difficult. But world would recognize statesmanship of Indian agreement to some kind of talks on range of differences with Pakistan. Amb Nehru then referred to last set of scheduled Indo-Pak talks which he said Paks had cancelled. Said GOI had been hopeful Rann of Kutch agreement forecast favorable turn Indo-Pak relations but then infiltrations began in Kashmir. Said India not seeking military solution India-Pak problems; but Pakistan was. Current fighting meant it would take long time arrange rational settlement. India wants to get unconditional cease fire and consider talks about many disputes with Pakistan afterwards.

Under Secretary then addressed himself to L.K. Jha's proposal for secret contingency discussions with GOI (New Delhi's 698).[5] (Amb Nehru unfamiliar with this matter. We explained it was confidential proposal put directly to Amb Bowles by L. K. Jha.) Under Secretary said we were not prepared undertake joint contingency planning at this time. Such discussions of what would be militarily effective against Chicoms would involve USG on side Indians and create ambiguity about US position in Indo-Pak conflict. If Chicoms attack, we would wish take another look at situation under consultation provision of Air Defense Agreement. In meantime we wanted Indians' best appraisal of situation through normal continuing discussions between US and Indian military in India.

Amb. Nehru inquired re Indian request for end US suspension MAP and sales shipments. Under Secretary replied he saw no possibility of US lifting suspension to India and not Pakistan, as Indians asked. Noted that this would destroy whatever influence US had with Pakistan and push Paks further toward Chicoms.

---

[5] Document 211.

Toward end conversation, Amb Nehru changed subject and asked, "why are you trying to starve us out?" Under Secretary replied this was matter we were currently looking into and we hoped have decision in one way or the other in day or two. Pointing to "extreme urgency" of food shipments, Ambassador said India needed resumption by Sept 25.[6]

At close conversation Amb Nehru said Education Min Chagla would be returning to Delhi Sept 19 and would probably come back to New York later. Said he had received no word that Swaran Singh planning special trip here but that presumably he would be coming for UNGA.

Rusk

---

[6] On September 19 Ball sent a memorandum to President Johnson recommending an extension of the existing P.L. 480 agreement with India for 1 month. He also recommended permitting purchase authorizations for Pakistan for 1 month. "This would hold them on a short tether and keep them worried." (Johnson Library, National Security File, Name File, Komer Memos, Vol. II) Telegram Aidto 392 to New Delhi, September 22, authorized the Embassy to negotiate an interim agreement with the Indian Government for 500,000 tons of wheat to meet urgent needs. It was anticipated that the agreement would cover 1 month of India's import requirements. (National Archives and Records Administration, RG 59, Central Files 1964–66, AID (US) 15–8 INDIA)

---

217.   Telegram From the Embassy Office in Pakistan to the Department of State[1]

Rawalpindi, September 20, 1965, 1200Z.

91. Indo-Pak crisis. I saw President alone at his request for 35 minutes beginning 1230 hours today. President showed strain from pressure of issues now bearing down on him. But he was calm, affable and outgoing although distressed. Following covers essence with secondary points to follow in septel.

He reaffirmed his deep conviction U.S. must play decisive role in surmounting present crisis and thereafter. Said Russians have been trying to seize settlement initiative, which should and still can belong

---

[1] Source: National Archives and Records Administration, RG 59, Central Files 1964–66, POL 27 INDIA–PAK. Secret; Flash; Limdis. Repeated to Karachi, USUN, London, New Delhi, CINCMEAFSA for POLAD, Tehran, Ankara, the White House, DOD, and CIA. Also passed to USIA.

to U.S. Thought U.S. actions recently have weighed heavily against Pakistan, although he knew it was not always intended that way. U.S. silence and inaction at various critical moments had also hurt. Chinese Communists expressing sympathetic sentiments in crisis which Paks do not want from ChiComs, and which had been expected from U.S. after events of Sept 6. Pak people bound to be somewhat influenced by contrasting ChiCom and Pak [U.S.?] records last two weeks despite their instinctive aversion for Communists. He said "Hindus" with their usual clever trickery and self-righteousness had given ChiComs opportunity to exploit tragic hostilities—opportunity which would never have arisen if Indians had not opened up international aggression for first time two weeks ago. Indians had again put Paks, rather than themselves, on spot with U.S. He regretted it had not been made clear to all before Sept 6 that international aggression was entirely different and more serious thing from clashes in disputed territory of Kashmir resulting from Kashmiri resistance to Indian oppression. If U.S. had warned early that any crossing of international boundary into territory proper of other by either India or Pakistan would not be tolerated, present dangerous opportunity opened up for Chinese Communists would never been created.

I focused conversation on implications of ChiCom ultimatum and on inescapable and imperative requirement for unconditional cease-fire under UNSC resolutions. I said without arguing background, position at this moment is that ChiComs have it within their power to put Paks in impossible situation unless GOP moves before expiration of ChiCom ultimatum to reject threatened Chinese intervention and implement unconditional cease-fire with India. Anything short of this would put Paks in position of seemingly abetting or at least passively benefiting from ChiCom aggression against India. This would be posture which USG and people could not accept. It would be impossible for Paks or anyone else to prove ChiComs had not been influenced in their decision by Pak failure to disassociate themselves. Such Pak position could not be defended before American Government and people, and I did not know how we could get back on our traditional basis after such a disaster. I asked President if he had been fully informed by Bhutto and Shoaib of my talks with them preceding day (based on Deptel 83 to Rawalpindi).[2] President said he had been fully posted and he understood the message.

President said he had just received partial report of UNSC action of last night. I said Sept 22 was shaping up as critical day, both as to acceptance UNSC resolution and as to ChiCom ultimatum. Pak action

---

[2] Document 214.

to disassociate itself from ChiCom designs needed to be taken before that time. I did not see how President Ayub and his govt could live down a failure to take this action. Even a semblance of Pak association with ChiComs in exertion of Communists military pressures on any free country would put Pakistan beyond reach of U.S. help.

President said with deep feeling that there was no Pak collusion or even consultation with ChiComs. There was no understanding between them and he had no knowledge of ChiCom intentions. All he knew of their moves was what he read in the world press. President then informed me that he had "recently" sent a message to Peiping telling ChiComs, "For God's sake, do not come in. Do not aggravate the situation."

I told him this information was significant, and I wanted to cite it in my report of the conversation. I asked him if he could expressly assure me that we had quite recently transmitted such a message to the Chinese Communists, and did he authorize me to quote him directly to this effect? President replied, "Yes, I do, except leave out 'for God's sake'."

I said way seemed open for President to follow through in the sense of his message to ChiComs and I urged him to do forthwith. He answered that he would give the most earnest thought to cease-fire decision to take effect next day or so. Great obstacle was Pak public opinion. He asked, "How can I survive an action which will look to the people as if we are giving up on Kashmir, just to help the Indians, with justice for the Kashmiris within our grasp?" "After all the sacrifices that have been made, how can I explain a decision to throw it all away with nothing but another UN resolution to show them?" He expressed grave concern that he and his government could not stand in the face of the expected violent public reaction. "The people would not understand." I told the President that if I knew anything about the people of Pakistan—their ideals, beliefs and convictions—after $3^1/2$ years here, I knew that they understood the inherent evil of Communism and its antipathy to every principle of Islam. I believed that even the rank and file Pakistani people without educational opportunities had learned from their mullahs that nothing good could come out of Communism. I believed the people would understand and reject the evil Communist motivation, which aimed at eventual disaster for Pakistan and Kashmir, as much as for India. I believed he could carry the people with him in a decision for national integrity and peace, and for the well being and continued development progress of the people of Pakistan in association with her true friends.

President said he agrees with my estimate of the inherent distrust of Communism on the part of the people and their understanding of its complete incompatibility with Islam. Still the people considered China to be less of a threat to Pakistan than were India and the USSR. He could not be sure that he could survive what would seem almost universally to be a decision to sacrifice the first national objective for the apparent purpose of helping an India which had not righted its wrongs.

I said the reality was far different and the people could be brought to sense this. I expressed a profound conviction that with his unrivaled place in the hearts and the confidence of the people of the country, he could carry them with him. I assured the President that the U.S. would do everything at its command to support him in any difficulties which might grow out of an affirmative decision by him on the UNSC cease-fire call and on the repudiation of ChiCom intervention. I told him that if it had ever seemed that the Kashmir settlement question was treated with a measure of resignation by the friends of Pakistan and India, it could never be so treated again after the fires through which we were now passing. President Ayub could count on a new sense of urgency in the international approach to this issue, if the GOP played its part in this hour.

In bidding me an affecting good-bye, President put his hand on my shoulder and said "God bless you," words which I repeated to him.[3]

McConaughy

---

[3] In the assessment of this conversation, sent to the Department in telegram 94 from Rawalpindi, September 20, McConaughy expressed concern that although Ayub seemed to be leaning in the direction of accepting a cease-fire "in a Hamlet mood he might find himself unable to make the decision." (National Archives and Records Administration, RG 59, Central Files 1964–66, POL 27 INDIA–PAK)

---

218. Telegram From the Department of State to the Embassy Office in Pakistan[1]

Washington, September 21, 1965, 12:19 a.m.

92. For Ambassador from Secretary.

1. You should seek an urgent appointment with Ayub on the grounds that you have reported your last conversation and have received further instructions.

---

[1] Source: National Archives and Records Administration, RG 59, Central Files 1964–66, POL 27 INDIA–PAK. Top Secret; Exdis; Flash. Drafted in the White House on September 20, and cleared by Ball, Handley, Deputy Assistant Secretary David H. Popper (IO), Komer, and McGeorge Bundy. Approved and initialed by Rusk. Repeated to New Delhi and USUN.

2. You should say to Ayub that his assurances with respect to his personal attitude toward Chinese Communist intervention have been received with great satisfaction in Washington. Unfortunately, the international political requirements cannot be met only by a private assurance alone. The U.S. public and world opinion too will inevitably assume Pak/Chicom collusion if the Chicoms move at a time when the Paks have not accepted the Security Council cease-fire demand.

3. The Security Council resolution is the product of intensive efforts by the U.S. delegate in which Indian and Soviet pressures were resisted sufficiently so that Kashmir is specifically mentioned in the preamble and SC consideration of how to reach a settlement is foreshadowed in operating Paragraph 4.[2] These two important changes are seen among best friends of Pakistan in Washington as providing the necessary footing for the Pak decision to accept the resolution. We regard Pak acceptance of this resolution as absolutely fundamental to restoration of peace in the area and do not see how Paks can get more until hostilities stopped.

4. The US supports every part of this resolution; so the GOP can be certain that, if the cease-fire is accepted, the US will not neglect its responsibilities under operative Paragraph 4. Indeed the US will expect to conduct its relations with the two parties with a careful eye to their own readiness to move forward with the efforts foreshadowed in that Article. However, you should avoid giving any impression that we are committing ourselves to support any particular form of negotiated settlement, or that we will cut off the Indians if they do not accept one. If necessary, you should make this very clear. What we are talking about is the readiness of the US to sustain the position that settlement of the underlying problem is needed, and that both parties should address themselves to that problem in good faith.

5. Without engaging the President directly, you should make it very clear that men closest to him here are convinced that Pak acceptance of SC resolution will clear the way for early man-to-man discussion between Ayub and President Johnson which could have most constructive effect on Pak/US relations. In fact, should President Ayub choose to couple visit to Washington with personal appearance at UN, we would warmly welcome this.

6. We do not fully understand significance of Bhutto visit to UN, but if Ayub should speak of Bhutto's mission in terms suggesting a

---

[2] Paragraph 4 of Security Council Resolution 211 of September 20 indicated that as soon as a cease-fire agreement was in effect the Council would consider the steps that could be taken to assist toward a settlement of the political problem underlying the conflict. (UN doc. S/RES/211)

last minute effort to change sentiment in the Security Council, you should leave him in no doubt that Bhutto is on a fool's errand. Ayub is his own best counsellor at this moment of decision.

Rusk

---

219. Telegram From the Ambassador to India (Bowles) to Robert Komer of the National Security Council Staff[1]

New Delhi, September 21, 1965, 1130Z.

Appreciate your cable[2] and also what I believe to be skillful Washington handling of extraordinarily complex situation which, although full of dangers, may offer certain opportunities for USG to promote its long-term interests in this area.

In regard to food situation I believe it is difficult for anyone not actually on ground fully to comprehend risks involved in further delay in authorizing shipments.

Right now 40 million Indians, most of them low income people living in large cities, are wholly dependent upon US foodgrains. In Calcutta in order to spread dwindling supplies daily rations have already been cut from twelve ounces to ten ounces. Inevitably story is spreading that this has been due to US decision to put squeeze on Indian people to force them to give in to Paks.

GOI and ourselves are doing everything possible to keep situation under wraps. However foreign and US press as well as Indian press are becoming aware that USG is stalling and serious gap in foodgrain supplies will soon result. Question has become not "Will this situation blow up?" but "How soon?"

When it does, impact here would constitute extremely serious blow to US influence at moment of great opportunity. Image in world press as well as in India of USG loaded with wheat putting squeeze on 40 million Indian slum dwellers in order to bring pressure to bear on Indian Govt which is faced with potential two-front war (while shipments continue to Pakistan) would be profoundly harmful; Communists will have a field day.

---

[1] Source: Johnson Library, National Security File, Country File, India, Exchanges with Bowles. Secret; Eyes Only. [text not declassified]

[2] Not further identified.

Very least we should do is to tell Indian Govt, hopefully within next 24-48 hours, that we are providing one million tons of grain and that we will do everything in our power to see that there is no break in arrival of food ships which now are scheduled to run out in late Oct. This arrangement does not have to be highly publicized. GOI would see advantage in treating it as routine matter.

Many thanks for all you have done and are doing.

Bowles

---

220. Telegram From the Embassy Office in Pakistan to the Department of State[1]

Rawalpindi, September 21, 1965, 1450Z.

98. Indo-Pak crisis. Following is advance summary several major points raised by President Ayub during our 40 minute meeting beginning at 5:30 p.m. September 21.[2]

Ayub's apology for mob action against U.S. nationals and facilities,[3] offer of restitution and assurances of future protection was earnest and categorical.

On cease fire he early made statement, "We don't know what decision we will take tomorrow. We must see what major powers really intend doing. That is why we have sent Foreign Minister Bhutto to New York to find out." Ayub said Bhutto was instructed on arrival during Tuesday night immediately to get in touch with Ambassador Goldberg and Soviet and other representatives of permanent members

---

[1] Source: National Archives and Records Administration, RG 59, Central Files 1964–66, POL 27 INDIA–PAK. Secret; Flash; Limdis. Repeated to USUN, London, Karachi, New Delhi, CINCMEAFSA for POLAD, Tehran, Ankara, the White House, DOD, and CIA. Also passed to USIA.

[2] A more detailed report of this conversation was sent in telegram 100 from Rawalpindi, September 21. In this report McConaughy noted that Foreign Secretary Aziz Ahmed was present during the conversation, which prevented the type of intimate, personal exchange that McConaughy had with Ayub the previous day. (Ibid.)

[3] Telegram 573 from Karachi, September 21, reported that the Embassy and the USIS Library were attacked by stone-throwing mobs on September 21. Glass was broken in the Embassy and the library was set afire and seriously damaged before police were able to disperse the mobs. (Ibid., POL 23–8 PAK) The Consulate General in Lahore also reported on September 21 that it had been attacked by a mob on the same day. The Consulate General and a nearby USIS building were damaged. (Telegram 24 from Lahore; ibid.)

of the Security Council. Bhutto was to find out what steps will be taken to move forward with the negotiation for a settlement of the Kashmir dispute. "What are permanent members thinking of doing?", Ayub repeated.

After presentation my message,[4] Ayub expressed gratification. He assured me that he would consider things most carefully and would not do anything irresponsible. He said that while U.S. had direct interest in the outcome, Pakistan's very existence was involved.

However, Ayub again stressed the need to have clarification on how U.S. and other permanent members "intended to proceed and how serious they are to assure a negotiated settlement of the Kashmir dispute." I could not shake him from the idea that he needed a special report from New York by Bhutto on these points before he could make his decision. Ayub said Bhutto would report to him by radio-phone before Security Council deadline for cease fire (3:00 a.m. Wednesday[5] EDT).

McConaughy

---

[4] Reference is to the message McConaughy was instructed to convey to Ayub in telegram 92 from Rawalpindi, Document 218.

[5] September 22.

---

221.   Telegram From the Embassy in India to the Department of State[1]

New Delhi, September 21, 1965, 1800Z.

734. L.K. Jha called tonight (1) to describe Indian position in regard to cease fire resolution and (2) to inquire urgently how US would react to an Indian acceptance in principle of Soviet proposal for mediation.

In regard to Security Council resolution Jha described Indian attitude in following terms:

1. India is worried about Chinese, wants nothing from Paks and is anxious to stop present fighting. Therefore it will agree to an immediate cease fire if the Paks will stop shooting at same time.

---

[1] Source: National Archives and Records Administration, RG 59, Central Files 1964–66, POL 27 INDIA–PAK. Secret; Flash; Limdis. Repeated to USUN, Karachi, London, Moscow, Hong Kong, and CINCMEAFSA, and passed to the White House, DOD, CIA, and USIA.

2. Although India has no desire to hold Pak territory, return to Aug 5 cease fire line without some safeguards creates serious problems. For one thing there should be an agreement in regard to infiltrators, two thousand of whom are still on Indian side of the line.

Moreover India is reluctant to give up positions it has won on Pak side of C.F.L. that cut off infiltration routes and prevent Paks from dominating key roads that are essential to supply Indian troops facing Chinese in Ladakh until some assurances can be provided that further Pak aggression will be prevented.

Jha believes these questions could be negotiated out either directly through Security Council or through General Nimo working with reps of the two nations on the ground.

Jha did not take an inflexible position. The GOI he said felt that while the issues involved were manageable, in view of recent developments they could not be ignored.

On the second point, i.e. Soviet proposal for direct negotiations in Tashkent between Ayub Khan and Shastri with Kosygin acting as mediator, Jha requested at earliest possible moment reactions of USG since it was necessary to give Soviets answer on Wednesday[2] well before Chinese deadline expires.

What, he asked, would we think of such a meeting? Would we consider it helpful, or would it seem to bring Soviets into a role that would not be in US interests? Shastri would appreciate getting our views on highly confidential basis soonest.

Jha added that Kosygin was pushing India hard for a favorable answer. There was a strong view within GOI that it would be advantageous to accept proposal on Wednesday in order to draw the USSR into a more favorable position vis-à-vis threatened Chinese attack.

However Shastri was hesitant to go the whole way. Just as we have shunned summit meetings for which there has been inadequate preparation so he feels confrontation with Ayub Khan in his present mood could not be expected to produce much. Nonetheless Shastri would like to say to the Soviets tomorrow (a) that he accepts in principle but that (b) he would like to carry discussions with Security Council in regard to a settlement somewhat further (c) reserving Kosygin's proposal for a later stage if needed.

I told Jha that although we could not take responsibility for his government's decisions on such a crucial question, we appreciated the Prime Minister's sensitivity for our views and interests, and I would ask my government to provide its informal and confidential evaluation

---

[2] September 22.

as soon as possible, hopefully by the opening of business Wednesday morning in New Delhi. If you can give me your reactions by then I will be grateful.[3]

Comment: Although difficult assess Soviet objectives, this gambit has advantage of bringing USSR into a constructive position vis-à-vis ChiComs. Since Paks likely to refuse, I judge proposal to be dead-end street. Nevertheless exercise demonstrates Indian willingness to negotiate.

Bowles

---

[3] The Department authorized Bowles to respond to Jha's questions concerning the Soviet offer to mediate by expressing appreciation for being consulted, and by indicating that the U.S. Government still considered that the best hope for solution to the conflict lay in action through the United Nations. (Telegram 535 to New Delhi, September 21; National Archives and Records Administration, RG 59, Central Files 1964–66, POL 27 INDIA–PAK)

---

222.   Memorandum From the White House Situation Room to President Johnson[1]

Washington, September 22, 1965, 7 a.m.

India–Pakistan

Pakistan announced acceptance of the UN cease-fire proposal at a dramatic last-minute Security Council meeting last night.[2] Pakistan Foreign Minister Bhutto announced Pakistani acceptance as the 3:00 AM UN deadline was reached. India had already accepted the UN proposal, but the Indian delegate to the UN asked that a new time be set for the cease-fire to become effective in the light of Pakistan's delay in announcing its position. The Security Council later announced that the deadline was extended 15 hours until 6:00 PM today.

Bhutto said Pakistan was giving the UN a "last chance" to settle the Kashmir question and stated that Pakistan would withdraw from the organization if it does not do so.

---

[1] Source: Johnson Library, National Security File, Country File, India, Vol. V, Memos & Miscellaneous, 6/65–9/65. No classification marking. Prepared by Briefing Officer Arthur McCafferty. A handwritten "L" on the memorandum indicates that the President saw it.

[2] USUN reported on this meeting in telegram 861, September 22. (National Archives and Records Administration, RG 59, Central Files 1964–66, POL 27 INDIA–PAK)

Prior to Bhutto's announcement, the US Embassy in Karachi reported that Ayub would have trouble with Pakistani public opinion if a cease-fire was announced. The Embassy noted that to some extent Ayub is a prisoner of the propaganda carried in the controlled Pakistani press in the past several days, but added that public opinion in Pakistan is subject to rapid shifts in sentiment. President Ayub will address his nation sometime this morning.

Replying to Peking's broadcast last night claiming that the Indians had attempted to destroy their old military works along the Sikkim border, the Indians have stated that none of their forces have crossed the Sikkim–Tibet border and that if the installations were destroyed, the demolition must have been done by the Chinese themselves.

Peking has as yet made no comment on the Pakistani acceptance of the UN cease-fire proposal.

Arthur McCafferty

223. Memorandum From the White House Situation Room to President Johnson[1]

Washington, September 23, 1965, 7:10 a.m.

India–Pakistan

The India–Pakistan cease-fire was honored without incident at 6:00 PM last evening and there have been no reported violations since it went it into effect.

Even in "peace" however, Indian and Pakistani statements continue to be diametrically opposed. Indian charges that Pakistan bombed Amritsar—killing 50 civilians a few hours after agreeing to a cease-fire—are refuted by Pakistani statements that the claims are baseless and in fact the Pak Air Force hit only military targets along the road to Amritsar.

Embassy New Delhi estimates that Pakistan has probably had 2,500–3,000 killed and 12,000–15,000 wounded during the fighting while India lost some 2,000 killed and 10,000 wounded.

---

[1] Source: Johnson Library, National Security File, Country File, India, Vol. V, Cables, 6/65–9/65. Secret. Prepared by McCafferty. A handwritten "L" on the memorandum indicates the President saw it.

UN Secretary Thant is wasting no time in gathering a 100-man team of military observers to send to the disputed area. So far Denmark and Canada have each agreed to send ten officers. The new observer group is to be known as UNIPOM, or United Nations India–Pakistan Observer Mission.

The Chinese Communists have allowed their deadline to pass without taking any action against the Indian frontier. Instead, an authoritative *People's Daily* observer article on 22 September claims that Peking's ultimatum has forced the Indians to comply with its demand that they destroy their "military works" on the Chinese side of the border.

The article attempts to keep open the threat of action by claiming that other demands—for a return of livestock and allegedly kidnapped border inhabitants—are still outstanding, and therefore, the "matter is far from closed and accounts must be settled." This language, however, is similar to claims made by Peking for years and does not carry with it the immediacy contained in the recent ultimatum.

The first signs of a relaxation in Chinese Communist military alert status in Western Sinkiang and Tibet may now be in evidence, according to field analysis of Chinese military communications.

[Here follows a brief report about developments in South Vietnam.]

Arthur McCafferty

---

224. Telegram From the Embassy in Pakistan to the Department of State[1]

Karachi, September 23, 1965, 1525Z.

607. Indo-Pak crisis: UNSC ceasefire resolution.

1. President Ayub telephoned me evening September 22 in Rawalpindi for post-ceasefire conversation. He informed me of his phone

---

[1] Source: National Archives and Records Administration, RG 59, Central Files 1964–66, POL 27 INDIA–PAK. Secret; Priority. Received at 2:05 p.m. Also sent to the White House, and repeated to USUN, London, Tehran, New Delhi, DOD, and CIA.

conversation earlier in the evening with President Johnson.[2] He said it was a fair connection and he clearly felt good about the way the conversation went. He expressed his gratitude for the kind sentiments the President had expressed in regard to the ceasefire decision and prospects for peaceful settlement. Ayub said President had very kindly mentioned possibility of his visiting US a few weeks hence when respective schedules might make it possible. Ayub said he had replied that he very much wanted to accept. He would be preoccupied for next two weeks or so with the aftermath of hostilities. But after that, he would need to confer with UNSYG U Thant in New York and he would like to combine that trip with a visit to the President in Washington. Indicated his hope to work such a visit out, although he made no attempt to be specific.

2. Ayub appeared grateful for US efforts to bring about ceasefire, but went out of his way to recall assurances I had conveyed that US would strongly support UN efforts for resolution of Kashmir problem. He said GOP would look seriously to US for significant action to encourage peaceful negotiation. He was confident US influence could be decisive. He said he would expect me as US representative here, who had played active part and knew situation well, to do full share in pursuing implementation of US assurances.

3. I told Ayub he knew we would stand by our assurances, but he also knew the limitations which we had stated. I jokingly upbraided him for keeping me in suspense until last moment as to whether he would agree to ceasefire. Ayub said he was sorry about this but he in truth could not be certain himself until almost the deadline because of his distrust of the Indians and his need for Bhutto's assessment from New York.

McConaughy

---

[2] The telephone call from Ayub in Rawalpindi was taken by Johnson in Washington at 10:55 a.m. Ayub placed the call to inform Johnson that Pakistan had accepted the cease-fire agreement. Ayub added: "We believe that you are a man of honor and a gentleman and will see that an honorable settlement is reached to prevent such unfortunate happenings occurring again." Johnson replied: "You may be sure of the readiness of the United States to support and sustain the position that settlement of the underlying problems is needed and is essential." He added, however, "I cannot give you any assurance of any particular form of settlement." Johnson concluded the conversation by inviting Ayub to visit the United States, and Ayub said that he would as soon as he could arrange it. (Johnson Library, Recordings and Transcripts, Recording of Telephone Conversation Between President Johnson and President Ayub, September 22, 1965, 10:55 a.m., Tape F65.05, Side A, PNO 2) Three slightly variant transcripts of this conversation are in the Alpha series, ibid. An additional transcript prepared in the White House by Juanita Roberts is ibid., National Security File, Country File, Pakistan, Vol. V, Memos, 9/65–1/66.

225. Editorial Note

On September 26, 1965, *Pravda* published a report on replies from Shastri and Ayub to Kosygin's September 17 good offices offer. Shastri expressed appreciation for the offer, but replied that the meeting proposed by Kosygin could only take place after the termination of military actions and the creation of a calmer situation. Ayub also expressed appreciation for Kosygin's initiative, but took the position that the necessary foundation for the meeting should be prepared through actions taken by the UN Security Council. (Telegram 1032 from Moscow, September 26; National Archives and Records Administration, RG 59, Central Files 1964–66, POL 27 INDIA–PAK)

226.   Telegram From the Embassy Office in Pakistan to the Department of State[1]

Rawalpindi, September 29, 1965, 1520Z.

121. Indo-Pak crisis: Sept 29 meeting with Pres Ayub.

A. Cease Fire and Withdrawal.

I met today with Pres Ayub for 55-minute discussion. Also present were FonSec and notetaker. Stull accompanied me. Ayub opened saying didn't know what Indians up to in current half dozen or more major cease fire violations. He said one instance Indians gave Pak frontline commander notice that if he didn't pull out would attack. Paks remained, Indians attacked and were driven back. Maintained GOP knows such Indian actions based on instructions from superior commanders. Said GOP has good info of continuing orders from superiors including Chavan and Chaudhury to Indian forces in Kashmir to press attack wherever possible. Cited one recent instance where Indian unit commander threatened with dismissal if he failed take Pak-held bridge. Asked what is GOI after?

Pres said, however unfortunate war has been, it inconceivable either side can retain international territory of other. Commented, "We are dealing with a diseased people and don't know how much control

[1] Source: National Archives and Records Administration, RG 59, Central Files 1964–66, POL 27 INDIA–PAK. Secret; Immediate. Repeated to Moscow, USUN, New Delhi, London, Hong Kong, Tehran, Ankara, Karachi, CINCMEAFSA for POLAD, Paris, the White House, CIA, DOD, and USIA.

exists at highest level. Chavan wishes to make history now but should have done so during serious fighting." Observed Indians nibbling here and there at cease fire. Referring Indian use air power yesterday in Rajasthan, said PAF desired retaliate soonest but he had responded, "Let's see what they are doing tomorrow." Said GOP dealing with very irresponsible people GOI. His expressed hope that early positioning UN cease fire observers would dampen current violations. Ayub responded GOP can't tolerate Indian actions if they continue too long. I urged Pak forebearance noting restraint would not be lost on world opinion. Ayub noted two-company size Indian attacks at Rajasthan and another Indian attack in southern sector in area where no fighting had occurred previously. Characterized Indians as cowardly enemy observing no rules of decency or of war. I told Pres we had relayed all info and cease fire violations passed US by GOP to Emb New Delhi. Said not surprisingly Indians had alleged violations initiated by GOP. Ayub cited Rajasthan violation, saying Pak forces had held area for two weeks. Stated military withdrawal is matter for mutual governmental agmt and is not local commanders' responsibility. Reiterated top Indian leadership irresponsible and castigated "little man Shastri." I interjected that UNSecGen fully apprised of seriousness cease fire violations, and his public reports should have some deterrent effect. Ayub argued GOP wishes observe cease fire but there must be some understanding between India and Pakistan about disengagement, some understanding as to how it must be regulated, controlled and supervised. Said given such understanding, carrying out those functions little more than routine military exercise.

I asked Pres Ayub whether he favored separate UNMOGIP and UNIPOM operations. Ayub indicated approval, saying Gen Nimmo too old, any event one man can't handle everything, and good idea that observer organizations separate but still interrelated. I observed effectiveness UN observers would depend importantly on caliber personnel and expressed passing hope Latin Americans would have good command English language. Ayub seized on this to suggest gratuitously that Alliance for Progress may have succeeded bringing Latin Americans well under U.S. influence.

I demurred re influence and noted had referred only English-language capability.

I asked Pres Ayub how he envisaged actual arrangements for mutual withdrawal. Ayub responded GOP has told SecGen and "among us" he has agreed that along with arrangements for military disengagement a body should be set up to arrange also for political solution. Ayub pointed to "good example for fruitful negotiations in Rann of Kutch precedent." Said some such sort of arrangement has to be laid on. However, "This thing bedeviled by four powers wanting to go together, and we do not know how that could work." Said small team of people necessary and pointed to British, "who know us" and to Americans, "who also know us a little." Commented French and Sovs appear more or less to agree and perhaps there could be understanding on inclusion a Frenchman. Added while latter would be ignorant of specific circumstances here, that would be all right. Said, "We want some such arrangement like that." I asked if suggested body would not always be under UN auspices? Ayub replied affirmatively (but without enthusiasm). Said UNSecGen should authorize such a team to go and negotiate. Commented skeptically he does not know how much relevant experience SecGen has. Noted "UK has more experience," and "Americans have some experience." Said some initiative necessary to break ice and get things moving gradually. Observed had not spelled out this concept in last week's telephone conversation with President Johnson, but had done so to PriMin Wilson. Reiterated Rann of Kutch good precedent and some such approach could create common ground and understanding for possible later Indo-Pak mtg. He referred Pres Johnson observation that Paks wish U.S. become directly involved, but UN must take that on. Commented, "That's all right with GOP." I asked Ayub if he had in mind something comparable to Dixon, Graham or contemplated Admiral Nimitz' mediatory roles but with broader mandate. Ayub replied, "That's it, that's it!" I asked if any mediation or good office effort would not have to take place after withdrawal. Ayub said, "No, now," adding, "if Indians can't agree, Paks can't either. Looking at future events, one can see that. What we want is withdrawal alongside cooling of tempers." I observed GOI could be expected disagree this Pak position. FonSec interjected if necessary go along with Indian position, there can be no agmt. Ayub said it's in SC resolution and SecGen is to arrange implementation that resolution. FonSec said resolution provides that after cease fire effective withdrawal will be considered and parties at same time will attempt find solution, and resolution calls on SecGen assist this process. Quoted Ayub, that "Military disengagement and political disengagement must go hand in hand. Withdrawal without a settlement will enable Indians procrastinate and preclude settlement."

Pres Ayub commented didn't think Indians for their part would actually withdraw, rather, intended stay in positions in Kashmir. Repeated present need is for cooling off arrangement alongside withdrawal. I asked Pres if he meant Indians would refuse withdraw from wrong side cease fire line. He replied, "Not in a hurry. They are diseased people, and I wouldn't put anything past them." I asked Ayub if he considered withdrawal from occupied national territory and from disputed territory (Kashmir) were separate questions. He replied, "Undoubtedly." I asked if he could envisage a phased withdrawal, and he replied, "That might well be so." I suggested Indians might well insist on single continuous procedure. Ayub replied, "That is why I said political and military must be side by side so both parties will know what is intended. After all, political and military aspects are combined and not separate watertight compartments. Without political arrangement India will not give up its military vantage points, and we will not give up our vantage points either." I remarked this could be interpreted by Indians as holding threat of force over any negotiations. Ayub replied GOP should be using that argument. Said, "I wouldn't be a bit surprised if meaning of these Indian cease fire violations is that GOI seeking to preclude political arrangements. Both we and they have to be reasonable." I interjected there must be concessions each side and Ayub agreed. I pointed out this always had been U.S. position and cited 1963 Ministerial discussions this regard. Ayub agreed and observed that with negotiated settlement one can't have all one wants. "That's why one negotiates." I stressed U.S. has no favorite solution Kashmir problem and Ayub replied, "We do hope you will stick to that position. We also hope you realize your objectives cannot be realized on the subcontinent without a settlement, and we hope you will help bring that about."

B. U.S.-Pak Relations.

President Ayub said, "It great misfortune that what we had been trying to do on your behalf to moderate ChiComs has not elicited word of appreciation from you. We may not have achieved, but we have tried and shall continue to try. These efforts may not be so fundamental, but they must also be considered. We got no credit, rather, I won't say bullying, but something akin to it. On top of that, solemn pledges were almost revoked." I commented US need make no apology concerning fulfillment its pledges to Pakistan. On contrary, US thinks it has fullfilled its pledges. Perhaps not in way evisaged by GOP but effectively and through UN. I told President Ayub what he had said was hard. I pointed out US had maintained many beneficial programs for Pakistan. Ayub continued, "We cannot become Communist, and we don't want to become Indians. The last thing we will accept is Indian dictation. We are prepared to be reasonable and to cooperate with India, but not to be subjected by her. Any policy which aims at the subjection of Pakistan by India we shall fight." I said of course that was fundamental, and we understood and respected this.

Pres Ayub referred to "rubbish of this scheme and that scheme," for example, published in British press (i.e., Victor Anante *Daily Telegraph* article). Asked what good can come for U.S. from saving ineffective weak governments? Said governments must be able to carry populace with them. Referred to unfortunate experiences as, for example, Vietnam escalation. States U.S. can never be driven out of Vietnam, but said question whether viable govt can be established there is bedeviling everybody and this despite military successes. Noted improvement military situation but questioned if also psychological improvement. Questioned if viable govt possible Vietnam and answered saying only possible if U.S. remains there for years. Concluded, "There are these lessons to be drawn about danger of rushing in." I said Viet Cong pressures must first be relieved before favorable psychological climate and stable govt can be assured. Ayub commented that entire structure Vietnam must be rebuilt which means U.S. must occupy country 15 to 20 years. I said "occupation" not accurate word to describe our assistance to Vietnam. Ayub stated it was evident that weak govt always heavily beset by extremist opposition. In civil conflict, he thought that side which has to enlist outside military support always loses. To bolster up govts with outside direct military intervention "always fails." They can be supported with material by outsiders, but they must fight their own battles on their own feet. He conceded my notation that South Vietnamese Army making a pretty good battle record now, and that govts weakened by military insurrections over period of years must have unusual help or be overwhelmed, as was GRC on mainland of China in 1949.

Comment follows in separate tel.[2]

McConaughy

---

[2] McConaughy provided his assessment of the conversation in telegram 123 from Rawalpindi, September 29. He noted that the stiff atmosphere of the discussion was a marked contrast to his meetings with Ayub the previous week. Ayub "seemed to be going out of his way to upbraid the US" for revocation of prior pledges of military support, for failure to appreciate Pakistani efforts to moderate the Chinese, and for something akin to "bullying" of Pakistan. McConaughy speculated on the reasons for Ayub's apparent change of attitude, but admitted that he was at a loss to do so with confidence. He concluded that the Kashmir dispute was the touchstone of U.S.-Pakistan relations. If the Kashmir dispute were resolved satisfactorily, U.S. relations with Pakistan would thrive. (Ibid.)

227.   Telegram From the Embassy Office in Pakistan to the
       Department of State[1]

Rawalpindi, September 29, 1965, 1455Z.

122. U.S.-Pak summit meeting. During meeting today with Pres
Ayub (reported separately),[2] I referred to my instructions follow up on
Sept 23 telephone conversation Presidents Ayub and Johnson with
regard possible Ayub visit to U.S. I said should Ayub go to UN we
would hope and expect he would also visit Washington for talks with
President Johnson along lines their telephone conversation. I invited
him to indicate what precise moves might be possible.

Ayub replied had discussed this matter previous night (presumably in Cabinet). Had decided would like ask UK agree to postponement long scheduled State visit owing to grave emergency situation
facing GOP. Said UK must surely understand reasons for postponement, and he believed President would understand need for postponement of trip to U.S. for same reason. Asked, "Please tell President
Johnson on my behalf my first duty is to my country. With popular
feelings as they are, and you know them, would be most difficult. We
have attempted to damp down these feelings. We have kept U.S. reaction our request for implementation defense agreement secret between
myself and FonMinistry. But, nonetheless, things could possibly get
out of hand. If President Johnson gives me six or eight weeks, I would
be flattered to come. This also what we telling UK. That visit has been
postponed so many times, but I just cannot go. I am not reluctant to
go. It is a question of my inability. President Johnson will understand; he
must understand this. As I told President Johnson during our telephone
conversation, this war is long distance from Washington but nonetheless he cannot leave U.S. My war is much closer to my country, and I
also cannot leave now." I interjected that of course his visit to U.S.
would not be extended State visit, but important short negotiating
discussion. Ayub said true and he certainly would not be going to
discuss economic affairs but only political matters. "The former are for
you to decide, not for me. They are your decision. Please explain to
President Johnson there is no reluctance toward visit on my part. You
must understand my problem. For example, only yesterday Indian Air
Force attacked, and our boys were eager to retaliate. Only I could make
decision not to retaliate. I must be here all the time and on top of

---

[1] Source: National Archives and Records Administration, RG 59, Central Files 1964–
66, POL 7 PAK. Secret; Immediate; Exdis. Repeated to the White House, London, New
Delhi, and Karachi.
[2] See Document 226.

everything. The people in Pakistan must also understand." I conceded that it would be difficult for Ayub leave country before cease fire fully effective. He said any day something can happen until real disengagement has taken place. Compared situation to a U.S.-Mexican war. I returned to his comment about visit possibility in six or eight weeks. He replied, "Yes, as soon as possible, but there are great difficulties and I must be on tap all the time."

I told President Ayub my great concern to get things off dead center in U.S.-Pak relations and observed in important respects meeting of two Presidents necessary to get things moving again. Ayub replied, "Of course, President Johnson can say what he likes in our discussions, and I shall speak frankly to him. But too I shall be reasonable. All we want is that you do not add to our problems."

Later in conversation when Ayub complained about lack U.S. appreciation his efforts, I underlined that all those matters argue for face-to-face meeting between two Presidents. (Ayub was referring to his efforts to exert moderating influence on ChiComs.) At conclusion of discussion, I promised report President Ayub's views on U.S. visit and expressed hope that in next few weeks it would be possible work out arrangements.

McConaughy

---

228.   Memorandum From the President's Deputy Special Assistant for National Security Affairs (Komer) to President Johnson[1]

Washington, September 29, 1965.

Pressure on Peshawar. Several days ago the Paks closed a small [*less than 1 line of source text not declassified*] installation [*less than 1 line of source text not declassified*]. On 22 September they forcibly closed a minor [*less than 1 line of source text not declassified*] acoustic installation [*less than 1 line of source text not declassified*]. [*1 line of source text not declassified*] This morning they closed two more small installations near Karachi.

Later today Pak guards barred our people from the airfield in Peshawar [*1 line of source text not declassified*]. No notice or explanation was given in any of these cases.

---

[1] Source: Johnson Library, National Security File, Memos to the President, McGeorge Bundy, Vol. 15, Sept. 23–Oct. 14 1965. Secret. A handwritten "L" on the memorandum indicates that it was seen by the President.

McConaughy raised the earlier incidents with Ayub this morning. Ayub professed total ignorance (cables on meeting attached)[2] but the Foreign Secretary knew all about it and indicated these installations were being used against Pak security. Since the installations closed have nothing to do with Pak/Indian matters, however, the pattern seems rather to point to a deliberate Pak effort to show us they have cards too, and as pressure to get us to resume aid.

If we can't get Kashmir for Ayub, our only lever to keep Ayub on the reservation is aid. If so, then we must keep convincing Ayub that unless he plays ball with us (e.g. on our installations), there won't be any. This suggests that we should quietly respond to the Pak squeeze on our installations by suspending at least some of the aid now in the pipeline. We have the following options:

A. Of the $264 million odd in FY'65 and prior aid now in the pipeline, about half is not yet covered by letters of commitment authorizing disbursements. AID could simply hold these up. It would take about a week for the Paks to catch on.
B. Once letters of commitment are issued, about six big US banks then issue letters of credit. A simple AID query as to how much credit remained to be drawn under these letters would get back to the Paks very quickly, and worry them.
C. We could go further and ask the banks not to issue any new letters of credit, and even to suspend any remaining disbursements under existing ones. This would get Pak wind up immediately.
D. This would leave only the aid goods already bought and perhaps in transit. Repossessing and/or diverting this entails many complications.
E. We could also hold up administratively the 175,000 tons of grain on which PA's were just issued.

Since the Paks are in a highly agitated frame of mind, it seems best we move carefully. Steps A and B above would put us in a good position, would worry the Paks, yet wouldn't entail early publicity. We also wouldn't want to trigger Pak closing of Peshawar before they had had a chance to digest the likely cost.

State probably will not have a recommendation before tomorrow. Among other things, we are worried over the possibility that Ayub is not fully master in his own house. Thus this memo is only to bring you up to date on the state of play.

R.W. Komer

---

[2] Attached were copies of telegram 122 from Rawalpindi (Document 227) and a telegram sent through special channels on September 29 in which McConaughy reported on the conclusion of his conversation with Ayub that morning. McConaughy protested against the actions described in Komer's memorandum to the President.

Mr. President:

My guess is that the State Department will come out recommending A. and B.[3] In this rather edgy situation, this seems enough to me. Any preliminary indication of your feelings would be helpful:

I am ready to do A. and B.

I will approve more if recommended

I want to be sure that we do not get into a debate on this, but simply act quietly and wait for Pak inquiries (I offer this last option because of the State Department's impulse to debate by cable.)[4]

McG. B.

---

[3] Komer sent a memorandum to Bundy later on September 29 in which he reported that "instead of quietly cutting off aid, NEA is recommending to Ball that we make one more try with Ayub, and ask him what he is trying to accomplish." Komer noted that he had "registered in spades our view that it was futile to try to talk with Ayub, and that I doubted he was out of control but was rather fully conversant with the squeeze play and for McConaughy, of all people, to go back and ask again what's up would simply invite Ayub retorting 'Restore MAP or we'll close Peshawar.'" (Johnson Library, National Security File, Name File, Komer Memos, Vol. II)

[4] No response by the President appears on the memorandum.

---

229. Memorandum From the President's Deputy Special Assistant for National Security Affairs (Komer) to the President's Special Assistant for National Security Affairs (Bundy)[1]

Washington, September 29, 1965.

Mac—

When I called BK Nehru to invite him for lunch with us Friday, he raised the question of a visit by the PM. Did we have in mind the same kind of quick visit to Washington as had been under discussion before the fighting or were we now proposing that if the PM went to the UN the President would be delighted to see him in Washington? I told BK that (1) we had no fixed view; (2) I couldn't speak for the

---

[1] Source: Johnson Library, National Security File, Name File, Komer Memos, Vol. II. Secret.

President, but assumed that with the aid bill now by us, the President would be happy to see the PM under either circumstance—it was a matter of working things out to their mutual convenience; (3) I had personally rather thought that with the issue before the UN, the PM would want to appear if he came to the US.

BK asked whether our feelers constituted a formal invitation. I replied that the situation was rather one of trying to work things out informally to the mutual convenience of the two leaders but that once this was done I was sure a formal re-invite was no problem. However, I recalled that BK himself had suggested the PM would like to make any formal visit to the US at a time when he could spend several days seeing the country, which of course was not possible during the present interregnum between Lok Sabha sessions. BK said he understood.

Mac, my understanding (particularly from the latest note from the President)[2] is that he'd be happy to see Shastri here in any way and any time that can be mutually worked out. Correct?

RWK

---

[2] Reference is to a September 24 note, attached to a memorandum from Komer inquiring about proposed visits by Shastri and Ayub. President Johnson agreed to a visit by Shastri and preferred that the visit take place before October 15. (Ibid., Memos to the President, McGeorge Bundy, Vol. 15, 9/23/65–12/23/65)

---

230. Memorandum From the President's Deputy Special Assistant for National Security Affairs (Komer) to President Johnson[1]

Washington, October 1, 1965, 6 p.m.

Pak/Indian Affairs. The situation is still confused. The *cease-fire* is still tenuously holding as more UN observers appear on the scene. But the latest Indian attack in the Chhamb sector is thoroughly arousing the Paks, and could lead to resumption of full-scale hostilities. We're pressing the SYG to act.

In any event *withdrawal to the 5 August positions* will be a tricky matter. The UK believes the UN must press for it immediately, lest the

---

[1] Source: Johnson Library, National Security File, Name File, Komer Memos, Vol. II. Secret.

war erupt again. The British feel the SC must take a tough stance, including sanctions if needed. But the Paks are insisting that withdrawal go hand in hand with the creation of machinery for Kashmir settlement. India's counterploy is to hint that the 1949 Kashmir cease-fire line is no longer valid.

Meanwhile Goldberg is conferring about an SC Commission of the four big powers (US, USSR, UK, France) to help the SYG work out a Kashmir settlement. The USSR is reluctant, and the Indians too.

Pak Attitudes. Ayub's attitude toward us seems to have hardened; we're not quite sure why. But he's now made clear he can't come here for 6–8 weeks at least; perhaps he wants to soften us up first through such devices as the squeeze on our installations.

Meanwhile, the Paks are allowing the almost wholly government-controlled media to feed the growing anti-US and pro-Chicom sentiment in Pakistan. Our Embassy and USIA reports US prestige is at an all-time low. The risk here is that Ayub may paint himself into a corner, and lose his ability to move back toward us even if he decides to do so. There is also a distinct risk that the frustrated die-hards may yet force Pakistan to go the Chicom route, even at the cost of US support. We are simply not in effective communication with Ayub at this critical moment, so if he's unable to come here it may now be important to send someone there.

Pressure on US Installations. The Paks have now closed up practically everything but Peshawar itself. There's evidence that we *did* use walkie-talkies illicitly from the Lahore sites in the early days of the war. But this was three weeks ago, so the consensus still is that the Paks are pulling a pressure play on us. Ball is still considering what retaliatory action, if any, to recommend; some argue that this is no time to goad the Paks further lest we help push them off the deep end, while others feel that a prompt, quiet reaction would cool the Paks off rather than the reverse.

Indian Attitudes. Embassy Delhi emphasizes that Indian success has united the nation and produced a new surge of nationalist fervor. Bowles and his UK colleague flatly assert that in this mood the Indians are highly unlikely to compromise on Kashmir. Instead continued hold-up of US aid is rapidly being interpreted as political pressure on India to give up Kashmir.

Embassy Delhi contends that if we hold up everything much longer it will dangerously stimulate the growing sentiment to go-it-alone in Delhi, which will only benefit the Soviets. According to Bowles, we face a critical opportunity either to maximize US influence in a newly self-reliant India or to face a rapid decline in this influence and an accelerating shift towards the USSR.

We here feel that Bowles' fears are probably premature, but that we do face a growing dilemma. There is little doubt that our decisions at this moment of truth in both India and Pakistan can have basic implications for our further influence for many years to come. We are trying to get the basic issues formulated to put before you, because we inevitably face some decisions shortly, whether or not Shastri or Ayub come here.[2]

R. W. Komer[3]

[2] A handwritten note by Johnson at the end of the memorandum reads: "Bob—Please see that Arthur Dean is kept fully informed and have him come here for consultation as often as advisable."

[3] McGeorge Bundy initialed below Komer's signature.

---

231. Telegram From the Department of State to the Embassy in India[1]

Washington, October 1, 1965, 9:19 p.m.

613. Aidto 407, info Karachi Aidto 555, Rawalpindi 118.[2] At meeting October 1 with Under Secretary Mann, Bhoothalingam said he understood "pause" in making good on pledge, but continued stoppage on new aid following ceasefire has come as shock. He emphasized need for very early non-project aid, including fertilizer. Said recent fighting had stimulated feeling of national unity and confidence in India which in midst very hopeful venture in economic development. Bhoothalingam wondered what would be result of irritation and frustration if Indian people felt let down by friends on whom they had counted. Said India's basic problem remains China and Indian defense needs must be considered that context.

---

[1] Source: National Archives and Records Administration, RG 59, Central Files 1964–66, AID (US) INDIA. Confidential. Drafted by Sober in SOA, cleared by Handley, and approved by Mann. Repeated to Karachi and Rawalpindi.

[2] Telegram Aidto 407 to New Delhi, September 30, summarized the meeting that day between Indian Finance Secretary S. Bhoothalingam and Acting AID Administrator William Gaud. Gaud told Bhoothalingam that the existing ban on new economic assistance loans to India and Pakistan would not be lifted automatically upon passage of the foreign assistance bill. Bhoothalingam protested that this action would cause serious problems in India, and that it was severe and out of proportion to the situation on the subcontinent. (Ibid.) Bhoothalingam was in Washington for meetings of the World Bank and the International Monetary Fund.

Mann referred to strong feeling in US that economic development incompatible with war. Said we have real problem in seeing that economic aid is not wasted in fighting. Referred to our own balance payments problems and strong Congressional concern over efficacy foreign aid programs. In concern over current appropriation bill, he noted Secretary had told Congress that Administration would consult with it before making new loans to India or Pakistan. Mann expressed hope we could find some way to get back to normal relationship on aid. Said our problem would be greatly eased if there were prospect of political solution satisfactory both India and Pakistan.

In response query how soon and under what conditions new loans would be resumed, Mann expressed hope we could see somewhat more clearly ahead in short time. Stated aid could only be effective in an otherwise favorable situation and emphasize we not intending put pressure on GOI. Said we need some more time and look forward to more talks with Indians on this issue.

Throughout conversation, Bhoothalingam and Ambassador B.K. Nehru (who also present) defended India's position vis-à-vis Pakistan re commencement of fighting and emphasized virtual insolubility political problem under existing conditions. They offered no positive response on hope expressed by Under Secretary that some progress toward political settlement might be in cards.[3]

Ball

---

[3] On October 6 Komer also attempted to explain to Bhoothalingam the problems involved in continuing a business-as-usual approach to economic assistance in the midst of a military confrontation over Kashmir. Komer emphasized the difficulties created by the conflict for foreign assistance legislation in Congress. He also noted, however, that during the past several months there had been some "deep soul searching as to what our aid program in the subcontinent had really been accomplishing." (Memorandum for the Record by Komer; Johnson Library, National Security File, Name File, Komer Memos, Vol. II)

232. Telegram From the Department of State to the Embassy in India[1]

Washington, October 2, 1965, 5:19 p.m.

619. Your recent tels such as 829[2] have given us most perceptive and useful view of atmosphere in India. Your recommendations touch fundamentals of US policy and are under study. In meantime, stance we are adopting with regard India takes into account this atmosphere and its implications for Indian policy. This stance is based on recognition that India has emerged from recent ordeal with strengthened unity, sense of national purpose, and status as the dominant power on subcontinent. This is distinct plus. At same time, however, believe we are justified in reminding India of its responsibility to help solve problems peacefully in troubled times ahead; this means that India must recognize that Pakistan has major problems in its relations with India which are being exploited by Chicoms. Therefore it is reasonable to ask India, in its own interest as well as ours, to engage in creative efforts to help lessen Pakistan's problems as a way of reducing Indo-Pak tensions and frustrating Chinese designs. It will be difficult for us to resume assistance until we are assured conditions exist on subcontinent which make development feasible.

With these thoughts in mind we have prepared following talking points for use by officials meeting Indians here in immediate future. Hope you will reinforce our efforts here in similar talks in Delhi.

India–Pakistan Dispute

1. We recognized that India is the larger power on subcontinent, with considerable force at its disposal.

2. Force, however, constitutes no solution in this day and age. As the larger power India in its own interest and in interest of world peace must take account of aspirations of people of Pakistan, quite apart

---

[1] Source: National Archives and Records Administration, RG 59, Central Files 1964–66, POL 27 INDIA–PAK. Secret. Drafted by Schneider, cleared by Laise and Popper, and approved by Raymond A. Hare. Repeated to Karachi, London, and USUN.

[2] Among the points made by Bowles in telegram 829 from New Delhi, September 29, in sketching the political environment created in India by the war was the "hard political fact that no Indian Govt. could agree to yield to Paks by negotiation what Paks have attempted and failed to gain by military force." He also noted that the Indian military would never yield the strategic Kashmir Valley to Pakistan, since that would cut their lines of communication with Indian-held Ladakh. Bowles emphasized that "no international pressure short of direct application of military force will induce India to yield on this particular question." (Ibid.)

from question of rights and wrongs. Recent conflict settles nothing and indicates Kashmir will not fade away. The longer it is allowed to fester, the more India runs danger of encouraging destructive Pakistan policies which can be exploited by Communist China.

3. We hope India will recognize desirability of availing itself of all the instruments of diplomacy to achieve better Indo-Pak relations and to give evidence of a willingness to do so.

4. We wish to assure India we recognize that a solution can only evolve from political compromise and accommodation of positions of both parties. It cannot be imposed from outside. However, we do consider that as fellow member of UN we have right to urge that process of unconditional talks within an agreed framework should be started in order to work toward peaceful settlement of outstanding differences. We all have stake in outcome.

Economic Assistance

1. Although we have been continuing shipments food and other commodities under our existing economic aid agreements, even with passage aid appropriation we are committed to consulting with Congress on situation in subcontinent in connection with making new economic aid loans or grants to either India or Pakistan. As we prepare for these considerations we will wish consider number of matters.

2. We will need to have idea of the effect of fighting on Indian economy.

3. Prospects for development will also be affected by future allocation of Indian resources between development and defense. We will also therefore need to know effect of GOI's proposed military expenditure on prospects for economic development.

4. More broadly, we will need to be assured that economic development in subcontinent, in which we have invested so heavily, is not again to be disrupted by fighting between India and Pakistan. It would appear to us therefore that there is a need for military disengagement and establishment of a process of negotiation which will provide a basis for peace in subcontinent.

5. Aside from new problems arising out of fighting, we are aware of the basic economic problems India faces in its development effort. We attach critical importance to policy measures India will take to make maximum use of its own resources and foreign assistance.

Military Assistance

We are committed to consulting fully with appropriate members of Congress regarding situation on subcontinent on conditions under which military aid might be resumed. We do not see how we can resume military aid or sales at the present time, particularly since fighting is still going on.[3]

Ball

---

[3] The Department sent a similar set of talking points to Karachi on October 5, urging a withdrawal from military confrontation and unconditional negotiations with India in search of a political settlement. The telegram also explained that resumption of economic and military assistance was contingent upon assurances that the assistance would not contribute to or be wasted in a military conflict on the subcontinent. (Telegram 595 to Karachi; ibid., POL PAK–US)

---

233. **Information Memorandum From the Assistant Secretary of State for Near Eastern and South Asian Affairs (Hare) to Secretary of State Rusk[1]**

Washington, October 5, 1965.

SUBJECT

　Indian Criticism of the United States Since the Cease-fire: The Question of PL 480 Wheat

Since the cease-fire there has been a steady obbligato of criticism of the United States in the Indian press, based largely on variations on the theme that we are showing partiality to Pakistan (the most recent was Defense Minister Chavan's Bombay speech yesterday). Not all comments on the U.S. have been critical, however, and on the whole we are being let off much lighter than, say, our British colleagues.

The main exception to this generalization is the recent uproar over alleged U.S. intention to use PL 480 wheat as a lever to extract concessions on Kashmir. It began with a public statement by the Prime Minister on September 26, in which he reportedly warned the great powers not to pressure India for concessions on Kashmir. He said "India may even have to face food shortages in case some countries stop food exports to India." Mrs. Gandhi on the 27th told a Jammu audience that India must be prepared to get along without aid rather

---

[1] Source: National Archives and Records Administration, RG 59, Central Files 1964–66, AID (US) 15–8 INDIA. Secret. Drafted by Carleton S. Coon, Jr.

than give in to pressure. These sentiments were fanned by reports from Washington correspondents of Indian newspapers following our September 29 signing of a one month PL 480 extension. The rest of the press picked up the theme rapidly and vigorously. The latest statement by an Indian official is Planning Chief Ashoke Mehta's on October 1 in which he warned against the use of aid, including food supplies, to exert pressure on India. He said that India has "alternate plans ready to go ahead without such aid."

During the last couple of days the issue has died down somewhat, perhaps the delayed effect of a statement on September 30 by an official GOI spokesman denying that short-term food agreements were meant as political pressure.

In effect, India's leaders have declared that India will tighten its belt and go it alone rather than trade concessions on Kashmir for American wheat. The Indian press has vigorously supported this position.[2]

---

[2] In telegram 636 to New Delhi, October 6, the Department expressed concern over statements by Indian leaders implying that the United States was using P.L. 480 wheat as a lever to extract concessions on Kashmir. The Embassy was instructed to make clear that the United States was not using food for political leverage. (Ibid., AID (US) 15 INDIA)

---

234.   Memorandum From the President's Special Assistant for National Security Affairs (Bundy) and Deputy Special Assistant for National Security Affairs (Komer) to President Johnson[1]

Washington, October 5, 1965, 8:45 p.m.

SUBJECT

India and Pakistan

This is one subject on which I think you may wish to have a brief meeting before you go to Bethesda. There are storm signals in both countries and we can do better in the next two weeks if all hands have up-to-date guidance from you.

---

[1] Source: Johnson Library, National Security File, Memos to the President, McGeorge Bundy, Vol. 15, Sept. 23–Oct. 14, 1965. Secret.

Moreover, your stay in Bethesda obviously puts off the time at which Shastri could come here, and, along with Ayub's unreadiness to move in a continued state of crisis, reduces the prospect that we can move forward by pressing for early conversations with you—although the Shastri possibility remains important and hopeful, perhaps for late October.

Meanwhile, there is a real danger that both Pakistan and India will misread our policy. The Paks may wrongly believe that their alternatives are crude pressure on us or a crude bargain with the Red Chinese—this is the way they are talking and acting. The Indians may wrongly feel that we are using food as a blunt instrument and that the only safe reply in Indian political terms is to move publicly and proudly toward isolation from the West. The Indians may also feel—again quite wrongly—that we intend to try to trade our assistance for their "surrender" on Kashmir.

These problems are compounded by the fact that our channels to Ayub and Shastri are clogged, both in Asia and in Washington. Except at the moment of truth on the ceasefire, your government has not succeeded in communicating sharply just what we do and do not want. In part this is the inevitable result of our decision to hold everything until Shastri and Ayub get here. But in part it is also the result of the very rapid changes in Pakistani and Indian thinking because of the enormous national crises into which they have steered themselves. We have not yet adjusted our responses to this new situation.

All of this, I suspect, is at least as clear to you as it is to us. But what we now need to do is to sort out our own thinking, and then make some sober and straightforward noises to the Asians.

Not as final answers, but as indications of the shape of the problem, we suggest the following principles and the following tactical conclusions:

A. Principles

1. India is more important than Pakistan and there is enough hope in India to justify continued support by food and economic aid if the Indians in turn are reasonable with us.

2. Within this priority we still need not lose Pakistan if we can show the Paks the emptiness of the Chinese route and the reality of continued Western economic support.

3. We should not kid ourselves about any early Kashmir settlement. American fidgeting over Kashmir will only make us trouble with India and arouse false hopes in Pakistan. The most we can do is what Goldberg is dong: press for acceptance by both sides of the process of peaceful discussion as against the process of trial by arms. (We emphasize this point because it would help wonderfully in this town if you

were to announce this conclusion as your own. Kashmir-fixers are a plentiful and dangerous commodity.)

4. We cannot tie our economic aid to positive progress on Kashmir. We can tie it to reasonable progress in the observance of the UN ceasefire resolution and to the acceptance of political process. We can also tie it to other basic US interests such as:

    a. Keeping the Paks out of Chinese arms;
    b. Keeping the Indians from unbalanced surrender to the Soviets (although Soviet help in itself is not intolerable);
    c. Keeping the Indians away from nuclear weapons;
    d. Pressing both countries toward better economic and agricultural policies.

B. Tactics

1. The thing which is giving us most trouble right now is the absence of dialogue. We are inclined to think that someone clearly speaking for you should be sent to these two countries within the next two or three weeks. This could be Arthur Dean, who begins work tomorrow, but if you want to give him more time to learn, you might want to send one of your own team. There is great advantage in sending someone who really speaks for President Johnson; whatever our other failings, we play your tune, and most people know it.

2. In due course, we should defuse the explosive issue of food as a political weapon. At the same time, we should not get back into long-term agreements. A shift in a couple of weeks from the current one-month basis to a quarterly basis, with appropriate agricultural assurances attached, would do us a lot of good and cost us nothing in terms of leverage.

3. The burden of our song to Ayub and Shastri should be a judicious mixture of firmness, concern, and continued readiness to help on reasonable terms. Specifically, to Ayub:

    a. We should drive home to the Paks the folly of threats and the still greater folly of switching to Peking.
    b. On Kashmir, we should maintain our commitment to a process, but make it crystal clear that the only real hope the Paks have here is in conciliation and not conflict with India. This is a fact of life, and their adventure this summer proves it.
    c. If the Paks are responsive, we are ready to start talking renewed economic aid, but as a simple fact it will be a long time before military assistance can begin again to either party. (These are warnings and expressions of willingness to negotiate—they should not be commitments, since these ought to be reserved both for a later time and a higher level.)

4. To the Indians, we would make it quietly clear that we accept and indeed support their primary role in the subcontinent, and that in particular we are not agents for Pakistan or supreme judges on Kashmir.

But, within this basic premise, we could and would press the Indians to recognize the necessity for political process and the advantage to them of gradual conciliation, since they too would lose if the Pakistanis made a fatal plunge toward China.

5. With respect to the UN Resolution, and political process, we should emphasize to both that unless there is a return to the methods of peace, it is a fact and not a theory that the whole future of US assistance will be gravely jeopardized. How can the American Congress justify long-range, large-scale efforts to people who cannot do what is needed to keep the peace? It is this test, not the test of a specific Kashmir settlement, which the American Congress will apply.

We have sketched these outlines of a policy, not because we are convinced it is the only one, but because we see a prospect of grave losses in both countries if we go forward in the coming weeks with no policy at all. It is this prospect which makes us urge a meeting even in these last hectic days before you go to Bethesda.

McG. B.

R. W. Komer

Set Up a Meeting

Speak to me[2]

---

[2] The memorandum contains no indication that Johnson responded to these options.

235.   Memorandum From the President's Deputy Special Assistant for National Security Affairs (Komer) to the President's Special Assistant for National Security Affairs (Bundy)[1]

Washington, October 7, 1965.

Mac—

Pak Gamesmanship. In addition to closing all our smaller facilities, some Paks have been up to other shenanigans of interest:

(1) Our Pak friends have sent pictures to Turkey of the way the Karachi mob damaged our USIS installation (show Turks how to deal with US facilities?).

(2) We know that in the hands of Karachi mob were handbills containing the Victor Anant *Daily Telegraph* article about how CIA started the war in an effort to get rid of Ayub.

(3) We have at least two indications that Bhutto himself fathered the Anant story (against Ayub?).

(4) Another report that Bhutto distributed 300 copies of *The Invisible Government* in the GOP.

(5) A report that the GOP originated a newspaper story in Pakistan claiming that the State Department instructed the US press to play down Indian defeats in an effort to make Congress think India could stand up to China.

[*1 paragraph (1-1/2 lines of source text) not declassified*][2]

McConaughy is in at long last with his evaluation of our facilities.[3] It doesn't tell us anything we didn't know. McConaughy doubts whether the GOP has an exaggerated idea any longer of the importance of Peshawar to the US, since the recent record of our aid hold-ups must convince them that they can't use Peshawar as a decisive lever on the US. McConaughy believes that the GOP will *not* now follow up against Peshawar though its prospects are directly linked with the outcome of the US/Pak relationship and Kashmir. He concludes that the smaller installations were apparently closed because of petty irritations, with no thought that they would strike at the heart of essential US interests in Pakistan or precipitate any Pak/US crisis.

I grant the risk that strong reaction to closure of our small facilities (actually 6 not 3) might convince the Paks that they are much more important than previously realized and that Pakistan had a larger lever than McConaughy thinks they believe. On the other hand, we are

---

[1] Source: Johnson Library, National Security File, Name File, Komer Memos, Vol. II. Secret.

[2] [*text not declassified*]

[3] Telegram 727 from Karachi, October 6. (National Archives and Records Administration, RG 59, Central Files 1964–66, DEF 15 PAK–US)

not going to convince the Paks to play ball unless we confront them continually with the prospect of losing all US support. Thus I see the small closings as an opportunity to drive this point home again.

However, the tactics are tricky. If we quietly clamp down on the aid pipeline, it might be some time before the Paks connected the two events. Therefore, it might be better to tell the Paks simultaneously that we felt they had committed an unfriendly act and were compelled to respond in kind.[4]

This could be done when Rusk sees Shoaib[5] this weekend.

RWK[6]

---

[4] Bundy added a handwritten marginal notation at this point that reads: "I'm not very keen on this now."

[5] Shoaib was in Washington for meetings of the World Bank and the International Monetary Fund. No record of this meeting has been found.

[6] Printed from a copy that bears these typed initials.

---

236. Memorandum From the President's Special Assistant for National Security Affairs (Bundy) to President Johnson[1]

Washington, October 19, 1965.

SUBJECT

Shastri visit and the Indian food pipeline

1. The attached cable from Bowles[2] shows that a great deal has been accomplished with Shastri by your policy of the last 3 or 4 months.

---

[1] Source: Johnson Library, National Security File, Memos to the President, McGeorge Bundy, Vol. 16, Oct. 15–Nov. 19, 1965. Secret. A handwritten "L" on the memorandum indicates that the President saw it.

[2] Not printed. Telegram 1025 from New Delhi, October 19, reported on a conversation between Shastri and Bowles on October 16. Shastri indicated that he was considering a brief visit to the United States following the adjournment of the Indian Parliament on December 10, if President Johnson wanted to see him. Shastri asked Bowles if it was true that U.S. policy toward India had changed, and if so why. Bowles responded that U.S. support for India was solid, but the Johnson administration was examining its aid program to all countries, and particularly its aid program for South Asia, which absorbed so much U.S. assistance. President Johnson wanted to know what the aid programs were accomplishing, how they could be improved, and whether the recipient countries were doing what they could to help themselves. Bowles stated that the only reason the flow of U.S. grain had been on a month-to-month basis was a concern that India was not doing enough to increase its own agricultural output. (Ibid., 9/23/65–12/23/65)

It also shows Bowles doing a good job of representing the U. S. and not India. It confirms what we have heard from B. K. Nehru and others—that Shastri is very eager to come and see you in December. In my judgment, it also confirms the prospect that such a meeting would be productive for us.

2. I have told Nehru that, for obvious reasons, no definite plans are now being made, and I think this will keep until you are ready to decide it.

3. The one thing which does need to be watched is the food pipe-line. On September 23 you authorized a one-month extension, and by the end of this week we will face that same problem again. While there is some sentiment in the bureaucracy for a longer agreement, my own feeling is that it is much better simply to renew for another month, on the same basis, thus keeping the situation as it is, with a short rein. The Indians understand increasingly that they really have not performed on their own side of the agricultural bargain, and as long as the pipeline does not actually break, I see no harm in this month-to-month process. I have discussed this matter with Clark Clifford, and he asked me to tell you that he strongly agrees with the month-by-month procedure for the present.

4. I am sending this memorandum by Jack Valenti so that he can get your judgment at the time most convenient to you.

McG. B.

237. Special National Intelligence Estimate[1]

SNIE 31–1–65   Washington, October 21, 1965.

INDIA'S NUCLEAR WEAPONS POLICY

The Problem

To estimate India's nuclear weapons policy over the next few years.

Conclusions

A. India has the capability to develop nuclear weapons. It probably already has sufficient plutonium for a first device, and could explode it about a year after a decision to develop one. (Paras. 1–3)

B. The proponents of a nuclear weapons program have been strengthened by the Indo-Pakistani war, but the main political result has been a strengthening of Prime Minister Shastri's position. We believe that he does not now wish to start a program and that he is capable of making this decision stick for the time being. (Paras. 4–14)

C. However, we do not believe that India will hold to this policy indefinitely. All things considered, we believe that within the next few years India probably will detonate a nuclear device and proceed to develop nuclear weapons. (Paras. 15–20)

[Here follows the 5-page Discussion section of the Estimate.]

---

[1] Source: Central Intelligence Agency, Job 79–R01012A, ODDI Registry of NIE and SNIE Files. Secret; Controlled Dissem. According to a note on the cover sheet, the estimate was prepared by the CIA and the intelligence organizations of the Departments of State and Defense, AEC, and NSA. All members of the U.S. Intelligence Board concurred in the estimate on October 21 except the representative of the Federal Bureau of Investigation, who abstained because the subject was outside his jurisdiction.

238. Telegram From the Department of State to the Embassy in Pakistan[1]

Washington, October 21, 1965, 8:24 p.m.

704. Following summary of conversation FYI and Noforn. It is uncleared and subject to amendment upon review.

Pak Foreign Minister Bhutto called on Secretary at Bhutto's request October 21 to discuss progress within UN on Indo-Pak situation.[2] Ambassador Ahmed and Counselor Farooq present Pak side; Ambassador Hare and Assistant Secretary Sisco on U.S. side. Bhutto appeared primarily interested get USG views on desirability further UNSC meeting, indicating Paks in favor. Meanwhile Paks prepared defer UNGA approach. Bhutto also emphasized desirability SYG visit to subcontinent. Secretary said we would want further reading from SYG before commenting on desirability SC meeting but reaffirmed that USG prepared join in maximum effort to give effect to entire September 20 resolution. *End summary.*

1. Bhutto said Paks still sorting out thoughts on further SC meeting. Said he thought French position on "constitutional problems" not too difficult and in any event had assured Paks this had nothing to do with substance of issue. Soviet position less clear and meeting might not be too good if Soviets were going to be sticky. All things considered he thought another SC meeting would be useful solidify cease fire, get progress on withdrawal and "perhaps a bit more." Bhutto agreed with Secretary on importance maintaining unanimity already achieved within Council.

2. Bhutto said unfortunately Indian position meanwhile was hardening and yesterday Paks had heard Indians intend launch new offensive in Rajasthan sector, probably similar earlier one in Tithwal. Indians had turned down proposal by UNSC President that Bhutto and Swaran Singh lunch together in New York. Indians' objective was to get the entire problem frozen again. Secretary commented September 20 resolution made it clear issue could not be frozen.

3. Bhutto concurred but asked how we proceed. In response to Secretary's query regarding Soviet Tashkent proposal, Bhutto said proposal still there but Soviets now saying it better for parties to talk directly.

---

[1] Source: National Archives and Records Administration, RG 59, Central Files 1964–66, POL 27 INDIA–PAK. Confidential. Drafted by Laingen, cleared by Sisco, and approved and initialed by Hare. Also sent to Rawalpindi, and repeated to London, New Delhi, USUN, and CINCMEAFSA.

[2] Bhutto was in the United States for the meeting of the UN General Assembly. His meeting with Rusk took place in the Department of State.

Added that Gromyko had invited him to visit Moscow en route back to Pakistan. Secretary said he thought Bhutto should know about comment he had made recently to Gromyko; telling him, when Gromyko had referred to Tashkent proposal, that for 17 years U.S. had had one dog chewing on one leg and another dog chewing on other and if Soviets wanted find out what it was like that was all right with us. Bhutto commented Paks would chew a little higher if they tried it on Russians.

4. Secretary said he hoped our position clear on Tashkent proposal. He had been somewhat negative in earlier comment on proposal with both Bhutto and Gromyko, but this had been with respect to outlook for settlement through that route and not to Soviet role in current consideration of problem. Secretary said that as prophet he could not be hopeful on ultimate outcome talks in Tashkent. On other hand he wanted Paks to understand we would not object to any step that might further prospects ultimate settlement; indeed U.S. would be happy to see talks in Antarctica if that would settle the matter. If Soviet proposal meant some forward movement on Soviet position from previous rigid stand on Kashmir issue that was all to the good.

5. Bhutto said he thought U.S. position clear and had also been emphasized previous day in talk with Ambassador Goldberg.

6. Secretary went on to say that for many reasons we see advantages proceeding within UNSC, especially if permanent members can continue act in unison. As of present, however, Secretary thought we did not have very precise indication what was in Soviet mind. Sisco commented it fairly clear Soviets not keen on four-power proposal idea but we not very clear on Soviet position over-all. Bhutto then inquired about possibility actions by SYG in context "in the meantime" clause of resolution; specifically visit by SYG to subcontinent. Sisco commented SYG focusing now on GOI and GOP replies to his message of October 14 on withdrawal; Bhutto said Paks thinking more in terms resolution as a whole, adding he felt it clear that SYG had independent mandate to proceed without further meeting UNSC. However if French and Russians felt it better to arm SYG with specific mandate there was no harm in that either from Pak viewpoint. Sisco interjected that we see effective cease fire as first requirement and withdrawal as next step, noting that "in the meantime" clause referred to what parties themselves might be able to do on underlying political problem, and that after first two steps implemented SC consider how to assist peaceful settlement.

7. Bhutto responded that even for purposes speeding withdrawal, visit by SYG to area may be needed. Paks had accepted resolution in its entirety and were prepared to fulfill their commitment. Unfortunately Indians were not, and there were many examples over the years to point to as evidence. GOP had made clear its willingness cooperate on withdrawal. Indians keep talking about need for effective cease fire and at

same time go on violating cease fire on one pretext or another, nibbling away at Pak territory they could not get by war. There was limit to Pak restraint. All this emphasized further desirability of SYG visit since he could see problem for himself. Since withdrawal would have to be negotiated at very high level, could also get views top-level GOP and GOI. Would also help put curb on "genocide" Indians practicing against Muslim villagers on their side CFL Kashmir. It also important that some UN movement take place before Soviet attitude hardens still more.

8. Bhutto noted Paks had been considering approach to UNGA, not as way of stymying things but to give stimulus to negotiating process. He had told Ambassador Goldberg Paks would not move to GA unless U.S. felt it useful. But if all concerned felt it best Paks wait, then there would very soon need to be some further endeavor in UNSC. Secretary said he could understand that if SC approach blocked then there would be some point in having UNGA throw its weight behind Council and he would think UNGA would be strongly inclined do so. Sisco said that if SC remedies exhausted, there would probably be considerable support in UNGA for kind of approach already taken by SC. Bhutto added that Paks had made fairly extensive analysis situation and thought they could get fairly good UNGA resolution, though not perfect one.

9. Bhutto wondered what Secretary would recommend if progress thwarted completely in UN forum. Secretary responded this was one of those questions where answer was so unsatisfactory he could only say that all concerned must work so that progress not thwarted. Prospect of renewed Indo-Pak hostility so appalling there must be progress within UN. In response further Bhutto question whether Secretary would then conclude that SC meeting now would be best thing to do, Secretary said U.S. would like to get further reading from SYG as to how he saw situation in light responses he has received to Oct. 14 proposal. It might well be that some meeting would be necessary at some point. In response Bhutto said Paks would cooperate and would do their best ensure that unanimity continued prevail in Council. Pakistan was not asking for the moon; all it wanted was some forward movement.[3]

Rusk

---

[3] In an October 22 memorandum to President Johnson, McGeorge Bundy reported that Bhutto had also raised with Rusk the issue of an Ayub visit to Washington. Bundy noted that Johnson had told Ayub in a telephone conversation that he wanted to meet with Ayub before Shastri. With Shastri also indicating a desire to visit Washington in December it became a question of which leader to see first. "Ray Hare and Bob Komer think Shastri first is better, both because India is more important and because if you see Ayub first, he is bound to press you to mediate Kashmir—and that is something we can't do in 1966." Bundy added that his feeling was that because the United States had so little to offer Ayub he ought to enjoy the small comfort of the first visit. (Johnson Library, National Security File, Memos to the President, McGeorge Bundy, Vol. 16, 9/23/65–12/23/65)

239. Memorandum for the Record[1]

Washington, October 27, 1965.

The President approved extension of the present food shipments to India for an additional 30 days. In doing so, however, he emphasized very strongly that we should make it clear to the Indians that we are not satisfied with their performance on their own agricultural program on their previous and existing commitments. He referred to a report he had received from Under Secretary Schnittker of the Department of Agriculture[2] which emphasized that (a) India has failed to live up to a commitment to this Government and to her own people in failing to reach her food production goals (b) India is not giving fertilizer and food production nor the investment promised in her plans and required by her people (c) India's key failures have been in fertilizer, pesticides, producer incentives, credit and seed varieties (d) fertilizer production is the crucial factor and (e) that the U.S. must use all possible leverage to improve India's performance.

The President noted the fact that the U.S. has been sending to India 20% of our wheat production and that India's relative position has been slipping back. These are matters which he will want to have some answers for and on which he believes the Indians should make some commitments with respect to actual performance.

---

[1] Source: National Archives and Records Administration, RG 59, Central Files 1964–66, AID (US) 15 INDIA. Confidential; Nodis. Prepared by Rusk.

[2] Schnittker's memorandum to the President is dated October 23. (Johnson Library, National Security File, Country File, India, Vol. IV, Memos and Miscellaneous, 9/65–1/66)

240.   Telegram From the Department of State to the Embassy in India[1]

Washington, October 29, 1965, 3:26 p.m.

800. Personal for Ambassador from Secretary. You will be receiving telegram authorizing you to negotiate thirty-day extension of food shipments to India.[2] I know this will be disappointing to you but I would like you to know that this decision has been made at the highest level and that limited extension is result solely of our grave misgivings regarding past performance and present plans of Government of India for increased food production. The decision to extend food shipments for only thirty days has nothing to do with Kashmir and is not to be construed in any way as political leverage to force India into a political settlement with Pakistan. It is based on evidence available to the highest authority that a longer term extension, or a new agreement on PL–480, should not be undertaken until such time as the USG has convincing evidence of the GOI's determination to put its food house in order.[3]

Rusk

---

[1] Source: National Archives and Records Administration, RG 59, Central Files 1964–66, AID (US) 15 INDIA. Confidential; Nodis. Drafted by Handley, cleared by Hare, and approved and initialed by Rusk.

[2] Telegram Aidto 598 to New Delhi, October 29, authorized the Embassy to negotiate an amendment to the Title I P.L. 480 agreement of September 30 to provide for an additional 500,000 tons of wheat/wheat flour. (Ibid., AID (US) 15–8 INDIA)

[3] On November 5 Bowles cabled that he had done his utmost to persuade the Shastri government that U.S. reluctance to negotiate a long-term P.L. 480 agreement was not an effort to bring political pressure to bear on India, but that "knowledgeable Indians do not find this line of argument persuasive," and "we ourselves are perplexed by it." Bowles noted that since the appointment of Subramaniam as Food Minister in 1964, the Indian Government had been very responsive to the Embassy's urgings that agriculture be given top priority among development goals. (Telegram 1201 from New Delhi; ibid.) In a short companion cable to Rusk urging him to read telegram 1201, Bowles stated that he understood the dilemma the Department faced, but "I badly need your guidance." (Telegram 1202 from New Delhi, November 5; ibid., AID (US) 15 INDIA)

241. Memorandum From the President's Deputy Special Assistant for National Security Affairs (Komer) to President Johnson[1]

Washington, October 30, 1965, 3 p.m.

Pak/Indian Roundup. While the two sides are still glaring at each other and sticking to rigid propaganda positions, there is considerable movement behind the scene.

There are many signs that the Paks are finally hoisting aboard that they have gotten themselves into a pretty mess, and that if hostilities resumed they'd take a licking. As a result they are now more eager for a withdrawal than for simultaneous talks on settling Kashmir.

This has also led to increasing Pak eagerness to get back in our good graces. Now Shoaib as well as Bhutto are signaling that Ayub is eager to come here soon; indeed Shoaib says Ayub now realizes that a considerable shift in Pak policy will be necessary to get back on a firm footing with us. We even have a report that Ayub intends to sack Bhutto in time.

So the Paks are moving our way. If we sit tight, Ayub should be ready to hear sweet reason within another month or two. However, the Paks are still threatening to move toward the Chicoms (and have leaked that Peiping has offered a tank factory). They also are still hinting that we must give Ayub something first, so he doesn't have to come here as a beggar.

The Indians, who regard themselves as victors, show less flexibility. Knowing they have the upper hand, they've been scaring the Paks with threats to reopen the war if Pakistan won't lay off Kashmir.

Meanwhile, they are refusing to even discuss Kashmir in New York on the grounds that the issue is closed. Their private and public utterances still indicate acute suspicion that the US and UK are trying to pressure them into giving up the fruits of victory. My own reading is that this mood will last until Shastri can hear from you personally where we stand. According to recent envoys, he's still eager to come around 10 December.

R. W. Komer

---

[1] Source: Johnson Library, National Security File, Memos to the President, McGeorge Bundy, Vol. 16, Oct. 15–Nov. 19, 1965. Secret.

242.   Telegram From the Department of State to the Embassy in India[1]

Washington, November 5, 1965, 7:21 p.m.

841. We note that on same day Security Council has adopted new resolution[2] strengthening appeal for effective ceasefire and strongly supporting SYG proposals for arranging withdrawals, Shastri (according Reuters) told Parliament ceasefire agreement "cannot stand in way of our troops regaining territories treacherously occupied by Pakistan after ceasefire came into effect." Shastri also quoted as saying "our taking remedial measures cannot be considered violation of ceasefire agreement." Other tickers report All India Radio and PTI as saying Pakistan troops "massing" on Rajasthan border. All this suggests Karachi's concern that Indians contemplating action along Rajasthan border may be well justified.

We believe GOI should be made aware in no uncertain terms our view that Shastri's position if accurately reported by Reuters, clearly inconsistent with SC resolution and Indian actions of type Shastri seems to contemplate would demonstrate India not now interested in reestablishment of peaceful conditions in which economic development of subcontinent can move forward. This would have inevitable effect upon current USG policy review regarding subcontinent. Indian failure respond to SYG proposal to send Sarmento to arrange withdrawal plans another indication that Indians not meeting their obligation to re-establish peace on subcontinent.

We count on you to get across these ideas soonest at place where it will do most good.[3]

Rusk

---

[1] Source: National Archives and Records Administration, RG 59, Central Files 1964–66, POL 27 INDIA–PAK. Confidential; Priority. Drafted by Schneider, cleared by Buffum, and approved by Handley. Repeated to Karachi, London, and USUN.

[2] On November 5 the Security Council adopted Resolution 215, which reaffirmed the September 20 resolution, requested the two parties to the conflict to observe fully the cease-fire, and demanded that representatives of India, Pakistan, and the Secretary-General meet to work out plans for withdrawal. (UN doc. S/RES/215)

[3] Bowles reported on November 7 that he had instructed a member of his staff to discuss Shastri's speech with L.K. Jha, using telegram 841 as a basis for his approach. Jha expressed surprise at the U.S. reaction to the speech, which he said was meant for domestic consumption and did not signal expanded hostilities. He stated that immediately after the cease-fire Pakistan had occupied a number of military posts in Indian territory in Rajasthan, and Shastri's speech was merely a "retrospective review" of Indian efforts to regain the territory. Jha said that India fully accepted the November 5 Security Council resolution. (Telegram 1207; National Archives and Records Administration, RG 59, Central Files 1964–66, POL 27 INDIA–PAK)

243. **Telegram From the Department of State to the Embassy in Pakistan**[1]

Washington, November 10, 1965, 4:31 p.m.

808. For Ambassador from Secretary.

1. I hope to be sending you instructions shortly about an Ayub visit. I agree fully with your recommendation that above all we must retain flexibility in our dealings with Ayub in period before visit and believe that you should know how we see things here.

2. While there are some signs of dawning Pak appreciation of their present plight and their need for improving their US relations, we agree with your assessment (Embtel 1011)[2] that even Shoaib's proposition represents lopsided view of realities in our relationship, i.e., GOP has no rational or comparable alternative to US political, economic and material support. As Ayub must be well aware, there are few foreign leaders anywhere to whom we have been more attentive and whom we have supported more consistently.

3. It is precisely to establish firm relationship based on such realities that makes it in Ayub's interest to have a meeting soon with President. While we recognize, as do you, that Ayub may seek some prior reassurances to reduce his political risks, it is up to Ayub to cope with visit's domestic implications which are after all his own creation. You have most patiently warned Ayub for years of danger inherent to his freedom of action in guiding Pakistan press and public opinion along a pro-Chinese and anti-US line.

4. We would expect summit meeting would encompass very fundamentals and future course of US–Pakistan relations. President desires to develop personal sense of what kind of relationship best serves our mutual interests. Concern here is to develop understanding of what constitutes workable relationship between aid donor and recipient. Aid is not a state of nature which US is bound to respect. We have obligations to our citizens to demonstrate our aid is achieving concrete results in terms of objectives aid is designed to serve. In Pakistan's case, what needs to be demonstrated to our satisfaction include the following:

a. *Actions showing Pakistan attaches priority to US and free world relationship.* Pakistan must disabuse itself of any notions that threat of turning to Chicoms will cause us to come running. This won't work

---

[1] Source: National Archives and Records Administration, RG 59, Central Files 1964–66, POL PAK–US. Secret; Priority; Nodis. Drafted by Laise; cleared by Handley, Hare, Ball, and McGeorge Bundy, and approved by Rusk. Also sent to Rawalpindi.

[2] Dated November 2. (Ibid., POL 27 INDIA–PAK)

and the sooner Paks stop using the tactic the closer we are to reaching a better understanding. What we seek is cooperative stance toward US. This does not rule out "correct" relations with China, but it does foreclose cozying up to China. In particular, positive steps to lower decibel count in Pakistan's denunciations of US policies are long overdue. Bhutto's distortions in New York re meetings with Ambassador Goldberg (USUN's 1753 repeated Karachi 174)[3] yet another example of GOP willful distortion of facts which has left sour taste here all too frequently over past years.

b. *Actions showing economic development has priority over dead-end policy toward India.* Past US policies of support were based on premise that Pakistan attached sufficient priority to economic development that Indo–Pak differences would not be allowed to escalate into war. This assumption was proved wrong. Until both countries take steps to defuse present explosive situation and start some processes to keep their tensions under control, we don't see possibility of fruitful long-term relationship with either country. What we want from Ayub is an indication that he is prepared to follow a course of reason on Kashmir, moderating his demands on India, so that economic development will not be sacrificed to a new Pak offensive on Kashmir and so that progress can be made toward settlement of Indo–Pak differences.

5. On broader subject of aid resumption, etc. we want it to be unmistakably clear to the Pakistanis that regardless of the actual and as yet unknown economic costs of their recent bout of warfare, it is widely accepted here by public, as reflected on the Hill and in the journals, that two nations we have helped considerably are frittering away scarce resources, both economic and military, as they bicker and fight. Aid resumption is going to be possible only if we can convince the Congress and the public at large that this is not going to happen again, and by "we" I include the Pakistanis as well.

Rusk

---

[3] Dated November 4. (Ibid., POL 15–1 PAK)

244. **Telegram From the Department of State to the Embassy in India**[1]

Washington, November 10, 1965, 4:32 p.m.

861. For Ambassador from Secretary.

1. Embassy's reporting on attitudes of GOI leaders regarding next steps in Indo–US relations, and particularly on Shastri's visit to USA, suggests that message we want to get across to them is just not getting through. Consequently believe you should know how we see things here as background for your negotiations re visit.

2. It appears that GOI leadership, in its present militant and go-it-alone mood, may have developed mistaken notion of relative weight of elements in equation of our relationship. While we do not discount either intrinsic importance of India to us or importance at this juncture in our relations that Shastri come here, we are not prepared to make overtures to get him here or to bargain with Shastri over conditions under which he will come. Given purpose of visit, it seems to us that it is of greater importance to Indians than to us that it takes place, and it is going to be a long, cold winter in our relationship unless he gets over here to sort things out with the President. We do not wish to encourage Indians to delude themselves regarding this basic point by our posture and our actions in period before meeting takes place. Moreover, while we recognize Shastri's narrow writ on Kashmir, it would seem from your reporting that he does have enough additional political strength these days to cope with any domestic political risks which he feels he may run in visiting US without prior understandings.

3. Our central concern will be to develop understanding of what constitutes workable relationship between aid donor and recipient. Aid is not a state of nature which US bound to respect. We have obligation to our citizens to demonstrate our aid is achieving concrete results in terms of objectives aid is designed to serve. In India's case, what needs to be demonstrated to our satisfaction includes following:

a. *Actions to turn swords into plowshares.* Present twilight state of no-war, no-peace threatens progress of economic development. Since India is larger country, special responsibility falls upon it to make every effort to restore peace and maintain security of subcontinent, along lines of SC Resolution of September 20. While movement toward reconciling Indo/Pak differences may be extremely difficult at this juncture, nevertheless

---

[1] Source: National Archives and Records Administration, RG 59, Central Files 1964–66, POL INDIA–US. Secret; Priority; Nodis. Drafted by Laise and Handley; cleared by Hare, Ball, and McGeorge Bundy; and approved by Rusk.

there is in present situation an unparalleled opportunity for India to steer Indo/Pak relations into new and more hopeful direction. At present time Pakistan is facing up to kind of hard realities and choices that would dispose it to come to terms with India on something less than plebiscite on Kashmir if India could provide way out. This means an honorable retreat for Pakistan into negotiations that will hold promise of easing its fears of Indian threat to Pakistan's security. Clearly this will involve Kashmir as well as other outstanding issues, and sorting out may take a long time. However, what is at stake is security of subcontinent and India's own larger interests vis-à-vis China. A serious and sustained process to find solutions to issues that divide India and Pakistan and to minimize thereby prospect of future war or exploitation by China is not too much for a friend interested in India's future to ask. And we intend to ask for such an effort while recognizing that settlement may be a long way off.

b. *Actions to translate economic promises to Indian people and to US into economic performance.* Most critical issue here is question of food production. My 800[2] and other messages have already spelled out nature of our concern over India's record to date and how this relates to future of PL 480 assistance.

4. On broader subject of aid resumption, etc. we want it to be unmistakably clear to the Indians that regardless of the actual and as yet unknown economic costs of their recent bout of warfare, it is widely accepted here by public, as reflected on the Hill and in the journals, that two nations we have helped considerably are frittering away scarce resources, both economic and military, as they bicker and fight. Aid resumption is going to be possible only if we can convince the Congress and the public at large that this is not going to happen again, and by "we" I include the Indians as well. As I told S.K. Patil when he came to see me, it was only by my assurances to the Congress that I was able to prevent legislative prohibitions on aid to South Asia.

5. As great Asian country, now alert to threat of expansionist Communist China, we believe India should be able understand and, indeed, give more support to efforts US and others making in Vietnam to thwart China's ambitions. We recognize GOI's difficulties, particularly with Soviet Union, in taking strong public position on this and that privately it does not wish see US pull out of Southeast Asia. But we consider that India's position and actions to date fall considerably short of what is possible.

6. In sum, Shastri should understand that President is interested in talking to him on wide variety of subjects in order to develop a personal sense of what kind of relationship between our two countries

---

[2] Document 240.

will best serve our mutual interests in years ahead, and that until this is accomplished we will not commit ourselves on numerous operational problems our two countries face. We do not intend to start out on journey until we know where we are going.[3]

Rusk

---

[3] Bowles responded that all of the issues raised in telegram 861 merited exploration during the proposed Shastri visit. He added, however: "if the tone of the message faithfully reflects the atmosphere in which the visit would occur I believe it would be a disaster." (Telegram 1270 from New Delhi, November 13; National Archives and Records Administration, RG 59, Central Files 1964–66, POL INDIA–PAK)

---

245.   **Memorandum From the President's Deputy Special Assistant for National Security Affairs (Komer) to the President's Special Assistant for National Security Affairs (Bundy)[1]**

Washington, November 11, 1965.

To add to our problems *we may have a major Indian food crisis on our hands.* Poor rains are apparently resulting in a very bad fall/winter crop. Last year's record production of 88 million tons was estimated earlier to be only 85 this year; new estimates are that it might be even less. Freeman's man, Brown, now in Delhi, has sent in Delhi 1244[2] attached, estimating that 10–15 million tons more grain imports from all sources may be needed to sustain India's millions to the next harvest. (I believe this figure includes our present shipments, which if continued at present rate would make up six million tons of this.)

The *Baltimore Sun* has been running a good series. Latest article attached.[3]

Am running this down and will be ready shortly to advise a course.

RWK

---

[1] Source: Johnson Library, National Security File, Name File, Komer Memos, Vol. II. Secret.

[2] Telegram 1244 from New Delhi, November 10, drew the conclusion that a poor monsoon pattern nationwide presaged a major food crisis, perhaps the most serious in recent history. (National Archives and Records Administration, RG 59, Central Files 1964–66, AGR 12 INDIA) In telegram 1248 from New Delhi, November 11, the Embassy reported that Food and Agriculture Minister Subramaniam had publicly estimated that the fall crop would be 3 million tons lower than the previous year's harvest, but the Embassy noted that independent observers had estimated the decline as closer to 6 million tons. (Ibid.)

[3] Not found attached.

246.   Telegram From the Embassy in India to the Department of State[1]

New Delhi, November 12, 1965, 0330Z.

1247. Yesterday at his request I called on L. K. Jha who said he wished to discuss the Prime Minister's visit to the United States.

After careful consideration it had been decided that any thought of a December visit should be abandoned. Parliament will not adjourn until the 10th of December and with the heavy agenda the session may drag on beyond that date which would leave almost no time before Christmas.

Therefore, the most convenient timing from the standpoint of the Prime Minister would be the first half of January, early enough to enable him to return by January 15 for the annual meeting of the All India Congress Committee in Jaipur on the 16, 17 and 18 of January.

Jha added that while the Prime Minister was anxious at some future date to spend more time in the US, he felt the current situation in India placed heavy demands on the Prime Minister and the visit should be a purely business occasion; he contemplated staying two or three days in Washington with possibly a day in New York. This would suggest the Prime Minister's arrival in Washington around the 10th of January and his return to India around the 14th, provided of course this fits the President's convenience. The Prime Minister was anxious that there not be any announcement of the suggested visit until a mutually agreed time in the future.

Jha then rather hesitantly stated that the Prime Minister and indeed the whole cabinet was deeply concerned about the outcome of the visit. India badly needed the US and if there is to be an independent non-Communist Asia with an effective block on Chinese expansionism the US also needed India. With so much at stake, Jha pointed out that the failure of the President and the Prime Minister to reach an understanding would have a catastrophic effect on the politics not only of India but of Asia at a very critical historic moment.

Therefore, did I see any discreet way of exploring on a preliminary basis the key questions that might arise and thus determine in some measure to what extent a meeting of the minds in Washington was likely? I said that I fully understood his concern but that I felt that with good will on both sides we can approach the meeting with confidence.

---

[1] Source: National Archives and Records Administration, RG 59, Central Files 1964–66, POL 7 INDIA. Secret; Priority; Exdis.

India's basic objectives and ours are very similar, i.e., India and America are equally anxious to block Chinese expansionism, and help maintain stability in Asia and Africa, to strengthen the UN, etc. The US also recognizes that a stable, economically viable, and democratic India with one-seventh of the world's population is absolutely basic to a stable and peaceful Asia.

For nearly twenty years we have been striving to create an Asian balance of power with almost no help from the major nations of Asia such as Japan, Indonesia, India and Pakistan.

This suggested a very key point of critical interest to us all: because we had no mass support for this essential effort we have been forced to fall back on relatively minor Asian powers such as South Korea, South Viet Nam and Taiwan and because these nations represented only 5 per cent of Asian peoples there has been no alternative but to introduce massive American military power into the equation.

One of the first questions the President might ask would be India's willingness and ability to work towards a more effective balance of power vis-à-vis China and thus to relieve some of the present pressures on the USA. To this Jha responded in a generally affirmatively although quite naturally non-committal manner.

Comment: We believe that it is of the utmost importance that this meeting go forward and I hope that the dates mentioned will be generally accepted. We also assume that we are as keenly aware as are the Indians that the failure of these discussions would have a profoundly adverse effect on US as well as Indian interests. It is my belief that in order to create a favorable and receptive mood the following steps are important:

1. As much as our policy will permit we should seek to relieve India of any reasonable suspicions that we are trying to take advantage of their food dilemna. We have made a vigorous rebuttal to these suspicions and in the effort we have had the powerful and effective support of Subramaniam.

It would be a master stroke for the USG to invite Subramaniam in the next 2 or 3 weeks to come to the US to discuss the Indian agriculture program and outlook. This suggestion would be received with warm approval in India and would put the Indian Government in a receptive mood for the kind of discussion which I am sure the President has in mind. If at the same time, we could release the non-profit fertilizer loans so that India could order the fertilizer urgently needed for the spring planting, Indian appreciation would be profound.

2. Here in India we could continue to impress on the Indians the need for curbing the careless and sometimes irresponsible statements of such Indian leaders as Indira Gandhi, Chagla, etc.

3. In New Delhi and in the UN we should press the Indians fully to carry out the cease-fire in spite of Pak provocation and to meet Pakistan more than halfway in regard to withdrawal. This will help lay the basis for a discussion of the long-term political problems facing the two countries without running head on into India's absolute determination not to give up the strategically important Kashmir Valley.

4. With the advice and guidance of the Department we would like gradually to proceed with more substantive discussions with Shastri and his advisors such questions as India's continued willingness to stand up to China, India's defense requirements under varying situations, the willingness of the Indians to give economic development the highest priority and the economic moves by India which encourage us to give India the support she requires to become self-sufficient in ten years.

There is every evidence that thoughtful Indians in and out of government are deeply conscious that many Indian criticisms of the US during the past months have been grossly unfair and there is evidence on every side of a desire to bring the situation back into balance. With careful handling in both Washington and New Delhi, we are confident this mood can be strengthened and a basis for successful negotiations in Washington established.

We would appreciate Department's response as soon as convenient, particularly in regard to Subramaniam visit[2] which will require some planning all around.

Bowles

---

[2] McGeorge Bundy relayed Bowles' suggestion concerning an invitation to Subramaniam in a November 14 memorandum to President Johnson. Johnson indicated his approval. (Johnson Library, National Security File, Country File, India, Vol. VI, Memos and Miscellaneous)

247. Telegram From the Embassy in India to the Department of State[1]

New Delhi, November 15, 1965, 1340Z.

1274. For Agr Sec Freeman from Bowles. Minister of Agriculture Subramanian is eagerly looking forward to opportunity to visit with you at FAO Conference in Rome where I understand you will both be on Nov. 19. The difficult agricultural situation with which Subramaniam is dealing, as you know, is now further complicated by what appears to be worst monsoon pattern in fifty or sixty years.

For the long haul GOI is deeply committed to an all out program of increased fertilizer output, better seeds, better use of water, expanded extension [service?], etc. Much of their new fertilizer and improved seed effort is to be concentrated on 30 million specially selected irrigated acres where they believe they can double present output in next five years.

Although we must of course continue to carry out the plans which they have laid down, it is also important that we convince Subramaniam that we have confidence in him personally. He is by all odds the ablest Minister in cabinet, vigorously pro-American and with great amount of courage. In the last two weeks he has performed valiantly answering attacks of left wing element who have charged that we have been using PL480 food as political lever. However, he is genuinely baffled when he reads statements in US press that his Ministry is not doing all it should in regard to agriculture since he has adopted just about every suggestion we have made in the sixteen months he has had job.

Therefore I earnestly hope you will encourage him and thank him for all he has done for India's future. He needs to feel that we are behind him. He has stuck his neck out politically in our behalf and his political career is committed to cooperation with the United States.

He will want to know from you about (a) outlook for a long-range PL480 agreement; (b) our ability to go beyond 500,000 tons per month if the supply situation becomes really desperate and (c) possibility of freeing some US foreign exchange to enable him to buy 700,000 tons of fertilizer (which we have been insisting upon) in time to affect crops which will be planted next June or July.

Although I know your time is short before you leave for Rome it would be most useful if you could arrange to bring Subramaniam back from Rome to Washington for further talks with some of the people

---

[1] Source: National Archives and Records Administration, RG 59, Central Files 1964–66, AGR 1 INDIA. Confidential; Immediate; Exdis. Passed to the White House.

there whe are not aware of what India has now committed itself to do and who are therefore genuinely sceptical that India will follow through on this effort.

If this not possible I would appreciate somehow arrange with Subramaniam to [visit] India to see for yourself what has been undertaken here since your last visit eighteen months ago and to share with GOI our thinking about what more they ought to be doing.

With considerable difficulty we have been sitting on the lid here for several months and I am confident that India is now at a turning point. It could move strongly in our direction but if we should twist the screws a bit too tight we may lose all we are seeking to gain. Do let me know whether you can invite Subramaniam back to Washington or if not, whether you might possibly be able to come to India yourself soon.

Regards.

Bowles

---

248.   Memorandum From the President's Deputy Special Assistant for National Security Affairs (Komer) to President Johnson[1]

Washington, November 16, 1965, 7 p.m.

Here are the papers Arthur Dean mentioned today.[2] Since aid to India and Pakistan is so central to the FY 1967 foreign aid problem now under review for you, we made a special effort. The attached papers are the result, and we are shooting them at your tough-minded friends.

---

[1] Source: Johnson Library, National Security File, Name File, Komer Memos, Vol. II. Secret.

[2] Reference is to a 29-page paper dated November 8 entitled "A United States Assistance Strategy for India," and a 21-page paper dated November 9 entitled "United States Assistance Strategy for Pakistan." There is no drafting information on either paper, but a covering memorandum by Komer, November 10, forwarding the India paper to the President states that it was drafted by "us 'soft on India' types." (Ibid., Country File, India, Vol. VI, Cables, Memos and Miscellaneous, 9/65–1/66) A copy of the India paper is ibid.; a copy of the Pakistan paper is in Washington National Records Center, RG 330, OASD/ISA Files: FRC 70 A 3717, 092 Pakistan)

We've made every effort to be hard-nosed, to put the alternatives coldly, and to give you a basis for choice. But we just can't get around two basic propositions: (1) that India is (with Japan) one of the two really key countries in Free Asia—so merits a comparable investment *almost despite the Indians;* (2) that Pakistan can complement our effort in India, or greatly complicate it if it goes the Chicom route.

Because these two big programs are the key variables, you may want to read parts of the argument before the aid review. If you wish to scan only the key portions, these are:

On India

pp. 5–7 which argue that India has actually done reasonably well with our money, and is basically going our way. Thus our real problem is less India's basic outlook than its performance.

pp. 8–10 on how we can't "buy" a Kashmir settlement, even if we throw all our aid in the balance. So we can't afford to make this the keystone of our policy.

pp. 16–19 which say that what we need is a new policy—not in content but in method—which would directly bargain continued massive aid for sharply improved Indian self-help. We would make this bargain self-enforcing by adjusting aid flow to Indian performance—especially in agriculture.

pp. 21–22 on how this sort of bargain can be struck by you and Shastri at the summit—the earlier the better.

On Pakistan

pp. 1–4 which describe our cruel dilemma—how just when our economic aid begins to pay off we find ourselves on divergent political courses.

pp. 7–11 on the urgent need for a meeting of minds at the summit and the political bargain we must insist on if our aid is not to be wasted.

pp. 16–19 on how it makes sense to support Pak development *if* we can reach a political understanding, and how tactically we might handle Mr. Ayub.

R.W. Komer

249.   Memorandum From the President's Special Assistant for National Security Affairs (Bundy) to President Johnson[1]

Washington, November 17, 1965, 11:15 a.m.

1. I spoke to Orville Freeman this morning about getting the Indian Agricultural Minister, Subramaniam, over here. Orville is going to an international agricultural meeting in Rome this week, and will be seeing Subramaniam there. He has undertaken to explore the matter fully, and he strongly supports the basic idea of the Subramaniam visit.

2. Orville pointed out that Subramaniam might find it difficult to come if there were no prospect that he could reach any understanding on help for Indian agriculture—because for him to go home empty-handed—as a well-known friend of the United States—might be politically tough. I told Orville that you were not ready to give any blank checks on this, and that I thought he should make his own estimate in the light of all the evidence as to whether it was likely that Subramaniam's visit would lay a base for a hard-boiled recommendation that limited interim assistance be given in such a matter as, for example, for fertilizer.

3. Orville and I agreed that your own freedom of action should be protected, but I pointed out that you had repeatedly emphasized in the last week that you were looking to the Department of Agriculture for determined efforts to make sure that every single action of the United States in the food aid field was effectively related to agricultural self-help by the receiving country. I said that I thought that since this was your position, you would be prepared to give due weight to a really well-considered and carefully limited recommendation growing out of a Subramaniam visit—if it had the signature of the Secretary of State for policy, the Secretary of Agriculture for food, the Secretary of the Treasury for dollar drain, and the Directors of AID and the Budget from their points of view. I said that the loans in question had no balance-of-payments import that I could see, so that I thought Freeman himself was the key figure.

4. On this basis, Freeman undertook to have a hard talk with Subramaniam in Rome and make a judgment on the visit at that time. We agreed to report this plan to you in case you had any objection to it.

5. I have since talked to Komer about my conversation with Freeman, and he believes that Subramaniam can fairly easily come here for a "planning" visit without taking any commitments home

---

[1] Source: Johnson Library, National Security File, Country File, India, Vol. VI, Memos & Miscellaneous, 9/65–1/66. Secret.

with him, if it seems better to you when the time comes to play it that way. Moreover, Komer thinks that in the light of the very bad Indian harvest, straight food shipments may turn out to be more important right now, both to the Indians and to us, than fertilizer. So I have agreed again with Freeman that he should be sure to give absolutely no assurance that a visit here would lead to a specific prize for Subramaniam.

6. Meanwhile, a cable[2] is going to Bowles telling him to explain politely to Shastri that while you would like to receive him at any time, and quite understand that he cannot come in December, the dates proposed in the first weeks of January are difficult for the reasons you stated to me yesterday. Bowles is requested to suggest to the Indians that Shastri propose himself for any date that is convenient to him after January 20.

7. We are also going forward to make sure that Ayub knows he will be welcome on agreed dates in December—if indeed he still wants to come then.[3]

McG.B.[4]

---

[2] Telegram 895 to New Delhi, November 18. (National Archives and Records Administration, RG 59, Cental Files 1964–66, POL 7 INDIA)

[3] Bundy sent a cable to the LBJ Ranch on November 26 to report that Ayub had proposed a visit to Washington December 14–16, following a speech to the UN General Assembly on December 13. (Telegram CAP 65753 from Bundy to the President; Johnson Library, National Security File, Country File, Pakistan, Ayub Visit, 12/12–16/65)

[4] Printed from a copy that bears these typed initials.

250.   Telegram From the Department of State to the Embassy in the United Kingdom[1]

Washington, November 23, 1965, 7:59 p.m.

2919. U.S.–U.K. talks conducted November 16–18[2] covered British assessment of situation in subcontinent, of positions of India, Pakistan, Russia and China, and consequences for British policy. Sir Patrick Dean led off for Brits in meeting with Acting Secretary Ball and tabled paper[3] which will be pouched. Purpose of talks and visit of Pickard and Belcher seemed to be to convey to U.S. that gravity of situation and special circumstances (including substantial investment) which characterize U.K. relations with India and Pakistan have led to British assessment that it is in our common interest for U.K. to move ahead with economic aid and selected military sales. One area of doubt was question of supplying Gnat components to India and on this point U.S. views were specifically requested. Implicit in British presentation was hope U.S. would relax its current aid policies in both India and Pakistan. In their view both countries realize U.S. arms embargo had had profound effect on Indo–Pak conflict which had greatly benefited India. Realities of this situaton necessitated at least sales of spares to Paks, particularly for Air Force.

Constant British refrain was pessimism about progress on Indo–Pak front and risks to Western interests of aid being used to extract political concessions. Brits held political pressure would, in present mood of two countries, be likely to drive each to act illogically and against its own national interest. Pakistan might move decisively toward China; India might elect economic stagnation and dependence on USSR. End result could be chaos and beyond retrieving by any efforts we might then make. Pickard thought situation in Pakistan already so explosive and Ayub under such severe pressures from military that it was difficult to see how satisfactory Washington conversations could take place unless Ayub were to go home with arms

---

[1] Source: National Archives and Records Administration, RG 59, Central Files 1964–66, POL 27 INDIA–PAK. Secret; Limdis. Drafted by Laise on November 20; cleared by Judd, Hare, and Handley; and approved by Ball. Also sent to New Delhi and Karachi, and repeated to USUN.

[2] Memoranda of conversation on these talks, which took place in Washington, are ibid., POL 27 INDIA–PAK, POL 2 ASIA, and POL 2 ASIA SE. The U.S. participants in the talks included Ball, Mann, Hare, AID Director Bell, and McNaughton (DOD/ISA). The British participants included Ambassador Dean, Cyril S. Pickard, Superintending Under Secretary for the Asia and Atlantic Division of the Commonwealth Relations Office, and Ronald H. Belcher, Under Secretary of the Asia Division of the Ministry of Overseas Development.

[3] Not found.

and/or guarantees against India and some agreement on Kashmir. If U.S. were to pay his price, however, impossible problems would be created for Shastri visit. U.K. has concluded it can best contribute to our common objective by maintaining complementary rather than parallel aid policies, thus trying to maintain what little influence it has and using it to reduce risks and to create reasonable political climate in which more massive U.S. leverage can be used to good effect.

Acting Secretary Ball stated that U.S. posture is to take very hard look at very important but complicated situation which exists on subcontinent. Before continuing to pour very large resources into subcontinent that makes development difficult for itself by its actions, we would want some assurance both on political side and on economic measures for self-help. We have had difficulty explaining to Congress why we were pouring our diminishing surplus stocks into an India that is not moving toward self-sufficiency. To continue to do so may be doing them a disservice. Pakistan has done better on this score but we still face problem of whether it is prudent and wise to provide resources to two nations which are more obsessed with each other than with their own development. These are questions which need answering.

Difference between U.S. and U.K. approach appears to be one of timing—how soon we should move and what should be understandings connected with these moves. Mr. Ball noted that U.S. is expecting Shastri and Ayub. He anticipated that visits would take place before February. We are very much looking forward to having frank talks. Out of these we will have clearer view of what we can expect of each other. We are not keen on rushing back and putting resources into an area where we do not know what is going to happen. Acting Secretary expressed hope that U.S. and U.K. could have sufficient agreement on requirements to move together. In light of this, resumption of sales of military equipment by U.K., particularly components for Gnats, frankly concerns us and it will intensify Pakistan anxieties. Therefore, it seemed desirable to reach some common conclusions on timing.

Throughout talks U.S. officials emphasized U.S. policy was unchanged for present and lack of parallelism of U.S.–U.K. policies would create problems for us. At conclusion of talks we confirmed to Brits that U.S. hoped U.K. would defer action on allowing sales of Gnat components to India until after Ayub, Shastri visits. In farewell conversation with Department officer Pickard stated on basis of what he had just learned about Indian deals with USSR and Czechs, he thought U.K. could pin holding line on Gnats to this new development.

Memcons follow.

Ball

251. Telegram From the Embassy in Italy to the Department of State[1]

Rome, November 26, 1965.

1377. Dept pass Texas White House—Eyes Only for President. From Secretary Freeman.

Estimates of Indian 1965–66 crop short fall have been carefully checked.

Earlier estimates appear optimistic in light of latest evidence. 1964–65 food grain production of 88 million tons will drop at least 10 million tons. Drouth most serious of this century. Virtually every area of India hit. Current actual consumption is estimated 174 kilograms of grain per capita, well below minimum FAO nutritional standards. If 10 million tons less food grains available, intake will drop to 152 kg per capita.

Prediction that 10 million tons cut in availabillity of food grains would result in substantial starvation appears to be valid.

Reinhardt

---

[1] Source: National Archives and Records Administration, RG 59, Central Files 1964–66, SOC 10 INDIA. Confidential; Priority; Exdis. No time of transmission is on the telegram. Received at 8:21 a.m. and passed to the White House at 8:56 a.m. Freeman was in Rome for meetings of the UN Food and Agriculture Organization.

---

252. Telegram From the Embassy in Pakistan to the Department of State[1]

Karachi, November 26, 1965, 1405Z.

1164. Subject: Indo–Pak Crisis: Shoaib on Current Problems.

1. During meeting with AID Director Williams in Rawalpindi, November 24, Finance Minister Shoaib stated that President Ayub had deep-seated suspicion that American CIA was attempting to undermine his position and bring about his downfall. Shoaib said he had been

---

[1] Source: National Archives and Records Administration, RG 59, Central Files 1964–66, POL 27 INDIA–PAK. Secret; Noforn; Limdis. Received at 1:04 p.m.

working with Ayub in preparation for the visit to Washington, but that he had not been able to remove Ayub's suspicion or even entirely plumb its full extent. It was a central point being actively played upon by those who advocated an alternative course in Pakistan foreign policy orientation, Shoaib said. He asked that this information be conveyed to the Ambassador and Secretary of State and he (Shoaib) recommended that reassurance to Ayub on this point be undertaken by President Johnson as "the first order of business" during the forthcoming visit.

2. Shoaib also said that the feeling was growing in Pindi that the US had let Pakistan down despite membership in SEATO and CENTO and specific pledges against Indian aggression. These points were being made in National Assembly and they were becoming harder to counter. US arms supplied to India had been used against Pakistan. Shoaib observed that he would meet again with President Ayub that evening and appeared to be inviting counter arguments. Williams replied that the US Government had fully met its pledge to come to Pakistan's assistance in a situation where the origin of hostilities was confused. We had produced the cease-fire at a time when it was desperately needed and we had "taken India's food supply by the throat," with short rein month-to-month approval, in support of the cease-fire. The ratio of US arms assistance was ten to one in favor of Pakistan over India and no country had received such generous economic assistance as Pakistan. The US was Pakistan's best friend by any standard of reasoning, AID Director Williams concluded.

3. Shoaib expressed concern about the increased military budget. He was afraid an enlarged army would become a permanent factor, but he said he was powerless to resist diversion of financial resources to defense, given the present mood and the need to replenish arms lost in the war. Williams hoped that no significant arrangement for arms from Communist China would be concluded before President Ayub's visit to Washington. Shoaib was visibly disturbed, saying that Pakistan had to replenish arms from somewhere; the Indians were building up and reportedly getting US arms from Israel and Formosa. Shoaib said he had kept out of the attempts to make alternative arrangements for arms, but he appeared to accept validity of the point that a major arms deal with Communist China would prejudice the success of Ayub's visit to the US.

McConaughy

253.   Telegram From the Embassy in Italy to the Department of State[1]

Rome, November 26, 1965.

1381. Dept pass Texas White House—Eyes Only for President From Secretary Freeman. Embtel 1373.[2]

Begin text:

Title: Agreement between Secretary of Agriculture Orville L. Freeman and Minister of Food and Agriculture C. Subramaniam, November 1965, Rome, Italy. End title.

It was agreed that it was very much to the benefit of both India and the United States to reverse the disturbing downward trend in per capita food production.

It was agreed that the quantity of resources allocated to agriculture has not been adequate in recent years.

It was agreed that:

1. Investment in agriculture during the fourth Five Year Plan (1966–67 to 1970–71) would be 2,400 crore rupees (nearly 5 billion dollars) or more than double the investment levels during the third plan period ending this year.

2. Investment in agriculture during the coming year (1966–67) would be increased by at least 40 percent above the current year even though the emergency might require cutbacks in other areas of investment.

3. Investment in agriculture next year (1966–67) will be 410 crore rupees as against 304 this year.

It was agreed that:

1. The Government of India will publicly announce and endorse the fertilizer consumption targets for the next 5 years agreed to by the Indian Ministry of Food and Agriculture. These quantities of fertilizer, to be made availabe through imports, if domestic production is inadequate, are as follows:

	N	P205	K20
	(million metric tons)		
1966–67	1.00	0.37	0.20
1967–68	1.35	0.50	0.30
1968–69	1.708	0.65	0.45
1969–70	2.00	0.80	0.55
1970–71	2.40	1.00	0.70

---

[1] Source: National Archives and Records Administration, RG 59, Central Files 1964–66, AID (US) 15–8 INDIA. Confidential; Priority. No time of transmission is on the telegram. Received at 2:24 p.m. and passed to the White House at 4:24 p.m.

[2] Not found.

2. Basic policy changes encouraging foreign private investment in the manufacture and distribution of fertilizer will be implemented.

A. The Government of India will announce a plan before January 1, 1966 to purchase any fertilizer produced in excess of market demand at world market prices.

B. The government of India will announce the removal of any geographic constraints on fertilizer marketing before January 1, 1966 to take effect as soon as fertilizer supplies are adequate, now expected in 1968–69.

C. The Government will reduce the role of the central nitrogen pool from its present near-monopoly position to one in which it handles only a minor part of the fertilizer supply. All manufacturers of nitrogenous fertilizer will be authorized to establish their own distribution arrangements.

3. That steps would be taken by the government to operate its own fertilizer plants at full capacity by allocating enough foreign exchange to ensure adequate supplies of raw materials and spare parts and by carefully reviewing periodically the level of management effectiveness.

4. That if modifications in the procedures for approving and licensing foreign private investment in the manufacture and distribution of fertilizer do not sufficiently shorten the time required for negotiations that futher administrative and procedural changes will be made.

5. A cabinet level committee, now chaired by the Prime Minister will make a continuing effort to see that bureaucratic procedures do not hinder or discourage private foreign investment in fertilizer production and distribution. It will also pass judgment on basic policy questions which if unresolved might hinder investment.

6. That there will be no tie-in between credit and distribution. That is, farmers will be given credit regardless of where they buy their fertilizer.

7. That the Government of India will not require government participation in the ownership of fertilizer plants in the private sector.

It was agreed that the current system of credit cooperatives was not adequate and that the following actions would be taken to remedy this:

1. A cabinet level committee on agricultural credit chaired by the Food and Agriculture Minister would explore alternative avenues of supplying credit to farmers.

2. The government will systematically review and test alternative credit possibilities. The following will be tested on a pilot basis.

A. The food corporation will supply credit to farmers against advances on their crops.

B. Current private credit institutions will be urged to extend credit availabilities and the possible need for credit subsidies will be evaluated.

3. The possibility of an all-India agricultural credit organization to supplement the credit supply of the cooperative sector will be actively explored.

It was agreed that new instrumentalities such as the agricultural production board, a committee of cabinet members and other key officials chaired by the Food and Agriculture Minister and vested with the authority to make binding decisions on matters of agricultural production, will be used to achieve the necessary allocation of resources to Indian agriculture.

It was agreed that:

1. 32 million acres of the most productive land farmed by the more efficient farmers will be designated for a crash production program with a target of 25 million tons of additional food grains by 1970 on this selected acreage.

2. The resources and inputs necessary will have the number one priority to wit:

A. The new fertilizer responsive varieties of food grains will be planted on well irrigated land, applying from 100 to 150 pounds of fertilizer per acre as compared with a national average of 3 to 5 pounds per acre. These new varieties, planted on the best irrigated land, would get the necessary fertilizer even though this might require a cutback on some other land if fertilizer were in short supply.

B. If the seed multiplication program for the new imported varieties (wheat from Mexico and rice from the International Rice Research Institute in the Philippines) falls behind schedule, foreign exchange will be made available for the import of additional supplies of suitable seed.

C. New irrigation techniques, going from the traditional flow method to controlled maximum irrigation, will be selectively applied. For this purpose resources will be made available wherever it is demonstrated practicable. In addition, adequate resources will be made available to develop minor irrigation sources to attain a water balance for multiple cropping. With this new intensive irrigation more and more land will be multiple cropped.

It was agreed that price policies will be reviewed periodically to ensure a continuing favorable relationship between the price of food grains and the price of purchased inputs such as fertilizer.

It was concluded that the new legislation establishing the food corporation and the recent amendments to the Defense of India rules along with the basic constitutional provisions did give the center government adequate authority to control the movement and distribution of grain between the states. The Minister made it clear that the central government now had the authority to develop and implement a rational food policy.

It was agreed that efforts to dramatize and mobilize public sentiment to demonstrate the urgency of action in agriculture would be made. Such actions as public statements by the President, Prime Minister and other leading public officials will be used even more in the future.

It was agreed that:

1. Highest priority will be given to agricultural development and allied programs in the fourth Five Year Plan. This priority will also apply to the allocation of foreign exchange to agriculture. It is noted that the agricultural program detailed above would require foreign exchange of the order of 2 billion dollars for the fourth Five Year Plan.

2. To meet food production targets the import of 500,000 tons of nitrogen fertilizer (in terms GF N) for the 1966–67 crop is essential. Out of this total quantity needed, arrangements will be made to import 100,000 tons from available resources. Every effort will be made to find the balance of the resources required to reach the target. Minister Subramaniam emphasized the critical importance of reaching this target, stating that in view of the severe limits on the availability of foreign exchange that immediate United States aid is imperative.

It was agreed that the Government of India will make the following food aid phase-out schedule an integral part of its fourth Five Year Plan for agriculture.

Year	Cereals Surplus (plus) or Deficit (minus)	Import Requirements for Buffer Stocks (in million tons)	Total Import Requirements
1966–67	(minus) 6.2	0.8	7.0
1967–68	(minus) 3.8	1.7	5.5
1968–69	(minus) 2.0	2.0	4.0
1969–70	(minus) 0.2	2.3	2.5
1970–71	(minus) 0.9	nil	nil

Signed Orville L. Freeman, Secretary of Agriculture, United States of America; C. Subramaniam, Minister of Food and Agriculture, India. Date November 25, 1965. *End text*.[3]

Reinhardt

---

[3] This agreement, subsequently referred to as the "Treaty of Rome," was hailed by John P. Lewis, Minister of Embassy in New Delhi and Director of the AID program in India, in a December 28 memorandum to Komer as more solid in content and promise "than any comparable program since Independence." Lewis' assessment was that the United States "has helped engineer what could be a breakthrough for Indian agricultural expansion." Lewis saw that expansion as an important part of an effort to speed up Indian economic growth, an effort being described by AID and the World Bank as "the Big Push." Lewis noted that the success of "the Big Push" would also depend on a revamped assistance program for India. (Johnson Library, National Security File, NSC History, Indian Famine, August 66–February 67, Vol. II)

254. Memorandum From the President's Deputy Special Assistant for National Security Affairs (Komer) to President Johnson[1]

Washington, November 27, 1965, 1 p.m.

Attached is Rusk's request for *another monthly 500,000 tons of food for India* and 175,000 tons for Pakistan.[2] Freeman's cables to you confirm that a new Indian food crisis is upon us. As a result, there will be pressure for a sharp increase in monthly shipments, perhaps from 500,000 to 700,000 tons. In fact, after Rusk's memo was drafted, we got an official Indian request for 650,000 tons (including 100,000 tons of milo) next month.

We're looking into this, but suggest going ahead on the old basis now and awaiting Freeman's recommendation on anything further. The reason for moving fast is that we've actually been taking five weeks to make each four week allocation, which means that we're really shipping at a slower rate when the problem is growing.

Freeman seems to have gotten quite an impressive set of commitments from Subramaniam (though without any reciprocal commitments on our part). Thus we're making progress on the long-term problem, though we still have the short-term food crisis to sort out. Freeman clearly wants to come to the ranch to report. Would you prefer to have us ask him to give his recommendations in writing first?

Approve India/Pak allotment

Ask Freeman to report in writing[3]

I'll handle Freeman

R.W. Komer[4]

---

[1] Source: Johnson Library, National Security File, Country File, India, India's Food Problem, Vol. I. Secret. A handwritten notation reads: "Rec'd Ranch 11–28–65, 8:30 p."

[2] Attached was a November 26 memorandum from Rusk to the President recommending the release of grain for India and Pakistan under existing P.L. 480 agreements.

[3] Johnson indicated his approval of this option by completing the sentence in his handwriting to read: "first and I'll see him as soon as possible." Komer noted in the margin: "I told Schnittker 29 Nov 65."

[4] McGeorge Bundy initialed below Komer's signature.

255. Memorandum From Secretary of Agriculture Freeman to President Johnson[1]

Washington, December 1, 1965.

SUBJECT

India—Food and Agriculture

I. For the first time the Indian Government through its Agricultural Minister Subramaniam has made concrete specific commitments to the United States which will if carried out vigorously significantly improve India's agricultural performance.

II. The critical question remains—How the United States can make certain that pledges are followed by performance.

III. It is expected that the Indian Government in the near future will make a public pronouncement on agriculture incorporating the agreed upon actions and targets with a commitment to accomplish them. Subramaniam indicated to me the likelihood that he would be speaking to the Council of State on December 8 to spell out a plan of action to meet the current crisis and that he would incorporate the commitments made at Rome in such a presentation.

IV. The public commitment by the Indian Government can be reinforced by the United States as follows:

(a) Length of Public Law 480 agreements can be conditioned to the performance of the Indian Government.

(b) The agricultural action commitments can be incorporated into the AID arrangements with disbursements conditioned on the Indian Government meeting its agricultural commitments. Precise detailed criteria to measure performance and insure action can be negotiated. Failure on the part of the Indian Government to perform will be surfaced under such a procedure and the appropriate action decision can be made accordingly.

V. The following sequence of actions might be followed:

(a) Communicate to Prime Minister Shastri that spelling out as the plan of the Indian Government the commitments made in Rome would be favorably received by the United States Government.

(b) United States announce another short term P.L. 480 agreement.

(c) Following Indian Government public commitment perhaps through Subramaniam's proposed December 8 speech to the Council

---

[1] Source: Johnson Library, National Security File, NSC History, Indian Famine, August 1966–February 1967, Vol. I. No classification marking.

of State, U.S. Government would then compliment the Indian Government on strong new efforts and announce the opening of negotiations for a further extension of P.L. 480 for a longer period (but still limited).

(d) When the U.S. Government resumes negotiations for economic assistance it will be made perfectly clear privately that assistance will be geared to the Indian performance in meeting their agricultural commitments and targets. In the alternative the President might direct that negotiations quietly resume prior to the Shastri visit. Such negotiations could provide a useful backdrop for the President's use at the time of the Shastri visit.

VI. Some personal observations:

Recent events and my meeting with Subramaniam in Rome encourage me where Indian agriculture is concerned.

1. It appears that the Prime Minister is at last convinced of the need to depart from traditional agriculture techniques and use modern inputs, such as chemical fertilizer.

2. It appears that the Prime Minister's attitude which hitherto might be described as Fabian Socialist toward agricultural development has changed. Today agriculture commands a position at the top rather than at the bottom of the totem pole in priorities.

3. Recent public statements by the Prime Minister substantiate the changed attitude and increased attention now given to agriculture.

4. Food and Agricultural Minister Subramaniam impressed me. He has drive and ability. He appears to hold a strong position in the Indian Cabinet and to have a good deal of political skill. He has been a steadfast supporter of the United States.

VII. Finally, it is my judgment, supported by the Indian specialists on my staff, that India can make the grade. It does have the physical resources. Its soils are for instance inherently far superior to those of Japan. Now that the Indian Government is targeting its goals and appears to be giving necessary priority in allocating its resources and we have some strong leverage to insist that they continue to do so, I believe significant progress can be made. It will be slow and tough, but it can be done.

256. Telegram From the President's Special Assistant for National Security Affairs (Bundy) and Deputy Special Assistant for National Security Affairs (Komer) to President Johnson in Texas[1]

Washington, December 1, 1965, 7:42 p.m.

CAP 65788. We've landed Shastri too. His private secretary has asked Bowles if the first week in February is convenient to you. This is in response to our suggestion that mid-January, as he earlier proposed, was bad for you but that any time after the 20th would be fine.

Shastri has apparently been maneuvered (by Ayub's acceptance) into going to Tashkent at the end of the year.[2] This is an added reason for his eagerness to sign up with you first lest we misunderstand. In fact, however, Tashkent may prove a blessing in disguise. When Ayub hits you on Kashmir, you can say work it out with Shastri at Tashkent. If (remote chance) the Soviets do work out a Kashmir deal, we'll gain as much from it as the Soviets. More likely, the Soviets will find themselves in the same box we've been in.

We suggest you take up Shastri visit with Rusk tomorrow, and decide on a firm date.

On Indian food, it looks as though a combination of the short rein strategy, Freeman's recent prods, and India's own desperate straits have finally made them think big. We like Freeman's strategy, but suspect that you'll want to keep Indians on a short rein tactically till you and Shastri strike the bargain. This is do-able, provided that our monthly interim shipments are big enough to keep India afloat till then. So we'd again argue for a quick monthly OK of as much as Freeman thinks desirable (plus the interim fertilizer loan—which we'd see as shrewd but not essential).

---

[1] Source: Johnson Library, National Security File, Country File, Pakistan, Vol. V, Memos, 9/65–1/66. Secret.

[2] According to press reports from New Delhi, Shastri announced on December 1 that he had agreed to meet Ayub at Tashkent in late December or early January. (Telegram 1401 from New Delhi, December 2; National Archives and Records Administration, RG 59, Central Files 1964–66, POL INDIA–PAK)

257.   Telegram From the Department of State to the Embassy in India[1]

Washington, December 2, 1965, 11:56 p.m.

976. For Ambassador from Secretary Freeman. Please communicate to Subramaniam that I have reviewed our Rome agreement with the President who is pleased with the steps taken and contemplated by the Indian Government to strengthen Indian agriculture. The President looks forward to Subramaniam's outlining his program including points agreed upon at Rome publicly as soon as possible, perhaps when he addresses Council of State as he suggested at Rome he would do soon.[2] Decision of PL–480, both extension period and amount, and fertilizer loan under active consideration.

Rusk

---

[1] Source: National Archives and Records Administration, RG 59, Central Files 1964–66, AGR 1 INDIA. Secret; Immediate; Exdis. Drafted by Freeman. The telegram bears a handwritten notation that reads: "OK/L," indicating that it was cleared with the President. Coon and Sober were informed.

[2] Bowles reported on December 3 that he had conveyed this message to Subramaniam who indicated that he intended to present his proposals for agricultural reform to the Cabinet and expected its approval. (Telegram 1413 from New Delhi; ibid.)

---

258.   Memorandum From the President's Deputy Special Assistant for National Security Affairs (Komer) to President Johnson[1]

Washington, December 6, 1965, 6 p.m.

India Food Catastrophe. Freeman's best expert is just back with the considered judgment of the people out there that the food crisis is even more catastrophic than previously estimated.[2] The shortfall will

---

[1] Source: Johnson Library, National Security File, NSC History, Indian Famine, August 1966–February 1967, Vol. I. Secret.

[2] The expert was Lester Brown, a staff economist in the Department of Agriculture and Freeman's adviser during his meetings with Subramaniam in Rome. On December 6 Freeman sent a portion of the report prepared by Brown after his trip to India to President Johnson. (Memorandum from Freeman to President Johnson; ibid.)

probably run as high as 20 million tons instead of 10–12 million (we're shipping at an annual rate of 6 million). *Some famine and starvation seem inevitable,* almost despite whatever we do. The whole crisis is now public, with major coverage in the Sunday papers here.

On the longer term front, you've seen Bowles' report (Delhi 1430)[3] that Indian cabinet bought almost all of the Subramaniam/Freeman recommendations. They will be announced Tuesday. India is also allocating $52 million equivalent to buying fertilizer.

Recommended US Response. We are already past the 4 December deadline if the pipeline is not to be interrupted. The tactics of our response should be to go big enough to seem generously responsive, yet limited enough to retain full bargaining leverage. The sheer magnitude of India's food crisis makes this easy.

A. *Make the next allocation 2 or 3 months.* The case for a longer period is to reduce panic and hoarding in India by showing that the US will come through. A secondary reason for 3 months is to carry us through Shastri visit, so he won't have to come beg. However, we could stick with 2 months or even one *if we went big on amount.*

B. 500,000 tons per month would now seem utterly incommensurate with the need (which may be *three times* higher). With some famine inevitable, should we open ourselves to accusations later that we share the responsibility for having shipped less than Indian capacity to receive? Given all the crisis publicity, our response won't look credible any longer if we keep shipments at 500,000 tons. However, port capacity gives us a ceiling well below the need; *thus, going to 750,000 tons would show responsiveness, while still making India come to us.* Even one month of this would look much better than 2–3 months at 500,000. Bell favors staying at 500,000 Title I but adding on 250,000 Title II disaster relief. We pay the freight on the latter, but it looks better and protects us against Krishna Menon-type allegations that we charged money for food when Indians were starving.

C. *$50 million Fertilizer Loan* will save 4 million tons of grain we'd otherwise be pressed to give later, though it alone will not meet the immediate problem in the months before the new crop comes in. Bell feels strongly that we should tie conditions to this loan which will force Subramaniam to carry out his promises.

---

[3] On December 6 Bowles reported that the Indian Cabinet had accepted the agreement reached at Rome with one minor exception relating to fertilizer distribution, which was to be studied by a subcommittee before final decision. (Telegram 1430 from New Delhi; National Archives and Records Administration, RG 59, Central Files 1964–66, SOC 10 INDIA) On December 7 Subramaniam made parallel statements in the Lok Sabha and the Raj Sabha reporting the Cabinet decisions concerning agriculture policy. (Telegram 1440 from New Delhi, December 7; ibid., AGR 1 INDIA)

If Subramaniam comes through publicly, we recommend a reciprocal *White House statement* (attached)[4] tailored to your decisions above.
It should get a good reaction here and abroad, make the Indians your
debtors, and usefully remind Ayub we won't play Kashmïr politics
with food. But it still leaves India's food crisis unsolved (and only we
can solve it), so keeps Shastri coming to you.

R.W. Komer[5]

---

[4] Not printed.
[5] Printed from a copy that bears this typed signature.

---

259. Special National Intelligence Estimate[1]

SNIE 31–32–65   Washington, December 7, 1965.

INDO–PAKISTANI REACTIONS TO CERTAIN US COURSES
OF ACTION

The Problem

To estimate the reactions to certain US courses of action by India
and Pakistan.

Scope Note

The problems of the subcontinent and US interests there are complex and interrelated. They are complicated still further by the deep
involvement of the USSR, China, and other powers. It follows that any
particular US action will produce different reactions according to the
overall international situation, and to the other decisions which accom-

---

[1] Source: Central Intelligence Agency, Job 79–R01012A, ODDI Registry of NIE and
SNIE Files. Secret; Controlled Dissem; Limited Distribution. According to a note on the
cover sheet, the estimate was prepared by the CIA and the intelligence organizations of
the Departments of State, Defense, NSA, and the AEC. All members of the U.S. Intelligence
Board concurred in the estimate on December 7 except the representative of the Federal Bureau of Investigation, who abstained because the subject was outside his jurisdiction.

pany it and set the general context of US policy. In order to render the problem manageable, we deal in this estimate with five general US courses of action, as given to us by the Department of State. It is recognized that many other combinations of policy decisions and many variations of emphasis are equally possible.

A Military Annex[2] incorporates our response to certain specific questions submitted by the Department of Defense concerning the effects of the US/UK arms embargo.

Assumptions

1. Communist China remains preoccupied with the war in Vietnam and does not launch a major military attack on India, though we do not rule out the possibility of limited military probes across India's northern border.

2. The USSR, while seeking to avoid an outbreak of Indo–Pakistan hostilities, continues its basic pro-Indian policy, including both economic and military assistance.

3. The formal cease-fire endures, but no political settlement is in sight and the Security Council remains the focal point of US acaction.

Discussion

I. The Current Situation

1. *Indo–Pakistani relations.* The two countries now regard one another with heightened suspicion and fear as a consequence of the recent war. Pakistan continues to press for negotiations and for a change in the status of Kashmir, i.e., one under which India would give up at least part of the area of Jammu and Kashmir it now holds. India remains adamant in refusing to do so; its determination has been reinforced by its awareness that its military superiority has been enhanced as a result of the recent fighting. The cease-fire is still shaky, and frequent violations continue. A renewal of major hostilities now seems unlikely, and the UN may be able to secure some token troop withdrawal over the next few months. However, there is, in this period, little likelihood that negotiations will make progress towards a political settlement.

2. *India.* India came out of the recent war with a new sense of self-confidence and pride and a heightened determination to hold on to Kashmir. Though many of its claims were exaggerated, the Indian Army in fact did well enough to erase many of the memories of its

---

[2] Not printed.

previous humiliations. The war's outcome has greatly strengthened Prime Minister Shastri's position and that of the Congress Party. However, the war aggravated India's already serious economic problems. For several years its rate of growth has been about 3–5 percent instead of the planned 7–8 perent, and the dislocations caused by the conflict have probably lowered this rate even further. Despite large food imports, very serious food shortages have existed. Shortfalls in this year's harvest now threaten India with a food crisis of major proportions. India's foreign exchange reserves are now at the minimum statutory level; at the same time, it has current foreign debt obligations of nearly $500 million a year.

3. *Pakistan.* The war brought on a similar mood of patriotic zeal in Pakistan, and most Pakistanis probably still believe their government's claim that Pakistan "won." Pakistani public opinion is now even more determined to force some progress on Kashmir. However, the military and government leaders probably know that India got the best of it in the war, and they now recognize that India is the stronger power. The fact that Kashmir remains in Indian hands is apparent to all. So far, Ayub's position and authority have not been threatened, but an increasing number of Pakistanis may come to blame him as it becomes clear that his recent policies have not weakened India's hold on Kashmir. The war has shaken business confidence and significantly reduced the level of private investment, a fact which is slowing Pakistan's heretofore impressive rate of economic growth. Its immediate economic problems, however, especially in the area of food supply, are not as critical as those of India.

4. *US Aid to the Subcontinent.* The US has provided military and economic aid to both India and Pakistan.[3] Over the past 15 years, the US has provided about $3 billion in economic aid to India and about $2.1 billion to Pakistan. In the same period, it also shipped PL 480 food grains worth some $3 billion to India and $1.1 billion to Pakistan. Military aid delivered to India (starting in 1963) has amounted to $92 million and to Pakistan (starting in 1954) $676.7 million. Since the outbreak of hostilities in September 1965, all US military aid has been stopped. No new US economic aid commitments have been made, but assistance already in the pipeline

---

[3] US economic aid (exclusive of PL 480) has been generally matched collectively by that of the other Western powers. The total amounts of economic aid received over the past several years by both countries from all sources—the US, the other Free World countries, and the Soviet Bloc—are given in Annex B. Amounts of military aid are shown in Annex C. [Footnote in the source text. Annex B and Annex C are not printed.]

still goes on. PL 480 food grains shipments continue, but are committed on a short-term basis.[4]

5. Both countries are now extremely worried about future US aid policies, though for different reasons. Pakistan, whose military power vis-à-vis India is now significantly weaker than it was before the recent war, wants military aid and sales resumed. Its armed forces, being almost completely dependent on the US for replacements and spare parts, have been weakened by attrition and the termination of US aid. India's leaders are concerned primarily with the resumption of US economic assistance. In particular, they need non-project aid to provide large amounts of fertilizer and other materials to increase agricultural output. Pakistan wants the US to use its aid to force India into a Kashmir settlement. India does not want the US to furnish Pakistan with military equipment under any circumstances.

6. *PL 480.* A highly important aspect of US aid to the subcontinent is the PL 480 food program which provides eight percent of the food consumed in each country. Its loss would hurt both countries, but Pakistan less than India. The Pakistani Government has built up relatively larger reserves of foodstuffs, and its domestic food grain production record is better than India's. Though short of foreign exchange, it could purchase the extra food needed for its 112 million population more easily than could India for its 484 million. Further, Pakistan could, more easily than India, arrange for equitable distribution throughout the country.

7. India's leaders fear a PL 480 cutoff. Were these shipments terminated, India would face a grave crisis. India does not grow enough food to be self-sufficient, its most recent harvest has been very poor,

---

[4] Mr. Thomas L. Hughes, the Director of Intelligence and Research, Department of State, believes that a more realistic and useful description of Indian and Pakistani views of US aid would read as follows: *The Subcontinent views US aid.* The US has provided military and economic aid (including PL 480) to India and Pakistan totalling about $10 billion. Because of the enduring hostility between the two countries, each assumes that the US has regularly considered this assistance program to each in relation to the other. India knows that despite its comparative size, international influence, democratic institutions, development potential and its increasing confrontation with Communist China, it has received only one-third as much assistance as Pakistan in per capita terms (roughly $6 billion including a small fraction of military aid as opposed to roughly $4 billion, one-sixth of it military). Pakistan undoubtedly assumes that this favorable past imbalance has resulted from a combination of its alliance status, its comparatively successful economic program, the provision of important facilities to the US, and India's persistent policy of non-alignment vis-à-vis the Soviet Union. In general, each probably considers that past US assistance to it would probably have been greater but for predictable US policy complications with the other. The Indians think this is especially true of the restraints on our supplying of military aid to them after the 1962 Sino-Indian hostilities. Both India and Pakistan are surely aware that as the US–Chinese confrontation in Asia grows, India's increasing hostility toward China, in contrast with Pakistan's expanding ties, are introducing major new factors into this situation. [Footnote in the source text.]

and it suffers from serious and continuing troubles in assuring equitable food distribution. These difficulties have already led to recent sharp price rises, hoarding, black marketing, and serious shortages in food deficit areas despite heavy PL 480 imports. Though India has minimal foreign exchange reserves, it could utilize its hard currency earnings (about $1.2 billion annually, mostly from the export of raw commodities) to buy food imports on the open market. However, it is doubtful that on a crash basis the Indian Government could divert the exchange and arrange for shipment. Even if it could, the diversion of several hundred million dollars of its export earnings would have a serious adverse effect on India's development program and its economy.

8. *The Subcontinent and Communist China.* Pakistan has developed progressively more cordial relations with Peking since the Chinese humiliated India in the border war of late 1962 and the US began military assistance to India. During the recent fighting, the ties between China and Pakistan became even closer. Though recognizing that China can provide little effective economic assistance and not enough military hardware, Pakistan views Chinese military power as a valuable asset in its confrontation with India. It sees considerable advantage India's fear of China's military power and the consequent deployment of major Indian forces along the Chinese rather than the Pakistani border. Moreover, Pakistan will wish to retain the option of seeking active Chinese intervention in the event of renewed Indo–Pakistani hostilities.

9. *The Role of the USSR.* Over the years, the USSR has been relatively hostile to Pakistan and has consistently backed India on Kashmir. Moscow has pledged over $1 billion of economic assistance to India; the latter will probably be utilizing Soviet bloc aid at the rate of $250–$300 million a year over the next several years. The USSR has also, since 1962, become a major arms supplier to India. The Soviets will almost certainly continue to view India as by far their primary area of interest on the subcontinent, continuing to grant economic aid and probably selling India additional military equipment. Recently, however, Moscow has apparently decided to improve its relations with Pakistan insofar as this is compatible with its position in India. This move has been made both possible and desirable by a series of developments: the deterioration of US–Pakistani relations; the growth of the Sino-Soviet dispute; the Chinese threat to India; and Chinese influence in Rawalpindi. Moscow now sees an opportunity to try to undercut both the Chinese and the US by seeking improvement in its relations with Pakistan.

II. Courses of Action

10. In general, the following possible US courses of action represent various means of attempting to influence the policy of India and

Pakistan by use of military and economic aid. Both countries urgently require such aid, though in different degrees. Neither country could wholly replace, from other sources, the types and amounts of aid previously received from the US. Therefore, both will be greatly affected by US policies in this respect.

11. There are nevertheless limits to the influence which the US can exert on either government by its aid policies. We do not believe that the basic antagonisms between the two countries can be significantly reduced by the influence of any outside power. India will remain hostile to Communist China, but will try to retain good relations with both the USSR and the US. India is unlikely to forego the option to develop nuclear weapons. For its part, Pakistan will almost certainly want to keep some sort of relationship with Peking as insurance against India, no matter how favorable its relations with the US may become. Pakistan believes it must have arms for protection against India and will seek such arms wherever it can.

12. Of the following courses of action, all except Course III differ significantly from those the US has followed in the past. Assuming that the US persisted for a long time in any one of these courses, the whole context of the situation would change. The balance of forces operating within the subcontinent would be different from what it is now, and the influence of the USSR, of Communist China, and perhaps of other powers would bear on the situation in ways largely unpredictable. This estimate does not attempt to trace out the numerous possible ramifications of such developments, or to assess their various meanings for the interests of the US. The following paragraphs set forth our judgment of reactions to the postulated courses in the fairly near future—a few months to a year or so—with only a few hints of some possible repercussions of wider scope or longer term.

13. Courses I, II, and III postulate continued economic aid from the US at approximately 1963–1964 levels to both countries. In Courses I and II, military assistance at 1963–1964 levels is provided to one country, while the other receives only "some military assistance"; in Course III, military assistance is resumed to both at 1963–1964 levels. The three courses differ not only in respect to amounts of military aid supplied, but also in the quid pro quo demanded of each country, and in the degree to which the US associates itself with the policies and aspirations of one or the other of the two. In respect to all five courses, reactions would to a considerable extent be determined by how the two countries interpreted US motives and long range objectives in each instance.

Course I: The US, convinced that a stable, influential, and economically viable India is the most effective Asian counterweight to

China, and that Pakistan's involvement with China can be held within acceptable limits, moves clearly toward India. In a variety of ways the US seeks a closer identification with India, resumes large scale economic and substantial military assistance to India and refrains from pressing India to make concessions on Kashmir. As part of this new relationship, the US would expect agriculatural and other economic reforms, closer Indian security collaboration with the US vis-à-vis China, and renunciation of an independent nuclear weapons capability. The US would bolster its new Indian policy by resuming economic aid at approximately 1963–1964 levels and some military assistance to Pakistan.

14. *India.* If the US should make such a definite choice favoring India, Indian good will toward the US would increase, particularly if there were a dramatic increase in US food shipments in time of threatened famine; however, this positive reaction would be tempered by the resumption of even limited arms aid to Pakistan. The US would be able to improve substantially its relations with the Indian Government. The prestige and primacy of Shastri and the Congress Party throughout India would be considerably enhanced, thereby contributing to Indian stability. Cooperation with the US in the security field, directed against China, would continue and probably increase. The Indian leaders would be more receptive to US advice in such fields as economic reform and improved food distribution. Their ability to carry out reform measures would continue to be limited, but the level of economic achievement would probably show some improvement. Although India's leaders would not formally and permanently renounce an independent nuclear weapons capability, they would probably be willing to give assurances that they would not order the manufacture of a nuclear device for some time.

15. At the same time, however, the Indians would hold fast to their policy of nonalignment between the US and the USSR. The Soviets would probably continue to provide India with substantial economic and military aid, and Indo–Soviet ties would remain close. In various areas of foreign policy, India would, from time to time, be at odds with the US.

16. *Pakistan.* We do not believe we can estimate with confidence the reaction of Pakistan. Important individuals would react in different ways, and conflicting emotions would be aroused. What Pakistan would do would depend in part on how the US actions were presented, on the actions and promises of other countries (including India), and on a variety of factors which cannot be foreseen. Many Pakistanis, probably including Ayub himself, favor closer Western ties and fear too close an association with Communist China. They realize the benefits of renewed US economic aid. They are also aware of their immediate need for even limited military assistance from the US, particularly badly needed spare parts for Pakistan's air

force.[5] Pakistan's government might therefore swallow its profound disquiet and resentment at US policy toward India simply on the grounds that it would prefer to have what US help it could get, distasteful as the whole situation was.

17. Pakistan's relations with the US, in such a case, would remain formally correct. Its CENTO and SEATO alliances would probably not be ended; nor would the principal US special facilities be likely to be closed down, though occasional harassments might take place. At the same time, Pakistan's leaders would make every effort to find alternate sources of military supply and hardware. Thanks to their expanding economy, boosted by the resumption of US and Consortium economic aid, they would be able to purchase substantial military equipment and hardware, though their requirements might be a good deal greater than they could fill by this means. Relations with China would probably be little different from what they were prior to August 1965, though public expressions of support for Peking would probably diminish somewhat. Pakistan would probably try to improve its relations with the USSR.

18. It is possible, however, that the Pakistanis would react in a truculent manner. They would soon become aware that the US had changed its earlier policies and had selected India rather than Pakistan as its principal associate in South Asia. This would come as a severe shock, diminishing Pakistan's hope of enjoying, in its own view, a position of security against India and achieving a favorable solution in Kashmir. Public opinion, already resentful of what it considers an unsatisfactory US role in the recent conflict with India, would be further inflamed. It would be difficult for any government in Rawalpindi, however strongly it desired renewed US military aid and closer ties with the West, to ignore or resist the pressures generated from below. Most of the top leaders themselves share at least some of these sentiments. In this situation, the Pakistan Government might lash out with extreme hositility to the US.

19. Were this to occur, Pakistan, while it would not break relations with the US, would react in such a manner as to make any normal relationship practically impossible. It would probably terminate the US special facilities in Pakistan, and quit CENTO and SEATO—even at the risk of losing US military and economic assistance. President Ayub's association with Pakistan's pro-US attitudes of the past would render him vulnerable to political attack, though he could probably sustain himself as the leader of a new policy based on denouncing the US and moving closer to those powers, particularly China, which are

---

[5] See Annex A for an analysis of Pakistan's military needs and procurement problems. [Footnote in the source text. Annex A is not printed.]

hostile to India. Whether Ayub remained or was replaced, Pakistani policies would take a more radical turn. Pakistan could throw in its lot with China and the radical Afro-Asians, perhaps leaving the UN, and embarking on a course similar to that which Indonesia has followed over the past several years.[6]

Course II: The US, convinced that Pakistan can once again be made a reliable ally at acceptable cost in terms of US–Indian relations, focuses its support on Pakistan. On condition that Rawalpindi will limit its relationship with China, the US resumes military and economic assistance, and presses hard for a Kashmir settlement satisfactory to Pakistan. The US would bolster this policy by resuming economic aid at approximately 1963–1964 levels and some military aid to India.

20. India. Indian reaction to a US course favoring Pakistan would be sharp and verbally violent. This would be particularly so in regard to renewal of substantial military aid to the country which India regards as the clear-cut aggressor in the recent hostilities. New Delhi would continue to see the USSR as its best potential source of sophisticated armaments, and relations with Moscow would remain excellent. Such a course would probably have little effect, one way or another, on India's nuclear weapons policies. Cooperation with the US in the security field against China might take at least a temporary downturn. However, India's leaders would want to count on US support against Communist China, particularly in the event of military attacks by the latter against India.

21. Moreover, the resumption of large-scale economic aid would be especially pleasing to India, which needs it far more than it does military aid. Especially at a time of threatening famine, India would welcome the assurance that PL 480 food would continue and that US assistance in a program to increase agricultural output would be

---

[6] Mr. Thomas L. Hughes, the Director of Intelligence and Research, Department of State, recognizes that either of the Pakistani policy choices set forth in paragraphs 16–19 is possible, but believes that on balance Pakistan would probably react in the more rational manner of paragraphs 16–17 rather than in the hostile manner of paragraphs 18–19. Even should it adopt a net posture of hostility, including, say, withdrawal from SEATO, he does not believe that termination of the facilities would automatically follow or even be probable. He believes this because of: (a) Pakistan's great dependence on US aid and its lack of satisfactory alternative sources, (b) Pakistan's probable assumption that the facilities have been and will remain a source of leverage for high US aid levels, as well as for continuing attempts to influence US policy toward India, and (c) the considerable practical utility which the large facility has for Pakistan itself as a result of the training its personnel receive as well as the exclusive enclave it has there for its own purposes—an asset which continued to be used uninterruptedly throughout the recent hostilities. He further notes that unlike CENTO and SEATO, the presence of the facilities has never been a public issue in Pakistan. He believes that in view of these fundamental considerations, the direct mechanical relationship which the estimate establishes in paragraphs 19, 23, 25, 28, and 29 between the level of US support on the one hand, and the continuance of the facilities on the other, is artificial and misleading. [Footnote in the source text.]

resumed. India's political system would be little affected; its economy would continue to show modest and unspectacular progress. Nonetheless, India would resent and vigorously resist US pressures on the Kashmir problem.

22. *Pakistan.* Pakistan would find distasteful the resumption of even limited US military aid to India. Rawalpindi would press for a formal guarantee of defense against an Indian attack, and would resent any negative US responses. Moreover, should US pressures on India fail to produce a Kashmir settlement (which would almost certainly be the case) Pakistan would become increasingly critical of the US. Pakistan would be likely to limit, though not to end, the relationship it has established with China over the past few years.

23. Despite these negative and adverse factors, however, US–Pakistani relations would be likely to show an overall improvement, particularly as it became clear that the US was indeed focusing its support on Pakistan rather than India. Special US facilities in Pakistan would be undisturbed, and those now closed would almost certainly be allowed to reopen. Pakistan's sense of security against India would be enhanced by the resumption of US military aid. However, the tensions caused by new Pakistani efforts to get a Kashmir settlement and the residue of distrust remaining from alleged US non-support during the recent war would prevent Pakistan from again regarding the US with the degree of trust or accepting the degree of dependence that existed during the mid-1950s.

Course III: The US, believing that its previous "even-handed" approach to the subcontinent still best serves its interests, resumes economic and military aid to both countries at approximately 1963–1964 levels and under the same conditions as before the hostilities. Simultaneously, while not taking the lead on matters relating to Kashmir, it encourages efforts in the UN and elsewhere to get negotiations for a political settlement underway. Without using aid as a sanction, it presses Pakistan to limit its relationship with Communist China and India to improve its agricultural program.

24. *India.* Renewed military aid to Pakistan would initially bring a sharp and angry Indian reaction. At least in official circles, however, this reaction would be somewhat softened by India's continuing need for US economic aid and support against Communist China. American pressures for an improved Indian economic performance, especially in the agricultural sector, would have some limited success. Various forms of cooperation against Communist China would continue. India would nevertheless be concerned by US military aid to Pakistan, and would itself seek a continuing high level of arms assistance from the USSR. This Moscow would almost certainly provide. The Shastri government, which would continue to dominate the political scene, would not abandon India's generally nonaligned posture in international affairs. The

course postulated would probably have little effect on India's nuclear policies.

25. *Pakistan*. US–Pakistan relationships would probably revert to something similar to what they were a year or so ago. However, the experiences of the war and its aftermath have had a considerable impact. Pakistan realizes, more than it did before, that it must for some time depend on the US to maintain an effective military capability. This would lead it to refrain from brusquely or needlessly antagonizing the US; the US special facilities would not be interfered with. Even so, Pakistan would probably still blame the US for not sufficiently pressuring India into negotiations or concessions. It would also criticize the US for continuing to supply arms to India. These major irritants, plus the belief of the Pakistani leaders that they cannot count on the US to save it from any further Indian "aggression" would lead them to seek to reduce this dependence on the US. Thus they would continue to try to maintain good—though perhaps more covert—relations with the Chinese. They would also seek to diversify their sources of arms supply to the maximum extent possible.

Course IV: The US, convinced that a lasting political solution can only be arrived at between the disputants themselves and that US participation in the negotiation process would be disadvantageous, adopts a wait-and-see policy. It resumes limited economic aid on a short-term basis and conditions longer term economic assistance on Indo–Pakistani tensions being kept under control, on Pakistan's self-imposed limitations on its relationship with Communist China, and on India's economic performance. Depending upon progress in limiting Indo–Pakistani tensions, the US may make available selected military hardware to both countries, but would avoid longer term MAP negotiations.

26. Regardless of US aid policies, the leaders of both countries would probably like to reduce the chances of renewed hostilities. The prospects for resumption of even limited US assistance would be attractive to each. We believe that the two governments would be able to reduce some of the tensions on the subcontinent over the next year or so. They would probably maintain the cease-fire and achieve some partial withdrawal of the military forces. Some modest progress would be likely in settling long standing disputes, such as the Bengali border enclaves and the large scale expulsion from Eastern India of Muslims claimed by India to be Pakistani citizens. In these circumstances, each would probably claim that it had fulfilled the necessary conditions for the resumption of aid.

27. However, there would be some formidable obstacles to the two disputants, on their own, making much substantive progress toward a lasting political solution in the subcontinent, or even towards setting up any effective process to keep Indo–Pakistani tensions under control.

Pakistan would find it almost impossible to stop insisting on a negotiated Kashmir settlement, and this would clearly inflame Indian public opinion. Pakistan, fearing Indian military power, would probably maintain some type of relationship with China directed against India. India, militarily stronger and already enjoying de facto control of Kashmir, might be willing to make minor readjustments on the cease-fire line, but it would make no major concessions on Kashmir.

28. For some months, US relations with India and Pakistan would probably remain much as they have been since the cease-fire of September 1965. There would probably not be much prospect for a substantial improvement in these relations, for the US would, in the Indian and Pakistani view, be obviously trying to pressure both countries into modifications of basic policies by denying them more than limited economic aid. Both nations would continue to suffer from relatively unsatisfactory economic conditions, though they should enjoy political stability. Their relations with other powers would probably remain unchanged. Though Pakistan might not move closer to Communist China, it would not abandon its present ties, and would continue to develop its relations with the USSR. It would probably make no move to close the US special facilities, but it might move in various ways to limit use of them. India would continue to have good relations with the USSR. At the same time, Indo–US cooperation in many fields would continue. This course of action would have no significant effect on a decision by India to manufacture a nuclear device.

Course V: The US concludes that Indo–Pakistani hostility is so profound as to be insoluble in the foreseeable future, thereby rendering previous levels of US assistance disproportionate to US interest in the subcontinent. Taking a calculated risk that India and Pakistan will increase their dependence on Communist and other support, the US adheres to modest programs providing limited PL 480 assistance, limited amounts of programs aid, but no new project assistance and no military aid.

29. Each side would at first probably view such an American decision as one similar to Course IV, intended to exert pressure on them to arrive at some mutual accommodation. In India the reaction would be much the same; in Pakistan, the response would be more severe because of the urgent need for US military assistance. Some pressure against the special US facilities could be expected. As time passed and the US action came to be widely understood, Pakistan would become increasingly concerned about the weakness of its position. It would almost certainly move closer to Communist China.

30. India would be extremely hard hit by such a course. Its concern for its security would be sharply increased. It would come to regard the USSR as its most reliable friend and would turn to the USSR for substantial new amounts of military hardware and economic aid, with

a good chance of success. It would be more likely than at present to undertake a nuclear weapons program in the near future. However, India's leaders would seek to avoid anything approaching an open break with the US, especially in view of their desperate need for PL 480 assistance.

31. Even if the USSR and some Free World countries continued to provide economic aid, the virtual termination of the US aid program would cause India's growth rate to fall below any level it has achieved in recent years. India would almost certainly default on some of its foreign debt obligations. Prime Minister Shastri and his government could probably rally the Indian public by taking an increasingly truculent line against Pakistan and denouncing the new US policy. Their position would probably not be threatened in the short run, for the Indian public would not hold them responsible for alleged US hostility towards India. A clearcut economic disaster could probably be avoided (assuming continuance of PL 480 aid) but as the economy settled into near stagnation, the Congress Party's position would become increasingly weak, and domestic stability might be threatened.

[Here follow Annex A, a 7-page assessment of "Indo–Pakistani Military Capabilities," Annex B, a chart detailing "Economic Aid Pledged to India and Pakistan," and Annex C, a chart outlining "US Military Assistance Value of Deliveries."]

---

260. Telegram From the Department of State to the Embassy in India[1]

Washington, December 9, 1965, 1:58 p.m.

Aidto 747. Joint State–AID message. Subject—PL 480 and Fertilizer Loan. President has just announced further extension PL 480 Title I program of 1,500,000 tons wheat for early shipment, that being equal to present monthly allocation on three months basis. President also announced $50 million loan for urgent import fertilizer tied to GOI

---

[1] Source: National Archives and Records Administration, RG 59, Central Files 1964–66, AID (US) 15–8 INDIA. Confidential; Flash. Drafted by Deputy Assistant AID Administrator Walter G. Farr, Jr., cleared by Handley, and approved by William S. Gaud.

expenditure like sum of own funds for fertilizer import.[2] President believes all nations capable of helping should assist meet India's present grave food problem and indicated USG would participate fully. Full text Presidential announcement following.

Inform Sen. Morse and other Senators and Congressmen in India of substance of Presidential announcement.

FYI. Pleased GOI announcement own plans import $79 million fertilizer. Every effort should be made assure AID loan entirely supplemental to maximum effort by GOI to import fertilizer with other than AID funds. Loan will also be tied in to overall agricultural program. By exchange of letters or otherwise, GOI will be expected agree to certain specific self-help efforts, particularly in private sector production and distribution fertilizer and other inputs. Detailed negotiating instructions follow. FYI.

Rusk

---

[2] Bill Moyers, the President's Press Secretary, made these announcements on President Johnson's behalf in Austin, Texas on December 9. (*American Foreign Policy: Current Documents, 1965*, p. 754.) An amendment to the existing Title I P.L. 480 agreement with India, providing for an additional 1.5 million tons of foodgrains, was signed in New Delhi on December 10. (Circular telegram 1133, December 11; National Archives and Records Administration, RG 59, Central Files 1964–66, AID (US) 15–8 INDIA)

---

261. Telegram From the Department of State to the Embassy in India[1]

Washington, December 11, 1965, 3:41 p.m.

1041. Personal for the Ambassador from the Secretary. Before leaving for a few days for NATO, I should like to emphasize one point mentioned in your 1466.[2] It is of the utmost importance that India make every possible effort to get additional food assistance from other countries if we are to be in a position to be of any substantial additional assistance ourselves. I was startled to learn just three days ago that

---

[1] Source: National Archives and Records Administration, RG 59, Central Files 1964–66, AID (US) 15–8 INDIA. Confidential; Exdis. Drafted and approved by Rusk.

[2] The Embassy reported in telegram 1466 from New Delhi, December 10, that the President's announcements were received with relief and gratitude and were having a tremendous impact throughout the country. (Ibid.)

B.K. Nehru was unaware of any approaches made to Canada, Australia, France, Argentina or others who could help. It seems to me that the Indian Government should put its diplomacy into high gear and get contributions from as many others as possible. Such contributions could include such items as fertilizer and shipping if food as such is not available. I am pleased that the Indian response to the President's most recent move has been good.

Rusk

---

262.   Memorandum From the President's Deputy Special Assistant for National Security Affairs (Komer) to President Johnson[1]

Washington, December 14, 1965, 11:30 a.m.

Here is the *inventory* of interim things we could do for the Paks if we were so disposed:

1. The safest thing would be to go ahead with the $39 million worth of loans already authorized during FY 1965. There are six of them—all relatively important. We could indicate that this was a parallel action to the $30 million in fertilizer for India.

2. We could make a new interim PL 480 agreement, which the Paks are requesting. It would be relatively small as Pakistan's current food picture is pretty good.

3. Military aid is much trickier, for the simple reason that it would be hardest for the Indians to understand at a time when the cease-fire and withdrawal on which we hinged such resumption have not yet firmed up.

  a. As Ball suggests, we could allow commercial sales to both India and Pakistan. This would help the Paks more because they could buy urgently needed spare parts.[2]

  b. We could quietly allow the Paks to buy from third countries (at present we are blocking US-origin sales).

  c. More important and, in my view, more desirable would be simply to indicate that if a good US/Pak relation can be restored, we

---

[1] Source: Johnson Library, National Security File, Memos to the President, McGeorge Bundy, Vol. 17, Nov. 20–Dec. 31, 1965. Secret.
[2] Komer added a marginal handwritten note at this point that reads: "they could buy then the C–130 starter motors."

would be prepared to discuss Pakistan's future security needs, including MAP and sales. I really don't think Ayub expects more.

d. Finally, the question of reassurances against India. Arthur Dean and I feel that reiteration of the fact that if Pakistan is allied to us, we would simply not stand by and let India take over Pakistan would be highly valuable to Ayub, given his present acute fear that the Indians have the upper hand. On the other hand, it would be imperative that you avoid the sins of yesteryear by making clear that our assurances simply could not be operative in a situation of other than unprovoked aggression. Ayub knows full well how cloudy the last case was.

R. W. Komer[3]

---

[3] Printed from a copy that bears this typed signature.

---

263. Memorandum of Conversation[1]

Washington, December 14, 1965, 1:16–1:30 p.m.

President Johnson said that he knew that he and President Ayub were running a little late since a luncheon was scheduled at 1:15 pm but that they both had wanted to use every possible moment. He said that, despite what the radio and newspapers had said, he and President Ayub were very good friends and that there was no one he admired more. He said that he and the President would arrange more meetings and that President Ayub had reassured him and convinced him, if he ever needed convincing, of the importance of Pakistan, of the friendship between Pakistan and the United States, and of the problems Pakistan has been facing. "Our people", the President said, "must be friends,

---

[1] Source: National Archives and Records Administration, RG 59, S/S Conference Files: Lot 66 D 347, CF 2569. Secret. Drafted by Handley on December 17 and 20. The memorandum is marked "Draft." Although it is dated December 15, according to the President's Daily Diary the meeting took place on December 14 in the Cabinet Room at the White House. President Ayub was in Washington for an official visit December 14–15. According to the President's Daily Diary, the other U.S. participants in the meeting were Ball, Hare, Handley, McConaughy, and Ambassador Lloyd Hand. The other Pakistani participants were Bhutto, Minister for Commerce Ghulam Faruque, Aziz Ahmed, Ambassador Ghulam Ahmed, Altaf Guahar, Secretary of the Ministry of Information and Broadcasting, Salman A. Ali, Director General of the Ministry of Foreign Affairs, and Minister of Embassy Iftikhar Ali. (Johnson Library)

we must find out what went wrong and erase it and we are going to do just that". The President was proud of the association between the United States and Pakistan and especially of President Ayub, one of today's truly great men.

President Ayub responded by saying that he had the greatest affection and regard for President Johnson. "The President when he was Vice President had no reason to take any note of me when I was here in 1961 but he invited me to his ranch and was so kind and generous that I will never forget it. The amount of kindness and affection he and Mrs. Johnson bestowed on me was unbelievable. The United States is very fortunate to have a man of his stature as President and I am truly happy the President is where he is. President Johnson is a man of very large heart."

President Ayub said that he and President Johnson talked about problems between Pakistan and the United States. They had recognized that there has been a certain amount of drift in the last few years. Pakistan's basic concern was its national security. United States policy had begun to change in 1959 when we had started reassessing the value of our pacts and alliances with various countries. It was during this period, with our changing views of the importance of pacts, that we had decided that we could do business with neutrals and that this had special application to United States relations with India. This was further stepped up when Communist China and India began to have border difficulties. The Indian military budget had been increased 300%. An army of a million had been established. It was difficult for him to understand how an army of this size could be used against China since there was no room for it given the difficulty of the terrain. He felt that this Indian buildup was directed principally against Pakistan. He stated that India had increased its divisions from 9 to 21. India was now raising 10 more divisions. Within the past four or five years the Indian military budget had increased from $600 million annually to $2.6 billion. He saw absolutely no requirement for such a large military establishment. If it were not for United States generosity India would be starving. On the other hand, if peace were possible, India and Pakistan could divert large sums to economic development. Pakistan intended to be reasonable about Kashmir with the hope that some kind of solution could be reached. After that, a reduction of forces could take place and then there would be freedom of fear from each other. If peace were to come United States interests would be promoted as would those of India and Pakistan. The question, of course, is how to bring this about. There was the United Nations. There was the possibility of a plebiscite or of arbitration where two or three eminent people might be asked to make the decision. With binding arbitration neither side would lose face. There was a precedent for this in the Radcliffe

Commission as well as the arbitration provision worked out for settlement of the Rann of Kutch border dispute.

Ayub said that he and the President had discussed United States–Pakistan relations, how attached both sides were to these relations and distressed to find that they had been adrift. The United States was the greatest power in the world and the United States should ponder how it could bring about the mechanics for moving India and Pakistan toward a settlement.

Ayub said that Pakistan was in a unique geographic position "with three major powers breathing down our necks".

Pakistan had to do what it could to maintain its security in the face of three powers whose motives were certainly questionable. For Pakistan, it was a compulsion of circumstances and they had therefore been trying to normalize their relations with China. As an indication of the dangers in Pakistan's geographic position, he said that the Soviet Union "had put an enormous amount of stuff in Afghanistan and that at the time of the Indian-Pakistan conflict that the Afghans had mobilized their resources against Pakistan". (Our information is that the opposite was true.)

Pakistan was made up of many races and tribes but they were all bound together by religion. There was no internal communism in Pakistan since the Communist Party had been banned.

He realized that the United States had its global problems and could recognize the difficulties facing the United States in trying to deal with DeGaulle, Viet-Nam, etc. But if the United States could make a gesture towards settling Indo-Pak disputes it would be enormously appreciated.

He concluded by saying that, if India and Pakistan were to clash, ruination would take place and then there would be no need for Communist China or the Soviet Union to bring communism to the subcontinent from the outside. Communism in such circumstances would surely come from within. United States interests in the subcontinent were, therefore, very much involved in having peace between India and Pakistan.

264. Memorandum of Telephone Conversation Between President Johnson and the Under Secretary of State (Ball)[1]

Washington, December 14, 1965, 6:40 p.m.

Ball told the President that he was seeing Ayub at 7:15 and wanted to ask if Pres had anything that he should stress. One thing Ball said he wanted to mention to Pres was that at lunch he had for Ayub,[2] Ayub mentioned to Ball his talk with Pres and was counting on talking with Arthur Goldberg. President said they had no discussion along this line.[3] President said Ayub expressed admiration for Goldberg. Ayub asked if Goldberg was in Cabinet room and Pres. said if not he would be at dinner tonight. Ball said he interpreted his talk with Ayub that Pres had agreed that possibly he could get together with Arthur and President and talk a bit. President said he intended to take him privately upstairs and spend a little time but did not intend to ask Goldberg. Ball brought up his conversation with Ayub concerning Tashkent visit at Russian invitation on January 4–5. Both Ayub and Bhutto asked what will happen if Tashkent fails on Kashmir question, meaning would we pick up ball? Ball thinks we should be extremely careful to give no indication that we will pick up ball because then they will make sure that Tashkent does fail. President said he did not raise that question with him. Pres. said Ayub thought there ought to be a plebiscite and failing that arbitration. President said he told Ayub that we did not have any more influence with Indians than we had with him—that we desired peace in that part of the world but could not achieve it. President said when he needed Ayub he was in Peking or Moscow. We regretted the situation. Ayub said he had no use for China but wanted to protect himself. He had nothing but friendship for us and said people of Pakistan and people of America could bring this about. President said he offered him no hope, no promises, no commitment, except that he said he hated for us to go along as we are now. The people that have been friends of Pakistan are disillusioned and do not understand his flirting with Chinese Communists and using the Chinese against us and India. President said the Indians are disappointing us as much as the Pakistanis. Ayub denied that he had been offended and said he

---

[1] Source: Johnson Library, Ball Papers, Presidential Telcons, 1/17/63–6/25/66. No classification marking. Transcribed by Theresa Dombroski.

[2] A memorandum of Ball's luncheon conversation with Ayub on December 14 is in National Archives and Records Administration, RG 59, Conference Files: Lot 66 D 347, CF 2569.

[3] Johnson was referring to the private conversation he and Ayub had prior to the meeting with their advisers on December 14; see Document 263.

sympathized with Pres and his problems. He put blame on UPI for stirring up everything.

President said he told him we are glad to see him go to Tashkent and if they can bring satisfactory results, fine, but if they can't, the problem we have is what we do with our people if he courts the Chinese. President said he told him he did not know where we could go in view of peculiar relationship with Chinese Communists because our people are trying to preserve Asia from Communism.

Ball said he was anxious about this one idea—he spoke to Goldberg who understands if he should talk to Ayub. Ball said we are not prepared to pick up pieces if Tashkent fails. President said it looks to him that this was discussion that leads nowhere. Ball said tomorrow after we have softened him up that we can inject a little more hope. Ball said he was subdued and spoke warmly of his conversations with President—they are verging on despair. President agreed that he appeared pathetic and spoke with inferiority complex. Ball agreed he has been chastened.

President told Ayub he is deeply disappointed at situation he finds himself in—our country is in position that it does not feel very sympathetic with any situation that involves allies of Chinese Communists. President said on hearing this Ayub jumped out of his chair and said he wants nothing to do with the Chinese but he is trying to prevent from being eaten up. Ball said Ayub has been in very difficult spot and he has his problems with his own people. President said that he told Ayub if he has any question with us that he needs no more to fear from President or our Government that Lady Bird does—that we feel very close to them. President mentioned that Ayub is free to change his own cabinet members—mentioning Bhutto. Ayub defended Bhutto saying that it was Bhutto who encouraged him to come to US and reaffirm their friendship etc. Ball said he thinks we ought to continue a pretty tough line tonight, that any give should come from the President. In the morning Ball said we can decide what element of hope we want to inject into the situation.

265. Memorandum of Conversation[1]

Washington, December 14, 1965, 7:15 p.m.

SUBJECT

    Visit of President Ayub Khan; Official Call by Acting Secretary Ball on H.E. President Ayub Khan

PARTICIPANTS

Americans	Pakistanis
Acting Secretary Ball	H.E. President Ayub Khan
Assistant Secretary Raymond A. Hare	H.E. Zulfikar Ali Bhutto, Minister for
Ambassador Walter P. McConaughy	Foreign Affairs
Deputy Assistant Secretary William	H.E. Ghulam Faruque, Minister for
J. Handley	Commerce
	The Honorable Aziz Ahmed, Secretary, Ministry of Foreign Affairs
	Ambassador Ghulam Ahmed, Pakistan Embassy
	Min. Aftab Ahmed Khan, Pakistan Embassy

Mr. Ball said that he had talked to President Johnson about the conversation between the two Presidents earlier in the day. The President said that he hoped to have another talk with President Ayub that night.

Mr. Ball said that Ayub certainly must have received the strongest impression that Viet-Nam is a major preoccupation for us. It plays a significant role in our attitude toward China. President Ayub should also know that our Viet-Nam policy has very strong support in the United States. Some people have wrongly inferred from anti-Viet-Nam demonstrations in the United States that our policy does not have full American support. Nothing could be further from the truth.

We understand Pakistan's geographic position vis-à-vis India, Communist China, and the Soviet Union. Yet Pakistan's policies have created anxieties here. We must realistically face the differences between the policies of our two countries which are based on the facts available to both countries. We have already gained a better understanding in the brief time that Ayub has been here of Pakistan's problems. Now we must see if we can find ways to identify our areas of common interest, welfare, and security.

---

[1] Source: National Archives and Records Administration, RG 59, S/S Conference Files: Lot 66 D 347, CF 2569. Secret. Drafted by Handley on December 20. The meeting was held at Blair House.

Mr. Ball went on to say that President Ayub should appreciate the high sensitivity of American public opinion about Communist China. Even though the press may have exaggerated matters we have indeed been concerned and disturbed about Pakistan's relations with Communist China and particularly about the possibility of a military alliance. During the moments that Mr. Ball had been speaking about Pakistan's relations with Communist China, President Ayub who had been listening intently, began to say softly and then in a rising crescendo, "No Sir, no Sir, no Sir."

President Ayub then went on to say that there was absolutely no military alliance between Pakistan and Communist China and that he had told the President the same thing that day. He said that Pakistan could only exist with the protection of a larger country. "We are in an alliance with the United States", he said. He hoped that this alliance would act as a deterrent to other countries seeking to dominate Pakistan. Pakistan's objective is to see that no one aggresses against it and her alliance with the United States is not intended to be a threat against any country but simply a deterrent to possible aggression.

Continuing, President Ayub said that Pakistan had never given a thought to a military alliance with China and that in any event Pakistan has always thought that Communist China "couldn't bring much against India." He said that he did not know the situation along the vast borders between India and Communist China but had difficulty reconciling India's military buildup with the dangers of Chinese aggression.

Mr. Ball said that he had talked to the President and that they had discussed the Tashkent meeting. We hope that something productive can come out of the meeting between President Ayub and Prime Minister Shastri. In our view the Soviets have a certain influence with India and he noted that the Soviets appear to be trying to increase their influence in Pakistan. There was, therefore, the possibility that the Soviets were beginning to use their influence to bring about an understanding between India and Pakistan. We welcomed an initiative of this kind and wished it well.[2]

At this point, Ayub commented that he had already understood this from a conversation between Ambassador Goldberg and Foreign

---

[2] On December 16 Ambassador Llewellyn Thompson told Soviet Ambassador Anatoliy Dobrynin that President Johnson had indicated to President Ayub that the United States welcomed the Soviet initiative in arranging talks between Pakistan and India at Tashkent. (Memorandum of conversation; ibid., Central Files 1964–66, POL 7 PAK) In a conversation with Walt Rostow on December 22, Dobrynin asked if the United States favored a particular Kashmir formula. Rostow indicated that it did not. Dobrynin said: "Be clear, we don't have a Kashmir formula either; and we don't propose to suggest a Kashmir formula at Tashkent." (Memorandum of conversation; ibid., POL US–USSR)

Minister Bhutto. He said that Pakistan was quite prepared to go along with this initiative of the Soviet Union since it was a member of the Security Council, but he hoped that the United States and Britain would also take an initiative. He hoped that we would judge our relationship with Pakistan on the basis of a fundamental common interest, i.e., peace on the subcontinent, and that we should consider using our influence to bring this about. Pakistan was not irrevocably attached to the plebiscite. Arbitration might be acceptable. He said that even if there were a Kashmir settlement but no general reduction in weapons there would be a waste of effort in both India and Pakistan and both countries would be impoverished. Should there be war, both societies would be shattered and internal Communism would have its day. He then went back to his earlier point that there was nothing to stop the United States from taking the initiative and that the United States has more of a stake in the subcontinent than the Soviet Union.

Mr. Ball said that if there were progress at Tashkent we might be able to help in improving relations between India and Pakistan. He said that even if it was only a modest step like disengagement it would be easier for other nations to do something constructive, hopefully through the United Nations and the Security Council but, if not, through other arrangements. We felt that Pakistan should approach Tashkent with the hope of achieving something. The signs were encouraging. In the past, the Soviets had blocked the Four Power Commission idea and their past attitude on Kashmir had been extremely one-sided. We were, therefore, most pleased that they were now taking the initiative. Mr. Ball said that we are pragmatic about this kind of problem and that we are not concerned with winning the Nobel Peace Prize. Ayub then laughingly said, "But you should want to win the Nobel Peace Prize."

Mr. Ball said that he had also been deeply concerned about the mounting spiral of military expenditures in the subcontinent and we hoped that a military buildup could be kept at a reasonable level. We had taken heart from Pakistan's economic performance and had been most pleased with the way Pakistan had used United States aid.[3]

Mr. Ball then raised the question of a communiqué. Ayub looked quite blank and turned to Ambassador G. Ahmed, who said he had had no instructions about working on a communiqué. Foreign Secretary Aziz Ahmed and later Foreign Minister Bhutto then spoke up against the idea of a communiqué, saying that this type of meeting was intended "to reduce the humps in the relations between Pakistan and

---

[3] Ball covered a broader range of issues affecting U.S. relations with Pakistan in a conversation earlier in the day with Foreign Minister Bhutto. A memorandum of that conversation is ibid., POL 7 PAK.

the United States" and that they saw the meeting as an opportunity for the two Presidents to develop better understanding about the other's problems and point of view. Under these circumstances they thought that a communiqué was unnecessary. Ambassador McConaughy and Assistant Secretary Hare spoke up in favor of a communiqué pointing out that at the very least the American press would speculate as to why none had been issued. At this point, Aziz Ahmed said that there would be no problems from the Pakistan standpoint since he had told a number of Pakistan editors that it was unlikely there would be a communiqué. The matter was left for further discussion the next day.[4]

---

[4] A joint communiqué was issued at the conclusion of the talks on December 15. Both Presidents indicated the importance they attached to a close and cooperative relationship and agreed on the need for a peaceful resolution of the outstanding differences between India and Pakistan. (Department of State *Bulletin*, January 3, 1966, p. 7)

---

266. Memorandum of Conversation[1]

Washington, December 15, 1965, 5:20 p.m.

President Johnson said that he and President Ayub had rehearsed and reviewed problems of both countries. He was very happy that President Ayub had been able to visit him and he wished that this visit had taken place earlier, a year or two before. He hoped that there would be another visit in the months ahead. He said that there was no leader with whom he had more rapport, understanding, or friendship. President Johnson said he and President Ayub had discussed in a completely frank way a number of serious matters which were of deep concern to both countries. For its part, the United States would do what it can do. He was praying that the upcoming Tashkent Conference would be successful.

---

[1] Source: National Archives and Records Administration, RG 59, Conference Files: Lot 66 D 347, CF 2569. Secret. Drafted by Handley. The memorandum is marked "Draft" and includes handwritten additions and corrections. The meeting took place in the Cabinet Room at the White House. According to the President's Daily Dairy, the U.S. advisers present included Ball, Hare, Handley, McConaughy, and Hand. The Pakistani advisers were Bhutto, Faruque, Aziz Ahmed, Ghulam Ahmed, Gauhar, Salman Ali, and Iftikhar Ali. The time of the meeting is also taken from the President's Daily Diary. (Johnson Library)

He was sure that there is nothing that Pakistan wants to do that is inimical to the United States. He had made it clear to President Ayub that if the Pakistani people are in danger of being "gobbled up" the United States would be there just as they are in Viet-Nam.

The President said that President Ayub had come asking for nothing but was going away with everything—with our friendship, our confidence, and our trust. "Indeed, everything we have got".

President Johnson said that he would like Mr. Arthur Dean to go to Pakistan, "as I did," to visit heads of government, and to make recommendations on how to improve the machinery.

He repeated that he believed and would say so to our people, that Pakistan would not do anything that is inimical to the United States.

He said that although nothing specific had been discussed or decided, he had told President Ayub that we are not going to let Pakistan say that we cannot feed India, adding that Pakistan had not asked any such thing. Nor were we going to let India think that we cannot protect Pakistan.

He did not know how two heads of State could leave each other with more feeling of brotherly love. He recalled his visit to Pakistan and said that he had never visited any country where he was treated better or that he loved more. Speaking directly to President Ayub, he said that "If your life (Pakistan) is threatened, ours will be also threatened".

President Ayub replied that he wished the United States had felt the same way a few months ago when Pakistan's life was being threatened. He went on to say that the conversation had done his soul a lot of good and that in spite of what he had read in the press, he and President Johnson had been able to have frank and friendly talks. He knew that Pakistan had no right to dictate United States policy to India or to other countries but that he hoped we would understand Pakistan's position. All Pakistan expects is an understanding of its position. Pakistan would never have any intention of doing any damage to the real interest of the United States. Pakistan is very deeply concerned about Viet-Nam because Viet-Nam is in Asia. He hoped that the Viet-Nam problem will come to a satisfactory end. Pakistan would be a force for moderation. He had stated in "sensitive places" (Peking) that the United States has a legitimate stake in that part of the world. At the same time Viet-Nam was of deep concern to Pakistan because it did affect its own security. He said that because of Viet-Nam and Chinese actions in Asia there seemed to be at the moment a strange coalition between India, the United States, and the Soviet Union.

In reiterating his deep satisfaction about his meeting with President Johnson he stressed the hope that the President could visit Pakistan sometime in the future.

267.   Record of Meeting[1]

Washington, December 15, 1965, 5:40 p.m.

PRESIDENT'S COMMENTS TO US ADVISERS CONCERNING PRIVATE MEETING WITH PRESIDENT AYUB

The President initially addressed his remarks to Mr. Arthur Dean. He said he wanted Mr. Dean to "go out there", and to see what has to be done. He should realize that Ayub felt himself threatened by India and was deeply afraid that Pakistan would be "gobbled up".

In discussing his afternoon's conversation with President Ayub, the President said that Ayub had told him that Pakistan's first obligation was to the United States. Ayub had no agreements of any kind with the Chicoms but what if the Indians were to try to gobble up Pakistan. The President replied that we would do what we did in Viet-Nam. We were not going to let anybody overrun them. Ayub said that was all he wanted to know. He did not want any economic or military aid at this point. Only the reassurance "you have given me."

The President philosophized about the spot in which Ayub seemed to find himself. Ayub felt hemmed in by powerful neighbors on all sides—China, Russia and India. At home he had his domestic problems with the Bhutto group and others. Ayub seemed almost to have a psychosis about India.

On Kashmir the President said he had told Ayub to do his best at Tashkent and that if Tashkent failed we would try something else as Goldberg indicated last night. But he should not be under any illusions that we can force a settlement. If we were able to we would have done so already.

The President told Ayub that we were not going to let Pakistan tell us how to handle India. We will give India food or anything else we want. Our Indian policy is our business. Ayub said he fully understood this but what if the Indians tried to knock us off? The President said we would not let them.

---

[1] Source: National Archives and Records Administration, RG 59, Conference Files: Lot 66 D 347, CF 2569. Secret. Drafted by Handley. The memorandum is marked "Draft" and contains handwritten revisions. The meeting took place in the Oval Office of the White House. The time and place of the meeting are taken from the President's Daily Diary; the memorandum itself indicates that Ayub and Johnson met between 4:30 and 5:30. (Johnson Library) The Daily Diary also indicates that the advisers present included Ball, McGeorge Bundy, Hare, McConaughy, Komer, Handley, Arthur Dean, Chief of Protocol Lloyd Hand, and Deputy Assistant Secretary of State for International Organization Affairs David Popper.

The President indicated that if Pakistan wanted close relations with us there could be no serious relationship with the Chicoms. We could not live with that. At the same time we understood certain relationships just as a wife could understand a Saturday night fling by her husband so long as she was the wife. Ayub got the point.

On aid, when the President started to talk about the possibility of providing some starters for Pakistani planes to deliver food to remote mountain areas and about the release of $40 million in 1965 loans for the Mangla transmission line, Ayub stopped him by saying he didn't want to talk about aid just now. Ayub said, "I don't want to ask for any aid, that's up to you."

The President said that Ayub had spoken at length about Pakistani public opinion which thought that the United States had stabbed Pakistan in the back and that the Americans favored India. The Paks thought this began when the United States gave military aid to India in 1962. Ayub mentioned that this had begun under President Kennedy and that he was reluctant to say anything bad about a decision made by a man who was now tragically dead.

The President told Ayub that Pakistan ought to give some of its rice surplus to India and open its ports to help relieve famine in India. If Pakistan would ship rice, we would replace it with wheat. Ayub said that the rice export was a possibility and that Pakistan had some of the world's finest rice. He also said that the two big Pakistan ports were already clogged with a backlog of ships, but thought that Chalna could be used although it would require lighters. Chalna was near Calcutta. If the Indians came to the Pakistanis and said that the United States wanted to use this port to help relieve famine in India, Ayub would approve, but the Indians would have to ask.

Ayub had said, "I know you won't believe it but those Indians are going to gobble us up." President Johnson had replied that if they tried this we would stop them and that he believed we could do this simply by telling India we would not allow it. We cannot believe that India would attack Pakistan if the United States were opposed.

The President said that we would like to have Pakistan troops in Viet-Nam under their SEATO Treaty but that we would not ask for them.

The President thought that Ayub was much chastened. He had gone on an adventure and been licked. He felt very uncomfortable now, so much so that the President commented that he hated to see a proud man humble himself so. Ayub was subdued, troubled, pathetic and sad. So much so that even Mrs. Johnson had commented on it.

The President told Ayub he would never try to upset him. Did Ayub believe it. Ayub said, yes, he did. The President said that Ayub had better be more concerned about his own people and not about us. Ayub defended Bhutto and said that Bhutto had wanted him to come much sooner to the United States. The President commented that anything Ayub had said about Bhutto would not offend Bhutto if he read it.

Ayub had complained that our Government officials were always more sympatico toward India. We always sent our best people to India, especially those who were closest to the White House e.g. Galbraith. The President recalled that in 1961 Ayub had begged him to ask President Kennedy to send one of the Bundy boys. The President commented that it would help a lot if we could send a good new Ambassador to Pakistan.

The President then emphasized how close he felt to Ayub. He understood him, his fears, his problems. He was impressed that Ayub had asked him for nothing specific and felt that good groundwork for the visit had been laid by Prime Minister Wilson and by our people in the field. Recognizing President Ayub's need for reassurance the President had told him that he would no more think about injuring Lady Bird than he would Ayub.

There ensued some discussion about the timing of the Dean mission, i.e. whether it should be before or after the Shastri visit. The general sense was that it should be after Shastri had visited Washington and that it should be to both India and Pakistan.

268. National Security Action Memorandum No. 339[1]

Washington, December 17, 1965.

MEMORANDUM FOR

The Secretary of Agriculture

SUBJECT

Critical Indian Food Situation

I am deeply concerned on humanitarian grounds with the near famine conditions which are developing in India, and which may require a dramatic rescue operation on the part of those nations able to assist. As you know, I have already announced that the United States would participate in such an effort.

---

[1] Source: Johnson Library, National Security File, NSAMs, NSAM 339, Critical Indian Food Situation. Secret. Copies were sent to the Secretaries of State, Defense, and Commerce, the Director of the Bureau of the Budget, the Administrator of the Agency for International Development, and the Special Assistant to the President for Science and Technology.

I further understand from my discussion with you that the key bottleneck may be less the availability of sufficient foodgrains from abroad than lack of available shipping, inadequate Indian port facilities, and inefficient food distribution facilities within India. These factors could critically hamper any international effort to get enough food to India's hungry.

Therefore, I request that you establish a special committee, including representation from the Departments of State, Defense, Commerce, the Agency for International Development, and such other Departments and Agencies as you deem necessary, to examine urgently how to cope with the looming Indian famine problem. I want you to regard all available resources of the U.S. Government as being at your disposal in planning for such an effort. After assessing the likely dimensions of the crisis and what would be required to meet it, you and your group should recommend whatever imaginative emergency techniques and devices which may be necessary to help prevent mass starvation in India.

I would like personally to review your recommendations as soon as they can be made available, before deciding what action I will take along with other interested governments.[2]

Lyndon B. Johnson

---

[2] Komer and Bundy recommended the text of NSAM No. 339 to the President on December 16, noting that it "puts the bee on Freeman to mastermind any famine rescue effort," drawing on the government's resources as necessary. (Ibid.) On December 27 Freeman sent a memorandum to the heads of the Departments of State, Defense, Commerce, the Agency for International Development, the Bureau of the Budget, and to Presidential Assistant Donald F. Hornig reporting on progress in response to NSAM No. 339. He noted that two inter-agency task forces had been established in response to the crisis in India. A food shipment operations task force was chaired by C.R. Eskildsen, Deputy Administrator of the Foreign Agricultural Service, USDA, and an agricultural productivity task force was chaired by Walter G. Farr, Jr., Deputy Assistant Administrator (NESA/AID). In addition, Freeman appointed Dorothy Jacobson, Assistant Secretary of Agriculture for International Affairs, to chair an executive committee to monitor progress, consider policy questions, and issue progress reports. (Washington National Records Center, RG 330, OSD Files: FRC 70 A 1266, India 1966)

269.   Telegram From the Department of State to the Embassy in
Turkey[1]

Washington, December 17, 1965, 6:08 p.m.

509. You should deliver following personal message from President direct to President Ayub during his stopover Ankara 3 pm tomorrow: "Mr. President: After reflecting on our candid talks I am convinced that we are back on an upward track in US–Pakistan relations. As a mark of my confidence, I have told David Bell to proceed with five loan agreements for the Mangla Dam Transmission Lines, the Lahore–Multan Highway, Sui Gas, Diesel Locomotives for your western railway, and a major loan for investigation and consulting services for the West Pakistan Water and Power Development Authority. We will not announce these now, but can do so at the time the loan agreements are signed. We are also looking urgently into the matter of starter motors and spare parts for your C 130's to deliver food in your northern areas. Again I must say that I regard our talks as a major step toward re-establishment of mutual confidence, and am very glad that you came.[2] Signed Lyndon B. Johnson."

Rusk

---

[1] Source: National Archives and Records Administration, RG 59, Central Files 1964–66, AID (US) 9 PAK. Secret; Flash; Exdis. Drafted in the White House, cleared by Komer, and approved by Hare. Repeated to Karachi.

[2] The Embassy in Turkey reported that the message was delivered to Ayub at the Ankara airport on December 18. (Ibid., Conference Files: Lot 66 D 347, CF 2569) On December 20 Ayub expressed his gratitude for the swift action on the loan agreements in a letter to Johnson. (Ayub's letter was conveyed in a letter from Ambassador Ahmed to Secretary Rusk, December 20; ibid., Presidential Correspondence: Lot 66 D 476, Lebanon thru Pakistan) The Embassy in India was informed of the decisions taken on these loans in telegram 1088 to New Delhi, December 20. The telegram noted that the loans had been previously authorized out of FY 1965 funds, and did not represent a new FY 1966 commitment. (Ibid., Central Files 1964–66, AID (US) 9 PAK)

270. Memorandum for Record[1]

Washington, December 20, 1965.

SUBJECT

President's Meeting with Indian Food Minister Subramaniam[2]

PRESENT

The President   Minister Subramaniam
Secretary Freeman   Ambassador B.K. Nehru
Mr. Komer

The President cordially welcomed Subramaniam, saying that he had looked forward to Subramaniam's visit. Secretary Freeman had filled him in on the Rome discussions and Subramaniam's program; in fact, Freeman was a wonderful public relations man on this matter.

Subramaniam said he brought the best wishes of Prime Minister Shastri, who looked forward to his February visit. Subramaniam too thought there had been good discussions in Rome. He felt that Agriculture now had first priority in India's Fourth Plan, and he appreciated the US support.

The President replied that he too looked forward to Shastri's coming. By then he would have submitted to Congress various proposals on food, health, population and other fields which would be of mutual interest. Freeman had reported how Subramaniam had exerted real leadership on India's food problem. This was very good. Perhaps Freeman should go out to India soon to see the situation for himself.

The President then mentioned the Ayub visit. He said that Ayub had made no criticism of anything we were doing for India. The President had deliberately authorized the $50 million fertilizer loan before Ayub came so that he wouldn't misunderstand our policy. In fact, Ayub realized that he couldn't write our Indian policies for us. Ayub didn't indulge in any ancient history, which made the meeting much easier. The President had asked him if he could use some of Pakistan's ports if necessary to move in food for India. Ayub had replied that if this was practicable, it would be manageable. The President thought that

---

[1] Source: Johnson Library, National Security File, Country File, India, Vol. VI, Cables/Memos/Misc., 1965–1966. Secret.

[2] Subramaniam was in Washington at Freeman's invitation to discuss the food crisis in India. Subramaniam also met with Freeman, Bell, Rusk, Vice President Humphrey, and a group of Congressmen. In his meeting with Rusk on December 22, Subramaniam said that the drought was the worst India had known since the 1890s, and that unless special measures were taken starvation was inevitable. (Memorandum of conversation; National Archives and Records Administration, RG 59, Central Files 1964–66, SOC 10 INDIA)

something along these lines would be an excellent means of promoting Pak-Indian rapprochement. Subramaniam agreed.

The President then developed his own thinking on how to help meet the Indian food crisis. We ought to look at everything we could do to help, not just at making food available. The whole problem of shipping, port facilities, transportation and internal distribution "ought to be attacked just as if we were in a war". He asked Secretary Freeman to move as fast as possible on these matters—and to talk to our best people in such fields. The President remarked that he had seen a press story about extensive storage losses in India. Subramaniam replied that this was overdone; it had actually been a local problem. He described the new "safe grains" movement to cope with this problem.

At this point the President described the motivations behind US policy. We were not interested in disciplining anyone, in becoming the masters of anyone, or in dominating anyone. All we wanted was India's friendship. Nor were we cocky about our own economic successes, because 25% of our people still had all sorts of needs. We had a poverty problem, a Negro problem, an urban problem, a health problem, etc. The President explained how he was trying to do something about all of them. And our interest did not stop at our boundary. We wanted to do something about health, education and poverty all over the world. One of the key things the President was going to try and do during his term of office was to achieve new results in the field of food and agriculture, health, population, and education abroad as well as at home. We would exercise whatever persuasion we could toward these ends. We wanted to provide incentives too. He told Subramaniam that "you gave us an incentive in your new program. If you can keep this program going we can help you more."

Subramaniam thanked the President. He then raised the special importance of taking extra care of children. They were the future. He felt that India should have a separate children's program in this crisis, so that India could say that children had equal opportunities. The President responded warmly to this idea.

The President then explained how his postponement of the Shastri and Ayub visits had nothing to do with Indian and Pakistani criticism of the US. He simply wanted to have his money in the bank before he talked aid matters. However, the postponement had led to misunderstandings. Both Subramaniam and B.K. Nehru assured the President that these were matters of the past and that there was no residue of concern at all.

The President mentioned three points which he thought were important to US-Indian collaboration. First, if we could find some way to get Kashmir considered and out of the way, this would help us to get on with much more important things. Second, he hoped that India would get other countries to help meet the food crisis. The more that others could do in some kind of international consortium the more helpful we could be. Third, he had to give the US people some hope that India would be able to take care of itself and even to help others in due time.

So the President urged that the Indians and ourselves put a food consortium together. This would help mightily with Symington and others in Congress. He was proud of the way in which he had gotten the aid bill through with fewer cuts than at almost any previous time. In fact, he had gotten about 85% of his legislative program through, but the honeymoon was over. The President also pointed out that he had never criticized Shastri. Indeed, the whole American press was remarkably free of criticism of India.

The President summed up by telling Secretary Freeman to see what we needed in a crash program, to see that our wheat and that of others got all the way to the Indian people who needed it most. We must try to avoid any holdup because of inadequate ports or distribution. He told Freeman to follow every sack of wheat from the US silo to the Indian stomach. Second, he said "let us get others in the act. Let us tell others what they can contribute." He thought that he might raise this matter with Erhard, and described his difficulties in getting the British and Germans to contribute to the Asian bank.

The President ended by urging Subramaniam to meet the press in the West lobby. He and Freeman should describe the general tenor of the discussions and also indicate that we had discussed some of the problems which would be taken up at the President's meeting with Prime Minister Shastri.

RWK

271.   Memorandum From the President's Deputy Special Assistant for National Security Affairs (Komer) to President Johnson[1]

Washington, December 20, 1965, 5:30 p.m.

We have a fascinating up-to-the minute report[2] [*1 line of source text not declassified*] that: (a) Bhutto seems to regard Ayub as having sold out on his US trip; (b) Bhutto may be planning to use some papers relating to a secret Pak/Chicom deal against Ayub; (c) Bhutto thinks he'd better quit—he actually dictated a letter of resignation to Ayub; (d) Bhutto believes that Aziz Ahmed has been won over to the American side, and that G. Ahmed is also on that side. The only mention of you is that Bhutto says you "back-patted Aziz Ahmed" a great deal (and apparently to good effect).

This report suggests that the visit (plus our hard line posture leading up to it) have really shaken the Paks, that changes in Pak policy are in the offing, and that Bhutto may be on the way out[3] (we don't know, of course, whether he actually did send his resignation to Ayub). This report also tends to confirm some older reports from the same source on a secret Pak/Chicom understanding.

R.W. Komer[4]

---

[1] Source: Johnson Library, National Security File, Country File, Pakistan, Vol. V, Memos, 9/65–1/66. Top Secret; Eyes Only.

[2] Not found.

[3] President Johnson discussed the subsequent resignation of Bhutto in a telephone conversation with former President Eisenhower on November 4, 1967. Johnson said that he had discussed Bhutto with Ayub during Ayub's visit to Washington in December 1965. [*text not declassified*] He told Eisenhower that he warned Ayub about Bhutto: "I just said to him—now, Mr. President, I know you rely on Bhutto just like I rely on Dean Rusk and like Eisenhower relied on Dulles, but you can't rely on him that way and I am not entering your internal affairs, but this man is damn dangerous as far as you are concerned and you are my friend and I am going to give you this warning and I know whereof I speak. [*text not declassified*]" (Johnson Library, Recordings and Transcripts, Recording of Telephone Conversation Between President Johnson and President Eisenhower, November 4, 1967, 10:05 a.m., Tape 67.14, Side B, PNO 40)

[4] Printed from a copy that bears this typed signature.

272. Telegram From the Department of State to the Embassy in India[1]

Washington, December 23, 1965, 6:13 p.m.

1122. For Bowles from Freeman. Reference our tel re Freeman–Subramaniam December 22 summary[2] letter text follows:

Dear Mr. Minister:

We were pleased that you could accept our invitation to come here on such short notice to discuss the food situation in your country. Your visit has made us intensely aware of the serious difficulties faced by your people and of the means by which our governments might cooperate in meeting these difficulties.

As you make your plans to speed the movement of grain into India, it would be most helpful if you could provide on a weekly basis information on the arrival of grain by ports as well as supply and distribution information on grain under the control of the Central Government. We also need more detailed information on a monthly basis, including the supply and distribution of grains held by the states. I understand that representatives of your Government and mine are in agreement as to the detailed format for this reporting. We would hope to be advised of any unusual situations which would affect the movement of grain.

We understand that you would welcome a team of US specialists to make a quick survey of the port and internal transport system, along with storage facilities. We are prepared to send such a team within a few weeks. The leader of the team, someone well acquainted with Indian agriculture and food problems, might be stationed in New Delhi working closely with you.[3] I might designate a Special Representative who would be on a more permanent basis. He would keep me posted on progress in implementing your longer-term agricultural development plans. If he could have access to you and be privy to your plans it would be very helpful.

---

[1] Source: National Archives and Records Administration, RG 59, Central Files 1964–66, POL 7 INDIA. Confidential; Immediate; Limdis. Drafted by E. T. Olson (USDA); cleared in USDA by Brown, Vickery, Eskildsen (FAS), and Freeman; cleared in State by Sober (SOA), and in AID/NESA by Donovan; and approved by Handley. Repeated to Karachi, London, Bombay, Calcutta, and Madras.

[2] Reference is to telegram 1121 to New Delhi, December 23, which summarized Subramaniam's meetings in Washington, and characterized them as "very useful." (Ibid., SOC 10 INDIA)

[3] On December 30 Freeman sent another telegram to Bowles in which he indicated that he planned to send a team of specialists to India for a 3-week survey beginning January 9. Freeman named C.R. Eskildsen, Associate Administrator of the Foreign Agricultural Service, to head the team. (Telegram 1155 to New Delhi; ibid.)

After current crop prospects, the short-fall in 1966 and the potential 1967 short-fall have been reviewed once more, we believe that an appeal should be made for external assistance to the "Community of Nations." This appeal should be made as quickly and dramatically as feasible. It would be well if it preceded the meeting between Prime Minister Shastri and President Johnson in early February. This might even take the form of an appeal by the representative of India to the United Nations.

It is also my understanding that you have begun to examine the possibilities of using large bulk carriers to discharge grain in midstream into smaller vessels and lighters for ultimate delivery to ports. In our discussion, there appeared to be certain problems in connection with the registry of the "liberty" type or smaller vessels which might be used for this purpose as well as the availability of such vessels. I trust you will be examining this situation further with the objective of increasing the overall discharge capacity at your ports as rapidly as possible.

We would like some help from you in overcoming certain problems we face in the United States. Internal rail transport and some ports are already in full use. If shipping requirements are increased, we may need to use facilities not normally used for shipments to your country. Your cooperation and that of your purchasing mission here in Washington in meeting these problems and limitations we face will be appreciated.

We are pleased with the progress that we have been able to make during our talks this week and we hope that we can continue our further close cooperation during the months ahead. Please keep us informed of any way in which we can be of further assistance.

You have done a splendid job here and left a strong favorable impression with everyone.

I have enjoyed coming to know you personally and look forward to a close and enjoyable personal and working relationship.

Sincerely yours,

Orville L. Freeman, Secretary of Agriculture

Rusk

273.   Telegram From the Department of State to the Embassy in India[1]

Washington, December 30, 1965, 8:02 p.m.

1170. Deptel 1071,[2] Cirtel 1242.[3]

1. Top levels here continue to view early organization by GOI of international effort to help India with food situation matter of highest priority. Request that you follow up with appropriate GOI officials this aspect Subramaniam visit immediately, discussing subject with them along following lines.

2. As President and Secretaries Rusk and Freeman made clear to Subramaniam, our readiness to provide food assistance over and above current level related to GOI willingness frankly to inform international community seriousness Indian food situation and to vigor with which it seeks international help. Organization of international effort will require considerable initiative and ingenuity. Subramaniam indicated that he recognized importance of such an effort, that he would discuss FAO role with Sen of FAO during Rome airport stop and would take up subject with PM and President upon return. We would be interested in results of such consultation.

3. As to how GOI effort should be organized, most urgent need is bilateral follow-up with countries in best position to provide help with respect immediate food needs. Especially important is effort, through diversions and other means, to utilize Indian port capacity to

---

[1] Source: National Archives and Records Administration, RG 59, Central Files 1964–66, SOC 10 INDIA. Confidential; Immediate. Drafted by R.H. Johnson and Handley; cleared by Farr (AID/NESA), Deputy Assistant Secretary Walter M. Kotschnig (IO), Laise, Terrell E. Arnold (E/TEP), Jacobson (USDA), and Special Assistant to the Secretary for Food for Peace Richard W. Reuter; and approved by Hare. Repeated to London, Ottawa, Canberra, and Karachi.

[2] In telegram 1071 to New Delhi, December 16, the Embassy was informed that U.S. readiness to provide special assistance to India over and above P.L. 480 assistance was related to the willingness of the Indian Government to inform the international community of the seriousness of the problem and the vigor with which it sought international help. The Embassy was instructed to make the U.S. position clear. (Ibid.)

[3] Circular telegram 1242, December 30, addressed to 13 posts in Europe and Asia, summarized Subramaniam's visit to Washington and emphasized the importance of a broad international effort to meet the food crisis in India. The Department indicated that it intended to call in representatives of the 13 countries to which India had made informal soundings asking for help. The Embassies were instructed to weigh in in support of that approach. (Ibid., AID (US) 15–8 INDIA) The Department sent additional messages to London, Ottawa, and Canberra stating that the United States considered that the United Kingdom, Canada, and Australia would play major roles in helping India meet its critical food needs. (Telegrams 3744 to London, 717 to Ottawa, and 504 to Canberra, all December 30; ibid., SOC 10 INDIA)

maximum possible extent next six weeks. As indicated septels, US is backing up Indian effort this regard through own bilateral approaches.

4. However, GOI should begin now effort to provide broader international framework for food and agricultural aid. This important to provide (a) framework within which countries unable to provide immediate food or shipping but able to provide fertilizer, seed and other aid for 1966 crop can be given reasonable assurance their contribution related to longer-term Indian effort deal with its basic agricultural problems; (b) means of coordinating international effort to ensure proper priorities and time phasing; (c) means of dramatizing international support. In broad terms emergency effort should be seen as means of dramatizing and moving toward international effort to support GOI solutions to longer term problem.

5. After having considered alternative approaches to organization of international effort, we believe best mechanism would be creation by GOI of coordinating committee of potential donor governments and donor international agencies, sitting in Delhi and including representation from FAO and World Bank. Indian designated to head international effort should be person of prominence, preferably Subramaniam himself. Other representatives on committee might be ambassadors in Delhi or special representatives sent to Delhi for purpose. Job of committee would be to support GOI efforts, as detailed para. 4, to muster international help of all kinds relevant to immediate crisis and next year's crop; to coordinate effort; and to dramatize international aspect. Chairman would play leading personal role.

6. In order achieve its important and urgent objectives, such an arrangement should be promptly established, hopefully within a week. With convening of US Congress, upcoming Presidential messages to Congress, etc., it essential that we have soonest some indication of GOI plans and initial actions so that US effort can be placed in broader international context.

7. Most important to any effort that GOI make clear to potential donors urgency of situation.

Rusk

274. Memorandum From the President's Deputy Special Assistant for National Security Affairs (Komer) to President Johnson[1]

Washington, January 4, 1966, 7 p.m.

Here is another brilliant, though awfully wordy, *report on India famine* by Freeman.[2] It boils down to the fact that *the most efficient and cheapest way to minimize famine (there will be some in any case) is to schedule an optimum flow into Indian ports before their capacity drops sharply when the rainy season begins in May.* Otherwise we and other donors will have to resort to expensive emergency measures at that time.

The 1.5 million tons have already been purchased and are being shipped as fast as possible. But there will be a gap in the pipeline and a sharp shortfall from the million tons a month we'd like to get in before the rains come unless we either (a) authorize at least another 500,000 tons shortly, or (b) at least tell the Indians privately we will, so they can firmly book shipping ahead.

Freeman reports that India is urgently requesting help from others, and getting some responses, but the evidence is that no one besides ourselves and Canada has much wheat (and Canadian ports get frozen over).

Frankly, one problem is that Freeman and the rest of us hesitate to hit you so soon again on Indian food.[3] However, would there be some appropriate place in the series of messages you are planning for a new dramatic announcement shortly?

Freeman is sending a technical mission to India Thursday and would like to go briefly himself around 20 January (perhaps en route to Vietnam). Would this merit a White House announcement along with another 500,000 or million tons of food?

Draft WH announcement

Draft para. for aid message

Tell Indians *privately* we'll allocate an additional million tons before Shastri comes[4]

R.W. Komer

---

[1] Source: Johnson Library, National Security File, Country File, India, Vol. VI, Cables, Memos, Miscellaneous, 9/65–1/66. Secret.

[2] Reference is to a January 4 memorandum from Freeman to President Johnson with a subject line that reads: "Follow up on Indian Food and Agriculture Situation." (Ibid., Cables, 9/65–1/66)

[3] McGeorge Bundy sent this memorandum to the President with an attached note that reads: "Bob Komer was scared to frame the specific recommendations on his covering memo here, but I told him that you were bolder than he on serious matters and that you were an admirer of honest advice. So here it comes with my courage and his wisdom." (Ibid.)

[4] Johnson wrote in the margin, in response to these recommendations, "See me."

275. Letter From Prime Minister Shastri to President Johnson[1]

Tashkent, January 6, 1966.

Dear Mr. President,

I was happy to get your message[2] which was conveyed to me by your Embassy in New Delhi just after Christmas. Minister Subramaniam told me about the warmth of the reception he had in Washington and of the generous offer of additional help to meet the critical shortage of foodgrains which we in India are facing due to the extremely poor monsoons that we had last year. We are doing everything possible to mobilise whatever assistance we can get from other countries, so that the entire burden does not fall upon you.

2. Ambassador Harriman saw me in Delhi[3] on the eve of my departure for Tashkent. I am greatly impressed by the determined effort which you are making to bring about a peace in Vietnam. Ambassador Harriman recognised that our own relationship with Hanoi was not such as to enable us to make a positive contribution by making any direct approaches to the Government of North Vietnam. He was, however, anxious that I could speak to Mr. Kosygin and I had a talk with him on the subject last night.

3. Mr. Kosygin's attitude was not negative. He emphasised, however, that the important thing was to find a basis for talks which was acceptable to Hanoi also and he welcomed the approach which Ambassador Harriman had made to the Government of Poland. He also indicated that the visit of Shelepin to Hanoi was intended to help the cause of peace.

4. My talks with President Ayub have just started. We are facing many difficult issues. I am hoping that both of us would subscribe to the principle of not having recourse to force for resolving them and I feel that once this has come about, there will be a different atmosphere in which it will be easier to resolve and reconcile our differences.

---

[1] Source: Johnson Library, National Security File, Country File, India, Shastri Correspondence. No classification marking. The letter was conveyed to the White House on January 6 under a covering note from Chargé P.K. Banerjee.

[2] In a message to Shastri transmitted to New Delhi in telegram 1133, December 24, Johnson indicated that he was looking forward to Shastri's visit to Washington and expressed his confidence in Shastri's determination to deal with India's food crisis. (National Archives and Records Administration, RG 59, Presidential Correspondence: Lot 66 D 294, Johnson/India 1964–1965) The signed letter, subsequently sent to Shastri, is dated January 4. (Johnson Library, National Security File, Special Head of State Correspondence File, India, 4/15/65–2/28/66)

[3] Harriman saw Shastri in New Delhi on January 2 and Ayub in Peshawar on January 3 to discuss Vietnam. Documentation on Harriman's brief visit to the subcontinent is in National Archives and Records Administration, RG 59, Central Files 1964–66, POL 7 HARRIMAN and POL 27 VIET S.

5. My wife and I are looking forward to our visit to the U.S.A. I hope that even before that, there will be substantial progress towards lowering of tensions in Asia.

6. May I once again express my deep appreciation for the timely and generous help you have offered in dealing with our food problem?

With warm personal regards,

Yours sincerely,

Lal Bahadur[4]

---

[4] Printed from a copy that bears this typed signature.

---

276. Memorandum From the Counselor of the Department of State and Chairman of the Policy Planning Council (Rostow) to President Johnson[1]

Washington, January 6, 1966.

SUBJECT

The Indian Food Situation: The Problem of Timing

I have been reading the history of the last great famine in India—in 1943—and discussing with experts the timing of various aspects of the Indian food situation this year.

Three facts emerge.

1. During February and March of this year there will be about 500,000 tons of unutilized Indian port capacity which could be used to build stocks if grain shipments get there on time. From April on port capacity will be tight.

2. If chemical fertilizers are to be applied in time to raise output in the November 1966 harvest, they must arrive in India by June.

3. If the food situation is as serious as all our experts tell us it will be, there will be certain signs of malnutrition and famine in the spring; but the most dangerous period will come in the months August–October 1966.

---

[1] Source: Johnson Library, National Security File, Country File, India, Vol. VI, Cables, 9/65–1/66. No classification marking. A handwritten "L" on the memorandum indicates that it was seen by the President.

From these facts, it seems clear that we ought to make a maximum effort now to use the 500,000 tons of idle port capacity available during February and March. That would be enough grain to feed something like 10 million people in the three critical months before the November harvest. Although we will be exploring with the Indians the possibility of extraordinary methods for food delivery, it is possible that what we lose in February and March will be lost for good.

So far as the U.S. is concerned, it may take a prompt decision by you to proceed with a PL 480 agreement beyond the 1.5 million tons in order to mobilize the wheat and the shipping in time to exploit the idle port capacity available in February and March.

In addition, it may be necessary for the Indians to put direct, very high-level pressure on the Canadians and Australians to divert some ships from their commercial traffic to Indian ports. I suspect only decisions by the Prime Ministers could force the special arrangements required to divert cargoes. We may wish Chet Bowles to call this possibility to Shastri's attention when he returns from Tashkent.

Frankly, what worries me, as a planner, is that a good many human beings may starve in those critical months before the next harvest because all of us didn't make the special urgent effort necessary to use the idle port capacity briefly available in the next several months.[2] (Probably 3 million Indians starved to death in the 1943 famine.)

A similar sense of urgency will be required to round up the chemical fertilizers and get them there by June. If they don't lay the fertilizer down in time, we could have a second thin harvest in 1966–67. In the case of fertilizers, pressure will probably have to be exerted on Japan, Germany and Britain, since I am told that our fertilizer production and shipping capacity are committed to the hilt. Again, the Indians should be leaning on them; and we should be backing their play.

Walt

---

[2] Komer sent a memorandum to President Johnson on January 8 in which he also stressed the importance of taking advantage of the opportunity to ship grain to India before Indian port capacity was cut by the onset of the rainy season in late May. (Ibid., Memos to the President, McGeorge Bundy, Vol. 18, January 1–8, 1966)

277.   Memorandum From Secretary of Agriculture Freeman to President Johnson[1]

Washington, January 7, 1966.

SUBJECT

India—Technical Team Visit

1. McGeorge Bundy has relayed to me your instructions.[2] The technical team will not leave as scheduled.

2. The team will stand by for further instructions. Bundy informs me that it is not your intention to cancel the team but rather to delay it until the Pakistan India Tashkent conversations have concluded.[3]

3. It is important that we keep as much pressure on Shastri in particular and the Indian Government in general as possible. To date they have conformed to our wishes in general terms. Public announcements implementing your expressions in your conference with Subramaniam and the Rome agreement have been made and a number of actions have been taken and instructions issued in New Delhi. However, that does not mean that the Indian Bureaucracy and the Indian States are acting. To the extent that we can measure the real commitment of the Indian Government and the Indian people by actions taken as well as announced, this should be done prior to the Shastri visit. We can make such judgments only from detailed information verified on the spot, not from generalizations. Hence the importance of getting the team to India and back as quickly as possible. They have been instructed not only to review and survey the Indian capacity for handling various

---

[1] Source: Johnson Library, National Security File, Country File, India, Vol. VI, Cables, 9/65–1/66. Administratively Confidential.

[2] Bundy sent this memorandum to the President on January 7 under cover of a memorandum that reads: "I had a talk with Orville this morning after my conversation with you, and this is the result. I hope you may find it more nearly what you want from him." (Ibid.)

[3] Freeman sent a cable to Bowles on January 7 informing him that the survey team would be delayed. (Telegram 1227 to New Delhi; National Archives and Records Administration, RG 59, Central Files 1964–66, SOC 10 INDIA) On January 8 Bowles replied to Freeman that the Indian Government, and Subramaniam in particular, were "severely let down" and concerned by the last-minute postponement for unspecified reasons. (Telegram 1173 from New Delhi; ibid.) Komer sent a cable to Bowles on January 8 in which he explained: "Might be helpful if I underline privately that failure GOI as yet to mount all-out effort to get famine aid from other countries is impeding our own response." (Johnson Library, National Security File, Country File, India, Exchanges with Bowles) Telegram 1247 to New Delhi, January 11, informed the Embassy that the trip had been rescheduled and the Eskildsen team was planning to be in India January 14–16. (National Archives and Records Administration, RG 59, Central Files 1964–66, SOC 10 INDIA)

volumes of grain (no commitments implied), but also to check thoroughly plans for the 1967 crop and how the long term Indian agricultural program is moving.

The team will be headed by Clarence Eskildsen, the Deputy Administrator of the Foreign Agricultural Service. He is a highly competent, experienced man. His rank is such that the team is clearly on a professional technical not a policy mission and there will be no basis for reading any commitment into it.

4. The Indians have been following up the possibility you suggested to Subramaniam that I might visit India before the Shastri visit. They have sent a number of inquiries this week about my plans. I expect I owe them a response one way or the other fairly soon.

Advantages

(1) Obviously I would be able to advise the President more solidly after following up the technical team's conclusions personally on the ground.

(2) Attention will be focused world-wide on the generosity of President Johnson and the U.S.A. where India's food needs are concerned.

(3) It may be that I could put more pressure on the Indians to take actions we might think are necessary prior to the Shastri visit rather than after. Commitments we may conclude are necessary which I could not get the President might require from Shastri at the time of the visit.

Disadvantage

An appearance by a Member of the President's Cabinet might well be interpreted as an overall commitment of the United States to provide whatever food is necessary in India in 1966. As you are well aware there has been considerable speculation to this effect already. We have done our best to prevent such speculation and to make clear that there is no commitment. Yet the very process of planning the logistics for the future (which we cannot afford to postpone) tends to stimulate speculative stories of U.S. commitment no matter how cautiously we proceed.

Recommendation

On balance I would recommend my visit to India wait until after the Shastri visit.

Additional pressure that we might be able to build up by a pre-Shastri visit would on balance, I think, be negated by the inevitable publicity which would carry an implication of a far-reaching commitment by the United States Government should I visit India this month. On the basis then that we will keep the most pressure on the Indian Government by withholding my visit until after the Shastri visit I would so recommend.

Action[4]

1. Postpone your visit until following Shastri.

2. Plan to go prior to the Shastri visit.

3. Discuss this with me further.

4. Send the technical team as soon as the Tashkent Conference concludes.

5. Talk to me further before you send the technical team.

---

[4] Options 1 and 4 are circled on the memorandum. It is not clear that the President made the markings, but the choices reflect the decisions that were made.

---

278. Editorial Note

President Ayub and Prime Minister Shastri met at Tashkent in the Soviet Union January 4–10, 1966, to discuss the conflict that had recently grown out of the long-standing Kashmir dispute. Soviet Chairman Kosygin played an active role during the talks in promoting the agreement that was signed on January 10. By the terms of the "Tashkent Declaration," India and Pakistan agreed to the complete withdrawal of all armed personnel of the two countries to the positions they held prior to August 5, 1965, this withdrawal to be achieved by February 25, 1966. Both countries reaffirmed their obligation under the UN Charter "not to have recourse to force and to settle their disputes through peaceful means." Against the backdrop of that statement, Kashmir was discussed, a discussion in which each side "set forth its respective position." Both countries expressed a "firm resolve to restore normal and peaceful relations," including commitments to repatriate POWs, restore normal diplomatic relations, consider measures aimed at restoring economic, trade, communications, and cultural relations, and "to discourage" propaganda directed against the other country. Both countries agreed to continue meeting as necessary "on matters of direct concern." For text of the Tashkent Declaration, see *American Foreign Policy: Current Documents, 1966,* pages 680–681.

Indian Prime Minister Shastri died in Tashkent on January 11 of a heart attack. Minister of Home Affairs G.L. Nanda was sworn in as interim Prime Minister. Nanda was not regarded in Washington as likely to maintain the position in the contest that would develop within the Congress Party to succeed Shastri. (Memorandum from Hughes to Rusk, January 10; National Archives and Records Administration, RG 59, Conference Files: Lot 67 D 305, CF 4)

---

279. Memorandum From the President's Deputy Special Assistant for National Security Affairs (Komer) to President Johnson[1]

Washington, January 12, 1966, 10 a.m.

What now on India? South Asia is so important to our larger interests vis-à-vis the USSR, and even more Red China, that I'd like to develop where I think we stand at the moment and where we might go from here.

Though our strategy has been upset by unexpected tragedy, any reappraisal ought to start with recognition that this strategy has worked remarkably well to date. As an early convert (though an initial sceptic), I'll argue this with anybody. But I'm more impressed with the conversion of the key people in State and AID, along with John Lewis and even Bowles in Delhi. The apparent pulling back which you began last April did force both Paks and Indians to start coming toward us. It also put us in a good position to capitalize on another tragic circumstance, the Pak/Indian war, by making both countries realize that they'd better stop such nonsense if they wanted massive US help. Then yet another circumstance, the approaching Indian famine, gave us even greater leverage.

In Pakistan's case, the "short-rein" policy of holding up economic and then military aid helped stop Ayub's drift toward China. It forced Ayub, when faced with the ultimate choice between Washington and Peiping in the final hours of the Pak/Indian war, to reject the Chinese tie lest it mean a break with us. This process culminated in Ayub's visit, which halted the downward slide in US/Pak relations. Though no aid commitments were asked or given, Ayub made clear that he regarded us as his ally and would not tie up with China, in return for your promise that we would not let India gobble up Pakistan. The game is by no means over, and could be upset if Bhutto got rid of Ayub rather than vice versa, or if the Paks saw in Shastri's death (as

---

[1] Source: Johnson Library, National Security File, Name File, Komer Memos, Vol. 2. Secret.

they did in Nehru's) another chance to gamble on Indian disunity. But the odds are favorable if we resume aid just fast enough to convince the Paks that full resumption is in the cards if they behave, yet do so slowly enough to force Ayub to match it with performance.

In India's case, our handling of PL 480 (plus the imperative of approaching famine) have produced the opening stgaes of an agricultural revolution. In the last two months India has taken more far-reaching steps toward self-reliance in food than in the preceding 18 years. If India is important, and it is, we must skillfully maintain this momentum by continued use of carrot and stick.

Yet the agricultural revolution is only part of the larger need to revolutionize India's approach to development—on the sound principle that a democratic, self-sustaining India serves our purposes in Asia (whether formally allied to us or not). There were abundant signs of a likely breakthrough here too, and that Shastri planned to say the right things when he saw you. Our getting off the hook of hinging our whole South Asia policy to the impossible goal of early Kashmir settlement powerfully stimulated this process (and was in effect accepted by Ayub in his talks with you).

Where now? We planned our Pak/Indian strategy around a series of benchmarks, most of them now passed. The September cease-fire was followed by Ayub's pilgrimage here and now the Tashkent agreements, which will hopefully begin an extended process of Pak/Indian reconciliation. But the culminating visit we envisaged before making the hard decisions on aid resumption has now been cast in doubt by Shastri's death. The nine months of education we invested in Shastri may have to be repeated with a less pragmatic and more nationalistic successor. Thus Shastri's death may turn out to be a major setback, though it is too early to tell.

So it is essential to start thinking about how to sustain the momentum of the enterprise. I'd prescribe a combination of generosity toward a nation in travail with continued emphasis on the imperatives of self-help and reconciliation with Pakistan, as most likely to keep the Indians coming toward us. They *must* do so for food at least—and no interim steps you authorize will really deprive us of much leverage here, since India's emergency need will grow faster than we can meet it.

The first requirement is to establish sympathetic contact with the new Indian Prime Minister once we know who he is (last time Nehru's successor was picked in 6 days). So I'd urge renewing the Shastri invite (perhaps for slightly later if it suited Indian convenience). The new Prime Minister might either be unable to come (his first priority must be to establish his own political base) or unable to make commitments if he did. Nonetheless, the gesture would be deeply appreciated.

If Shastri's successor cannot come soon, then you might consider sending Art Dean (and perhaps myself) quietly to Delhi as well as Karachi around mid-February to get some feel for how firmly the new leadership is prepared to follow the Shastri line. Depending on Dean's report, we could then decide on what *interim* steps, e.g. aid resumption, to take pending a later visit by the new Indian prime minister.

In sum, I urge that we not let our Pak/Indian enterprise falter—despite our preoccupation with other pressing matters. South Asia is so important to us—especially at a time of growing confrontation with Red China—that we can't afford to do so unless there is no other alternative. If the general thrust of this paper makes sense to you, I will draw up (with State) a more detailed scenario.[2]

R.W. Komer

I generally approve—go ahead

Let's wait till the picture clarifies[3]

---

[2] Bundy wrote a marginal notation on the last page of the memorandum that reads: "RWK This memo is an unusually good one. McGB"

[3] Johnson did not respond specifically to either of the options listed by Komer, but he added a handwritten note that reads: "Mc & K—See me as soon as P.M. is selected in India and we will formulate our plans. L"

---

280. **Telegram From Secretary of State Rusk to the Department of State[1]**

New Delhi, January 13, 1966, 1837Z.

Secto 12. Vice President and Secretary met with Prime Minister Nanda for half hour morning January 13.[2] Ambassador Bowles and Nehru present, also on Indian side Foreign Secretary C.S. Jha, Secretary to Prime Minister L.K. Jha and Surendra Sinh, and on American side DCM Greene. Following is uncleared memorandum of conversation,

---

[1] Source: National Archives and Records Administration, RG 59, Central Files 1964–66, POL 32–1 INDIA–PAK. Secret; Priority. Repeated to Bangkok for the Secretary.

[2] The meeting took place during Vice President Humphrey's and Secretary Rusk's trip to India for the funeral of Prime Minister Shastri. Also in the party were Senator John Sherman Cooper and former Ambassador John Kenneth Galbraith.

much of which dealt with Tashkent meeting and communiqué, and which was supplemented by further half hour with L.K. Jha.

In reply Secretary's question whether Shastri's death would affect Tashkent agreement, Nanda said he has tried to make clear that as far as he is concerned Shastri's word is the word of the nation. Vice President said this encouraging note will be welcomed in Washington. Nanda continued that he felt spirit on both sides is that Tashkent agreement will be fulfilled and that this is a moral commitment. He said India will need the help, wisdom and understanding of all concerned to see it through.

Following brief recapitulation of communiqué, Indians emphasized that its major obligation is that henceforth negotiation not force will be relied on to deal with questions between India and Pakistan.

Foreign Secretary observed that Pakistan High Commissioner is already back in New Delhi and said that Indian High Commissioner would proceed to Karachi on Monday. Following elaboration of chain of events leading to communiqué (see below), Prime Minister noted that Socialists and perhaps others in India will oppose agreement but this is to be expected.

Secretary Rusk called Prime Minister's attention to President's State of Union message as reflecting powerful feeling of President's preoccupation to be able to devote our resources to economic and social development at home and abroad, certainly in India. But U.S. needs peace in the world to be able to do this; hence the most recent diplomatic efforts to find a basis for peace. Secretary noted he had told Gromyko that since 1947 the United States has spent $800 billion on defense, and the Soviets proportionately more; he had said that the Governments of both the United States and Soviet Union owe it to their people to lift this burden.

Nanda said Vietnam struggle is in the way of achieving these goals and eludes solution in the terms suggested. Vice President emphasized U.S. capacity to help people at home and abroad is limited by amount we have to spend on resisting aggression in Southeast Asia. President Johnson has made clear that he wants to get on with development in Southeast Asia, including North Vietnam.

In response to Prime Minister's general agreement on need to start talking, Vice President agreed and pointed out that U.S. sets no conditions on talks; we want to get disputes out of the area of violence and into the area of reason. When this is done, then we will be able to do the things we want to do for the people in all countries.

Nanda said India also wants peace and equally wants democracy; latter requires defeating poverty and providing food and better life and equal society for all.

Vice President responded that we are committed to same goals and wish people of all Southeast Asia would understand that we would rather use our resources for pursuing these goals than for war.

Nanda noted India had made progress despite problems and tensions confronting it; Vice President agreed and said U.S. supported effort at Tashkent and that he had told Kosygin of President Johnson's gratification at the outcome of the Tashkent meeting.[3] If we could get the same kind of assistance from Kosygin on the Vietnam issue as he had given at Tashkent, it would be helpful. Certainly the U.S. is ready.

L.K. Jha recalled that Shastri's major impression from talk with Kosygin at Tashkent about Vietnam had been the difference from the hostility and suspicion toward U.S. which he had encountered in May. This time Harriman mission seems to have had a favorable effect, and Kosygin had specifically commented favorably on Harriman having first seen the Poles who had been in touch with Hanoi. Kosygin had also said that the big problem is China.

The conversation with the Prime Minister concluded with his good wishes that the present American efforts for peace would be successful.

Following account of Tashkent meeting emerged from Foreign Secretary's remarks during meeting with Nanda and L.K. Jha's subsequent more detailed account.

Talks began well. Ayub in each of personal meetings he had with Shastri, took position that he wanted to live in peace and earnestly implored Shastri to make it possible. Indicated willingness agree to almost anything but said he could not return to Pakistan without something he could show as a gain. On central issue of Kashmir Ayub seemed to be looking for an opening toward a settlement acceptable in Pakistan. Shastri had told him he could not move from well known position. Thereafter Ayub suggested deferring the Kashmir issue and it did not again come up in their conversations; from this Shastri concluded Ayub was prepared not to let Kashmir issue stand in way of restoring good relations between India and Pakistan.

According to L.K. Jha major problem for Shastri was that he could not agree to withdrawal along Kashmir cease-fire line without adequate assurances that infiltration would not recur; accordingly he pressed for either or both of "no war" pact and clear affirmation of respect for cease-fire line. On all other points there seemed to be no substantial controversy.

---

[3] A record of the meeting that Humphrey and Rusk had on January 13 with Kosygin was prepared by Rusk and transmitted to Washington in telegram Secto 10, January 13. The meeting was largely devoted to Vietnam. (National Archives and Records Administration, RG 59, Central Files 1964–66, POL 7 US/HUMPHREY)

Next phase, which Foreign Secretary described as "low point", started with Indians giving Paks draft of a "no war" treaty of friendship. Ayub countered with a one sentence statement to effect both sides agree to seek peaceful solutions of their differences; at Shastri's suggestion he readily added phrase "without recourse to force."

Then, on January 8, Indians took hand at draft communiqué calling for respect for cease-fire line and no resort to force. Ayub sent High Commissioner Hussain to Jha with message rejecting both Indian treaty draft and communiqué as entirely unacceptable. This looked like complete breakdown.

Until this point Kosygin had confined his activities to exploring the ground privately and separately with Shastri and Ayub but had made no proposal of his own. After Ayub's rejection of both formulations, Kosygin asked Shastri whether he should take a hand and Shastri had encouraged him to try as long as it was clear that the effort was entirely Kosygin's.

Starting at 9:00 in the morning on January 9 and continuing until 12:30 next morning, Kosygin went back and forth, working from his own draft of communiqué, which was close to Indian first draft. Ayub apparently felt he could defend the language that resulted regarding non use of force as a reaffirmation of an obligation already entered into, not as a new obligation. From Indian point of view language was acceptable as reiteration of well known position.

On cease-fire, Paks first tried to confine language to commitment to observe cease-fire along cease-fire line; Shastri said this did not go far enough in covering problem of infiltrators, and result was obligation to observe terms of cease-fire on cease-fire line. Hardest decision of all for Shastri was to accept this as adequate assurance on which to base agreement to withdraw from Haji Pir Pass.

Jha considers that Paks found their anxieties to establish machinery for settling all questions, including Kashmir, met by provision for continuing dialogue. He sensed it was an unspoken assumption on both sides that Kashmir will figure again at a summit meeting after the dust settles. He also believes that when Kosygin sounded Ayub on a Kashmir settlement based on partition along cease-fire line with adjustments, he got a strong negative reaction and dropped the matter. Nevertheless, Shastri continued to feel Paks do not wish resume fighting.

Jha commented that follow through could stumble over several matters, including definitions, e.g. what constitute "internal affairs." Nevertheless, he was hopeful agreement will be regarded by both sides as charting course for the future, even though both will have some domestic problems. He expressed disappointment that only thing Paks would not agree on explicitly was restoration of property seized during the conflict, but would only agree to talk about it. Indians had felt there could not be a break over this issue.

Vice President and Secretary urged that GOI maintain momentum established by agreement at Tashkent.

L.K. Jha in second meeting also gave further account of Shastri talk with Kosygin about Vietnam. This is being reported in septel.

At conclusion, Jha referred to Shastri's planned visit to U.S. and said he doubts very much new Prime Minister will be able to leave India on the planned dates. The budget session of Parliament and the budget itself will necessarily occupy his full attention. He went on to make case that India's economic and particularly foreign exchange difficulties are reaching such a critical stage that further delay in alleviating them could be dangerous. He said he realized that new American commitments to assist in India's fourth 5-year plan may have to wait, but urged that dangers of further factory closings and unemployment, especially from mid-February onward, be averted by lifting freeze on new U.S. commitments already pledged.

The Secretary said he hoped it would be possible to work this out by consulting together and strongly urged that new Prime Minister not himself freeze on position he could not get to Washington. Secretary said he and Vice President would consult President Johnson. He recalled major political problem, indeed crisis, which had arisen in Congress over further aid to the sub-continent and said that the two countries which received roughly one-third of all U.S. aid have a political constituency in U.S. they have to nourish. He noted the new Prime Minister and President Johnson will have to get in touch to work out the answer to the question Jha had raised.

Meeting concluded with Vice President and Secretary again congratulating GOI on encouraging success at Tashkent, which Vice President noted President Johnson had found very constructive.

Rusk

281. Telegram From the Embassy in India to the Department of State[1]

New Delhi, January 14, 1966, 0830Z.

1795. 1. Vice President, Secretary and Ambassador met January 13 with Subramaniam. Vice President and Ambassador joined meeting after it had started due prior engagement with Kamaraj.[2]

2. Others present on Indian side were Asoka Mehta, B.K. Nehru, Bhoothalingham, Dias and Surendra Sing; on American side, Senator Cooper, Reuter, Handley and Weiss.

3. Following is summary principal points.

4. In response Secretary's question, Subramaniam indicated that crop figure still somewhat in question due uncertainty of rains. He hoped to have clearer idea by end of month.

5. Subramaniam stated major new element of uncertainty has entered picture due presumption that as result Shastri's death scheduled Washington talk with President Johnson was now unsure. GOI had been counting on these discussions to clear up outstanding questions and to provide urgently needed decisions on food and other assistance.

6. Secretary cautioned GOI not to make decision on cancellation Washington talks until President and new PM had opportunity to consult.

7. Subramaniam agreed but expressed doubts would be possible proceed with talks as originally scheduled. He noted new PM will have to organize the government and take hard decisions on budget for upcoming budget session of Parliament. This will take time.

8. He stressed that GOI could not afford additional time for decisions on assistance. Its need for immediate commitments of additional food supplies was most urgent. GOI wished to test to the full, as U.S. had urged, its capacity to unload and distribute food supplies and thus was essential avoid any gap in supply line.

9. He also noted that in anticipation additional supplies would be made available, GOI had chartered 300,000 tons shipping in February over and above existing million and a half tons of grains committed by the U.S. He expected 125,000 tons to be provided by Canadians

---

[1] Source: National Archives and Records Administration, RG 59, Central Files 1964–66, POL INDIA–US. Confidential; Priority. Repeated to Athens, Belgrade, Bonn, Buenos Aires, Canberra, Copenhagen, Karachi, London, Moscow, Oslo, Ottawa, Paris, Stockholm, The Hague, Tokyo, Vienna, Wellington, USUN, and Rome.

[2] Kumaraswamy Kamaraj Nadar, Chief Minister of Madras, 1955–1964, elected President of the Congress Party in January 1964.

under their recent commitment, leaving 175,000 tons of shipping yet uncovered by any supply commitments.

10. Subramaniam stressed GOI would need new commitments of PL 480 supplies by beginning February if gap in supply were to be avoided.

11. He and Dias also noted GOI taking risks in running down its stocks on assumption additional supplies would be forthcoming. They emphasized difficulty of planning stock utilization and distribution supplies without some immediate, additional and longer run commitments. They also urged immediate commitments in order take full advantage of most favorable shipping season prior onset of monsoon around next June.

12. Subramaniam also emphasized urgency of additional assistance to provide non-food aid, alluding to unfulfilled 1965 U.S. consortium pledge.

13. Subramaniam noted constructive results achieved at Tashkent in reducing tensions between India and Pakistan and helping bring about rapprochement between them. Alluding to our understandable desire avoid dissipation of U.S. aid in wasteful conflict between the two countries, he believed Tashkent agreement answered one of our major concerns against providing economic aid to India.

14. In view Tashkent and India's pressing needs which could no longer be postponed, Subramaniam strongly urged U.S. proceed promptly even in absence Presidential–PM talks (a) to release substantial additional PL 480 supplies of food and (b) to make available other U.S. aid already "committed" (that is, U.S. 1965 consortium pledge).

15. After extended discussion, reported below, of steps taken by GOI to mobilize assistance from other countries, Secretary noted that Tashkent and tragedy of Shastri's death were two new developments which we would have to take into account. He stated that while he could not make any specific commitments at this time, there was general disposition on part of his government to take current Indian crisis seriously and to be helpful. He indicated that when Vice President and he returned to Washington, they would discuss the matter with President and try reach decision on the two requests put forward by Subramaniam.

16. In response query by Vice President and Secretary, Subramaniam summarized major efforts GOI making to obtain assistance from other countries, he presented memorandum[3] describing in detail these efforts and results to date. (Handley carrying memorandum.) He also reaffirmed his intention to convene shortly meeting of Ambassadors

---

[3] Not found.

in Delhi to highlight Indian situation and solicit aid. (Calling of meeting is subject approval interim Prime Minister.)

17. Vice President and Secretary expressed gratification at efforts GOI making and urged GOI keep pressure up. Vice President stated that best we could do to help may not be enough. For this as well as other reasons everyone should pitch in.

18. Vice President particularly stressed approach to Japan. He stated there had been some helpful indications recently of Japanese interest and willingness to assist other countries in Asia. He felt this was thus propitious time to contact Japanese for aid, especially shipping and fertilizer. Vice President also urged Indians to press West Germany for assistance.

19. Vice President and Secretary also urged FAO be prompted to help. Secretary specifically suggested that Sen, Director-General FAO, be approached.

20. Subramaniam had no objection but noted views expressed by U Thant that FAO not proper forum. He repeated what he had previously told Embassy that U Thant had indicated his intention take advantage of January 18 meeting world food program to urge assistance to meet India's urgent food requirements.

21. Secretary suggested that FAO could at least send note to member governments calling attention to India's food needs. Subramaniam agreed and said he would try to get this done.

22. In regard to questions about Russian participation, Reuter noted he had informed Dias in earlier conversation that U.S. had no objection to GOI's approaching Russians for assistance. Secretary agreed, and noted that if Russians could send food to Cuba, why not to India?

23. Vice President and Secretary inquired about reports of great losses food grains due rodents and other wastage and asked what was being done about this. While acknowledging there some wastage, Subramaniam and Dias stated these stories greatly exaggerated. They described some of steps GOI taking to reduce what losses there were, including construction modern storage facilities and campaign to reduce rodent population. Dias noted GOI now has 2.7 million tons of modern storage capacity and has program underway for construction another 2.5 million tons.

24. Vice President and Secretary were pleased to hear of measures being taken. In order to counter alarmist statements and adverse U.S. publicity, they urged GOI get information to the press on true magnitude problem and steps it was taking.

25. Subramaniam and B.K. Nehru noted GOI had gotten such information out but unfortunately it wasn't as newsworthy as alarmist reports. They agreed make further efforts to make the facts known.

26. Dias noted that in shipments in the last three months some 90 percent of Indian imports of PL 480 wheat was weevil infested. Previously weevil infestation had been around 21–22 percent.

27. Vice President expressed surprise at high rate and indicated U.S. should do something about it.

28. Secretary asked whether there would be any difficulty on part of new Indian Government in continuing present GOI agricultural program and priority to food. Subramaniam replied he anticipated no difficulty. He stressed that program he had announced was Cabinet decision and was made to the Parliament, which would thus expect program to continue. In support of Subramaniam Asoka Mehta noted GOI had already made allocations of funds giving highest priority to agriculture.

29. In response Vice President's inquiry, Subramaniam indicated GOI had requested for current calendar year 10 million tons of wheat and 1 million milo. Of this amount GOI hoped 4 million could be obtained under Title II and 7 million under Title I.

30. Vice President suggested that when new Prime Minister comes into office, he should make new official request of India's needs from U.S. Subramaniam agreed to have this done.[4]

Bowles

---

[4] In telegram 1796 from New Delhi, January 14, Bowles referred to Subramaniam's conversation with Humphrey and Rusk and appealed to Rusk, Humphrey, and President Johnson for a decision within the week on a new P.L. 480 agreement to ensure the continuous flow of grain to India. (National Archives and Records Administration, RG 59, Central Files 1964–66, AID (US) 15–8 INDIA)

---

282. Memorandum From the President's Deputy Special Assistant for National Security Affairs (Komer) to President Johnson[1]

Washington, January 18, 1966, 5:45 p.m.

Here are Freeman's new recommendations on India famine relief.[2] He proposes (1) announcing a new 1.5 million ton allotment in your

---

[1] Source: Johnson Library, National Security File, Country File, India, India's Food Problem, Vol. I. Secret. A handwritten note on the memorandum reads, "Rec'd 5:50 p."
[2] Reference is to a January 18 memorandum from Freeman to the President. (Ibid.)

foreign aid/food message, or alternatively as a gesture of confidence as soon as the new Indian PM is elected; (2) making 1/5th of such allotments *feedgrains*, as a means of pressing India to do more on agriculture; (3) hitting other countries harder to share the burden; and (4) authorizing him to reimburse India out of later allocations for dollars it spends now to keep the pipeline full (this last gives us a lot more maneuverability).

The above seems sensible. I'd favor holding any allotment till your food message, rather than acting now, because it will probably lead the new PM to write you. We ourselves should also prod other countries harder now to contribute, especially since the Delhi government will be temporarily disorganized. This point is worth covering in your food message. But no matter how hard we and the Indians push, I frankly doubt that we can get others to contribute as much as 1/5th of India's needs (as Freeman suggests). Let's exhort like hell, but any such arbitrary formula would only tie our own hands.

RW Komer[3]

Approve Freeman package

Make new allotment now

Discuss with me further[4]

---

[3] Bundy initialed below Komer's signature.

[4] Johnson checked this option. He also sent a note to Komer on January 18 in which he wrote: "Please try to get Freeman to quit giving stuff away." (Johnson Library, National Security File, Country File, India, India's Food Problem, Vol. I)

283. Telegram From the Department of State to the Embassy in India[1]

Washington, January 18, 1966, 8:55 p.m.

CAP 66028. For Ambassador. Deliver following message soonest to new Prime Minister[2] from President Johnson. "Dear Madam Prime Minister: Let me offer my warm congratulations on your appointment and wish you every success as you assume leadership of the world's largest democracy. The relations between our two countries are firmly grounded in our common dedication to the principles of human dignity, human welfare, democratic institutions, and peace. Under your leadership I look forward to a broadening and deepening of this community of interests, and pledge our friendship and cooperation to this end.

You know how much I had been looking forward to seeing Prime Minister Shastri, under whom your government made such great efforts to bring a better life to India's millions. I will be delighted if you can come on February 1, but realize that your new burdens of office may make this difficult. If you cannot come then, I hope that we can reschedule your visit for an early date, so that we can discuss the many momentous problems we both face. Mrs. Johnson and I remember with much pleasure our earlier meetings with you, and look forward to seeing you again soon."[3]

---

[1] Source: National Archives and Records Administration, RG 59, Central Files 1964–66, POL 15–1 INDIA. Limited Official Use; Immediate. Drafted by Komer and Officer in Charge of India, Ceylon and Nepal Affairs Carleton S. Coon, Jr.; cleared by Handley, Public Affairs Adviser Daniel Brown (NEA), and Special Assistant Joseph W. Reap (P); and approved by Hare. A note attached to the telegram indicates that it was erroneously assigned a White House message number in the White House Situation Room, and consequently was not given a Department of State telegram series number. The same note indicates that McGeorge Bundy cleared the message with the President.

[2] Indira Gandhi, Minister of Information in the Shastri government, was elected Prime Minister at a meeting of the members of Parliament of the Congress Party on January 18. The final vote was 355 for Gandhi and 169 for Morarji Desai. Prime Minister Gandhi and the members of her Ministry were sworn in on January 24. The new government included Gulzarilal L. Nanda as Minister of Home Affairs, Sachindra Chaudhuri as Minister of Finance, and Asoka Mehta as Minsiter of Planning. Swaran Singh, Y.B. Chavan, and Chidambara Subramaniam retained their portfolios as Ministers of External Affairs, Defense, and Food and Agriculture, respectively.

[3] Printed from an unsigned copy. Gandhi returned a letter to Johnson on January 24, expressing her appreciation for the message of congratulations. She accepted the invitation to visit the United States but noted that it would be a few weeks before she felt free to go abroad. There were, she noted, decisions pending with regard to problems facing India which required urgent attention, and she asked Johnson to receive Ambassador Nehru to discuss them. (Johnson Library, National Security File, Special Head of State Correspondence File, India, 4/15/65–2/28/66)

284. Telegram From the Embassy Office in Pakistan to the Department of State[1]

Rawalpindi, January 19, 1966, 0615Z.

286. President Ayub on Tashkent.

1. During Jan 18 call on Pres Ayub I told him Pres Johnson and Secretary Rusk had instructed me to convey their great appreciation for Ayub's high statesmanship in reaching Tashkent agreement and undertaking to follow promising but not easy course in relations with India. I further told Ayub I was instructed to say US will follow developments stemming from Tashkent with interest and sympathy and with a disposition to do everything possible to support and help in conciliatory course he is following.

2. Pres Ayub said Prime Minister Shastri had realized necessity of peace for both India and Pakistan, and Ayub thought Shastri had also realized need for some resolution of Kashmir dispute. According Ayub, at Tashkent Shastri initially suggested freezing the Sept 23 cease-fire line but Ayub has opposed this as lacking in principle and had emphasized that this and other aspects Indo–Pak relations must be based on recognized principle. Here Ayub said Russians were helpful in moving Indians along in reasonable direction. Ayub stressed US also can play important role of helping bring India along. This not question of forcing Indian decision, which he agreed with Pres Johnson not feasible. Nonetheless, he said, US has role to play, and its influence on India could promote consolidation of Tashkent spirit. Any event, GOP will keep us informed about Tashkent follow-on negotiations with India. I said hoped new Indian Prime Minister could go promptly to Washington and believed this important to Pakistan as well as India and US. Ayub agreed reiterating importance of US influence on India. If that influence used, US policy objectives will be advanced, according Ayub. Ayub said Kosygin worked night and day at Tashkent and had expressed hope Paks would not feel USSR favoring India. To this Ayub said he replied that he hoped Kosygin would thoroughly understand position of Pakistan as well as India. According Ayub, Russians played big role in Tashkent agreement. For example, he said, right at the end India had pressed for no-war declaration but in this as other matters Kosygin had been able to exert constructive influence. Ayub then remarked "I think US can now play much bigger role." Ayub impression was that Kosygin a big man, reasonable and open to argument.

---

[1] Source: National Archives and Records Administration, RG 59, Central Files 1964–66, POL 32–1 INDIA–PAK. Secret; Priority. Repeated to USUN, New Delhi, London, Karachi, Moscow, Tehran, Ankara, and Kabul.

3. I remarked that statement on non-use of force in Tashkent declaration was in line with UN Charter and predicted that Pak people will surely come to understand reason behind it. Ayub agreed they would understand and observed that, in any event, he couldn't act contrary to Pak national interests. He added, "If they want someone else, I am willing." I probed with observation Ayub apparently being supported on Tashkent by east wing and civil servants, business and bulk of rural populace, but he did not take the bait.

4. I observed it tragic irony that every time Pakistan appears to be making progress with Indian leader he passes on, as in case Gandhi, Nehru and now Shastri. I inquired if there any private understandings with Shastri at Tashkent to which his successor might not be privy. Ayub said had feeling Shastri relieved after signature Tashkent declaration. At following private luncheon Shastri had suggested to him both sides should take visible actions that would have impact on their peoples, e.g., meetings of Indo–Pak military leaders on withdrawal, prompt exchange of high commissioners, perhaps revival of air transit rights. Ayub said they also discussed such problems as shootings along East Pak–Indian border. Ayub said he noted all East Pakistan under one administration while West Bengal under several, and had proposed all border control West Bengal be put under single military commander.

4. [sic] After Shastri's death Ayub said he promptly convened Shastri's advisors and passed on to them what Shastri had indicated to him privately. These advisors included Defense Minister Chavan, Fon Min Swaran Singh, Fon Secretary Jha, High Commissioner to Pakistan Kewal Singh and two or three others. I expressed hope nothing in way of specific understandings had been lost in process, and Ayub said he hoped same.

5. Ayub said Defense Minister Faruque, who attended Shastri funeral, had reported from Delhi that population there seemed relieved to see him, although, Ayub added, one doesn't know how Indian Government feels. I said there appeared be good general reception of Tashkent declaration in India, although no doubt some dissatisfaction bound be present on both sides.

6. During brief exchange on Indian succession, Ayub indicated considerable reservations about leading candidate Indira Gandhi. He seemed to think she an extremist who, being a woman, might embark on adventures. While believing she perhaps better than Morarji Desai, Ayub said he apprehensive lest she be dominated by Krishna Menon.

McConaughy

285. Telegram From the Embassy in India to the Department of State[1]

New Delhi, January 20, 1966, 1345Z.

1865. 1. Although I was invited to visit Mrs. Indira Gandhi at her home early last evening following her election, I thought it wiser to postpone my presentation of the Pres's invitation[2] until this morning when she might have more of an opportunity to talk. I called on her at 11:30 (local) Thursday and talked with her for 35 mins on a wide range of subjects.

A. Mrs. Gandhi expressed her appreciation for my congratulations and for Mrs. Bowles personal call on her last evening and admitted deep personal satisfaction over her election. If she had taken over following her father's death, she said, it would have been properly written off as an emotional carry-over of the Nehru name. Although the present circumstances were tragic she was now accepted by the party in her own right and this meant a great deal to her.

B. Mrs. Gandhi spoke in a friendly manner of Morarji Desai; while deploring his rigidity she said he had great courage and she particularly appreciated his generous remarks following her election. (*Note:* There are many rumors and counter-rumors here regarding Desai becoming a member of Cabinet in either Home or Finance Ministries. Many people in and around the govt favor this move because of his demonstrated ability to carry one-third of the parliamentary group along with him while others argue that he is too disruptive a personality or that he would not accept if asked.)

C. Mrs. Gandhi was much pleased with the Pres's letter and invitation; also with the letter from the Vice Pres.[3] In view of all the fence mending and political decisions that lay ahead she did not see how she could get away during the first week in Feb before the budget session of Parliament started. She was hopeful however that after the budget message is delivered (Feb 28) there might be a lull which would permit her to accept the Pres's invitation at that time. She stressed her desire to visit US as soon as it was humanly possible.

D. Mrs. Gandhi expressed concern over stories which she said had appeared in the US press stating that she leaned towards the USSR

---

[1] Source: National Archives and Records Administration, RG 59, Central Files 1964–66, POL 15–1 INDIA. Secret; Immediate. Repeated to London, Karachi, Moscow, and USUN and passed to the White House at 1:45 p.m. McGeorge Bundy passed a copy of the telegram to the President on January 20. (Johnson Library, National Security File, Memos to the President, McGeorge Bundy, Vol. 19, 1/3–2/23/66)

[2] See Document 283.

[3] Not found.

and was a close friend of Krishna Menon. She asked for my personal cooperation in clearing up what she described as a gross misunderstanding.

E. Mrs. Gandhi stated that she had deep respect and affection for the US and was a great personal admirer of Pres Johnson. She understood the importance of US assistance, and was profoundly grateful for what we had done. While India was also helped by the USSR she was under no illusions about the totalitarian nature of Soviet society nor was she unaware of Soviet long-term objectives in regard to India.

F. In regard to Krishna Menon the stories of his alleged political connection with her were simply not true. Indeed he had done more to harm her during the past difficult week than any other single individual. He had worked relentlessly for Nanda and had done so in a manner designed to discredit her personally. While Krishna Menon still had followers among the younger people because of his speaking ability and personal charm, he would have no part in her administration; she had come to look on him as an adversary and not as a friend.

2. In response, I urged her to relax in regard to her relationship with the US. She had many good friends and admirers there and Pres and Mrs. Johnson were eagerly looking forward to her visit. Most thoughtful Americans understood India's desire to build a bridge between the US and USSR and were hopeful that the new govt under her direction would be increasingly successful along these lines.

3. I added that there was however some feeling in America that GOI neutrality in recent years had been bent towards the Soviet Union and I was hopeful that this impression could be corrected during coming months. As I saw it the formula for good relations with us involved three basic points:

A. Continue fully to support the Tashkent settlement and do everything in India's power to implement not only withdrawal portion but also proposals for dealing with outstanding disputes.

B. Maintain a genuine and positive neutrality in regard to US and USSR assisting us wherever possible in our efforts to move the Soviet Union towards a more constructive world position which would enable us to go forward on such questions as disarmament, stabilization of trouble areas, etc.

C. Key India's requests for US aid to pragmatic economic policies which take into account the recent successful experience of such countries as Japan, Italy, Mexico, etc. giving high priority to agriculture, education, and population planning and assigning a major developmental role to the private sector.

4. Mrs. Gandhi expressed her appreciation of my personal assurances and stated she could not take exception to any of my comments

in regard to Indian policy in the context of the India–US relationship. If this was in fact the essential formula for a good working relationship between India and the US it would be an easy matter for her to follow it.

5. In an obvious further effort to reassure us in regard to her general economic and political posture, Mrs. Gandhi spoke in the highest terms of Subramaniam whom she described as ablest man in the Cabinet and also went out of her way to praise Asoka Mehta and Chavan for whom she knows we have a high regard.

6. She also expressed her appreciation of Pres Johnson's effort to find a basis for peace in Viet Nam and stated that her govt would do everything in its power to assist us to that end.

7. Mrs. Gandhi added that in economic matters she thought her new govt would be significantly more action-minded than the previous one. Although she had the greatest admiration for Mr. Shastri, she would insist on more young people in the govt and would press hard on such programs as family planning.

8. *Comment:* Throughout this informal and relaxed exchange Mrs. Gandhi was calm, articulate and assured. Indeed I sensed a significant change in her personality which was reflected in a new appearance of personal security and a willingness to comment freely on controversial matters.

9. We still have no hard info in regard to the new Cabinet except for the assurance that Subramaniam will probably stick with Agriculture but that if he should move to Finance someone in whom he personally has total confidence will take his place.

Bowles

286. Memorandum From Secretary of State Rusk to President Johnson[1]

Washington, January 28, 1966.

SUBJECT

The Next Step on Food Aid for India

I strongly support Orville Freeman's recommendation to you for a new allocation of 1.5 million tons of PL 480 foodgrain for India. My recent visit in New Delhi and what I have learned since my return convince me that we should make the new allocation of grain as soon as possible.

There is no lessening of the Indian need. On the contrary, Minister of Food and Agriculture Subramaniam states that the crisis is now developing rapidly and that there is considerable suffering in some areas.[2]

Mrs. Gandhi, in her new role as Prime Minister, has already emphasized how important the food issue looms among her Government's problems. The new Government needs the nation's confidence in its ability to avert widespread famine.

Meanwhile, the Indians have been moving ahead on the self-help requirements we have had in mind for both the long run and short run:

—In reappointing Subramaniam as Food and Agriculture Minister, Mrs. Gandhi has assured him of her firm support for what he is trying to do to place Indian agriculture on a more solid basis for the years ahead. She has specifically expressed her support for the detailed understanding which he and Orville Freeman have worked out. The Indians have already taken first steps on this front by liberalizing the terms under which new private foreign investment in fertilizer can operate, and by increasing their own allotment for fertilizer imports for this year.

---

[1] Source: Johnson Library, National Security File, Memos to the President, McGeorge Bundy, Vol. 19, Jan. 19–Feb. 4, 1966. Confidential. McGeorge Bundy sent the memorandum to the President on February 1 under cover of a note in which he wrote that he was sending Rusk's memorandum without comment "because I know you will not need any further advice on the opinions of our local Indians." (Ibid., Country File, India, India's Food Problem, Vol. I)

[2] On January 23 Bowles reported on a conversation with Subramaniam in which Subramaniam stated that acute shortages were developing in Rajasthan and Madhya Pradesh, and that in Kerala the Communists were taking advantage of the shortages to attack the government and Subramaniam personally. (Telegram 1883 from New Delhi; National Archives and Records Administration, RG 59, Central Files 1964–66, SOC 10 INDIA)

—The Indians are also doing what we asked them to do to help themselves to meet the immediate crisis. They have stepped up sharply the rate of shipment of the 1.5 million tons of grain which you authorized on December 9. The last shipment under that allocation should leave the United States within a month. At the same time, the Indians have responded to our urging that they recognize the true dimensions of their problem and plan ahead to meet it. They have booked an additional 200,000 tons of ocean freight for use in February and are planning to go into the market within the very near future to begin booking 900,000 tons of shipping for the month of March. This is being done on faith in our intentions to make additional food available in time. A further allocation of grain is needed very shortly so that the Indians will be able to use the additional shipping and keep up the maximum rate of movement in the period while the weather remains favorable.

—The Indians have also moved with unusual vigor to enlist international support in their current crisis. Canada, the United Kindom, Sweden, Austria, Greece and The Netherlands have already promised aid, and various other countries are now considering how to help. More countries need to come on board, but the returns to date (see attachment)[3] indicate the chances are good for a reasonably broad international program of emergency food aid.

There thus seem to be urgent economic and political reasons why we should move ahead promptly with another 1.5 million tons of grain. This would be a limited and interim action, keeping our aid on a fairly short rein and leaving us with ample options on how to react to the Indian crisis as time goes on.

Dean Rusk

---

[3] A 3-page attachment, undated, entitled "International Responses to Indian Appeal," is not printed.

287. Memorandum From the President's Deputy Special Assistant for National Security Affairs (Komer) to President Johnson[1]

Washington, February 1, 1966, 5:30 p.m.

Pak/Indian Interim Steps. Here is the list you requested today of the interim steps I'd suggest taking now with both countries. I'll also work up the best formula on food sharing that I can.

These proposals may be more forthcoming than your own thinking as of this moment, but I feel that the momentum we've achieved in moving Paks and Indians our way (Tashkent, troop withdrawal, new Indian agriculture program) is so promising that we ought to show just enough responsiveness to keep the process going.

A. *Steps to help Ayub.* We ought to do enough for Ayub to avoid undermining his position that his visit here was successful, especially when his Tashkent reconciliation policy is under fire. So I'd favor the following steps parallel to whatever we do for India:

1. *An interim PL 480 agreement.* Pakistan is much better off than India, but is pressing for food too as it sees India getting so much. We could move pronto with an $18 million extension of the old agreement, or make a new 3 month deal for $26 million (300,000 tons wheat and 25,000 tons of oils).

2. *$50 million program loan* for fertilizer and raw materials to speed up Pak economy would be a major gesture and good economics too. We'd tie stiff *economic* conditions (same as for India below).

3. *Ease up on military sales.* Ayub himself just raised this issue. The Pak military are hurting and disgruntled; we want to ease their pressure on Ayub and guard against the Paks buying a lot from the Chicoms. It's hard to justify restoring MAP yet (this would also be ticklish with Congress). But we could lift our ban on *non-lethal* military commercial sales, plus telling Ayub we'll entertain requests for *MAP credit sales* once the 25 February troop withdrawal takes place (the Paks want to buy two civilian C–130s, have about $3 million in orders for commo equipment stacked up, and need a lot of spare parts).

4. *Hornig Medical Mission* you promised Ayub will leave soon, and be a good gesture hopefully costing mostly surplus rupees.

This package should hold Ayub for at least two months (till after a Gandhi visit), but still leave at least $30 million in FY '66 aid, $85 million from EXIM for the Karachi steel mill, and more PL 480 to be

---

[1] Source: Johnson Library, National Security File, Memos to the President, McGeorge Bundy, Vol. 19, Jan. 19–Feb. 4, 1966. Secret.

doled out later. I'd dress it up via a letter to Ayub. Later you could send out Arthur Dean to discuss terms and conditions prior to further help.

B. *Package for India.* The following is carefully graduated to give Mrs. Gandhi a clear sense now that we want to help, but again save the bulk of our AID money and PL 480 for later bargaining. So when BK Nehru comes in tomorrow with an urgent plea for famine relief and emergency economic aid to keep India's faltering economy going, you could respond with:

1. *Another interim PL 480 Allocation.* Mrs. Gandhi will doubtless have told BK to plead for a pledge covering the whole emergency period.[2] Our problem is to be responsive enough so that no one can say we're being niggardly, but not let India off the hook. So I'd tell him you'll allocate 1.5 to 2 million tons to keep the pipeline full, and may seek a Joint Resolution endorsing a major US anti-famine effort if others will join in appropriately. But you could emphasize that any *further major US contributions will depend on what others do.* We can't carry the whole load. So India better get humping.

2. *$100 million Program Loan.* India's industry is running down badly owing to lack of raw materials. So a loan now would reap dividends, while still reserving the bulk of our aid ($85 million from FY '65 and earlier, at least $70 million from FY '66 and massive PL 480) for later parleying with Indira. As a means of bringing home what we expect, we'd tie on stiff conditions: (a) India must match our $100 million; (b) the money must be used for revving up existing capacity, not to start new projects; (c) reassurance that India won't siphon off too much for defense; and (d) reopening of India's dialogue with the World Bank, which is our ally in getting better Indian performance.

3. *Ease up on military commercial and MAP credit sales.* This will help Pakistan more than India, but ought to be symmetrical.

4. [5 lines of source text not declassified]

5. Last, I'd *authorize Freeman to tell the Indians that we'd reimburse them* out of any future PL 480 if they go ahead now and buy wheat with their own foreign exchange. This involves no commitment or added cost, since we're going to give them some future PL 480, but has the great virtue of getting them off their duffs instead of sitting

---

[2] The magnitude of the emergency was underscored by the report of the food grain survey team that was submitted by C. R. Eskildsen to Freeman on January 31. (National Archives and Records Administration, RG 59, Central Files 1964–66, AID (US) 15 INDIA) Freeman summarized the report in a memorandum to President Johnson on February 1 and noted that India's request for 11 million tons of food grains to meet the emergency was accepted by the team as a "bare bones minimum." (Johnson Library, National Security File, Country File, India, India's Food Problem, Vol. I)

around waiting for a handout. This isn't a gimmick to get more food for India—in fact it lets us play a tougher game.

The above steps are in accord with current State,[3] DOD, and AID thinking. We've had remarkable success to date in Pak/Indian policy and made both countries sing our tune. I'm convinced, as your guy who watches South Asia closely, that the time has come to ease up enough to keep Paks and Indians moving the right way, while retaining plenty of chips to play yet another hand when Indira comes. And we'd tie everything to performance.[4]

R. W. Komer

---

[3] Department of State proposals for policy initiatives relating to India and Pakistan were outlined in two February 1 memoranda sent to the White House entitled "Scenario for Pakistan: Next Steps in Our Relations" and "Scenario for India: Next Steps in Our Relations." The tenor of the proposals in the memoranda accords with Komer's recommendations. (Ibid., Country File, Pakistan, Vol. VI, Memos, 1/66–9/66 and Country File, India, Vol. VII, Cables, 1/66–8/66, respectively)

[4] McGeorge Bundy added a handwritten note under Komer's signature that reads: "This is quite a package, but I am strongly for it—sooner or later we'll have to show a carrot to match our stick, and compared to the size of our whole strategy and our *planned* commitments, these are small decisions." Johnson responded with a handwritten marginal note that reads: "I don't agree—Don't make any promises to anyone until we can talk further."

---

288.   Editorial Note

President Johnson had a long telephone conversation with Secretary of Agriculture Freeman on February 2, 1966, in anticipation of Johnson's meeting later that day with Indian Ambassador Nehru. In the course of that conversation, Johnson touched on the problems he found in managing the direction of policy toward India, as well as the course he wanted that policy to take.

"I'm getting awfully skittish on the India thing because I get any contact—a burnt child dreads the fire—and any contact I have on it I'm misunderstood. I'm by implication committed to underwrite the famine, by implication committed to give them 10 million tons, by implication committed to do it all between now and the first of May. Then I get 14 memos from everybody in the government. It starts with Bowles, and then it goes to State, and then it goes to every Indian lover in town, and then it goes to all the do-good columnists, and then to Agriculture, and then Bob Komer, and then Bundy, and so on and so forth. Now I don't want to do it that way. And that makes me just immediately, just to save myself, feel like they're getting ready to rob my bank. I have to put up the bars and close the doors, and wait til it dies down, or until I can get it started. Now what I want to tell Nehru today is very simple. I'm not going to make any big commitments, I'm not going underwrite anything. I'm going to say to him today just what I said a long time ago. I'm waiting to see what kind of a foreign policy we can have with your people. It's not going to be a one-way deal. I'm not going to just underwrite the perpetuation of the government of India and the people of India to have them spend all their goddamn time dedicating themselves to the destruction of the people of the United States and the government of the United States."

Johnson sketched the kind of discussion he intended to have with Ambassador Nehru.

"Now we're going to sit down and have a good free discussion. I'm ready to do it for Shastri. I'm pretty sensitive about your trying to bludgeon me on account of the visit. You were wrong on that and I don't like it. And you didn't help yourself a damn bit with it. And if you want to go to Russia, there's nothing I'd welcome more. I'd just give you a certified check and publicly applaud it. Just like I did the Tashkent agreement. I'm not in the slightest concerned about your getting help from Russia. Get every damn dime of it you can. This business of 'the Communists might help you a little therefore I've got to give you everything I've got' doesn't appeal to me. Now maybe I'm wrong. But if I am I'm going to be wrong for three more years, and that's that."

Johnson went on outlining the hypothetical conversation.

"I do think you got a problem. I do think you need help. I do want to help. But it's not going to be a unilateral thing when I do it. When I do it I'm going to say to Congress that I think they have a food situation here, and I think these people need help."

But Johnson resisted the notion of massive assistance to India without any tangible return on the investment.

"All we're going to do, as far as I'm concerned, we're not going to make all these economic grants that we've been making, we're not going to make these loans. We're just going to sit here until they find it to their interest to come and discuss and negotiate, to outline what it is they want us to do. And if all they got to propose to me is a way for me to deliver some money to them, then I'm not going to be interested in it. I'm interested in their helping us too. How can they help us? What can they do to help us?"

The theme runs throughout the conversation.

"But I want to see how this balances out on the scale. When I put my wheat down here, and it costs me a few hundred million, I want to see what you're putting on the other side. And if it's just a bunch of bullshit and a lot of criticism of the President that's a different thing." Johnson was particularly sensitive to Indian criticism of his policies in Vietnam.

"I would think they could help us if they could understand our objectives in the world and our viewpoint, and try to be a little more sympathetic in recognizing them. I don't say just rubber-stamp anything we do, but I don't think they need to denounce us every day on what we're doing in Vietnam."

Johnson nonetheless was willing to address the food crisis in India.

"I'd like to have a message written to the Congress and a bill introduced and passed, which will be known as the Indian food bill, Indian relief bill, for the relief of the Indian nation, or something of that kind."

But Johnson was not prepared to go forward with a food bill for India until after he had met with Prime Minister Gandhi.

"I asked her to come. I thought she'd come in the last part of January. There's some indication she's coming in the early part of February. I'd like to add it today. But I don't want to set it up until I get some kind of agreement out of them. What are they going to do for the United States?" (Johnson Library, Recordings and Transcripts, Recording of Telephone Conversation Between President Johnson and Secretary of Agriculture Freeman, February 2, 1966, 10:01 a.m., Tape F66.03, Side B, PNO 1)

---

289. Memorandum for Record[1]

Washington, February 2, 1966.

SUBJECT

President's Meeting with Indian Ambassador Nehru

The President greeted Ambassador Nehru warmly, saying that he thought the new cabinet was off to a good start. He well understood India's succession problem, having gone through the same tragic situa-

---

[1] Source: Johnson Library, National Security File, Country File, India, Vol. VII, Cables, 1/66–8/66. Secret. The meeting took place at the White House on February 2 but the memorandum is dated February 3.

tion himself. Nehru replied that Mrs. Gandhi was touched by the President's message[2] and sent warm greetings to him. The President commented jocularly that with a woman Prime Minister in India, the pressure was now on us. We would have to do something more for our women. Nehru riposted that the women of India were "impossible" now.

Commenting that talks were long overdue, the President was anxious to see Mrs. Gandhi as soon as possible. He was troubled because he had an incipient revolt on his hands in Congress. He did not want to go to Congress on future aid to India till he had talked things over further with Mrs. Gandhi. In the meantime he had asked our best people to get up a program; then he would ask the Congress to join in it. The President wanted to go this route because he was getting tired of the charges that he was running everything, even though he kept asking for Congress' views (as on Vietnam).

The President then discussed multilateralizing our aid, including food. He didn't wholly agree with Senator Fulbright on doing everything via multilateral rather than bilateral means. The best argument against multilateralism, as the AID people kept claiming, was that we didn't get credit for the aid we gave. Yet given the UN's success in dealing with the Pak/Indian cease fire, he wondered if it might not be best to use the multilateral route in meeting Indian food needs. We might make a substantial contribution to the World Food Program or the UN itself and ask every other country to come in appropriately. We put in 50% of the World Food Program now. We could even say that we would increase this proportion if others would do the same, not necessarily in wheat alone but in its equivalent. The Ambassador commented that the US was the only country which had food to spare, and it didn't cost the US anything to send it abroad. The President bridled at this, retorting that we *did* have to pay for every nickel's worth of wheat or other commodities. He had just seen figures from the Budget Bureau indicating that we had to pay $60–80 per ton for wheat.

The President wanted to sit down with the new Prime Minister and discuss what he could do for India as well as vice versa. Then he would tell the Congress what he wanted to do in bushels and dollars. This had not been budgeted yet. He noted that he was being severely criticized right this minute for feeding Vietnam refugees, while cutting out $600 million in military construction here. We could get results from the Congress if we consulted it. Congressman kept claiming that they were not consulted enough. Senator Fulbright kept saying that

---

[2] See Document 283.

when the President acted without the Congress he was being ostentatious and dictatorial.

The President then raised the question of promises vs. performance. He described how in 1961 we had committed $300 million to Brazil for social projects. The Brazilians were to do several things in return. They passed a number of resolutions, but didn't perform on a single one. Then he, President Johnson, had doubled aid to $550–600 million, but Senator Morse claimed that we were less liked in Latin America now than ever. The President suspected that a good deal of this problem was our "image", created by Vietnam and the Dominican Republic. So we had to figure out—the quicker the better—what to do for India and then put it up to the Congress. He was trying to get a five-year authorization for aid, but doubted that he would get it in an election year.

The President told Nehru to evolve—with Komer and others—a sensible program. Then we would send our people—including Secretaries Rusk, Freeman and Gardner—up to testify. The first program we would undertake under the new AID/Food Message was the Indian emergency. At the moment the President thought we should act through the UN, perhaps after an interim allocation to keep things going. Senator Fulbright was right that we got no credit for what we did bilaterally.

Ambassador Nehru interjected that handling food this way was difficult. But economic aid had to be given with conditions, which were more acceptable if exacted through multilateral agencies. Mrs. Gandhi had asked him to say that she would like to come in the second half of March. The Indian Parliament would still be in session then, but she thought she could get away. The President asked the Ambassador to tell her that there was no one in the world who understood her problem in taking over better or with more sympathy. Mrs. Johnson and he would see her on no notice at all, at any time she could come. It was essential that they meet as early as possible so he could get ahead with what he wanted to do. Nehru should tell Mrs. Gandhi just to wire when she was coming.

The Ambassador mentioned that Mrs. Gandhi had asked him to tell the President how much she appreciated the peace moves on Vietnam. She was greatly disappointed at the lack of response. Nehru commented on India's contribution through talking with Kosygin at Tashkent. He added, "I don't know if you know yet, but we also made some approaches through our Consul General in Hanoi." However, the North Vietnamese were not responsible [responsive?]. We also sent our ICC Chairman to Hanoi. He reported that there were two parties in the NVN Government. The moderates were gaining ground but were still in the minority. Nehru repeated that Mrs. Gandhi was "very distressed" at the lack of response to these approaches.

The President then explained at length our decisions on the pause and the many efforts we had made to establish contact and generate a response. He explained how the Soviets and others had said something would come of a pause if we stopped ten days or so, but it didn't work. He "appreciated very much" what Shastri said at Tashkent with Kosygin. However, the net of the whole exercise was that the President was worse off than a month ago. His basic problem was not with the peace lovers but with those who argued for a yet tougher line.

The President indicated that he was "terribly proud" of what India did at Tashkent in moving toward reconciliation with the Paks. "Shastri died the right way in the cause of peace, not at the end of a gun barrel." Ambassador Nehru replied that Mrs. Gandhi had asked him to tell the President that "India was going all-out to make Tashkent work." The Indians hoped to withdraw well before 25 February. They were also proposing resumption of ministerial meetings and of transit overflights. Meanwhile, anti-Pak propaganda had been stopped.

The President discussed Ayub's problems, remarked that one of these was that he had ended up almost an "advocate of India". But Ayub had many difficulties with his own people. When he came to the US he was a chastened man, but also a proud one. He didn't rebel or even argue, when the President told him he had to settle with India. Nehru remarked that what the President had done with Ayub had had considerable effect on Tashkent. The President hoped that Ayub wouldn't lose his job as a result; Bhutto and others seemed to be a serious threat. Nehru said that the Indians realized they had to help Ayub, but India had a few problems of its own at home with hard-liners.

The Ambassador then made "two specific emergency requests." The first was food. The US had given India 1.5 million tons in December, and the last would be shipped this week. Could the US give a firm public commitment on more, to cover at least till the end of June? If the US were unable to make a public commitment, it would promote hoarding and riots—as in Kerala. Of course, the Kerala crisis was partly food and partly politics. He explained that if the Indian people lacked confidence that sufficient wheat was coming, they would not give up their own stocks of rice and wheat for distribution. If India could have 5 million tons of wheat now, "it would take us up through June." Second, the Ambassador claimed that there had been a freeze on all US aid, including what was pledged last year—about $500 million was outstanding. The Indian economy was running out of raw material. Factories were operating way below capacity and unemployment was up. Since it took eight months between the signing of a loan agreement and the actual arrival of the goods involved, India's economic problems were bleak unless aid was started up again. These two problems were so urgent that the Prime Minister had asked Nehru to take them up right away. India also intended to talk with the World Bank shortly about its broader economic problems.

The President replied that he understood the urgency of these matters. His problem was whether he could borrow on his own prestige by going ahead without the Congress on these matters. He didn't know how soon this bank would run out. So his judgment was that he should make no commitments till there was an understanding between our two countries, and till he got the approval of the American people via the Congress. Otherwise, he was just asking for more problems. So on food in particular, he desired to send a message and legislation to the Congress on what we could do and what we thought others should do. To act in any other way would jeopardize the future relations between our two countries—and the President's own relations with the Congress.

Nehru asked how India's short term emergency needs could be met in the meantime. The President replied that he might take some action before the Congress moved, but could only afford the utter minimum. He did not want to make new agreements until he could both touch his Congressional base and talk with Mrs. Gandhi. Nehru pointed out that if Shastri hadn't died, he would have been in Washington this very day. Circumstance had prevented a US/Indian meeting of minds. The President reminded him that we had planned on the 1.5 million tons carrying us till Shastri came, and pointed out that it had lasted till this time. However, he thought that we might be able to make another interim allotment to carry us past the time when the Prime Minister came, because he didn't want her to be under pressure to come here. He would get the appropriate Congressional leaders together before the week was out, and then announce an interim allotment.[3] The President thought that the American people would come through, but the Indian people had to understand that we Americans had our problems too. If the President sent a message to Congress[4] and there was full public discussion Indians must realize that they

---

[3] On February 4 the White House announced authorization for an extension of the P.L. 480 agreement with India to provide an additional 2 million tons of wheat and 1 million tons of sorghum. (Johnson Library, National Security File, Country File, India, India's Food Problem, Vol. I) An amendment to that effect to the existing P.L. 480 agreement was signed on February 5 in New Delhi. (Telegram 2009 from New Delhi, February 5; National Archives and Records Administration, RG 59, Central Files 1964–66, AID (US) 15–4 INDIA)

[4] On February 10 President Johnson sent a message to Congress "On Food for Freedom." The message addressed the problem of hunger worldwide and the things the United States could do to help meet the problem and to help the hungry nations of the world become self-sufficient. For text, see Department of State *Bulletin*, February 28, 1966, pp. 336–341.

were going to be criticized during this discussion. Nehru thought that Indians would understand.

The President then re-emphasized that the Prime Minister should come—the sooner the better. The two of them could work out an understanding. The President would get a food message up to Congress right after, and we would get it through in thirty days.

Nehru again made a plea for economic aid; "defreezing" economic assistance was as important as food. The President said he would talk with Nehru again on this. He had made up his mind that there would be no new aid till we had agreed on a new course with both India and Pakistan. He thought he had such an agreement with Ayub, but had been holding up any new initiatives with Pakistan till the Indians could visit. Indeed, he believed that his talk with Ayub had more to do with the success of Tashkent than almost anything else. Ayub knew from his talks here that war with India or ties with China were "inimical to US interests". Ayub had said that he would not do anything inimical to the interests of the US.

The President then said that he would deal with the Kerala problem (another interim food allotment) without Mrs. Gandhi asking him. He was going to treat Mrs. Gandhi as he would want her to treat him. He knew her problem better than she might think he knew it, since he had gone through a similar succession crisis. The President then walked Ambassador Nehru out through the Lobby.

R. W. Komer

---

290.   Memorandum From the President's Deputy Special Assistant for National Security Affairs (Komer) to President Johnson[1]

Washington, February 4, 1966, 3 p.m.

Pakistan too. If we announce another India PL 480 allotment, State and AID urge that we at least make a private gesture toward Pakistan too. Pak needs are far less than those of India, but Ayub is under fire

---

[1] Source: Johnson Library, National Security File, Memos to the President, McGeorge Bundy, Vol. 19, Jan. 19–Feb. 4, 1966. Confidential. A handwritten note on the memorandum reads, "Rec'd 4:30 p."

and has to show that we aren't neglecting Pakistan after he came here.[2] The minimum sensible (which would require no publicity) would be to tell the Paks we will shortly begin talks for a new interim PL 480 deal to cover their needs through spring (perhaps 200,000 tons of grain and 25,000 tons of oil). We could also invite the Pak Agriculture Minister (a friend) to come here next month, to match the Subramaniam visit. This step commits us to little, while covering our Pak flank. We could spin out negotiations and terms as much as needed. Here is yet another "gimme", but I can't avoid making these pleas. I'm unfortunately the staffer responsible to you for half the beggars in the world.

Approve[3]

Hold up

R.W. Komer

---

[2] In a February 5 telephone conversation with Vice President Humphrey, President Johnson noted that Ayub had run a political risk in taking the stand he did at Tashkent. Johnson felt that Ayub had reached an accommodation with India in good part in order to maintain his credibility with the United States. Johnson consequently felt that the United States should do what it could to help Ayub weather the political storm. (Johnson Library, Recordings and Transcripts, Recording of Telephone Conversation Between President Johnson and Vice President Humphrey, February 5, 1966, 10:15 a.m., Tape F66.04, Side B, PNO 1 40)

[3] President Johnson checked this option.

---

291. Letter From Prime Minister Gandhi to President Johnson[1]

New Delhi, February 8, 1966.

Dear Mr. President,

Ambassador B.K. Nehru has reported to me the talk he had with you on the 2nd February. I am grateful to you for receiving him immediately after his return to Washington and for the patient and sympathetic hearing you gave him. Even more, I thank you for your immediate

---

[1] Source: Johnson Library, National Security File, Special Head of State Correspondence File, India, 4/15/65–2/28/66. No classification marking. Another copy of this letter is attached to a covering transmittal note from Ambassador Nehru indicating that the letter was transmitted to the White House on February 9. (National Archives and Records Administration, RG 59, Presidential Correspondence: Lot 67 D 262, President—India 1966)

response in making available another three million tons of foodgrains under your P.L.–480 Programme. This sets at rest our immediate anxieties on the food front. We are intensifying our efforts to make other countries join more meaningfully in the international effort which you have initiated to help us.

There is one matter which is still causing me concern. It is so urgent that I feel I must write about it straightaway as it cannot wait until I am in a position to visit you in Washington which would be some time in the later half of March.

Following the unfortunate conflict with Pakistan, there had been a pause in the flow of U.S. aid to India. You have been good enough to release some of this aid recently to help us to meet our fertilizer needs. The cause of our present deep anxiety is that the suspension of non-project aid has left most of our industries desperately short of essential raw materials, components and spare parts for which they have been relying on U.S. sources of supply. Production and employment in many units have already been affected. In another few weeks, we apprehend large-scale unemployment and closure of factories all over the country. I do hope, Mr. President, that this matter will receive your attention in the immediate future as to keep it pending till I am able to come to Washington would only prolong the period for which men and machinery will be kept idle.[2]

With warm regards,

Yours sincerely,

Indira Gandhi

---

[2] In a February 9 memorandum to the President, transmitting the letter from Prime Minister Gandhi, Komer wrote with regard to her request for economic assistance: "The $100 million program loan should prove a more than adequate answer when the Vice President reaches Delhi." (Johnson Library, National Security File, Memos to the President, McGeorge Bundy, Vol. 20, 1/3/66–2/23/66)

292.   Letter From President Johnson to President Ayub[1]

Washington, February 10, 1966.

Dear Mr. President:

Thank your for your letter of January 22,[2] which was delivered to me on February 4 shortly before I left for Honolulu. I have greatly admired what you and Prime Minister Shastri did at Tashkent in the cause of peace. It was a remarkable demonstration for all the world to see of how good will and good sense can overcome the dictates of fear and the passion of war.

Neither side lost at Tashkent. Both Pakistan and India have surely gained in the hard work of securing peace on the subcontinent. I well realize that there are those in Pakistan who think Tashkent did not go far enough. But I share your hope that Tashkent will enable both India and Pakistan to turn a new leaf so that there can now be real progress toward removing the differences that have for so long troubled relations between two great friends of the United States.

What has happened since Tashkent leads me to see real basis for this hope. I have been deeply impressed with the way you are seeking to convince your people of this. I am also greatly encouraged by what Mrs. Gandhi has said both publicly and privately about her determination to see that the Tashkent Declaration is carried out.

What you and India can do to keep the spirit of Tashkent alive will greatly affect what we as friends of both countries can do to help. You know how much we cherish the goal of a real peace in South Asia. We will not shirk doing what we can to help bring that about.

As a result of our own discussions and the auspicious developments at Tashkent, I have asked Vice President Humphrey to take up with you certain reciprocal steps which we feel able to take at this juncture.[3] I am delighted that he will have the opportunity to visit with you, primarily on events in Southeast Asia. I was greatly heartened by our talks in Honolulu with the leaders of South Viet Nam, and he will want to tell you about what was accomplished there and what more

---

[1] Source: Johnson Library, National Security File, Head of State Correspondence File, Pakistan, Vol. 2, Pres. Ayub Correspondence, 1/1/66–12/25/67. Confidential.

[2] Ayub wrote to Johnson on January 22 to make the point that the popular reaction to the Tashkent agreement in Pakistan bore out Ayub's contention that the Kashmir issue lay at the heart of the troubled relations between Pakistan and India. Ayub reiterated his opinion that early steps to settle the Kashmir dispute were essential to the establishment of good relations between the two countries. (Ibid.)

[3] Vice President Humphrey was scheduled to arrive in Karachi on February 15, following stops in Saigon and Bangkok. Humphrey visited Pakistan February 15–16; he visited India February 16–17.

can be done to find a way to bring peace to the people of Viet Nam. In this our determination is undiminished, despite the hostile response from Hanoi.

Mrs. Johnson and I send our warm personal regards.

Sincerely,

Lyndon B. Johnson

---

293.   **Telegram From the Department of State to the Embassy in Vietnam**[1]

Washington, February 10, 1966, 10:07 p.m.

2342. For the Vice President. Subject: Interim Aid for India and Pakistan.

1. President has authorized negotiations for economic commodity loans of $100 million for India and $50 million for Pakistan subject to agreement on economic policy conditions. President would like Vice President initiate discussion these matters Karachi and Delhi including application necessary economic conditions. Memorandum[2] which President approved in substance given to Mr. Bundy for VP. New Delhi Aidto 1109 and Karachi Aidto 1306[3] provided additional details re contemplated conditions which in summary call for:

    a. priority to development and its corollary avoidance of diversion of resources to arms race

    b. emphasis on using aid and at least matching amount own resources for imports for full utilization of existing capacity, as opposed to use for building new capacity or increasing reserves, and

    c. In case India, resumption discussions with IBRD on economic policy changes.

---

[1] Source: National Archives and Records Administration, RG 59, Central Files 1964–66, AID (US) INDIA. Confidential; Exdis/VP. Drafted by Director of the Office of South Asian Affairs in AID C. Herbert Rees; cleared by Macomber, AID Administrator David Bell, Stoddard (DOD/ISA), Komer, and Handley; and approved and initialed by Rusk. A handwritten marginal notation, in an unknown hand, reads: "OK/L" indicating that the telegram was also cleared by the President. Also sent to New Delhi, Karachi, and Rawalpindi.

[2] Not found.

[3] Neither found.

2. President also authorized greater flexibility to permit some commercial sales and MAP credit sales of non-lethal military equipment, subject to continued satisfactory moves toward peace (e.g. actual troop withdrawal). VP asked advise governments of this new policy, indicating it to be administered on selective limited case by case basis with decisions clearly related to events on subcontinent.

3. We here concerned that public announcement loans at time VP in South Asia might appear as bribe related Vietnam, therefore contemplate that appropriate announcements concerning economic loan negotiations be made after completion South Asia visits. No public announcement on military sales policy contemplated.

4. Suggest that VP, in telling Mrs. Gandhi and President Ayub of above decisions mention following:

a. President well impressed with new movement toward establishment peace on subcontinent symbolized by Tashkent troop withdrawal, and other moves toward Pak/Indian reconciliation;
b. This frees U.S. to take interim steps, i.e., the loans, to help prevent undue run-down of Indian and Pak economies;
c. Undertakings sought in return are part of increasing emphasis on self-help essential to justify such aid resumption to the Congress. In Delhi suggest VP add that President looks forward to seeing Mrs. Gandhi as soon as convenient for her, to reach meeting of minds at summit which will facilitate resumption of mutually beneficial relation. In both capitals would also be most valuable to underline basic view that President eager to help those who help themselves and who respond in kind. He determined that our relations must be a two way street.

5. In this connection, the President suggests that you develop with Mrs. Gandhi the theme that he must balance in the scales what each people can do for the other. More and more, public sentiment in both countries must be taken into account in our relations. The President intends to lead the American people into carefully weighing all the ways in which we can contribute to furthering our friendship with almost 500 million Indians. We believe we can help in many ways—in food, economic aid, education, health, and in maintaining peace in the world. In return, the President hopes that Mrs. Gandhi, before she comes here, will explore ways in which her 500 million people can be helpful to 200 million Americans. This doesn't mean that we want India to ally itself with us, much less adopt our economic system or philosophy. Nor do we insist on total Indian support of our foreign policies. But when the US is under attack in the UN or other forums it would be immensely helpful if the Indians could occasionally at least stand up and say "stop, look and listen—let's try to understand what the US is doing before we criticize it." Last but not least, one immediate thing the Indians could do would be to find ways of helping to promote peace through the ICC (septel will follow on ICC matter).

6. Septels will also be prepared on administrative details economic loan documentation and on military sales matter.[4]

Rusk

---

[4] Telegram 2374 to Saigon, February 12, conveyed additional points that the President suggested Humphrey might take up, including informing Gandhi of the prompt decision to authorize a $100 million program loan to India as his response to her urgent request. He encouraged Humphrey to get an up-to-date feel for India's food problems but warned that he could offer no further help until he had consulted with Congress. Johnson was inclined to favor announcement of the program loans in Karachi and New Delhi, and telegram 2374 recommended that Humphrey issue a statement at the end of each visit setting forth the decision to negotiate the loans. (National Archives and Records Administration, RG 59, Central Files 1964–66, AID (US) INDIA)

---

294.   Telegram From the Department of State to the Embassy in Pakistan[1]

Washington, February 12, 1966, 12:38 p.m.

1225. Joint State/Defense. [Refs] (a) Deptel 1417 to Delhi, 1184 to Karachi, 331 to Rawalpindi; (b) Deptel 1410 to Delhi, 1120 to Karachi, 328 to Rawalpindi;[2] (c) Deptel 1467 to Delhi, 1213 to Karachi, 340 to Rawalpindi, 2342 to Saigon.[3] Notal.

Subject: U.S. Military Sales Policy re India/Pakistan.

1. In light of prompt and effective movement by India and Pakistan to implement withdrawal provisions of pertinent SC Resolutions and

---

[1] Source: National Archives and Records Administration, RG 59, Central Files 1964–66, DEF 12–5 INDIA. Secret; Priority; Limdis. Drafted by William L. Simmons and Schneider (SOA), and Stoddard (DOD/ISA); cleared by Komer, Hoopes, Warren, Officer in Charge of Politico-Military Affairs (NEA/NR) Lieutenant Colonel Billy W. Byrd, and Dwight M. Cramer (G/PM-MC); and approved by Handley. Also sent to Rawalpindi, New Delhi, and Saigon and Bangkok for the Vice President. Repeated to CINCMEAFSA, CHUSMSMI, and CHMAAG Pakistan.

[2] Telegrams 1410 and 1417 to New Delhi deal with unrelated matters. The references are in error and have not been further identified.

[3] Document 293.

Tashkent Declaration, USG has concluded that our objective in imposing *total* ban on military shipments to India and Pakistan has been largely accomplished and that retention of this policy would not serve U.S. interests or objectives in either country. At same time, there have been fundamental changes in our relationship with subcontinent and phasing and substance of future military shipments to India and Pakistan must take this into account.

2. President has therefore authorized more flexible policy to permit some commercial sales and MAP credit sales of nonlethal military equipment. Policy will be administered on selective, limited, case-by-case basis with decisions clearly related to events on subcontinent and subject to continued satisfactory moves toward peace, e.g. actual troop withdrawal.

3. New policy, which Vice President will convey both Governments, designed to (a) relieve some of the pressures on both leaders, but particularly Ayub; (b) ease pressures on India and Pakistan to turn to Soviet and Chicom sources of supply respectively and give us stronger basis for action designed prevent such dependence; (c) indicate U.S. understanding of security problems facing both countries; (d) enable us to retain military relationship with both, and most important (e) indicate U.S. approval of India's and Pakistan's movement toward reconciliation their differences at conference table. Specific sales under this policy will be concluded only upon satisfactory completion of withdrawals; i.e., presumably February 25.

4. We plan to approve export military items gradually, at least at outset, and with special attention to political and military effects of each approval given circumstances on subcontinent. At outset we will look with greater favor on straight sales than credit sales, getting into latter as and when situation on subcontinent continues improve. (We anticipate GOP will wish to take advantage of opportunity to place their purchases on a credit sales basis. If this matter is raised GOP should be advised that we are prepared discuss further steps in implementing a credit arrangement.)

5. *Definition of Nonlethal:* Includes transport, observation, trainer aircraft, and unarmed helicopters and support equipment and spares;

Trucks, trailers, and miscellaneous wheeled vehicles and spares;

Communications, radar and signal equipment (includes Star Sapphire, but not grant aid at this time);

Engineer equipment (including Border Roads Organization support), medical and Quartermaster equipment;

Training;

Excluded from the foregoing are armed or armored vehicles such as tanks and APC's, infantry weapons, artillery, ammunition, armed helicopters, and combat aircraft. Spare parts in support these items also excluded.

Machine tools for defense production not on Munitions List and non-lethal but there likely be problem availability since in any event surplus U.S. tools being diverted to U.S. munitions industry for priority Vietnam needs.

6. *Execution:* USG prepared to accept cash and credit sales requests (i.e. either new orders or requests for revalidation orders presently suspended) through medium of USMSMI and MAAG Pak for items and services identified as non-lethal in para 5 above. It should be emphasized, however, that each such request will be treated on case-by-case basis and willingness of U.S. to acquiesce in sale must necessarily be weighed against conditions prevailing at time on subcontinent. Further relaxation of U.S. policy to permit resumption of some grant aid and possible sale of lethal items not predictable at this time.

7. We consider that opening up of our sales policy to both India and Pakistan gives us opportunity to re-establish measure of cooperation and rapport between MAAG Pakistan and USMSMI and their host country's military colleagues. Accordingly, we consider it of utmost importance that items requested by India and Pakistan be submitted through MAAG Pakistan, USMSMI and CINCMEAFSA channel for validation.

8. Most appropriate initial items (in addition to exceptions already made ref b) seem to us to be in field communication equipment; e.g. Pakistan, Electro-Craft radios of value $3 million; India, AN/PRC–25 radios from RCA (we willing offer credit for these since delivery unlikely until mid-year in accordance our request to Indians to give up early delivery in favor our needs Vietnam).

9. Request Country Team comments on initial military items falling under non-lethal definition para 5 to be released soonest. For time being you should not discuss this with third country missions, i.e., British, Canadian, Australian.

10. New policy should not be conveyed to Governments until visit of Vice President. At that time each Government should be informed policy applies equally to other. No public announcement should be made and we would expect GOI and GOP follow similar course. We will inform U.K., Canada and Australia of new policy after it has been conveyed to both Governments.

11. For Karachi/Rawalpindi: We are informing Pak Embassy here that Department has Electro-Craft problem under active review, and

that we assume GOP will take this into consideration before pressing further to break contract.[4]

Rusk

---

[4] Telegram 1485 to New Delhi, also sent to Karachi as telegram 1229, February 12, expanded upon a primary concern conditioning policy considerations in Washington: "As we begin to move back selectively toward new economic aid and supply of military items to India and Pakistan, their level of military expenditure is high among the issues of concern to us. In brief, our concern stems from belief that overspending on defense endangers progress by both toward accommodation and causes them unduly divert their resources and energies from task of internal economic development." (National Archives and Records Administration, RG 59, Central Files 1964–66, DEF 1 INDIA)

---

295. Telegram From the Embassy in Pakistan to the Department of State[1]

Karachi, February 16, 1966, 1420Z.

1626. Following is brief of uncleared memorandum of conversation between VP Humphrey and President Ayub in Karachi Feb 15/66 (full text being pouched[2]):

Summary. Vice President Humphrey met for nearly two hours February 15 with President Ayub to discuss United States Vietnam policy with particular attention to Honolulu Conference results, and to inform Ayub of United States decisions: (1) to negotiate economic commodity loan of $50,000,000; (2) to negotiate shortly interim PL–480 agreement; (3) to relax ban on military shipments to permit some commercial and MAP credit sales of non-lethal military equipment.

Ayub expressed hope for success of efforts launched at Honolulu to promote social and political progress in Vietnam, but stressed formi-

---

[1] Source: National Archives and Records Administration, RG 59, Central Files 1964–66, POL 7 US/HUMPHREY. Secret; Immediate; Exdis/VP. Repeated to New Delhi and passed to the White House at 11:10 a.m.

[2] The memorandum of conversation was transmitted to the Department as an enclosure to airgram A–511 from Karachi, February 25. (Ibid.) A transcript of this conversation is ibid., Conference Files: Lot 67 D 305, CF 6A. The transcript indicates that the meeting began at 5:35 p.m. and ended at 7:25 p.m. It also lists the participants in the meeting as Humphrey, Harriman, Valenti, McConaughy, Ayub, Bhutto, and Shoaib.

dable obstacles which Indo–Pak confrontation imposes upon Pak capability offer assistance other than continuing attempts counsel moderation on Soviet and Chinese Communist leaders, which Ayub indicated readiness to do as opportunities arose. Ayub was appreciative of United States aid decisions noted above, pointed to critical Pak requirements for replacements for range of United States origin military equipment, and underlined felt threat to Pakistan of growing Indian military capability. Throughout, Ayub stressed desire for peace and Pak intention carry out Tashkent declaration provisions in "letter and spirit." *End of summary.*

Vietnam

After conveying President Johnson's good wishes to Ayub, and with reference President Johnson's letters of Feb 10[3] and 11[4] to Ayub, Vice President Humphrey gave long and detailed account of American diplomatic and military effort with respect Vietnam and related events of recent Honolulu Conference. VP described root problem of moving local govt towards social progress and recognition of South Vietnamese leaders of this problem and its magnitude. VP noted South Vietnam Govt had developed program which intended meet military needs and reconstruction goals and coordinate them at provincial level, emphasizing self-help aspect. Program not perfect and hour late, but in US view program can be effective and deserves support. Military situation manageable and improving. It is political-social problems which loom large. Other countries can help with non-combatant support in this struggle for development and social progress which in Pak of particular concern. Moreover, whole struggle in Southeast Asia in US view is vital for all. VP described total program of Communist attack on Southeast Asia, noting that in President Johnson's view this large-scale challenge must be faced now: otherwise it will be necessary meet it elsewhere at other time. US must show determination and strength, and believes its actions this regard tie directly into Pak security. While recognizing each nation's sovereignty, US feels strongly factual case is as stated.

Governor Harriman gave strong support VP's presentation elaborating on reasons which impelled resumption of bombing. He adverted to possibility Ayub might impress upon Communist China, Moscow, Hanoi desirability of moderation; stress particularly to Soviets sincerity

---

[3] Document 292.

[4] Johnson's letter to Ayub of February 11, transmitted to Karachi in circular telegram 1531 of that date, conveyed Johnson's impressions of the recent Honolulu conference on South Vietnam. (National Archives and Records Administration, RG 59, Central Files 1964–66, POL 27 VIET S)

with which US seeking peace; consider contribution of medical team or other contribution to Vietnam struggle.

Ayub expressed thanks for explanations, and appreciation to President Johnson for keeping him informed. He said, "I know you face great difficulties, are doing your best, and I hope you succeed." He noted 35 years of terrible continuing war in area had resulted in tremendous problem. Good deal depends upon how much local people prepared to sacrifice. Problem also of growing nationalism in area. But key is willingness undertake social reform, then outside forces can assist.

In response to remarks by Governor Harriman, Ayub noted that Indian pressure of 1.2 million men under arms fantastically reduces Pak abilities enlarge its military and political commitments. Pak very security at stake. Pak greatly interested in Vietnam situation. In Peiping and Moscow, Ayub pointed out US had interests in Asia as world power. Pak will continue at least plead for moderation. Anytime ChiCom or Sov leaders pass through "we shall certainly continue these efforts." Regarding matter of contribution Ayub noted that if Pak to do so it would incur enmity of Sov Union and Chinese and put itself in impossible situation with India as avowed enemy while US unable really underwrite Pak liabilities. (FonMin Bhutto noted parenthetically that following resumption of bombing GOP had not issued any adverse statement although India, member of ICC, had.)

Elsewhere Ayub noted Pak has accepted commitments and risks far beyond its military and economic power, vide instance U–2 incident. For sake US friendship Pak incurred wrath of USSR despite latter's capacity destroy Pak. Pak was asked in 1961 contribute battalion for Laos and replied with offer of brigade. Unfortunately owing present problem with India, Pak ability do anything like that greatly reduced.

Ayub went on delineate difficulty Pak situation geographically split with 1400 miles of "not very friendly India" between wings. India constant open threat. If any of Pak's big neighbors move, Paks in difficulty. Then too Pak is ideological state bordered by Communist neighbors USSR and China. Security important, but also a country must have good social and economic programs. Pakistan has been cited by many as outstanding example of effective economic development. US has been major contributor and Pak deeply grateful.

Tashkent, Indo–Pak Relations and Arms

Pak bedeviled by problem of how to find peace with India. Tashkent declaration (TD) good start which requires diplomatic followup. Pak has every intention follow through. Tashkent in interest whole region. Pak wants live in peace and only hopes India does too. But what is sense of fabulous Indian expenditures for armaments? Before 1962 India had ten divisions. Now has 21 plus three recently organized and talking about additional seven. Indians spending $2.6 million [*billion?*] for military purposes. Much of military equipment not suitable for use in Himalaya against Chinese. Some reduction in armed forces indicated in interests of all. In another connection Ayub enjoined VP tell Indians Paks "want peace" and indicated great achievement for all would ensue if US could persuade India be reasonable.

VP reminded Ayub of US gratitude concerning statesmanlike Tashkent. He pledged US would do everything possible to insure implementation of UNSC Sept 20 resolution and TD provisions. US does understand Pak problem and President Johnson greatly disturbed at possibility of arms race on sub-continent. [garble—He feels] India committed to TD and that India concerned over possibility ChiCom attack.

Economic Aid

VP noted President Johnson told him he wished contribute to Pak progress and TD implementation. US prepared negotiate $50 million dollar economic commodity assistance at this time and to open up discussion further economic assistance that may be needed. VP indicated stipulation concerning priority for economic development and application of loan to imports for existing plant capacity.

PL 480

VP indicated US readiness negotiate shortly interim PL 480 agreement and discuss longer-term food requirements. Doubtful that US able fill all Pak requirements although would like to in view drought and Pak achievements in agricultural development field.

Military Supplies

VP informed Ayub of US decision to relax ban on military shipments to permit some purchases non-lethal equipment. Ayub wondered what Pak to do with its fighters when US had given only three months supply of spare parts. "We can't leave Pak defenseless; no country can allow that. If we can't get what we must have from you then we must go elsewhere." VP noted US taking look at whole picture and that as Tashkent proceeds it can take new look. US not trading but working with reality. We can take further look this spring or early summer and spring is just around corner.

Purposes in India

VP noted for Ayub's info he intended in India: (1) emphasize importance Indo–Pak relations along TD lines; (2) inform PM Gandhi of US and Pak views this regard; (3) discuss 100 million dollar commodity loan to India in similar terms as $50 million dollar loan to Pak.[5]

McConaughy

[5] Humphrey issued a statement to the press on February 15 following his conversation with Ayub in which he announced the $50 million loan and the offer to negotiate an interim P.L. 480 agreement. (Telegram 1614 from Karachi, February 15; ibid., POL 7 HUMPHREY) The Embassy reported on February 16 that the Pakistani press had headlined the announcements concerning the loan and the P.L. 480 agreement. The Embassy noted that it was the best press the United States had received in Pakistan in months. (Telegram 1625 from Karachi; ibid.)

296. Telegram From the Embassy in India to the Department of State[1]

New Delhi, February 17, 1966.

2136. Dept pass priority AmEmbassy Canberra for Vice President. For the President from the Vice President. I have had a useful and full schedule in India. We stopped first in the Punjab and spent half a day touring their agricultural university and experiment station, an accelerated agricultural production project, a health center and family planning clinic and a Peace Corps project. I was impressed by the way the Indians are adapting the knowhow learned from US in agricultural research, education and production.

In New Delhi I saw President Radhakrishnan and Vice President Husain last evening and today saw Ministers concerned with economic affairs and agriculture, Foreign and Defense Ministers, and the Prime Minister.

In all these meetings I stressed our concern that Tashkent Declaration be followed up effectively. The President, the Prime Minister, and the Ministers all said this is their firm intention.

I also went into detail about the Honolulu meetings and their significance for the future of both the military and social-economic efforts in Vietnam. I made clear we asked only for peace and freedom

[1] Source: National Archives and Records Administration, RG 59, Central Files 1964–66, POL 7 US/HUMPHREY. Secret; Priority; Nodis. No time of transmission appears on the telegram, which was received at 3:31 p.m. and passed to the White House at 4:35 p.m.

of choice for the people of Vietnam. We urged the Indians to recognize our common interest in the success of these efforts and to give us any views of theirs in private but not in public. We also urged that GOI use its influence with the Soviets directly and in ICC to encourage them to be helpful in bringing the North Vietnamese to the negotiating table. I asked them to consider medical or other humanitarian assistance to SVN.

The response was generally affirmative about working on the Russians, which they say they will continue to do even though they do not anticipate much give there in the immediate future. The President in particular expressed his willingness and desire to work on the Russians.

Response on public postures was qualified by their concern to retain influence in Moscow and to acquire influence in Hanoi, both of which they feel require that they not be seen to be leaning too far towards US. They appear to feel this approach will serve our mutual interest in the objective of containing and frustrating the Chinese.

I explored in detail their food needs and economic prospects and I am satisfied that their planning for the budget which is to be presented on February 18 gives top priority to agriculture measures agreed to with Secretary Freeman. This confirmed by Prime Minister. Also GOI will confine defense expenditures to the limits previously agreed to with Secretary McNamara.

Indian Ministers detailed efforts being made by GOI to mobilize assistance from other countries to meet their present food emergency. I am satisfied that the Indians are making a major effort in seeking other country assistance.

They also reviewed in detail the disastrous effect which foreign exchange shortage is having on the economy. They were grateful for our interim assistance and recognized that further talks would be necessary between you and Mrs. Gandhi before an understanding on a longer term program could be reached.

I told Mrs. Gandhi how much you were looking forward to seeing her to continue discussions on all these matters and it appears that she is thinking of coming shortly after the 15th of March.

Additional information on my conversation with Prime Minister will be sent from Canberra. All items in my instructions from Rusk covered in these talks. Feel progress made.

Bowles

297. Telegram From the Embassy in New Zealand to the Department of State[1]

Wellington, February 20, 1966.

490. To the President. From the Vice President. Subject: Notes on the Vice President's visit with Prime Minister Gandhi at her home Thursday evening, February 17, 1966.

Present were Prime Minister Gandhi and Foreign Minister Swaran Singh and Ambassadors Harriman, Bowles, and the Vice President.

The earlier conference, 3:00 to 5:00 p.m.,[2] which covered all aspects of our economic and political relations with India, left some matters indefinite and requiring a more responsive and definitive answer from the Prime Minister and her Ministers. Earlier in the day we had met with the Ministers of Agriculture, Planning, Finance, and subsequently with the Minister of Defense and the Chief Military Officers, and the Minister of Foreign Affairs. In each of these conferences I had reviewed in detail the Honolulu Conference, my observations on Vietnam, my discussions in Thailand, Laos, and Pakistan. I had underscored the growing threat of Chinese Communist militancy in all of Southeast and South Asia. I had further emphasized the importance that President Johnson placed upon the development of human resources and the concept of self-help. I had pointed out that we were going to give particular emphasis to education, training, health and health facilities, agricultural production and the modernization of agricultural techniques through technical assistance and education. I had emphasized the importance of the allocation of greater resources by the respective countries to these fields. I made it manifestly clear that the quantity

---

[1] Source: National Archives and Records Administration, RG 59, Central Files 1964–66, POL 7 US/HUMPHREY. Top Secret; Flash; Literally Eyes Only for the President. No time of transmission appears on the telegram, which was received at 2:23 p.m. and passed to the White House at 3 p.m.

[2] In his earlier conversation with Gandhi, Humphrey had discussed the food crisis in India, and had informed her that the United States was prepared to negotiate a $100 million non-project loan with India. He also indicated that he told the Defense Minister and the Chiefs of Staff that the United States was prepared to consider commercial and credit sales of nonlethal military equipment, and that if progress in the spirit of the Tashkent Declaration continued, it might become possible to discuss other aspects of military assistance. The conversation was mainly devoted to a discussion of developments in Vietnam. Humphrey stressed the danger of Chinese aggression and asked that India use its good offices whenever possible to try to facilitate negotiations to bring an end to the fighting in Vietnam. He asked Gandhi to restrain judgmental public pronouncements by Indian officials on the conflict. The United States was not asking for an endorsement of its policies in Vietnam, and it welcomed private exchanges concerning the conflict, but Humphrey said it affected relations between the two countries if Indian officials continued to throw "dead cats at the U.S." (Memorandum of conversation, February 17; ibid.)

of our aid would be related directly to the amount of self-help undertaken by the respective countries.

Of course, there was a detailed discussion of the Communist activities in all of these areas, and particularly the intrusion of North Vietnamese troops and trained political cadres into the Southeast Asian area.
In each conference we had spelled out our conviction that the attack
in Southeast Asia was but the first manifestation of Communist militancy in a war-like posture which could easily spread to other areas.
In other words, there was and continued to be a threat to all Asian
countries from the aggressive militant attitude and policies of the Chi-
Com regime. In our earlier conference with the Indian Prime Minister
and her advisers, I had the feeling that she was aware of these matters
but that her young adviser, Mr. Singh (not the Foreign Minister), was
more or less an apologist for a neutrality that leaned to the Russians and
even tried to explain away some of the Chinese Communist activities in
Southeast Asia. It should be clear that all Indians were very much
aware of the Chinese Communist threat to India. But their thinking
had not taken them to the position that the ChiCom threat extended
all the way across the bottom of Asia to the southeast. I pounded away
at the interrelationship of Communist activities in the subcontinent
and Southeast Asia.

Now, in order to pin all of this down, and particularly to get some
specific positions by the Indians on a number of matters, I asked Mrs.
Gandhi to sit with me on the occasion of the dinner at her home to go
over a few matters. Here are some of the questions I asked and here
are the answers:

1. I pointed out to Mrs. Gandhi that we had reviewed in detail
the matter of Indian commitment to improved agricultural production.
This had been discussed with the Ministers of Agriculture, Finance
and Planning. I asked her directly, "Will you support the position
of your Minister of Agriculture on the allocation of resources to the
agricultural sector, and will you give your commitment to support the
agreements arrived at between Secretary Freeman and Indian Agricultural Minister Subramanian?" Her answer was a clear and unequivocal
yes. She added that the GOI would not only do this, but was actively
supporting family planning and also actively supporting agricultural
research in new crops and expanded production.

I explained to Mrs. Gandhi that there was a limit to what India
could expect from the public treasury of the United States. We had
serious problems on foreign aid. In fact, I made it clear several times
during the day that while India had her problems with her parliament,
we had ours too. I also said that what India needed was capital and
techical know-how. Most of this was available in the private sector of
our country and other countries. Therefore, does India welcome and,

indeed, encourage the injection of inclusion of private resources into her economy? Has India revised her laws and regulations so as to create a favorable environment for private investment? This, of course, refers to investment in fertilizer plants, machinery, and other lines of equipment. The Prime Minister assured me that the necessary changes in laws and regulations had been made to create a favorable environment. I asked for specific answers. She and the Foreign Minister promised us a paper which would outline in detail the several changes in laws and regulations which added up to a favorable environment for investment by private capital from other countries. I made it clear that I was not speaking for U.S. capital alone, since we were concerned about the outflow of U.S. capital and its effect on our balance of payments deficit. What I was talking about was a general policy which could and should encourage private investment from Japan, Germany, France, England, etc., as well as the United States. The Prime Minister and the Foreign Minister gave an affirmative response. The Prime Minister did add that it was the feeling of their own people that insofar as possible, Indian resources should be used and outside capital should be a supplement. With this we had no disagreement. She mentioned the problem of foreign exchange required for repatriation of profits. I replied that if the enterprise was profitable and investment climate friendly, the companies would most likely reinvest profits in India.

2. Now on Vietnam. During the late afternoon conference we had a long discussion on Vietnam. I was not fully satisfied with the responses of the Prime Minister and her advisers. I had a feeling that Mrs. Gandhi recognized that India should be cooperative with the U.S., but her young adviser, Mr. Singh, seemed to indicate doubt and at times a contrary attitude. Therefore, I admonished Mrs. Gandhi and her advisers that the least India could do if she disagreed with some of our policies was to express that disagreement discreetly in the channels of diplomacy rather than in public statements and in the press. Both Averell and I spent a great deal of time going over our position in Vietnam—why we were there, our objectives, namely the right of people to make their own choice; and that we were going to stay until the job was finished. We made it unqualifiedly clear that America was committed to the defense of South Vietnam. I pointed out that we did not seek to escalate the war. To the contrary, we were using limited power for limited objectives. Our bombing of North Vietnam was under very careful control, directed at routes of infiltration, military depots, bridges, etc. I assured her that you personally were giving daily attention to all military operations in order to avoid any act that might precipitate confrontation with either the Chinese or the Russians. I did stress, however, that we were determined to resist and beat the aggression. We would not retreat. I informed Mrs. Gandhi the opposi-

tion in the U.S. was mainly vocal—a limited number, and in no way represented the majority view of the American people. These assurances seemed to satisfy her and she appreciated the burdens you were carrying and our desire for peace.

She then asked what India might do to be of help. And I responded that we would appreciate their good offices with the Soviets and if possible to use their contacts in Hanoi. I reminded Mrs. Gandhi that India was a member of the ICC and we wanted India to act fairly and objectively in that capacity. She and her Foreign Minister insisted they were acting fairly, but did point out that if India was to have any influence on the Russians, she would have to be wise and somewhat quiet in her ICC role.

Mrs. Gandhi expressed deep concern over Communist China's aggressive policies. I reminded her that it was the same Communist China that attacked India which was aiding North Vietnam and the Vietcong. She agreed to this. And, therefore, I suggested that we had a common cause in stopping Red China. I asked her to think through what India would do if Communist China should attack us in Vietnam. Would India move her forces into Tibet as a diversion? Would India continue to pin down large Chinese armies on her frontier by maintaining or increasing India's military forces on her northern frontier? I asked for no immediate answer, but simply wanted to have the Indian officials think through some of these potential situations. In other words, I faced the Indian Prime Minister and the Foreign Minister with some hard realities.

It is my view that Mrs. Gandhi is yet somewhat uncertain in her leadership position. She depends a great deal on her Ministers. Our friends in Australia who know her, however, say that in a short time she will be in command. She is bright, experienced in the ways of politics, tough-minded, and knows how to use power. This is the view of Lord Casey, Governor General of Australia, who has known her a long time.

I informed Mrs. Gandhi that she had to be prepared for some frank, down-to-earth discussions when she arrived in Washington. I told her we were deeply committed to Indian freedom and independence and Indian security, but we would expect the same commitment on India's part to the U.S. It would be well for her and her Ministers to think through the cooperative relationships between India and U.S. in the defense against Communist China in Southeast Asia and the subcontinent.

I would say the visit was helpful. The President of India is a realist. He promised to use his good offices to bring pressure to bear on the Soviets to exert more influence on Hanoi for peace. He is well aware of the Chinese Communist threat and plans. He is friendly to the U.S., and our Australian allies have a high regard for him.

Favell

298. Memorandum From Secretary of Agriculture Freeman to President Johnson[1]

Washington, March 4, 1966.

SUBJECT

Review of the India Food Situation

Official estimates of foodgrain production in India are still holding at 76 million tons. Grain imports from all sources are expected to average about a million tons monthly in March, April, and May.

Grain procurement and efforts at belt tightening are moving slowly. Rationing programs instituted thus far cover 34 million people or 7 percent of the total population. An additional 20 million may be added by June 1, bringing the total up to 11 percent. This will cover most of the major urban centers but very little of the country outside these centers.

The riots in Kerala protesting the lack of rice have subsided for the present, but scattered food protests and demonstrations are occurring elsewhere in India.

Dissatisfaction with food policies

At the annual convention of the Congress Party, the Government's food production and distribution policies came under fire. Minister Subramaniam, as Minister of Food and Agriculture, bore the brunt of the attack.

At times the Party Leaders nearly lost control of the convention delegates who were loudly demanding the abolition of the food zones. Most of the criticism came from the deficit states, which this year outnumber the food surplus states by about 3 to 1.

At one time Minister Subramaniam threatened to resign. This is not the first time he has used this threat, but there is probably a limit to the number of times this tactic can be effectively used. There is little doubt but that Subramaniam's position has been weakened somewhat by the current crisis and the unrest and dissatisfaction it has generated.

Subramaniam appears to be fighting hard to implement the policies agreed upon in Rome. Despite the fact he got Cabinet and Parliament concurrence, he has been facing some strong opposition. At the annual convention of the Congress Party, Subramaniam was openly reprimanded by Congress Party Chief Kamaraj for having signed an overly generous agreement with an American firm permitting it to construct

---

[1] Source: Johnson Library, National Security File, Memos to the President, Walt W. Rostow, Vol. 21, 3/3/66–3/30/66. No classification marking.

and operate a fertilizer plant. Subramaniam insisted that the Indian Government must live up to its agreement and he prevailed.

Subramaniam was also criticized by Kamaraj for the recent decision to permit foreign private investors to price and market their own fertilizer. Again he held his ground and won out. Kamarj later partially retracted his criticism of Subramaniam, saying that in fact this decision was made by the Government of India.

The 1966/67 crop

We are thinking ahead to the 1966/67 crop in India. Historical records indicate that crop production does not usually recover completely after a serious monsoon failure such as that experienced this past year, even if the next monsoon is a good one.

Reports of serious and worsening power shortages indicate water levels in irrigation reservoirs are far from optimal.

Scattered readings of soil moisture levels indicate these are far below normal throughout most of the Indian subcontinent.

Fertilizer supplies for 1966/67 crop

A third key factor affecting the 1966/67 crop and on which we already have some information is fertilizer supplies. As things now stand, supplies of all three major nutrients will be well below the levels for 1966/67 agreed upon in Rome.

Nitrogen fertilizer supplies are expected to range between 700,000 and 800,000 tons. This is up from the 550,000 tons used in 1965/66 but far short of the 1,000,000 ton level agreed upon in Rome. We do not have complete data on phosphate and potash supplies for 1966/67 but the shortfalls may be even greater than for nitrogen.

The Indians have used all of the $50 million loan you announced on December 10. They more than matched that loan with foreign exchange of their own as they had agreed they would. Even so, they are falling far short of targets. Several factors account for this.

Fertilizer prices have risen sharply over the past several months. Our $50 million loan did not go nearly as far as it would have a year or two ago.

World supplies of fertilizer raw materials, particularly sulphur, are in short supply. The inability to obtain adequate supplies of raw materials coupled with the failure to allocate enough foreign exchange for spare parts has prevented domestic plants from operating at anything near full capacity.

Getting fertilizer consumption up to target

It now seems quite clear that fertilizer consumption will be well below target in 1966/67 unless strong action is taken. We might very well press Mrs. Gandhi to find enough foreign exchange to get fertilizer consumption up to the agreed upon levels. It appears that Subramaniam could not carry the point alone again. From a political point of view, it would be very desirable to involve Mrs. Gandhi more directly in agricultural policy making. This would take some of the direct pressure off Subramaniam.

I recommend we use every way possible to get them to free enough of their own foreign exchange to get fertilizer consumption up to target. If this does not work, I would suggest we urge them to go again to some of the other advanced countries such as West Germany and Japan asking them to supply specific quantities of fertilizer on concessional terms so they can meet their consumption targets. These additional fertilizer needs would total about $100 million. After all, they did not have any great qualms about asking us for $750 million worth of foodgrains.

If we decide none of these will work, you might want to consider an additional $100 million loan to be used specifically for fertilizer, fertilizer raw materials and spare parts. One pound of fertilizer produces on the average 10 pounds of grain. Fertilizer supplied now will reduce the amount of grain we will be asked to contribute next year. If we let them off this year, it will be almost impossible to get them back on target in subsequent years.

Preparing for Mrs. Gandhi's visit

Later this week I am sending Les Brown, my key India expert, to India to take a last reading of conditions there before Mrs. Gandhi comes here. He will take a close look at the progress, or lack of it, in getting new fertilizer plants under construction, and in carrying forward the Rome agreement.

Brown will also be investigating the feasibility of attempting to shift cotton land into the production of foodgrains in India. If this proves feasible, we could work off some of our heavy cotton stocks under P.L. 480 while reducing their import needs for U.S. wheat.

This proposition seems logical on the face of it, but will need to be examined in terms of the economic implications, particularly to the producers involved, as well as the political overtones.

The fact that Poage brought this up in an open hearing and that it got in the newspapers means it has already reached India. It may have created political problems for Subramaniam and will possibly create more if we try to move in this direction.

Nonetheless, I have discussed it with leaders in the cotton industry and also cotton Congressmen and Senators and we will thoroughly investigate it.

I will send you a complete up-to-date report when Brown returns.

299.   Memorandum From Secretary of State Rusk to President Johnson[1]

Washington, March 16, 1966.

SUBJECT

Possible Assurances and Nuclear Support Arrangements for India

India may, at any time, decide to embark on a nuclear weapons program. While we do not expect such a decision soon, barring major unexpected changes in the situation the US Intelligence Board estimates that on balance India probably *will* do so within the next few years. I concur in this assessment. At the same time, it remains in the interests of the United States to curb nuclear proliferation, and an Indian decision to manufacture nuclear weapons would increase the probability that other countries would also decide to do so.

I believe that we should, therefore, attempt to head off an Indian decision to produce nuclear weapons. To do so, we might in time have to be more responsive to Indian security needs, preferably in some way that will minimize our own commitment. However, we must recognize that this response would almost certainly involve an increased and more specific US commitment in the subcontinent and would entail important costs in terms of probable reactions of other states. The enclosed staff study[2] reviews briefly our efforts to deal with this problem, defines the issue and sets forth the broad alternatives, and outlines some illustrative arrangements that could be considered if it is eventually decided to offer some form of nuclear sharing to India. I do not propose that you should now decide upon any one of these alternatives. These alternatives, including the possible nuclear sharing arrangements, are intended merely to illustrate for your background the possible general lines of action which may have to be considered.

I propose that when Mrs. Gandhi comes to Washington you let her know that we are sympathetic to her policy of using nuclear energy for peaceful purposes only, and to her efforts to give priority to India's economic needs and development.

I believe you should indicate that you agree that nuclear powers should try to work out some arrangements to safeguard the security interests of non-nuclear powers. As she is aware, we have raised the

---

[1] Source: Johnson Library, National Security File, Country File, India, Gandhi Visit Papers, 3/27–30/66. Top Secret; Limited Distribution.

[2] The attached undated 12-page paper, entitled "Possible Assurances and Nuclear Support Arrangements for India," is not printed.

matter privately with the Soviet Union, and it has also been a subject of continuing discussion at Geneva.

I believe you should also say that in any case if a growing Chinese Communist nuclear capability should ever pose a serious threat to India, you hope she would frankly discuss the question with us so that we could examine together possible means to meet that threat without nuclear proliferation and without Indian assumption of the heavy economic and other burdens of a nuclear weapons program.

Implicit in the over-all question of assurances to India is the basic issue of what degree of nuclear support the United States is willing to proffer to non-nuclear nations. In this connection I recommend that you not offer India any bilateral nuclear assurances at this time.

You might also wish to tell Mrs. Gandhi that we are prepared to make available to her periodically (as we did for Prime Minister Shastri) intelligence on the Chinese Communist nuclear capability.

Secretary McNamara and Mr. Foster concur in this recommendation. (The Joint Chiefs of Staff would prefer not to offer India at this time any nuclear assurances beyond those given by you in October, 1964.) We would of course wish to continue to examine other possible arrangements outlined in the enclosed study. We will continue to study these alternatives.[3]

Dean Rusk

---

[3] Airgram A–256 to New Delhi, March 29, instructed the Embassy to report all indications of possible Indian nuclear weapons activity. (National Archives and Records Administration, RG 59, Central Files 1964–66, DEF 12–1 INDIA; also available on the Internet, National Security Archive (www.gwu.edu/~nsarchive), Electronic Briefing Book No. 6, "India and Pakistan—On the Nuclear Threshold," Document 8)

300.   Telegram From the Department of State to the Embassy in India[1]

Washington, March 18, 1966, 6:49 p.m.

1751. Deptel 1561, Paris 44.[2] Indian Food Crisis.

1. We believe Mrs. Gandhi should be aware before her departure of our continued concern with Indian efforts to obtain maximum assistance from other countries and that we expect to discuss this with her. We understand GOI reluctance to appear at home to be unable manage food problem without massive foreign assistance but do not think this should affect vigor of Indian effort to organize assistance from other governments. Impression here that GOI is relying heavily on U.S., is discounting capability or willingness of other countries to help, and is not sufficiently aware our determination that other countries share burden. Items which disturb us are failure to establish donor country coordinating committee, which we believe strongly favored by other major donors, lack of Indian initiative on bilateral basis in seeking more than token contributions from industrial countries, about which Australians also greatly concerned, and disinclination make high level approach to other governments as they have promised they would do. We would hope that Mrs. Gandhi would take opportunity to ask for something better than present meager French contribution when she sees President deGaulle.

2. Leave to your discretion best way of insuring GOI officials and Mrs. Gandhi well briefed; it also desirable that you bring back full report on GOI recent efforts and present intentions regarding international effort, including any renewed approaches to third countries.

Rusk

---

[1] Source: National Archives and Records Administration, RG 59, Central Files 1964–66, SOC 10 INDIA. Confidential; Priority. Drafted by Arthur C. Bauman (NEA/SOA) on March 17; cleared by Laise, Officer in Charge of Economic Affairs Guy C. Mallett, Jr. (NEA/SOA), Horbaly (USDA/FAS), Officer in Charge of Indian Affairs in AID's Office of South Asian Affairs Walter C. Furst, Economic Officer in Charge of French-Iberian Affairs Edgar J. Beigel (EUR/WE), and Alan D. Berg (M/FFP); and approved by Hare. Repeated to Paris.

[2] In telegram 1561 to New Delhi, February 19, the Department noted what was perceived in Washington as a "let-up" in the effort of the Indian Government to obtain maximum support from third countries to meet the crisis in food requirements. The Embassy was instructed to urge a greater effort on India's part. (Ibid.)

301. Memorandum for Record[1]

Washington, March 22, 1966.

President's meeting with Ambassador B.K. Nehru. The President's Tuesday (March 22) appointment with B.K. Nehru was quite informal and largely social in character. The President first took Ambassador Nehru on a long tour of the White House grounds, during which he met several of Mrs. Johnson's luncheon guests, and then had Ambassador Nehru to lunch with Secretaries Rusk and McNamara and members of the White House staff.

During this period the President made several points to Nehru along the following lines. First, he said that he was not asking India to go into the Dominican Republic or Vietnam; all we wanted was greater Indian understanding of our problems in such areas and such help as they could give in bringing peace. We did not want to command or direct the Indian Government, nor even to make a "trade" with it.

However, there were two things which we needed in order to be able to help India. After all, we needed the support of the U.S. Congress, especially on food. It was essential to get other countries to help meet India's famine needs so that the Congress would not feel we were being called upon to do the whole job. We needed to be able to say to our people that we and the Indians had explored all other avenues. Moreover, we had to make an equitable proposal to the Congress—we could start out by saying that we would do half the remaining job if others would contribute half. If this didn't work we could say we would do two-thirds. If this didn't prove feasible, then we might have to do yet more.

The second essential prerequisite was *self-help.* Anyone we were working with must be able to demonstrate that they were doing the most that they could for themselves. Subramaniam had made a big impression here by describing what India intended to do for itself in agriculture. Now the President wanted to move at Mrs. Gandhi's pace. But he had to be able to convince our people that Mrs. Gandhi was doing the best for her country first. Ambassador Nehru replied that India was doing more for itself than any other country in the free world. He offered to prove to the President that India was financing more of its own development effort than any other country, and was receiving far less per capita aid than most.

The President said that he had to prove three things to the Congress: first, that others were fully participating in help for India; second,

---

[1] Source: Johnson Library, National Security File, Country File, India, Vol. VII, Cables, 1/66–8/66. Secret. Prepared on March 25.

that India was doing everything that she could do for herself; and third, that in providing aid for India and Pakistan, we were not fueling an arms race.

On the political side, the President said that he understood the Indian position on China and wanted India to understand ours. In order to support Mrs. Gandhi we wanted to throw all of her enemies off balance. To this end, we would do the opposite of what people were claiming we were going to do in terms of pressing India. Ambassador Nehru replied that India was prepared to accept the World Bank's advice if the World Bank were prepared to put up the cost. He explained briefly how India would need a cushion of aid if it were to liberalize the economy.

The above were the highlights of a rather disjointed conversation. Later Ambassador Nehru left with Mr. Komer a set of charts which he had planned to give to the President to demonstrate that India's own development effort was extensively self-financed; that India's economic progress had indeed been substantial; and that India's recent economic growth compared quite favorably to that of Pakistan. He also left a memo[2] on Indian aid requirements for the Fourth Plan which called for gross consortium aid during the 5-year period of $8.65 billion; deducting debt service charges of $2.6 billion during the period left a net aid requirement of roughly $6 billion.

RWK

---

[2] Not found.

---

302.   **Memorandum From the President's Acting Special Assistant for National Security Affairs (Komer) to President Johnson**

Washington, March 23, 1966, 7:10 p.m.

[Source: Johnson Library, National Security File, Memos to the President, McGeorge Bundy. Top Secret; Sensitive. 1 page of source text not declassified.]

303.   Memorandum From the President's Deputy Special Assistant for National Security Affairs (Komer) to Secretary of Agriculture Freeman[1]

Washington, March 24, 1966.

India Food Message. In discussing the food problem with Secretary Rusk, Ambassador Bowles, and myself[2] today, the President expressed the following views.

1. We should be ready to go with a message by Tuesday.

2. He does not want to make any more interim allocations prior to putting the whole matter before the Congress.

3. He believes that we must propose specific quantities in the message, as otherwise it will get amended in this sense on the Hill.

4. His own current thinking is to request on the order of 2.5 million tons of wheat, a million tons of milo, and some cotton—all to be included in the message. By not asking for any more we would keep up the pressure on other countries to contribute.

5. He is open-minded on the subject of a formula.

I am sure that the President would be prepared to hear argument on these points, but I wanted to be sure you had his current thinking.

R.W. Komer[3]

---

[1] Source: Johnson Library, National Security File, NSC Histories, Indian Famine, August 1966–February 1967, Vol. I. Confidential. Copies were sent to the President's Special Assistant Joseph A. Califano, Jr., and to AID Administrator David E. Bell.

[2] Jack Valenti was also present and prepared handwritten notes on the meeting. His notes indicate that he did not participate in the discussion. (Ibid., Office of the President File, Valenti, Jack, Meeting Notes (Handwritten) 2/26/66–4/6/66)

[3] Printed from a copy that bears this typed signature.

304. Memorandum From Secretary of State Rusk to President Johnson[1]

Washington, March 26, 1966.

SUBJECT

The Economic Bargain with Mrs. Gandhi

Discussions held since the submission of our strategy and talking points papers[2] have indicated the desirability of restating in brief and specific terms the economic bargain we hope to strike with Mrs. Gandhi, if we reach the desired understanding on political issues.

In sum the proposition is this:

1. On the economic front the basic issue is confidence: confidence on our part that India will press forward aggressively to accelerate its economic development through liberal economic policies and emphasis on agriculture; and confidence on Mrs. Gandhi's part that the U.S. can be counted on to provide necessary financial support.

2. We believe Mrs. Gandhi is prepared to make the following points:

a. India plans to liberalize its import control policies and its internal price, marketing and other business controls and to adjust its exchange rate and tax policies to support such liberalization. If assured of U.S. support, India is ready to work out the details of these measures with the World Bank and IMF and to take the necessary actions this spring.

b. In order to move rapidly toward self-sufficiency in food production, India will follow through on emphasizing agricultural development, including making adequate fertilizers available to farmers and vigorously seeking to attract foreign private investment in fertilizer production.

c. India has already made a good start on family planning and will accelerate its efforts to control population growth.

3. We would recommend the following U.S. response:

We realize that a liberalized import program is possible only with assurances of substantial Consortium financial support. The U.S. will provide its share of that support in coordination with the World Bank and the rest of the Consortium. We suggest that India's key finance and planning people come to Washington as soon as possible to work out the details with the World Bank and the IMF. We will work with them and talk to our key consortium partners.

---

[1] Source: Johnson Library, National Security File, Country File, India, PM Gandhi Visit Papers, 3/27–30/66. Confidential.

[2] The strategy and talking points papers, prepared as background for the Gandhi visit, are ibid.

[Our financial support for FY 1967 would involve about $385 million A.I.D. loans and $50 million EX-IM loans—the same levels as pledged in recent years—and $35 million as the U.S. share of readjustment of Indian debt. In future years A.I.D. loans may go up a bit, if Indian performance warrants.][3]

4. While the foregoing would be the key points in any bargain, the following points are also important:

a. We are disappointed that India has not moved forcefully enough to attract foreign private investment in fertilizer production. No special financial backing is needed for action on this score; and the vigor of Indian performance in seeking fertilizer investments will certainly affect our judgment as to how vigorously we can expect India to move on other economic fronts. We do not expect India to accept unreasonable terms from foreign investors, but we do expect India to make every effort to tap this large resource of financing and know-how. We are not doctrinaire on the public sector-private sector question; we have financed public sector plants and may well again, but only after we are sure India is doing all it can to capitalize on available private resources.

b. Congratulations might be offered on India's promising initiation of its family planning program.

Dean Rusk

---

[3] Brackets in the source text.

305. Telegram From the Embassy in Pakistan to the Department of State[1]

Karachi, March 26, 1966, 1600Z.

1805. Dept pass White House. Ref: Embtel 1804[2] and Deptel 1340.[3] Conversation with President Ayub re Indo–Pak relations.

1. In same March 24 conversation with President Ayub, I took up, pursuant to reftel, recent unsatisfactory development of Indo–Pak relations. I discussed forthcoming Washington visit Indira Gandhi, confirming that we would seek to promote acceptance by GOI of need for peaceful solution of all essential Indo–Pak issues as a necessary contribution to security of India as well as Pakistan. We were urging both parties to seek constructive atmosphere for continuation of bilateral ministerial talks, with recognition that each side would have to show some flexibility in every round if momentum was to be maintained. Urged Paks to seek progress on all fronts where essential interests of two countries touched, including trade, arms limitation, refugees, and territorial disputes, as well as Kashmir. I said that, in all candor, we felt disappointment that Paks apparently had shown needlessly rigid and negative attitude in recent first round of Ministerial talks at Rawalpindi, particularly citing apparent GOP unwillingness to negotiate restoration of various services and relationships interrupted by war.

2. President Ayub denied that Pakistan had been the cantankerous party in the talks. He said the Indian refusal to engage in even prelimi-

---

[1] Source: National Archives and Records Administration, RG 59, Central Files 1964–66, POL INDIA–PAK. Secret; Immediate. Repeated to Rawalpindi, New Delhi, and London. Passed to the White House at 1:45 a.m.

[2] In telegram 1804 from Karachi, March 26, McConaughy reported on that part of his conversation with Ayub on March 24 that dealt with an impending visit to Pakistan by a delegation of senior Chinese officials. McConaughy expressed regret at what he described as the unfortunate aspects of the visit, particularly in that it coincided with Prime Minister Gandhi's visit to the United States. Ayub represented the visit as the logical outgrowth of his visit to China in 1965, and part of the process of normalizing Pakistan's relationship with a potentially dangerous neighbor. He noted that the Chinese trip had been planned well in advance of the announcement of the Gandhi visit. (Ibid., POL 7 CHICOM)

[3] Telegram 1340 to Karachi, March 10, expressed the Department's concern about the outcome of the first round of Ministerial talks between Indian and Pakistani officals growing out of the Tashkent agreement. The talks took place in Rawalpindi March 1–2 and did not proceed beyond the Pakistani insistence on a full discussion of the Kashmir dispute. The Indians refused to discuss the substance of the issue and the talks broke off. The Department instructed the Embassy to make the point to the Government of Pakistan that if the Tashkent process was to lead to peace, each side must approach the bargaining table with some flexibility, and not allow its tactics to become a stumbling block that threatened the entire process. (Ibid., POL INDIA–PAK)

nary discussion of mechanism for later Kashmir negotiations had torpedoed the Ministerial talks, not any Pak intransigence. He condemned Indian self righteousness in pretending they were the wholly reasonable party and Pak stubborness entirely responsible for lack of accomplishment. President said GOP would not refuse to consider restoration remaining usual operating connections between the two countries, but he felt that restoration was relatively small matter which could not provide any basic solutions and that routine questions should not be mixed at Ministerial level with the matters which did fundamentally matter, which he identified as settlement of basic dispute (Kashmir) and arrangement to live with each other in peace and security without threat posed by excessive military capability. President said Indians were as delinquent on issue of arms build-up as on Kashmir. Pakistan could have no feeling of confidence or security about the future in such circumstances and would have to condition its posture on that of India, which was unyielding as to Kashmir and threatening as to arms build-up. Ayub felt that we were over-estimating the importance of day to day relationships such as trade, bilateral air services, communications and travel between the two countries. He said that existence of these facilities had not prevented the outbreak of war in 1965 and restoration would not solve the current deep difficulties in Indo–Pak relations. He was not sure that a normalization of ordinary relationships would be timely or appropriate at this juncture. The tragic losses inflicted during the war were only a few months back and people could not and should not forget them and go about ordinary day to day business as though nothing had occurred.

3. I said we felt that it was right and proper to go about the healing process as rapidly as possible, beginning with modest measures if that was the best that could be done at the moment. We thought that restoration of any and all normal ties and reestablishment of the fullest possible intercourse between the two counties would accelerate the healing process, tending to lower the barriers of hate and misunderstanding, some of which grew out of ignorance and disruption of normal links.

4. I told President we thought it was possible that GOI might be prevailed upon in a later bilateral session to agree to discussion its national security requirements as to Kashmir, and to consider the Pak view of its national security requirements as affected by the Kashmir issue. I suggested that in a pre-election year, this might be about all the Indians could realistically be expected to do and it might be the forerunner of a broader joint exploration of other aspects of the Kashmir issue later on. I suggested that a joint Indo–Pak examination of defense requirements and ceilings might also be undertaken. I probed to see how receptive the President might be to this approach.

5. Ayub was less than lukewarm to this suggestion, indicating that while national security of Kashmir was of major importance, it could hardly be separated out from other aspects of the issue, all factors being closely inter-related. He was not willing to say that he saw promise in this approach but he indicated he would think about it. I told him that some such exchange could be construed by each side as the "visible effort" that needed to be made by each party. I told Ayub we were watching closely the performance of each side, and as Vice President Humphrey had intimated, the willingness of both India and Pakistan to make accommodations in the spirit of Tashkent would have a bearing on our ability to reestablish our economic and technical assistance programs on a fuller scale. Tactics by either side incompatible with their responsibility for maintenance of peace and negotiating progress would militate against our ability to restore our aid programs in the way that we would like to.

6. President Ayub expressed GOP willingness to do full part to contribute to peace and maintain progress along lines Tashkent declaration but asserted corresponding Indian willingness was so far missing. He cited alarming scale of Indian rearmament, including recent acquisition large number Communist tanks, not suitable for use in Himalayas, and certainly intended only for employment against Pakistan. He referred to swollen Indian military budget and large diversion of Indian resources to arms purchases, facilitated by foreign economic assistance. He said Indians were well aware of domestic political difficulties posed for him after Tashkent by their talk about Kashmir and their commitment to arms race. Nevertheless, he was willing to continue ministerial talks and expected to schedule another round some time after Washington talks.

7. Ayub said Indians were greatly encouraged to follow aggressive course by sympathetic and generous attitude they are encountering from aid-giving counties. He said Indians felt they were riding high and "Indian balloon needs to be pricked." He said this could only be done by one of the major foreign powers, obviously referring to US and Soviet Union. He said Indians would come down to a realistic negotiating basis very quickly if only one of their great power friends would prick the balloon.

8. I told President we were fully aware that Indira Gandhi talks in Washington would have bearing on Pak interests as well as Indian, and we expected to have something to communicate about the outcome of the talks later on. President affirmed his particular interest.

McConaughy

306. Memorandum From the President's Deputy Special Assistant for National Security Affairs (Komer) to President Johnson[1]

Washington, March 27, 1966, 3 p.m.

Final Notes on Gandhi Visit. This is my valedictory as your Mid-East hand, but fittingly so because I don't think there's been a more important *substantive* meeting since Kennedy met Khrushchev in Vienna. The flow of people and memos citing this as a historic opportunity to settle on a new course with 500 million Asians suggests that this is more than a Chet Bowles promotion.

Moreover, I think that we finally have the Indians where you've wanted them ever since last April—with the slate wiped clean of previous commitments and India coming to us asking for a new relationship on the terms we want. Circumstances helped (famine and the Pak/Indian war), but seldom has a visit been more carefully prepared, nor the Indians forced more skillfully to come to us (note how little press backlash about US pressure tactics—when it's been just that for almost a full year).

The proof is that India is now talking positively about buying all the World Bank reforms; its line is now that it *wants* to go boldly in this direction, but can only do so if the consortium will help pay the inevitable cost. This is precisely where we wanted to maneuver the Indians—into saying they'll help themselves if we'll respond in turn.

The Nature of the Economic Bargain. This is aptly described in Dean Rusk's memo[2] at Tab A. I'd only add two points. First, I'd break away from the old *pledge* figure (435) and talk *privately* in terms of around a half billion dollars from all US sources—it sounds more generous while the arithmetic is the same—plus at least half a billion in food. This is over $1 billion—a generous response in anyone's league.

Second, I'd stress that this can be a *self-enforcing bargain*—in two critical respects. Most of our dollar loan aid plus debt rollover (and the consortium's as well) can be tied directly to import liberalization, as we did with the Paks. If India doesn't liberalize to our taste, it just doesn't get the dough. Similarly, you have already proved how our holding back on PL–480 can force India into revolutionizing its agriculture. Once the famine is licked, I'm for continuing to ride PL–480 with a short rein—it will be painful but productive. If these points don't add up to requiring self-help, I'll eat them.

---

[1] Source: Johnson Library, National Security File, Country File, India, PM Gandhi Visit Papers, 3/27–30/66. Confidential.

[2] Document 304.

That tough-minded *George Woods and the World Bank* are with us is reassuring. You've read the VP's report on his talk with Woods,[3] and at Tab B is Gaud's memo[4] on his views. Woods talks about "double or nothing" being the only sensible course on India aid, and it's true that on any per capita basis our aid to India is very low (less than a dollar per person ex-food), while India's own self-help contribution to its development is higher than that of almost any other LDC (twice that of Pakistan).

But as I explained the other day I think we can get real results in the next two years without going to Congress for a lot more money. *Debt rollover* is the backdoor financing key, and it's the same as aid. If India takes off as a result of our strategy, then we'll have a solid case to take to the Hill.

Political Conditions. We're not going to get as much from Indira on the political side, especially on Vietnam and Pakistan. She's new at being PM, scared of the coming elections, and lacking as yet in the confidence in her own position which would let her talk big. But we have a strong ally moving India toward us on these matters—Mao Tse-tung. Just as he forced the Soviets in our direction, he's done the same with India. So the Indians are increasingly serious about China, and all we need do is nudge this trend along.

On *Pakistan*, the one thing that really gravels Indians—Dinesh Singh and B. K. Nehru are prime examples—is that we "equate" 500 million Indians with 100 million Paks. If you would just tell Mrs. Gandhi that we can count, it would reassure her enough about our basic intentions, that she'd stop any carping about our aid to the Paks.

If she raises *military aid*, I'd short circuit this by saying that it's far less important than economic issues and we plan no decisions for a while, beyond perhaps allowing *sales*. Nor do we intend to re-arm Pakistan to where it can threaten India. In fact, we favor both countries putting a ceiling on military outlays; we don't intend to finance an arms race indirectly via US economic aid. But India too must realize that forcing the Pak military to depend on Peking for arms would be folly from India's own viewpoint.

She's also ready to say in spades that India has no intention of taking over Pakistan. Get her to say so, and you can use it as powerful reassurance to Ayub. It's the best you can get him, because she simply

---

[3] Not found.

[4] In a March 25 memorandum to the President, Gaud summarized World Bank views on India. He noted that if the Indian Government agreed to liberalize import controls, proceed vigorously with the new agricultural program, and keep up the momentum on population control, the World Bank would lend full support. (Johnson Library, National Security File, Country File, India, PM Gandhi Visit Papers, 3/27–30/66)

can't give anything now on Kashmir (and it only creates useless trouble for us to try).

Emergency food is the trickiest problem. What's needed is both to give her reasonable confidence that Uncle Sam will help generously and to keep enough pressure on her to seek other help and push on with reforms. The best bet is to say you'll put it up to the Congress. But you should know that all your Executive Branch advisers are deeply worried lest Hill debate get out of hand, and create a sour aftermath to a successful visit. Even the sober Ellsworth Bunker reminded me of the 1951 experience when Mr. Truman went up for a $190 million food loan to India; Bunker said the violent criticisms voiced in the debate set back our political relations far more than the food helped fill bellies. Ellender talking about sacred cows certainly won't help. You might ask Bunker about this.

You're the judge on Congress. I'd only urge that we design the message to create the least flap and give you the most room to maneuver. This means avoiding tight formulas which box us in, since the worst of the famine is yet to come. Also, what happens if you ask for only 3.5 million tons of wheat/milo, and then want to authorize another tranche around September when Congress is out of session?

Visit tactics. All those who know her urge you see her alone first, put her at her ease, and then trigger her spiel by asking where she sees India going.

If she says the right things, you have a whole range of responses. I'd be *generous but general,* telling her that if she does what she says we'll respond in kind. We'll abide by what India works out with the World Bank (up to around a half billion—including debt rollover and EXIM).

The experts say there's a strong case for *moving quickly* in May/ June, before India gets caught up in its election campaign and Indira loses room to maneuver. So you might urge that *she send her economics ministers pronto to talk with the World Bank.*

I'm also sending up State's briefing books, which have all the facts and background. You might want to reread the *Strategy* and *Talking* papers. I'll have an agenda for tomorrow's 10 a.m. pre-briefing session, at which we can clear up any last-minute points.

R.W. Komer

307. Summary Record of Conversation Between President Johnson and Prime Minister Gandhi[1]

Washington, March 28, 1966.

At approximately 12:35 p.m., the President and Mrs. Gandhi returned to the assembled group of advisers[2] in the Cabinet Room and reported briefly on their talks as follows:

The President said they had had a pleasant and most helpful exchange of views and they discovered they had many things in common. In fact, he hadn't realized how numerous these were. Prime Minister Gandhi faced some of the same problems which he had after the death of President Kennedy—demanding internal problems, difficult international issues, and elections. He said that they had been talking about her needs and our needs. She had told him of the agricultural agreements that had been reached between Minister Subramaniam and Secretary Freeman, and mentioned the fact that they had to go before her Parliament. He had told her that we had a similar requirement and were taking a message to Congress. We wanted to be able to say to the IBRD as soon as it gets other countries pulled together that we will do what we can. He said he wanted to ask Congress to support this and also the food program. He hoped a message would go up this week, then the Prime Minister can have her economists meet with George Woods to work out the details. He and the Prime Minister had not gone into detail.

The President said they also talked of the need for peace in that part of the world and said they understood each other and agreed to do everything possible to be helpful to each other. He then asked Mrs. Gandhi if she had anything to add.

Prime Minister Gandhi said the President had summed up things very well. They had indeed found they had much in common. The President had said how worried he is about the problem of getting support from people who are opposed to paying out large sums of aid to India. She had replied that India can be a great force for peace and

---

[1] Source: Johnson Library, National Security File, Country File, India, Vol. VII, Memos & Miscellaneous, 1–8/66. Secret. No drafting information appears on the record, but an April 5 note from Saunders to Bromley Smith indicates that Handley and Laise prepared it. (Ibid.) Prime Minister Gandhi visited the United States March 27–April 1; she was in Washington March 28–29.

[2] The group included Rusk, Hare, Bowles, Valenti, Komer, Handley, Ambassador Nehru, L.K. Jha, C.S. Jha, and Minister of Embassy P.K. Banerjee. A memorandum of their conversation before Johnson and Gandhi joined them, which was devoted almost entirely to Vietnam, is in National Archives and Records Administration, RG 59, Central Files 1964–66, POL 27 VIET S.

that India is, of course, grateful for the material help of the United States, but it needs even more the understanding of the United States. She said she told the President he is admired in India because India sees him as someone trying to translate the ideals of the United States' Constitution into reality; he was someone who believed in it sincerely. Asia is in an explosive state; now that independence has been gained, people have come to expect something more than the past has offered; new horizons have opened up which are still beyond their reach. They are impatient for change to take place. Mrs. Gandhi said she told the President India is in a position to use its aid much better; it is making an effort to be better organized and more efficient, drawing in younger, more energetic groups. She said India had a record of achievement, but mistakes had also been made. One of the significant facts was that among the educated group of people—and although this was still small, it was an increasing group in India—they had achieved a fair amount of excellence. These people are now being called upon to get greater efficiency and more movement. She believed that between the United States and India there could be a good working partnership.

The President said he had also asked the Prime Minister to give us from time to time recommendations for procedures to get peace in Vietnam and the rest of the world. He said he had made no request; he had expressed appreciation for their ICC service and hoped somehow we could find the answer to peace. He had told Mrs. Gandhi that we are generally agreed that we want to do what we can and what the Congress will let us do to support George Woods' efforts in India's economic development. He thought that arrangements could best be made between technicians. The President then said that they had gone on to discuss generally the question of family planning, agriculture and peace planning, but no details. He said he thought it had been a very enjoyable talk.[3]

The Secretary reported briefly on the exchange of views that had taken place among the advisers during the course of the Presidential

---

[3] In a telephone conversation later in the afternoon with Rusk, Johnson observed that he had not gotten much out of his conversation with Gandhi. "I just sat there and listened to what I consider to be a rather limited and superficial discussion of problems." He could discern no sense of urgency in Gandhi's description of the problems facing her nation. Rusk said that he had had a similar experience during a luncheon conversation with the Prime Minister. Both Johnson and Rusk noted that Gandhi had taken no initiative in the discussions. Johnson said that when he suggested that famine in India might lead to widespread starvation and death Gandhi had responded that no one would die from the famine. She indicated that malnutrition was the worst specter faced by the Indian people. In Johnson's view, Gandhi had not made a strong case for U.S. assistance. (Johnson Library, Recordings and Transcripts, Recording of Telephone Conversation Between President Johnson and Secretary Rusk, March 28, 1966, 4:44 p.m., Tape F66.13, Side A, PNO 232)

talks. He noted that he thought the discussion had been beneficial and that it had been possible to go into detail on our attitudes toward peaceful settlement in Southeast Asia and how this might be brought about. The Indian delegation had also reported on the worsening of the Tashkent atmosphere. The Secretary thought we had laid groundwork for further useful discussions and we had, therefore, employed our time very usefully.

Prime Minister Gandhi intervened with one further thought which she termed her pet idea: she mentioned that on the subject of achieving better Indo-Pak relations she had been wondering if there could be some major economic project, like the Mekong, which might help to improve relations. She thought common involvement in a constructive effort might contribute to lessening of fears and tensions. The Secretary observed in a sense this is the way the Saar problem was solved. Ambassador Bowles noted that harnessing the Brahmaputra was just such a project. The Secretary said we would be happy to hear more about how this might be brought about. The President closed the conversation by saying we would leave it to our imaginative Ambassador Bowles to come up with ideas.

308.   Memorandum of Conversation[1]

Washington, March 29, 1966, 10 a.m.

SUBJECT

    Indo-U.S. Talks: Food, Disarmament and Nuclear Policy

PARTICIPANTS

    India
    Prime Minister Gandhi
    His Excellency B.K. Nehru, Ambassador of India
    Mr. L.K. Jha, Secretary to the Prime Minister
    Mr. C.S. Jha, Foreign Secretary, Ministry of External Affairs
    Mr. P.N. Haksar, Deputy High Commissioner of India to the U.K.
    Dr. P.K. Banerjee, Minister, Embassy of India
    Mr. Ashoke Chib, First Secretary (Political), Embassy of India
    Mr. Krishna Rao, Treaties Division, Ministry of External Affairs

---

[1] Source: National Archives and Records Administration, RG 59, Central Files 1964–66, POL INDIA–US. Secret. Drafted by Laise on March 31, and approved in S on April 4. The meeting took place at the Blair House guest residence. The time of the meeting is taken from Rusk's Appointment Book. (Johnson Library)

United States
The Secretary
Ambassador Raymond A. Hare, Assistant Secretary, Bureau of Near Eastern and
    South Asian Affairs
Ambassador Chester Bowles, Ambassador to India
Miss Carol C. Laise, Director, Office of South Asian Affairs

The Secretary opened the discussions by asking what would be the principal questions Prime Minister Gandhi would face in Parliament about her visit here. Mrs. Gandhi said it would be, "have I sold the country?" The Secretary noted the dilemma concerning the public presentation on food. It shouldn't be such as to frighten people in India, but on the other hand the need must be seen to be real in the United States. Mrs. Gandhi observed that the need is real. The Secretary said things may be said here that will be uncomfortable for India. Mrs. Gandhi suggested that the subject might be treated as a localized matter. Mr. L.K. Jha observed that this won't help either of us. He said that the disturbance on the Indian side arose out of the Pope's public appeal, which led to the belief that there were dead bodies in the streets. He thought the case should be presented as this being the year in which famine was averted; it was a natural calamity and we are all doing our best to meet it. Ambassador Nehru commented that this was too much an understatement; if we don't get the wheat, there will be a famine. The situation in the United States is that to get a response, the need must be somewhat overplayed. Mr. C.S. Jha said "let's emphasize the positive." The Secretary replied that maybe emphasis should be on prevention rather than cure. He thought it would be helpful to publicize information on the caloric content of the diet, i.e. there is a need for more food because people are eating more.

The Secretary said there are three central questions in Congress: (a) the character of the need; (b) what is India doing for itself? and (c) what are other countries doing? He noted, for example, that although Canada had increased its contribution to India, it had also announced another million and one-half ton wheat sale to China. This somewhat negated the effect of their gift to India. However, he recognizes that there was nothing India could really do about this. Prime Minister Gandhi observed that surely if China is being helped this is all the more reason to give wheat to India. The Secretary acknowledged this was a good answer, but the question in Congress will be why isn't Canada, a fellow member of the Commonwealth, as good a friend of India as the United States.

The Secretary then asked if food came up in Paris. The Prime Minister replied that it was mentioned. The French had said that they would look into it. They had noted that it is a long time since the last harvest and the stocks have already been committed to sales; August is the harvest month.

The Secretary changed the subject to the Geneva Conference and disarmament. He said that following the test ban treaty we had been in frequent contact with the U.S.S.R. in an effort to go forward. It was heavy weather but we had been beginning to turn down military budgets by mutual example; Vietnam led this to be put aside. Nevertheless, there should be a chance to move ahead on nonproliferation. As a matter of policy, we and the U.S.S.R. agreed on limitation, but things are snagged at the moment on what they say about nuclear cooperation in NATO. If they would concentrate on nonproliferation, we could satisfy them. Nothing contemplated in NATO is as potentially dangerous as the existing arrangements. The Soviets have understandable nervousness as long as they don't know what the West intends to do with its nuclear forces. They don't like NATO or anything that ties the U.S. to Europe. They don't like any arrangements to share in NATO or to enhance Germany. On this we can't help them. Maybe the importance of this would wither away in time. If we think solely of proliferation, we can help meet that problem. As regards the non-nuclear powers, we are interested in the Indian views.

Prime Minister Gandhi said that India is interested in nonproliferation; "we are sure we don't want to go into the manufacture of nuclear devices or bombs." Mr. L.K. Jha asked whether part of the Russian anxiety wasn't the fear of the German finger on the trigger. The Secretary replied that if there were any reality underlying this fear, we would be on the Russian side. We are utterly opposed to sharing nuclear weapons. The prime example of this is France. We paid a price for our policy; we can't let anyone help fire U.S. nuclear weapons. From the point of view of the U.S.S.R., that should be satisfactory. It isn't because they don't know the details of any arrangements we might reach, but it is simply because we haven't worked out the details ourselves. The Secretary noted that conventional forces could set off the chain of nuclear war, so the problem of a German finger on the trigger is not a real argument. We need Russian help if we are to avoid development of the wrong kind of a nationalist Germany. The Secretary said that he felt the Russians believed our statements were made in good faith but they think we are wrong about the steps that will follow. He hasn't abandoned hope. Mr. Krishna Rao asked about the recent amendments which we had submitted in Geneva and wondered if this would help solve the problem. The Secretary said the amendments would help close the gap, although the Russians had rejected them. Nevertheless, Gromyko had indicated interest, which would perhaps be picked up after the Moscow meeting of the Communist Party. The Secretary went on to note that we are also concerned about lesser countries. These countries seem to show great concern about disarmament of the major powers, but show little concern about it as it affects themselves. When the UN was debating disarmament, 70 countries were lining up to buy arms from us. This extends to Latin America, Africa and the Middle East. We hope to have movement on the nuclear free zone in Africa and Latin America and have talked to Russia about it in the Near East. We feel strongly that the Geneva efforts should continue and we should gnaw away at the problem.

Ambassador Nehru asked the Secretary to develop his ideas about security of the non-nuclear states. The Secretary said this is a complex question for all of us. It is not inconceivable that the U.S.S.R. and the U.S. might act jointly, but there is no disposition on the part of the U.S.S.R. to talk. This raises the question as to whether the U.S. and U.K. should take on the obligation and, if so, wouldn't this require some sort of an alliance, and does India want an alliance? Mr. C.S. Jha replied, "No"; Prime Minister Shastri had gone into all this and the Indian Government had concluded that the U.S.-U.K. guarantee would not work. The Soviet position is that the guarantee should involve all powers and it doesn't want to indicate willingness to use nuclear weapons against nuclear powers. A general prohibition is what they want. The difficulties with the treaty as Mr. Jha saw it are (1) differences among the nuclear powers, and (2) the attitude of the non-nuclear powers. India goes along with the position of the Eight. The two main points here are (a) the question of balance of obligations. What this would be is a matter for negotiation; India doesn't know. Cutting down stockpiles raises a question of inspection and the U.S.S.R. is not prepared for this; (b) some kind of assurances to the non-nuclear powers. As far as India is concerned, it is China that looms large. Some solution should be found. The Soviets have come out with the prohibition on the use of nuclear weapons and the proposal that no nuclear power will use the nuclear weapons first. He understood that this gives the U.S. problems. The Secretary observed that if we could get balanced reduction of armaments, we could compromise on the first strike problem. Mr. Jha asked what was the significance of the latest U.S.S.R. statement that they are prepared to consider IAEA safeguards? The Secretary responded that the U.S.S.R. has moved on the question of safeguards and this is possibly of significance, particularly in the Near East. This could reduce fear in the area. Maybe we could move here in lieu of the nonproliferation treaty. We had the impression at the time of the signing of the nuclear test ban treaty that the U.S.S.R. had China very much on its mind. In regard to the issue of fingers on the trigger, we have pointed out to the Russians that on the two key arrangements there are safeguards. The more fingers that are added, the greater will be the inertia and, therefore, the U.S.S.R. has less cause for worry. Mr. Jha observed that when the Indians were in the U.S.S.R., Kosygin had said that Germany is a more serious problem for the U.S.S.R. than Vietnam is for the U.S.

Mr. Jha said he had one point to raise on the question of a matter of balance. The Indian Government (i.e., the Ministry of External Affairs) had been giving thought to this; they did not insist on the assumption of too much of an obligation by the nuclear powers; all they sought was a beginning. He asked what the U.S. reaction would be to a nonproliferation treaty that does not spell out the balance but contains a promise by the nuclear powers that they would come to some arrangement to cut back. After two years there would be a review and if the nuclear powers had not been able to make progress toward balanced reduction, the treaty would fall to the ground. The Secretary assured the Indians that the U.S. was interested in nuclear disarmament, reduction in production of fissionable materials, etc. The snag is inspection; the U.S. is very forthcoming on this. One of the difficulties, however, is that inspection asks the Soviets for a unilateral concession. The U.S. is an open society, the U.S.S.R. is not. It is not just a question of trust and faith; if we are to prevent deep fear in this country, we have to be able to say we know whether the Soviets are keeping their word. We need inspection, therefore, from a military and a psychological point of view. A good many things can be done without intrusion on the U.S.S.R. On the comprehensive test ban, we have sought to deal with it as a matter, not of policy, but a technical problem of detectability. If we could conduct joint inspections, progress would be possible, but the U.S.S.R. objects on political grounds.

Mr. L.K. Jha said he wished to reinforce what the Prime Minister had said about India not going nuclear. He warned, however, that one factor should be mentioned: over the last three or four years there has been public questioning of this policy. Unless there is greater speed in negotiations, India as a have-not nation may find the situation getting out of hand politically. The possibilities of preserving balance should not get so much weight so long as the direction is right. The Secretary noted it would be sometime yet before there is any significant deployment of Chinese weapons; we have good evidence of this. We would like to move on general disarmament. The U.S. has spent $850 billion in defense since 1947; such sums could be more constructively used for other purposes. The same is also true of the Soviets. Both of us are anxious to disarm.

Mr. C.S. Jha referred to the Secretary's mention of the smaller countries acquiring arms. He noted that this worries India when it sees Saudi Arabia buying $300 million worth from Britain, and the U.S. also selling large quantities to Saudi Arabia and to Iran. India has heard and fears some of this may eventually be passed on to Pakistan. They know Pakistan has put out tenders in the world market. Chinese arms are going into Pakistan. All this creates problems and he hoped the arms-selling countries would develop some standards and norms other than profit. Otherwise instability will grow. There was then a brief exchange on controls which the U.S. exercised over transfer of our matériel to third parties, with the Secretary noting that such control exists on military aid but it is more difficult to exercise the same control over sales.

Mr. C.S. Jha asked whether we had made any assessment of recent U.S.S.R. statements and whether we saw a trend back to Stalinism developing in the Twenty-third Congress. The Secretary said we had not had a chance to analyze Brezhnev's speech, but he would try to get a preliminary assessment to convey to Mr. Jha that evening at dinner. However, the U.S. impression is that the Soviet policy will continue to move in a moderate direction. The reaons are pressures in Eastern Europe and internal problems of allocation of resources. Mr. Jha again rephrased the question by asking whether we would think this new Soviet pronouncement might result in a shift toward China. The Secretary replied that it was much too soon to say. Undoubtedly there are different elements functioning in the Kremlin; however, most of our Eastern European contacts indicate that the dynamics are such that it would be impossible for the U.S.S.R. to move toward Peiping by acceding to Peiping's views on doctrine. We may be in a rather dangerous period as far as China is concerned.

Prime Minister Gandhi asked what we saw as the major external problem of China. The Secretary thought it was their failures in Indonesia, Africa and at Algiers. Mrs. Gandhi wondered whether they looked at them as failures. The Secretary replied that they must be aware of the facts. In addition they see U.S. power committed to Southeast Asia. They must realize their policy is unprofitable, although they keep saying revolution is inevitable.

The Secretary raised the question of Peiping's UN membership and said the question is what is to be done about Formosa; beyond the Assembly is the Security Council. Many countries which are supporting the admission of Communist China would not expel Formosa. One of the questions is whether other Asians want Peiping to exercise the Asian veto in the Security Council. Mr. C.S. Jha replied that the CPR wielding the veto is not a comfortable prospect. Nevertheless, he felt that it would be easier to tame the Chinese in the UN than outside. He thought they would not be likely to have things their own way. In addition he said there is a case for the reconstitution of the Security Council and he thought India had a good case for a seat as one of the permanent members. Ambassador Nehru asked the Secretary why in view of the enlargement that is taking place in the Security Council the number of vetoing countries couldn't be enlarged? The Secretary replied that if this were done we would hope that there would be a reduction in the veto power.

309. Summary Record of Conversation Between President Johnson and Prime Minister Gandhi[1]

Washington, March 29, 1966.

Following the five o'clock meeting between the President and Prime Minister Gandhi, the President reported to the assembled group of advisers[2] in the Cabinet Room that he had gone over the food message to Congress with the Prime Minister. He indicated that he would review the message with the Senate leaders at 6:15 p.m. that day and with the House leaders the next day. He hoped to get it approved for submission by noon on the thirtieth. The President reported that the Prime Minister had read the message but had not commented on it. He asked Ambassador Nehru to review it.

The President, the Prime Minister and the advisers reviewed and approved the draft Communiqué,[3] with the addition of a paragraph in which Mrs. Gandhi formally extended an invitation to President Johnson to visit India. The President thanked Mrs. Gandhi for her invitation and expressed the hope that conditions here and in India would permit acceptance of it.[4]

---

[1] Source: Johnson Library, National Security File, Country File, India, Vol. VII, Memos and Miscellaneous, 1–8/66. Secret. No drafting information appears on the record, but according to an April 5 memorandum from Saunders to Bromley Smith, Handley and Laise prepared it. (Ibid.)

[2] For a list of the advisers involved, see footnote 2, Document 307.

[3] For text of the joint communiqué issued on March 29, see Department of State Bulletin, April 18, 1966, pp. 603–604.

[4] On March 31 Johnson sent a personal message to Gandhi in New York expressing his pleasure in their conversations in Washington and adding "how much we value your friendship." (Telegram 2324 to USUN; National Archives and Records Administration, RG 59, Central Files 1964–66, POL 7 INDIA)

310. Memorandum From the President's Special Assistant (Komer) to President Johnson[1]

Washington, March 29, 1966, 10:15 p.m.

George Woods is eager to start working over the Indians on a self-help and aid package as soon as he knows where we stand. Therefore, if you are satisfied as a result of your talks that Mrs. Gandhi intends to adopt the major economic reforms that we and the World Bank have been seeking, the best way to move ahead might be for me to tell Woods on your behalf. State, AID and I suggest we tell him the following, which protects us with plenty of caveats:

1. You have concluded from your talks that she is prepared to liberalize India's import control policies as well as internal price, marketing and other business controls which have been inhibiting economic growth, provided the necessary financial support is forthcoming. Additionally, she is prepared to adjust exchange rates and tax policies to support liberalization.

2. In order to move more rapidly toward self-sufficiency in food production, Mrs. Gandhi has assured you that India will follow through in emphasizing agricultural development, making adequate fertilizer available to the farmers and vigorously seeking to attract foreign private investment in fertilizer production.

3. She has also spoken to you of India's efforts in the family planning field and of her determination to accelerate these programs.

4. In turn you have indicated to Mrs. Gandhi your realization that the liberalization program described above can be implemented only with assurances of substantial financial support. You are prepared to say informally that if India actually takes the necessary steps to the satisfaction of the World Bank and the other consortium donors (including ourselves) we are prepared to help provide needed support for such a program in phase with its execution, subject of course to Congressional appropriations.

5. You currently believe that we will be able to support the Indian economic reform program in FY 1967 with about $385 million of AID loans (if Congress meets your aid request) and $50 million of EX-IM Bank loans—the same levels as pledged in recent years. Of this amount you are prepared to extend an increased proportion in the form of program lending. You also understand that the economic reform program will require a debt rescheduling in which the U.S. will take

[1] Source: Johnson Library, National Security File, Memos to the President, Walt W. Rostow, Vol. I, 4/2–5/26/66. Confidential.

its share—approximately $30 million for FY 67 (much less than the Europeans). All this is, of course, conditioned not only on India's actually following through with its reform program, but also on the willingness of other consortium members to bear an appropriate portion of the burden.

6. Finally, in view of our continuing wish to provide our support in coordination with the World Bank and the other members of the Indian Consortium, you have suggested that Mrs. Gandhi have her senior financial and planning officials come to Washington as soon as possible in order to work out an agreement with the World Bank and the IMF regarding the details of the economic reform program and the financial backstopping arrangements. We expect the Bank to take the lead in coordinating the necessary consultations between India and the governments of the consortium members.

This package is the real McCoy—much more so than emergency food. If George Woods, with our backing can drive the tough bargain which he contemplates, we will have accomplished more in moving India via our aid leverage than in the last six years combined. And we will have done so at little if any greater out-of-pocket cost than in 1963 or 1964. I stress again that this is a *self-enforcing bargain*—if India doesn't make the reforms we and the Bank want, it doesn't get most of the dough. This puts the choice squarely up to them. I may be over-enthusiastic, but I see this as a major foreign policy stroke, affecting 500 million people in the largest country in the Free World.[2]

R.W. Komer

Tell Woods

See me[3]

---

[2] A handwritten postscript by Komer reads: "We'd keep all of this very quiet for the time being, leaving it to the Indians to make the first move."
[3] Johnson checked this option.

311. Memorandum From Secretary of State Rusk to President Johnson[1]

Washington, March 30, 1966.

SUBJECT

Food Assistance for India

I strongly endorse the amounts and types of food assistance to India listed in your message to the Congress.[2] India has an urgent need for this help. It needs it soon: the next allocation of food grains should be made by April 15 at the latest if the pipeline is to be kept full.

While the Indian Government is confident that it can stay on top of a very difficult supply problem if the rate of grain arrivals is maintained, delays will cause an acute crisis for Mrs. Gandhi. Her Government has not yet consolidated its position and is beset by serious internal problems, only one of which is food. Inability of the Indian Government to feed its people (especially in Kerala and the major cities such as Calcutta where rioting has already occurred) would undermine the Government's ability to maintain order during the coming election year. This could deter Mrs. Gandhi from moving ahead to solve her longer-run economic problems.

Dean Rusk

---

[1] Source: Johnson Library, National Security File, Country File, India, India's Food Problem, Vol. I. No classification marking. A handwritten "L" on the memorandum indicates that it was seen by the President.

[2] President Johnson's March 30 message to Congress addressed the pressing problem of drought and famine in India. Johnson noted that the United States had supplied 6 million tons of food grain to India during the previous fiscal year and 6.5 million tons during the current fiscal year. India needed an estimated 6 or 7 million tons of grain to meet its minimal requirements through December 1966. Johnson proposed that the United States provide 3.5 million tons of that total, with the remainder to be provided by other contributing nations. For text of the message to Congress, see Department of State *Bulletin*, April 18, 1966, pp 605–607.

312.   Circular Telegram From the Department of State to All Embassies and Legations[1]

Washington, March 30, 1966, 3:52 p.m.

1894. From Secretary to Ambassador. You should expeditiously bring to the attention of host government, at level and in manner you deem most effective, the message by President Johnson on Food for India conveyed on wireless file today. If you judge host government has capacity to provide food or money to buy food, you should urge it to respond generously and quickly to the great humanitarian needs in India resulting from severe drought conditions.

Rusk

---

[1] Source: National Archives and Records Administration, RG 59, Central Files 1964–66, SOC 10 INDIA. Limited Official Use. Drafted by Deputy Executive Secretary John P. Walsh, cleared by Handley and Schneider, and approved by Rusk. A draft copy of this telegram bears a handwritten marginal notation by President Johnson which reads: "Good—ask for and have assembled replies from all countries for me to see." (Johnson Library, National Security File, Country File, India, India's Food Problem, Vol. I)

---

313.   Memorandum From the President's Special Assistant (Rostow) to President Johnson[1]

Washington, April 3, 1966, 5 p.m.

We now have first-round *reactions to your food message,* which our ambassadors have delivered in almost every foreign capital. A spate of local holidays has prevented a number of governments from responding yet, but we have enough answers to form a clear pattern. The sampling you asked to see is attached.[2]

The most striking aspect of these answers is how many countries are themselves on the emergency list. They draw a graphic picture of the world's food problem!

Nevertheless your message has been well received. Even some of the marginally poor nations want at least to send India token help. A

---

[1] Source: Johnson Library, National Security File, NSC History, Indian Famine, August 1966–February 1967, Vol. I. Confidential.

[2] Not printed.

number of the wealthier ones are cranking up more substantial responses, and some that have already given are considering more.[3]

To capitalize on this momentum, I have asked *State to organize our follow-up.* We don't want any potential donors to slip off the hook. We also need to get the Indians involved in this follow-up. The big danger is that they will sit back and relax, figuring that we have now assumed leadership—something we had insisted they do.

It will still be an uphill job to get others to match our 3.5 million tons of grain, though we may well get more than equivalent dollar value (about $210 million) in other commodities and services.

I will report again later when results are firmer.[4]

Walt

---

[3] Rostow added a handwritten marginal notation at the end of the memorandum that reads: "5 considering, 12 giving, 8 token."

[4] President Johnson's handwritten notation on the memorandum reads: "Walt see me and get Nehru in at once." At an April 5 meeting at the White House, at which the President, the Vice President, Rusk, McNamara, Rostow, and General Taylor were the principal participants, the issue of food for India was discussed. President Johnson instructed Rusk to meet with Ambassador Nehru and "put the heat on" for help from other countries. (Johnson Library, Office of the President File, Valenti, Jack, Meeting Notes (Typed) 12/21/65–4/6/66) Johnson put pressure on Nehru personally in a telephone conversation on April 5. He ran through the U.S. survey of potential contributors and suggested that Nehru work with Rusk in a joint effort to solicit additional support. (Ibid., Recordings and Transcripts, Recording of Telephone Conversation Between President Johnson and Ambassador Nehru, April 5, 1966, 4:59 p.m., Tape F66.14, Side A, PNO 1)

---

314. Telegram From the Department of State to the Embassy in India[1]

~

Washington, April 6, 1966, 5:13 p.m.

1895. Following summary of conversation April 5, 1966 between Secretary and Indian Ambassador B.K. Nehru FYI and Noforn. Handley also present. It is uncleared and subject to amendment upon review.

1. Following successful Senate Agriculture Committee Hearing on President's program for food to India at which Secretary Rusk and

---

[1] Source: National Archives and Records Administration, RG 59, Central Files 1964–66, SOC 10 INDIA. Confidential. Drafted and approved by Handley. Cleared by Staff Assistant Peter T. Higgins in AF. Repeated to Lagos.

Secretary of Agriculture Freeman testified,[2] Secretary called in Indian Ambassador B.K. Nehru. Secretary gave him run-down on Agriculture Committee Hearing and told him that Committee had unanimously reported out House Resolution and that Senator Ellender expected that final Senate action will be taken April 6. Secretary then went on to say that at request of President, he wanted to mention one matter of some urgency. Secretary said that at the public hearing before the Senate Agriculture Committee and privately he had been pressed hard by a number of Senators as to what other countries were doing to contribute to India. He expressed his and the President's particular interest in learning from India exactly what it had done to contact other countries and what results had been obtained.

2. The Secretary said that on our part, we had contacted 113 countries and of these 23 had offered contributions, 13 were considering offers, 33 had given no firm response, and 44 were unable to contribute. The Secretary said that total contributions from other countries up to now could be valued at about $150 million.

3. Among the countries contacted was Nigeria which had expressed interest in providing some aid although not very much. Moreover, the Nigerians did not want to appear to be intruding in other people's business and would also have some practical problems regarding transportation. But, the Secretary added, our report from Nigeria indicated that the GON had not taken any initiative because they had received no request from the GOI.

4. The Secretary went on to emphasize that even though token contributions might not be important to the GOI they were of the utmost importance to us since it was essential to the American Congress and American people that our contribution, although large, be part of a large scale international effort. The Secretary pointed out that since India was suffering from the results of an extraordinary drought, he did not think that Indian initiatives to secure contributions from other countries would be a derogation of Indian prestige. Some of the countries contributing might feel that in another year under similar conditions they too could turn to India and other countries for help without loss of prestige.

5. He urged on the Ambassador the importance of the closest possible contact between India and the US in sharing information and a "box-score" as to which countries might be able to help and on follow-up. He said we would furnish the Indian Embassy a list of all

---

[2] A transcript of the hearing before the Senate Committee on Agriculture and Forestry on April 5 is ibid., AID (US) 15 INDIA.

countries we had contacted and the reactions we had received. He urged on the Ambassador the need to reciprocate.

6. Amb. Nehru expressed appreciation for the role played by the USG, particularly the President's, in this effort and indicated gratification over the action of the House and Senate Agriculture Committee. He said that his Embassy would furnish the Dept. all available information on GOI's contacts with other countries and agreed on the importance of keeping closely in touch with each other.

7. Amb. Nehru went on to say that there was a recent report from the Ministry of Food and Agriculture indicating that overall wastage of grains produced in India was now estimated at between 14–16% instead of an alleged 50% as had been given wide publicity. This included losses in the field, from threshing, from rodents, etc. He added that losses in government facilities were less than 1%.

8. The Secretary gave Amb. Nehru the text of the Resolution approved by the Senate Agriculture Committee which included the two amendments adopted by the House. One of these amendments the Secretary pointed out, dealt with the need to make sure that food was being given to the destitute. The Secretary suggested that it would be very important for the Embassy and the GOI to give publicity to measures being taken to make sure that food was being made available not only to those who could afford to buy it but also to the very poor. Ambassador Nehru agreed and said he would follow through on this point.

Rusk

---

315. Telegram From the Department of State to the Embassy in India[1]

Washington, April 6, 1966, 6:29 p.m.

1897. As results Gandhi visit begin stand out in clearer perspective, following points worth passing for your guidance:

---

[1] Source: National Archives and Records Administration, RG 59, Central Files 1964–66, POL 7 INDIA. Confidential; Limdis. Drafted by Handley and Farr in AID/NESA, cleared by Rostow and Saunders, and approved by Handley. A note by Saunders on a draft of this telegram indicates that it was based on a conversation between President Johnson and Rostow on April 3. (Johnson Library, National Security File, NSC Histories, Indian Famine, August 1966–February 1967, Vol. II)

1. While atmosphere very cordial, no concrete agreements reached. This not unexpected. However, difficult to get any sure sense exactly what Indians intend to do. While Gandhi party appeared understand nature economic deal we and IBRD have in mind, we still not sure they intend to go through with it. Decisions left to be made in Delhi.

2. In this connection, we see danger euphoria of visit, President's strong message to Congress and resumption consortium activity will lull Indians back into secure feeling US ready to shoulder Indian burdens. Crucial this not happen because, while we do not intend to abandon Indians, we mean what we say about self-help. We want to bring Indians back to earth gently but quickly.

3. Indian performance will be main criterion for our next moves. For instance, we expect Indians move quickly to accept Woods' invitation begin discussions with IBRD. We expect Indians begin hot pursuit fertilizer investors with propositions carefully prepared to be responsive to reasonable investor needs.

4. In short, next move up to Indians. Since it essential they realize this, suggest you make clear appropriate levels we consider ball now in Indian court. We have promised understanding help when they move. They should expect little more from us until they do.

Rusk

---

316.   Memorandum From the President's Special Assistant (Rostow) to President Johnson[1]

Washington, April 14, 1966, 12:45 p.m.

With the Gandhi visit behind us, it is time to begin shoring up the Pakistan side of our affairs in the subcontinent.

A first step is to tell Ayub what you said to Mrs. Gandhi about Indo-Pak relations and Kashmir, since we promised to keep him informed. Kashmir is still his chief concern, and he will be watching sharply for signs that we are favoring India. The attached letter[2] assures him that

---

[1] Source: Johnson Library, National Security File, Memos to the President, Walt W. Rostow, Aides File, Vol. I, April 1–30, 1966. Confidential. A handwritten note on the memorandum reads, "Rec'd Ranch 4–16–66, 5:00 p."

[2] Document 317.

you pressed Mrs. Gandhi on this subject as hard as you pressed him. While we cannot report any specific progress, it will reassure Ayub to know that you have not forgotten your promise to him to say the same hard things to the Indians that you said to him. It is also a chance to let him know gently that we are watching the Chicom visit.

I recommend you take an especially close look at the State Department text. Because most of your talk with Mrs. Gandhi was private, they were drafting partly in the dark. Knowing what you told both her and Ayub, you may want to put your personal stamp on this one. The only caution is that we do not want to say anything the Paks could leak to our disadvantage in India.

Secretary Rusk will soon be sending you recommendations for possible next steps with Pakistan on the economic side. Ayub's finance minister will be here next week for informal talks with the World Bank and AID. Ayub is still pressing for resumption of military aid, and we will have recommendations on that in a few weeks. But we are ignoring both the economic and military questions in this letter in order to preserve your flexibility, while still maintaining a little movement.

WR

317. Letter From President Johnson to President Ayub[1]

Washington, April 17, 1966.

Dear Mr. President:

Thank you for your letter of March first[2] and for the understanding it conveys of our effort in Vietnam. Vice President Humphrey has reportedly fully on his discussions with you.

I would like in this letter to share with you some of my views on the good talks I had with Prime Minister Gandhi. You may already have seen some of the public statements that Mrs. Gandhi and I made, but in the event you have not, I am asking Ambassador McConaughy to make a set available to you.

---

[1] Source: Johnson Library, National Security File, Head of State Correspondence File, Pakistan, Vol. 2, Pres. Ayub Correspondence, 1/1/66–12/25/67. No classification marking. The letter was transmitted to Pakistan in telegram 1475, April 17. (National Archives and Records Administration, RG 59, Central Files 1964–66, POL 27 VIET S)

[2] A copy of this letter, which deals with Vietnam, is ibid.

These statements I think provide a good summary of our talks, but I want to assure you personally that we discussed frankly the subjects which concern you most. I stressed to Mrs. Gandhi the importance we attach to the restoration of peace on the subcontinent and the continuation of the process of reconciliation begun at Tashkent. I explained to her the difficulty my government will have in providing sustained assistance unless we can be reasonably sure that India and Pakistan are now able to concentrate on peaceful development. I urged her to keep up the effort to resolve the underlying issues which divide India and Pakistan, including Kashmir.

I can report to you that I found Mrs. Gandhi to be firm in her commitment to carry out fully the Tashkent Declaration. At the same time, her views on relations with your country were moderate and constructive. She explained to me in complete candor the domestic political and economic problems she faces as her Government prepares for next year's elections. Both you and I have submitted ourselves and our Governments to the electorate in the recent past and I believe that you can appreciate, as I do, her very real problem in this regard.

I have read with concern of recent charges by both Pakistan and India that the other side is violating the Tashkent accord. I have also been troubled about the effect the visit of the Chinese Communist leaders might have on relations between the two great nations of the subcontinent. But I was heartened to read of the exchange of messages between you and Mrs. Gandhi as she returned to New Delhi from abroad. I earnestly hope that the moderation and keen sense of realism you both possess will keep alive the spirit of reconciliation so encouragingly begun at Tashkent.

Sincerely,

Lyndon B. Johnson

---

318.   Memorandum From the President's Special Assistant (Rostow) to President Johnson[1]

Washington, April 18, 1966, 4:30 p.m.

State of play in India and Pakistan. As soon as she returned to New Delhi, Mrs. Gandhi scheduled her Planning Minister (Asoka Mehta)

---

[1] Source: Johnson Library, National Security File, Country File, India, Vol. VII, Cables, 1/66–8/66. Confidential.

to fly to Washington today to begin talks with the World Bank this week.[2] By coincidence, Ayub's Finance Minister (Shoaib) arrives today for similar talks.[3]

The difference between these two missions is that the Indians are working from your assurance to Mrs. Gandhi that if they meet the Bank's terms, we will help. The Pakistanis are still waiting to find out where they stand. Secretary Rusk will have recommendations on next aid steps for Pakistan in the next day or two, and we may suggest that you see Shoaib for a few moments to pass your current feelings direct to Ayub.

The stumbling block with Pakistan is more political than economic. Pakistan made its deal with the Bank two years ago. The problem is that, since Ayub's visit here, he has feted Liu Shao-chi, paraded Chicom military hardware, blocked any progress on non-Kashmir issues at the India-Pak ministerial meeting, failed to reopen our closed facilities and permitted some use of the US as a whipping boy in connection with the Chicom visit. On the other hand, Ayub himself has been quite restrained during the Chicom tour and is carefully sending Bhutto to both the CENTO and SEATO ministerial meetings (he missed last year). The question Secretary Rusk will be putting to you is whether you are willing anyway at least to spell out the economic and political terms of an aid deal or whether you feel Ayub's performance requires us to hold off on any offer now.

We are still a couple of weeks from having a recommendation for you on next steps on military aid. However, State and Defense are working on details, and we are already tying it in with the economic talks by trying to establish ceilings on defense expenditures.

Worldwide responses to your Indian food message are still coming in, and we will give you a more detailed report as soon as B.K. Nehru gives us a late reading on India's own approaches. In short, we now figure that other donors have come up with about $165 million in a variety of contributions—or within about 20% of matching the value of your 3.5 million ton offer ($210 million at world prices).

Walt

---

[2] Mehta visited Washington April 18–May 6.
[3] Shoaib visited Washington April 18–29.

319.   Memorandum of Conversation Between the President's Special Assistant (Rostow) and the Pakistani Finance Minister (Shoaib)[1]

Washington, April 19, 1966.

After I explained broadly our concerns about Tashkent and military expenditures, Shoaib made the following points.

1. He will take up with George Woods two multinational projects on which Pakistan is prepared to move now with India: the export of natural gas to India from the fields of West Pakistan; and the joint development and exploitation of the waters of the Ganges–Brahmaputra–Teesta rivers. Shoaib says that, in the past, the Indians were unwilling to become "dependent" on Pakistan gas. And they have also been unwilling to discuss the joint development of the river waters. He hopes George Woods can interest the Indians in proceeding on these two fronts quietly but promptly.[2]

2. He will also take up with George Woods a possible World Bank role as third party in India–Pak negotiations to limit over-all military expenditures between the two countries. He says Ayub is prepared to settle for Pakistan military expenditures between one-fourth and one-third of Indian military expenditures.[3] In any case, Shoaib has been financing the increase in Pak military expenditures by increased taxation and is determined to preserve the level of development expenditure in Pakistan, earning the additional foreign exchange necessary for additional military expenditures by a special export drive. But this assumes that the old economic aid level to Pakistan will be restored.

3. Shoaib says the biggest single thing that we could do to restore U.S.–Pak relations would be to finance the steel mill.[4] He will be seeing

---

[1] Source: Johnson Library, National Security File, Country File, Pakistan, Vol. VI, Cables, 1/66–9/66. Confidential.

[2] Rostow sent a copy of this memorandum of conversation to the President on April 19 with a covering note in which he stated that Shoaib's message was important if true. He noted that in the past Pakistan had insisted upon movement on the Kashmir problem before considering economic collaboration. Rostow suggested that George Woods of the World Bank be encouraged to follow up on the constructive moves Shoaib had indicated Pakistan was prepared to make and lean on the Indians to cooperate. (Ibid.)

[3] Shoaib discussed Pakistan's military budget with Secretary McNamara on April 22. In the course of the discussion, Shoaib pointed to Pakistan's pressing need for spare parts for U.S.-supplied aircraft and tanks. (Memorandum of conversation; Washington National Records Center, RG 330, OSD Files: FRC 77–0075, Memos of Conversations Between Sec McNamara and Heads of State (other than NATO))

[4] Shoaib also discussed financing for the Karachi steel mill with Under Secretary of State Mann on April 25 in the course of a wide-ranging discussion. (Telegram 1522 to Karachi, April 25; National Archives and Records Administration, RG 59, Central Files 1964–66, POL 7 PAK)

Harold Linder as well as Dave Bell on this. The management will be done by the National Steel Company of the U.S. The energy will come from natural gas. The raw material will be mainly U.S. scrap metal. National Steel, as well as Shoaib, believes it will be an efficient operation, making a profit.

WR

320. Editorial Note

On April 19, 1966, President Johnson signed into law House Joint Resolution 997, "To support United States participation in relieving victims of hunger in India and to enhance India's capacity to meet the nutritional needs of its people." Johnson noted that the legislation supported and endorsed his recent offer to enlarge food shipments to India to help offset the worst drought of the century. He called upon the governments of other countries to join in the effort to meet the disaster. For text of P.L. 89–406, issued as 80 Stat. 131, see *American Foreign Policy: Current Documents, 1966*, page 688.

321. Memorandum From the President's Special Assistant (Rostow) to President Johnson[1]

Washington, April 20, 1966, 11:15 a.m.

The *next step in shoring up the Pakistan side of our affairs in the subcontinent is to decide what kind of aid deal we offer.* You established common political ground with Mrs. Gandhi and told her we would help Indian development within our means if her planners would come to terms with the World Bank on economic policy. Ayub's political performance since he was here, while not all bad, leaves us uncertain as to whether we are on common ground. So it is harder to decide where to go on aid. But Finance Minister Shoaib is here talking with the Bank this week, and we must make at least a tentative decision.

---

[1] Source: Johnson Library, National Security File, Country File, Pakistan, Vol. VI, Memos, 1/66–9/66. Secret.

The *choice is between two courses,* which the attached paper from State[2] spells out in more detail:

1. Taking *a hard line,* we could promise Shoaib nothing. We could tell him that Pakistani political performance still does not justify the full-scale development aid that its economic performance could warrant. The Pakistanis have received Liu Shao-chi and, worse, substantial quantities of Chicom tanks and jet fighters. Although they agreed to troop withdrawal at Tashkent, they blocked further progress at the Indo-Pak ministerial meeting. The press still uses us as a whipping boy. The government still has not reopened our closed facilities. Until we see more compatible behavior, we can not move on any aid but a limited holding-operation.

2. *Meeting Ayub half-way,* we would accept a Pak-Chicom relationship on about the present plane, even including modest Chicom military aid. We would tell Shoaib (as State recommends in the attached memo) that we are ready to resume development aid through the World Bank consortium at about the FY 1965 level of $140 million in non-project loans *provided that Pakistan:* limits defense expenditures (we will ask the same of India), moves ahead with India, respects our Asian interests and cooperates with us to a reasonable extent and accepts World Bank terms.

The central issue is how you want to treat Ayub. Do you feel in the light of your talk with him that you must continue to stonewall to bring him around? Or do you feel that you have a satisfactory understanding with him on limiting his relationship with Communist China and promoting peace with India that permits you now to meet him halfway?

State's "Recommendation 1" provides an offer to meet Ayub halfway on grounds that, if we do nothing, Ayub will have no choice but to move closer to China. However, it spells out strong enough political conditions that Ayub would still have to accept that it does not get us back into full-scale aid until we hear from him. *Alternative* would be saying nothing now.

State's "Recommendation 2" offers a six-month PL 480 deal now. The *Alternative* would be more measured pace, promising to discuss a new deal when we have a clearer idea of requirements.

State's "Recommendation 3" is to say that, if all goes well, we would be ready to talk about project loans (and more PL 480) in December. The *alternative* is to leave this carrot for later.

---

[2] Reference is to an April 19 memorandum from George Ball to the President entitled "An Aid Deal for Pakistan." (Ibid., Memos to the President, Walt W. Rostow, Vol. I, 4/2–5/26/66)

My own feeling is that "Recommendation 1" gives us enough control to justify going that far now. It still keeps our aid in six-month slices. But I would prefer the alternatives to the other recommendations. I do not believe we ought to sacrifice the fruits of your painful but successful tough posture of the past year by rushing into new promises until we hear again from Ayub.[3]

Walt[4]

---

[3] There is no indication of a response from Johnson on the recommendations, but see Document 323.

[4] Harold Saunders signed for Rostow.

---

322. Minutes of Meeting of the 303 Committee

Washington, April 22, 1966.

[Source: Johnson Library, National Security File, Intelligence File, India's Unconventional Warfare Force. Secret; Eyes Only. Extract—2 pages of source text not declassified.]

---

323. Memorandum From the President's Special Assistant (Rostow) to Secretary of State Rusk[1]

Washington, April 23, 1966.

In the course of a review of various foreign policy problems before him, the President made the following decisions:

1. Project loans for India.[2] The President would prefer to see our resources at this time going to agriculture rather than to projects of

---

[1] Source: Johnson Library, National Security File, Files of Walt Rostow, Non-Vietnam, April–July 1966. Top Secret.

[2] In an April 13 memorandum to the President, Secretary Rusk recommended resuming negotiations on four AID project loans, which were suspended when a hold was placed on new economic commitments to India and Pakistan. The loans in question were to support minerals exploration and thermal power plant extensions at Dhuvaran and Durgapur, and to help finance the construction of the Beas Dam, designed to provide irrigation for 6.5 million acres in western Rajasthan. The total dollar amount was $85.3 million. (Ibid., Memos to the President, Walt W. Rostow, Vol. I, 4/2–5/26/66)

this type. He would wish to know to what extent the electric power projects would actually contribute to agriculture. If, however, it is impossible to transfer these resources more substantially towards use in support of agriculture, the President approves the opening of negotiations on these projects with the Indians at an early appropriate moment.

2. Pakistan aid strategy. The President first wishes to know if the proposed two-tranche project loan assumes that we will get from the Congress the full amount we have asked. What do we do if Congress cuts our request? Within the limits set by the answer to that question and by Pak compliance with conditions set forth in the memorandum to the President of April 19, recommendations 1 and 2 are approved.[3] The President reviewed the history of the steel mill[4] negotiations with Pakistan over recent years. He observed that we appear to have something like a moral obligation in this matter. If AID and the Export-Import Bank agree, they may proceed with this project loan.

[Here follow summaries of Presidential decisions unrelated to South Asia.]

W.W. Rostow[5]

---

[3] Concerning the recommendations in Under Secretary Ball's April 19 memorandum to the President, see Document 321. Recommendation 1 of Ball's memorandum proposed the resumption of AID commodity lending in 6-month segments beginning in July at the level needed to support Pakistan's development program and self-help policies. Ball proposed the resumption provided that the other members of the Pakistan consortium contributed a proportional share and that Pakistan limited its defense expenditures to agreed levels, made a conscientious effort to maintain the "spirit of Tashkent," demonstrated a satisfactory level of cooperation with the United States and appreciation of U.S. interests in Asia, and accepted the conditions advocated by the Pakistan consortium relating to import liberalization and Pakistan's development program. Recommendation 2 proposed negotiation a new P.L. 480 agreement, subject to the understanding that Pakistan would make a greater effort to promote agricultural output. (Ibid.)

[4] Reference is to the proposed steel mill to be built at Karachi.

[5] Printed from a copy that bears this typed signature.

324.   Memorandum From the President's Special Assistant
        (Rostow) to President Johnson[1]

Washington, April 25, 1966, 4:20 p.m.

SUBJECT

India/Pakistan Aid, Tashkent, and Military Expenditures

I should like you to know that I have told State and AID that they should not read your relatively benign attitude on the India/Pakistan aid papers the other day as a signal that you were not deeply concerned about Indian and Pakistan performance with respect to the normalization of their relations and the limitation of military expenditures.

I am a little concerned that unless we keep the heat on, they might begin to resume assistance without sufficiently concrete performance in these two respects.

The problem is to find specific actions which represent progress.

With respect to Tashkent and normalization, there are two things that might be done:

—a new round of ministerial meetings between India and Pakistan;
—the beginnings of some work on multi-national India/Pakistan projects which would commit them to interdependence. Pakistan gas to India and Indian coal shipments to Pakistan are one possibility; the Ganges–Brahmaputra–Teesta River complex is another.

With respect to military expenditures, we apparently reached an agreement with the Indians some time ago about their overall military budget. The Paks are trying to get agreement that they should position themselves at a level somewhere between 25% and 33% of the Indian expenditures; say, 2/7.

On the whole, this is probably too high for both of them. But, given the agreement, it may be difficult to get India down right away, which George Woods would like to do; but at the minimum, we should make sure that the present Indian (and Pak) military budget levels do not continue to rise, but level off.

Walt

Is this the right line to take?[2]

Is it wrong

See me

---

[1] Source: Johnson Library, National Security File, Country File, India, Vol. VII, Memos & Miscellaneous, 1–8/66. Secret.
[2] Johnson checked this option.

325. Telegram From the Department of State to the Embassy in India[1]

Washington, April 25, 1966, 9:06 p.m.

2041. 1. Indian Planning Minister Asoka Mehta met Secretary April 25. Following report based on uncleared memcon. It is FYI, Noforn and subject to amendment upon review.

2. Mehta said talks with IBRD have been going well so far. He would like to reach specific agreement regarding current Indian fiscal year and broad understanding regarding Indian needs for Fourth Five-Year Plan as a whole. Current economic situation very bad but program to liberalize imports could have very good effect and India needs to do it. GOI also anxious to finalize Fourth Plan. Secretary observed we were also in turbulent period in that annual Congressional review of aid program taking place.

3. Mehta described India's current economic difficulties. He noted that although production this year abnormally low, Indian economy has achieved diversification and degree of sophistication giving potential for very rapid growth. He observed India's current tribulations having salutary effects:

(a) Psychology of Indian farmer completely changed. He now wants fertilizer, electricity, improved seeds, etc. This has become political issue. Healthy development but can recoil on GOI if nothing done.

(b) Broad-based demand for family planning. Program going very well, proportionately even better in some states like Punjab than in Taiwan.

(c) Since foreign exchange pinch currently felt throughout country, general awareness has developed of need for intensified and sustained export drive. State Chief Ministers now display clear understanding this requirement and what it means to them directly.

(d) State Chief Ministers have recently unanimously decided raise taxes in this pre-election year rather than cut back development. As they are close to people, this is good sign of new commitment of ordinary Indians to concept of development and a most important psychological change.

4. Mehta recounted recent GOI measures to attract foreign private investment in fertilizers and observed that if his talks with Bank and Fund succeeded, GOI could "push this all the way." He also noted US companies being invited join Indians to set up distribution companies for improved seed.

---

[1] Source: National Archives and Records Administration, RG 59, Central Files 1964–66, POL 7 INDIA. Confidential. Drafted by Coon, cleared by Handley, and approved by Laise. Repeated to Karachi, London, and USUN.

5. Secretary referred to importance of peace in subcontinent and asked about prospects for Indo-Pakistani cooperation in development field. Mehta, noting that Prime Minister Gandhi expressed support for this concept to President, stated that GOI welcomed Indo-Pak economic development cooperation in principle and said he had so informed Woods of IBRD. In response Secretary's question, Mehta said he had not seen Pak MinFin Shoaib on present visit but would be happy to meet him.

6. Secretary asked whether GOI considering further ministerial talks pursuant Tashkent agreement. Mehta said first ministerial discussions not fruitful. Subsequent Chicom visit to Pakistan and Pakistan display Chinese arms not taken very well in India; Mehta implied it best to allow cooling off period prior starting new round of ministerial talks. Secretary noted importance of continuing to work on these problems. Mehta said it might be easier move first on economic side. Referring again to Indo-Pak political problems, Secretary drew analogy of US-Soviet problem over Berlin, noted he had spent two years discussing Berlin with Russians, and stressed that important thing was to keep communications going.

7. Secretary said basic question in US now regarding aid to subcontinent was peace.[2] Two questions important: chances for future hostilities and levels of defense expenditures by each government. Mehta said Indian public had completely accepted Tashkent and India's mood was opposite of belligerency. He noted that if one examined closely circumstances of last year's two hostilities, it clear Paks started each. Taking longer view, he noted that before Chicom attack only two per cent of India's national income devoted to defense. Need for new equipment for mountain fighting, road construction, etc. thereafter forced this percentage up but it has since remained fairly steady. As long as need to defend against China remains, India will not be able to reduce level of its defense expenditures very much. Mehta said, however, that if there should be some reduction in Pak defense outlay, India would be willing to match it. Such Indian reduction could not however be "mixed up" with need for defense against Chinese.

8. In response to Secretary's question on Binational Foundation,[3] Mehta said if we could agree on permanent Indian Chairman and

---

[2] Rostow also stressed the importance of a rapprochement between India and Pakistan in a conversation with Mehta on April 27. (Memorandum for the record, April 28; Johnson Library, National Security File, Country File, India, Mehta Visit, 4/19–28/66)

[3] Reference is to the binational educational and cultural foundation Bowles proposed in March 1964. As envisioned by Bowles, the foundation was to be funded by rupee bank deposits held by the United States in India as a result of funds generated from the repayment of development loans and P.L. 480 proceeds. (Letter from Bowles to Moyers, March 12, 1964; Johnson Library, National Security File, Country File, India, Exchanges with Bowles)

majority of Indian members, Indian public would find it easier to accept idea as genuinely Indian institution.

9. On internal stability, Mehta discounted severity of problems in Punjab and Naga-Mizo Hills. Punjab problems sorted out. Discussions with Nagas going well, and in any case troubles there should be seen in perspective (India successfully assimilating 25 million other tribals).

10. In conclusion, Mehta held forth prospect of very rapid progress in India, given sufficient external aid to permit the necessary structural changes.

11. At the Secretary's suggestion, Mehta agreed another meeting would be desirable shortly before his return to India, i.e., May 4.

Rusk

326. Memorandum From the President's Special Assistant (Komer) to President Johnson[1]

Washington, April 26, 1966, 6 p.m.

Who Welshed on Whom? I know you'll forgive an old Pakistani (who likes Ayub too) for saying that we need not feel we failed to honor any commitment to the Paks. The shoe is on the other foot.

As Dean Rusk said, we've insisted from the outset that CENTO and SEATO were anti-communist alliances. But the Paks have always regarded them as reinsurance against India, and tried to get them skewed around this way. True, our arming India against China helped push the Paks toward China, but our policy here was quite consistent with the anti-communist purpose of our alliances. Thus, while one can't *blame* the Paks for being unhappy with us, it isn't because we betrayed them; it is because their own policy of using us against India has failed. They know full well we didn't give them $800 million in arms to use against India (but they did).

Even so, we have built up Pakistan's own independent position and sinews—to the tune of almost $5 billion in support. We've protected Pakistan against India; we had more to do with stopping the war Ayub started than anyone else (just in time to save the Paks). In return, all

---

[1] Source: Johnson Library, National Security File, Memos to the President, Walt W. Rostow, Aides File, Vol. I, April 1–30, 1966. Secret. A copy was sent to Rostow.

we've gotten is a bit of quite valuable real estate (yet *four* of our installations are still closed).

So if there's any history of broken moral commitments, it's on the Pak side—not ours. There is even a good case that the Paks lied to us about China; for example, did Ayub tell you about getting MIGs and tanks? But this is history. Our need now is to keep the Paks from going off the deep end. But if we just return to business as usual (and let Bhutto convince Ayub again that he can have his cake and eat it too), we'll fall into the same trap all over again. We can't afford to let Ayub return to thinking that he can both get arms from China (and use China against India), while still getting massive economic aid from the US. The answer is to keep dangling the carrot (as you did last December), *but to give only enough to whet Pak appetites that they can get back into our good graces if they start playing ball.*[2]

Granted that this is risky, and that we might lose Ayub (our best hope). But it is less risky than past policy, because if Pakistan keeps sliding down the slippery slope we'll lose Ayub anyway and Pakistan to boot. This has been the trend, and it was only your *tough* policy since April 1965 that slowed it down. So I'm for impressing on Shoaib (our best friend and pipeline to Ayub) that sizeable US aid, including military, depends on Pakistan avoiding Chicom arms or ties. In fact, it might be most effective for you to call Shoaib in *privately* and tell him just this.[3]

R.W. Komer

---

[2] According to a memorandum for the record prepared by Rostow on April 26, President Johnson decided at a meeting with his principal advisers on April 25 to make U.S. assistance to Pakistan conditional on additional requirements. Johnson decided that some movement by Ayub on issues of importance to the United States, such as the closed installations, would be necessary before he would proceed with the loans cited in the April 23 memorandum from Rostow to Rusk (Document 323). The President also decided that an agreement to sell spare parts to Pakistan would be dependent upon an understanding on Pakistani limitations on military expenditures. (Johnson Library, National Security File, Country File, Vietnam, Vol. 50, Memos (A), 4/1–8/66)

[3] At the end of the memorandum Komer wrote: "I'll work with Walt Rostow on this matter." Johnson responded with a handwritten notation that reads: "Walt—bring this to McNamara's attention." Rostow sent a copy of Komer's memorandum to McNamara on April 27 with a covering note indicating that the President wanted him to read it. (Washington National Records Center, RG 330, OSD Files: FRC 70 A 4443, Pakistan 1966) In a May 2 memorandum from Townsend Hoopes to McNamara commenting on Komer's memorandum, Hoopes noted that he and John McNaughton proposed to make economic assistance to Pakistan dependent upon a Pakistani promise to stop the flow of military assistance from China, and to make military assistance dependent upon a promise to terminate Chinese assistance. (Ibid.) Hoopes stated in a May 2 memorandum to McNaughton that he had discussed their recommendations with McNamara, and McNamara had commented that he did not see how the United States could avoid providing essential spare parts to Pakistan unless it was prepared to see Pakistan ally itself completely with China. (Ibid., OASD/ISA Files: FRC 70 A 6648, 000.1–400)

327. Memorandum From the President's Special Assistant (Rostow) to President Johnson and Secretary of State Rusk[1]

Washington, April 27, 1966, 7 p.m.

SUBJECT

Conversation with Pakistan Minister of Finance Shoaib

The following points arose in my discussion with Shoaib this afternoon.

1. *U.S. Installations.* After Secretary Rusk raised this question[2] he sent an immediate urgent message to President Ayub, expressing his personal shock at the fact these installations were not yet open. He hopes for a reply before he leaves on Friday.

2. *Ganges–Brahmaputra–Teesta Project.* He has talked with Mehta as well as the IBRD about this. The World Bank is prepared to take the initiative. Woods may now be looking in England for a third man to work with the Paks and Indians. It could form an item on the agenda of the next Ministerial meeting between the Paks and Indians.

3. *Military Expenditures.* These will take time to reduce. What is needed now is an agreed level for Pak military expenditures in relation to the Indian program (which is fixed by agreement between the U.S. and U.K.). We talked of the possibilities of introducing a political and psychological environment in both countries which would permit their leaders to get away with reduced military budgets. One method would be agreement between the Pak and Indian military to thin out the forces on the Pakistan-Indian frontier and substitute for them paramilitary and border guard units. Shoaib says Pakistan has such forces. He does not believe the Indians now have them. In any case a discussion on this question might form an item for the next Ministerial meeting.

4. *Next Ministerial Meeting.* The Indians would have to agree, without in any way changing their public position on Kashmir, to let the Pakistani talk about Kashmir as an item on the agenda. It would be understood that at some agreed moment—perhaps after one morning on the subject—they would proceed to the other two items. They might be: military arrangements; the Ganges–Brahmaputra–Teesta joint project.

---

[1] Source: Johnson Library, National Security File, Country File, Pakistan, Vol. VI, Memos, 1/66–9/66. Secret.

[2] Shoaib met with Rusk on April 26. A report of that conversation was transmitted to Karachi in telegram 1536, April 26. (National Archives and Records Administration, RG 59, Central Files 1964–66, POL 7 PAK)

5. *China.* I raised with Shoaib the political difficulties we face with the Chinese equipment and the visits. I said that the problem was real and political even though the President had known in advance from President Ayub about them. He asked what, at the present stage, Pakistan should do about China. I said: "Nothing. Keep your relations with China as quiet and inactive as possible." I went on then to explain the depth of the problem of what appeared to be close China–Pakistan ties at a time when the Chinese Communists were actively encouraging Hanoi to continue a war in which our men were being killed every day. It was not impossible for us to understand Pak policy and the reasons for it. But the Pak Government must be conscious that every pro-China move they make throws a heavy political burden on our relations.

6. *A Story.* In great confidence Shoaib said he would tell me of a recent incident in the Pak Cabinet. Ayub said: "I want it understood that never again will we risk 100 million Pakistani for 5 million Kashmiri—never again."

I said that in equal confidence I would tell him that one of the reasons we were so anxious to end the war between India and Pakistan was we feared a military set-back for the Paks which might destroy the morale of the nation and Ayub. He said: "It was close—very close."

Walt

---

328. **Memorandum From Secretary of State Rusk to President Johnson**[1]

Washington, April 27, 1966.

SUBJECT

An Aid Deal for Pakistan

We have told Mrs. Gandhi that we are prepared to do our part in support of an economic reform program, which is now being worked out between Indian Planning Minister Mehta and the IBRD. We must urgently decide how to proceed with Pakistan. Our economic decisions for Pakistan are complicated, however, by political problems.

---

[1] Source: Johnson Library, National Security File, Memos to the President, Walt W. Rostow, Aides File, Vol. 1, April 1–30, 1966. Secret.

Pakistan's Finance Minister Shoaib leaves Washington April 29. I will be seeing him shortly before his departure and would like your permission to present to him the aid deal indicated below. Shoaib must present his budget in early June and therefore his economic policies must be set within the next six weeks. The IBRD has taken the lead in formally promoting the economic aspects of the aid package recommended below, and to support our effort to achieve an understanding on defense expenditures.

On the political side of the problem there are two basic policy questions: (1) Has President Ayub violated his understanding with you in acquiring Chinese Communist military equipment? (2) Has Ayub's political performance since his talks with you justified return to economically justifiable development lending?

Our recommendations assume that the steps so far taken do not represent a breach of your understanding and that we need to reach a combined economic-political bargain in order to help Ayub balance the pressures pushing him toward Communist China.

Recommendation 1: That you authorize us to describe to Pakistan's Finance Minister Shoaib the following bargain: We are ready to resume AID commodity lending in six-month slices beginning in July at a level needed to support Pakistan's development program and self-help policies (about the FY 1965 annual rate of $140 million) provided other members of the IBRD Consortium do their fair share and that Pakistan: (1) limits its defense expenditures to a level to be agreed upon (we will seek a comparable understanding with the Indians); (2) demonstrates a conscientious effort to maintain the "spirit of Tashkent" and to contain the intensity of India-Pakistan disputes; (3) demonstrates a satisfactory appreciation of basic U.S. interests in Asia; (4) maintains a satisfactory level of cooperation with the United States; and (5) accepts the economic conditions advocated by the IBRD Consortium to restore the funding level of its development program and restore and extend import liberalization. These conditions are defined more fully under U.S. requirements below.

Recommendation 2: That you authorize us to tell Shoaib that after we know the results of this spring's wheat harvest, we will agree to negotiate a PL–480 agreement and provide shipments for six months, subject to the understanding that the GOP would take further steps to promote greater agricultural output.

Recommendation 3: Within the context of these two decisions to resume aid, we recommend that you authorize us to tell Shoaib at the same time, as a further carrot to performance, that we will proceed to cost out the Karachi Steel Mill and, assuming that the political climate continues to be satisfactory and that costing problems prove to be manageable, we will look forward to a favorable decision within perhaps three to four months on a U.S. contribution of not over the $120 million level ($85 million EXIM Bank; $35 million AID) earlier contemplated.

We have concluded that there will be adequate funds to finance this package. The first slice of commodity aid can be financed from money already appropriated. The second slice is only about half of the new money for Pakistan included in your appropriation request for this year. The $35 million for the steel mill would leave a margin of $40 million.

Administrator Bell concurs; Secretary Freeman concurs in those recommendations concerning food aid.[2]

Background:

Pakistan-Communist Chinese Relationship: Fear plus India's attitude on Kashmir operate to pressure Pakistan to seek unqualified political support from a major power. The continuing Indian military build-up pressures Pakistan to seek suppliers of military hardware. The current power alignments and our withholding of MAP cast Communist China in both roles. Pakistan has recently received a number of MIG–19's (the best estimate cites 22 out of a reported planned total of 100) plus medium tanks from the Chicoms, who are offering substantial additional matériel. During the visit of China's President to Pakistan last week, the public theme of Chicom-Pak solidarity against India was intensified. But President Ayub appears to have resisted Chinese lures which would place impossible strains on Pak–U.S. ties. Ayub instructed Shoaib to tell us there has been no change whatsoever in the discussion and understandings which Ayub reached with you last December.

Ayub's Domestic Problems: In the present atmosphere, it is as impossible politically for Ayub to abandon his efforts to resolve the Kashmir dispute with India as it is for Indira Gandhi to make meaningful concessions to Ayub before the elections in 1967. If he is to retain his power base, which has been weakened by recent events, Ayub has few options. He must continue a hard line against India, maintain his ties with the Chicoms, and seek to replenish his military stockpile.

U.S. Requirements:

1. Our requirements are peace and stability in the subcontinent and Pakistan respect for basic U.S. interests in Asia; we assume that the Chinese objectives are the precise opposite. Therefore, we need to

---

[2] President Johnson approved each of the three recommendations. The decisions were conveyed to Shoaib before he left Washington, and a summary of the talks with Shoaib in which the understanding concerning economic assistance was outlined was transmitted to Karachi in telegram 1564, April 30. (National Archives and Records Administration, RG 59, Central Files 1964–66, POL 7 PAK)

have continuing evidence from Pakistan that in managing its relationship with China it is meeting our requirements; e.g.,

—*Maintenance Spirit of Tashkent:* Pakistan must make an evident effort to restrain the intensity of India-Pakistan disputes. It must be willing to continue the dialogue with India at whatever levels necessary to achieve progress in resolving "matters of direct concern to both countries." Pakistan must be willing to seek agreement on other outstanding issues, particularly those left over from last September's conflict, without conditioning settlement on progress on Kashmir, although we recognize that for its part, India must be willing to *discuss* Kashmir with Pakistan. Willingness to agree to cooperative joint India–Pakistan economic projects would be evidence of a desire by Pakistan, as India, to maintain the spirit of Tashkent.

—*Satisfactory Appreciation of Basic U.S. Interests in Asia:* This should be reflected in the Pakistani attitude on the U.S. effort in Vietnam, and in Pakistan's continued adherence to the SEATO and CENTO alliances.

—*Satisfactory Level of Cooperation with the U.S.:* This should be reflected in the continued operation of the U.S. special facilities at Peshawar, Pakistan (which represent [*less than 1 line of source text not declassified*] of our intelligence needs in Pakistan and which have continued in operation without interruption); in continuing a satisfactory pace of negotiations for the reopening of our two Atomic Energy Detection Stations [*1 line of source text not declassified*]; and in building a climate (e.g., through restraint and accuracy in public statements and the controlled press) which is conducive to friendly relations with the United States.

2. *Limit on Defense Expenditures:* We will require an understanding with Pakistan, as we also will with India, on limiting military expenditures. We have examined various approaches to this problem and have concluded that the most realistic way to proceed is to do what we can this year to reduce the level of defense expenditures in both countries, starting from bargaining positions outlined below. We recognize, however, that, given the current state of India–Pakistan relations and political pressures in both countries, immediate results will be limited. Therefore, we will put the weight of our effort on achieving a downward trend in defense spending over the years by conducting with India and Pakistan an annual review of defense expenditures in connection with consideration of our economic aid program. We would ask both countries to disclose to us, at least in general terms, what equipment they are receiving from Communist China and the Soviet Union. We would also say that if they are unable to sit down together to work out an agreed limitation on defense expenditures, we would hope at least that each would ensure that the other learns of the steps it is taking to cut back on defense spending so as to encourage reciprocal cuts.

For discussions with Pakistan and India this year, we would start from negotiating positions as follows:

Pakistan: For the fiscal year about to begin, Pakistan should limit its over-all defense expenditures to $3^1/2\%$ of estimated GNP for a total of about $400 million (expenditures during the past year total $525 million and constitute approximately 5.3% of GNP), and limit its foreign exchange expenditures to $84 million, this figure to include the value of aid from all sources (expenditures in foreign exchange during the past year have been about $147 million).

India: For the fiscal year just begun, India should reduce its actual defense expenditures from its budgeted level of $2081 million to no more than last year's actual expenditures ($1972 million or about $3^{1}/2$% of estimated GNP) and should reduce its foreign exchange expenditures to no more than $286 million, counting Soviet equipment on the basis of deliveries rather than payments. (The $286 million figure comes from a Memorandum of Understanding we negotiated with the Indians in 1964, but the Indians have been counting Soviet equipment, which they get on long-term rupee credit, on a payments basis. On this basis they are probably within the ceiling, but on a deliveries basis they will be $50–100 million over it. We propose a change since it is the deliveries of large quantities of Soviet equipment which is an important stimulus to the extensive Pakistani military procurement program.)

3. *Economic Requirements:* We will also seek a restoration by Pakistan of its previous priority and funding to economic development in FY 1967, agreement to a resumed and extended import liberalization program by July and steps to increase further agricultural production, including active pursuit of potential foreign investors in fertilizer production.

Dean Rusk

---

329. Memorandum for the Record[1]

Washington, April 27, 1966.

The President in a talk with Rusk and Rostow yesterday expressed these feelings about aid to India and Pakistan:

1. He recognizes it will be hard to get concrete progress on our two conditions—progress on Tashkent and defense ceilings—immediately. So he is willing to move ahead cautiously. We can maintain

---

[1] Source: Johnson Library, National Security File, NSC Histories, Indian Famine, August 1966–February 1967, Vol. II. Secret. Prepared by Saunders.

control by meting out our aid in two tranches and making it clear the second tranche—but not the first—will depend on concrete progress by late in the year on these two fronts. In Pakistan, he feels reopening our facilities is something the Paks could move on quickly.

2. He feels we have a moral commitment to finance the Karachi Steel Mill. However, he realizes we need a political context. So we might move ahead with recosting now but hold off final commitment.

3. He feels we are morally obligated to sell spare parts for military equipment we have already given Pakistan.

H.S.

---

330. **Memorandum From the Deputy Assistant Secretary of State for Near Eastern and South Asian Affairs (Handley) to Secretary of State Rusk**[1]

Washington, April 28, 1966.

SUBJECT

President's Talk with Pakistan Finance Minister Shoaib

Bill Gaud and I went to the White House this afternoon for the President's meeting with Finance Minister Shoaib who was accompanied by Ambassador Ahmed. The President first saw Shoaib with only Walt Rostow in attendance. This session lasted about one-half hour. Ambassador Ahmed, Bill Gaud and I joined the President, Shoaib and Walt Rostow for a brief round-up session in which the President made the following points:

1. He continued to have the greatest respect and regard for President Ayub and had asked Minister Shoaib to convey this message to him.

2. He understood Pakistan's difficulties but even with this understanding we too have our problems. He spoke particularly about problems caused by Pakistan's relations with China and India. He emphasized the problems of Pakistan/Chinese relations at a time when American boys were dying in Viet Nam and said that it would be very hard for Americans to understand the kind of relationship that seemed to be developing between the Pakistanis and Chinese when Pakistan

---

[1] Source: National Archives and Records Administration, RG 59, Central Files 1964–66, POL 7 PAK. Secret; Exdis.

is supposed to be an ally of the United States. We too might someday like to give the Chinese leaders a "parade" but we were a very long way from that at the moment. On India/Pak relations, he said we simply cannot finance a war between these two countries and he hoped that men in India and Pakistan would find some way to bring about a lasting peace. There might be joint economic projects, there might be a river to be dammed and shared, for example.

3. He said that Ayub knows how he feels about Kashmir and he doubted that he would be as restrained as Ayub has been about this matter. But settlement of these problems takes time and understanding.

4. He said that Secretary Rusk would be meeting with Mr. Shoaib tomorrow and would be discussing the conditions under which we would be prepared to help Pakistan to join with the World Bank in helping Pakistan in its economic programs. He looked with sympathy on the steel mill and felt that we should help Pakistan in this project.

5. The President spoke with some emotion about the closing down of the facilities. He said he didn't understand this because it seemed to him Ayub would have reopened them after their talks in December and he did not know why this problem had not been straightened out.

6. The President emphasized the importance of limiting military expenditures. He said that he talked with India's Prime Minister Gandhi and Food Minister Subramaniam about this problem. India cannot expect to continue to build MIGs and steel plants and at the same time continue to get help from us for food and economic programs. India has got to be able to feed itself and has to see this as its major priority.

7. The President concluded his summary by emphasizing his great admiration for President Ayub. He recalled that President Kennedy had told him that Ayub was a truly great statesman and he wanted Minister Shoaib to know that he has never met a head of state for whom he has greater respect and admiration than he has for Ayub. He knew Ayub's problems and he knows Pakistan's problems. Pakistan happened to choose some "lulus" for neighbors including Russia, China and Afghanistan, but that was not Pakistan's fault.

At the end of our meeting with the President Walt Rostow asked all of us to join him for a few minutes in his office where he emphasized to Minister Shoaib and Ambassador Ahmed the President's great concern about the facilities and the need to have them reopened. He said the President saw this as a possible breakdown between him and Ayub and he was troubled by it.[2] Minister Shoaib got the point but Ambassador Ahmed considerably less so.

---

[2] The Department emphasized this concern in telegram 499 to Rawalpindi, April 30. The telegram summarized the portion of Johnson's conversation with Shoaib that dealt with the closed installations. (Ibid., DEF 15 PAK–US)

Walt Rostow has told me that the President, in his initial talk with Minister Shoaib, followed the attached memorandum[3] he had prepared for the visit. You will see from this that the President has made it very clear to Shoaib what general understandings we must have before we can resume assistance to Pakistan. The President did not, however, get into the specifics of aid figures and military levels. It would seem, therefore, in your meeting with Shoaib that this is the subject on which you might wish to concentrate.

---

[3] Not attached. The April 28 briefing memorandum from Rostow to the President listed a number of suggested points the President might want to make in his meeting with Shoaib. (Johnson Library, National Security File, Memos to the President, Walt Rostow, Aides Files, Vol 1, April 1–30, 1966)

---

331.   Letter From President Ayub to President Johnson[1]

Saidu Sharif (Swat), May 1, 1966.

Dear Mr. President,

I thank you for your letter of April 17, 1966.[2]

I am grateful to you for informing me of your discussions with Prime Minister Mrs. Indira Gandhi and, in particular, for urging her to keep up the effort to resolve the underlying issues which divide India and Pakistan, including the dispute over the State of Jammu & Kashmir.

We in Pakistan earnestly desire to implement the Tashkent Declaration with a view to restoring peace in the sub-continent. However, unfortunately, we have not as yet seen any tangible signs, barring verbal professions of peace, of a like desire on the part of the Indian Government and its leaders. On the other hand, plans for a major expansion of the Indian armed forces continue to be implemented as a matter of great urgency. In the meantime, the Soviet Union has decided to resume supplies of heavy military equipment to India. All this is bound to increase tension in the sub-continent.

We are not oblivious of the domestic political and economic problems which the Indian Prime Minister faces in her country in prepara-

---

[1] Source: Johnson Library, National Security File, Head of State Correspondence File, Pakistan, Vol. 2, Pres. Ayub Correspondence, 1/1/66–12/25/67. No classification marking. The letter was sent from President Ayub's camp in Saidu Sharif (Swat), Pakistan.
[2] Document 317.

tion for the forthcoming general elections in India. However, I do not see why progress towards removing the underlying cause of the India-Pakistan conflict should adversely affect her election prospects. In my judgment it should strengthen her position.

You have expressed concern about the possible effect of the recent visit of the Chinese leaders to Pakistan on relations between Pakistan and India. As you know, Chairman Liu Shao-chi came to Pakistan in response to a long-standing invitation extended to him during my visit to China last year. I see no reason why this visit should come in the way of implementing the Tashkent Agreement by either country.

With warm personal regards,

Yours sincerely,

Mohammad Ayub Khan

---

332. Memorandum From the President's Special Assistant (Rostow) to President Johnson[1]

Washington, May 2, 1966, 9 a.m.

Ambassador Bowles has asked that two long cables of his be called to your personal attention. They are attached.[2] But let me try to summarize them.

First, he sees us entering a period of acute competition with the USSR for leverage in India.

Straws in the wind indicate that the Soviets are trying hard to undercut the new Indo-US cooperation generated by Mrs. Gandhi's visit here and subsequent progress on economic programs. The attack focuses on the wide range of economic reforms we and the World Bank are pressing, which the Soviets and their Indian backers see as a threat to socialism. While we have a lot of momentum, Soviet prestige is high, and many Indians are uncertain of our intentions, so the battle will not be one-sided.

---

[1] Source: Johnson Library, National Security File, Country File, India, Vol. VII, Memos & Miscellaneous, 1–8/66. Secret.

[2] Reference is to telegrams 2914 and 2931 from New Delhi, both April 28, which were retyped for the President and attached to this memorandum. Copies are also in National Archives and Records Administration, RG 59, Central Files 1964–66, DEF 19–8 US–INDIA and POL 1 INDIA–USSR, respectively.

Second, Bowles sees military aid as an important key to this struggle. This is where the USSR can put the heat on most effectively, and where the Indians are most sensitive. We think Soviet deliveries of military equipment have already slowed. Bowles fears resumption of US military aid to Pakistan would play right into Soviet hands.

Third, Bowles has long felt that our military aid to Pakistan has been a mistake. India is the big power in the subcontinent, and it opposes China. He feels we muffed our opportunity in 1963–64 after the Chicom invasion by not moving into India with large-scale military aid to pre-empt the Russians, and he feels our unwarranted concern for the Paks led us down that false path. He would like to see us resume limited military aid to India now, but says that resuming lethal aid to Pakistan—even spare parts—would undo all the progress we have made with India in the last few months. He would not resume any military aid to the Paks unless they renounce Chicom aid and cooperate in the defense of the subcontinent against China.

Our view is: 1, India is, indeed, more important than Pakistan. But 2. It is the Indian interest as well as ours to keep a Western option open to Ayub.

In this spirit Secretary Rusk is considering an instruction to Bowles (which he will check with us) suggesting he discuss frankly with the Indians how we keep that door open for Ayub without endangering India. The Indians have to recognize that our dilemma is theirs because they have a bigger stake than we do in where Ayub and Pakistan go.

Most of the town feels we will have to get back into at least selective sales to both sides when we have established a better political and economic framework, and agreed force levels.

We are not, therefore, asking you for a decision now. We will wish to make some concrete progress towards limiting military spending on both sides before we put some operational choices to you.

Walt

333.   Memorandum for the Record[1]

Washington, May 4, 1966.

SUBJECT

Summary Record of the President's Meeting with Indian Planning Minister
Asoka Mehta

The President met with Indian Planning Minister Asoka Mehta
and Ambassador B.K. Nehru this morning at 10:45 am. Messrs. Bell,
Rostow and Handley were present.

The President began the meeting by saying how delighted he was
to meet with Minister Mehta. He said that he had had good reports
about the Minister's discussions in Washington and invited him to tell
him about what was going on in India. The President added that there
was no area or people in which we were more interested or more
concerned about. He said that the recent visit of Prime Minister Gandhi
has been applauded in the United States and that we were inspired by
what India was doing.

Minister Mehta made the following points:

(1) He had just returned from Canada.

(2) While the United States was building a "Great Society", India
was embarked on a "Great Change." He spoke of the transformation of
the structure of production and of the changes taking place in the minds
of so many Indians. These changes kept people like him going. He spoke
at length about progress in agriculture, family planning, and about the
way younger people were coming to the fore. Farmers want to break
away from traditions, putting pressure on him for electricity, fertilizer
and irrigation. They are "clamoring for changes." He mentioned a recent
meeting to discuss how best to celebrate the 100th anniversary of Gandhi's birth and he said that it was virtually unanimous that the best monument to Gandhi would be a program for rural electrification. (The President recalled that a substantial part of the talk he had with Prime Minister
Nehru when he visited India concerned rural electrification.)

(3) He said that the supply of fertilizers is the chief subject the
Chief Ministers of the various Indian states discuss with him these
days. They say they cannot go back to their states without some commitment on this subject.

(4) In discussing family planning, he said that in 1965 there were
more vasectomies than in the preceding 10 years. In five states annual

---

[1] Source: Johnson Library, National Security File, Country File, India, Planning Minister Mehta Visit, 4/19–28/66. Secret. Drafted by Handley.

targets for "the loop" had been reached within five months. Twenty-nine million IUD's would be fitted within the next five years.

(5) There were subtle changes taking place in the Indian society which gave him great confidence. India is no longer an under-developed country, although still not fully developed. Within a few years India would be largely self-reliant in transportation and power. India's power program for the next five years was of the same order as that of Great Britain. At the end of the British rule in India, there were 35,000 miles of railroad but only 2.5 million kilowatts of power. In 1966–67 alone India was adding 2.5 to 3 million KVA's.

(6) When he told the Ministers of the various states that they had a choice between cutting development planning or raising taxes, they decided to raise taxes. India is collecting 8–900 million dollars additional taxes this year, the worst year in terms of economic and food problems in recent history.

The President then made the following points:

(1) We were in a heavy budget year. He had moved the budget from $99 billion to $113 billion this year and with add-ons by Congress, Viet Nam and other things it may well go over $120 billion.

(2) We had made no request of the Prime Minister or Subramaniam nor had we demanded conditions. He thought that relations between India and the United States had moved forward.

(3) Subramaniam had made quite an impression on Secretary Freeman, our technicians and on himself. He felt that India was genuinely trying to face up to its problems.

(4) He had seen in the newspapers that we had demanded concessions from the Prime Minister but this was not true. He had demanded no concessions but had listened to her and was inspired by what India was doing.

(5) Americans were pleased with Tashkent. He realized that this was an election year in India—we had ours too—and therefore, he could understand certain problems. But we longed for both India and Pakistan to "bend a little" so that their resources would not be used for war. He pointed out there will be difficulties but that Tashkent was an important achievement and should be carried forward.

(6) He hoped that Minister Mehta would go over economic criteria with George Woods, Secretary Rusk and AID Administrator Bell. While he could proceed on the general assumption that the Prime Minister and Subramaniam had demonstrated India's needs and what India was doing to cope with its problems, we had to take into account certain standards and criteria since we had commitments to others, e.g. Pakistan, the Western Hemisphere, etc.

(7) He thought that the talks with Subramaniam and the Prime Minister had fully justified his decision last year to wait until the Aid Bill was out of the way. There was now a complete atmosphere of trust and confidence between India and the United States.

(8) He was grateful to Prime Minister Shastri for his efforts with Kosygin to get Hanoi to the peace table. He had understood that Shastri's letter to him on this subject[2] was probably the last he had written to a chief of state.

(9) The visit of Prime Minister Gandhi was as perfect as any visit could be.

(10) Despite the advice of some of his best friends and advisers, he had sent a special message to Congress on the Indian food problem and other matters. Congress had come through with a unanimous vote of confidence and was now part of the program. He attributed much of this success to the effect of the visits of Food Minister Subramaniam and Prime Minister Gandhi.

(11) He had made no request of the Prime Minister or of India on Viet Nam. All we want is peace. If India can help, she will find that the United States and this administration would lean over backwards to achieve a lasting peace.

(12) He invited Minister Mehta to attend the Diplomatic Reception tonight and hoped that they would be able to find a few minutes to talk together. He then said that since he was already late for his appointment in Detroit for the funeral of Senator McNamara ("funerals don't wait even for Presidents of the United States"), he would like to see Minister Mehta again before he returned to India.

Following the President's departure the group adjourned to Mr. Rostow's office. A second meeting between the President and Minister Mehta was tentatively set up for 5:30 pm, May 5.[3] Minister Mehta in reviewing his schedule noted that he was having luncheon on the Hill tomorrow with Senator Morse and others.

In responding to a question from Mr. Bell and Mr. Rostow, Mr. Mehta said meetings at the Bank were going well, although they were only now getting to the heart of the problem. He said that the extent of India's economic liberalization depended on assistance that would be available from the Bank and other donors. He was seeing Mr. Woods this afternoon and hoped that they would come to grips with this problem at this meeting.

---

[2] Document 275.

[3] According to the President's Daily Diary, there was a meeting between President Johnson and Mehta at 2:54 p.m. on May 5. (Johnson Library) No other record of this meeting has been found.

334. Letter From the Ambassador to India (Bowles) to President Johnson[1]

New Delhi, May 5, 1966.

Dear Mr. President:

It occurred to me that you might like a first-hand report of the impact here in India of your discussions with Mrs. Gandhi. Here in brief is the way the situation has been shaping up:

1. Mrs. Gandhi and her close associates were enormously pleased with the visit. They returned with glowing accounts of your courtesy and understanding and the warm response of the American press, and people.

2. As a result the already significant group of U.S. supporters within the Government has been materially strengthened. With the exception of the Communists and Congress Party left-wingers there has also been a very warm response from the press, Parliamentarians and the public in general.

3. However, the Soviet Union, the Moscow branch of the Communist Party and the fellow travelers in the left wing of the Congress Party, recognizing the enormous political significance of the closer Indo–U.S. relationship, have launched a well organized and, I must admit, rather effective counter attack.

Led by Krishna Menon and K.D. Malavia in Parliament and strongly backed by such Soviet-financed publications as *Blitz*, *Link* and the *Patriot*, this group has been taking shrewd advantage of recent dope stories from Indian correspondents in the United States which have provided the Indian public with a dismally pessimistic view of the economic discussions now under way in Washington. The extreme left has also picked on the Indo-American Foundation as evidence of a new U.S. drive to "take over India" and warned that Mrs. Gandhi and her Government are prepared to sell India out to the United States.

4. However, Mrs. Gandhi, instead of ducking this political challenge as many feared she might do, has met the left wing attacks head on with a vigorous defense of India's relationship to the United States. In so doing, she has boldly staked her political future on a closer understanding with the United States and the Western powers and on the increased flow of foreign exchange which India requires to become economically self-sufficient within a ten or twelve year time span.

5. Mrs. Gandhi, recognizing that she has a hard political fight on her hands, is right now placing her highest priority on strengthening

---

[1] Source: Johnson Library, National Security File, Country File, India, Exchanges with Bowles (cont.). Secret.

her own position with the Indian people. Thus she is launched on a series of speaking appearances (which include as many as four appearances a day) plus regular radio talks over a nationwide network.

Some observers feel that she is paying too little attention to Parliament and the Congress Party political leadership. However, I believe that she has deliberately chosen to build her strength first of all with the people, so that she may have a solid public base for the political struggle with the leftist groups (supported on some issues by the extreme right) that lies ahead.

6. If Mrs. Gandhi and her associates stick with their present vigorous economic pragmatism and if, with the help of the World Bank, we are able to provide the support required to insure the necessary increase in India's economic growth, I believe that the positive economic and political results by the end of this year will be clearly evident.

For instance if the current negotiations with Asoka Mehta are successful and if the foreign exchange needed to increase India's imports of maintenance items is made available the rise of factory production and employment will be significant. At the same time as you know vigorous steps are being taken to provide more fertilizer, water, improved seeds, etc. With a fair break in the monsoon this is expected to provide a 20% to 25% increase in food grain production in this fiscal year.

7. If this economic breakthrough does in fact occur it will I believe open the doors to a *political* revolution in India which may have historic consequences for the entire free world.

Since Independence 19 years ago the old guard who lived and worked under Gandhi and Nehru has dominated the Congress Party. These men for the most part are conservative, unimaginative, uncreative and in many ways doctrinaire.

If Mrs. Gandhi's effort to create a new economic and political climate succeeds the door will be opened wide to men and women in their 30's, 40's and early 50's who have thus far largely been shut out of active participation in Indian public life.

8. In response to Mrs. Gandhi's "new look" and in anticipation of this political awakening younger people are already beginning to speak out with renewed vigor and confidence. Indeed some observers sense a growing feeling in the air which is reminiscent of the early days of the New Deal.

9. If this political and economic evolution does in fact take shape a new generation of Indians will be taking over following elections next February, a generation which is more pragmatic, flexible, imaginative and increasingly aware of India's potential role as a stabilizing force in Asia. The Cabinet which Mrs. Gandhi will select next February will reflect this political switch.

Thus, the decisions which we face in regard to India take on an important new dimension; i.e., it is not simply a matter of assuring a solvent Indian Government but of assuring the *political* success of the most promising government that India has had since Independence.

10. However, a note of caution is in order. There are at least three developments which could stand in the way of the development of which we have such high hopes:

A. A second drought comparable to the one last year. (As last year's was the worst in 65 years, it is unlikely to repeat itself this year.)

B. A failure on our part to understand the acute sensitivity of the Indian political situation in an election year. (The pressures we have brought to bear on the Indians up to now have been dramatically effective and we have largely won our objectives. Now as the political temp rises we must be careful not to expose Mrs. Gandhi to the leftist charge that her policies are directed by the U.S. Government in Washington and administered by the U.S. Embassy in Delhi.)

C. A direct Pak–Chinese attack on India or a major stirring up of the Himalayan border areas through "national liberation" techniques. (This is worrisome but not likely.)

We have come a very long way in our relationship with India since you and I reviewed the situation in your office in May of 1965. At that time I suggested that the U.S. may be forced within the next few years to choose between three possible courses of action in Asia:

a. We can get out of Asia leaving it to the tender mercies of the Chinese and/or Russians (which would be unthinkable);

b. We can continue to increase our military inputs in an effort to bolster our severely limited political power base (the Asian nations which are now directly associated with us total no more than 6% or 7% of the Asian people);

c. We can work tactfully and pragmatically for the development of an *indigenous Asian counterweight to China* (since India has more than half the non-communist population of Asia it must inevitably play a key role) which we can effectively support with a much smaller investment of American resources.

In the last year we have, I believe, made far greater progress towards this third choice than is generally recognized.

The tactics which you chose to clarify the political-economic issues here in India have been dramatically successful. India has responded and accepted in large measure the suggestions and conditions which we have advanced.

Most important of all Mrs. Gandhi has emerged as a politically competent, liberal-minded democratic leader who appears to recognize the communist-left as her primary domestic enemy and who understands the crucial importance of the U.S. in providing the support required to make India economically self-sufficient and politically viable.

If the situation develops as we hope it may, there is reason to expect that by Christmas a new economic and political dynamism will begin to be evident here in India that will be clearly recognizable at home. If this occurs we will have the beginning of a new power balance in Asia which well be greatly to our advantage and for which you can take great personal credit.[2]

With my warm regards,

Sincerely,

Chet Bowles

---

[2] Johnson added the following handwritten marginal notation to the letter: "Bill M—Give substance to Phil Potter." Reference is to Bill Moyers and Phillip Potter, the Washington bureau chief for the *Baltimore Sun*.

---

335. Memorandum From the President's Special Assistant (Rostow) to President Johnson[1]

Washington, May 7, 1966, 9 a.m.

Ambassador Ahmed of Pakistan gave me verbally the following message:

1. President Ayub had not understood in his conversations with you that he had undertaken a personal commitment to reopen the closed facilities.

2. Since this is your understanding, he will now give the matter his urgent personal attention.[2]

Walt

---

[1] Source: Johnson Library, National Security File, Memos to the President, Walt M. Rostow, Vol. 2, May 1–15, 1966. Confidential. A handwritten note on the memorandum reads, "Sent by wire to President."

[2] McConaughy met with Ayub on May 5 to discuss Shoaib's visit to Washington and the Ayub government's response to the conditions involved in reestablishing U.S. assistance to Pakistan. During the course of the conversation, Ayub took up the issue of the closed installations. He could not recall discussing the issue with Johnson in Washington, and he noted that newspaper leaks in U.S. papers concerning the stations complicated the issue in that the Soviet Union and China were more likely to react to the reopening of the stations. Nonetheless, Ayub said, a Foreign Office draft proposal for reopening would be given to McConaughy for comment within the week. (Telegram 2032 from Karachi, May 6; National Archives and Records Administration, RG 59, Central Files 1964–66, POL 15–1 PAK)

336.   Telegram From the Department of State to the Embassy in India[1]

Washington, May 8, 1966, 12:20 p.m.

2170. Joint State/AID message. Subject: Indian Planning Minister Mehta's Visit to Washington.

1. Mehta left Washington May 6 after two and a half weeks of discussions with IBRD and USG. In addition to talks with Bank and senior USG officials he met with President twice (May 4 and 5). Mehta expects be back in New Delhi by May 10.

2. *Mehta's Discussion with Bank.* We maintained stance throughout visit that Mehta was here to work out understanding with Bank and USG was not party these negotiations. Discussions were in fact Bank operation in which we did not participate. Following conclusion Mehta's talks with IBRD, he informed us that there had been general policy agreement between him and Bank. IBRD has confirmed this to us. We also understand that Mehta told Bank his position represented that of GOI. Bank informs us that extensive details remain to be worked out. We understand procedure will be for GOI to submit series of memoranda to Bank indicating Indian line of action with regard each of reforms.

3. While in Washington Mehta also had discussions with a variety of high-level USG officials. During these discussions Mehta generally stressed new GOI emphasis on agriculture and family planning, and good prospects for general economic breakthrough given adequate external support. (See Deptel 2041[2] for example of Mehta's general line.) For our part we attempted in these talks to clarify for Mehta the considerations we held of particular importance for establishing the general framework within which our aid relationship could develop along mutually beneficial lines given a satisfactory GOI understanding with the IBRD.

a. We made it clear to Mehta how we felt about the problem of peace on the subcontinent. We told him we wanted concrete evidence that India and Pakistan were gradually settling their differences, and in this connection asked whether a new round of ministerial talks might not produce enough agreement to improve climate. We told Mehta Shoaib felt the ball was in India's court. Mehta responded noncommittally.

---

[1] Source: National Archives and Records Administration, RG 59, Central Files 1964–66, POL 7 INDIA. Secret; Priority; Exdis. Drafted by Coon, cleared by Macomber and Rostow, and approved by Handley. Repeated to Karachi and Rawalpindi.

[2] Document 325.

b. We also told Mehta we wanted some sort of ceiling on domestic and foreign military spending and asked that accounting of Soviet aid be on delivery basis. As in conversation reported Deptel 2041, Mehta's response was generally to effect GOI was in fact holding line on defense budget, GOI loath to divert funds from development to military, etc. Indian reps claimed that only arms coming from Soviet Bloc are naval equipment and assistance in building aircraft factory.

4. Following conclusion discussion with Bank, Mehta raised subject of amounts of nonproject and project aid with USG officials. Stated Indians accepted Bank's analysis of $900 million requirement of nonproject aid for first year and required assurance that adequate support will be available throughout Fourth Five-Year Plan. Mehta also attached great importance to continuation project aid, noting that progress on projects had been virtually nil for past year. Apparently adding what he understood had been available from US for projects in FY 66 ($110 million) to amount he believed necessary from FY 67 ($150 million), he indicated need for coming year for $260 million in project aid from US.

Bank indicated optimism about raising $900 million non-project aid (including debt adjustment and including $100 million US nonproject loan now under negotiation.)

USG indicated imminent release of four loans already authorized. Also said that $260 million was substantially more than would be available for DL projects because 1) we are not recognizing the $110 million carryover and 2) we wished to give a sharp priority to program lending. We did mention the possibility of announcing the availability of a fixed amount of extended risk guarantees in support of private US project financing.

5. In concluding session with Mehta,[3] USG informed him that we aware of problems facing India, felt deeply about them, and wanted to do our part to support India's economic program. We said that the way GOI was approaching its problems meets our complete approval. We reminded Mehta of our inability commit our Congress and that what we could do depended on funds Congress made available. But we assured Mehta we recognized consequences of proposed Indian action and would do our part to best of our ability. We reemphasized importance we attach to peace on subcontinent and problem of military expenditures.

Comment: IBRD tells us informally that Indians have proposed economic policy changes to be accomplished over two year period which Bank finds acceptable. IBRD/GOI agreement is contingent on

---

[3] On May 5, Mehta met with Rusk, Bell, Handley, and Laise. A memorandum of this conversation is in the National Archives and Records Administration, RG 59, NEA/INC Files: Lot 70 D 314, India 1966, Visits—Asoka Mehta.

GOI working out suitable arrangements with IMF which are also acceptable to IBRD. This presumably to be done during coming week by Mehta associates remaining here. IBRD plans to communicate promptly with major creditors to transmit proposals and to seek assurances of support.

We are sending by separate telegram statement which we worked out with Mehta and which we agreed that he could make to Parliament on Friday May 13, if agreement with IMF consummated by that time. Our understanding that no public statement of this kind be made prior May 13. In intervening period Indian comment is expected to be to effect that Mehta had useful talks here and is now reporting to GOI. Essential that no substantial comment be made prior to May 13 as we will be consulting with Key members of Congress.

We hope Mehta statement will meet Prime Minister Gandhi's political requirements for the present. You should clearly understand that IBRD/GOI agreement is contingent on subsequent agreement with IMF and on success of consultations with creditors.

Rusk

---

337.   Letter From Prime Minister Gandhi to President Johnson[1]

New Delhi, May 12, 1966.

Dear Mr. President:

More than a month has gone by since I had the pleasure of visiting your great country and enjoying the warm hospitality with which you received me. I am writing to you today not because I have any specific problem to put to you but because I feel that an occasional letter at a personal level might be a useful way of sharing thoughts about matters of common concern.

One of the things which had impressed me most was your complete understanding of what I would call the political side of aid as distinct from its economic aspects. The reluctance with which aid-giving countries view the prospect of finding large sums of money to help developing countries on the road to progress is understood by everyone.

---

[1] Source: Johnson Library, National Security File, Memos to the President, Walt Rostow, Vol. 3, 5/6–26, 1966. No classification marking.

What is not so easily or widely appreciated is the reluctance and some-times even resentment with which aid is accepted by the recipient. Ever since my return, I have been asked searching questions in Parliament and by the Press to discover whether I have been pressurised by you or the World Bank to do things against our better judgement. I do not mind this. Indeed, I welcome it because in part the questioning reflects the spirit of self-respect and dignity which survives in our people inspite of the many problems of poverty. This is a source of strength to me.

However in part these questions are prompted by political factors of a different nature. With elections not many months ahead, every political party is anxious to take up positions which are critical of the party in power, and even within my party, there is the usual struggle for nomination which is a phenomenon which you understand far more than I do. My critics have specially chosen the Indo–U.S. Foundation as the spring-board for a personal attack on me, even though the basic idea had been agreed long before I came to office. Such criticism, inspired on personal or party motivation, does not worry me. What has distressed me a little is that many people in academic life with no political motives have also expressed some apprehensions. I am hoping to meet them personally with my Education Minister in the next few days. I should like to give the fullest consideration to their viewpoint and to allay their anxieties as far as possible. It is only after this meeting has taken place that detailed discussions on the draft will start with your Embassy here. I hope that in these talks, there will be fullest understanding of our problems.

You will doubtless want to hear a little about the food situation in India in which you have taken a personal interest. The reporting in the press, both in India and abroad, tends to be exaggerated one way or the other. On the one hand, an impression is given in some sections of the foreign press that there is no great shortage and we are giving an exaggerated picture. On the other hand, constant allegations are made in Parliament and elsewhere of starvation deaths. The actual position is somewhere in between the two extreme views. There is an acute shortage of foodgrains, because of the complete failure of the monsoon last year. There are also certain areas, mostly in the States of Maharashtra, Gujarat, Mysore and Orissa, which have always been scarcity pockets. Their plight this year is undoubtedly precarious. The timely movement of imports under PL-480 as well as from other sources has averted a calamity. We have begun relief works to give employment to the people in the scarcity areas. I recently returned from a tour of a district in the State of Maharashtra where conditions were distressing. I was heartened to see the energetic measures, both short-term and long-term, taken by the State Government and local farmers. Tomorrow,

I am visiting some areas in the State of Orissa to see for myself what more can be done to provide relief. One of the most difficult things to combat is the shortage of drinking water in areas which have poor communications. In our Fourth Five-Year Plan we have to pay special attention to the problem of water supply in the remote rural areas.

The reports which we have from Pakistan are far from encouraging. The entire trend of publicity through the press and radio, the part which Pakistan is playing in fomenting trouble in the hill tracts on our Eastern borders, the kind of rapport that it has established with China—all these indicate a complete negation of the spirit underlying the Tashkent Declaration. But perhaps you know much more about the true state of affairs in Pakistan than we do, since our diplomats have limited opportunity to acquire information about what goes on in Pakistan for obvious reasons.

The latest explosion in China of a nuclear device is a matter of deep concern for us. There has been a growing demand in this country for developing a nuclear device of our own. We have stood firmly against this. But each fresh report of China's activity in this regard strengthens this demand and attracts new adherents to it.

Mr. Asoka Mehta, our Minister for Planning, returned from the United States on Sunday, the 8th morning, and the same evening, he gave me an account of the talks he had with the World Bank and Members of your Administration, as well as of the two meetings he had with you. He told me of your kind words about me and also of the deep human sympathy with which you viewed the problems of this subcontinent and the efforts we are making to lift nearly 500 million people out of poverty, ignorance and disease. I came away from the United States convinced of your friendly support and cooperation in our endeavor. I am glad you could find time to see Mr. Mehta and that you gave him an indication of your support for our Plan.

I have little doubt that Mr. Mehta is also going to be criticized and attacked for what he has done or what he is supposed to have done. Controversy is the spice of democratic life. I hope that American journalists who may not be used to our hot food and hot climate will not use too many hot words in their despatches to the U.S. Press!

What a thoughtful gesture it was to send me the pen with which you signed one of the many documents which reflect your friendship for my country.

With kind personal regards to you and Mrs. Johnson,

Yours sincerely,

Indira Gandhi

338. **Telegram From the Embassy Office in Pakistan to the Department of State**[1]

Rawalpindi, May 18, 1966, 1520Z.

639. Joint State/AID message.

1. I met this morning with Fin Min Shoaib and Fin Sec M.M. Ahmad for discussion of aide-mémoire delivered by MFA May 17 (Embtel 636).[2] Acting AID Director Bee accompanied. Shoaib introduced subject himself by saying he wanted provide Bee with copy of aide-mémoire which he knew had been given to Embassy by MFA.

2. I said that I was disappointed by tone and content of aide-mémoire. Shoaib countered with view that aide-mémoire should meet requirements of US Government and pave way for early decisions on aid. While phraseology might not be ideal in all respects, he considered note contained several distinct achievements in substance. He thought statement regarding GOP willingness to participate with GOI in a ministerial meeting was positive and forthcoming. He also thought that mention of reducing military forces of both countries as topic for bilateral discussion along with Kashmir was also a significant gain. Finally, he considered statement welcoming a World Bank initiative for discussion of eastern rivers problem to be a major step forward.

3. When I stated that we found the indicated two to one ratio of military forces to be troublesome, Shoaib countered that this was a military judgement which he was unable to question; that is, if India attacks Pakistan, Pakistan would need to have force at least half the size of Indian force in order to defend itself successfully. Shoaib went on to stress, however, that aide-mémoire did not bless this military judgement which he said Pakistan could not financially support. Limitations of Pakistan's resources and need for development were such as to permit expenditure allocation to defense of only rs. 225 crores, or less than one-fourth of current Indian budget. Thus, he said, key word to stress in this paragraph is "nevertheless."

4. Shoaib pointed out it had been by no means easy to get agreement within GOP on defense budget figures in aide-mémoire, and he clearly considered it an achievement to have these figures recorded in government document. As regards level of defense spending for current fiscal year, Shoaib stated he simply could not at this juncture give a

---

[1] Source: National Archives and Records Administration, RG 59, Central Files 1964–66, AID (US) PAK. Secret; Immediate; Limdis. Repeated to Karachi, New Delhi, and Taipei and passed to the White House at 2:35 p.m.

[2] The text of the aide-mémoire was transmitted in telegram 636 from Rawalpindi, May 17. (Ibid.) The aide-mémoire is summarized in paragraph 11 of the telegram printed here.

figure, but that he still feared it might reach as high as rs. 268 crores. He stressed that costs of war plus major equipment replacements had to be borne in the current year. He also stated that it was not possible to segregate foreign exchange expenditures for defense as between fiscal years 1965/66 and 1966/67.

5. I pointed out, in accordance Deptel 543,[3] that US was deeply troubled by level of Pak defense expenditures currently envisaged, and expressed hope it would be possible to bring them down to levels cited during Washington discussions. Shoaib protested that, while he knew US would like lower figures, figures used in aide-mémoire were within framework of discussions he had had with Bell in Washington. Moreover, he stressed, GOP would be willing to move down from these levels if the Indians were to reduce their budget.

6. I then referred Shoaib to article in this morning's Pak *Times* by Z.A. Suleri (see separate telegram)[4] and asked whether this forecast public discussion of range of important issues two governments were dealing with. Shoaib, after reading article, stated that GOP definitely did not wish to get involved in public debate. In fact, he thought public ventilation would be embarrassing and undesirable from standpoint of GOP. He feared that there would be some further leaks on both sides and he urged utmost be done to avoid them. In this connection, he said there were some fairly embarrassing articles (for GOP) which appeared in *Washington Post* and other US papers at the time of his visit to Washington. Shoaib added that destructiveness of public debate on this issue clearly shown by difficulties Mehta and GOI now having with Indian Parliament.

7. As illustrative of continuing press problems, I called to Shoaib's attention PPA article which appeared in most Pakistan papers May 16 regarding alleged downing of Chinese plane over ChiCom territory. He indicated that he had not seen this article, but agreed that tone was nasty. (See para 3 Karachi's 2087[5] to Dept.)

8. As regards Pakistan's relations with China, Shoaib said that wording of final paragraph (consideration 5) was meant only to reaffirm GOP policy toward China as outlined by Ayub to Pres Johnson in December and in Ayub's recent statements to Ambassador McConaughy (Karachi's 2032).[6]

---

[3] Dated May 13. (Ibid., POL 15–1 PAK)

[4] Not found.

[5] Dated May 16. (National Archives and Records Administration, RG 59, Central Files 1964–66, POL 31–1 CHICOM–US)

[6] In his conversation with McConaughy on May 5, reported in telegram 2032 from Karachi, Ayub stated that there had been and would be no deviation from the understandings concerning Pakistan's relationship with China that had been reached during his talks with Johnson in Washington on December 14 and 15. (Ibid., POL 15–1 PAK)

9. Shoaib stressed that he would need to have US answer soon. Budget speech is scheduled for June 11 and budget must go to printer around end of May. He earnestly hoped it would be possible to conclude deal before end of month and thereby achieve major step forward toward normalization US–Pak relations.

10. Following meeting, I spoke to Shoaib privately and reminded him there was key item to which aide-mémoire was not addressed, namely, reopening of closed AEDS installations, and that this matter clearly must be resolved and emphasized that we were awaiting MFA response. Shoaib said he understood this, adding that he had sent Ayub memo emphasizing need for GOP to move ahead on this issue.

11. *Comment:* In essence, GOP aide-mémoire: (a) has accepted upper budgetary limitation on defense expenditures conditional upon similar Indian restraint; (b) has reiterated Pak willingness to discuss with India Kashmir settlement and arms reduction; (c) has indicated would welcome World Bank initiative for discussions of eastern waters; and (d) has reasserted Pak–ChiCom relationship is not inimical to other countries.

12. In our judgement GOP aide-mémoire can barely be considered minimal response to US proposals and this only provided GOP comes through on AEDS issue. Question is whether US should reject GOP aide-mémoire as inadequate and seek to negotiate more favorable language or proceed with aid package. We recommend against rejection unless, of course, GOP should itself reject by failure to agree to reopening of AED Stations. Outright US rejection would at this juncture be serious blow to positive elements and windfall for destructive forces in Pakistan, possibly tip delicate East-West policy balance here, and probably invite wave of charged anti-American public reaction. While it may be possible to obtain more forthcoming language by negotiation, we very much doubt if substantive result would be net improvement and justify delay and risk of giving opposition another opportunity to sabotage this effort to rebuild relations.

13. Accordingly, we recommend US, upon GOP agreement to reopen AED Stations, promptly advise GOP of willingness proceed with aid program as discussed with Shoaib.

Cargo

339. Letter From President Johnson to the Ambassador to India (Bowles)[1]

Washington, May 20, 1966.

Dear Chet:

I am grateful for your firsthand report of May 5th[2] on the situation in India. I am pleased that Mrs. Gandhi seems to have enjoyed her visit here and sensed our authentic interest and understanding of her problems.

It is good that she has shown the courage to carry forward her economic program in the face of pressures from the Left and Right.

We shall be doing all we can to back the IBRD plan, within the limits of the resources Congress finally grants. As you know, we shall not have an easy time with AID legislation this year.

I am impressed with what Mehta said—and with what you say—about the potentialities for an economic upsurge in India in the years ahead.

I would underline for you two problems with which your letter did not deal.

First, the question of military expenditures. George Woods will undertake to assess the military expenditures of India and Pakistan and try to get them moving downward. Neither country can afford to go on spending so much either of its own resources or its foreign exchange for defense. In both countries the issue is politically sensitive; and we cannot expect radical reductions immediately. But if we are to generate the resources they need to accelerate economic and social development, we cannot be complacent about this issue.

Whether Indian and Pakistani political leaders can afford to reduce military expenditures depends, in turn, on progress in the normalization of their relations. In this connection, I pointed out to Mehta the responsibility borne by the larger country in this kind of tense bilateral problem. I told him how hard we have had to work to make it possible for Mexico to live with us in an atmosphere of inner confidence and self-respect. India has a parallel responsibility.

I do not believe that India can become "an indigenous Asian counterweight to China" unless India regards it as part of its own responsibility to work actively towards the normalization of its relations with Pakistan.

Far too much of India's diplomatic energies and military resources will be focussed on the Pak problem for it to emerge as a major constructive force unless the subcontinent as a whole is peaceful.

---

[1] Source: National Archives and Records Administration, RG 59, Central Files 1964–66, POL 2 INDIA. Confidential.

[2] Document 334.

I understand that this transformation cannot be brought about in days or months. I also understand Mrs. Gandhi's election problems. Nevertheless, India cannot safely be passive with respect to its commitments at Tashkent.

Only those on the spot can work out what the next steps might be; but you should understand that nothing would ease our problems more in getting the resources necessary for Indian development than a forthcoming Indian position with respect to normalization of relations with Pakistan.

Among the next steps, I would urge you to take up with the Indian Government the possibility of their assuming the initiative in mounting a second Ministerial meeting.

Our next Ambassador to Pakistan, the distinguished lawyer and businessman Eugene Locke, will be working under similar instructions in Rawalpindi.

Again, Chet, let me thank you for your report and for the great work you are doing in a critical region.

Sincerely,

Lyndon B. Johnson

---

340. Memorandum From the President's Special Assistant (Rostow) to President Johnson[1]

Washington, May 27, 1966, 4:30 p.m.

In November you tentatively approved a recommendation from Sect. Rusk, McNamara and Raborn for establishing contingency alternatives for our intelligence facilities in Pakistan. But you felt we ought to hold final decision until after you talked with Ayub. Then we held further until after Tashkent and the Indian visit.

Now State, Defense and CIA have reviewed their October recommendations and (with minor updating) feel we should go ahead. They emphasize that this is not a proposal to relocate most of the present activities from Pakistan or to duplicate them. They propose to develop minimum space and install basic equipment so we can diversify some of these activities and be in a position to move them all on short notice with little intelligence loss if need be.

---

[1] Source: Johnson Library, National Security File, NSAMs, NSAM 348, Alternatives to U.S. Facilities in Pakistan. Top Secret; Sensitive. Another copy is ibid., Memos to the President, Walt W. Rostow, Vol. 5, May 27–June 10, 1966.

To refresh your memory, they recommended we: (a) increase existing [*less than 1 line of source text not declassified*] facilities in Embassies Tehran and New Delhi; (b) add one floor to a planned warehouse in the embassy compound in Tehran; (c) acquire land outside Tehran for eventually developing a more satisfactory permanent installation (including dependent quarters) if needed; and (d) explore the possibility of developing facilities in India.

Costs of (a) and (b) would be about $1.5 million; time about 9 months. Cost of (c) is approximately $5 million with eventual cost depending on how extensively we develop that site; time about 18 months. Cost of (d) is uncertain until we have a concrete plan but less than the $8–36 million they projected last fall when they suggested shipborne coverage in the Bay of Bengal (which did not prove out in a later test).

As general guidelines, they recommend (a) no further investment in Pakistan; (b) as new facilities come into being, we transfer some of those now in Pakistan to reduce the leverage any one country holds over us; but (c) unless you decide otherwise or the Paks kick us out, we retain a substantial portion of our present Pak activities.

They also recommended certain sweeteners for Iran to develop the favorable political climate essential to expansion. Your recent approval of the new military sales package has brought those up to date.

The balance of payments impact would be minimal; all equipment would be US-built. One-time real estate and construction costs would be about $6 million, and annual recurring costs about $750,000 (much of which would be offset by reduction of Pak facilities).

I believe it makes sense to go ahead with this program now. Since we no longer have the kind of close relationship with Pakistan we had prior to the Chinese attack on India, we would be well to reinsure.

If you still approve, I recommend you *sign the attached.*[2]

Walt

---

[2] Johnson wrote "OK" on the memorandum and signed the attachment, which was issued on May 30 as National Security Action Memorandum 348. NSAM No. 348, addressed to the Secretaries of State and Defense and the Director of Central Intelligence, was entitled "Alternatives to US Facilities in Pakistan," and reads as follows:

"I have reviewed your 22 October 1965 Memorandum to me in response to NSAM 337 as updated by the Department of State's 17 May 1966 Memorandum to Mr. Rostow and by my approval on May 23 of the new military sales package for Iran.

"I approve your recommendations as updated subject to the usual review by the Bureau of the Budget before expenditures are authorized." (Ibid.) For text of NSAM No. 337, see Document 168. Rusk's October 22, 1965, memorandum to Johnson, and Benjamin Read's May 17, 1966, memorandum to Rostow, both of which contained recommendations for the implementation of NSAM No. 337, are in the Johnson Library, National Security File, NSAMs, NSAM 348, Alternatives to U.S. Facilities in Pakistan. For Johnson's approval of a sales package for Iran, see *Foreign Relations, 1964–1968*, Vol. XXII, Document 144.

341. **Telegram From the Embassy in India to the Department of State[1]**

New Delhi, May 27, 1966, 1229Z.

3261. Pass White House and Dept of Defense.

1. We share concern expressed in Deptel 2311[2] over recent deterioration in relationship established at Tashkent. We also agree that the next few weeks in Indo–Pak relations will be critical.

2. On May 25 and 26, Carol Laise and I spent a total of more than four hours with Mrs. Gandhi, L.K. Jha, C.S. Jha and Swaran Singh during which the question of Pak–Indo relationships was the primary subject. The mood on the Indian side was extremely moderate with a genuine concern over the situation which has been developing since Tashkent combined with an equally genuine uncertainty as to what to do about it.

3. The general theme which we developed in these conversations was (a) that India with its large population, growing industrial strength, and democratic base has a wide open opportunity to become the major force for peace, progress and stability in Asia and (b) that this objective can be reached only if India's economic growth rate can be stepped up sharply and a way found to keep Pakistan from diverting India from its crucially important, overriding national goals.

4. As in previously reported conversations with the two Jhas and with other members of the govt I also stressed:

A. Since the last Pak–India meeting was held in Rawalpindi it is India's responsibility to take the initiative in inviting Pakistani reps to India;

B. A ministerial level conference at this time will create the same old confrontations between the same old professionals with little hope of progress; the wiser course therefore lies in meeting between Mrs. Gandhi and Ayub Khan.

5. While agreeing with my general thesis, L.K. suggested that in the present context a top-level meeting was risky since a failure at the summit would seem to close the door to further progress. Mrs. Gandhi later remarked that several of her staff associates had advanced this thesis.

---

[1] Source: National Archives and Records Administration, RG 59, Central Files 1964–66, POL INDIA–PAK. Secret; Priority. Repeated to Karachi, Rawalpindi, London, Moscow, USUN, Bombay, Calcutta, and Madras, and CINCMEAFSA and passed to the White House and DOD at 2:55 p.m.

[2] Dated May 25. (Ibid.)

6. I disagreed with this conclusion on the grounds that no one could legitimately expect a miracle from the first meeting between Ayub and Mrs. Gandhi; indeed Mrs. Gandhi's invitation could state that the purpose was to exchange views on current difficulties and to establish some system of communication through which future progress might become possible.

In his first meeting with Mrs. Gandhi, Ayub Khan would almost certainly be restrained and since Mrs. Gandhi herself would be anxious to create a feeling of goodwill we could expect a minimum of conflict and a maximum of constructive atmospherics.

7. Although neither L.K. Jha nor Mrs. Gandhi responded directly to this proposal both stressed that they are searching for an effective approach and that my suggestion had not been ruled out. (*Note:* When I next see L.K. Jha I shall suggest that the tangible outcome of a meeting between Mrs. Gandhi and Ayub might be an agreement on a series of regular monthly meetings between personal reps of Mrs. Gandhi and Ayub similar to our Warsaw meetings with the Chinese. Through these meetings the two parties could keep the dialogue open and maintain a regular channel for exploring current problems which in turn could provide the basis for meaningful negotiations.)

8. During our meetings with the two Jhas, Singh and Mrs. Gandhi the Indian view which was presented with varying emphasis was as follows:

A. At Tashkent Ayub seemed generally anxious to find a solution to the Pak–India impasse and at no time insisted that Kashmir must be settled before progress could be made on other issues. In his opening remarks at the Rawalpindi meeting, Ayub had continued this friendly and open-minded approach. However, shortly thereafter the mood abruptly changed and at the close Ayub spoke in very different terms. The assumption was that during this interval Bhutto had somehow managed to increase his influence over Pak policy.

The GOI seems genuinely to believe that Ayub is a moderate in search of a reasonable settlement. Bhutto is considered a reckless and intensely ambitious man comparable in some ways to Subandrio.

B. The Chinese would now like to use the Paks as they are using North Vietnamese as an instrument of Chinese policy and if necessary to do their dying. Pakistan in its turn has eagerly seized on this opportunity to bring pressure to bear on the US and USSR as well as on India.

C. Bhutto is promoting thesis that India is about to disintegrate. This reflects the Peking view which in the case of China is explained by the isolated position of its leaders.

D. Although they find this situation profoundly disturbing with no ready answers, the Indians assert that they will continue to do their best to break the impasse.

9. In our talks with L.K. Jha and C.S. Jha I brought up the problem of Kashmir by expressing the hope that though problems between India and Pakistan will require persistence and time, India could simultaneously move to straighten out their relationship with the Kashmiris and thereby eliminate basis for Pak charge of oppression.

To this suggestion L.K. Jha, as in the past, responded affirmatively again hinting that some answer might be found before or during elections next February. However, C.S. Jha said he saw no hope whatever for progress through Sheik Abdullah whom he loosely described as pro-Chinese and pro-Pak.

10. In our talk with L.K. Jha I also brought up the question of military equipment to Pakistan. I pointed out that without spare parts from the US many of the Pak F–86's were inoperative and that if we fail to provide these parts there will be additional pressure on the Paks to procure MIG 19s from China (which the Indians know is a superior plane).

11. To this and other references to military aid to Pak L.K. Jha expressed profound distress and opposition. He stated that to give arms to Paks at a time when they were openly threatening India, drawing closer to China and pressing US to increase their military capacity for use against India would be not only self defeating but dangerous.

Such a move, he said, would enable the Paks to raise their price to the Chinese (which the Chinese would almost surely meet) and would accomplish none of the objectives which we seek. A modest amount of military aid would be wholly ineffective in easing out the Chinese and would only lead to Pak demands for much more aid; if we then raised ante we would increase the likelihood of war. Swaran Singh vigorously reiterated this position the following day; in addition he said such a move would directly and adversely affect India's ability to initiate moves to reduce Indo–Pak tensions and resolve outstanding differences.

12. We believe that India is earnestly seeking some appropriate gesture that might help to ease the current tensions and strengthen hand of Ayub. There is every evidence among Indian leadership of a moderate though worried mood. At the All India Congress Committee meeting in Bombay the subject of Pak–India relations was carefully sidetracked in order to avoid provocative speeches. Although news stories occasionally headline border incidents Indian editoral comments have been consistently sober.

13. L.K. Jha indicated India is searching for a concrete proposal or proposals for economic cooperation which might signal their desire to reduce tensions. In this connection he acknowledged Beru-Bari transfer might provide useful gesture towards reconciliation. (Subsequently

David Scott, Acting UK HICOM reported that during his trip to Pakistan Aziz Ahmed had indicated this kind of move would not be acceptable GOP.) This morning's headlines state that GOI is moving unilaterally to permit normal trade relations with Pakistan.

14. We shall continue to work along above lines not only in our conversations with GOI but also with the many friendly and cooperative members of the Indian press. However, in one sense, we are leaning against an open door since the Indians are already persuaded of dangers; the question is how best to deal with them.

15. I suggest this is an important time to bring all appropriate pressure to bear in Karachi and Rawalpindi to meet India at least part way and above all to take advantage of Mrs. Gandhi's genuine good will before pre-election mood takes over here in India and she loses her political flexibility.

16. Although the GOI mood now is affirmative there are three developments which would abruptly destroy whatever hopes there may be for a rational settlement of Pak–Inida differences.

A. An aggressive border action by the Chinese. This could foreclose any conciliatory move by the Indians on ground that such a move would make them appear to be giving ground to Paks in the face of Chinese pressure;

B. Intensification of Pak disruptive efforts in Kashmir and in eastern hill areas.

C. A decision by USG before Indian elections next February to provide military supplies to Pakistan, particularly in face of ominous internal developments in Pakistan such as increasing influence of Bhutto and input of sizeable amounts of Chinese military equipment. In the politically charged pre-election atmosphere here this resumption of US military supplies would absolutely foreclose any Indian initiative on the Pak question, undermine the political leadership of Mrs. Gandhi and the moderates, greatly strengthen both Krishna Menon and the fellow travelers on the left, and the extremists on the right and destroy current prospect for a significant economic and political breakthrough in this critical and strategically-placed nation.

Although it is impossible accurately to foresee the situation that we will face next winter, by that time the answers to some questions at least will be a lot more clear.

Bowles

342. Letter From President Johnson to Prime Minister Gandhi[1]

Washington, May 30, 1966.

Dear Mrs. Gandhi:

Your letter[2] was a source of strength and satisfaction to me.

We are both leaders of a democracy and must put our policies to the test of national elections and carry our parties with us in the process. That means we are almost always at work in a sea of troubles. Understanding that, it is good to share our thoughts as we try to solve the problems we face.

I have been reading with admiration the reports of your spirited defense of your policies against political attack—most recently at the Congress Party meeting at Bombay.

As you may have gathered, I am also meeting my critics at least half way as we enter our congressional campaign.

We learned much from Planning Minister Mehta about your plans for moving India ahead to faster economic progress. I was particularly pleased—even moved—by his account of the gathering energy and determination in evidence from the farmers in the villages to the new generation of ingenious and determined young industrialists.

It was also good to hear directly from him of his encouraging discussions with the World Bank. As I told him, I wish to be as helpful as possible to you and to your government in the period that lies ahead.

I feel the state of relations between our two countries is bright and promising. I know we both are seeking much the same thing: practical ways of achieving an economy of abundance with social justice and freedom from exploitation.

Against the background of this generally hopeful picture, I share your concern about one matter of great importance to the future of free Asia—indeed, of the whole world community. That, of course, is the present state of relations between Pakistan and India.

I well know how difficult it is for democratic leaders to be conciliatory and moderate in the face of critical public opinion. But it seems to me extremely important that communications be maintained between the two countries, with the objective of creating a firmer basis of peace.

---

[1] Source: Johnson Library, National Security File, Special Head of State Correspondence File, India, 3/1/66–12/31/66. Secret. Transmitted to New Delhi for delivery to Prime Minister Gandhi in telegram 2357 to New Delhi, May 31. (National Archives and Records Administration, RG 59, Central Files 1964–66, POL 15–1 INDIA)

[2] Document 337.

The process begun at Tashkent must not wither and die.

Quite apart from the overriding need for peace, any thought that last fall's hostilities might recur would provide a ready argument to political leaders in this country who are opposed in principle to any substantial aid program. More important, it would plant doubts among even the strongest supporters of our foreign assistance. This could strengthen efforts to cut back the next aid bill in general and more particularly to block the resumption of economic aid to India and Pakistan on the scale that you and I know is necessary.

As a concrete means of reversing a dangerous arms buildup, it seems to me crucial that India and Pakistan find some way of limiting their defense expenditures and starting them on parallel downward paths. This is essential to both peace and development. I know from our own experience with the Soviet Union how difficult this is to do. However, before Viet Nam both we and the Soviets—without ever talking about it—had begun a series of unilateral but seemingly reciprocal cutbacks in our spending.

Let me add that I remain as convinced as ever of the genuineness and depth of your own dedication to the cause of peace with your neighbor. The knowledge of your commitment to peace is a source of encouragement and strength to me as I ask the American people to help in India's development.

You suggested you might be interested in my view of the current state of affairs in Pakistan. It does seem that Pakistan is going through a difficult period. The government there is under considerable political pressure to demonstrate some achievement on Kashmir. It is hard to predict where these pressures will lead, but I believe we both have an opportunity to influence future events.

As I told you when you were here, I have confidence in President Ayub, and I believe that he intends to maintain friendly ties with the Free World. As you know, I am about to send a new Ambassador to Pakistan, a trusted and capable colleague, Mr. Eugene Locke. He has clearly in mind the necessity of peace on the subcontinent and the requirement of responsibility and flexibility on the part of both countries. I shall be most interested in his thoughts as to how the U.S. and Pakistan can go about working out a relationship that is best for all of us. I shall keep in touch with you and will hope for your support during the weeks ahead.

I have often thought, late in the night, of the burden of history and political pressure borne by you and my friend Ayub in this matter. I have only two observations: first, as I told your Minister of Planning, we have learned from our experience with Mexico the special responsibility that the larger partner must bear in making it possible for the smaller nation to live in confidence and dignity as a neighbor; second, in working forward from our present difficult position, you may have to take small steps, each then understanding the political problems of the other, each fighting loyally before his own public opinion for whatever limited agreements can be achieved.

From this distance it would appear that a forthcoming invitation for high-level talks might now be timely.

I was interested in your remarks about the Indo-American Foundation. I know from my own experience that even a project as intrinsically worthy as this one can become a source of political controversy; it is not the first time, nor will it be the last, that a good project has been strongly questioned and vigorously debated as a part of the democratic political process. Working together, however, and with a full understanding of the problems which confront us both, I am sure that we can find a way to launch the Foundation in a form which will preserve its essential character and its ability to stimulate Indian education as we both intend.

Your observations on the food situation in India were helpful to me and, on the whole, heartening. As you are aware, I am following this matter personally. Congress reacted favorably to the message I sent it toward the end of your visit here, and we will continue to do our part to help you weather this difficult season. However, our own stocks of wheat have dropped more rapidly than expected, and I have recently had to increase wheat acreage here. That will not increase our anticipated stocks until 1967.

My prayers are joined with yours that the coming rains are bountiful.

The political disturbances in Viet Nam have been disquieting. But I am convinced, in the phrase I quoted in my African talk the other day, they are "growing pains." They are part of the process by which the Vietnamese people are working out their political future in their own way. We are using our limited influence to persuade them to work these matters out by discussion rather than by violence.

The Vietnamese government has made clear its continuing commitment to elections before the middle of September and the work of the committee set up to prepare for these elections is going forward. We support the government's commitment to these elections and we continue to believe that in this way and in other ways the process of building a truly free nation in Viet Nam will go forward.

As for the war, we shall apply that minimum of our great military power necessary to convince those responsible in Hanoi that the aggression should cease, while searching every day to bring the matter from the battlefield to the negotiating table.

Before closing, let me say that I admire your courage in sticking to a policy of foregoing nuclear weapons. I think this is a wise and a good policy. I cannot believe, knowing the costs and limitations of small national nuclear systems, that they represent the wave of the future in this increasingly interdependent world.

With warm personal regards,

Sincerely,

Lyndon B. Johnson

343.   Memorandum From the President's Special Assistant (Rostow) to President Johnson[1]

Washington, June 2, 1966, 4:30 p.m.

Secretary Rusk recommends we take another step in our relations with Pakistan.

In your conversations with Ayub in December and with Shoaib in April, you reached a general understanding that we would resume economic assistance if they would meet certain political conditions.

The Secretary now thinks we should move forward with our side of the understanding.[2] He proposes that we:

a. Release $70 million for commodity aid about 1 July.

b. Indicate a readiness to release a second slice of $70 million six months later, if our relationship is proceeding satisfactorily.

c. Meet our obligation on the Karachi steel mill ($85 million Ex-Im and $35 million from AID *if* the Paks decide to go ahead and are ready to meet any additional costs resulting from revised estimates.

He recognizes that going ahead now on this six months' basis is to take a calculated risk, because the Paks have not yet fully met the political conditions we set.

—They are not bringing military spending down as far as we recommended, though they have come down some.

—They may be planning limited new agitation in Kashmir.

—They have paraded—not just accepted—Chicom military equipment.

—They are negotiating hard on reopening the small atomic energy detection stations, [1 line of source text not declassified].

---

[1] Source: Johnson Library, National Security File, Country File, Pakistan, Vol. VI, Memos, 1/66–9/66. Secret. A handwritten note on the memorandum reads, "Rec'd 6 pm."

[2] Rusk outlined his proposal in a May 30 memorandum to the President. (Ibid.)

We can have no illusion that, by resuming aid, we will now get all we want.

The Secretary thinks the risk is worth taking. George Woods urges that we go ahead: it fits his strategy with the Paks.[3] He will be working on them steadily to get military expenditures down further. Bell concurs.

Before making my recommendation to you, I sought independent answers to the following questions:

1. *How serious is Pakistani involvement in disturbances along the Indo/ Pakistani border?*

The CIA prepared a detailed memorandum[4] which concludes:

—With respect to the Mizo and Naga tribal rebels (whom the Paks aided before Tashkent) there is no conclusive evidence that this aid continued after Tashkent. The possibility of some limited assistance cannot be precluded. If so, it has been very limited.
—With respect to infiltration into Kashmir, some intelligence and clandestine operatives may have been sent across into Kashmir in early May. They were not armed for combat, and their number is probably fairly small.

This is not good business; and we shall have to watch it carefully; but I do not think it sufficient to keep us from going forward along our track with Ayub.

2. *In the matter of the small stations, is Ayub violating his pledge to you that he will not do things contrary to U.S. vital interests?*

I have looked carefully into the terms of the negotiation. It appears that what they are negotiating hard about concerns legitimate Pak interests in the installations; [1 line of source text not declassified]. This is a trend in installations in many parts of the world. I conclude it is not a violation of Ayub's pledge to you.

3. I have talked with George Woods. He is getting deeply into the business of military expenditures in both India and Pakistan. The Pak military budget for this year should be less than it was for last year. Bringing down the military budgets of the two countries will be a process rather than an immediate decision, interwoven with any constructive diplomacy we can generate between India and Pakistan. I conclude in this matter that we are doing at the moment as well as we could expect; we are lucky to have George Woods in the middle of the affair.

4. *Can we hold up this package or any part of it for Gene Locke to give as an initial gift to the Pakistani?*

---

[3] David Bell sounded out Woods on June 1 on the question of proceeding with program loans on Pakistan. (Memorandum from David E. Bell to Walt W. Rostow, June 1; ibid.)

[4] Not found.

Shoaib must present his budget on June 9. With knowledge of our aid package, he can underline the utility of the U.S. relationship and implicitly demonstrate the virtues of restraint towards India. Without knowledge, he cannot put forward a bold development budget. Moreover, Ayub, without a public announcement of our assistance, will have difficulty holding back his radicals, who are progressively undermining Tashkent and creating an atmosphere in which a meeting with India will be politically unviable for him. An affirmative aid decision will strongly, if indirectly, support the voices of reason and moderation within the government of Pakistan. And it is urgent that this element be added to the Pak military equation.

I then probed as to whether we could leave the Karachi steel mill for Gene Locke to give them.

Macomber considers this of uncertain value. It is a substantial project, but it is quite uncertain at the moment. National Steel is reviewing the cost figures, and these will not be clear until six weeks to two months from now. After these figures are known (which may boost the cost to some $70 million foreign exchange over what we are planning to contribute), there will have to be negotiations between the government of Pakistan, the U. S. Government, ExIm, etc. The Paks may even have to do some negotiating with West Germany for some part of the overrun. It is, therefore, far from neat or clean. Indeed, there may be some backfires because costs will have risen and we will not be increasing our contribution to cover them fully. Ambassador Locke perhaps would be better out of this one.

My feeling is that Gene Locke will not need any presents. In his person and his connection with you, he is the greatest present you could give Ayub.

On balance, therefore, I recommend you approve the Secretary's proposal. I believe it is right that we release our aid on a 6-month basis. This will give us an opportunity to see how the politics of the situation evolves and retain continuing leverage.

I also believe we should consider, shortly after the release of this package, a letter to Ayub like the one you have just dispatched to Mrs. Gandhi.

Walt

Should we prepare an Ayub letter?

Yes[5]

No

---

[5] Johnson checked this option.

344.   Telegram From the Department of State to the Embassy
        Office in Pakistan[1]

Washington, June 6, 1966, 3:57 p.m.

610. Subject: Aid Bargain with Pakistan. For Chargé. This message
contains instructions for use by Ambassador Locke[2] with Ayub in conveying steps President has now authorized on US side of economic
aid bargain presented to Shoaib during April visit here. Ambassador
Locke will convey this information to Ayub immediately following
presentation credentials. Chargé should inform Shoaib in advance that
Ambassador will be under instructions seek substantive conversation
with Ayub at time he presents credentials, in order convey next steps
USG prepared take in economic aid.

   A. Background

   1. GOP response to conditions of Pak performance in bargain is
less than we had hoped for. GOP has accepted concept defense budget
ceiling and indicated an intention reduce over-all spending next year.
But its continuing efforts to expand armed forces, including Chicom
procurement, add to arms race potential in subcontinent and we have
no certain assurance of downward trend defense spending in either
Pakistan or India. Pakistan is clearly keeping up the pressure on Kashmir and its frustration on this score could lead it to new efforts of
agitation with real risk for peace on subcontinet. The result could be
that events might negate or undermine what we otherwise believe to
be determined GOP efforts to resume economic development program
and restore import liberalization.

   2. We recognize that renewed US economic aid in these circumstances involves a calculated risk. Nevertheless we have concluded
that on balance the situation justifies decision resume aid on short-
leash basis. In doing so we would be affirming to Ayub and other
friendly elements in Pakistan that we are prepared do our part to
rebuild our relationship on new and firmer ground. But we would
condition our follow-through in aid bargain on same elements of performance that we originally posed to Shoaib and thus serve new notice

---

[1] Source: National Archives and Records Administration, RG 59, Central Files 1964–
66, AID (US) PAK. Secret; Priority; Limdis. Drafted by Laingen on June 4; cleared by
Schneider, Rees (AID), Wriggins, Handley, in draft by Hoopes, and in substance by
Horbaly (Department of Agriculture); and approved by Handley. Also sent to Karachi
and repeated to New Delhi, USUN, and London and pouched to CINCMEAFSA, Ankara,
Tehran, and Bangkok.
[2] Ambassador McConaughy left Pakistan on May 15. Cargo served as Chargé until
Ambassador Locke arrived. Eugene M. Locke was appointed Ambassador May 27 and
presented his credentials June 9.

that we intend keep these elements under careful, continuing review as our relationship evolves.

B. *Action Instructions*

1. We want Ayub to be directly aware of importance we attach to economic aid steps we now ready to take. We want him and GOP to understand that these steps are intricate part of process begun with Ayub's visit here and our subsequent talks with Shoaib at highest level.

2. You should preface your remarks to Ayub on this subject by recalling President's satisfaction over growing sense of confidence in our relationship begun in his talks with Ayub in December and strengthened as result meeting he had with Shoaib here in April. As evidence of our desire strengthen this trend, and our confidence in similar intentions Ayub and GOP, President asked that you go out immediately to Pakistan and to convey directly on his behalf information as to several steps USG now prepared take in economic aid field with Pakistan, despite some uncertainties that remain as to trends in subcontinent. FYI: What you should get across here (in fairly low key with Ayub but more strongly to Shoaib in subsequent conversation) is point that our decision move ahead was not easy one in view response we have had from Paks on conditions we posed, and that as consequence we intend keep these conditions under continuing review as our relationship evolves. End FYI.

3. You should state President has authorized us begin negotiations immediately on $70 million commodity loan, on assumption GOP prepared follow through this month on economic aspects of aid bargain; i.e. announcement of budget with restored priority to development and return to import liberalization. In addition President has authorized us tell GOP we prepared consider further $70 million commodity loan in fall after Congress has acted on aid bill, if review at that time indicates continued progress in our relations and economic performance. USG also prepared meet its commitments on Karachi Steel Mill ($85 million EXIM and $35 million AID) provided GOP decides go ahead with project after reviewing revised cost estimates when these available and provided Pakistan meets any added costs. We will also be prepared begin negotiations on Pakistan's food needs under PL 480 for balance CY 66 after returns spring wheat harvest assessed.

4. You should indicate to Ayub that these actions on our part and our follow through on them depend on several factors. Above all there is need for peace on subcontinent and conditions in which development efforts can proceed with maximum effect, including downward trend in defense spending. You should note the highest importance the President continues attach to efforts by both India and Pakistan find ways to deal peacefully with problems between them, including Kashmir. You should indicate great weight President

personally attaches to reaffirmation conveyed to him by Shoaib of understanding reached between Ayub and the President on our respective interests in Asia. And you should say that we believe it incumbent on both of us to seek ways to improve atmosphere in which we conduct our bilateral relations, an objective that is of highest importance to you as you begin your mission.

5. You should frame your remarks on small facilities (AEDS stations Lahore and Malir) problem in context our desire improve bilateral relationship; noting our satisfaction that negotiations underway, that you believe basis for agreement exists and that you assume this problem will be resolved. You should also say that you believe it in interest both of us that reopening and refurbishing of stations not be delayed pending final signature agreement. FYI: We hope GOP will agree interim reopening stations but do not wish make actual reopening condition for first steps on aid.[3] End FYI.

6. Following your talk with Ayub, you should go over same ground with Shoaib but in greater detail as to our requirements, emphasizing the difficulty of our decision and making perfectly clear that we intend keep situation under continuing review as we take each step in economic aid; i.e. we will expect tangible, continuing evidence that Pakistan:

a) will stick to a course of moderation and negotiation with India;

b) will assure a downward tend in its defense spending (reasserting points Embassy will have made pursuant Deptel 604);[4]

c) will continue demonstrate appreciation US interests Asia;

d) will follow through quickly in negotiations begun on small facilities (making strong pitch on reopening);

e) will indicate, in its budget presentation June 11, top priority to development, agricultural self-help and restored import liberalization and will follow through in subsequent actions.

---

[3] On June 7 Cargo reported that Additional Foreign Secretary Agha Shahi had called him in and told him that the Ayub government was certain that it would encounter serious political and military repercussions if it agreed to reopen the stations. (Telegram 737 from Rawalpindi; National Archives and Records Administration, RG 59, Central Files 1964–66, DEF 18–8 PAK) Howard Wriggins sent a copy of the cable to Rostow on June 7, noting that it was not certain whether the position taken by Pakistan represented the situation as actually perceived by the Ayub government or was a bargaining ploy. (Johnson Library, National Security File, Country File, Pakistan, Vol. VI, 1/66–9/66)

[4] Telegram 604 to Rawalpindi, June 3, repeated to New Delhi as telegram 2383, expressed the Department's continuing concern over the high levels of military spending by Pakistan. The Department instructed the Embassy in Pakistan to pursue the issue of restraint in military expenditure with members of the Ayub government. The Department noted that restraint on the part of Pakistan was conditioned upon similar restraint on the part of India. (National Archives and Records Administration, RG 59, Central Files 1964–66, AID (US) PAK)

f) and will move promptly to release seized AID and MAP cargos impounded last September and reimburse USG for unlocated cargos.

7. FYI: We are also considering follow up Presidential letter, content of which would depend in part on report of conversations with Ayub and Shoaib. End FYI.

Ball

---

345. Telegram From the Department of State to the Embassy in India[1]

Washington, June 7, 1966, 3:25 p.m.

2404. Ref: Deptel 2383 to New Delhi (Notal).[2] Subject: Indian Defense Expenditures.

1. Assistant Secretary Hare called in Indian Ambassador Nehru June 6 to discuss with him question of defense expenditures and to bring our discussion this subject with GOI to level of specifics we have already reached with GOP.

2. In brief remarks on Indian devaluation, Amb. Nehru described Mrs. Gandhi's decision as "very courageous," expressed some surprise that GOI would have made this move so far in advance of any foreseeable consortium pledging session, and suggested that devaluation will be good move only if India can "get a lot of money" to make it work prior to elections.

3. Ambassador Hare then briefly informed Amb. Nehru of Amb. Locke's departure for Pakistan evening of 6th. Amb Hare expressed view that Amb Locke's appointment at this time will turn out to be useful not just for US-Pak relations but useful from a subcontinent point of view. Amb Nehru agreed and expressed hope he and Amb Locke would be able to meet when Amb Locke returns in a week or two.

4. Ambassador Hare then reviewed results of Mehta mission here, specifically focussing on need to reduce defense spending. He stressed

---

[1] Source: National Archives and Records Administration, RG 59, Central Files 1964–66, DEF 1 INDIA. Secret. Drafted by Herbert G. Hagerty in SOA, cleared by Hare and Schneider, and approved by Handley. Repeated to Rawalpindi, Karachi, London, Bonn, and CINCMEAFSA for POLAD.

[2] See footnote 4, Document 344.

our view that peace and development in the subcontinent require that there be reasonable limitation on defense expenditures and indicated as well our unwillingness, through economic aid, to finance indirectly an arms spiral in South Asia. He then referred to Soviet military assistance which, he noted, Amb Nehru had described as not very substantial during Minister Mehta's talk with the Secretary. Amb Hare said information gleaned from only public sources such as press and GOI statements in Lok Sabha indicates that program has an overall value of more than $250 million and that it has included large number of transport aircraft, three squadrons of MIG–21's (in addition to production facilities acknowledged by Amb. Nehru earlier), surface-to-air missile complexes, and large number of helicopters and tanks. Amb Hare also mentioned submarines and noted that this information could well be partial since certain info of this character is often kept confidential.

5. Amb Hare said our point in raising this matter and clarifying our position is that this substantial Soviet assistance feeds fears in Pakistan and contributes to arms spiral on basis of its *arrival* in South Asia rather than on basis of stretched out *payments*. For that reason we believe that costs of Soviet military assistance should be thus reckoned on basis of deliveries.

6. Amb. Hare indicated that we had also pressed Paks hard on question of reducing defense expenditures, and he suggested that if India, as the larger power, could initiate first steps toward reduction defense spending, then it would be helpful in getting Pakistan, as smaller, to come along as well.

7. Finally, Amb Hare made point that in our annual aid reviews, we would be assigning considerable weight to subject of defense spending and to need for downward trend. He said he hoped GOI and GOP might get together on this, but if that not possible, then cooperation by independent example might have same effect.

8. Amb Nehru responded saying he had no instructions this regard and his remarks should be interpreted as his and not necessarily GOI's. He spoke briefly of 1964 Memorandum of Understanding,[3] indicating that while he agreed US would not want to fuel arms spiral, that memorandum appeared to him to have been broken by our suspension of military assistance.

9. More important, he said, is fact that GOI wants to spend no more than is absolutely necessary to meet the two-fold threat to its security. Prior to 1962, GOI spent too little on defense; now GOI needs forces deployed against the threat from China regardless of cost to other important needs. Second threat comes from Pakistan which "suf-

---

[3] See footnote 2, Document 53.

fering from some kind of lunacy" that its security is threatened by India. He said GOI needs no more than parity on Pak side to protect Indian security on that front. If GOP is willing reduce forces, then GOI would be willing to reduce anti-Pak component its forces on man-for-man basis, but anti-Chicom component of Indian forces would still be very large. He went on to say there is no question of a ratio between the two armed forces since the threats they face differ; neither ratio nor costing basis is relevant. Main point, Amb Nehru said, is the threat.

10. Amb Nehru asked Amb Hare what response US had from Paks. Amb Hare pointed out Pak interest in reducing arms load and in keeping heavy emphasis on economic development. Amb Nehru said GOI has same view. GOI, he said, has already put lid on defense spending; current defense budget essentially same as last year's, with no increase in real terms due to war. GOP's has doubled. GOI is most interested, he emphasized, in reducing arms spending and focussing not on "military glory" but on economic progress, but GOI finds it necessary to defend itself against "psychotic Pakistan" which has allied itself with China.

11. Ambassador Hare noted that we agree GOI defense budget has not gone up appreciably, but it was precisely for that reason that we had made point about costing basis for Soviet bloc assistance, since deliveries which heighten Pakistan anxieties are not accurately reflected in current GOI defense budget.

12. Ambassador Hare recapped points he wished leave with Amb Nehru, summing up by noting that while we recognize difficulties, we consider it simple proposition. An arms spiral in South Asia causes such difficult problems for us that we believe it is essential to get the arrows pointed down rather than up. Ambassador Nehru agreed on the importance of a downward trend, saying he would report this conversation to his government and assuring Ambassador Hare that the GOI will do all it can to limit defense spending, but not below the level of the threat the GOI feels it faces.

13. *For New Delhi:* Embassy should, at appropriate time and level, reinforce message on defense spending Ambassador Hare conveyed to Amb Nehru.

Ball

346. Summary Notes of the 558th Meeting of the National Security Council[1]

Washington, June 9, 1966.

The Problem of Indian Nuclear Weapons

The President: indicated that this was the first of a series of NSC meetings to be devoted to the discussion of complex problems requiring careful exploration before they were to come to him for discussion. He expressed his concern about the growing pressures in India favoring the nuclear route. Its own economic progress and the stability of the whole area depended on India not going nuclear. The Paper[2] admirably summarized the problems. He invited Mr. Ball to lay out the issues.

Mr. Ball: briefly summarized the Interdepartmental paper of June 7, 1966, on this subject, giving the pros and cons of the suggested alternatives[3] (Plowshare[4] was not mentioned). Although his presentation was even-handed, he appeared to favor some form of multilateral approach which attempted to deal with India's real security problems.

He recommended further—and urgent—staff studies.

Mr. McNamara: agreed and thought recommendations could come forward for Presidential consideration within two to three weeks.

Mr. Foster: Stressed the urgency, since disarmament meetings resume in Geneva in June, and the U.S. must have an improved position within a month or six weeks at the outside. He thought the two or three principal alternatives now under study (in the Committee of Principals) could easily be staffed out and recommended within a month.

---

[1] Source: Johnson Library, National Security File, NSC Meetings File, NSC Meetings, Vol. 3, 6/9/66, The Problem of Indian Nuclear Weapons. Secret/Sensitive; For the President Only. Those attending the meeting, in addition to the President, included the Vice President, Ball, McNamara, Rostow, Raborn, Bell, Goldberg, Treasury Secretary Henry Fowler, ACDA Director William Foster, AEC Director John Palfrey, USIA Director Leonard Marks, and JCS Chairman General Earle Wheeler. (List of attendees for the 558th NSC meeting; ibid.)

[2] Reference is to an interdepartmental policy paper entitled "The Indian Nuclear Weapons Problem: Current Issues," which was circulated to NSC members June 7 under a covering memorandum from NSC Executive Secretary Bromley Smith. (Washington National Records Center, RG 330, OSD Files: FRC 70 A 4443, India 471.61)

[3] The alternatives suggested in the policy paper as having the potential to restrain the development of an Indian nuclear device included economic pressure the United States could bring to bear, the dampening effect that an arms control agreement between the United States and the Soviet Union would have on an Indian nuclear program, and a bilateral or multilateral security arrangement to guarantee India against a nuclear attack.

[4] Plowshare was the program being developed to demonstrate the peaceful potential of controlled nuclear explosions.

Mr. Marks: Urged (a) a conference of world intellectuals to stress the economic costs and security liabilities of nuclear weapons; (b) using the 20th anniversary of the Baruch proposals[5] as the occasion for a bold new U.S. initiative.

The Vice President: Stressed how little additional expenditure would be necessary beyond that already invested for India to go nuclear. He preferred a UN umbrella with private U.S. reassurances to India. This leaves the door open to the Soviets without forcing either the Indians or Russia to take a public stand.

Ambassador Goldberg: Stressed the urgency of deciding on any such arrangement, since it would require soundings with the Russians well in advance of the opening of the UNGA in September. Also necessary would be precise commitments to the Indians.

Mr. Foster: Cited Minister Banerjee, the Indian Minister who had officially indicated that "for a period, a General Assembly resolution would be adequate."

Mr. Rostow: Urged:

a. the urgency of our own explorations but reminded the Council of the complexity of decisions countries must face before they chose to go nuclear. Our problem was to buy time until the Indians came to accept the necessity for Western assistance;
b. the nuclear issue was so complex that it could not be dealt with solely by the specialists concentrating on arms control or by the country or area specialists. We must find ways of combining these two types of specialists in the study of this problem.

The President: Instructed the Department[6] to speed the study of the Indian nuclear problem and said he would issue a NSAM shortly.

Howard Wriggins[7]

---

[5] Reference is to U.S. proposals for the international control of atomic energy put forward in a statement on June 14, 1946, by Bernard M. Baruch, the U.S. representative on the UN Atomic Energy Commission. For text of the statement, see *A Decade of American Foreign Policy: Basic Documents, 1941–1949*, pp. 865–871.

[6] An apparent reference to the Department of State. See Document 359.

[7] Printed from a copy that bears this typed signature.

347. National Security Action Memorandum No. 351[1]

Washington, June 10, 1966.

TO

The Secretary of State

SUBJECT

Indian Nuclear Weapons Problem

At the meeting of the National Security Council on June 9, 1966,[2] the President noted the increased urgency of dealing with the Indian nuclear weapons problem following the third Chinese Communist nuclear test. He has directed the Secretary of State, in collaboration with the Secretary of Defense, the Director of the Arms Control and Disarmament Agency and heads of other departments and agencies, as appropriate, to study in greater depth the following interrelated issues emerging from the National Security Council review of the Indian nuclear weapons question:

a. The extent to which it might be in the U.S. interest to use our economic leverage more explicitly to discourage an Indian national nuclear program.

b. The effect which various arms control agreements might have on Indian nuclear intentions, and what price the U.S. should be prepared to pay for such agreements.

c. How far it is in the U.S. interest to go in meeting Indian security concerns, what form such action might take, and what the optimum timing might be.

d. Whether there are other approaches to the problem which need to be pursued.

The study should balance the price of each of these suggested courses of action against the damage resulting from India's choosing the independent nuclear path. For the purpose of this study, no change in our present position on a non-proliferation treaty should be assumed.

The study should result in specific recommendations to the President as to measures which the U.S., in its own interest, should take to delay or prevent India's choosing that path.

The President requests that the first report of recommendations for his attention be presented to him no later than July 15, 1966.

WW Rostow

---

[1] Source: Johnson Library, National Security File, NSAMs, NSAM 351, Indian Nuclear Weapons Problem. Secret; Exdis. Copies were sent to McNamara, William Foster, Wriggins, U. Alexis Johnson, and Helms.

[2] See Document 346.

348.   Telegram From the Embassy Office in Pakistan to the Department of State[1]

Rawalpindi, June 9, 1966, 1329Z.

753. Ref: Deptel 610 to Rawalpindi.[2]

1. My presentation of credentials followed by private meeting between President Ayub and myself took place in satisfying atmosphere.

2. DCM Cargo, General Rafi, and Chief of Protocol were present during credentials presentation phase. President Ayub spoke in warmest terms of his relationship with President Johnson and expressed his strong desire to maintain best possible relationship with United States. He stated his conviction that the long range interests of United States and Pakistan coincided. He stressed difficulties of Pakistan's strategic and geographic position—with three great powers "breathing down our necks". It was necessary for Pakistan to strive for friendly relations with these powers, although India was not yet prepared for this. Indian hostile intentions, Ayub added, were not imaginary; they had been demonstrated in fact last September. Nevertheless, he hoped that friendship would be attained with India and asserted his desire for peace on the subcontinent. He said that Pakistan and India both needed 15 years of peace and that, for Pakistan, this would mean an opportunity to carry forward economic development that had already made great strides. Reverting to his comments on Pakistan's relations with great powers, Ayub said that the United States was the only great power that had no designs on Pakistan and friendship with the United States was highly valued. Ayub expressed hope for our understanding of the difficult problems faced by Pakistan in its relations with its neighbors. He said he understood the compulsions of US global policies and that Pakistan was a small element in this large picture. But he hoped the United States did not consider Pakistan expendable. (I interjected that we indeed did not consider Pakistan expendable but, on the contrary, an important friend.) President Ayub concluded his remarks by very graciously welcoming me to Pakistan in my capacity as President Johnson's representative here.

3. Credentials presentation was followed by 45 minutes private meeting between President Ayub and me in which I covered ground of reftel.

---

[1] Source: National Archives and Records Administration, RG 59, Central Files 1964–66, POL 15–1 PAK. Secret; Priority; Limdis. Repeated to New Delhi and Karachi.

[2] Document 344.

4. President Ayub expanded on his statements reported in para 2. above with particular reference to his friendship for United States, his desire for peace on the subcontinent, his desire to reduce military expenditures, and his hopes for discussions with Indian leaders. On latter point, he thought that GOP representatives could be helpful in encouraging Indians to suggest meeting, but indicated that GOI should take initiative in moving toward further Indo–Pak meetings.

5. I said we hoped that Pakistan could reduce its military expenditures, that figures were not going down as much as we would like them to, although they were being reduced to some extent. Ayub replied that military expenditures were being reduced to a considerable extent, and indicated that Pakistan would be prepared for further reductions, linking this, however, to parallel action by India. I told him that we were likewise encouraging Indians to reduce their military outlays.

6. I told Ayub that we were encouraging Indian leaders to resume discussions on all problems they faced with Pakistan, including Kashmir. We spoke of other matters to be considered such as the Ganges/Bramhaputra control and development, and levels of military expenditures.

7. Ayub made no particular comment, although he did not dissent, when I expressed the desirability of a reduction of forces along both sides of the Indo–Pak border and the cease-fire line. I said I thought the ultimate objective should be a U.S.–Mexican type of border arrangement and that this could involve para-military forces which should be under strict operational control of the central government authorities.

8. During our private discussion Ayub reaffirmed promises he had made to President Johnson during his visit to Washington that he would do nothing to hurt the interests of United States. He said President Johnson had told him that we would do nothing to hurt the interests of Pakistan. Ayub followed this by commenting that he had told his Ministers on his return from Washington to stay away from Vietnam questions in their speeches and that he had passed advice to the press to stay away from anti-U.S. statements about Vietnam and other topics. Ayub said he thought this had been followed up reasonably well. (I believe that this comment by President Ayub gives me a good basis to take up press problems with him if the situation should warrant.)

9. In describing problems that he faced Ayub adverted to the question of spare parts. He indicated he did not take position that United States was wrong in cutting off military supplies. However, he observed that since all his equipment was of U.S. origin, he could not obtain parts except at exorbitant prices (noting parenthetically that we were urging him to lower his military budget) and that this put Pakistan at a disadvantage in comparison with India. India, he said, does not

have such a problem, because it could and did procure its military supplies and equipment from other sources. Ayub made no specific request to me on subject of spares but he clearly wanted me to understand that he had a problem.

10. I told Ayub what we were prepared to do on the matter of economic aid. I let him know that this was not an easy matter for us and that we had taken this decision on the basis of statements by himself and Shoaib to President Johnson and of our understanding and expectation that Pakistan would follow through with efforts to maintain peace on the subcontinent, resolve its differences with India, improve its bilateral relations with the United States and continue its emphasis on economic development. I mentioned also the importance we attach to import liberalization and to release of seized cargoes and compensation for those that could not be returned. On matter of compensation, Ayub agreed in principle and said GOP would be prepared to negotiate that matter with us, presumably on amounts involved. Ayub was obviously pleased at this word and the indication it conveyed of U.S. readiness to take affirmative steps to build strong U.S.–Pak ties.

11. I am reporting separately my discussion with Ayub on the reopening of the small technical facilities.[3]

12. I am seeing Finance Minister Shoaib at 6:30 this evening and will go over some of these points in greater detail with him.

Locke

---

[3] Locke reported on this part of his discussion with Ayub in telegram 754 from Rawalpindi, June 9. In light of the importance the United States attached to the reopening of the facilities, Ayub indicated that he was prepared to negotiate an agreement to reopen them if they could be made less conspicuous by moving them into the Peshawar complex. If that was not acceptable to the United States, Ayub said that he would consider reopening them where they were if they were manned by Pakistani personnel. (National Archives and Records Administration, RG 59, Central Files 1964–66, POL 15–1 PAK) The Department replied, in telegram 640, June 13, that it could accept the bases for negotiation put forward by Ayub. (Ibid., DEF 18–8 US)

349.   Memorandum From the President's Special Assistant (Rostow) to President Johnson[1]

Washington, June 11, 1966, 6:15 p.m.

Mrs. Gandhi has taken the first big step in the economic program Mehta worked out with George Woods. She has devalued the rupee. This has triggered strong opposition within her own party, from the Left, and from Indian business men.

She needs the prompt response of aid donors to permit import liberalization and to underscore the positive part of her program. That is why George Woods is pressing the consortium hard for prompt action.

The politics of our bargain are in pretty good shape.

—She is angling through diplomatic channels for another meeting with the Paks. Gene Locke is working the other end of the line. While this will probably not produce anything dramatic, it should keep the Tashkent process going.

—The effort to get a grip on military spending is less advanced. But George Woods is working actively on this, as you know; and State is pressing the Indians to take our concern seriously.

We are pleased with Mrs. Gandhi's boldness; a bit worried about the tightrope she's on; and feel we should go ahead now with our part of the economic deal.

Woods has promised to let her know by 15 June—next Wednesday—how much the consortium will contribute toward the World Bank target of $900 million in non-project aid. She has committed herself to announce further steps on import liberalization by about 20 June. She cannot do this without the Woods package. The consortium meets on Tuesday.

Dave Bell accepts the World Bank's $900 million target and would like your approval:

To put in a U.S. planning figure up to $335 million at the consortium negotiating session Tuesday. This is in addition to the $100 million you approved for the Vice President to take with him in February. Our planning figure would include: (a) an immediate new program loan of $150 million available from FY 66 funds and (b) up to another $185 million to be made contingent on Congressional approval.

Bell would start bargaining with a low U.S. figure of $280 million (plus the earlier $100 million) to press other donors to give more and would go up to the full $335 million only if necessary to get the maxi-

---

[1] Source: Johnson Library, National Security File, Country File, India, Vol. VII, Memos & Miscellaneous, 1–8/66. Confidential.

mum out of the others. AID can handle the higher figure with what it has already asked of Congress.

Woods is pressing the Germans to increase the $62 million they plan to put into the consortium; and to increase within that figure the present amount (about $45 million) of their program lending. We shall be on to the Indians to press home George's point.

Bell recommends the package[2] and has consulted the Congress.

State concurs.

Bureau of the Budget concurs in an attached memorandum.[3]

Secretary Fowler is in dissent as his attached memorandum[4] to you indicates.

He makes three points:

—He believes 42 percent rather than 48 percent is the "Appropriate share" for the United States;
—He regrets that the debt rescheduling for India will be delayed by the World Bank until the fall;
—He generally opposes continued non-project lending to India unless we can establish a more favorable bilateral trade balance with India.

I have looked carefully into these points.

With respect to shares, the 42 percent is an historically accepted figure covering both project and non-project lending. It is not the relevant figure for this package, which is wholly non-project. In fiscal 1965—the last year for a full consortium package—the non-project share of the United States was as high as 35 percent. It is, thus, true that in the sensitive area of non-project lending we are making progress in getting others to do more.

Moreover, our share looks bigger than it is. We are being allowed by the World Bank to count the $100 million non-project loan to India which we granted via the Vice President, as part of this year's consortium package, although it represents funds which under normal circumstances we would have lent India last year. The other members of the consortium did not break off the assistance to India as we did during the war period. They are not getting credit this year for the contributions they made last year.

Therefore, on this point I conclude that our share in this non-project package is "appropriate."

---

[2] Memorandum from David E. Bell to the President, June 10. (Ibid., NSC Histories, Indian Famine, August 1966–February 1967, Vol. II)

[3] Reference is to a June 11 memorandum from Charles L. Schultze to the President.

[4] Reference is to a June 11 memorandum from Henry H. Fowler to the President.

With respect to debt rescheduling, all of us would like to see that take place as soon as possible. It requires, however, complicated prior negotiation. George Woods believes he cannot get it organized until the fall. He has, however, accepted and will try to press on the others, a principle greatly to our advantage; namely the principle that we will take the debt rescheduling "off the top." This means that those who, in the past (mainly Europeans), lent on hardest terms will bear the greater burden in the rescheduling; we will deduct this from the $900 million; and we shall divide up the balance according to the agreed percentages. It is just that this principle be accepted; but it is also to our advantage. And it is worth our while to let George Woods fight this battle for us between now and the autumn, which is his recommendation.

With respect to the commercial balance, it is true that we buy more from India than they buy from us. However, this does not bear directly on the present loan package. All of it is tied. We are working hard—and should work harder—to increase our exports to India. We are making some progress. But we cannot count on having even bilateral trade balances with every country. Moreover, of the other major trading partners of India: the pound is in worse trouble than the dollar; the Germans are no longer building reserves; and we have good balance of payments arrangements with Japan. The Indians trade little with the French.

I conclude, therefore, that while we wish to go further in increasing our exports to India as to other countries, there is no balance of payments pain in this loan package; and there is not even much pain in India's favorable trade balance with us.

Therefore, I concur in the recommendation of AID, State, and the Bureau of the Budget.

The $900 million is the minimum necessary to carry Mrs. Gandhi over import liberalization and her political crisis.

Economically, our balance of payments will not be damaged.

And we are getting about as much equity from the consortium as one is likely to get in an imperfect world.

I recommend you approve the AID package as presented.

Walt

Approve AID package[5]

Disapprove

See me

---

[5] Johnson checked this option.

350.   Telegram From the Department of State to the Embassy in India[1]

Washington, June 14, 1966, 10:46 p.m.

2477. 1. The President has approved the following US position regarding aid to India:

(a) We accept the requirement of $900 mil non-project aid as calculated by the World Bank (U.S. $100 mil commodity loan announced by VP in Febr. is counted toward this total);

(b) we are prepared to negotiate an immediate non-project loan in the amount of $150 mil;

(c) we are prepared to make further non-project loans to India after Congressional action in order to meet share in financing India's non-project aid requirements for the year, and we now contemplate an additional loan in the amount of $130 mil. This latter loan would be subject to Congressional action. We now contemplate that this would complete our contribution bringing U.S. total to $380 mil or 42 perent,[2] which U.S. share recent years total pledges.

2. As a fall back position, the President has further authorized us to increase the contingent portion of our contribution to be provided after Congressional action, by an amount up to $55 mil which could be financed by AID, or by a combination of AID and Export-Import Bank resources. This total package assumes India sustains economic liberalization, avoids arms race and pursues peace on sub continent.

3. Subsequently, Macomber conveyed to Woods points (a), (b) and (c), further qualifying (c) as subject to appropriate burden sharing by other donors. Woods indicated he did not expect have word from British regarding their contribution until June 15. By that date Woods estimates contributions of US, UK, Canada (which he now contacting) and Bank will total somewhat over $700 mil. He plans to convey this figure to Indians June 15 noting US conditions of Congressional action and appropriate burden sharing.

4. Woods' position as we understand it is that if Indians require immediate response to their query regarding resources to support reforms, figure of $700 mil is best Bank can do at this time. Additional contributions will take more time.

5. Principal problem Bank has encountered so far in rounding up contributions has been with Germans. Woods has informed us in

---

[1] Source: National Archives and Records Administration, RG 59, Central Files 1964–66, AID 9 INDIA. Secret; Priority; Exdis. Drafted by Schneider; cleared by Macomber (draft), Wriggins, and EUR/GER; and approved by Handley. Repeated to Rawalpindi and Karachi.

[2] Reference is to the percentage of assistance pledged by the members of the India consortium.

confidence that in response to his latest query German Minister of State Westrick (please protect both sources) has replied as follows:

"We are, as I explained to your collaborators, in very hard budgetary discussions. It seems to me impossible to come to a final decision regarding the aid for India within short time. I hope that we will continue in principle to support the Indian economic development but we cannot give assurances at the present time."

6. Bank as yet has no report from Japanese who next most significant contributor. Bank meeting June 7 asked early report from all including smaller donors but no reports yet in.

7. In our view while $700 mil figure is far from what we or Indians had hoped for, there is reasonable prospect for reaching goal of $900 mil given time. For example, if, on top of $700 mil from Bank, UK, Canada and US, others only match their last year non-project pledge the total would be over $810 mil. Obviously look for increased non-project contributions from others, particularly Germany, Japan and Italy. Principal problem, of course, is the Germans and it is up to Indians, at least in the first instance, to press the Germans for early adequate contribution. We are making this point to Indians here. Japanese are also rather unknown factor since Bank has not yet made serious individual effort with them.

8. Above information is FYI for the present. White House has authorized us to convey points (a), (b) and (c) to Indians, but we believe we should defer this until after Bank has given its overall response. We will notify you by Immediate telegram when this has been done.[3]

Rusk

---

[3] On June 15 the Department informed the Embassy in New Delhi that the World Bank had informed the Indian Embassy about the projected levels of economic assistance. The Embassy was authorized to discuss the U.S. assistance package, as outlined in telegram 2477, with the Indian Government. The Embassy was instructed to point up the qualifications listed in paragraph 2, and to make clear that U.S. ability to proceed with additional non-project loans, as indicated in paragraph 1 (c), was dependent on Congressional action and proportionate burden sharing by other donors. (Telegram 2479 to New Delhi; National Archives and Records Administration, RG 59, Central Files 1964–66, AID (US) INDIA) The Department issued a press release on June 15 that stated that, in conjunction with the members of the consortia on India and Pakistan, the United States was in the process of resuming economic assistance to India and Pakistan. (Telegram 659 to Rawalpindi; ibid., AID (US) PAK)

351. Telegram From the Embassy in India to the Department of State[1]

New Delhi, June 15, 1966, 0758Z.

3462. Ref: Deptel 2447.[2]

1. As reftel points out, the US has a major interest in heading off arms race in subcontinent and in containing Chinese threat to both India and Pakistan. The guidelines for discussion with GOI regarding Indian military expenditures and relationship to Paks outlined in reftel impress me as both useful and sound. As previously reported we have been pressing GOI on this subject and will continue to do so.

2. Thus far informal response by GOI officials to proposition that both India and Pakistan should agree to discuss a ceiling on their military budgets has been generally affirmative. Although there is considerable uncertainty in regard to procedures I believe, as a starting point, that GOI would agree to a confidential inquiry by the World Bank to establish the facts in regard to defense budgets of both nations.

3. The critical difficulty would be the development of an acceptable formula for limiting military establishments on both sides. As Indians see it they have four-and-one-half times the population of Pakistan and well over four times the GNP. More than that they face two formidable military threats along a land frontier of over 9000 miles: First in importance are the Chinese who attacked in 1962 and second are the Paks who attacked in 1965 against an obligation [sic] of Chinese ultimatum. Although most moderate Indians agree that Pak fears of an Indian attack on Pakistan may be genuine, they believe such fears to be utterly irrational and hence unlikely to be significantly affected by what Indians may say or do at the negotiating table.

4. In regard to the current flow of Soviet equipment the Indians point out that they turned to the USSR in August 1964 only when it

---

[1] Source: National Archives and Records Administration, RG 59, Central Files 1964–66, DEF 19–8 US–INDIA. Secret; Exdis. The Embassy suggested that the cable be repeated to Rawalpindi, Karachi, and CINCMEAFSA as desired.

[2] In telegram 2447 to New Delhi, June 10, the Department expressed concern over the Indian Government's apparent lack of understanding of the impact of its extensive arms procurement program on the military policy of Pakistan. The Embassy was instructed to discover what the Indian Government proposed to do about a situation that could lead to China becoming Pakistan's major supplier of military equipment. The Department suggested that India should recognize that it would be far better for Pakistan to maintain its existing U.S.-supplied forces from either U.S. or other Western sources of supply. (Ibid.)

became clear that they could not secure the military equipment they needed from the US. Of the $396 million that the Indians anticipated from US and Western sources in the first three years of the 1964 agreement only $140 million was made available. In a conversation at my home last week, General Chadhury suggested that the difference of $256 million is roughly comparable to the amount that India has since committed for equipment from the USSR. (Chadhury stressed that we had inadvertently forced India to turn to the Soviets which they did not want to do.)

5. There are two steps that might persuade India to cut back on its current defense spending, both of which present difficulties: (a) clear recognition by the US of the Chinese threat to India and a pledge within limits imposed by our Constitution that we would provide all feasible assistance to India in event of another ChiCom attack (possibly as a reaffirmation or extension of the air defense agreement); (b) a statement by GOP that it is prepared to sign a no-war agreement as the first step toward the limitation of respective military establishments. Because both of these assurances appear unlikely under present circumstances, I am not particularly hopeful that India will agree to a further reduction below the levels to which we and they agreed to in June 1964. However, if Paks were willing, it may be possible to work out some reductions in that portion of Indian military establishment for defense against Pakistan in return for reductions in Pak establishment.

6. Despite these difficulties I believe Mrs. Gandhi will continue to seek some kind of dialogue with Paks on all problems of mutual interest; indeed I suspect that this may be the next item on her agenda once devaluation-liberalization program is on tracks and Punjab situation settles down.

Major question within GOI now appears to be appropriate level of the talks. After failure at Rawalpindi Mrs. Gandhi is genuinely anxious to assure forum which will be potentially most productive or, at a minimum, least risky.

7. We have already pointed out (Embtel 3281)[3] the damaging impact we will face in India if US provides lethal military supplies to Pakistan regardless of how they may be financed. Further conversations with GOI officials, talks over the weekend with Indian military at Defense Staff College in south India, and widespread evidence of all-out Communist–Mennonite campaign to destroy Mrs. Gandhi because of her growing relationship with US confirm our belief that these fore-

---

[3] In telegram 3281 from New Delhi, May 31, the Embassy recorded its objections to the resumption of the supply of lethal weapons to Pakistan. (Ibid., DEF 19–8 US–PAK)

bodings have not been overdrawn. Thus we continue strongly to support conclusions reached in Pindi's 675[4] and our 3281.

8. As a consequence of the war last August and September against an American-equipped Pak army and air force we are dealing here in India with an emotional, highly charged, gut issue which will not respond to reason. Even such sympathetic and sophisticated GOI officials as L.K. Jha could not be persuaded that US is serving long-range Indian/US interest by resuming its old role as supplier of lethal military equipment to Pakistan even on a moderate scale. Without exception such individuals are deeply convinced that any US move in this direction would again encourage unreal expectations in Rawalpindi and consequently greater inflexibility on part of Paks, while simultaneously undercutting US relationship with India at a time when they have personally staked their positions within GOI on improved understanding.

9. A large majority of Indian public, prodded by shrewd and far-reaching left wing campaign, would react with the utmost vigor to the resumption of lethal US spares for Pak fighter planes which even our best friends within GOI and press point out can only be [garble—used?] against India. Our loss in public esteem and distrust of US policy and judgment would be massive.

10. Adverse Indian reaction underscored by emotional political attacks and an extremely bad press would create counter reaction in the US with further danger to the excellent relationship developed during Mrs. Gandhi's visit.

11. At the same time resumption of US lethal military supplies to Pakistan would undermine for some time to come our capacity to foster an accommodating Indian attitude toward Pakistan. An essential element in the delicate exercise of persuading India to consider a limitation on its military establishment vis-à-vis Pakistan is India's trust in both reliability and good judgment of USG.

12. Another likely casualty of US lethal equipment to Pakistan would be whatever ability we may still have to keep India on non-nuclear path at least long enough to offer some hope of a world-wide non-proliferation agreement. Mrs. Gandhi's government would never accept credibility of US assurances regarding nuclear threat if we appeared at same time to be joining Communist China in arming Pakistan against India.

---

[4] Telegram 675 from Rawalpindi, May 26, transmitted the Embassy's assessment that the sale of lethal spare parts to Pakistan would not win enough points with the Pakistani military to counterbalance the anticipated cost to the U.S. relationship with India. The Embassy recommended no direct sales of lethal spare parts or equipment to either India or Pakistan. (Ibid.)

13. I agree with Rawalpindi's 675 on wisdom of our standing aside when Paks seek to buy elsewhere in the West the equipment which they feel they need. There is no good reason why we should discourage these purchases as long as they come within previously acknowledged budgetary limits, hopefully set in agreement with India.

14. I believe that for foreseeable future we must choose between two courses of action regarding arms policy toward India and Pakistan:

A. We can resume a lethal military supply relationship with Pakistan and as a consequence see a sharp deterioration in our position in India which because of its size and political orientation is the only realistic starting point for the building of an indigenous Asian counterweight to China.

B. We can limit our military supplies to both countries to non-lethal categories (if anything at all) and continue to press both India and Pakistan to focus their energies on economic development and to move toward a realistic and tolerable mutual accommodation with regard to their respective military establishments.

15. We are now striving to make B. work. I strongly urge that we continue to do so.

Bowles

---

352. Memorandum From the Joint Chiefs of Staff to Secretary of Defense McNamara[1]

JCSM–403–66   Washington, June 15, 1966.

SUBJECT

The Problem of US Military Assistance to India and Pakistan

1. (U) Reference is made to a memorandum by the Assistant Secretary of Defense (ISA), I–23952/66, dated 8 June 1966[2], subject as above.

2. (U) The Joint Chiefs of Staff have completed a review of the staff study forwarded by the reference and do not concur in the thrust

---

[1] Source: Washington National Records Center, RG 330, OSD Files: FRC 70 A 4662, Pakistan 091.3, MAP. Top Secret.

[2] On June 8 John T. McNaughton sent a memorandum to McNamara, attaching a study prepared in DOD/ISA on "The Problem of US Military Assistance to India and Pakistan." McNaughton noted that the study concluded that a policy of lethal sales to either India or Pakistan would produce major disadvantages for the United States and no clear advantages. (Ibid., OSD Files: FRC 70 A 4443, Pakistan 091.3 MAP–MAAG)

of the study nor in its conclusions and recommendations except as noted in the Annexes[3] hereto.

3. (S) The Joint Chiefs of Staff note that there is a segment of international influence which contends that as a result of a more amicable Soviet/US relationship, together with the apparent Soviet/ChiCom ideological split, the US policy should be based on cooperation with the Soviets. The Joint Chiefs of Staff believe that it must be kept foremost in mind, and as the basis of US objectives and policy, that the USSR is still the primary adversary of the United States and that US efforts throughout the world should not encourage or accommodate the Russian design or goal any more than that of the ChiComs.

4. (S) In developing US policy objectives for the subcontinent, it must be recognized that what the United States may consider as illogical or irrational attitudes and policies on the part of India and Pakistan are, in fact, the controlling elements upon which US actions will have to be predicated. These include the following:

a. Pakistan's fear that the fundamental Indian goal is the conquest of Pakistan.

b. India's intransigence on the Kashmir issue for fear of losing face before the world (as opposed to acquiring face in accord with its support of international goals for peaceful settlement of issues).

c. Maintenance of armed forces by India and Pakistan in excess of their legitimate needs which neither country economically can afford.

d. Refusal of India and Pakistan to realize the great advantages that would accrue to them (and the world at large) if they both could agree on a policy in the subcontinent which would provide for their national security and economic-sociological development.

5. (TS) The United States also must correlate its role in the subcontinent with other areas. With Pakistan, the United States must consider not only its bilateral agreements, particularly regarding critical, special facilities in Peshawar, but also its position in relationship to CENTO, SEATO, and the Moslem world. With India, the United States must take into account Indian/ChiCom hostility and the attitudes and policies of both India and Communist China in relation to Southeast Asia, to include Indo/Soviet and Soviet/North Vietnam relationships and the positions of each nation toward world peace. A US strategy of assistance to India which results in ChiCom expansion into Pakistan, with a concomitant weakening of CENTO and SEATO and a loss of US special facilities in Pakistan, would be self-defeating. The losses thereby incurred would exceed any anticipated gain to the United States and India—particularly if India should become encircled with a ChiCom-dominated Sino/Pak alliance. It, therefore, is in the national interest

---

[3] Annexes A–G are not printed.

of both the United States and India to make every effort to improve relations with Pakistan so that Chinese ingress in the subcontinent may be pre-empted.

6. (S) US national interests are best served by maintaining a stable, economically sound, and secure subcontinent. The military postures of both India and Pakistan prior to the 1962 ChiCom aggression reflected an acceptable military situation from the US point of view. However, significant change now has been induced, and reversion to the status quo ante 1962 is highly improbable. Therefore, a new balance for the subcontinent must be achieved. The most desirable is one wherein:

a. Pakistan maintains its CENTO role and serves as an anchor on the "containment" flank of the West.

b. Pakistan co-exists with India and rejects any close relation with the ChiComs.

c. India rejects closer ties with the Soviets and continues to deter the ChiComs.

d. India achieves a modus vivendi with Pakistan.

7. (S) The Joint Chiefs of Staff recommend that the following military assistance policy be adopted to further US objectives in the subcontinent:

a. Expand the present policy on sale of nonlethal items to permit cash and credit sales of spare parts for US-supplied equipment in both countries without regard to lethality.

b. Offer a grant-aid program of in-country and CONUS training to India and Pakistan.

c. Resume grant-aid selectively on a case-by-case basis for projects which are in the US strategic interest.

d. Attempt to gain, as a long-term US strategy, Indo/Pak agreement on the minimum force structures, military manpower ceilings, defense spending limitations, and foreign exchange diversions. The United States should use all available and potential leverage to promote this strategy.

e. Be prepared to discuss modernization of the forces of both countries in the interest of security of the subcontinent provided India and Pakistan achieve a mutual agreement, as set forth in subparagraph d, above, acceptable to the United States.

For the Joint Chiefs of Staff:

Harold K. Johnson[4]
Acting Chairman
Joint Chiefs of Staff

---

[4] Printed from a copy that indicates Johnson signed the original.

353. Telegram From the Department of State to the Embassy in Pakistan[1]

Washington, June 24, 1966, 8:53 p.m.

701. Following is summary memcon. It is FYI, Noforn, and subject to amendment upon review.

1. Pakistan Ambassador Ghulam Ahmed called on Secretary June 23. Assist. Secy. Hare also present. Ambassador stated he was under instruction to clarify personally to Secretary GOP's position on question reopening AEDS stations Lahore and Karachi. Cited problems in political, psychological, and military areas which reopening could cause for Pakistan vis-à-vis Soviets; presentation virtually identical Shahi démarche to DCM June 7 (Rawalpindi's 737).[2] Ambassador added that Soviet Ambassador Washington continually questions him about "American bases" near Peshawar; said Soviet Deputy Prime Minister Mazurov had raised this specifically with Ayub and said he hoped AEDS stations would not be reopened. All this raised considerable dilemma for Paks, both in context Kashmir issue and in area military supply where Pakistan had no indication US intention resume deliveries and Soviets had at least indicated they willing discuss supply to Pakistan. Added he did not know whether actual talks had begun with Soviets this subject.

2. Secretary said he was glad to have Ambassador's clarification. Said some of considerations cited by Ambassador were peripheral to small stations in question which primarily concerned with detection process serving nuclear test ban treaty requirements. Secretary said we would be considering problem further, and would be discussing with Ambassador Locke prior his return Rawalpindi.

3. Secretary asked Ambassador re prospects for Indo–Pak talks. Ambassador stated he not fully informed; thought talks likely to take place although Mrs. Gandhi's Moscow visit might delay them a bit. He understood there had been considerable amount US persuasion on both parties to get talks going. Secretary said we hoped very much talks could begin and that there would not be undue delay for discussion agenda. Cited our own experience with Russians where we had found it often useful not have any agenda but simply to start talking.

Ball

---

[1] Source: National Archives and Records Administration, RG 59, Central Files 1964–66, DEF 15 PAK–US. Confidential; Limdis. Drafted by Laingen; cleared by Laise, McCracken, and in substance by Spain; and approved by Hare. Also sent to Karachi and repeated to New Delhi and Moscow.

[2] See footnote 3, Document 344.

354.   National Intelligence Estimate[1]

NIE 31/32–66   Washington, July 7, 1966.

THE FOREIGN POLICIES OF INDIA AND PAKISTAN

The Problem

To examine possible developments, over the next year or two, in the relations between India and Pakistan and between them and the major powers.

Conclusions

A. In view of the mutual suspicions and animosities on both sides, there is little prospect of any substantial improvement in Indo-Pakistani relations in the foreseeable future. India will remain basically unyielding on Kashmir, while Pakistan will continue to seek movement toward a solution. Pakistani pressure on this issue probably will involve some infiltration into Kashmir, but Pakistan, recognizing Indian military superiority, will be careful to avoid actions which it thinks might develop into major fighting.

B. Pakistan considers that it must improve its forces to be able to defend at least West Pakistan in any future hostilities. India is determined to be able to cope simultaneously with Pakistan and China. In the current year, both are spending substantial sums on defense—$569 million or about 5.5 percent of GNP in the case of Pakistan and $2.1 billion or four percent in the case of India—and both will continue to give defense requirements a very high priority.

C. India will remain hostile to China and will seek to remain nonaligned between the US and USSR. India has already made a number of economic reforms urged by the US, in order to get renewed economic aid. It is concerned by the Soviet Union's gradual move away from uncritical support of India. To inhibit further movement, and to continue receiving economic and military aid, New Delhi will take pains to avoid offending the Soviets whenever possible.

D. Pakistan will continue to try to balance its relations with the US and China. It is aware that a close association with the latter would jeopardize its relationship with the US. At the same time, it needs arms, and China appears to Pakistan as the one country which is willing to

---

[1] Source: Central Intelligence Agency, Job 79–R01012A, ODDI Registry of NIE and SNIE Files. Secret; Controlled Dissem. According to a note on the cover sheet, the estimate was prepared by the Central Intelligence Agency and the intelligence organization of the Departments of State and Defense, NSA, and AEC. All members of the United States Intelligence Board concurred in the estimate on July 7 except the representative of the Federal Bureau of Investigation, who abstained because the subject was outside his jurisdiction.

provide, apparently at modest cost, the types and amounts necessary to rearm and improve Pakistan's military posture.

E. Both India and Pakistan are aware that US provision of economic aid will be tied to performance on matters of importance to the US, such as limiting military spending and giving priority to economic development. In a general way, we believe that India will probably meet US requirements somewhat better than will Pakistan.

[Here follows the 9-page Discussion portion of the Estimate.]

---

355. Telegram From the Embassy in Pakistan to the Department of State[1]

Rawalpindi, July 9, 1966, 0953Z.

82. Separatist Movement in East Pakistan.

1. During July 7 call on S.M. Yusuf in his new capacity as Foreign Secretary, I called attention to accusations of American involvement in East Pak separatist movement being given currency in Pak press and also in public statements of GOP officials, and cited:

A. Articles in Dacca newspaper, *Paigam*, of April 30 and May 1, 1966 in which headlines alleged "Unholy Alliance of American Circles with Advocates on "[Six?] Points" and "Six Points Nourished by American Injection" and in which assertion was made that U.S. "has purchased one particular party in West Pakistan" and given this party its six points;

B. East Pak newspaper *Janata* June 23, 1966 alleging that U.S. is "creating a secessionist trend in East Pakistan" and that U.S. "wants to use East Pakistan as a springboard in world strategy";

C. A resolution of ad hoc working committee of East Pak Muslim League of June 23, 1966, alleging that "certain foreign elements" attempting to fan autonomy movement in East Pakistan "with a view to serving their own global interests"; and

D. National Assembly speech on June 29, 1966 by Communications Minister Sobur alleging that East Pak "autonomy movement could not conceal its own alliance with some hostile powers, those who for their global interests want to drive a wedge amongst the solidarity of the people."

That these indirect accusations were also against the U.S. was clear, I said, from use of expression "foreign powers with global interests."

---

[1] Source: National Archives and Records Administration, RG 59, Central Files 1964–66, POL PAK. Secret; Limdis. Repeated to Karachi, New Delhi, and Dacca.

I noted, and Foreign Secretary indicated agreement, that in Pakistan "power with global interests" meant the United States. We had no doubt on basis of reactions we had received that people of Pakistan clearly understood such articles and statements were intended to be charges against U.S.

2. I said such allegations were completely false, and that to give them currency in press and in public statements by GOP officials could only have a depressing effect upon efforts to maintain and develop atmosphere of collaboration and understanding which would strengthen US–Pak relations. I developed at some length illogic of any assumption that U.S. policy would now seek to fragment Pakistan when we had devoted extensive efforts and resources over period of years, and were so now doing, to help build, in collaboration with GOP leaders, strong and unified Pakistan as source of stability in subcontinent and as barrier to Communist penetration. I noted that, with this basic and long-standing policy, U.S. could not conceivably favor separation of East Pakistan from Pakistan, process which would occasion political strife, economic dislocation, and popular unrest, promoting serious instability in sub-continent and offering temptations and opportunities for Communist China. it would not be reasonable to assume U.S. would work against its own interests and its own policy objectives by seeking to press [for] political disintegration of Pakistan. Nor could it be alleged that the right hand did not know what the left hand was doing and that U.S. was in fact pursuing two policies with respect to East Pakistan. I said U.S. policy in Pakistan is policy of the President of U.S. and that he and his representative in Pakistan, the American Ambassador, have responsibility and authority to assure U.S. policies and objectives are supported by all branches and agencies of U.S.G. I told Secretary that this in point of fact was the situation in practice and would continue to be the situation governing American actions in Pakistan. I summarized by saying that U.S. policy toward Pakistan continues to be based on need for an independent, strong, and unified Pakistan; that U.S. does not support separatism in East Pak; and that constitutional arrangements for the two wings and question of greater autonomy for East Pakistan are internal matters to be worked out by Pakistan in accordance with its own processes.

4. Secretary Yusuf said he welcomed assurances as to U.S.G. policy with respect to unity of Pakistan and our attitude on question of separatism in West Pakistan. He then referred to the conversation between Ambassador Locke and President Ayub on June 16[2] at which he had

---

[2] Locke's meeting with Ayub on June 16 was reported in telegrams 803, 805, and 806 from Rawalpindi, all June 17. (Ibid., DEF 19–8 US–PAK, AID (US) PAK, and POL INDIA–PAK, respectively)

also been present. Yusuf noted that Ayub had initiated this topic and had cited reports which GOP continued to receive about conversations between American officials in Dacca and opposition political figures. Foreign Secretary said there were numbers of such reports. He admitted there was high degree of sensitivity about East Pakistan on part of GOP officials which he attributed to GOP conviction that India is promoting East Pak separatism. Amplifying this point, Yusuf said that radio stations from India were beaming separatist propaganda into East Pakistan seven or eight hours each day and also that pamphlets and leaflets urging East Pakistan separatism were printed in India and brought into East Pakistan for distribution. (According UK HICOM Pickard, East Pakistan Governor Monem Ekhan cited these same points in discussion with him last week in Dacca.)

5. Yusuf wondered whether American officers in East Pakistan were on all occasions as discreet in their choice of contacts as they should be. He said GOP did not take position that all opposition leaders were beyond the pale. GOP considers an opposition necessary. Some opposition figures accepted the premises of Pakistan's constitutional system. (Yusuf in fact referred to them as the "loyal opposition.") However, other opposition leaders were "disruptionists," seeking to promote disintegration of Pakistan and separate existence for East Pakistan or a Bengali state. Yusuf said he was making no assertion as to facts, but that if American officials were in frequent contact with opposition leaders of the disruptionist type, this would certainly give rise to misunderstanding.

6. I responded that I was certain there was not such a pattern of contacts by our people in East Pakistan, that they of course talk with opposition political leaders as part of their normal functions as political officers of U.S.G., but that in such conversations they did not take positions on controversial domestic issues, much less lend support to separatist elements in East Pakistan. I said that the pitfalls with respect to kinds of reports he had been talking about were well known to both of us as were pressures which might affect their credibility. Yusuf acknowledged this and remarked that Ayub "did not credit all these reports."

7. Foreign Secretary said Secretary Rusk in Canberra had raised topic of allegations about American activities with respect to East Pakistan in conversation with Additional Secretary Shahi. Secretary Rusk had suggested joint inquiry into this problem. Yusuf quickly added that GOP did not think joint inquiry would be useful approach.

8. Foreign Secretary undertook to explain rationale by which some Pakistanis might believe that U.S. "global interests" would be served by separatist movement in East Pakistan. He entirely disassociated himself from such view, but said was useful to broad understanding

of problem. Rationale which he developed was that U.S. support of India was basic U.S. policy, part of its global strategy; India was now in great difficulty because of its limited access to Assam, routes across East Pakistan being not now open to India; Indian position vis-à-vis China would be strengthened by more ready access to Assam; therefore U.S. might be prepared encourage East Pakistan separatist movement. I said that such line of reasoning was fantastically erroneous, adding that I had noted Foreign Secretary did not accept it. As I had outlined earlier, our estimate was that separate East Pakistan would be great factor of instability in South Asia.

9. Foreign Secretary again stated his belief that Indian policy is directed toward detaching East Pakistan. I said I found it impossible to believe Indian policy in fact pointed in this direction, that persons following this view would be clearly misguided, since, if successful, it would result in enormous pressures being brought to bear on India with respect to Bengal and would be advantageous only to China. I added that so far as I could see only one country would stand to benefit, in terms of its known goals, from East Pak or Bengali separatism and that country was Communist China. Yusuf made no comment on this remark.

10. I told Secretary Yusuf that Embassy was acutely aware of sensitivity to GOP of issues relating to East Pakistan and that we had very responsible officers serving in East Pakistan. I said we would be ready at any time to discuss with Foreign Secretary any reports of charges as to alleged American actions in East Pakistan. I reiterated again our concern as to harmful effect of press charges and public allegations by GOP officials and asked him to let this be known to appropriate authorities of his government.

11. *Comment:* Allegations that U.S. is fomenting separatism in East Pakistan are extremely difficult to deal with effectively because of:

A. Politically tense situation there and in Pakistan generally which moves Pak officials to be sensitive, suspicious, alarmist;
B. Short-run utility to Pak political leaders of being able to attribute pressing difficulties to nefarious foreign influence;
C. Pattern and style of government and society which assume deviousness and anticipate intrigue;
D. Vulnerability of U.S., which is widely accepted here as having capability for large-scale under-cover manoeuvre.

For these reasons, such allegations are to certain extent inherent in situation which can be expected to continue.

12. Nonetheless, I believe there are measures which we can take with some prospect of blunting these allegations. This is particularly true to extent such allegations reflect concerted campaign of defamation, instigated or abetted at various levels of Pak Government. In my judgment, best tactics in private discussion are:

A. Unreserved assertions of the complete falsity of the allegations;
B. Confident statements that there is no evidence to support them; and
C. Persuasive arguments that they are totally illogical.

The core counter-argument here is that East Pak separatism would be entirely contrary to United States interests, and inconsistent with United States policy toward Pakistan.

13. My discussion with Foreign Secretary took place in good atmosphere and, I believe, illustrates the utility of getting this subject out in the open in discussions with GOP officials. It is also evidently much more possible to have a reasonable discussion on this question with the present Foreign Secretary than with his predecessor.

Cargo

---

356. Memorandum From the President's Special Assistant (Rostow) to President Johnson[1]

Washington, July 11, 1966.

SUBJECT

Message from Secretary Freeman on East Pakistan's Food Problems

Attached is an interesting message from Secretary Freeman.[2]

The Pakistanis are having problems with food prices in East Pakistan. Drought has cut production about 5% and there is a price push because food stocks are lower than usual at this time of year, the opposition is badgering the Government, and the administration has

---

[1] Source: Johnson Library, National Security File, Country File, Pakistan, Vol. VI, 1/66–9/66. Secret. A handwritten "L" on the memorandum indicates it was seen by the President.

[2] A retyped copy of telegram 221 from Karachi, July 11, was attached to the memorandum. The telegram, sent eyes only for the President from the Secretary of Agriculture, is ibid. In telegram 221 Freeman reported on his July 11 conversation with Ayub in which they discussed agricultural developments in Pakistan and prospects for a new P.L. 480 agreement in addition to the East Pakistan discussion summarized by Rostow. Freeman arrived in Pakistan on April 11 for a 3-day visit. That visit was followed by a 2-day visit to Afghanistan and a 3-day visit to India. The Embassy in Rawalpindi reported on what it saw as a successful visit by Freeman to Pakistan in telegram 167, July 16. (National Archives and Records Administration, RG 59, Central Files 1964–66, ORG 7 AGR) The Embassy in New Delhi offered a similar assessment of Freeman's visit to India in telegram 1155, July 22. (Ibid.)

not handled what stocks it has on hand to best advantage. Ayub has brought the price pressure to Freeman's attention, and they have discussed the possibility of diverting to East Pakistan several ships waiting to unload at Indian ports.

Our specialists in Agriculture are hard at work reviewing the figures to see what East Pakistan's real needs are. They are also looking into the logistical problems of diverting ships from Indian to East Pakistani ports. State is for it as a helpful political gesture.

Freeman would like to explore the matter further, which is fine. He also asks authority to make a prompt announcement of whatever agreement he reaches after discussions with the Indians. In our view this is premature. The politics of Indo-Pak relations are so tricky that nothing must be said until we are sure it is feasible; and if they can work it out, it may be better to have the Indians and the Pakistanis make their own announcement, without our being publicly engaged. State has therefore told him to explore the matter, but to make no public announcement until further clarification.

Walt

---

357.   **Memorandum From Secretary of Agriculture Freeman to President Johnson**[1]

Washington, July 19, 1966.

SUBJECT

Agriculture on the Scene Inspection and Review—Japan, Pakistan, Afghanistan, India

[Here follows the section of the report on Japan.]

Pakistan

A. Political

President Ayub Khan, as reported in my cable from Pakistan,[2] was cordial and friendly. He recalled his visit with you with pleasure. He realizes how important agricultural development is to Pakistan. The

---

[1] Source: Johnson Library, National Security File, NSC Histories, Indian Famine, Vol. V, August 1966–February 1967. Confidential.

[2] See footnote 2, Document 356.

Pakistani agricultural minister is weak, so I plan to communicate directly with Ayub.

Foreign Minister S.H. Yusuf. I had two long talks with this career public servant of wide experience and now the ranking man in the Foreign Ministry following Bhutto's departure.[3] He seemed friendly and reasonable. He reflected genuine fear of India, citing the Goa takeover. He seemed to be more relaxed about Kashmir than I expected, although bitter that the Indians would not permit a plebiscite. The fact that after twenty years India hadn't earned the loyalty of the people was frequently repeated. Reference to the Chinese was guarded, but he evidenced no great enthusiasm. The India-Chinese clash he described as a border confrontation. The merits of each side he described as confusing. When I asked about the Russians at Tashkent, he said they had performed earnestly and well. He described Kosygin as running back and forth from Shastri to Ayub like an errand boy, spending an hour or two repeatedly with each. On balance, I would evaluate his attitude as "let bygones be bygones and go on from here." As he put it, the fact we can't agree on everything shouldn't mean that we must be unpleasant.

Ayub and Yusuf expressed high regard for you. It would be my judgment that personal communication with Ayub should be maintained to the extent possible.

B. Indian PL 480 Wheat to Pakistan

As I cabled you in my "eyes only" cable, I had hoped we might please Ayub—bring Pakistanis and Indians closer at no cost to the United States.

Ayub reportedly has a nasty political problem in East Pakistan, triggered now by a crop shortage from flood and drought with sharply rising rice prices. Immediate relief could be had by diverting 50,000 tons of wheat to East Pakistan in ships now waiting to be unloaded in India. Replacement can be made to India from wheat committed but not yet shipped to Pakistan.

It was my estimate that maximum U.S. benefit would come from the U.S. openly arranging the switch. Otherwise, I feared the Pakistanis would be too sensitive to accept help from India. I was advised that the U.S. should stay in the background and let the Indians and Pakistanis come together. I proceeded accordingly and got Subramaniam to agree to make the 50,000 tons available immediately provided that Pakistan would ask for it publicly. Our Embassy at Rawalpindi has been so informed. At this writing, Pakistan is unwilling to ask. We are

---

[3] Foreign Minister Bhutto resigned on June 19.

urging them to do so. I fear the United States has lost a good opportunity.

C. *Food Situation*

U.S. arrivals under PL 480 have been cut in half, dropping from 1.5 million tons in 1963 and 1964 to about 660,000 tons in fiscal 1966. Pakistan has suffered drought and flood and has experienced a crop short fall. Supply figures and crop estimates are still fuzzy. I arranged for the necessary joint U.S.-Pakistan procedures to review them and develop the best possible members so some solid judgment can be reached quickly. Negotiations for a PL 480 agreement for the balance of calendar 1966 should be undertaken very soon. I hope to send negotiating instructions to Rawalpindi within a week. I am also reviewing the possibility of promptly increasing the current 300,000 ton wheat agreement to 400,000 tons. This would please Ayub and as a practical matter would be charged against the amount to be negotiated for the current calendar year. A final judgment on this should, I think, be withheld until we see what happens on the wheat exchange between Pakistan and India.

D. *Agricultural Economic Development*

The Pakistanis have made encouraging progress. SCARP, the salinity reclamation project developed and supported by the United States near Lahore, which I believe you visited, is an unqualified success: (1) water table lowered 10 feet, (2) 425,000 acres reclaimed, (3) yield up 30 to 150 percent (wheat 15 to 55 bushels, corn 16 to 70 bushels per acre), (4) land value up from $50 to $1,000 per acre since I visited it in 1961. The Pakistan agricultural growth rate has climbed to 3.5 percent annually, but with a 2.7 percent population increase and an expanding economy the increase is soaked up each year. They must reach 4 percent to hold and 5 percent to gain ground on the food problem. The Pakistanis realize this.

They have a vigorous program, have sharply increased agriculture's share of the budget, and made more foreign exchange available. Ayub asked us for a list of chemical firms because pesticides are very short. A new 200,000 ton fertilizer plant has been contracted with ESSO. Fertilizer is in short supply. The agricultural sector of the economy is vigorous and in my judgment currently meets the self-help standard of the Food for Freedom Act.[4] I believe we should keep the pressure on and provide all the technical assistance that can be effectively used

---

[4] President Johnson requested this legislation in a February 10 message to Congress. (Department of State *Bulletin*, February 28, 1966, pp. 336–341) Congress enacted the Food for Peace Act on November 11, 1966. (P.L. 89–808; 80 Stat 1526)

to help them. However, we must be alert to ensure that the agriculture sector in their economy continues to command first priority (after defense) on the nation's resources. PL 480 ought not to be extended at this time beyond the calendar year.

[Here follows the section of the report on Afghanistan.]

India

   A. Political

The Prime Minister's absence (she was visiting the Soviet Union) inhibited conversation on the world political situation. They are, of course, anti-Chinese. S.K. Patil (Boss of Bombay) went way out of his way to be seen with me publicly. He is a former Minister of Agriculture and an old friend. His primary message was that the climate is good to improve U.S.-India relations. He emphasized his strong support for the Prime Minister (heretofore he has been cool) and even praised Subramaniam (a decided change). Patil is one of the top Congress party political operators (allegedly the No. 1 money-raiser), so I was pleased at his outspoken support for the current Indian Administration.

It would be my evaluation that it is correct as generally reported that Subramaniam is very close to and extremely influential with the Prime Minister. He described for me privately (not bragging or name-dropping) the agony of that decision on devaluation. Clearly, he was a strong prime mover in accomplishing it.

President Radnakrishnan sends his warmest personal regards. He urges that the United States unilaterally and without any commitment cease bombing North Vietnam. Then, he argues, the *rest of the world* would, through the force of world opinion, bring about negotiations. I questioned him fairly closely about this, but could detect no basis for his estimate other than his own subjective opinion. As we prepared to leave him he asked that I carry a message of sympathy to you for the burdens you carry and the extreme difficulty of the situation in Vietnam. He described his feeling of the situation in terms of the Hindu god Shiva—the Power god who takes many poses. One pose is called Nila Kantha or Blue Throat; to wit: the god has a blue throat—if he throws it out he will destroy the world—if he swallows it he will destroy himself.

A public statement I made on arrival in Delhi commanded a lot of attention and dominated my press conferences. To my surprise the Indians have been of the opinion that they would have a five-year grace period under the current soft currency sale terms of PL 480 before shifting to the long-term low-credit conditions of the Food for Freedom program. I think they understand now that although exceptions can be made they will be in extreme circumstances only such as a localized disaster or where the United States itself needs local currency. This has caused some apprehension by the authorities worried about India's debt load, but even they acknowledge that it makes sense. They are requesting that we make an exception for India, but I was very firm in insisting that the time had come when India must pay in dollars but at generous terms. I think they understand.

B. *Food*

The shortfall of food caused by the monsoon estimated last December to be 18 million tons has proved accurate. When Subramaniam came to Washington he said that India would tighten its belt to the extent of 5–6 million tons, and he asked 11 to 12 million tons of grain. As of this date the United States has committed 8 million tons. We have exceeded one-million ton a month arrivals several months. India with our help has raised 1.2 million tons of grain from other sources and the equivalent of 1.5 million tons of grain in money, fertilizer or other commodities for a total value approximately $150,000,000. If the 11 million ton figure requested was a minimum to be reached it will be necessary to make available yet this calendar year 1.8 million tons more of food grain. Subramaniam asked for 2 million tons of wheat and strongly urged that we make several hundred thousand tons of rice available by September plus some vegetable oil and cotton. I carefully outlined the current wheat supply situation in the U.S., emphasizing the loss of an estimated 150,000,000 bushels by drought and frost this spring. The contrast between 1961 when I first visited India as Secretary of Agriculture with 1.5 billion bushel carryover, and now with 500 million bushels made the point that we must be frugal.

Last December we set down three requirements if the United States was to give India the necessary assistance. First that the grain be handled expeditiously and reach the needy. Second, that strong and effective steps be taken pursuant to the Rome agreement to strengthen Indian agriculture. Third, that a real effort be made to get help from other countries. It was emphasized that the self-help requirement would be a stern one. On all three counts it is my judgment that India has lived up to her commitments. One of the greatest food movements of all times taking almost 600 ships is being accomplished.

Not all of the agricultural development targets set out last fall have been reached, but the specific actions agreed on have been taken. I am impressed with Subramaniam's top staff. They are sharp and hard driving. Although very much remains to be done yet by any reasonable standard, I am pleased to report that Subramaniam has fulfilled the economic development commitments he made in Rome. I am not as satisfied with the effort to get help from other countries. France, a wheat surplus nation, denied help. The USSR's contribution is only 5 million dollars. However, it does appear that a real effort was made and 150 million contribution from some 35 other nations is a creditable accomplishment.

It would be my recommendation then, that the United States promptly begin negotiations to meet the needs of India for the balance of this calendar year. Our supplies of wheat are adequate for this amount. We should withhold agreement for the last half of the current fiscal year to be certain India continues to give agriculture top priority in her economic planning. Then we will have a more clear picture of the Indian need and our supply, both of which are currently subject to uncontrollable contingencies.

---

358.   Summary Notes of the 562d Meeting of the National Security Council[1]

Washington, July 19, 1966, 11:45 a.m.–12:45 p.m.

The World Food Problem

The President: This discussion on the current world food problem was called because: 1. The war on hunger is as important as any national security problem we face; 2. The size and urgency of the problem requires us to move rapidly to organize a worldwide attack on hunger; and 3. U.S. public opinion polls show a resistance to our assisting foreign countries in the fields of health, welfare, education, and food.

Secretary Rusk: The Development Assistance Committee is meeting in Washington this week. We plan to alert those who are assisting foreign countries to the urgency of the food problem. Up to now, the food producing countries have been looked to to solve the serious world food problem. However, the fight on hunger must include nations other than the food producing nations. We must work out a combination of means to fight hunger. We are disappointed in what the developing states have done to increase their food production. We have also been disappointed by what the donor states in DAC have done in providing food aid.

AID Director Bell: Summarized the Aid paper (copy attached).[2] He used the charts attached to the paper to illustrate the magnitude

---

[1] Source: Johnson Library, National Security File, NSC Meetings, Vol. 3, 7/19/66. Confidential/Sensitive; For the President Only. An attached list shows that 18 attended the meeting in addition to the President, including Humphrey, Rusk, McNamara, Ball, Helms, Fowler, Freeman, Bell, Gaud, Rostow, and Hamilton.

[2] Reference is to a discussion paper entitled "The World Food Problem," signed by Bell on July 15.

of the problem and to emphasize that an agricultural program must be integrated into the national economy of every developing country.

Secretary Freeman: India is doing what it said it would do in improving seed, developing water resources, and increasing the use and production of fertilizer. Famine is not likely now in India but we must get tough with the Indians to ensure that they achieve a five percent agricultural growth rate. As to U.S. domestic production, we should return additional U.S. acreage to food production. We need enough food to ensure that famine will not occur in the future. The Indians have lived up to their commitments and we must live up to ours. (Secretary Freeman's paper and table referred to are attached.)[3]

The Vice President: We should increase the amount of wheat carried over into the next year in order to block the speculators and to use it as a means of holding down inflation.

Secretary Freeman: A final decision on the increase in U.S. acreage must be taken no later than Labor Day.

The President: Every official taking part in the Development Assistance Committee meeting this week (the Vice President, Secretary Rusk, Secretary Freeman, Ambassador Bell) should make clear that the United States is deadly serious about a worldwide effort to fight hunger and that it is in the interests of all advanced countries to help to the fullest extent that they can.

Secretary Rusk should prepare plans for a State–AID–Agriculture–BOB effort to prepare studies and recommendations as to the next steps to be taken in the war on hunger.

A major objective of this Administration is the export of food, health, and education. Top priority must be given to getting Congress to authorize adequate resources for this purpose.

Secretary Fowler: The export of U. S. goods and services is desirable if it is done in such ways as to avoid displacing commercial markets. The export of cash is not. We must get on a burden-sharing basis with other countries because of the effect on our balance of payments position of the movement abroad of U.S. resources. We must insist that international organizations find ways to transfer abroad our resources with the least effect on our balance of payments.

Bromley Smith

---

[3] A July 19 paper entitled "Review of the World Food Situation," and eight tables illustrating the U.S. wheat situation were attached.

359. Memorandum From Secretary of State Rusk to President Johnson[1]

Washington, July 25, 1966.

SUBJECT

Report to the President on the Indian Nuclear Weapons Problem

In accordance with NSAM 351[2] there is transmitted herewith a report on the Indian Nuclear Weapons Problem.[3] The report has been approved by the Senior Interdepartmental Group, by the Secretary of Defense and by the Director of the Arms Control and Disarmament Agency.

The report recommends no dramatic steps to discourage the Indians from starting a nuclear weapons program; this is because we have been unable to devise anything dramatic which would not cost us more than any anticipated gain. The report does, however, recommend that a number of further studies be made, as this is a developing rather than a static situation. We have all agreed that our purpose with respect to the Indians is to buy time during which, hopefully, we can move forward on broader fronts to bring under more permanent control the dangers inherent in the proliferation of nuclear weapons.

Dean Rusk

---

[1] Source: Johnson Library, National Security File, NSAMs, NSAM 355. No classification marking.

[2] Document 347.

[3] This undated report, prepared by the Senior Interdepartmental Group, is summarized in Document 363. Documentation on the preparation of the report and its consideration by the Senior Interdepartmental Group is in the Johnson Library, National Security File, Agency File, SIG, Vol. I, 12th Meeting, 7/15/66.

360. Telegram From the Ambassador to India (Bowles) to the President's Special Assistant and Chief of Staff (Moyers)[1]

New Delhi, July 25, 1966.

5618. I have just sent an Exdis cable[2] to the President and Secretary Rusk pointing out the profoundly adverse impact that U.S. Mission in India believes a resumption of U.S. supplies of lethal military equipment to Pakistan will have on our position in India at this critical stage.

In this private message to you I would like to add that I have a deep personal involvement in this issue which I cannot wish out of existence.

In 1952 when it was first proposed that we arm Pakistan in the face of clear evidence that Pakistan wanted the equipment for use against India rather than the Russians or Chinese, I was able (in my first assignment as Ambassador here) to persuade President Truman to veto the idea.

When Secretary Dulles picked up the plan in the fall of 1953, I wrote him stressing that if arms we gave Pakistan were ever used in combat, it would not be against China or Russia but only against India, and that even if they were never used, their effect would be to upset the power balance in South Asia, to cloud our relations with India which is potentially the most important non-Communist power in Asia, and to open the door to a much closer Soviet relationship with India. Unhappily these concerns have been fully justified by events.

In the intervening years, President Eisenhower, Ambassadors Bunker, Galbraith and myself assured India over and over again that this U.S. equipment would never be used against her. Yet when the attack came last August and September, it was clear that there was no way that we would prevent their use.

As a result we were faced with a very strong public reaction here in India growing out of deep resentment that young Indians were being killed by the equipment we had given the Paks. In an effort to contain these feelings, I told the Indian government, public and press on several occasions that I could not imagine my government resuming a policy

---

[1] Source: Johnson Library, National Security File, Country File, Pakistan, Vol. VI, Cables, 1/66–9/66. Secret. No time of transmission is on the telegram. An attachment indicates that the telegram was sent [text not declassified].

[2] Telegram 1307 from New Delhi, July 25. (National Archives and Records Administration, RG 59, Central Files 1964–66, DEF 19–8 US–INDIA) Bowles was responding to a personal message sent to him by Rusk on July 24 to tell him that a consensus was building in Washington in favor of altering policy on military assistance to allow sales of lethal spare parts to India and Pakistan. Bowles was invited to comment. (Telegram 14123 to New Delhi, July 24; ibid.)

which had proven so costly for everyone concerned unless the Pakistanis could be persuaded to join India and the U.S. in opposing the Chinese.

My objective is not to add to the concerns of the President at this difficult time but rather to relieve him of problems wherever I possibly can. However, past events have given me a personal involvement on this issue which I thought you should know about.

Warm regards.

---

361. Memorandum From the Ambassador to Pakistan (Locke) to President Johnson[1]

Washington, July 26, 1966.

Mr. President:

1. My jobs are to:

A. Keep India and Pakistan from fighting;
B. Keep Pakistan from being too close to China.

2. From point of view of doing these jobs, Ayub best man U.S. can have as President of Pakistan. He doesn't want to get too close to China, perhaps for reasons of personal survival. But he may be forced toward China if he can't otherwise obtain security against India. Some leading generals do not see dependence on China as threat to Pakistan.

3. Many leading Pakistanis, particularly in Army, feel U.S. would sacrifice Pakistan for India. Ayub does not at this time, primarily because of friendship for President Johnson. He believes Bowles would sacrifice Pakistan and *made strong pitch for Bowles' removal*, with man "strong enough to stand up to India". I shall meet Bowles next week in Hong Kong or Bangkok.

4. Ayub has shown his good faith by

A. Firing Bhutto
B. Conduct at SEATO meeting
C. Not particularly warm reception of Chou En-lai

---

[1] Source: Johnson Library, National Security File, Country File, Pakistan, Vol. VI, Cables, 1/66–9/66. No classification marking. Locke returned to Washington for consultations following his first 10 days as Ambassador. According to a July 25 briefing memorandum prepared for President Johnson by Rostow, Locke was scheduled to meet with Johnson on July 26. (Ibid.) No record of that meeting has been found. Locke probably gave his memorandum to Johnson at that meeting.

D. Cut off of any Assembly remarks on Hanoi and Haiphong bombing.

5. We need to keep faith with him by helping him feel secure against India without his getting closer to China. This means first furnishing spare parts.

6. We also need to get India–Pakistan talks started on arms limitations and other matters. These talks must include Kashmir. Real progress on Kashmir can only be achieved, however, by secret meetings. Many believe Kashmir insolvable. I believe we must try to find solution, as otherwise no chance of lasting peace on subcontinent. Talks must be bilateral secret talks between the two countries at first; but, if at some later time settlement can be achieved by heavy handed U.S. approach, we should not hesitate.

Eugene M. Locke[2]

---

[2] Printed from a copy that bears this typed signature.

---

362. Telegram From the Department of State to the Embassy in India[1]

Washington, July 26, 1966, 2:06 p.m.

15058. Eyes only for the Ambassador from the Secretary. I much appreciated your thoughtful 1307.[2] I have no doubt that Indian reaction would be sharp but there are certain factors in my mind which were not discussed in your telegram on which I would appreciate your further comments.

1. In present circumstances, India is moving toward a complete military domination of the subcontinent. Her own military production capability plus very substantial increments of Soviet equipment puts her in the position of saying that it is all right for India to build up its armed forces from the Soviet Union but not all right for Pakistan to acquire even spare parts from the United States.

---

[1] Source: National Archives and Records Administration, RG 59, Central Files 1964–66, DEF 19–8 US–INDIA. Secret; Nodis. Drafted and approved by Rusk and cleared by Hare.
[2] See footnote 2, Document 360.

2. India should be concerned about any Chinese military influence south of the Himalayas. If the United States does not supply spare parts to Pakistan, Pakistan will be impelled to take more and more from Peking. Is this in India's interest? This is the other side of the coin of the Indian view that spare parts from us to Pakistan would constitute joint action by Peking and Washington to build up Pakistan at India's expense.

3. India's conduct over the past twenty years with regard to Kashmir is difficult to accept. Her view that this is not a dispute but a closed question runs counter to repeated actions by the United Nations and bumps into the long standing and instinctive American policy that the wishes of the people concerned should have a paramount influence on such political questions.

4. Do you really think that there is one chance in a thousand that India would take any action to be a counter-weight to Communist China in Asia unless India itself were attacked? I find it hard to believe that India would lift a finger against mainland China in any other circumstance. Relevant to this point is the outrageous departure from non-alignment which Mrs. Gandhi accepted in Moscow.

5. Although I accept that Pakistan stimulated the events of last year by sending infiltrators into Kashmir, it is nevertheless true that India, without consultation, escalated the conflict immediately by sending her own armed forces across the cease-fire line. She has been very critical of the United States over more or less drastic steps that we have taken in the face of North Vietnamese escalation. Had we reacted as forcefully as India did to Kashmir infiltrators, India would have been horrified. Accepting Pakistani responsibility for the infiltration, India must accept its share of responsibility for the scale and pace of escalation.

6. I am personally troubled by the point that the United States, having furnished ninety percent of the equipment of the Pakistan armed forces, has an obligation not to deny spare parts so long as India and Pakistan are prepared to live at peace with each other.

7. Finally, I doubt that we should move toward reliance upon India as our sole partner in the subcontinent because I do not believe that India would accept or play that role.

8. Did Mrs. Gandhi get a commitment from the Russians not to supply arms to Pakistan? Was that the price she received for the deep compromise of her non-alignment? If not, what would be Indian reaction to Soviet supply of arms to Pakistan? My guess is that they would accept it in relative good grace but still be deeply offended if we were to do the same.

Is there not basic inequity in the Indians' expectation that we would refrain from a policy now being followed by the British? Of course, the British policy favors India many times over in terms of arms purchases by India and Pakistan.

9. My conclusion is that when all of the pretence is cast aside, the general Indian attitude is that "what India wants India gets." The same India which preaches to others has no problem about throwing an armored division into Hyderabad, seizing Goa and calling Kashmir a closed question.

10. I fully recognize the cogency of the views put forward in your 1307 but I am concerned about the prospect that India, with all of its other problems, would find itself facing a Chinese-Pakistan combination with all of the possibilities for trouble through wars-of-liberation techniques around the frontiers of India. I would feel better about the situation if India seemed to be willing to make any substantial moves on its side to make peace with Pakistan.

I have fully noted your point about the Indian elections and the impact upon pro-American ministers such as Mehta and Subramanian. But if you have additional observations on the points above, I would appreciate it.[3]

Personal regards.

Rusk

---

[3] Bowles responded with a personal telegram to Rusk on July 28. He answered Rusk point-by-point, arguing that India by virtue of its size and military strength would inevitably dominate the subcontinent, and that the United States was compelled to recognize that fact and shape its policies accordingly. On the sensitive issue of the sale of spare parts, Bowles wrote: "experience has led GOI to conclude that if the finger on trigger is Pakistani US military equipment is just as threatening to Indian security as Chinese equipment." (Telegram 1479 from New Delhi; National Archives and Records Administration, RG 59, Central Files 1964–66, DEF 19–8 US INDIA)

363. Memorandum From the President's Special Assistant (Rostow) to President Johnson[1]

Washington, August 1, 1966.

SUBJECT

Follow-up on NSC Discussion of the Indian Nuclear Weapons Problem

Secretary Rusk has sent the paper[2] you requested at the NSC meeting of June 9 on the Indian nuclear problem. He sees no dramatic steps to discourage the Indians from starting down the nuclear route that would not cost us more than any likely gain would be worth. However, his paper, agreed around town, does recommend a number of steps which together provide some hope of discouraging or delaying an Indian decision.

In the economic field, it recommends a number of steps to impress on the Indians the costs—in development, manpower and Indo–Pakistan relations—of going nuclear. It also suggests we keep an eye on ways to link possible larger economic assistance in the future to a firm Indian commitment not to go nuclear.

To meet legitimate Indian security worries, it proposes sharing more systematically our intelligence analyses of the Chinese nuclear threat and the difficulties the Chinese face in making it effective. It also recommends seeking Soviet cooperation in a UN assurance to non-nuclear countries and suggests we continue efforts to achieve arms control agreements which might delay an Indian decision to go nuclear.

It asks for a number of studies, including how best to deal with Chicom "blackmail" of India or an overt Chicom nuclear threat to India, how to bolster the credibility of private security assurances to India and how to react if India does go nuclear.

The report also recommends a number of steps to bolster the technological and political prestige of those states which could go nuclear but refrain from doing so.

It requests that a high priority be assigned to gathering and analyzing relevant intelligence, and recommends a long-term contingency study of what we should do in the event that India decides to undertake a national nuclear program.

---

[1] Source: Johnson Library, National Security File, NSAMs, NSAM 355, Indian Nuclear Weapons Problem, further to NSAM 351. Secret.

[2] Reference is to the enclosure to the July 25 memorandum from Rusk to Johnson; see footnote 3, Document 359.

You will find these recommendations spelled out in the attached[3] (pp. 1–4). They do not solve the Indian nuclear problem, but they do represent a good blueprint for making the most of the assets we have. If you approve continuing along these lines, I will sign the attached NSAM to keep the departments moving down this path.

Walt

Approve[4]

See me

---

[3] The attachment is a copy of the July 25 memorandum from Rusk to Johnson and the attached report.
[4] Johnson checked the approval line.

---

364.   National Security Action Memorandum No. 355[1]

Washington, August 1, 1966.

TO

The Secretary of State

SUBJECT

The Indian Nuclear Weapons Problem, further to NSAM 351[2]

The President has approved the recommendations contained in the Secretary of State's memorandum to the President of July 25, 1966,[3] concerning the Indian Nuclear Weapons Problem, as requested in NSAM 351. These recommendations are attached.

He asks that the Secretary of State assume responsibility for implementing these recommendations. Where appropriate, the Secretary may, in consultation with other agencies, delegate to these agencies responsibility for implementing specific recommendations.

Within one month, I would appreciate it if the Department of State could report to this office the assignment of operational respon-

---

[1] Source: Johnson Library, National Security File, NSAMs, NSAM 355, Indian Nuclear Weapons Program, further to NSAM 351. Secret. Copies were sent to McNamara and the Directors of ACDA, CIA, and USIA.
[2] Document 347.
[3] Document 359.

sibility for the specific tasks called for by these recommendations. By November 1 we would hope for the first progress report on implementation.[4]

WW Rostow

---

[4] A progress report was sent to Rostow on October 31 by Benjamin Read. The report dealt largely with the establishment of an interdepartmental working group, the gathering of data, and ongoing studies of the problem. (Johnson Library, National Security File, NSAMs, NSAM 355, further to NSAM 351) There was nothing in the report judged important enough by Wriggins to pass on to the President. (Memorandum from Wriggins to Rostow, November 4; ibid.)

---

365. Memorandum From the President's Special Assistant (Rostow) to President Johnson[1]

Washington, August 8, 1966.

SUBJECT

Military Supply Policy for India and Pakistan

After lengthy discussions, State and Defense have finally agreed on how to approach the problem of military supplies to Pakistan and India.

Since providing lethal spares to Pakistan will promote difficulties in India for us and for Mrs. Gandhi, and not providing them will create difficulties for us and Ayub in Pakistan, the paper[2] does not make a specific recommendation today on whether or not to sell spares for Pakistan now.

Rather, it seeks to put the narrow problem of spares for Pakistan within the much larger and more important issue of getting both India and Pakistan together (or separately) to agree on limiting their defense outlays. It proposes that Gene Locke explore with Ayub how he will limit his relationship with China and enter serious talks to reach agreed arms limitations with India, while we study with him the problem of

---

[1] Source: Johnson Library, National Security File, Country File, India, Vol. VII, Memos & Miscellaneous, 1/8/66. Secret.

[2] Reference is to a joint State/Defense memorandum to the President, August 1, entitled "Military Supply Policy for India and Pakistan." (Ibid., Memos to the President, Walt Rostow, Vol. 9, July 16–31, 1966)

spares and possible free world, third country sources of indispensable military equipment. Simultaneously, Chet Bowles would make clear we are above all seeking to get the two countries to agree on an arms limitation and to restrain the Pak-Chicom relationship. But to do this we have to explore with Pakistan their need for spares. This step should help to allay their growing fear of India and give India, Pakistan, and the U.S. time to promote a more active dialogue on agreed arms limitations.

You are, in short, being asked to authorize parallel explorations in both capitals. A final decision on actions to be taken will depend on the results of these explorations.

If they are conducted with finesse and luck is with us, we could make substantial progress. If our political opponents in either country wish to, they could use the mere fact of our explorations to raise some dust. Even starting the explorations will net us sharp criticism in India, as Sig Harrison's premature story in the *Washington Post*[3] demonstrates.

This approach will keep our hand in the game in Pakistan and may provide one handle for tackling the arms limitation problem. The Indians should not take so desperately seriously a possible U.S. program of roughly $8 million. If their reaction is profound and sustained, we can still decide what to do later on.

Both Secretaries recommend you proceed with this exploratory step, and I concur.

W.W.R.[4]

Agree to explore in both Pakistan and India[5]

See me

---

[3] On July 29 Selig Harrison reported that the United States had taken a "guarded first step" toward resuming the supply of spare parts to Pakistan's armed forces. (*Washington Post*, July 29, 1966, p. 1)

[4] Printed from a copy that bears these typed initials.

[5] Neither option is checked.

366. Telegram From the Embassy in Pakistan to the Department of State[1]

Rawalpindi, August 9, 1966, 1930Z.

435. 1. Amb Bowles and I had fine meeting for 2½ hours in Bangkok. We agree such meetings are highly desirable.

2. On Kashmir Amb Bowles and I agree it would be desirable to have secret meetings between trusted emissaries of Mrs. Gandhi and Pres Ayub who might be named at exploratory meeting between these Chiefs of State. Amb Bowles doubts however that actual results will flow from such meetings until India sorts out relations with Kashmiris.

3. Amb Bowles and I agree problem of Indo–Pak relations is broader than Kashmir and discussions should involve other subjects. Perhaps Ayub and Mrs. Gandhi, or their emissaries, could settle on framework for discussing together subjects. We agree I should discuss with Ayub whether and where he will meet with Mrs. Gandhi and his version of modalities of future discussions between the two countries.

4. Amb Bowles and I agree on importance of preventing arms race on subcontinent. To this end it is my belief we should seek to bring about secret discussions on arms limitation between representatives of both countries chosen by their respective Chief of State. I desire to discuss with Ayub his willingness to authorize such discussions.

5. Amb Bowles does not believe GOI will hold meaningful discussions if U.S. provides lethal spare parts for Pakistan and unless (A) Pakistan renounces use of force in regard to Kashmir and (B) U.S. offers some tangible assurance of assistance to GOI in event of ChiCom and/or Pak attack. He believes if we do not furnish spares to Pakistan India might be persuaded as first step to agree to assessment of size of its own and Pak military establishments by World Bank. I believe bilateral discussions between representatives of the two countries probably will be more fruitful. If such discussions cannot now be brought about, I believe we should seek to promote same objective of stable military force relationship through separate discussions between U.S. and each country.

6. Amb Bowles and I do not reach any broad agreement on complex of issues relating to U.S. military policy toward subcontinent. We agree Pak military dependence on ChiComs would be disastrous for India, and one of our prime objectives with respect to India is to prevent

---

[1] Source: National Archives and Records Administration, RG 59, Central Files 1964–66, POL INDIA–PAK. Secret; Immediate; Exdis. Repeated to Saigon for Bowles and to Karachi. Passed to the White House at 7:04 p.m.

Pakistan from growing closer to ChiComs. Amb Bowles believes Indian leaders would agree with this and would also agree China is main threat to India. He indicates that principal fear of Indian leaders is possibility of ChiCom–Pak military combination. However, Amb Bowles considers that (A) Pakistan will not move closer to China even if Pakistan fails to secure lethal spare parts because Ayub and landowners supporting him will not tolerate further closeness to Communism; (B) we can in any event prevent such a development by threatening to shut off economic aid to Pakistan; and (C) ChiComs would not increase military aid to Pakistan to any extent because of their own requirements.

7. On sale of equipment to Pakistan by friendly third countries, Amb Bowles says he will do everything he can, using argument U.S. not responsible for what other sovereign nations do, to manage what he expects will be serious problem to Indian reaction.

8. Ambassador Bowles may have further comments.

9. For my part, with respect to these critical questions of U.S. military policy in this part of world, I remain convinced for reasons I set forth in Washington that course outlined in draft memorandum for President entitled "Military Supply Policy for India and Pakistan" is right.[2] I believe it most important I be able to talk to Ayub along lines of this memorandum shortly after his return from Dacca August 12. The security of India will not be advanced if Pakistan is continually pressed toward China by Indian military weight. In my judgement this vicious circle must be broken.[3]

Locke

---

[2] See Document 365. Locke sent his comments on the memorandum to the President in a memorandum dated July 25. (Johnson Library, National Security File, Country File, Pakistan, Vol. VI, Memos, 1/66–9/66)

[3] Bowles transmitted his comments on his meeting with Locke in Bangkok in telegram 3200 from Saigon, August 11. Bowles stated that Locke's account accurately reflected the meeting. His only qualification was to note that he had been pressing the Indian Government for a heads of state meeting not, as Locke reported, to settle Indo–Pak differences, but to create a positive atmosphere in which to discuss differences and find solutions. (National Archives and Records Administration, RG 59, Central Files 1964–66, POL INDIA–PAK) Rostow sent copies of both Ambassadors' accounts of the meeting in Bangkok to President Johnson on August 11. Rostow's advice was that "we ought to move very cautiously about spare parts for Pakistan; but move very strongly via our two Ambassadors and George Woods towards getting India–Pak agreement on the level of their military budgets." (Johnson Library, National Security File, Country File, Pakistan, Vol. VI, Memos, 1/66–9/66)

367.   Memorandum of Conversation[1]

Washington, August 17, 1966.

SUBJECT

India–Pakistan Problems

PARTICIPANTS

The President
His Excellency B.K. Nehru, Ambassador of India
Ambassador Raymond A. Hare, Assistant Secretary, Bureau of Near Eastern and
   South Asian Affairs
Mr. W. Howard Wriggins, National Security Council

At his request, Ambassador Nehru called on President Johnson at 12:30 p.m., August 17. The Ambassador delivered a letter which he had brought back from Prime Minister Gandhi.[2] The President accepted it without opening it and asked if this was the message which had been mentioned in the newspapers. He then inquired about the monsoons, to which the Ambassador replied that things were all right so far but it was too early to be sure. The President then commented that he understood India has political problems (based on Ambassador Nehru's conversation with Walt Rostow[3]) and noted that we did also.

The Ambassador said that he was depressed by what he had observed during his trip to India. There was a prevailing "ugly mood" growing out of frustration, anger and annoyance both inside and outside the Congress Party. It was alleged that Mrs. Gandhi was submitting to foreign pressure, especially on the devaluation issue, in order to get aid. The attitude seemed to be that, if getting aid meant surrender of sovereignty, this was unacceptable. He noted that this was what people say whether or not they mean it. But the way in which they were saying it was very virulent. This was particularly true in the context of devaluation because the rupee was regarded as a strong currency, not like a lot of the Latin American currencies. The Ambassador observed that the brunt of the criticism is falling on Food Minister Subramaniam, Finance Minister Chaudhuri, Planning Minister Mehta and the Ambassador himself.

---

[1] Source: National Archives and Records Administration, RG 59, Central Files 1964–66, POL INDIA–PAK. Confidential; Limit Distribution. Drafted by Laise on August 18 and approved by Wriggins on August 24. According to the President's Daily Diary, the meeting took place at 12:35 p.m. at the White House. (Johnson Library)

[2] See Document 368.

[3] Rostow's memorandum of his conversation with Nehru on August 12 recorded Nehru's "well-known gloom about the Indian scene." (Johnson Library, National Security File, Country File, India, Vol. VII, Memos and Misc, 1/8/66)

The President replied that it is the best people who always get attacked. Citing the U.S. situation, he noted that Secretaries Rusk and McNamara are two of the most peaceful men in town, yet they are the ones here who are under the gun. He also recalled the extreme criticism of Lincoln. This made it possible, the President said, for us to understand what the Indians are enduring. Ambassador Nehru noted, however, that our two systems are different. The Indian Prime Minister can be thrown out "at the drop of a hat" whereas the President was in office for an elected term. Reassuringly the President observed that he does not believe the worst will happen. He noted we had the same type of problems and hoped Mrs. Gandhi would come through. He understood that the Indians don't want to be dictated to and in this context he mentioned the Indo-American Foundation. He told Ambassador Nehru that we would be flexible, but we couldn't disown the parentage.

Going on to other matters, the President stressed the need to face the population and fertilizer problems and said he admired what the Indians had done. He was sure it would pay off in the end.

But on Pakistan, India should do better. India is the larger country and with that went responsibility. There is no use in telling the Paks to go to hell, they won't go. The President said he appreciated Tashkent. The need now is to get back to talking and in this context he recognized the difficulties created by the Indian elections. He again drew the parallel to the Vietnam situation, saying we want to talk but the others won't react. Indicating that he understood that peaceful gestures sometimes are misunderstood domestically, he noted that his own poll of popularity had gone down after the pause in bombing in Vietnam. People just didn't understand it and regarded it as weakness.

Ambassador Nehru said that India is "desperately anxious" to come to terms with Pakistan but couldn't yield on Kashmir. The idea of Tashkent was to put Kashmir in "cold storage." Reading at random from a message he had just received discussing the Pak conditions for talks, he presented a picture of the Pak position as being that no meaningful talks could take place without concrete steps on Kashmir; all other issues were peripheral and these other things could not be settled until Kashmir was settled. The Ambassador stressed that India is ready to get together on everything, including arms, but the Pakistanis keep saying "after Kashmir."

The Ambassador went on to say that India was hoping for a reduction in the relations between Pakistan and the Chinese. The presence of Chinese advisers, hints of nuclear cooperation following Ghulam Faruque's visit to China and other such developments give no indication at all of Pakistan moving away from the Chinese. The result is that India is left under double pressure, from both China and Pakistan. At this point Mr. Wriggins injected the observation that conditions prior to conversations are often exaggerated for bargaining purposes and this in itself need not inhibit talking. The Ambassador noted India was ready to talk without conditions, but reiterated that the Paks won't talk until after Kashmir.

The President undertook to see what we could do and said he would welcome suggestions. After some hesitation, the Ambassador ventured the opinion that he didn't really know what we could do since he didn't know about our relations with Pakistan. He went on to add that there were two things that the U.S. could do for India: (1) "Don't crowd us," let matters take their own course since democracies are not rational before elections; and (2) give all the wheat possible so people can be fed. Frankly, the importance of wheat is essentially political and short term. In the long term, as he had previously observed to Ambassador Hare, India has to face up to the realization of starvation or the solution of its own problems.

In closing the President said let's talk things over and see what we can do. The Ambassador promised to follow up with Ambassador Hare.

---

368. Memorandum From Howard Wriggins of the National Security Council Staff to President Johnson[1]

Washington, August 19, 1966, 9:20 a.m.

SUBJECT:

Mrs. Gandhi's letter[2] in brief

1. This rather long letter covers a lot of ground.

2. It is a dignified, poised effort to resume the dialogue which she must feel was impeded by her slip in the Moscow communiqué.[3] (B.K. Nehru has reported it was a staff snafu; even the Foreign Minister didn't see it before it was published.)

---

[1] Source: Johnson Library, National Security File, Head of State Correspondence File, India, Vol. 1, PM Gandhi Correspondence, 1/11/66–9/12/67. Secret. A handwritten note on the memorandum reads, "Rec'd 9:45." A handwritten "L" indicates it was seen by the President.

[2] Prime Minister Gandhi's 5-page letter to President Johnson was dated August 7. (Ibid.)

[3] In the communiqué signed on July 16 at Moscow at the conclusion of her visit to the Soviet Union, Gandhi ageed to language calling for an end to the U.S. bombing of North Vietnam. (*American Foreign Policy: Current Documents, 1966*, pp. 689–693)

3. *On economic matters,* she underlines the high priority on food production, the trickiness of the rains this year, the desire of her government to be economically independent in ten years. She makes no complaint about devaluation but stresses that hard economic decisions are difficult enough before an election—doubly so if "there is the slightest suspicion of external pressure, whether from foreign countries or international institutions. It is very largely for this reason that the decision to devalue was met with such violent opposition, even within my own party."

4. *Her visits* to Cairo, Brioni and Moscow were "very useful." In October she will receive Tito and Nasser; (and we can expect strong neutralist noises from her guests. But she must receive them well to prove her loyalty to "non-alignment" before the election). New countries require strongly nationalist regimes if they are to have enough popular support to make the necessary economic decisions.

5. *She regrets* any *misunderstanding* there may have been over the Moscow communiqué and hopes her subsequent statements clarified our doubts.

6. *On Vietnam,* their policy is to find a way to get from the battlefield to the conference table "where the parties concerned can find a solution in peace." She believes you and she were agreed on these fundamentals—and she says that Nasser, Tito and Kosygin also agree on this objective. "China, of course, thinks differently."

7. *India* is also *in touch with Hanoi.* Ho won't meet on any terms which "could be construed as a sign of weakness." She believes if we stopped bombing the north, her peace efforts would be strengthened.

8. *She passes on to you Kosygin's view* that if U.S. forces cross the 17th parallel, "it would not be possible to avoid escalation of the conflict into a larger war."

9. *On Indo-Pak relations,* she alleges closer Chicom relations with the Paks, and a possible second Pakistani try at infiltration and disruption with Chicom connivance. (Intelligence is checking this again at our request. Previous similar reports have proved highly exaggerated.) Talks with Pakistan are stalled because the Paks "seem still to insist that the question of Kashmir must be settled" first.

10. *Talks on defense expenditures* will be on the agenda if talks are begun.

11. She concludes with a reference to Luci's "glittering" wedding and how much you will miss Luci. "What a lovely girl she is. Seeing her reminded me how incomplete a family is without a daughter."

12. (State is preparing a draft reply which we will have this weekend.)

Howard
Bromley Smith

369. Telegram From the Embassy in Pakistan to the Department of State[1]

Rawalpindi, August 20, 1966.

599. For the President.

1. Following is text of letter dated August 20 for President Johnson from President Ayub. MFA passed letter to Embassy at 1715 hours August 20 stating Ayub desired letter be sent by Embassy communications to ensure rapid receipt by President Johnson.

Begin Text. 20th August 1966

Dear Mr. President,

Ambassador Locke has seen me. We understand from him that your government will be taking a decision shortly on the question of resumption of supply of defence equipment and spare parts to Pakistan.

In this connection I would like to share with you some of our fears at the situation developing in this region which has serious implications for Pakistan. As you are no doubt aware, India has mounted a steadily growing propaganda campaign against Pakistan accusing it of all kinds of nefarious intentions including collusion with a foreign power in order to obtain atomic weapons for military purposes and preparing for, what the Indians call, a second round of fighting. The Indian Government has, we understand, gone to the extent of issuing a warning to the United States Government that a resumption of arms supplies to Pakistan would be a "very serious threat to the security of India," and that it would be regarded as an unfriendly act by the Government of India which would put a severe strain on US-Indian relations.

This wholly unwarranted Indian propaganda campaign is directed at thwarting the establishment of greater rapport between the US and Pakistan. Furthermore, it provides a cover for India's own large scale military preparations including the development of nuclear capability for military purposes. In this connection I take the liberty of recalling what you, Mr. President, said in our meeting last December that United States would not allow India to dictate US policy towards Pakistan, nor would they allow Pakistan to dictate US policy towards India.

---

[1] Source: National Archives and Records Administration, RG 59, Central Files 1964–66, DEF 19–8 US–PAK. Secret; Immediate; Nodis; Privacy Channel. No time of transmission appears on the telegram, which was received in the Department at 10:03 a.m. Passed to the White House. Howard Wriggins summarized Ayub's letter in an August 23 memorandum to the President. (Johnson Library, National Security File, Head of State Correspondence File, Pakistan, Vol. 2, President Ayub Correspondence, 1/1/66–12/25/67)

I wish to make it clear that Pakistan remains willing to enter into purposeful negotiations with India for the settlement of all outstanding disputes and differences between the two countries. We have kept United States Government informed of our discussions with the Government of India on this subject. India while ostensibly expressing its willingness to discuss all outstanding issues between the two countries has made it very clear that it will not alter its stand on Jammu and Kashmir which it claims to be an integral part of India and for whose complete integration it is taking one measure after another. The Government of India is now deliberately building up an atmosphere of tension along the cease-fire line and elsewhere and uttering threats of renewed hostilities. I am sure you will appreciate that in the circumstances it is not possible for my government to accept at face value the Government of India's professed desire to improve the climate of relations and foster good-neighbourly ties between our two countries.

We understand from Ambassador Locke that the US Government wishes to follow an "even handed" policy towards Pakistan and India. This is perfectly understandable. At the same time I would be less than frank if I did not draw your attention to the fact that the denial of arms replacements and spares to Pakistan would seriously impair her ability to defend herself which surely could not be your intention. Denial of these facilities means complete write off of the American equipment which we hold in large proportion. Its replacement from other sources would put a fearful burden on our resources. Thus our need for spares etc. stands on a different footing to that of India which is not dependent on American equipment to the same extent.

We earnestly hope that in reaching the decision which your administration is to take shortly in this vital matter, our fears and the problems will get the considerations they deserve. Please accept, Mr. President, my warmest regards and best wishes for your continuing good health.[2]

---

[2] Ambassador Locke commented on Ayub's letter in telegram 601 from Rawalpindi, sent marked for the President on August 22. Locke stated that Ayub's letter underscored his conviction that affirmative action on Pakistan's request for spare parts, tied to Pakistan's willingness to limit its arms purchases from China and discuss arms limitations with India, was of critical importance in preventing a closer relationship between Pakistan and China. India, he argued, "should not be permitted to bluff US from action which is in her own vital interest and which is essential to put US–Pakistan relations on proper basis for foreseeable future." (National Archives and Records Administration, RG 59, Central Files 1964–66, DEF 19–8 US–PAK) Bowles transmitted a contrasting view of the issue in telegram 2673 from New Delhi, August 19. He argued that to provide the spare parts necessary to reactivate Pakistan's F–104s, B–52s, and Patton tanks "would have a devastating long-term effect" on relations between the United States and India and between India and Pakistan. He stated that the Indian Government was convinced that any military equipment the United States provided to Pakistan would be used against India, and that the reactivation of U.S. supplied planes would tip the military balance against India. (Johnson Library, National Security File, Country File, Pakistan, Vol. VI, Cables, 1/66–9/66)

Yours sincerely, Mohammad Ayub Khan

End Text.

Locke

---

370. **Memorandum From Howard Wriggins of the National Security Council Staff to President Johnson**[1]

Washington, August 23, 1966.

SUBJECT

Military Policy toward India and Pakistan

We are coming down to the wire on military supply policy toward Pakistan and India. The Bunker/Dean report[2] is now in, and the meeting with Secretary Rusk and McNamara will be for the purpose of reviewing their findings.

In sum, they recommend that we undertake a limited and carefully phased program of sale of spares to Pakistan, on rather clear conditions, with carefully phased interpretative initiatives in India.

They propose that *in Pakistan* Gene Locke enter into very private and exploratory talks with Ayub to see how far he will be willing to go in (a) limiting his relationship with China, and (b) undertaking serious and forthcoming discussions with India on outstanding issues, particularly arms limitation. As we become reassured on these points, we would assist him in finding sources of spares in western markets for his aircraft and other U.S. supplied equipment. Those parts he could not find there we would sell to him directly. The extent and duration of such a policy would depend upon his continued reasonable approach to India, his determination in seeking arms limitation and willingness to limit his supply and political relations with China.

In India, we would make clear that we were examining with Ayub ways to explore arms limitation, his relations with China, and other

---

[1] Source: Johnson Library, National Security File, Name File, Wriggins Memos, 1966. Secret.

[2] Reference is to an assessment done by Ambassadors Ellsworth Bunker and Arthur Dean of the joint memorandum on military supply policy for India and Pakistan produced by the Departments of State and Defense on August 1; see footnote 2, Document 365. Their assessment, which has not been found, was summarized in greater detail in an August 24 memorandum from Wriggins to the President. (Johnson Library, National Security File, Name File, Wriggins Memos, 1966)

matters of interest to India. We would also, however, indicate that a small program of the sale of spares was in question. We would reassure the Indians that this did not mean a return to our earlier policy of massive assistance to Pakistan, but represented an effort to retain some influence in Pakistan to improve the chances of a reasonable Pakistan policy towards India and limit China's penetration into the subcontinent.

If the proposed policy works, in six months we should find that pressures in Pakistan toward a closer Chinese relationship will have been reduced; with considerable luck and a good deal of careful but inconspicuous management, direct and private talks between India and Pakistan will have led to a halt in the arms race and perhaps even a down turn in defense expenditures. The chances that this will be possible are perhaps less than even; but if they succeed, it will be very much to our interest.

On the other hand, we will have become the object of considerable political antagonism in India as Mrs. Gandhi's opponents on the Left and the Hindu Right both attack her for allowing their Muslim neighbor to receive military supplies from the United States. And we can expect Mrs. Gandhi herself to have to criticize us directly if she is to hold her own in the political scramble. This will adversely affect Congressional attitudes toward aid to India and will make Ambassador Bowles' position more difficult, but we cannot tell for how long.

There are risks in this policy. The Pakistanis could accept our spares and then resume their earlier adventurist policies toward India—though this is generally conceded to be highly unlikely; our enemies in either India or Pakistan can surface confidential conversations before they have come to fruition, precipitating greater hostility of both against us. Both sides may enter talks and emerge more bitter than ever. The Indian political opposition can so distort our intentions and our actions as to make Mrs. Gandhi's position more difficult.

But no action also has its obvious costs: Postponing this approach to Ayub until after the Indian election would avoid difficulties for us—and for Mrs. Gandhi—in India. But it would lead Pakistanis to believe we had succumbed to India efforts to veto our policy toward them, would weaken Ayub, strengthen the hand of the more extreme Generals and Airforce Colonels, and generally encourage a more instransigent policy toward India and closer ties with China. It will also make Gene Locke's problems as a new Ambassador more difficult.

Your Ambassadors differ sharply on what should be done. Ambassador Locke believes he can gain substantial advantages from a policy which is more forthcoming toward Pakistan's desires than the Dean/Bunker approach; but this will provoke even more difficulties in India than the course proposed. Personal messages to you from your Ambassador and Ayub are attached.[3] Most of the Pakistani specialists in town feel Ambassador Locke overstates the advantages to be gained if we follow this course and he somewhat overstates the costs if we do not.

In New Delhi, Mr. Bowles argues that any such course will be bound to create the most profound difficulties for us in India. He believes the political backlash will be virtually impossible to contain. In a number of personal communications, he has strongly expressed his dire fears. India specialists in Washington believe he substantially overstates the liabilities of the proposed course—and also the advantages of choosing India instead of attempting to work with both India and Pakistan, as this proposal seeks to do.

Thus, the policy being recommended by the Department has built-in contention. No one is enthusiastic, except perhaps Ambassador Locke, but it appears to be the least costly policy we can design.

I therefore recommend that you accept the Department's proposals as set forth in the attached memorandum.[4] I would urge the following caveats:

(1) the talks in Pindi should not be started until after the present session of the Indian legislature closes in early September;
(2) Secretary Rusk should be charged with a particular responsibility to monitor these negotiations with especial care to ensure that both Ambassadors follow their delicate instructions with precision.

Howard Wriggins[5]

---

[3] See Document 369 and footnote 2 thereto.

[4] Not found attached. An apparent reference to the State–Defense memorandum cited in footnote 2 above.

[5] Printed from a copy that bears this typed signature.

371. **Memorandum From Howard Wriggins of the National
       Security Council Staff to President Johnson[1]**

Washington, August 24, 1966.

SUBJECT

Next PL 480 Agreements for India and Pakistan

State, Agriculture and AID recommend you approve now the next PL 480 agreements for India and Pakistan.[2] Although the monsoon leaves a big question mark, we expect these agreements to carry us through January or February, leaving one more agreement to sign before India's February elections.

The departments recommend for India 1.2 million tons of wheat and up to 800,000 tons of coarse grains; for Pakistan, 200,000 tons of wheat and 200,000 tons of corn or milo.

The wheat picture is pretty bleak. The departments have carefully reviewed Indian and Pak requests against the background of our own very tight wheat supply—4 million tons less for PL 480 than last year, a 25% drop. The painful fact is that we just will not have enough wheat to send all the two governments feel they need, even though half of our total PL 480 wheat this fiscal year is earmarked for those two countries.

We will be answering India's request for 7.8 million tons of wheat in FY 1967 with only 5 million and Pakistan's request for 2.2 million tons with only 830,000. But after thorough study, the departments have done the best they can by these two—and better than by most other PL 480 recipients this year.

We can offer coarse grains to help fill the gap. The departments propose 2.3 million tons in FY 1967 for India (the Indians asked only for 1.5 million) and 330,000 for the Paks (they are expecting much less, if any). However, the Indians after a major effort to increase consumption have said they couldn't handle much more—even if we can't make up the difference in wheat. The Paks are willing to try a small quantity for the first time, but we don't know how that will work out.

Despite short supply, we will be able to complete our 1966 emergency program and see *India* through her harvest, though she will still be hard pressed to meet ration levels with the wheat we can send. The

---

[1] Source: Johnson Library, National Security File, Country File, Pakistan, Vol. VI, Memos, 1/66–9/66. Confidential.

[2] Reference is to a joint August 22 memorandum to the President from Rusk, Freeman, and Gaud. (Ibid., NSC Histories, Indian Famine, August 1966–February 1967, Vol. III) A copy is also in National Archives and Records Administration, RG 59, Central Files 1964–66, AID (US) INDIA.

serious pinch could come next spring, especially if this fall's crop is below average. That is when stocks must be built against the shortage period before next fall's crop. So we have to hold back now to save as much wheat as possible for that potentially critical time and to make our pre-election agreement as large as possible. If you approve this agreement, we will have committed 3.6 million tons of wheat so far for FY 1967, leaving only 1.4 million tons more to send through June.

While the Indian agreement could be signed any time in September, we ought to move immediately in *Pakistan*. Hoarding has become a problem, and promise of new shipments should turn loose stocks already in the country. So we want to ship as much as we can now without losing flexibility next spring. Approving the departments' recommendation would bring our FY 1967 total to 580,000 tons of wheat, leaving only 250,000 tons for the rest of the year.

I recommend you approve the departments' recommendation. We will continue diplomatic efforts to explain fully the facts of our own wheat situation.

Howard

Approve India

Approve Pakistan

See me[3]

---

[3] Johnson checked this option. On the August 24 covering memorandum from Bromley Smith to the President, which Smith used to transmit the Rusk–Freeman–Gaud memorandum and the Wriggins memorandum to the President, Johnson wrote: "We must hold onto all the wheat we can—send nothing unless we break an iron bound agreement by not sending. See me." (Johnson Library, National Security File, Country File, Pakistan, Vol. VI, Memos, 1/66–9/66)

372. Letter From President Johnson to President Ayub[1]

Washington, August 30, 1966.

Dear Mr. President:

Thank you for your letter of August 20[2] which arrived at a time when my closest colleagues and I have been reviewing the manner in which our own policies and actions in South Asia can best contribute to our common goal of peace and security. One of the elements of this review is, of course, our military supply policy. Your letter underscores the complexities of this problem, and you may be sure we have the concerns you express very much in mind.

We ourselves are troubled over what appears to be a growing atmosphere of mistrust and apprehension between Pakistan and India. I am especially concerned that this will make it harder for India and Pakistan to avoid an arms race which could threaten the development of your nations and compound our problems in helping. I am glad to know from you that Pakistan remains committed to negotiations with India as the way of solving the many troublesome issues that cause this situation. I believe that is Prime Minister Gandhi's intention as well. I can only encourage you to persist in seeking to establish the kind of trusted communication between you and Mrs. Gandhi that will build confidence between your governments and make possible a more rational approach to the issues that now set you at odds.

Ambassador Locke has told me of the good talks he has had with you. I deeply appreciate the warm welcome you have given him.

With warm regards,

Sincerely,

Lyndon B. Johnson

---

[1] Source: Johnson Library, National Security File, Head of State Correspondence File, Pakistan, Vol. 2, President Ayub Correspondence, 1/1/66–12/25/67. No classification marking.

[2] See Document 369.

373.   Letter From President Johnson to Prime Minister Gandhi[1]

Washington, August 31, 1966.

Dear Mrs. Gandhi:

After I talked with Ambassador Nehru about his visit to India, I read with deep interest your letter[2] which he delivered to me personally.

I understand the serious domestic problems which you are facing in your pre-election period. You know you have my friendship and sympathy as you confront them.

Secretary Freeman has also given me a firsthand report of his recent trip to India. I was encouraged by what he had to say about your resolute efforts to increase agricultural production and reduce the rate of population increase. The problems you face in these areas are formidable, but I am confident that you and your nation are on the right track and that you will overcome them. I join those who are praying that the next harvest in India will be bountiful.

As you know, we have also had a drought and our harvest is not expected to be good. We will do what we can to help you through the difficult food situation you face in the months ahead, although the help we may be able to give may not be as much as we both would want.

I admire the courage you showed in devaluing the rupee and embarking on a program of import liberalization. I share your hope that this program will be successful.

Few problems in this troubled world have given me more cause for concern during the past year than your country's relations with Pakistan. You know how highly I value my personal relationship of confidence and trust with you and President Ayub. You also know that I want to contribute constructively to the material progress, dignity, and security of both India and Pakistan. As I told you when you were here, it is painful for all of us when two friends are forced by history into a relationship with each other such as that which now exists between India and Pakistan.

I am particularly concerned at what appears to be growing mistrust within each country regarding the intentions of the other. I fear that the result will be that both you and President Ayub will face increasing problems with your own citizens in maintaining a public atmosphere which would make possible a process leading to reconciliation. I very much hope that both you and President Ayub will try to avoid or

---

[1] Source: Johnson Library, National Security File, Special Head of State Correspondence File, India, 3/1/66–12/31/66. No classification marking.

[2] See Document 368.

deflate public charges and countercharges which further dissipate the political climate achieved at Tashkent. Public statements about military force levels increase the difficulties you both face in avoiding the arms race that neither of you wants.

Some Pakistanis may still cling to the false notion that their objectives in Kashmir can be obtained by force. I believe that President Ayub does not subscribe to such a view and his signing of the Tashkent agreement gives you this assurance. I have always found him to be a man of honor.

Our information does not support the statement that Pakistan is preparing for radical action against India. Nor do I have the impression that relations between Pakistan and Communist China have altered significantly toward closer cooperation during the last few weeks. This is, of course, a matter about which I share your concern. But strained relations between India and Pakistan increase Pakistani receptivity to improving its relations with China. On the other hand, improved India-Pakistan relations could become a guarantee that Pakistan would not move further in a direction we both deplore.

Therefore, I would urge both you and President Ayub to bend every effort to reestablish trusted communications between your representatives which will lessen the present spiral of apprehension and make possible a more rational approach to many specific issues that now set you at odds.

In this connection I greatly welcomed your expression of willingness to see arms levels discussed. If you believe we could be helpful in bringing about the opening of such a dialogue, we would, of course, welcome any suggestion you might have.

I note that your talks with President Nassser, President Tito, and Chairman Kosygin led you to conclude that they, like our two governments, are in basic agreement on moving the Viet Nam problem to the conference table. The crucial question, of course, remains how this objective can be brought about. India is in a position to be of help in resolving this issue, which thus far has stubbornly resisted our most intensive and searching efforts and those of our friends in many countries.

You mention that you are in touch with Hanoi. We will give the closest attention to whatever concrete indications that channel may produce that Hanoi has come to a genuine and realistic interest in finding a mutually acceptable basis for talks. A reduction of hostilities, including a cessation of bombing, is possible if matched by reciprocal action by the other side. This action need not be of a formal or declared nature. It could take any of a number of possible verifiable forms which, as you put it, need not necessarily be construed as a "sign of weakness" on Hanoi's part. We are not looking for signs of weakness from Hanoi, but rather for a genuine desire on its part to end this conflict.

Thank you for your gracious words about my daughter. The problems and feelings of parents the world over are, indeed, much the same.

With warm personal regards,

Sincerely,

Lyndon B. Johnson

---

374. Memorandum From the President's Special Assistant (Rostow) to President Johnson[1]

Washington, September 2, 1966, 10 a.m.

SUBJECT

Indian and Pak PL 480 Agreements

After our talk yesterday morning about the relation between our domestic bread prices and our India-Pak PL 480 programs, I asked the Budget Bureau informally for an opinion. The Bureau has headed the interagency operation of which I spoke.

The attached[2] strikes me as a good updated analysis based on the facts developed during the July inter-agency review of our wheat situation. It is not a formal memo checked with Agriculture. I believe you will wish to read it.

The argument is that we set the FY 1967 PL 480 planning figure only after reviewing domestic projections of consumption, exports and the carryover necessary to keep prices in line. Speculation in the market has kept prices unexpectedly high. But this is a largely irrational element on which cutting PL 480 shipments would have almost no significant effect. It might even have the contrary effect by indicating panic about the domestic position.

Therefore, though the reaction of speculators is impossible to predict, it looks to me as if these Indian and Pak agreements would have no effect on domestic prices. I would hate to hold the small Pak agreement up much longer; and I believe the pared down proposal for India

---

[1] Source: Johnson Library, National Security File, Country File, India, India's Food Problem, Vol. 1. Secret. A handwritten "L" on the memorandum indicates it was seen by the President.

[2] Reference is to a September 1 memorandum from Assistant Director of the Bureau of the Budget Charles J. Zwick to Rostow, entitled "Effect of P.L. 480 sales on domestic wheat prices."

is about as far as we should go, given their pre-harvest and pre-election requirements and our commitments. That proposal—only running through February—gives us the chance to make a fresh assessment after the Indian November harvest is in.

But if you still feel uncomfortable, we might hold back on the larger Indian deal—I propose delaying signing until late September anyway—and ask for a formal Agriculture–Budget answer to your question.

Walt

I'm satisfied; go ahead with your approach on both India and Pakistan

Go ahead with Pakistan now; ask for a formal Agriculture-Budget analysis on India[3]

See me

---

[3] Johnson checked this option.

---

375.   Telegram From the Embassy in Pakistan to the Department of State[1]

Rawalpindi, September 2, 1966, 1450Z.

835. Ref: State 38151.[2] Meeting with Pres Ayub.

1. I met with Pres Ayub for 45 minutes Sept 2 with FonMin Additional Sec Agha Shahi and notetaker Piracha also present. After reading letters from Mrs. Johnson and Sec Freeman,[3] Ayub carefully studied reftel communication from Pres Johnson.

2. I elaborated on: (a) need for peace on subcontinent, for conditions favoring economic development and for downward trend defense spending; (b) importance Pres Johnson attaches to Indo–Pak moderation and efforts deal peacefully with problems including Kashmir; (c) improvement in US–Pak bilateral relations and mutual recognition

---

[1] Source: National Archives and Records Administration, RG 59, Central Files 1964–66, POL INDIA–PAK. Secret; Immediate; Exdis. Passed to the White House.

[2] Telegram 38151 to Karachi and Rawalpindi, August 30, transmitted the text of President Johnson's August 30 letter to President Ayub. (Ibid., Presidential Correspondence: Lot 66 D 476, Lebanon thru Pakistan) For text of the letter, see Document 372.

[3] Neither found.

respective national interests; (d) US understanding of Pak security concerns expressed in Ayub's Aug 20 letter to Pres Johnson;[4] (e) US concern at harmful effects of Indo–Pak propaganda escalation including military tension; (f) US confidence in Pak and Indian top leadership; and (g) possibilities for secret Indo–Pak discussions.

3. Ayub indicated: (a) readiness to establish "trusted communications" with Mrs. Gandhi preferably covering full range Indo–Pak issues; (b) scepticism about utility Indo–Pak arms limitation discussions separate from consideration of political differences; (c) conviction India already has acquired excessive arms while Pakistan does not plan, and cannot afford, further arms acquisition.

4. Ayub interrupted my comments on propaganda escalation to read report from Pak HICOM New Delhi stating current Indian purpose in generating tension is to justify possible postponement of Indian elections desired and discussed in Congress Party circles. Pak HICOM recommended GOP not reply to Indian propaganda. Ayub asked me what GOP should do in such cases since Pak public exposed to Indian propaganda does not know what to think, and internal situation requires some reply.

5. I referred to Sept 6 Defense of Pakistan Day which I hoped would not be occasion for new round of Indo–Pak charges and counter-charges. This regard, I cited anti-Indian press release for Sept 6 (Rawalpindi 813)[5] which I hoped would not set tone for celebration. (Press release subsequently withdrawn per Rawalpindi 828).[6] Ayub stressed Defense of Pakistan Day intended commemorate achievements of armed forces and left impression he wishes avoid strong anti-Indian orientation.

6. I suggested establishment trusted communication between Ayub and Mrs. Gandhi might best be through personally known confidants, not anti-Indian or anti-Pak, preferably without political ambition but with negotiating experience and, on arms problems, perhaps with military experience. Ayub volunteered perhaps somebody like Jai Prokash Narain or Raja Gopalacharian on Indian side.

7. Ayub balked when I said hoped could report to Washington that he willing undertake secret Indo–Pak military discussions with or without concurrent consideration other differences. Ayub professed see no purpose in separate military discussion but left open possibility GOP might nonetheless go along if pressed. Ayub asked if US would

---

[4] See Document 369.

[5] Telegram 813 from Rawalpindi, September 1, transmitted the text of a press release prepared by the Press Information Department entitled "India's Wanton Aggression." (National Archives and Records Administration, RG 59, Central Files 1964–66, POL 32–1 INDIA–PAK)

[6] Dated September 2. (Ibid.)

participate any such talks? I said had not contemplated this and I didn't know. I added that discussions concerning level of forces might be more relevant to mutual security than less precise approaches through defense budgets and gross national products percentages.

8. When I pointed to possible utility of trusted military officers as confidants on both sides, Ayub appeared have no objection but said generals would have to turn to political leaders to ascertain conditions determining military requirements. For example, he said, defense requirements would vary with Kashmir solution. I attempted to counter Ayub's scepticism about working separately towards arms limitation with suggestion India and Pakistan begin from current force levels and through discussion seek to establish some understanding of mutually tolerable military relationship.

10. *Comment:* (A) My impression is Ayub might go along if we insisted on separate arms discussion with India, but he does not think such an approach can accomplish anything under present political conditions. Accordingly, I believe we should promptly sound out Mrs. Gandhi on willingness to establish "trusted communications" channel, i.e., secret talks between confidants of Ayub and Mrs. Gandhi on all topics, including Kashmir and arms limitations.

(B) I believe we need to know more specifically what would contribute to subcontinental security. This regard, it would be useful if Washington could proceed with military studies concerning reasonable defense establishments in India and Pakistan. These could serve as basis for separate US supporting discussions with GOI and GOP.

(C) I suspect Ayub may interpret Pres Johnson's letter and my presentation to signify likely postponement of US decision on lethal spare part sales to Pakistan until after Indian elections. While a little doubt may be healthy, I do not believe we should permit Ayub to draw too pessimistic a conclusion in this regard. In my judgement, best interests of US would be served by informing Ayub promptly after adjournment later this month of present session of Indian Parliament, and certainly well before Indian elections, of US willingness to discuss lethal spares with him in connection with Indo–Pak arms limitation and Sino–Pak military supply relationship.[7]

Locke

---

[7] In a follow up conversation on September 3 with Additional Foreign Secretary Agha Shahi, Locke pointed out that the emphasis during his conversation with Ayub on the difficulties faced by the United States with regard to military supply policy was not intended to foreshadow a negative decision. He reported that his purpose was to prevent Ayub from making decisions based on the mistaken notion that the United States had decided against him in the critical national security field. (Telegram 847 from Rawalpindi, September 3; ibid., POL INDIA–PAK)

376. Memorandum From the President's Special Assistant
(Rostow) to President Johnson[1]

Washington, September 15, 1966, 7:30 p.m.

SUBJECT

Effect of Indian PL 480 on US Wheat and Bread Prices

I now have from Agriculture, the Council of Economic Advisers and the Budget Bureau the formal analysis you requested of the relation between the proposed next PL 480 agreement for India and our own wheat and bread prices.[2]

No one can predict with absolute certainty that US wheat prices have leveled off for good after their June rise (though August held steady) or that speculators will not jostle the market again. However, these studies do conclude that:

—Stopping this India agreement for 1.2 million tons of wheat through February would have a negligible effect on wheat prices here.

—Even cutting off the whole PL 480 program probably would not reduce bread prices, because wheat accounts for only 14–15% of the retail price of bread. If bread prices rose, it would be largely for other reasons which slightly lower wheat prices (if they were possible) could only partly offset.

—Our own wheat crop will come in 1.8 million tons (56 million bushels) higher than we estimated when, back in July, we allocated 11.3 million tons (413 million bushels) to PL 480 worldwide in FY 1967. So we will have more of a buffer than we decided then would be adequate to keep prices stable.

—In general, there is no logical reason for wheat prices to move significantly higher, although there is always some risk that the speculators will read the signs otherwise. Agriculture will continue to tailor PL 480 programs carefully to the classes of wheat in better supply and to spread out purchase authorizations to minimize market effects. World wheat output is expected to be higher this year than last; the Soviet crop is better, lessening the pressure on Free World supplies; and the prospective crop from our own increased acreage allotments should begin to influence prices toward the end of the year.

---

[1] Source: Johnson Library, National Security File, Files of Walt W. Rostow, Meetings with the President, April–Dec. 1966. Confidential

[2] The analysis was in a September 12 Bureau of the Budget memorandum from Zwick to Rostow. (Ibid.)

Because of our clear commitment to India and the negligible influence of this program on our own market, I recommend we go ahead now with the Freeeman–Rusk–Gaud program of 1.2 million tons of wheat and 800,000 tons of sorghum (their memo attached).[3] An agreement signed in the next two weeks will just barely keep the pipeline flowing. If you approve, I will ask Secretary Freeman to try to stretch this as far into January and February as feasible unless unexpected Indian developments cause us to take another look.

Walt

Approve[4]

See me

---

[3] See footnote 2, Document 371.

[4] Neither option is checked. Rostow raised the issue again in a September 20 briefing memorandum for a Tuesday luncheon meeting. He noted that the Departments of State and Agriculture were pressing for a decision on P.L. 480 for the subcontinent. (Johnson Library, National Security File, Files of Walt W. Rostow, Meetings with the President, April–Dec. 1966) On September 23 Vice President Humphrey sent a memorandum to the President in which he added his weight to the judgment that the proposed P.L. 480 agreements with India and Pakistan could go forward without any predictable impact on the price of bread in the United States. (Ibid., Name File, Vice President, Vol. I)

---

377. Memorandum From the President's Special Assistant (Rostow) to President Johnson[1]

Washington, September 26, 1966, 1 p.m.

SUBJECT

New Indian PL 480 Agreement

The last shipment of wheat under the current agreement is now scheduled to leave the US by 31 October. It should arrive in India about 1 December, give or take a few days. These October shipments will include 327,000 tons of wheat and 150,000 tons of milo. Milo shipments will continue with 150,000 tons each in November and December.

---

[1] Source: Johnson Library, National Security File, Country File, India, India's Food Problem, Vol. 2. Secret.

It takes about 9 weeks between Washington decision and arrival in India for negotiation, procurement, movement of grain to port and transit (30–40 days). Counting back 9 weeks from the beginning of December indicates there will be a gap in December arrivals if we don't go ahead with the new agreement in the next week.

A 1–2 week gap probably wouldn't cause difficulty. The Indian government would begin to get nervous but could chalk the slippage off to bureaucratic delay.

But somewhere between 2 and 4 weeks from now, it will become obvious to the Indian grain dealers and politicians that there will be a gap in December. With arrivals of US wheat running about 345,000 tons in October and 202,500 in November, little or no wheat arriving in December would raise questions.

No one argues that Indians would starve. Not even the Indian government knows how much food may be tucked away in that vast nation. But the one clear indicator we have shows that government grain stocks have been drawn down from 1 million tons on 1 June to 738,000 on 1 September. This is a little more than one month's average off-take (600,000 tons).

This indicator operates in the Indian market much like our carryover here. When it drops, speculation increases and prices rise. The government, with short stocks, has no large quantities to release to force prices down.

Even harder to measure is the effect of unexplained delay on the high-level Indian's view of our dependability. Mrs. Gandhi's reliance on US and World Bank advice has become a major political issue. We don't want to give her opposition an opening to argue that we don't back our promises with performance, especially since the World Bank consortium is already falling $20 million short of its $900 million target.

The ideal on pure foreign policy grounds would be to go ahead now. But if you are still uneasy about U.S. prices, I'd suggest this course:

—Wait 1–2 weeks to confirm what now looks like a break in U.S. price levels. The price in the Kansas City wheat market fell 12¢ per bushel in the week of 16–23 September. The price had hung around $1.97 since mid-June (a jump from the $1.79 of 10 June) until last week's drop to $1.85.

—Then if we have to delay longer we ought to give the Indians confidentially some hint of why we're delaying (though we wouldn't want this to get back to our farmers). We might also let the Indians begin purchasing against the new agreement and promise to reimburse them later (Agriculture has a procedure for this).

This may come up at lunch tomorrow. However, if not, we will need your decision on whether (a) to go ahead now with the original

Freeman–Rusk–Gaud proposal of 1.2 million tons of wheat and 800,000 tons of coarse grain, or (b) to hold off for another couple of weeks.

Walt

Go ahead now with Freeman–Rusk–Gaud proposal

Keep an eye on wheat prices and come back in a week[2]

See me

---

[2] Johnson checked this option, and added the following handwritten comment: "Freeman recommends holding."

---

378. Memorandum From the President's Special Assistant (Rostow) to President Johnson[1]

Washington, September 28, 1966.

Mr. President:

The attached note from Marvin asked for my analysis of Eugene Locke's letter to you. (Tab A)[2]

1. Locke argues that if we do not provide Ayub with military equipment he will turn to China.

2. This would have the following effects:

—Give China a base south of the Himalayas;
—Put pressure on India which would lead her to ask for a U.S. military guarantee.

3. He meets the argument that military dependence does not necessarily mean alliance by citing the fact that Pakistan is more vulnerable to becoming an ally of China than, say, Indonesia, because of Pakistan's fear of India.

---

[1] Source: Johnson Library, National Security File, Country File, Pakistan, Vol. VII, Memos, 10/66–7/67. Confidential.

[2] Attached was an undated letter to President Johnson from Ambassador Locke, with a September 27 covering note to Rostow from Special Assistant Marvin Watson.

4. With respect to India, Gene argues that the bad effects would only be temporary. India badly needs our aid and our role as a balance to Russian influence, on the one hand, and the Chinese threat, on the other.

In general, he regards the spare parts issue as critical to our relationship with Pakistan and urges that he be permitted to inform Ayub that we will proceed. Only in the last paragraph does he say, "Of course what I have said about Pakistan's military needs is said in the context of reaching understandings at the same time about limitations on arms from China and about an attempt to reach some arms limitation understanding with India."

Comment: In some ways Gene Locke's view is the mirror image of Chet Bowles' who argues that if we supply spare parts to Pakistan, we will throw India still deeper into the arms of the Soviet Union. Chet will also recall the following facts:

—India is 5 times as large as Pakistan and our major interest on the subcontinent;

—India stands against our enemy—Communist China;

—He correctly warned that a Soviet military relationship with India would come about if we did not meet India's military requirements a few years ago.

I talked with Sect. Rusk this morning about where he stands on this problem. He urges the following, with which I strongly agree:

We must urge Chet to use maximum influence on India to negotiate an arms limitation deal with Pakistan and be prepared to listen to the Paks on Kashmir. It is not good enough to threaten Washington with a deepened India-Soviet arms relation. There is no future unless India-Pak relations improve and we keep for India a moderate Pakistan. This is basically an Indian responsibility. Therefore, Chet should concentrate on bringing it about.

Walt

379.   Memorandum From the President's Special Assistant
(Rostow) to President Johnson[1]

Washington, September 28, 1966, 9:15 a.m.

SUBJECT

Pending Decision on Military Supply for Pakistan: A Message from Gene Locke

Gene Locke cables you and Secretaries Rusk and McNamara asking that he be authorized to explore with Ayub the returns we might gain, however limited, if we sold him military spares for equipment originally procured from the United States.

In this cable, the text of which is attached,[2] Gene says we are losing our chips in Pakistan by our indecision. He reports that the sale of spares is the number one issue with the Pakistan government and he believes it could be used to promote Indo-Pakistan arms limitation discussions and limited Pakistan arms purchases from China. Further waiting (a) encourages Ayub's domestic opponents, (b) promotes the belief that the US does not care about Pakistan's security and (c) permits both the Government of Pakistan and India to conclude that India can dictate our policy toward Pakistan. He reminds us that further waiting is in itself a decision.

As background, you will recall that before Gene left for Pakistan in July, staff papers were prepared on this subject. They would have authorized him to explore with Ayub how the sale of spares might be used to define more precisely Ayub's relations with China and encourage him to enter serious discussions with the Indians on arms limitation.

Ambassador Bowles' reaction was so strong that Secretary Rusk held the recommendation for further thought. Newspaper leaks led Indian officials to protest publicly in the Indian Parliament.

You requested Ellsworth Bunker and Arthur Dean to look into the matter. They reported to you in mid-August, recommending we go ahead, but with somewhat more caution than the earlier proposal.

Since then, no decision has been reached. Secretary Rusk has been reluctant to proceed until he talked with Ambassador Bowles. Secretary McNamara has not yet focused on the problem but his Deputy for International Security Affairs, opposes the idea.

---

[1] Source: Johnson Library, National Security File, Country File, Pakistan, Vol. VII, Cables, 10/66–7/67. Secret.

[2] Telegram 1148 from Rawalpindi, September 27. A copy is also in the National Archives and Records Administration, RG 59, Central Files 1964–66, DEF 19–8 US–PAK.

I agree that further delay in a decision is eroding our position, and we should face this one shortly, perhaps toward the end of Chet Bowles' visit.

Walt

I agree, ask Secretary Rusk to review the bidding and give me DOD/ State recommendation—agreed or split—by October 5[3]

Meet Gene Locke's difficulty and approve the Dean/Bunker recommendation

Tell Gene now we can't sell spares to Pakistan

See me

---

[3] Johnson checked this option and amended it with a notation indicating that he wanted recommendations on the issue from Bunker, Katzenbach, Eugene Rostow, and Arthur Dean. He added a further handwritten notation that reads: "Let's discuss this weekend—Take to David." Reference is to Camp David, the Presidential retreat in Maryland where, according to the President's Diary, President Johnson spent the weekend of October 1–2 with Rusk, McNamara, Katzenbach, Walt Rostow, and Eugene Rostow. (Johnson Library) A list of decisions taken by the President during the weekend, apparently drafted by Walt Rostow, indicates that Johnson authorized Rusk to draft instructions to the two Ambassadors to try to get India and Pakistan to agree on arms limitations. A decision on the spare parts issue was postponed. (Ibid., National Security File, Files of Walt W. Rostow, Meetings with the President, April–Dec 1966)

---

380. Memorandum From the President's Special Assistant (Rostow) to President Johnson[1]

Washington, October 15, 1966, 10:30 a.m.

SUBJECT

A Sidelight on Indian PL 480

The attached from John Schnittker[2] explains release yesterday of another 250,000 tons of wheat for India. This is just an administrative

---

[1] Source: Johnson Library, National Security File, Country File, India, India's Food Problem, Vol. II. Confidential. A handwritten note on the memorandum reads, "Rec'd 10–15–66, 1:30 p."
[2] The attachment was an October 14 memorandum from Acting Secretary of Agriculture Schnittker to the President.

device for completing shipments you promised in your March message to Congress.

The reason for a special action is that, while your approvals are written in tons, PL 480 agreements are written in dollars. When US prices rose, the dollar totals in the 27 May agreement would not cover the total tonnage you authorized. The shortfall became evident when Agriculture and the Indian Supply Mission totaled all the purchases under the May agreement.

This means there will be 200–250,000 tons more in the pipeline than we thought earlier this week. While this will carry Indian shipments into November, delaying our decision on the new agreement until you get back[3] will still cause shipments in November and December to dip.

I think the most important element to weigh against domestic concerns is how delay will affect Mrs. Gandhi's feelings about our promises of support. We made milestone economic and food deals with her, saying we'd stand behind her as long as she did her share. There have been some gaps in the Indians' performance, but overall they've made the right decisions.

These deals have become a major issue in India's election campaign. The question is whether Mrs. Gandhi can show that US aid pays off or whether her opposition makes stick its charge that she's sold India's dignity for a mess of pottage.

---

[3] Reference is to the trip the President was scheduled to make to meet in Manila October 24–25 with the heads of the other six governments with military forces in South Vietnam.

I don't predict disaster if we hold off. This is a political judgment which you are best suited to make. I'd be more comfortable about the Indian end if we went ahead now.

Walt

I still think we ought to hold off[4]

OK, go ahead

---

[4] Johnson checked this option.

---

381.   Telegram From the Ambassador to India (Bowles) to the President's Special Assistant (Rostow)[1]

New Delhi, October 19, 1966, 1256Z.

6752. On my return to India I find that the food situation has worsened seriously in comparison to a month ago. In several key areas the vitally important rains of early October have not come and consequently estimates of output for this crop year are down by at least four or five million tons.

In Bihar, parts of Uttar Pradesh, Rajasthan and Madya Pradesh the late rains had been largely lacking and a desperate situation is in the making. Several of our people who have recently visited Bihar and Uttar Pradesh report that if anything the GOI is underestimating the danger. Asoka Mehta, Subramaniam and others are now visiting the area and it is my guess that we will be faced shortly with a request for an additional shipment of milo to meet this new situation.

In the meantime I am being pressed very hard since my return in regard to recommendation to President for two million tons—1.2 of wheat and 800,000 of milo—which are now pending in Washington. When I left the US the President was waiting for a report on India's agricultural performance under the terms of our general understanding. I have just read the report[2] put together by the Department of

---

[1] Source: Johnson Library, National Security File, NSC History, Indian Famine, August 1966–February 1967, Vol. III. Confidential. The message was sent [text not declassified].

[2] Not found.

Agriculture, AID, and the Department of State; it seems to me to be completely factual, balanced and accurate. Under the circumstances I will be grateful to you personally if you can give me your private estimate of where the situation stands and how soon we may expect a decision on the pending requests[3]

Regards,

---

[3] On October 31 the Country Team in India expressed its increasing concern "at adverse impact in an explosive political period of further delay in signing new agreement." (Telegram 6340 from New Delhi; National Archives and Records Administration, RG 59, Central Files 1964–66, SOC 10 INDIA)

---

382. Telegram From the Department of State to the Embassy in Pakistan[1]

Washington, October 21, 1966, 6:33 p.m.

71125. Joint State/Defense message. Subject: Military Supply Policy for India and Pakistan. For Ambassadors Locke and Bowles.

1. This message contains instructions relating to continuing review being conducted here of our military supply policy for India and Pakistan.

2. Our premise is that it is vitally important for US interests not to be forced to choose between these two countries, as their current tactics are designed to get us to do. Our continuing objective is to build both sound US-Indian and sound US-Pakistan relations; we do not intend to permit either to veto what serves our policy interests in the other.

3. Our problem, however, is that both India and Pakistan are now pursuing policies that divert their own limited resources from development, dilute the massive economic aid we are providing each of them, and cause a dangerous drift toward greater dependence in the military field on Communist China and Soviet Union. Neither GOI nor GOP

---

[1] Source: National Archives and Records Administration, RG 59, Central Files 1964–66, DEF 12–5 PAK. Secret; Exdis. Drafted by Laingen and Coon on October 6; cleared by Hare, Spain, Heck, Handley, Warren, Macomber, Hoopes, and Walt Rostow; approved by Secretary Rusk. A handwritten notation on the telegram reads: "OK/L" suggesting that the telegram was also cleared by the President. Also sent to New Delhi and London and repeated to CINCMEAFSA.

appears sufficiently to recognize serious consequences this situation has had and will continue to have for their own interests in relations with us and our ability in practical terms to help them meet their problems. Neither seems aware that public and Congressional reaction to last fall's tragic Indo-Pak war, diminished resources for foreign aid overall, and our bed-rock commitment in Viet-Nam could make it impossible for us to do what we believe needs to be done even in area economic aid (not to mention security field) unless some more constructive element than now exists is introduced into Indian-Pakistan relations.

4. We believe this situation requires bilateral discussion with leadership both countries, on frankest possible terms, to consider what we can do toward curtailing arms race between them and at same time serve other US interests, including prevention Communist influence (particularly Chicom) from eroding our own position further. In first instance this requires that we begin exploratory conversations with GOP and subsequently with GOI, in order better ascertain whether and how a change in our current military supply policy might better serve US interests in subcontinent.

5. Against this background, action addressees authorized undertake action along following lines:

(a) *For Rawalpindi:* You should arrange fully private session with Ayub for frank and exhaustive review of where we stand in our relationship. You should reaffirm our strengthened confidence we on right track in rebuilding sound US/Pak bilateral relationship. You should then go on to review our growing concern over difficulties India and Pakistan having in coming to grips in meaningful way with their problems, new evidence arms buildup, and risk this poses for peaceful and steady growth stronger economies and better life people both countries.

(b) You should say that you have therefore been instructed to talk frankly with Ayub in order consider together what might be done to build basis for more durable peace in subcontinent. (If asked by Ayub you may indicate that Ambassador Bowles is being instructed do the same in New Delhi.)

(c) You should go on to describe what we believe is our common interest with Ayub in the peaceful resolution of Indo–Pak issues and in curbing the arms race potential in subcontinent now, before new and even more costly round of arms procurement ensues. We would like to know from Ayub what he is prepared to do to further these objectives. You should say that present trend in both countries strikes us as strongly counter-productive and that we see heavy responsibility on leadership both sides to act now to curb this trend before it too late. You should explore with Ayub his arms supply relationship and intentions with Chicoms, noting that while asking us for decision on spares he has never taken us into confidence to any degree on his intentions arms procurement generally, including possible deal with Soviets. (FYI—This designed elicit expression Ayub's intentions re Soviet supply. Even though it would not raise same problems for us as does Chicom source, it has bearing on prospects for further arms spiral. End FYI.)

(d) You should also explore with Ayub on what basis he prepared support efforts achieve understanding on force levels, matériel procurement, and defense spending, that would head off arms spiral in subcontinent while protecting legitimate security requirements of each country. (FYI—Important thing is to get something going, preferably with India, but at least with us. End FYI.) What specifically would Ayub be prepared to do in this area? You may wish reinject idea of secret Indo-Pak talks in this context, suggesting to Ayub that for our part we see merit in idea that he and Mrs. Gandhi designate individuals who have their confidence and trust and who could explore in non-public discussion, preferably outside South Asia, what might be possible in arms limitation and other problems, including Kashmir. (Further elaboration this point was contained State 16670.)[2]

(e) You should tell Ayub we can appreciate his security concerns, as spelled out in his letter to President August 20.[3] But Ayub should recognize that we have our problems too and that what we can do to help him meet these concerns depends on what he can do to help us. Specifically it depends heavily on genuine, determined efforts on Pakistan's part to lower tension and to demonstrate its intentions on arms limitation and resolution other Indo–Pak problems. Ayub must also realistically recognize that any modification our present arms policy would assume acceptable limits on his arms supply and political relations with Chicoms. Moreover Ayub should know that we frankly see real problems in any modification our current arms sales policy because of disruptive risks for Indo–Pak reconciliation process and he should fully understand our belief this consequence can only be avoided if there is in fact forward movement Pak-Indian relations.

(f) In sum, we want Ayub to know that we appreciate fact that his past dependence on US equipment puts him in present circumstances in difficult position, that we are not oblivious to his security problem, that we currently reviewing possible modification our military sales policy, but that in view misuse our equipment in 1965 we can assist in reactivating US supplied equipment only if he will help create conditions which give promise of peace in subcontinent and no recurrence of events 1965 and help head off arms race. Until we have some better

---

[2] Dated July 27. (Ibid., POL INDIA–PAK)
[3] See Document 369.

idea of what he is prepared to give on his side of the bargain we have little basis on which to act. He should also be fully aware that any leak of this exploratory conversation would obviously increase the obstacles to a modification of US arms policy.

(g) FYI—Above is as far as you should go with Ayub in first round in suggesting possibility some give in our present arms sales policy. Our thinking however is that if Ayub's response is considered satisfactory after assessment in Washington, we would subsequently indicate to Ayub that we are ready discuss with him GOP's legitimate military requirements and how they might be met, it being understood any US supply role would be limited to cash sales lethal spares for previously supplied US equipment not readily available from other Western sources and sales of non-lethal equipment. To extent lethal spares are available from non-US Western sources, we would prefer that Pakistan rely on such sources in future and we would be prepared help facilitate this in ways open to us. To extent such spares not available these sources, we would discuss with Paks what supplementary amounts might be available from us. We have in mind limited, transitional level of spares from US. (We presently envisage $8 million as ceiling figure for all spares, lethal and non-lethal.) Finally, although we do not intend resume supply lethal end items, we would indicate readiness over longer term to help GOP in arranging for procurement justifiable new equipment of this nature from other Western sources. End FYI.

(h) *For Delhi:* We recognize that because of risk of leaks, there should be minimum delay between time our first démarche to Ayub and corresponding representations Delhi. But we believe we cannot authorize those representations until Washington has assessed Ayub's response. Precise nature our instructions to you for representations with Mrs. Gandhi will depend on nature Ayub response. Tentatively, however, we see your initial representations along following lines:

(1) Refrain from discussing precise nature our initial approach to Ayub on arms limitation and possibility some degree relaxation arms policy.

(2) Instead, stake out general contours of the way we see our strategic interests in Asia and how US and Indian interests coincide.

(3) Within this context discuss what we both can do to minimize Chicom presence and influence in Pakistan, when issue of Pak security is paramount factor.

(4) Explore options available to us. As we see it these boil down to actions on India's part involving willingness to talk, to compromise, and to make concessions on basic problem such as arms control and Kashmir; and/or US actions to maintain moderating influence in Pakistan. Extent to which India can or cannot move on former has bearing on what US will need to do on latter.

(5) Urge GOI that now is time to move decisively on arms balance and limitation. This is process which larger power must effectively initiate, failure do so serves only interest of Chicoms. This means India

as well as Pakistan must unilaterally exercise restraint now in arms acquisition and it also means that start must be made toward eventual bilateral understanding that will encompass matériel acquisitions and force structure as well as defense expenditure levels.

(6) Underscore for GOI that our economic and military supply policies are related to this objective. We do not intend under foreseeable circumstances return to military supply relationship we had with Pakistan (or India) prior September 1965. However, some flexibility on our sales policy should be maintained. Regardless of our policy Pakistan as sovereign state is going to insist on meeting what it considers its minimum security requirements. Indeed, Indian recognition of this will reduce GOP fears that India desires to undo partition.

(7) Discuss with GOI how to maximize India's public understanding and minimize India's public misinterpretation of US actions. In context present realities Indians should understand that India is central to our interests in Asia; security of subcontinent is essential element of this interest; and our future policies, including those relating to military supply, will reflect this.

(i) *For both Rawalpindi and Delhi:* Both approaches when made should take note of representations we have already made during economic aid discussions on risk of arms race and urgency downward trend defense spending. They should note that same basic concern is fundamental in approaches you now making on broader issue of arms limitation and imply without specifically saying so that magnitude and kind of future US economic aid will be related to efforts each makes in arms limitation.

(j) *For London:* You should inform HMG in closest confidence of kind of explorations we undertaking first with GOP and then with GOI. Rawalpindi and Delhi should similarly inform High Commissioners, bearing in mind that any leaks would jeopardize whole operation.

6. It is important that all concerned recognize that our efforts at this stage purely exploratory in nature and that we making no commitment as to specific policy decisions. We see steps outlined above as first in series exploratory steps with both leaders, aimed at achieving progress toward understanding on arms balance and limitation which could encompass wide variety of approaches. We are aware any progress will be slow and that there are clear limitations in degree influence we can hope to have through limited military supply policy we envisage. Essentially our purpose at this stage is to learn more than we now know how our policies as a whole can effectively help contain arms race, reduce dependence either country on Communist sources supply and at same time promote fundamental need for continuing patient Indo–Pak dialogue. Where we go from here, including role British might play, will depend heavily on nature your first approaches to GOI and GOP and your own recommendations.

Katzenbach

383.   Telegram From the Embassy in Pakistan to the Department of State[1]

Rawalpindi, November 1, 1966, 1254Z.

1667. Dept pls pass Harriman. Discussion with President Ayub: Military Supply Relationships.

1. During meeting of Governor Harriman[2] and myself today with President Ayub I conveyed in brief discussion of about fifteen minutes military supply relationship approach as set forth SecState 71125.[3]

2. Ayub's response was moderately encouraging although still in general terms. Ayub indicated Pakistan already had received nearly all military equipment contracted under current arms deals with China. He added Pakistan is also seeking obtain some matériel from USSR but indicated he is not "pushing" Russia as he hopes hear from US first.

3. Ayub implied both arms limitations and arms sources are appropriate subjects for discussion and indicated Pakistan continues deeply desire limit armaments. This regard, Ayub charged India had built up military much more than Pakistan and had obtained massive quantities of equipment which unsuitable for deployment in mountainous terrain fronting China and therefore aimed only at Pakistan. He added Pakistan has no intention of attacking India and simply wants to survive as integrated and stable country. Ayub authorized Foreign Minister Pirzada and Foreign Secretary Yusuf who also were present to explore general subject further with me.

4. Given primary purpose of meeting to discuss Manila Conference, and Governor Harriman's tight schedule, it proved impossible to discuss subject in greater detail this occasion. I intend take matter up further with Pirzada and Yusuf as suggested by Ayub. Presumably Embassy Delhi may wish to defer action pending further soundings here.

Locke

---

[1] Source: National Archives and Records Administration, RG 59, Central Files 1964–66, DEF 12–5 PAK. Secret; Priority; Exdis. Repeated to New Delhi.

[2] Harriman was in Rawalpindi to brief Ayub on the results of the Manila Conference. He sent his report of the discussion with Ayub on November 1 to President Johnson and Secretary Rusk in telegram 1958 from Tehran, November 1. (Ibid., POL 7 US/HARRIMAN) Harriman's account of the discussion with Ayub focused on Vietnam. He also sent an account of the meeting he and Bowles had with Gandhi on October 31. That conversation also focused on Vietnam, and Harriman reported that the Prime Minister was assertive, insisting that the United States stop the bombing of North Vietnam without prior conditions. (Telegram 1959 from Tehran, November 1; ibid.)

[3] Document 382.

384. Telegram From the Embassy in Pakistan to the Department of State[1]

Rawalpindi, November 6, 1966, 1545Z.

1751. Ref: State 71125.[2] Subject: Military Supply Policy for India and Pakistan.

1. In meeting with Foreign Secretary Yusuf at 1700 hours November 6, called at his request on military supply policy, he stated he had talked with President Ayub following my meeting with Yusuf in Karachi on November 3 (Pindi tel 1716).[3] The following is statement of Government of Pakistan. (Yusuf had hand-written statement, quite possibly prepared by Ayub, which he read to me and from which I took notes):

A. Pakistan does not want arms race with India. It wants only minimum deterrent force consistent with safety and security of country. Since minimum force depends on nature of threat, Pakistan would welcome agreement with India on arms limitation. To that end Pakistan would be willing to enter into secret talks with Government of India at place and level to be fixed by mutual consent.

B. Pakistan believes best place for talks is Delhi. The reasons are (1) that in its view this would cause less speculation than meeting by high level representatives of two countries in a third country and (2) that this would remove usual Indian ploy of delaying months to await non-existent instructions from Delhi.

C. Pakistan believes talk should be held within the framework of a political settlement and that it is therefore essential that talks on political issues (which I interpret to mean Kashmir) should proceed simultaneously with arms limitation talks. However the talks need not be by the same representatives or in the same location.

D. The Government of Pakistan has stated in the past and reiterates that it has no offensive or defensive alliance with China. The present arms agreement with China has a fixed financial limit and will be allowed to run its course. The bulk of Chinese equipment has already

---

[1] Source: National Archives and Records Administration, RG 59, Central Files 1964–66, DEF 12–5 PAK. Secret; Priority; Exdis. Repeated to New Delhi.

[2] Document 382.

[3] Locke's November 3 meeting with Yusuf was a follow up to the discussion of military supply policy with Ayub on November 1. Locke asked for a commitment by Pakistan to engage in secret arms limitation discussions with India, expressed concern over the level of defense expenditures in India and Pakistan, and asked for assurances that military supply agreements with China would be limited. (Telegram 1716 from Rawalpindi, November 3; National Archives and Records Administration, RG 59, Central Files 1964–66, DEF 12–5 PAK)

arrived, only a small portion is yet to come. The arrival of the remainder will be spread over a period of time.

E. To the extent Pakistan obtains military equipment from the United States in the future, her need to tap other sources will be correspondingly reduced. Pakistan would prefer equipment of U.S. origin as its people are conversant with it. They are seeking military equipment from Russia, but have not pushed this, preferring to wait to determine what may be available from United States. In view of the limitation on Pakistan's resources, terms on which arms are supplied will be an important consideration.

F. There is now a major deficiency in Pakistan's military equipment. This consists of (1) losses in the last war not yet filled and (2) additions to equip increased force raised since war and necessitated by Indian expansion. Pakistan does not desire equipment for expansion above its present armed force level, but only adequately to fill out equipment for Pak forces that exist today.

G. Pakistan will be willing to talk in terms of exact figures and numbers when she discusses her requirements in the event the United States determines to help her meet those requirements.

H. The President cautions that while Pakistan will enter into talks with India in good faith, these talks by their very nature can be protracted and the outcome uncertain, and she cannot delay her procurement until such time as agreement is actually reached.

I. The President again wished to raise the question of the tanks to be purchased from Germany. (Pindi tel 1615).[4] These tanks are not additive to the tank force but are for replacement purposes. Most of Pakistan's tanks are Sherman tanks which are no longer being made and spare parts for which are difficult to obtain. It is Pakistan's desire to phase out these tanks, replacing them with tanks of the kind requested. Because they are excess with Germany and she has no place for them, they can be obtained for a reasonable price. Yusuf does not have numbers available but they will depend on how many Sherman tanks are to be phased and when. Yusuf can get us estimates of numbers if we desire.

2. President Ayub leaving for London morning of November 13. I am prepared return from Dacca to Karachi to talk with him about any message received from Department before that time. (Importance attached by President Ayub this subject indicated by fact Secy. Yusuf

---

[4] In telegram 1615 from Rawalpindi, October 28, the Embassy reported that Pakistan was seeking U.S. approval of the purchase of M–41 and M–47 tanks and 155 mm. cannon from West Germany. The Germans were reported willing to sell but only through a third party and with U.S. acquiescence. The Foreign Ministry noted that India had obtained Seahawk aircraft from Germany through Italy in a similar fashion. (Ibid.)

telephoned me yesterday and asked me to postpone my trip to Dacca one day in order to hold above reported meeting with him.)

Locke

---

385. Memorandum From Secretary of Agriculture Freeman to President Johnson[1]

Washington, November 7, 1966.

SUBJECT

Review of the Indian Situation

I. Current Crop Prospects

The more recent reports from New Delhi, estimating the coming foodgrain harvest at 80–85 million tons, indicate a much smaller foodgrain harvest than was anticipated by Indian government officials a few months ago. It now seems quite likely that India's food situation will continue to be precarious throughout the coming year and that grain import needs will continue to be high. This is due in part to a very poor monsoon and in part to shortcomings in this year's agricultural development effort.

II. An Evaluation of this Year's Agricultural Effort

The nature of the monsoon continues to be the overwhelming factor determining the level of food production on the Indian subcontinent. The second most important factor is the use of fertilizer. In this area, the Indians have performed well on some counts but poorly on others. They have willingly allocated scarce foreign exchange for the import of fertilizer in order to meet the agreed upon targets for fertilizer availability. However, last year because of delays in financing much of the fertilizer was not ordered on time.

Efforts to increase foreign private investment in the production of chemical fertilizer in India have been quite successful compared with any previous efforts but not adequate when related to the scale of

---

[1] Source: Johnson Library, National Security File, Country File, India, India's Food Problem, Vol. II. Confidential. Rostow forwarded Freeman's memorandum to the President on November 9 under cover of a memorandum in which he noted that Rusk endorsed Freeman's recommendation. Rostow added his own endorsement of the recommendation. (Ibid.)

India's needs. A similar shortfall exists for investment in pesticides and the multiplication and distribution of improved seed varieties.

Minister Subramaniam seems to be doing his utmost to achieve the objectives for Indian agriculture which he and I mutually agreed upon several months ago. But private foreign investment in fertilizer is moving slowly. The reason is, at least in part, that both sides (the Indian Government and the foreign investors) are trying to get the best deal possible for themselves and are willing to delay in order to get it. The follow-through necessary to complete complicated negotiations is lacking on the Indian side. We believe that the solution to this problem of ensuring the necessary action for foreign private investment can only be accomplished by the Prime Minister herself. Somehow she must be made to realize this. Reaching agreement with Minister Subramaniam, however competent and influential he may be, is not enough. The Prime Minister, however, is deeply pre-occupied with the campaign for the General Election to be held in February. The key figures in politics are jockeying for position in anticipation of the formation of a new cabinet in February.

We are also concerned about the reluctance of the Indian Government to ease controls and regulations in the agricultural sector. Two years ago I went to India and helped them to set up a Foodgrains Corporation, comparable to our Commodity Credit Corporation, which would have the responsibility for supporting farm prices at a level which would make the use of modern inputs profitable. It now appears that the Government of India is using the Foodgrains Corporation to procure foodgrains at below market prices, thus discouraging food production rather than stimulating it with proper pricing as was originally intended. However, procurement prices have recently been raised in four states. We are planning to send to India, within the next week or two, a member of the team who originally helped establish this corporation to evaluate its performance.

III. *Proposed Action on PL 480 Interim Agreement*

These matters and some others that we are checking out need to be taken into consideration before allocating any substantial quantities of food assistance. We will be prepared to review with the Indians a progress check list in detail when negotiations take place in Decmber for the balance of fiscal 1967. In the meantime I would urge that we go slowly and make only the minimum necessary allocation to avoid breaking the pipe line.

We can expect no substantial policy changes before the Indian elections in late February and our negotiations in December should be kept quiet so as to avoid providing ammunition to those who attack the present government for being too subservient to U.S. wishes. But in the December negotiations we can and will explore a number of self-help measures which could improve India's agricultural performance and impress upon Indian leaders how gravely we view performance shortfalls.

We recommend therefore that we go ahead at this time with 1.2 million tons of wheat and 800,000 tons of grain sorghum on an interim basis, meanwhile preparing for detailed top level negotiations in December. By early December we should have more detailed information on the nature of shortcomings of this year's agricultural effort as well as the first report on our own wheat acreage.

State and AID concur in this analysis and recommendation.

---

386. Telegram From the Department of State to the Embassy in India[1]

Washington, November 7, 1966, 1:37 p.m.

80047. Literally Eyes Only for Ambassador from Secretary. Re your 6660,[2] I believe I should let you know very privately that we have some major problems back here about reproducing in 1967 anything like the food shipments we made to India during 1966 and that we should not let the Indian Government take it for granted that we can be a source for such food in advance of any decisions actually made.

It comes as a deep disappointment that "imports from abroad must at least equal those of calendar year 1966." The following questions are going to be highly relevant back here:

1. How good is Indian performance on their own commitments? Your 6660 is most helpful but indications of any failure to make the maximum effort could be very damaging here.

---

[1] Source: National Archives and Records Administration, RG 59, Central Files 1964–66, AID (US) 15 INDIA. Secret. Drafted by Rusk on November 6, cleared by Hare and Katzenbach, and approved by Rusk.

[2] Telegram 6660 from New Delhi, November 4, was sent by Bowles to the President and Secretaries Rusk and Freeman to put the "critical Indian food situation" in clear perspective. In the 10-page cable, Bowles described the crisis facing India and the need for U.S. help to avert a tragedy. He credited the Indian Government for its strenuous efforts to improve agricultural output and concluded that only repeated failure of the monsoon rains prevented a significantly expanded harvest. Bowles argued that the "short-tether" policy governing U.S. food shipments was self-defeating in that it created the impression of political pressure and gave leverage to an opposition seeking to unseat the Gandhi government with which the United States had worked closely in attempting to modernize Indian agricultural methods and open up the Indian economy. (Ibid., SOC 10 INDIA)

2. Our own prospective supply situation is not encouraging in terms of repeating next year what we did this year. Quite apart from actual production and wheat stocks, it was necessary for us to be much more restrictive on a number of other countries this past year because of Indian requirements. It will not be easy for us to continue this policy without deep injury in other places.

3. What are the prospects for India's obtaining substantial amounts of food from other sources? In this case, it will not be very agreeable here for the Indians to use their available foreign exchange to buy in other markets and leave it to us to come forward with major concessional food shipments. They at least ought to offer to buy in our market. If, for example, they purchase large quantities of grain from the Soviet Union on relatively hard terms, it would create serious questions as to why they should not buy in our market on similar terms. Similarly, it will be important for them to get concessional help of substantial amounts from others. What do you know about Indian plans in this regard?

4. While we must avoid the overt impression of political conditions, the truth is that India has a political constituency in the US which it must nourish if it expects substantial concessional help. This is simply a political fact of life since the President has no resources except those made available by Congress and this in turn is affected by the general political atmosphere. I am sure you realize that the gratuitous departure of India from a position of non-alignment in Viet-Nam does not help at all. I cannot understand why the Indians cannot simply support the Geneva Agreements of 1954 and 1962 and the idea of a peaceful settlement. The Moscow Communiqué and the demand for a unilateral cessation of bombing are complicating factors which should not be underestimated.

I mention these factors because they bear upon paragraph eleven of your 6232.[3] It would be most unfortunate if the government leadership should proceed on the basis that they can somehow rely upon us at the end of the day to come through with whatever is required. If they face a repeat of their 1966 situation, they have some formidable problems to solve and should not be in the mood to take us for granted. Anything that you can send us on the above or other related points will be greatly appreciated.

Warm regards.

Rusk

---

[3] Dated October 27. (Ibid., AID (US) 15–8 INDIA)

387. Telegram From the Department of State to the Embassy in India[1]

Washington, November 8, 1966, 7:16 p.m.

81259. Ref: Rawalpindi's 1751[2] and 1759;[3] Delhi's 6698.[4] Subject: Military Supply Policy.

1. We believe discussions with Ayub and Foreign Secretary Yusuf have now reached point where corresponding representations should begin with GOI. We are encouraged by nature Ayub's response and believe it both tactically and psychologically desirable we move promptly exploit that response.

2. Accordingly you should seek earliest possible opportunity open discussions with Mrs. Gandhi along lines Para 5(h) State 71125.[5] These could be natural follow-up to highly opportune exchange you had with C.S. Jha reported Embtel 6698. We continue feel it best for present not spell out precise nature talks with Ayub. However you authorized describe our démarche in general terms and to say we are encouraged by both his stance on future Chicom procurement and readiness find way to begin exploratory talks with GOI, urging Mrs. Gandhi as you did Jha to "try it out" with Ayub. (As indicated Pindi's 1759, Pak Hicom Delhi reportedly instructed take up idea of secret talks with GOI.)

3. *For both Delhi and Rawalpindi:* Given Ayub's upcoming visit UK appreciate knowing reaction your British colleagues to our current efforts.

Rusk

---

[1] Source: National Archives and Records Administration, RG 59, Central Files 1964–66, DEF 12–5 PAK. Secret; Priority; Exdis. Drafted by Laingen; cleared by Spain, Coon, Wriggins, Handley, Kitchen, Hoopes, and Deputy Assistant Administrator in AID/NESA Walter G. Farr, Jr.; and approved by Hare. Repeated to Rawalpindi, Dacca for Locke, and London.

[2] Document 384.

[3] In telegram 1759 from Rawalpindi, November 7, Locke reported that Foreign Secretary Yusuf had indicated that his government had received a feeler from Indian Foreign Minister Singh concerning the possibility of secret talks. Yusuf noted that the Pakistani High Commissioner in New Delhi had been instructed to follow up on the opening. (National Archives and Records Administration, RG 59, Central Files 1964–66, DEF 12–5 PAK)

[4] Telegram 6698 from New Delhi, November 5, reported on a conversation between Bowles and C.S. Jha. In the course of discussing relations between India and Pakistan, Bowles noted that the current political environment in each country effectively precluded a public dialogue. Jha agreed and was receptive to Bowles' suggestion that secret talks without an agenda offered the only good prospect of improving relations. (Ibid., POL INDIA–PAK)

[5] Document 382.

388.   Telegram From the Embassy in India to the Department of State[1]

New Delhi, November 8, 1966.

6826. For the Secretary from Ambassador Bowles. Reference: New Delhi 6660;[2] State 80047.[3]

1. I appreciate your strictly eyes only cable on the Indian food situation. As you point out, we are facing heavy demands from many directions and something has to give. Against this background I shall take up your points one by one.

A. Our cable 6660 on India's current agricultural performance is the result of a thorough study by all elements of our mission here plus lengthy discussions with everyone we could find in India who might have an enlightened opinion or reliable knowledge of Indian agriculture. Our analysis was specifically checked against the broad knowledge of Bernie Bell, who has been in India for the last sixty days heading the World Bank Study Group which has been exhaustively studying the Indian economic and agricultural situations since September 1964 and which will soon report to the consortium. Bell himself fully supports our findings as does Sir John Crawford, the eminent Australian agricultural economist now in Delhi as a member of the World Bank team. Both Bell and Crawford will underscore these views when they reach Washington in the next two or three weeks following the consortium meeting in Paris. I suggest you talk to them and judge for yourself.

B. Frankly and confidentially what particularly worries me is the fact that the most sober and balanced analysis we can develop here has on several occasions been undercut by hearsay reports by people who had not been here or whose information is fragmentary. For instance when I was in Washington the President told me he understood that India is falling down badly on its fertilizer program. When I ran this down I discovered that this story grew out of someone's interpretation of India's reluctance to extend its March 1, 1967 deadline for the special incentives to new private sector plants, a reluctance which I explained in our 6660 as reflecting India's judgement that by holding to this date for the time being it might induce quicker decisions by the fertilizer companies.

---

[1] Source: National Archives and Records Administration, RG 59, Central Files 1964–66, AID (US) 15 INDIA. Secret; Nodis: Eyes Only. No time of transmission appears on the telegram.

[2] See footnote 2, Document 386.

[3] Document 386.

C. May I repeat that our report on the unprecedented revolution now occurring in Indian agriculture is an accurate, balanced and considered one, fully supported by the findings of every foreign agricultural expert whom we know in India. India's recent performance, while not perfect, is substantially ahead of anything we anticipated. In the language of Bill Gaud's memordandum to Walt Rostow of October 7, 1966,[4] it is "incomparably better than in any previous year."

2. I am aware of and concerned by the shortages in our own available stocks of wheat and other claims on our resources.

A. The needs here are desperate and are so recognized by everyone concerned. As far as priorities are concerned we must take into account the possibility of India disintegrating under the economic and political pressures set in motion by the adverse monsoon throughout most of India last year and compounded by a monsoon this year which has failed even more dismally in an area inhabited by 100 million people.

B. It should be stressed that India is prepared to take large amounts of milo, which I understand we have in substantial supply as well as any other edible grains. I hope that with our existing supplies we will be able to meet India's minimum requirements during the first half of 1967, and that by the latter half increased supplies as result 30 per cent expansion US wheat acreage will be sufficient to satisfy remaining needs until the harvest a year from now. While I fully appreciate our desire to avoid any further reduction in our foodgrain stockpile, we may have to weigh the adverse implications of such temporary reduction against the importance of keeping people alive and avoiding the disintegration of the largest and most strategically placed non-Communist nation in Asia.

3. Last night the Canadian High Commissioner told me that Canada had been asked to provide 2 million tons of wheat and that it was his impression that his government would agree. He thought that one million tons would be on an outright grant basis as in the case of Canadian shipments this year and the second million would be on long term credit. The Australians and French also tell me they have been asked for wheat. The French Ambassador said he thought his government would react favorably. I hope that the Australians can also be persuaded to provide assistance in view of their favorable crop.

A. I recognize the political problems that would be created by India purchasing large amounts of grain for hard currency from others while receiving grain on a concessional basis from US. I have no knowl-

---

[4] Reference is to an October 8 memorandum from Gaud to Rostow assessing Indian agricultural performance. (Johnson Library, National Security File, NSC Histories, Indian Famine, August 1966–February 1967, Vol. III)

edge of what the Soviet Union will do. However, since they have had a good crop, I would not be surprised to see them come up with some well-timed gesture.

B. India will obviously have to secure whatever she needs by whatever means. We must remember that we have a crucial stake in seeing that the foreign exchange required to keep India's economy moving is not completely diverted into famine relief; Soviet political interests, as they see them, may lie in precisely the opposite direction. In any case, we have never allowed the greed and short-sightedness of other nations to set a ceiling on our performance, and this is no time to start.

4. I know you will agree that no nation, however enlightened its leadership, can change its foreign policy overnight. Thirty years after our own isolationist policies had become irrelevant, Congress voted to deny France and Britain the military equipment necessary to defend themselves against the Nazis. Similarly, India is still clinging doggedly to the sterile premises of the Bandung Conference. The so-called Non-Aligned Summit Meeting here in Delhi was a ridiculous performance: there will probably be more silly gestures in the future.

A. However we should not underestimate the progress we have made in India on foreign policy matters. The biggest circulation dailies [garble—invariably?] criticized the Moscow communiqué: criticism of the recent Yugoslav–UAR–India communiqué was even more devastating. In the last year, partly due to our own efforts here, a large number of key Indian journalists have visited East Asia including Viet-Nam. As far as I know their reports in every instance have been strongly sympathetic with our interests in Asia. Under separate cover I shall send you recent articles which reflect this profound shift in thinking.

B. There is no doubt in my mind that if we get into a war with China, India will, reluctantly to be sure, be dragged in on our side much as we were dragged into two world wars in support of the French and the British. In the meantime India will continue to be frustrating, difficult and inconsistent reflecting the inner conflicts of a new nation facing staggering problems and possessing, not unnaturally, a vast sense of insecurity and a realization of its own relative weakness.

C. While the Indians look to us hopefully for support, they are by no means taking us for granted. They are keenly aware of the inadequacy of our supplies and of our emphasis on performance as a precondition for assistance. They have experienced the suspension of our aid and our short-tether policy of doling out PL480 a few months at a time, a policy which whatever its advantages has made rational long-term planning in India impossible. As we reported, the GOI has come under extremely heavy attack for its so-called dependence on the US for PL480 and other assistance. As a consequence, the government has been extremely hesistant to approach us for additional assistance; if anything, it has recently underestimated its needs in dealings with us.

5. Tomorrow I shall send a cable to you and the President outlining my deep anxiety about the political and economic situation here.[5] I do not exaggerate when I say the the future of India, with its democratic promise and economic potential, is hanging in the balance. What is at stake is not only India's stability but its future relationships with US and other Western nations; these will be profoundly affected by developments in the next six months.

6. The 2 million tons of wheat and milo which I recommended in late August is still being held in abeyance. Even if the President approves it today a significant slowdown in the arrival of food ships here will be inevitable by mid-January, which is the very time when the food shortage will be most critical and with the election only one month away political tensions most acute.

7. It is absolutely essential, Dean, that we keep these food grains flowing and that we take a fresh long term look at the importance of a stable friendly India to American security interests in Asia. If India lapses into chaos or antipathy, and in my opinion these are very real possibilities, the massive sacrifice we are making in Vietnam will lose much of its meaning. I know that we can count on you to do everything possible at what I really believe to be a crucial moment. With warm personal regards.[6]

Bowles

---

[5] Telegram 6843 from New Delhi, November 9. (National Archives and Records Administration, RG 59, Central Files 1964–66, SOC 10 INDIA)

[6] In a November 9 memorandum to the President, Rostow characterized this cable from Bowles as a "vivid, somewhat overstated, but essentially accurate account of the nature and seriousness of the situation created by the crop failure in the state of Bihar and neighboring areas." He added that Ambassador Nehru had called him to warn that starvation was expected in India by February unless the flow of U.S. grain was resumed. (Johnson Library, National Security File, Country File, India, India's Food Problem, Vol. II)

389. Editorial Note

On November 10, 1966, President Johnson told Secretary of Agriculture Freeman that he was disappointed with the memorandum Freeman had sent to him on November 7 (Document 385). In the course of a telephone conversation, Johnson said: "You must've had two men write this memo. You gave the best damn arguments I ever saw for not giving it to them. You said they hadn't kept their agreement on investment and fertilizer. That it's moving slowly. That they're jockeying to try to get a deal that's better for themselves. That they're delaying. That they don't have the follow-through necessary to do what they agreed to do. . . . That they're easing regulations and controls in the agricultural sector, which we're concerned about. That the government is using the Foodgrains Corporation to procure them at below market price, discouraging food production rather than stimulating it as agreed to. . . . Therefore, I recommend we give them 1.2."

Johnson drew a different conclusion: "That's going to get me in trouble. I can't take a recommendation like yours, and Rusk who just says 'me too' on any goddamn thing you can dream up. I can't do that and feed India another year. I'm not going to unless Congress does." He told Freeman to send his study group to India. "In the meantime, I'd urge we go slowly. . . . Tell them we can't act 'til the Congress comes back. And send your man over, and take each thing they agreed to do, and study damn carefully, because these give-away days, they voted them out of office last Tuesday." He told Freeman to tell Bowles "that we have completed our commitments. That we've given them $1 billion. That these billions come hard these days. . . . And that these matters need checking out." (Johnson Library, Recordings and Transcripts, Recording of Telephone Conversation Between President Johnson and Secretary of Agriculture Freeman, November 10, 1966, 3:36 p.m., Tape F66.31, Side A, PNO 1)

Johnson did not feel that he could get a balanced appreciation of the situation from Bowles. He described Bowles to Vice President Humphrey as "the Ambassador from India not to India." (Ibid., Recording of Telephone Conversation Between President Johnson and Vice President Humphrey, November 24, 1966, 9:40 a.m., Tape F66.31, Side B, PNO 336)

Johnson was seriously concerned about "give-aways" at a time when the grain surplus in the United States was depleted and he was facing the prospect of a $135 billion budget. In a follow-up conversation with Freeman on November 11, Johnson said that in future food allotments he wanted to know what the United States was going to get in return for its food. "Usually we just get kicked in the pants. That's what she [Gandhi] does to us. She'll call old Tito or somebody else and just give us hell. I don't want to write her foreign policy, but it looks to me the least they could do, right before our election, is quit kicking us." (Ibid., Recording of Telephone Conversation Between President Johnson and Secretary of Agriculture Freeman, November 11, 1966, 8:59 a.m., Tape F66.31, Side A, PNO 158)

390.   Telegram From the Department of State to the Embassy in India[1]

Washington, November 11, 1966, 7:40 p.m.

83625. For Ambassador from Secretary Freeman. Ref: State 83624.[2] Please pass following message from me to Subramaniam:

Begin Text.

1. We are much disheartened here by the reports of another poor crop in India. Coming after last year's near disastrous crop, it poses exceedingly difficult problems. We also face difficult supply, domestic food price and political problems here.

2. This Administration is deeply concerned over the failure of major food producing countries other than Canada to contribute foodgrains to India on a meaningful scale.

3. The new food aid legislation requires that we carefully assess agricultural performance in countries requesting food aid. At the direction of the President I am therefore sending immediately two of my top economists to India to undertake a quick on-the-spot assessment of the agricultural production effort, particularly the functioning of the Foodgrains Corporation, private investment in the production of fertilizer, the extent to which the 6.5 million tons target of additional foodgrain production is being achieved under the High-yielding Varieties Program, and other jointly agreed targets which help to determine whether the self-help requirement of our new legislation is met.

---

[1] Source: National Archives and Records Administration, RG 59, Central Files 1964–66, SOC 10 INDIA. Confidential; Priority; Exdis. Drafted by Lester Brown in Agriculture; cleared by Farr (AID), Wriggins, and Secretary Freeman; and approved by Handley.

[2] Telegram 83624 to New Delhi, November 11, also for Bowles from Freeman, provided more background detail on the mission Freeman proposed to send to India to assess the food crisis. Freeman noted that the utmost urgency was attached to the assessment. (Ibid.)

4. This team of economists, consisting of Martin Abel and Art Thompson, have worked with you and your staff previously. They will be joined by Assistant Secretary Dorothy Jacobson the week of November 20.

5. Since our short supply situation has resulted in increased Congressional concern, we would like to have several members of Congress from both houses and both parties join us in order to confirm to their elected colleagues India's need and the seriousness of the effort being made. We realize this may be a delicate matter particularly at this time in your political timetable. But you can be sure that the President would not propose it unless he felt it essential here. We would welcome your suggestions as to how this could be kept as low key as possible as they join the team the week of November 20.[3] *End Text.*

Rusk

---

[3] In a personal cable to Rusk, Bowles described this message as "extraordinarily insensitive" and complained that sending economists from Washington to assess the situation in India constituted an indictment of the Embassy's competence and judgment, which he felt to be "unjustified and unacceptable." Bowles argued that Freeman's message suggested a totally unfounded relationship between a second poor crop year and Indian efforts in agriculture. He stated that he did not intend to deliver Freeman's message to Subramaniam unless directed to do so by Rusk or the President. (Telegram 6998 from New Delhi, November 12; ibid., AID (US) 15 INDIA) Rusk responded in telegram 83747 to New Delhi, November 12, that the dispatch of a special mission to India was not intended as a vote of no-confidence in the Embassy's judgment. Rusk noted that the larger objective of the experts from Agriculture and the later Congressional delegation was to enlist the cooperation of Subramaniam and the Indian Government in redoubled efforts to meet the crisis and to persuade them not to take for granted action by the United States. (Ibid.) In telegram 83787 to New Delhi, November 13, Rusk instructed Bowles to make an oral presentation to Subramaniam along the lines of Freeman's message, but softened somewhat to take account of Indian sensibilities. (Ibid., SOC 10 INDIA)

391. **Letter From Howard Wriggins of the National Security
Council Staff to the Ambassador to India (Bowles)**[1]

Washington, November 12, 1966.

Dear Chet:

By now you will have received cables indicating that two agricultural economists from the USDA will be on their way to Delhi Monday[2] evening. Several Congressmen and Senators will be coming later, early in December, since it has not been possible to alter the schedules of the key Members of Congress at this short notice.

This mission should be seen as an earnest of the President's deep concern for India's plight. The past several mornings he has come in with a new angle, so you can be assured he is deeply concerned. From the urgency of your messages, he suspects that we are in for another really tough year in India and that the Congress will have to be asked to come through handsomely again, even though we argued this year that such high requirements were quite exceptional. He therefore feels it absolutely necessary to build a base in Congress which can only be done by (a) a really cool review, sponsored by Washington, of Indian agricultural performance and (b) adequate Congressional participation so that the members can reassure their elected colleagues. The President knows Mrs. Gandhi's political difficulties, particularly the last distressing weeks, but he has his problems, too. Without such a quick look now, he does not believe he can get Congress cranked up sufficiently. He is even unable to move on the interim 2 million tons until this team of experts reports.

The Department of State, with Freeman's concurrence, is also asking Doug Heck to plug into the agricultural team's immediate investigations. It is important that he go along insofar as he can in order to get a rather precise view of the political implications of pressing the agricultural changes Subramaniam has agreed to and we have been urging. And on his return, he will be able to interpret to us all verbally, as our discussions proceed, the broader context and experience of the specialized economic mission.

The attached is a rough outline[3] of the kinds of information we think we will need. It may not all come out in the report of Secretary Freeman's experts, but it suggests the total picture we think we will eventually have to provide and send it to you as the best indication

---

[1] Source: Johnson Library, National Security File, NSC Histories, Indian Famine, August 1966–February 1967, Vol. III. Confidential; Eyes Only.

[2] November 14.

[3] Not printed.

of our thinking here now. I am sending a copy to John Lewis to impress on him the need for a broad view in this exercise.

This is in haste. You can imagine how distressed we are that the Government is having its present difficulties. It is particularly discouraging for those of us who have been plugging India's bright future for so long. But I personally think it will come through this time of troubles, though it may be a close thing.

All the best—and be of good cheer. Don't the British say, "Keep your pecker up"?

Sincerely,

Howard Wriggins[4]

---

[4] Printed from a copy that bears this typed signature.

---

392. Telegram From the Embassy in India to the Department of State[1]

New Delhi, November 14, 1966, 1322Z.

7055. Ref: State 83787.[2]

1. At 10 am Nov 14 AID Director John Lewis and I called on Subramaniam to outline our plan for urgent review of Indian food situation first by experts from USDA, second by Congressmen. Dias, Secretary, Dept of Food, also attended meeting. We are forwarding by separate cable[3] aide-mémoire which outlines conversation in detail and which we have conveyed to Subramaniam.

2. After hearing our presentation Subramaniam stated he would welcome any action that would create a better understanding of India's food problem and effort India is making to meet its needs as a basis for continued assistance.

3. As noted in aide-mémoire, Subramaniam promptly brought up question of India's urgent and immediate needs. In November 1,200,000

---

[1] Source: National Archives and Records Administration, RG 59, Central Files 1964–66, SOC 10 INDIA. Confidential; Priority.

[2] See footnote 3, Document 390.

[3] Telegram 7056 from New Delhi, November 14. (National Archives and Records Administration, RG 59, Central Files 1964–66, SOC 10 INDIA)

tons of foodgrains would be landed. In December he expected roughly one million tons. Unless additional shipments can be arranged very soon, arrivals in January will drop to 500,000 tons. This will mean reduced rations in all major cities just one month before national elections.

4. Under these extreme circumstances he expressed hope that we would agree to release, on interim basis the additional 500,000 tons required to keep pipeline full until first of February. If an agreement were not signed in near future, India would undertake to pay for this emergency grain with its own foreign exchange.[4]

5. I told Subramaniam we would convey his request to Washington and inform him as soon as we receive reply. As Dept knows from our previous cables, we do not feel that Subramaniam overstates extent of the emergency. We are therefore hopeful that it will be possible allow India obtain an additional 500,000 tons of food grain immediately either through prompt amendment to present PL480 agreement or under reimbursable procedure which was used earlier this year (Deptel 2119, May 2).[5]

Bowles

---

[4] Rostow passed on this request in a November 14 memorandum to the President. (Johnson Library, National Security File, Country File, India, India's Food Problem, Vol. 2) The Embassy was informed, in telegram 86882 to New Delhi, November 17, that urgent Indian cash purchases of grain would be shipped expeditiously so that deliveries would continue. (National Archives and Records Administration, RG 59, Central Files 1964–66, SOC 10 INDIA)

[5] Telegram 2119 was sent to New Delhi on May 3. (Ibid., AID (IBRD) 9 INDIA)

---

393. Editorial Note

On November 27, 1966, Secretary of Agriculture Orville Freeman called President Johnson to discuss the report of the experts Freeman had sent to India to assess agricultural developments. Freeman said he was preparing a memorandum for the President summarizing the report. Johnson observed that such a memorandum would be politically sensitive, and he was concerned about leaks to the press in the Department of Agriculture. He told Freeman to give him an oral summary of the report and not to submit the memorandum. Freeman noted that his experts had gone to India with instructions to determine how well India was living up to the agreement Freeman and Subramaniam had signed in Rome. The experts concluded that "their batting average was about 80 per cent. That on the things they said they'd do, they pretty well delivered on." On balance, the experts gave the Indian Government an "A" for effort.

Freeman went on to assess the new food crisis that was complicating the Indian Government's efforts to live up to the agreement. "This monsoon failure took place in central India. It came on very quickly with an almost complete failure of rainfall in the last six weeks." In some ways, he noted, the new crisis posed a more difficult problem than the subcontinent-wide crisis of the previous year: "this time the shortfall is concentrated in a very limited area that involves about 150 million people which is a long way from the seacoast and which, unfortunately, is in an area in India which has the worst government in terms of the state government. And they seem to be having just a hell of a time getting the local leadership in that area—the chief ministers, as they call them—to move." Freeman observed that without food supplies from abroad there was a serious danger of starvation.

In response to a question from Johnson, Freeman stated that the anticipated grain harvest in India would produce some 85 million tons, approximately 10 million tons less than expected before the failure of the monsoons. Johnson asked how the projected 85 million ton total compared with the amount of grain produced in India the previous year. Freeman responded that India had produced 74 million tons during the previous famine year. Johnson asked how much grain had been supplied to India from abroad during the previous year, and Freeman indicated that India had received approximately 11 million tons, of which the United States had supplied 8.5 million. Johnson found it difficult to understand why India needed grain from abroad if it was going to produce as much as it had gotten by on during the previous year:

"I just don't see why they ought to call Uncle Sam. They got eleven million more tons of production this year than they had last year when we gave them ten. Themselves. Now, they haven't had a goddamn big failure. They've just produced eleven million more than they had last year. But they're just on that tit and they want ten million free tons, and we want it for our farmers and so nobody here is stopping."

Freeman explained that the problem in India was one of uneven distribution. Some of the Indian states would enjoy grain surpluses, but in the wake of the famine it was difficult to persuade people to part with that surplus. One of the options being considered by the Gandhi government, if grain from abroad could not be found to meet the new crisis, was to use the army to compel a redistribution of grain. Freeman noted that with a general election pending in India, the experts in the Department of Agriculture felt that such a move would probably lead to the fall of the government. Another option would be to use the limited foreign exchange reserves India had to buy grain on the international market. To do so, however, would impact heavily on the economic development program the United States was supporting in India. Johnson was skeptical about how India was spending its foreign exchange reserves: "I'd bear in mind that they got two hundred million of currency that they can buy all the damn wheat they need, instead of airplanes." He also had difficulty sympathizing with the distribution problem Freeman had described:

"It's just a hell of a note for me to say to India that I've got a big surplus in Texas but I haven't in Maine so you got to ship it up to us for Maine, India, because I won't take it from Texas. That don't make sense. The only reason I got to ship it is because they won't use their own."

Johnson was also dubious about the advice he was getting on India: "I've got more damn people that are working for the Indians and fewer working for the Americans than anybody I ever saw." With that reservation, he asked Freeman to outline the immediate problem. Freeman noted that significant quantities of wheat were scheduled to be shipped from the United States to India in December and January. Between 800,000 and 900,000 tons were to be shipped in December and some 200,000 more in January. From the middle of January until the beginning of April, however, Freeman stated "they are going to be naked." Except for the United States, Canada was the only other country contemplating emergency grain supplies for India, and Canada was hampered by frozen ports. In light of the serious nature of the crisis, Freeman suggested that Johnson authorize an additional 2 million tons of grain to bridge the shortfall until the new crop was harvested in India in April.

Johnson was not prepared to make the kind of commitment proposed by Freeman without authorization from Congress. He was concerned over the prospect of a $20 billion budget deficit, and he felt he had to give priority to financing the war in Vietnam. "Now, goddamn it, I've just got to stop something. And I don't know anything easier to stop than the Indian wheat." He was prepared to contemplate an additional 500,000 tons, at a cost of approximately $35 million, to supplement the more than 1 million tons already scheduled for shipment, but beyond that he wanted Congress to be consulted. His concluding instruction to Freeman was to arrange for a draft resolution bearing on the food crisis for Congress to consider when it came back into session in January:

"I think if you just tell Rusk on this, or Nick, or whoever you are dealing with in the morning that we want to get a resolution ready and, as soon as they do, why, Congress gets back, we'll have one of the first meetings, like we did last time. We'll follow the same procedures. Unless there is something that I'm not aware of, I don't want to go up into the dozens of millions of dollars on commitments unless I got these Congressmen and other folks behind me." (Johnson Library,

Recordings and Transcripts, Recording of Telephone Conversation Between President Johnson and Secretary of Agriculture Freeman, November 27, 1966, 7:30 p.m., Tape F66.32, Sides A and B (entire tape))

---

394.   Telegram From the Ambassador to India (Bowles) to the President's Special Assistant and Chief of Staff (Moyers)[1]

New Delhi, November 28, 1966, 1106Z.

7126. 1. Because I felt that we have done all that we can do through regular channels to communicate the importance to U.S. interests in India of keeping the grain pipe line full and because USDA team is now making its report, we have been sending in only routine reporting cables.

2. However as this emergency grows I am taking the liberty of cabling you directly and privately because I want to be absolutely sure that those close to the President and the President himself understand the agonizing political-economic situation which is building up here in India. In view of the turmoil of Manila, the US elections, the continuing Viet-Nam crisis and some unpleasant surgery, it would not be surprising if the full implications of our messages have failed to filter through.

3. Here is the situation as briefly and soberly as I can state it: by next Wednesday or Thursday the Indian Cabinet will have to decide whether or not to cut the already meager rations on which some 120 million people largely in the urban areas are living in order to spread the available supplies over a longer period.

Under the very best of circumstances the moderate pro-democracy Congress Party is bound to face severe losses in the elections in February. If the already inadequate daily foodgrain ration to these 120 million people is cut these losses will be significantly greater and the prospect of a government emerging which is closer to the U.S. will diminish sharply.

4. I have been making a vigorous and continuing effort through background talks with the Indian press and key Indian officials to

---

[1] Source: Johnson Library, National Security File, Country File, India, Exchanges with Bowles. Secret; Eyes Only. The message was [text not declassified] addressed to the White House, Eyes Only Bill Moyers.

temper the current fears, insecurity and distrust. Thus far the Indian press and GOI spokesmen, including Mrs. Gandhi,[2] have been remarkably moderate. However as starvation deaths grow significantly and the electioneering climate takes over, such restraints will be cast aside and moderation will go by the board.

5. Although I do not know the real reasons for the delay I surmise from newspaper dope stories out of Washington and from various visitors that several factors are involved. Following are some of them with my comments:

A. India is not doing enough to help herself. Although India after 200 years of stagnation is not doing everything it should in agriculture, it is doing far more than we dreamed it could do two years ago. This is the concensus of every qualified observer who has had a first hand look (including experts for the Ford and Rockefeller Foundations, the World Bank and our own mission). India's water development still lags and adequate credit facilities are lacking in many areas but even here the prospects for progress are encouraging.

Unless I am profoundly mistaken India will be close to foodgrain self-sufficiency by 1971 and in a balanced food position by 1975.

Although it may properly be charged that the Indians should have given agriculture a much higher priority several years ago we ourselves carry a certain responsibility for the delay.

In the 1950's the economic assistance policies of the USG in India were not designed to make India self-sustaining in foods but consciously or unconsciously to preserve India as a dumping ground for PL 480 food surpluses which at that time seemed limitless. It has only been during the last three years that the USG has itself faced the Indian food situation realistically and attempted to deal with it vigorously.

B. India should ask others besides Uncle Sam. India has been pressing all nations in a position to help vigorously in the last few weeks, and some of these nations will probably come through (Canada, Australia, perhaps even Soviets). However, no nation other than U.S. is in a position to keep the food grain pipe lines full during the next crucial 90 days.

---

[2] The Associated Press reported from New Delhi on November 26 that Prime Minister Gandhi told the Press Club of India that India had been forced to seek food from other parts of the world because of a delay by the United States in signing a new P.L. 480 agreement. She said the delay was purportedly because India was not making sufficient efforts to increase its food production, but she denied that this was the case. As a result of the reduced flow of grain from abroad, she said that the government was considering a cut in grain rations to the Indian people in order to provide more food for the drought-affected areas of the country. (Ibid., NSC Histories, Indian Famine, August 1966–February 1967, Vol. III)

C. The necessary food is available in India, if only the surplus states would give it up to the needy areas. This story, which seems to have originated with a Warren Unna article, is based on gross misinformation. The Indian Government has been vigorously procuring in the few surplus states in desperate effort to maintain rations in large urban areas throughout India and at the same time boost deliveries to faminetorn Bihar and up.

D. Mrs. Gandhi is unfairly critical of U.S. policies in Viet-Nam. I more than almost anyone else can sympathize with the President's frustration over the vagaries and contradictions of India's foreign policies; the Moscow communiqué was particularly irritating as I told Mrs. Gandhi in a blunt personal letter the day after the communiqué was signed. However, this situation is not new. India's non-alignment evolved out of the independence movement and has been in full bloom now for nineteen years. (*Note:* It took us Americans forty years and two world wars to learn the folly of isolationism.)

Moreover if we can avoid undue strain on our relations with India now I believe that there is a better than even chance that the new government which will be formed after the elections will adopt a posture more favorable to us in Southeast Asia and elsewhere.

Many key Indian political leaders, some of whom may emerge with greatly enhanced influence following the election, already have a keen appreciation for what U.S. is trying to do there. Last week *Blitz* and the Communist press were in an uproar because the Indian Government told the North Viet-Nam representative here in India not to release a statement critical of the U.S. which had been prepared for the press.

In any event, the appearance that U.S. is delaying food shipments because of displeasure with India's Viet-Nam policy which has been created by leaked news stories out of Washington simply sets off a strong chauvinistic reaction here which plays into the hands of those who most strenuously oppose our policy.

6. Nevertheless, even if one were to concede these arguments and, I must emphasize that all but the last run wholly counter to the evidence available to us and the qualified analysts and observers who have recently gone over the ground, one absolutely fundamental question remains: is the United States with its traditional commitment to human welfare going to stand by idly in the face of a major and increasingly apparent human disaster in India and permit that disaster to occur? This question will necessarily be answered by our action, or inaction, in the next ten days. Whatever we decide to do thereafter, no matter on what scale or priority, will come only after starvation has become inevitable to an unknown number of people barely living today in the Bihar area. It will not be long before our TV screens and front pages will be overflowing with grim pictures and stories of this tragic situation.

7. As far as India is concerned our failure to act will provide a bonanza political opportunity for the Communists and lose us the respect and confidence of even the moderate groups in one of the few remaining democratic nations in Asia and Africa, confidence which hae been painstakingly built up over the past two decades. With all our power and wealth we simply cannot permit our moral leadership, to which the President has personally contributed so much, to be gravely and perhaps irreparably damaged by allowing Indians to starve while we wait for still more facts.

8. By now Martin Abel of the Department of Agriculture, who knows India well and who, as you know, has been making an intensive study of the food situation here during the last ten days, has reported to Orville Freeman who I assume will then report directly to the President. Unless I am mistaken, Abel's analysis and also Dorothy Jacobson's will coincide in most respects with our own.

9. I earnestly hope that based on this additional information the President will release the emergency grain necessary to maintain the pipeline flow at least well into March. This will see us beyond the election and through a dangerous crisis period in which both we and they can be grievously hurt, and leave time for a sober consideration of our 1967 Indian food plan. If we are forced to cut down this coming year on our shipments to India let's do it next fall and not now.

10. One possible approach that might allow us to meet the current emergency while protecting our Congressional rear is as follows:

A. Announce soonest that we are releasing 500,000 tons of wheat and milo on an emergency basis with the understanding that the Indians will pay for it with their own money if we should decide to discontinue the food aid program.

B. Ask the Congressional delegation headed by Bob Pogue and Walter Mondale which is coming out here in two weeks to give the President their judgment immediately following their visit of the importance of extending this emergency program by an additional million and a half tons of foodgrains. This would cover period until President can consult in early January with Congressional leaders or secure a new joint resolution if this is indicated.

C. Postpone decision on the 1967 food aid program for India until after Congress has had an opportunity to take suitable action in January. The 2 million tons will alleviate need for further decisions until late January.

11. If this personal message adds nothing new to what the President already knows please file and forget it. However if you feel it can be helpful in further clarifying the situation please use it as you think best.

12. Believe me, Bill, I would not send this personal plea for action if I were not very deeply concerned by what may be ahead.

395. Memorandum From Secretary of Agriculture Freeman to President Johnson[1]

Washington, November 28, 1966.

SUBJECT

India—Analysis Team Report—Recommendation

ENCLOSURE

Team Report[2]

1. The enclosed is self-explanatory. The team sought to make it objective and quantitative with a minimum of subjective evaluations. Particular attention was given to measuring whether India had met the commitments made by Minister Subramaniam at Rome. In certain cases commitments as to action were implicit rather than explicit. In these cases the effort applied was evaluated accordingly.

The sections on the *Food Situation* include both objective evaluation and some judgments.

The political situation is more in the area of State than Agriculture. Nonetheless, I felt you would welcome opinions from the last credible source "on the ground."

2. My *evaluation* of the Report is as follows:

A. The Indians have met their clear cut commitments. The record is not a complete 100 percent where results are concerned but they have come close and have, I believe, sincerely tried to deliver.

B. The food situation is grave. Two million tons of grain must come from somewhere between mid-January when the pipeline runs out and April, when the spring crop comes in. (How much relief the spring crop will give remains to be seen.) Otherwise there will be starvation in India during that period. The balance of the year will have to be considered separately.

3. Alternatives—There are four possible ways to get the 2 million tons of grain:

A. It is possible, but unlikely, that the Indians could get it by the use of military force internally to procure in the surplus states. But this would postpone, not lessen, the total requirement for imported grain

---

[1] Source: Johnson Library, National Security File, NSC Histories, Indian Famine, August 1966–February 1967, Vol. III. No classification marking.

[2] Attached was a November 27 report from Martin E. Abel and Arthur T. Thompson to Freeman entitled "Evaluation of Agricultural Self-Help Efforts and Review of Food Situation in India."

in 1967. The President can best judge the politics of such a course of action. Subramaniam's analysis is carried in the Report.

B. It is possible that Canada could ship some in time to help. Australia is another possibility. So far neither France nor Russia have given encouragement. It is not likely that any combination of these could get the 2 million tons needed in the next few months.

C. India might buy commercially. One hundred million dollars would buy about 1.5 million tons of wheat and a third more grain sorghum. India's free foreign exchange reserves are estimated at 150 to 200 million dollars. The President can best judge the practicality of India using these reserves in light of the economic development program.

D. The United States. However, the logistics of moving grain from the U.S. are such (6 weeks at a minimum) that there is a real threat of famine if we wait to see what other countries do, and whether India will take the necessary steps to procure internally or buy outside commercially.

The Team reported to me that Minister Subramaniam outlined his three alternative courses of action:

A. A contribution from the United States at the level of recent months.

B. A reduced contribution from the United States supplemented by a commercial purchase.

C. Use military force for internal procurement and supplement by commercial purchase.

He stated that he knew exactly what he would have to do under each alternative. He asked that the U.S. make up its mind so he would know what alternative to follow.

4. Political

I do not feel competent to pass judgment on the political situation not having been exposed directly for 6 months. Mrs. Jacobson who is an experienced political observer reports that it is most sensitive and that the current government will likely stand or fall on the food question and whether the U.S. acts promptly. The Team reported to me that Subramaniam said that the present government would be defeated if the Army was used for compulsory procurement. He precicts that under such circumstances he would not be re-elected.

5. Recommendations

A. I would recommend that an interim allocation be made promptly. On the record the Indians have met their commitment made to the U.S. at Rome. They are trying hard. Agriculture today is clearly the number 1 item (perhaps as much as defense) in their planning and budgeting.

In 1965 the U.S. allotted 6 million tons of food grain to India. The Indian "self-help" effort in 1966 merits, in my judgment, a continuation of shipments at least at that level. We have shipped 3.2 million tons so far in this fiscal year. The 2 million tons I recommend be allotted between now and mid-February would fall within the 6 million ton level of 1965. Such an allocation could be made at once or in two segments—1 million tons immediately and the second million could be made subject to the confirmation of the Congressional team that India is making an adequate agricultural effort and couldn't get the grain from any other source in time to prevent disaster.

B. Any allocation should be made under strict conditions. It should be clear that the continuation and strengthening of self-help efforts is a condition. Negotiations on self-help should begin soon to be completed following the Indian election. Any further allocation should depend on clear and definite Indian commitments to take further specific steps to strengthen their agriculture.

---

396.   Memorandum for the Record[1]

Washington, November 28, 1966.

SUBJECT

Telephone Call from the President on Indian Wheat (from the Ranch, 10:43 a.m.)

In summary, the President instructed that:

1. We provide him with a December–January–February schedule of absolute "minimum" requirements.

2. Irrespective of the above, we will not provide *any* wheat unilaterally, without substantial contributions from Canada, Australia, and France. Goldberg should have a hard go at them to see what they are prepared to do.

3. If we can get substantial contributions from the other producing countries, the President would be willing to provide a few hundred

---

[1] Source: Johnson Library, National Security File, NSC Histories, Indian Famine, August 1966–February 1967, Vol. III. Secret. Drafted by Francis M. Bator, the President's Deputy Special Assistant for National Security Affairs.

thousand tons prior to any Congressional action—if they do $1/2$ million tons we might do $1/2$ million tons. ("Get me a program which involves other donors, and for a U.S. amount of not over $1/2$ million tons.")

4. For anything more than that, we must get a Congressional resolution. The President is prepared to make this the first order of Congressional business in January.

FMB

---

397. Telegram From the President's Special Assistant (Rostow) to President Johnson in Texas[1]

Washington, November 28, 1966, 2338Z.

CAP 661088. To the President from Walt Rostow. State wants your clearance on the following deal.

1. The Canadians would put up 21 million dollars in special food assistance to India as a pure grant. They may be announcing this in any case this afternoon or tomorrow morning. It consists of 150 thousand tons of wheat plus $9 million worth of flour, milk concentrates, etc.

2. We would put up 500 thousand tons of grain valued at $35 million on concessional terms (PL 480 Title I).

3. The Indians would agree to buy either from us alone (or from us and the Canadians) an additional 500 thousand tons of grain. (The Canadians may take the view that it is inappropriate, given the Indian foreign exchange position, to buy grain now. Besides, they may think that it would fudge up their normal commercial marketing arrangements. In that case, the 500,000 ton order would come to us.)

4. This would be the nut of the deal. Are we empowered to put this deal to the Indians, once we have confirmed the Canadian $21 million grant offer?

5. In addition, we would go out promptly to the Australians and ask them to put up 200,000 tons of grain on concessional terms. Our people think we might end up getting 100,000 tons, but it will take time for two reasons. First, the Australians are only now gathering in their harvest

---

[1] Source: Johnson Library, National Security File, Country File, India, India's Food Problem, Vol. II. Confidential.

and don't quite know where they stand. Second, they haven't yet moved over like the Canadians to the idea of concessional grain. State does not think the deal should be held up until the Australians come round.

6. We would also go out to the French with a request that they put up some grain on concessional terms. We are not optimistic.

7. For your information, the last grain ship carrying wheat under present agreements from the U.S. to India will leave on December 7 and arrive by mid January.

Grain arrivals from all sources now look as follows: October 918,000 tons; November 820,000 tons; December 320,000 tons; January 564,000 tons; February zero.

In short, no grain arrivals are yet firmed up between mid January and the end of February.

8. The best estimate we have for the current harvest is 78.5 million tons, not 84 million tons. The Indians are projecting higher figures in order to avoid panic and to get through their elections.

---

398.   Memorandum From the President's Special Assistant (Rostow) to President Johnson[1]

Washington, November 29, 1966.

SUBJECT

The Next Step in Pakistan: a second $70-million Loan

When you sent Gene Locke out for his initial meeting with Ayub last spring, you authorized him to say we would resume our AID lending in six-month slices provided the Paks would do certain things. We wanted them to limit their defense expenditures, to make an honest effort to maintain the "spirit of Tashkent," to demonstrate a satisfactory appreciation of our interests in Asia, to cooperate on arrangements for our facilities and to live up to the economic conditions laid down by the World Bank Consortium.

Locke feels that Ayub has done an honest job of living up to his share of this bargain. I recommend you read the attached excellent

---

[1] Source: Johnson Library, National Security File, Country File, Pakistan, Memos, 10/66–7/67, Vol. VII. Secret. A handwritten note reads, "Rec'd at Ranch 11–30–66, 9:20 a.m." A handwritten "L" indicates the memorandum was seen by the President.

memo from Secretary Rusk detailing our conditions and Pak performance.[2] Of course, there is room for improvement in relations with India, but we at least have both capitals thinking about quite substantive talks, though probably not until after Indian elections. On all the economic and bilateral issues, Pak performance looks pretty good.

Now is the time to go ahead with the next six-month slice—a second $70-million commodity loan through the Consortium—if you are satisfied that Ayub has lived up to your understanding with him last December and the conditions you laid down in April. Secretary Rusk recommends that you approve.

Charlie Schultze finds that their economic performance has been good, their need clear, and that our share of total assistance is declining.[3] This loan fits within the reduced Development Loan authorized by Congress for FY 67 and leaves room for a U.S. loan to help finance U.S. equipment sales on the Karachi Steel Mill, for which your authorization will be sought later.

This $70-million loan will be for purchases in the U.S. Secretary Fowler concurs.

My own feeling is that we are back on an even enough keel to warrant taking this second step. Ayub has responded well to your sending a personal friend as Ambassador, and his removal of Foreign Minister Bhutto was a major step in rooting out the anti-American tone which characterized Pak policy in 1964 and 1965. Our policy on military spares may be the next big test in our relationship. Going ahead with this economic step now shows that we consider our relations still to be on the upgrade and gives us a firmer base for working toward the tough resolution of the military aid problem.

I recommend you authorize the proposed loan.

Walt

Approve

Disapprove

Call me[4]

---

[2] The memorandum from Secretary Rusk to the President is dated November 21.

[3] Schultze recommended approval of the loan in a November 28 memorandum to the President. (Johnson Library, National Security File, Country File, Pakistan, Memos, 10/66–7/67, Vol. VII)

[4] Johnson checked this option. Rostow noted in a December 13 memorandum to the President that he did not receive word of the President's response until December 12. He asked if Johnson wanted to make a decision at that point. There is no indication on the memorandum of the President's response to Rostow's question. (Ibid., Files of Walt W. Rostow, Meetings with the President, April–December 1966)

399.   Memorandum for the Record[1]

Washington, December 9, 1966.

The President last night authorized Walt Rostow to convey the following points to B.K. Nehru:[2]

1. It is counter-productive to leak stories to the *press* and to pressure the President on the food problem. The President is the best friend the Indians have. By working through the press, they make it harder for him to do what he did during their emergency last year and what he may have to do again this year.

2. The Indians should give equal priority to *buying wheat commercially* in the U.S. It does not set well for us to read of larger purchases elsewhere when we are carrying the bulk of the concessional burden. (I asked WWR whether the President knew that the Indians intended to buy 50,000 tons and whether we should read his comment to imply that they should buy more. WWR said yes.)

3. The *President can not move until his Congressional group comes back* on 23 or 24 December. (However, the President has USDA lining up fast ships to move as quickly as they can after he makes a decision.)

4. The President is assured that India will be covered for January. He will be in a position to help in *February* if he gets a favorable report from his Congressional delegation. He can make no commitment now but the Indians should keep quiet and have some faith.

Rostow planned to see Nehru in New York this afternoon.

H.S.

---

[1] Source: Johnson Library, National Security File, NSC Histories, Indian Famine, August 1966–February 1967, Vol. III. Secret. Drafted by Saunders.

[2] In a December 8 conversation with Katzenbach, Johnson complained about a number of news stories he had read suggesting that the U.S. supply of grain to India was dwindling. "This whole mess that the pipeline is going to dry up in January is just a damn lie." Johnson noted that the pipeline was currently full, and that 1 million tons of grain would be delivered to India in January. He felt that Nehru was contributing to a false impression through his contacts with a number of major papers. He said he was "damn tired of them treating me this way." He also enjoined Katzenbach to "get out your damn baseball bat" and do something about the people in the State Department who he thought were attempting to put pressure on him on India policy by leaking information to the press. (Ibid., Recordings and Transcripts, Recording of Telephone Conversation Between President Johnson and Under Secretary of State Katzenbach, December 8, 1966, 10:26 a.m., Tape F6612.01, Side B, PNO 34)

400.   Message From the President's Special Assistant (Rostow) to
the Ambassador to India (Bowles)[1]

Washington, December 10, 1966.

Chet:

Assure you President is deeply concerned regarding Indian food needs, but he is determined to establish a sound political position to support our share of the massive needs you report for next year. January arrivals are now covered in part from Canada and Australia, as a result of our unwillingness to rush in. Decisions regarding February and beyond can't be taken until after Congressional delegation[2] returns and after considering their recommendation and other problems here. Friday, December 9, I discussed this with Bijou,[3] on President's instructions, sketched the above, and reiterated the four key points in our policy that (a) there must be evidence of effective high priority on agriculture; (b) there must be equitable burden-sharing internationally—others must contribute substantially grant foodstuffs or cash for food purchases; (c) there must be a Congressional base for food aid; (d) commercial purchases should be made on an equitable basis—we, too, are an important market for cash sales of grain and we hope the GOI Treasury officials will come to consider grain purchases here as high a priority as purchases in Australia and Canada.

Bijou understands these points. I also stressed the counter-productivity of his Embassy or any other US or Indian governmental official attempting to use the press in an effort to stampede us. Sect. Rusk will have more of the flavor for you when you meet shortly.[4]

Walt[5]

---

[1] Source: Johnson Library, National Security File, Country File, India, Exchanges with Bowles (cont.). Secret; Eyes Only. A handwritten note indicates that the message was sent as [text not declassified].

[2] The Congressional delegation scheduled to arrive in India on December 14 to assess the food situation was composed of Senator Jack Miller, Congressman W.R. Poage, and Congressman Robert Dole.

[3] Ambassador Nehru.

[4] On his return from a trip to Vietnam, Rusk made a refueling stop in New Delhi on December 12 and met at Palam airport with Bowles and Foreign Minister Chagla. Rusk and Chagla discussed the situation in Vietnam and the food crisis in India. Chagla stated that the unwillingness or inability of the United States to help India meet the food crisis would cause resentment among the Indian people who would be unable to understand the U.S. rationale no matter how valid it might be. Rusk responded that Chagla's comment was unfair. He noted that the United States had sent food to India on a massive scale while help from other countries had been minimal. (Memorandum of conversation by Bowles, December 12; National Archives and Records Administration, RG 59, Central Files 1964–66, POL INDIA–US) On December 14 Bowles sent to Rusk the answers to a number of questions raised by Rusk in his December 12 conversation with Bowles concerning the food crisis. (Telegram 8634 from New Delhi; ibid., SOC 10 INDIA)

[5] Printed from a copy that bears this typed signature.

401. Circular Telegram From the Department of State to Certain Posts[1]

Washington, December 13, 1966, 1:23 p.m.

101529. For Ambassador from Acting Secretary. Indian Food Crisis

1. U.S. Government is seriously concerned over food situation in India which for second year in row is faced with drought and substantial short-falls in food production. Situation is aggravated this year by near-famine conditions in northeastern India involving approximately 75 million people. While India has made considerable progress in its agriculture development program, this effort has been undermined by unfavorable weather. Until next major crop is harvested in October 1967 India's need will be great.

2. To meet last year's crop failure, we supplied eight million tons of foodgrains (about $500 million). Our response to India's needs last year was facilitated and endorsed by a Congressional resolution which authorized President to provide these PL–480 foodgrain shipments to India. The last shipments under that authorization are expected to arrive in India in January.

3. To cope with its pressing needs, Indian Government has approached us and several other major food-producing countries for further assistance. Canadian Government has already responded generously with $21 million food grant. It plans seek appropriation of another $75 million for food assistance, involving total grant of a million tons of wheat. We have hopes Australia will also supply wheat on grant or generous concessional terms.

4. We wish to do what we can but supplying India's needs this year will strain our diminishing foodgrain resources. Our wheat carryover is lowest in years. We have had to expand acreage under cultivation to meet additional demands at considerable budgetary cost. It is apparent another long-term foodgrain assistance program will require Congressional support. Accordingly we consider it important that all industrial countries, especially members of India Consortium, as well as food-exporting countries generally share in this responsibility.

---

[1] Source: National Archives and Records Administration, RG 59, Central Files 1964–66, SOC 10 INDIA. Limited Official Use. Drafted by Heck on December 12; cleared by Handley, Macomber, Wriggins, Deputy Assistant Secretary of State for Congressional Relations H.G. Torbert, Jr., and Brown (USDA), and in substance by Fried; and approved and initialed by Acting Secretary Katzenbach. Sent to Ankara, Athens, Bangkok, Bern, Bonn, Brussels, Buenos Aires, Canberra, Copenhagen, The Hague, Helsinki, London, Madrid, Mexico City, Oslo, Paris, Rangoon, Rome, Stockholm, Tokyo, Vienna, and Wellington and repeated to Karachi, Moscow, New Delhi, Ottawa, USUN, and Paris for the Secretary.

5. Actions such as India's self-help efforts, Canada's, and hopefully Australia's, are steps in this direction. Foodgrain-exporting nations however cannot be expected carry entire load. Industrial countries generally should be expected assist, not merely by token shipments of food, etc., but also by contributing funds to buy wheat or other grains in world market or by providing shipping, fertilizer, etc.

6. You should consult with your Indian colleague and support his efforts to obtain assistance from host government. FYI: GOI is being urged to issue such instructions.[2] End FYI. If your Indian colleague seeks your support you should urge host government to respond generously and quickly with food, money to buy food or equipment and supplies. Capability of USG to continue to extend substantial food assistance to India will depend to considerable degree on India's self-help efforts to buy foodgrains and solicit assistance from others and on response of latter to humanitarian crisis which India faces.[3]

Katzenbach

---

[2] The Embassy in India reported on December 15 that Food Secretary Dias had offered assurances that India would explore every genuine source of assistance. (Telegram 8648 from New Delhi; ibid.)

[3] On December 19 Benjamin Read sent to Rostow a summary report on the replies received in response to circular telegram 101529. Read's covering memorandum characterized the responses as disappointing. (Ibid.)

---

402. Memorandum From the President's Special Assistant (Rostow) to President Johnson[1]

Washington, December 16, 1966.

SUBJECT

Next PL 480 Agreement with Pakistan

The time has come to decide whether to take the next step with Ayub. When you sent Gene Locke out in June, he took with him your promise to resume economic and food aid for six months and to con-

---

[1] Source: Johnson Library, National Security File, Country File, Pakistan, Memos, 10/66–7/67, Vol. VII. Secret. A handwritten note on the memorandum reads, "rec'd 12–16–66, 3:15 p."

sider another six months in December or January provided Ayub met certain conditions.

You now have before you (a) Secretary Rusk's recommendation[2] for a $70 million non-project loan for the last half of FY 1967, and (b) the attached Schnittker–Gaud recommendation[3] for meeting urgent Pak requests for further food aid.

The main decision is how you want to deal with Ayub. Secretary Rusk feels that he has come far enough in meeting our conditions to warrant our going ahead for another six months. Locke feels Ayub has kept faith, though performance has not been perfect.

If you want to keep the heat on, the AID loan is the better vehicle for discussing progress on our political conditions. Holding off our PL 480 decision would generate greater political pressure on Ayub than delaying the AID loan because sharply rising food prices (20% in November alone) are fast becoming his top political problem. However, I don't believe you want to use food that way.

There are good reasons for treating the Pak food program separately from India's. First, while the Paks suffered from drought this year too, their needs are smaller—about 700,000 tons for the rest of FY 1967. Second, they have already rounded up almost 500,000 tons— about 25% of this year's total import needs—through purchases here and elsewhere and from other donors. They have spent 10% of their scarce foreign exchange to do this. Third, they are already performing well in agriculture. Charlie Schultze's memo (attached)[4] details what the Paks need and have done.

John Schnittker and Bill Gaud recommend (attached) that you give a go-ahead in the next week on 250,000 tons of wheat and 250,000 tons of coarse grains ($36 million) in time to negotiate an amendment to the current agreement before 1 January. Ships would have to begin leaving around 15 January to get our wheat in during the critical March–April pre-harvest period. By waiting until 1 January we would lose valuable time negotiating a totally new agreement under the unfamiliar procedures required by the new law.

If you prefer to hold off until next week when you get US harvest figures, that would cause no harm. But if they're satisfactory, I would recommend letting the Pak negotiations proceed unless you wish to convey a completely negative political signal.

Walt

---

[2] See footnote 2, Document 398.
[3] Attached; dated December 12.
[4] Attached; dated December 16.

Go ahead now

Check with me when US harvest figures are in

Hold until after India decision[5]

See me

_____

[5] Johnson checked this option. A handwritten note reads: "Jake Jacobsen telephoned Mr. Rostow, 9:25 am 12/20/66 and said Pres. wants to hold PL 480 and program loan until makes India announcement."

---

403. Memorandum From the President's Special Assistant (Rostow) to President Johnson[1]

Washington, December 16, 1966.

SUBJECT

Important CARE Food Program in India

Bill Gaud with Agriculture agreement is prepared to go ahead with a $25 million special nutrition program for 5–7 million children under 12 and expectant and nursing mothers in the worst drought areas of India. The program would be run by CARE and other relief organizations would participate to the limits of their ability. It would be under Title II (emergency programs) of PL 480.

The Indian government initially requested a program which would cost about $60 million. The $25 million would give them a start on a revised program for mixing in India a composite food including Indian ingredients and those from other donors that would provide an alternative source of high protein which is much cheaper than milk powder.

Gaud has the authority to approve this kind of program but thought you ought to see it first because it is relevant to the whole Indian problem.

It seems to me there's little question of our giving CARE a go-ahead on this. However, I wonder whether there wouldn't be considerable

_____

[1] Source: Johnson Library, National Security File, Country File, India, India's Food Problem, Vol. II. Confidential. A handwritten note on the memorandum reads, "Rec'd 12–16–66, 7:25 p."

advantage for you in announcing it. To be sure it isn't the main grain sale they're awaiting, but reaching 5–7 million children and mothers is no small program. If you could release it tomorrow, it would hit the Sunday papers (draft release attached[2]). If you do, it would be a good idea if I could call B.K. Nehru in advance.

Walt

Approve White House release

Let Gaud announce it[3]

---

[2] Not printed.

[3] Neither option is checked. A telephone message from the LBJ Ranch concerning the memorandum, relayed to Rostow on December 17 by Jake Jacobsen reads: "I would not do a thing on that now. I want to personally approve every item for India. Tell Gaud I want to approve and do all." The message is summarized in an attached handwritten note.

---

404.   Memorandum From the President's Special Assistant (Rostow) to President Johnson[1]

Washington, December 20, 1966.

Poage, Miller and Dole, whom I warned not to talk about recommendations in India, have sent via CIA channel the following message asking Freeman to be informed.

"Replying to Freeman telegram[2] detailed letter will be hand delivered to Freeman Thursday morning which recommends 1.8 million tons of grain be furnished Government of India with maximum amount donated under Title II of PL 480 before December 31 or under Title II of new act[3] immediately after January 1."

---

[1] Source: Johnson Library, National Security File, Country File, India, India's Food Problem, Vol. II. Secret; Eyes Only. A handwritten note on the memorandum reads, "sent to Ranch via wire CAP 661271.

[2] On December 19 Freeman sent a cable to New Delhi for Poage that reads: "Please cable to the President from India your preliminary report on India's food needs and agricultural performance and your recommendations to the President regarding the need for an interim allocation of grain." (Telegram 105400 to New Delhi; National Archives and Records Administration, RG 59, Central Files 1964–66, LEG 7 POAG)

[3] Reference is to the Food for Peace Act, adopted by Congress on November 11. (80 Stat. 1526)

405.   Letter From Representatives Poage and Dole and Senator
       Miller to Secretary of Agriculture Freeman[1]

New Delhi, December 20, 1966.

Dear Mr. Secretary:

Pursuant to your request, we, the undersigned, have travelled throughout India and have made on-the-spot visits to drought-stricken farming areas and, appropriate storage and transportation facilities. We discussed food problems with Indian officials at all levels and U.S. Government and voluntary agency people.

We were impressed by the magnitude of economic progress, especially in agriculture, by the severity of the drought in northern India, and by the awesome prospect of human suffering which is certain to follow if no help is forthcoming. We wish to emphasize that we were impressed by programs and progress toward Indian self-sufficiency.

A most urgent decision is required if food aid from the United States is to arrive in an orderly manner during February, March, and April. More deliberate planning for follow-up assistance should be firmed *up by March.*

Based on figures available to us at this time and considering our declining U.S. reserves, we recommend that 1.8 million tons of grain (at least 30% sorghum) be furnished the Government of India, with maximum amount donated under Title II of P.L. 480 before December 31, or in the alternative if legally more expeditious under Title II of the new Act immediately after January 1, with announcement of such action at once. The donation should be: (1) based on emergency drought relief for the people of India from the people of the United States; (2) require that to the maximum extent possible the United States donated grain be distributed free to needy persons or proceeds be used for their relief; and (3) the announcement should express the hope of the United States that the USSR and other countries will join the United States, Canada, and Australia in helping India meet her food and fertilizer shortages. A portion of the 1.8 million tons should be considered for Title III distribution through voluntary agencies.

Donations to GOI appear more advantageous than concessional sales (1) because of excessive United States holdings of rupees in India; (2) in order to enable GOI to more effectively negotiate help from the USSR and other countries; (3) to follow examples of Canada and Australia; and (4) to help persuade GOI officials and the Indian press

[1] Source: Johnson Library, National Security File, NSC Histories, Indian Famine, August 1966–February 1967, Vol. III. No classification marking.

to move more quickly toward the United States position regarding Vietnam and to change open criticism of U.S. military strategy to one of condemnation of communist aggression.

We expressed to some GOI officials our belief that the American people feel that some Indian spokesmen have been unfair to both the United States Government and to a majority of the Indian people by their undue criticism of the United States policy in Vietnam. Yet, we have never been welcomed more enthusiastically or hospitably than we were during this visit.

We draw your attention to Section 103(i) of the new PL 480 Act which requires the President to promote progress toward assurance of an adequate food supply by encouraging countries with which agreements are made to give higher emphasis to the production of food crops (such as grain) than to the production of non-food crops (such as cotton) as are in world surplus. In view of large U.S. holdings of rupees, we suggest that in negotiating long-term agreements concessional sales for local currency be replaced by sales on credit eventually repayable in dollars as early as economic conditions in India permit. In view of rapid population growth in India, we urge that any new agreement further emphasize and support efforts to expand agricultural production and technology while implementing effective family planning programs.

We suggest that no new long-term agreements with India under Titles I and IV be concluded until the matters we have discussed herein have been resolved. However, a long-term agreement should be concluded by March 1967.[2]

Sincerely yours,

WR Poage

Jack Miller

Bob Dole

---

[2] Freeman summarized the Congressional delegation's recommendations in a telephone conversation with President Johnson on December 22. Johnson indicated that he was not prepared to accept the 1.8 million ton recommendation. He interpreted the delegation's recommendations as covering India's needs through February and March and agreed to cover India's needs through February because Congress was not in session and could not act in time to get food to India to meet the requirements for February. He authorized Freeman to make a low-level announcement that the United States would send 450,000 tons of wheat and 450,000 tons of feed grains to cover February. Johnson indicated that he would leave the March requirements for Congress to address once it came back into session. He stated that what the United States would do to meet the continuing need would depend on Congress, and on what other countries would do to contribute proportionate amounts to match the U.S. contribution. (Ibid., Recordings and Transcripts, Recording of Telephone Conversation Between President Johnson and Secretary of Agriculture Freeman, December 22, 1966, 11:07 a.m., Tape F6612.03, Side A, PNO 90)

406. Telegram From the President's Special Assistant (Rostow) to President Johnson in Texas[1]

Washington, December 21, 1966, 2053Z.

CAP 661283. If and when you are ready to make your Indian food decision, you may wish to check this rundown of the related decisions on India and Pakistan you also have to work with.

1. At the top of the list is the $25 million CARE special nutrition program in India for expectant mothers and children in the worst drought areas. This is a significant effort which could reach 5–7 million of the most vulnerable people, and you could well couple it with whatever announcement you make on the major feeding program. (I sent you a memo[2] and draft press release Friday.)

2. PL 480 for Pakistan is the next priority since we ought to sign a new agreement next week to keep their pipeline going. I don't recommend specifically linking this to the Indian program. Ayub resents our linking his programs with India's and there's no need to rub in the fact that we have to think of them together. The Paks have already done a good job buying here and elsewhere to cover their own gaps and their agricultural performance has been good. But if we delay a substantial decision too long, they will feel impelled to use so much of their scarce foreign exchange that import liberalization and other desirable development policies will have to be sacrificed. Simply going ahead with the Pak program as soon after the Indian decision as you are ready ought to make your point that these are all parts of the worldwide food problem you are trying to dramatize.

3. The Pak $70 million loan is the most flexible, though we don't want to wait too much longer. This is the other important part of Gene Locke's second round steps to keep your relationship with Ayub developing.[3]

---

[1] Source: Johnson Library, National Security File, Country File, India, India's Food Problem, Vol. II. Secret. Received at the LBJ Ranch at 3:51 p.m.

[2] Document 403.

[3] Telegram 108416 to Rawalpindi, December 24, informed the Embassy that the commodity aid loan for Pakistan had been approved. (National Archives and Records Administration, RG 59, Central Files 1964–66, AID (US) 9 PAK)

407.   Telegram From Secretary of Agriculture Freeman to President Johnson in Texas[1]

Washington, December 22, 1966, 1837Z.

WH 60790. I have conferred with Rostow and Katzenbach pursuant to your instructions that the India announcement be made on a low key basis. The following statement has their concurrence.

"It was announced today that an allocation of 900,000 tons of grain, 50 percent wheat and 50 percent sorghum, has been made to India. Immediate shipment will be made with arrivals during the month of February and early March. Combined with earlier U.S. authorizations, purchases by India and grants by Australia and Canada, grain arrivals in India will continue to be around the record million ton per month level. Substantial stocks of privately owned and CCC wheat and grain sorghum are positioned in Atlantic, Gulf and West Coast ports to speed shipments."

As directed, I plan to hold a press backgrounder prior to releasing the statement.[2] That backgrounder will emphasize the following points.

1. That grain arrivals in India in February will maintain the million ton record level.

2. That other countries are joining with us in meeting India's needs. I will repeat what I said in Austin that a 50–50 proportion with other countries around the world is not unreasonable.

3. That progress has been made by India in strengthening her agriculture. The self-help criteria are being met.

4. That the President does not want to go any further in connection with grain allocations to India than is absolutely necessary until Congress has had the opportunity to consider the matter.

5. That purchases have been made by India on a commercial basis in the U.S. and that the proportion between the commercial and the concessional is improving.

Each of these points will be developed as effectively as possible during the course of the backgrounder.

---

[1] Source: Johnson Library, National Security File, Country File, India, India's Food Problem, Vol. II. Unclassified.

[2] Rostow cabled the President on December 23 that Freeman had made the statement and held the backgrounder for the press as planned on December 22. (Telegram WH 60792 to the LBJ Ranch; ibid., Memos to the President, Walt W. Rostow, Vol. 17, 12/14–31/66)

408. **Memorandum From the President's Special Assistant (Rostow) to President Johnson**[1]

Washington, January 2, 1967, 4:45 p.m.

SUBJECT

Progress Report on Message to Congress on Food for India

1. We have made progress in giving shape to your idea of (a) internationalizing food aid to India and (b) other countries matching in food and additional agricultural inputs what we provide in food. A consensus has developed with Agriculture, AID, and State that the World Bank India consortium is the best place to do the job.

2. I have explored the idea at length with George Woods. He is now strongly for it; and his senior staff has been exploring the implications with our people.

3. Amb. Nehru is for it as the most efficient multilateral forum. He also thinks it will be a more dignified way to deal with food aid than rushing about the world with a "begging bowl." We don't yet know how the Indian government will react. They would probably like to keep things as separate as possible; but I'm confident they'll go along once they know that you have decided food and agricultural aid should be treated as hard and multilateral.

4. The next consortium meeting is scheduled for about mid-March. This is a good time to come to grips with the new policy:

—it is this session which, in any case, must make a fresh start on India's next five-year plan, with its new high priority for agriculture;
—we will have by that time a clearer fix on India's 1967 food requirements;
—the Indian elections will be over and blunt talk by donors will be less politically explosive.

5. The critical problem we face is to reconcile two policy requirements:

—the need to make by about January 15 at the latest a decision on a further Indian grain allotment, in order to keep the pipeline full in March and April; and
—the need to bring Japan, Germany, Italy, Britain, etc. along on the new method for handling Indian agricultural aid. (Canada wants to move this way; and we shall also wish to bring Australia formally into the India consortium.)

---

[1] Source: Johnson Library, National Security File, Country File, India, India's Food Problem, Vol. III. No classification marking.

6. Ideally we would wish to announce the new policy at the time of the next Indian grain allotment. And this remains one option. But those dealing with the India consortium feel that we have a better chance to bring the industrial countries along if, before we firmly announce our position, we send abroad a first-class team to explain:

—food aid is now hard and we are going to treat it that way from now forward;

—the U.S. and Canada, in the consortium, Australia and the USSR, outside the consortium, have, in effect, been giving extra hard aid to India to meet the emergency;

—since the common goal is Indian food self-sufficiency at the earliest possible time, it is possible and right for the other industrialized countries of the world to contribute more in chemical fertilizers, pesticides, etc.;

—we are prepared to work on a 50–50 matching basis to keep Indians from starving and to hasten Indian self-sufficiency in food if Indian self-help efforts are adequate;

—we believe the World Bank consortium is the proper place to negotiate out such a policy—along with other aspects of India aid—and propose that it be taken up at the mid-March consortium meeting.

7. The background for this feeling that prior consultation is wise is that some of the other donors feel we have acted somewhat unilaterally in the past with respect to the Indian and Pak consortium arrangements; and they are inclined to use that as an excuse for contributing less, rather than more, to the development of the subcontinent. A further step which they regard as unilateral might make a hard job harder.

8. On this view, the idea would be to send abroad, say, E.V. Rostow (or Ellsworth Bunker) and Bill Macomber to prepare the ground for the new approach in mid-March.

9. This would mean, however, that we would have to make another Indian grain decision under the new legislation before the new policy was fully and publicly announced, debated and supported by Congress.

10. There are, therefore, three options as follows:

Option one. You could *let go with both barrels* in an early detailed message at the time the next India food allotment was made. It would describe the need to share the burden; to increase aid in fertilizers, etc.; and set forth in some detail how you think this could be done. It would contain specific figures of what we would offer; define targets for what other countries must do to match us; and authorize 1.5 million tons interim to carry through far enough to permit serious and tough negotiations with the new government to be formed in April. This message would be issued after prompt consultations with the returned Congressional mission and Congressional leaders. If we are to expect some cooperation from other members of the consortium, at a minimum we must give them the gist of your general approach *before* your message and commit ourselves to send a negotiator to discuss these matters in detail with them after your message, but before the consortium meets in March.

Such a message is being drafted.

Its advantages:

—before you make another interim allocation for India, this approach formally defines for Congress and our people how you would like to proceed, including international matching, the Bank's role and what you expect others to do;

—it dramatizes your concern for Indian agriculture, and your determination to have the burden shared more equitably.

Disadvantages:

—our agriculture specialists and those knowledgeable on the consortium are doubtful others will match us unless we make a substantial advance diplomatic effort (or are prepared to fudge the figures). This approach does not leave time enough ahead of your message to make a maximum advance effort. If there are not full discussions in advance, the Europeans and Japan are likely to resent our effort and be even less helpful.

Option two. You could make a low-key interim allocation now and present a major message to Congress only in February, after careful advance consultations with consortium members. (Joe Califano prefers this date for other reasons.)

After consultation with the returned Congressional mission and with Congressional leaders, you could authorize a second interim allocation of, say, 1.5 million tons, under the new Food for Freedom legislation, by January 15. This would carry the pipeline far enough so that the real negotiations could be with the new government which takes office in April. It could count as part of your proposed bargain for the balance of 1967. You could indicate to Congressional leaders in low-key private talk how you were proceeding; and that you were determined to have our food aid treated as "hard" and matched in the consortium. Secretary Rusk could then push urgent high-level exploratory talks with prospective European and Japanese donors. After these conversations, we could sense more accurately what we might expect of the others, before you deliver a detailed message to the Congress.

Advantages:

—it would protect you in Congress from getting too far committed to specific matching formulae which may be unrealistic;

—it would give our consortium specialists and George Woods time to soften up other members.

Disadvantages:

—you would be making a new allocation for India without formally consulting Congress and getting a resolution;

—you would be some way down the road before officially notify-
ing Congress of your intentions;
—most aspects of the deal would become publicly known before
your detailed message went to the Congress.

Option three. After consultations with the returned Congressional
delegation and Congressional leaders, you could perhaps combine the
advantages of both options by sending a short message to Congress
on January 15, sketching in general terms your intent about internationalizing and finding ways to augment agricultural assistance while sharing the burden more equitably. You could then indicate you were authorizing negotiations under the new legislation for a 1.5 million ton
interim shipment. You could promise a more detailed message later in
the session. After careful negotiations with prospective donors, a more
accurate detailed message could be submitted.

Advantages:

—such a two-stage approach would permit you to lay out your
general strategy without having to specify so early in the calendar year
figures or matching formulae;
—it would put the world on notice of your general approach
without publicly putting the finger on any specific countries before
your staffs had had a shot at winning them over privately.

Disadvantages:

—if Congress insists on extensive discussion before it gives you a
resolution, Bill Gaud, Gene Rostow and Orville Freeman will have to
tip most of your hand before the consortium meeting in any event.

11. I myself feel Option two is best at the present time, if you feel
informal Congressional consultations would meet your criteria of what
is right and necessary before making an additional interim allocation.
Option three sounds good and statesmanlike; but we're liable to fall
between two stools: the message would be too thin to be impressive;
too substantive to avoid appearing to force the Japanese and European
hands unilaterally and without consultations.

My impression is that the way you have handled the Indian food
situation in the past several months—and especially your success in
smoking out Canada, Australia, and the USSR—have proved popular
at home as well as educational abroad. I suspect quiet Congressional
consultations could cover you on the next interim India allocation, if
you were to indicate the direction of your policy; but only you can
assess the matter properly.

12. I recommend, therefore, that you have an early session with
Orville Freeman; Sec. Rusk and Gene Rostow; Bill Gaud and Bill Macomber to go over the track; directly hear the argument; and choose
your option.

13. A final issue arises out of the work we have done, which you will also wish to consider; namely, the likely size of the Indian food deficit and our proper share in meeting it.

There are various estimates about as to what India will require by way of food imports for calendar 1967. They run from a high of 11 million tons to a low (Indian Embassy, Washington) of 8 million tons.

About 2.3 million tons have already been granted, loaned, or bought for 1967. That leaves somewhere between 5.7 and 8.7 million tons to be covered.

Subtract from that the 3 million tons you are willing to put up and have matched by others. That leaves between 2.7 and 5.7 milllion tons to be found elsewhere.

Here are the best figures we can now estimate—or guess—for what others might contribute on a concessional basis, over and above grants already made in 1967:

Canada	900,000 tons
Australia	100,000 tons
USSR	500,000 tons
Others	100,000 tons
	1,600,000 tons

This will be a million tons short of the minimum deficit and might be 4 million tons short of the maximum which your experts are now inclined to think is the more realistic figure.

More chemical fertilizers will not cover it; although they would help in 1968.

The books then could be balanced by:

—properly prorated commercial purchases of grain;
—an additional U.S. PL 480 contribution, above 3 million tons;
—further Indian belt-tightening;
—or some combination of these elements.

The trouble with commercial food purchases is that they run down Indian foreign exchange and endanger the whole program of liberalizing their domestic economy and getting the bureaucrats off the neck of the private sector, slowing up their domestic development. The World Bank, the IMF, and the whole consortium pushed India hard in this direction last year.

Also, I am told, Agriculture is worried again about piling up surpluses and lowering domestic prices—with the new wheat acreage—if we only move an additional 3 million tons to India this year.

14. The best way to balance the books, of course, would be for the other industrialized countries to put up extra money for India and

have India use some of it to purchase U.S. and other grain, without cutting foreign exchange available for other aspects of development. In effect, our negotiators and George Woods will, in one way or another, be pushing for some such over-all increase in non-food-producers aid to India.

15. I have the strong feeling that I am telling you nothing you don't already know; and that you discounted all this when you laid down the 3 million tons as a guideline. I have no recommendation to make; but I did wish you to know the bureaucracy will probably be pressing you for a figure higher than 3 million tons when the time comes to negotiate for matching in the consortium.

Walt

409.   Memorandum of Conversation[1]

Washington, January 9, 1967.

SUBJECT

   Indian Food

PARTICIPANTS

   Senator Jack Miller
   Congressman W. R. Poage
   Orville L. Freeman, Secretary of Agriculture
   Dorothy H. Jacobson, Assistant Secretary, Agriculture
   Clarence R. Eskildsen, Deputy Asst. Secretary, Agriculture
   Eugene V. Rostow, Under Secretary for Political Affairs, Department of State
   Alan R. Novak, Special Assistant to Under Secretary Rostow
   Walter G. Farr, Jr., Deputy Asst. Administrator, Bureau of Near East and South
      Asia, Agency for International Development

Mr. Rostow opened the meeting, stating that the Administration was seeking advice on the Indian food problem from members of Congress who had been to India and who were members of the Agriculture Committees. There were a number of questions: When should a Presidential Message be sent to the Congress? Should a resolution accompany the Message? When should there be hearings? When should there be action by the Congress? When should an interim allocation

---

[1] Source: Johnson Library, National Security File, Country File, India, India's Food Problem, Vol. II. Secret. Drafted by Novak.

be made to keep the pipeline full? How large should this interim allocation be? Senator Miller thought that it would be better not to send a resolution to the Congress at the time of the Message. He proposed that the President say in his Message that a draft resolution would shortly follow, or perhaps even better, leave it to the Congress to draft an appropriate resolution. Senator Miller said it was important that we avoid specifics in the Message such as the actual figures on a final allocation since this would serve to attract Congressional attention and criticism, which might affect the outcome of the upcoming Indian elections. He recommended that there be no hearings or other Congressional action until after the elections.

Secretary Freeman raised the question of timing of the interim allocation. He pointed out that the pipeline will run out in the middle of March and that ideally an interim allocation should be made by next week. He also raised the question of how big the interim allocation should be. Congressman Poage suggested that the real question was what the President wanted to do. Secretary Freeman agreed and said he thought the President was inclined to try for the minimum interim amount. Senator Miller said he thought an interim allocation of less than 1.8 million tons, assuming 200,000 tons more was contributed by the Soviet Union, would keep the pipeline full until the end of May. Secretary Freeman pointed out that there was an additional problem. The monsoon season would make it impossible to ship in as much grain in June as in earlier months and that the interim allocation might therefore have to be slightly larger to take this into account. He also pointed out that the interim allocation should be large enough to hold us until the Consortium had time to act.

Secretary Rostow agreed, pointing out that the Consortium was unlikely to act immediately, since these countries, like ourselves, also had legislatures to deal with. Congressman Poage addressed himself to the principle of matching in the Consortium. He said it was his understanding, on the basis of last Friday's[2] meeting at the White House, that the President wanted matching on a 50–50 basis over the next two fiscal years. Senator Miller agreed. Senator Miller and Congressman Poage both agreed that such matching did not have to start until the second half of calendar 1967 and if we divided the calendar year in half, assuming India needed ten million tons for the year, five million in the second half would have to be matched—2.5 million by the U.S. and 2.5 million from elsewhere. They agreed that in the first six months of 1967 something less than 50–50 would do. But Congressman Poage stressed that he felt that the President was

---

[2] January 6.

very serious about the principle of 50–50 matching and that if others stopped contributing, we should stop contributing. Secretary Freeman agreed that the President would want to go as far as possible to achieve this goal.

Congressman Poage then asked why we should be optimistic about this Consortium approach and wanted to know what would be its appeal. Mr. Farr stated that we had two objectives here: one was to make food shipments like any other kind of aid—like dollars—and the other was to gain acceptance for this principle in order to get additional burden-sharing from the other members of the Consortium.

Congressman Poage then asked why we should do the begging. Mr. Rostow replied by pointing out that, in the last analysis, if we don't support India's diplomatic efforts in what will be a difficult negotiating situation at best, we will find ourselves at the end of the year in the same position that we were at the end of this year, and we will not have achieved our objective. Senator Miller agreed we must help solicit but he stressed his feeling that the Indians should do still more than they have been doing. Secretary Freeman, in summarizing the discussion, said there was agreement that the principle of matching should go into effect in the second half of calendar 1968 and that the Indians must be pressed to work hard at getting additional contributions. It was left that the Congressmen would talk with Congressman Dole, discuss the matter with the leadership of both Houses, and then make recommendations to the President within the next day or two on the basis of the understandings reached at this meeting.

In discussions the following day between Senator Miller and Mr. Eskildsen, it became clear that the Congressional group wanted particularly to keep the interim program amount to a bare minimum. They apparently agreed that there was little likelihood of Congressional and Consortium action and a new agreement by the end of March (which would get foodgrain in volume to India only by very late May). However, they relied upon a document they saw in India to make an estimate of 800,000 tons as the minimum monthly requirement, and as their memorandum[3] indicated, they felt matching could begin before July 1. This accounted for a smaller estimate of the interim allocation than that formulated by the Executive Branch.

---

[3] Document 405.

410. Memorandum for the Files[1]

Washington, January 10, 1967.

SUBJECT

India discussions in late 1966 and early 1967

On Friday, December 2, the President called me by telephone to discuss the India situation in regard to grain exports. Marvin Watson or Jake Jacobson also called on or near the same day. The President suggested the possibility of exporting half-million tons of wheat and half a million tons of grain sorghum in late December and wanted to know how this could be handled.

On December 3, Saturday, I met for most of the morning with Eskildsen, Jaenke, and Moseley to put together a memorandum detailing the amount of wheat and sorghum that were in position to be exported and also the estimated India arrivals in January, February, and March based upon a possible million-ton authorization from the U.S., plus old authorizations not yet fully shipped.

I was instructed, on Sunday morning by telephone from Texas, to send this memorandum to the President as fast as possible. I did this by wire[2] thru the situation room and found later some impatience on the part of the President's staff that "some eyes in the situation room might have seen the memorandum". About mid-afternoon on Sunday, December 4, I was called by the President who again reviewed the situation including a lot of the material that was in the memorandum which he apparently had not seen although I had delivered it personally to the White House about 12:00 noon. It was in this conversation that I pointed out to him the great difficulty of locating ships that could be loaded quickly with cargos for India when decisions to authorize additional grain to India are made at a very late date. I explained the problem of the U.S.S. Manhattan which was known to be leaving India about December 4, and which was available to be booked but might within a few days head for the Middle East to pick up a cargo of oil. The President by telephone authorized me to take an option on the U.S.S. Manhattan which I did by calling Eskildsen who by late evening of the same day told me that the Manhattan was in the Bay of Bengal and it had been arranged that she would arrive on the West Coast about Christmas Day.

---

[1] Source: Johnson Library, National Security File, NSC Histories, Indian Famine, August 1966–February 1967, Vol. V. No classification marking. Drafted by John Schnittker.
[2] Reference is to telegram CAP 661170 from the White House to the LBJ Ranch, December 4. (Ibid., Vol. III)

Also in this telephone conversation with the President, we reviewed January arrivals which were represented to be 964,000-tons including 714,000-tons from the United States and some grain from Canada and Australia. (Looking back, it's now clear that this should have been 564,000-tons, not 714,000-tons. We did some double counting, thus bringing the January arrival figure to about 150,000-tons higher than could be realized.)

The President also asked about the crop conditions in the Southwest and spoke of the drought in Texas.

He instructed me to call a message to Miss Fehmer later that day recapping the January arrivals expected in India and telling him what the highest rates of unloading ever achieved in India were in the past. By the time I called Miss Fehmer she had some additional questions from the President which I responded to but made no record of.

On December 6, I recapped all this material in a confidential memorandum to the President.[3] Either On December 5 or 6 in telephone conversations with the President and with Marvin Watson, and Jake Jacobson, I indicated in response to their questions that I preferred December 15 as the date for a final decision on additional allocation to India. I pointed out that with a Congressional team arriving back in the United States on the 21st or 22nd, I understood it would be rather difficult to make a decision on the 15th while the Congressional team was in India.

Also on December 5, I talked with Watson and Jacobson about using Sen. McGee as a substitute for Sen. Mondale who could not make the trip to India with Mr. Poage, Dole, and Sen. Miller of Iowa. The White House staff specifically concurred with the appointment of McGee even though he was in a different time table. I cabled McGee in Delhi[4] asking him to look at the agricultural situation to the extent possible while he was in India.

His cable[5] came back on December 6, indicating that he had already done this.

On December 14, we briefed the Poage mission before they headed for India.

On December 16, in a telephone conversation with the President I again reaffirmed the need for a one-million ton decision at the earliest possible date, and again reviewed the difficult shipping situation with him. It was at this time that the President agreed that we should proceed

---

[3] Not printed. (Ibid.)

[4] Telegram 47019 to New Delhi, December 5. (National Archives and Records Administration, RG 59, Central Files 1967–69, LEG 7 MCGEE)

[5] Telegram 8204 from New Delhi, December 6. (Ibid.)

to option some ships even though this was a matter which India usually handled. The next day, December 17, which was a Saturday, Ray Ioanes reported to the Secretary and me at noon that they had optioned about 100,000-tons of shipping on a 72-hour basis and that it could be "rolled over" for several days, although some ships might be lost in the process.

On December 20 we learned that the Poage report[6] would recommend that the President go ahead with an interim allocation to India. We also made tentative arrangements with Watson and Jim Jones for a personal report to the President on the 22nd. These later collapsed when we learned that they had issued a brief press statement in Delhi before departure and that Dole would be bringing back a written report[7] from the team.

About December 20, after staff meeting, I authorized Ioanes and Jaenke to load the *Manhattan* completely, even though this would delay her departure by several days. Originally it had been planned to load only 77,000-tons on this ship which carried 102,000-tons. Actually we felt very good about the fact that the *Manhattan* had slipped only about a week from the original plan for arrival in India—from about January 30 to February 6.

January 6, I met with Minister Kaul at the request of Ioanes and Eskildsen to review the arrivals of grain to India and the departures from the United States. By this time it had become clear that arrivals in January were slipping to approximately 750,000-tons and that arrivals in February could not quite reach the 1-million ton mark. The Secretary directed that everything possible be done to make arrivals in February reach the million ton mark (I have dictated a separate memo[8] on that.)

Also on late Friday, January 6, the President met with the Secretary, Poage, Dole, and Sen. Miller to review the India situation, following a week of discussions within the Executive Branch on the kind of message that ought to be sent to the Congress on India.

---

[6] See Document 404.
[7] Document 405.
[8] Not found.

411. Memorandum From the President's Special Assistant (Rostow) to President Johnson[1]

Washington, January 12, 1967.

SUBJECT

The Indian Food Package

We now have a Rusk–Freeman–Gaud proposal for internationalizing the Indian food problem (Tab A)[2] and a recommendation from Congressman Poage's group (Tab B)[3] on the size of an interim allocation pending Congress' response. I am also attaching State's draft message to Congress (Tab C)[4] describing your Indian program as the next important step in your War on Hunger. We'll edit the message and adjust the numbers further once we have your guidance. Here are the main points in this complex set of recommendations:

1. The Secretaries propose to throw *Indian food aid into the World Bank's India consortium,* and the Congressmen generally agree. If you approve, I'll have to get final and formal agreement from George Woods and we'll have to get the Indians and other consortium members aboard.

2. The Secretaries underscore the *importance of careful consultations with India and other consortium members* before we publicly announce this approach. They have two reasons:

a. Other consortium members resent unilateral action. The chances of persuading them to take on food in the consortium will be greater if we tackle them privately first.

b. Quite frankly, Bill Gaud feels chances of getting as much as we're asking from other donors are slim. We all feel you should have a realistic picture of the odds before you take a strong public stand.

The Congressmen naturally do not address this operational point, but it is crucial in launching your program the right way. The big sticking point will be the consortium members who have avoided food aid so far. We may be able to move Germany, if it counts against the offset, to which State and Defense are agreeable. But the others will be tough. With the Bank doing the accounting, we would try to *persuade other aid donors to match* our special emergency food contribution in the

---

[1] Source: Johnson Library, National Security File, NSC Histories, Indian Famine, August 1966–February 1967, Vol. IV. Secret.

[2] Reference is to a joint memorandum sent to the President on January 11; not printed.

[3] Reference is to a letter sent by Senator Miller and Congressmen Poage and Dole to Freeman on January 11. Poage sent a copy to Rostow on the same day; not printed.

[4] Undated; not printed.

second half of CY 1967 by giving food, fertilizer or cash. We would expect their contributions to be over and above: (a) their already planned pledge in the Indian consortium and (b) their contribution to IDA replenishment. The special contribution in new aid for food would be at least $120 million in this calendar year.

It will take some pretty *tough high-level arm-twisting* to persuade these already strapped governments to do that much more. Therefore, the Secretaries *recommend you send scouts to sound out the consortium capitals before you send your message to Congress.*

Since this will require the highest-level emissary we can field, I'd suggest trying to get Doug Dillon. If he's not available, Gene Rostow's responsibilities and intensive work on this problem in recent days would make him a natural. Whoever goes will have to get going this week.

3. *The Secretaries believe we should plan on 4.4 million tons more for the rest of CY 1967.* The Congressmen do not specifically address the total CY 1967 need since they'll address this later when they have your message. However, they have figured their interim allocation from the same 10 million ton estimate of Indian need that the Secretaries use.

The Secretaries looked hard at 3 million and seriously doubt it would do the job:

—They believe the higher figure is necessary to give us a workable negotiating posture with our consortium partners. They feel that asking other donors to increase their total aid to India while we stay at the same level in economic aid and cut our food aid in half (8.3 million in 1966 to 4.6 this year—1.6 already approved plus 3) is an untenable negotiating position. They know it will be an uphill fight to get any more aid at all, so we need to put ourselves in the best negotiating position possible.

—If we gave 3 million tons and others matched us, the total of 8.3 million (including 2.3 million already on the way) would still fall short of India's estimated need of 10 million. A low figure now could have adverse political effects in India before the election and could discourage US farmers from planting.

—With 4.4 million tons, we'd still be reducing our proportion of food aid from 90% in 1966 to 60% in 1967; and, with luck, we would be laying the foundation for moving to 50–50.

—The higher figure of 4.4 looks reasonable, yet is still pretty tough to match. If you wish to stick to an overall US figure of 3 million tons now, you could buy some flexibility by promising a mid-summer review after our crop is in; although that would weaken our negotiating posture and worry the Indians as they go to the polls.

4. The Secretaries agree with Poage and his colleagues that *an interim allocation is urgent.* The Secretaries propose 2 million tons to cover the pipeline while we're swinging the World Bank into action and waiting for the new Indian government to be formed. To do this we would have to cover Indian needs at least through the end of May,

because we won't be able to negotiate an agreement with the new Indian government until mid-April. The Congressmen urge 1.7 million.

The Secretaries could live with 1.7 million provided we recognize that the Congressmen's figure will not carry through to the end of May unless there is more grain available from the spring crop than we anticipate or unless India receives unexpected contributions from other nations. (The Congressmen are figuring that India needs 800,000 tons a month—a figure from a public Indian document—while Subramaniam privately fixes the need at 900,000.)

5. Whichever figure you approve, *timing will be important.* Here are the main alternatives:

—Postpone your message until the end of January, well before the Indian elections, but late enough so we can complete consultations and so the Congress won't have to let it be unanswered too long. (We won't want Congressional debate before the election.) To delay this way, we would have to announce an interim allocation immediately. The main advantage of this approach would be to settle the pipeline problem for awhile and give us ample time to complete high-level talks and still avert a new round of press speculation about the pipeline. The Congress would like it too because it does not want to hold off acting on your message too long.

—Send your message as soon as we can warn other capitals and announce the interim allocation in the message. We could probably get a preliminary reaction from other consortium members by about 23 January, but we couldn't expect anything firm. Chance of press leaks increases once we start talking in other capitals.

In either case, the Secretaries favor a message before the Indian election, though we would want to avoid Congressional debate in the first two weeks of February right before the Indians vote.

Here, then, are the decisions to be made:[5]

1. Get George Woods' final and formal agreement to take on Indian food aid.

2. If Woods agrees, get the Indians aboard and then start talking with other consortium members.

3. For this mission:

Try to get Dillon
Send Gene Rostow[6]

4. Set a planning level for the rest of CY 1967.

—As Freeman–Rusk–Gaud recommend: 4.4 total, 2 million interim and 2.4 later

---

[5] Johnson approved recommendations 1 and 2.
[6] Johnson checked this option.

—Alternative to bow to Congressmen: 1.7 interim and 2.7 later[7]
—Your initial thought: 3 million in the message with promise of a summer review

5. Timing.

—Interim allocation immediately, rest in the message 23 January or later
—Interim allocation and total figure both in the message by 23 January[8]

Walt

---

[7] Johnson circled "1.7 interim" among the choices at this option.
[8] Johnson checked this option.

---

412.   Memorandum From the President's Special Assistant (Rostow)[1]

Washington, January 14, 1967.

MEMORANDUM FOR

Secretary Orville L. Freeman
Agriculture Department

Under Secretary Nicholas deB. Katzenbach
Department of State

Mr. William S. Gaud
Administrator, AID

SUBJECT

January 12, 1967 Meeting with the President on the Indian Food Package

It is my understanding that at last evening's meeting with the President, it was agreed:

---

[1] Source: National Archives and Records Administration, RG 59, Katzenbach Files: Lot 74 D 271, The President. Secret. Sent under cover of a January 13 memorandum from Rostow to Katzenbach, Freeman, Eugene Rostow, and Gaud, which stated that it represented Rostow's understanding of what had been agreed the previous evening regarding Indian food. He asked them to notify Wriggins promptly whether it also reflected their understanding, and welcomed any suggestions. According to the President's Daily Diary, the meeting took place at 7:30 p.m. in the Cabinet Room at the White House and included, in addition to the President, Freeman, Katzenbach, Walt Rostow, Eugene Rostow, Gaud, Macomber, and Wriggins. (Johnson Library)

1. to firm up our understanding with George Woods that the India consortium will assume responsibility for food aid;

2. to develop plans on the assumption of a 10-million ton Indian import requirement for CY 67, of which the U.S. might provide 6 million tons (including amounts already allocated); but no commitment could be made to such a U.S. contribution until Congressional review;

3. to go hard for 50–50 sharing by May or June, although it was recognized we might not be able to do it on a regular basis;

4. to send scouts to India to win Indian acceptance of this general approach and then to Western Europe immediately to see how near we could come to 50–50 shares;

5. to prepare a message to go to Congress by January 23rd, after we receive a preliminary report from our scouts. It would announce an interim allocation of 1 million tons (1/2 wheat and 1/2 sorghum) and the $25 million CARE Title II request. It was recognized that a positive message would help in the Indian elections, but a disappointing proposal could adversely affect the outcome;

6. that hearings on the message would not start until after the Indian election;

7. that a second interim allocation of 1 million tons more before a long term agreement, was not entirely out of the question, but could not be made without a recommendation from relevant Members of Congress;

8. that Under Secretary Katzenbach and Secretary Freeman will renew soundings with Congressional leaders and members of the Appropriations Committees, including Members Ford, Mahon, Rooney, Russell, Ellender.

W. W. Rostow[2]

---

[2] Printed from a copy that bears this typed signature.

413.   Circular Telegram From the Department of State to Certain
Posts[1]

Washington, January 13, 1967, 6:17 p.m.

118255. For Ambassador from Secretary. Subject: Indian Food Crisis. Ref: Cirtel 101529.[2]

1. Dept cirtel 101529 outlined our concerns over food situation in India and our interest in wider sharing of responsibility for meeting India's food aid requirements. Response to this effort has been encouraging and as a result of our efforts and those of GOI several countries have increased their contributions. So far, in this current drive India has received grants of 150,000 tons of wheat from Australia, 150,000 tons from Canada, 200,000 tons from USSR, and 35,000 tons from World Food Program (FAO). Sweden and Norway are also considering significant grants of fertilizer and France is considering grants of dried milk. In addition, India has purchased 150,000 tons of wheat from Australia, 50,000 tons from US, and plans to buy another 50,000 tons from US. GOI also buying rice from Burma and Thailand. On December 23 we supplemented these contributions and purchases with 900,000 tons of PL 480 foodgrains for immediate delivery.

2. This effort and shipments already in pipeline provide India with its required food imports of over 800,000 tons monthly through March. Much more needs to be done to tide India over until summer crop is harvested about October/November.

3. We are urgently reviewing additional steps to close this gap while encouraging GOI down road to greater food sufficiency. To this end President is planning another message to Congress before end of January on Indian food crisis which would make following points: (a) The burden sharing should be further internationalized on a much larger and more comprehensive and systematic scale than any yet attempted in order to achieve a genuinely multilateral program to handle India's food problem; (b) To enlist the participation of others on more organized basis, food assistance should be placed along with economic aid, under World Bank

---

[1] Source: National Archives and Records Administration, RG 59, Central Files 1967–69, SOC 10 INDIA. Secret; Immediate; Exdis. Drafted by Heck on January 12; cleared by Handley, Farr, Wriggins, Deputy Assistant Secretary for International Resources Edward R. Fried (E), Country Director for Germany Alfred Puhan, Country Director for Canada Rufus Z. Smith, Country Director for France and Benelux Robert Anderson, Country Director for Italy, Austria, and Switzerland Wells Stabler, Deputy Assistant Secretary for European Affairs Walter J. Stoessel, Jr., Country Director for Japan Richard L. Sneider, Country Director for the United Kingdom J. Harold Shullaw, and Eskildsen; and approved by Eugene Rostow. A handwritten notation on the telegram reads "OK/L," suggesting that it was cleared with the President. Sent to Bonn, London, The Hague, Paris, Rome, Tokyo, and Brussels and repeated to New Delhi, Ottawa, and Vienna.

[2] Document 401.

Consortium. We feel time has come to add food as another responsibility of the Consortium. This is sound economics, fair burden sharing, and provides a proper channel for incremental food and food-related aid of donors who have not previously been involved in this effort; (c) As incentive, we are considering pledging substantial amount of foodgrain to the Consortium to be matched by other nations either in food, fertilizer, pesticides, shipping, etc. or by additional program assistance. These contributions would of course be additional to regular Consortium pledges; (d) To keep food flowing while these arrangements being worked out, another allotment of undetermined amount for immediate delivery to India would be authorized; (e) We remain vitally interested in Indian performance and in GOI efforts to improve its agricultural production.

4. To indicate priority President places on this effort, to highlight importance we attach to this multilateral program and to enlist support of those in best position to increase their contribution, the President is sending Eugene Rostow, Under Secretary for Political Affairs as his representative to discuss our proposals with appropriate officials of host government. He will acquaint them with President's thinking and dimensions of our plans and seek indications of their position and extent to which we can count on their participation. President will want to review their soundings before message goes to Congress.

5. In undertaking this campaign we are fully conscious of demands being placed on our partners, all of whom have their Indian problems. As members of Consortium they are already confronted by substantially higher level of regular requirements. In addition IDA is seeking substantially increased contribution much of it to be earmarked for India. We estimate their share of emergency matching food program based on prorated share of Consortium pledges will total another $95 million divided roughly as follows: UK $26 million, Germany $27 million, Japan $20 million, Italy $12 million, France $6.5 million, Netherlands $3.5 million, Austria $1.25 million, Belgium $.75 million.

6. In meantime Rostow and State/AID USDA team plans depart for New Delhi January 15 stopping in Tokyo enroute and proceed immediately thereafter to other posts. Exact schedule follows. Request you inform host government of Rostow's impending arrival, begin set up meetings with appropriate key officials at highest levels and prepare background papers on host government AID programs to India, financial situation and other relevant facts useful to negotiations. Pass info to Rostow in New Delhi.

7. In separate message[3] we are asking New Delhi to inform GOI of foregoing and to have latter instruct appropriate Indian representatives

---

[3] Telegram 118378 to New Delhi, January 13. (National Archives and Records Administration, RG 59, Central Files 1967–69, SOC 10 INDIA)

accordingly so that they will remain in step with us. In view of delicate consultations now necessary it is important that no leaks occur on detail or substance of these proposals. Press guidance follows.

Rusk

---

414. Memorandum From President Johnson to the Under Secretary of State for Political Affairs (Rostow)[1]

Washington, January 14, 1967.

The purpose of your mission to Asia and Europe as my special emissary is to explain the United States position on future food aid to India and to win agreement of the Indian government and the members of the World Bank's India consortium for a systematic international program to help India achieve its goal of self-sufficiency in food grains at the earliest possible date and to cover ad interim India's food deficits. In India, you should stress the importance of India's taking the lead in making its own case in other capitals.

I. The U.S. Position

I regard our approach to the problem of India as a major component of the policy on food and population stated on January 10, 1967 in my State of the Union Message.[2] You should make clear my grave concern that the world's food production is falling sharply behind population growth—that vast areas have for the past 20 years been losing the capacity to feed themselves. You should emphasize that the United States has brought its own domestic food surpluses under control and can no longer be counted on to provide an inexhaustible reservoir of food grains for the hungry as a by-product of domestic policy. Grain stocks elsewhere have also tended to fall in recent years. You should

---

[1] Source: National Archives and Records Administration, RG 59, Central Files 1967–69, POL 7 US/ROSTOW. Secret. The draft instructions were sent to the President on January 14 by Walt Rostow under cover of a memorandum in which he stated that the instructions were moderately detailed to give Eugene Rostow a clear sense of how far he could go in revealing the administration's plans. (Johnson Library, National Security File, Files of Walt Rostow, Eugene Rostow Trip, Jan 1967) The instructions, as sent to Rostow, were revised slightly in Johnson's hand. The instructions were transmitted to Rostow in telegram 118911 to Tokyo, January 15. (National Archives and Records Administration, RG 59, Central Files 1967–69, POL 7 US/ROSTOW)

[2] For text, see *Public Papers of the Presidents of the United States: Lyndon B. Johnson, 1967*, Book I, pp. 2–14.

explain the significance of the new Food for Freedom Program whereby the United States decided to use appropriated funds to encourage farmers to produce extra food for food aid programs in countries determined to master their own agricultural problems. You should state that the United States now expects all the other nations of the world—rich and poor alike—to shoulder their share of the world's fight against hunger and malnutrition. You may cite my view that failure of other nations to join this effort now will leave the world on the road to intolerable suffering.

II. Our Proposal

You should outline my proposal that future food and agricultural aid for India be planned and allocated insofar as possible through the India consortium of the World Bank. With the permission of Mr. George Woods, you may say that the Bank has agreed to accept this responsibility. You should explain our reason for this choice: (a) the interconnection between agricultural and industrial development; and (b) the desirability of assuring that food and agricultural aid complement and, if possible, not undercut aid supporting India's overall economic development. You may reassure your listeners that this proposal is in no way meant to pre-empt important efforts in other world organizations to find solutions to the world's agricultural problems.

III. Your First Objective

You should obtain the agreement of the governments of India and the major members of the India consortium to this course. If they cannot give you their final assent, you should take away with you the best sense you can of their probable decision and emphasize the importance of a firm decision within two weeks.

IV. Interim Arrangements[3]

You may inform those governments in strictest confidence that I plan to announce by the end of January an interim additional allocation of 1 million tons of food grain. Thereafter, I will be guided by the sense of Congress and the response of our associates in determining further emergency allocations. We will expect other governments to help as they can with emergency measures to keep India's pipeline full during this interim period.

---

[3] Johnson deleted an initial proposed sentence in this paragraph that read: "You are authorized to say that the U.S. is willing to keep food flowing to India by continuing emergency food deliveries through May–June until the consortium can organize its effort." After marking that deletion, Johnson noted that the remainder of the paragraph was "OK."

V. Burden-sharing

Our goal for the second half of calendar 1967 and thereafter is to establish a system whereby the U.S. provides no more than half of India's concessional food aid requirement. This will require other donors—in the consortium and out—to match the U.S. contribution with an equivalent value in food, fertilizer, cash or other materials essential to agricultural production on concessional terms. This aid must be additional (a) to economic aid required to meet consortium goals this year, and (b) to donors' contributions to IDA replenishment. *Your second objective,* therefore, is to secure promises of as much additional aid as possible, to estimate how much added aid we can expect and to report to me your impression of how quickly we can move to a full 50–50 split of the food aid burden. You may make clear that this proposal for sharing the food aid burden is not intended to alter already established patterns of assessing proportionate shares of other economic aid within the consortium.

VI. Indian Requirements and U.S. Share

For planning and talking purposes only, you are authorized to say that they (Indians) now estimate India's import requirements for CY 1967 at about 10 million tons. Without implying any commitment, you may, if you feel it will improve your bargaining position, indicate that the United States might[4] be willing—with the approval of the Congress—to provide as much as 5 or 6 million tons under concessional terms total in CY 1967 (including 1.6 million already approved) provided other donors do their fair share. You must make clear that these are planning figures which will necessarily be refined as we gain a more accurate picture of India's spring crop and our own crop later in the summer.

VII. Report

You should report your findings in each capital as you go. I will expect a final recommendation from you on the program to be outlined in my message to Congress about 23 January, or as soon thereafter as possible.

VIII. German Offset

Before your arrival in Bonn, you will receive separate instructions on the extent to which you are authorized to offer to count additional German contributions of agricultural aid against U.S.-German offset arrangements.

---

[4] Johnson underscored the word "might" and changed the text to read "to provide as much as 5 or 6 million tons" from the original reference to 6 million tons.

IX. Publicity

You should caution the governments with which you talk against premature public or press disclosure of the substance or details of your discussions. You should, however, inform them that the U.S. government tentatively plans to state its position publicly soon after your return.

LBJ

---

415.   Telegram From the Department of State to the Embassy in India[1]

Washington, January 16, 1967, 4:57 p.m.

119084. Please deliver following message from the President to Prime Minister Gandhi as soon as possible: "Dear Mrs. Gandhi: Your message to me conveying New Year's greetings was most welcome.[2] We certainly face grave problems in the months ahead. But I fully share your hope and expectation that we shall overcome them, and that cooperation between our two governments and peoples will grow still closer.

We continue to give serious thought to your government's problems in providing enough food for your people. We see your difficulty this year as reflecting a larger fact: quite apart from your particular problems of drought, the developing regions of the world are losing the ability to feed themselves. We foresee a somber future if the world fails to reverse this trend by concerted and determined action.

I profoundly hope that India will take the lead in inspiring and urging all nations—rich and poor alike—to join a truly world wide effort to bring population and food production back into balance. We believe you realize the day is past when the United States can bear this burden alone. We count on the Government of India to become

---

[1] Source: National Archives and Records Administration, RG 59, Central Files 1967–69, POL 17–4 US. Confidential; Priority; Limdis. Drafted by Coon; cleared by Macomber, Wriggins, and Mary S. Olmstead (NEA/INC); and approved by Handley. Repeated to Tokyo for Rostow.

[2] In her New Year's message to President Johnson, December 31, Prime Minister Gandhi expressed her thanks for the assistance rendered by the United States in helping India to deal with the critical situation caused by a second successive year of drought. The message was conveyed to the White House under cover of a note from Ambassador Nehru on December 31. (Ibid.)

an example of what a determined people can do for themselves. We count on your government also to dramatize to all nations of the world the depth of this problem.

It is my earnest hope that your own representatives in other capitals will press your case with their host governments—an effort we will support but for which your government will, of course, wish to take responsibility.

At the same time I realize with the utmost understanding that the problems you face in the months ahead cannot be solved entirely by your own efforts. Joint effort of all nations able to help will be required to avert what you rightly describe as a human tragedy; and they will be needed equally to hasten the day when Indian agriculture can meet India's requirements.

I wish you to know that I am deeply concerned that this aid be forthcoming in as sufficient and timely a fashion as we can justify to our people. However, as I said in my recent State of the Union message, I am convinced that this problem is a responsibility of the international community, and will have to be met by a truly international effort.

To explain my thoughts more fully, I am sending Mr. Eugene V. Rostow our Under Secretary of State for Political Affairs as my personal representative to discuss this problem with you and with the leaders of other friendly and interested countries. He will be arriving in New Delhi shortly after you receive this letter.

In closing, may I again express my hopes that 1967 will see progress on this and the many other grave problems we face.

With warm personal regards. Sincerely, Lyndon B. Johnson"

We do not intend to release this letter, and we assume GOI will not.[3]

Rusk

---

[3] Gandhi responded on January 23 in a letter to Johnson that she regretted not being able to meet with Rostow during his visit to India because of her campaign schedule. She applauded the effort he was making to help enlist additional assistance for India, and stated that India would do all it could to second that effort. She reiterated the commitment of her government to increase food production and to control population growth. (Johnson Library, National Security File, Special Head of State Correspondence File, India, 1/1/67–4/30/67)

416. Telegram From the Embassy in India to the Department of State[1]

New Delhi, January 19, 1967, 1313Z.

10326. Pass White House. From Rostow and Schnittker.

1. At meetings today with Chaudhuri, Subramaniam, Mehta and ranking civil servants: 1. The Indian Government confirmed that it fully concurs in our approach to the solution of the Indian emergency food problem for this calendar year and succeeding years. It has instructed its Embassies in the capitals we shall visit to make appropriate representations. 2. FinMin Chaudhuri conveyed an expression of regret from the Prime Minister who was unavoidably out of town campaigning. Chaudhuri indicated her great appreciation for the President's letter[2] and for the effort the President has undertaken in India's behalf, and Chaudhuri expressed his own appreciation of the President's interest. 3. We discussed whether we should aim for a single consortium meeting, or two meetings, one devoted to food and the other to the broader program of economic assistance. The merits of these alternatives might be explored during the week with the staff of the IBRD. We explained that this was a question we would keep in mind during our remaining consultations. 4. A fuller list of detailed points raised will be reported later by Embassy.

Bowles

---

[1] Source: National Archives and Records Administration, RG 59, Central Files 1967–69, SOC 10 INDIA. Secret; Exdis. Passed to the White House at 10:55 a.m. Rostow's party included Heck, Schnittker and Martin Abel from Agriculture, and Walter G. Farr of AID/NESA.

[2] See Document 415.

417. Telegram From the Embassy in Italy to the Department of State[1]

Rome, January 20, 1967, 0837Z.

3769. Pass White House, AID, USDA/AmEmbassy New Delhi. From Rostow and Schnittker. During a private conversation Thursday evening with Messrs. Subramaniam and L.K. Jha, the Ambassador and Leonard Weiss also being present, our tentative planning figures from American participation in the 1967 food delivery program for India were revealed in strict confidence. Both Jha and Subramaniam strongly urged an interim allocation at least sufficient to carry India's minimal food deliveries through June, taking other sources of supply into account.

Problem of deliveries during second quarter of CY 67 also arose several times during our earlier discussions with Indians. They made point that all food deliveries in sight during first quarter totaled 2.3 million tons which is below target of 850,000 tons per month. To compensate for these shortfalls and reduced offloadings during monsoon GOI requires million ton arrivals monthly between April and June to meet 10 million ton target for year.

As of now, with exception of Canadian offer and indicated interim US allocation no deliveries in sight after March. Subramaniam estimated needs during second quarter to be 3 million tons and both he and Jha urged that an interim allocation of only one million tons announced now would be politically dangerous especially for officials and ministers closely identified with economic liberalization policies.

Pending assurance of supplies for April–June GOI considering a further cut in allocation to states during February which would reduce quotas to Bihar and in ration areas to 700 calories a day. Other subjects discussed during conversation will be covered in telegrams from Embassy Delhi.[2]

Reinhardt

---

[1] Source: National Archives and Records Administration, RG 59, Central Files 1967–69, SOC 10 INDIA. Secret; Exdis. Passed to the White House at 8 a.m.

[2] In a January 23 memorandum to Freeman, Schnittker also reported he found that Subramaniam and other Indian officials had grave reservations about supporting the idea of funneling food assistance to India through the India consortium. They were also concerned about the self-help requirements of the new Food for Peace legislation. (Johnson Library, National Security File, NSC Histories, Indian Famine, August 1966–February 1967, Vol. V)

418. Memorandum From the Under Secretary of State for Political Affairs (Rostow) to Acting Secretary of State Katzenbach[1]

Washington, January 27, 1967.

SUBJECT

Indian Food Mission

Our party returned late Wednesday[2] night from Tokyo, New Delhi, Rome, Paris, Bonn, London, The Hague and Brussels.[3] The list of capitals includes all the members of the Indian Aid Consortium except Austria and Canada. Austria has been consulted by the Ambassador, and Canada has been briefed in advance.

Our posture throughout was that we were appearing in support of requests made by the Government of India, whose Ambassadors did in fact appear in each instance, and make the necessary case for aid. We explained that we were undertaking confidential consultations, as part of the process through which our Government and others could reach decisions on emergency food aid to India. We told the host governments that the President was considering a message to Congress on the subject, but would make no decision and take no action until this round of talks was concluded. His decision, we said, would turn in considerable part on the views of other governments.

Except for Bonn, which will report its views within a few days, all the governments we saw authorized us to report:

1. That feeding India during the period of its transition to self-sufficiency in food should be accepted as an international responsibility;

2. That the consortium is a practical and successful device which should be used at this time;

3. That the emergency food plan for India should not be allowed to diminish the flow of resources coming forward under other development programs, but should be considered additional to the targets for each country suggested by the I.B.R.D.;

---

[1] Source: National Archives and Records Administration, RG 59, Central Files 1967–69, POL 7 US/ROSTOW. Secret. Concurred in by Schnittker. Sent to the President under a January 27 memorandum from Katzenbach, stating, "I am authorized to say that Secretary Freeman and Administrator Gaud approve the recommendations in the report, as I do."

[2] January 25.

[3] Reporting telegrams from Rostow detailing the progress of his mission, which began in Tokyo on January 16, are in National Archives and Records Administration, RG 59, Central Files 1967–69, POL 7 US/ROSTOW and SOC 10 INDIA.

4. That in general the arithmetic we suggested seemed acceptable as a working basis for consideration, although it should be stressed that no government made a firm promise to meet its consortium quota. Each did, however, promise to make its best efforts to find the necessary funds indicated by the consortium plan, within the limits of existing or politically possible budgets.

5. All agreed that food aid should be planned on a relatively long-term basis, in the context of India's general economic plans, so as not to interrupt progress under those plans, or to justify a suspension of India's trade and investment liberalization measures. Everyone agrees that if the Indians have to use a good deal of their foreign exchange for food, they will be required to suspend their trade liberalization programs, as Pakistan has done.

So far as Germany was concerned, no key ministers were in town when we arrived. We had a thorough briefing with officials and junior ministers. Their preliminary reaction was positive, despite the obvious restraint of Dr. Strauss' budget. We were assured an early decision, both in terms of the general idea, which they found attractive, and with particular reference to the offset possibility.

The talks with the Government of India were positive. The doubts represented by Ambassador Nehru's position here were much in evidence. But at a meeting with Indian Ministers, we were told the Government of India was entirely satisfied with our explanations, and would take full responsibility for our position. Their main concern, in terms of their own planning, and their election, was that we publicly announce a sufficient interim allocation to assure minimal food supplies for the year. We were told that rations in Bihar and Utter Pradash will be reduced to 700 calories a day.

We gave the figures about our own probable participation in the program only to Agriculture Minister Subramanian and to L.K. Jha over drinks at the Ambassador's house at the end of the day. The thought that we should now make an interim allocation of only 1 million tons fell like a stone. They said it would be exploited badly in the election. "Look", people would say, "those candidates have relied on the Americans, and this is all they could get." Subramanian emphasized that the pipeline would run out in March, and that there was literally nothing in sight for him to plan on at the moment except for what we could do now, and Canada later.

With these considerations in mind, we strongly recommend a present interim allocation of 2 million tons. Anything less might spoil the political effect of the message in India; weaken Subramanian and other staunch friends; and, in some Indian minds, justify undoing trade liberalization.

We believe the results obtained in these talks justify going forward with the proposal as planned in the earlier drafts of the message. If the message is to be released early next week, we should inform each of the consortium governments in advance, as well as Australia. We should also explore the possibilities of approaching the U.S.S.R. A separate message should go to the Government of India. We expect that follow-up work by the Indians and by our Embassies, together with the effect on each government of the favorable decision of others—notably the German commitment for $35 million, which we hope to obtain soon—should help move the total level of commitments towards a reasonable pattern of sharing.

We are not able at this time to estimate these contributions with any degree of certainty; the most we can say is that food assistance mobilized under the Consortium will not be effectively translated into significant food grain deliveries before the second half of calendar 1967, and may, although substantial in amount, even then fall short of our goal of $120 million.

The group accompanying me on the trip worked extremely well and enthusiastically. And the help of our Ambassadors and Embassy staffs was superb. They had prepared the way with imagination and zest, and I am sure they will follow up well.

Recommendations:

We recommend:

1. That the President proceed with his message to Congress for an international and additive effort to meet India's food needs under the general supervision of the World Bank Consortium.

2. That he announce in the message an interim allocation of 2 million tons of food grains to help fill the food gap of the next few months,[4] avoid endangering Subramaniam and others we support, and permit India to plan without suspending its trade liberalization measures. (Note. Under Secretary Schnittker calls attention to the alternative possibility of providing an interim allocation of 1 million tons now and another 1 million tons a month from now.)

3. That he also announce the approval[5] of a $25 million grant under the PL–480 Title II for distribution by CARE and other voluntary agencies. The mission was asked about this program in New Delhi and its need seems clearly indicated.

---

[4] Another copy of this memorandum was revised by President Johnson to read: "1 million tons of food grains . . . of the next month" (Johnson Library, National Security File, Country File, India, India's Food Problem, vol. 3)

[5] Johnson changed recommendation 3 to read "That he also ask for the approval . . ."

4. That the President authorize the initiation of interim allocations of food grains by reimbursable Purchase Authorizations (PAs) so that shipments can begin immediately even though it will take several weeks to complete an agreement with India.

5. That we be authorized to proceed forthwith to work with the I.B.R.D. in planning the next meeting or meetings of the consortium, and in following up all member governments with Bank help to get government positions as firm as possible before the meeting.

Eugene V. Rostow

419. Memorandum From the President's Special Assistant (Rostow) to President Johnson[1]

Washington, January 27, 1967, 7:15 p.m.

SUBJECT

India Food Decisions

Gene Rostow's report (Tab A)[2] lays the foundation for your message to Congress. He did not, of course, come back with signed pledges from the other consortium members for full matching. He did get agreement in principle, including agreement to go to work via the World Bank Consortium on the basis you outlined. The next step is to surface your program publicly via your message to Congress and to get the Congress aboard. Simultaneously, we'll push for a consortium meeting as soon after India's elections as possible.

We have a draft message (Tab B)[3] as cleared by Freeman and Katzenbach. It could use some editing and shortening, but is a serious piece of work.

Before editing, however, you will have to decide the key questions as follows:

1. *Size of the interim allocation.* At our meeting on 12 January you preferred 1 million tons. Gene's report in effect asks you to reconsider

---

[1] Source: Johnson Library, National Security File, Country File, India, India's Food Problem, Vol. III. Secret.

[2] See Document 418.

[3] Dated January 27.

and recommends 2 million. When he discussed this in strictest confidence with Subramaniam and L.K. Jha, they told him that the smaller allocation would cut the ground out from under those leaders who have staked their positions on following the agricultural and economic policies we're pushing.

The argument for 2 million tons, in addition to the political, is that we will need time to get the machinery Gene has activated into full swing. The Indians should unload about 5.3 million tons before the monsoon starts in late June. That means they need 3 million tons beyond what is in the pipeline; and it is most unlikely we can move to full sharing quickly enough to do the January–June job. Gene feels that we'll have greater leverage with the other consortium members if we don't appear to be unloading India all at once.

2. *Sharing the burden for the rest of the year.* Secretaries Rusk and Freeman and Bill Gaud have recommended (Tab C)[4] that we use a planning figure of 6 million tons total U.S. contribution for CY 1967. They recommend that we phase into proportional burden sharing this way:

—2.3 million tons are already in the pipeline—1.6 U.S. and 0.7 other.

—2 million tons at the time of your message would help keep the pipeline flowing, but India would still need to pick up another 1 million tons before 30 June.

—4.7 million tons would be needed July–December, and we would plan to do half.

Congressman Poage's recommendation[5] was similar to this—moving to matching by the second half of the year.

In the message, we have deliberately described this formula vaguely—"a further allocation provided that the other countries of the world contribute their proportionate share." This way, we don't tip our hand on amounts for the rest of the year and we don't tie our hands with the Congress. Gene made clear to our consortium partners what we expect; but it seems wise in a prolonged negotiation of this kind to maintain maximum flexibility.

3. *What we ask Congress for.* Charlie Schultze has explored the possibility of seeking an appropriation. As I understand him, he fears that approach will severely limit your maneuverability and recommends you consider alternative ways to meet your objective. I will send you Charlie's memo setting out the alternatives as soon as he has signed off.[6] You will want to read it carefully.

---

[4] See footnote 2, Document 411.

[5] See footnote 3, Document 411.

[6] Memorandum from Schultze to the President, January 27. (Johnson Library, National Security File, NSC Histories, Indian Famine, August 1966–February 1967, Vol. IV)

4. *The CARE program* is tentatively included in the draft message, and we need your final yes or no on this.

5. *Reimbursable purchases.* If you plan to hold this message past the first of the week, Secretary Freeman would like to tell the Indians to start buying grain and booking ships on a reimbursable purchase basis, if and when Congress acts.

6. I recommend a meeting tomorrow (Saturday) for you to hear argument and decide these matters, if you so wish.

Walt

Set up a Saturday meeting[7]

See me

---

[7] Johnson checked this option.

---

420. Circular Telegram From the Department of State to Certain Posts[1]

Washington, February 2, 1967, 3:38 p.m.

129901. Subject: Indian Food Aid. Ref: Depcirtel 127928.[2]

1. Rostow mission presented its report on results of trip to President Johnson January 28.

2. Today President has sent message to Congress reviewing situation and outlining our next steps.[3] (See Wireless File for summary.) U.S. will provide two million tons grain under PL–480 for interim allocation. President asked Congress approve U.S. commitment to share fully in international effort and proposed U.S. allocate up to three

---

[1] Source: National Archives and Records Administration, RG 59, Central Files 1967–69, SOC 10 INDIA. Secret. Drafted by Mary S. Olmsted (NEA/INC); cleared by Handley, Heck, Deputy Assistant Secretary George S. Springsteen (EUR), O'Neill (USIA/IAN), Hirsch (USIA/IPS/EO), and Wriggins; cleared in draft by Fried, Novak, and Farr; and approved and initialed by Eugene Rostow. Sent to Bonn, Brussels, The Hague, London, Paris, Rome, Tokyo, Vienna, Canberra, and Ottawa and repeated to Cairo for Ambassador Battle, New Delhi, Moscow, and Rawalpindi.

[2] Circular telegram 127928, January 30, sent to the same posts as telegram 129901, circulated an interim report on the Rostow mission. (Ibid., POL 7 US/ROSTOW)

[3] For text, see *American Foreign Policy: Current Documents, 1967,* pp. 757–763.

million tons more provided that it is appropriately matched. President also recommended approval of allocation of $25 million emergency program in drought-stricken areas to be administered by CARE and other voluntary agencies.

3. Presidential message strongly stressed: (a) Self-help—"I am convinced that the War on Hunger can be won only by the determined efforts of the developing nations themselves." "India must herself take prompt steps to increase her fertilizer investment and production and improve distribution." (b) Multilateral approach—"We must support the Indian Government's efforts to enlist the aid of other nations in developing a systematic and international approach to the problems of Indian agriculture." (c) Coordination through the Aid India Consortium organized under the chairmanship of the IBRD. (d) Additive nature of food aid so that this program will not diminish flow of resources for other development programs. (e) Matching—Additional foodgrain will be allocated "provided it is appropriately matched."

4. These are all points accepted in principle by countries visited by Rostow mission. Now that USG has laid its cards on table we hope other countries will begin to translate their agreement in principle into action by series of announcements of donations of food, fertilizer, shipping, or added program assistance. You should approach host Government to inform them of Presidential message and leave no doubt that we now expect other countries to do their share.[4]

Rusk

---

[4] Bowles reported on February 3 that the reaction to the President's message in India had been excellent. He stated that key Indian leaders deeply appreciated the vote of confidence in their efforts. (Telegram 11129 from New Delhi; National Archives and Records Administration, RG 59, Central Files 1967–69, SOC 10 INDIA) On February 6, Congressmen Poage and Dole introduced resolutions in the House of Representatives supporting the President's message on food assistance for India (House Joint Resolutions 262 and 267), and Senators Miller and Gale McGee introduced a similar resolution in the Senate (Senate Joint Resolution 29).

421. Memorandum From the President's Special Assistant (Rostow) to President Johnson[1]

Washington, February 16, 1967.

SUBJECT

Releasing Second Half of Indian Program Loan

Last spring you authorized an overall pledge of up to $335 million in non-project loans to India as part of George Woods' deal to persuade the Indians to devalue the rupee and liberalize import controls. We pledged only $280 million and released the first slice of $150 million last summer. India's self-help performance since then has been quite good in spite of the problems Mrs. Gandhi faces. Now AID is about ready to go with the second slice once Bill Gaud and Treasury agree on a few balance of payments details.

Bill's normal timetable would be to authorize the loan sometime next week and to have the signing ceremony a couple of weeks after that. The Indian election will be over by 21 February, and there is no one time better than another in the next month. Therefore, I see no foreign policy reason for not letting him go ahead. However, you may prefer to hold off until after the Congressional resolution on food, which may not pass until just before the Easter Recess, even though this loan is not part of our food effort. I'd appreciate your guidance.

Just for your information, the second $70 million slice of the Pakistan loan which you approved right before Christmas should also be ready for signature within a week or two, but I see no problem there.

Walt

Go ahead with India signing when ready

Wait till after the Congressional resolution[2]

---

[1] Source: Johnson Library, National Security File, Country File, India, Vol. VIII, Cables, 9/66–2/67. Confidential. A handwritten note on the memorandum reads, "Rec'd 2–18–67, 1:20 p." A handwritten "L" indicates that it was seen by the President.

[2] Johnson checked this option.

422. Telegram From the Department of State to the Embassy in Pakistan[1]

Washington, March 3, 1967, 6:51 p.m.

148588. 1. Deputy Chairman Planning Commission MM Ahmad accompanied by Ambassador Hilaly met with Agriculture Under Secretary Schnittker and Assistant Secretary Jacobson March 2 with requests for 250,000 tons wheat for FY '67 (Hilaly) and 1.5 million tons for FY '68 (Ahmad) with deliveries of latter to commence in June.[2]

2. Schnittker agreed to look into both requests. In regard to FY '68 request and timing of these deliveries Schnittker said, in the context of U.S. supply situation and forthcoming consideration of global requests, that "we'll do our best on the timing."

3. Ahmad's presentation of food situation followed same lines as earlier talk with Gaud (reported separately) and he provided same Aide-Mémoire.[3] He stressed two additional points (1) GOP approval of policies and resources for agricultural production which would enable FY 1970 to be last year of concessional wheat imports, and (2) provisional decision to shift to local currency convertible payment as follows: FY '68 one-third, FY '69 one-half, FY '70 three-fourths.

Rusk

---

[1] Source: National Archives and Records Administration, RG 59, Central Files 1967–69, AID (US) 15–8 PAK. Confidential. Drafted by Guy C. Mallett (NEA/PAF); cleared by Horbaly (USDA/FAS), and Palmer (AID/NESA); and approved by Spain. Repeated to Lahore and the Embassy Office in Karachi.

[2] During his visit to Washington Ahmad pressed his request for food assistance for Pakistan in meetings with Eugene Rostow on March 6, with Wriggins on March 6, and with Jacobson on March 10. (Ahmad's meetings with Rostow and Jacobson were reported in telegrams 150823 and 153129 to Rawalpindi, March 8 and 10 respectively; ibid.; his meeting with Wriggins was summarized in a March 6 memorandum from Wriggins to Walt Rostow; Johnson Library, National Security File, Country File, Pakistan, Vol. VII, Memos, 10/66–7/67)

[3] Not found.

423. Telegram From the Department of State to the Embassy in Pakistan[1]

Washington, March 11, 1967, 1:13 p.m.

153467. For Ambassador. Ref: Rawalpindi's 3349,[2] New Delhi's 12963.[3]

1. We are troubled at what appears to have been abrupt cold shoulder by GOP to Indian initiative picking up Ayub's public call for reduced arms expenditures and renewed effort lower Indo/Pak tensions. Paks can be skeptical of Indian motives if they like and can hold rigidly to insistence that "political" talks and arms limitation discussions must proceed simultaneously. However, we and other friends of Pakistan can hardly be expected to have much sympathy for policy that has effect of precluding any and all movement toward what we consider vital objectives (i.e., arms limitation and reduced defense spending).

2. We believe you should now seek opportunity convey our position to Ayub directly. You should say that USG regrets apparently negative attitude conveyed by Yusuf on an Indian proposal that rests on commendable public initiative on Ayub's part. You may say that we can appreciate GOP's determination not to be taken in by a "gambit". We also recognize Pakistan's problem in wanting to be able to point to some movement on Kashmir.

3. Pakistan cannot expect its friends however to go along with position that in effect rejects possibility movement almost anywhere

---

[1] Source: National Archives and Records Administration, RG 59, Central Files 1967–69, POL INDIA/PAK. Secret; Priority; Limdis. Drafted by Coon and Laingen on March 10, cleared by Spain, and approved by Handley. Also sent to New Delhi and repeated to London, Moscow, and CINCMEAFSA.

[2] In telegram 3349 from Rawalpindi, March 10, the Embassy reported that Foreign Secretary Yusuf had discussed a letter received by Foreign Minister Pirzada from Indian Foreign Minister Chagla. Chagla's letter, a copy of which was conveyed to the Department on March 15 by the Indian Embassy, was written in response to the opening offered by Ayub in a speech on January 28 at the Pakistan Institute of International Affairs in which he spoke of the need to divert the resources being used by India and Pakistan for the production of arms to the production of food and the necessities of life. Chagla expressed agreement with the sentiments expressed by Ayub and, on behalf of his government, suggested a meeting to discuss the question. Yusuf noted that his government had responded that it was prepared to discuss arms limitations, but only in the context of related political problems, in particular Kashmir. (Ibid.) The text of Chagla's March 2 letter was transmitted to New Delhi in telegram 156560, March 16. (Ibid.)

[3] Telegram 12963 from New Delhi, March 9, summarized a discussion on March 8 between Bowles and C.S. Jha. Jha reviewed India's efforts to initiate discussions with Pakistan following Tashkent to improve on the spirit of the agreement. He read to Bowles the letter written by Chagla to Pirzada on March 2. Bowles commented to the Department that the Indian Government seemed to be making a genuine effort to resolve its differences with Pakistan. (Ibid.)

unless something done simultaneously on Kashmir. Such position applied to issue as vital to Pak security as arms buildup strikes us as particularly unfortunate and counter-productive Paks own interest. Moreover, we find GOP position hardly one likely contribute to any flexibility in future Indian Government, whether Chagla stays on or not. USG hopes strongly that last word has not been said on Indian proposal by either party.

4. We do not believe you should link GOP response directly to policy problems in South Asian security field still pending with us here. But we hope you can find way discreetly to remind Ayub that what we can do for Pakistan (and India) is not unrelated to impression created official Washington of degree to which both countries genuinely interested in limiting arms race, irrespective but without prejudice to progress on other bilateral issues.[4]

5. *For New Delhi:* You authorized take appropriate opportunity convey to MEA our encouragement at Indian initiative and our hope GOI will persevere in effort but you should not inform Indians our exchange on subject with GOP.

Rusk

---

[4] Locke reported on March 15 that he discussed the Chagla letter with Ayub and made the points suggested in telegram 153467. Ayub indicated that he was unaware of Chagla's letter and said he would discuss it with Yusuf. He ruled out as politically impossible arms limitation talks with India that did not involve discussion of the Kashmir question. He did not rule out the possibility of secret talks however. (Telegram 3428 from Rawalpindi; ibid.)

424. Editorial Note

The general elections held in India February 15–21, 1967, returned the Congress Party to power with a somewhat reduced majority. A number of prominent political figures were not reelected, most notably Minister of Food and Agriculture Chidambara Subramaniam. Indira Gandhi formed a new government on March 13. The most significant addition to her cabinet was Deputy Prime Minister and Minister of Finance Morarji Desai. M.C. Chagla, Swaran Singh, and Y.B. Chavan continued as Ministers of External Affairs, Defense, and Home Affairs, respectively. Jagjivan Ram replaced Subramaniam as Minister of Food and Agriculture.

425. Memorandum From the President's Special Assistant (Rostow) to President Johnson[1]

Washington, March 16, 1967.

SUBJECT

Military Supply Policy for Pakistan and India

As a follow-up to our "Tuesday luncheon" of Monday, March 13, Nick and Secretary Rusk would like to send out the attached telegram explaining the full military supply package for both India and Pakistan.[2] It is their understanding that on Monday the total package was agreed to. It is my recollection, however, that you agreed only to the spares for Pakistan, because of Gene Locke's change of plans.

Proceeding with spares for Pakistan is necessary to fulfill our understandings with Ayub. But the South Asia specialists, as well as the Secretary, believe that to do something only for Pakistan at this time would be a mistake. We *must* balance this with meaningful steps

---

[1] Source: Johnson Library, National Security File, Country File, Pakistan, Vol. IX, Memos, 5/68–11/68. Secret. A handwritten note in the margin reads, "Rec'd 11:35 a."

[2] As ultimately approved, the telegram was sent to New Delhi and Rawalpindi on March 31 as telegram 166539, Document 431.

in India particularly when we're also working on the Indians to sign the NPT. Secretary Rusk believes the total package should be approved and acted on, though the exact timing of each component should be left to the discretion of those closest to the problems on the subcontinent, depending upon progress made toward arms limitation.

In addition to the spares for Pakistan, Secretary Rusk recommends the following as part of our overall effort to limit arms expenditures on the subcontinent:

(a) withdraw the MAAG and USMSMI missions in Pakistan and India to dramatize that we are not, repeat not, returning to our earlier relationship with Pakistan. Adequate follow-on supervision could be provided through the military attaché's office;

(b) discourage the sale by third countries to India and Pakistan of equipment produced with U.S. technology, co-produced with us, or produced in the U.S.;

(c) re-institute training slots for key Indian and Pakistani military personnel;

(d) disperse remaining obligated '67 credit sales funds only where these will contribute to U.S. security interests, e.g. for Star Sapphire ground radar in India or to support the general policy on arms limitation;

(e) permit credit sales on non-lethal items for both countries only on a case-by-case basis, depending on progress toward arms limitation, up to but no higher than $75 million for FY 68, a figure which would be not a target but an absolute ceiling and would not be communicated to either country.

They argue that only if State has such chips to play in both countries will we have a real hope of getting commitments to limit arms. A piece-meal approach won't do; the whole must be available as part of the talk from the beginning.

State and DoD agree on this balanced package. But Tom Hughes in INR, like Chet, worries about the Indian reaction and Dave Linebaugh in S/P thinks we are counting on getting too much from the Pakistanis for what is too small and too late.

Nick is confident that the problem on the Hill is entirely manageable, although there have not been advance soundings because of the classification problem.

In my view, we are not likely to get a more balanced or carefully thought-out package. As Secretary Rusk says in the attached recommendation[3] to you, "I believe the problem was thoroughly reviewed,

---

[3] Reference is to an advance copy of a March 17 memorandum from Rusk to the President, sent to endorse the attached recommendations of the Senior Interdepartmental Group concerning military supply policy toward Indian and Pakistan. (Johnson Library, National Security File, Country File, India, Vol IX, Memos and Miscellaneous, 3–7/67)

taking into account all the relevant points of view held within the Government." I think we should go ahead.[4]

Walt

Approve whole package

See me[5]

---

[4] Rostow added a handwritten postscript that reads: "Given your letter to Ayub, this should ideally move forward very soon."

[5] Johnson checked this option and added the following handwritten note: "Let's talk about this on plane going out." His reference was to an impending trip to Guam to meet with officials of the South Vietnamese Government on March 19–20.

---

426. Circular Telegram From the Department of State to Certain Posts[1]

Washington, March 18, 1967, 5:31 p.m.

158201. India Food.

1. Passage of Congressional Resolution[2] supporting President's India Food Program should be signal for renewed diplomatic activity in all country posts where possibility of obtaining food or food-related contributions to match food grains offered by U.S. Our objective to maximize commitments forthcoming at April 4 Consortium Meeting in Paris.

2. It should be stressed that overwhelming support from both houses of Congress for President's program demonstrates depth and seriousness of U.S. commitment to this program.

3. Government of India asked to begin new round of diplomatic representations in coordination with our own efforts.

---

[1] Source: National Archives and Records Administration, RG 59, Central Files 1967–69, SOC 10 INDIA. Confidential. Drafted by Rostow's Special Assistant Alan R. Novak, and approved and initialed by Under Secretary Rostow. Sent to Bonn, Brussels, London, Paris, New Delhi, Rome, The Hague, Tokyo, Canberrra, Ottawa, Vienna, Helsinki, Stockholm, Oslo, and Copenhagen.

[2] House Joint Resolution 267, "To support emergency food assistance to India," was adopted as P.L. 90–7 on April 1. (81 Stat. 7) Printed in *American Foreign Policy: Current Documents, 1967*, pp. 763–764.

4. Previous support diplomatic efforts by Australians and Canadians most helpful. Effort should be made to enlist their help again.

5. Stress that various kind contributions acceptable so long as additive and helps free Indian foreign exchange for food purchases. Point out debt relief favorable contribution if on good terms and to be encouraged.

Report progress as it develops.

Rusk

---

427. Telegram From the Department of State to the Embassy in India[1]

Washington, March 22, 1967, 3:43 p.m.

160135. Eyes Only for the Ambassador from the Secretary. Just a personal comment on the occasion of the passage of the India Food Bill. It now becomes extremely important for India herself to put on a major diplomatic effort to mobilize resources from other governments. Although we shall try to be helpful, India must take the primary responsibility. Quite frankly, our own political capital is running out where we go soliciting other governments for financial help for somebody else. Further, India should discover for herself where the responsibility will lie if President Johnson's courageous action should fail to produce the necessary resources. It would be helpful if you could keep us closely informed as to the progress of India's diplomatic effort so that we can coordinate our own desire to be helpful.[2]

Personal regards.

Rusk

---

[1] Source: National Archives and Records Administration, RG 59, Central Files 1967–69, SOC 10 INDIA. Secret; Exdis. Drafted and approved by Rusk and cleared by Handley. A marginal notation reads: "OK/L," suggesting that the cable was cleared by the President.

[2] On March 23 Bowles reported that he had met with Subramaniam's successor Jagjivan Ram to discuss the food crisis. In the course of the conversation, Bowles stressed the importance of a vigorous diplomatic initiative by India to solicit contributions from other nations to match the food being contributed by the United States. (Telegram 13819 from New Delhi; ibid., POL 15–1 INDIA)

428. Telegram From the Embassy in India to the Department of State[1]

New Delhi, March 28, 1967, 1320Z.

13991. For President and Secretary Rusk from Ambassador Bowles.

1. Mrs. Gandhi's new government stands at critical crossroads in domestic economic policy and in its relationship with USG. Variety of forces including determined and substantially strengthened parliamentary opposition, persisting food crisis, slow down in industrial growth, lag in exports and need to decide finally on size and shape of fourth plan, are forcing GOI to undertake fundamental reappraisal of its economic goals and policies required to achieve them.

2. That this reappraisal should occur on heels of recent election setback is neither surprising nor contrary to our interests. Indeed, on the plus side, we will be dealing with a strong Finance Minister who is favorably inclined toward us and generally well-disposed to economic policies we have been urging. Moreover, very magnitude of problems facing GOI has created a badly needed sense of urgency.

3. Major question mark among new leadership is ability and willingness of USG to support GOI's effort to speed rate of economic growth and particularly push forward with liberalized economic program which was adopted following devaluation.

4. Unfortunately, atmosphere in which estimate of future US stance is being made is heavily fogged by widespread public and parliamentary uneasiness regarding admitted and alleged CIA activities,[2] persistent rumors about renewed US military supplies to Pak-

---

[1] Source: National Archives and Records Administration, RG 59, Central Files 1967–69, POL 15 INDIA. Secret; Priority; Exdis.

[2] Bowles attributed the political furor that developed in India over alleged CIA activities in part to Soviet-sponsored forgeries designed to exacerbate U.S.-Indian relations. (Telegram 13640 from New Delhi, March 21; ibid., POL INDIA–US) CIA Director Richard Helms sent a letter to Rusk on March 24 in which he noted that during the course of a debate in the Indian Parliament on March 23 on the CIA in India, several members of the Lok Sabha referred to statements made by former Ambassador Galbraith in his article on the CIA in *The Washington Post* on March 13. In that article, Galbraith wrote that CIA activities in India "were generally known to and involved no conflict with local authorities." (Ibid., Rusk Files: Lot 72 D 192, Secretary's Misc Correspondence) Helms sent a memorandum to the President on March 28 in which he noted that he had discussed with Galbraith the impact of his article in India. He told Galbraith that that article had "raised unshirted hell in India and has provided the central point of an acrimonious debate in the Lok Sabha." Galbraith professed surprise and dismay, and promised to be more discreet in future. (Central Intelligence Agency, Job 80–B01285A, DCI (Helms) Files, Chrono Jan–July 1967)

istan,[3] and general concern about ability of USG to maintain required level of assistance here in view of demands in Vietnam.

5. Against this background it is important for us to make it clear to GOI and its leaders that we mean to do all we can to assist new government to get India on the move. Since leadership can move towards more liberal economic policies only if they feel confident about resources available, a US declaration of intent, perhaps by Gene Rostow in consortium context or in personal letter from the President to the Prime Minister, will provide a major shot in the arm.

6. In concrete terms I am hopeful (a) that we will be as forthcoming as possible at the critical India consortium meeting early April and (b) that we will make earliest possible decision in regard to additional food shipments before public and parliamentary anxiety again becomes focused on diminishing flow through pipeline.

7. Regarding consortium I am keenly aware of problems in respect to aid legislation. However, I believe that it is essential, in addition to non-project assistance required to sustain import liberalization program, that we provide a substantial amount from Ex-Im Bank for projects. (*Note:* until 1965 the Ex-Im pledged India about $50 million per year; since then it has contributed next to nothing.) Ex-Im project loans of say $150 million for each of next two years, on top of adequate [garble] non-project assistance to sustain import liberalization, would help give Indian economy and national confidence boost they urgently need at this stage.

8. In regard to food shipments pipeline appears assured through early June. While I recognize that additional 3 million tons approved in Congressional Joint Resolution are tied to appropriate assistance from other nations, I believe we should somehow come through with our full share early enough to avert another food price crisis which would have grave impact on central government and state-center relationships both of which are now extremely fragile. Three million tons would take India through the middle of September. By that time we expect that more normal rains and new technology will assure harvest which, with additional assistance from other nations (hopefully including Soviets), should cover all or almost all of rest of 1967.

---

[3] In telegram 13994 from New Delhi, March 28, Bowles added the following observation: "I am assuming that we do not intend to embark on a policy which would provide lethal military supplies to Pakistan. If we should do so we would utterly destroy the very real hope of negotiating the Indo–Pak arms ceiling which we have been pressing for so many months. In present atmosphere of doubt and suspicion engendered by sharp public and parliamentary reaction to CIA revelations, it would also jeopardize our relations with a new government which, with our support and a little luck, could emerge as more realistic and U.S.-oriented than any since independence." (National Archives and Records Administration, RG 59, Central Files 1967–69, AID (US) 15 INDIA)

9. While fragile is appropriate word to describe present situation here and while Mrs. Gandhi's government faces acute new political problems on top of perennial economic ones, I believe ingredients for dramatic economic progress are also at hand. Such progress will require our timely, substantial and astute assistance. It would, in turn provide a new and I believe more stable and mutually satisfactory basis for Indo–US relationships.

Bowles

429. Memorandum From the President's Special Assistant (Rostow) to President Johnson[1]

Washington, March 30, 1967.

SUBJECT

Instructions for Our Delegation to the India Consortium

George Woods' consortium meets 4 April (a) to nail down matching food aid from other donors, and (b) to round up enough additional general economic aid to keep India's import liberalization program going until the consortium's October pledging session.

Agriculture will top the agenda, but Woods will also use the meeting to keep up our end of the broad economic bargain he and Mehta made last spring with your backing. Woods concludes that the Indians have stuck to the terms of that deal, and meeting his targets is essential to keeping it alive.

That general economic program plays an important role in the success of agricultural reform. It's essential to India's buying or producing its agricultural requirements, but it's also important to the politics of reforming the agricultural system. Mrs. Gandhi's new government faces hard bargaining with recalcitrant states to get them to go along with reasonable food-sharing programs. Her leverage comes from having outside resources to allocate to best developmental and political

---

[1] Source: Johnson Library, National Security File, NSC Histories, Indian Famine, August 1966–February 1967, Vol. IV. Confidential. A handwritten notation reads, "Rec'd 10:36 a." A handwritten "L" indicates the memorandum was seen by the President. Sent to the President at the LBJ Ranch in Texas as telegram CAP 67230, March 30. (Ibid., Country File, India, Vol. IX, Cables, 3–7/67)

advantage and from her ability to produce the results consortium aid promises.

Woods' main goal at this meeting—apart from rounding up matching food contributions—is to make a breakthrough in softening the terms of other donors' aid. This beginning attack on India's debt burden is crucial to forcing others to share the aid burden more fairly. If we don't soon solve that problem, India will be repaying some donors more than it gets in new aid, and our aid will just go to pay India's European creditors.

The attached memos from Schultze and Gaud[2] spell out a two-step strategy which includes a $33–48 million non-project Ex-Im loan on newly flexible terms and the offer of an early $50 million AID non-project loan (from FY 1967 funds) against our FY 1968 program. Gaud would come back to you before determining the size of that overall pledge and our share next fall.

What they are asking you for now is authority to make these two limited offers. Since we've already made our big food offer, we're proposing just enough more in strategic forms to improve our leverage on both the Bank and other donors. Gene will lead our delegation and is fully aware of your overall objectives. We think this will give him enough to negotiate with.

I recommend you use Schultze's memo (attached) as your decision document, since it details our conditions.[3]

Walt

---

[2] Reference is to a March 26 memorandum from Gaud to the President and a March 28 memorandum from Schultze to the President, both entitled "The India Aid Consortium Meeting." (Ibid., India's Food Problem, Vol. IV)

[3] Schultze's memorandum indicates that President Johnson approved the two proposed loans on April 2.

430.   Telegram From the Department of State to the Embassy in
India[1]

Washington, March 31, 1967, 10:46 a.m.

166136. Personal for Ambassador from the Secretary.

1. You and Gene Locke should shortly be receiving a statement
on our new policy regarding military supplies to India and Pakistan
as well as instructions on how this policy should be implemented. On
the instructions of the President, Secretary McNamara, AID Administrator Gaud and I, as well as other key officials have given long, serious
and careful consideration to all aspects of this new policy. Your views
have been taken into account by all concerned.

2. This has not been an easy decision but I am confident that what
we are proposing is the right course for the United States to follow in the
months ahead. We do not seek a military buildup in the subcontinent.
There is too much of that already and India is far from being without
blame. In fact our new policy has just the opposite objective. We believe
that, together with our diplomatic, economic and food efforts, it is an
essential element in our endeavor to divert Indian and Pakistani energies
and substance from the arms race and channel them instead towards
economic programs which could within a few years substantially improve prospects for economic and food self-sufficiency. We realize we
cannot by our own actions bring this about. We will therefore enlist the
help of the Bank, our allies, and, if at all possible, even the Soviet Bloc.

3. We fully agree with you that our objective in all this is an arms
agreement between these two countries. Our efforts should be in that
direction and we think we will be more influential in this process if
our policy is broad enough to give us a wide range of inducements
and incentives especially with the GOP.

4. We all recognize that our new policy could cause us immediate
problems in India, but I urge you not to be defensive with the Indians.
There is much in the new policy that should appeal to them. For
example:

A. We will be terminating grant military assistance to Pakistan
and ending a basic military relationship we have had with that country
since 1954.
B. The withdrawal of MAAG from Pakistan (and USMSMI from
India) will be publicly announced at an appropriate moment.

---

[1] Source: Johnson Library, National Security File, Memos to the President, Walt W.
Rostow, Vol. 25, April 1–15, 1967. Secret; Nodis. Drafted by Handley on March 30; cleared
by Battle, Heck, and Spain; and approved by Rusk.

C. The package will include funds for completion of Star Sapphire on terms far more concessional than we are offering elsewhere at present as well as a substantial credit sales program for non-lethal equipment.

D. We are in fact reverting to a military relationship with both countries similar to the one we had in the fifties with India (when it was on friendly terms with Communist China and the Soviet Union).

E. By being in a position to sell military spares to Pakistan, we will have an opportunity of slowing down the re-equipping of Pakistani military forces. Were we to continue to prevent Pakistan from maintaining for the time being its American supplied military establishment, we would surely be running the risk of a major, sudden expensive change-over and modernization process which would almost certainly be detrimental to Indian interests.

The fact is that by this new policy we will be doing no more and indeed less than other suppliers of military equipment to India and Pakistan, i.e. Britain, France, Italy, Germany, Communist China and the Soviet Union. Moreover, we know we will be less forthcoming than other military suppliers because we intend to scrutinize requests more carefully than they do.

5. It seems to me that the GOI should see our new policy in the perspective of our total relationship with India, a relationship in terms of economic, food, political and other support that is clearly based on USG conviction that India is central to our interests in South Asia. Since World War II four US administrations have steadfastly supported the independence of India as well as massive American assistance to India's economic development. In the days immediately ahead we will be moving forward on a number of fronts and these should not be ignored or discounted. They include:

A. $25 million total package for voluntary agencies.

B. A non-project loan of $132 million.

C. Project GROMET.[2]

D. AID level discussions at the Consortium meeting in early April.

E. Another tranche of PL–480 Title I shortly after the Consortium meeting.

F. Continued diplomatic efforts to mobilize an international food program for India.

6. In the light of our changed relationship with Pakistan and considering the totality of our relations with India, I am confident that you can explain our new policy in such a way that the Indians will appreciate our objectives and will not forget the advantages that accrue to them through their overall relationships with the United States.

Rusk

---

[2] Project GROMET was the code name for an Indian rain augmentation project initiated with U.S. support at the end of 1966.

431.   **Telegram From the Department of State to the Embassy in India[1]**

Washington, March 31, 1967, 5:28 p.m.

166539. For Ambassador from the Secretary.

1. After full consideration of alternatives, we have concluded that the US should follow a policy toward India and Pakistan designed to limit arms acquisition, to restrain military expenditures, to reduce the possibility of military confrontation, and to encourage highest priority allocation of resources to agricultural and economic development. The United States should use all useful leverage at its disposal to further this policy, including its bilateral economic assistance, its participation in the World Bank and in aid consortia, and end-use controls over US military equipment supplied directly or indirectly to third countries.

2. The supply of military equipment by the United States should be governed by this policy. The United Kingdom, the Federal Republic of Germany, France and the Soviet Union should be urged to follow similar restraints in their military supply policies toward India and Pakistan.

3. Initial implementation of this policy should include:

A. Withdrawal of MAAG (Pakistan) and USMSMI, making alternative, limited arrangements for providing such military representation, inspection and supervision of sales and training as may be required; the Joint Chiefs of Staff to be a party to such arrangements.

B. Steps to prevent the sales by third countries to India and Pakistan of military equipment which (a) includes US technology and components; (b) is produced in the US or (c) is co-produced with the US, except when the US has determined that such sales contribute to arms limitation or reduced defense expenditures.

C. Indicating to India and Pakistan that, although the US remains unwilling to contribute to the augmentation of the military establishment of either country through the sale of lethal military equipment, it is willing to consider on a case by case basis the sale of spare parts for previously supplied lethal equipment when there is a clearly established critical need and when such sales contribute to arms limitation or reduced military expenditures and the maintenance of a reasonable military balance between the two nations. The question is not now before us as to replacing an end item of US origin should that item be

---

[1] Source: Johnson Library, National Security File, Country File, India, Vol. IX, Cables, 3/67–7/67. Secret; Exdis. Drafted by Handley on March 14, cleared by Katzenbach and Rostow at White House, and approved by Rusk. Also sent to Rawalpindi.

totally destroyed through accidental loss. That contingency will be considered when it arises.

D. Indicating to India and Pakistan our willingness to reinstitute training in the US for a limited number of key Indian and Pakistani military personnel under MAP.

E. Disbursement of remaining obligated FY–67 credit sales funds only where such expenditures will contribute to US security interests (e.g. Star Sapphire) or to support of the general policy of arms limitation. Credit sales shall be for non-lethal items only.

4. FY–68 credit sales planning for India and Pakistan should be predicated on the preceding paragraphs. The relevant figure in the 1968 budget should be $75 million with the following provisions:

A. The figure is to be classified.

B. It is to be an absolute ceiling, not a target.

C. It should under no circumstances be communicated to the Governments of India and Pakistan without specific approval of the Secretary of State.

D. Proposed credits will be reviewed case by case for their contribution to arms limitations.

5. After we have consulted with Congress you will be receiving instructions on implementation of this policy, and timing and manner of presentation. We recognize that situation will differ between New Delhi and Rawalpindi and that certain current problems including NPT may have bearing on timing of presentation in New Delhi.

Rusk

432. Memorandum From the President's Special Assistant (Rostow) to President Johnson[1]

Washington, April 2, 1967.

SUBJECT

Wheat and Oil Agreement for Pakistan

Here is the wheat agreement Gene Locke probably mentioned to you. He is paying his farewell calls[2] on Pakistan's senior economic ministers early tomorrow morning and would like to give them an answer then. This would necessitate getting a cable out to him early this evening. If that's cutting it too close, we can get it to him easily—if you approve—for his final call on Ayub Friday.[3]

Charlie Schultze's memo (attached)[4] lays out the figures. In a nutshell, Pakistan has asked us for an added 250,000 tons of wheat now to help break a rapid rise in prices stemming from drought shortages. Freeman and Hall propose 200,000—half to be charged against any FY 1968 US allocation for Pakistan.

I recommend approval. Pakistan has done a sound job in agriculture. Approving this program now would help Ayub with a tough economic-political problem. Even doing this wouldn't take us beyond average past levels (1.5 million tons) for this year.[5]

Walt

---

[1] Source: Johnson Library, National Security File, Country File, Pakistan, Vol. VII, Memos, 10/66–7/67. Confidential.

[2] Locke resigned his post as Ambassador to Pakistan effective April 16. He was replaced by Benjamin H. Oehlert, Jr., who was appointed on July 27 and presented his credentials on August 16.

[3] April 7.

[4] Dated April 3, Schultze's memorandum to the President dealt with the proposed P.L. 480 agreement with Pakistan.

[5] Johnson's marginal handwritten response reads: "OK, for either 200 or 250—I'd give him 250 but notify Locke at once."

433. Telegram From the Department of State to the Embassy in Pakistan[1]

Washington, April 5, 1967, 9:14 a.m.

168709. Ref: State 166539.[2] Subject: Military Supply Policy for India and Pakistan. Following are your instructions covering military supply policy conveyed by reftel:

1. We desire implement decision as soon as Congressional consultations, now underway, are complete; telegram will inform you of completion. While we recognize Ambassador Bowles will need some elbow room on timing of approaches to GOI, there is some urgency for Ambassador Locke to inform GOP. We understand meeting with Ayub now set for April 7; we believe GOI should be informed as soon after that as possible to assure shortest gap possible between presentations. Basic elements of new policy should be communicated as stated reftel, omitting references to internal USG operations.

2. Both posts should emphasize that new policy reflects intensive review over long period time and with involvement highest levels USG. Both should also insure it clearly understood we do not under foreseeable circumstances intend return to supply relationship we had prior September 1965.

3. Our new policy recognizes that fundamental historical changes have taken place. Our purpose is to establish a new relationship that takes into account legitimate defense requirements both countries but rests primarily on conviction that basic security and economic well being of both countries depends on their finding way to lessen tensions between them and thus to reduce share of their resources going to military expenditures.

For Rawalpindi: 4. In conveying policy package to Ayub you should say we were encouraged by his response to our representations on arms limitation in November (Rawalpindi's 1751).[3] On assumption that that response remains basis for GOP arms policy, we now prepared do following within context of stated policy (i.e., only when such actions will contribute to arms limitation or reduced defense expenditures):

---

[1] Source: National Archives and Records Administration, RG 59, Central Files 1967–69, DEF 12–5 INDIA. Secret; Immediate; Exdis. Drafted by Spain, Laingen, and Heck on March 27; cleared by Handley, Macomber, Captain Asbury Coward (G/PM), Katzenbach, Townsend Hoopes, AID Acting Deputy Assistant Administrator for Near East and South Asia Alfred D. White, and Wriggins; and approved by Rusk. Also sent to New Delhi and repeated to London, Tehran, and CINCMEAFSA.

[2] Document 431.

[3] Document 384.

(a) entertain specific requests for cash purchase in US of lethal spares on case-by-case basis;
(b) continue to consider requests for credit purchase of non-lethal end items;
(c) discuss his other problems of military supply, including requests for purchase from third countries of US-controlled equipment, but only within policy context stated reftel;
(d) resume limited grant training program, if GOP so desires.

5. Before we able to address Pak request for our concurrence in M-47 tank deal with Germans (Rawalpindi's 3489),[4] we need know: (a) effect of prospective purchases of US tank spares on level operational tanks of US origins; (b) how proposed German deal would further affect tank strength levels; (c) number Pak tanks of Chicom origin; and, (d) effects of foregoing tank strengths on overall armed forces structure.

6. In conveying policy package to Ayub we hope you can get across that we are prepared to help him meet his legitimate security requirements but that manner in which GOP deals in coming weeks and months with recent GOI offer begin talks on arms limitation (State 158121)[5] could have decisive impact on way we able to respond to GOP requests.

For New Delhi: 7. We recognize difficult task you face in getting Indians to see that their own interests served by our new policy. There are a number of elements in package designed help meet your problem (i.e., permanent MAAG withdrawal, credit sales, training). We believe it would be useful highlight following points:

(a) This decision terminates grant military assistance to Pakistan and substantially results in the end of a military relationship we have had with Pakistan since 1954;
(b) the withdrawal of MAAG from Pakistan (and USMSMI from India) symbolizes this new policy;
(c) need for some degree of flexibility in our sales policy if we are to have any influence on Pak position regarding arms limitation;
(d) fact that military supply is only one element of larger USG policy designed contribute to security, integrity, and economic well being of South Asia as a whole; the record speaks for itself as to what we have done and are ready to do for India, a country that is central to our interests in area;

---

[4] In telegram 3489 from Rawalpindi, March 17, Locke reported that Ayub reiterated Pakistan's need for M–47 tanks and interest in obtaining them from the Federal Republic of Germany. (National Archives and Records Administration, RG 59, Central Files 1967–69, DEF 12–5 PAK)

[5] In telegram 158121 to New Delhi and Rawalpindi, March 18, the Department expressed mild encouragement over recent developments in Indian-Pakistani relations. The Department cited, as grounds for this encouragement, Chagla's offer on March 14 of talks with Pakistan without preconditions, and Ayub's expressed willingness to consider secret talks concerning arms limitations. The Embassies were instructed to encourage both governments to build on these openings. (Ibid., POL INDIA–PAK)

(e) specific benefits for India include (1) $17 million on 3 per cent and ten year repayment basis for completion of Star Sapphire project. This is a special concessional rate, no longer available elsewhere and is provided in recognition of importance of completing this project; (2) authority to continue our credit sales program on case-by-case basis (currently on 5¹/2 per cent and 7 year terms); (3) limited grant training program.

8. We believe it would also be useful for you to reiterate in this context our strong satisfaction over recent Chagla letter to Pirzada[6] on arms limitation talks, adding that we continue believe special burden responsibility rests on India as larger power if progress to be made in such talks.

For both posts: 9. Para 3 C reftel states policy on replacement items, i.e., the question is not now before us as to replacing an end item of US origin should that item be totally destroyed through accidental loss. That contingency will be considered when it arises.

10. Both GOI and GOP should understand what while we are prepared to discuss arrangements for carrying out our new policy, including handling of any public announcements, decisions of timing and tactics will have to be our own, influenced particularly by Congressional requirements. You should stress most strongly that we intend handle this matter in as low key as possible and will look to both Governments for their cooperation. We would prefer for present to avoid any kind of public announcement or comment on new policy but recognize difficulty doing so for very long. FYI: We believe it preferable to make low key announcement which focuses on MAAG and USMSMI withdrawal instead of reacting to leaks. This announcement would be made as soon as possible after Ambassador Bowles talks to GOI and might be followed up with backgrounder in Washington with selected journalists, possibly including Indians and Paks who resident here. Will keep you informed. End FYI. Contingency press guidance being prepared.

11. If asked about timing MAAG/USMSMI withdrawal, you should say this still being worked out. FYI: We envisage July 1 as target date. End FYI.

12. FYI: We recognize that conflicting approaches GOI (willingness talk with GOP on all subjects but without recognizing existence dispute on Kashmir) and GOP (willingness talk GOI all subjects but only if Kashmir dispute also discussed) will continue complicate our efforts achieve arms limitation. We believe you should continue take every opportunity urge both sides to moderate their preconditions. Mean-

---

[6] See footnote 2, Document 423.

while, we are prepared for time being to see what we can accomplish bilaterally. End FYI.

13. We intend brief Ambassador Hilaly and Chargé Bannerjee as soon as we know approaches made to Governments.

For London: 14. As soon as scenario for presentations in Rawalpindi and New Delhi has been worked out, we expect to authorize you to convey new policy to HMG at appropriate level and in closest confidence. In doing so you should say that we will wish consult further on what we might be able to do together to achieve progress toward arms limitation subcontinent.

Rusk

---

434. Memorandum From the President's Special Assistant (Rostow) to President Johnson[1]

Washington, April 8, 1967.

SUBJECT

Preliminary Report on the Paris Indian Consortium Meetings[2]

The meetings appear to have been highly successful. The Consortium has agreed to include food aid in its planning and pledging; it sustained the non-food requirement of $900 million foreign exchange aid; and it has already made additional commitments virtually matching our 3 million tons of food.

There are three types of additional assistance: (a) direct food equivalents, now totalling approximately $70 million; (b) accelerating European pipelines to release real resources this year which normally would not have come forward for a number of years, amounting to roughly $50 to $70 million additional; and (c) debt relief, over and above what donors agreed to do to meet the $900 million foreign exchange requirement. We won't know the exact debt relief figure until April 25th when

---

[1] Source: Johnson Library, National Security File, Country File, India, Vol. IX, Memos & Miscellaneous, 3–7/67. Confidential. A handwritten note on the memorandum reads, "Rec'd 4/8/67, 12:30 p." A handwritten "L" indicates it was seen by the President.

[2] Eugene Rostow, who headed the U.S. delegation to the meetings of the India consortium in Paris, April 5–6, reported on the results of the meetings in telegrams 15622 and 15623 from Paris, both April 6. (National Archives and Records Administration, RG 59, Central Files 1967–69, SOC 10 INDIA)

representatives come to Washington for a wrap-up meeting to make final commitments. This may total some $139–141 million more.

The Paris delegation recommends that we now release 1.5 million of the 3 million additional tons of food approved by the Congressional resolution. They want to hold the second 1.5 million as leverage until after the April meeting firms up debt relief arrangements.

We'll report in greater detail when we've talked to the people who were there, but the preliminary report looks good.[3]

Walt

---

[3] Rostow added a handwritten postscript that reads: "in short, it looks as if Gene may have got more than the extra $190 million."

---

435.   Telegram From the Embassy in Pakistan to the Department of State[1]

Rawalpindi, April 8, 1967, 1000Z.

3788. Ref: State 166539[2] and 168709.[3]

1. Conveyed contents reftels (omitting USG internal and New Delhi instructions) orally to President Ayub in forty-five minute conversation April 7.

2. President Ayub reaffirmed statements passed to me by Foreign Secretary Yousuf November 6 (Rawalpindi 1751).[4] Particularly he said tanks and other equipment are to "fill gaps" and replace worn out obsolete equipment, not to increase force levels.

3. President stated GOP has replied to Chagla note about arms limitation meeting, and Foreign Office instructed to furnish us copy. Ayub said meetings should be secret and at diplomatic level at present,

---

[1] Source: National Archives and Records Administration, RG 59, Central Files 1967–69, DEF 12–5 INDIA. Secret; Priority; Exdis. Repeated to New Delhi, London, Tehran, and CINCMEAFSA.

[2] Document 431.

[3] Document 433.

[4] Document 384.

since any Ministerial meetings which got in press would only increase Indo–Pak tensions.

4. Ayub was optimistic about meetings. He said senior Pak officer (most probably G. Mueenuddin) recently went to India for wedding and saw B.K. Nehru, an old friend of his, and subsequently Indira Gandhi. Nehru said politically impossible seriously discuss Kashmir. Mrs. Gandhi said she prepared to listen to Pak officer but would make no comment. Ayub said conciliatory public statements by Indians on arms limitation and other subjects are purely for US consumption. Ayub noted that while Pak military budget reduced this year, India budget increased to about 969 crore. He said much hidden in EA budget because of India's ordnance production. Pakistan estimates real Indian defense expenditures 15 to 20 per cent greater than above figure. Ayub reiterated that way to obtain arms limitation is for US to talk independently to each country as British did in Rann of Kutch dispute. He reiterated Pakistan wants arms limitation, Pakistan can never have anywhere near as large army as India, which is sapping India's economic strength; Pakistan merely wants to be able to defend itself adequately.

5. I noted our need for list of Pak spare part requirements and requirements for purchases from third countries, including information prerequisite for consideration German tank purchase. My impression is Ayub prepared to make requested information available, at least against specific possibility obtain desired tanks.

6. We discussed possibility of Defense Minister Khan travelling to US soon to talk with Defense and State Departments.

7. *Comment:* Review of public and private statements by Ayub and senior responsible officials over past several months demonstrates consistency in GOP position reflected anew in Ayub's remarks today. Principal elements are GOP: (a) willingness in principle to reduce defense expenditures and limit arms; (b) requirement for some degree of motion on political issues; (c) scepticism about Indian sincerity and concern at possible GOI press leaks and public exploitation of talks; (d) preference for secrecy exploratory talks via diplomatic channels and for US bilateral approaches with each side. Emphasis varies but all elements remain central to Pak position.

8. It now most important to develop GOP confidence in political and military feasibility of new US policy. Immediate requirement this regard is expeditious US response to Pak lethel spare parts request.

9. Absolute discretion all parties essential with respect to existence and content Indo–Pak talks and regarding any military strength figures supplied to US. Would appreciate opportunity review any proposed press release re US military support policy.

10. Please advise your reactions to Khan visit. We recommend he come and that opportunity be used to begin rebuilding relationship between US and Pak armed forces.[5]

Locke

[5] Locke reported on April 11 that he had followed up his discussion with Ayub on April 7 by covering the same ground with Defense Minister Admiral Khan, Foreign Minister Pirzada, Foreign Secretary Yusuf, and Air Marshal Nur Khan. (Telegram 3788 from Rawalpindi; National Archives and Records Administration, RG 59, Central Files 1967–69, DEF 12–5 INDIA) At Admiral Khan's request, the Embassy prepared and sent to him on April 12 a memorandum outlining the new military supply policy for India and Pakistan. (Telegram 3862 from Rawalpindi, April 12; ibid.) Locke's judgment was that the Ayub government found the new U.S. military supply policy to be moderately satisfactory and, under the circumstances, an understandable modification of U.S. policy. (Telegram 5007 from Karachi, April 14; ibid., DEF 12–5 PAK)

---

436. Letter From Prime Minister Gandhi to President Johnson

New Delhi, April 10, 1967.

[Source: Johnson Library, National Security File, Special Head of State Correspondence File, India, 1/1/67–4/30/67. No classification marking. 3 pages of source text not declassified by the Indian Government.]

---

437. Telegram From the Embassy in India to the Department of State[1]

New Delhi, April 10, 1967, 1430Z.

14747. Dept pass CINCSTRIKE/USCINCMEAFSA, AmEmbassy London, AmEmbassy Rawalpindi, AmEmbassy Tehran. Ref: State 166539[2] and 168709.[3]

[1] Source: National Archives and Records Administration, RG 59, Central Files 1967–69, DEF 12–5 INDIA. Secret; Priority; Exdis.

[2] Document 431.

[3] Document 433.

1. I decided it best convey contents reftels to Foreign Minister Chagla rather than Prime Minister Gandhi since once she took position it would be government policy, whereas we retain some flexibility by making approach to Chagla. I also decided to convey our position in writing and accordingly handed him aide-mémoire at beginning our meeting. Full text aide-mémoire transmitted next following telegram.[4] While meeting was conducted in polite terms, there was no doubt that Chagla and Bajpai, who was also present, were deeply concerned over effects of our decision.

2. After reading aide-mémoire Chagla stressed that GOI policy is to attempt to prevent arms race which is harmful to both India and Pakistan. GOI is prepared for serious talks. I asked if he had yet had reply to his letter to Foreign Minister Pirzada. He replied in the negative but stated he understood reply was about to be received and Indian HICOM in Pindi was returning tomorrow to Delhi and he expected he would be carrying reply with him.

3. Chagla said the question was how far U.S. policy would contribute to achieving our shared objective of preventing an arms race. He pointed out GOI was worried not merely about arms that the Paks obtained from all over the world but about the arms that were going to Pakistan through Iran, Turkey and Saudi Arabia. in this connection he cited unusual circumstance of Iranian planes recently taking part in Pakistani National Day celebrations. He said he would be going to Tehran in a few days and wanted to have a frank talk with the Shah.

4. Chagla said deep concern would be aroused by resumption of provision of spare parts for lethal equipment in hands of Paks even on sales basis since this would understandably strengthen Pak military capacity. I pointed out that we were simply readjusting our policy so that it would now be consistent with that of other Western countries. He believed new policy strongly favored Paks and reminded me that they had previously told us Paks would use our weapons against India. We had been unable to prevent Paks from using such equipment against India.

5. Chagla was concerned that effect of resumption spare parts supply for Pakistan lethal equipment would inevitably lead to a step up in arms race. It was felt that the timing of our move was "singularly unfortunate" coming immediately before anticipated reply of Paks to Chagla letter. Our new policy it was feared would encourage Pak intransigence. He pointed out that criteria of limitation of military

---

[4] Telegram 14748 from New Delhi, April 10. (National Archives and Records Administration, RG 59, Central Files 1967–69, DEF 12–INDIA)

expenditures means that Paks will be able to obtain more equipment within the same expenditure ceiling.

6. Chagla asked if we agreed that the Indians should discuss arms limitations irrespective of Kashmir, and I told him we understood that the Kashmir problem could not be solved first.

7. Bajpai expressed grave concern which Chagla shared that proposed announcement April 12 would have extremely damaging effect not only on Indian public attitudes but also on L.K. Jha's visit to Washington. They strongly urged that announcement be held up at least a few days.

8. In closing Chagla agreed with my suggestion that the value of this policy would be determined by the manner in which we implemented it and added that if it helped the Indo–Pak dialogue it was all well and good, if not, all India's efforts to establish a dialogue would be for naught. We agreed that we would again be in touch in a few days after they had had an opportunity to give a thorough study to our aide-mémoire.

9. During meeting I also handed Foreign Minister on separate paper text of proposed press statement. I did not give him text of contingency questions and answers. Bajpai pointed out that the press statement as presently drafted draws major attention to our provision spare parts for previously supplied equipment to Paks and fact India also included as Chagla put it was "SOP with no real meaning", since we have not in past provided lethal items to Indians on anywhere near scale provided Paks.

10. Effect of proposed press statement he said will be highly damaging our interests in India. (*Note:* I am sending separate message April 11 containing suggested redraft of press statement which is attempt to place our policy in perspective that would help diminish difficulties here.)

11. Action requested: As Chagla will undoubtedly be calling me back in day or two for further discussion, I would like to be able to assure him catagorically that if Paks give a negative response to Chagla letter[5] calling for arms limitation, and by negative response I include a reply indicating prior necessity to settle Kashmir, that I be authorized assure GOI in such circumstances we would not proceed authorize sale spare parts for previously supplied lethal military equipment. Anything further I could say to effect Paks agree not go to ChiComs for additional equipment would be helpful.

Bowles

---

[5] C.S. Jha told Bowles on April 11 that Pakistan had just rejected the proposal in Chagla's letter. Jha stated that the Pakistani response would amplify the negative reaction in India to the decision taken by the United States on military supply policy. (Telegram 14899 from New Delhi, April 12; ibid.)

438. Telegram From the President's Special Assistant (Rostow) to President Johnson in Texas[1]

Washington, April 15, 1967, 2326Z.

CAP 67295. For the President from Walt Rostow. Subject: L.K. Jha and the NPT.

Against the background of the following letter from Mrs. Gandhi, I had a talk this morning with L.K. Jha,[2] one of her closest and most responsible advisors and B.K. Nehru.[3] You will see from her letter that she hopes Jha will be able to see you—he leaves town on Wednesday.[4] There are three issues:

Firstly, Soviet and U.S. assurances to India and others who sign the NPT: He has just come from Moscow where he appears to have made substantial progress in getting out of the Russians the beginnings of an assurance. According to him, the Russians are prepared to make a declaration when the NPT is signed to the effect that the nuclear powers have a responsibility to act quickly through the Security Council if a non-nuclear signatory of the NPT is subject to unprovoked nuclear threat or attack. There would also be language permitting a nuclear power to act in fulfillment of that assurance without waiting for Security Council action, freeing it from a possible delay as a result of a Security Council veto. According to him, they are ready to do it simultaneously with us, even though our respective assurances would not necessarily be identical.

We do not yet have the formal Soviet text. But Jha has a reputation for care and accuracy. If he is nearly accurate, this could represent a real breakthrough.

We will be studying a paper[5] he has drafted combining our views and Russia's, as he understands them. He recognizes that we can't give him anything definitive until we see the Russian text, but he hopes for some sign from us of a serious interest in privately exploring with the Russians an assurance paralleling what he thinks they are ready to declare.

---

[1] Source: Johnson Library, National Security File, Head of State Correspondence File, India, Vol. I, Prime Minister Gandhi Correspondence, 1/11/66–9/12/67. Confidential.

[2] Jha visited Washington April 12–19.

[3] A memorandum of this conversation, prepared by Rostow, is in the Johnson Library, National Security File, Country File, India, Vol. 9, 3/67–7/67.

[4] April 19.

[5] A copy of this undated paper is in the Johnson Library, National Security File, Head of State Correspondence File, India, Vol. I, Prime Minister Gandhi Correspondence, 1/11/66–9/12/67.

Secondly, we discussed briefly our new arms policy toward the subcontinent. They fear that our selling spares to Ayub will make him less willing to reach agreement with them, and make it more difficult for them to hold the line on defense expenditures. I stressed our intention to look at military supply on a case by case basis in the light of particular transactions' effect upon the level of expenditures.

Third, we discussed the problem of at least holding the line, and preferably, reducing arms expenditures. They argued we should force the Paks to reach an arms agreement with them by not selling spares until they agreed (for his part, Ayub wants us to act as middle man, so that we can pressure the Indians on Pakistan's behalf). I urged them to press forward in all possible ways their effort toward secret talks, preferably between military and financial specialists in both countries in an effort to find a way to prevent a further arms race, which we did not intend to finance. They shouldn't be discouraged if the Paks didn't respond quickly—after all, India was by far the larger, stronger country. Pakistan has no arms production and no source of supply like India's from Russia.

Prime Minister Gandhi leans heavily on L.K. Jha's judgment. It is important that he go home with a clear knowledge of our interest in his brokerage effort between us and Moscow. He saw Kosygin when there, and before he came here, his government asked if you could receive him.

In view of the possibility that we may be on the verge of a break-through on the NPT, and the importance of strengthening his hand in New Delhi against the Hawks who want to go nuclear, I recommend you try to see him on Tuesday or Wednesday.

Have Marv set up an appointment.[6]

Consult with me on this

[Here follows the text of Prime Minister Gandhi's April 10 letter to President Johnson; see Document 436.]

---

[6] Neither option is checked on the telegram. Johnson did, however, meet with Jha on April 19; see Document 440.

439. Letter From the Deputy Ambassador-designate to Vietnam (Locke) to President Johnson[1]

Djakarta, April 18, 1967.

Dear Mr. President:

Enclosed is an "Aide-Mémoire on the U.S. Government's Arms Policy For Pakistan and India"[2] which President Ayub handed me when I lunched at his house April 15. He asked me to send it to you.

The Aide-Mémoire discusses not only the military supply policy, but economic aid as well.

With respect to our military supply policy, all government officials with whom I have talked recognize that it is an improvement over the current situation. They do not believe, however, that it adequately recognizes their defense needs. I believe that it does, if properly interpreted and implemented. They agree, but have no confidence in our interpretation or implementation. For this reason it is extremely important that:

1. We handle spare parts requests expeditiously and do not debate for long periods whether they are in "critical need" or contribute to "reduced defense expenditures." Obviously all spare parts not on hand are "critically needed" and to buy them from us is cheaper than to buy them from gun runners, thus reducing defense expenditures. We should only assure ourselves that the supply of parts requested is of reasonable quality.

2. We handle requests for permission to buy end items from third countries promptly and with understanding. If these items are actually for replacements and to fill in gaps, as claimed, and not for expanded forces, they should be allowed. Requests in this category should be considered as reducing defense expenditures, because these tanks are less expensive than new ones from other countries which would otherwise be bought. The key question should be whether or not the requested tanks are necessary to an adequate defense within existing force levels.

3. We use economic pressure to prevent the Indians from fueling an arms race.

Some of the reasons Pakistan is suspicious of our proper implementation of the new policy are:

---

[1] Source: Johnson Library, National Security File, Country File, Pakistan, Vol. VII, Memos, 10/66–7/67. Confidential. Ambassador Locke left his post as Ambassador to Pakistan on April 16, and was passing through Indonesia en route to his new post as Deputy Ambassador to Vietnam.

[2] The enclosed aide-mémoire, prepared in the Ministry of Foreign Affairs and dated April 15, laid out a variety of reasons for concluding that "the new U.S. arms supply policy affects Pakistan adversely." The aide-mémoire also argued that "U.S. policy towards Pakistan in the economic field gives rise to concern."

1. We appear to them to have bought the Indian "status quo" on Kashmir and to be trying by our policy to force them to accept it. This they will never do.

2. We said when I first came to Pakistan that we were requiring India, like Pakistan, to keep her defense expenditures in line and avoid an arms race; yet the Indian defense budget has gone up, where Pakistan's has gone down somewhat; and the balance of forces has increased considerably in favor of the Indians since the 1965 War.

3. In November, pursuant to State Department message, I asked President Ayub certain questions with respect to his intentions about arms limitations, talks on all subjects (including Kashmir), and arms sources (especially Chinese and Russian), and left the thought that our degree of responsiveness to his defense needs would depend on our assessment of his answers. His answers, I believe, were satisfactory from our point of view, yet our action was delayed five months, and then given in the form of a policy which on its face does not appear to recognize his needs, although it can be interpreted to do so. (*As above stated, our declared policy—properly interpreted and implemented—will properly recognize his needs, and it is this prompt and proper interpretation and implementation that is important.*)

The paper's comments with respect to economic matters are not completely balanced. We cannot be more forthcoming on Tarbela at this time than we have been, and they understand the reason. We have been reasonably forthcoming both as to amount and timing on consortium aid and food, at least as compared with India. It is difficult for Pakistan to understand, however, although I have tried to explain why it takes so long to get a commitment issued on the $70 million loan, after you authorized it some time ago. Also they still feel we should have been more responsive in meeting their request to send 250,000 tons of wheat before the end of the year in response to President Ayub's personal letter to Secretary Freeman;[3] the wheat was eventually committed and sent, but not in time to avoid Pakistan buying more with its own foreign exchange and being forced to suspend the free list. And it is true—as they charge—that they have spent many times per capita more of their foreign exchange on food than India, and India's greater famine may be principally due to India's failure to use the same self-help measures as Pakistan. In other words, we have been *very* responsive to many of their requests, but they have been frustrated and their economic progress has been slowed and liberalization prevented by a combination of slowness in consortium aid and their necessity to spend so much foreign exchange on food grain—whatever the cause.

---

[3] Not found.

It is true that if we could be more responsive from a timing point of view on all kinds of aid, we could build more good will without giving more in the total. But of course we have our own problems, and Pakistan has not always been quick in solving some of our minor troubles in Pakistan.

There will be a tendency in reading the enclosed report to be a little aggravated by what appears to be Pakistan's failure to see our problems and appreciate our help. But we should resist this tendency. We should seek to understand and be sympathetic to their frustrations—whatever the cause. Pakistan's orientation toward the West is extremely important to us (and to India as well) and we should not be diverted from our major foreign policy goals by emotional reaction.[4]

Faithfully yours,

Eugene M. Locke[5]

---

[4] Locke expanded his analysis of the Pakistani aide-mémoire in another letter to the President, sent from Bangkok on May 1. He noted that his first reaction to the aide-mémoire was one of anger, for it did not show any appreciation for U.S. actions with respect to Pakistan's security and food problems. Upon reflection, he decided that the aide-mémoire did not accurately reflect the attitudes of Ayub and his principal advisers. As he saw it, the Pakistani leadership viewed the new U.S. military supply policy as a step forward and recognized the importance of U.S. economic assistance. Locke felt that the Pakistanis did not question the fact that they received their fair share of economic assistance, but had problems with the timing of the assistance. Locke attributed the aide-mémoire to pressure from the "China lobby" in the government and in the press. (Johnson Library, National Security File, Country File, Pakistan, Vol. VII, Memos, 10/66–7/67)

[5] Signed for Locke by Ambassador to Indonesia Marshall Green.

440.   Memorandum of Conversation[1]

Washington, April 19, 1967, 11–11:50 a.m.

THOSE PRESENT

President Johnson
Ambassador B.K. Nehru
L.K. Jha
Mr. V. Sarabhai
W.W. Rostow
Howard Wriggins

After welcome by the President and exchange of pleasantries, L. K. Jha indicated that he had come at the request of the Prime Minister on a visit to the Soviet Union and Washington, to explore the question of security assurances connected with the NPT. The Soviet reply had been positive and he hoped the U.S. too would be able to move ahead.

The President said that he had just received the text[2] this morning, that it looked very interesting. From earlier statements, the Indians could know generally how interested we were in this problem; we will have to look at it with care; but we will get right at it. (He asked Mr. Rostow to be sure the staff work was ready for tomorrow's meeting.)

L.K. Jha said that the Prime Minister also wanted him to thank the President for all his help on so many fronts, including food and economic aid. If he should find it possible to come to New Delhi, the President would receive a very warm welcome.

The President replied that he had enjoyed his earlier visit and learned a great deal, particularly in the countryside, where he saw so much progress being made. Perhaps it would be possible to think about a trip for sometime next year, but he couldn't make a commitment now for so far ahead. He pointed out that Ambassadors Cooper, Gal-

---

[1] Source: National Archives and Records Administration, RG 59, Central Files 1967–69, POL 7 INDIA. Secret. No drafting information appears on the memorandum, but it apparently was drafted by Wriggins. A typewritten notation on the memorandum indicates it was uncleared. The time of the meeting, held in the Oval Office at the White House, is from the President's Daily Diary. (Johnson Library)

[2] The undated text of a draft Soviet declaration concerning assurances to non-nuclear nations in the event of aggression by a nuclear power, as conveyed to Washington by Jha, is attached to an April 20 memorandum from Kohler to Rusk. (National Archives and Records Administration, RG 59, Central Files 1967–69, POL 7 INDIA; also available on the Internet, National Security Archive (www.gwu.edu/~nsarchive), Electronic Briefing Book No. 6, "India and Pakistan—On the Nuclear Threshold," Document 14) Secretary Rusk and Soviet Foreign Minister Gromyko discussed the Soviet draft on June 23. The memorandum of conversation is printed in *Foreign Relations, 1964–1968*, vol. XI, Document 198; it is also available on the Internet, National Security Archive Electronic Briefing Book No. 6, Document 16.

braith, and Bunker had all been so well received they had been made converts to India's cause; perhaps if he went, he would be converted too. L.K. Jha said he hoped that would be so.

The President indicated that he had appointed Ambassador Bunker, whom the Indians had trained, to Vietnam in the hope that some way could be found to end that conflict satisfactorily. Perhaps the Indians, who knew Ambassador Bunker, would now be able to help a bit more. Despite numerous efforts to reach agreement with North Vietnam, none of our many initiatives had elicited Ho's willingness to talk. No Administration had done more to ease relations with the Soviet Union: Space Treaty, East/West trade; Consular Agreement, etc. We were not rigid on anything except running out on our contracts. What a disordered world it would be if others came to assume the U.S. word was worthless!

The President wanted the Prime Minister to know how much he had enjoyed having her here; he had worried about the painful political steps she had had to go through. But after all both of them were better off than such former leaders as Erhard, Macmillan and Khrushchev. Her country had many friends in the U.S.; he had had trouble getting the support she needed; but in the end, as a result of the Congressional resolution and other steps, things were likely to come out all right.

Everyone who has been out there feels that India is part of our future, and that we are part of theirs. "And so do I," he said.

In conclusion, the President reiterated his interest in having the Russian text examined with great care and indicated we would be back to them shortly with our reactions.[3]

---

[3] Jha also met with Secretary of Defense McNamara on April 18. They discussed the need for assurances to India against nuclear threats, U.S. resumption of the sale of "lethal spares" to the subcontinent, and the Non-Proliferation Treaty. The memorandum of conversation is in the Washington National Records Center, RG 330, OSD Files: FRC 72 A 2468; also available on the Internet, National Security Archive (www.gwu.edu/~nsarchiv), Electronic Briefing Book No. 6, "India and Pakistan—On the Nuclear Threshold," Document 15.

441.   Letter From President Johnson to Prime Minister Gandhi[1]

Washington, May 9, 1967.

Dear Madame Prime Minister:

The frankness and informality of your letter[2] and of my recent meeting with Mr. L.K. Jha recall the warmth of our talks during your visit here a year ago. I agree wholeheartedly that there is no subsitute for these personal exchanges.

This is why I am especially tempted by your gracious invitation to visit India again. No journey could give me greater pleasure, for Mrs. Johnson and I treasure memories of our last visit. Regrettably, I think it unlikely that we shall be able to make this trip in the months immediately ahead. As we look a bit further into the future, however, I hope it may be possible.

The year since your visit has been exceedingly busy for us both. We have each had our share of satisfactions and disappointments. These are inevitable given the problems we face.

Your letter suggests that perhaps your greatest satisfaction these past twelve months has been the mature, responsible way in which so many million Indians demonstrated the strength and vitality of Indian democracy by participating in India's fourth general election. You have a right to be proud, especially in view of the natural calamity which has afflicted many regions of India. I know the drought has added greatly to your burdens and caused you great personal sorrow.

All friends of India share both your pride and your grief.

I continue to follow closely your food situation. The Consortium meeting in Paris was an important step in meeting both the short range and longer term aspects of this problem. While you still have much to do in encouraging other governments to participate fully in both the food and the economic aid programs, I believe you have started down a new path which offers hope. We will continue to work at your side and expect soon to release additional wheat now that others have taken substantial steps toward matching our effort.

You must also find satisfaction in the measures your government has taken during the past year to give greater emphasis to agriculture, to carry out massive countrywide family planning programs, to liberalize

---

[1] Source: Johnson Library, National Security File, Head of State Correspondence File, India, Vol. I, Prime Minister Gandhi Correspondence, 1/11/66–9/12/67. No classification marking. Transmitted to New Delhi in telegram 192874, May 11. (National Archives and Records Administration, RG 59, Central Files 1967–69, POL INDIA–US)

[2] Document 436.

imports and to relax controls over industrial investment and production. I am confident that pressing along the course set by these new policies can bring India to its goal of a self-reliant economy and a rising standard of living.

My government will continue to do its share in the international effort to support India. But I am sure you know that our ability to help will depend in considerable measure on whether both India and Pakistan can contain—and even reduce—military spending. Further increases in defense spending by your government and Pakistan's would make it far more difficult for me to mobilize support for economic development in either country. I know you want to hold down defense spending, and I believe President Ayub is motivated by a similar resolve.

On my side, I think that my greatest satisfaction recently has come from those signs which hold out the possibility of a relaxation of world tensions—even a slight relaxation. We have concluded the Outer Space Treaty[3] and made some progress in negotiating a non-proliferation treaty. In this great effort—which will help determine the kind of world in which our children and grandchildren will live—we welcome the constructive support of India.

That is why we were especially glad to see Mr. Jha at this time. As you know, I have long been aware of India's security problems vis-à-vis hostile China. Obviously, your country's concern has increased since October 1964, when the Chinese exploded their first atomic device. I stated publicly then that the United States is willing to extend its strong support to any country which has chosen not to use its nuclear technology to build weapons if that country should be threatened with nuclear weapons. I can understand why you have raised the question with the major nuclear weapons states of making clear their concern and intentions in this connection.

As I told Mr. Jha, I am deeply interested in the trend of his discussions in Moscow, including the illustrative text of a possible Soviet declaration on nuclear assurances. My advisers and I are carefully exploring the possibilities in this approach, and we will be in touch with you.

Our great and continuing disappointment in this past year is that the relentless efforts we have made to find a peaceful and honorable resolution of the Vietnam conflict have thus far failed to evoke a corresponding response from the other side. The United States stands for peace and justice with honor, and I shall continue to pursue peace. A

---

[3] Reference is to the treaty on principles governing the activities of states in the exploration and use of outer space signed in Washington, London, and Moscow on January 27. The treaty entered into force on October 10. (18 UST 2410)

just solution, of course, cannot be one which denies the right of our Vietnamese friends to independence and self-determination, without external coercion. I would hope that those nations which share a stake in these precious principles would support my country's efforts to find an honorable peace.

With warmest good wishes.

Sincerely,

Lyndon B. Johnson

442. Memorandum From the President's Special Assistant (Rostow) to President Johnson[1]

Washington, May 10, 1967.

SUBJECT

Next Step on Indian Food

We can now consider releasing some of the 3 million tons offered in your food message and endorsed by the Joint Congressional Resolution. The Consortium has accepted food aid as an integral part of its work and has incorporated food targets in its overall economic goals. We have firm matching food-related aid for $97.6 million—about half of the $190 million target. Therefore, Secretary Freeman and Bill Gaud recommend (Tab A)[2] releasing 1.5 million tons costing about $100 million (375,000 tons of that in sorghum) plus $12 million in vegetable oil.

Our main debate has been over whether to release all three million tons now. Secretary Freeman earlier recommended (Tab C)[3] that we go ahead with the whole amount in order to boost our domestic market and take some of the steam out of farmers' criticism that the Administration deliberately increased wheat acreage last year to drive prices down. The fact is that excellent crops in Canada and elsewhere have undercut prices, but Freeman has had a hard time selling that to the farmers. However, he agrees that we should go with only half that amount now provided we release the rest early this summer.

---

[1] Source: Johnson Library, National Security File, Country File, India, Vol. IX, Memos & Miscellaneous, 3–7/67. Confidential.

[2] Not found attached.

[3] An April 17 memorandum from Freeman to the President was attached at Tab C.

We have good prospect of getting pretty firm matching aid for the rest of the 3 million tons by the end of June. Because food is not available for this purpose, we have devised new ways of breaking loose special financial aid that the Indians can use in buying food. These are frankly pioneering ventures in the Consortium, and we can measure their success only by seeing whether they actually make it possible for India to buy additional food. We understand that the Indians are already placing orders for 745,000 tons of grain and plan to spend another $50 million as soon as some of this financial aid is firm. But we will have a clearer idea when the Consortium working group meets again in June to pin down final arrangements for debt relief and for freeing other pledged money for food purchases.

I know this second half of our matching effort may look a bit fuzzy to you at this stage. However, after reviewing the figures (see Schultze's memo attached),[4] I regard it as an honest effort to achieve matching aid that is truly additional to regular economic aid. We're still in midstream, so I would not mislead you by saying that our job is done. But this is a sound effort in which I think you can have faith.

Arrival figures definitely dipped between January and May but will pick up again in June.

January—685,900	May—608,000
February—821,000	June—980,000
March—654,000	July—523,000
April—678,000	

Releasing 1.5 million tons now on top of expected Indian purchases should keep the Indian ports full for at least another three months and give us time after the June Consortium meeting to assess further matching, Indian purchases and best timing for our final release.

Meanwhile, we are approaching the peak of the famine in Bihar. State, Agriculture and AID will shortly recommend a new CARE disaster program of about $50 million. I have insisted on a careful study which will not be along for several days. However, I wanted you to be aware of that additional proposal as you make this decision.

The other recommendation in this package is to authorize $50 million program loan (Tab B)[4] as the first slice of our own economic aid. India's fiscal year began 1 April and the Consortium pledging season will not take place until October. One of our objectives at the April meeting was to encourage as much early pledging as possible. Before that meeting, you authorized our offering this $50 million pro-

---

[4] Not found attached.

vided the Consortium meet all the targets it set for itself then. Because the food matching and debt relief questions are still pending, we have not actually met those targets. However, Gaud feels progress was good enough that holding off on this loan will not substantially increase our leverage. On the other hand, no one feels under great pressure to rush it through now. Gene's feeling is that everybody has done a good job, that we want India to get moving and that we should let this go now. On balance, I recommend approving.

I suggest you use Charlie Schultze's detailed rundown (attached) as your decision document.

Walt

---

443. Telegram From the Department of State to the Embassy in India[1]

Washington, May 13, 1967, 2:04 p.m.

194039. For Ambassador from the Secretary.

1. You have seen the President's statement in his most recent letter to PriMin Gandhi (State 192874),[2] that further increases in Indian and Pakistani defense spending would intensify his difficulties in mobilizing support for economic development in either country. I am counting on your making sure that the proper people in the GOI have fully considered the implication of our position and that this will be reflected in the budget to be presented May 25. I know you have already done missionary work on the subject, but hope that during the critical days ahead you will do everything you can to persuade the GOI that the new defense budget should clearly demonstrate India's intention to limit and cut back its defense spending.

2. I am well aware of the hazards of asserting this kind of influence. You may assure the Indian Government that we have no desire to embarrass it; while there is no secret about our general position on Indian and Pakistani defense spending, we consider the specific repre-

---

[1] Source: National Archives and Records Administration, RG 59, Central Files 1967–69, POL INDIA–US. Secret; Exdis. Drafted by Coon on May 12; cleared by Heck, Spain, Handley, and Battle; and approved by Rusk. A handwritten marginal notation reads: "OK/L," suggesting that the telegram was cleared with the President. Repeated to Rawalpindi.

[2] See Document 441.

sentations I am asking you to undertake, and the President's letter, as highly privileged information. Obviously whatever steps both governments take in this regard, they will want to present them as their own considered decisions and not the result of our pressures.

3. You may assure the Indian officials to whom you make these representations that we are working on their Pakistani friends with equal vigor. You might point out, however, that since the Indian budget will be the first of the two to be presented, the Indians through chronological necessity will have to set the pattern: a unilateral cutback, not made publicly contingent on a matching Pakistani response.

4. Should the GOI raise questions such as the interrelationships of this matter to Kashmir, Pak-Chinese collusion etc., you should indicate we are also sensitive to these issues but tying them together deflects us from the matter at hand: defense budget levels. We must start somewhere and this is the time and place to begin to break the vicious circle.

5. I hope that the GOI is correctly interpreting the care with which we are looking into their proposed purchase of U.S.-equity Hawker Hunter aircraft from the UK as another sign of the seriousness of our intention to implement our new military supply policy towards both Pakistan and India in a manner that will inhibit either from actions that could fuel an arms race.[3]

6. FYI: Ambassadors Nehru and Hilaly will be called in next week to be given the same message.[4] End FYI.

Rusk

---

[3] In telegram 16938 from New Delhi, May 18, Bowles responded that he and the rest of the Embassy staff had been pressing the Indian Government for several months to reduce military spending. He added that on receipt of the Secretary's cable he had met with Morarji Desai for another discussion of the subject. Desai agreed with the arguments put forward concerning the importance of reducing military expenditures, but pointed to the difficulty of doing so as long as China remained a serious threat and Pakistan maintained an unyielding attitude on the issues which troubled relations on the subcontinent. (National Archives and Records Administration, RG 59, Central Files 1967–69, DEF 1 INDIA)

[4] Assistant Secretary Battle called in Ambassador Hilaly on May 20 to discuss Pakistan's defense expenditure. Battle referred to upcoming Indian and Pakistani budgets as a unique opportunity for both nations to begin cutting defense spending. He stressed long-standing U.S. concern on the subject at the highest levels, and pointed out that any increase in Pakistan's defense spending would make the task of mobilizing support in Congress for economic development funds for Pakistan very difficult. (Telegram 199452 to Rawalpindi, May 22; ibid., DEF 1 PAK)

444. Telegram From the Ambassador to India (Bowles) to the President's Special Assistant (Rostow)[1]

New Delhi, May 17, 1967, 1224Z.

Although I am sure that you are doing all that you can do to help keep the Indian food program moving, I would like in this private and personal message to underscore the critical nature of the food situation here.

Because of unseasonal rains there is increasing hope of scraping by without mass tragedy. But this is wholly dependent upon uninterrupted maintenance of food supplies. While we are encouraged that the situation has been managed better and has deteriorated less than we feared, a large number of highly responsible people, including Steb,[2] who have recently visited drought-stricken areas have come back with appalling stories of great human misery and malnutrition.

These reports come to us at a time when we are at a point, if we are not already past that point, where another drop in our food grain arrivals can no longer be prevented. When the experts assured us last fall there would be no slow down in the pipeline, they turned out to be wrong. Grain unloadings for the month of January were a little more than half of what they might have been. Even if we act today to ship whatever share of the 3 million tons the President is willing to approve there is a serious question whether a similar interruption will not be inevitable.

I would also like to emphasize my concern about our recommendation for an additional $75 million worth of Title II foodstuffs. This would enable volunteer agencies which are doing a magnificent job in critical areas to increase the food ration from 5 ounces to 8 ounces, to extend the coverage to many desperately needy people who are trying to survive on roots, bark and grasses and keep the volunteer agency program going into December.

As to the stories, which I understand appeared in the *Washington Star*, about Indian confusion and indifference, I can only say they are grossly inaccurate and irresponsible. When we first came to realize last fall that Bihar and U.P. would be in deep trouble we agreed that a disaster of this kind could not have hit in a worse place. In Madras, Maharastra, Gujerat, or the Punjab a crash relief effort could be handled with great effectiveness. However Bihar and U.P. are the two most

---

[1] Source: Johnson Library, National Security File, Country File, India, Exchanges with Bowles. Secret. The message was [text *not declassified*] addressed to the White House.

[2] Mrs. Bowles.

backward and poorly administered states in India. Nevertheless the government employees in that area, ably supported by the volunteer agencies and by steadily increasing numbers of dedicated volunteers, students and others, have been putting on a really remarkable performance in the face of enormous difficulties. The story of the diversion of Canadian milk is also a gross distortion. In fact the transfer was a temporary one which was approved by the Canadian Government to be made up later. The supply is already en route.

I don't like to trouble you, the President and the Secretary with emotional appeals at a time which I know is difficult for all of you. However, I would be failing in my responsibility if I did not tell you that the situation is desperately serious and is sure to grow worse before it gets better. If you could secure some prompt decisions for us a great many people here would begin to breathe a bit easier.[3]

---

[3] Bowles sent a similar appeal to Katzenbach on May 24 in telegram 17293 from New Delhi. (National Archives and Records Administration, RG 59, Central Files 1967–69, SOC 10 INDIA)

---

445. Telegram From the Department of State to the Embassy in India[1]

Washington, May 18, 1967, 9:39 p.m.

197663. Eyes Only for Ambassador from the Secretary. I have just received a FBIS excerpt (embargoed until morning May 19) reporting a message for Ho Chi Minh's birthday from Prime Minister to Ho Chi Minh, expressing the hope that "the Vietnamese people will have the good fortune of having Ho Chi Minh's wise and dedicated leadership to guide them." We cannot, of course, expect India to agree with every view of ours in international affairs. But we do expect, where vital interests of the US are concerned, that India would at least take a non-aligned position. If Mrs. Gandhi thinks that we are just good guys and will take a lot of punishment without reaction, she is underestimating the mood of the American people while we are carrying such heavy burdens. If she feels that she must slant her "non-alignment" in favor

---

[1] Source: National Archives and Records Administration, RG 59, Central Files 1967–69, POL INDIA–US. Secret; Immediate; Nodis. Drafted and approved by Rusk.

of the Communist world in order to keep her credentials clear with Moscow, she cannot maintain her credentials with the US. The general mood in this country does not permit us to act like an old cow which continues to give milk, however often one kicks her in the flanks. No one has spent more time and energy and political capital in trying to help India than has President Johnson. No one is carrying a greater burden in serving one of India's vital interests, namely, in organizing a durable peace in Southeast Asia, than the President and the young men in this country who are being killed in Viet-Nam.

If Mrs. Gandhi's message to Ho Chi Minh is as I have reported on the basis of preliminary information, I do hope that you will find some way to let her know that the interests of this country are not being served by this kind of cringing and that the US can be just as tough as everybody else in deciding whether relations are to be friendly, correct and cool, or on a basis of active opposition. I hope our early information is wrong. I have met with Congressional groups five times during the first three days of this week trying to carry some of the burdens of such policies as supporting India. Just today I faced in the House Foreign Affairs Committee a demand for a full debate on the floor of the House of Representatives of the exact amounts and terms of our aid to India in the light of India's own policies.

Perhaps my struggle here makes me a bit edgy but I really do think that those who pretend to be non-aligned should in fact be non-aligned and stay away from questions on which they are not prepared to take any serious responsibility. Mrs. Gandhi has no constituency in North Viet-Nam and Ho Chi Minh has no constituency in India but Mrs. Gandhi surely does have a major constituency among the American people and she had better give some thought on how to nurse it from time to time. Her own personal relations with the President of the US are perhaps the most important single aspect of India's future safety and viability. The President has not spoken to me about this but you and I know that this, too, is something which Mrs. Gandhi should think about.[2]

Rusk

---

[2] Bowles cabled in response that he understood and appreciated Rusk's strong reaction to Gandhi's birthday greetings to Ho Chi Minh. He characterized the decision to send such greetings as "silly, stupid, and misguided." Bowles felt, however, that it would be a mistake to take up the issue with Gandhi, who he said was in a tense mood with a variety of problems pressing upon her. Desai was unavailable, so Bowles took up Rusk's complaint with P.M. Harsar, who had become Executive Assistant to the Prime Minister following the resignation of L.K. Jha. Harsar agreed that the dispatch of such a message and its public release were embarrassing errors, which he attributed to disorganization and bias in the Ministry of Foreign Affairs. He anticipated taking action that would prevent similar incidents in future. (Telegram 17034 from New Delhi, May 19; ibid.) Rostow sent copies of Rusk's cable and Bowles' reply to President Johnson on May 24. (Johnson Library, National Security File, Country File, India, Vol. IX, Cables, 3–7/67)

446. Telegram From the President's Special Assistant (Rostow) to President Johnson in Texas[1]

Washington, May 29, 1967, 1829Z.

CAP 67484. I am sorry to do this by wire, but the World Bank's Pakistan consortium meets Wednesday[2] morning in London, and I would like to clear our position with you today if possible.

The Freeman–Gaud memo[3] I have recommends: (1) We announce our willingness—subject to Congressional appropriations—to consider providing non-project aid at the same level as last year ($140 million). (2) We agree to negotiate a loan for $25 million of that $140 million now from FY 1967 funds for fertilizer imports. (3) We inform the Government of Pakistan that we are prepared to provide 1 million tons of wheat as an initial agreement against FY 1968 targets.

There is no question that Pakistan's general economic and agricultural performance make it one of the most deserving of our aid recipients. As you read in Dick Gilbert's memo,[4] we're looking for a major breakthrough in grain production in the next year or two. Moreover, Ayub will read our ability to announce a positive response Wednesday as an important signal of your intent to continue rebuilding our relationship.

Our $140 million would be 40–47 per cent of Pakistan's overall requirement for $300–350 million in non-project aid, which the consortium is expected to endorse. This will support continued import liberalization.

The 1 million tons of wheat would permit Pakistan to import quickly against a projected need for about 2.25 million tons this year. Moving quickly would help undercut price increases. We would take a reading later in the year on Pakistan's remaining needs after its crop is in, but would include now about $24 million in cotton, oil and tallow.

I recommend your approval of the basic package; Secretary Fowler and Charles Schultze are aboard.

---

[1] Source: Johnson Library, National Security File, Country File, Pakistan, Vol. VII, Memos, 10/66–7/67. Confidential. A handwritten "L" on the telegram indicates it was seen by the President.

[2] May 31.

[3] Reference is to a May 25 memorandum from Gaud to the President concerning the Pakistan aid consortium meeting. Gaud noted in his memorandum that the Department of Agriculture concurred in the recommendations. (Johnson Library, National Security File, Country File, Pakistan, Vol. VII, Memos, 10/66–7/67)

[4] Reference is to a May 9 memorandum dealing with the assistance programs for India and Pakistan prepared by Richard V. Gilbert, an economist and specialist on South Asia. (Ibid., Memos to the President, Walt W. Rostow, Vol. 29, May 25–31, 1967) Rostow recommended Gilbert's analysis to President Johnson in a May 25 memorandum. (Ibid.)

There are two additional issues on which we need your judgement:

1. Freeman and Gaud recommend that we make clear to the Pak Government that we expect half of Pakistan's remaining FY1968 commercial wheat purchases to be made in the US. Treasury endorses this recommendation. State recognizes that we have applied this formula to the huge Indian program but recommends against generalizing this condition to apply to other PL 480 agreements. Charlie Schultze supports State's position because he fears that gain in sales under this small program (at most 250,000 tons or $15 million) is not worth the risk of being charged with bad faith under the Kennedy Round food aid and grain agreement. As you recall, all exporters agreed there not to preempt specified shares of commercial wheat markets as a condition for giving food aid. This was part of the price we paid to get other nations to share the food aid burden.

My compromise of this would be to let the Paks know our feelings but not tie them to any percentage. I understand your purpose in the Indian case which is so large as to be in a class by itself. But we probably ought to be careful in the smaller programs. They have already placed FY 1968 orders for 200,000 tons here.

Approve your compromise[5]

Approve strict 50 percent tying

Call me

2. Bill Gaud tried to get Harold Linder[6] to come in on the consortium offer, at least to the extent of a $20–25 million non-project loan for added fertilizer imports. Harold refused, so there is no such recommendation before you. But I have been trying at every turn to get the Ex-Im Bank more fully engaged in our more promising less developed countries. Given our hopes of making Pakistan the next success story both for our aid program and for the war on hunger, this seems an excellent opportunity to bring Ex-Im along. However, at this stage the only way we could do that would be for me to call Harold on your instruction and ask him to reconsider. I would listen to his arguments but try to persuade him. Pakistan itself has delayed its steel mill—for which Ex-Im had set aside $85 million—to concentrate on agriculture. I think using some of that money to help the Pak fertilizer program would be a fair reward for good sense.

You may tell Linder I would like to offer

---

[5] Johnson checked this option.

[6] President and Chairman of the Export-Import Bank.

$20–25 million unless there are overriding arguments against

See if you can persuade him; just say I asked you to inquire[7]
don't press this round

---

[7] Johnson checked this option.

---

447. Memorandum From the President's Special Assistant (Rostow) to President Johnson[1]

Washington, May 30, 1967.

SUBJECT

Status of Indian Aid Requests

As I wired you Saturday,[2] the Indian Government via B.K. Nehru's firm promise has agreed to place 50% of its remaining commercial grain orders in the U.S. this year. On the strength of your Monday approval, we have let the Indians begin buying against their next PL 480 agreement on a reimbursable basis. But the following Indian aid decisions still await your approval:

1. Release 1.5 million tons of wheat and sorghum ($100 million) plus some vegetable oil ($12 million) as recommended by the Freeman–Gaud memo of 10 May (Tab I–A).[3] Our consortium effort has so far produced firm matching for $97.6 million, so the 1.5 million tons have been evenly matched under the terms of your February message to Congress. We stand a good chance of matching the whole $190 million when George Woods completes his debt relief exercise next month, but the famine is reaching its peak, and the pipeline is thinning out. Moving

---

[1] Source: Johnson Library, National Security File, Memos to the President, Walt W. Rostow, Vol. 31, June 13–20, 1967. Confidential.
[2] Reference is to White House telegram 67449 to the LBJ Ranch in Texas, May 27. (Ibid., Vol. 29, May 25–31, 1967)
[3] None of the tabs was attached.

this half of our offer now would keep the Indian ports full as well as help our own market situations.

Release now[4]

See me

2. A $50 million famine relief program for Bihar state, where the famine is worst. This is mainly to broaden the CARE program you launched in your food message to provide nutritional supplement to about half the children and mothers with babies. But we would also tell the Indians this would more than compensate them for the freight differential ($2–3 million) on their extra commercial purchases here. (Tab II)

Approve

See me

3. A $50 million program loan from FY 1967 money recommended in Bill Gaud's memo of 4 May (Tab I–B.) This is the first slice of our non-project loan to support this year's consortium effort to bolster quickly India's exchange reserves and to keep the Indians on the import liberalization route.

Approve

See me[5]

---

[4] Next to this option Rostow wrote: "Under conditions set by the President." Rostow probably annotated this memorandum after reading President Johnson's handwritten response on a May 31 memorandum he sent to the President again making the case for the release of 1.5 million tons of grain to India. The President wrote "OK" on that memorandum but added a note of concern about the fact that only half of the target goal of $190 million of pledges from other donors had been met: "This doesn't smell good—Better get India busy on other 1/2." (Johnson Library, National Security File, Country File, India, India's Food Problem, Vol. IV)

[5] Neither option under paragraphs 2 and 3 is checked on the memorandum.

448.   Memorandum From the President's Special Assistant
(Rostow) to President Johnson[1]

Washington, July 21, 1967, 5:25 p.m.

Mr. President:

In the attached, Messrs. Schultze, Freeman and Gaud[2] recommend
that you authorize an agreement for one million tons of PL–480 wheat
for Pakistan. (The agreement would also contain small quantities of
tallow, oil, cotton and dry milk.) This wheat was part of the package
you approved as our pledge at the May meeting of the Pakistan Aid
Consortium.

Schultze's memorandum (Tab A) gives a good summary of the
case for the agreement and the things the Paks have agreed to do in
return—*including buying most of their commercial wheat purchases from
the United States.*

I recommend you approve.

Walt

Approve[3]

Disapprove

Speak to me

---

[1] Source: Johnson Library, National Security File, Country File, Pakistan, Vol. VII,
Memos, 10/66–7/67. Confidential.

[2] Reference is to a July 5 memorandum to the President from Freeman and Gaud,
and a July 11 memorandum to the President from Schultze.

[3] Johnson checked this option and added a handwritten notation that reads: "Notify
new ambassador Oehlert who is still here."

449.   Memorandum From the President's Special Assistant (Rostow) to President Johnson[1]

Washington, July 28, 1967, 5:20 p.m.

SUBJECT

Ammunition sales to Pakistan

At Tab A is a draft cable,[2] approved by Katzenbach and Nitze, which further defines our policy on arms sales to India and Pakistan. Because of the current problems on the Hill, I thought you would want to review it.

You will recall that last April we announced a new arms policy for the Sub-Continent. Essentially, we:

—pulled our large military advisory teams out of India and Pakistan, replacing them with small attaché-type offices;
—stopped all grant military aid to both countries, except for a little training;
—banned U.S. sales of military end items to either country;
—announced our intent to stop any third-country military sales to either country over which we had some control, unless such sales contribute to stabilization and/or decline in their military expenditures;
—agreed to make cash sales to both countries of spare parts for equipment we have previously supplied.

Neither country threw its hat in the air about his policy, but both accepted it with reasonable grace. The Paks immediately gave us a list of spare parts they want to buy. The Indians asked to buy some machine tools for an ammunition factory and some books and technical manuals about ammunition manufacturing. We agreed to the small Air Force and Navy spare parts request for Pakistan, as well as the sale of machine tools to India. *The decision now is whether to agree to the larger ($9.2 million) parts request for the Pakistani Army and the technical data request from the Indians.* After a careful analysis, Defense has concluded that the Pak Army request is reasonable, and that the release of information to India on ammunition-making will cause us no problems.

Paragraph 1(a) of the cable raises one additional question—should ammunition be sold under the "spare parts" rule? You know the arguments; if one is willing to supply a breech mechanism necessary to fire a rifle, he looks silly refusing to provide ammunition, which is just as necessary. This must be weighed against the fact that ammunition sales

---

[1] Source: Johnson Library, National Security File, Country File, Pakistan, Vol. VII, Memos, 10/66–7/67. Confidential.

[2] Not printed.

may present a tougher public relations problem than ordinary spare parts. After much soul-searching, Katzenbach and Nitze have decided to recommend that we agree to consider ammunition requests on a case-by-case basis.

On balance, I agree with the recommendation. These are *cash* sales—not the credit sales the Congress is most upset about. They are to be made under an announced policy which has been greeted pretty favorably in the press and on the Hill. If we refuse to follow through, we will lose much of our influence on military policies and expenditures in Pakistan. We would also cost Ben Oehlert a large part of the initial fund of good will he needs in dealing with Ayub. I would advise you to approve the message.

We have *not* checked this move on the Hill. With arms sales a hot issue, the chances of a leak and a distorted story are no worse than even. If you think it necessary, however, I can ask Katzenbach to do some soundings with the appropriate people.

Walt

Approve message[3]

Have Katzenbach check on the Hill and then come back to me

O.K. on the spare parts, but tell the Paks we can't sell ammunition

Disapprove

Speak to me

---

[3] Johnson checked this option and the message was sent to Rawalpindi and New Delhi on July 29 as telegram 14208. (National Archives and Records Administration, RG 59, Central Files 1967–69, DEF 12–5 PAK)

450.   Memorandum From the President's Special Assistant (Rostow) to President Johnson[1]

Washington, August 2, 1967, 1 p.m.

SUBJECT

Food Aid for India—*Act II*

At Tab A is a complicated memorandum from Gaud and Free-man[2]—supported by Rusk and Fowler—recommending a new PL 480 agreement to supply India with a million tons of wheat, along with other minor odds and ends. The memorandum is complex because it is very hard as a technical matter (1) to define precisely what we mean by "matching", and, whatever our definition, (2) to be sure how much matching is actually going on. Your advisers have concluded that by any measure we now have enough matching to justify another one million tons of U.S. wheat.

The Matching Problem

You will recall that your India food message—and the Congressional Resolution which followed—spoke in terms of 3 million tons of additional wheat this calendar year if we got "appropriate" matching from other donors. By May, we had collected pledges totalling $97 million in new food or food-related aid from the others. Therefore, you authorized a first agreement providing for 1.5 million tons of wheat, worth about $95 million.

We now have a further $122 million in aid pledges from other donors—most of it in the form of debt relief. (See table at Tab B for breakdown.)[3] Both the World Bank and the Indians argue that this is more than enough in matching pledges to justify releasing another 1.5 million tons, completing the full 3 million tons contemplated in the Resolution.

However, our matching proposal was designed to draw *additional* aid resources from the other donors—resources that otherwise would not have been supplied to India. Neither we nor the Indians gain anything from ear-marking aid as food-related which is clearly not over and above what these countries have traditionally provided through the

---

[1] Source: Johnson Library, National Security File, Country File, India, India's Food Problem, Vol. IV. Secret. A handwritten note on the memorandum reads, "Rec'd 3:32 pm."

[2] Memorandum from Freeman and Gaud to the President, August 1. (Ibid., Memos to the President, Vol. 37, August 1–10, 1967)

[3] The table, which lists the offers of food assistance on a country-by-country basis, is ibid., NSC Histories, Indian Famine, August 1966–February 1967, Vol. IV.

consortium anyway. We just don't know how much of this "new" $122 million is additional. (Indeed, we know that some of it definitely is *not* additional—the British have told us outright that their contribution will be subtracted from their consortium pledge.) Until we see what our brethren do at the consortium meeting in October, we just won't know whether they are really providing something extra or whether they are simply putting new labels on old benefits.

Despite a hot debate, your advisers have not been able to agree on precisely how much more U.S. wheat we can provide now without threatening the matching principle. But they do agree that we can clearly justify at least a million tons. The acid test of additionality is how much new grain from non-PL 480 sources the Indians have come up with since our last PL 480 agreement was authorized. Any new grain from other donors is clearly eligible for matching. Any Indian purchases beyond what they had programed in May reflect the Indians' belief that the new aid they have received has freed more of their foreign exchange for buying food. This is not a foolproof method of measuring additionality. The Indians may be diverting money from their development budget to buy food, or they may just be wrong about what the new aid will do for them. But our people doubt that much diversion is going on, and they point out that there are tremendous pressures on the Indians to be right about their foreign exchange situation.

Applying this test, we find that India has scared up 1 million tons in new grain from non-PL 480 sources since last May. They have a new Australian donation of 150,000 tons, 200,000 tons in the process of being donated by the Soviet Union and 650,000 tons in additional Indian commercial purchases. (There is some question about whether the Russians will come through, but the Indians have officially informed us that they will buy enough more themselves to cover any Russian shortfall.) Accepting the tough principle that the best proof of additionality is how much a new non-PL 480 grain the Indians actually import, we can clearly justify another million tons from the U.S. This is what your advisers recommend.

The Need

The Congressional Resolution and the entire matching exercise are aimed at an overall target of 10 million tons of grain imports into India this year—through food aid and commercial purchases—without forcing India to slow down her development program. According to our latest estimates, she may be able to squeeze by with 9.5 million tons without mass starvation. Even with her greatly expanded commercial purchases (44% more than last year), this will require the full 3 million tons from us mentioned in the Resolution. The central Government's stocks are now down to about two weeks' supply and dropping. Food shortages are very important factors in touch-and-go political situations in several major states. The outlook for the next four months is bleak at best. Without our grain it is hard to see how Mrs. Gandhi could handle it without completely derailing the fertilizer imports and other development expenditures which will stimulate larger Indian crops in the future.

And the timing is urgent, as usual. The 1.5 million tons authorized in May will be fully delivered by the middle of September. Because of the closing of Suez and the strain on tanker supply, it now takes six weeks' leadtime to book ships, rather than 3–4. Thus, if the pipeline is not to break, we need a decision this week.

The Politics

The political case for food aid to India is neither better nor much worse than when you last reviewed it. The Indians played an irritating and often stupid role in the Middle East crisis. Internally, Mrs. Gandhi remains as weak and indecisive as ever; her party is having more and more difficulty maintaining its power in the states. Nobody is certain how long she can hang on. However, there is a powerful case that this makes food aid more rather than less imperative. If change is to come to India, it is very much in our interest that it be as peaceful as possible. But peaceful change is most unlikely in a context of starvation.

The major immediate political point is that if we do let the pipeline break, our relations with the Gandhi government—and any successor— will turn very sour indeed. And our public explanation of why we didn't come through (presumably because we don't think we have been matched) would not be supported by the World Bank or other "neutral" observers. We could also expect some trouble at home.

The Alternatives

You should know that this recommendation is the result of careful examination of four alternatives:

1. Do nothing until after the October consortium meeting.
2. Do a million tons now and worry later about the additional half-million tons required to meet the 3 million tons mentioned in the Resolution.
3. Do 1.25 million tons now, on condition the Indians buy the other 250,000 tons.
4. Do 1.5 million tons now, arguing that we have matching for at least 1 million tons and that we are not committed to 1–1 matching. (On this alternative, we would have at least 6–5 matching for the full year.)

No. 1 was dismissed as impossible in view of the urgent need and the dangers of delay. No. 3 was rejected as too time-consuming and too likely to force India to dip into development funds to pay for wheat. No. 4, strongly favored by State and AID, was rejected because Fowler and Freeman believe it would amount to abandoning the matching principle.

That left us with No. 2 as the lowest common denominator. Its principal drawback is that it leaves us with a further 500,000 ton requirement late this year for which we now have no matching prospects in sight. The choice between Nos. 2 and 4 (1 million tons versus 1.5 million tons) reduces to whether we want a 1.5 million ton package now with an unmatched component or risk a half-million ton package later with no matching at all. You may wish to consider going ahead with the full 1.5 million now.

Indian Purchases from the U.S.

The Indians have taken the procurement lesson to heart. Their commercial grain purchases in the U.S. this year will be at least four times[4] what they bought last year. And they are following through on their promise to buy at least half of all their commercial grain from us, beginning last May.

All of the self-help conditions we have worked out for the earlier agreement would also apply to this one.

Recommendation

I recommend you approve the Gaud–Freeman memorandum.[5]

Walt

Approve Gaud–Freeman memo (1 million tons)

I want to hear more; set up a meeting for me with Rusk, Freeman, Gaud, etc.[6]

No

See me[7]

---

[4] Johnson circled "four times" and wrote in the margin "How much?"

[5] Rostow added a handwritten postscript that reads: "We started out to match $190 million. We have matched somewhere between (say) $160 million and $219 million. We are taking the lower figure here. In fact, the exercise has been more successful than we could have hoped."

[6] Johnson checked this option.

[7] Johnson checked this option and added the following handwritten note: "Get me someone to argue the other side please." On August 4, in response to the President's instruction, Rostow sent him three memoranda drafted by the NSC Staff that made the case for three options: no more food now, one million tons now, and 1^{1}/2 million tons now. (Johnson Library, National Security File, Country File, India, India's Food Problem, Vol. IV)

451.   Special National Intelligence Estimate[1]

SNIE 31/32–67   Washington, August 3, 1967.

THE INDO-PAKISTANI ARMS RACE AND ITS ECONOMIC IMPLICATIONS

The Problem

To estimate the military capabilities of India and Pakistan over the next several years in conflicts: (a) India against Pakistan; (b) India against China, (c) India against Pakistan and China; and to assess the economic implications of present and probable future force levels in India and Pakistan.[2]

Scope Note

This estimate considers only the relative military capabilities of India, Pakistan, and China in a conventional war. It does not discuss the numerous domestic and international problems which would be engendered in any such conflicts.

Conclusions

A. India's arms buildup began after the Indo-Chinese war of 1962, and was initially directed to improving India's military capabilities against China, particularly in mountain warfare and air defense. Since the 1965 Indo-Pakistani war, India has further expanded its forces and has strengthened units facing Pakistan. India is now modernizing its armored units and its air force, and appears assured of a steady supply of modern military equipment over the next several years, mainly from the USSR.

B. Pakistan, with substantial US assistance, started to modernize its armed forces in the mid-1950's. At the start of the 1965 war, Pakistan's ground forces were one-fourth the size of India's. Pakistan is seeking to bring them up to one-third India's size, and has made some progress. Achievement of this goal is, however, likely to be considerably delayed. Since 1965, China has been Pakistan's principal supplier, though considerable matériel has been ordered from France and various

---

[1] Source: Central Intelligence Agency, Job 79–R01012A, ODDI Registry of NIE and SNIE Files. Secret; Controlled Dissem; Limited Distribution. According to a note on the cover sheet, the estimate was submitted by Deputy Director of Central Intelligence Rufus Taylor, and concurred in by the U.S. Intelligence Board on August 3.

[2] In the Annex we examine the economic implications of a specific reduction of the armed forces of India and Pakistan as outlined by the Department of Defense. [Footnote in the source text.]

sources in Western Europe. Over the next few years, Pakistan appears less likely than India to have an assured source of large quantities of modern armaments and will probably fall further behind in this respect.

C. We believe that India would win any war with Pakistan alone. India could also probably repel a Chinese attack before it could reach the Indian plains. We believe that India's armed forces would be able to prevent a major breakthrough by combined Chinese-Pakistani forces equipped with conventional weapons, though they might have to yield ground in Ladakh and northeastern India.

D. The arms race has aggravated the economic difficulties of both India and Pakistan. In real terms, India's defense spending is about 100 percent, and Pakistan's about 70 percent higher than in 1961. But for both countries, the greatest burden has probably been the drain on foreign exchange. This includes the expenditure of hard currency for military items, and in the case of India, the export to the USSR of commodities which would otherwise have earned hard currency. Such outlays by both countries are now about three times what they were in 1961. This has caused cutbacks in development programs and in imports for civilian production.

[Here follow the 11-page Discussion section of the estimate and a 1-page annex entitled "Implications of a Force Reduction."]

452. Notes of Meeting[1]

Washington, August 8, 1967, 1:25–2:50 p.m.

NOTES OF THE PRESIDENT'S MEETING
WITH
SECRETARY McNAMARA
UNDER SECRETARY KATZENBACH
GEORGE CHRISTIAN
WALT ROSTOW
JOE CALIFANO

At the Tuesday luncheon

The following areas were discussed at the meeting:

1. Indian Wheat

The President said he had just completed discussions with Ambassador Chester Bowles,[2] who reported that large quantities of wheat had been damaged by rains.

The President pointed out that he was unsure what course of action we should follow about additional requests for aid to India.

Mr. Rostow said he was forwarding to the President a set of alternatives for his consideration. The President said it would appeal to him if some other nation would recognize their responsibilities in this nation, even the Russians.

[Here follows discussion unrelated to South Asia.]

---

[1] Source: Johnson Library, Tom Johnson's Notes of Meetings, Aug. 8, 1967—1:25 p.m., Tuesday Luncheon Group. Top Secret; Literally Eyes Only. Prepared by White House Deputy Press Secretary Tom Johnson. According to the President's Daily Diary, the luncheon took place in the White House. (Ibid.)

[2] Bowles was in Washington for consultations and met with the President at noon on August 8. No other record of that meeting has been found.

453. Memorandum From the President's Special Assistant (Rostow) to President Johnson[1]

Washington, August 10, 1967, noon.

SUBJECT

Wheat for India

At Tab A, Messrs. Katzenbach and Gaud restate for you the options on India food.[2] In addition to the three choices presented at last Saturday's meeting (no food now; 1 million tons; and 1.5 million tons), this memorandum adds two more variants:

—Do a million tons, but announce it as a cut in the 3 million ton target established in the Congressional Resolution. That is, the emphasis in our announcement would be that budgetary problems had forced us to cut back from the 3 million tons set out in the Resolution to 2.5 million tons. Since we have already supplied 1.5 million tons, this leaves 1 million.

—Authorize no new agreement now, but allow the Indians to buy wheat in the United States on the understanding that the bill will be paid either through a new PL 480 agreement later, or from Indian foreign exchange.

The first variant reflects the only way we have been able to devise whereby this decision could be presented as consistent with your cuts in domestic spending. A 500,000 ton cut in the wheat target we announced in the Message and the Resolution might compare favorably with the cuts you must make in domestic food programs. On the debit side, it would make it impossible for you to come up with more wheat later in the year if the Indian situation gets desperate, and it would probably subject you to international criticism that we had committed ourselves to go to 3 million tons if matched and then gone back on our word.

The second new option is a stopgap designed to get the food into India while we decide the terms. But you should know that if you approve this it will be very difficult to avoid picking up the tab for whatever the Indians have contracted for between now and whenever we decide what more we are willing to do through PL 480. In any event, the 600,000 tons your advisers suggest would buy us only about a month before the question would come up again.

---

[1] Source: Johnson Library, National Security File, Country File, India, India's Food Problem, Vol. IV. Confidential. A handwritten note on the memorandum reads, "Rec'd 2:15 pm."

[2] Reference is to an August 9 memorandum from Katzenbach and Gaud to the President. (Ibid.)

At Tab B is a short discussion of debt relief[3]—what it is and how it relates to other forms of aid.

At Tab C is a paper you asked Ed Hamilton to do outlining how we might go at the others for more matching funds,[4] assuming we are unwilling to accept debt relief. Hamilton emphatically does *not* recommend this. He has supplied it at your request.

The Katzenbach/Gaud memo ends with a recommendation of a flat *1.5 million tons now.* That is, and has always been, the State/AID preference. Fowler and Freeman support *1 million tons now,* and are strongly opposed to going any further. Katzenbach and Gaud would *not* strongly object to this solution.

In my bones, I think we should do the 1.5 million tons now if we are going to have to do that much by the end of the year. If the domestic politics of the budget problem simply won't permit that amount, I think you should approve 1 million tons now, covering it in a public announcement by slamming the door on the last 500,000 tons mentioned in the Congressional Resolution.

Walt

1. Go ahead with 1.5 million tons now.

2. Go ahead with 1 million tons now. Our public posture should be that further authorizations will be considered as necessary.

3. Go ahead with the 1 million tons, but slam the door in public on the last half-million tons in the Congressional Resolution.

4. Tell the Indians to go ahead on the reimbursable basis. We will decide later what we can do through PL 480.

5. I want to have another go at the other donors. Give me a detailed proposal filling out the scenario at Tab B.

6. Tell the Indians we can do nothing more for them now.

7. See me.[5]

---

[3] Reference is to an undated memorandum drafted by Eugene Rostow entitled "Debt Relief as Matching." (Ibid., NSC Histories, Indian Famine, August 1966–February 1967, Vol. IV)

[4] Reference is to an August 10 memorandum from Hamilton to the President. (Ibid., Memos to the President, Walt Rostow, Vol. 37, August 1–10, 1967)

[5] Johnson checked this option and added the following handwritten note: "We must get State and Gaud nearer to our problem. They are in the sky."

454. Memorandum From George W. Ball to President Johnson[1]

Washington, August 15, 1967.

I have reviewed the supplemental memorandum with regard to the India Food Aid Program, submitted by Bill Gaud and Eugene Rostow,[2] and have the following comments.

The basic question emerged clearly from our Saturday[3] morning discussion: should you stretch the concept of matching beyond what the average man (including the average Congressman) would ordinarily understand by the term in order to send an additional 1.5 million tons of grain to India?

In answering the question one must take into account a number of considerations:

a. Would Congress believe an assertion that other nations have met the matching test? If not, what effect would this have on your other programs?

b. Has the Indian political performance been such as to justify our stretching a point to provide them additional grain?

c. Have other donor nations been led to offer additional help on the assumption that, on the basis of their offers, we would now put up the remaining 1.5 million tons?

d. How seriously would India's development be prejudiced by the need to pay for all or part of the 1.5 million tons from its own resources?

You might wish to ask State and AID to submit answers to these questions. In appraising their answers I would suggest that the following considerations be kept in mind:

1. The question of providing grain should not be determined as though it were a humanitarian matter. It is not a question of whether Indians starve but of how the Indian Government uses its finite store of resources. We know that it is now using some of those resources injudiciously—for an inflated defense budget and some unrealistic development schemes. If they had the will to do so, the Indians should be able to fund the additional 1.5 million tons by simply cutting out some of the floss.

---

[1] Source: Johnson Library, National Security File, Country File, India, India's Food Problem, Vol. IV. Secret. Ball left his position as Under Secretary of State on September 30, 1966, and was counsel with the law firm of Cleary, Gottlieb, Stein and Hamilton, and chairman of Lehman Brothers International, Ltd., in New York. Rostow sent Ball's memorandum to the President on August 16 under a covering memorandum. (Ibid.)

[2] Reference is to an August 8 memorandum from Gaud and Rostow to the President, entitled "India Food Aid Program." (Ibid.) Johnson sent a note to Rostow on August 10 instructing him to send the memorandum to Ball for comment. (Ibid.)

[3] August 12.

2. The Indians have been characteristically bloody-minded about the Middle East (their active support of Nasser) and about Vietnam (Ho Chi Minh's birthday telegram). They have certainly not earned the right to special consideration on the basis of performance.

3. I would not worry much about the reaction of other donor countries. We have carried this burden for a long time and they have done damn little.

4. A credible case has not been made that other donor nations have met the matching test *by any qualitative standard.* This becomes clear if one asks the following questions:

a. Could we expect Congress to agree that the World Bank's willingness to grant a one-year postponement of $50 million of debt repayment is the equivalent, for purposes of "matching," to an American offer of $50 million of wheat on PL 480 terms? The same question can be asked with regard to the "debt relief offers" of $33.6 million made by the United Kingdom and $14.5 million made by West Germany; in fact, 80 percent of what is represented as "matching" comes in the form of debt relief.[4]

The critical point, it seems to me, is that, in view of India's hopeless repayment schedule, most of this debt will have to be rolled over anyway, and this raises the point that has haunted us so long: since we have furnished help on a long-term basis while other countries have provided assistance on a shorter term basis, the Europeans constantly get credit for additional aid by extending old debts while we have to put up new money.

b. Should the Administration take the position that there has been matching when some items are clearly not additional and we cannot know whether others are additional until after the October Consortium meeting?

I would be inclined to answer the foregoing questions in the negative, without meaning in any way to diminish the achievement of Gene Rostow and others in the Government who have certainly obtained concessions that donor countries would not otherwise have made.

Clearly there has been matching with respect to the first step of 96.7 million dollars, but most if not all of the rest is arguable and ambiguous and I heartily disagree with the implication in the Gaud–Rostow memorandum that we can rest any part of our case for matching on the ground that *the Indian Government and the IBRD consider* that contributions by others have "more than matched" our 190 million dollar offer. They are scarcely disinterested parties.

---

[4] Ball sent another memorandum to President Johnson on August 18, expressing second thoughts about what constituted matching contributions. He suggested that before making a decision, Johnson get a good appreciation of what had been agreed upon with the other donors concerning the standards governing matching contributions. (Johnson Library, National Security File, Country File, India, Vol X, Memos and Miscellaneous, 8/67–2/68)

On the other hand, I would agree with Messrs. Gaud and Rostow that you are not legally bound by the fifty–fifty matching principle. The decision must be made in terms of what is the wisest course after all the issues have been balanced. I think Congress would accept your decision to go ahead with *some* additional food aid to India (I would stop short of the full 1.5 million tons). But if you decide to do this, I would recommend that you do not overstate what has been done by other donor countries although the Administration should certainly take credit for inducing other nations to grant aid and make concessions that would not otherwise have been forthcoming.

The realistic option, it seems to me, is either to provide no additional wheat or to offer perhaps one-half or two-thirds of the 1.5 million tons requested. This would make clear to Congress that you are not accepting the matching performance of other donor nations at face value but are discounting it on qualitative grounds. Nonetheless, it would be a generous offer and should go far toward enabling India to meet her food requirements while still protecting her development program.

GWB

---

455. Memorandum From Edward Hamilton of the National Security Council Staff to President Johnson[1]

Washington, August 21, 1967.

SUBJECT

George Ball's Recommendation on Food for India

1. Ball's memorandum (Tab A)[2] recommends that you:

—authorize 750,000–1 million tons now;
—tell the Congress that we do *not* accept at face value the debt relief offered by other donors. Therefore, we have discounted it in calculating how much more grain we can supply under the matching principle.

---

[1] Source: Johnson Library, National Security File, Country File, India, India's Food Problem, Vol. IV. Confidential. A handwritten note on the memorandum reads, "Rec'd 2:05 pm."
[2] Document 454.

2. The advantage of Ball's plan is that we could move now and still have some protection from the charge that we had accepted debt relief as matching before we knew (i) on what terms debt would be rescheduled, and (ii) whether the debt relief would be additional in regular consortium contributions.

3. The problems with the Ball proposal are that:

—our discount would have to be arbitrary. There is no rationale for counting debt relief as 50% eligible for matching, as distinguished from 70% or 30% or 0%.

—it would discredit debt relief as a form of aid. Up to now we have joined the World Bank in pushing the Europeans to re-schedule India's enormous debt burden. As a practical matter, it is easier to get this kind of aid than to push large appropriation bills through parliaments. We are going to need it badly in the years ahead.

—it would be seen abroad as welshing on our commitments. It was made clear at every stage of the matching exercise that we *would* accept debt relief as matching—in Gene Rostow's testimony, in the US position at the March consortium meeting, and in the consortium press release following the April meeting.

—it would make it impossible for us to supply any more wheat this year if the Indian situation becomes desperate. (The consensus among your advisers is that we probably will have to do more.)

4. After reading the Ball proposal, you asked that we put together a package of about 750,000 tons, supported by an air tight matching argument along the Ball line.

5. The plain fact is that we *cannot* justify more than about 400,000 tons on a one-to-one matching basis without using debt relief. Nor is there any prospect for further matching contributions this calendar year.

6. Therefore, *if* we must decide now whether and how much we have been matched, I am afraid I can offer you no choices other than the ones you have already heard.

7. There is, however, one further alternative I would suggest as superior to Ball's, though still less attractive, in my judgment, than the earlier proposals. Essentially, you might:

—authorize a million tons now.

—tell the Congress that we do not know at this point precisely how much we have been matched, and we will not know until after the October consortium meeting.

—we don't want the Indians to starve and the subcontinent to dissolve into political chaos while we are determining precisely how much we have been matched.

—therefore, we are going ahead with this tranche of grain *on the explicit understanding that we will deduct from our consortium pledge any shortfall between the cost of this grain and the amount of "matching" funds we discover are real and additional.*

8. Advantage of this approach is that it puts off the decision on the precise amount and additionality of matching until the time when

we are better equipped to make such a finding. It also protects us from any charge that we are spending one penny more than we believe has been matched. At the same time it would let us move the wheat *now*. It would put maximum heat on the Indians and the other donors to make sure that the European consortium contributions are as generous as possible. It might even bail us out of a difficult situation at the consortium meeting, since the slashes in the Foreign Aid Bill will put us in a poor position to come up with a large consortium pledge in any event.

9. The disadvantge of this approach is that it might add the last straw to an already over-burdened camel. The consortium is in serious danger of falling apart. Everybody is tired; everybody is unhappy with the Indians; and everybody has budget problems. It is possible that the European reaction to our loading on this additional threat would be to wash their hands of the whole business. We could expect George Woods and company to be pretty upset as well. In both cases, however, the reaction would be much less violent than what we could expect if we refused to accept debt relief as matching.

10. On balance, Mr. President, I am still in favor of the proposals you reviewed last week. But I understand and share your displeasure with the Indians. And I know that there are problems to which those of us who aren't elected are too apt to be insensitive. Thus, if we cannot go ahead with the earlier recommendation I would vote for the "we'll deduct it from our consortium pledge" approach instead of George Ball's plan.

EKH

1. Tell State I want to go ahead with the Ball plan at 750,000 tons _____;
at 1 million tons _____.

2. Tell State I want to take the "we'll deduct it from our consortium pledge" line at 750,000 tons _____; 1 million tons _____.

3. Go ahead with as much as we can claim has been matched without using debt relief (about 400,000 tons).

4. Go ahead with 1 million tons as originally recommended.

5. Speak to me.[3]

---

[3] None of the options is checked on the memorandum.

456.   Memorandum From the President's Special Assistant (Rostow) to President Johnson[1]

Washington, August 31, 1967, 11 a.m.

SUBJECT

India Food

After careful consideration, it seems to me that there are four criteria your India food decision should meet:

1. It should combine:

—enough more wheat to avoid in India the most serious political unrest and human misery associated with food shortages—or at least to counter the argument that disaster followed directly from U.S. parsimony, and

—enough conditions and limitation to keep the pressure on the Indians to produce and the other donors to come across at the October consortium meeting in such a way that their matching debt roll-overs prove to be additional.

2. It should be consistent with our commitments to other donors throughout the matching exercise. (Specifically, I am afraid this means that we cannot now refuse to accept—or decide to discount by some percentage—debt relief as eligible for food matching.)

3. It should provide a matching argument which the average Congressman with other things on his mind can understand and accept (see Tabs A and B).[2]

4. It should give you maximum protection from both the domestic political dangers:

—the danger of maintaining wheat shipments to India while cutting expenditures for domestic food distribution programs; and

—the partially conflicting danger of the political heat from falling U.S. farm prices and the charge that you are cutting P.L. 480 to take the costs of fighting inflation out of the hide of the American farmer.

I don't pretend to have a perfect solution. But I believe the following formula comes as close as we can:

1. Authorize one million tons of wheat now.

2. Announce that we will be constantly reviewing the need for more, particularly in the light of our very difficult budget problem. (We could try here to establish the fact that when wheat prices are falling it does *not* help the budget to cut P.L. 480—indeed, it hurts.)

---

[1] Source: Johnson Library, National Security File, NSC Histories, Indian Famine, August 1966–February 1967, Vol. IV. Confidential.

[2] At Tabs A and B were undated draft matching arguments.

3. On matching, take the line that we do not yet know with precision the extent to which we have been matched with additional resources. We shall only know after the October consortium meeting—but even then, with a margin of uncertainty. But there is substantial evidence that we have been matched—at least up to the cost of one million tons—and we don't want the Indians to starve while we make absolutely sure.

4. To assure that the principle of matching is preserved, the amount of our 1967 consortium contribution will not be final until we are certain how much of the aid and debt relief which has been generated since last May is *real* and *additional* to ordinary consortium contributions. (We would leave the strong implication that any shortfall between the cost of this wheat and the total of real additional aid will be deducted from our consortium contribution.)

5. Before the announcement, have Freeman, Katzenbach, and Gaud brief the Congressional leadership, the Chairmen, and ranking minority members of the foreign affairs committees, the agriculture committees and the appropriations committees. If there is a howl of protest, they should report back to you before making the announcement.

This solution would:

—leave it open for you later either to ship more wheat or to cut back for domestic political reasons;
—keep the heat on the Indians and the other consortium members; and
—give you maximum protection—though none too much—with the Congress.

I think all your advisers would support this plan, though you may wish to check it with Secretary Rusk.

A final word, Mr. President.

With all its imperfections, this has been a remarkable exercise you have mounted. These are the results.

1. Australia entered and Canada confirmed the legitimacy of being in the food-aid business—ending the notion once and for all that food aid was a question of U.S. surpluses.

2. France, Japan, Germany, Scandinavia, Belgium, the U.K., the Netherlands, and Italy accepted the legitimacy, in principle, of their contributing to food aid with either food production resources or money.

3. At the time of great difficulty in generating aid funds, we all managed somehow to keep enough foreign exchange flowing to permit India to continue the relaxation of bureaucratic controls.

4. We have embedded in Indian policy firmly a top priority for agriculture.

5. We have engaged the World Bank for the first time in the food aid business on the consortium principle and have a basis for keeping it there on that principle—which guarantees reasonable burden-sharing in the future.

6. If you wished to proceed with the full 1.5 million tons for, say, domestic price reasons—I believe a viable case could be made.[3]

Walt

---

[3] Jim Jones added a handwritten note on the memorandum that reads: "Appeals to me. Do not mention w prices." The quote apparently reflects President Johnson's response to Rostow's recommendation to authorize the shipment of 1 million tons of wheat. On September 1 the White House released a statement to the press that confirmed the President's decision to authorize the shipment of an additional 1 million tons of wheat to India. For text, see *American Foreign Policy: Current Documents, 1967*, pp. 765–766. When he was informed of the decision, Ambassador Nehru's response was "thank God." (Memorandum from Walt Rostow to the President, September 1; Johnson Library, National Security File, Memos to the President, Walt Rostow, Vol. 40, September 1–10, 1967) On September 9 Indian Minister for Food and Agriculture Jagjivan Ram wrote to Secretary Freeman to express the gratitude of his government for the shipment of grain. (Ibid., Vol. 41, September 11–14, 1967)

---

457.   Telegram From the Department of State to the Embassy in India[1]

Washington, September 7, 1967, 1819Z.

33331. Subj: U.S. Policy Toward Indo-Pak Relations and Our Bilateral Security Relations with Each Country.

1. As addressee posts are aware, recent months have seen gradual evolution in U.S. policy toward military supply relations with India and Pakistan, flowing from policy changes announced last April. Some of these changes have at least implicitly intersected with broader ques-

---

[1] Source: National Archives and Records Administration, RG 59, Central Files 1967–69, POL INDIA–PAK. Secret; Limdis. Drafted by Coon on August 30. Cleared by Heck, Spain, Handley (draft), Vice Chairman of Policy Planning Council Joseph A. Yager, Linebaugh (S/P), Wolf (G/PM), Brown (IO/UNP), Roy (EUR/SOV), Rees (AID/NESA), and Deputy Assistant Secretary of Defense for Near East and South Asia Harry H. Schwartz. Approved by Rusk. Also sent to Rawalpindi and repeated to London, Moscow, USUN, and CINCSTRIKE.

tions; e.g., recent discussion (State 14083)[2] of how far we should go in telling each Government what we are doing with the other involves to some degree question of comparative priority we attach as between efforts to resolve or reduce Indo-Pak disputes and our efforts to strengthen our bilateral security relations with each.

2. Posts have made valuable contributions to the policy discussion which has preceded and accompanied these changes. New Delhi's 16350,[3] for example, flagged desirability of our all agreeing amongst ourselves on assumptions underlying our actions and posture in subcontinent. This in turn led to recent SNIE[4] on military threat and force level questions. Although results necessarily somewhat limited, SNIE has established certain conclusions which we can accept and build on.

3. The policy conclusions set forth below are designed serve as guideposts for further operational decisions in coming months. (We are deliberately omitting for present any consideration of nuclear question; NPT draft has just been tabled in Geneva, and it unusually difficult right now to predict how questions of nuclear weapons and security will interrelate with other subcontinent security questions.)

A. Indo-Pak reconciliation remains an important U.S. goal; its achievement would greatly facilitate achievement of important U.S. bilateral and regional objectives. Experience has shown, however, that our resources and influence operate at maximum disadvantage when directed toward goal of reconciliation; in fact good historical case can be made that under present circumstances we cannot bring about reconciliation no matter how hard we try. It follows that our efforts should usually be directed more toward strengthening our bilateral relations with each country than toward bringing them together. There are however certain regional issues we must continue to address, viz.:

1) Renewed conflict: We have clearly indicated that if the two countries insist on fighting each other again they will be dealing us out of picture as significant supplier of resources. This is a solid and uncomplicated position which we should all continue to recognize and enunciate as a fundamental element of our policy.

2) Arms race: We have no intention of fueling an Indo-Pak arms race either directly or indirectly and we intend to continue to apply diplomatic and perhaps other pressures toward persuading each Government to hold line and in due course reduce its defense expenditures.

3) Regional initiatives: Our desire not to be caught in middle should not inhibit initiatives, particularly in economic areas which might bring the countries together or head off issues that might evolve in the political or security fields. As example of former we are examining possibility of encouraging an initiative by a third country to seek

---

[2] The reference is in error and has not been further identified.
[3] Not found.
[4] Document 451.

to restore normal links between the two countries in telecommunications, air, road and rail services, and trade and transit rights. An example of latter might be effort solve Eastern waters problem and thereby avert casus belli through IBRD or other third party initiative.

B. This means that while we will continue to counsel each Government to follow moderation and restraint in its dealings with the other we should, except under currently unforeseeable circumstances, avoid taking substantive positions or otherwise become substantively involved on Kashmir or other Indo–Pak issues not cited above.

C. Each Government can be expected to continue to press with imagination and vigor its ongoing efforts to embarrass our relations with the other. We should discourage such efforts as actively as we can without causing significant damage to our bilateral relationships.

D. The reasons why it is in our interest to strengthen our bilateral relations in security matters differ as between India and Pakistan. With India we have a more immediate threat of military pressure from China; the Chinese threat in Pakistan from our view is more of a political nature at this time. In each case we have additional important interest of strengthening our ability to help keep down defense spending. Strategically our Indian interest is stronger but we cannot afford to pursue it so single-mindedly as to destroy or severely restrict our Pakistani interest. It would be most desirable if GOI could be brought at least implicitly to recognize that it was in their interest too that we maintain a constructive relation with Paks. Indians should understand this relationship based on our conviction that we should seek avoid isolating Pakistan, and thereby driving her closer to Chicoms. We also believe Pakistan's political stability and economic progress sufficiently significant for long range security of sub-continent to justify our continued support and encouragement.

E. Since we are not going to revert to major military supply role in either country in foreseeable future our assets for strengthening our security relationships will remain restricted. But they will not be negligible, and skillful orchestration of a variety of different activities can, as suggested in New Delhi's A–14,[5] increase our total effectiveness. Our role as economic and food aid supplier will provide underlying strength to our efforts in security field though economic aid leverage can usually be applied with precision only in cases where the objective we seek is directly related to the purposes for which aid is being provided.

F. Task that lies ahead in each country is difficult per se and further complicated by inevitable impact of what we do in either country on the other. Very few of decisions that will face us will be clear-cut; this

---

[5] Dated July 6. (National Archives and Records Administration, RG 59, Central Files 1967–69, POL 1 INDIA–PAK)

makes it all the more important that we continue operate on same wavelength.

Rusk

---

458. Telegram From the Department of State to the Embassy in India[1]

Washington, September 15, 1967, 2327Z.

38363. Subject: Morarji Desai's visit to Washington.

1. Indian Deputy Prime Minister Morarji Desai left Washington for New York September 14 after three crowded days of discussions here. Visit went well and frank and useful discussions were held in cordial atmosphere. Only jarring note was Desai's tactlessness at press conference which antagonized most of journalists present. On other hand, *Washington Post* commented favorably editorially on visit.

2. During course of September 11–13 visit Desai saw President, Vice President, Secretaries Rusk, McNamara,[2] Fowler and Freeman, as well as Gaud, Linder, Governor Harriman and George Woods. He met with members of Senate Foreign Relations Committee, addressed National Press Club and had several sessions with press.

3. The discussions were wide ranging and covered India's agricultural problems and policies, political developments in India, outlook for aid and debt relief, family planning, India's relations with Southeast and East Asia, China, Vietnam, Middle East, nuclear policy, NPT and security assurances.

4. No proposals were advanced by either side and none were expected. Each of foregoing topics was discussed in some detail at least once and several, such as China and Vietnam, were covered several times. For the most part Desai followed the GOI position on these issues. He was inflexible on the Middle East and voiced well-known Indian ob-

---

[1] Source: National Archives and Records Administration, RG 59, Central Files 1967–69, POL 7 INDIA. Secret. Also sent as telegram Toros 59. Drafted by Heck, cleared by Special Assistant to the Under Secretary for Political Affairs Thomas O. Enders, and approved by Handley. Repeated to Bombay, Calcutta, Madras, Hong Kong, Kathmandu, London, Moscow, Ottawa, Tokyo, Rawalpindi, and CINCSTRIKE.

[2] Desai met with Rusk and Humphrey on September 11, with Johnson on September 12, and with McNamara on September 13. Records of these meetings are, respectively, ibid.; ibid., NEA/INC Files: Lot 71 D 174, Economic Affairs (Gen.), Morarji Desai Visit; Johnson Library, National Security File, Name File, Vice President, July 1, 1966, Vol. II; ibid., Country File, India, Vol. X, Memos and Miscellaneous, 8/67–2/68; and Washington National Records Center, RG 330, OSD Files: FRC 73 A 1250, India 121.6.

jections to NPT. He discounted efficacy of security assurances. He strongly reaffirmed policy of present Congress Government of foregoing nuclear weapons.

5. Desai recognized the need for further Indian initiatives to improve relations with countries of Southeast Asia and with Japan and Australia. He expressed concern over China's continued threat to India. The subject of relations with Pakistan came up inferentially and Kashmir was not raised by either side.

6. Desai was given a full briefing on Congressional and public attitudes to aid and on U.S. resources that may be available for India next year. He was told not to expect more than 250 million additional DL funds.

7. Desai departed from his script most notably when discussing Vietnam. He displayed considerable interest in our views and in developments in North and South Vietnam. Much of his questioning reflected concern that South Vietnamese might become restive and withdraw their support of U.S., thereby putting us in awkward position. He readily agreed to proposition that we could not expect to discontinue bombing in North while North Vietnamese continued their infiltration and aggression in South Vietnam. He repeated this view on TV show September 13, stating with regard to our bombing policy "we do want that these operations of destruction stop, and not stop only on one side, they have to stop on both sides."

8. We believe that Desai left with clear picture of our views on topics covered and on aid prospects. Two proposals emerged during discussions with Secretary and with McNamara: (a) to undertake strictly private, informal periodic meetings for full exchange of views on mutual problems and policies in order identify areas of agreement and disagreement and understand why we disagree when we agree to do so. Desai suggested these talks include parliamentarians and private leaders who have confidence of their government; (b) to consider a cost-effectiveness study of Indian defense spending with the aim of buying same amount of security with less money. This arose during discussion with Secretary McNamara who said we would help whenever asked. Desai expressed interest in concept.

9. We will be following up on both suggestions and in meantime welcome Embassy's comments on how best to get them going.

10. Septels report details on discussions on aid and economic matters[3] and on military and security subjects.[4] Memcons follow.

Rusk

---

[3] Telegram 37916 to New Delhi, September 15. (National Archives and Records Administration, RG 59, Central Files 1967–69, POL 7 INDIA)

[4] Telegram 38829 to New Delhi, September 16. (Ibid.)

459. Memorandum From the President's Special Assistant
(Rostow) to President Johnson[1]

Washington, October 5, 1967, 2 p.m.

SUBJECT

Situation Report: Selling Wheat to Pakistan

As you look ahead to decisions on the full range of food aid, I thought you would want to know the specific considerations we have to take into account in a case like Pakistan's.

The Paks calculated their food import requirements for FY 1968 at *2.25 million* tons of wheat. We have already provided 1.25 million. They purchased another 200,000 tons. They're getting 66,000 tons from Canada and Australia. That leaves *734,000 tons* for them to get.

Of this *734,000 tons*, we have told them we will provide 500,000 tons under PL 480. As you instructed, we have offered to provide half of the final 234,000 tons if the Paks would match it with cash purchases. This means we sell them *117,000* tons for about *$9 million*.

When the instruction to sell the 117,000 tons went to Ben Oehlert, he cabled back his deep concern. (His cable is at Tab A.)[2] The AID economists share his feelings. The argument goes like this:

—The Paks have already bought 200,000 tons, and they have squeezed their foreign exchange budget to the bone. (Pakistan's foreign exchange now stands at $166 million—enough to finance five weeks of imports. Most countries are very uncomfortable with anything less than enough foreign exchange for four months' imports.) In the last two years they have tripled their cash food buying in world markets.

—Their wheat *reserves* are dangerously low. Their target is a reasonable 950,000 tons. They are now at 300,000 tons. With scheduled imports—including our 734,000 tons, if they get it all—they will only raise reserves to 500,000 tons by June 1968.

—If we play our cards well, we have a good chance of a *big* package of wheat for Pakistan—purchases and PL 480—for the whole of calendar 1968. The total might run over 3 million tons ($195 million). With that kind of bait, we might get them to agree to a much higher level of purchases, starting within the next three months. If we use the time between now and the abundant new Pak harvest (December) wrangling about this small portion, we may lose the opportunity for

---

[1] Source: Johnson Library, National Security File, Country File, Pakistan, Vol. VIII, Memos, 8/67–4/68. Secret. A handwritten note on the memorandum reads, "Rec'd 10/5/67, 4:15 p." A handwritten "L" indicates that the President saw it.
[2] Reference is to telegram 1074 from Rawalpindi, September 29. (National Archives and Records Administration, RG 59, Central Files 1967–69, AID (US) 15–8 PAK)

the large deal which would really help our domestic wheat price and our balance of payments.

—The Paks will need every penny of foreign exchange to back up the import reform planned for January 1968. AID and the IMF have encouraged this reform. The Paks badly need to devalue. They need to simplify import controls to let market forces work freely and take up slack in the economy. They also need to provide more incentives for exports. The hard fact is that our forcing even a small additional outlay (the $9 million we're asking them to spend on our wheat) might strengthen the factions in the GOP who oppose reform so that the January package would be canceled.

—Finally, we must look at the wheat bargain in terms of our overall negotiating position with the Paks. Our large, important intelligence installation at Peshawar comes up for renegotiation in mid-1968. The current betting is no better than even money that Ayub can hold off his neutralists well enough to sign a renewal. Whether he can will be largely determined by the tone of our relations over the next few months. The wheat business certainly won't kill the Peshawar renewal, but it will be one more irritant and one less generosity which we could cite next year as evidence of our reliable good will. (This is particularly true in light of the fact that we have been urging the Paks to conserve foreign exchange to maintain their economic health.)

Despite these concerns, Oehlert is carrying out the instruction we have given him to try to work out a sale and will see Ayub Friday morning. We have given him firm instructions along the lines you directed (Tab B).[3] Judging from Ben's effectiveness so far, we just might do it—however adamant the Paks (below Ayub) seem, and however reluctant Ben and people here in town are about this particular deal. Ayub might well conclude that even a big sacrifice now—and helping you when you need it—will pay dividends in the long run.

Meanwhile, we have been playing the same tune with the Pakistan Finance Minister who is now in Washington. I told him Wednesday[4] about the staggering load you carry with the budget, and how important even small wheat sales are to your ability to go on financing programs in the poor countries.

We certainly have to look carefully at this whole range of questions before we come to you for food decisions. I am not convinced, for example, that Pakistan *should* devalue right now. I have commissioned a study to examine this problem in a new light. Maybe the Paks will just put us off until 1968, taking only 617,000 tons now with a promise to buy the 117,000 in next year's deal. They just might take that risk with their food stocks.

---

[3] Reference is to telegram 49058 to Rawalpindi, October 5, in which Oehlert was instructed to "stick to 500,000 ton offer." (Ibid.)

[4] A summary of Rostow's conversation on October 4 with Finance Minister N.M. Uqaili was sent to Rawalpindi in telegram 49050, October 5. (Ibid., POL 15–1 PAK)

I take your time with all this because it is reasonably typical. I've got the "sell wheat" message loud and clear, and I think the bureaucracy is getting it too. But I thought you would want to know what kinds of judgments are involved. I will have papers to you within the next few days looking toward an NSC meeting on the whole food outlook. The meeting is now scheduled for next Wednesday (October 11).

Walt

---

460. Memorandum From Edward Hamilton of the National Security Council Staff to the President's Special Assistant (Rostow)[1]

Washington, October 6, 1967, noon.

SUBJECT

Indian Arms Purchases from the Soviets

We have disturbing new evidence this morning that the Indians are dealing from the bottom of the deck on arms purchases. The story goes as follows:

1. Last June, after considerable soul searching, we granted permission to the British to sell 24 Hawker–Hunter fighters to India on explicit GOI assurances that:

—these would be *replacement* aircraft which would not increase total Indian combat capacity; and

—that the Indians would *not* buy any aircraft from the Soviet Union. (There had been rumors for months that the Indians were trying to swing a deal for a large number—perhaps 200—of SU–7 fighter bombers.)

2. British-Indian negotiations have been underway ever since, and the Indians have become more and more concerned that the British are not a dependable source of supply—e.g., it now appears that the Brits have only 17 planes to sell rather than the 24 the Indians wanted.

3. We had a cocktail party rumor last week that the Indians and the Soviets were about to sign a contract providing for 200 SU–7's at $1 million each. (Hawker–Hunters cost $200,000 per copy.)

---

[1] Source: Johnson Library, National Security File, Country File, India, Vol. X, Memos and Miscellaneous, 8/67–2/68. Secret.

4. Yesterday our DCM in Delhi spoke to the Defense Ministry official who had given the original assurance against SU–7's (copy of the message at Tab A).[2] The conversation was imprecise, but the gist of it seemed to be that: (i) the Indians are going to buy SU–7's from the Soviets; (ii) they believe this is necessary because of the short supply of British fighters, the need for a fighter bomber for use in the north, and the fact that the Paks have Mirage fighter bombers; and (iii) they will argue that their June assurance was limited to "fresh procurement" and that this does not represent bad faith. (It is not at all clear what "fresh procurement" means. It may mean that any aircraft purchased for replacement purposes is not covered by the assurance. In any event, it is clearly a transparent attempt to circumvent a promise which couldn't have been more categorical.) I don't need to lecture you on the idiocy of this action. It would represent bad faith with us, escalation of the arms race on the subcontinent, serious complication of our relations with the Paks, and a further blow to slim hopes we now have for generating some enthusiasm in the Indian Aid Consortium. (Aside from the distaste every donor feels for the worsening of Indo–Pak military problems, this contract—if it is anything like the size it is rumored to be—would certainly result in considerable diversion from development to defense.) In addition, we could expect real trouble on the Hill. Senator Symington knows and has followed the Hawker–Hunter deal very closely and could certainly be expected to reflect his displeasure with this development in an amendment to the Foreign Aid Appropriation Bill.

State has the following steps in train to head this off:

1. A strong cable to Bowles to read the riot act to Mrs. Gandhi.[3] (She leaves Monday for Eastern Europe, so this will have to be over

---

[2] Telegram 4150 from New Delhi, October 5. (National Archives and Records Administration, RG 59, Central Files 1967–69, Central Files, DEF 12–5 INDIA)

[3] Reference is to telegram 50373 to New Delhi, October 6. (Ibid., DEF 19–6 USSR) Bowles cabled on October 9 that he was unable to take up the issue of the SU–7s with Prime Minister Gandhi because she was leaving for a trip to Eastern Europe. He took up the issue instead with Morarji Desai. Desai's initial reaction was one of "sharp but unfocused irritation." India, he said, was confronted with a serious security threat in China and could not allow foreigners to judge the strength India needed to meet that threat. He also noted that Pakistan was building up its air force with purchases from Iran, Germany, and France. Bowles pressed the importance of reducing defense expenditures, and Desai agreed to raise the question of the purchase of the SU–7s with Defense Secretary Shankar. (Telegram 4310 from New Delhi; ibid.) Bowles met with Shankar on October 10, and Shankar defended the purchase of SU–7s as an agreement negotiated with the Soviet Union in February or March 1966, well in advance of the assurances offered the United States in June 1967 concerning additional purchases of Soviet aircraft. In response to Bowles' question concerning the size of the purchase, Shankar said that the number of SU–7s involved was much smaller than the rumored 200. (Telegram 4432 from New Delhi, October 11; ibid.)

the weekend.) I transmitted to the drafters my own view that no language is too strong for use in this cable.

2. An immediate meeting between Secretary Rusk and B.K. Nehru.

3. Talks with the British, both here and in London. (We don't yet know precisely where the Hawker–Hunter negotiations stand and whether they could be reversed.)

4. A Monday meeting between McNamara and Swaran Singh,[4] the Indian Defense Minister. Singh is in town for other reasons, but we can certainly take advantage of his presence for this.

I think these steps are fine as far as they go. But they may not be nearly enough. The Indians have been debating this problem and probably negotiating quietly with the Soviets for months. I doubt that it will be possible to turn them around at this point with anything less than our biggest guns. If we don't seem to be making progress over the next few days, I would suggest a Presidential letter—or perhaps even a quiet visit by a special emissary of the President. In the present mood of the Congress, a great deal hangs on whether we are able to turn this off. I think it is fair to say that public knowledge of a deal of this size at this time would almost certainly cost us a very sizeable chunk of our foreign aid appropriation—perhaps enough to eliminate aid to India.

I will keep you informed.

EH

---

[4] McNamara met with Singh on Monday October 9 and discussed the importance of holding down India's defense expenditures. He did not bring up the issue of the SU–7 fighter bombers, however. (Memorandum of conversation, October 9; Washington National Records Center, RG 330, OSD Files: FRC 77–0075, Memoranda of conversation between Secretary McNamara and Heads of State (other than NATO))

461. Memorandum From the President's Special Assistant (Rostow) to President Johnson[1]

Washington, October 10, 1967, 6 p.m.

SUBJECT

NSC Meeting on Food Aid (Noon, Wednesday, October 11)

I think this meeting can serve two useful purposes:

—to give you a clear picture of the outlook for food aid; and
—to give you a chance to instruct us on what kind of food aid programs we should try to put together in the major customer countries, particularly India and Pakistan.

Papers

Attached are two Freeman–Gaud papers which have been prepared for this meeting. At Tab A[2] is a response to your request to the Secretary of State to examine each of our present food aid programs to find ways to move more wheat. At Tab B[3] is a special memorandum on India which recommends a large wheat program in 1968 and spells out your major options on amounts, conditions, and matching arrangements.

The Wheat Picture

Orville Freeman's PL 480 wheat target for FY 1968 is about 11 million tons. We have a little less than 6 million tons now contracted or under negotiation. An additional 2 million tons will be provided through our donation programs. *The immediate problem is to find ways to move another 3 million tons in the next 8 months.* It is clear that we can't hope to do it without big programs in India and Pakistan—the potential elsewhere won't add up to more than 500,000 tons.

We also have a longer term problem. The PL 480 target for FY 1969 is also 11 million tons, and we must try to meet that in a year of bumper crops in India and Pakistan. Thus, it is to our advantage to do our bargaining for all of CY 1968 *now,* when our clients need the wheat, rather than wait until next summer when they are rolling in their own. (Obviously, our own concern about domestic wheat prices is not going to decline between now and next November.)

---

[1] Source: Johnson Library, National Security File, Memos to the President, Walt W. Rostow, Vol. 45, Oct. 10–15, 1967. Confidential. Drafted by Hamilton.

[2] Reference is to an October 10 memorandum from Gaud to the President entitled "P. L. 480 Program Possibilities." (Ibid.)

[3] Reference is to an October 10 memorandum from Freeman and Gaud to the President entitled "Food Aid for India in 1968." (Ibid., Vol. 46, Oct. 16–20, 1967)

You should know, however, that Freeman and Schultze think that meeting our PL 480 targets will probably *not* lead to any dramatic rise in domestic wheat prices. The grain traders know what our targets are. They have taken them into account in deciding what price to offer. The only prediction we can make with confidence is that if we do *not* meet our targets, the wheat price will fall further.

India

How we handle India will largely determine how much wheat we move. The monsoon is holding up well; chances look better and better for a bumper crop of 95 million tons of food grains. We don't know precisely how much the Indians will need to import, but nobody is guessing higher than 7–8 million tons. Estimates of how much they really *must* import range as low as 3–4 million tons. *We have settled on a PL 480 target for India of a little more than 6 million tons during calendar 1968.*

It seems to me that we have three objectives to serve in designing this year's approach to food aid to India:

—to move as much wheat as possible;
—to get the Indians to take the policy steps necessary to make use of the economic lift provided by a good harvest; and
—to preserve the matching principle.

These objectives are at least partially conflicting. For example, if we insist on full matching of every bag of wheat by other donors, it is the unanimous consensus of your advisers that we will not move more than 1 million tons.

There is an additional complication this year in that 1–1^1/2 million tons of the total we can move will be for government-owned buffer stocks that allow the GOI to run a CCC-type price support program, and provide for internal food emergencies. This grain would go directly into the hands of the Food Corporation of India for storage and use from time to time as required. (We would hope to get the GOI to match it with their own domestic buying which in itself would serve to support producer prices and help to avoid a sharp price drop which could undo much of the economic benefit of the bumper harvest.)

The paper at Tab B sets out three policy options for next year:

1. insist on full matching;
2. a one-year agreement to provide a base amount of wheat (say the 3^1/2 million tons we supplied last year), plus an amount for building buffer stocks (1–1^1/2 million tons)—all this *without matching*. In addition, we would offer to match any contributions from other donors. (The estimate is that these would be about 1 million tons in such contributions. This would result in our moving upwards of 6 million tons.)

3. A six-month agreement providing for a base amount (again $3^1/2$ million tons) plus 1 million for buffer stocks, with *no* matching requirement and no commitment on what we would do in the last half of 1968. (We would justify the fact of no matching requirement on the ground that the International Grains Agreement is scheduled to take effect on July 1, 1968, and provides that other donors must provide 2.3 million tons of wheat per year to poor countries. Our pitch would be that this guarantees the matching principle.)

Even with our best efforts, option 1—full matching—would move only about 1 million tons of wheat during 1968 and make it impossible for us to meet our target either in this fiscal year or in next fiscal year. It would eliminate any leverage we might have to get the Indians to reform their economic policies.

Option 2 would probably result in our moving about 6 million tons, of which 1 million tons would be matched by other donors. It would give us a reasonable shot at getting the Indians to make the reforms.

Option 3 would result in moving about $4^1/2$ million tons of grain in the first half of 1968 and leave room for more. It would give us some basis for negotiating the reform package. *This is the option recommended by Freeman and Gaud.*

You should be aware that both options 2 and 3 would probably lead to charges that the Administration, having built the matching principle into a major political asset, has abandoned it as soon as it became clear that other donors wouldn't play. We would have a reasonable defense. But there might well be some heat. (Of course, it is not at all certain that it will be in anyone's interest to make this a cause celebre in an election year.)

The timing of our approach to the Indians is critical. The argument in the attached is that if we go at them with a six- or twelve-month package *now* before their big harvest hits the market, we have a reasonable chance of moving a lot of wheat and getting a reasonable quid pro quo in terms of economic reforms and commercial sales. If we string it out piece by piece, our bargaining position will suffer as the immediate need for food declines. *Thus, the recommendation is for a relatively long-term agreement to be negotiated within the next six weeks.*

In light of the above and the discussion tomorrow, we need your general guidance on the following questions:

—How large an India food package should we put together? One month, six months, or a full year?
—How should we treat matching? Should we insist on dollar for dollar matching; should we confine matching to grain above and beyond a base amount and a contribution for buffer stocks, or should we finesse the problem by maintaining that matching is taken care of by the International Grains Agreement?

Pakistan

You will recall commissioning Ben Oehlert to see whether he could sell some wheat to Ayub on the basis that we would match new sales with PL 480. Oehlert had a good meeting with Ayub last week. There was no specific pledge to buy wheat—Ayub said he had to talk to his Finance Minister—but he was friendly and did promise that if he bought wheat from anybody, he would buy it from us. Oehlert sees him again tomorrow morning; we may get an answer then. (This conversation involves only about 120,000 tons—value: $9 million.)

Pakistan's crop outlook is at least as good as India's, probably better because they have more than 2 million acres sown with the new high yield wheat seeds. Our estimate is that the best we can do under PL 480 in CY 1968 is about $1^{1}/_{2}$ million tons, of which 500,000 tons would be for buffer stocks. (There is not as much groundwork in Pakistan as in India on the buffer stock proposition. All we have is an educated guess that they will agree to establish such stocks.)

Our bargaining problem in Pakistan is the same as in India—if we can get a large agreement negotiated before the new crop comes to market, we have a fair chance of moving a lot of wheat and of using the deal to get the Paks to agree to an import reform package which we think is very important. If we can't move quickly, we will be selling a less and less attractive product.

The question on Pakistan is the same as for India: how large a package shall we prepare for immediate negotiation? *The recommendation is that you authorize a CY 1968, full-year package calling for 1.5 million tons.*

Other Customers

The memorandum at Tab A reflects a careful canvass of all our PL 480 clients looking for ways to substitute food for AID dollars or otherwise to move more wheat usefully. *This review has come up largely empty.* The proposals made at Tab A, taken together, will not increase wheat shipments by more than 500,000 tons at the outside—most of what would be accomplished by expanding our donation programs. The non-donation increases result from conservative re-estimates of the "usual commercial marketings" of the wheat exporters—including the U.S.—in these countries. (We have to be very careful about this; in cases like Korea, every cut we make in usual marketings cuts directly into *our* commercial markets. It does us no good to substitute PL 480 shipments for dollar sales.)

The truth is that ways have not yet been found to make substantial substitution of wheat we have in abundance for dollars we don't. *My own recommendation would be that you tell the group you consider this an interim report, and send them back to work on a final report to be submitted to you by the end of next week.*

Summary Recommendation[4]

I would vote that you give us the following instructions tomorrow:

1. Begin talking to the Indians in terms of a six-month, $4^1/2$ million ton wheat package, to be negotiated immediately. This package would not mention matching on the ground that it is taken care of by the coming into effect of the International Grains Agreement.

2. After the current wheat-sale proposition is settled, begin talking to the Paks about a CY 1968 package of 1.5 million tons.

3. Accept the memorandum at Tab A as just an interim report on the question of substitution of wheat for dollars. Ask for a final report to reach you by the end of next week.

W.W. Rostow[5]

---

[4] There is no indication on the memorandum of the President's response to these recommendations.

[5] Printed from a copy that bears this typed signature.

---

462. Telegram From the Department of State to the Embassy in Pakistan[1]

Washington, October 10, 1967, 0058Z.

51282. Following were main elements meeting between President and Pakistan Foreign Minister Pirzada,[2] October 5. Ambassador Hilaly, Mr. Walt Rostow, and Handley were present.

Pirzada began meeting by saying that President Ayub had asked him to convey warm greetings to the President. The President replied that he hoped Pirzada would remember him to President Ayub for whom he had great admiration.

---

[1] Source: National Archives and Records Administration, RG 59, Central Files 1967–69, POL 7 PAK. Secret; Limdis. Drafted by Handley on October 6. Cleared by Spain and Hamilton (White House) and approved by Handley. Repeated to New Delhi, London, USUN, and Moscow.

[2] Pirzada visited the United States October 5–6. A summary of his meeting with Rusk on October 6 was transmitted to Rawalpindi in telegram 49679, October 6. (Ibid.)

In response to President's question about the situation in UN, Pirzada said on the Near East question he had found things settling down and that situation was far less "agitated" than it was at summer session ESSGA. He thought that a solution was now possible. He said that Ayub had done his best to persuade the Arabs to make a settlement and he believed that most of the Arab countries were now willing to accept the resolution worked out between the U.S. and the Soviets. Everyone was now looking to U.S. He thought that a solution would be entirely possible if something could be done about the refugees and Jerusalem. He said that Pakistan, as a Moslem nation, had very special interest in Jerusalem question. When pressed as to what kind of status he envisaged, he replied that it should be the same as it was on June 4, even though this meant the city would be split. He thought that arrangements could be worked out for access to Jewish holy places. They had found in Moscow that the Soviets were prepared to continue to support the resolution they had discussed with the USG if this were satisfactory to the Arabs.

The President noted that he had heard about the good economic progress being made in Pakistan and wondered if this were continuing. Pirzada replied that they were proud of their economic development and very grateful for assistance given by the U.S. which had made this progress possible. He said that construction of Tarbela, which is now insured by U.S. support, will go a long way to making Pakistan prosperous. He thanked President for his decision to send a team to study Pakistan's watershed problems. The President said that we were pleased to help Pakistan since we were very fond of their people.

Pirzada said that the dedication of the Mangla Dam would take place on November 23 and he hoped the USG would accept the GOP's invitation to send a high level delegation to it. He said that GOP was very pleased with the performance of the American contractor, the Guy F. Atkinson Company, and noted that this company was now bidding for construction of Tarbela.

In response to question on Indo/Pak relations, Pirzada said there can be no relief from tension until the Kashmir hurdle is removed. Kashmir, he said, was considered non-negotiable by the Indians. Meanwhile, the situation in Kashmir had become very serious, with riots taking place and with repression and cruelty being inflicted on people of Kashmir. Every effort should be made to try to bring India to the conference table on Kashmir. The President noted that it would be indeed wonderful if the Kashmir question could be solved. In commenting on post-Tashkent contacts with India, Pirzada did not attribute much importance to the reported upcoming telecommunications meeting. He said there had been a lot of foot dragging on the part of the Indians and that the meeting would be simply to ratify points that had been earlier agreed to by experts on each side. He noted that up to now there had been no firm decision on the delegations since the Indians had delayed for three months in working out the details, but nevertheless he felt sure that the meeting would take place.

The President said that we were very pleased with the reductions in the Pakistan defense budget. Pirzada said that has not been easy since India has increased its budget and is buying submarines, tanks, and sophisticated weapons. That is why, he said, Ayub had gone to Moscow. He had told the Soviets that if they wanted peace in the subcontinent they must stop shipment of sophisticated weapons.

The President and Pirzada briefly discussed the fighting between India and Communist China on the Sikkim border and agreed that at this stage it seemed "inconsequential".

In discussing other aspects of Ayub's visit to Moscow, Pirzada said that Kosygin had been greatly impressed with his visit to the U.S. and his talks with the President. In answer to a question from the President about what the Soviets had said on Viet Nam, Pirzada replied that the Soviets had the impression that if the bombing were stopped, negotiations might take place. The President commented that this was just an impression.

In discussing the food situation Rostow mentioned that he had had a talk with Finance Minister Uquaili the day before regarding commercial purchases of U.S. grain. Hilaly said that Pakistan was in a tight foreign exchange position and would be very reluctant to make additional commercial purchases. Rostow then said that, in all candor, he had to explain the difficult budget and fiscal situation facing the President. He understood their difficulties but the President's problem is also very serious and that at a time when he might be considering the possibility of cutting down on school lunch programs in the U.S., it would be difficult for the American public to understand why additional commercial purchases by Pakistan were not possible.

As the meeting ended, Pirzada said that Ayub had asked him to thank the President for the sale of spare parts for the Pakistan Air Force. Ayub had also asked him to remind the President that Pakistan had made an official request to purchase replacements for aircraft and tanks. The President said that this request was under study, that we were anxious to help but that he had grave difficulties with the Congress on the question of military supplies. He pointed out that even today the Senate and House conferees on MAP had not been able to reach a decision and he was very uncertain as to what the outcome would be. Pirzada then added that Pakistan's request for purchase of spares for the Army had not yet moved. Handley expressed some surprise at this and agreed to look into it.

Rusk

463. **Summary Notes of the 576th Meeting of the National Security Council**[1]

Washington, October 11, 1967, 12:10–12:40 p.m.

U.S. Food Aid

The President: The PL–480 program was initiated as a surplus food program in an attempt to raise the price paid U.S. farmers for their products, principally wheat. It has become an AID problem because we must now substitute bushels of wheat for those dollars which the Congress is not giving us to use in assisting foreign countries economically.

AID Director Gaud: The PL–480 program has gone through three stages. The first stage involved disposal of surplus commodities. Our agreements provided for very easy terms. In the second stage, we made our conditions tougher. In the third stage during which surpluses became shortages, we were unable to do what we wanted to. The present stage involves the usage of the surpluses we have while retaining specific self-help actions we require of countries receiving assistance.

There are four identifiable issues:

1. Do we insist on specific clauses covering marketing requirements or should we be flexible on this point, deciding on a case-by-case basis? It is recommended that we stretch the marketing requirements and keep the clauses covering this issue flexible.

2. Without jeopardizing our long-term objectives, we must decide whether we can increase food aid to fill the gap left because of the reduced AID funds appropriated by Congress. Specific countries involved are Ceylon, Colombia, and Chile.

3. Should we use food aid to build up buffer stocks in the recipient countries?

4. Should we soften the terms and the amount of down payment now being required in existing agreements? Two countries particularly involved are Brazil and Colombia.

The President: Why doesn't Brazil want our wheat?

AID Director Gaud and Secretary Freeman: Our terms are too high in their opinion. They believe our wheat will cost them too much.

Secretary Freeman: The wheat situation in the U.S. has turned around. Availabilities may well be down if current crop estimates are

---

[1] Source: Johnson Library, National Security File, NSC Meetings, Vol. 4, 10/11/67. Confidential/Sensitive; For the President Only. Drafted by Bromley Smith. An attached list of those attending indicates that, in addition to the President, Rusk, McNamara, Helms, Fowler, Freeman, Schultze, Gaud, Rostow, and Hamilton participated in the discussion. (Ibid.)

correct. Food agreements have been tightened up with a view to forcing recipient countries to carry out self-help measures. Our wheat exports dropped because the worldwide harvest is good. The wheat market overreacted. We now have checked the downward price trend. The bushel price may be $1.50. Our policy should be to move out PL–480 wheat rather than to force commercial wheat sales.

The present estimate is that we will have to move 400 million bushels to get a domestic price of $1.40 to $1.50 a bushel. Current sales are estimated at 300 million bushels. The only place to sell additional quantities is in India.

The President: If India goes out in the open market to buy wheat, it should buy from us.

Secretary Fowler: The question boils down to the Indian problem. Given the domestic supply situation, if we push wheat sales, we face the prospect of eroding the self-help provisions in our agreements and affecting the commercial market. Among the options listed in the Freeman–Gaud paper (copy attached),[2] an option not listed would provide that the condition of our sale would depend upon agreement of India to purchase 500,000 tons of U.S. wheat. We would insist on other countries matching what we did. In general, we should insist that food aid be included in the total aid picture insofar as matching is concerned. Our present domestic supply problem should be handled in such a way as not to weaken the matching principle in future years.

Walt Rostow: We have a chance to break down zonal restrictions involving the movement of food in India. To do so would be a real plus and is worth a try. When the Indian Consortium is negotiated in November, we should try to get our food aid counted as part of our contribution.

Secretary Rusk: We should ask the Senior Inter-Departmental Group to look at our various food and AID policies.

The President: Recommendations should be sent to me. If food recipient countries must buy wheat in addition to the amounts they are receiving from donors, they should buy from the United States.

Bromley Smith

---

[2] Reference is to an October 10 memorandum from Freeman and Gaud to the President entitled "Food Aid for India in 1968." (Ibid.)

464. Telegram From the Embassy in Pakistan to the Department of State[1]

Rawalpindi, October 13, 1967, 0720Z

1269. Ref. Rawalpindi 1197[2] and 1241.[3] Subj: Military Supply. Please pass White House.

1. At social function October 6, Defense Minister Admiral Khan requested I call on him following morning on urgent matter.

2. Next morning he had with him Defense Secretary Ghias Uddin Ahmed. After pleasantries, they made following statements, with the Minister doing most of the talking.

A. Next to President Ayub, they and the military establishment are the best friends USG has in Pakistan;

B. They offer their assistance in connection with any problem our Embassy here might have, even if not within sphere of their Ministry;

C. They do not know what USG desires might be with respect to continuation of Peshawar, but are anxious to help fulfill whatever they might be; and

D. They badly need 200 tanks, reciting usual statistics about originally agreed force levels requirements, battle losses, and obsolescence, emphasizing "mad arms build up of GOI" and Pakistan's need to be equipped for 30-day holding action in the event of GOI attack to allow time for U.N. and friendly countries to halt hostilities. They explained increase in GOP request from 100 to 200 tanks by saying Pakistan really needs 600 to 700 and previous fiscal limitations of 50 for FY 68 and 50 for FY 69, have now been relaxed to 100 each year. They added, Ayub, despite dedication to security, continues to give economic development first priority.

3. In response, I mentioned U.S. overall and subcontinental arms policy as well as current Congressional situations. When I referred to gratifying though small reduction in percentages in GOP and GOI budgets devoted to arms, they alleged GOI budget is meaningless, since it [garble] being adhered to and GOI is arming feverishly and has purchasing missions scouting in many countries including Czechoslovakia. They claimed all this was directed against Pakistan, since GOI well aware ChiComs have no intention attack or conquer India where they would encounter almost unsurmountable logistical and terrain problems.

---

[1] Source: National Archives and Records Administration, RG 59, Central Files 1967–69, POL PAK–US. Secret; Exdis. Repeated to New Delhi.

[2] In telegram 1197 from Rawalpindi, October 9, the Embassy asked for a rundown on the talks in Washington with Foreign Minister Pirzada. (Ibid., POL 7 PAK)

[3] Telegram 1241 from Rawalpindi, October 11, reported that Oehlert's tentative appointment to meet with Ayub that evening had been postponed until Ayub returned from France. (Ibid., POL 12–5 PAK)

4. I said Minister and Defense Secretary seem to have more information about arms buildup in India than I, and they volunteered to furnish me "documented statistics".

5. I pointed out that:

A. We have no solid information from GOP regarding number of ChiCom tanks Pakistan has received or which might still be committed and

B. We have no assurance that if US-manufactured tanks became available GOP would not seek more elsewhere.

6. Defense Minister and Secretary responded that:

A. They would be glad to welcome a technical group and show what material Pakistan has and needs and why; and

B. Firm asurances would be given that if Pakistan acquired 200 tanks requested no more would be sought or acquired elsewhere.

7. Defense Minister and Secretary said while they will prepare report for me on alleged GOI arms build up, it would be better for me to discuss with Ayub the points in paras 5 and 6 above, adding it would be a good idea to do it "in cool of evening over couple of scotch-and-sodas". They would set up date for me at 1930 hours October 11, and I should confirm with Ayub's Military Secretary, General Rafi.

8. Rafi was in Lahore and did not return until evening of Oct. 9. I was subsequently informed Ayub had previous commitment for evening October 11 and would see me to discuss these matters after his return from France, Romania, and Turkey October 31.

9. This approach by Defense Minister and Secretary suggests several pregnant speculations including that:

A. It is opening ploy in campaign to relate US military supply to Peshawar continuance. Although only tanks were mentioned it seems probable ante will be raised to encompass at least all pending requests for military supplies (including aircraft, artillery, rifles) and will be related to Pakistan's continuing requirements for lethal end items replacement and modernization to maintain desired military posture vis-à-vis India;

B. Ayub returned emptyhanded from Russia with respect to USSR military equipment for GOP and reduced assistance for GOI, although possibility exists he obtained some assurances of help insufficient to Pak needs, and he wishes to see can be done with USG; and

C. Postponement of suggested discussion until Ayub's return from France indicates he wishes defer our conversation until he explores possibility of obtaining military equipment from France.

10. Range of above speculations could be extended almost indefinitely, but I believe we shall be on firmer ground in this regard after my next meeting with Ayub, during which I hope mostly to find out what he may have in mind. Meanwhile, Washington may wish to consider implications from its perspective, of apparent Pak inclination to link military supply and Peshawar.

11. I would appreciate benefit Washington's preliminary views for my background prior to seeing Ayub.[4]

Oehlert

---

[4] In assessing the Pakistani request for tanks, the Department stressed that the vital factor in deciding how to respond to the request would be the number of tanks supplied or committed to Pakistan by China. (Telegram 55550 to Rawalpindi, October 18; ibid., POL 12–5 PAK)

---

465. Memorandum From the President's Special Assistant (Rostow) to President Johnson[1]

Washington, October 18, 1967, 2:30 p.m.

SUBJECT

Food Aid to India

As you instructed at last week's NSC meeting, Messrs. Freeman, Gaud and Schultze have put into writing their joint proposal on wheat for India. Their memorandum is at Tab A.[2] It argues for:

—a six-month agreement providing for $3^{1}/_{2}$ million tons of wheat (plus minor amounts of other commodities as appropriate);
—very tough self-help conditions;
—acceptance of the International Grains Agreement formula as sufficient guaranty of matching by other donors;
—an informal but tough line on commercial purchases, making it clear that it is important to us that the Indians buy American if they buy any wheat abroad;
—no new approach to the Congress;
—immediate commencement of negotiations. (Our negotiating leverage declines as the Indians move closer to a bumper harvest.)

Nick Katzenbach has reviewed and approved this proposal. Joe Fowler has decided to write a separate memorandum (Tab B).[3] He argues that:

---

[1] Source: Johnson Library, National Security File, Country File, India, India's Food Problem, Vol. IV. Confidential. A handwritten "L" on the memorandum indicates it was seen by the President.

[2] October 17 memorandum from Freeman, Gaud, and Schultze to the President entitled "Food Aid for India." (Ibid.)

[3] October 17 memorandum from Fowler to the President entitled "Food Aid for India." (Ibid., Memos to the President, Walt Rostow, Vol. 46, Oct. 16–20, 1967)

—we should condition our PL 480 wheat on Indian agreement to buy at least 500,000 tons from us for cash;

—we should not accept the Grains Agreement formula as fulfilling the matching requirement for the first half of 1968, since the Grains Agreement does not come into effect until July 1 of next year. In the meantime, if we can't get any more matching resources, we ought to insist that our food be counted as dollar aid in the Indian Consortium.

The rest of us have been over Fowler's points very carefully. He may well be right on his *second* count, but we don't need to decide that issue here. If Passman & Company gut the AID appropriation bill, it is very unlikely that we will have to insist that at least part of our food be counted as dollar aid. (There are some costs to this—e.g., the Canadians and the Australians will take a similar stand and cut down their dollar aid accordingly—and there is a serious risk that the Consortium might dissolve under such pressure.) But we don't need to face this question directly until we know how much AID money we will have. We will come back to you when that decision needs to be made, and Fowler will have a full voice in the recommendation. Making this decision now does *not* mean that you are overruling him on this point.

Joe's *first* point is tougher. Everybody wants to sell as much grain as possible. Freeman would be delighted to back any tactic he thought was likely to extract more commercial sales. But the truth is that the Indians are very unlikely to buy *any* wheat abroad in a year of record domestic harvests and severe foreign exchange shortage. They certainly aren't going to buy anything like 500,000 tons, and the leverage of this PL 480 offer is not nearly sufficient to get them to do so. They didn't buy quite that much from us last year in the second consecutive year of the worst drought in recent history. This year's Indian grain crop will be nearly 20 million tons more than last year's. The prospect of another $3^1/2$ million tons in imports just isn't attractive enough to make them spend scarce foreign exchange on wheat.

Joe's proposal has other drawbacks:

—a flat condition such as he proposes would be a clear violation of our pledge in the International Grains Agreement not to tie any PL 480 sales to cash sales. (The language in the Freeman/Gaud/Schultze memo is already right on the borderline in this respect; some State lawyers are concerned that even this may be too strong.)

—if such a condition became widely known in the diplomatic community—and it would become widely known—the Canadians and Australians, from whom we now expect upwards of a million tons of food aid to India, would either scrap those plans or insist upon the same conditions we impose. The result might well be no wheat sales for anybody, and the others, particularly Australia, would be very bitter;

—such a condition would rob us of all our leverage to get the internal policy reforms we want from the Indians. They would see it as a straight commercial proposition which they would almost certainly refuse. But even if they bought it, they certainly wouldn't feel they owed us anything on the policy front.

Thus, although everybody agrees with Fowler's objectives, the rest of us would argue that his condition would: (i) keep us from moving the wheat we have to move if we are to meet our FY 1968 PL 480 targets and support domestic prices, (ii) weaken our influence on Indian internal agricultural policy, (iii) sour the other donors on helping India, and (iv) get us into international legal trouble which could sink the Grains Agreement before it is even ratified.

My vote is with the Freeman/Gaud/Schultze recommendation at Tab A.

Special Note:

In considering this decision, you should know that we have considerable evidence that the Indians are going back on their promise not to buy Soviet fighter-bombers. They told us last June that they would not buy Soviet planes if we let the British sell them 24 Hawker–Hunters. We gave the British the go ahead. It is now becoming clear that the Indians have some sort of bargain with the Soviets to buy a substantial number—perhaps 100—SU–7 fighter-bombers at about $1.7 million per copy. Secretary Rusk has already called in B. K. Nehru and sent Bowles in to Morarji Desai to demand an explanation. We haven't yet got any straight answers.

If these reports are true, we will want to rethink our whole posture on aid to India—and the Congress may want to as well. But our position in the food negotiation gets less advantageous with each day we wait. Thus, I would suggest we:

—start the food negotiation with the specific caveat that all bets are subject to change if the aircraft problem turns out as rumored;
—hold off on the *dollar* side of our aid to India until we get satisfaction on the aircraft.

Walt

Start negotiations on basis Freeman/Gaud/Schultze memo (Tab A)[4]

Use Fowler's formula—3 million tons in PL 480 if they agree to buy 500,000 tons commercially from us

Speak to me

---

[4] The President approved this option after adding the first four words by hand.

466.   **Telegram From the Department of State to the Embassy in India**[1]

Washington, October 22, 1967, 2001Z.

58064. For Ambassador from Secretary.

1. President has asked me convey following to you:

A. A message[2] going forward to you outlines elements of a food package we are asking you discuss with GOI. This is a large program involving three and one-half million tons of foodgrains and some $250 million of U.S. resources. Its dimensions are yet another indication of our determination to work with the Indians to meet their food shortages and help them on road to self-sufficiency in foodgrains. This effort on our part is particularly significant as it occurs at a time when aid resources we can offer India and other countries are declining.

B. In putting this proposal to Indians you should also make crystal clear to them that our ability to continue to be forthcoming on the whole range of our assistance relations with the GOI is closely related to India's performance in reducing diversion of resources from economic to defense expenditures.

C. Our decisions on aid will be closely related to a satisfactory resolution SU–7 matter (State 56877).[3]

D. We do not propose at this time to make our food package contingent on reduction in defense budget but Indian actions in this field will weigh heavily in decisions we will be making shortly on division of aid appropriations, future PL–480 agreements, Consortium meeting and other forums which contribute to India's growth. Indians should realize their performance will have important bearing on these decisions, on Congressional attitudes, and on efforts we are making to get Pakistanis to cut back their defense spending.

Rusk

---

[1] Source: National Archives and Records Administration, RG 59, Central Files 1967–69, SOC 10 INDIA. Secret; Immediate; Exdis. Drafted by Heck on October 20. Cleared by Handley, Spain, Wolf, AID's Assistant Administrator for Near East and South Asia Maurice J. Williams, and Walt Rostow, in substance by Reid (OSD/ISA) and Freeman. Approved and initialed by Rusk.

[2] Not found.

[3] Dated October 19. (National Archives and Records Administration, RG 59, Central Files 1967–69, DEF 19–6 USSR–INDIA)

467. Telegram From the Department of State to the Embassy in India[1]

Washington, October 27, 1967, 0017Z.

60510. New Delhi 4882.[2] Subject: Memcon with B.K. Nehru on Food.

1. Following is uncleared summary of memcon prepared by Secretary Freeman of October 21 talk between President, Ambassador Nehru and Secretary Freeman. Full memcon[3] being pouched.

2. Nehru thought commercial grain question could be worked out although he expressed concern about relations with Australia and Canada.

3. Nehru said Chief Ministers recently concluded they could not liberalize food zones at this time and certainly could not abolish them. Assuming a crop of 95 million tons (which by no means assured) and imports of 7.5 million tons, Nehru said per capita intake would be somewhat less this year than in 1964, allowing for seed, feed, private stocks, and general attrition. Therefore, Nehru said, India not in strong enough position to abolish zones. (USDA estimates indicate per capita availability in 1967/68 virtually identical to that of 1964/65, with same assumptions re imports, private stocks, etc.)

4. Freeman acknowledged political problem in abolishing zones but pointed out danger in not abolishing them. Argued that bold step at this time would tend to counteract downward pressure on prices from big crop in the most productive states. Producers increasingly adopting new techniques and methods. Sharp drop in prices to producers could disillusion Indian farmer and set back entire agricultural effort seriously. Continuation of zones would have that effect and now is time to abolish them. With two million tons of GOI reserves clearly attainable, plus at least an increase of 2.5 million tons in private hands, this is time to move.

5. Nehru discussed necessity to listen to local decision-makers and democratic process which would reflect itself in demands of people to abolish food zones should the above contingencies take place.

---

[1] Source: National Archives and Records Administration, RG 59, Central Files 1967–69, SOC 10 INDIA. Secret; Priority; Exdis. Drafted by Mary S. Olmsted (NEA/INC) on October 25, cleared by Heck and Hamilton at the White House, and approved by Handley.

[2] In telegram 4882 from New Delhi, October 23, Bowles asked for a report on the President's conversation with Ambassador Nehru. (Ibid.)

[3] A copy of the memorandum of conversation was sent by Freeman to Rusk on October 24. (Ibid.)

6. Freeman replied sometimes people in democracy must lead rather than count noses and issue of zones or no zones was not, and was not likely to become, political question on which Indian people could express themselves.

7. Nehru replied that should move in direction of abolishing zones be made, there ought to be more than six months' assurance of grain from U.S.

8. Conversation ended with directive by President that Secretary Freeman review his analysis of India situation and confirm his strong position that food zones in India should be completely abolished now and a maximum amount of pressure brought to bear to accomplish that goal or explain any adjustments that might be called for.

9. Nehru was asked to communicate with GOI and see what could and would be done by them to abolish food zones.

Rusk

---

468. Memorandum From Edward Hamilton of the National Security Council Staff to the President's Special Assistant (Rostow)[1]

Washington, October 27, 1967.

SUBJECT

The Arms Problem in India

We talked briefly on Tuesday about the fighter-bomber dispute in India. The following is a summary of where we stand now and what directions I would like to see us take in the future:

Facts:

1. In June, we gave the British permission to sell the Indians 24 Hawker–Hunter fighters. We insisted upon two conditions:

—that they be replacements, not additions to Indian air power, and
—that India assure us she would *not* follow through on the purchase of 200 Russian SU–7 fighter-bombers which was rumored to be under negotiation.

---

[1] Source: Johnson Library, National Security File, Country File, India, Vol. X, Memos & Miscellaneous, 8/67–2/68. Secret.

2. Over the last month it has become increasingly clear that:

—the Indians are in the process of buying 150–200 SU–7's from the Soviets at $1–1.7 million apiece;

—they knew of this purchase at the time they assured us they wouldn't (most of the planes were apparently contracted for by October 1966); and

—they are going ahead with the deal regardless of our views.

3. We have already used some of our big diplomatic guns to nail down the facts and to urge the Indians against going through with the deal:

—Bowles has called on Morarji Desai, pursuant to a very strong cable from Rusk pointing out that this Indian action would be the worst combination of bad faith, bad resource allocation, bad strategy vis-à-vis Pakistan, and bad U.S. politics upon which continued massive U.S. aid to India depends;

—Rusk has called in B.K. Nehru and made the same points;

—Jerry Greene, our DCM in Delhi, has had several conversations with the No. 2 man in the Indian Defense Ministry, who gave us the original assurance and who is now the source of most of our information about what they are actually doing;

—Bowles was instructed to make it clear that the atmosphere created by the handling of the SU–7 problem would affect the full range of our aid relations with India, including the wheat deal. (We did *not* threaten to revoke the wheat deal if we didn't get satisfaction on the SU–7's.)

5. Bowles, obviously upset, is urging that we not allow the SU–7 problem to poison our overall relations with India. He argues that India is now at a crossroads ("watershed" is his term), and that a tough démarche from us on the SU–7's could well turn her away from the West and away from concentration on economic progress. He agrees the incident is regrettable and that it will probably cause some trouble in the Congress. But he argues strongly against doing much, if anything, about it.

6. Senator Symington—along with an unknown number of other members of Congress—knows the history of the problem up to but not including the details we have picked up in the past month. Luke Battle has mentioned to him a couple of times that we have a problem and that he wants to give him a full briefing soon. Symington has always been very strongly anti-India (and pro-Pak); he is sure to point to this as yet another shameful example of Indian untrustworthiness (and the facts will lend considerable support to his case).

7. The Indians argue that:

—the assurance applied only to new procurement, not to old orders;

—British footdragging on the Hawker–Hunters made it clear that India could not depend on this aircraft as its workhorse for the period between the phasing out of their older planes and the phasing in during the 70's of Indian-manufactured MIG 21's;

—the five-year defense plan worked out in 1964 and agreed to in principle by the U.S. provided for an air requirement which the SU–7's will help to meet. There is no desire to exceed the 1964 plan, but India can't afford any shortfalls, particularly since the Paks are not getting Mirage fighter-bombers.

The first proposition is transparently false. The assurance was clear. The second and third are now the objects of a study being carried out by DIA and INR. (Of course, even if the study shows that the Indians are not doing anything more than the 1964 plan prescribed, we will have to decide whether the 1964 plan—which was followed by the Indo-Pak war—still represents our concept of what Indian security demands.)

8. We are now engaged or about to be engaged in five separate negotiations with the Indians, most of which are for their benefit:

—a PL 480 wheat package totalling 3.5 million tons ($250 million);
—a mid-November meeting of the Indian Consortium at which under normal circumstances we would pledge upwards of $380 million;
—a $17 million Star Sapphire project providing for an early warning radar system against the Chinese;
—a $25 million private deal under which the Bendix Corporation would join with an Indian corporation to build an airplane factory;
—Negotiation of parallel U.S.-Soviet security assurances for non-nuclear signers of the NPT, particularly India.

Implications

1. If it leaked that India is buying 150–200 Soviet fighter-bombers after we received specific assurance that she would not do so, I think there is an excellent chance that the Congress would pass an amendment to the AID appropriation bill cutting off dollar aid to India unless and until the deal were revoked.

2. If we let the Indians get away with this reneging without penalty, it would be very hard for us to convince them we mean what we say in future arms policy negotiations. This would be a real credibility gap.

3. We have clandestine information that the Paks already know about the SU–7 deal. They are so short of foreign exchange that they have not yet done anything about it. But publicity will put them in a very different political situation, and we can expect heavy pressure to help them regain "parity."

4. However, it is the combined judgment of our Mission in Delhi and NEA/Washington that no amount of U.S. pressure is likely to get Mrs. Gandhi to call off the SU–7 deal entirely. Any direct threat to cut off aid to India would probably have the reverse result—she would do a Sukarno rather than bend under pressure. (In fact, she probably

doesn't have the political weight to carry the Cabinet in any other direction.) The result would be dissolution of the Consortium, failure to make use of the economic recovery promised by the good harvest, and a heavy blow to any hope of rapid economic growth in India for some time to come.

Action Program

In summary, the Indians have been lousy. It makes sense for us to try to get them to undo the damage, but the chances aren't really very good. It is very hard on our interests—both short and long-term—to cut off the help we are giving them, particularly grain. Yet it is terribly important that we have very soon a palatable story to tell Symington and other interested parties if we are to head off the problem in the Congress before it guts the Aid Bill. Any direct tying of aid to the SU–7's alone would probably drive India into going through with the bargain and scuttle their development programs as well.

I have suggested that our policy be built along the following lines:

1. The SU–7 problem is directly tied to the Hawker–Hunters. We should immediately suspend our approval of the Hawker–Hunter deal until we get satisfaction on the SU–7's. (It is particularly important to have done this by the time we talk to the Congress.)

2. We should agree with the Indians that the SU–7 problem cannot be looked at alone—that the real problem is what amount of resources should be allocated to defense, measured against an agreed concept of Indian security needs. We are willing to join India in a hard look at that whole question, starting as soon as they like.

3. In the meantime, however, the defense budget problem is so important to the overall development outlook in India that we do not feel we can move ahead with our Consortium pledge until there is substantial agreement on the broad question of the proper size of the defense effort.

Tactics

The current plan—which has not gone yet beyond the sixth floor[2]—is to put this line into a letter from Rusk to Mrs. Gandhi. (This is entirely appropriate because Mrs. Gandhi is Foreign Minister as well as Prime Minister at the moment.) We would try to do it diplomatically, and we have some basis for the joint study line in that the Indians themselves proposed general defense talks a few months ago. The cancellation of the Hawker–Hunter approval is not really likely to bother her much, although it probably will force her to make an explicit review and

---

[2] Reference is to the sixth floor of the Department of State; the Secretary of State and his deputies have their offices on the seventh floor.

decision on whether to go ahead with the SU–7 proposition. The Consortium pledge threat may also be less powerful leverage than we would normally expect because she knows that we are now in a freeze on all new commitments and that the Congress is thinking seriously about cutting off the water. But it should be serious enough to get her to agree to the talks and perhaps to some modification of the SU–7 arrangement. (Obviously, we would push hard to get the SU–7 deal turned around completely if the discussions give us a substantive case against it.)

Perhaps most important, this letter would be a basic document we could show the Congress as evidence that we take this perfidy seriously and that we are doing something about it. When we have sent it, I would argue that Battle should have quiet talks with Symington and other interested parties on the Hill. I think it is much better to go to them than to let them be surprised by a headline. They may insist that we aren't being nearly tough enough—that we ought to cut the Indians off entirely until they make good on their promise. But I think early consultation is the tactic best calculated to head this off if it can be headed off.

These are my thoughts. The letter is now in preparation in NEA, but I have no assurance that the Secretary will agree to go along. I will keep you informed.

EH

---

469. Telegram From the Department of State to the Embassy in Pakistan[1]

Washington, October 30, 1967, 0032Z.

61581. For Ambassador. Ref: Rawalpindi 1269.[2] Subject: Military Supply.

1. FYI: The temptation to try to "buy" an assured future for the Peshawar facility with one or two hundred tanks is very real. However, we concur with para 9 reftel that to recognize linkage military supply

---

[1] Source: National Archives and Records Administration, RG 59, Central Files 1967–69, DEF 12–5 PAK. Secret; Immediate; Exdis. Drafted by Spain and Prescott. Cleared by Battle, Handley, Heck, Wolf, Schwartz (DOD), Williams (AID/NESA), and Hamilton at the White House and approved by Katzenbach. Repeated to New Delhi and CINCSTRIKE.

[2] Document 464.

policy with Peshawar would probably result in intolerable pressures from GOP for more and more hardware. Furthermore, we convinced such recognition would destroy the foundation of that policy which has its justification in its own separate objectives. Therefore, we believe it best during your October 31 conversation with Ayub for you to make no mention of Peshawar. From standpoint our interests we feel it still too early begin negotiations on this question. When we are ready these will have to be played out against background of totality US–Pak relations, of which our military supply policy is only part—although we hope in Pakistan's eyes a valuable part which it will wish preserve. End FYI.

2. We believe it would be useful, therefore, for you in your meeting with Ayub to review our whole military supply policy in order (A) prevent any misunderstanding by GOP on this important aspect our relationship, and (B) to impress on him value to Pakistan of this policy.

3. You should point out that since new policy began in April, 1967, we have approved for purchase $23 million in ammunition and spare parts. Air Force and Navy spare parts already being received in Pakistan. Despite Pirzada complaint to President, GOP has only within present month begun to submit specific purchase requests for Army spares, which we assume will also begin reach Pakistan soon. During same period, we have also approved $5 million jeep sale on very favorable three per cent–ten year credit terms and sales of assorted other non-lethal items. Military training program, for which we paying cost, has already been reestablished with 17 officers expected to take courses in US this year.

4. You may add that, while there will inevitably be delays resulting from our Vietnam priorities and manufacturers' lead times, as long as spare parts and other matériel requirements remain within framework our policy, we as interested as GOP in working out speedy and effective handling, including possible arrangements for filling all spares needs on yearly basis. This high priority business for General Geary.

5. On tank question, you should say that original request for 100 tanks has been actively considered. GOP had first indicated West Germany would be source and we understand from ForMin Pirzada this possibility still remains despite public FRG denials. For Ayub's information only, we also believe it possible some excess M–47s may be generated in Italy or France. However, we have never received formal request from any of these countries for sale to Pakistan. You may tell Ayub that we will understand it if the GOP decides to consult discreetly with possible sources of tanks to determine whether or not and what kind of a deal it can make with one of them.

6. You should remind Ayub again that Congressional and public concern makes the whole subject of military supply an extremely sensi-

tive one. You can tell him that we would be prepared examine carefully any request for approval of 100 tank sale we might receive from Germans, French, or Italians. However, you should make clear that we would have to consult at the appropriate time with the Senate and House Committees concerned and that we cannot guarantee either concurrence or that a leak which might cause difficulties would not take place. Even for such consultation we would have to make sure that any request served the objectives of our military supply policy. To do this, we would have to have a clear understanding that: (a) number of tanks received or on order from Red China has not resulted in net increase Pak armour and that no further deliveries from this source expected; (b) GOP not planning purchases of tanks from other sources (e.g., France or Soviet Union); (c) for each US-controlled tank acquired one obsolete tank would be scrapped from Pak tank inventory; and, (d) Pakistan advise us of what, if any, major arms acquisitions of other kinds it foresees in reasonable future and justification therefor.[3]

7. FYI: We believe frank understanding on above conditions essential as we cannot afford be caught in another equivocation as with India on the Hawker Hunter/SU–7 deal and because, as we see it, main justification for tank sale, should it be approved, would be prevention excessive defense spending and/or introduction new weapons system which would follow from Pak acquisition expensive French AMX tanks or greater numbers Chinese or Soviet tanks. If possible therefore you should obtain from Ayub (1) total number of Chinese tanks held or expected; (2) which other major items military material Pakistan has acquired or is seeking from non-US sources; and, (3) some indication whether or not he prepared accept above conditions. End FYI.

8. We believe action should be completed on original request for 100 tanks before moving on to decisions on other lethal end items. However, should subject come up, you may tell Ayub we remain prepared consider on case-by-case basis any third country requests for sale to Pakistan of US-controlled equipment provided such sale meets objectives our military supply policy. Request for second hundred tanks is in this category and we willing to discuss it when question of first hundred has been satisfactorily disposed of. Direct US sales of artillery or any other lethal end-item are out of question at this time.

---

[3] Oehlert and Ayub discussed the tank issue when they met in Karachi on November 1. Oehlert asked for the assurances concerning alternate sources of supply outlined in telegram 61581. Ayub, "after some sparring," agreed that if his minimal requirements could be met with U.S.-originated equipment, he would undertake to scrap one obsolete tank for each new one acquired, and he would not seek or accept additional equipment from other sources. (Telegram 807 from Karachi, November 1; National Archives and Records Administration, RG 59, Central Files 1967–69, POL 27–14 VIET)

9. On replacement aircraft (Rawalpindi 332,[4] 968[5]) you may indicate our understanding that most of aircraft requested (four F–57Bs and two F–104As) were lost during 1965 war. We cannot consider replacement for these aircraft. Only real accidental loss would appear to be one RB–57A which reportedly lost in landing washout at Risalpir in May, 1967. You may tell Ayub that while we have not yet investigated availabilities we willing in principle give consideration to request for purchase replacement this aircraft.

10. You should indicate to Ayub our gratification at relatively moderate approach he has taken thus far in seeking acquire military hardware. Without this approach, including modest reduction this year's Defense Budget, we doubt that we would have been able sustain our current military supply policy even this far. We consider it of the greatest importance that he maintain this moderation and that Pakistan and the US have completely frank understanding on military supply problems. Should he be interested, we would be prepared at appropriate time have some of our experts discuss with his officers our own "cost effectiveness" approach to problem of getting maximum capability from minimum expenditure.

Rusk

---

[4] Telegram 332 from Rawalpindi, August 5, reported on a request from Defense Minister Khan for "replacement" of 4 F–57B, 1 RB–57A, and 2 F–104A aircraft. (Ibid., DEF 12–5 PAK)

[5] In telegram 968 from Rawalpindi, September 23, the Embassy reported on a letter from Defense Minister Khan in which he reiterated Pakistan's desire for 200 M–47 tanks, 4 F–57B, 1 RB–57A, and 2 F–104A aircraft. (Ibid.)

470. Telegram From the Embassy in Pakistan to the Department of State[1]

Rawalpindi, November 25, 1967, 0710Z.

2019. Govto 12. 1. By appointment at 1100 hours Friday morning November 24, our delegation[2] with Ambassador Oehlert presented to Ayub the map case as the President's gift. He received it with appreciation.

2. Immediately thereafter the Ambassador and I met with Ayub alone for well over an hour. Foreign Secretary Yusuf was also present and took voluminous notes.

3. I presented Ayub with the original of President Johnson's letter[3] which I had read at the dedication services the previous day. He expressed warm appreciation of the President's message and referred to his long friendship beginning with the visit as Vice President. The letter had scooped in the press the messages from all other countries and the handwritten postscript was featured.

4. We first discussed Vietnam, which I will report in septel.[4]

5. Raising the Middle East problem, I expressed our encouragement by the unanimous approval [of] the British resolution by the Security Council, including Soviet support. Although Ayub said he had received the British draft from New York, he read carefully paragraph by paragraph a copy I handed him. I suggested that it would be useful for him now to encourage King Hussein who had made a good impression in the US. Unfortunately, Nasser had repudiated Hussein's position. Ayub agreed to support the efforts of the UN representative Gunnar Jensen, although he suggested that we not press the Arabs too hard. He pointed to the wide interpretation that could be

---

[1] Source: National Archives and Records Administration, RG 59, Central Files 1967–69, POL 7 US/HARRIMAN. Secret; Priority; Limdis.

[2] The telegram was from Ambassador at Large Averell Harriman, who was head of a Presidential delegation that attended the dedication ceremonies at the Mangla Dam on November 23. The delegation included Senator E. L. Bartlett of Alaska, Representative Delwin M. Clawson of California, Governor Kenneth M. Curtis of Maine, and Governor Calvin L. Rampton of Utah.

[3] Reference is to a November 20 letter from Johnson to Ayub in which Johnson lauded the Ayub government and the people of Pakistan for the signal accomplishment represented by the construction of the Mangla Dam. (Johnson Library, National Security File, Head of Correspondence File, Pakistan, Vol. 2, President Ayub Correspondence, 1/1/66–12/25/67)

[4] In telegram 2016 from Rawalpindi, November 25, Harriman reported that he had explained to Ayub President Johnson's urgent desire that pressure be exerted on North Vietnam to negotiate a peaceful settlement. Ayub agreed to do what he could in his contacts with Communist countries to promote a settlement. (National Archives and Records Administration, RG 59, Harriman Files: Lot 71 D 461, Pakistan Trip)

given the phrasing of the resolution. I replied that all we wanted was the basis for peace along the lines of the President's five points. He agreed that a basis for a permanent peace was essential and recognized that the resolution was an important step forward, underlining the value of Soviet support. He made no bones about Soviet long-term intentions in the area, but thought that they did not want renewed hostilities. Jerusalem came up later in my talk with him at luncheon. He stated that his prople would demand independent status for the Moslem holy places, which were revered second only to Mecca. He agreed, however, the subject should be kept apart from the other Arab-Israel problems.

6. As Ayub had mentioned the need for cooperation by the advanced countries to the developing countries, I gave him a copy of the President's Science Advisory Committee's report on hunger, which included detailed analyses of Pakistan's problems. I said I thought that approach of increased food production within an over-all expanding economy as proposed by this report was receiving increased attention in the US and elsewhere.

7. Ayub then brought up the question of tanks in the following manner: (A) he propounded the view that India had lost its ideology; since the death of Gandhi India had abandoned its principle of non-violence; since the death of Nehru, it had abandoned its policy of non-alignment; bigotry was now becoming more and more rampant in India; the elections were showing this type of candidate was winning; the present government was weak and could not last. Yet, India was developing vast military strength as a result of our past help and present Soviet assistance. This was obviously directed at Pakistan. He genuinely feared the possibility of another attack from India, and Pakistan must be prepared to meet it. (B) He said Pakistan badly needed 500 tanks to replace obsolete Shermans, but was presently requesting only 200. This is in line with prior statements made by him and the Minister of Defense to Ambassador Oehlert. (C) He reaffirmed previous statements made to Amb. Oehlert that he would scrap obsolete tanks on a one-for-one basis if he could receive tanks from or through US. (D) He expressed an understanding of our inability to make direct sales of tanks but expressed the hope that our government would take the initiative with countries where M–47 tanks under our control were known to exist in surplus and obtain offer of sale to Pakistan on appropriate terms. At this point I asked Amb. Oehlert to restate our present position with respect to tanks. He reminded Ayub that in previous conversations it had been pointed out: first, that we could not undertake direct sale; second, that we could not consider approving transfers through any intermediate government; third, that we could not take any initiative in undertaking to be purchasing agent for GOP; fourth,

that we had under consideration only 100 tanks although we did not foreclose the possibility of considering a second 100 after the first 100 was disposed of one way or another and if justification could be established adequate to make it possible to undertake such consideration; and that if GOP established the availability of 100 tanks in some other country for purchase on acceptable terms USG would give earnest consideration to their request to approve sale of such tanks directly to Pakistan. Ayub stated he must have reconstructed tanks, as he could not afford new ones. Although I admitted we were unhappy at size of India's military budget, we didn't believe Indian aggressive intentions toward Pakistan. I admitted weakness Indian Government and many internal problems, but asked whether this wasn't what had been expected as inevitable after Nehru's death, and expressed the opinion it was too early to predict political future. I underlined our respect for Pakistan's economic development and considered use of resources for further economic expansion as wiser investment for Pakistan security than extravagant military outlays. However, I agreed to report his concern.

8. Conversation broke off in order to prepare for luncheon at which Ayub entertained all visiting delegations. He asked me to express his high respects to the President.

Oehlert

---

471.   Memorandum From the President's Special Assistant (Rostow) to President Johnson[1]

Washington, November 28, 1967, 5 p.m.

SUBJECT

PL 480 Grain for India

You will recall authorizing Freeman and Gaud to start negotiations with India on the basis of a 3.5 million ton package to cover the first six months of 1968. The Indian side of the bargain was a strong self-help package headed by abolition of the inefficient zonal boundaries which now restrict movement of food between stages. The package

---

[1] Source: Johnson Library, National Security File, Country File, India, Vol. X, Memos and Miscellaneous, 8/67–2/68. Confidential.

also contained other important steps to keep farm prices up, get the central government into a position to smooth out price fluctuations, and continue to build up imports of fertilizer, pesticides and improved seeds. You asked them to report back to you when the results of the negotiation were clear and before anything was signed.

At Tab B,[2] Freeman and Gaud report that they have been able to get Indian agreement on every aspect of the package *except* immediate elimination of food zones. The Indian Food Minister has told us that he wants and intends to eliminate the zones, but that it would be political suicide to try to do it before next fall when the current crop is in and there is a fairly solid estimate of next year's crop. Freeman and Gaud are inclined to agree. They recommend that we go ahead with the package on the assurance that the Indians will move next fall if conditions improve as expected. Charlie Schultze supports this conclusion; his memo (Tab A)[3] is a good summary of the proposal. (You will note that this step would involve *no* additional budgetary costs.) Joe Fowler asked us to tell you that his views haven't changed since October (he would like to see more contributions from others and a specific quid pro quo on commercial sales), but he is not inclined to press them again now.

Congressional Attitudes

As agreed in October, Freeman's Congressional consultations have been limited to the people you sent to India last December. Congressmen Poage and Dole support the proposal as recommended, but Senator Miller would prefer to insist on full matching from other donors and to cut down the size and/or extend the duration of the agreement. (Miller's suggestions are discussed on pages 2–3 of the Freeman/Gaud memo at Tab B.) Freeman does not believe Miller can be persuaded to agree to his proposal, but he states that "he has no reason to believe" Miller will make a public fuss if we go ahead.

On the merits of Miller's first suggestion, Freeman and Gaud believe—and I agree—that if we insist upon matching from other donors, we won't move much more than 1 million tons of wheat to India in all of 1968. The result would be lower U.S. wheat prices, higher CCC costs, and no pressure on India to make agricultural policy reforms. We have a matching rationale for 1968 in the Kennedy Round Grains Agreement which requires the Europeans to provide 2.3 million tons of grain per year in food aid beginning July 1, 1968. We can represent

---

[2] Reference is to a November 22 memorandum from Freeman and Gaud to the President entitled "Food Aid for India in 1968." (Ibid.)

[3] Reference is to a November 27 memorandum from Schultze to the President entitled "Food Aid for India." (Ibid.)

that Agreement as the multilateral matching formula we have been after, replacing our 1967 insistence on bilateral matching. Miller is right that this would result in much less than even matching of U.S. food aid. But if we want to come anywhere near the 11 million tons of wheat Agriculture wants to move next year to support domestic prices and keep CCC costs within reason, we must have a policy which allows us to provide much more to India than the other donors—rightly or wrongly—are willing to provide. Even so, the Freeman/Gaud memorandum pledges that we will keep the heat on the others as much as possible.

Miller's other suggestions would (a) cut the new agreement to 2 million tons over four months or (b) keep it at 3.5 million tons but make it cover all of 1968 rather than just the first six months. The Indians might accept the first, but only at the price of eliminating some or all of the policy reforms promises they are now prepared to make. They would consider the second totally inadequate to provide a resource base for the buffer stock/price support operation we are trying to get them to set up—and they would be right. In either case, negotiations would drag on for weeks and perhaps months, during which we would not be shipping any grain and our negotiating position would be deteriorating as the bumper Indian crop hit the market.

For these reasons, Freeman recommends we proceed without further contact with Miller.

Timing of Announcement

There is one other small issue. Freeman and Schnittker want to announce our offer immediately to get a domestic price effect. Gaud & Company would rather wait a day or two to nail things down with the Indians. It would be better international relations to wait until we have solid agreement with the Indians, but it would not cause us major problems to announce now if you agree that the domestic price needs an immediate jolt.

Walt

1. Approve Freeman/Gaud/Schultze proposal[4]

2. Freeman to have another talk with Miller, but to go ahead whatever Miller says

3. Freeman to have another talk with Miller and report results to me before my decision

4. Disapprove

5. Speak to me

---

[4] Johnson checked this option.

472.   Telegram From the Department of State to the Embassy in India[1]

Washington, December 7, 1967, 0213Z.

80797. State/AID/DOD message. Ref: (a) New Delhi's 5487;[2] (b) Rawalpindi's 1886.[3] Review of US Military Supply Policy to India and Pakistan.

We have reviewed US military supply policy which was defined and announced last April. Review was conducted in light of (1) our experience to date, (2) comments from addressees, notably per reftels, and (3) totality of our interests in subcontinent as we see them evolving under pressure of developments such as presently diminishing economic aid availabilities. Our principal conclusions, set forth below, are general in nature, reflecting broad nature of our review. Separate guidance will follow regarding more specific operational questions such as next steps re SU–7's and Hunters.

I. Conclusions

(A) Present US military supply policy toward India and Pakistan has proven flexible and useful tool supporting variety of US interests.

(1) We should therefore continue to monitor US sales of lethal spares and third-country sales of US controlled lethal end items on case-by-case basis. Policy guidelines governing individual decisions should remain as set forth in previous messages.

(2) We should continue our diplomatic efforts, both bilaterally and through Consortium, to persuade each country to exercise restraint in its defense spending, recognizing that our initiatives to this end must be carefully calculated if they are to be acceptable and credible.

---

[1] Source: National Archives and Records Administration, RG 59, Central Files 1967–69, DEF 12–5 INDIA. Secret; Limdis. Drafted by Coon on November 22; cleared by Battle, Prescott, Colonel Fredericks (NEA/RA), Wolf, Heck, Charles A. Kiselyak (H), Rees, Director for Near East and South Asia Brigadier General Henry C. Newcomer (DOD/ISA), and Bromley Smith. Also sent to Rawalpindi and repeated to London and CINCSTRIKE.

[2] In telegram 5487 from New Delhi, November 6, from Bowles to Rusk, Bowles stated that he was convinced that the military assistance policy the United States was following with regard to the subcontinent was not achieving its objectives. In his view, the United States was attempting to control key elements of a complex and politically sensitive situation that was largely beyond its control. He urged a careful review of the military assistance policy to bring it into better harmony with the situation that existed in the subcontinent. (Ibid.)

[3] Oehlert offered his assessment of the military supply policy in telegram 1886 from Rawalpindi, November 18. He recognized that the policy was not "tidy, comfortable nor fully consistent." On the basis of the evidence in hand, however, Oehlert judged that the policy had already achieved a measure of success in Pakistan, and concluded that, if firmly and realistically implemented, it offered a better prospect for success than any alternative which had been put forward. (Ibid., DEF 12–5 PAK)

(3) As opportunities arise we should also continue to counsel restraint on other countries which are actual or potential suppliers of military equipment to subcontinent.

(B) Present reaffirmation our policy does not imply we expect it to produce miracles.

(1) On contrary, it is evident we lack decisive influence over either country's decisions on defense spending and arms acquisition, and can at best hope to maintain a restraining influence on each.

(2) We recognize that India and Pakistan, as major states (with India facing direct security threat from China) are going to maintain armed forces which have at least some first-line combat aircraft and other sophisticated equipment, plus total force levels at least somewhat consistent with external threat to their security as they perceive it. Their maintenance of such forces is not necessarily inconsistent with our longer-term strategic interests; though present development and resources considerations dictate US posture of restraint, our posture should not foreclose future US options involving greater degree of cooperation in security field.

(C) Another major caveat: There is an underlying relationship between magnitude of our economic aid commitment to each country and extent to which we can effectively press that country's government to exercise restraint in defense spending.

(1) As long as we remain major provider of economic resources to both countries we have inescapable responsibility to do what we can to restrain each from actions leading to arms spiral between them that diverts scarce resources from development without adding to net security of either.

(2) Assuming this year's aid will be cut very substantially, we should continue to oppose an arms race but should recognize that our capability to exercise a restraining influence on defense spending has been diminished.

(3) If, despite our best efforts, we can get no more money from Congress next year for FY '69 aid than we appear likely to get this year for FY '68, it may be prudent to withdraw to quieter, less insistent role in dealing with GOI and GOP on defense expenditures.

II. Discussion: Basic US Policy Options

As we see it there are three basic policy options at least theoretically open to us. At one extreme would be some variant of highly restrictive policy such as we maintained immediately after 1965 war. At other extreme would be French-style approach of selling either country anything it wanted that it could pay for. Third or intermediate option would involve efforts to keep lid on arms race through combination of general suasion and flexible posture on individual sales cases.

(A) First option, involving no lethal sales to either country, has obvious advantages and disadvantages.

(1) Advantages:

(a) It would constitute simple and readily comprehensible stance, avoiding disputes over interpretation, putting us at least superficially squarely on side of peace and plowshares (though Paks would regard it as pro-Indian betrayal).

(b) It could in some cases (where US-controlled equipment significantly cheaper than comparable items from other sources) operate in direction of increasing cost of armament and hence of increasing fiscal pressures for restraint; and

(c) It would be applauded by significant Congressional elements.

(2) Disadvantages:

(a) Except under circumstances such as Indo-Pak war and immediate aftermath it would seem unsound for us arbitrarily to renounce any and all use of major and established instrument of national policy capable of furthering our subcontinental interests. Our ability to carry on meaningful military supply relationships with India and Pakistan has been and continues to be such an instrument.

(b) On Indian side our flexibility in using this instrument in recent months has furthered our interests in a variety of ways (see below).

(c) On Pakistani side it seems evident our flexibility has played an important role in enabling Ayub to contain his country's relations with China and thereby in supporting US strategic interests in subcontinent as defined para 3 (D) of State 33331.[4] It has also made possible small but significant cut in GOP's recent current defense budget.

(d) Reversion to highly restrictive policy at this stage would do incalculable harm to our interests in Pakistan and hence to our larger interests in subcontinent.

(B) Second extreme option, of selling anything to anyone willing and able to pay, also has attractive features and basic weaknesses.

(1) Advantages:

(a) It would save us painful moralizing with both India and Pakistan (though Indians would regard it as pro-Pakistan);

(b) It would eliminate recurrent problems bedeviling our relations with HMG and other Western allies;

(c) It would help ease balance of payments pressures; and

(d) It would put us in stronger position to reduce Indian military dependence on USSR and Pak recourse to China.

(2) Basic weakness is that such policy would undermine our present policy of actively opposing Indo-Pak arms race. Latter policy has been strongly affirmed cornerstone of our broader policy toward subcontinent at least since President's press backgrounder in November 1965. We believe active opposition to an Indo-Pak arms race is essential element of any US commitment to support Indian and Pak economic development in major way. Thus despite its attractive features, laissez-faire policy, like highly restrictive first option, is not satisfactory instrument for advancing current US interests in region. This leaves some

---

[4] Document 457.

variation of middle-of-the-road approach as only feasible course under present circumstances.

III. Discussion: Pros and Cons of Middle-of-Road Approach

Middle-of-the-road option combines (a) case-by-case reviews under certain understood ground rules of military sales cases which we control and (b) diplomatic suasion of more general nature, in which we implicitly or explicitly relate Indian/Pakistani restraint on defense spending to future economic aid availabilities.

(A) Case-by-case review procedure:

(1) As pointed out in ref A and also in State 207414[5] and previous, case-by-case review procedure suffers from weakness that we do not control all supply sources, thus objections on our part to given sale we control may simply drive customer to second source we do not control. We continue however to believe that with careful handling we can exploit relative convenience and economy of India/Pakistan purchasing items which we control as opposed to comparable items from other sources, in manner permitting us to exert marginal restraining influence. This has in fact proven case. Despite difficulty over SU–7's, for example, we retain GOI's firm commitment to retire obsolete aircraft on at least a one-for-one basis as and when GOI phases in Hunters.

(2) A second problem involved in case-by-case review procedure is critical public and Congressional attitude towards arms supply of all kinds to LDC's. This has made it necessary even within terms of our policy to move cautiously, as with GOP request for tanks. Together with problems that inevitably grow out of discussions concerning a country's military inventory, this situation has definite potential for irritation, as ref (A) suggests.

(3) On positive side, our review procedure has been providing essential underpinning in each country for continuing dialogue on security matters. Last July Embassy New Delhi ably described importance of our developing and maintaining such dialogue with Indians (A–14:[6] India: Growth and Security). One of few felicitous consequences of SU–7 affair has been GOI offer review force levels with us. Recent conversation with Pak Defense Minister (Pindi 1724)[7] well illustrates value such dialogue on Pak side.

---

[5] Dated June 2. (National Archives and Records Administration, RG 59, Central Files 1967–69, DEF 12–5 INDIA)

[6] Airgram A–14 from New Delhi, July 6. (Ibid., POL 1 INDIA–US)

[7] Telegram 1724 from Rawalpindi, November 9, reported that Defense Minister Khan had asked whether Pakistan might approach Iran with regard to Iran's surplus M–47 tanks, which could meet Pakistan's needs. Khan said that Iran was willing to provide the tanks to Pakistan if the United States agreed. (Ibid., DEF 19–8 US–IRAN)

(4) As noted elsewhere, our ability apply general suasion on defense spending levels could be diminished should forthcoming aid levels be sharply reduced. Case-by-case review procedure would not be materially affected by any such limitations.

(5) Foregoing arguments appear equally applicable to case-by-case review of direct US sales cases (lethal spares) and third country lethal end item sales cases. Seems to us that direct US sales have in fact been proceeding smoothly and have contributed to advancement of our objectives in both countries. Only hitch that has developed has been in our efforts to monitor sales of third-country lethal end items, specifically Indian prevarication regarding SU–7's. On other hand our efforts to develop and apply criteria on third country lethal end items has clearly contributed to our dialogue with each government regarding its security plans. This has been particularly true in the case of Pakistan, where we have been applying rather more stringent criteria rather more successfully than has been the case in our discussions with the Indians. In Pak case, our policy in this regard succeeded for example in inhibiting German sale of Patton tanks (in period before publicity caused FRG to back down anyway). We conclude there is no more basis at this time for changing our policy with respect third country lethal end items than there is with respect to US-supplied lethal spares.

(B) General Suasion re Defense Levels:

(1) We know from experience that Pakistanis and particularly Indians tend to react viscerally and strongly to any démarche on our part which they construe as US effort to influence their national security decisions by threatening to reduce economic aid. We have also learned from experience that amount of leverage we obtain from given aid input varies not only with amount of aid, but also and more directly, with closeness of relationship between kind of aid we are putting in and kind of decision or policy we are trying to influence. It is therefore likely to be far more risky and difficult to apply econ aid leverage to decisions on defense spending than, say, it is to apply food aid leverage to decisions on agricultural policy. GOP and particularly GOI could have especially acute problems in heeding our advice were public opinions within their countries to learn extent and nature our efforts.

(2) Another limitation economic aid lever suffers from is its credibility. Current Congressional action will almost inevitably result in sharp cuts in FY '68 development aid to India and Pakistan but we doubt whether either GOI or GOP will conclude these cuts result primarily from any specific failure on their part to accommodate themselves to recent USG démarches re defense spending. However it is in

928 Foreign Relations, 1964–1968, Volume XXV

our interests to impress GOI and GOP of Congressional sensitivities such as those reflected in Conte amendment.[8]

(3) Despite these limitations we should continue to impress upon both governments that they each have constituency here, and way they handle that constituency, including their decisions on defense spending, will ultimately determine character of their bilateral relations with us. It is difficult to use this argument effectively in specific field of defense spending without overstepping bounds of either propriety or credibility, but we have to continue to do best we can, as long as we continue to play major role as provider of economic resources. While it may never be in our interest actually to invoke econ aid sanction, our aid input remains of considerable importance to India and provides underlying strength to our position. Our efforts will be helped to extent we can persuade each government of inevitability and legitimacy of link between our role as restrainer on defense spending and our role as free world econ aid leader.

(4) In particular we need to impress on Indians that we are going to have extremely difficult task next year in obtaining FY '69 aid appropriation sufficient to support aid level to India that we both agree situation calls for to support shared growth objectives; and that when we approach Congress we need to be armed with understanding with GOI on expected defense spending levels. Such understanding might best emerge from general defense talks Indians have recently proposed.

Rusk

---

[8] Reference is to the Conte–Long Amendment to the Foreign Assistance and Related Appropriations Act of 1968. The amendment, being debated in December 1967, was adopted as Section 119 of the Appropriations Act on January 2, 1968. The amendment directed the President to withhold economic assistance in an amount equivalent to the amount spent by any underdeveloped country other than Greece, Turkey, Iran, Israel, the Republic of China, the Philippines, and Korea for the purchase of sophisticated weapons systems. (P.L. 90–249; 81 Stat. 936)

473. **Telegram From the Department of State to the Embassy in Pakistan[1]**

Washington, December 21, 1967, 1803Z.

87856. Ref (Notal): (a) Rawalpindi 1269;[2] (b) State 61581;[3] (c) Karachi 807;[4] (d) Rawalpindi 1724;[5] (e) Rome 3081;[6] (f) Teheran 2471;[7] (g) Rawalpindi 2279;[8] (h) Teheran 2502;[9] (i) Bonn 6251;[10] (j) Rawal-

---

[1] Source: National Archives and Records Administration, RG 59, Central Files 1967–69, DEF 12–5 PAK. Secret; Immediate; Exdis. Drafted by Spain and Lewis D. Junior (G/PM) on December 15; cleared by Heck, Country Director for Iran Theodore L. Eliot, Jr., Rockwell, Handley, Edwin D. Crowley (EUR/GER), Stabler (EUR/AIS), Edgar J. Beigel (EUR/FBX), Battle, Williams, and Hamilton, and in draft by Wolf, Newcomer, and Major Wix (DOD/ISA); and approved by Katzenbach. Repeated to Tehran, Rome, CINCSTRIKE, CINCEUR, Brussels, and Bonn.

[2] Document 464.

[3] Document 469.

[4] See footnote 3, Document 469.

[5] See footnote 7, Document 472.

[6] Telegram 3081 from Rome, December 11, reported that the Italian Ministry of Defense was prepared to refurbish and sell 200 M–47 tanks to Pakistan if authorized to do so by the United States. (National Archives and Records Administration, RG 59, Central Files 1967–69, DEF 12–5 PAK)

[7] Telegram 2471 from Tehran, December 10, from Oehlert who was visiting Iran, reported on his conversation that day with Defense Minister Khan, who was also visiting Iran. Khan was at the point of returning to Pakistan following a "tank tour," which took him to Belgium, Italy, and Iran. He felt that the terms offered by Iran were the most favorable available. Oehlert turned the conversation to the question of the extension of the agreement governing the U.S. communication facilities at Peshawar. Khan said that the Foreign Ministry would oppose an extension, but that he favored one and intended to press his viewpoint with Ayub. He anticipated that Ayub would agree with him. (Ibid.)

[8] In telegram 2279 from Rawalpindi, December 12, the Embassy reported that Defense Minister Khan had reviewed the price and availability of M–47 tanks from Italy, Belgium, and Iran and indicated a preference for dealing with Iran. (Ibid.)

[9] In telegram 2502 from Tehran, December 13, the Embassy expressed its reluctance to concur in the transfer of refurbished M–47 tanks from Iran to Pakistan. The Embassy noted that the proposed transfer would contribute to the problem of attempting to persuade the Shah to avoid heavy expenditures for new tanks. (Ibid.)

[10] In telegram 6251 from Bonn, December 13, the Embassy reported that the Foreign Office had been impressed by a briefing provided by the Embassy concerning Congressional sensitivities with respect to arms transfers, particularly transfers to the subcontinent. (Ibid., DEF 19–8 US–GERW)

pindi 2019;[11] (k) Teheran 2563.[12] Subject: Military Supply, M–47 Tanks, and Peshawar.

1. While some loose ends remain, principal pieces involved in Pak tank problem now seem on table. We wish to (a) move to decision ASAP and (b) avoid possibility of misunderstanding among several parties involved in complicated procedure. US position must rest on following basic points, which Embassy Rawalpindi authorized convey (except as noted FYI) to GOP.

2. We are prepared in first instance to act only on up to 100 tanks and request to us from any seller country should be so presented. When contractual agreements are completed for the first 100 tanks, we would be willing to consider other requests including second 100 tanks. This is as responsive as we can be at this time.

3. We have now received from GOP assurances that (1) it will scrap obsolete tanks (M–24s) one-for-one for any US-controlled tanks acquired (ref d, para 3 and ref j, para 7c); (2) that GOP has total of 150–160 Chicom tanks with no additional tanks on order from Chicoms (refs d, para 3 and g, para 3); and that (3) GOP will procure no additional tanks from any source without consultation USG.

4. Approval by us of any sale would be conditioned on absolute and unequivocal confirmation of 3 above. Should it become apparent after approval that Pakistan had already arranged, by contract or other less formal mode, for more than the stated 150–160 Chicom tanks we would have to withdraw our approval. Embassy Rawalpindi should now ask for such confirmation. In addition we believe that you should reiterate importance we place on continued reduction in defense spending in both Pakistan and India which is basic objective whole military supply policy.

5. While we are gratified at close and cordial relationship between Iran and Pakistan underlying the Iranian offer described by Admiral Khan (ref f, para 2c), we strongly prefer in light current USG arms

---

[11] Document 470.

[12] In telegram 2563 from Tehran, December 18, from Oehlert, he expressed sympathy with the concerns outlined in telegram 2502 from Tehran. He noted, however, that the United States had indicated to Pakistan that it would give serious consideration to a third-country request to transfer 100 tanks to Pakistan if the terms were favorable, with the possibility of a subsequent transfer of an additional 100. The terms offered Pakistan by Iran were the most favorable of the offers presented, and Oehlert was concerned that if the United States did not authorize the sale by Iran there would be resentment in Rawalpindi. In the event that the Iranian sale could not be authorized, Oehlert asked for permission to inform the Ayub government that the United States would look with favor on a request from Belgium to transfer 200 tanks to Pakistan, provided that the price was favorable. (National Archives and Records Administration, RG 59, Central Files 1967–69, DEF 19–8 US–GERW)

discussions with Iran that GOP go to European source rather than to Iran.

6. FYI: We do not wish to make an issue of Iranian offer with GOP and believe above is as far as you should go in explaining our negative reaction re Iranian sale. In fact, however, we would appreciate all possible efforts your part to steer GOP away from involvement with Iran in this matter. The GOI has recently informed US of plans to embark on a large new five-year military procurement program at a time when we are having difficulty in meeting our existing MAP and credit sales commitments because of Congressional action. In our efforts to persuade the GOI to reduce the scale of its military program, we believe we have been successful in persuading the Shah at least tentatively to avoid heavy expenditures for new tanks by rehabilitating older M–47s. We cannot, therefore, approve Iranian tank sales to Pakistan and an Iranian request would be extremely embarrassing to us at this time. End FYI.

7. Information we have to date on European sources, costs, condition of tanks and delivery times is as yet incomplete and in part contradictory. Subject to closer look when more facts are in, terms offered to date do not seem preclude our approval of sale.

8. Should GOP wish us act on Italian proposal, it will be necessary clarify discrepancies between ref f, para 2, in which first 50 tanks are said to be Italian owned with remainder to be procured from Germany and ref e, para 1b, which indicates all tanks to be from surplus stocks in Germany. We do not exclude possibility of Italy acquiring and rehabilitating up to 100 German tanks for GOP, but all parties concerned should understand before the event that if later pressed we will have to indicate we knew and agreed that tanks sold by FRG to Italy were to facilitate Italian sale to Pakistan.

9. FYI: Re possible FRG role, we note (ref i) that FonOff now considering whether Cabinet and Bundestag might agree to direct sale tanks to Pakistan. We would appreciate Embassy Bonn's prognosis. End FYI.

10. Paks stated second preference as M–47 source, Belgium, might be most acceptable from all points of view. If GOP seriously interested it should stimulate Belgian request to USG, complete with info on costs, condition of tanks, and projected delivery schedule. FYI: If current negotiations with Italians for cooperative logistics agreement are successful, we might prefer Italians as best source. End FYI.

11. In sum, if GOP wants action on tanks, it should: (a) unequivocally confirm assurances paras 3 and 4 above; (b) cast request in terms of 100 M–47s; (c) select optimum supply source, hopefully giving full weight to foregoing considerations; and (d) get source government to submit request to USG for approval to sell to GOP, such request to be

accompanied by data on costs, condition of tanks, financing terms and delivery schedules to permit our response. FYI: We would prefer not to be faced at the same time with active requests from more than one country. End FYI.

12. FYI: We assume you will probably wish make above points to President Ayub or MOD Khan who has represented GOP in bulk of discussion this subject. We expect, however, to be filling in Pak Embassy here as well and wonder if it would not be good idea for you to touch base with MFA (perhaps Pirzada himself) in Rawalpindi also. Our views re connection between military supply and Peshawar which has appeared in discussions with Admiral Khan (refs a and f) follow in septel[13] which should be read with this message as guidance for further handling that matter. End FYI.

Rusk

---

[13] Document 474.

---

474.   **Telegram From the Department of State to the Embassy in Pakistan**[1]

Washington, December 21, 1967, 1803Z.

87857. Ref: (a) Rawalpindi 1269;[2] (b) State 61581;[3] (c) Tehran 2471.[4] Subject: Military Supply and Peshawar. For Ambassador.

1. We believe time has come to try establish certain basic principles for our efforts ensure continuance Peshawar Communications Station. Department's views on these follow and we would welcome your comments on them. Throughout Peshawar discussion, we will wish leave you maximum discretion on timing and tactics but feel that following points should be made clear to GOP soon at time and in manner you deem most appropriate:

---

[1] Source: National Archives and Records Administration, RG 59, Central Files 1967–69, DEF 15 PAK–US. Secret; Immediate; Exdis. Drafted by Spain; cleared by Heck, Richard E. Curl (INR/RCI), Handley, Wolf, General Newcomer, Major Wix, and Hamilton at the White House; and approved by Katzenbach. Repeated to CINCSTRIKE.

[2] Document 464.

[3] Document 469.

[4] See footnote 7, Document 473.

(a) The Peshawar Communications Station remains of great and undiminished importance to the US and we wish to keep it—though not at any price.

(b) Peshawar is integral part totality USG–GOP relationship and must not by us or GOP be specifically linked to military supply policy (ref (b), para 1).

(c) Military supply policy is in itself of considerable continuing value to GOP (ref (b), paras 2–5 and ref (d)[5]) and we assume GOP wishes preserve it. (FYI: GOP requests for tanks and extension leases for naval vessels, if approved, will be further evidence this.)

(d) Any GOP attempt, such as Admiral Khan may have in mind to use Peshawar to force change in military supply (refs (a) and (c)) will not be successful and would only put strain on USG–GOP relations.

2. We believe following additional points (which should not be communicated to GOP) important to our own (i.e., USG) thinking on Peshawar matter.

(a) While we prepared look as favorably as possible on GOP requests designed increase its own capability at Peshawar (e.g., recent "shopping list" submitted [less than 1 line of source text not declassified]), there are limits to what we can do in this field in terms both our own technical security requirements and our inability make major direct contribution to GOP capabilities directed against neighbor who is also friend of ours. In any event, degree our forthcomingness this field not likely be decisive in future Peshawar.

(b) Bearing in mind 1 (c) and (d) above, MOD Admiral Khan's indications of desire support continuance Peshawar are welcome. However, final discussions and decisions will have to be with Ayub[6] in terms (a) and (b) above, and MFA will likely play significant role. In order try minimize danger of issue, which is one of broad national interest to both USG and GOP, being framed in terms of inter-ministry squabble within GOP, and on assumption we our own best advocate, we wonder if it would not be useful for you ease into subject of Peshawar with Pirzada at early date.

Rusk

---

[5] The telegram does not include a reference (d).

[6] Oehlert met with Ayub on December 22 and informed him, as instructed, that the Peshawar facility remained of undiminished importance to the United States. Ayub agreed that Peshawar was an integral part of the relationship between the United States and Pakistan, and he also agreed that the question of the renewal of the agreement should be discussed well in advance of the expiration of the 10-year agreement governing the facility in order to avoid "crash decisions." (Telegram 2443 from Rawalpindi, December 22; National Archives and Records Administration, RG 59, Central Files 1967–69, POL 15–1 PAK)

475.   Memorandum of Conversation Between President Johnson and President Ayub[1]

Karachi Airport, December 23, 1967.

President Johnson summarized to me the operational result of his talk with President Ayub as follows:

1. We shall look urgently into the possibility of an additional PL 480 allocation of vegetable oil to Pakistan.

2. We shall look urgently at possibility of additional 500,000 tons of wheat for Pakistan, of which 400,000 would be PL 480 and 100,000 commercial purchase. The purpose would be to build up Pakistani stocks in this generally favorable environment.

President Ayub said that with some exertion they could store this additional shipment.

3. President Johnson agreed to look into the possibility of replacing the 500 obsolescent Sherman tanks with Pattons. In addition to agreeing to sales from third countries (e.g., Italy and Turkey), he wanted us to examine whether we could not sell these directly to Pakistan if the Shermans were taken out of action.

---

[1] Source: Johnson Library, National Security File, Country File, Pakistan, Vol. VIII, Memos, 8/67–4/68. Secret. Drafted by Rostow. A note on the memorandum reads: "(Partial)." Although the memorandum is dated December 22, the President's Daily Diary establishes that President Johnson met with President Ayub during a 1-hour refueling stop at the Karachi airport on December 23. (Ibid.) President Johnson was returning to Washington from a trip to East Asia that included stops in Australia and Thailand. He did not stop in India, but sent a message to Prime Minister Gandhi from Air Force One on December 23 expressing regret that the press of time precluded a stop to meet with her. (Telegram 89247 to New Delhi; National Archives and Records Administration, RG 59, Central Files 1967–69, POL 7 US/JOHNSON)

476.   Telegram From the Embassy in Pakistan to the Department of State[1]

Rawalpindi, December 27, 1967, 0857Z.

2492. Ref: (a) State 87857;[2] (b) Rawalpindi 2443.[3]

1. In Pindi reftel reported Ayub conversation of December 22 re Peshawar.

2. With further reference to State 87857:

A. Regardless of what we say about not linking Peshawar specifically to military supply policy (para 1(b), State 87857) it will be impossible to divorce the two from each other in the minds, tactics, and strategy of GOP and it is a fact that both negotiations must be conducted in the same time frame. The key word of the above reference is "specifically" and we will be so guided.

B. The GOP will not be greatly convinced of the "considerable continuing value to GOP" of USG military supply policy (State 87857, para 1 (c)) unless either or both:

I. Such policy produces reasonable quantity end items for GOP on a case to case basis;
II. Such policy results in measurable reductions in GOI offensive strength.

C. Admiral Khan's reference to tanks and Peshawar in same conversation can be construed not as attempt to "force change in military supply policy" (para 1 (d) State 87857) but rather as expectation that positive results will be forthcoming under that policy on a case to case basis.

D. While it is agreed that we must make clear to GOP that there are limits to what we can do in the field of increasing GOP capacity at Peshawar, this proposition should rest on terms of our own technical security requirements and not on our inability to make major direct contribution to GOP capabilities [6½ lines of source text not declassified]

3. Pursuant to conversation with Ayub will be talking next week both to Khan and to Pirzada. Both will have a substantial intervention in the decision and we intend maintain dialogue with both as well as with Ayub.

Oehlert

---

[1] Source: National Archives and Records Administration, RG 59, Central Files 1967–69, DEF 15 PAK–US. Secret; Exdis.

[2] Document 474.

[3] See footnote 6, Document 474.

477.   Memorandum From the President's Special Assistant (Rostow) to President Johnson[1]

Washington, December 28, 1967.

SUBJECT

Tanks for Pakistan

I have looked into two questions you raised after your conversations with President Ayub:

1. If they are clearly for replacement, why don't we sell tanks directly to Pakistan, rather than fuss with a complicated deal in which the Europeans sell them to Pakistan with our permission?

2. Whatever the purchase arrangements, why are we talking about 100 tanks when Ayub wants 200?

There are two stock arguments against a direct U.S. tank sale to Pakistan. First, we have no tanks of the M–47 model Ayub is seeking in Europe. This was the Korean war tank we stopped making in 1954. It has long since disappeared from our active inventory and our MAP shelf.

However, we do have a considerable number of newer M–48 tanks in inventory. This is an improved version of the M–47—no more armor or fire power, but better mechanical performance and electronic equipment. Moreover, Defense estimates a cost of roughly $45,000 per copy for our M–48's which compares favorably with the estimated $80,000 per copy the Europeans will charge Ayub for reconditioned M–47s. Thus, taking the question of supply alone, it appears that we could offer Ayub better tanks than he is seeking (although not enough better to give the Indians real trouble) for less money than we would have to pay the Europeans for the inferior model—and make ourselves some foreign exchange in the bargain.

But we must also weigh the second argument against direct sale: that it would undermine the policy on arms sales in South Asia we announced last April. That policy is designed to exert maximum restraint on defense spending while at the same time keeping both countries, particularly Pakistan, from being forced to rely solely on the Soviets and the Chicoms as arms suppliers. The centerpiece of our policy is a ban on U.S. sales of new weapon systems to either side and a stated intent to discourage other suppliers from such sales except where clearly for replacement. This gets us out of the arms sales busi-

---

[1] Source: Johnson Library, National Security File, Country File, Pakistan, Vol. VIII, Memos, 8/67–4/68. Secret.

ness in South Asia, except for spare parts, without slamming the door on Pakistan's need to maintain and modernize her largely U.S.-equipped forces.

This policy is partly a reaction to past and present Congressional unhappiness with arms sales to poor countries. (You will recall the flak when U.S. tanks were firing at each other from both sides of the line during the Indo/Pak war in 1965.) It has already saved us a number of requests for planes and other sophisticated weapons from both sides. It has been the framework for substantial pressure—and some success in Pakistan—for reductions in Indo–Pak defense spending. Still it is not an entirely tidy answer. It did not, for example, keep the Paks from buying 150 tanks from the Chinese nor the Indians from buying jets from the Soviets. Indeed, it is sufficiently untidy to cause Bowles to send a strong cable[2] recommending an immediate policy reassessment with a view to a ban on all U.S. sales to both sides of all lethal equipment—spare parts and end items. (You will recall instructing us, pursuant to the Bowles cable and a rejoinder from Ben Oehlert,[3] to conduct a thorough review of arms sales on the Subcontinent. That review is completed and State has instructed Bowles and Oehlert that we will continue for the present with our present policy.)[4]

The Congressional side of the problem has worsened considerably with the passage of the Conte amendment to the foreign aid appropriation bill which calls for reductions in foreign aid equal to poor countries' spending on sophisticated weapons. We haven't yet determined whether we must consider tanks "sophisticated." If so, the President must find the tanks deal "vital" to U.S. security and waive the effect of the amendment, or he must cut AID development loans to Pakistan by an amount equal to spending for tanks. If the past slate were clean, it is a moot point whether we would get a better reaction on the Hill to such a waiver if we were making the sale as against the Europeans doing it. But in the light of our announced policy—which would be clearly violated by any direct sale—an offer of U.S. sale would produce a situation almost precisely parallel to the F–5 problem in Latin America. We could probably expect much the same results with Henry Reuss and other liberals in both Houses.

Beyond this, there is the question of credit terms. We have no unused authority to offer Ayub time payments. He can probably do better with the Europeans.

---

[2] See footnote 2, Document 472.
[3] See footnote 3, Document 472.
[4] See Document 472.

In short, if we sell these tanks directly, we will violate our own announced policy against selling arms on the Subcontinent; we will thereby open ourselves to requests for other sophisticated weapons—including aircraft—from both sides; and we will do these things in the heat of Congressional displeasure with all sales of sophisticated weapons to poor countries. We will also draw heavy fire from the Indians, with whom we hope to start general defense talks in the next few weeks. Most important, we will burden the aid bill with another heavy albatross to carry in an already tough year. In spite of the advantages, therefore, I would recommend against our offering to make the sale ourselves.

The question of why 100 rather than 200 tanks is a matter of international and Congressional tactics. The original Pak request was for 100, although it was clear that this was the first in a series of actions designed eventually to replace all of the 500 Sherman tanks Ayub mentioned to you. The Paks later raised the request to 200 because their foreign exchange situation loosened a bit so that they thought they could afford more. Our object is to keep the modernization process to a slow and steady pace which doesn't divert resources from development. On the Congressional side, Luke Battle talked to the Senate Foreign Relations Committee in terms of 100 tanks and got grudging approval precisely, in part, because the allowance was smaller than the request. If we wanted to do 200, we would probably have to return to Fulbright & Co. and we could not expect a pleasant reception.

All things considered, I would vote that we keep talking in terms of 100 tanks to be purchased from the Europeans, probably from Italy or Belgium.[5]

Walt

---

[5] A marginal note on the memorandum by Jim Jones reads: "I want to talk to him about this," apparently quoting the President's response to Rostow's memorandum.

478. Telegram From the President's Special Assistant (Rostow) to President Johnson in Texas[1]

Washington, December 28, 1967, 1638Z.

CAP 671199. Subject: Wheat for Pakistan. We have some confusion in the ranks about your wishes on a new PL480 wheat agreement for Pakistan. I thought we had better check with you directly.

1. In October you made two decisions on wheat for Pakistan.

—First, you authorized immediate negotiation on 500,000 tons of wheat plus oil and other commodities. It was the signing of this agreement that you saw on the ticker on Tuesday.[2]

—Second, you instructed Oehlert to try to work out a deal for another 250,000 tons of which we [they] would buy half and we would supply half through PL480.

2. Just before we got to Pakistan last week Ayub's people gave Oehlert their answer to the half-and-half proposition put to them in October. Their counter-offer is to buy 100,000 tons if it is part of a package containing 400,000 tons in PL480 wheat. In short, they have responded to our proposal of a 1–1 ratio between purchases and PL480 with a counter-offer of 4–1. It is this package, totaling 500,000 tons, that Ayub discussed with you.

3. Oehlert recommends we accept Ayub's counter-offer. Freeman and Gaud support that recommendation.

I support the recommendation that we accept Ayub's proposal, but I want to be sure that we are following your wishes in accepting a somewhat less favorable proposition than you instructed us to put to the Pakistanis. Oehlert rightly points out that they are in a rough foreign exchange position, and that even this proposal is generous in a bumper crop year. I don't think we will do any better by pushing, although we may be able to move some more PL480 wheat for buffer stocks in 1968. For now, I recommend you authorize us to accept the Ayub proposition.[3]

---

[1] Source: Johnson Library, National Security File, Country File, Pakistan, Vol. VIII, Memos, 8/67–4/68. Confidential.

[2] December 26.

[3] The President approved the recommendation.

479.   Telegram From the Department of State to the Embassy in India[1]

Washington, December 28, 1967, 1929Z.

90381. State/AID/DOD message. Ref: State 80797.[2] Defense Talks with GOI.

1. Final passage of aid legislation with resolution House–Senate differences close to lower House levels has underscored importance of obtaining better understanding with Indians than we have been able to achieve to date regarding where they are planning to go over next several years in their defense spending and military force levels. As indicated last para State 80797 we need to have some such understanding in hand to administer FY '68 funds as well as when we discuss crucially important FY '69 aid bill with Congress. FYI: Inclusion of Conte[3] and Symington Amendments[4] in FY '68 aid bill has added to importance of achieving such understanding, as indicated below. End FYI.

2. It is clearly sense of Congress that US economic aid resources shall not be used to support regional arms races. Congressional attitudes toward our economic aid program are influenced by degree to which such arms races are in fact taking place. As major developing country and largest aid recipient, manner in which India handles its Congressional constituency here regarding its defense spending can have important bearing on Congressional attitude toward aid as a whole. At present Congress is disturbed by reports of Indian re-equipment on extensive scale and is far from convinced that pace-setter India is genuinely anxious to hold down defense spending and avoid arms spiral with Pakistan. Evidence of Indian restraint could thus prove critical factor influencing FY '69 aid bill.

3. Meanwhile we have immediate question of applicability of Conte and Symington Amendments to current aid to India. Dept. is studying interpretation and application of amendments, and will

---

[1] Source: National Archives and Records Administration, RG 59, Central Files 1967–69, DEF 1 INDIA. Secret; Limdis. Drafted by Coon on December 27; cleared by Heck, Wolf, Kathryn N. Folger (H), and in draft by Spain, Acting Assistant Legal Adviser for Economic Affairs Knute E. Malmborg, Williams, and Colonel Black (DOD/ISA); and approved by Handley. Repeated to Rawalpindi, London, and CINCSTRIKE.

[2] Document 472.

[3] See footnote 8, Document 472.

[4] The Symington Amendment, Section 620 (s) of the Foreign Assistance Act of 1967, was adopted on November 14 and required the President to withhold assistance if in his view the recipient country excessively and unnecessarily diverted resources to military expenditures. (P.L. 90–137; 81 Stat. 445)

shortly instruct the field thereon. In any event, we will soon be talking to Congress about current and proposed Indian acquisitions of sophisticated military equipment from abroad in more detail than ever before. Whatever Indians may think about Conte and Symington Amendments we hope that they will at least privately recognize it is in their interest that when we go to Hill we are familiar with Indian plans and rationale.

4. In light foregoing we believe Embassy should take early occasion get talks started with Indians. Fact that GOI officials have already expressed interest in such talks (reftel) should provide useful opening wedge. We believe Country Team has adequate manpower resources for type of talks we envision and Washington or CINCSTRIKE deputation unnecessary, but willing reconsider if you disagree.

5. Believe we should recognize both among ourselves and with GOI that main purpose of talks will be to help prepare us for administering aid in FY '68 and for next round of aid legislation and that this should determine character and subject matter of discussions. We would thus hope that talks would give us better understanding of rationale behind current GOI defense spending levels and provide us better basis for balanced independent judgement which we could support with Congress as to degree of restraint Indians showing in total defense spending. To extent it should become clear GOI intends under currently foreseeable circumstances to cut this year's defense expenditures and hold line on defense budgets for next several years, so much the better. We would also hope GOI could give us reasonably detailed picture of current and planned acquisitions of individual items of sophisticated equipment, foreign exchange costs and rate of payment of such acquisitions including estimated foreign exchange equivalent of rupee payments to Bloc, and, most important, rationale for their acquisition. Inevitably this will involve some discussion of threat estimates and force levels as well as budgetary data but we do not foresee anything on that scene comparable in detail and comprehensiveness to exercise preceding 1964 memo of understanding.[5] (Incidentally it would be helpful if Indians would come to share our sense that 1965 war completely changed the rules of the game, that questions we are interested in now relate to general trends in defense spending and to how specific planned acquisitions relate to current and prospective threat, not to whether current and planned budgets and acquisitions are consistent with a five-year plan formed in another era.)

6. We recognize and sympathize with Embassy New Delhi's reluctance engage in discussions with GOI regarding Indian force levels vis-à-vis Pakistan, particularly to extent this involves estimates of Pak

---

[5] See footnote 2, Document 53.

threat. Unfortunately we fail to see how we can examine only half a defense establishment in a sufficiently coherent way to enable us to form the kinds of judgements we are seeking here. We hope that by laying our cards on table with GOI at outset of talks we can arrive at the kinds of understandings we need without excessive diversions into blind alleys of debate regarding Pakistani intentions, capabilities, etc.

7. Recognize you may have further thoughts regarding strategy, tactics, and terms of reference. Hope we can work these out soonest and get talks started by mid-January. Timewise, fuse on Capitol Hill is likely prove short.[6]

Rusk

---

[6] Bowles reported on January 8 that he discussed the issue of India's defense expenditures with Desai on January 2, stressing the limitations placed on U.S. policy by the Conte and Symington Amendments. Desai indicated that he remained determined, for a variety of reasons, to hold defense expenditures to the minimum consistent with security requirements. Bowles noted, however, that it would be unrealistic to expect India to violate understandings with foreign suppliers in order to provide the detailed information the United States required. (Telegram 8089 from New Delhi; National Archives and Records Administration, RG 59, Central Files 1967–69, DEF 1 INDIA)

---

480.   Telegram From the President's Special Assistant (Rostow) to President Johnson in Texas[1]

Washington, January 12, 1968, 1638Z.

CAP 80307. For the President. Subject: Wheat for Pakistan. You will recall that you authorized us to accept President Ayub's offer of a 500,000 ton wheat deal, 100,000 tons in CCC sales and 400,000 tons on PL 480 terms. That decision was conveyed to Ben Oehlert.

Last night Oehlert advised us[2] that (1) he understood you to instruct him to put together a program totalling one million tons of wheat (not 500,000); (2) he has put together a package proposing a one million ton program—all PL 480—to cover the rest of calendar '68; and (3) he wants to give this proposal to Ayub at 9:30 tonight Ranch time.

---

[1] Source: Johnson Library, National Security File, Country File, Pakistan, Vol. VIII, Memos, 8/67–4/68. Confidential. Received at the LBJ Ranch at 11:45 a.m.

[2] Telegram 2692 from Rawalpindi, January 11. (National Archives and Records Administration, RG 59, Central Files 1967–69, AID (US) 15–8 PAK)

Everybody wants to move as much wheat to Pakistan as possible but we need organized recommendations on two questions raised by the Oehlert proposal. First, do we want to bless the calculations of wheat requirements contained in Oehlert's memorandum? (Once we sign on to these, we will have pretty well settled the limits on our 1968 PL 480 program.) Second, do we want to offer Ayub the full million tons on PL 480 terms? (This proposal involves a one-to-ten ratio between CCC sales and PL 480, rather than the one-to-four ratio represented by the proposal you approved last month.)

We know of no reason why a delay of a day or two to pull the government together on these questions should cause any problem in Pakistan. Therefore, we have instructed Oehlert not to deliver his proposal until he gets further instructions.

We expect to come to you for a decision on this matter in the very near future. But I thought you would want to know how we are handling Oehlert's request. If you wish, of course, we can simply tell him to go ahead now.[3]

---

[3] A handwritten note on the telegram by Jim Jones reads: "I said I'd give 400 and sell 100 and do it again—give 800 sell 200. But I would give all if necessary." The quote is apparently the President's response to Rostow's comments. Another handwritten note reads: "Jones told Rostow."

---

481. Letter From Secretary of State Rusk to the Ambassador to India (Bowles)[1]

Washington, January 19, 1968.

Dear Chet:

Many thanks for your letter of December 22[2] reviewing the background of Indian defense planning. I certainly agree that in judging

---

[1] Source: National Archives and Records Administration, RG 59, Central Files 1967–69, DEF 1 INDIA. Secret. Drafted by Schaffer in NEA/INC on January 11.

[2] A copy of Bowles' December 22, 1967, letter to Rusk is ibid. He also sent a copy to McNamara who responded on January 17 along the lines of Rusk's response. He too felt that the 1965 war had changed the situation on the subcontinent and that the 1964 Memorandum of Understanding with India had been overtaken by events. From that perspective, McNamara felt that the "SU–7 incident was most unfortunate and we must make it clear to the Indians that such actions seriously inhibit our ability to support legitimate economic and military requirements." (Washington National Records Center, RG 330, OSD Files: FRC 72 A 2468, India 1967)

Indian activities in the arms field we must not allow ourselves to be governed by our exasperations with India's uncandid behavior. I think I can say in all sincerity that these exasperations, vexing as they were, have not influenced our consideration of the issues involved.

In discussing the buildup of the Indian Air Force, you suggest that acquisition of the SU–7 and other aircraft is in accordance with the Indian 5-year defense plan (since stretched to 7 years) which was adopted with our approval in 1964. As you know, the Indians both here and in New Delhi have argued from this position. I recall that it was the burden of one of B.K. Nehru's last calls on me. B.K. went so far as to produce the plan itself to demonstrate that we have no reason to object to the SU–7s.

The argument would have considerable force if we could conclude that nothing significant had happened since May 1964 to call into question the relevance of the Plan in the context of Indo-American relations. I cannot agree that this is the case. The Indo-Pak conflict in 1965 has fundamentally changed the situation and has led us to a basic recasting of our arms supply policy toward the subcontinent. The 1964 Defense Plan, developed against a background of significant US assistance to the strengthening of India's defenses, cannot at this late date determine our approach to Indian defense expenditures.

This fundamental difference between 1964 and 1968 is further underscored by the mood of Congress. The lawyers are still studying the Conte and Symington Amendments and we have not yet come to a definite conclusion as to how we will interpret them in the administration of our foreign aid programs. What is definite, however, is that both amendments reflect the distaste of Congress toward the acquisition by developing nations of advanced weaponry and a determination on its part to prevent indirect American financing of such weapons.

I am reasonably certain that were we to try to ignore history and the mood on the Hill and seek to justify Indian arms acquisitions in terms of the conditions which prevailed in 1964 our effort would be a non-starter with Congress. I think that influential Congressmen, perhaps even more than we here, recognize that the old pre-1965 era in Indo-American relations is over and that we must work toward a new relationship.

I would hope that one of the achievements in working out this new relationship will be a restoration of candor between the two sides and a frank discussion of where India is going in the defense field. Our telegram 90381[3] spells out at some length how important it is, in

---

[3] Document 479.

terms of the administration of FY68 funds as well as our discussion with Congress of the FY69 aid bill, that we reach a better understanding of what the Indians mean to do.

I hope that you will devote all your skill toward developing a meaningful dialogue and, particularly, to relating it to the need for restraint on the Indians' part in total defense spending.

With best regards,

Sincerely,

Dean

482. Memorandum From the President's Special Assistant (Rostow) to President Johnson[1]

Washington, February 2, 1968, 7 p.m.

Mr. President:

Herewith a longer get well message to Ayub.[2] It mentions both the wheat and the tanks you discussed with him at the Karachi airport.

On *wheat* we are moving ahead with the first 500,000 tons you discussed. We will go ahead with the second 500,000 tons as soon as the first agreement is signed.

On *tanks* the Paks have approached Belgium—with our blessing—to accept the Belgian offer of reconditioned tanks at a reasonable price. In the meantime, however, the Belgian Foreign Office has caught wind of what their defense ministry is doing and is trying to get the Prime Minister to revoke the offer. If they succeed, the Italians are panting to step into the breach.

---

[1] Source: Johnson Library, National Security File, Memos to the President, Walt W. Rostow, Vol. 59, February 1–6, 1968. Confidential.

[2] The message approved by the President was transmitted to Rawalpindi on February 3 in telegram 109738 for delivery to President Ayub. (National Archives and Records Administration, RG 59, Central Files 1967–69, POL 15–1 PAK) On February 16 the Embassy confirmed reports that Ayub had suffered a heart attack. (Telegram 3421 from Rawalpindi; Johnson Library, National Security File, Country File, Pakistan, Vol. VIII, Cables, 8/67–4/68)

However this comes out, it looks as though Pakistan will get the tanks. But I think it would be unwise for you to get very far out on a limb in promising them.

W. W. Rostow[3]

Approve[4]

Disapprove

Call Me

---

[3] Printed from a copy that bears this typed signature.
[4] None of the options is checked.

---

483.   Telegram From the President's Special Assistant (Rostow) to the Ambassador to India (Bowles)[1]

Washington, February 10, 1968, 2349Z.

CAP 80402. For Ambassador Bowles from Walt Rostow. We were delighted to receive your message reporting Morarji Desai's assurances on the Conte amendment.[2] It is very good to know that we will not have a serious problem on this score at least through the end of the fiscal year.

As you know, both the Conte and the Symington Amendments reflect deep concern among the Congress and the people that we exert all the influence we can against arms races between poor countries, particularly Latin America and South Asia, and against diversion of resources from economic to military purposes. I know that nobody feels these concerns more deeply than you do.

---

[1] Source: Johnson Library, National Security File, Country File, India, Vol. X, Cables, 8/67–2/68. Secret; [text not declassified].

[2] In telegram 9881 from New Delhi, February 1, Bowles referred to the assurance offered by Desai that no contracts or agreements for acquisition of military equipment of the type envisioned by the Conte Amendment had been entered into or were comtemplated from January 2 to June 30, 1968. (National Archives and Records Administration, RG 59, Central Files 1967–69, AID (US) 5)

I would hope, therefore, that this successful experience on the Conte issue can be followed up with a special effort to make it clear to Morarji that our ability to come through with the economic aid we all agree India needs depends heavily on the shape of the defense budget he will announce on February 29. The President has just sent to the Hill an aid request $600 million higher than what he got last year despite (1) serious risk that it will be sharply cut, and (2) crying domestic needs for which he has a better chance of getting the money he requests. To make this act of courage worthwhile we will need equal courage in Delhi.

I know that U.S. influence on Indian budget decisions is a very touchy problem. Still, I think it is very important that we try to find a private way to get across one simple fact of life: If the Indians could possibly manage a decrease in the defense budget this year, we would have an additional major weapon in fighting for the foreign aid appropriation we need. If, on the other hand, there is a major increase, we will put a powerful weapon in the hands of those who would have us abandon India to her fate. I realize that Morarji has already ruled out a decrease in a public speech, but I wonder whether your personal intervention might not get him to reconsider. In any case, we should make certain he is absolutely clear on the importance of restraint in terms of the situation here.

Once the budget is announced, I would hope we could follow through with the general defense talks that you and Morarji have discussed in days past. The Conte–Symington business is not, I am convinced, a transitory phenomenon. Both we and the Indians are going to have to get used to sharing our knowledge and our planning on these delicate matters. The sooner we start, the better.

My best to you and Steb. I know things must be hectic with UNCTAD in town. Elspeth sends her regards.

484. Memorandum From the President's Special Assistant (Rostow) to President Johnson[1]

Washington, February 20, 1968, 3:15 p.m.

SUBJECT

Possible Ayub Visit

Ben Oehlert has had a feeler[2]—which he thinks is premeditated and serious—from one of the caretaker military leaders who is minding the store in Pakistan while President Ayub recovers from what we now believe were two successive heart attacks. The suggestion is that Ayub would make a visit to Britain and the United States during his convalesence.

The public reason for the trip here would be medical, but the private reason would be a face-to-face negotiation with you about renewal of our important intelligence facility at Peshawar.

Oehlert reports he was "completely non-commital about a U.S. trip both generally and during any particular time frame." He has asked for guidance on whether we would welcome such a trip and, if so, when.

At Tab A, *for your approval,* is a draft reply which says:

—We would be happy to provide Ayub with any medical help he wants in the United States.
—The President would want to see Ayub.
—For Oehlert's information, we would prefer a private visit as part of Ayub's recuperation, but we would try to arrange an official visit if Ayub strongly prefers it.
—In any event, we want to avoid the impression that we are deeply worried about the Peshawar negotiation. (The renewal need not be effective until the end of June. We should try to keep our cool as long as we can.)

---

[1] Source: Johnson Library, National Security File, Country File, Pakistan, Vol. VIII, Cables, 8/67–4/68. Secret.

[2] In telegram 3451 from Rawalpindi, February 18, Oehlert reported that Defense Minister Khan had suggested that the issue of Peshawar could best be decided by Ayub and Johnson in a face-to-face meeting that might take place in the United States during a trip planned as a part of Ayub's convalesence. (National Archives and Records Administration, RG 59, Central Files 1967–69, POL 15–1 PAK)

I think this is about right. Ben is certain to deliver the message with the warmth I know you would want.

Walt

Approve message[3]

Disapprove

Call me

---

[3] Johnson checked this option and added the handwritten notation "as amended." He amended the proposed message to delete a reference to possible scheduling problems. The gist of the message remained as outlined in this memorandum and was sent to Rawalpindi in telegram 118643, February 21. (Ibid.)

---

485. Memorandum From the President's Special Assistant (Rostow) to President Johnson[1]

Washington, February 28, 1968, 1:45 p.m.

SUBJECT

Tanks for Pakistan

In the attached (Tab A)[2] Katzenbach recommends that you authorize formal notice to Italy that we approve their sale of 200 M–47 tanks (100 now and 100 later) to Pakistan. This would meet the immediate need Ayub discussed with you at the Karachi airport. McNamara and Gaud join in the recommendation, and Luke Battle has raised the general proposition of a third-country sale with Senator Symington's Subcommittee of the SFRC (with Fulbright in the room) and got no objection.

This is the result of a lengthy effort to get Ayub his tanks without sinking the arms policy for South Asia we announced last April and thereby provoking another storm on the Hill which could scuttle the

---

[1] Source: Johnson Library, National Security File, Country File, Pakistan, Vol. IX, Cables, 5/68–11/68. Secret; Exdis.

[2] Reference is to a February 27 memorandum from Katzenbach to the President entitled "Approval of Italian Sale of M–47 Tanks to Pakistan." (Ibid.)

Aid Bill. The Italians would make the sale pursuant to a general franchise we are negotiating under which they will be our agents in Europe for buying, rehabilitating, and reselling used tanks. The preliminary price ($40,000–$50,000) quoted to the Paks is reasonable.

In return for your approval, Ayub has promised to scrap old tanks on a one-for-one basis, to give us a full rundown on their present armor (including their Chicom tanks), not to buy any more Chicom tanks, and not to buy any more tanks from anybody without consulting with us.

At Tab B[3] are State's findings that neither the Conte nor the Symington Amendments—dealing with poor-country arms purchases—affect this sale.

I recommend you approve.

One issue of tactics remains. The present thinking in State and Defense is to tell Ben Oehlert that you have approved 200 tanks but authorize him to tell Ayub about only 100. The argument is that we are better off to see how he performs on his end of the bargain before telling him about the second tranche. There is some merit to this case, but the effect on Ayub would be considerably different if we told him about all 200. He has dealt with our bureaucracy for a long time; he would know there is a connection between the larger number and your Karachi conversation.

Walt

Approve Katzenbach memo

Disapprove

Call me

Tell Ayub about the first 100 tanks only

Tell Ayub about all 200 tanks[4]

---

[3] Not printed.
[4] Johnson checked this option.

486. Memorandum From the President's Special Assistant
(Rostow) to President Johnson[1]

Washington, February 29, 1968.

SUBJECT

$115 million AID Loan to Pakistan

In the attached (Tab A),[2] Messrs. Gaud and Zwick recommend that you approve an AID loan to Pakistan of $115 million. Joe Fowler concurs.

The loan is to finance irrigation equipment, pesticides, industrial raw materials, and other goods necessary to maintain the excellent economic performance Pakistan has shown for the past five years. Together with the $25 million supplied last June, this will meet our $140 million Consortium commitment to Pakistan for FY 1968.

The timing is particularly urgent because the Paks have agreed to undertake a new liberalized import policy effective tomorrow (March 1). They need the foreign exchange cushion provided by this loan, both to quiet fears that they couldn't stand a run and to meet any pressures on foreign exchange which do arise because of the new ground rules. Ben Oehlert is afraid that if we don't get a firm approval to the Paks today, they may scuttle the import reform, with serious damage to our relations with Ayub.

I recommend you approve. At Tab B is a State/AID paper[3] advising you that in their judgment there is no requirement that you take any step to withhold aid from Pakistan under the terms of the Symington Amendment which deals with military expenditures by poor countries.

Walt

Approve package[4]

Disapprove

Call me

---

[1] Source: Johnson Library, National Security File, Country File, Pakistan, Vol. VIII, Memos, 8/67–4/68. No classification marking.

[2] Attached were a February 20 memorandum from Gaud to the President entitled "Production Loan to Pakistan," and a February 24 memorandum from Zwick to the President entitled "Proposed $115 Million Development Loan to Pakistan."

[3] Not printed.

[4] Johnson checked this option.

487.   Memorandum From the President's Special Assistant (Rostow) to President Johnson[1]

Washington, March 4, 1968, noon.

SUBJECT

Indian Debt Relief

In the attached Messrs. Gaud, Zwick and Fowler recommend you approve a U.S. role in a debt relief package for India.[2] The World Bank has proposed a relief package of $100 million per year for three years. Our share would be less than $9 million per year.

In short, in return for a minor rescheduling of a 1951 wheat loan to India, this exercise would reschedule a good part of the backbreaking load of European debt the Indians now face. There must be such a rescheduling of European debt if we are to avoid a situation within five years in which all our aid to India will go to pay back European loans. Charlie Zwick's memorandum (Tab A) is a good, concise summary of the proposal. It requires no action by Congress.

You will note in the Zwick memorandum that we have some evidence that India is making another arms deal with the Soviets. Although as a matter of law the Conte Amendment does not apply to debt relief, we would make it very clear that any suggestion of a violation of the letter or the spirit of the assurance Morarji Desai has given us to satisfy the Conte Amendment will affect our ability to provide debt relief just as it will affect all other forms of aid. I think this gives us a defensible position on the Hill if the Indians do something stupid. We still have plenty of time to reverse ourselves on debt relief if need be because the first repayments are not due until June.

I recommend you approve.

This one has a very short fuse. The debt relief meeting began today in Paris. The Japanese—who would have to forego about $20 million a year—are taking a very strong position against the principle of debt relief and they have some support from the Italians. The World Bank needs our help if there is to be any chance of turning the Japanese around. If you approve, we need to let our negotiators know this afternoon.

---

[1] Source: Johnson Library, National Security File, Country File, India, Vol. XI, Memos and Miscellaneous, 2/68–10/68. Secret.

[2] Memorandum to the President from Zwick, February 27.

My apologies for the rush. We have spent almost a week digging this out of the Treasury.

Walt

Approve package[3]

Disapprove

Call me

---

[3] Johnson checked this option.

---

488. Telegram From the Department of State to the Embassy in India[1]

Washington, March 16, 1968, 1823Z.

131690. Ref: (A) New Delhi's 10954;[2] (B) New Delhi's 10955.[3] For the Ambassador. Subject: Conte/Symington Amendments.

1. We agree with thrust of reftels that India has reasonable case under Symington amendment. On other hand, as reftels suggest, application Conte amendment poses complex problems. A fundamental

---

[1] Source: National Archives and Records Administration, RG 59, Central Files 1967–69, DEF 12–5 INDIA. Secret; Priority; Exdis. Drafted by Coon on March 14; cleared by Battle, Heck, Wolf (G/PM), Clark (AID/PPC), Williams, Warnke, and in draft by Hamilton, Handley, Spain, Sober, and Folger; and approved by Katzenbach. Repeated to CINCSTRIKE and Rawalpindi.

[2] In telegram 10954 from New Delhi, February 5, Bowles reported that the Indian Government confirmed reports that it was contemplating the purchase of an unspecified number of MIG–21 fighters from the Soviet Union to compensate for delays in production of MIGs in India. The Embassy raised the issue of the Conte Amendment, and the government recognized that assistance to India might have to be reduced as a result of the legislation. Accordingly Bowles suggested that $25 million be withheld from pending production loans to India to offset what he stated was the maximum estimate of the cost to India of no more than 25 MIG fighter planes. (Ibid.)

[3] Bowles sent telegram 10955 from New Delhi to Rusk on February 5 to argue that the United States should not overreact to the discrepancy between the assurances offered by Morarji Desai and the subsequent revelation that the Indian Government intended to purchase additional MIG fighters from the Soviet Union. Bowles urged that concern over the discrepancies should not be allowed to obscure U.S. national interest in supplying urgently needed economic assistance to India. (Ibid.)

difficulty is that while we are committed by law as well as policy to relate our economic aid to recipient's decisions on defense expenditures, GOI appears equally committed to view that our economic aid gives us no charter to know or question its decisions in security field. We respect your judgment that if GOI is confronted with stark choice between forefeiting our aid or submitting to what it sees as our dictation on basic security decision, GOI will choose former. Such a confrontation as you rightly point out could have incalculable consequences. Nevertheless, it may not be easy to avoid.

2. Part of difficulty arises from evident failure of GOI to appreciate seriousness of our commitment. Relation we draw between economic aid and recipient's defense program has become a matter of law, as expressed in Conte and Symington amendments. We have assured Congress we take these amendments seriously and intend to implement them in spirit in which they were legislated. Furthermore, we are planning on probability that these amendments or others like them, possibly more stringent, will be with us for some years to come. Thus cosmetics and figleafs with which GOI has approached problem so far (insofar as it has even recognized problem existed) are totally inadequate basis our relations.

3. GOI has not tailored its actions to any perceptible degree to meet reality of Conte and Symington amendments. Evidence of Indian bad faith—no matter how unintended or necessary from GOI's point of view—is far more troublesome here than any transaction of which we are informed. Thus there has been erosion of our confidence in value of GOI's assurances which began with SU–7 "misunderstanding" and has been compounded by need to "amend" Morarji's recent assurances.[4] It simply will not do to offer "amendments" whenever we discover behavior doesn't correspond to words. What assurance have we that GOI will not adopt such tactics in future? One instance involving substantial U.S. aid commitment on false basis could well sink all aid to India.

4. We know you have these problems very much on your mind and will continue to do your best to persuade GOI to improve. But record suggests that since it is USSR, not U.S., that supplies bulk of India's defense imports, GOI is likely as matter of conscious policy to find ways to avoid leveling with us about specific procurement activities in which we are not directly involved. On the other hand, prospects

---

[4] On February 28, Hamilton sent a memorandum to Rostow in which he noted that reports had been received indicating that, despite Desai's assurance that India would make no purchases of sophisticated weapons between January 2 and June 30, an Indian mission to Moscow had reached an agreement to buy 25 MIG–21 fighter planes at a cost of $37 million. (Johnson Library, National Security File, Country File, India, Vol. XI, Memos and Miscellaneous, 2/68–10/68)

should be more hopeful of developing and sustaining a reasonably candid and useful dialogue with GOI on its overall defense spending and force levels. Your recent conversations with Swaran Singh and B.R. Bhagat reinforce this judgement. If this is case, we should consider adjusting our tactics to aim for a relationship which might attain this minimum objective.

5. As we see it eventual objective would be achievement of a workable understanding with GOI based on Indian recognition of legitimacy of our interest, as major supplier of economic and food aid, in India's gross force plans and defense spending levels, including foreign exchange outlays for sophisticated weapons systems. As long as India stayed within such mutually agreed gross force and defense spending levels we would resign ourselves normally to take up with GOI only those individual defense procurement transactions in which we were directly involved, either because we were supplier ourselves or because we exercised control over third country supply.

6. Strictly FYI, we have been considering possible approaches to immediate problem of how to apply Conte amendment to India partly in context of their potential contributions to achievement this relationship. Following possible options have not been fully staffed out. They are suggested here for your background and to elicit your comment. No decision has been taken to pursue any of them.

(A) Formal Conte Waiver: We could recommend formal Presidential waiver under Conte amendment, either now for FY '68 aid or later, say for FY '69. This course poses number of problems including fact that law as presently written would require determination that Soviet equipment in Indian hands is vital to U.S. national security. Do you think waiver which would become public would (a) serve our overall purposes, including that of holding down Indian defense expenditures, or (b) create political problems for Indians?

(B) Deduction under Conte amendment: We are considering your suggestion to dock India $25 million this fiscal year. We recognize some such action may prove only feasible way to handle immediate problem; nevertheless, in evaluating available alternatives, believe following factors ought to be considered:

(1) The amount deducted will become matter of public knowledge and final responsibility for determining said amount rests with us not GOI. We must of course act on basis most reliable information available. To extent our sensitive intelligence data differ from those supplied by GOI or available publicly, we may face numerous sticky problems arising from need to avoid jeopardizing sources, from desire to avoid public speculation as to what GOI is really up to, from questions of GOI good faith, etc.

(2) Deduction under Conte amendment could tend to fix ceiling for annual aid level to India and make it more difficult to carry out our present plan for additional commitments to India at end of fiscal year.

(3) More fundamentally, we are somewhat troubled by possible long-term effects on Indian attitudes of formal invocation Conte amendment, even though amount of penalty may not be large enough significantly to affect development program. We understand that reasons for our pressure on Indian defense spending may not have gotten fully across, in sense that many Indians assume our pressure reflects interest in maintaining regional Indo-Pak arms balance accompanied by lack of interest or sympathy for India in its defense against China. To extent this generalization valid, seems to us that formal action under Conte amendment could strengthen misconception we no longer cared about Indian security problems with China; result could be continuing erosive effect on Indian confidence in U.S. and on value India places in maintaining good relations with U.S. as hedge against China. This could relate to our future ability influence India on NPT, moderation toward Pakistan, and other issues with security implications. Please comment. End FYI.

7. Regardless of course of action we decide on, it is clear that MIG deal has seriously complicated our relations. We realize GOI had considered deferring MIG deal and decided against it but believe it possible GOI might reconsider if it were fully apprised of nature of our concern and especially of our objective as defined para 5.

8. Accordingly you should approach GOI at appropriately high level along following lines, unless you have serious reservations you wish discuss with us first. (Presume you will want to make your approach at Ministerial level, perhaps at joint meeting of Deputy PM and Defense Minister, which would have advantage of removing any doubts on our side that MOD has been short-circuiting Finance Ministry.)

(A) USG remains committed to support of Indian economic development. India is in fact receiving increasingly high proportion of total US aid resources. For FY '69 we hope obtain resources from Congress which will constitute substantial increase over current FY level for India and provide major stimulus toward level of economic activity in India we have both been working towards for many years.

(B) We remain as convinced as we were in 1963 and 1964 that US and India share a vital interest in opposing the hostile ambitions of Communist China. We recognize India's role as defender of a long and sensitive border with China. We therefore fully appreciate India's need for an adequate defense establishment.

(C) We are also concerned that Indian expenditures on defense acquisitions can cut into resources available for development and to that extent undercut resources we provide. Furthermore, Conte and Symington amendments have incorporated into law principle that we must relate our aid to recipient's defense program, in sense of precluding us from indirect support of certain defense expenditures.

(D) We shall continue to want as much detailed information as GOI feels free to give us that will help us to administer Conte and

Symington amendments, although of course we shall have to make final determinations ourselves on basis all information available to us. But we would like at least to work out understanding, based on GOI's recognition of legitimacy our interest, as major supplier of economic and food aid, on India's gross force plans and defense spending levels, including foreign exchange outlays for sophisticated weapons systems. We would normally raise with GOI only those individual defense procurement transactions in which we were directly involved, either because we were supplier ourselves or because we exercised control over third country supply.

(E) An immediate problem we face arises from need for time in which to seek better relationship which hopefully would not bring Conte/Symington amendments into play. This constrains us request GOI to place a temporary moratorium on post-January 2 agreements for acquisition sophisticated military equipment. (This would include specific proposed transaction AID Director Lewis recently discussed with Finance Secretary Patel.) Duration of moratorium would be short, several months at most, and purpose would be limited to that of giving us time to work out problem in its broad outlines, and to try to establish understanding as to how we can together best manage question of aid-defense relationship for longer pull.

(F) Favorable GOI response to this suggestion will be extremely helpful in context immediate decisions we face regarding pending program loan and PL 480 agreements, which we hope we can proceed on shortly. If GOI cannot in all conscience respond favorably we shall do our best to keep our relations on an even keel, but task will be considerably more difficult, as well as time-consuming.

9. FYI. We intend to call in Ambassador Jung in the next couple of days to convey same message here.

Rusk

489.   Telegram From the Embassy in India to the Department of State[1]

New Delhi, March 20, 1968, 1524Z.

11697. Ref: State 131690.[2]

1. Morning March 20 I met with Morarji Desai to discuss problems arising from Conte amendment and particularly our concerns as outlined in reftel. In order to make sure Morarji thoroughly understood pertinent points we prepared carefully sanitized version of reftel, including language best calculated to emphasize (a) our understanding of GOI predicament, (b) severe legal restrictions under which we are now operating, and (c) genuineness of our efforts to find mutually acceptable way out of impasse.

2. Morarji started to read the document, but soon stopped to challenge what he termed "US right to know" Indian force levels and other military matters. He asserted "One thing must be clear: no matter how much money you give us, we can not compromise our right as a sovereign nation to make our own decisions regarding military defense. If this has become a condition of US aid, we shall have to get along without it."

3. I urged Morarji to finish reading before expressing his views, which he did with exception of single comment challenging suggestion that India may be motivated to maintain good relations with USG as "hedge against China." Morarji asserted that basis for Indo–US relations is much broader than this: we are two democracies struggling to sustain common values and objectives, etc.

4. After reading entire "cable" carefully, Morarji made following points:

(A) USG must recognize India is faced with major military threat. Two years ago, contrary to our repeated prediction and assurances, Pakistan, supported by Communist China, attacked India. China is now starting a campaign of organized insurgencies, through north Burma, toward east India and GOI views this as a continuing and growing threat. Consequently, highest single priority for GOI is defense and it must be sole judge of what is required.

(B) USG must know that India is not militaristic nation bent on conquest. On contrary, with India's massive developmental needs in mind, he personally begrudges every rupee going into military expend-

---

[1] Source: National Archives and Records Administration, RG 59, Central Files 1967–69, DEF 12–5 INDIA. Secret; Priority; Exdis.

[2] Document 488.

itures. He has been under heavy pressure from Defense Ministry Sharply to increase present budgets but has flatly refused to do so. However, whether we continue aid or not, India will maintain present force levels, which are minimum required for its defense.

(C) Morarji stressed that even those Cabinet members friendly to us are adamant on this subject. For instance, there had been strong opposition to acceptance of our offer to help India with military cost-effectiveness on grounds this would be entering wedge by USG and would lead to US influence over GOI military development and priorities.

(D) In 1963 and 1964 GOI had hoped and even assumed US would be willing help modernize India's defense establishment. However, because of Pakistani pressure we had not only refused to assist India, thereby forcing GOI to turn to USSR, but had implied that we could offer no guarantee of support in case of non-nuclear Chinese–Pak attack.

Even now, he said, in spite of Pak flirtation with China, we are helping Pakistan, directly and indirectly, "through Iran and other sources." This assistance is for a Pak military establishment that is openly designed to fight India. Moreover, although SEATO and CENTO have no relevance to present Asian realities we still speak of Pakistan as our "ally."

(E) In regard to Indian determination to withstand pressure on what it believes to be its sovereign right to make its own decisions, GOI, he said, had taken identical position with USSR when Soviets suggested that if India did not sign NPT they would have to review entire aid commitment. GOI had refused to knuckle under to Soviets on this point and now must react similarly to USG's request, which would be interpreted as effort to control levels and patterns of Indian defense expenditures.

(F) Morarji added that he fully understands pressures under which President Johnson, Secretary Rusk and others are operating, that he personally supports US position in Vietnam, and that he feels future of Asia depends on close working relationship between USG and GOI. If, despite these personal convictions, we are unable to develop working relationship with him, he is certain that many other key GOI leaders, whose political views are opposed to both ours and his own, would find a close USG–GOI relationship impossible.

5. In reply I stressed that all points he made were well understood by myself and Dept., as he could see from reading cable. However, we face legal problem from which we cannot escape. It is our hope that the acute siuation presented by Conte amendment is temporary; if we can muddle through next few months some acceptable measures may be found to meet our common objectives.

6. I then asked Morarji to give me whatever facts he could on MIG deal on personal and off-the-record basis. He replied that purchase of these planes is direct result of failure three MIG plants in India to meet Soviet-set production schedule. Under special provision of original agreement if MIG's were not produced on time in India Soviets would supply them on fly-away basis. He stated that while no MIG's have yet been delivered there is a chance they will arrive in India sometime in June (i.e., before June 30). As matter of principle, he cannot stall their delivery or affect it in any manner. However, there will be no payment to USSR until one year after actual delivery, which means that nothing will be paid under this contract before June or July 1969. Payments will be in rupees over ten year period which Soviets will use to purchase various commodities in India.

7. Again spelled out our legal dilemma. Morarji replied that he fully understood and only wished he could go to US next week to talk it out with President Johnson. He stated India has strong case in regard to China–Pakistan threat and he has full confidence that he could convince any responsible American Senator or Congressman of rightness of GOI position.

8. I told Morarji that visit to US would be timely and worthwhile and I know he would be listened to carefully. He replied that in view of budget session and his responsibility as Finance Minister it would be impossible for him to leave until session adjourns on May 10, after which he would be delighted to make the trip if there is any prospect of its being effective. He would, however, need some plausible excuse so that true nature of his visit would not become evident. I asked if an honorary degree from some good university would be adequate and he replied affirmatively.

Comment and recommendations follow by septel.[3]

Bowles

---

[3] Bowles commented on his conversation with Desai in telegram 11696 from New Delhi, March 20. His assessment was that neither Desai nor other members of the Indian Government would budge from the position relating to the Conte Amendment outlined in telegram 11697. He recommended that the administration seek a waiver to the amendment and anticipated that the effect of such a waiver would be to encourage voluntary Indian cooperation on the question of military expenditure, which pressure could not achieve. (National Archives and Records Administration, RG 59, Central Files 1967–69, DEF 12–5 INDIA)

490. **Telegram From the Embassy in Pakistan to the Department of State**[1]

Rawalpindi, April 6, 1968, 0901Z.

4396. Please pass White House and concerned agencies. From Ambassador.

1. Pursuant to appointment sought by him I called on Foreign Minister this morning. Yousuf and Piracha were present.

2. The Minister handed me a letter terminating the Peshawar Agreement. The text of the letter follows:

"I have the honour to refer to the agreement concluded on 18th July, 1959, between the United States of America and Pakistan relating to the establishment of a communication unit in Pakistan and to state that the Government of Pakistan have decided to terminate the said agreement (when it expires on 17th July, 1969). Therefore, in accordance with Article 12 of that agreement, I hereby convey to you notice of termination on behalf of the Government of Pakistan.

"I avail myself of this opportunity to renew to your excellency the assurances of my highest consideration." Signed Syed Sharifuddin Pirzada, Foreign Minister of Pakistan.

3. Following delivery of notice the following statements were made, with Yousuf doing most of the talking:

A. When the Minister and Secretary Rusk met in Washington last fall the Secretary noted that USG–GOP relations are now normal with former special circumstances no longer present including the 1965 cessation of arms supply;

B. GOP now normalizing friendly relations with all major powers;

C. This means that their relations with each power must be bilateral with nothing directed against any third power;

D. Peshawar has been and continues to be a serious liability in GOP relations with both USSR and ChiComs;

E. Renewal would not be appreciated by USSR or by ChiComs or by "our own people";

F. Because of recent technical development such as satellites USG really no longer needs Peshawar;

G. USSR and ChiComs can do many things to harm GOP, including in her relations with GOI;

---

[1] Source: National Archives and Records Administration, RG 59, Central Files 1967–69, DEF 15 PAK–US. Secret; Immediate; Exdis. Rostow sent a copy of this telegram to the President under an April 6 memorandum. (Johnson Library, National Security File, Country File, Pakistan, Vol. VIII, Memos, 8/67–4/68)

H. GOP anxious to maintain good relations with USG free of strain and hopes that "they can continue to go up and up as they have recently";

I. GOP sincerely hopes that this termination will have no adverse effect on either USG–GOP aid relations or on the recently improved military supply situation;

J. The USG and USSR have mutually been seeking a détente with each other and continuance of Peshawar would cast a shadow on those efforts;

K. GOP hopes, especially in view of recent Viet-Nam relationship, that USG will evolve a new ChiCom relation which would be made more difficult by Peshawar continuance.

4. Following the above exposition I expressed surprise at the abruptness and apparent finality of this notice and discourse to which Yousuf responded that they wanted USG to have as much notice as possible and felt that in 15 months USG could effect adequate and satisfactory substitute arrangements.

5. I noted that USG probably did have the technical, geographic and financial capacities to adjust to a new situation but the necessity to make such an effort would put a heavy strain on USG–GOP relations not only because it would be extremely costly but also because it would be interpreted in many USG circles as an indication that GOP preferred cooperative relations with USSR and ChiComs more than with USG.

6. I then stated that I would of course report this development to Washington and would seek instructions. At this point I observed that I assumed that the subject was still open to discussion and negotiation. The response was affirmative.

7. I then reviewed briefly the salient reasons why it would not be in the interests of GOP to insist on a July '69 closing of this operation, as follows:

A. GOP is itself getting a useful take;

B. GOP has the continuing benefit of valuable training;

C. The Peshawar area enjoys a very valuable economic benefit from the operation;

D. If indeed USG, albeit at great expense and inconvenience, substituted other operations, then this means that neither USSR nor Chi-Coms would benefit from termination;

E. The known existence of the operation had not prevented continual improvement in GOP relations with USSR or ChiComs;

F. The existence of Peshawar gives GOP bargaining power with USSR and ChiComs whereas its elimination would remove that leverage and decrease Communist interest in GOP.

8. Yousuf responded:

A. GOP is not getting any worthwhile info from operation largely because USG does not share its take except in unimportant items and all important areas are taboo;

B. GOP own oeration is very marginal. GOI is aware of it and has objected to it thus putting a further strain on GOP–GOI relations;

C. Training is very limited and can be had under other available arrangements;

D. The economic benefits are of no great order;

E. Whether or not Communists would be in improved situation without Peshawar they press very hard for its discontinuance and GOP does not consider it as a lever but rather as a hardship, noting that Communists constantly refer to both Peshawar and CENTO as representing special treatment of USG in violation of GOP's avowed policy of bilateral even-handedness;

F. GOP relations with Communists have continued to improve despite Peshawar because GOP has been becoming more and more non-aligned and USSR and ChiComs have grudgingly accepted Peshawar during its original term but would feel quite differently about a renewal;

G. Peshawar is directed against USSR and ChiComs but GOP does not engage in any operations directed against USG;

H. GOP is apprehensive about military build-up of GOI and must obtain assistance somewhere but Communists always cite Peshawar and CENTO as reason not to aid GOP militarily and USG has changed its own arms policy toward GOP except for recent opening up of spare parts program and possible third country tank aquisition.

9. I then observed that in addition to the points I had previously made GOP should consider that, having in mind first that GOP was usually aligned against USG position in international problems and second that there was very little GOP could do for USG to show its friendship other than to refrain from a Peshawar eviction, USG would be entitled to draw its own conclusions regarding the genuine interest of GOP in maintaining, let alone improving, present relations between our two countries.

10. The conversation then turned to matters of the press, which has been pushing for some statement. It was agreed that it was in the interest of both governments to minimize press coverage and that no statement would be made by GOP other than the observation that discussions are taking place.

11. Yousuf noted that the GOP National Assembly meets May 3 and that questions would undoubtedly be put to the government from the floor.

12. The meeting broke up on the note that further conversations would be held, at my initiative, when I had received instructions.

13. *Comment:*

A. It is not surprising that formal notice of termination would have been delivered. This would understandably be logical way for GOP to initiate discussion;

B. It is not surprising that notice would have been delivered shortly before the expected arrival of Kosygin;

C. It is worthy of note that GOP placed such stress on:

(1) Exclusion areas and lack of GOP take which we consider to be a red herring; and
(2) Military supply.

14. It is my judgment that no further response should be made to GOP prior to Kosygin arrival and departure other than for me to express, and Washington to express to Hilaly, the great surprise and deep concern of Washington a the abruptness and indicated inflexibility of the GOP position coupled with a statement that we will initiate further discussions following full appraisal of the effects of a continued GOP inflexible posture on USG–GOP relations. Please confirm or comment.

15. Would appreciate development of guidelines on:

A. Minimum acceptable period of continuance beyond July '69;

B. Degree to which exclusion areas may be reduced or eliminated;

C. What line should be taken with respect to:

(1) Maintenance and/or enlargement of scope of present military supply policy now limited to spare parts and third country acquisition of 200 tanks;
(2) Possible effects on future aid policy; and
(3) Other potential effects on GOP–USG relations.[2]

Oehlert

---

[2] The Department instructed that no further response should be made until a full assessment of the situation was completed in Washington. (Telegram 143051 to Rawalpindi, April 6; National Archives and Records Administration, RG 59, Central Files 1967–69, DEF 15 PAK–US)

491. Memorandum From the Assistant Secretary of Defense for International Security Affairs (Warnke) to Secretary of Defense McNamara[1]

Washington, April 11, 1968.

SUBJECT

Peshawar Communications Facility

We have received official notification (Tab A)[2] this past week from the Government of Pakistan stating its intentions to terminate the Peshawar agreement when it expires on 17 July 1969. The original agreement governing the establishment of a facility at Peshawar was concluded on 18 July 1959 and was to remain in force for a period of ten years, and for a second period of ten years thereafter unless either party gives written notice to the other at least twelve months before the end of the first ten year period of its desire to terminate the agreement. I recommend we proceed as set forth below.

We know the President discussed the matter with Mr. Katzenbach and Mr. Helms last Saturday morning. A consensus apparently was reached that the USG should remain silent for the present. A period of silence is, in our opinion, the best tactic. I believe, furthermore, we should not initiate conversations with the Pakistanis until we know exactly what we want to say and why. I also believe we should be noncommittal with the Press.

Approve

Disapprove

I believe there is a pretty good chance the facility can be maintained beyond 1969, but that this will require careful and thorough identification and consideration of the problems involved. There are several elements of DoD with interest in these facilities and of course other government agencies. Accordingly, I recommend my office be the focal point for DoD participation in this problem.

Approve

Disapprove[3]

Paul C. Warnke

---

[1] Source: Washington National Records Center, RG 330, OASD/ISA Files: FRC 72 A 1498, 680.1 Pakistan. Secret.

[2] Reference is to telegram 4396 from Rawalpindi, Document 490.

[3] Deputy Secretary of Defense Nitze initialed his approval of both recommendations on April 13.

492. Memorandum From the President's Special Assistant (Rostow) to President Johnson[1]

Washington, April 22, 1968, 5:30 p.m.

SUBJECT

AID Program Loan to India

Herewith, Messrs. Gaud and Zwick recommend a $225 million AID loan to India. This loan will provide all the AID capital assistance now planned for India during FY 1968.

Charlie Zwick's memorandum (Tab I)[2] is a reasonably short summary of requirements, self-help performance, balance of payments effect, and relation to Indian military expenditures. Gaud's memorandum (Tab II)[3] gives you somewhat more detail.

I think the economic case for the loan is clear. India is now in the first stages of a massive economic recovery, led by her record grain harvest. If she can find the foreign exchange required to get and keep her slack industrial capacity moving, she can start a cycle of growth which would be the most hopeful event in the history of our foreign aid efforts. If she can't find that foreign exchange, we can expect not only severe economic pressures, but much larger burdens on an already creaking—though still democratic—political system.

As you know, we have had our problems with the Indians of late on the NPT and on their military expenditures. I think it would be a mistake, however, to withhold this loan on either count. We seem to be having somewhat more luck in establishing conversation with the Indians on the NPT precisely because we are not threatening aid cutoffs, whereas the Russians are apparently taking a very hard line which includes such threats. On the Conte amendment and military spending, we would propose to hedge the disbursements of this loan against the possibility that we will learn later that the GOI is playing fast and loose with us. As of now, we are fairly certain that no arms payments will be made during the period we have been assured that they will not. But we are prepared if we find out otherwise.

This loan, like all our aid to India, would be made within the multilateral context of the consortium, in which our share will drop

---

[1] Source: Johnson Library, National Security File, Memos to the President, Walt W. Rostow, Vol. 72, April 12–23, 1968. Secret.

[2] Memorandum from Zwick to the President, April 12, entitled "AID Program Loan to India." (Ibid.)

[3] Memorandum from Gaud to the President, April 10, entitled "$225 Million Production Loan to India." (Ibid., Country File, India, Vol. XI, Memos and Miscellaneous, 2/68–10/68)

this year to about half the bilateral contributions. The loan would involve no balance of payments outflow.

W. W. Rostow[4]

Approve package
Disapprove
Call me[5]

---

[4] Printed from a copy that bears this typed signature.
[5] This option is checked and the date April 23 is written next to this line in an unknown hand.

---

493. Telegram From the Embassy in Pakistan to the Department of State[1]

Rawalpindi, April 22, 1968, 1320Z.

4635. From Ambassador. Please pass White House. Subject: Tanks.

1. German Ambassador to Pakistan returned to Pindi on Friday[2] from Bonn consultations. Saw him socially over weekend and he asked to see me ASAP re tanks. We met 1200 hours today. More on this subj later this tel.

2. At 0900 hours today GOP Defense Minister and Secretary informed me that they were convinced that no tanks would be forthcoming for GOP from FRG through Italy because:

A. FRG would in all probability not make a sale to Italy on basis which would permit tanks to come to GOP; and B. even if they were ultimately proved wrong in this respect Italy would not agree to acceptable terms.

3. Defense Minister and Secretary went on to say that there is a vital tug-of-war going on within top GOP levels re their short and long term relationships vis-à-vis USG, USSR and ChiComs. They said that in that context:

---

[1] Source: National Archives and Records Administration, RG 59, Central Files 1967–69, DEF 12–5 PAK. Secret; Immediate; Exdis.
[2] April 19.

A. GOP military and other elements urging closer USG relationships including Peshawar renewal for additional three years;

B. "Enemies" of USG including powerful elements of MFA among others contending that USG is pro-India and anti-Pakistan, citing:

I. 1962 and 1965 developments;

II. Apparent unwillingness apply Conte–Symington Amendments to India despite heavy Indian rearmament program;

III. No spare parts have been shipped despite fact program was announced a year ago. *Comment:* The reasons for this delay are understandable to us but not readily explained to GOP military and certainly not to elements already convinced that we are dragging feet and will continue to;

IV. Breakdown of tank deal after tank deal, for one reason or another, also being used against us as additional evidence that we are not being helpful but are rather causing delays behind the scenes.

4. German Ambassador informed me that:

A. There is no tank agreement between FRG and either Government of Italy or Italian firms;

B. He strongly doubts that FRG can now make any tank agreement which would permit tanks to go from FRG to GOP through Italy because:

I. India exerting strong pressure against such a transaction including threat to recognize East German Government;

II. Publicity given fact that some German tanks would probably end up in Pakistan has strengthened hands German Socialist Party which is opposed to cooperation re arms for GOP, which represents approximately 40 per cent of parliamentary coalition and to which FRG Foreign Minister belongs.

5. Whatever the reasons, it is a fact that no spare parts have yet been forthcoming.

6. Whatever the reasons, it is a fact that tank possibility after tank possibility has evaporated.

7. Whatever the reasons, it is a fact that the Germany to Italy to Pakistan transaction remains an enigma shrouded in mystery.

8. It is a fact that first through spare parts and second through approval of tanks, under strict conditions, from third countries we have been moving towards arms policy liberalization here in order to:

A. Maintain some reasonable forces balance on subcontinent;

B. Counter Indian indigenous production capacity and USSR pipe line;

C. Maintain and improve our influence here; and

D. Hold at present levels or better yet diminish both USSR and ChiCom influence here.

9. During their visit here Hamilton, Spain and Heck indicated that there could be further liberalizations if necessary to obtain needed tanks and possibility limited quantities other hardware.

10. It is my considered judgement that the moment of truth has arrived and that some prompt and positive steps must be taken to:

A. Convince GOP of sincerity and effectiveness our policy; and

B. Forestall GOP moves for either or both profligate spending as per France and/or diminishing influence with corresponding increase influence USSR and/or ChiComs.

11. Our prior decision to see to it that GOP does get 200 tanks in early time frame and on reasonable terms is not adversely affected by Peshawar termination notice. On the contrary, I view such a notice as an added reason why we should speed up effectuating that decision at least with respect to the first 100 tanks.

12. Depending on how Peshawar comes out we may or may not be prepared to be forthcoming on the second 100 tanks and/or other items.

13. It is therefore urgently recommended that we wait no longer for the evolving of a complicated Tinker to Evers to Chance triple play but that on the contrary, we at once inform GOP that pending further evolution of arrangements with Germany, Italy and/or Belgium, they can have 100 tanks in either following ways:

A. By purchase from Iran;

B. By direct purchase from our own inventories; or

C. From German inventory which we would reclaim from Germany and sell to GOP. The German Ambassador assures me his government would have no problems with such an arrangement.

14. By confirming publicly our agreeability to having GOP receive tanks under our control we have already invited any Indian or Congressional displeasure which might be inherent in the situation. It is difficult to see how either problem would be seriously further complicated by following any of the courses recommended in paragraph 13 above.

14. Respecting the Iranian possibility it is observed that:

A. The Shah has the means and probably the determination to get the number and quality of tanks he wants—if not all from us then from some other source;

B. He might be persuaded not to raise his sights re new acquisitions because of a sale of M–47s or 48s to GOP;

C. It is far more important to protect vital interests here and to thwart those of USSR and ChiComs than it is to place any particular limitation on the number of new tanks the Shah purchases, especially since we may not be able to control that anyway.

Oehlert

494. Memorandum From the President's Special Assistant (Rostow) to President Johnson[1]

Washington, May 8, 1968, 4:15 p.m.

SUBJECT

AID Loan to India

Two weeks ago you instructed us to hold up on the $225 million AID program loan proposed for India. This loan would fill out our share of Consortium aid for Indian fiscal year 1968, which ended in April.

As you know, India's economic performance and prospects are better now than ever. We have tried to use the delay to find ways to use the loan as political leverage with Mrs. Gandhi and to impress on her how painful it is to get these large sums for a country that isn't always as helpful as we could wish. I am afraid we have come up empty. Bill Gaud and Nick Katzenbach concur in the following analysis and recommendation.

Setting

We must start with two unpleasant but very real facts:

1. *From the Indian point of view we would be trying to exert more pressure with substantially less aid.* Our total capital aid to India in FY 1968, including this loan, would be about $290 million, about $100 million less than last year. Thus, as the Indians see it, we are cutting back by more than 25%. This is particularly painful now because India is in an economic recovery, led by the bumper harvest, which will cause very serious foreign exchange pressure in the Fall. And the Indians have not forgotten that we were among the leaders in the Consortium who assured them in 1966 that they would get $900 million per year in non-project aid if they agreed to devalue and make other economic reforms. They went through with the reforms. But this year, because of our cut and the delay in IDA replenishment, they will get less than $600 million in non-project aid. This adds up to a poor base for more arm-twisting.

2. *The Government of India is in a particularly weak and delicate political position.* Mrs. Gandhi presides over a loose confederation of worried politicians. She is not strong enough to crack the whip over them, and

---

[1] Source: Johnson Library, National Security File, Country File, India, Vol. XI, Memos and Miscellaneous, 2/68–10/68. Secret.

they are not strong enough to withstand heavy nationalist pressures from the Parliament. This problem has been aggravated lately by the lobbying on the Non-Proliferation Treaty in which the Russians (or so the Indians say) have threatened to cut off aid unless India signs. Predictably, Mrs. Gandhi and Morarji Desai have responded with a number of belligerent statements, public and private, to the effect that anybody who tries to blackmail India with aid can take a flying leap. Whether we like it or not, we are clearly in a position where the slightest hint of an attempt to use aid as a direct lever outside the economic field will produce an outraged and counterproductive reaction.

Possible Quids Pro Quo

There are three major areas in which we might press the Indians to be more helpful:

1. *Indian Military Spending:* The Indians keep about one million men under arms. They have made several recent deals with the Russians for aircraft, frigates, submarines, and other equipment to modernize their forces. They argue that this is all needed for defense against China, and they are in fact within their 1964 defense plan worked up with our cooperation. We tried to get them to keep their military budget from rising this year, but they announced an increase of slightly less than 5%. In fact, because of price rises, this probably works out to a very small increase in real terms, but it still causes concern in Pakistan and could lead to another round or reciprocal defense increases in both countries.

We have also been having trouble with India with respect to the Conte Amendment which requires us to cut economic aid in the same amount that poor countries spend on sophisticated weapons unless the President finds the arms purchase vital to U.S. security. To be brutal, the Indians have lied to us twice—once before the Conte Amendment and once after—about what aircraft they are buying from the Soviet Union. Both cases seem to be products of ignorance rather than intentional deception, and the second case does not now appear to be an actual violation of the Conte provision. But we need much better cooperation in the future.

Our preferred solution to this range of problems has been formal Indo-U.S. defense talks in which we would get the information we need to administer the Conte and Symington Amendments. In theory, we might ask for such talks as a quid pro quo for this loan. But this proposal was explicitly and indignantly rejected in March by Morarji Desai during the last go-around on Conte violations—though, characteristically, he informally gave us the information we wanted in the same session. It is Chet Bowles' judgment, with which we concur, that any new approach now would not only queer any chance for military conversations, but might also derail current plans for general U.S.–GOI policy talks (proposed by the Indians) in Delhi in July where we hope to make some headway on this subject.

2. *The NPT:* Most Indian politicians are frightened of the NPT. They overstate the public sentiment against the Treaty (Morarji likes to say that 99% of Indian public opinion opposes it), but they do know that nobody who counts is really strongly for it and they are afraid that anybody who gets out on a limb will have it chopped off. The Cabinet has taken a formal and public decision against signing the Treaty "in its present form." But the Indian UN Representative is not lobbying with other countries against the Treaty; he is sitting quietly and observing.[2]

It is conceivable that we could try subtly to tie this loan to the Treaty. But again our judgment is that this tactic would hurt us far more than it would help. Mrs. Gandhi and Desai have staked out their position on Russian blackmail; we could expect them to be at least as tough with us. Indeed, a frontal attack from us might well make it so juicy a political plum to oppose the Treaty that it would tip the final balance against it.

3. *Economic Reforms:* The Indians have done every major thing we have asked them to do in the economic sphere. They made agriculture their top investment priority. They devalued and liberalized imports. They are holding to the import liberalizations in fiscal year 1969 despite the prospect of serious foreign exchange shortage. They are building food buffer stocks and have agreed to make the Food Corporation into the CCC-like entity we advised. They have moved to keep farm prices at incentive levels despite the bumper crop. They have begun to relax the food zones which separated states. In short, we simply don't have any major changes in economic policy to which we could tie this loan even if the loan would provide enough leverage to get them adopted.

On the other hand, if the Indians do *not* get this loan, economic conditions will force them to turn away from the rapid-growth, free-market track we have urged them to take. Their present balance of

---

[2] Telegram 13839 from New Delhi, May 7, reported a conversation with Homi Sethna of the Indian Atomic Energy Commission and Babha. Sethna expressed his objections to the inspection provisions in the Non-Proliferation Treaty and commented that he "did not foresee an Indian signature to NPT 'unless Mrs. Gandhi wants to commit political suicide.'" (National Archives and Records Administration, RG 59, Central Files 1967–69, AE 6 INDIA–USSR; also available on the Internet, National Security Archive (www.gwu.edu/~nsarchiv), Electronic Briefing Book No. 6, "India and Pakistan—On the Nuclear Threshold," Document 17)

payments prospects are very bleak, even assuming this loan is made promptly available. If it is not, they will very soon be forced to put the clamps back on imports and put a damper on what could be the best economic year since Indian independence. We cannot say that this loan will guarantee the economic success we seek. We can say that success is impossible without this loan—and soon.

Conclusions:

We conclude that we can find nothing to be gained from delaying this loan. We have all learned many a lesson from you in years past about dealing with India. But this time there is nothing we want from her which we haven't already received or could possibly receive if we needle her with this loan. (I think this is true with respect to Vietnam negotiations as well.)

On the other hand, there are very great costs to delay. The economic recovery led by the bumper grain crop is the most hopeful event in the developing world in at least five years. If the Indians can find the foreign exchange to take advantage of it, we could get sustained growth in the subcontinent on a scale we have only dreamed about in the past. If they cannot find the foreign exchange, we will not only have missed a great economic opportunity, we will have discredited the economic policy line we have worked many years to sell; we will face serious economic stabilization problems in India; and we will have aggravated the current political unrest by adding a host of potent economic issues.

The Aid/India Consortium meets in Washington May 23–24. Only the U.S. has not formally announced an aid pledge for the Indian fiscal year just ended. (This meeting is actually supposed to be about *next* year's money.) It will be very embarrassing for our representative if we have not announced this loan before then. But our problems will far transcend embarrassment. The other Consortium members have maintained their contributions at historical levels despite the fact that it was obvious that the Congressional cut would force us to cut back. If we don't come through now with even our reduced contribution, we will (1) undermine efforts to raise the necessary funds for next year, and (2) make it crystal clear that we are holding out for some quid pro quo which the Indians will assume is political and may hotly denounce—probably with the support of the other Consortium members.

None of this denies or excuses the fact that the Indians can be irritating and uncooperative. Nor does it excuse the fact that they have often been less than helpful on Vietnam. But I think that this is one of those times when we must swallow our discontent and go ahead with the treatment despite the patient's behavior. I recommend that you approve the loan.

W. W. Rostow[3]

Loan approved[4]

Let's hold off a while longer

Loan disapproved

Call me

---

[3] Printed from a copy that bears this typed signature.
[4] Johnson checked this option.

---

495. Telegram From the Department of State to the Embassy in Pakistan[1]

Washington, May 14, 1968, 2311Z.

164030. 1. Ambassador Hilaly at his request called on Assistant Secretary Battle today. He opened conversation by describing changing South Asian situation brought about by UK decision to leave the area and Russian move to fill this vacuum. Referring only briefly to Indian arms buildup, he explained GOP decision reassess Pakistan's defense requirements in light these developments.

2. Hilaly then stated GOP had drawn up list of "minimum defense requirements to insure Pakistan's security." He presented "austere list" which included four hundred 106 recoilless rifles, one hundred twenty-five 175mm guns, various types ammunition, thirty armored recovery vehicles, four maritime aircraft, sixteen patrol boats with missiles, eight F–104s and various types of electronic counter measure and signal equipment. He said he understood from MOD that Embassy Rawalpindi had also been informed of list.

3. Ambassador Battle expressed appreciation for GOP's constructive attitude in making list available and applauded restraint shown

---

[1] Source: National Archives and Records Administration, RG 59, Central Files 1967–69, DEF 12–5 PAK. Secret; Limdis. Drafted by David A. Macuk (NEA/PAF), cleared by Spain and in substance by Schaffer and Reed (DOD/ISA), and approved by Battle. Repeated to New Delhi and CINCSTRIKE.

by GOP in its defense spending. Battle asked whether matériel listed encompassed total requirements from all sources including Red China and Russia, noting we had heard Pakistan might be receiving SU–7s from USSR. He also inquired how long a period the list was intended to cover. Ambassador Hilaly replied list covered needed supplies from all sources, explaining he had not been informed of any plans for SU–7 deliveries and that the requirements were for "now" but he assumed they would be good for two or three years. Battle promised review list noting a substantial portion of the items were already obtainable under our current policy. He promised we would be in touch as soon as our study had been completed.

4. Hilaly pointed out that "lethal" weapons on list as well as all other matériel were defensive in character and suggested USG should reconsider ban on sale of lethal end items to Pakistan. He added list was designed to bring Pak defense forces up to, but not to augment, present capacity.

5. In closing Ambassador Battle and Country Director Spain mentioned our concern over recent flurry of interest by press representatives about information newsmen claimed to have that GOP had given USG notice termination of Peshawar communications agreement. Mentioned indications that information was supplied to other correspondents by *Dawn* Washington correspondent Ejaz Hussain. Hilaly first indicated doubt that leak could be attributed to Hussain or Pakistan Embassy sources; but later conceded that such was possible and he planned investigate.[2] He argued however that in such matters it was unrealistic to hope that secrecy could be maintained for any length of time.

Rusk

---

[2] In a May 20 letter to Battle Hilaly wrote that Foreign Minister Arshad Husain, who succeeded Pirzada on May 1, made the following statement on May 20 in the National Assembly in response to a question: "The agreement for establishment of a U.S. communications unit near Peshawar is to run for a period of ten years and is automatically renewed for a further period of ten years unless notice of termination by either side is served at least twelve months in advance of expiry of the first ten year period. The Government of Pakistan gave notice of termination to U.S. Government on April 6th, 1968. This step is in keeping with our policy of developing bilateral relations of friendship and mutual understanding with all countries. We can have friendly relations with U.S.S.R., China, and U.S.A. without these being at the cost of any of the others." (Ibid., DEF 15–4 PAK–US)

496. Telegram From the Department of State to the Embassy in Pakistan[1]

Washington, May 21, 1968, 0044Z.

167508. For Ambassador Oehlert from Battle.

1. Pakistani Foreign Minister's public statement re termination Peshawar arrangement[2] causing deep concern here with respect to possible implications this statement on aid bill. I appreciate your vigorous efforts to prevent or moderate statement[3] and recognize that it will be difficult undo damage. Nevertheless, in event opportunities occur I want you to be aware serious concern at high levels in Executive Branch re implications for whole aid program and trust you will do what you can to bring these home to top levels GOP.

2. We expect to have technical study completed by Executive Branch in next few days evaluating relative importance Peshawar and will be in touch with you again then.[4]

Rusk

---

[1] Source: National Archives and Records Administration, RG 59, Central Files 1967–69, AID (US) 1 PAK. Secret; Exdis. Drafted by Battle on May 20, cleared by Spain, and approved by Battle.

[2] See footnote 2, Document 495.

[3] Oehlert reported on these efforts in telegram 5169 from Rawalpindi, May 20. (National Archives and Records Administration, RG 59, Central Files 1967–69, DEF 15 PAK–US)

[4] In a May 23 memorandum to Rostow, Hamilton summarized the conclusions of the study. The primary conclusion was that the Peshawar installation was much less important than it had been in previous years. The study recommended against a major effort or a quid pro quo to keep the facility. (Johnson Library, National Security File, Files of Walt Rostow, Visitors—1968)

497. Information Memorandum From the President's Special Assistant (Rostow) to President Johnson[1]

Washington, May 23, 1968.

SUBJECT

India Debt Relief

You directed us in March to join in negotiation of a debt relief package for India, as recommended by the World Bank. Our two primary goals in the negotiation were: (1) a formula assigning the largest share of relief to countries whose aid has been on hardest terms; and (2) $100 million in total annual relief for the next 3 years.

We have come out with a good bargain which meets those goals. The package is scheduled to be formally blessed by the other donors at the India Consortium meeting here today. Below is a table showing the agreed annual payments to be postponed. The U.S. share is $8.7 million per year, less than 9% of the total and less than any other major donor.

Amount of Debt Relief
($ millions)

Donor	Annual Share
Germany	$ 27.5
United Kingdom	18.0
Japan	16.8
World Bank	15.0
United States	8.7
Italy	5.5
France	5.2
Austria	0.9
Belgium	0.9
Canada	0.8
Netherlands	0.8
Total	$100.1

This package will commit the Indians to press the Soviets for comparable relief and to adopt prudent limits in accepting future credits. We're still not satisfied that all the Consortium donors are giving relief on as easy terms as they might. Therefore, though this is nominally a 3-year arrangement, we plan to participate with a firm commitment for only one year to preserve our leverage for the next two.

---

[1] Source: Johnson Library, National Security File, Country File, India, Vol. XI, Memos, 2–10/68. No classification marking. A handwritten note on the memorandum indicates it was received at 11:11 a.m.

All in all, other donors have been much more forthcoming than most of us expected. This package does not increase their total aid to India, but it makes what they do provide much more useful in economic terms. More important, it establishes the principle that those who insist on hard loan terms end up bearing the burden of debt rollover—a point we have been trying to get across for years.

The U.S. amount is below the cutoff calling for Presidential review, but I thought you would be pleased to know that a fair bargain has been struck.

Walt

---

498.   Telegram From the Embassy in Pakistan to the Department of State[1]

Rawalpindi, May 31, 1968, 1245Z.

5405. Ref: State 173271.[2] Please pass White House. From Ambassador.

1. Yesterday Chief of Army Staff General Yaqub gave General Geary the following information:

A. GOB[3] offering only class 5 tanks, which are wrecks requiring complete overhaul.
B. As is price dollars twelve thousand including ten thousand USG residual (at which residual Yaqub expressed disappointment).
C. Overhaul quoted at dollars fifty thousand not including parts (which would vary from dollars ten to fifteen thousand) or engines (which would cost dollars twenty to twenty-five thousand).
D. Cost to get tanks here estimated at dollars five to seven thousand.
E. Therefore total cost delivered here would range from dollars ninety-seven thousand to dollars one hundred nine thousand.

2. Price is therefore double limits previously established by USG.

3. Paks indicated to General Geary that they could not contemplate such a transaction.

---

[1] Source: National Archives and Records Administration, RG 59, Central Files 1967–69, DEF 12–5 PAK. Secret; Immediate; Exdis.

[2] Telegram 173271 to Rawalpindi, May 29, instructed Oehlert not to take a specific position concerning renewal of the agreement governing the Peshawar facility during his scheduled conversation with Ayub. Such a position, the Department noted, had yet to be defined. (Ibid., DEF 15 PAK–US)

[3] Government of Belgium.

4. When I arrived at President's house this morning I was ushered into an ante-room where I was immediately joined by the Defense Secretary, General Yaqub and General Rafi, who informed me that President Ayub had just overruled them and decided to purchase 100 Belgian tanks "as is" for dollars twelve thousand each and rehabilitate them here. The Secretary and Yaqub said that they hoped USG would waive or substantially reduce its dollars ten thousand residual. At that point I was called into Ayub's office.

5. I had previously decided that I would not request Ayub to clarify the conflicting positions to me of his MFA and MOD, but would rather only ask him if I could give President Johnson a message from him that if President Johnson should subsequently have any suggestions about Peshawar the door would be open for future discussions. I had reached this decision because I felt that if I confronted him with a ministerial conflict his only options would be:

A. To refuse to answer: or
B. To disavow one or the other ministry's position.

6. When I was ushered in both Foreign Secretary Yusuf and Presidential Adviser Fida Hassan were present, which confirmed in my mind the wisdom of not posing a ministerial confrontation.

7. After the usual exchange of pleasantries, he asked me to convey to President Johnson his deep appreciation for the arrival of the second watershed management team.

8. President Ayub then informed me that he had overruled his military people and decided to accept the 100 Belgian tanks as is and to rehabilitate them in this country. He said the tanks were really junk but that he was desperate, had to have some equipment and had no other place to turn. He said that whereas six months ago tanks had been available from Iran they no longer were because the Shah had decided to keep all his M–47's and M–48's and rehabilitate them himself. Ayub stated that he still needed more tanks than those first 100 and that there being no other source, he hoped that USG would sell him 100 directly.

I made no response to this except to say first that I would convey his message and second that I thought he realized how difficult such a thing would be in view of our present Congressional posture.

9. I then asked him if he had any other messages for me to convey to President Johnson.

10. He responded that he would appreciate it if I would convey to both the President and to Lady Bird his sincerest affection, his sympathy for the crushing burdens which the President bears, and his prayerful good wishes for the President's success, good health and happiness.

11. I then stated that there was one message I would be pleased to be permitted to carry to President Johnson, namely: that if the President should subsequently have any suggestions about Peshawar the door would be open for future discussions.

12. For the first time in my fairly frequent contacts with him he showed visible signs of agitation. (Otherwise, in health, bearing, appearance and attitude he was his old self.)

13. He made a long and somewhat agitated statement that he had given the Peshawar matter the deepest of consideration, that he recognized its great importance to USG, that he had no desire to do anything to harm the USG, that he had the deepest affection for President Johnson, Vice-President Humphrey, Mr. McNamara and many other warm American friends, that he had been a comrade to arms with the American military and admired and respected them all (naming among others Admiral Radford and General Twining), but that the security of his country required that Peshawar be closed. He went on to say that at the time of the Powers U–2 incident Russia threatened him with nuclear attack; that at the time of the Cuban missile crisis the Russians informed him that if a conflict broke out Pakistan would receive one of the first waves of atomic missiles, and that the Russians had recently made it clear that if he permitted Peshawar to continue his country would be in grave danger. He then besought my sympathy for and understanding of his position and requested me to make that position clear to President Johnson and to express to the President Ayub's hope and concern that the President too would sympathize and understand. It is to be noted that during this lengthy monologue he did not answer my question either affirmatively or negatively. It is also interesting to note that he did not mention China.

14. At the end of his dissertation, I repeated the question in somewhat different phraseology.

15. He responded with an almost identical soliloquy.

16. I rephrased the question a third time.

17. He stood up, held his head, and said that while he had not consulted any of his advisers about what he was about to say, the only possibility which he had been able to think of was that the facility might be installed on a smaller and less visible basis, in a different location, under complete Pakistani control.

18. Given the circumstances and my several instructions, I did not see my way clear to respond forcefully to Ayub's presentation.

19. I rose again to take my leave, thanking him for the interview even though "the outcome had not been to my liking." He asked me to remain for another cup of coffee, but the conversation was confined

to platitudes about my wife, children and grandchildren, the USG presidential election, etc. etc.

20. He accepted my third attempt to leave, but once more repeated his observations of paragraph 17 above.

21. It is my considered opinion that Ayub has not chosen an MFA position over a MOD position but rather that the MFA position was Ayub's position.

22. It is also my considered opinion that Ayub is convinced that closing Peshawar is required by his bilateral policy, and that:

A. He will suffer punishment or lose reward from Russia, or both, if he lets Peshawar remain open even for a short time after July 17, 1969; and

B. He will suffer no retribution from USG if he closes it.

23. It is further my considered opinion that Ayub will not modify his position unless he becomes convinced, either or both, that:

A. He will suffer massive aid punishment if he closes it; and/or

B. He will receive very substantial military equipment, but probably on a purchase basis, if he leaves it open for a time.

24. It is additionally my considered opinion that:

A. We should not either threaten (A) above or withdrawal present spare parts program unless we mean to carry it out:

B. We should not promise (B) above unless

(1) We consider it in our national interest to do so regardless of Peshawar; or

(2) The final evaluation of Peshawar is so high that we consider we must save it for at least a few years.

25. Present schedule is to leave Pindi noon Monday for Karachi and to leave Karachi 0600 hours Thursday for New York arriving Washington for consultations Monday June 17.

26. Please advise ASAP:

A. If wish further representations made to Ayub before departure; or

B. If wish me to postpone departure; or

C. If wish me arrive for consultations prior June 17.

27. Reference State 173125,[4] I feel most strongly that under all the circumstances we should not respond in any way in Washington or here

---

[4] Telegram 173125 to Rawalpindi, May 29, summarized a conversation between Pakistan Country Director Spain and Pakistani Ambassador Hilaly that dealt largely with the recent visit of Soviet Premier Kosygin to Pakistan. At the conclusion of the conversation, Hilaly asked for an early response to the hardware list he left with Assistant Secretary Battle on May 14. (National Archives and Records Administration, RG 59, Central Files 1967–69, POL 7 USSR) For the list referred to by Hilaly, see Document 495.

to the hardware list until after a full posture on both Peshawar and military supply policy has been evolved, hopefully during my consultations.

28. At 0830 hours tomorrow morning I will deliver a letter to MOD reading as follows:

"Dear Mr. Secretary:

As you know, President Ayub informed me this morning that a decision had been taken to purchase 100 M–47 tanks from Belgium in 'as is' condition for $12,000.00 each. Reference is made to my letter of May 9[5] addressed to the Minister of Defense, particularly to the following portions:

1. Reference to previous undertakings on page 1.
2. Reference to estimated price on page 1.
3. Comments on pages 3 and 4.

I assume that this mission will in due course receive a formal communication from your government confirming its intention, setting forth estimated cost of purchase and rehabilitation, confirming the previous undertakings referred to on page 1 of my letter of May 9, and requesting the approval of my government for the indicated transaction."

Oehlert

---

[5] Not found.

---

499. Memorandum From the President's Special Assistant (Rostow) to President Johnson[1]

Washington, June 22, 1968, noon.

SUBJECT

Your Questions on the Aid Fertilizer Package for India[2]

I have looked into the two questions you raised. Bill Gaud and Charlie Zwick concur in the observations that follow:

---

[1] Source: Johnson Library, National Security File, Country File, India, India's Food Problem, Vol. IV. Confidential. A handwritten note on the memorandum indicates that it was received at 2:50 p.m.

[2] The fertilizer package included a loan of $37 million for a major expansion of an Indian fertilizer plant and a loan of up to $30 million to finance Indian imports of U.S. fertilizer. Johnson posed the questions in response to a June 19 memorandum from Rostow recommending approval of the loans. (Ibid.)

1. Would we be criticized for shoveling out money in June?

Gaud doubts that we would. He told the House Appropriations Committee this spring that he would cut corners elsewhere at the end of the year to lessen the $100 million gap in Indian fertilizer financing caused by last year's aid slash. There was no objection.

In any event, we have a very strong case against any such critic:

—AID's FY 1968 appropriation was signed January 2, 1968, the latest ever. Congressional slowness crammed virtually all the Agency's loan obligations into less than six months.

—Nevertheless, AID will commit a lower percentage of its 1968 Development Loan funds in June than ever before. If you approve the India package and a few other loans now on their way to you, AID will commit only about 23% of its loan money in June, compared to 32% in 1967 and 53% in 1966.

—Including this package, only about 18% of AID loans to India in 1968 would be committed in June.

—Most of this money—the $37 million for the fertilizer plant—will be expended slowly as the construction proceeds. The bulk of it will not be spent for 2–3 years and the last of it probably won't be disbursed in less than 4 years. Expenditures from both loans in FY 1968 will be nil, so that it can't be argued that we are trying to spend the money before the $6 billion cut comes into play.

2. If we don't commit this money now, will we have it for next fiscal year?

Technically these loan funds *would* remain available next year if we didn't commit them now. In fact, however, unobligated loan money would be Passman's most powerful "evidence" that Congress was right to cut the aid bill to ribbons last year and that it should cut even more deeply this time. This is not to say that he would not push such cuts in any event, but experience suggests that this is the best argument he could have. (We may not be able to avoid giving Passman some such ammunition this year. There may be a substantial—$35–50 million— unobligated balance in Alliance for Progress Loan funds. But we should present as small a target as possible.)

You should also consider the following points:

—The fertilizer financing need in India must be met now, in June and July, if the ground is to be prepared for next spring's crops. India should let contracts for at least $95 million in fertilizer imports by the end of August, $33 million in June alone. The second of these loans provides some of the foreign exchange necessary to do that. If we don't commit this loan now, yet we want to help get fertilizer on the land before the spring crop, we would need to commit the money very early in FY 1969—in July or August.

—This money comes from AID's Development Loan account. Along with the Alliance appropriations, this is the most important development instrument we have. It is also the most vulnerable on the Hill. Last year it was cut nearly in half—down to $435 million for loans around the world ex Latin America. This is the place we can least afford to give Passman an opening by ending the year with unobligated balances.

Recommendation

Delaying these loans would not save on 1969 expenditures unless AID is to abandon further help to the fertilizer program in India for this crop year. Even then, it would not save more than $20–$30 million in FY 1969. On the other hand it would weaken our support for the most hopeful current advance in the poor world—the agricultural revolution in India—and, at the same time, give Passman another potent weapon to beat the aid program.

I recommend you approve the loans.

Walt

Loans approved[3]

Loans disapproved

Call me

_____

[3] Johnson checked this option.

_____

500. **Memorandum From Edward Hamilton of the National Security Council Staff to the President's Special Assistant (Rostow)[1]**

Washington, June 26, 1968.

SUBJECT

Military Supply Policy for South Asia (To be discussed at SIG Meeting scheduled for Thursday, June 27)

The Problem

You should try to read through the attached State papers—both the issues paper and the NEA position paper.[2] They are better than most.

_____

[1] Source: Johnson Library, National Security File, Agency File, SIG, Vol. V, 40th Meeting, 6/27/68. Secret; Sensitive. A handwritten note on the memorandum reads: "Mr. Rostow did not attend SIG meeting."

[2] "The Issues" was the subtitle of an undated 3-page paper drafted by Spain on June 21 and entitled "U.S. Military Supply Policy for India and Pakistan." The NEA position paper was an updated 7-page paper drafted by Spain, Prescott, and Coon on June 21 and entitled "US Military Supply Policy for South Asia: NEA's View." (Both ibid.)

You know our present military supply policy in South Asia, announced in April 1967. We do not sell lethal end-items to either India or Pakistan; we do sell spare parts (which is meaningful only to Pakistan) and we concur in third-country sales on U.S.-controlled equipment, on a case-by-case basis, when we think the sale will not contribute to an Indo-Pak arms race or seriously disrupt the power balance on the subcontinent. We have used this policy to sell modest amounts of spare parts, including ammunition, to Pakistan and to approve two third-country sales—British jet aircraft to India, and Italian or Belgian-owned tanks to Pakistan.

Nobody argues that this is a tidy policy. Both countries resent the arms embargo; it neither suppresses arms appetites nor effectively cuts off arms supplies in either country; it has encouraged both countries to turn very largely to Communist arms suppliers, with some undeniable political complications for us; it is especially hard on the Paks because they are American-armed and because the Indians have the political clout to close off all other suppliers except the Chinese and perhaps the French. When combined with the stresses induced by the Conte Amendment, this adds up to a constant and powerful irritant which is clearly poisoning our political and economic relations with both countries.

The main question at issue now is whether this situation would improve if we change our policy to permit direct U.S. sales of end-items on a case-by-case basis. Ben Oehlert very strongly favors such a change, largely on the ground—formidable, in view of our experience—that third-country sales simply don't work as a means of keeping Ayub supplied with the arms he has to have to keep his throne and maintain some leverage with India. Chet Bowles argues precisely the reverse: that we should extend the embargo to spare parts and third-country sales and put our chips on helping the two countries toward self-sufficiency in arms production. NEA proposes a compromise solution weighted toward the Oehlert end of the spectrum: that we should permit direct sales where we can get substantial arms-limiting conditions—such as a ceiling on defense spending—and that we should make a positive technical assistance effort to encourage self-sufficiency in arms and introduce cost effectiveness analysis into both military programs.

Merits

I think everybody agrees that, all other things being equal, it would be very pleasant if the President had unfettered authority to make arms sales to India and Pakistan when and if they made sense. Most of us also agree that this authority would help, not hurt, our efforts to get both countries to be sensible about their military spending.

Unfortunately, other things are far from equal. As matters now stand:

1. Even if we wanted to, we could not sell any jet aircraft or other sophisticated weapon to either country without making an equal cut in economic aid unless the President determined it to be vital to our security. This would be difficult in the case of India. It would be next to impossible for Pakistan.

2. Even if we wanted to, we would not be able to make *credit* sales—which are necessary if we are to be competitive on most items—after June 30 unless the military credit sales bill or equivalent authority is enacted. Even if it were enacted, the money we have requested is fully earmarked for other countries (Korea, Iran, etc.) where we have outstanding commitments.

3. There is no sign that the Congressional tide which last year produced a rash of amendments limiting arms sales to poor countries has run its course. Indo–Pak tension was an explicit and oft-cited example of the kind of thing the Congress is concerned about. However wrong-headed they may be about how to go about dampening arms races, we must face the fact that we have not persuaded them that arms sales are a good instrument to this end. As a practical matter, therefore, we could expect real trouble on the Hill if we proposed to make sales on the subcontinent.

The question is whether we eliminate one of several major barriers to arms sales to India and Pakistan—and, whether the removal of one will strengthen or weaken the others. The scenario might well run as follows:

1. We would presumably make our policy public in connection with the sale of the second 100 M–47 tanks which we are now committed to try to get for Ayub. The reaction in India would be immediate and very strong. Our main argument to justify the Italian/Belgian deal for the first 100 tanks has been that we don't want to fuel Pakistani paranoia directly, but that we are prepared passively to concur when Ayub can be persuaded to buy old, cheap, U.S.-controlled equipment from others rather than new stuff from the French or the Chinese. This has consistently been labeled a smokescreen by many Indians; this change would expose it as just that. Bowles (overstating the case) now argues that the third-country tank deal may well "kill us" in India. Certainly, it is fair to say that a subsequent direct sale would cut our political influence—though perhaps not our economic policy influence—to the vanishing point.

2. The Paks would see this as a door thrown wide and would rush in with any number of requests for *credit* sales of high-powered weapons, particularly aircraft. (They have already given us a list of items they feel they must buy somewhere in the near future.) When

confronted with the constraints presented by the Conte Amendment, the military credit sales problem, and the general attitude on the Congress, they and we would rapidly discover that all we can really do in the way of major sales are M–47 tanks. We could not, for example, supply the F–5's and F–104's Ayub wants. The resulting frustration could very well nullify whatever advantages flow from our policy change.

3. If and when the specific irritation of the tank sale to Pakistan settles down and the Indians looked seriously at the new policy, they would, in my judgment, probably still conclude that it was heavily weighted toward Pakistan. India is now almost entirely dependent on Soviet weapons systems for modern arms. She is committed to the maintenance procedures and systems involved. However much many Indians would like to balance things a bit, it would not make much economic sense for India to take on new and wholly different major weapons systems—even if we could make them available. Beyond that, U.S. cash sales couldn't possibly compete with Russian barter arrangements, which spread payment over 10 years. The real effect of the amendment would be to permit us to sell largely to Pakistan, which has no competitive alternatives—and no real threat other than India. In short, we could expect very little if any softening of the Indian position over time. Indeed, we could expect strengthening of forces in Indian politics which argue that we are out to rebuild Pakistan into a military threat and that India must build even greater military superiority over Pakistan. The result: higher Indian defense budgets—followed by higher Pakistani defense budgets.

4. Our determination to help the two countries become self-sufficient in arms—much as I wish it weren't—would be superfluous with respect to India and infinitesimal with respect to Pakistan. India now has about 30 ordnance factories, including a plant to manufacture MIG–21's. Pakistan doesn't even produce her own steel: it would be many years, even with heavy American aid, before she would be in a position to produce the weapons that worry us and worry the Indians. The current proposal talks only of technical aid. It is a nice gesture, but we can't expect it to be taken very seriously by either country. At best, it would worry the daylights out of the Paks.

I suspect it is clear that I just can't see what benefits we could get through direct sales which would be worth the costs in the subcontinent and in the Congress. We should not delude ourselves; for the foreseeable future, the question reduces to whether we amend our overall policy in order to get 100 tanks into Pakistan. We cannot go a single step beyond that without knocking down other barriers which are largely beyond our control.

I am a devout supporter of the proposition that a workable policy in South Asia depends on some means of getting a minimal flow of modern weapons into Pakistan without forcing a substantial reduction in U.S. economic aid. I am just as irritated and frustrated as anyone else by the delays of third-country bargaining. But it seems to me far preferable to try to make that approach work better with the second 100 tanks than to buy more trouble in India and on the Hill by offering direct sales. I do not believe it can be shown that U.S. interests have yet been badly hurt by Communist military sales to either country, or that, even if they have been, we are going to be in a position any time soon substantially to reduce those sales. Nor do I think it important to our interests, for example, to "be in on the ground floor" of the build-up of a largely superfluous Indian navy. The only real benefit involved is the expediting of the tank deal with Pakistan. I just don't think it is worth it.

Timing

We are all agreed that now is not the time to announce a change even if we decide on one. The aid bill would be severely threatened by an announcement; Katzenbach's upcoming talks in Delhi would be blown out of the water; and we don't need to provide the second 100 tanks immediately. Any announcement should wait until the Congress adjourns.

One other timing factor occurs to me. I would argue that it would be a considerable disservice to a new President to inherit the situation I think this change may stimulate. If possible, I think we should let a new administration build its own policy in South Asia without this albatross.[3]

EH

---

[3] The Senior Interdepartmental Group met on June 27 to consider, inter alia, the question of a military supply policy toward the subcontinent. Ambassadors Bowles and Oehlert, both in Washington for consultations, participated. Bowles argued for the suspension of both direct and third-country sales of lethal weapons, and Oehlert argued for a more flexible military supply policy that would countenance direct sales where the situation dictated. Battle contended that, in light of the impending change of administrations and problems with Congress, it was a bad time to contemplate a change in policy. After discussion, the SIG agreed to recommend maintenance of the existing policy, and to encourage the tank sale by Belgium to Pakistan to meet Ayub's immediate problem. (Summary of discussion and decisions at the 40th SIG meeting, prepared by Katzenbach on July 5; ibid.) The SIG discussion and recommendations were summarized by Katzenbach in a July 3 memorandum to the President. (National Archives and Records Administration, RG 59, Central Files 1967–69, DEF 12–5 PAK)

501. Memorandum From the Under Secretary of State (Katzenbach) to President Johnson[1]

Washington, July 5, 1968.

SUBJECT

U.S. Communications Facility at Peshawar, Pakistan

Recommendation:

That Ambassador Oehlert be authorized to indicate to President Ayub your recognition of his problems and your willingness, despite the damage it will do to our interests, to agree to close out the Peshawar station, asking at the same time that in order to reduce the damage we be given adequate time beyond July 18, 1969, to close out the station along the lines suggested in the last two paragraphs of this memorandum.[2]

The Deputy Secretary of Defense, the Director of Central Intelligence, and the Chairman of the Joint Chiefs of Staff concur in this paper.

Discussion:

President Ayub told Ambassador Oehlert in the course of a long and agitated statement on Peshawar on May 31 that the security of Pakistan requires that the United States communications station there be closed. Ayub's position confirmed the earlier delivery of a note by the Pakistani Ministry of Foreign Affairs and a public statement by the Pakistani Foreign Minister to the National Assembly that the GOP intended to terminate the communications facility when the present ten-year agreement expires on July 18, 1969. Ayub's statement seemed to overrule previous hints from the Pakistani Ministry of Defense that a way could be found to preserve the station—especially if United States military supply policy were to be changed to permit direct arms sales to Pakistan. When pressed by the Ambassador, Ayub said the only possibility he could think of, apart from complete withdrawal, was replacement of the present Peshawar station by a smaller, less visible installation in a different location under complete Pakistani control.

---

[1] Source: National Archives and Records Administration, RG 59, Central Files 1967–69, DEF 15 PAK–US. Top Secret. Drafted by Spain and Major Wix on July 1 and cleared by Wolf, Battle, Curl (INR/RCI), and [*text not declassified*] (CIA).

[2] The memorandum does not indicate the President's response to the recommendation. A handwritten note by Harry Brock of S/S notes that the President's response to the recommendation was contained in his July 14 letter to Ayub which was transmitted to Rawalpindi in telegram 202058; see Document 503.

The [*less than 1 line of source text not declassified*] Peshawar [*less than 1 line of source text not declassified*] is still important to the United States intelligence community and we would like to retain it as long as possible. A recent comprehensive technical assessment prepared under the cognizance of the Director of Central Intelligence indicated that Peshawar is substantially less important now than it was a few years ago and that the loss of intelligence on [*less than 1 line of source text not declassified*] can, to an acceptable degree, be offset provided that we can find alternative facilities elsewhere in the area, Iran being the most promising. From a technical viewpoint, [*1 line of source text not declassified*], but there is no realistic substitute facility available to obtain the information now derived on certain targets in [*less than 1 line of source text not declassified*]. This information, though desirable, is not vital in itself.

Development of these alternatives presents certain technical and political problems. A contingency facility planned for Iran, for example, could not be ready before the spring of 1970 and we might not find it advisable to introduce into Iran the full number of personnel planned for this facility in accordance with the contingency plan for Peshawar (NSAM 348).[3] However, it appears at present that alternatives are likely to be available at least to the degree where it would not be in our interests to offer a substantial price to Pakistan in an effort to maintain the facility at Peshawar.

For this reason, and because we feel that our basic policy decisions on economic aid and military supply should be made on the basis of broader United States interests vis-à-vis Pakistan, we do not believe that any major change in these policies is likely to be desirable for the specific purpose of affecting the Pakistani position on Peshawar. Ambassador Oehlert will, of course, make continued tactical use of our military sales and of our AID program in ways designed to help us get the most advantageous possible settlement of the Peshawar question. However, we do not believe prior decisions are necessary either to give Ayub something beyond that permitted by our present military supply policy in order to save Peshawar or to deny him something otherwise possible under this policy or under our economic aid program in order to pressure him into meeting our requirements on Peshawar.

Within this framework, our purpose is to hold as much as we can at Peshawar as long as we can. Probably the most acceptable arrangement would be one in which we accepted Pakistani termination of the ten-year agreement as of July 18, 1969, but sought to arrange an

---

[3] See footnote 2, Document 340.

indefinite additional period during which we would actually move out. During this period we might dismantle some of the antenna which are not essential to us, seek other ways to reduce the visibility of the activity, see whether or not the Pakistanis would be interested in some of the equipment which we do not want to relocate, and attempt to eliminate or greatly reduce our exclusion area so that the Pakistani presence on the base could be complete. Should Ayub insist on setting definite dates for completion of the move, we might first ask for a maximum of three years, aim at getting two, and settle for the most we get.

The possibility of establishing some kind of smaller United States-operated facility, [1 line of source text not declassified] agreeable to the GOP, will also be explored. Ayub himself has already mentioned the possibility of Pakistani continuation of a part of the Peshawar operation in a smaller, less visible facility in a different location completely under GOP control. This too will be investigated.

Detailed supporting guidance for Ambassador Oehlert's discussions with President Ayub is now being prepared.

Nicholas deB Katzenbach

---

502. Telegram From the Embassy in Pakistan to the Department of State[1]

Rawalpindi, July 9, 1968, 0901Z.

6039. Please pass White House. From Ambassador.

1. Spent an hour with Ayub after twenty minute session with McCormack and Griffith of COMSAT.

2. Several matters discussed will be covered septel.[2]

3. Except for a few brief flashes of his old energy Ayub seemed disinterested and lethargic. He has lost more weight. He has definitely retrogressed since my last visit with him.

---

[1] Source: National Archives and Records Administration, RG 59, Central Files 1967–69, DEF 12–5 PAK. Secret; Exdis.

[2] In telegram 6040 from Rawalpindi, July 9, Oehlert reported on the effort he made in the conversation with Ayub to point up the problems being experienced by a number of U.S. companies trying to compete in the Pakistani economy. (Ibid., FN 9 PAK–US)

4. Upon departure COMSAT representatives Ayub said "The Foreign Minister is waiting. Would you mind terribly if I asked him to come in?" I responded "Mr. President, as you know, I had asked to see you alone but of course the decision is yours." He then said "It would save me having to take notes and repeat the conversation." He then sent for the Minister who came in with Mohiuddin Ahmad, the successor to Mansur Ahmad on the American desk, who took copious notes.

5. With respect to tanks, I assured him that the Belgian deal was still very much alive, pointing that:

A. There had been bureaucratic delays due to the changes of government; and

B. That the Belgians felt no particular incentive because they wouldn't make any money and had no public excuse such as they would have if the transaction provided work and profit.

6. I then suggested that he consider:

A. Sending for the Belgian Ambassador and impressing on him both Ayub's deep personal interest and the needs and merits of the situation; and

B. Offering to have half of the tanks rehabilitated in Belgium in order to provide incentive and to lessen burden of rehabilitation on GOP.

7. He seemed a bit vague about the status of the Belgian deal, commenting that the Belgians had indicated that they want to talk again but that so far they had not been willing to discuss reasonable prices and terms for rehabilitation.

8. He did not commit himself either re whether or not he would send for the Belgian Ambassador what response would be given to the alleged Belgian desire to talk again or what his reaction was to a half and half deal.

9. I did not indicate that if the Belgian deal fell through we would seriously consider a direct sale because I felt that to do so would cause him to drop the Belgian transaction in favor of direct purchase.

10. During the course of the conversation I pointed out the significance of the Conte–Long amendment, mentioning specifically that it would require us to make a deduction from aid for the acquisition of sophisticated weapons unless the President certified to Congress that the acquisition was in the national security interests of the USG, emphasizing that of course he could not do so with respect to weapons acquired from a Communist country so that such acquisition would mean in effect that GOP would have to pay a double price for such weapons.

11. On the Peshawar question, not having received my expected guidelines, I had nothing to try to sell so I contented myself by saying that:

A. President Johnson had been greatly disappointed in the way the termination notice had been handled; did not and never had wished to embarass Ayub unduly since he fully understood Ayub's problems; but believed that the matter could be handled to the satisfaction of the USG and GOP; and

B. My government had been interested in Ayub's suggestion of "A smaller less visible installation in a different location under complete Pakistani control" and had requested me to explore that possibility fully.

12. At that point the Minister spoke up for the first time and said "Mr. President, may I make a comment?" Ayub acquiesced, whereupon the Minister said "While I was not present at the previous meeting I have studied the record very carefully and, Mr. President, you did not state the matter as the Ambassador has suggested."

13. With a flash of his former self Ayub said, somewhat heatedly "Oh yes, he did. That's exactly what I said. The Ambassador has quoted me exactly."

14. The Minister did not speak again on the subject.

15. Ayub then took up the conversation, saying:

A. He had said exactly what I said he did, and he had meant it, but that there had been fresh developments since then;

B. The Russians had since predicted that USG would suggest a smaller, less visible installation in a different place under GOP control, but that the USSR would know all about it at once and would consider it a very hostile act; and

C. Therefore, sorry as he was about it, he could no longer consider that possibility.

16. After pleading surprise since the suggestion had been Ayub's own, I closed the conversation by noting that under the circumstances I would have to seek new instructions.

17. *Comment:* It seems clear to me that:

A. Ayub's health has deteriorated;

B. He has been carefully hemmed in by his Ministers and Secretariat (see septel re other matters brought up in which he would previously have shown great interest but which today he merely asked me to take up with Agriculture Minister Doha and Commerce Minister Hoti); and

C. His Foreign Ministry is most hostile to USG. I have no doubt that someone in the Ministry, and I personally suspect the Minister himself, leaked to the Russians the suggestion Ayub had made at our previous meeting.

18. When I receive guidelines about "phasing out" I will of course seek a further audience to present them. FYI: Ayub's schedule calls for departure to Lahore and Karachi July 13, to Iran 20, to the UK 22.

19. Today's developments emphasize importance of a good word from Iran and Turkey, as suggested in Rawalpindi 6038.[3]

Oehlert

---

[3] Oehlert suggested, in telegram 6038 from Rawalpindi, July 9, that Ayub's visit to Tehran July 20–22 would offer an opportuity for Iran and Turkey to encourage Ayub to extend leniency to the United States with regard to the facility at Peshawar. (Ibid., POL 7 PAK)

---

503. Telegram From the Department of State to the Embassy in Pakistan[1]

Washington, July 14, 1968, 0009Z.

202058. For the Ambassador. The following letter from President Johnson should be delivered promptly to President Ayub.

"Dear Mr. President: In the spirit of honesty and frankness that has always been at the heart of our relationship, I feel I must tell you of my deep concern over the reports I have received during the past several weeks from Ambassador Oehlert about your Government's attitude toward our communications facility at Peshawar. I have delayed writing to you personally until now because I hoped that some mutually acceptable solution could have been worked out by this time.

I was surprised and disturbed that your Government saw fit publicly to announce its position on the Peshawar facility before any real discussion between our two Governments was possible. And it was particularly distressing to learn that your Government's action may have been taken because of threats and demands by another power.

I had thought that you and I shared a conviction that our own security—as well as the security of many other nations—was well served by our cooperation in maintaining the Peshawar facility. Accurate technical and scientific information on the intentions and capabilities of others can, as you know, be a stabilizing element in the present uncertain state of the world.

---

[1] Source: National Archives and Records Administration, RG 59, Central Files 1967–69, DEF 15 PAK–US. Secret; Immediate; Nodis. Drafted by Katzenbach; cleared by Helms, Nitze, and Rostow at the White House; and approved by Samuel G. Wise (S/S-O).

In all frankness, the actions of your Government do not seem to me to be appropriate to the close relationship that has existed for so many years between our two countries and which has been manifested in our contribution of more than $3½ billion in aid to Pakistan.

I accept, of course, your right to terminate the 1959 Communications Agreement,[2] although I would hope that even now you could reconsider that decision. I do want you to know, simply and unequivocally, that the closing down of the Peshawar facility in July 1969 will give us real problems.

In this connection, I must point out that this facility is a complex one. Some of its elements can be moved relatively easily. Others will take more time. Their hasty removal could result in significant gaps in our understanding of the intentions of others and thereby diminish the sense of security we both seek.

If, however, your decision is firm, I would hope and expect that you might allow our representatives to discuss an arrangement whereby the various elements of the facility can be phased down and closed out in an orderly way during a period beyond the formal termination date of July 17, 1969. I have asked Ambassador Oehlert to convey these views to you and to be prepared to enter into full discussion of them at an early date.

I cannot hide from you the fact that the loss of the Peshawar facility will be a real blow to what I believe to be our mutual interests. But I do think that if we can agree to arrangements that will permit a reasonable withdrawal period it will lessen the impact. Such arrangements, if arrived at through imagination and good will on both sides, would make the transition easier to accomplish. I do not think, old friend, this is too much to ask.

Sincerely, Lyndon B. Johnson."

Rusk

---

[2] For text of this agreement, signed in Karachi on July 18, 1959, see 10 UST 1366.

504. Telegram From the Department of State to the Embassy in Pakistan[1]

Washington, July 16, 1968, 0001Z.

202781. Ref: Rawalpindi 6173.[2] Subject: Peshawar Communications Facility.

1. Please deliver Presidential letter to Ayub[3] ASAP.

2. As you know, now appears likely Belgian–Pak deal will go through. We will take up matter with GOI at appropriate time. Language announcement virtually agreed. Anticipate we will be able handle Belgian desire be even-handed with Indians more or less along lines para 3 Rawalpindi 6174.[4] However, there can always be additional last minute snags and in any event we wish see how Ayub reacts to Presidential letter on Peshawar. If Ayub queries on this subject, therefore, you should not go beyond already stated position that Belgian tank arrangement seems be in last stages and we remain hopeful it will be consummated under terms and conditions previously discussed.

3. We agree would be useful to get Shah and Turks to put in good word with Ayub at proper time, but here too would rather wait; if possible, until after we have had chance assess Ayub's reaction to Presidential letter. Also, the more people who know details of our Peshawar problems, the more chance there is for information to get to Russians who would use for additional mischief-making. We propose, therefore, defer action on this item at least for few days.

4. You may draw on following in attempting to get maximum possible phase-out period from Ayub:

(a) We of course wish to remain in operation as long as we reasonably can in order to reduce the damage to our interests from termination of Peshawar. During the phase-down period, we can dismantle and remove some antenna which will make our preparations for departure obvious. Alternatively, should Ayub prefer, we can leave most general

---

[1] Source: National Archives and Records Administration, RG 59, Central Files 1967–69, DEF 15 PAK–US. Secret; Immediate; Nodis. Drafted by Spain, Wolf, Wix, and Sheldon on July 15; cleared by Curl, Country Director for Turkey John M. Howison, NEA Deputy Assistant Secretary Stuart W. Rockwell, Country Director for Iran Theodore L. Eliot, Jr., Heck, Nitze, and Helms; and approved by Katzenbach. Walt Rostow was informed.

[2] In telegram 6173 from Rawalpindi, July 14, Oehlert indicated that he was reluctant to deliver the President's letter to Ayub without guidelines concerning the position to take in discussions concerning the future of the facility at Peshawar. (Ibid.)

[3] See Document 503.

[4] In paragraph 3 of telegram 6174 from Rawalpindi, July 14, Oehlert suggested that Belgium be informed that U.S. military supply policy applied equally to India as well as Pakistan, on a case-by-case basis. (National Archives and Records Administration, RG 59, Central Files 1967–69, DEF 19–8 US–BEL)

purpose antenna intact, even after we've ceased to use them, so that they could be inherited by Paks. (FYI: Exactly which antenna could go first will have to be worked out with US technical authorities. End FYI.)

(b) To further reduce visibility, we can begin to remove personnel and some miscellaneous equipment on a schedule to be worked out with GOP. This could include relinquishing off-base housing, removing dependents, and cutting back on support activities.

(c) FYI: Present estimate is that 12 months is desirable for orderly withdrawal with about 6 months possible on crash basis. Should you believe it worthwhile, in terms our objectives keeping as much as possible as long as possible, we could begin phasedown schedule to take effect before July 17, 1969, but we would hope to decide finally on this only after further discussions with GOP. End FYI.

(d) FYI: Only exception to 12 months period above, as far as retention priorities are concerned, DOD considers Sugar Tree most important for continued operation until mid-1971, if possible. End FYI.

(e) We can grant Pakistanis permanent possession of communications electronic equipment now on loan to them, and possibly some additional similar items. However, most of our equipment at Peshawar will be needed for other US requirements because of stringent budgetary restrains on new procurement. For security reasons we must remove all our sophisticated equipment, which would not be usable by Paks anyway.

(f) Re exclusion area, if it would be helpful, we will use our best efforts to make entire base accessible to Pakistanis with, of course, exception communications center.

(g) After thorough consideration, our conclusion is that we not prepared pay additional rental for any time extension.

(h) Some additional quid might be available through consideration of what removable non-technical property to which Paks not legally entitled we could leave in Pakistan upon departure. (FYI: This depends on DOD requirements elsewhere and may not be very large. See 40 USC 512. End FYI.)

5. We recognize foregoing alone not likely persuade Ayub on extension, which likely depend more on his reaction to Presidential letter. In light Ayub reaction, we will provide further guidance.[5]

---

[5] Printed from a copy without a stamped signature. Oehlert delivered the Presidential letter to Ayub on July 17. He reported that he had no opportunity during a brief meeting with Ayub to make the additional points contained in telegram 202781 to Rawalpindi. (Telegram 6235 from Rawalpindi, July 17; ibid., DEF 15 PAK–US)

505.   Letter From President Ayub to President Johnson[1]

Rawalpindi, July 19, 1968.

Dear Mr. President,

I thank you for your message of July the 16th,[2] delivered by your Ambassador in Pakistan and appreciate very much the directness and candour with which you have referred to the issue of the US communications facility near Peshawar.

2. In a spirit of equal honesty and frankness I would like to explain to you the position as we see it.

3. To the best of our knowledge, the Peshawar facility monitors a variety of activities and operations. Or to put it in your own words, it provides "accurate technical and scientific information on the intentions and capabilities of others". I concede that this facility is valuable to your country but by its very nature it lays us open to the hostility and retaliation of powerful neighbours.

4. The close relationship between our two countries in the security field, to which you have alluded in your letter, Mr. President, has progressively been whittled away. Only last year when your Ambassador communicated to us the new United States arms supply policy, he said that "a fundamental and historical change" had come about in our relationship. Your Secretary of State told our Foreign Minister last October in Washington that there was now "no special relationship" between Pakistan and the United States.

5. We in Pakistan cannot remain unmindful of the swift changes which are taking place in the world and especially around us today. We cannot ignore the threats which are developing to our existence, particularly from the feverish arms build-up in India. The arms supply policy of your country provides us with no comfort. If anything, it aggravates the imbalance between India and Pakistan.

6. The Peshawar facility on our soil in no way contributes to our security useful though it may be to your country. For us it constitutes a danger.

7. Changes in world politics make it imperative for Pakistan to improve its relations with neighbouring countries and for this purpose to remove irritants and obstacles to the development of friendly relations. I believe this is an objective to which your own Administration

---

[1] Source: Johnson Library, National Security File, Head of State Correspondence File, Pakistan, Vol. 3, President Ayub Correspondence, 12/31/67–[sic]. No classification marking. Delivered to the White House by the Pakistani Embassy on July 31.

[2] See Document 503.

is dedicated and I recall with satisfaction the many significant steps which you have taken for achieving détente and a lessening of tension around the world. The Peshawar facility negates the attainment of this objective. It would have been logical in the light of circumstances to which I have referred above for Pakistan to request that it be given up a long time ago. But on the contrary we decided to carry out our commitments under the agreement fully in an honourable manner even though thereby we have run the risk of damage to our political interests and national security.

8. You, Mr. President, have referred to the aid which your country has been generous enough to give to Pakistan over the years. We have always gratefully acknowledged the valuable role which this assistance has played on our economic development. Pakistan–United States amity and co-operation has in no small measure contributed to the maintenance of stability in this important region of Asia and there is no doubt in my mind that the removal of the Badaber facility will not come in the way of our close co-operation in the field. It is, therefore, with faith in your statesmanship and far-reaching vision that I ask you to appreciate the problems of a small country which is hemmed in by powerful neighbours.

9. I have directed my officers to start immediate discussions with your representatives on the mechanics of dismantling the Peshawar facility so that the operation may be carried out in a smooth and orderly manner.[3]

With best regards and good wishes for your continued health,

Yours sincerely,

Mohammad Ayub Khan

---

[3] Ambassador Hilaly called on Rusk on August 2 to follow up on the delivery of Ayub's letter. He said the decision not to renew the agreement concerning the Peshawar facility had been a "heart-rending" one, and he attributed it in part to Ayub's need to protect his domestic political position. (Telegram 214843 to Rawalpindi, August 3; National Archives and Records Administration, RG 59, Central Files 1967–69, DEF 15 PAK–US)

506.   Telegram From the Ambassador to Pakistan (Oehlert) to the President's Special Assistant (Rostow)[1]

Rawalpindi, July 24, 1968, 0709Z.

334. 1. When I left your office at approximately 1700 hours on Friday, June 28, you and I, along with Nick Katzenbach and everyone else concerned at State, Defense, Joint Chiefs and the intelligence community, were in full and complete agreement that we should move heaven and earth to insure that the Belgian tank deal went through as immediately as possible.

2. After considerable delay on the part of the Belgians, Brussels sent its 8001[2] on July 12 setting forth the bases on which the Belgians were prepared to move.

3. There were no conditions in the Belgian proposition that we had not discussed in advance and agreed we should comply with. In fact, we were willing to go much further than the Belgians required.

4. Thirteen days have now gone by with no response to Brussels from Washington, despite two intervening messages from me to Washington.

5. I can understand why Washington would be interested in Ayub's response to President Johnson's letter,[3] but on the other hand we ought to be willing to look at the other fellow's side of it, which may be briefly outlined as follows:

A. Our April 1, 1967 announcement of a new military supply policy encouraged GOP to believe that at long last it would be able to obtain some American-made equipment.

B. The Paks then worked up a deal with Germany, which we refused to approve because instead of selling direct, the Germans insisted on selling through a third country. Admittedly, there was a difference between this proposal and our new policy, but it didn't appear to the Paks to be a difference of substance.

C. Nevertheless they accepted our position and worked out a deal with Iran which was precisely in accord with our policy. Nevertheless,

---

[1] Source: Johnson Library, National Security File, Country File, Pakistan, Vol. IX, Memos, 5/68–11/68. Top Secret. Sent [text not declassified] from Ambassador Oehlert to the White House for Walt Rostow.

[2] In telegram 8001 from Brussels, July 12, the Embassy outlined the grounds on which the Belgian Government was prepared to proceed with the sale of tanks to Pakistan. The Embassy noted that the only new element of importance among the Belgian conditions was the Belgian desire to inform India that Belgium was prepared to sell tanks to India on similar terms. (National Archives and Records Administration, RG 59, Central Files 1967–69, DEF 19–8 US–BEL)

[3] See Document 503.

we refused to approve this deal for reasons which the Paks could never be expected to understand. It was precisely in accord with our policy and our only reason for rejecting it was because we did not want the Shah to spend too much of his own money buying equipment from us, even though such sales would be to our labor, profit, taxation and balance of payments interests.

D. We then put the Paks in touch with the abortive Italian-German deal which many of us knew from the beginning could not possibly succeed because:

I. The Italians had no tanks of their own, but had to acquire them from Germany;

II. The Italians would not move until they had customers for all the 750 tanks;

III. The Italians were insisting on outrageous prices;

IV. The Germans insisted on a clause in the Italian contract which would prohibit resale to Pakistan.

6. Then we steered the Paks to Belgium. We have every reason to believe that the Belgians have indicated to the Paks that they are ready and willing to proceed, but that we are dragging our heels, which, in fact, we are. Under all these circumstances, I think we should have some appreciation of Ayub's difficulty in making any affirmative response to President Johnson's letter.

7. We are committed to the tanks. We all recognize that. We should fulfill our commitment. We can not expect any Peshawar success unless we do, nor can we expect to have any credibility or influence with the Paks unless we do.

8. I am counting on you, personally, old friend, to break this deadlock in accordance with our agreement.[4]

---

[4] President Johnson considered and accepted Oehlert's advice at a luncheon meeting on July 24 with Rusk, Clifford, Helms, Rostow, and Generals Earle Wheeler and Maxwell Taylor. (Memorandum for the record by Rostow; Johnson Library, National Security File, Files of Walt Rostow, Meetings with the President, May–June 1968)

507. Memorandum From Edward Hamilton of the National Security Council Staff to President Johnson[1]

Washington, August 5, 1968.

SUBJECT

Wheat for India

Herewith Messrs. Freeman, Gaud and Zwick recommend a $169 million PL–480 agreement with India. Zwick's memorandum (Tab A)[2] is a concise summary of the proposal. The more detailed Freeman/ Gaud memorandum is at Tab B.[3]

This agreement would provide for the second half of calendar 1968. Last December you approved a $216 million bargain providing 3.5 million tons of grain to cover the first half. This agreement will provide another 2.3 million tons of grain, along with small amounts of tallow, milk and tobacco. Total: 5.8 million tons of grain to India in 1968—about the same as last year.

The development case for providing the food is strong. The Indians have moved on all the self-help measures called for in the December agreement and are ahead of schedule on the important ones. The new wheat would go primarily to build buffer stocks to back the CCC-type price support operation we have been pushing the Indians to adopt. Taken with India's own bumper grain crop, this will provide the best grain supply situation and outlook in recent Indian history. However, this agreement gives us little new political leverage because the Indians aren't in the dire need of the famine years.

The most compelling argument for the agreement is our domestic wheat situation. Despite reduced acreage the 1968 U.S. crop will be another record, and the wheat price has now dipped under $1.25 for the first time in a decade. Freeman frankly does not expect to reach our wheat export target of 750 million bushels for this crop year. But this agreement is the core of any fighting chance he may have.

---

[1] Source: Johnson Library, National Security File, Country File, India, Vol. XI, Cables, 2/68–10/68. Confidential. A handwritten note on the memorandum indicates it was received at the LBJ Ranch on August 6 at 8:30 a.m.

[2] Reference is to an August 3 memorandum from Zwick to the President entitled "P.L. 480 Agreement for India." (Ibid.)

[3] Dated July 26 and entitled "PL 480 Program for India." (Ibid.)

Commercial Purchases

India now plans to acquire 1.5 million tons of grain in 1968 beyond the amounts we provide through PL–480. At least one million tons of this will come in food aid from other donors. This leaves 500–700,000 tons to be bought on the world market. We have pushed hard to get the Indians to buy as much as possible from the U.S. So far this year they have bought 146,000 tons from us (and 200,000 tons from others). We hope to get another 200,000 tons or so.

Cuban Problems in the Wings

As you consider this, you should know that we have evidence of a new transaction by an Indian firm in Cuba. An Indian engineering company has contracted with the Castro Government to do the plans for a metal refinery which will probably process products of an expropriated American mine. The Indian involvement is entirely private, so there is no legal restriction on PL–480 or other aid. But it is hard to believe that the aid-haters on the Hill would let this one slip by if it caught their attention. The deal has been in the Indian press but not, so far as we know, in the American papers. It may pass unnoticed, but it may also give us real trouble.

We have made it clear to the Indians that we are unhappy about this, and that the Congress is likely to be more so. They have listened politely and explained that it is a private transaction over which the Government has no control. In fact, of course, the GOI could make it practically impossible for the firm to go ahead. But the Government would take a lot of political heat. State's judgment—which I share—is that the Indians aren't about to pay that political price to safeguard wheat they don't really need for immediate consumption. If we push them and make the wheat a condition, my guess is the only effect will be that we won't move the wheat.

Recommendation

I recommend you approve the agreement.

EH

Agreement approved

Agreement approved but hold off announcement until Congress is out of town

Disapprove[4]

See me

---

[4] Johnson checked the disapproval line. A handwritten note on the memorandum by Jim Jones, reads: "Hold this long as possible then disapprove"; this note is apparently a quote from the President. On August 7 Freeman, who had been informed of the President's decision by Hamilton, sent a memorandum to the President expressing his concern over the decision. He noted that the 2.3 million tons of wheat involved was important to India to build up its buffer stocks of grain, but he argued that the proposed grain sale was critically important to the United States in light of the record U.S. wheat crop. (Ibid.) Bowles saw the proposed P.L. 480 agreement as an opportunity to reverse the gradual erosion in U.S.-Indian relations. In an August 29 letter to Rusk, Bowles stated that if the President had decided to disapprove the P.L. 480 agreement, "it is a blow that could scarcely come at a worse time." (Department of State, NEA/INC Files: Lot 72 D 132, AID 15–1, PL 480 General)

---

508.   **Telegram From the Ambassador to Pakistan (Oehlert) to President Johnson[1]**

Rawalpindi, August 5, 1968, 1051Z.

5602. 1. When you posted me here you told me to feel free to communicate directly with you when I believed the circumstances justified it.

2. It is fair to say that I have not abused that privilege.

3. The circumstances do now justify it.

---

[1] Source: Johnson Library, National Security File, Country File, Pakistan, Vol. IX, Memos, 5/68–11/68. Top Secret; Immediate; Eyes Only for the President. An interim acknowledgment of this telegram on August 6 by Bromley Smith at the White House [*text not declassified*]. (Ibid.)

4. Our national interests in this country—indeed in this part of the world—have reached a crisis.

5. Having, unsuccessfully, used every other means at my command to resolve this crisis, I have no other resource except to place the problem on your overburdened but broad shoulders.

6. Whatever its troubles may be with some of its East European satellites, the USSR has made and is making great progress in this part of the world:

A. It has attained its century-old ambition to reach warm waters;

B. The strength of its Mediterranean fleet grows apace;

C. It has made a captive of the more belligerent Arab states, especially the UAR, Syria, Algeria and Iraq;

D. It has obtained a naval presence in the Indian Ocean, the Arabian Sea and the Persian Gulf;

E. It has made India largely dependent upon it because of military supply;

F. It has largely outflanked the friendly Arab states of Jordan and Saudi Arabia;

G. It has at least partially outflanked Iran and Turkey.

7. It is clearly contrary to our national interests for Pakistan to move into the Russian orbit—not only because of Pakistan itself but also because of the effect upon Iran, Turkey, and Saudi Arabi.

8. The following has happened with respect to Pakistan:

A. Our liberalized military supply policy of April 1967 has not obtained Pakistan any end items:

I. Efforts through Germany, Italy and now Belgium have all failed;

II. The failures have been due in large measure to Indian pressure.

B. We have seen the first visit in history of a Russian head of state to Pakistan.

C. We have seen the first visit of a Russian naval vessel (a squadron) to Pakistan;

D. We have received the termination notice on Peshawar;

E. The USSR has indicated a willingness to sell lethal end items to Pakistan despite strong Indian protests.

9. If Pakistan is forced to rely on Russia for arms, Peshawar is lost and all of our other vital interests in this part of the world, including Iran, Turkey and Saudi Arabia, are jeopardized.

10. Time is of the essence.

11. Pakistan prefers U.S. made arms for logistical and ideological reasons but has been unable to come by them.

12. Our commitment to third party sales dates back to April 1967.

13. Our commitment of "one hundred tanks now and one hundred later" dates back to March 1, 1968.

14. All of the heat we might expect from the Congress, the press, or India has already been taken by our declared willingness to see Pakistan get tanks from Italy etc.

15. Our commitment of those tanks was conditioned on:

A. No further acquisition of tanks or other lethal end items by Pakistan from anyone without consultation with us;
B. Scrapping the present tank inventory on one for one basis;
C. Purchase price and terms acceptable to us.

16. Our commitment of those tanks was not conditioned upon any Peshawar extension. In fact, my positive instructions were not to link the two.

17. During my June 1968 Washington consultations all responsible officials to whom I talked in State, Defense, Joint Chiefs and the intelligence community agreed that if the Belgian tank deal fell through we should sell the tanks directly if need be.

18. The only reservation to the above was one of timing because of a concern for Congressional reaction.

19. During my consultations I met with the Georgia delegation, the Florida delegation, the Zablocki Subcommittee in executive session, and an informal group of members of Senate Foreign Relations and Armed Services Committees at the invitation of Dick Russell.

20. All, and especially Russell and Senator Symington, were strongly in favor of a change in military supply policy for the subcontinent to allow direct sales of lethal end items on a case by case basis. Such a policy modification, or at least a special exception to the present policy, for the two hundred tanks committed would not be an embarrassment to the next administration.

21. On the contrary, it is the only way to keep the next administration's options open. With all the other problems facing it, it will be at least a year from now before the next administration can fix on a subcontinent arms policy. It will then be too late. Peshawar will be gone and the Paks will be in Russian hands. By moving now we can prevent this from happening without in any way committing or binding the policy of the next administration.

22. I beseech you, Mr. President, to move forcefully and immediately to get Ayub his tanks.

23. It may not even be necessary to make a direct sale. Iran is ready, able and willing to provide the tanks. Ayub knows this. If we do not allow it, he will certainly conclude that we do not want him to have any tanks and never did.

24. An Iranian sale would be 100 percent in accord with our present policy. It would need no modification of or exception to that policy. It would not represent the slightest deviation in principle from our al-

ready expressed willingness to approve a sale by Germany, Italy or Belgium.

25. The only reason ever advanced for not approving such a sale when the possibility first arose last December has been that if we do approve it, the Shah will want to buy more M–60's from us than our experts think he should in the interest of his own budgetary considerations.

26. It is the Shah's own money. He is no longer receiving aid.

27. For him to buy more M–60's from us is in our own interests:

A. Employment-wise;
B. Profit-wise;
C. Tax-wise;
D. Balance of payments-wise.

28. It can not please the Shah to refuse to allow him to do this.

29. If the Shah wants more modern tanks he will get them—if not from us then from the French or the Russians—which would not be in our interests.

30. If we let the Shah sell Ayub the tanks our balance sheet would look like this:

A. Assets:

I. The Shah will be pleased;
II. Ayub will be pleased;
III. The Russians will be slowed down in Pakistan and in all of South Asia and parts of the Middle East;
IV. Our financial interests will have been served;
V. Peshawar retention will be helped;
VI. We will have fulfilled our commitment.

B. Liabilities:

None.

31. Mr. President, on December 23, 1967, in Karachi, in your presence I told Ayub that Pakistan was not my client but that my only client was the USG. I told him that while I had great respect for him and for his government and for their accomplishments and hoped that I could often be of assistance to his government's interests, I had come here only to serve my own government. You will remember the context in which those remarks were made.

32. I have not changed.

33. I give not one fig for Pakistan except as its interests are ours.

34. My earnest request to you to approve Iran and if for some unforseen reason that should fail then to make a direct sale, is based exclusively on our own national interests.

35. I know that the greatest American I have ever known will forgive me for plagiarizing him—I am a free man, an American and an Ambassador of the United States of America in that order.

36. It is in those three contexts, Mr. President, and only those three, that I seek your action.[2]

_____

[2] Hamilton and Bromley Smith sent a copy of this telegram to President Johnson in Texas on August 6. (Memorandum to the President; ibid.) They also sent a copy of telegram 17737 from New Delhi, July 31, in which Bowles pressed for a reversal of the decision to countenance the sale of tanks to Pakistan in light of the purchase of Chinese tanks by Pakistan, the impending purchase of Soviet arms including tanks by Pakistan, and the adverse impact on U.S.-Indian relations of even an indirect sale of U.S.-originated tanks to Pakistan. (Ibid., Memos to the President, Walt Rostow, Vol. 90, August 1–10, 1968) On August 9 Battle sent a cable to Oehlert assuring him that every effort was being made to facilitate a third country sale of tanks to Pakistan. He noted, however, that an Iranian sale continued to pose significant policy problems. (Telegram 217963 to Rawalpindi; National Archives and Records Administration, RG 59, Central Files 1967–69, DEF 12–5 PAK)

_____

509. Memorandum From the Under Secretary of State (Katzenbach) to President Johnson[1]

Washington, August 8, 1968.

SUBJECT

Indo-US Talks, July 26–28, 1968[2]

As you know, I have just finished a week in India launching the first in a series of annual planning talks with the Indians. During the week—in addition to three days of talks—I visited the huge Bakhra–

_____

[1] Source: Johnson Library, National Security File, County File, India, Vol. XI, Memos and Miscellaneous, 2/68–10/68. Secret.

[2] Katzenbach headed a team that visited New Delhi for the first in a projected series of annual bilateral consultations between the United States and India. Included in Katzenbach's party were Battle, Heck, Assistant AID Administrator Maurice Williams, and Hamilton of the NSC Staff. The Indian delegation at the talks was headed by Minister of State for External Affairs B.R. Bhagat. While in India, Katzenbach, accompanied by Battle, Heck, and Bowles, met with President Zakir Husain, Prime Minister and Foreign Minister Gandhi, and Deputy Prime Minister and Finance Minister Desai. Katzenbach reported on his meeting with Gandhi in telegram 17455 from New Delhi, July 25. (National Archives and Records Administration, RG 59, Conference Files: Lot 69 D 182, CF 313) A memorandum of his conversation with Husain on July 27 is in Department of State, NEA/INC Files: Lot 73 D 24, India 1968, India/US—Informal Talks. A brief report on the talks was transmitted to Washington on July 29 in telegram 18664 from Paris. (National Archives and Records Administration, RG 59, Central Files 1967–69, POL INDIA–US) A more complete summary report on the talks was transmitted to Washington in airgram A–1390 from New Delhi, August 13; ibid., POL 1 INDIA–US.

Nangal Dam, a family planning center and an agricultural research station. In addition, I had private talks with Mrs. Gandhi, President Husain and Deputy Prime Minister Desai.

I came away with the following impressions and conclusions:

—India is managing its affairs far better than I had suspected. Vast problems remain, but I was continually struck by the spirit of determination and self-confidence of all.

—There has been a very real and exciting break-through in agriculture. The Indians now are giving agricultural production the priority it deserves. Sustained progress will, of course, require sustained Indian effort and both support and policy monitoring by the aid consortium. You can be proud of your personal role in reducing the threat of a massive Indian famine and malnutrition.

The talks themselves went well. The atmosphere was good; the discussion informal and relaxed. By agreement, we both stuck to the larger issues and did not push too hard on touchy subjects.

South East Asia

The most significant outcome of the talks was an Indian indication that they have decided to take on a more active role in Southeast Asia. In the short run this means improving their relations with the countries of the region. For the post-Viet-Nam period they suggested that they—with other SEA countries—promote a regional group which would assume greater responsibility for the problems of the area. The Indians hope the neutrality and security of this grouping would be recognized and supported by the US and others.

The idea certainly has not been thought out in detail, but the significant point is India's initiative to involve itself in an area it has long overlooked. We told the Indians to try the idea out on others, including the Russians, with whom they plan similar talks next month.

Surprisingly, the Indians did not exclude Pakistan from this regional grouping. I also was interested to hear that the Indians are now surplus in small arms production. One of the roles they might play in promoting their scheme would be to supply modest military assistance (both equipment and training).

China

I returned with a far better understanding of India's problems with China. The Indians are extremely troubled by Chinese pressures, and have built up a substantial force to cope with any conventional military threat (including Chinese support for insurgents along the northeastern borders). Morale among the Indian armed forces is high and—unlike 1962—they should be able to give a good account of themselves. As we total up our security assets in Asia, I think we can look upon this force as a net plus against China

Pakistan

Tanks for Pakistan came up at various times, but the Indians did not belabor the subject as they had earlier threatened to do. This is, as you know, an extremely complicated problem, so I will send you a separate memo on it.

Aid

Not surprisingly, the Indians are troubled about aid cutbacks, but are adjusting to the blow. They were particularly worried about prospects for IDA, since continuation of their import liberalization program is dependent upon IDA funds.

Gandhi Trip

I learned that Mrs. Gandhi will visit South America in September and October. She expects to stop overnight in New York on October 14 on her way back, and would, I suspect, like to see you informally while she is in the US. You may want to invite her to a private lunch at the White House on October 15. I personally believe it would be a useful move.[3]

Nicholas deB. Katzenbach

---

[3] Another copy of this memorandum included a typed marginal notation indicating that the President's response to this suggestion was "Hold off for now." (Ibid., POL INDIA–US)

510. **Telegram From the Department of State to the Embassy in Pakistan[1]**

Washington, August 23, 1968, 1745Z.

226368. For Ambassador. Ref: (a) Rawalpindi 6575,[2] (b) State 214860,[3] (c) State 202781,[4] (Nodis).

1. You are authorized meet with Akhbar and Yusuf to present proposal for withdrawal Peshawar along lines paras 2–6 below.

2. *Personnel:* (A) USG proposes begin phase-out technical operational personnel in January 1969. Withdrawal of total of about 800 operational personnel would be completed by December 1969, at which time all USAF operational activities would end. Under planned month-by-month personnel withdrawals, about half of total operational personnel would be out in July 1969. Army Sugar Tree unit (approximately 30 personnel) would remain in operation until final close-out of Peshawar.

(B) Approximately 500 support personnel would begin departures before July 1969 with final evacuation to be completed by July 1, 1970. Since many of these personnel would be involved in final clean-up after operations ceased in December 1969, bulk of them would depart in monthly withdrawals between January and July 1970.

(C) In sum, we would have about 30% present authorized personnel out by July 1969, another 30% by December 1969, with remaining 40% completely out by July 1, 1970.

3. *Technical Equipment:* (A) As operational personnel are withdrawn as outlined above, the equipment and associated matériel which they have been using would be crated and readied for shipment. The exact movement schedule from the station would depend on availability of transportation, but, in any event, it would all be out before July 1, 1970.

(B) Antenna dismantling would begin in January 1969 with the antenna associated with Placid I (Bankhead), including the 15-foot dish

---

[1] Source: National Archives and Records Administration, RG 59, Central Files 1967–69, DEF 15 PAK–US. Secret; Exdis. Drafted by Spain on August 15; cleared by Heck, Handley, Wolfin (G/PM), Curl (INR), Robert H. Neuman (L/NEA), Sheldon (CIA), Hero (OSD/OGC), Wix (DOD/ISA), and Bromley Smith at the White House; and approved by Katzenbach. Repeated to CINCSTRIKE.

[2] In telegram 6575 from Rawalpindi, August 1, Oehlert reported on a conversation with Foreign Office Director General Piracha in which Piracha pressed for action on the pending tank sale. (Ibid., DEF 19–8 BEL–PAK)

[3] Telegram 214860 to Rawalpindi, August 3, informed Ambassador Oehlert that he could expect a proposal regarding the termination of the Peshawar facility shortly. (Ibid., DEF 15 PAK–US)

[4] Document 504.

inclosed in the 21-foot radome, two 6-foot dishes inclosed in another radome, the corner reflector and four log periodic-type antenna. Dismantling and removal of these could probably be completed in ninety days. Other UHF and special antenna would be removed from January through June 1970, or earlier.

(C) Equipment for the 12 positions presently being used by the Pakistanis would be turned over to them in the event of a favorable Pak response to the USG phase-out plan. The high frequency antenna systems would be left to them in any event.

(D) In sum, some of the most visible antenna would be dismantled well in advance of July 17, 1969. Dismantling of the remainder of that which we would remove would span the January 1969–July 1970 period. The Pakistanis would receive title to the equipment for the 12 positions they now have plus the high frequency antenna.

4. *Non-technical equipment and facilities:* Physical plant, including residential and office buildings and recreational facilities worth approximately $10 million will be left behind for the GOP. Since individual items are not covered in the 1959 agreement, disposition of these would be worked out between USAF and Pak authorities. (FYI: In the event of a favorable Pak response to the USG phase-out plan we would be prepared to be helpful by leaving Peshawar a valuable and readily usable installation to the GOP. Since the 1959 Agreement is silent on residual value, we are in poor negotiating position on this subject. However, believe point that valuable installation will accrue to Pakistanis should subtly be made known. End FYI.)

5. *Dependents:* Dependents would normally depart with their sponsors according to schedules outlined paras 2(A) and 2(B) above. We would anticipate that about 50% of the approximately 400 dependents would be withdrawn by July 1969 and that all would be out by January 1970. (FYI: If absolutely necessary, we could undertake to remove maximum possible number earlier in 1969 making it possible at that time also to abandon base housing and to reduce and consolidate support facilities such as commissary, school, and hospital. End FYI.)

6. *Exclusion Area:* As part of proposed phase-out plan, we would be prepared to eliminate the US Exclusive Use Area at once. We would need only time to accomplish necessary physical adjustments which would probably be done in about two weeks. We would still require, of course, a separate small area under special security protection for our communications center. (FYI: 6937th Sp. Commander should be able provide you with description physical implications such change, e.g., number of additional square feet added to joint US/GOP area. End FYI.)

7. FYI: *Tactics and Timing:* Our objective remains to get as much time as possible beyond July 1969, but it now seems to us here that

one-year is most practical target to shoot at. There will remain some flexibility on a variety of specifics, but above proposal incorporates elements package discussed earlier (ref (c)) and is designed to make one year "moving-out" period beyond July 1969 as palatable as possible to Pakistanis. Should it turn out that one year period is unobtainable, we would then prefer total close-out by July 1969, including the withdrawal of US equipment used in the Pakistani exclusion area. Implementation such plan would have to begin soon, and, therefore, it is important that we determine as quickly as possible whether or not above proposal viable.

8. On this question, we still believe basic GOP attitude as reflected in and affected by recent exchange Presidential letters will be more important than specifics of withdrawal plan, but wish do anything possible present most attractive proposal. We hope paras 2–6 above will give you enough to open discussions. Should it become clear proposal is workable, one or more officials from agencies most directly concerned would come to Rawalpindi to help refine specifics.

9. We realize atmosphere for discussions could be improved by affirmative action on tanks and that it may be desirable wait additional week or so to see how current initiatives play out before coming to grips with Yusuf and Ahkbar on Peshawar plan. We will inform you on tanks ASAP.

10. Question of offering additional cash "rent" for period July 1969–July 1970 has been reexamined and para 4 (g) ref (c) is reconfirmed. We are prepared continue but not increase present rent. End FYI.

Rusk

---

511. **Telegram From the Embassy in Pakistan to the Department of State**[1]

Rawalpindi, August 24, 1968, 0705Z.

7085. From Ambassador. Subject: USSR Military Supply for Pakistan.

1. This morning the Defense Minister and Defense Secretary informed me that USSR has agreed in principle to sell GOP any hardware it wants, including tanks.

---

[1] Source: National Archives and Records Administration, RG 59, Central Files 1967–69, DEF 19–6 USSR–PAK. Secret; Exdis.

2. They added that last night President Ayub had asked the Minister to inform me that he is reluctant to act on this agreement because:

A. From an economic viewpoint he would prefer to acquire cheaper, second-hand material;

B. From a logistical viewpoint he would prefer to acquire U.S.-produced material;

C. Most importantly, he wished to avoid, if possible, any increased dependence on USSR.

3. They then stated that despite Ayub's reluctance, he would be forced to move in the Russian direction unless he could be assured early-on that U.S. manufactured sources would be forthcoming.

4. They then alluded to Iran, stating that this was, from their viewpoint, the cheapest, quickest and most certain source.

5. After explaining our Congressional problem vis-à-vis Iran, I informed them, without in any way identifying the countries, that we were having discussions with two other possible sources and hoped to have determined their position within the next several weeks.

6. They reverted to Iran, suggesting that USG, GOP and GOI could have a private, gentlemen's agreement among a very limited number of people in each government, that tanks would be forthcoming from Iran after Congress adjourns—for delivery next calendar year. I depreciated the practicabilities of such an agreement, including the prospects that it could remain secret.[2]

Oehlert

---

[2] The Department confirmed in telegram 231334 to Rawalpindi, August 31, that the proposed "gentlemen's agreement" was not feasible. The Department indicated that negotiations with Turkey concerning the sale of U.S.-originated tanks by Turkey to Pakistan were underway, with the prospect of an agreement in September. Oehlert was instructed to avoid replying to Admiral Khan's approach if possible until the negotiations with Turkey were concluded. (Ibid., DEF 12–5 PAK)

512. Action Memorandum From the President's Special Assistant (Rostow) to President Johnson[1]

Washington, September 23, 1968, 6 p.m.

Mr. President:

The attached memorandum and file (Tab 1)[2] are, in a sense, a reclama from Secretaries Rusk and Freeman, Bill Gaud, and Charlie Zwick on your decision of August 5 on India. (See Tab 2)[3] The history is as follows.

—We reported firmly and clearly to one and all that you wished to make no further decisions on India in your administration.

—In examining the political and economic consequences of this judgment, Sec. Rusk, for one set of reasons, Sec. Freeman, for another, Bill Gaud and Charlie Zwick, for a third, all felt that they had a duty to lay the matter once more before you on the following basis: What absolutely minimal decisions on Indian aid were required to keep alive the political and economic assets which you had built up there through your policies. (Sec. Freeman's anxiety has another dimension which is wholly familiar to you.) They concluded by raising for your decision:

—A $50 million fertilizer loan (as opposed to $200 million in general AID funds) because, as Zwick's memorandum says: "Failure to order this fertilizer now will mean a serious shortage of fertilizer for India next year which cannot be made up later."

—Similarily, this minimal program would cut the proposed 5.5 million tons of wheat to 1.5 million tons: the reason "If there is a break in PL 480 shipments from August through next March, we are all concerned that the buffer stocks will be drawn down to a point where the Indian government will be unable to move ahead in breaking down the food zones that prevent building a national agricultural market."

Secretary Rusk, I gather, is prepared to make this case to you on political grounds.

Since you know so well the arguments surrounding Indian aid, I forward the attached file unsigned by me: another signature is of no help. I do feel it is my duty, however, to make available to you this proposed minimal package which is, in the judgment of your responsi-

---

[1] Source: Johnson Library, National Security File, Country File, India, Vol. XI, Cables, 2/68–10/68. Confidential. A handwritten note on the memorandum indicates that it was received on September 24 at 9:10 a.m.

[2] Zwick pulled together the positions of Rusk, Freeman, and Gaud in a September 12 memorandum to the President dealing with aid to India. (Ibid.) The file cited by Rostow was his tabulation in a September 23 memorandum to the President of the remaining decisions relating to India. (Ibid.)

[3] See Document 507.

ble advisers, the recommended course of action in the light of your well understood reservations.[4]

Walt

---

[4] A handwritten note on the memorandum by Jim Jones reads: "Walt—Talk to Pres. about this. Pres. didn't say no more decisions. He said no more gifts."

---

513. Telegram From the Department of State to the Embassy in Pakistan[1]

Washington, September 25, 1968, 2333Z.

245135. Ref: Rawalpindi 7675.[2] Subject: Peshawar Negotiations. For Ambassador.

1. We are encouraged by your report of Akhbar's assurance we will be able continue operations through July 17, 1969 with dismantling and withdrawal to take place later. However, legal opinion here unable find any solid base for us to claim such right in agreement itself, and we cannot plan on that basis without written confirmation.

2. We must emphasize that time is running out for decision one way or another. Operating agencies need maximum lead time for orderly phase out of facility.

3. While we agree desirability avoiding visible alteration normal operations and personnel procedures prior to negotiations with GOP, USAF has already had to cease sending dependents not now on orders and we foresee other steps required soon. You should, therefore, initiate negotiations ASAP after your return to Pindi in accordance with State 226368[3] in order to achieve an early decision.

---

[1] Source: National Archives and Records Administration, RG 59, Central Files 1967–69, DEF 15 PAK–US. Secret; Priority; Exdis. Drafted by Spain and cleared by Mouser (NEA/INC), Neuman (L/NEA), Wolf (G/PM), Austin and Curl (INR), and Colonel Kravitz (DOD/ISA). Repeated to CINCSTRIKE.

[2] In telegram 7675 from Rawalpindi, September 18, Oehlert noted that Ayub was preoccupied with preparations for a trip to East Pakistan and that the time was not ripe to approach him on the Peshawar issue. Oehlert also noted that it would not be good strategy to make such an approach without a resolution of the Pakistani tank request in hand. He felt that until the opportunity to discuss Peshawar with Ayub was more propitious, it would be wise to rely on the assurance offered by General Akhbar that the Peshawar facility could be operated until the termination date and then dismantled. (Ibid.)

[3] Document 510.

4. Should it become evident that extension to 17 July 1970 is not feasible with proposed package, you should attempt obtain written confirmation of Akhbar's undertaking to permit full operation through July 17, 1969 and dismantling and removal thereafter. Such arrangement would, of course, be preferable to complete evacuation and turnover by July 17, 1969.

Rusk

514. Memorandum of Conversation[1]

Washington, October 4, 1968, 12:37–1 p.m.

SUBJECT

 Meeting between the President and Morarji Desai, Deputy Prime Minister of India[2]

PARTICIPANTS

 President Lyndon B. Johnson
 Morarji Desai, Deputy Prime Minister of India
 His Excellency Nawab Ali Yavar Jung, Ambassador of India
 Ambassador S. Jagannathan, Economic Affairs at Indian Embassy and Executive Director for India at the World Bank
 William J. Handley, Acting Assistant Secretary of State for Near Eastern and South Asian Affairs
 Harold E. Saunders, NSC Senior Staff

Deputy Prime Minister Morarji Desai called on the President for a twenty-minute conversation at 12:40 p.m. on Friday, October 4. After a brief exchange of pleasantries, the President and Deputy Prime Minister exchanged remarks on the following subjects:

When the Deputy Prime Minister commented that the President had had a difficult time since they last met, the President said that we

---

[1] Source: Johnson Library, National Security File, Country File, India, Vol. XI, Cables, 2/68–10/68. Secret; Exdis. Drafted by Saunders and Handley on October 30. Approved by the White House on November 22. The time of the meeting, which was held at the White House, is from the President's Daily Diary. (Ibid.)

[2] Desai visited Washington September 28–October 5 to attend meetings of the International Monetary Fund and the World Bank. While in Washington he met with Freeman, Fowler, and Rusk, in addition to President Johnson. A memorandum of his conversation with Rusk on September 28 is in National Archives and Records Administration, RG 59, Central Files 1967–69, POL 1 INDIA–US. The results of Desai's visit were summarized in telegram 251579 to New Delhi, October 8. (Ibid., POL 7 INDIA)

had had lots of problems but that we had also found lots of answers. We had not found answers for all of our most difficult problems but we had been blessed by progress in a number of fields. For instance, just this week, the President had had occasion, on signing several bills, to review our progress in the field of conservation, and he was very proud of what had been accomplished during his administration. On the other hand, we have still not been able to find an answer to the difficult problems of Vietnam.

Continuing on Vietnam, the President said that others had a different view of the problem from his but he felt, after looking at the problem from every possible angle and hearing every possible viewpoint that doing anything other than what we have done would have led to conditions far more difficult than the ones we face now.

He said Czechoslovakia had been a disappointment—indeed frightening—and he was quite concerned. The U.S. and the U.S.S.R. had been just on the verge of sitting down and making progress on limiting offensive and defensive weapons, on Vietnam and on the Middle East. "Then just before we got on the elevator, they invaded Czechoslovakia."

The President said the Middle East is quite troublesome. "We can't get either side to cooperate." At home, the economy is in excellent condition. People are expressing discontent, but a lot of this is artificially stirred up.

In sum, the President said there are pluses and minuses on our record. Then he asked the Deputy Prime Minister to tell him about conditions in his country. The President particularly inquired about the recent rainfall and the condition of the next Indian crop.

The Deputy Prime Minister said that the rain last year had been good and the crop a record one. The rains this year are less and the crop will be smaller, though it will be the end of October before anyone can make a sound estimate of just how big it may be. He noted that the industrial sector of the economy had begun to recover. In response to the President's inquiry whether India's changes in agricultural policy have paid off, the Deputy Prime Minister said that they definitely had. In spite of the possibility of poor rains this year, he tentatively estimated that the crop would not fall below 90 million tons because of the stronger production base that had been established as a result of changes in agricultural policy. There followed a brief discussion of the nature of what the October rains contributed to each of the Indian crops in comparison to the relation of the rains to harvesting and planting in Texas.

The President asked about Prime Minister Gandhi, B.K. Nehru, and former Agriculture Minister Subramaniam. The Deputy Prime Minister replied that Mrs. Gandhi was well into her Latin American tour but would have to cancel her scheduled visit to Peru because of the coup. He said that B.K. Nehru was in Assam and that Subramaniam was now head of the Committee on Aeronautics and had been in the United States a few weeks ago. The President said he was sorry he had missed Subramaniam and expressed admiration for the job Subramaniam did as Agriculture Minister.

The President said that a lot of problems had come together in the past few months—the war, Congressional difficulties, and the United Nations. The Deputy Prime Minister responded by saying that he doubted the President's successor could change many of these problems and that he would be confronted by pretty much the same pressures. He also said that he had the greatest admiration for the way the President had stood up to his problems.

The President said he was concerned over the turn in recent months in the American people's attitude toward other nations. He said this has been a familiar pattern in American history. After World War I we had had the Washington Naval Conference and scrapped a lot of our war material. Then we got into World War II and after that we demobilized and then came the Korean War. Now we are in Vietnam. Throughout this period, we have had other problems such as Greece, Turkey and the India–Pakistan war. A lot of the American people say that we should not try to be the World's policeman. The President did not feel that was the issue. If a child was sick with smallpox next door, he didn't see how anyone could justify not going to its aid on the ground that one shouldn't "mess with other people's business."

The President also said that his "enemies" say that we are "messing" too much in other people's affairs. What they mean by this, the President said, is that our policies are costing too much money. He felt that this was unrealistic and he was proud of how we have worked with a number of other countries, especially India. He said that India was doing better and so was Latin America and Africa. He said that some people were talking about bringing our troops back from Europe and he thought this had been an invitation for the Soviets to do what they had done in Czechoslovakia. He could not understand the new mood of isolation in the United States. It is in both parties, but his own party was worse than the other.

The Deputy Prime Minister asked whether it would be possible to release the remainder of this year's PL 480 shipments now. The President said he was not going to make many decisions on consequential matters between now and the election, which is just a month off. Then we would have a new President-elect. "Anything you do in your last few days in office, people suspect you of ulterior motives." The President said anything the new President could do, he wanted to let him handle.

The Deputy Prime Minister responded by saying that this decision "has already been done earlier by you; it is not a new decision." The Deputy Prime Minister went on to say that the President had already sent 3.5 million tons, and 2.3 million tons of the total approved remained. He said it would "come in handy" right now. India needs to build its buffer stocks, and it now appears that it has to look forward to a crop smaller than last year's.

After a noticeable silence, the President asked how long the Prime Minister was going to be in Latin America. After the Deputy Prime Minister's short response, the President asked whether India was any closer to the solution of the Kashmir problem. The Deputy Prime Minister responded that they were "neither closer nor farther" from the solution. The President asked how President Ayub was. He said that Ayub was "very distressed with us." Ambassador Jung said, "Why?" The President said Ayub felt that we haven't treated Pakistan fairly. We have helped India more than we had Pakistan. The President said he felt Ayub was "disillusioned and disheartened." The President said he was "sad about this."

When the Deputy Prime Minister said that he couldn't understand Ayub's feelings since we had done much more for Pakistan than for India, the President pointed to a photo of his family and said in essence that the Deputy Prime Minister's remarks make him think that while member of a family loved each other and worked together, there were times that each child thought the other was getting more than its share.

The Deputy Prime Minister presented the President with an album of Gandhi commemorative photos and, after a picture-taking session around the gift, the meeting broke up with an exchange of best wishes. The President hoped that Mr. Desai would have a good visit to Washington and said that he had lots of admirers in this country, especially Secretary Rusk who had been "vociferous" in praising him.

515.   Telegram From the Department of State to the Embassy in
Pakistan[1]

Washington, October 9, 1968, 2339Z.

252851. Subject: Visit to Washington of Pakistan Foreign Minister.[2]

1. Talks with Pakistan Foreign Minister Arshad Husain went
smoothly.

2. In pre-lunch informal private meeting October 8 with Acting
Secretary Foreign Minister asked that President Ayub's best wishes
and best regards be conveyed to President Johnson. Acting Secretary
undertook do so, mentioned Ambassador Hilaly's effective role as
Pakistan Ambassador here, and indicated high respect President Johnson and Department have for Ambassador Oehlert. Acting Secretary
also took opportunity to mention to Foreign Minister importance which
we attach to negotiations on Peshawar which would begin October
11 in Rawalpindi and to express hope these negotiations would be
successfully concluded.

3. Acting Secretary gave luncheon in honor of Foreign Minister
at 1 pm, after which discussions continued until 6:30 p.m. Participants
on Pak side were Foreign Minister, Ambassador Hilaly and Minister
Farooqi from Pakistan Embassy. Finance Minister Uquaili and Finance
Secretary Ghulam Ishaq Khan joined in for economic assistance topic.
In addition to Acting Secretary, US side included Deputy Secretary of
Defense Nitze, Assistant Secretaries of State Hart and Bundy, Assistant
Secretary of Defense Warnke, and other State and DOD officers, as well
as AID Assistant Administrator Williams for economic topic.

4. Main topics covered were:

(a) *Economic Aid Level:* Pak concern about economic aid cutbacks
came up several times. Main argument was that US aid had enabled
Pakistan make significant progress in the development field but that
a serious reduction in aid levels at this time would jeopardize whole

---

[1] Source: National Archives and Records Administration, RG 59, Central Files 1967–
69, POL 7 PAK. Secret; Limdis. Drafted by Spain and Prescott (NEA/PAF); cleared by
Handley, Macomber, and Country Director for India Christopher Van Hollen (NEA/
INC), cleared in substance by Glenn Lee Smith (NEA/P) and Deputy Assistant Secretary
of Defense Harry H. Schwartz (DOD/ISA); and approved by Katzenbach. Repeated to
New Delhi and USUN.

[2] Husain was in the United States for the session of the UN General Assembly. He
met with Rusk in New York on September 30 in addition to the meetings in Washington
on October 8 chaired by Katzenbach, and a meeting with Rostow on October 9. A record
of Husain's meeting with Rusk is ibid., POL PAK–US. Records of the meetings on October
8 are ibid., POL 27 INDIA–PAK, AGR 12 PAK, and DEF 1 PAK. A record of Husain's
meeting with Rostow is in the Johnson Library, National Security File, Country File,
Pakistan, Vol. IX, Memos, 5/68–11/68.

development effort. Paks recognized that some cuts were necessary as a result of Congressional action but expressed hope level would not fall below $100 million. Paks also raised question whether US would approve Pak sale of approximately 500,000 tons rice which would help Paks make up for short fall in economic aid. Acting Secretary recognized superior Pak development performance and said that we would do the best we could with what Congress allocates but that the outlook was definitely not good. On rice question, it was suggested this matter should be raised with Secretary of Agriculture Freeman.

(b) *Military Supply:* Foreign Minister said that Secretary Rusk had promised him that a decision on subject of tanks might be reached before he left the US. Acting Secretary explained Congressional and public opinion problems on arms sales and traumatic effect on US attitudes of 1965 Indo–Pak war. Recognized that present policy unsatisfactory in many respects but problem was to find alternative. Said that he had hoped to be able to give specific answer on tanks but was unable to do so. He expected have an answer soon, however, and would be in touch. FonMin indicated desire GOP continue rely on US as primary source military supply. Brought up problem of aircraft replacement and indicated a Pak decision on future sources of supply would probably have to be taken within next six months. Acting Secretary said US understood GOP problem but that it was difficult to make a decision on this kind of problem at this time. Amb mentioned delays in spare parts shipments. DOD representative indicated this not likely be major problem and undertook be in touch with Embassy. Amb also raised questions regarding procurement Sidewinders in Europe and asked for US "helpful hints" this regard.

(c) *Kashmir:* FonMin reviewed efforts for Kashmir settlement. He recognized disadvantages of continuing hostility and indicated that President Ayub had instructed him do anything possible to seek a settlement. India, however, refused recognize Kashmir as a dispute. FonMin indicated that GOP may have to go back to UN, was not asking for anything now but would seek US advice when this point reached. In reply to question, FonMin said that Soviets had not followed up on Tashkent agreement.

(d) *Farakka:* FonMin said present inclination of GOP was to run out technical and Secretarial level talks in hope some way could be found settle Farakka issue. If no solution found, GOP would have to go to UN, World Court, or elsewhere to try to find way out. He said Soviets had raised question of Farakka with GOI. US side expressed hope talks would be constructive and indicated that from US viewpoint outside intervention might be counterproductive.

(e) *Mid-East:* Foreign Minister stressed importance of Jerusalem to Muslim world and urged compliance with Jerusalem Resolution.

Said he believed Arabs willing undertake settlement but had nothing new to offer and did not indicate he was thinking of any initiatives in the UN on this subject.

(f) *Communist China:* FonMin not very forthcoming on this subject and confined his remarks to his personal observations. US side expressed thanks for Secretary Yusuf's efforts in North Korea and China.

(g) *Soviet Union:* FonMin believed that Czech crisis posed a two-fold problem for Soviets: (1) ideological—whether Communist movement should be polycentric or monocentric, and (2) strategic—protection of Soviet spheres of influence.

5. Ambassador Hilaly's small stag dinner for FonMin evening October 8 attended by Acting Secretary, Senator Sparkman, and key Department and DOD officials was warm, relaxed and informal. FonMin made apparent his awareness great US contribution to Pakistan's progress and well-being and his appreciation for it.

6. October 9 lunch hosted by House Foreign Affairs Subcommittee Chairman Zablocki was marked success. Speaker McCormack attended and paid personal tribute to President Ayub. Despite fact that House had been in continuous session for 26 hours, many House members, including Committee Chairman Morgan and Congressman Sikes attended "working lunch" and participated in spirited discussion with FonMin on his views Communist China, Indo-Pak problems, and Pakistan's development progress. This followed by session in Senate Foreign Relations Committee room with Acting Committee Chairman Senator Sparkman and Senator Hickenlooper. In both cases FonMin handled himself well and obviously left good impression on key Congressmen and Senators.

7. Throughout visit discussions were easy, friendly, and smooth flowing. FonMin expressed general agreement with US views on world situation, Soviet Union and Communist China. He indicated privately he completely satisfied with Washington visit and that his confidence in US sincerity and good-will of highest.

8. *Press Guidance:* Department used following guidance for press inquiries: "We are pleased that Pakistan's Foreign Minister has been able to come to Washington. During the Foreign Minister's brief visit he met Acting Secretary Katzenbach and other senior officials for an exchange of views on a wide range of topics including matters of world interests and bilateral concerns. Specific inquiries are to be answered with 'I have nothing further to add.'" This guidance adhered to throughout. Press play here so far low key and uncontroversial.

Rusk

516.   Telegram From the Embassy in Pakistan to the Department of State[1]

Rawalpindi, October 11, 1968, 1400Z.

8406. From Ambassador. Ref: State 252292.[2]

1. Following letter from Akhbar to McCloskey, dated 9 October, was received late Wednesday: [3]

"Thank you for your letter dated 3 October 1968.[4] It is correct that I had given the US authorities assurance that as long as the Peshawar communication unit agreement remains operative, we will afford you all the necessary support stipulated in the agreement. I am glad to know that you found this support satisfactory.

The Government of Pakistan has served notice for the termination of the agreement on 18 July 1969. It therefore follows that all the provisions of the agreement will lapse on that date. You will also recall that apart from the notice given by the Government of Pakistan, I had been giving the US authorities hints and indications on the termination of the agreement many months before hand. You will therefore agree that every opportunity has been given to enable you to plan an orderly and smooth evacuation of the base, as it will cease to operate as a communication unit on 18 July 1969. The agreement and all its provisions will lapse on the above date.

You are therefore advised to dismantle and ship out of the country any removable property by 18 July 1969 as the provisions of the agreement exempting such property from inspection, search and seizure would lapse on that date and the US Government will have no further rights in the matter.

The evacuation of any movable property left over in the base after 18 July 1969 may be subject to separate negotiations between the two governments."

2. Impossible yet to be certain, even after today's meeting, whether this repudiation of Akhbar's previous assurances, obviously fathered by Yusuf, represents merely a gambit of a tough opening bargaining position or a deep-seated decision of GOP not to yield one inch—at least sans tanks.

---

[1] Source: National Archives and Records Administration, RG 59, Central Files 1967–69, DEF 15 PAK–US. Secret; Immediate; Exdis.

[2] The Department, in telegram 252292 to Rawalpindi, October 9, welcomed the opening of negotiations on Peshawar scheduled to begin on October 11 and recognized the importance the sale of tanks to Pakistan could have on the negotiations and indicated that vigorous efforts were being made to facilitate such a sale. (Ibid., DEF 12–5 PAK)

[3] October 9.

[4] Not found.

3. Today's meeting attended on our side by Oehlert, Rogers, Mc-Closkey and Nastoff. On theirs by Yusuf, Akbar, Piracha and Farooqi.

4. Presented aide-mémoire (copy being pouched along with transcription of meeting notes)[5] which first addressed itself to exchange of McCloskey/Akhbar letters pointing out that next to last paragraph of letter sounded like a threat to seize any USG property remaining on base after July 17, 1969.

5. Their side flatly and firmly denied any such threat was intended and indicated they considered it subject to negotiations because they do not consider that agreement conveys any such rights. However they did not give categoric assurance in form satisfactory to us that we can operate through termination date and then dismantle and ship in orderly fashion.

6. If further negotiations indicate that GOP will not back down from position Akbar letter then I would regard this as not only unfriendly but actively hostile since it is tantamount to a threat to confiscate USG property unless we accept a close-down substantially in advance of date called for by the agreement. The agreement guarantees USG right to operate base as a communications unit and to use equipment through July 17, 1969, and also specifies that title to removable materials, equipment or property will remain in USG and "may be removed freely by the USG at any time."

7. It is my prayerfully arrived at conclusion that we should refuse to submit to any such threat which contravenes the provisions of the agreement, repeated oral assurances previously given, and the accepted standards of conduct between friendly nations.

8. I therefore recommend that, if GOP remains intransigent on this point, and if necessary to overcome such intransigency on the part of GOP, we be prepared to discontinue both economic aid and the supply of military spare parts.

9. More than Peshawar is at stake. In *Friends Not Masters*[6] Ayub states that each bilateral negotiation "would be determined by the limits of tolerance of third parties . . . to illustrate, the United States would not be too eager to provide us with unlimited economic and military assistance if we were to establish bilateral relations with major Communist powers without regard to American interest of strategies in Asia. If we cannot in an unlimited way identify ourselves with

---

[5] Airgram A–607 from Rawalpindi, October 14. (National Archives and Records Administration, RG 59, Central Files 1967–69, DEF 15 PAK–US)

[6] Reference is to Mohammed Ayub Khan, *Friends Not Masters* (London: Oxford University Press, 1967).

American interests, we must learn to do with less than unlimited American assistance." (Pages 118–119.)

10. In a conversation last week with Chargé Rogers and Admiral King, Piracha stated and emphasized the doctrine of "limits of tolerance."

11. It seems clear that the GOP is testing the limits of tolerance of the USG. If we show a high threshold of tolerance in this matter then we can never hope again to win GOP support for any policy of ours which is opposed by either USSR or ChiComs unless we are then willing to face a confrontation. To back down would be an almost irreparable show of weakness. To stand firm might win the day. At worst it would clarify the situation and we would know how far GOP has committed its policy toward its Communist neighbors without regard to USG interests, policy or sensibilities. Such a confrontation is bound to come sooner or later unless the USG is content to continue economic aid and military spare parts regardless of GOP preferential treatment of Communist interests without regard to USG interests.

12. Although of course I did not raise such issues at today's meeting, I repeated my recommendation of paragraph above for the longer haul. In addition to the strategic concerns supporting those recommendations, any action by GOP to seize USG property would cause justifiable US political tempest, particularly if aid or sales to GOP continued, and also would raise a serious legal question concerning the applicability to our economic aid program of Section 620 (e) of FAA—the Hickenlooper amendment. While that provision could be read as not covering expropriation of USG property, we believe it would be anomalous to construe it as applicable to cases of seizure of US citizens' property but inapplicable where property of USG is involved. At our meeting today, I brought to the attention of GOP the possible applicability of Section 620 (e) to any expropriatory action.

13. Balance of aide-mémoire, which was discussed at some length, covered:

A. Review of antecedent events of termination notice, President Johnson's letter to President Ayub of July 14,[7] latter's letter to President Johnson dated July 19,[8] and Piracha's information of appointment of Yusuf/Akbar committee;

B. A recognition of GOP's previous support of base, the need for the base, its irreplaceability, its importance, the unfavorableness to USG interests of the GOP termination notice and its attendant circumstances; and

---

[7] See Document 503.
[8] Document 505.

C. A proposed phase out schedule which tracks that covered by my instructions except that for bargaining purposes I added six months to each time phase.

14. Throughout discussions second portion aide-mémoire GOP side maintained strong stance that base must cease all operations on 18 July 1969, but:

A. Indicated it would be helpful to them if we would ostentatiously dismantle some elements prior to July 18, 1969, which we indicated we could and probably would do; and

B. Stated that they would need to consider and discuss aide-mémoire proposals before taking a position.

15. Neither our aide-mémoire nor our conversation indicated any equipment we would be willing to give them in return for some extension and they did not raise the question.

16. Next meeting set for October 18 at time to be agreed upon. Would hope at that meeting to obtain acceptable assurances our rights of removal of property.

Oehlert

---

517. Telegram From the Embassy in Pakistan to the Department of State[1]

Rawalpindi, October 20, 1968, 0900Z.

8628. Subject: Peshawar/Tanks. Please pass White House. From Ambassador.

1. Last evening President Ayub phoned me to say that he had decided to "take a calculated risk" and agree to some extension of base operations along the lines of my previous proposal.[2] He emphasized

---

[1] Source: National Archives and Records Administration, RG 59, Central Files 1967–69, DEF 15 PAK–US. Secret; Immediate; Exdis. The text of this telegram was sent to President Johnson at the LBJ Ranch in telegram CAP 82588, October 20. (Johnson Library, National Security File, Country File, Pakistan, Vol. IX, Cables, 5/68–11/68)

[2] When Oehlert met with Foreign Secretary Yusuf on October 18, Yusuf informed him that the U.S. proposal to phase out operations at the Peshawar facility gradually following the termination of the base agreement on July 17, 1969, had been considered, but the Pakistani Government position was that all operational activities at the facility must be terminated on July 17, 1969. (Telegram 8589 from Rawalpindi, October 18; National Archives and Records Administration, RG 59, Central Files 1967–69, DEF 15 PAK–US) Oehlert expressed his disappointment over the position taken by the Pakistani Government in a conversation with Ayub on October 19. He told Ayub that the decision to force the closure of the facility on July 17, 1969, would be seen by many in Washington as evidence that Pakistan attached greater importance to its relations with China and the Soviet Union than with the United States. (Telegram 8625 from Rawalpindi, October 19; ibid.)

that he was willing to take such a risk because he was anxious to be helpful to USG in any way he could.

2. He added that he had instructed Secretary Yusuf to get in touch with me and work out the details.

3. Ayub then said that there was another matter he had meant to discuss with me the evening before. He reminded me of his conversation with President Johnson and me in Karachi last December 23[3] about "horses", said he greatly appreciated all the efforts which had been made in that direction, and that he hopes that those efforts would be carried forward to early fruition because he badly needed the "horses."

4. I assured him that every possible effort was being made.

5. Pursuant to appointment I met with Yusuf at 1000 hours this morning. He handed me an unofficial unsigned aide-mémoire[4] reading as follows:

A. Dismantling, packing and removal of the facilities, installations and equipment shall commence in January 1969. This will be accompanied by a staggered thinning down of personnel.

B. All facilities, installations and equipment not dismantled by the cut-out date (i.e. 17 July 1969) will be dismantled not later then 31st December 1969 in accordance with a fixed monthly programme.

C. All dismantled facilities, installations and equipment shall be packed and crated and be removed from Pakistan as early as possible and in no case later than 28th February 1970. All remaining base personnel will be evacuated completely by the same date.

6. Attention is called to the reference to "a fixed monthly program" in paragraph 5 (B) above. Yusuf and I agreed that we would meet again on Monday, October 28.

A. For him to receive our formal response to the above proposal (I would hope and urge that it be accepted, since it covers all desired points except for Sugar Tree operation for some months after 31 December 1969); and

B. If possible for US to submit a proposed fixed monthly schedule although it was agreed that there could be an exchange of notes along the lines of the aide-mémoire with the fixed monthly schedule to be furnished later. Would hope to be able to submit the schedule on October 28 and would appreciate guidance along those lines ASAP.

7. There was one disturbing element in the Yusuf conversation, but I do not consider it insurmountable. He stated that, in addition to an exchange of letters embodying the point of the aide-mémoire, there should be a verbal understanding that all antenna would be down by July 17, 1969.

---

[3] See Document 475.
[4] Not found.

8. I told him that, while I was not technically informed, I believe that such a requirement would negate the intention for us to be able to operate selected equipment through 31 December since I did not believe that the equipment was operable without antenna.

9. He responded that what they wanted was continued use in "a discreet manner" with all antenna indoors if possible or at least as unobtrusive as possible.

10. The gist and tone of the conversation was such that I believe they will not insist on the antenna point provided much of the most obtrusive elements are down by July 17 and further progress in that direction is evident thereafter.

Oehlert

---

518. Telegram From the Ambassador to Pakistan (Oehlert) to President Johnson[1]

Rawalpindi, October 25, 1968, 0811Z.

500. 1. President Ayub's personal intervention in the Peshawar matter and his instructions to his Foreign Office to work out a time extension along the general lines of our request evidences his desire to accommodate our wishes in such matters to the extent he deems possible and to improve relationships between the two countries.

2. A breakthrough on tanks would greatly strengthen our hand and make it possible to us to continue working in the direction of those objectives.

3. Most respectfully but most urgently I request you to give the deepest consideration to the possibility of either:

A. Sweetening the pot to the extent necessary with Turkey, or
B. Authorizing a direct sale of tanks either as an exception to the present military supply policy or in connection with a liberalization thereof.

---

[1] Source: Johnson Library, National Security File, Memos to the President, Walt W. Rostow, Vol. 101, October 23–28, 1968. Secret. [text not declassified]

519.   Action Memorandum From the President's Special Assistant (Rostow) to President Johnson[1]

Washington, October 25, 1968, 3:45 p.m.

SUBJECT

Tanks for Pakistan

At Tab A[2] Nick Katzenbach advises that we have reached the decision point in the nagging year-old effort to find Patton tanks for Ayub. If you feel strongly about this obligation, he recommends that we pay the cost ($3 million) of arranging an interim sale through Turkey, the only feasible third-country deal we've been able to turn up. Failing a Turkish deal, Katzenbach thinks we should tell Ayub we have honestly done our best and he will have to look elsewhere. With the support of his SIG colleagues, Nick lays out your main options:

1. *Turkish sale:* The Turks apparently won't sell 100 M–47's to Pakistan unless they can get 100 refurbished M–48's for themselves in the bargain. This will cost us about $3 million; Nitze is prepared to find the money within current budget limits. But this would take care of only half of the 200 tanks Ayub wants. Defense is not ready to chip in another $3 million for another round of the Turk-to-Pak tank switch. Katzenbach and Co. recommend you can and should leave the second 100 tanks for your successor. One hundred now at $3 million and 100 left hanging is the preferred course.

2. *Iran:* The Shah will sell 100 old M–47's to Ayub if we replace them with new M–60's. This would add $22 million to Iran's planned purchases. Thus it would fly in the face of our budget-cutting advice to the Shah and probably raise a storm on the Hill. No one recommends this alternative.

3. *Change policy for one-time exception:* You could lift the current ban on direct U.S. weapons sales to the subcontinent just to sell Ayub these tanks. Your advisors think this would be the worst of worlds. It would mock a policy we've all defended up to this moment, be certain to bring an outcry from the Hill, and deeply embitter the Indians,

---

[1] Source: Johnson Library, National Security File, Country File, Pakistan, Vol. IX, Memos, 5/68–11/68. Secret/Sensitive. A handwritten note on the memorandum indicates it was received at 4 p.m.

[2] Reference is to an October 22 memorandum from Katzenbach to the President entitled "Tanks for Pakistan." (Ibid., Memos to the President, Walt Rostow, Vol. 101, Oct. 23–28, 1968) A copy is in National Archives and Records Administration, RG 59, Central Files 1967–69, DEF 12–5 PAK.

who have always feared that we didn't mean our even-handed policy following the 1965 war. Chet Bowles feels strongly that it's far better to remove the arms ban for good—whatever flak this would bring in India—rather than try to carry off a one-time exception for Pak arms clearly aimed at the Indians.

4. *Reverse current policy:* You could lift the South Asian arms ban altogether because of (a) the demonstrable argument that third country sales just don't work, and (b) the policy judgment that arms sales are the only way to get the seat we want at Pak and Indian tables to influence—and, hopefully, restrain—their inevitable military spending. As with all military sales, we would be deciding sales to India and Pakistan case-by-case on the grounds of legitimate need and aiming at ultimate limitation of arms spending.

Nick would like to see us do everything we can to make the Turkish sale work because removing the ban altogether will surely present us with a sizeable and expensive shopping list from the Paks. And though they would make righteous noises at first about our policy switch, the Indians would also soon be pressing to buy. Certainly we could call the shots on what we even consider selling. But no one can be sure that lifting the ban, arousing expectations, and then turning down numerous requests wouldn't leave us with less leverage on the Indians and Paks than we have now. Whatever its effect abroad, a change in policy would bring sharp reaction from the Hill.

Despite these strong arguments against lifting the ban, Nick and his colleagues feel that if the Turkish deal is unworkable—and you personally feel a commitment to Ayub—the next best way to get him the tanks would be to change present policy across the board. We hoped third-country purchases would add enough flexibility to our policy to make it livable. If that door just won't open, then we have to make the hard choice between abandoning the military field in the subcontinent altogether and staying in the game. Nick would argue for staying in the game, but he'd prefer to see that choice left to your successor. That's why he thinks it's worth $3 million to make the Turkish deal work.

Indian Reaction

It goes without saying that any of the above actions which get Ayub his tanks will make us unpopular in India for awhile. Even though the Indians have made major purchases from the Soviets, even if the tanks got to Ayub via a third country entirely in the context of our current no-favorites arms policy, and even though we approved a British sale of Hawker–Hunters to the Indians under the same policy provision, this deal would be our first involvement in a major Pakistani arms purchase since the 1965 war.

Peshawar Negotiations

Nick believes—and I tend to agree—that the tanks should be kept separate from Peshawar talks. Ben Oehlert has long felt that the tanks would enable us to make the best of our withdrawal from the base. You should know, however, that it looks as if Ayub has already turned around and largely met our request for an extension of certain facilities several months beyond the July 1969 close-out of the agreement. Ayub will see this as a major concession; Ben points out (Tab B) that Ayub talked about tanks in the same breath.[3]

Recommendation

This is a mixed bag. Following Nick's recommendation and offering $3 million in replacement tanks to the Turks is clearly the easiest way out. But we should consider that we are only prolonging the agony in South Asian arms policy. It could be argued that this is the time to scrap current policy as plainly unworkable, take the public heat and let the new Administration see if open sales can work at all. Your successor would probably find it easier to clamp back on the ban than to take it off.

On balance, my own vote goes with Katzenbach to make the Turkish deal work.

Walt

Try Turkish deal with sweetener as last effort[4]

Turkish deal with sweetener but fall back to changing policy

Change policy now

One-time exception

Let Turkish deal ride; tell Paks to come back to my successor

Call me

---

[3] The reference should be to Tab C. Rostow added a handwritten note at this point that reads: "At Tab C is Oehlert's personal message to you—arrived today back channel." For the text of Oehlert's message, see Document 518.

[4] None of the options is checked. A handwritten note on the memorandum by Jim Jones indicates the President's response: "Jim—Set up meeting soon to discuss this."

520. Telegram From the Department of State to the Embassy in Pakistan[1]

Washington, October 26, 1968, 1754Z.

262361. Ref: Rawalpindi's 8628.[2] For Ambassador.

1. You authorized inform GOP at October 29 meeting that USG agrees generally to Peshawar withdrawal proposal presented in Foreign Secretary Yusuf's October 20 Aide-Mémoire as reported para 5 reftel. You should indicate USG would like formalize understanding through exchange of notes. Proposed text of USG note in para 4 below.

2. Believe you should reiterate orally to Yusuf that, while dismantling of most conspicuous antenna will begin well before July 17, 1969, we will wish maintain selected antenna to December 31, 1969. You may wish also to point out that, if GOP should wish, we are prepared to leave some antenna on departure.

3. FYI: If proposed arrangement concluded satisfactorily, we are prepared cease Sugar Tree operations also by December 31, 1969. End FYI.

4. Following is proposed text USG note for presentation October 29 meeting:

Begin Text: Excellency: I refer to recent discussions between representatives of our two Governments regarding the forthcoming termination of the Agreement on the Establishment of a Communications Unit in Pakistan, signed at Karachi, July 18, 1959. As a result of these discussions, it is agreed that:

A. Dismantling, packing and removal of certain facilities, installations and equipment shall commence in January 1969. This will be accompanied by a staggered thinning down of U.S. personnel.

B. All of the facilities, installations and equipment remaining on July 17, 1969 shall be dismantled no later than December 31, 1969, in accordance with a fixed monthly program which shall be separately agreed.

C. All dismantled facilities, installations and equipment shall be packed and crated and be removed from Pakistan as early as possible and in no event later than February 28, 1970. All remaining base personnel will be evacuated completely from Pakistan by the same date.

D. The rights, privileges, and immunities which the Pakistan Government has previously accorded to U.S. personnel and property at

---

[1] Source: National Archives and Records Administration, RG 59, Central Files 1967–69, DEF 15–10 PAK–US. Secret; Immediate; Limdis. Drafted by Spain on October 24; cleared by Handley, Wolf, Curl, Van Hollen, Robert H. Neuman (L/NEA), Colonel Kravitz (DOD/ISA), Admiral Showers (DIA), Sheldon, and Saunders; and approved by Katzenbach. Repeated to CINCSTRIKE.
[2] Document 517.

the Peshawar facility will be extended to cover the period from July 18, 1969 until February 28, 1970.

Upon the receipt of a note from you indicating that the foregoing proposal is acceptable to the Government of Pakistan, the Government of the United States of America will consider that this note and your reply constitute an agreement between the two Governments on this subject, the agreement to enter into force on the date of your note in reply.[3]

Accept, Excellency, et cetera. *End Text.*

Rusk

---

[3] Oehlert met on October 29 with Foreign Secretary Yusuf and General Akbar and presented the note. Yusuf and Akhbar indicated that the U.S. response appeared to be satisfactory. (Telegram 8845 from Rawalpindi, October 29; National Archives and Records Administration, RG 59, Central Files 1967–69, DEF 15–10 PAK–US) The Foreign Ministry returned a note to the Embassy on November 1 accepting the Embassy's note as the basis for agreement. (The texts of both notes were transmitted to Washington as enclosures to airgram A–641 from Rawalpindi, November 14; ibid.)

---

521. Telegram From the President's Special Assistant (Rostow) to President Johnson in Texas[1]

Washington, November 4, 1968, 1505Z.

CAP 82673. Secretary Rusk urged me this morning to lay before you the Pak tank and India aid decisions.

The following paper presents the two issues.

1. Ayub's Tanks. The issue is whether to:

A. Spend $3 million in military aid funds to try to persuade Turkey to sell 100 M–47's to Pakistan. We would replace them with 100 M–48's. Nitze says he can find the money.

B. Or remove the ban on arms aid to the subcontinent altogether and sell the tanks directly to Ayub. If the Turkish deal falls through,

---

[1] Source: Johnson Library, National Security File, Country File, India, India's Food Problem, Vol. IV. Secret.

this would be the only practical alternative to get Ayub even 100 tanks. My earlier memo and Nick Katzenbach's are attached.[2]

2. Indian Aid. You asked me to lay out for you alternative aid packages.

These facts should be taken into consideration:

—There is no pressing food shortage in India. But the Indians need:

A. Food imports to keep prices down and to help them continue their promising program of agricultural reform.
B. They need fertilizer imports for next spring's harvest. If they cut back here, they will not get the full advantage of the miracle seeds now in place.

—The Indians fear a sharp cutback in foreign development aid. They expected a commitment of $200 million from IDA by now. They can no longer count on this. Second, they are completely in the dark about the U.S. program. Normally we would have pledged our aid for fiscal 1969 in a consortium meeting held in late summer or early fall. There has been no meeting because of uncertainty about what the Congress would appropriate.

A. The danger is they may over-react by overcautious budgetary decisions—which they are in process of making now—they could in effect put their whole development program in suspense.
B. Whether they over-react or not, the sharper the cutback in available foreign exchange, the sharper the cutback they will have to make in development investment.

These are the alternatives:

A. Food aid only. This could range from one million tons to the 2.3 million tons we originally proposed. One million tons would reopen the pipeline and give the Indians some confidence. The 2.3 million ton figure (which would bring our 1968 shipments up to the 1967 level) would give them the best chance of getting a grip on their agricultural price and supply problems.

B. Food aid plus an interim loan commitment. Building from the food aid decision, we would add say $100 million as a loan commitment now. This would be large enough to have a good psychological impact and would still leave roughly half the fiscal 1969 appropriation for decision by your successor. Perhaps half the loan money would be for fertilizer and the rest for industrial imports. Bill Gaud would have to decide on the mix in light of the total program.

C. Food aid plus the total FY 69 aid appropriation for India. This would mean food aid plus an estimated $195 million in loan money. (We gave $285 million last year.) The main argument for committing the full

---

[2] See Document 519 and footnote 2 thereto.

amount now is that it would do the most good now. It would have the greatest impact on Indian budgetary decisions and on their fertilizer procurement policy. It would give them some margin to gamble that IDA may still come through by the middle of 1969. Your successor would still have the decision to make on calendar 1969 food aid and time to work out the next India consortium pledge and get it through the Congress.[3]

---

[3] A handwritten note on the memorandum by Jim Jones quotes the President's response: "Give them the 2.3 mill. tons that you proposed plus the $195 mill. loan and announce it this afternoon. Also give Ayub some food or something. LBJ/JRJ"

---

522. Telegram From the President's Special Assistant (Rostow) to President Johnson in Texas[1]

Washington, November 4, 1968.

After clearing with Freeman, Gaud and Katzenbach, in response to your request, I propose you make the following announcement this afternoon on India food:

"The President today authorized the negotiation of a PL–480 agreement with India to provide for the sale of approximately 2.3 million tons of wheat and wheat flour, 90,000 tons of tallow, and other agricultural commodities, totalling a current export market value of $169 million. This program will help India carry out its new agricultural policies which are moving Indian agriculture toward modernization and a decreasing dependence on food aid."

We propose not to include the economic loans in this announcement. Bill Gaud still needs to work out the details over the next few days, and we will instruct him to go ahead at a level of up to $195 million.

On the Pak side, we don't believe there will be much reaction to another food deal for India. The tanks—what they most want—do not lend themselves to public announcement because we still have to make our deal with the Turks and even then it will be an arrangement between the Turks and Paks. As for an economic cushion, we think a quiet word

---

[1] Source: Johnson Library, National Security File, Country File, India, India's Food Problem, Vol. III. Confidential. Sent to Jim Jones for the President and repeated to Tom Johnson in San Antonio. A handwritten note on the telegram indicates the message was sent as White House telegram CAP 82682.

in the next few days from Ben Oehlert on outstanding Pak requests should more than satisfy Ayub. Thus we propose the following:

1. An immediate telegram to Ankara trying to wrap up the tank deal with the Turks as outlined in our earlier memo[2] to you.
2. Over the next week we will have for Pakistan:

a. A development loan package up to $70 million, if you approve.[3] This is this year's aid level. The recommendation will be on your desk this week.

b. Word that we are ready to consider sympathetically their PL–480 request of about $20 million. At the same time, we would tell them that we are ready to make concessions on their usual marketing requirement that would indirectly enable them to increase their earnings from rice exports. The Paks are doing so well agriculturally that they do not need much food aid.

We believe these steps will balance adequately on the Pak side.

There is one final option to consider. John Schnittker wishes you to know that the Indians have today requested 100,000 tons of rice. They need it, and we have abundant supplies. We have not gone into rice for India for several years because of the implications for our rice acreage allotments. Schnittker himself would recommend against doing this now, but he did not want to foreclose it on his own. If you wished to do this, we would include the following as a new second sentence in the announcement: "In addition, the President noted a recent request from India for a quantity of rice which he said would be given careful consideration." I do not recommend this unless you have reasons for it.

---

[2] Reference is to Document 519.

[3] In a November 18 memorandum to the President, Rostow endorsed a recommendation from Gaud and Zwick for a $71 million development loan package for Pakistan. Johnson initialed his approval. (Johnson Library, National Security File, Country File, Pakistan, Vol. IX, Cables, 5/68–11/68)

523.   Telegram From the Embassy in Pakistan to the Department of State[1]

Rawalpindi, November 7, 1968, 1210Z.

9165. Literally eyes only for President Johnson from Ambassador.

1. In any change of administration time is required for the identification and analysis of problems and for the decision making process.

2. With a change of parties this process will take longer than usual and will be complicated by the fact that the Executive and the Congress will be of different parties.

3. I seriously doubt that we can stem the tide here of drift toward reliance on the Communist world for the time required without the encouragement of a few tanks.

4. Mr. President, on last December 23 you told Ayub and me that you were sick and tired of the India lovers in the State Department.

5. I am too.

6. In the intervening months they have resorted to every excuse, every delay, every strategem to thwart your wishes with respect to tanks for Pakistan.

7. I pray you not to let them get away with it.

8. In the immortal words of John Nance Garner, Mr. President, "Let's strike a blow for freedom."

9. Alice joins me in thanking you for the opportunity of service to our country and to you personally which you have given us and we extend our affection to you and Lady Bird. We expect to follow you into private life shortly after January 20 and will look forward to the privilege of enjoying your company both in Palm Beach and on the shores of the Pedernales.[2]

Oehlert

---

[1] Source: Johnson Library, National Security File, Country File, Pakistan, Vol. IX, Memos, 5/68–11/68. Top Secret; Cherokee. The Cherokee communications channel was established on November 5 for the exchange of literally eyes only messages between the Secretary and an Ambassador. (Circular telegram 267318 to all Embassies, November 5; National Archives and Records Administration, RG 59, Central Files 1967–69, DEF 12 CHEROKEE)

[2] A typewritten note attached to the telegram, dictated by President Johnson on November 7 reads: "Write Oehlert a good, strong wire and tell him I am really doing what he wants done." Rostow did so on November 7 in an eyes only cable to Oehlert in which he called attention to telegram 268175 to Ankara. (White House telegram CAP 82740 to Rawalpindi; Johnson Library, National Security File, Country File, Pakistan, Vol. IX, Memos, 5/68–11/68) Telegram 268175 to Ankara, November 7, instructed the Embassy to reiterate continuing high-level U.S. interest in the sale of M–47 tanks by Turkey to Pakistan, and the urgent need for a response. If necessary the Embassy was authorized to indicate that the United States was prepared to make available to Turkey 100 rehabilitated M–48 tanks to replace 100 M–47 tanks sold to Pakistan. (National Archives and Records Administration, RG 59, Central Files 1967–69, DEF 12–5 PAK)

524. Telegram From the Embassy in Pakistan to the Department of State[1]

Rawalpindi, November 16, 1968, 1445Z.

9454. From Ambassador. Ref: State 272942.[2]

1. At lunch today I handed President Ayub, Foreign Minister Arshad and Presidential Advisor Fida Hassan a letter[3] patterned after the appropriate parts of my May 9 letter to Defense Minister, and strongly stating secrecy requirement. Copy being pouched.

2. Additionally, I stated orally that during past several months there had been reports of Pak acquisition of additional tanks from USSR and/or ChiComs, that reports had been source of concern to us and that both in connection with a Turkish transaction and the Conte–Symington amendments we would need to know the validity of those rumors.

3. Ayub responded that they had no agreement with ChiComs re arms and that the only lethal items being acquired from USSR were "ammunition, spare parts and things like that."

4. Ayub then said that he had understood that there were to be 200 tanks.

5. I responded that in March we had indicated to them that, subject to certain conditions, we were prepared to approve third country sale of "100 tanks now and 100 later"—that the word "later" had not been defined and that there was no longer time to work out the details of the first 100 and tackle the problem of the second 100 before our change of administration so that the question of the second 100 would have to be taken up with the new administration.

6. Ayub then asked what the price of the tanks would be. I told him that, except for our residual value, the matter was between GOP and GOT.

7. He showed a marked reluctance to bargain with Turkey, taking the position that US really owned the tanks, that they had no value over and above our residual, and that, that should be the price.

---

[1] Source: National Archives and Records Administration, RG 59, Central Files 1967–69, DEF 12–5 PAK. Secret; Immediate; Exdis. Repeated to Karachi.

[2] Telegram 272942 to Rawalpindi, November 16, authorized Oehlert to tell Ayub that the United States and Turkey had agreed in principle on the sale of 100 M–47 tanks by Turkey to Pakistan. Oehlert was instructed to point out that final approval of the sale was dependent upon Pakistan's acceptance of the conditions set forth in Oehlert's May 9 letter to Admiral Khan. (Ibid.)

[3] Not found.

8. I said that as I saw the procedure his and the GOT military should identify a particular 100 tanks, we would appraise their residual value, and that the price, if any, over and above that would be a matter of negotiation between GOP and GOT.

9. He seemed unhappy about that and the meeting ended with his comment that they would consider my letter and give me a reply.

10. At no point was any question raised about any of the conditions restated from the May 9 letter.

11. Would appreciate ASAP:

A. Re our transfer of 48s to GOT do they pay us anything? Previous telegrams make clear only that rehabilitation cost will not be passed on;
B. Is GOT expecting to charge a higher price than residual value;
C. Under present proposal do we keep residual value or pass it on to GOT?

Oehlert

---

525. Telegram From the Ambassador to India (Bowles) to President Johnson[1]

New Delhi, November 19, 1968, 1259Z.

850. 1. I hesitate to introduce any more controversial problems at a moment when your plate is already full. However, I feel impelled in good faith to express to you directly my deep personal concern over what the press states is a pending agreement to encourage the Turks to sell Patton tanks to Pakistan under US license.

2. Although we have reviewed the background on numerous occasions it may be useful briefly to consider the chain of events which brought us to present difficulties:

A. Since John Foster Dulles made his so-called "alliance" with Pakistan in 1954 we have provided Pakistan with nearly $800 million in military equipment, most of it on a grant basis. The very nature of this aid indicates that Pakistan never intended it for use in the mountains against the Chinese or Soviet forces but rather on the Punjabi plains against India.

---

[1] Source: Johnson Library, National Security File, Country File, India, Exchanges with Bowles. Secret. [text not declassified]

B. Between 1954 and 1965 two American Presidents and several Ambassadors (including myself) assured the Indians that we "would never allow this US equipment to be used against India."

C. In 1963–64 following the Chinese war, after providing limited assistance to India, we rejected its request to help modernize its defense establishment at a rate of about $75 million annually because of fear of upsetting our relationship with Pakistan. In return for this assistance the Indians had been prepared: (1) to agree not to buy lethal weapons from the Communist nations, (2) to negotiate a military force level agreement with Pakistan, and (3) to work with us on a political basis to establish greater stability in Asia and Southeast Asia.

D. Only in August 1964 when it became clear that we were not prepared to give India this assistance, did India turn to the Soviet Union as its major source of military equipment.

3. As the Indo-Pak crisis developed in early August 1965 the Paks sent some 6,000 armed guerrillas into Kashmir on the mistaken assumption that they would receive the support of the Kashmir people. When this effort failed the Paks sent an armored brigade to cut off India's vulnerable supply lines into Kashmir. After this column had penetrated some 12 miles into Indian territory and to relieve the pressure the Indians moved into the Pakistan Punjab. Whatever the fault of India in raising the tension which led to this three-week war, the 3,000 or so Indians who lost their lives were killed by American weapons, which we had repeatedly and officially assured the Indians would never be used against them.

4. Since then I and my associates have felt strongly that we should refuse to give lethal equipment either to Pakistan or India. I have taken this position in recognition of the complexity of our relationship with Pakistan and in spite of the threat to the integrity of the Indian nation by a Chinese movement across north Burma through Nefa or through the Chumbi Valley between Bhutan and Sikkim.

5. It is my conviction that the only realistic way to move the Chinese and Soviet military influence out of the subcontinent is not to provide lethal equipment to the two governments, but to help both to become as self-sufficient as possible in regard to their defense requirements. This will not be accomplished overnight.

6. India's present tank strength is 1,282 and Pakistan's is 965; a ratio of only 4 to 3 in India's favor. This is considered by the Indians a bare minimum considering the two-pronged threat they face. If under these circumstances we provide new tanks to Pakistan we will further escalate and fuel a subcontinental arms race and the Indians will surely increase their inventory to maintain this ratio. At this critical point this will have a profoundly adverse effect on the relationship of India and

Pakistan and our relationship with democratic India, which has a major potential role to play in Asia.

7. I am keenly aware of the pressures Pakistan is bringing to bear, and I also share the irritation we often feel when India fails to take constructive positions on international issues. Nevertheless, I must call to your attention the enormous investment we have made in India in the last 15 years, the increasing dynamism which is becoming apparent in the Indian economy and the solid basis for hope that India within a few years may become a major force for stability in Asia.

8. Therefore, I recommend with all the earnestness at my command that no lethal military assistance be given either Pakistan or India under present circumstances.

9. After dictating this cable, I had a difficult talk with Foreign Secretary who is deeply concerned about the sale of tanks. This discussion is reported in New Delhi 22700.[2]

Bowles

---

[2] Dated November 19. (National Archives and Records Administration, RG 59, Central Files 1967–69, DEF 12 PAK) On November 25 Rusk sent a personal cable to Bowles in which he stated that the message Bowles sent had been carefully reviewed but the decision was to assist Pakistan to buy tanks from a third country. (Ibid., DEF 12 CHEROKEE)

526. Telegram From the Department of State to the Embassy in India[1]

Washington, November 23, 1968, 0156Z.

276950. Subject: U.S. Military Supply Policy. Ref: New Delhi's 22784.[2]

1. We know of your strong views on tanks for Pakistan but for reasons you are aware, decision has been made to proceed if Pakistan and Turkey can work out arrangements. For reasons set forth in previous communications, most recently in report of Hart/Jung conversation (274522),[3] we do not believe long-pending tank transaction poses problem of major proportion, unless GOI decides to exaggerate its significance. We do not believe tank deal should logically contribute to escalation of arms race, any more than U.K. sale of Hawker–Hunter aircraft to India contributed.

2. We appreciate fact GOI is aroused by prospects of sale and they fear that tanks might somehow encourage Pakistanis to some adventure against India. Judging, however, by your conversation with Kaul (New Delhi's 22700)[4] there may also be element of self-justification for impending Indian arms purchase from Soviet Union, negotiations for which were under way well before tank deal with Pakistan was revived.

3. We have reviewed points made in para 4 of reftel. As you know, our present military supply policy would exclude direct U.S. sale of light tanks, armored personnel carriers and armored reconnaissance airborne assault vehicles to India. Our policy would permit, however, case-by-case examination of third country arrangements for sales these three items, if and when we are approached. Current policy would also

---

[1] Source: National Archives and Records Administration, RG 59, Central Files 1967–69, DEF 12–5 PAK. Secret; Exdis. Drafted by Grant E. Mouser (NEA/INC) on November 22; cleared by Van Hollen, Colonel Kravitz (DOD/ISA), and General Doyle (DOD/Joint Staff/J–5), and in draft by Schmelzer and Spain; and approved by Handley. Repeated to CINCSTRIKE/USCINCMEAFSA.

[2] In telegram 22784 from New Delhi, November 20, from Bowles to the Secretary, Bowles reiterated his conviction that the United States should not sell or countenance the sale of lethal weapons to India or Pakistan. If, however, the sale of Patton tanks by Turkey to Pakistan was irreversible, Bowles stated that the impact of the sale in India might be muted somewhat by a concomitant decision to sell or authorize the sale of lethal weapons to India. (Ibid.)

[3] Telegram 274522 to New Delhi, November 20, reported on a conversation on November 19 between Assistant Secretary Hart and Indian Ambassador Jung in which Jung registered his country's concern over reports of a sale of U.S.-originated tanks to Pakistan. Hart noted that the sale remained to be consummated, but stated that if it occurred it could serve the purpose of preventing Pakistan from becoming completely dependent upon Communist sources for military equipment. (Ibid.)

[4] See footnote 2, Document 525.

exclude licensing arrangement for indigenous production of fighter-interceptor aircraft (though defense production projects such as Varangaon acceptable). In all cases, we would want to examine each purchase request carefully in order to avoid any escalation of subcontinent arms race and unnecessary diversion of resources from economic development.

4. We will keep you posted regarding tank transaction[5] and meanwhile hope you can use points made to Jung to temper Indian reaction. Our comments on sale of 106 mm ammunition under existing policy (DRI 837 68 of 20 Nov)[6] will be forwarded separately.

Rusk

---

[5] On December 26 Oehlert reported that he had learned from the Pakistani Foreign Office that the Foreign Ministers of Pakistan and Turkey had reached agreement on the sale of Turkish tanks to Pakistan. (National Archives and Records Administration, RG 59, Central Files 1967–69, DEF 12–5 PAK)

[6] Not found.

Afghanistan

527. Letter From President Johnson to King Zaher[1]

Washington, January 2, 1964.

Your Majesty:

I have asked my good friend, Sargent Shriver,[2] to bring you my warm personal greetings. He will of course be looking into the activities of the Peace Corps, but I particularly wanted him to have the opportunity to meet with you.

All of us have watched with admiration the accelerated pace of Afghan economic and political advance under your wise direction. Your friends were also very pleased when normal relations were restored between your country and your neighbor, Pakistan.

I regret that a mission abroad prevented me from seeing you and Her Majesty in Washington. However, President Kennedy told me of the great pleasure your visit gave him and of the candid and fruitful discussions he had with you. While you and I share a common loss at his passing, let us build together on the friendly relationship you and he began. Should you have any thoughts you would like me to have, I hope you will speak as freely to Mr. Shriver as you would to me.

I have asked Sargent Shriver to convey to you our deep appreciation for your warm welcome to the 33 Peace Corps Volunteers in your country. Since its birth under President Kennedy, I have regarded the Peace Corps as one of the most imaginative instruments ever devised for capturing the idealism of youth and putting it to work in the cause of world peace and understanding.

Our Volunteers have benefitted enormously from their experience in your country. The United States will also benefit as they return, with broader horizons and greater understanding of the world, to take their places in our society. They will add a new dimension to American life. I only hope that they have contributed in some small way to the well-being of your people and to their understanding of us.

---

[1] Source: Johnson Library, National Security File, Special Head of State Correspondence, Afghanistan, 11/23/63–10/1/66. No classification marking.

[2] Peace Corps Director R. Sargent Shriver was in Kabul January 21–22 during a trip to several Middle East and South Asian countries. Documentation on Shriver's trip is in National Archives and Records Administration, RG 59, Central Files 1964–66, POL 7 US/SHRIVER.

Please accept my thanks for your receiving Sargent Shriver, and rest assured of the continued great interest of the United States in the independence and prosperity of your country.[3]

Sincerely,

Lyndon B. Johnson

---

[3] In his reply of April 15, King Zaher assured the President of his "sincere desire to maintain our existing friendship on a basis of mutual understanding and goodwill." (Ibid., POL AFG–US)

---

528.   National Intelligence Estimate[1]

NIE 37–64   Washington, January 22, 1964.

AFGHANISTAN

Conclusions

A. For the last decade, Afghanistan has been undergoing a substantial economic and social modernization. Since the removal from office of Prime Minister Daud in March 1963, modernization has started in the political field as well, under a cabinet which for the first time in 30 years is not headed by a member of the royal family.

B. The new cabinet has no political base save in the support of the King and royal family, who remain the source of power. For the moment at least, they favor political reform. The question is how they will react to increasing pressure for change, as and when modernizers within and outside the government wish to move farther and faster than the monarchy deems prudent. We believe there is at least an even chance that the monarchy will stay sufficiently abreast of the times to avoid violent upheaval.

C. The Afghans will continue eager to take assistance from both Bloc and West, but will make every effort to see that neither acquires inordinate influence. They have done this successfully for ten years

---

[1] Source: Central Intelligence Agency, Job 79–R01012A, ODDI Registry of NIE and SNIE Files. Secret; Controlled Dissem. According to a note on the cover sheet, the estimate was submitted by the Director of Central Intelligence and concurred in by the U.S. Intelligence Board on January 22. A table of contents and map are not printed.

and should be able to continue, despite the fact that virtually all military assistance has come from the Bloc. Under the new government, tolerable relations with Pakistan have been restored, and both sides will try to keep tensions under control, though flareups are always possible and can, as recent experience shows, have damaging consequences for Afghanistan.

D. If further large-scale foreign aid is forthcoming, as seems likely, Afghanistan should make increasing economic progress, on the base of a substantial infrastructure created over the past decade. But it is still a very underdeveloped country and will long be hampered by lack of trained people and shortage of domestic revenue. The USSR, which has in recent years become Afghanistan's chief trading partner and its major source of aid, will continue in these roles, but this will probably not be translated into decisive political influence.

[Here follows the 9-page Discussion portion of the NIE.]

529. Airgram From the Embassy in Afghanistan to the Department of State[1]

A–238   Kabul, December 26, 1964.

SUBJECT

Interview with Dr. Abdul Zaher, Deputy Prime Minister

Dr. Abdul Zaher became Deputy Prime Minister during my absence in the United States. I thought it fitting to call on him as a matter of courtesy in connection with his new responsibilities after my return to Kabul. Dr. Zaher's long acquaintance with the United States in connection with his medical training there has always inspired him to retain a very lively and sympathetic interest in the United States. He therefore was interested in talking at some length about the recent U.S. domestic political scene, the outcome of the elections, etc.

The conversation then turned to the current scene in Afghanistan. I remarked that, while gratified with many of the signs of progress and current developments in Afghanistan, I could not help but be concerned over the RGA's greatest problem—the financial crisis. We

---

[1] Source: National Archives and Records Administration, RG 59, Central Files 1964–66, POL 1 AFG. Confidential. Drafted on December 24 by Ambassador Steeves. Repeated to Karachi.

talked at some length as to what was causing the current instability, the dangers of inflation and the measures which I had heard were being taken to solve the current problems.

During the period when Dr. Zaher was President of the National Assembly, his very sympathetic ear was one that could be used to express certain opinions that one would hesitate to present to certain others less sympathetically inclined. One of these subjects that I have discussed with Dr. Zaher in the past was Afghanistan's military posture. In connection with their financial straits, this subject arose again. With some apology in talking about a delicate matter, I pointed out to him that a good bit of their budgetary difficulties now were undoubtedly being caused by the heavy commitments the RGA was making both to current and projected military plans and development. I expressed the view that although one could well understand progressive measures to increase the efficiency and effectiveness of forces whose responsibility it was to maintain good internal security, the outside observer could not help but wonder what justification there could be for vast sums being spent for the latest model of fighters, tanks and missiles which were of dubious use. Afghanistan's posture was one of maintaining the protective coloring of neutrality. Their policy was one of the reconciliation and amicability with all of their neighbors. While this posture was understandable, it was difficult to reconcile this stance with continuing high expenditure on arms. The exercise became all the more questionable when it was quite obvious that lack of budget and facilities often meant that this sophisticated equipment deteriorated sitting in place. What therefore was the purpose and how could Afghanistan possibly get itself out of its financial difficulties with these obligations staring them in the face?

In response I was treated to a rather unusual performance by Dr. Zaher. His attitude could well be explained that now being Deputy Prime Minister he must hew to the accepted line, but he pointed out with some emotional fervor that Pakistan's unfriendly attitude unwilling to cease and desist in its program of bringing under complete control the tribal areas Afghanistan simply had to be prepared for any eventuality. He felt that if Pakistan went so far as to take punitive action against any of the tribal people within Afghan territory, they simply could not be left impotent. At this point in the conversation I quickly recalled that Colonel Abdul Wali[2] had used the same argument with me some months previously. Dr. Zaher's argument was largely based upon the political necessity of showing their people so exercised

---

[2] Colonel Abdul Wali, the King's son-in-law and Chief of Staff of the Afghan Central Forces.

over the Pushtunistan issue[3] that they were physically ready to retaliate should Pakistan take extreme steps. No amount of persuasion or argument could budge him. I pointed out the ultimate folly which would result from preparing for an unfriendly confrontation with Pakistan rather than devoting themselves to the further advancement of the already begun thawing processes and the dialogue which could bring about understanding. While he agreed to this in theory, he felt that gestures from Pakistan plus the step-up in Pakistan's armed strength left Afghanistan with no alternative but to be in a position to offer at least token resistance. I, of course, discussed with Dr. Zaher at some length where such a program would lead. It would make them more dependent upon the Soviets, who were the suppliers of this hardware. It was hardly a practical view of the future (in view of Afghanistan's neutrality) to look upon this type of alignment with any equanimity. I made some reference to the fact that some of the recent happenings, such as the Cairo Conference[4] and Afghanistan's activity in the United Nations on the Congo,[5] looked dangerously like Afghanistan's becoming more unneutral. This latter subject he simply refused to discuss.

At the conclusion of the discussion in which I pointed out to him the grave danger of becoming too beholden to the Soviets, I asked him if this were a price that the Afghans would eventually be willing to pay in order to carry on their stiff posture toward the south. He replied rather gravely, "We wouldn't, but our successors would." He went on to explain that no government in Kabul could possibly exist without giving real substantive support to the Pushtunistan issue. If they were ever overthrown for slipping in their fidelity to the national purpose, radicals would take over from them and might indeed be just that unwise. In summation, he pointed out to me that as I well knew Afghanistan passionately desired U.S. support, sympathy and understanding. He said they had the same attitude towards Germany and were now hopeful of getting more sympathetic treatment from Great Britain. He alluded to past history in pointing out that the United States

---

[3] The Pushtunistan issue, which had troubled relations between Afghanistan and Pakistan since the creation of Pakistan, involved a dispute over the future of the Pushtun tribes living along the Pakistan side of the boundary between the two countries. Afghanistan's continued advocacy of self-determination or statehood for these people had been consistently opposed by Pakistan.

[4] The Second Conference of Heads of State or Government of Non-Aligned Counties, held in Cairo on October 5–10 called for the United States to lift its commercial and economic blockade of Cuba and negotiate the evacuation of Guantanamo Naval Base. The text of the Cairo declaration is printed in *American Foreign Policy: Current Documents, 1964*, pp. 691–698.

[5] On December 1 Afghanistan joined 21 other countries in requesting an urgent meeting of the Security Council to discuss the situation in the Democratic Republic of the Congo caused by the military rescue operation launched in Stanleyville and in other parts of the Congo by Belgium and the United States. (UN doc. S/6076 and Add. 1–5)

had not been as forthcoming with Afghanistan as we might have been while we were arming Pakistan to the teeth. They really had no alternative but to look after their selfish interests.

While his attitude throughout was extremely cordial and we parted on a very friendly note, I did come away with the impression that I had never had a more serious presentation of this feeling from a person of Dr. Zaher's nature who before has been much more flexible in his viewpoint. He may have been speaking as the new Deputy Prime Minister, he may have been talking to me in the hopes that word of their determined stand would filter back into Pakistan or he may have been speaking again as the frontiersman, which he is, from a province bordering on Pakistan, but whatever the reason, he revealed a firmness and a dedication to the so-called Pushtunistan issue such as I had never received from him before.

JM Steeves

---

530.   Telegram From the Embassy in Afghanistan to the
        Department of State[1]

Kabul, March 3, 1965, 5 p.m.

481. Governor Harriman accompanied by Ambassador called on PriMin Yusuf March 2 for more than hour's discussion bilateral problems and world issues.[2] PriMin expressed concern at slow rate progress Helmand Valley development and made strong plea for budgetary support assist RGA in its current financial difficulties. PriMin told Harriman he was concerned re continuing inflation and felt perhaps commodity loan assistance to soak up excess currency in circulation would be desirable. Yusuf added he aware USG concerned RGA spending inordinate amount on army and military procurement but noted only neighbor with which Afghanistan had any problem was Pakistan which had received considerable military assistance from USG.

---

[1] Source: National Archives and Records Administration, RG 59, Central Files 1964–66, POL 7 US/HARRIMAN. Confidential. Repeated to Karachi and New Delhi.

[2] Under Secretary of State for Political Affairs W. Averell Harriman visited Kabul March 2–3 en route to the Far East Chiefs of Mission Conference in Baguio, Philippines. His March 16 report to the President is in the Johnson Library, National Security File, Country File, Israel, Harriman Israeli Mission II. Harriman also called on the King on March 2. A report of this conversation is in telegram 480 from Kabul, March 3. (National Archives and Records Administration, RG 59, Central Files 1964–66, POL 7 US/ HARRIMAN)

Governor Harriman told PriMin question budgetary support was unpopular subject with Congress who had to derive funds from taxes levied on American people. He told PriMin we are continuing to see if there is any more efficient way of approaching our mutual aid problems, notably in the Helmand Valley. Harriman said he already aware RGA concern at pace HVA development, hoped to carry out aerial inspection of Helmand Valley March 3 prior leaving for New Delhi, and would upon his return Washington personally investigate whether anything more could be done to speed up work on the HVA project.

In response Governor's question, PriMin stated Afghan relations very good with Soviet, ChiCom and Iranian neighbors. He added relations with Paks improving, noting this connection March 2 signature new five-year Pak–Afghan transit agreement. PriMin said he was not fully satisfied with agreement but felt it represented acceptable compromise.

Governor Harriman conveyed President's greetings to PriMin and outlined President's domestic programs and success President has had in promoting them. PriMin responded Afghans had great respect for what President has been able accomplish domestically and singled out action on civil rights for special approval.

In general discussion world problems, Harriman drew on his extensive experience with Soviets, explaining Communism has made industrial progress, but that system has conspicuously failed produce adequate food. Governor speculated this was due character farm work which requires hardworking individuals with personal stake in operation, rather than hourly paid factory hands paced by machine. PriMin commented he impressed by effectiveness cooperatives which he had seen during his recent visit India and remarked he also understood Egyptian cooperatives highly effective. Harriman replied Egyptians would be better off if Nasser spent more time on internal matters and less on foreign adventures such as assistance Congo rebels. PriMin noted Tshombe highly unpopular among non-aligned states. Harriman told PriMin Tshombe was probably in fact second most popular Congolese among his countrymen, most popular being Lumumba who dead. Whether or non-aligned states doubted Tshombe's internal popularity or disliked him personally was no excuse for intervention in Congolese internal affairs. To drive this point home Harriman asked PriMin how he would take it if intruders tried to promote his removal in Afghanistan. PriMin Yusuf got the point and did not have any reply. PriMin opined effort should be made reach political settlement, to which Harriman responded this had been consistent USG objective but fact was OAU had proved ineffective so far. We were hopeful of results from new Nouakchott group.

On Vietnam, Harriman stressed as he had in press statement on arrival that problem would be solved if North Vietnamese would stop intervening in SVN affairs. PriMin took standard RGA line expressing concern at possibility widening conflict and hope political settlement could be worked out.

Comment: Conversation was frank but cordial throughout. PriMin was unabashed in his presentation for additional USG economic aid which constitutes further indication country's current difficulties. Believe opportunity provided by Governor's visit for extended wide-ranging talks such as foregoing, which continued at dinner residence evening March 2 with PriMin and six members Cabinet, most useful in underlining USG views on world problems to highest levels RGA.[3]

Steeves

---

[3] In a follow-up telegram to Secretary Rusk from New Delhi, Harriman observed that U.S. relations with Afghanistan were developing satisfactorily, but that the major problem was delay in AID program decisions, which the Afghans interpreted as indicating a lack of genuine U.S. interest, and which they contrasted with "prompt and open handed decisions" by the Soviets. He added, "There is no doubt that the King and other ministers look on us as strong anchor to windward. However, Prime Minister is, I feel, a bit too trustful of Soviets' continuing friendship and goodwill." (Telegram 2485 from New Delhi, March 4; ibid., POL AFG–US)

---

531. Memorandum of Conversation[1]

Washington, April 28, 1965.

SUBJECT

    Afghan Aid Request

PARTICIPANTS

    Mr. Mir Mohammed Siddik Farhang, Deputy Minister of Planning of the
        Afghan government and Leader Grantee
    His Excellency T. A. Majid, Ambassador
    Mr. Phillips Talbot, Assistant Secretary—NEA
    Mr. William J. Handley, Deputy Assistant Secretary—NEA
    Mr. Frank E. Schmelzer, Afghanistan Desk Officer—SOA

Farhang said that the Afghan economy would remain a problem for the next few years because of long-term structural weaknesses. The price of Afghanistan's major export to western markets, karakul, had

---

[1] Source: National Archives and Records Administration, RG 59, Central Files 1964–66, AID (US) 8 AFG. Confidential. Drafted by Schmelzer on May 6.

remained about the same since 1939, whereas the price of manufactured goods imported from the West had increased 300 per cent in this time. The present Afghan aid request[2] grew out of the short-term financial crisis, but he was glad to report, as he had heard from Kabul the day before, that the deficit for the fiscal year ending March 20, 1965 had been 600 million Afghanis rather than the one billion which it had been feared to be. Farhang said that the attention of the government had been concentrated on political and social reform with the thought that the government could revert to economic problems later. Now, however, the attention of the government is concentrated on the current economic problems, and the government has learned that it must tackle political and economic problems simultaneously. The government hopes that it will not suffer politically during the election period in October as a result of present economic problems.

Mr. Talbot said that the U.S. would await the results of the IMF mission talks in Kabul before deciding what we could do to help Afghanistan. Mr. Handley asked what the Afghans themselves could do to improve their situation.

Farhang replied that recently the government had convened successfully a congress of landowners to persuade them to agree to an increase in land taxation. The government hoped to do a number of other things to overcome structural weaknesses: (1) to process karakul in Afghanistan, perhaps with U.S. assistance, which could increase the income from this source by 50 per cent; (2) to set up a wool scouring plant; (3) to sell fruit in the Middle East particularly Kuwait. The fruit presently sold to Pakistan and India is sold on bilateral account and does not earn foreign exchange; (4) eventually, to export cotton goods. Farhang said that the Textile Mill is in better shape now because Abdul Majid Zabuli,[3] its moving force, had returned to Afghanistan and because the government was giving it additional assistance. Farhang commented that he hoped that the private sector would play a stronger role perhaps after five years. The government planned to help selected enterprises, and the new legal system would facilitate the development of private enterprise as a whole.

Referring to his discussion April 26 with Mr. Macomber of AID, Farhang said that he had reported to his government Mr. Macomber's suggestion that Afghanistan would be best advised to give up one or more projects now contemplated under U.S. assistance in order to better handle the present financial problem. Farhang said that he did not

---

[2] The Embassy reported in telegram 563, April 2, that it had received a letter from Minister of Planning Yaftali requesting U.S. assistance to help solve Afghanistan's financial crisis. (Ibid., FN 1–1 AFG)

[3] Abdul Majid Zabuli, President of Bank-i-Milli.

know how his government would react to this suggestion. He himself felt that it would be better to continue with the projects contemplated; otherwise, workers and machinery becoming available as other projects are finished would remain unused, and there would be an imbalance in Afghan development if new American projects were not taken up (Soviet projects would continue).

Mr. Talbot said that he hoped Mr. Farhang would take back with him the knowledge that the United States is very much interested in the constitutional and economic development of Afghanistan. Many Americans were interested in these developments, particularly since the visit of Their Majesties to the U.S. in 1963. Mr. Talbot said he was glad to meet Farhang again, this time in Washington. Farhang expressed appreciation of American interest and assistance, and concluded that he hoped that he could also take back with him to Afghanistan American agreement for assistance to meet the current need there.

---

532. Telegram From the Embassy in Afghanistan to the Department of State[1]

Kabul, May 6, 1965, 1200Z.

660. Ref Embtel 659.[2] For Secretary from Ambassador. Reftel reports watershed session I had with PriMin May 5. While I most reluctant add extraordinarily heavy burdens you are carrying feel I would be derelict my duty were I not to call to your personal attention implications PriMin's position for future US-Afghan relations.

If we are to be prevented by our own regulations or other factors from stepping up assistance on Helmand Valley project, with which we have been so closely associated for fifteen years, Afghans quite likely request us terminate this major US activity here. Since many key Afghan officials, such as MinFin and MinInt, have been personally

---

[1] Source: National Archives and Records Administration, RG 59, Central Files 1964–66, POL 33–1 AFG–IRAN/HELMAND. Secret; Exdis.

[2] In telegram 659 from Kabul, May 6, Ambassador Steeves reported on his conversation with Prime Minister Yusuf, who informed him that he and his cabinet had decided to give top priority and assign whatever resources might be required to accelerate the Helmand Valley project. Yusuf asked for a definite answer as to U.S. plans "for the completion of the project." Following a lengthy discussion, they agreed to defer further deliberation until after their joint technical planners could meet to consider what could realistically be achieved in the Valley. (Ibid.)

identified with Helmand Valley in past and it is in a very real sense seen here as heart our economic program, Afghans are likely regard any such development as "abandonment" by USG. This would set in train here developments gradually curtailing our position and influence.

We presently undertaking joint US–Afghan technical discussions see whether goals envisioned by PriMin feasible but I am not sanguine outcome unless we able to do more ourselves than so far authorized. Accordingly, before curtailment along lines above suggested takes place, believe policy determination required as to whether maintenance our existing satisfactory position here of sufficient importance USG, and to its CENTO allies Iran and Pakistan, to warrant us making special effort provide forthcoming response to PriMin and thus maintaining major and productive US presence in Helmand Valley development to which Afghans now giving highest priority.[3]

Steeves

---

[3] In telegram 326 to Kabul, May 11, the Department of State commented: "Ambassador can be sure we will take his warning signal seriously. We do not intend to let US–Afghan relations deteriorate but neither can we ignore our own aid standards and political requirements. We will seek to resolve our problems with Afghanistan in order to enable us to do what is required to maintain an effective U.S. presence there." (Ibid.)

---

533. Telegram From the Embassy in Afghanistan to the Department of State[1]

Kabul, May 13, 1965, 1215Z.

679. Ref Embtel 675.[2] Embassy Econ Counselor saw IMF team for one hour just prior team departure Kabul. After very difficult discussions last forty-eight hours, including lengthy meeting with PM Yusuf, team left with signed letter committing RGA to program fiscal and financial reform, which team feels will be acceptable to Fund directors as basis extension standby facility. Team felt that commitments obtained were well above minimum latitude their instructions and were unani-

---

[1] Source: National Archives and Records Administration, RG 59, Central Files 1964–66, FN 10 AFG/IMF. Limited Official Use.
[2] Dated May 13. (Ibid.)

mous in expressing opinion that acceptable commitments would not have been forthcoming without US–FRG "pressure" position linking in tying consideration future extraordinary assistance to favorable outcome IMF consultations.

Despite tough negotiations and undoubtedly painful concessions made by RGA, Afghan sources report that team earned respect of Afghans and that Ministry of Finance officials are privately saying that IMF visit will result in enactment of reform measures which they have long advocated but never had sufficient political strength to carry out.

Team plans to file RGA statement of undertaking and their report immediately upon return Washington this weekend, and estimate that if Fund directorate approves RGA proposals, agreement could be reached within three weeks and drawings commence soon thereafter.

CT comments on consultations and recommendations for subsequent U.S. action now under preparation.[3]

Brewer

---

[3] On May 15 the Country Team in Afghanistan recommended consideration of a commodity assistance loan. They commented that the IMF team had succeeded in establishing fiscal responsibility as a condition for additional aid and that acceptance by the Afghan Government of IMF controls represented a victory for the advocates of a Western presence in the country. (Telegram Toaid 1331 from Kabul, May 15; ibid., AID (US) 9 AFG)

---

534. Telegram From the Embassy in Afghanistan to the Department of State[1]

Kabul, June 12, 1965.

734. Joint Embassy/USAID Message. Ref: Deptel 342;[2] NESA action memorandum May 25;[3] Embtel 732.[4] I had two hour session with Prime

---

[1] Source: National Archives and Records Administration, RG 59, Central Files 1964–66, AID (US) AFG. Confidential. No time of transmission is on the telegram.

[2] Telegram 342 to Kabul, May 28, from Ambassador Steeves, who was in Washington for consultations, described the program for aid to Afghanistan that had been tentatively agreed upon and suggested the Embassy request that the Afghan Government withhold any policy decisions on the Helmand Valley until after his return. (Ibid.)

[3] Not found.

[4] In telegram 732 from Kabul, June 10, Ambassador Steeves reported that the package agreed upon during his Washington consultations had been favorably received by the Prime Minister and his associates. (National Archives and Records Administration, RG 59, Central Files 1964–66, AID US–AFG)

Minister Yusuf morning June 10 to outline agreement in principle on Afghan aid program reached in Washington during my consultations. MinPlan Yaftali and Farhadi (FonOff) were with PriMin, and HVA head Wakil joined us for discussion HVA. DCM Brewer and AID Director Nucker accompanied me.

Began by explaining to PriMin I had been asked return Washington view completion IMF study, Nucker's presence there and fact I already relatively near in Western Europe. Told Yusuf we had been able reach general agreement in three main areas and fourth miscellaneous category future USG aid RGA and said would like outline entire package prior discussing details. PriMin agreed.

Re PL 480 wheat, I reminded PriMin Afghanistan about only country in world still on Title II[5] basis. We had agreed this would be continued for another year with program up to 150,000 tons if detailed studies supported. I noted questions higher deposit price, storage and transportation were among problems on which technicians would have to reach agreement and suggested this working level study begin promptly. PriMin expressed pleasure at news.

Re loan program, I referred request Yaftali letter[6] and said we favored selective project commodity loan which would make maximum contribution in areas USG already assisting such as agriculture on which MinAg had appealed to me month ago. We also hoped such loan would encourage small industries in private sector. However, both imagination and administrative machinery would be required implement program properly. I suggested we get down to technical studies right away to determine how best use $2 million which being made available as first tranche but noted program capable of increments as need shown. PriMin asked whether as much as $4 million might be available in coming year if RGA could justify. Nucker explained details, adding if $2 million orders from farmers and businessmen right away then more possible. Yusuf expressed gratitude but noted program would not help foreign exchange problem. American prices were higher than elsewhere. I interjected American goods also better. PriMin agreed but added had hoped loan could be used for consumer goods. I told Yusuf frankly this was not possible but of course our suggested help would give RGA greater flexibility in use other funds. Nucker stressed our approach could be used soak up Afghanis from private sector and at same time assist agricultural and industrial development. I added use agricultural or industrial bank might result establishment of some sort revolving fund which might then prompt interest some American

---

[5] Title II of P.L. 480 authorized the transfer of surplus agricultural commodities on a grant basis.

[6] See footnote 2, Document 531.

bank consider lending additional help. Told Yusuf we had been promised first priority on assignment advisor who could sit with bank manager and show him how make this program work. PriMin asked whether advisor might come soon to which Nucker replied as soon as RGA desired. PriMin indicated expert should come now.

Remaining three-quarters our discussion largely devoted HVA, I told PriMin we suggesting four-pronged approach: (a) special case re Arghandab; (b) equipment loan for ACU[7] which might illustratively work in Shamalan; (c) BuRec team proceed in Darweshan and elsewhere prepare basis for subsequent loan applications; and (d) agreement in principle on Kajakai power. Informed Yusuf that, as rapidly as we could prepare drainage map Arghandab and get data on which contractor could base bid, we were willing get this going on special basis. We would also need examine irrigation gates and sluices so that both supply water and drainage regulated. PriMin asked who might do required survey. Nucker replied we thinking several experts might be added J.G. White contract save time. PriMin asked whether USG funds available for survey and construction. Nucker affirmed re survey but said construction would be on loan basis.

Re ACU equipment loan, I stressed urgency so ACU could get to work on HVA areas Afghans might choose. PriMin felt ACU work should be supplementary to that of US contractor brought in later. I agreed, assuring him funds would be available for equipment loan. Response Yusuf's query re amount, Nucker said $4–5 million had been discussed. I told PriMin it was in this area that we would look to RGA provide men and money enable ACU start work on semi-classified land such as Shamalan. PriMin remarked he would have two thousand men trained as machine operators by next month, but said ACU could only help in total picture on limited supplemental basis.

Re BuRec, I told PriMin we would expect team continue work in other areas such as Darweshan on basis original concept full land classification needed justify subsequent incremental loans. However, we could be working on Arghandab and ACU on Shamalan at same time.

Turning Kajakai power, I informed PriMin USG agreement in principle loan this project. Nucker explained following steps: (1) as soon as RGA requested, we prepared make loan approximating $1 million for two 1500 kw diesel generators Kandahar; (2) in August pair experts would arrive work with RGA resolve problems remaining from Beck report and develop loan application for Kajakai power units; and (3) power distribution line, which already funded, going forward with

---

[7] Afghan Construction Unit.

Washington starting work with Harza re contract for project. PriMin said troubled lest whole power development be dependent on agreement particular arrangements re organization and foreign scholarship training. I commented Beck report total set recommendations some of which might not need be immediately implemented. PriMin stressed RGA unprepared spend substantial sums on loan basis on foreign scholarships. I cautioned him total program must incorporate enough of Beck and related suggestions to assure that power system we were helping provide could be operated. PriMin stressed need begin construction immediately rather than waiting five years and opined Beck schedule should be accelerated. With USG agreement in principle now in hand he felt necessary technical details could be worked out. I urged Yusuf not dismiss training aspects project lightly. Yaftali asserted in the past training had always been on grant basis.

Re miscellaneous category, told PriMin I had feared foregoing might have required sacrifice something else in program but was happy assure him this not so. HIQ[8] and AID could go forward on schedule.

Additionally, where RGA had development schemes which required equipment for exploitation, such as coal mines, USG prepared under certain conditions consider equipment loans. One condition would be some American management. I mentioned both Dar-e-Suf and Herat locations and said we happy discuss if RGA interested.

In subsequent general discussion PriMin sought fix clearly in mind what USG proposal meant in terms HVA. Said he accepted proposals re Arghandab and need for ACU equipment loan application but asked what proposed re other HVA areas including Shamalan, Darweshan, Nadi Ali, Marjeh and Tarnak. I replied additional investment Nadi Ali probably unjustified. Tarnak and Darweshan would require land classification as prelude loan application. Wakil noted quality Arghandab land similar Darweshan–Shamalan. Difference was more settlers Arghandab with greater skill. Would be pity tackle Arghandab now and "forget about" Darweshan and Shamalan. Nucker commented Arghandab had Washington approval in principle, since land being preserved required different technical and legal tests than undeveloped land. Re-equipped ACU could get started on Shamalan with our guidance while elsewhere land classification and project planning would be down. Soon as ten thousand acres or more found meet USG legal requirements development loan application could be submitted.

Yaftali asked whether private contractor could not do Darweshan survey. Nucker replied yes on loan basis. PriMin stressed RGA would not apply for loan for survey work. Wakil argued for private contractor

---

[8] Herat–Islam Qala road.

do survey work as most efficient. Brewer noted past disappointing rate BuRec progress in large part due failure HVA lend proper support. Nucker felt BuRec could be instructed concentrate its efforts and, with necessary HVA support, would do as well as private contractor. I said would be difficult shift from BuRec entirely without creating confusion and misunderstanding. Wakil replied BuRec could oversee quality contractor's work. PriMin emphasized RGA concerned lest work be delayed as in past. Inquired how long survey Arghandab would take. Nucker replied should not take excessive length of time. Wakil disagreed, noting permeability study and similar work needed in addition to drainage pattern. PriMin again inquired why private contractor could not do work under BuRec supervision. Wakil added could not understand why grant money available for BuRec survey but not for survey by private contractor. Yaftali cited fine RGA experience with private contractors such as MK and AHC.

I told PriMin we had great faith in entire package and accordingly hoped RGA would leave to us matter of assuring BuRec moved with appropriate speed and momentum. PriMin wondered whether contract could be drawn up with either BuRec or J.G. White giving timetable within which work to be finished. I remarked might be possible get Arghandab out of way in three years. Nucker added elsewhere might do twenty thousand acres a year. PriMin seemed satisfied and inquired re steps to be taken following this meeting. Nucker said staff would spend considerable time with HVA and would ascertain who should make Arghandab study and how long it would take.

In summing up, PriMin expressed hope program would be workable as proposed. While it did not meet all RGA had asked, it showed USG good will and cooperative spirit. He was pleased some work could start promptly to overcome frustrations all sides had experienced. Work would be done certain areas as outlined with remaining land being completed on basis twenty thousand acres a year.

PriMin then said Herat–Kandahar road would be open in two months and inquired re status HIQ. Nucker replied detailed specs being prepared Livorno and hoped contractor might mobilize during winter, start construction next spring and finish in one year. PriMin expressed appreciation and again said how pleased he was work could start promptly on HVA.

Comment: While obviously not meeting RGA wishes on all points, believe our presentation package did succeed convincing PriMin USG determination move ahead more rapidly than in past, notably re HVA which to him is all important. Afghans still would prefer faster rate development which they think possible through private contract arrangement. They have, however, accepted our proposals as basis for moving forward. We can now get down to detailed work and I would hope will be able demonstrate on continuing basis that any further delays in implementation will be RGA responsibility, not ours. To this end, CT will do all it can see foregoing schedule carried out, and I urge maximum continued support appropriate Washington agencies to achieve this end.

Steeves

535. Airgram From the Embassy in Afghanistan to the Department of State[1]

A–249   Kabul, June 2, 1966.

SUBJECT

The Ambassador's Audience with King Zahir Shah on June 1

I was received in audience by His Majesty Mohammad Zahir Shah at the palace this morning at my initiative to discuss with him several subjects of mutual interest on my return to Kabul after leave in the United States. As on the occasion of previous audiences (Emb A–107, October 30, 1965[2] and A–189, March 10, 1966[3]), I brought along Second Secretary Eric Neff to serve as interpreter in French. The following is a record of the conversation except for one subject which is being reported separately.

I opened the conversation by saying how pleased I was to see the King again and how much I had enjoyed our association over the years. I added that, as the King perhaps knew, I would be leaving Afghanistan in about six weeks to take up my new assignment and, although the exact date of my departure had not yet been fixed, I thought it would be about July 15. The King replied that he, too, had very much enjoyed our relationship and that he would be sorry to see me go.

Briefly recounting my recent leave in the U.S., I commented that I had brought back with me many expressions of goodwill for the King and Her Majesty from all those they had met during their last visit to

[1] Source: National Archives and Records Administration, RG 59, Central Files 1964–66, POL 2 AFG. Confidential. Drafted by Eric Neff and William F. Spengler of the Political Section, and approved by Steeves.

[2] Airgram 107 from Kabul, October 30, 1965, reported a meeting on October 13 between the Ambassador and the King. (Ibid., POL 2 AFG)

[3] Airgram 189 from Kabul, March 10, reported a meeting on March 1 between the Ambassador and the King. (Ibid.)

the U.S. I added that these expressions of esteem and goodwill came not only from the highest echelons of government but also from all those down the line who had the pleasure of meeting them. In this connection I specifically mentioned former Governor Welch of Indiana who had written me that he considered the King's visit to his state as one of the high points of his tenure as governor. I also mentioned how pleased I had been to have been able to attend the University of California's presentation to Ambassador Majid of an Honorary Doctorate—adding how popular and well regarded the Ambassador was in Washington.

I then raised the question of Prime Minister Maiwandwal's working visit to Washington (Emb A–248),[4] adding that the exact date was now in the process of being worked out and wondering if he thought that about November 1 would be convenient. The King replied that he was very pleased about the visit, adding that the Prime Minister would be especially busy during the next few months, but thought that November would probably be the best time. I then commented that the visit not only reflected my government's interest and concern for Afghanistan, but also was an expression of high regard for the Prime Minister himself. The King indicated that he appreciated this, and left me with the impression that he, too, approved of the job the Prime Minister was doing.

Referring to the forthcoming opening ceremonies for the new Kabul/Kandahar road, constructed with American assistance, I said that I hoped the King would be able to officiate. I added that the exact date would depend on the engineers and the climate, but I thought the project would be completed by July 18. I also mentioned we were exploring the possibility of having Vice President Humphrey attend the opening. The King replied that, of course, he would be delighted to attend the opening ceremony and that he would be most happy if the Vice President could also be present.

I discussed our concern about the slow progress of the Helmand Valley development project. I pointed out that the United States had made a major investment in the project and was prepared to do more, but he should know we were unhappy with the way the project was being administered. I mentioned in passing the shortage of local funds allocated for repairing and cleaning the canals, and said that while I did not want to burden him with details, I did want him to be aware that problems exist and of our concern in this regard. The King replied that he was grateful for our assistance and was very much aware that problems existed. In fact, he was aware of them in detail. He added

---

[4] Dated June 2. (Ibid.)

that he would keep in mind what I had told him. I then said that I had discussed the matter last week with the Prime Minister and had subsequently sent a memorandum to him[5] describing some of the difficulties which had arisen.

I then told the King that, as he well knew, ever since my arrival in Afghanistan I had worked to improve the climate for private investment which I and my government believed could make a major contribution to the development of the country. I referred to the recent visit here of a group of American business leaders and representatives of the Department of Commerce, and specifically mentioned a promising project that had been proposed by Mr. Mariani, a member of the group and president of one of the largest fruit and nut processing companies in the U.S., to establish a canning industry in the Kandahar–Helmand area. I had discussed the project with the Prime Minister who had expressed great interest in it. I also left with the King a copy of the proposal which I had given the Prime Minister. The King responded that he and his government were very much interested in attracting private investment into Afghanistan and would certainly continue to support this effort.

I closed the conversation by thanking the King for the trees and bushes he had given for the new chancery grounds and said that I hoped that my new assignment as Director General of the Foreign Service might enable me to attend the dedication ceremonies of the new chancery. I told the King I would be paying a final farewell call on him sometime nearer my actual departure.

JM Steeves

---

[5] Not found.

536. Telegram From the Embassy in Afghanistan to the Department of State[1]

Kabul, July 25, 1966, 1220Z.

379. Subject: Secy Freeman's Discussion with RGA. Ref: State 11304.[2]

1. Details Kabul–Kandahar road openings being submitted by airgram[3] and general impact Secy Freeman's visit by septel.[4] This message covers Secy's meeting July 13 with PriMin Maiwandwal and key Cabinet members which only official discussion with RGA during short visit. Following account based on oral report by Amb Steeves (only Mission official present).

2. Secy observed privately before meeting that Afghan performance in tackling basic agric problems appeared shockingly inadequate. RGA spokesmen at meeting did nothing overcome this impression. Meeting related solely to Afghanistan's agric problems and foodgrain situation. Afghans described problems and plans in general but largely failed provide convincing info.

3. In response, Secy avoided being hypercritical but did not conceal awareness of Afghanistan's failure take effective measures alleviate agric problems. When Afghan official estimated 200,000 tons as foodgrain import requirement for coming year, Secy observed pointedly that raising ante progressively from original 50,000 ton program suggested Afghanistan going backward rather than making progress in meeting food problem. (As far as we know, specific quantities not otherwise discussed and Secretary emphasized fact of limited stocks of US foodgrains available for export this year.)

4. Re prospects future US foodgrain assistance, Secy stressed Title II no longer possible. Explaining course of new legislation in Congress, including pressures for cash dollar sales or loans, Secy foresaw more restrictive law probably most closely resembling present Title IV.

---

[1] Source: National Archives and Records Administration, RG 59, Central Files 1964–66, POL 7 US/FREEMAN. Confidential.

[2] In telegram 11304, July 20, the Department requested additional details on the Kabul–Kandahar road opening, including Secretary Freeman's talks with Afghan Government officials, and the general impact of his visit on U.S.-Afghan relations. (Ibid.)

[3] Airgram 19 from Kabul, July 28, described the July 13 ceremonies opening the Kabul–Kandahar highway, built under an AID development grant. Secretary of Agriculture Orville L. Freeman attended as special representative of the President. (Ibid., IT 7–16, AFG)

[4] In telegram 415 from Kabul, July 27, the Embassy reported that Freeman's visit had dramatized U.S. interest in Afghanistan, and that, although no substantive actions or decisions were taken, the Secretary's discussions with top Afghan officials helped place the U.S. aid prospects in better perspective. (Ibid., POL 7 US/FREEMAN)

5. This context, PriMin admitted that RGA, in urgently requesting further Title II assistance, hoped beat enactment of new legislation. Secy saw little chance success such tactic. (See also Embtel 274.)[5]

6. In discussion of possible domestic effects of future Afghan food-grain purchases, Secy asked if RGA had considered direct subsidy in reselling to consumers; Afghans did not object this suggestion. Secy also raised possible substitution of coarse grains for wheat; response inconclusive.

7. Secy emphasized throughout that it squarely up to Afghans to meet own problem by taking effective measures produce more food—e.g. adoption of prices providing adequate incentive to Afghan farmers and importation of more fertilizer.

8. In subsequent conversation with Amb Steeves, PriMin stated he regarded Secy very sympathetic and understanding man. PriMin added he anxious visit US as best means of communicating Afghan sense of "dependence" on USG for substantial and timely aid, though he believed he had conveyed general idea to Secy.

9. Understand staffers Brown and Walsh attended discussion, took notes for records of Secy and White House, respectively. Department might obtain more complete account from them if desired.

Blood

---

[5] Dated July 18. (Ibid., AID (US) AFG)

---

537. Telegram From the Embassy in Afghanistan to the Department of State[1]

Kabul, November 19, 1966, 1010Z.

2015. Joint Embassy/USAID message.

1. In view present competition for limited US aid funds, Country Team believes it useful recall significance continuing bilateral economic assistance as principal instrument for assuring type of US presence needed to secure our over-all objectives in Afghanistan.

2. Such presence was found imperative when RGA was much less responsive to popular aspirations than it is now. Major political

---

[1] Source: National Archives and Records Administration, RG 59, Central Files 1964–66, AID (US) AFG. Confidential.

transformation of recent past renders it even more vital to our interests. In CT view, therefore, USG cannot afford lower its sights in Afghanistan re level of presence on grounds that present government is "safely" Western-oriented. CT does not view this simply as problem of giving aid and comfort to a friendly government somewhat frightened by prospects it has opened up through Western-type political liberalization. More important problem is to make sure our total program, at this juncture, does not fail express to growing sector of populace which politically alert that US has creative and dependable interest in their progress.

3. Central role of technical assistance in providing this assurance is obvious. However, benefits are gradual and long-term in nature. Advice alone is not enough to secure popular confidence. To assure continuation of presence adequate to accomplish our objectives, CT convinced US must keep up momentum in certain sensitive sectors where any open invitation to Soviets or ChiComs to take over in areas of past US efforts could tip balance and render our past investment ineffectual. This need not mean abdicating our incentives to self-help and other program criteria. It does mean we must move on an adequate number of projects which combine economic development potential and political benefits for US.

4. In this context, CT has following views on currently pending program issues:

A. Food and Agriculture

(I) Re Food for Peace, CT believes current US posture is in Afghanistan's own best interests and should be carried through despite emotional shock being experienced by RGA. Essential positive element US posture is, of course, continuing readiness supply fertilizer, equipment and technical assistance to assist RGA's intensified food production program.

(II) We must recognize, nevertheless, that in recent years Afghans have regarded PL–480 support (of type now being phased out) as primary form US assistance. Its transformation will inevitably shift public attention more acutely upon Helmand Valley development, where our present image is unsatisfactory, as well as upon economically stagnant area Kandahar which also traditionally associated with US aid effort.

B. Helmand Valley

For this reason, it fortunate we are now in position move ahead with Kandahar diesel-electric power project, and that we are on point of financing badly-needed new equipment for HACU.[2] This new movement will be all to the good. But we must recognize that Helmand–Kandahar

---

[2] Helmand Authority Construction Unit.

agricultural development as we conceive it can show results only gradually. CT proposes continue restraining RGA ambitions for land development at uneconomic pace. This underscores urgency of proceeding with long-deferred Kajakai hydro project. CT convinced that, among various proposals for US action in Afghanistan, this is one where both economic and political factors clearly show it in our interest to carry out. In view foregoing circumstances, timing of final US commitment to project has become more critical than ever. Thus, CT has received with extreme concern, even dismay, indication (per Aidto 532)[3] that AID/W considering further deferment Kajakai loan as well as possibility stopgap alternatives. Separate message on specifics reftel will follow soonest.

Although Helmand long thought of as US preserve, Soviet or ChiCom offers to build on our foundations are by no means out of question if we allow matters drift too much. We may question their economics, but Soviet-aided Nangarhar project and ChiCom-aided Parwan project show that both powers are prepared enter this type activity in Afghanistan and possibly expand it (viz. new ChiCom survey Farah Rud Valley, west of Helmand).

C. Civil Aviation

In this sector, takeover our predominant role by another power would be particularly harmful to US reputation, and takeover by Communists a signal defeat. Despite progress, we are not yet near point where Afghans can go it alone in civil aviation. CT believes Boeing jet project justified on economic grounds. If it should prove to be borderline case, however, CT wishes point out that rejection loan would deny US another case where economic and political factors fortuitously combined to constitute a real opportunity for US. Turndown would in fact mean we paid political price: population would eventually draw conclusion that, at critical time, US was unprepared share with Afghanistan its special genius in commercial jet transport.

Bush airline idea has potential for increasing national cohesion and encouraging responsiveness by RGA to population in remote areas. If friendly Western power such as Canada should prove willing finance foreign exchange costs such venture from outset, CT would regard this as in harmony US interests. If not, it will be only natural for RGA to look to US. Project is not yet sufficiently developed to pose specific programming issues. Our attitude, however, should be sympathetic if feasibility studies should show that Bush operations of specified scale could be conducted on economic basis or something close thereto (as has been done in some other LDC's).

---

[3] Not found.

D. Ministry of Justice Proposal

CT will need further study before able give outline initial response to CA–1063[4] re Title IX Foreign Assistance Act. However, should mention that CT has serious doubts about going ahead with project for reorganization Ministry Justice and overhaul legal code. RGA is not pursuing initiative with any enthusiasm. Present leadership Ministry Justice totally inadequate for realization benefits. Even if this changed, doubtful that request, if resumed, would be confined to just the kind of activity we would want to involve ourselves in. Risks are abundant in view intertwining Islamic law with present system. If anything went wrong with project, public much more likely find fault with our role than give US credit for involvement more constructive aspects.

E. Roads

For reasons already suggested (particularly section C above), we may want to concern ourselves in future with targets opportunity re road-building in north. There is no doubt about impact on rural populace of highways already built here by US and Soviets, or about increased mobility afforded to urban populations. Activity along roadsides testifies to how such roads can change lives of people and, in their minds, point the way to the future.

This longer-run US interest affects issue of increasing aid loan to permit widening roadbed Herat–Islam Qala road. CT believes decision to economize by building 5.5 meter road ([garble] meters including shoulders) was mistake which, if not rectified, will plague us in future. Since Kabul–Kandahar–Herat road is 7 meters wide (10 meters including shoulders) and IBRD-financed road from Nrshed to Afghan border will apparently have roadbed 9 meters wide, it seems inevitable that HIQ link with narrower roadbed will, in words one astute official US observer who recently visited here, turn out to be "monument to niggardliness." Here is prime case where we have ability respond quickly at cost which seems reasonable in light our total stake in Afghanistan. Because cost of widening will increase with every day of construction, CT believes widening HIQ road most urgent of program issues confronting US in Afghanistan and urges immediate approval before AHC gets any further down road.

Blood

---

[4] Reference is incorrect; CA–1063, December 3, concerned a different subject. (National Archives and Records Administration, RG 59, Central Files 1964–66, FN 1–1 LAOS)

538. Memorandum From the President's Special Assistant (Rostow) to President Johnson[1]

Washington, March 25, 1967.

SUBJECT

Background for Maiwandwal Visit Tuesday, March 28 at 12:00 noon[2]

Our main reason for inviting the Afghan Prime Minister is to reassure him that we're still behind him in his delicate balancing act between the West and the USSR. So far Afghanistan has kept the Western door wide open, even though we've put in less than half the Soviet level of aid. The Afghan King, in a private talk with President Kennedy in 1963,[3] opened his heart on his fear of going completely under Soviet domination. Maiwandwal probably doesn't know this, but it's typical of most Afghan leaders' real sympathies. We want to encourage them.

But staying out of Soviet clutches is an uphill fight. Economically, Afghanistan is increasingly linked with the Soviet economy, and the USSR provides all its military equipment. But we have a near-monopoly of assistance to its whole educational system. PanAm has built its airline and is minority co-owner. Most of the Cabinet is clearly pro-Western. Maiwandwal himself is an old friend and knows the U.S. well, but he has to avoid further criticism that he's in our pocket.

The main thing he wants from his visit is a sense that we're not backing away. He and his colleagues are leery of our increasingly tight approach to aid. (FY 67 $34 million, FY 68 $18 million.) We can't make a long-term commitment to his new Five Year Plan, though it's a good one worked up with Bob Nathan. But we are ready to go ahead with

---

[1] Source: Johnson Library, National Security File, Country File, Afghanistan, Visit of Prime Minister Maiwandwal, 3/28/67. Secret. A handwritten note on the memorandum reads, "rec'd 3/25/67 1:50 p."

[2] Prime Minister Mohammed Hashim Maiwandwal visited the United States March 25–April 9. While in Washington March 28–30, he met with President Johnson and other U.S. officials. For the exchange of greetings, exchange of toasts, and joint statement issued on March 28, see Department of State *Bulletin,* April 17, 1967, pp. 627–632. A summary of Secretary Rusk's conversation with Maiwandwal is in telegram 165557 to Kabul, March 30. (National Archives and Records Administration, RG 59, Central Files 1967–69, POL 7 AFG) Briefing papers and other material relating to Maiwandwal's visit are ibid., Conference Files: Lot 67 D 587, V.26 and V.27.

[3] For a record of this meeting, see *Foreign Relations,* 1961–1963, vol. XIX, Document 327.

several projects (described in Secretary Rusk's memo).[4] We believe these plus your normal warm hospitality will do the job.

I recommend you read Secretary Rusk's memo and the scope paper (General Tabs A and C attached).[5] The economic charts (background Tab B) prepared especially for you suggest the main contours—low overwhelmingly agricultural GNP, exports growing but going mainly to the USSR, elementary industry growing slowly—the very first steps of development. Above all, you will be interested in the description of Afghanistan's new experiment with parliamentary government which Maiwandwal is trying to make work (background Tab A). Maiwandwal is running into familiar problems of student unrest, party building, how to make an archaic bureaucracy function rapidly. His bio is at Bio Sketches Tab A, and we'll have talking points for you Monday night.

Walt

---

[4] In a March 24 memorandum Rusk recommended that the President indicate to Maiwandwal U.S. support for Afghanistan's economic development program, and inform him that the $4.6 million loan for equipment for the Helmand Valley was nearly ready for a signature. Rusk suggested that Maiwandwal also be told that a decision was expected in 30 days on his request for a $13 million AID loan for hydroelectric power at the Kajakai Dam site in the Helmand Valley, and that Afghanistan's application for an Export-Import Bank loan of $7.5 million was still under consideration. (Johnson Library, National Security File, Country File, Afghanistan, Visit of Prime Minister Maiwandwal, 3/28/67)

[5] Tabs A, B, and C are not printed.

---

539. Memorandum of Conversation[1]

Washington, March 28, 1967, 12:40–12:54 p.m.

SUBJECT

The President's Conversation with Afghan Prime Minister Maiwandwal

PARTICIPANTS

United States
The President

---

[1] Source: National Archives and Records Administration, RG 59, Central Files 1967–69, POL 7 AFG. Confidential. Drafted by Spain, approved in S and by Saunders on June 19. The President and Prime Minister Maiwandwal met privately in the Oval Office from 11:50 a.m. to 12:35 p.m.; the part of the meeting printed was held in the Cabinet Room at the White House. (Johnson Library, President's Daily Diary)

Secretary of State Dean Rusk[2]
Mr. Walt W. Rostow, Special Assistant to the President
Mr. Howard Wriggins, Executive Office of the President
Ambassador Symington, Chief of Protocol
Acting Assistant Secretary William J. Handley, NEA
Ambassador Robert G. Neumann, U.S. Ambassador to Afghanistan
Country Director James W. Spain, Pakistan-Afghanistan Affairs

Afghanistan
His Excellency Mohammad Hashim Maiwandwal, Prime Minister
His Excellency Abdullah Malikyar, Ambassador of Afghanistan
His Excellency Nur Ali, Minister of Commerce
Secretary Farhadi, Council of Ministers

After the President and the Prime Minister joined the other members of the party, the Prime Minister thanked the President for the opportunity which his visit to the United States provided to renew old friendships.

Secretary Rusk noted that the Secretary General of the United Nations had just made public his proposal on Vietnam and that the USG had commented favorably on it. He added that he understood Hanoi's reaction was negative.

The President said he had discussed the announcement with the Prime Minister and told him of our disappointment at Hanoi's negative reaction. He said we had earlier consulted with our allies on the proposal and responded affirmatively. We had done this a dozen or so times in the past on other proposals. However, Hanoi's reaction to the Secretary General was that this was none of his business.

War is everybody's business, the President said, and the U.S. is prepared to consider anybody's suggestion for ending it. He said he had asked Mr. Rostow to check the time and manner of our consultations on U-Thant's latest proposal and that he wanted to show this data to the Prime Minister.

The President added that he felt more strongly then ever that the people of Vietnam should be allowed to have free elections and that after that, if they wanted us out, we would be happy to leave. The money we are spending for bullets we would be happy to spend instead for bread. We would even be willing to help Ho Chi Minh.

He stressed, however, that we were not going to surrender or pull out of Vietnam, saying that if agreements were no good there, they were no good anywhere. He said we are still ready to go toward peace. Our answer is Yes. Hanoi's is still No.

The Prime Minister observed that the Secretary General is going abroad again and suggested that perhaps he would be having further consultations on Vietnam during his trip.

---

[2] The Prime Minister also met with Secretary Rusk on March 28. (National Archives and Records Administration, RG 59, Central Files 1967–69, E 5 AFG/Five Year Plan)

Secretary Rusk noted that U Thant had seen two North Vietnamese diplomats in Rangoon and thought it possible that those discussions had been taken into account in the Secretary General's present proposal. The Secretary told the Prime Minister that we knew of his interest in the cause of peace in Vietnam. He added he did not know whether or not the Prime Minister had any way to explore privately further moves; he remarked that he thought public approaches were not likely to get very far at the present time.

The Prime Minister agreed that public approaches were not apt to be effective and said that the rigid public stands which both sides have taken makes this difficult. He noted that Afghanistan has always stood by the April, 1964 recommendations of the seventeen non-aligned countries. In response to a question from Secretary Rusk as to how much attention the Vietnam problem attracted in Afghanistan, the Prime Minister said that it attracted a good deal of attention and now that there is democracy in the country it was sometimes used by the politicians for their own purposes. He expressed his concern over the problem describing it as an explosive situation which he feared might escalate into a bigger danger.

---

540.   Memorandum of Conversation[1]

Washington, March 29, 1967.

SUBJECT

Afghan Prime Minister's Comment on His Talk with the President

PARTICIPANTS

His Excellency Mohammad Hashim Maiwandwal, Prime Minister of
    Afghanistan
Mr. James W. Spain, Country Director, NEA/PAF

Before Prime Minister Maiwandwal's departure from Blair House today for his luncheon with the Secretary of State, I had the opportunity to ask him for his understanding of his discussion with the President yesterday.[2] My query was prompted by some remarks the Prime Minis-

---

[1] Source: Johnson Library, National Security File, Country File, Afghanistan, Vol. I, Memos and Miscellaneous, 12/63–4/68. Secret. Drafted by Spain.

[2] See Document 539.

ter made to me last evening which I thought suggested a possible misunderstanding. This turned out not to be the case.

The Prime Minister said that his discussion with the President had been thoroughly enjoyable and constructive. He felt that he and the President had come to grips with some major problems and understood each other very well indeed. He said that the point he had been trying to make in response to the President on Vietnam was that a number of other countries in the world, specifically including Afghanistan, did not see the Vietnam situation in exactly the same way we did. He said that he had tried to point out to the President that the United States had a tendency to be unduly concerned at different times with different problems; some years ago it had been organizing the northern tier into CENTO to defeat Communist aggression; earlier it had been the Marshall Plan and the Korean war; now it was Vietnam. The interests of Afghanistan and of other non-aligned Asian countries did not change as did those of the United States. This was the reason why they were not able to come as far as we would like them to at any given time on Vietnam, CENTO, the Korean war, etc.

On more specific subjects, the Prime Minister indicated that he had discussed the Ariana Airline request for a loan from the Export Import Bank and understood the situation as it had been explained to him by Ambassador Neumann in New York and by the President. He was content and he would wait.

On Afghanistan's present food needs, he said that the President had told him that the U.S. would do what it could to help on as generous terms as possible, specifically that cost would be repayable in 40 years.

On the Kajakai project, he said that the President was sympathetic and had said that the papers were being prepared. He understood that the President had not made a commitment and that the President expected that he (Maiwandwal) would not discuss the matter publicly at this time.

He said that the President had also mentioned the upcoming loan for land improvement equipment in the Helmand Valley and that they both understood that action on this was virtually completed.

I asked the Prime Minister for his views as to timing of any future steps on the Kajakai project. He said that he would very much like to be able to announce it together with the next food agreement shortly after his return to Kabul, April 15. He said that if the food agreement were to be ready sooner, he would like to withhold announcement until after his return. He added that the Kajakai loan was particularly important to him personally and that he deduced from his conversation with the President that an announcement shortly after his return home would probably be possible.

541.   Memorandum From the President's Special Assistant (Rostow) to President Johnson[1]

Washington, April 17, 1967.

SUBJECT

Afghan PL 480 Agreement

Secretary Freeman is ready to go ahead with the $4.4 million wheat and oil agreement you mentioned to Prime Minister Maiwandwal.[2] Sharply rising food prices have triggered demonstrations in Afghanistan over the past two weeks, and Ambassador Neumann recommends we go ahead as soon as possible. Maiwandwal has just returned and can make good political use of a go-ahead to dampen fears of shortages.

His one comment under pressure at the Press Club[3] remains an isolated incident. His public statements on the rest of his tour were quite moderate. Now that a couple of weeks have elapsed, we should probably go ahead now unless you are strongly opposed.

Charles Schultze's economic analysis is attached.[4]

Walt

Approve[5]

See me

---

[1] Source: Johnson Library, National Security File, Country File, Afghanistan, Vol. I, Memos & Miscellaneous, 12/63–4/68. Secret. A handwritten note on the memorandum indicates that it was received on April 18 at 5:05 p.m.

[2] In an April 7 memorandum to the President, Secretary of Agriculture Freeman and AID Administrator Gaud recommend negotiation of a P.L. 480 agreement with Afghanistan. (Ibid., Memos to the President, Walt Rostow, Vol. 26, April 6–30, 1967)

[3] In response to questions on Vietnam following a speech at the National Press Club on March 30, Maiwandwal stated that peace talks were impossible as long as the United States continued bombing North Vietnam, and he urged an unconditional end to the bombing. (Memorandum from Wriggins to Rostow, March 30; ibid., National Security File, Country File, Afghanistan, Visit of Prime Minister Maiwandwal 3/28/67)

[4] The April 15 memorandum to the President from Schultze noted the self-help measures undertaken in Afghanistan in the past year and recommended that the President authorize negotiation of the proposed P.L. 480 agreement due to Afghanistan's urgent need for wheat and oil.

[5] Both options are checked; apparently Johnson checked "See me," and Rostow checked the approval after consulting with him. A notation in Rostow's handwriting reads: "Call Nick," presumably Under Secretary of State Nicholas deB. Katzenbach. Telegram 185010 to Kabul, April 29, states that 40,000 tons of wheat for Afghanistan was approved that day. (National Archives and Records Administration, RG 59, Central Files 1967–69, AID (US) 15–8 AFG)

542. Telegram From the Embassy in Afghanistan to the Department of State[1]

Kabul, April 28, 1967, 0815Z.

4366. Kajakai and Wheat Announcements.

1. In my 4209[2] and previous messages I urged immediate US announcement next PL–480 wheat tranche.

2. In ensuing days furor caused by allegations of Afghan student against CIA (Hotaki case)[3] has increased markedly in intensity as result spate of strident comment in local press (Kabul 4365).[4] PriMin's belated confrontation with Parliament likely occur Tuesday May 2, at which time PriMin will be hard put to defend his recent trip to US and indeed value US–Afghan ties in light suspicion cast on US motives toward Afghanistan because of Hotaki case (Kabul 4322).[5]

3. We are whistling in the dark if we do not face up to fact that Hotaki case has not only seriously jeopardized Maiwandwal govt but also has caused substantial deterioration in US position here. In one week much of profit of Maiwandwal visit has been erased.

3. [sic] We have one action within our power which holds some promise of helping retrieve situation. We can and should announce new PL–480 wheat sale and intention to proceed with Kajakai before PriMin's appearance at Parliament expected May 2.[6] PriMin, through Farhadi, informed DCM today that timely announcements would be immensely helpful.

---

[1] Source: National Archives and Records Administration, RG 59, Central Files 1967–69, AID (US) 15–8 AFG. Secret; Priority; Limdis.

[2] Dated April 18. (Ibid., AID (US) 15 AFG)

[3] Reference is to an Afghan living in the United States who made charges of CIA activities in Afghanistan that received publicity in the United States, including an article in the April issue of *Ramparts* magazine. ("Three Tales of the CIA," *Ramparts*, Vol. 5, No. 10, April 1967, pp. 23–24) Hotaki's charges were summarized in a March 11 memorandum from Read to Rostow. (Johnson Library, National Security File, Country File, Afghanistan, Vol. I, Memos and Miscellaneous, 12/63–4/68) On April 24 the Embassy reported that the Hotaki case had "erupted with a vengeance here creating critical political problem for PriMin Maiwandwal." (Telegram 4293 from Kabul; National Archives and Records Administration, RG 59, Central Files 1967–69, ORG CIA)

[4] Telegram 4365 from Kabul, April 28, reported that the "eruption" of the Hotaki case "continues with increasing intensity amid mounting public criticism, now spurred by heavy press play, reflecting adversely on Maiwandwal government and USG." (Ibid.)

[5] Telegram 4322 from Kabul, April 25, reported on the postponement of the Prime Minister's confrontation with Parliament. (Ibid.)

[6] In telegram 4548 from Kabul, May 9, the Embassy reported that the furor over the Hotaki affair appeared to be subsiding following a persuasive speech in Parliament by Maiwandwal, in which he declared the accusations were unsubstantiated rumors. (Ibid., POL 15–1 AFG)

4. I strongly urge immediate announcement of these two evidences US cooperation with Afghanistan not because we wish defend Maiwandwal (he may already be past saving) but because it is essential we offer proof of disinterested US help at moment when US under heavy attack and suspicion for carrying out covert operations of "imperialistic and neo-colonialist" nature.

Neumann

---

543. Memorandum From Harold H. Saunders of the National Security Council Staff to the President's Special Assistant (Rostow)[1]

Washington, May 2, 1967.

SUBJECT

Further Aid for Afghanistan

Now that we have broken loose the PL 480 for Afghanistan, we ought to look forward to the two remaining aid items on the Afghanistan agenda:

1. The big one, of course, is the Kajakai Dam loan. This has now worked its way almost all the way through the AID loan machinery and will come to us sometime in the next week or two.

2. There is also a $4.6 million loan for earthmoving equipment to be used in the Helmand Valley, largely for irrigation works. This is already to go and would not normally come to the President because it is less than $10 million. However, in view of the President's general freeze on Afghanistan aid, AID is asking whether it can go ahead on its own. I agreed to sound you out since you have talked recently with the President.

If the President does not feel strongly about this any longer, you may want me to give AID a go-ahead on the small loan. The Kajakai loan will have to come to the President later anyway. If you feel the President would not like anything to go ahead without his knowing, we can hold the small loan a week or two until we are ready to

---

[1] Source: Johnson Library, National Security File, Files of Harold H. Saunders, Afghanistan, 4/1/66–1/20/69. Secret.

check the Kajakai project with him and simply make the smaller one a paragraph in that memo.

Hal

Go ahead with the equipment loan

We'd better check it with the President later[2]

---

[2] Rostow changed the second option to read: "We'd damned well better check it with the President," and added, "See me, WR."

---

544. Memorandum From the President's Special Assistant (Rostow) to President Johnson[1]

Washington, June 7, 1967.

SUBJECT

Afghanistan—Loan for Kajakai Hydroelectric Plant

Here is the request for your formal approval of a $12 million loan to Afghanistan to finance the installation of additional generating equipment at the Kajakai dam in the Helmand Valley, with which we've been associated for many years. When Ambassador [*Prime Minister*] Maiwandwal was here in early April, you advised him we would decide on the loan within thirty days, but AID has given it a most thorough going over.

After careful review, they concur that it is economically sound. If you approve this loan, actual construction will not be started until satisfactory progress is made toward improving accounting procedures, the rate structure and the collection of payments in their electrical industry.

Secretary Fowler agrees the balance of payments effects of the loan are minimal.

It would create a political problem if we turned it down now. We have done three feasibility studies and already in 1965 told them we "agreed in principle" to finance it.

---

[1] Source: Johnson Library, National Security File, Memos to the President, Walt Rostow, Vol. 30, June 1–12, 1967. Confidential.

Charlie Schultze agrees with Bill Gaud we should go ahead.[2] I recommend you approve.[3]

Approve Kajakai

Disapprove

See me

AID has also been holding off on a $4.5 million equipment loan for earth-moving machinery to be used in building irrigation works in the Helmand Valley. This small a loan would not normally come to you, but AID has held it up ever since you put a freeze on all Afghan aid. They would like to go ahead now. I recommend we proceed.

Yes on small loan

Disapprove

See me

W.W. Rostow[4]

---

[2] Schultze recommended approval in a May 29 memorandum to the President. (Ibid.)

[3] In both cases, the last option is checked and 6/8/67 is handwritten in the margin. Telegram 214155 to Kabul, June 22, states that the two loans had been approved. (National Archives and Records Administration, RG 59, Central Files 1967–69, AID (US) 9 AFG)

[4] Printed from a copy that bears this typed signature.

---

545. Telegram From the Embassy in Afghanistan to the Department of State[1]

Kabul, November 27, 1967, 1545Z.

1. Interview Harriman with PM Etemadi[2] Nov. 25, and subsequent dinner for delegation hosted by PM, were conducted in atmosphere unusual warmth. PM and Afghan Ministers present gave impression

---

[1] Source: National Archives and Records Administration, RG 59, Central Files 1967–69, POL 7 US/HARRIMAN. Confidential; Priority. Repeated to Belgrade and Bucharest for Harriman, and to Rawalpindi and Tehran. Ambassador at Large W. Averell Harriman made a trip to Pakistan for the dedication of the Mangla Dam November 21–27 and stopped in Kabul on the return journey for talks with the King and Prime Minister Etemadi. A record of Harriman's meeting with the King is in telegram 1577 from Belgrade, November 26. (Ibid.)

[2] On October 11 Prime Minister Maiwandwal resigned, and on November 1 the King appointed Foreign Minister Nur Ahmad Etemadi as Prime Minister.

they felt occasion offered them important opportunity set forth problems faced by new government and express views and hopes.

2. Also present at interview were Yaftali (Deputy PM), Hamed (Min Planning), Farhadi (MFA), Amb Neumann, Spain and McClure.

3. PM opened by saying vote of confidence in new [garble—government] showed democratic experiment proceeding successfully. Key to dealing with Parliament was frankness and sincerity.

4. PM felt by far most serious problems facing him were economic. He anticipated need for austerity, and was concerned about new 5-year plan. Afghanistan needed understanding and cooperation from friends, particularly U.S. Appreciated report of Agricultural Review Team,[3] but needed assistance, particularly wheat. Achievement self-sufficiency in wheat in 5 or 6 years, he felt, depended both on political stability and continued foreign aid. In passing, PM noted his belief there had been some hoarding of good 1967 wheat harvest because of what he considered to have been lack of political stability in recent past.

5. Yaftali stressed financial problems. Said RGA realized it must do more about tax and fiscal reforms, but insisted foreign aid was essential. Expressed concern about debt repayment to USSR. In response Harriman's question about extent to which gas would meet this problem, he said it would really help only after full production rate reached in 2 or 3 years.

6. Both PM and Yaftali emphasized that top priority for RGA efforts was in agriculture.

7. When Yaftali mentioned that fertilizer loan funds had been diverted to HIQ road, PM interjected that completion of road was very important for Afghanistan, particularly for development trade with outside world through Iran. Added that RGA also hoped connect with projected Iranian road to port of Bandar Abbas, but would need foreign technical and financial aid to pave necessary 200 kilometers.

8. Yaftali said RGA was trying encourage more private sector activity (he cited light industries and textiles as export possibilities). Said RGA had already removed some export taxes and planned to do more. When he referred to discussions with IMF, Harriman commented IMF recommendations are usually very sound.

9. Yaftali then turned to plea for indication of general extent prospective US assistance during 5-year plan period. Referred to "shopping

---

[3] A U.S. Agricultural Review Team was sent to Afghanistan June 20–July 20 to advise the Afghan Government on measures to achieve agricultural self-sufficiency. (Telegram 4725 from Kabul, May 20; National Archives and Records Administration, RG 59, Central Files 1967–69, ORG 7 AGR) On October 2 President Johnson sent a letter to Prime Minister Maiwandwal enclosing the report and recommendations of the agricultural experts. (Ibid., POL 15–1 AFG)

list" transmitted some months ago. PM said Parliament was demanding such indication, and parliamentary approval of plan depended considerably upon RGA's ability to furnish meaningful answer. Later in conversation, he said fact that of 180 deputies who spoke in recent debate on government a great number had talked about plan showed intensity of public interest and expectations re planned development. He acknowledged past assistance, and said both RGA and Afghan people recognized depth of American good will for their country. This was why he felt he should be fully frank during visit (a friendly gesture in itself, which he highly appreciated) about what was really needed from US. One thing, he said, was wheat, which RGA needed soon, partly to impart a sense of security throughout country after what happened in local wheat market last winter and spring.

10. Asked about other aid donors, PM said USSR had already committed itself to support plan. Delegation was going to Moscow shortly to firm up specific projects. French were expanding technical assistance, and were considering some industrial projects; he estimated French aid contribution at about $15 million. Germany was helping too. However, Afghanistan counted mainly on US and USSR.

11. Gov Harriman replied that USG certainly wanted to help. Some assistance would undoubtedly be possible, but we could not be sure just how much. Congress was severely reducing the resources available. Long-term commitments were more of a problem than ever. Harriman said he could therefore not answer some of PM's questions, except to say that USG had deep respect for PM and RGA and desired be helpful. He personally appreciated fact that Afghanistan was at a turning point in economic development. Added that USG believes strongly in importance of agriculture for countries like Afghanistan and realizes its development is slow process.

12. On other subjects, exchanges were equally friendly and frank.

13. PM spent what we felt was inordinate amount of time on Pushtunistan issue. Said this was only major problem in way of brotherly relations with Pakistan with which Afghanistan has so much in common. Recalled at length Afghan restraint and support of Pakistan in 1965 war. But he insisted both countries had to face issue, and both would gain immensely if true will of Pushtun people expressed. PM emphasized pressures upon RGA from Parliament. He expressed considerable bitterness about Ayub's recent book,[4] saying it undid years of careful work to improve relations.

---

[4] Reference is to Mohammed Ayub Khan, *Friends Not Masters* (London: Oxford University Press, 1967).

14. When asked for specific proposals, PM said it was simple; will of Pushtun people must be expressed. As practical matter, main thing needed was statement of intention by Pakistan willingness to discuss subject.

15. In further discussion, PM mentioned incidentally that UN had been helpful in cause of peace, but Afghanistan had no intention take Pushtunistan issue to UN. Harriman said Pushtunistan was bilateral problem. US regretted its existence, hoped relations among parties would improve, but did not see how we could usefully get involved. USG did, however, have greatest respect for and interest in Afghanistan. PM concluded what Afghanistan needed on this issue was understanding.

16. PM stressed gratitude his government and many Afghans for USG kindness in providing medical care for former PM Maiwandwal.

17. Re Iran, PM said relations were very good and improving daily. Poor relations of past were due mainly to mutual lack of knowledge. Today there was no political problem, only technical one on distribution Helmand waters.

18. Re Communist China, PM said after some prodding that relations remained "correct." Projects under loan proceeding satisfactorily. He added with smile we should really ask our Pak friends about this, since they were very close to Chinese.

19. On Middle East, PM said he shared Harriman's gratification that UN resolution adopted unanimously by SC.[5] PM also characterized King Hussein as "wise and courageous." On Cyprus, Governor and PM agreed situation tragic, Greece and Turkey must eventually get over emotional approach to problem.

20. On Vietnam, Harriman stressed President Johnson's desire for peace negotiations, shared by almost all countries including USSR. Hanoi misjudging attitude of American people and determination see matter through. PM expressed thanks for this and previous expositions US position. Said Geneva agreements were obvious basis for solution.

21. Governor expressed appreciation for PM's frankness and obvious readiness face realities. PM made clear throughout conversation his appreciation for visit by delegation.[6]

Neumann

---

[5] Reference is to UN Resolution 242 passed by the Security Council on November 22, 1967. For text, see *American Foreign Policy: Current Documents, 1967,* pp. 616–617.

[6] On December 9 Ambassador Neumann called on the Prime Minister to expand on Harriman's November 25 conversation. He stressed the importance of self-help measures by Afghanistan and explained the restrictions imposed by Congress on the availability of total resources. (Telegram 4266 from Kabul, December 11; National Archives and Records Administration, RG 59, Central Files 1967–69, POL 15–1 AFG)

546. Telegram From the Embassy in Afghanistan to the Department of State[1]

Kabul, February 21, 1968, 1130Z.

3185. Subject: PL–480 Title I: RGA Proposal of 8/30/67.

1. We are concerned about consequences further delay authority negotiate new Title I agreement PL–480. If unable proceed by March 1 at latest, anticipate deterioration prospects solution troublesome economic matters outstanding between USG and RGA, with consequent unfavorable effects RGA self-help efforts.

2. Would remind Dept RGA request has been pending with USG almost six months. Washington approval negotiation appeared imminent last December and again mid-January. Deliveries wheat Kabul can hardly now be made current crop year. This however, is less significant than role of new agreement in total American aid package for Afghanistan and hoped-for impact of latter on Afghan economic policies. In light other developments affecting US assistance Afghanistan, if we appear hesitate further on PL–480, RGA will surely begin wonder whether basic change American policy toward Afghanistan has occurred.

3. RGA has recently completed economic negotiations with Soviets which in Afghan eyes appear have been in many respect less troublesome than negotiations with US—particularly re commodity assistance. However, our main concern lies in other areas.

4. RGA at last appears ready move on long-term solution vexatious trust fund problem. We can hardly imagine RGA going through with this, however, until we have made firm offer on PL–480.

5. Deadlines for RGA budget decisions FY beginning March 22 are rapidly approaching. We understand RGA plans to include trust fund payments in budget from now on. Early assurance on PL–480 will be essential to assure such item included in budget. Moreover, anticipated proceeds proposed PL–480 agreement will play important role in determining magnitude next development budget. Loss of confidence our intentions could lead to serious cutback overall level RGA development spending, at time when economy in doldrums, and could even lead to cuts in RGA's top-priority agricultural production program.

6. We therefore urge prompt authorization negotiate.

Blood

---

[1] Source: National Archives and Records Administration, RG 59, Central Files 1967–69, AID (US) 15–8 AFG. Confidential; Priority.

547. Memorandum From the Director of the Bureau of the Budget (Zwick) to President Johnson[1]

Washington, March 27, 1968.

SUBJECT

Proposed P.L. 480 Agreement with Afghanistan

Orville Freeman and Bill Gaud request your authority to negotiate an $8.2 million P.L. 480 agreement with Afghanistan (Tab A).[2] The agreement would provide 90,000 tons of wheat and 6,000 tons of vegetable oil on 40-year dollar credit terms, with a 10-year grace period. To help the U.S. balance of payments, it would require that the first $750,000 be paid over 10 months beginning on June 30.

The amount of wheat proposed for this agreement is quite generous in view of Afghanistan's recent good crop. However, I feel that it is warranted by our desire to move wheat and by the additional self-help leverage which we can get from a larger P.L. 480 program. This agreement would bring to $12.5 million the amount of food aid provided in FY 1968. Our dollar aid is limited to technical assistance and is estimated at $7.5 million this fiscal year.

Self-help. Afghanistan has taken a number of important steps to increase agricultural production, with a view to self-sufficiency in wheat and edible oil by the early 1970's. The last P.L. 480 agreement, signed in July, contained general self-help conditions designed to reinforce the Government's commitment to that goal. This agreement would require additional specific and sound measures, in particular (a) the establishment of a wheat price high enough to provide incentives to farmers, and (b) improvement of fertilizer distribution by turning it over to the private sector.

Military Expenditures. Afghanistan's military supply situation presents a particularly thorny problem. Although about half of its military hardware was provided under contracts concluded prior to 1961, the country's defense establishment is out of all proportion to its economic situation or any realistic appraisal of the current threat. Almost all of Afghanistan's military equipment has been supplied by the Soviets. The current inventory includes an estimated 335 tanks, 55 or more

---

[1] Source: Johnson Library, National Security File, Country File, Afghanistan, Vol. I, Memos and Miscellaneous, 11/63–4/68. Secret.

[2] Tab A, not printed, is a March 6 memorandum from Freeman and Gaud to the President. (Ibid., Memos to the President, Walt Rostow, Vol. 69, March 25–31, 1968)

surface-to-air missiles, 250 anti-tank missiles, and 96 MIG fighters. (A background paper on military expenditures is attached at Tab B.)[3]

In spite of this situation Gaud feels, and I agree, that a close reading of the Symington amendment[4] does not require you to make a finding that Afghan resources are being diverted to unnecessary military expenditures to a degree which materially interferes with economic development. The rationale for this approach is essentially two-fold:

—Since three-fourths of the equipment is provided on a grant basis, *actual expenditures* amount to only about 20% of the budget and are not out of line with neighboring India and Pakistan.

—These expenditures in themselves probably *do not unduly interfere with development.* Lack of technical skills and workable institutions constitute a more serious bottleneck to Afghan development.

There are also two strong practical reasons for not invoking the Symington amendment now:

—Our aid program in Afghanistan helps to counterbalance a much larger Soviet presence. In 1963, King Zahir embarked upon an experiment in parliamentary democracy which probably would not have been possible without our influence and support.

—In Afghanistan as elsewhere, the Symington and Conte/Long amendments[5] can be quite useful for purposes of persuasion, but they lose their utility once they are applied. Our relatively small aid program may not enable us to convince the Afghans to reduce their future defense expenditures in any event, but to precipitately cut off all U.S. assistance clearly would not achieve this objective.

On the other hand, I do not think we can simply conduct business as usual in the face of this problem. There is a reasonable chance that the U.S., by building on the dialogue which Ambassador Neumann has begun, can induce some restraint in the Afghan military budget. Moreover, if we ignore the spirit of the Symington amendment in Afghanistan, we lay ourselves open to charges on the Hill that we are not serious about its application and will not put any teeth into our policy anywhere in the world.

On balance, *I recommend that we go ahead with this proposed P.L. 480 agreement,* but that in negotiating it the State Department be instructed

---

[3] The attachment, entitled "Review of Proposed PL 480 Agreement with Afghanistan per Section 620 (S) of the Foreign Assistance Act, as Amended," undated, is not printed.

[4] The Symington Amendment to the Foreign Assistance Act of 1967, adopted November 14, 1967 (P.L. 90–137; 81 Stat. 445), directed the President to terminate development loans and P.L. 480 assistance to nations that diverted such assistance to military expenditures or diverted their own resources to "unnecessary" military expenditures "to a degree which materially interferes" with their own development.

[5] The Conte–Long Amendment to the Foreign Assistance and Related Appropriations Act of 1968, adopted January 2, 1968 (P.L. 90–249; 81 Stat. 936), directed the President to withhold an equivalent amount of economic assistance from any underdeveloped country other than Greece, Turkey, Iran, Israel, the Republic of China, the Philippines, and Korea, that used its own resources to purchase sophisticated weaponry.

to make a vigorous effort, both here and through Ambassador Neumann in Afghanistan, to get across to the Afghans the following points, agreed to by Bill Gaud and Luke Battle:

—While we recognize that it is difficult for one country to pass judgment on the national security problems and military structure of another, it is our best judgment that Afghanistan's present military structure and expenditures need serious reexamination in the light of the present military threat and what we all know to be the country's economic needs.

—U.S. law now requires that we take future developments on this front fully into account in thinking about any further P.L. 480 assistance or dollar loans or continuation of our technical assistance program.

—We strongly urge Afghanistan to seek ways to reduce the burden of military expenditures upon its economy. The Afghan Government should know that, under present circumstances, increases in the defense budget or new contracts for additional military equipment will make it extremely difficult for us to provide assistance in the future.

Charles J. Zwick

Approve P.L. 480 sale; instruct Ambassador and State Department to take strong line with RGA

Disapprove[6]

---

[6] This option is checked and next to it a typewritten note reads: "N.B.: The Disapprove decision was made on March 29, 1968. On April 23, 1968 the President reversed his decision and agreed."

---

548.   Memorandum From the President's Special Assistant (Rostow) to President Johnson[1]

Washington, April 22, 1968.

Mr. President:

We have had a serious failure in communicating your decision on the attached PL 480 package for Afghanistan. As the note indicates, Miss Nivens telephoned, as is usual, your decision to the staff member working the area, Roger Morris, who was acting in Ed Hamilton's

---

[1] Source: Johnson Library, National Security File, Country File, Afghanistan, Vol. I, Memos and Miscellaneous, 12/63–4/68. Secret.

absence. He heard her relay of your decision as "approved" rather than "disapproved."

He communicated the decision, as is usual, to State which notified our man in Kabul.

We discovered the mistake a few days later and flashed Kabul (Tab C)[2] but it was too late to catch our Ambassador before he had (1) delivered the lecture on military spending (reporting cable at Tab D),[3] and (2) delivered the news that we were ready to go ahead with the PL 480 deal (Tab E).[4]

Thus, due to our error, I am afraid there will be some broken crockery if we back out now.

We have two choices:

—The President can withdraw our offer to make this agreement on the grounds that the Symington Amendment is not being complied with:

—or we can accept the consequences of our error and let the PL 480 package go through.

As you can see from the cable at Tab D, our Ambassador believes that his lecture on military spending has begun a serious rethinking of the Afghan military budget. He would certainly argue that cutting off the food aid now would be self-defeating. It would also cast doubt on our $8.2 million AID program in Afghanistan, since the Symington Amendment leaves the President no leeway once he decides that aid should be terminated because a country is spending too much on defense.

To assure that this will not happen again, I have made arrangements that all decisions will be communicated twice: to the relevant member of my staff; and to the Secretariat at the Department of State.

Walt

Proceed to withdraw offer on Symington Amendment grounds

Let PL 480 deal proceed[5]

Call me

---

[2] Not printed; telegram 148514 to Kabul, April 17.
[3] Not printed; telegram 3775 from Kabul, March 30.
[4] Not printed; telegram 4072 from Kabul, April 18.
[5] This option is checked; Johnson added a handwritten note, "No choice."

Index

ISBN 0-16-049945-3

90000

9 780160 499456